D1697153

NORTH AMERICA | CENTRAL AMERICA | CARIBBEAN | SOUTH AMERICA

IMPRINT

The Deutsche Bibliothek is registering this publication in the Deutsche Nationalbibliographie; detailed bibliographical information can be found on the internet at http://dnb.ddb.de

ISBN 978-3-938780-56-5
Copyright 2008 by Verlagshaus Braun
www.verlagshaus-braun.de

The work is copyright protected. Any use outside of the close boundaries of the copyright law, which has not been granted permission by the publisher, is unauthorized and liable for prosecution. This especially applies to duplications, translations, microfilming, and any saving or processing in electronic systems.

1st edition 2008

Editor in chief: Michelle Galindo
Editorial coordination: Kristin Kress, Franziska Nauck
Editorial staff: Fabricio Astua, Claire Chamot, Wiebke Friedrich, Robin Hermann, Paola Hernández, Anna Hinc, Eyal Moran, Annika Schulz, Sophie Steybe, Antonia von Tschurtschenthaler
Text editing: Alice Bayandin, Erin Cullerton, Eyal Moran
Graphic design: ON 2D | Tom Wibberenz, Michaela Prinz
Imaging and Pre-press: Bild1Druck GmbH

All of the information in this volume has been compiled to the best of the editors knowledge. It is based on the information provided to the publisher by the architects offices and excludes any liability. The publisher assumes no responsibility for its accuracy or completeness as well as copyright discrepancies and refers to the specified sources (hotels, architects offices). All rights to the photographs are property of the photographer (please refer to the picture).

1000 x
ARCHITECTURE
OF THE AMERICAS

BRAUN

1000x
CONTENT

0006 **PREFACE**

0008 **NORTHERN AMERICA**
0010 **CANADA**
0130 **USA**

0632 **CENTRAL AMERICA**
0634 **BELIZE**
0635 **COSTA RICA**
0640 **GUATEMALA**
0641 **HONDURAS**
0642 **MEXICO**
0768 **PANAMA**

0774 **CARIBBEAN**	0782 **SOUTH AMERICA**	1018 **INDEX ARCHITECTS**
0776 **BARBADOS**	0784 **ARGENTINA**	1021 **INDEX PROJECTS**
0777 **JAMAICA**	0805 **BRAZIL**	
0778 **PUERTO RICO**	0921 **CHILE**	
0780 **TRINIDAD & TOBAGO**	0988 **COLOMBIA**	
	0993 **ECUADOR**	
	1002 **PERU**	
	1016 **URUGUAY**	
	1017 **VENEZUELA**	

PREFACE

1000 x Architecture of the Americas features 1000 outstanding and creative projects recently built and under development in the Western Hemisphere by acclaimed and emerging architects established in the American continent. Comprised of varying typologies and split by numerous economic, cultural and historical differences, North, Central and South America offer a plethora of innovative up-and-coming trends in the field of contemporary architecture. The projects featured range from the domestic scale illustrating a wide variety of houses to the mega metropolitan scale, including museums, religious institutions, schools, office buildings all the way to stadiums and airports, each influencing the architectural climate throughout the continent.

This book explores the powerful diversity of the architecture of today from Canada to Chile as an evolving phenomenon, where the design varies depending on the climate conditions, economics, materials, building regulations, architects' approach and style.

The cultural and economical influences are seen from one extreme to the other. While in Canada and the United States the building regulations are stricter and architects have to work around the code to shift and encourage urban trends, Central and South America present an interesting condition for architects where most of its developed area is built up without the professional intervention of architects and the creative interpretation of a weak code create a series of spaces and opportunities to negotiate. Moreover, the urban and political conditions strongly influence their work patterns and shape the avant-garde architecture.

The material palette ranges from digital fabrication techniques, which open up investigations into the limitations and potentials of the architectural surface to traditional indigenous materials making architecture a 'field of constructive experimentation'.

Today, an ever-increasing body of talented architects in the Americas, including many practitioners showcased within these pages, strives to explore sustainable systems, landscape design and urban planning in a nimble dance between builder and designer beyond the limits of architecture in their region. Taking their inspiration from visions of the future and traces of the past, these are the people who are defining the aesthetics of tomorrow's architecture.

621x

NORTHERN AMERICA

0010 **CANADA**
0032 **MONTREAL**
0073 **TORONTO**
0115 **VANCOUVER**

0130 **USA**
0140 **AUSTIN**
0284 **LOS ANGELES**
0364 **NEW YORK**
0473 **PHOENIX**
0530 **SAN FRANCISCO**
0565 **SEATTLE**

CITY Alban (ON)
COUNTRY Canada
REGION North America
TYPOLOGY Culture
COMPLETION –
WEBSITE www.bsnarchitects.com
ARCHITECTS Baird Sampson Neuert Architects

FRENCH RIVER VISITOR CENTRE

The Centre is designed as a journey through the site and across the history of the nation's first Canadian Heritage River. Conceived as a landscape promenade, both found and constructed, it reveals, through movement, key themes and understandings of the river's essence. Visitor arrival and site services are organized within the landscape to unfold from Highway 69, and culminate at an exterior waterfall introducing the theme of water. Natural materials, views, and board-formed concrete walls extend the river's landscape through the ramped exhibit hall back out to orientation terraces connecting to hiking routes.

01 Exterior view 02 Exhibit 03 Teaching terrace 04 Exterior view of elevated exhibit hall 05 Visitor centre floor plan

Photos: Tom Arban Photography

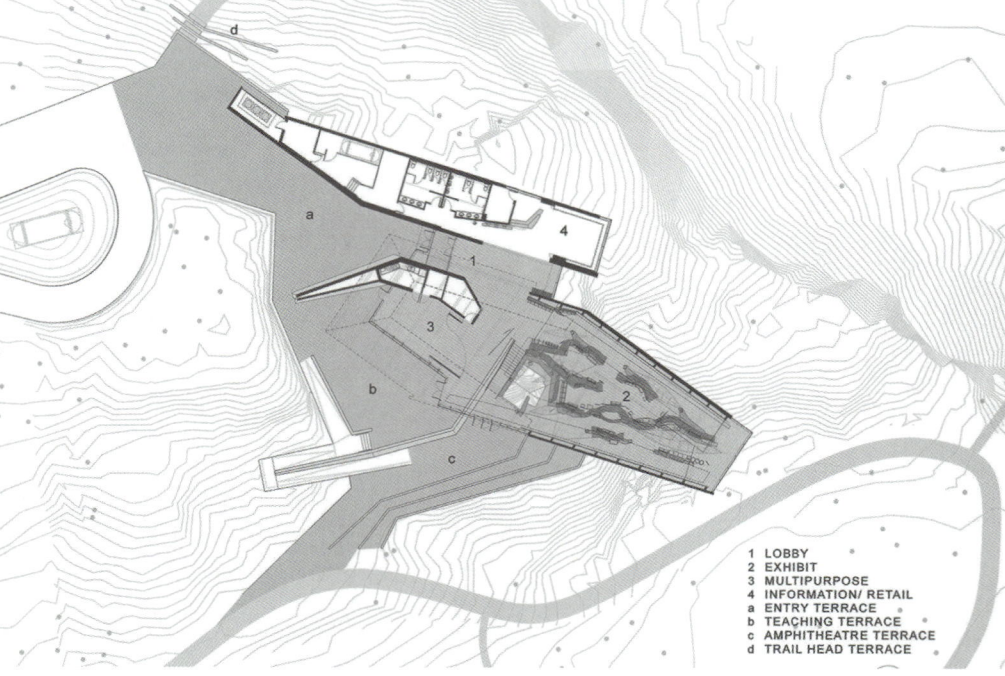

1 LOBBY
2 EXHIBIT
3 MULTIPURPOSE
4 INFORMATION/ RETAIL
a ENTRY TERRACE
b TEACHING TERRACE
c AMPHITHEATRE TERRACE
d TRAIL HEAD TERRACE

BRAMPTON SOCCER CENTRE

The indoor 'Soccer Centre of Excellence' project nurtures youth and adult soccer to a high level. The building is designed to be a full site community and soccer 'Landmark Destination'. Four indoor fields are paired into two masses and shifted to create a zone of sky-lit circulation. These masses frame a civic corner 'Activity Space' and an inner site 'Arrival Space'. Interlocked floating planes with metallic outer shells and cedar lining comprehensively organize the site by forming clerestory towers and hooded overhangs, allowing light and views into the building while endorsing the sport and its community.

01 Façade glazing with laminated glass graphics **02** Main entrance **03** Glazing bays allow views into fields **04** Groundfloor **05** Lobby with cedar lined interiors

Photos: Tom Arban Photography

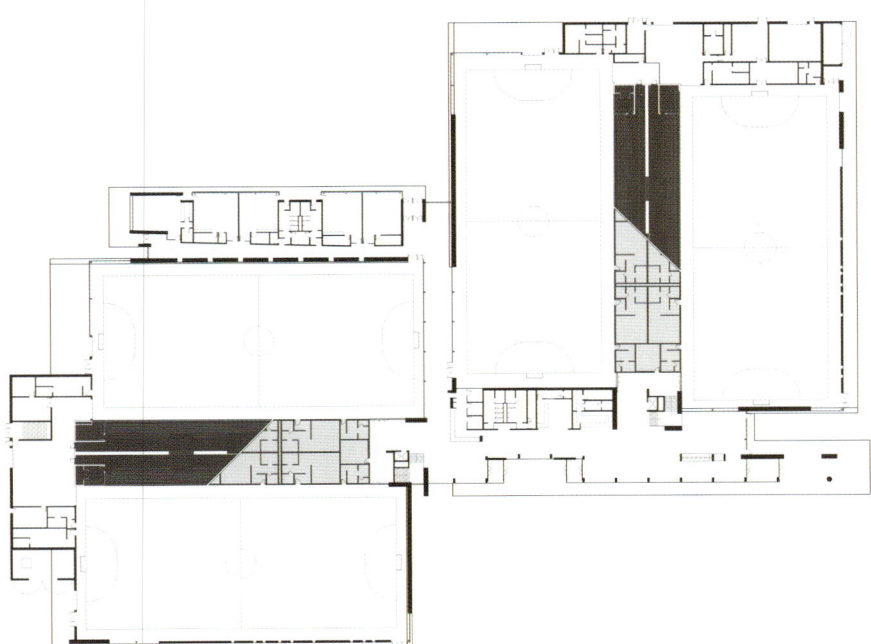

CITY: Brampton (ON)
COUNTRY: Canada
REGION: North America
TYPOLOGY: Leisure / Sports
COMPLETION: 2007
WEBSITE: www.mjmarchitects.com
ARCHITECTS: Maclennan Jaunkalns Miller Architects

CITY Brantford (ON)
COUNTRY Canada
REGION North America
TYPOLOGY Education
COMPLETION 2004
WEBSITE www.strattonarchitects.com
ARCHITECTS G. Bruce Stratton Architects

W. ROSS MACDONALD SCHOOL FOR THE BLIND

W. Ross Macdonald School for the Blind is a facility uniquely geared towards primary school education and life-skills training. Lighting flexibility, texture differences, physical guides, and audible clues are carefully controlled elements designed to enhance the student's independence, correlating to non-visual cues that will guide them in their daily activities. The floor is where materiality becomes a physical feature, where changes adjacent to the walls alert the user to encroaching barriers and transitions of programmatic elements. Students are therefore quickly able to navigate based almost solely on sound and texture.

01 View to music room and two-story multi-purpose room behind **02** Façade with coloured laminated glass **03** Cross and atrium section **04** Poured concrete wall, view at fully glazed study rooms

Photos: Steven Evans

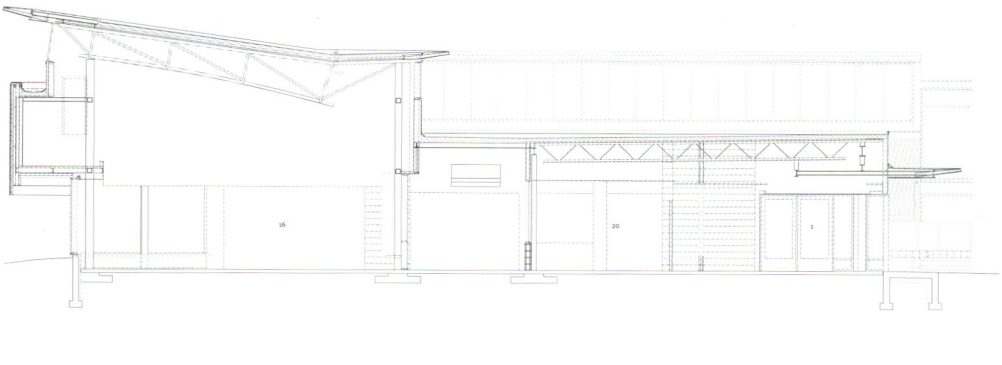

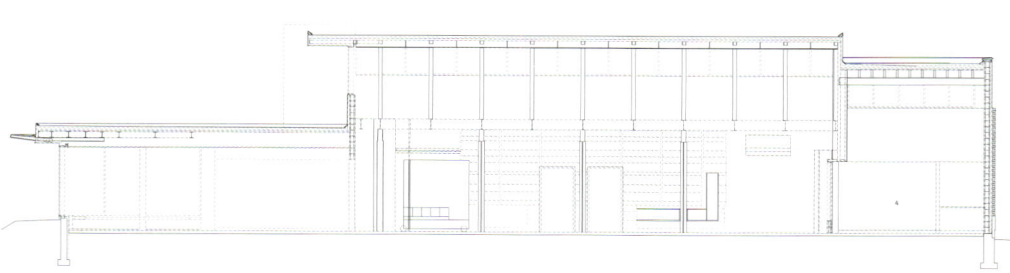

DISCOVERY LANDING

Discovery Landing was conceived by the City of Burlington as a major building block of its downtown revitalization program which focuses upon design excellence as a means of establishing a memorable community destination. Integrating architecture and landscape, the project establishes a continuous, unfolding topography for recreation and engagement that extends into the City and lakefront. This new topography creates an experientially rich urban landscape that concentrates and intensifies interaction along the water's edge, while supporting major events and festivals within the adjoining parkland.

01 View to the lake **02** Staircase leading to lake **03** Lake view **04** Entrance hall **05** Site plan

Photos: Tom Arban Photography

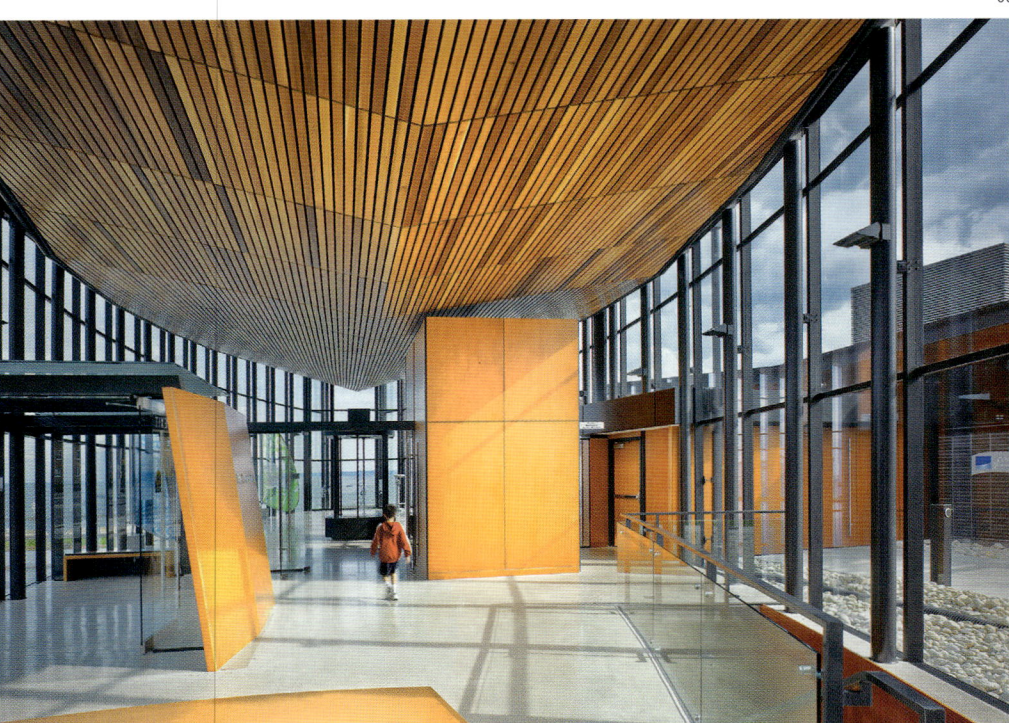

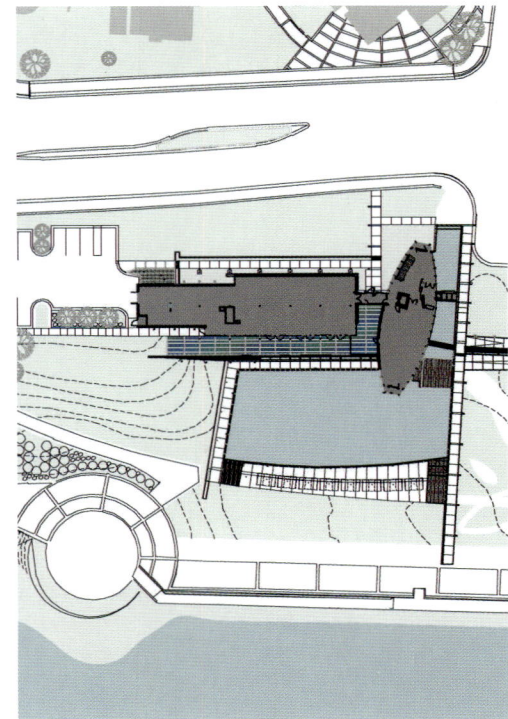

CITY Burlington (ON)
COUNTRY Canada
REGION North America
TYPOLOGY Public
COMPLETION 2006
WEBSITE www.bsnarchitects.com
ARCHITECTS Baird Sampson Neuert Architects

CITY Burlington (ON)

COUNTRY Canada

REGION North America

TYPOLOGY Public

COMPLETION 2005

WEBSITE www.teeplearch.com

ARCHITECTS Teeple Architects

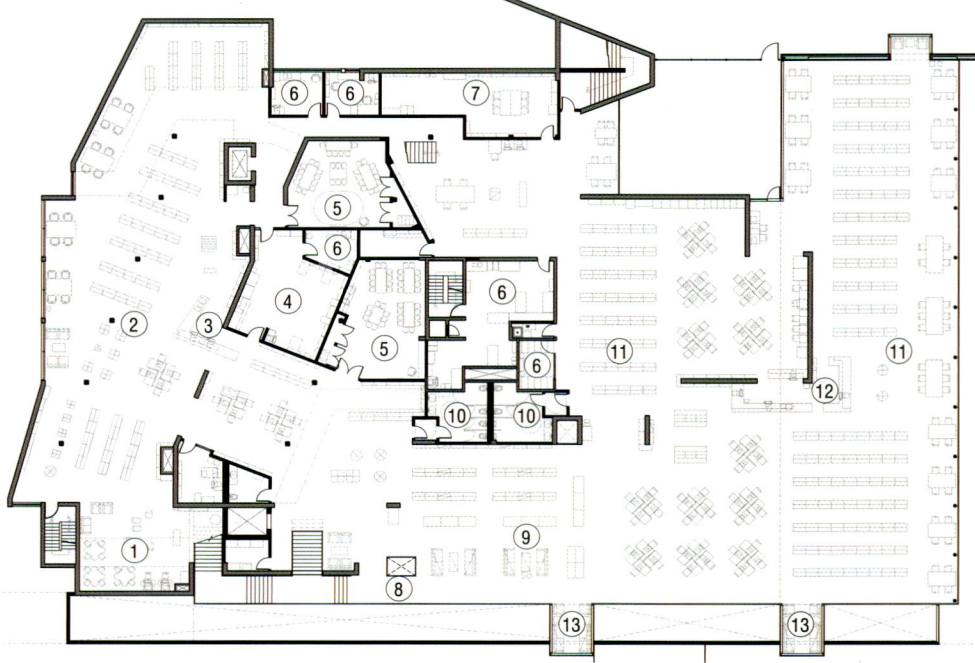

BURLINGTON CENTRAL PUBLIC LIBRARY

This project involves the renovation of the existing Burlington Public Library, located in Burlington's Central Park, originally built in the 1960's. The public spaces of the library have been functionally re-organized to provide main public entrances and a circulation desk at the lower level, a large functional second floor with a new two-storey reading room, a renovated third floor, and a new Children's Discovery Centre. The lobby, which includes a café and display areas, is the main orientation point. It faces an old row of trees from the original farm property, and allows western views from the park beyond.

01 Lobby with display areas **02** Three-story lobby west addition **03** Main level plan **04** General view by night **05** Circulation desk

Photos: Tom Arban Photography, Michael Awad

FIELDING ESTATE WINERY

Fielding Estate is a small winery producing limited batch wines through traditional methods. Located on 18 acres atop the Niagara Escarpment, the design maximizes the amount of arable land and optimizes views across the landscape. Two distinct program elements, a production area and a retail bar, resulted in a parti of a long shed under an open gabled roof, with the bar overlooking the winemaking process. Sustainable design features include a gravity-fed septic system and treatment bed, a central skylight with operable vents allowing lighting and passive ventilation, a permeable granular drive, and a storm water retention pond.

01 Floor plans **02** Exterior view **03** Production area **04** Exterior view by night

Photos: Tom Arban Photography

CITY Beamsville (ON)
COUNTRY Canada
REGION North America
TYPOLOGY Retail
COMPLETION 2005
WEBSITE www.superkul.ca
ARCHITECTS superkül inc | architect

CITY
Calgary (AB)

COUNTRY
Canada

REGION
North America

TYPOLOGY
Office

COMPLETION
2005

WEBSITE
www.mdbworld.com

ARCHITECTS
Eleven Eleven Architecture

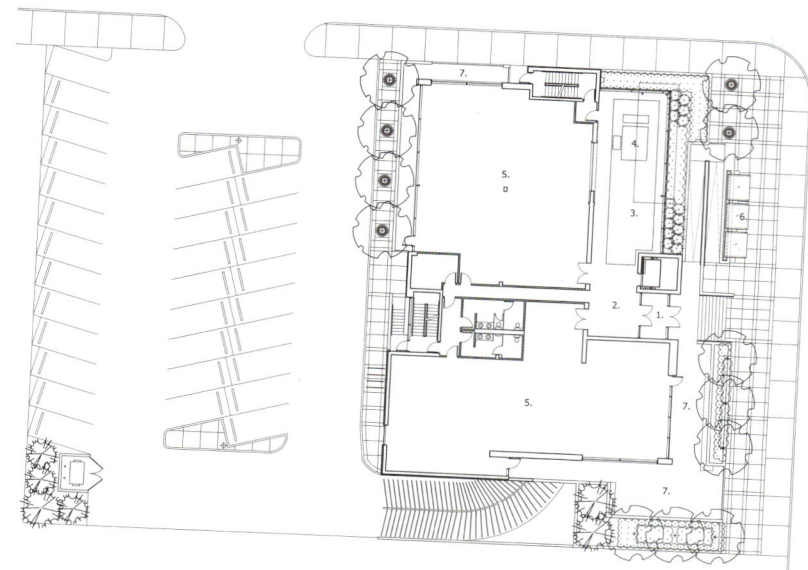

MTECH BUILDING

MTech Building is a contemporary design that evokes the sense of optimism, where the designers set out to redefine the normative notion of the speculative office building with a dynamic, balanced composition. The exterior consists of a careful composition of pre-cast architectural concrete, pure white composite metal panels, and a series of stacked meeting rooms clad in a ceramic fritted glass hovering within the four-storey atrium. The interior can be thought of as a series of spaces interconnected both vertically and horizontally, allowing for numerous simultaneous visual and spatial experiences of the building's layered complexity.

01 Southwest view **02** Northeast view **03** Site plan and main floor plan **04** Façade elevation **05** North elevation façade with concrete and metal panels **06** Atrium main entrance area

Photos: Robert Lemermeyer

1830 BANKVIEW

The design of this project provided the client "Luxe Developments" with a sophisticated solution to a restrictive inner city lot in a cosmopolitan neighborhood of a typically conservative city. Placed within a contained linear site, this project operates as a series of four vertical townhouses. Each of the four units' three stories includes terraces with panoramic views of the city, double-storey entrances, and large expansive windows. The ultimate result of the design is a large, glazing, natural light and terraces that punctuate the articulation of the elevation to provide a measure of rest and contemplation throughout each unit.

01 Four vertical townhouses with southern exposure **02** Units with double-sotry entrances **03** Living space with fireplace **04** Guestroom **05** Bathroom

Photos: Ric Kokotovich

CITY Calgary (AB)
COUNTRY Canada
REGION North America
TYPOLOGY Living
COMPLETION 2007
WEBSITE www.orda.ca
ARCHITECTS Office of Richard Davignon, Architect Inc. (ORDA)

CITY Cambridge (ON)
COUNTRY Canada
REGION North America
TYPOLOGY Culture
COMPLETION 2007
WEBSITE www.kongatsarchitects.com
ARCHITECTS Kongats Architects

HESPELER LIBRARY

This redevelopment in the historic textile town of Hespeler, Ontario, wraps a 1922 Carnegie Library within a generous glass case. The new building envelope has modulated ceramic frit patterns on glass that weave around the building, creating varying degrees of transparency that respond to interior activities. Automatic operators within the glass panels naturally ventilate the interior, while a layering of hand-woven nylon thread and linen paper drapes complete a final filtering of sunlight to wash the interior with a soft light. The fine scale of the building's glass wrapper defers to the scale of the existing Carnegie Library.

01 New buidling envelope with frit patterns on glass **02** Fine glass façade with view into existing library **03** Degrees of transparency in building case **04** Main floor plan **05** Interior view of library

Photos: Ben Rahn/A-Frame Inc., Steve Payne (02)

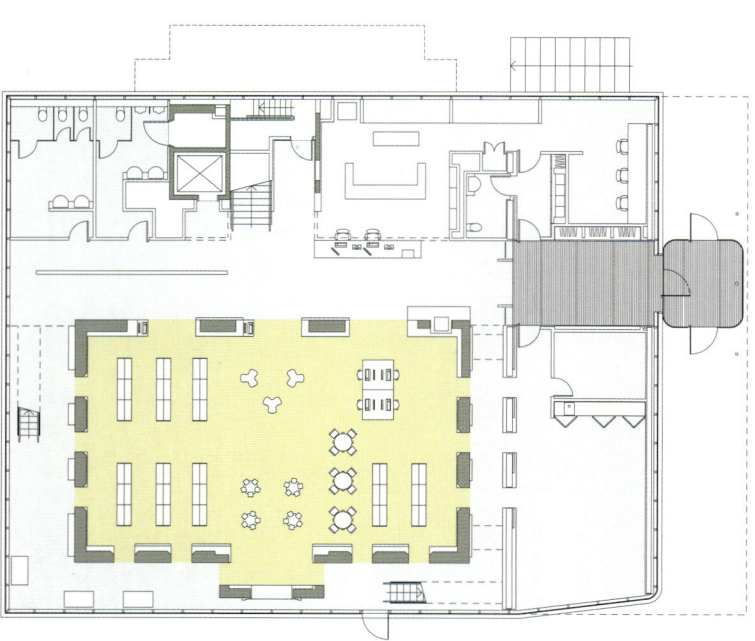

JOSEPH STUDIO

Working in the vernacular of Ontario's outbuildings, this oil-painter's studio has a beautiful opening to an intimate group of shaded residential gardens. Private entry from the street along a flagstone path is framed by a textured wood storage wall and another narrow garden. Exposed structure and storage shelving of Douglas fir are day-lit with large areas of clear thermal glazing, while the direct summer sun is shaded by large black walnut trees along the western edge of the site. High efficiency mechanical systems combine with passive solar heat gain and natural ventilation to minimize energy consumption.

01 Exposed structure and storage shelving of Douglas fir
02 Private entry from the street **03** View inside the studio
04 Clear thermal glazing **05** Isometric

Photos: Paul Dowling, Catherine Dowling (02)

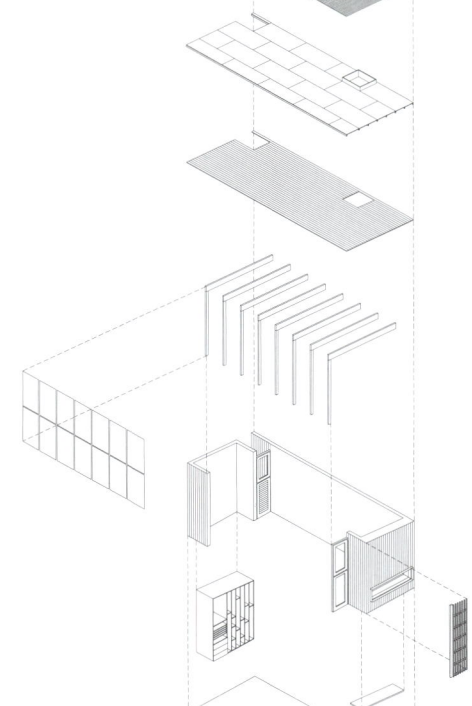

CITY Dundas (ON)
COUNTRY Canada
REGION North America
TYPOLOGY Culture
COMPLETION 2005
WEBSITE www.lillepolddowling.com
ARCHITECTS Lillepold Dowling Architects

CITY Drag Lake, Haliburton (ON)
COUNTRY Canada
REGION North America
TYPOLOGY Living
COMPLETION 2004
WEBSITE www.mafcohouse.com
ARCHITECTS Molenaar (Dan & Diane Molenaar)

PAVILION HOUSE YM

Pavilion House YM is a symbolic divider between the world of mechanized convenience taken for granted and the wilderness. Located on an isolated stretch of Canadian shield, north of Haliburton, Ontario, the house is accessible only by boat or in the winter across the frozen lake. The dimension was directed by the size of the bronze tinted glazing that clad the entire Douglas fir superstructure, to retain contact with the surrounding granite, forest, and lake. Visitors feel that this simple edifice, with its reflective surfaces is floating, due in part to the sheer strength of the pier system and the cabins strategic placement.

01 Pier system on contour of site **02** Douglas fir superstructure cladded with bronze tinted glazing **03** Cross ventilation **04** Kitchen **05** Floor plan

Photos: Christopher Wadsworth (01), Joseph Franke (02, 04), Paul Orenstein (03)

01

02

03

04

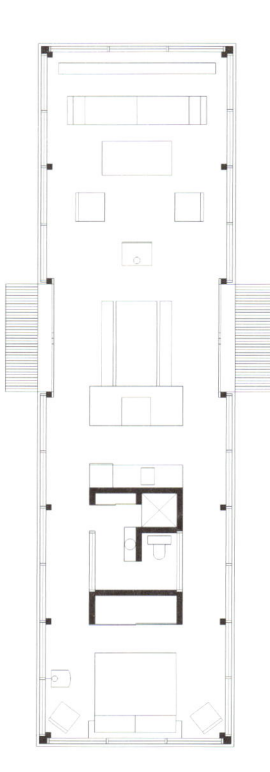
05

NEW VARSCONA THEATRE

This added renovation to the busiest experimental theatre in Canada is located in the Strathcona district of Edmonton, renowned for its cultural life and outdoor festivals. The project focuses on the "front-of-house", providing entry foyer, ticket office, beverage and food services, lounge, and coat space. A landscape of concrete benches, lit from underneath, is appreciated visually in all seasons and occupied informally or as performance seating. The theatre design is a catalyst for the public engagement of this cultural district, activating what is typically mono-functional space into the necessary space of the public realm.

01 Concrete benches as performance seating **02** Front façade **03** Longitudinal section **04** Floor plan main level **05** Outdoor performance interacting with street audience

Renderings: Marc Boutin / Mauricio Rosa

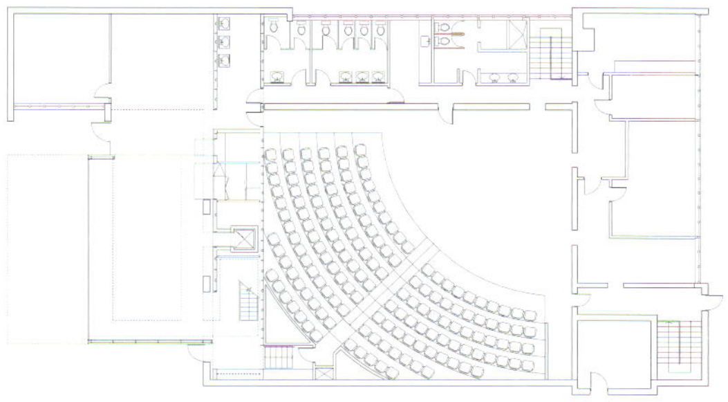

CITY Edmonton (AB)
COUNTRY Canada
REGION North America
TYPOLOGY Culture
COMPLETION in progress
WEBSITE www.the-mbac.ca
ARCHITECTS Marc Boutin Architectural Collaborative

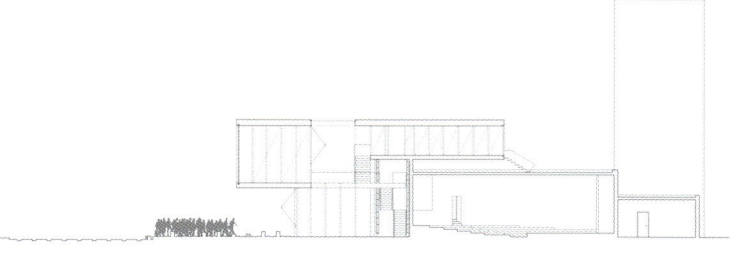

HOUSE ON HURRICANE LAKE

This house sits on a steeply sloped site on the Canadian Shield overlooking Hurricane Lake in Halliburton, Ontario. The land is shaped by severe glaciations from ice scraping the pre-Cambrian rock clean after the last ice age. The relationship of the contained outdoor terrace and lake below dramatizes the distinction between the new constructed ground and the exquisite natural surroundings. The distinction of these spaces also flattens the spatial depth between the house and the lake. The landscape is compressed and drawn up into the space of the house, becoming a seamless experience of interior and exterior.

01 Exterior view Cor-ten steel wall **02** Exterior view of front elevation **03** Interior view of the living room and kitchen **04** Floor plans **05** Elevation

Photos: James Dow, Bob Gundu (02)

CITY Halliburton (ON)
COUNTRY Canada
REGION North America
TYPOLOGY Living
COMPLETION 2005
WEBSITE www.shim-sutcliffe.com
ARCHITECTS Shim-Sutcliffe Architects

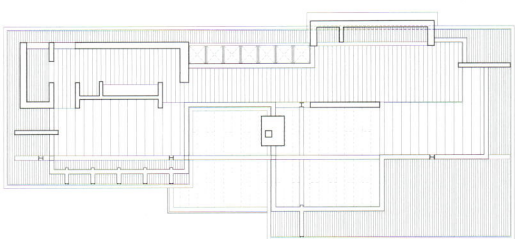

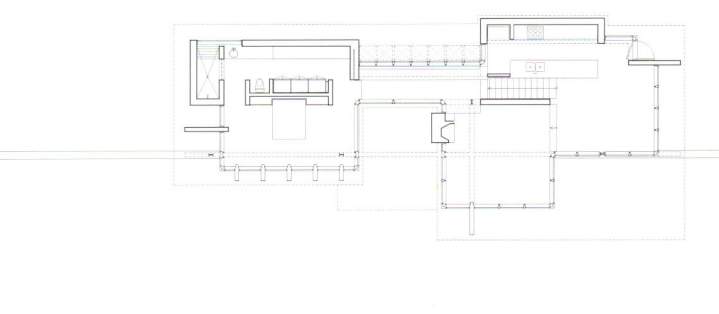

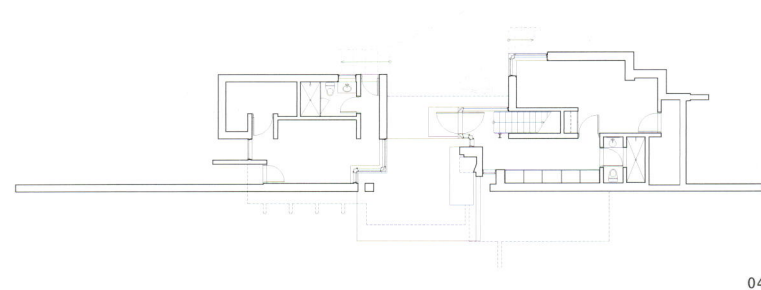

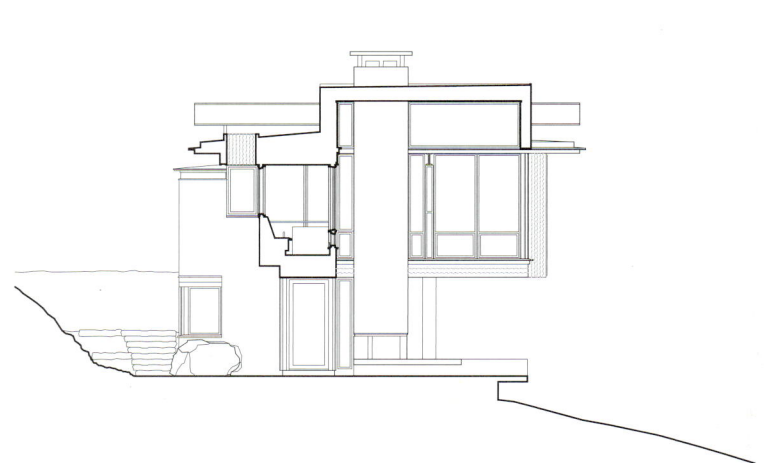

KLEINBURG POOL PAVILION

This 460 square foot 'light box' is situated along the edge of a four and a half acre residential property in Kleinburg, Ontario. Governed by an existing organic-shaped pool, this intervention defines the eastern edge of a nested retreat, resting between the residence to the north and a forested landscape to the south. The natural character of the site inspired the extensive use of wood as the structure's primary building material. Beyond its function, the pavilion intensifies one's sense of the immediate and distant environments by playfully exploring the relationship between interior and exterior.

01 Exterior-interior connection through wooden façade
02 Terrace dining space **03** Pavilion illuminated at night
04 Floor plan

Photos: Tom Arban Photography

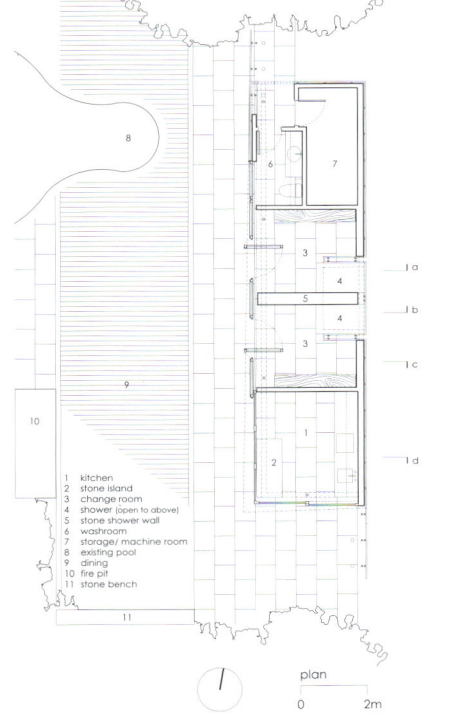

CITY Kleinburg (ON)
COUNTRY Canada
REGION North America
TYPOLOGY Living
COMPLETION 2005
WEBSITE www.michaelamantea.com
ARCHITECTS Michael Amantea

CITY: Kamloops (BC)
COUNTRY: Canada
REGION: North America
TYPOLOGY: Living
COMPLETION: 2003
WEBSITE: www.darcyjones.com
ARCHITECTS: D'Arcy Jones Design Inc.

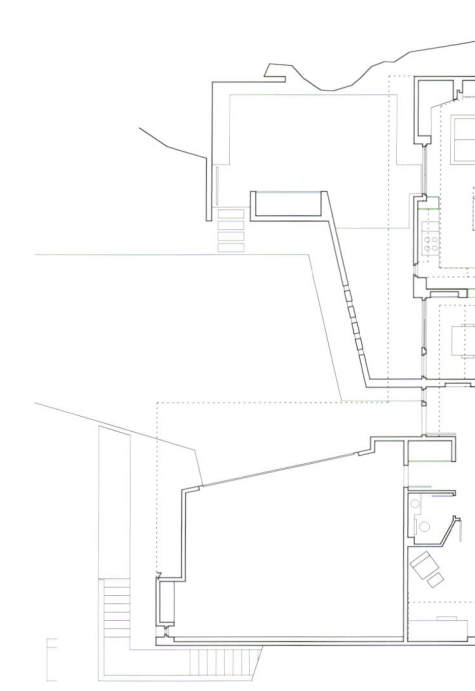

MOSEWICH HOUSE

Crouching on the edge of a steep slope, this sculptural suburban home is surrounded by a mix of housing styles. The front yard is filled with existing Ponderosa pines, sagebrush and bunch grass, in-filled with new indigenous plantings. To merge interior spaces with the landscape, a private courtyard unites the kitchen and dining areas, while intimate views of rock outcroppings contrast with long views to the river valley below. No structural steel was used in the construction of the house, but rather was built using conventional North American wood-frame construction, finished with cement stucco.

01 Exterior from treed forest below **02** Main floor plan **03** Exterior view from street **04** View of river valley from living area **05** Fireplace and living area hovering over the forest

Photos: Undine Pröhl

QUEENS UNIVERSITY - BEAMISH - MUNRO HALL

This 80,000 square foot facility for six faculties of engineering takes the form of a terraced central atrium flanked on three sides by innovative learning environments. The facility is instrumented as a working laboratory so students can see structural elements that are usually hidden, and monitor air quality, heating, lighting and cooling systems using specially designed software. It has received "4 Green Leafs" status in the BREEAM/Green Leaf program for eco-efficiency and an 2005 Award of Excellence during in the Innovation in Architecture category from the Royal Architectural Institute of Canada.

01 Main entrance **02** Terraced atrium classrooms **03** Site plan **04** Structure detail **05** Entrance by night

Photos: richardjohson.ca

CITY Kingston (ON)
COUNTRY Canada
REGION North America
TYPOLOGY Education
COMPLETION 2004
WEBSITE www.bharchitects.com
ARCHITECTS Bregman + Hamann Architects

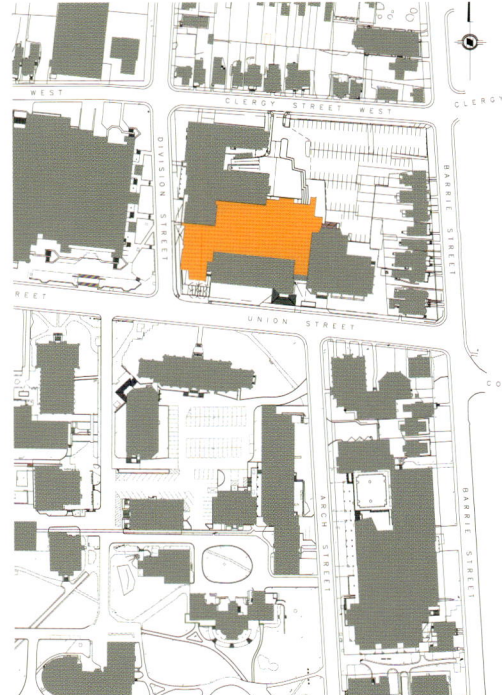

CITY Lake Simcoe (ON)

COUNTRY Canada

REGION North America

TYPOLOGY Living

COMPLETION 2004

WEBSITE www.taylorsmyth.com

ARCHITECTS Taylor Smyth Architects

SUNSET CABIN

This private retreat is a single 275-square-foot room, with all components including bed and storage cabinets built in. The floor of the cabin extends outside towards the lake to become a deck with access to an outdoor shower. Three walls of the cabin are floor to ceiling glass, wrapped by an exterior horizontal cedar screen for privacy and shade. A cutout in the screen is carefully located to provide spectacular views of the sunset, while at night, the effect is reversed and the cabin glows like a lantern. A green roof allows the cabin to blend into the landscape, due to its visibility from the main cottage at the top of the hill.

01 Site plan **02** View at dusk **03** View to lake side
04 Cedar screen for privacy and shade

Photos: Ben Rahn/A-Frame Inc., Taylor Smyth Architects (03, 04)

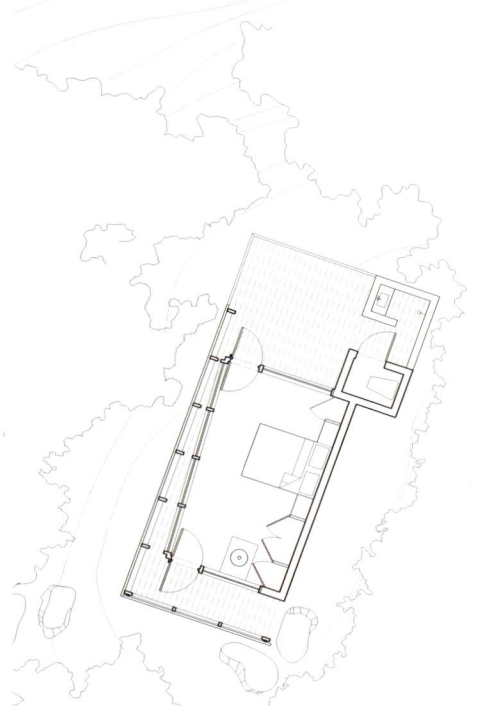

HOUSE ON LAKE ERIE

A lakeside house is connected to a guesthouse with a garage below. The progression from the garage to the lakeside opens both visually and through the use of materials from a u-shaped stone-walled court, enclosed on the fourth side by a hill, through the corrugated metal clad house, culminating in a façade of glass overlooking the lake. Wood, paneling, stone and glass are selectively featured on the exterior. Facing the court, the massing is unified and solid, while towards the lake, multiple stacked volumes open their floor-to-ceiling windows to take in the lake views.

01 Exterior view **02** Stone façade **03** Living room **04** View into two-story private library **05** Elevations

Photos: Dave Whitaker

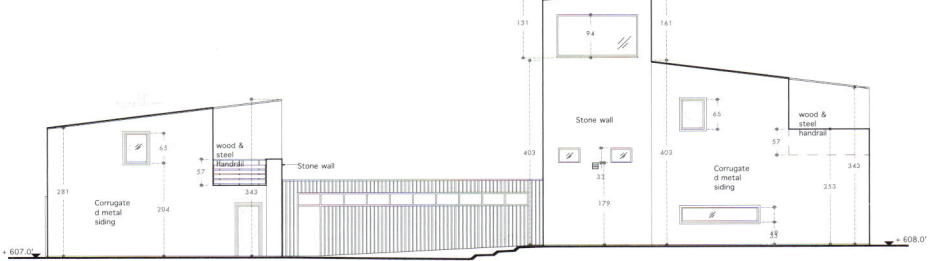
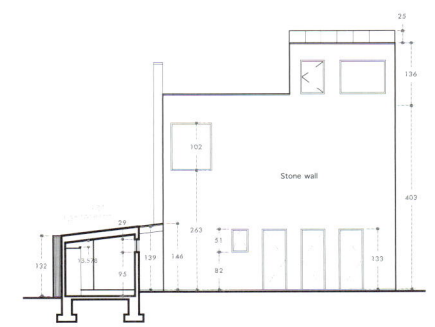
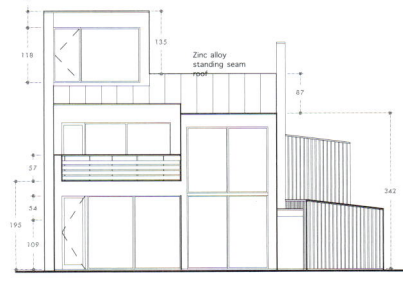

CITY Lake Erie (ON)
COUNTRY Canada
REGION North America
TYPOLOGY Living
COMPLETION 2004
WEBSITE www.efmdesign.com
ARCHITECTS EFM Design

CITY Lake Muskoka (ON)
COUNTRY Canada
REGION North America
TYPOLOGY Living
COMPLETION 1999
WEBSITE www.shim-sutcliffe.com
ARCHITECTS Shim-Sutcliffe Architects

MUSKOKA BOATHOUSE

Located on the southwestern shore of Lake Muskoka, north of Toronto, this boathouse consists of two indoor boat slips, one covered outdoor boat slip, storage for marine equipment, sleeping cabin with kitchenette, shower area, bedroom/sitting room, and outdoor porches. Surrounded by Pre-Cambrian granite rock formations of the Canadian Shield, the distinctly modern boathouse exists in a rich cultural landscape of ornate Victorian cottages, pioneer log cabins and custom wooden boats. This "sophisticated hut" in the wilderness attempts to strike a balance between modernism and the vernacular, building and nature, light and dark.

01 Outside alleyway **02** Wooden façade with storage for canoe **03** Section **04** View to the lake **05** Interior with fireplace

Photos: James Dow (01, 05), Ed Burtynsky (02, 04)

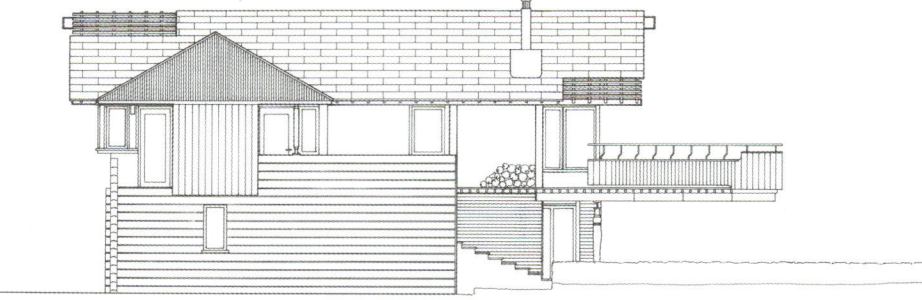

FOREMAN POINT COTTAGE

The two-level modern lakeside cottage has staggering levels in the direction of the waterfront, resulting in a split level of varying ceiling height. The ground floor, housing the guest suite and the living area, is flanked on two sides by an open deck and a screened porch. The two bedrooms are on the upper floor. Local materials were used in the construction of the house – Douglas fir and pre-finished pine and birch on the exterior, birch and slate on the interiors and cedar for the outdoor decks.

01 Exterior view **02** Interior **03** Rear view **04** Floor plan
05 Living space with fireplace

Photos: Jonathan Savoie

CITY Lake Muskoka (ON)
COUNTRY Canada
REGION North America
TYPOLOGY Living
COMPLETION 2005
WEBSITE www.altius.net
ARCHITECTS Altius Architecture (Trevor McIvor)

01

02

03

04

05

CITY: Mississauga (ON)
COUNTRY: Canada
REGION: North America
TYPOLOGY: Health
COMPLETION: 2005
WEBSITE: www.farrowpartnership.com
ARCHITECTS: Farrow Partnership Architects Inc.

THE CREDIT VALLEY HOSPITAL

The Carlo Fidani Peel Regional Cancer Centre and Ambulatory Centre, The Credit Valley Hospital Farrow Partnership Architects Inc. designed The Credit Valley Hospital's 320,000 square foot Cancer Care and Ambulatory Care facility, which includes features such as Complex Continuing Care, Rehabilitation, Maternal Child Care, Laboratory Services, and Emergency Room renovations. These recently completed renovations and additions are only phase one of a larger three-phase, $349 million dollar project, designed to serve the future health care needs for the people of Mississauga. The dramatic spaces and warm materials of the new facility promote humanistic healing practices among patients and staff.

01 Exterior view by night **02** Site plan **03** Glass façade **04** Wooden construction **05** Lobby

Photos: Shai Gil (01, 03), Peter Sellar, KLIK Photography

ABSOLUTE

The last two phases of the project were the product of an international design competition, in which the winning entry was submitted by MAD from Beijing, China. Burka Architects designed the structure, internal layout of the towers, the podium, spearheaded the approval process, and created the construction documents. The project occupies the most significant corner in Mississuaga, Ontario, and is regarded as a landmark design. The floorplans are designed to rotate as the buildings rise, creating a playful shape that changes from every angle, while public spaces provide a transition between the ground plane and the towers.

01 General view **02** Exterior view to towers **03** Aerial view **04** View by night

Renderings: Burka Varacalli Architects

CITY Mississuaga (ON)
COUNTRY Canada
REGION North America
TYPOLOGY Live-work
COMPLETION in progress
WEBSITE www.bvap.net
ARCHITECTS Burka Varacalli Architects

ITHQ – TOURISM INSTITUTE OF QUEBEC

The ITHQ – Tourisme Institute of Quebec, a much-maligned Montreal landmark, had been cited as the worst example of the architectural legacy of the seventies. The ITHQ renewal project involved bringing the building up to operational and technical standards, and updating its envelope, systems, and student-service facilities. The key to changing public perception of the building was to give it a "second skin." The result is a building reborn; what was once pallid, gray and impenetrable is now colorful, luminous and limpid; a change that mirrors the new life the ITHQ has brought to Quebec's hospitality industry.

01 New building's second skin **02** Façade structure **03** General view **04** Front view from street

Photos: Michel Tremblay, Michel Brunelle

CITY Montreal (QC)
COUNTRY Canada
REGION North America
TYPOLOGY Education
COMPLETION 2004
WEBSITE www.aedifica.com / www.lapointemagne.ca
ARCHITECTS AEdifica + Lapointe Magne

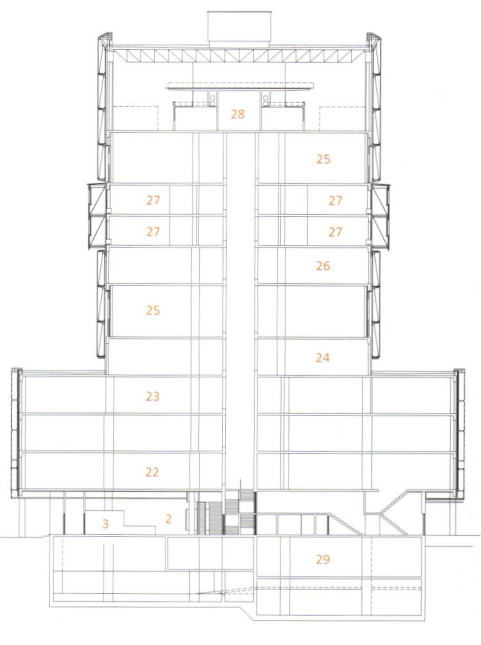

MARCHE D'ALIMENTATION ADONIS

Installed in Montréal since 1970 as a simple market, le Marché Adonis saw an important growth in recent years. Contrary to typical North American supermarkets where a systematic implantation of a predefined model spreads around the landscape of our cities and its suburbia, le Marché Adonis is uniquely designed to blend harmoniously in the surrounding urban fabric. This architecture explores the traditional market through its inclined roof floating on top of the voluminous market space, and by its open facades that assures a maximum transparency and communication between the exterior and the interior.

01 Exterior view by night **02** Floor plan **03** Stairs to administration office **04** Market hall **05** Coffe-shop

Photos: Robert Etchevenny

CITY Montreal (QC)
COUNTRY Canada
REGION North America
TYPOLOGY Commercial
COMPLETION 2005
WEBSITE www.boutrospratte.com
ARCHITECTS Boutros + Pratte

01

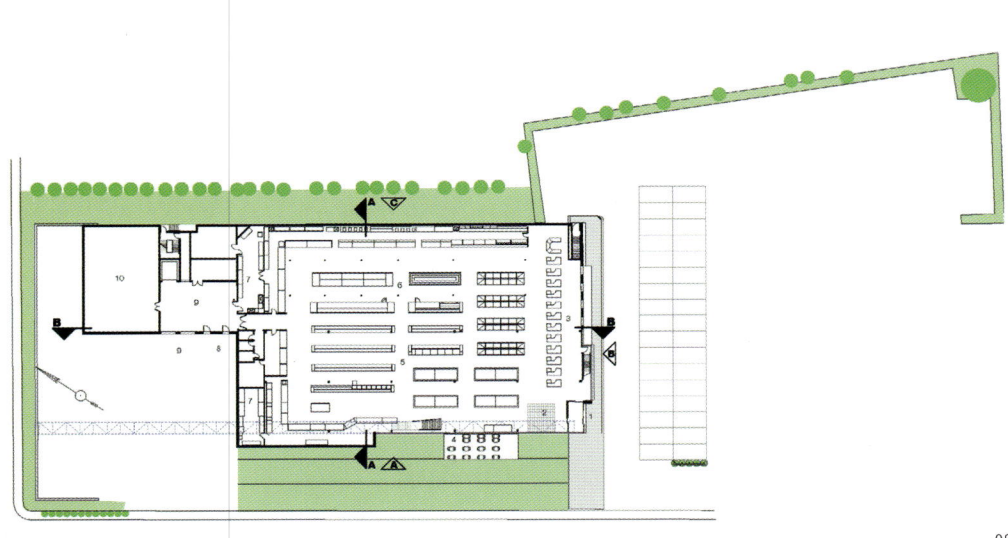
02

03

04

05

CITY Montreal (QC)
COUNTRY Canada
REGION North America
TYPOLOGY Living
COMPLETION 2006
WEBSITE www.brieregilbert.com
ARCHITECTS Brière, Gilbert + associés architectes

'COOPÉRATIVE D'HABITATION AU PIED DU COURANT'

The approach for this housing complex was inscribed in a logical interrelation between architecture and urban design. The project qualifies the interactions between each of its four site limits and the surroundings by an 'L' shape building with voids, volumes and color. The conceptual intentions were closely linked with the quality of social interaction as well as a future relationship with its urban and social environment. All apartments have views front and back and take advantage of natural lighting. Each kitchen, living room, and dining room is in relation with an exterior terrace with access to the common courtyard.

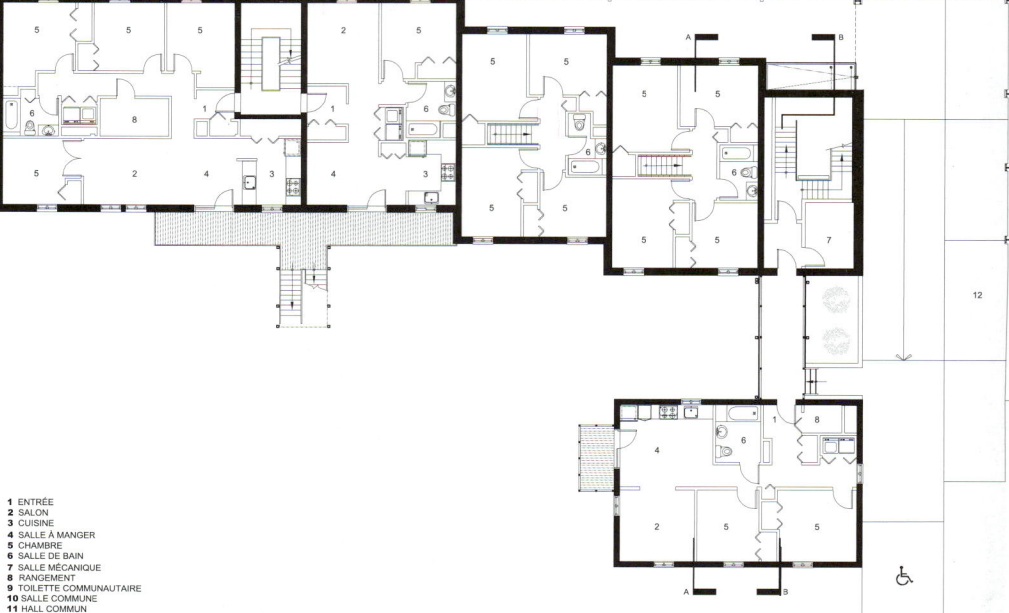

01 Exterior view to garden **02** Voids, volumes and colors
03 Common courtyard **04** Main floor plan

Photos: Christian Perreault

1 ENTRÉE
2 SALON
3 CUISINE
4 SALLE À MANGER
5 CHAMBRE
6 SALLE DE BAIN
7 SALLE MÉCANIQUE
8 RANGEMENT
9 TOILETTE COMMUNAUTAIRE
10 SALLE COMMUNE
11 HALL COMMUN
12 STATIONNEMENTS

NORMAND MAURICE BUILDING

The Normand Maurice Building is an office headquarters, warehouse and armory storage for the Department of National Defense, the Royal Canadian Mounted Police, Canada Customs and several other public bodies. Using an integrated design team, synergies between mechanical, electrical and other building systems were exploited, resulting in operating costs 35% lower than comparable facilities. The integration of sustainable strategies resulted in reduced CO_2 emissions, which came out to approximately 800 tones less per annum. For its achievement, the building is expected to receive the LEED Gold Certification.

01, 02 Exterior view by night **03** Sections **04** Rooftop
05 Front façade **06** Green roofs and louvers

Joint venture architects: ABCP Architecture & Urbanisme and Beauchamp-Bourbeau Architectes

Photos: Nic Lehoux

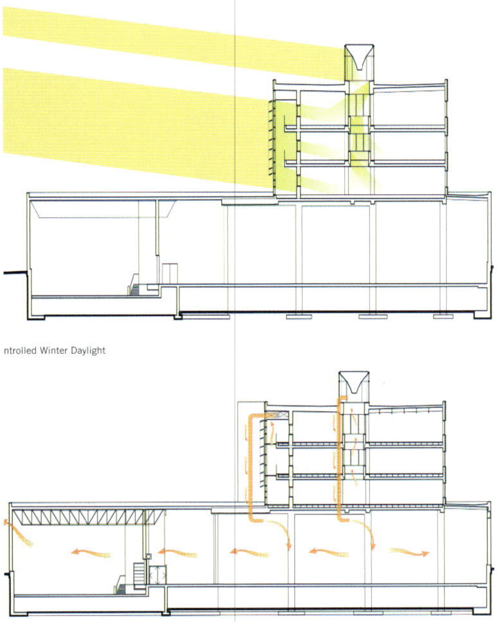

CITY Montreal (QC)
COUNTRY Canada
REGION North America
TYPOLOGY Office
COMPLETION 2006
WEBSITE www.busbyperkinswill.ca
ARCHITECTS Busby Perkins + Will Architects Co.

115 STUDIOS POUR LE CIRQUE DE SOLEIL

Performers from all around the world converge to the Cirque du Soleil headquarters in Montréal for a short period of training before touring with the company. This project consists of 115 studios, complemented with all the services required. The project explores the notion of dynamic equilibrium in the same way that jugglers, contortionnists, and trapezists play with the weight of things to defy gravity. Its expression of stacked containers reflects the transient nature of the building's nomadic occupants as well as the tension existing between the individual and the collective in the company.

01, 02 Stacked modules **03** Atrium **04** Sections **05** Interlocking spaces

Photos: Steve Montpetit

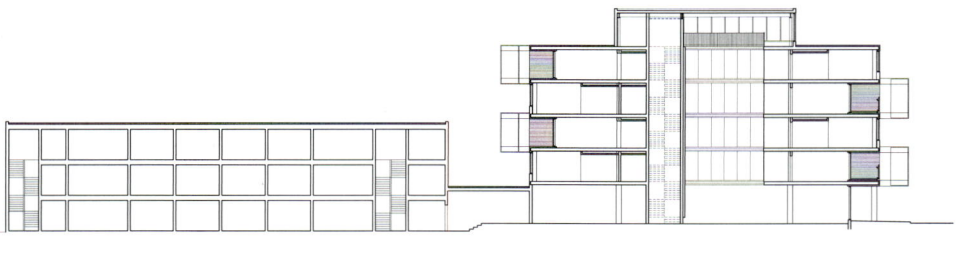

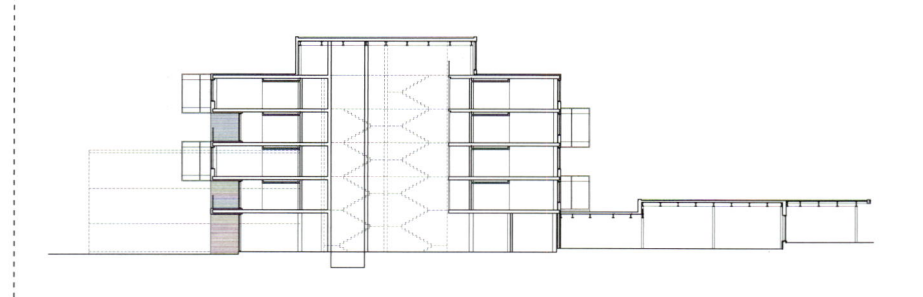

NEW THEATER – DAWSON COLLEGE

The project is an addition to the historic house of the Congrégation de Notre-Dame in Montréal where Dawson College moved in 1988, and was driven by the need to provide its theatre and photography departments with more adequate facilities. The project occupies the southeastern courtyard of this H shaped building over new photo labs and studios laid underground. It acts as an object within a field of tension, an induction copper coil that houses a small theatre linked horizontally to the existing building by a glazed café area. The exterior is clad in copper that will age naturally like the adjacent roofs.

01 Main entrance **02** Classrooms **03** Cafeteria **04** Site plan **05** Auditorium

Photos: Steve Montpetit

CITY Montreal (QC)

COUNTRY Canada

REGION North America

TYPOLOGY Culture

COMPLETION 2007

WEBSITE www.arch-fabg.com

ARCHITECTS Les Architectes FABG

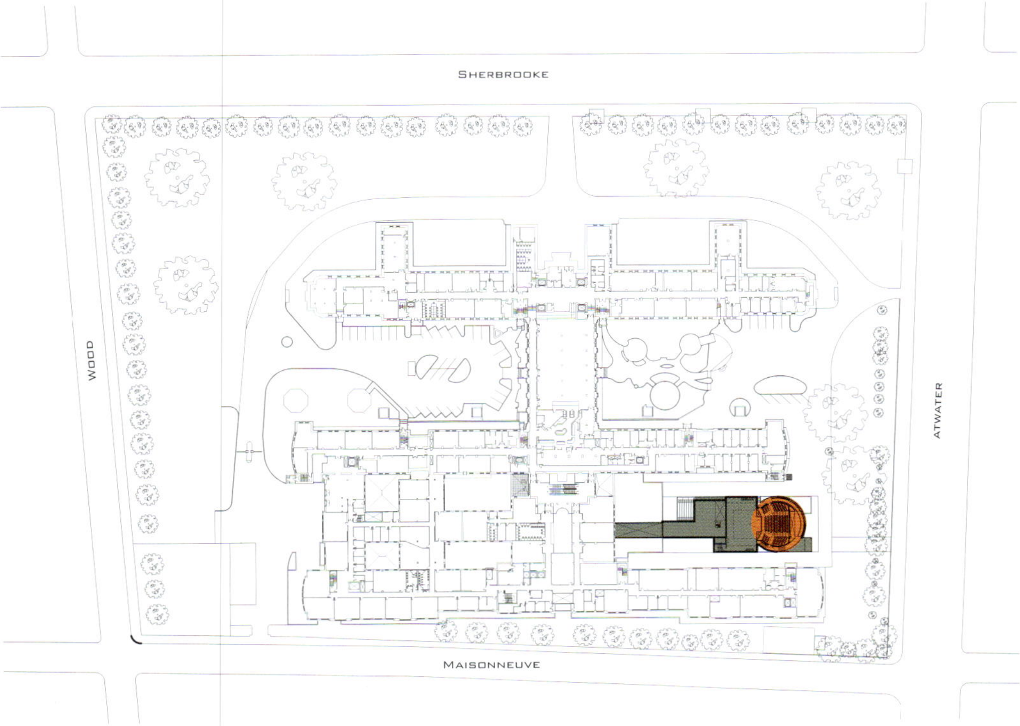

CITY	Montreal (QC)
COUNTRY	Canada
REGION	North America
TYPOLOGY	Culture
COMPLETION	2004
WEBSITE	www.halingberg.com
ARCHITECTS	Les architectes Tétrault, Dubuc, Saia Barbarese Topouzanov architectes, Hal Ingberg architecte (independant architectural consultant)

PALAIS DES CONGRÈS, MONTRÉAL

Hovering above the gash created by an urban expressway, the original Palais des Congrès de Montreal constituted an important psychological barrier separating Old Montreal from the modern city. The new and innovative project repairs the damaged urban tissue while grafting itself onto the four pre-exiting buildings. This is done in such a way as to always retain an equivalence of height with respect to this context. Therefore, in spite of its many dramatic characteristics, the surface profile of the new Palais des Congrès is highly contextual, and oddly enough, almost chameleon-like.

01 Projection of colored light onto stainless steel wall
02 Entrance hall **03** Canopy detail at side of main entrance
04 Main façade

Photos: Hal Ingberg

OPUS HOTEL

Opus Hotel Montreal is a unique boutique hotel blending contemporary style and design with a nod to the historic. The original avant-garde structure, built in 1914 by Joseph-Arthur Godin, was the first poured concrete building in North America. Created in an Art Nouveau style, the building featured little ornamentation, saved for a signature curving staircase. This simplicity of design is reflected in the unmistakably modern concrete addition, created by architect Dan Hanganu of Montreal and interior designer Yabu Pushelberg of New York, both winners of the prestigious 'Platinum Circle Award'.

01 General view by night **02** Lounge **03** Presidential suite **04** Interior room

Photos: Courtesy Opus Hotel

CITY
Montreal (QC)

COUNTRY
Canada

REGION
North America

TYPOLOGY
Hospitality

COMPLETION
2007

WEBSITE
www.hanganu.com

ARCHITECTS
Dan Hanganu
(interior designer:
Yabu Pushelberg)

REGION North America
COUNTRY Canada
CITY Montreal (QC)
TYPOLOGY Education
COMPLETION 2004
WEBSITE www.msdl.ca
ARCHITECTS Menkes Shooner Dagenais LeTournex Architects (in joint venture with Saucier and Perrotte Architects)

SCHULICH PAVILION OF THE MCGILL UNIVERSITY FACULTY OF MUSIC

The new pavilion for the McGill Faculty of Music is located at the eastern edge of the campus. It houses a multimedia performance and practice space large enough to accommodate a full symphony orchestra and choir, which is the heart of the program. The building is outfitted with recording studios exhibiting the latest technology, a practice room for operas, a media and technology space, a recital hall, and laboratories for interdisciplinary research on music. Built around the concept of box within a box, the program's technical challenges were met through a four level volume, achieving perfect acoustics.

01 Music library **02** Entrance **03** Recital hall **04** Four level volume façade **05** Longitudinal building section

Photos: Marc Cramer

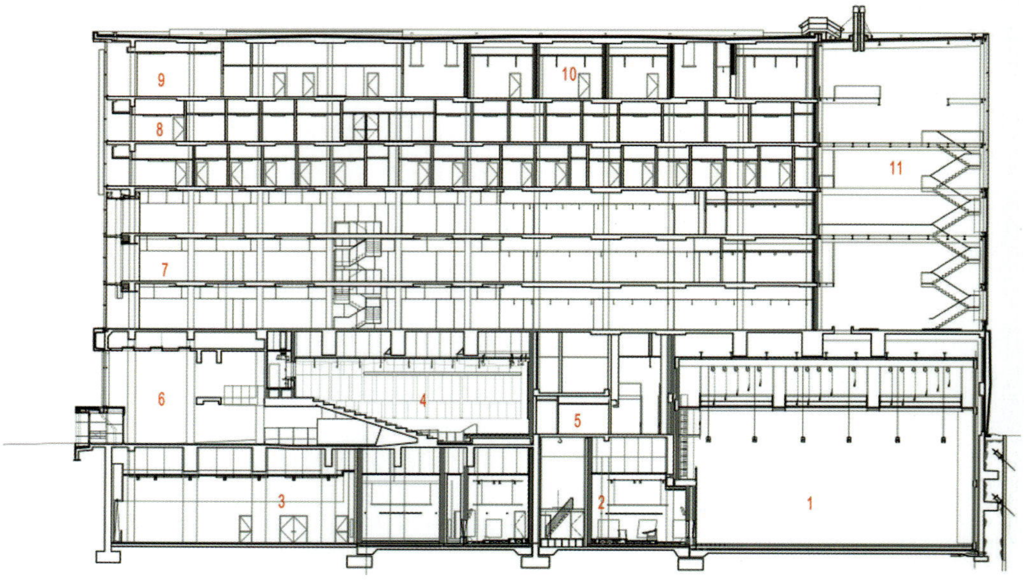

LASSONDE PAVILIONS, ÉCOLE POLYTECHNIQUE

Located on the the University of Montreal Campus and bordering the Polytechnic school of engineering, this building intended to illustrate by example an environmentally responsible construction. Several amphitheatre type classrooms were designed including eight large rooms with a capacity of over 100, and seven rooms with a capacity of 65 to 75. Research groups in diverse disciplines (nano-robotics, telecommunications, biomedical automations, robotics, micro-electronics, micro-waves and spatial electronics) have access to laboratories equipped with specialized furniture and cutting edge technology.

01 Terrace from laboratories **02** Circulation passages **03** West elevation **04** View by night into classrooms and laboratories

Architects in consortium: Saia Barbarese Topouzanov Architectes / Desnoyers Mercure & associés

Photos: Guy Lavigueur (01, 04), Marc Cramer

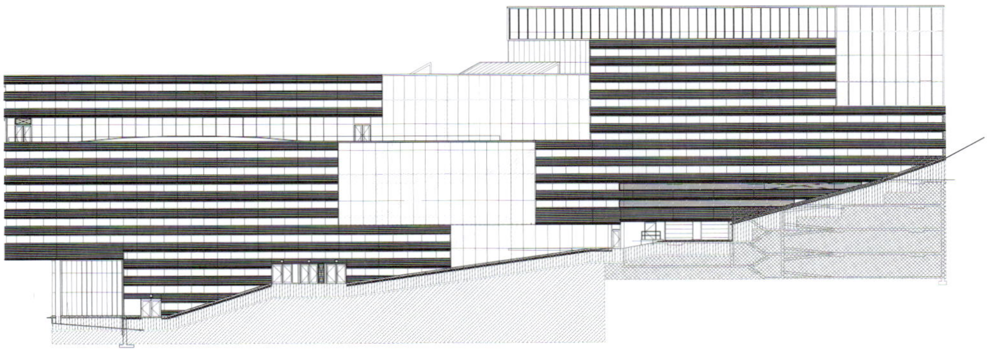

CITY Montreal (QC)
COUNTRY Canada
REGION North America
TYPOLOGY Education
COMPLETION –
WEBSITE www.msdl.ca
ARCHITECTS Menkes Shooner Dagenais Le Tournex Architects

CITY
Montreal (QC)

COUNTRY
Canada

REGION
North America

TYPOLOGY
Education

COMPLETION
2006

WEBSITE
www.sbt.qc.ca

ARCHITECTS
Saia Barbarese Topouzanov architectes (in consortium with Tétreault Parent Languedoc et associés)

MASTERPLAN, PIERRE DANSEREAU SCIENCE COMPLEX, UNIVERSITY OF QUÉBEC IN MONTREAL (UQAM)

Bounded by four streets in Montreal's downtown core, the UQAM Science complex occupies a distinctive urban block within the city's vibrant festival district. A field of green enclosed by buildings all around, evolves into a series of structures interlaced by courtyards, gardens and pathways. The master plan reveals a renewed notion of campus as a sanctuary for learning, while rejuvenating its spirit by restoring and uniting old structures in harmony with three new ones. The plan is woven into its urban fabric by extending adjacent streets, where careful massing brings light into the courtyards.

01 Exterior view **02** Master plan **03** Garden elevation **04** Exterior view entrance

Photos: Fred Saia (01), Marc Cramer (03), Alain Laforest (04)

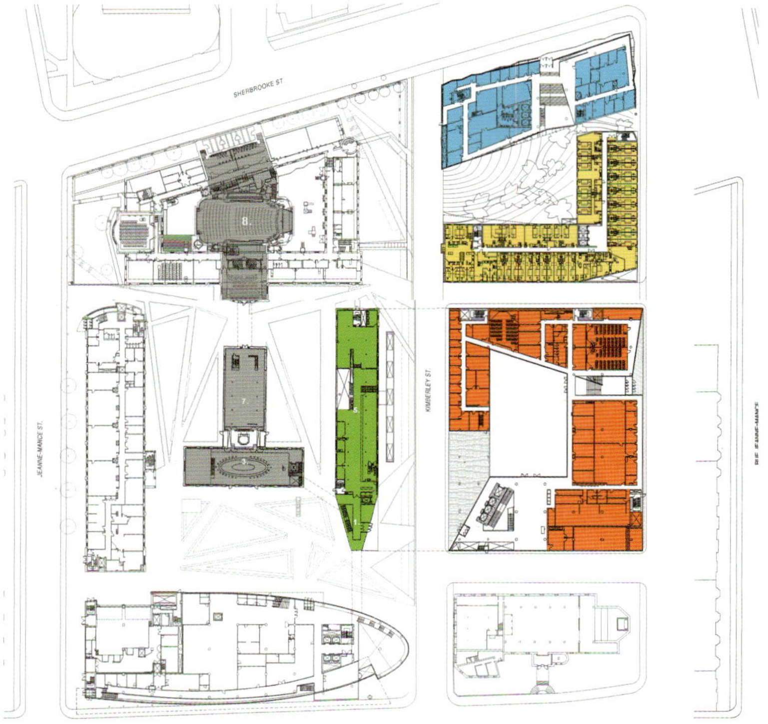

ÉCOLE PRIMAIRE MONT-JÉSUS-MARIE

Situated behind a convent, this school building took form in a garden of nearly two hundred trees. This setting and its urban context dictated the plan and orientation of the building and its numerous playgrounds. The concern for harmonizing the school with the landscape and the community further inspired its design, which embraces principles of green architecture. The classrooms are clustered around courtyards creating spaces for learning and play, which are sheltered from the elements and have exceptional views. The Mont-Jésus-Marie elementary school has brought new life to a once forgotten garden.

01 Courtyard **02** View into library **03** Gymnasium and auditorium **04** Ground floor plan **05** Main entrance

Photos: Steve Montpetit

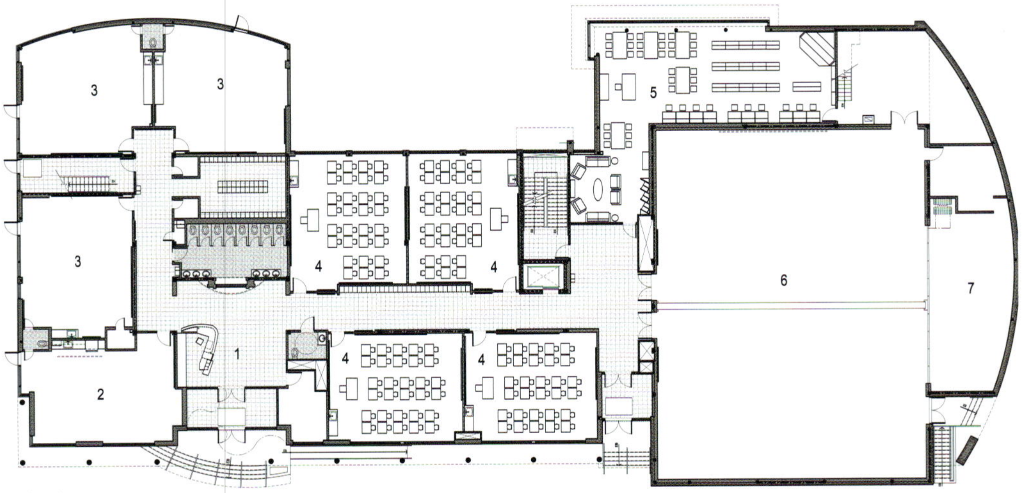

CITY Montreal (QC)
COUNTRY Canada
REGION North America
TYPOLOGY Education
COMPLETION 2005
WEBSITE –
ARCHITECTS Consortium Atelier d'Architecture Saroli Palumbo et Bergeron Thouin

BIOLOGICAL SCIENCES BUILDING, UNIVERSITY OF QUÉBEC IN MONTREAL (UQAM)

A complex site wrapped by both large-scale and residential projects, this project volumetrically acknowledges its context while reinforcing a distinct sense of "campus". As part of the UQAM Science Complex, this state-of-the-art pavilion includes teaching and research facilities in addition to a business incubator component. The pavilion adopted green construction principles including: rehabilitating a vacant city lot by using recycled or low volatile organic compound materials, storing rainwater for toilets and gardening, disposing of construction site waste, selection of a reflective energy efficient roof, and heat recovery.

01 Buff-colored and dark grey brick façades **02** Translucent and transparent tinted glass **03** Entrance **04** DNA patterns façade

Photos: Marc Cramer

CITY Montreal (QC)
COUNTRY Canada
REGION North America
TYPOLOGY Education
COMPLETION 2006
WEBSITE www.sbt.qc.ca
ARCHITECTS Saia Barbarese Topouzanov architectes (in consortium with Tétreault Parent Languedoc et associés)

CDP CAPITAL CENTRE

A major urban renewal operation was initiated when the Caisse de dépôt et placement du Québec decided to relocate all its Montreal subsidiaries under one roof within the new international district. It became the area's development catalyst with 728,469 square feet of office and commercial space. This horizontal skyscraper restores vital street and pedestrian connections, reweaving the urban fabric. This civic gesture encompasses numerous innovations in the fields of bio-climatic and energy efficiency, offering a better control of the environment, and a pioneering example of sustainable development.

01 Night view across Place Riopelle **02** Atrium view to the East **03** Bio-climatic principles section diagram **04** Atrium view to the West

Photos: Stéphane Poulin, Alain Laforest (02)

CITY
Montreal (QC)

COUNTRY
Canada

REGION
North America

TYPOLOGY
Office-commercial

COMPLETION
2003

WEBSITE
www.daoustlestage.com

ARCHITECTS
Gauthier Daoust Lestage inc. / Faucher Aubertin Brodeur Gauthier / Lemay et Associés

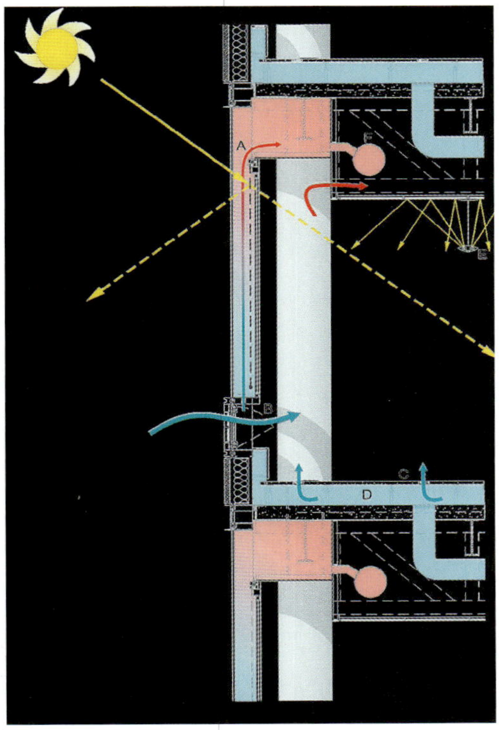

CITY Montreal (QC)
COUNTRY Canada
REGION North America
TYPOLOGY Education
COMPLETION 2006
WEBSITE www.sbt.qc.ca
ARCHITECTS Saia Barbarese Topouzanov architectes (in consortium with Tétreault Parent Languedoc et associés)

SCIENCE HEART, UNIVERSITY OF QUÉBEC IN MONTREAL (UQAM)

The "Science Heart" project features a foundry, a boiler room, and industrial workshops of the former École Technique. In turn with the renovation of the Sherbrooke Pavilion amphitheatre, these elements are integral components of the "Cœur de Sciences", and the sector in its entirety is primarily dedicated to the exchange and promotion of scientific knowledge. Located in the center of the campus, this core, condensed with an industrial heritage, is celebrated by a translation into the contemporary scientific domain. This area's program includes a library, café/bar, conference centre, reception/exhibition area, and multimedia space.

01 Library with reading spaces second floor 02 View into amphitheatre 03 Library entry hall 04 Silk-screened glass façade

Photos: Marc Cramer (01, 03), Alain Laforest (02), Fred Saia (04)

MCGILL UNIVERSITY – THE MONTREAL GENOMICS AND PROTEOMICS CENTER

The new pavilion for the McGill University Faculty of Music is located at the eastern edge of the campus. It houses a multimedia performance and practice space large enough to accommodate a full symphony orchestra and choir, which is the heart of the program. The building is outfitted with recording studios exhibiting the latest technology, a practice room for operas, a media and technology space, a recital hall, and laboratories for interdisciplinary research on music. Built around the concept of box within a box, the program's technical challenges were met through a four level volume, achieving perfect acoustics.

01 Street side view **02** Entrance view **03** Staircase
04 Interior **05** Elevation

Architects in joint venture: Kuwabara Payne McKenna Blumberg Architects (KPMB)

Photos: Courtesy Fichten Soiferman Architects

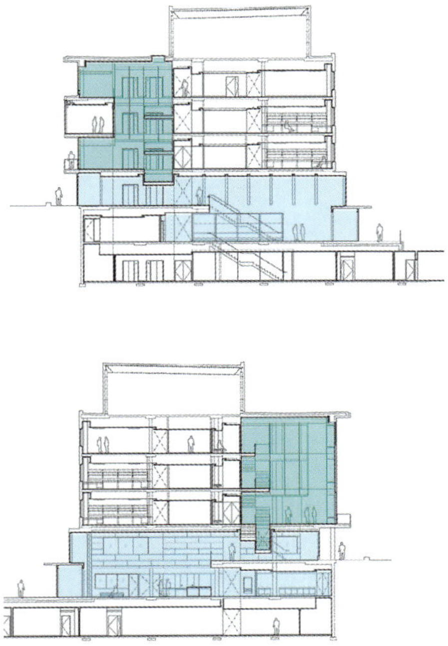

CITY Montreal (QC)
COUNTRY Canada
REGION North America
TYPOLOGY Education
COMPLETION 2003
WEBSITE www.fsa-arch.qc.ca
ARCHITECTS Fichten Soiferman Architects

CITY: Montreal (QC)
COUNTRY: Canada
REGION: North America
TYPOLOGY: Transportation
COMPLETION: 2009
WEBSITE: http://arcoparchitects.com
ARCHITECTS: Arcop Architects

RENOVATION AND EXPANSION OF PIERRE-ELLIOTT-TRUDEAU - MONTREAL INTERNATIONAL AIRPORT

The PCJA consortium was formed by four Montreal firms who participated in all phases and provided full services including space programming, concept design, and on-site supervision. The project entailed the expansion and re-planning of the existing airport in order to bring it to international standards and meet the traffic needs for 2009. A large portion of the building had to be renovated and brought up to code, as the existing facilities were at the core of the installations. Some of the major projects included the Northeast domestic sector, baggage rooms, international and transborder jetties, and public arrival halls.

01 Ceiling detail **02** Exterior view **03** Interior view **04** Exterior view **05** Interior detail

Photos: Marc Cramer

CENTRE COMMUNAUTAIRE INTERGÉNÉRATIONNEL D'OUTREMONT

The formal, spatial, and organizational concept was a response focused on integrating the building with its context of joining old and new. The L-shaped extension wraps around two of the arena's blind façades, assuming its place in the urban fabric by filling out the structure's footprint and enhancing its volume. Inside, it meets the existing arena via an interstice, showcasing the arena through glass panes set into its reconstructed west wall. The programs facilities include athletic, cultural and artistic activity rooms, a large hall for 300 people, and the offices of the borough's recreational services department.

01 General view **02** Façade and glass panes **03** Athletic room **04** Corridor **05** Site plan

Photos: François Bastien

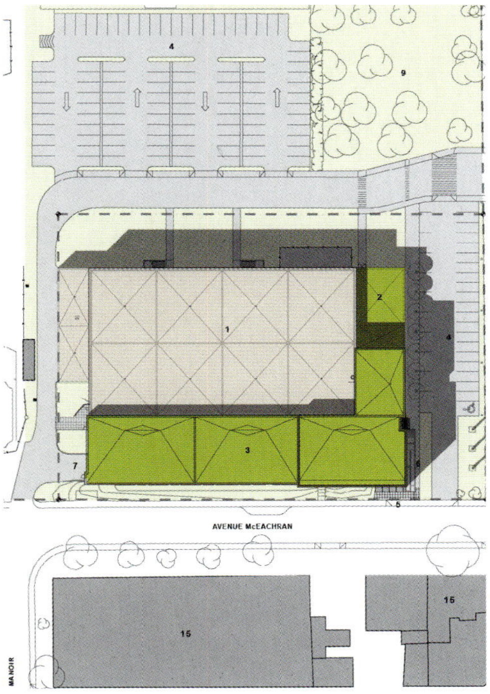

CITY Montreal (QC) (Outremont)

COUNTRY Canada

REGION North America

TYPOLOGY Cultural

COMPLETION 2006

WEBSITE www.cardinramirez.com

ARCHITECTS Cardin+Ramirez & Associés Architectes

CITY Naramata (BC)
COUNTRY Canada
REGION North America
TYPOLOGY Living
COMPLETION 2004
WEBSITE www.allenmaurer.com
ARCHITECTS Allen + Maurer Architects

MAURER HOUSE AND STUDIO

Maurer House and Studio, located above Okanagan Lake in Western Canada, is composed of four small pavilions. Surrounded by existing trees, the buildings form a private, tranquil garden where native grassland thrives. To reduce heat gain in summer and make air conditioning unnecessary the design was guided by the principle "form follows physics": Simple shed roofs, large overhangs, metal cladding, extensive glazing and large sliding doors allow the house to be flooded with daylight and fresh air.

01 View into the pavillions **02** Shed roofs with large overhangs **03** Metal cladding and sliding doors **04** Site plan **05** Dining room

Photos: Florian Maurer, Stuart Bish (02)

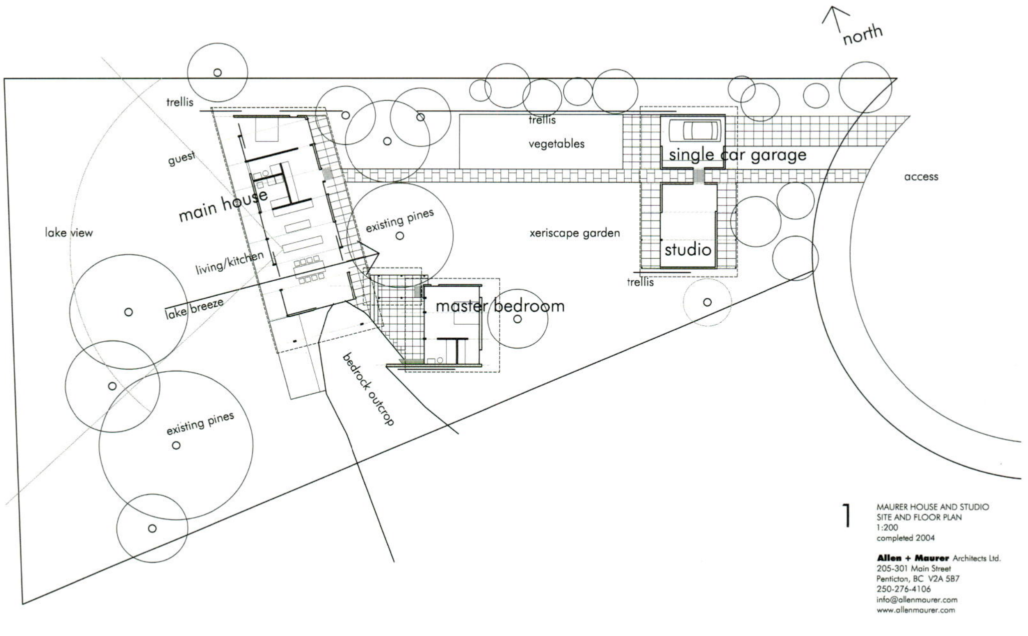

MINTON HILL HOUSE

Located in Quebec's Eastern Townships, the Minton Hill House strikes a delicate balance between the engaging of its panoramic hilltop position and the provision of a protective domestic environment. Created in cedar, slate and glass, the house is at once an environmental filter, a view-framing device, and a series of interior and exterior gardens and courts. Detached from the grounded elements of the house, the floating roof is the project's defining symbol – it celebrates the house's hilltop position with a spread-wing profile that gently separates land and sky.

01 Cedar, slate and glass façade **02** Ground floor plan
03 Floating roof and exterior gardens **04** Living space

Photos: Marc Cramer

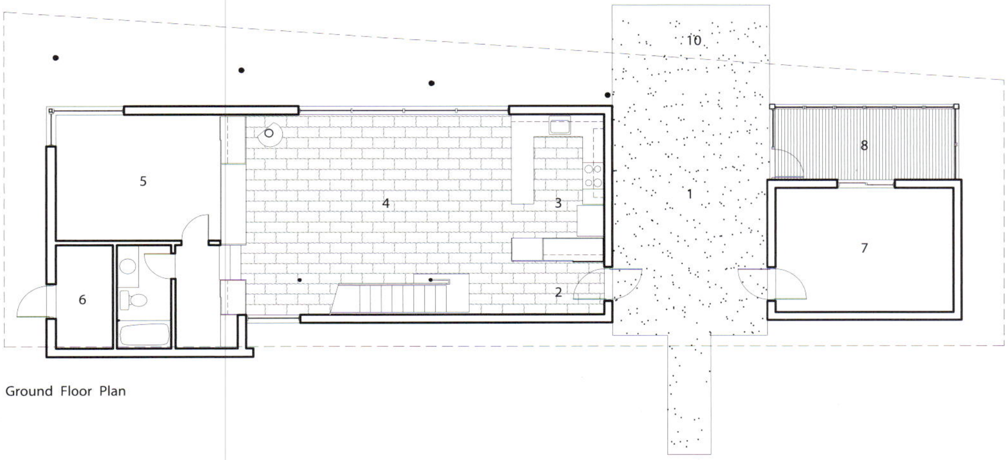

Ground Floor Plan

CITY North Hatley (QC)
COUNTRY Canada
REGION North America
TYPOLOGY Living
COMPLETION 2004
WEBSITE www.affleck-delariva.ca
ARCHITECTS Affleck + de la Riva Architects

REGION North America | **COUNTRY** Canada | **CITY** Osoyoos (BC)
TYPOLOGY Culture | **COMPLETION** 2006 | **WEBSITE** www.hbbharc.com | **ARCHITECTS** Hotson Bakker Boniface Haden architects + urbanistes

NK'MIP DESERT CULTURAL CENTRE

Located in the most endangered landscape in Canada, the design is a specific response to the building's unique context – the spectacular Canadian desert found south of the Okanagan Valley in British Columbia. This 1,600-acre parcel of land, belonging to the Osoyoos Indian Band, features indoor/outdoor exhibits that honor the Band's cultural history. The desert landscape flows over the building's green roof and is held back by the largest rammed-earth wall in North America. Constructed from local soils mixed with concrete, the wall retains warmth in the winter and allows for substantial thermal mass cooling during the summer.

01 Building's context in desert **02** Wall materials: local soils mixed with concrete **03** Site plan **04** Exterior exhibit of the Osoyoos Indian Band wigwam

Photos: Nic Lehoux

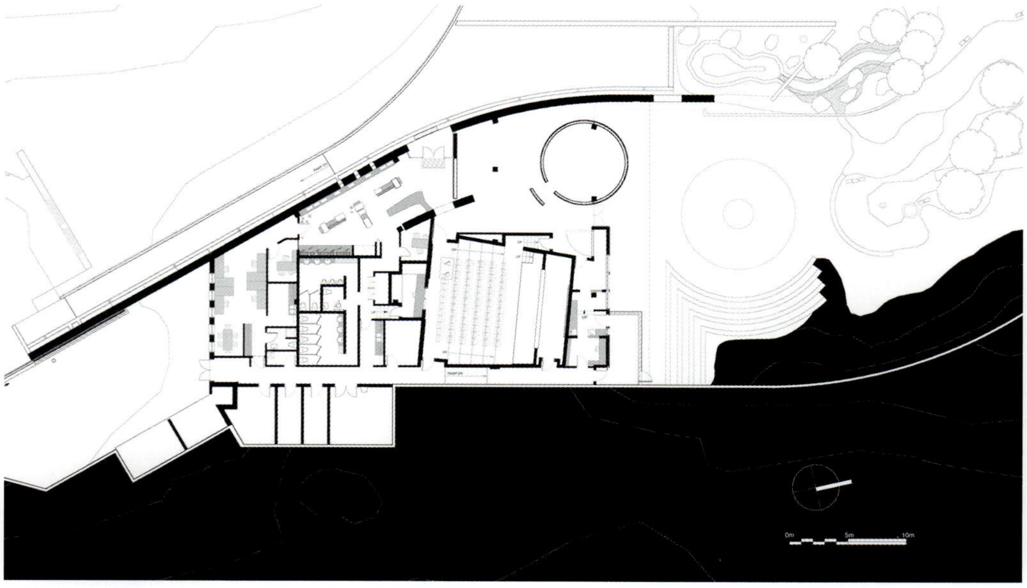

CANADA AVIATION MUSEUM

The Museum expansion project includes the addition of an aircraft storage facility and library/administration facility to the existing building. The site is organized at three different scales to reveal the museum complex and enhance visitor experience. The architectural language is simple and bold, creating a clear and identifiable symbol of the power and grace of flight. The gently curved and sloping building forms unify the new complex, while the simple modulated, reflective metal skin contrasts with the muted colors of the surroundings, dramatically increasing visibility from the parkways.

01 General view 02 Metal skin 03 Museum view into parkways
04 Site plan 05 Exhibition space 06 Exterior building angle

Photos: Marc Cramer

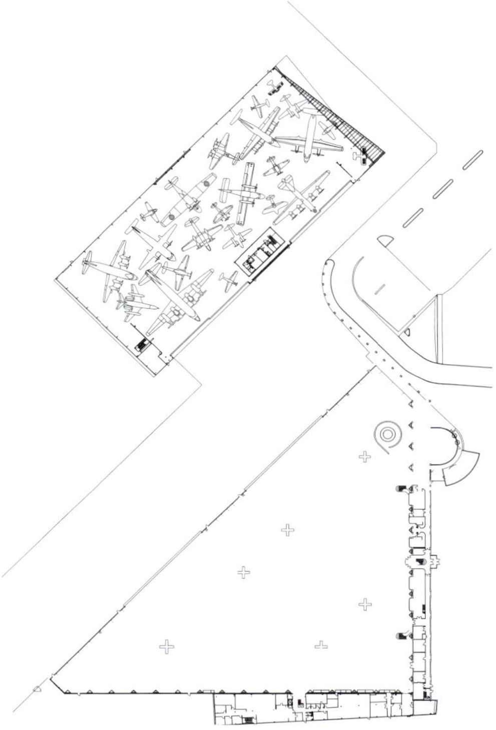

CITY: Ottawa (ON)
COUNTRY: Canada
REGION: North America
TYPOLOGY: Culture
COMPLETION: 2004
WEBSITE: www.arcop.com
ARCHITECTS: The ARCOP Group

CITY Ottawa (ON)

COUNTRY Canada

REGION North America

TYPOLOGY Culture

COMPLETION 2005

WEBSITE www.mtarch.com

ARCHITECTS Moriyama & Teshima Architects (in joint venture with Griffiths Rankin Cook Architects)

CANADIAN WAR MUSEUM

Regeneration embodies the sequences of devastation, rebirth and adaptation. War destroys nature, yet it regenerates as the power of life prevails: a process that rekindles faith and courage. The New Canadian War Museum emerges from the bank of the Ottawa River, rising eastward to engage the cityscape and pay homage to the Parliamentary Precinct. The overall expression of the building is horizontal, with a rooftop of wild grasses. It expresses the sublime strength of the Canadian landscape, the ambiguities of war and sacrifice, and that intangible quality that is integral to our identity as Canadians.

01 Museum exterior view **02** Lobby **03** Indoor sky-lit court **04** Memorial space **05** Floor plans

Photos: Tom Arban Photography

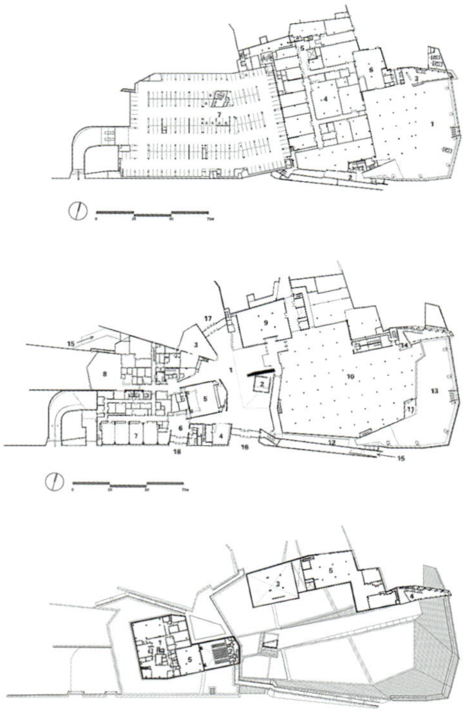

LANGUAGE TECHNOLOGIES RESEARCH CENTRE (LTRC) UNIVERSITY OF QUEBEC IN OUTAOUAIS (UQO)

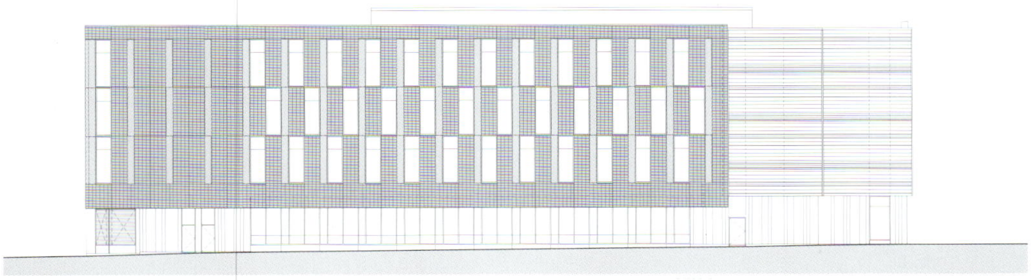

This new pavilion of the University of Quebec in Outaouais constitutes, by its situation, a frontier between the cemetery and the existing university buildings. Dedicated to research, this four-story building includes offices, laboratories, conference rooms, a general-purpose room, a library with a resource centre, and a café. The building is designed around the organization of a voluntarily simple circulation axis, punctuated by external vistas. External space thus marks users' movements, while the atrium is skirted by the main circulation axis, which is modulated by sights crossing the offices and the vertical garden.

01 Exterior view **02** Garden area **03** East elevation **04** North elevation **05** Detail of window and façade **06** Indoor sky-lit corridor

Architects in collaboration: Fortin Corriveau Salvail Architecture + Design

Photos: Michel Brunelle

CITY Outaouais (QC)
COUNTRY Canada
REGION North America
TYPOLOGY Education
COMPLETION –
WEBSITE www.msdl.ca
ARCHITECTS Menkes Shooner Dagenais LeTournex Architects

CITY: Peterborough (ON)
COUNTRY: Canada
REGION: North America
TYPOLOGY: Education
COMPLETION: 2005
WEBSITE: www.teeplearch.com
ARCHITECTS: Teeple Architects

TRENT UNIVERSITY CHEMICAL SCIENCES BUILDING

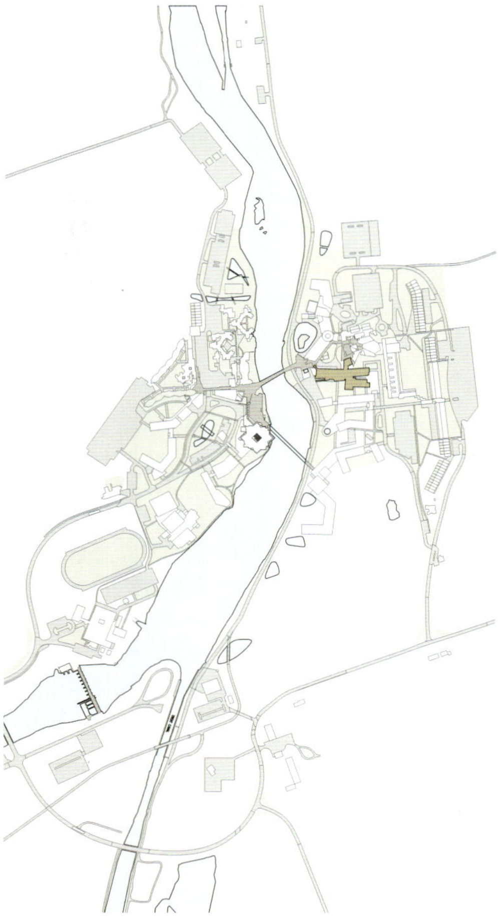

The science centre is conceived as a promenade, both architectural and natural that brings the users into repeated contact with the Otonabee River – the central focus of Ron Thom's Trent University campus. The promenade weaves between the existing Science Centre Precinct and its +15 circulation system, presenting views of Trent's unique river landscape to students as they move through the campus and building. The river is the constant reference point, while the project provides a highly regularized, flexible system of teaching labs that can be combined, as required, into various research projects. .

01 Night view **02** Site plan **03** Promenade linking ground floor to existing science precinct **04** Building in direction towards river

Photos: Tom Arban, Shai Gil

BIRD STUDIES CANADA HEADQUARTERS

Located next to a World Biosphere Reserve, the Bird Studies Canada Headquarters has a distinct presence without disturbing the site's natural heritage. Two elemental wood building forms create a backdrop for the existing farmhouse and courtyard. Clad in dark cedar siding, the buildings are neutral objects, their appearance changing with the light and weather. The two buildings are connected by a glazed entry that functions as an entry to the headquarters, a gateway to the larger property and as a frame to views of the adjacent wetlands.

01 Rear view **02** Entry **03** Site plan **04** Exterior view by night **05** Lecture hall

Photos: Steven Evans Photography

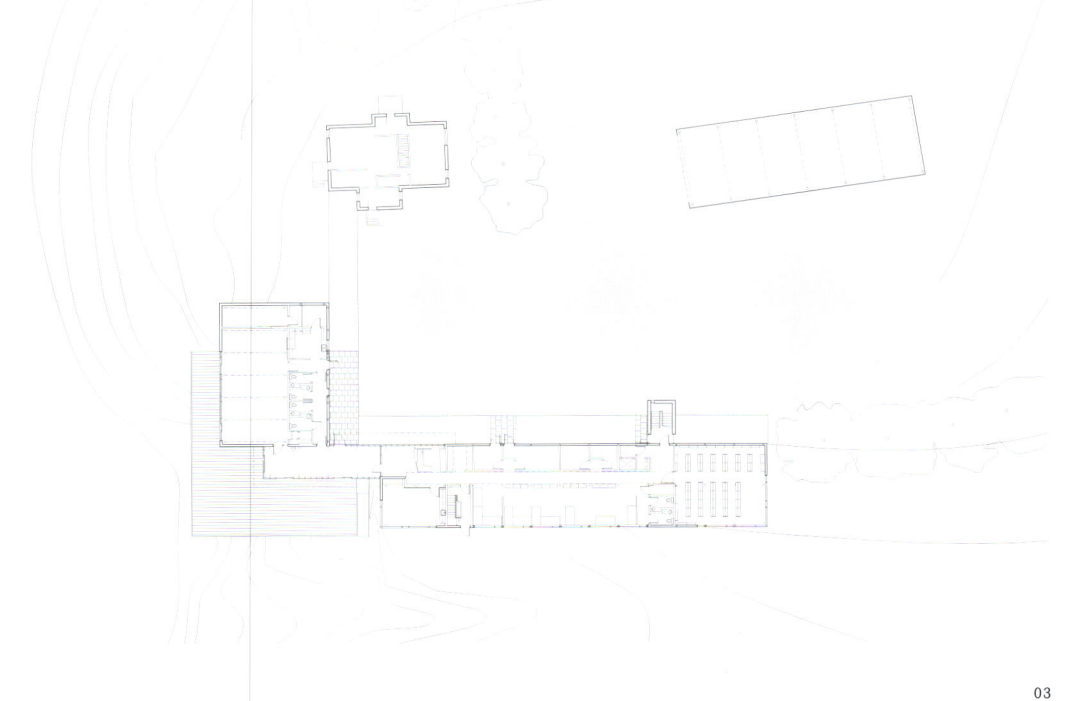

CITY Port Rowan (ON)
COUNTRY Canada
REGION North America
TYPOLOGY Education-office
COMPLETION 2003
WEBSITE www.montgomerysisam.com
ARCHITECTS Montgomery Sisam Architects Inc.

CITY: Pointe-au-baril
COUNTRY: Canada
REGION: North America
TYPOLOGY: Living
COMPLETION: 2007
WEBSITE: www.mos-office.net
ARCHITECTS: MOS: michael meredith, hilary sample

FLOATING BOATHOUSE

This project intersects a vernacular house typology with the site-specific conditions of this unique place: an island on Lake Huron. The location on the Great Lakes imposed complexities to the house's fabrication and construction, as well as its relationship to the site. Annual cyclical change related to the change of seasons, compounded with escalating global environmental trends, cause Lake Huron's water levels to vary drastically from month-to-month, year-to-year. To adapt to this constant, dynamic change, the house floats atop a structure of steel pontoons, allowing it to fluctuate along with the lake.

01 House in context **02** Dock **03** Bridge **04** Side view of deck **05** Section

Photos: Florian Holzherr
Drawings: Mos

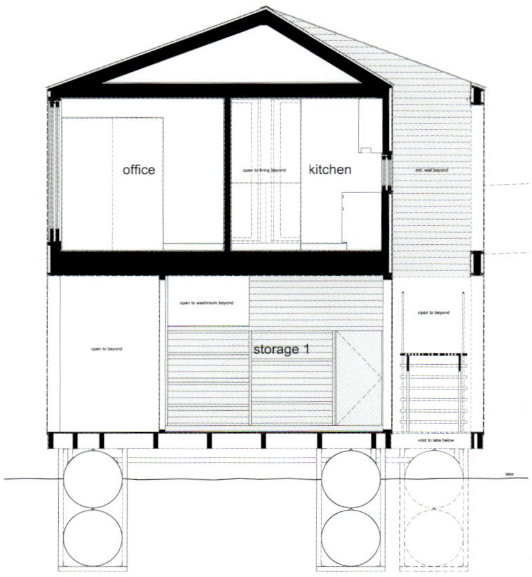

PAVILLON GENE H. KRUGER
QUEBEC LAURENT GOULARD

Incorporating both research facilities for the wood industry and undergraduate teaching space for 200 students and faculty in an 8,000-m² building, this all wood construction is located on the edge of Université Laval's suburban Québec campus and linked to the existing buildings of the Faculty of Forestry and Geometrics. The objective of the design was to demonstrate the potential of an all wood construction in a large scale building and to create the university's first building according to the principles of sustainable development, concentrating on the reduction of operating costs, especially energy consumption.

01 Exterior structure **02** Hallway **03** Interior **04** Floor plan **05** Detail

Photos: Laurent Goulard

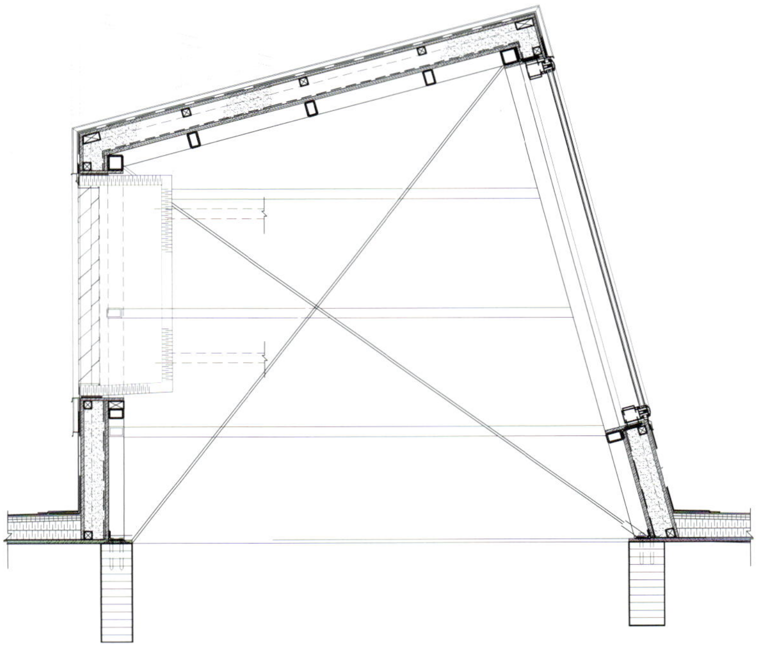

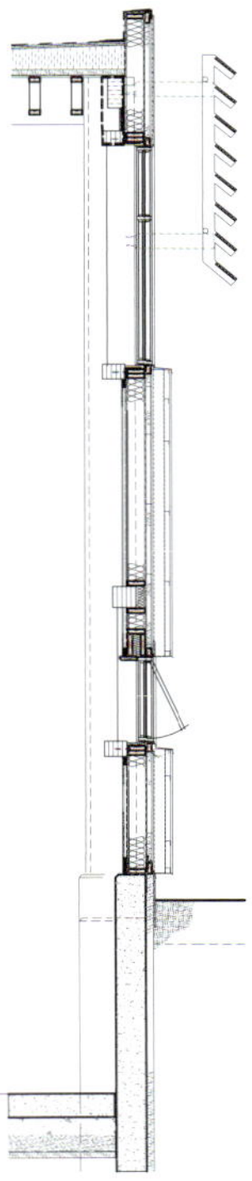

CITY Quebec (QC)
COUNTRY Canada
REGION North America
TYPOLOGY Education
COMPLETION 2005
WEBSITE www.bbgl-intl.com
ARCHITECTS Architectes Gallienne e Moisan

BIBLIOTHÈQUE DE CHARLES-BOURG

Marked by a red color presence, the project is located on a natural site where each stage is inter-connected and profits from the natural light coming from the higher stage. Vertical circulation acts as an element of connection between the three levels, as well as being the element of progressive discovering. Two large openings make it possible to create such a vast screen with a connection to the external world. The situated private location allows for beautiful views while being withdrawn into the quietude of the setting, where on the top level, the main room opens to a vast terrace localized with tree-heads.

01 Entrance area by night **02** Interior view of the library **03** Extension of building **04** Façade louvers **05** Floor plan

Photos: Benoit Lafrance, Chantal Gagnon (02)

CITY Quebec (QC)
COUNTRY Canada
REGION North America
TYPOLOGY Education
COMPLETION 2006
WEBSITE www.croftpelletier.qc.ca
ARCHITECTS Croft Pelletier architectes

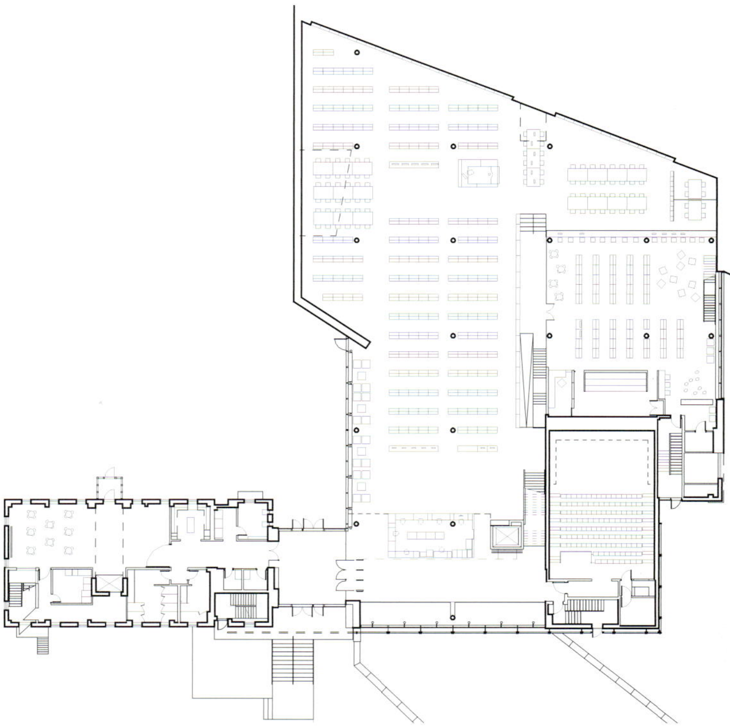

RICHMOND CITY HALL

The development of the 120,000 square foot Richmond City Hall is designed in association with Kuwabara Payne McKenna Blumberg, and is comprised of four major building components, which go on to create an ensemble of public spaces. The complex strcuture, interiorly and exteriorly, have been carefully designed to ensure the public will recognize and appreciate Richmond City Hall as an inviting and accessible public resource. Its siting incorporates sound design just as the architecture integrates it as well, while environmental and sustainability principles are able to achieve above average performance trends.

01 Exterior view by night **02** Glass façade and balconies
03 Floor plan **04** Galleria by night

Photos: Martin Tessler

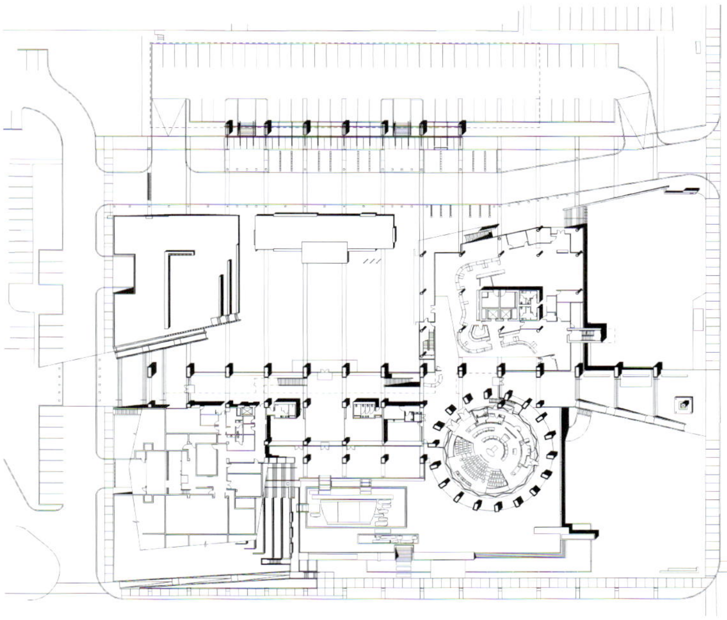

CITY
Richmond (BC)

COUNTRY
Canada

REGION
North America

TYPOLOGY
Institution / Technology

COMPLETION
2006

WEBSITE
www.hbbharc.com

ARCHITECTS
Hotson Bakker Boniface Haden architects + urbanistes

CITY Richmond (BC)
COUNTRY Canada
REGION North America
TYPOLOGY Living
COMPLETION 2007
WEBSITE www.lmal.ca
ARCHITECTS Larry McFarland Architects

JOHN MS LECKY UBC BOATHOUSE

Situated on the Fraser River, this two-story floating building provides a training facility for rowing and paddling programs and an event hall for receptions and conventions. The distinctive form of the boathouse is a deliberate step away from the typology of boathouses built in the past century. The design was inspired by elements of the sport of rowing; the curved shapes and repeating modules of the building speak to the rowing motion and to the form of the rowing shell. Like a rowing shell, the floating building leaves little impact on the surrounding environment.

01 Boathouse situated on Fraser River **02** Building at twilight **03** Cedar screens framing the outdoor decks **04** Sections

Photos: Derek Lepper

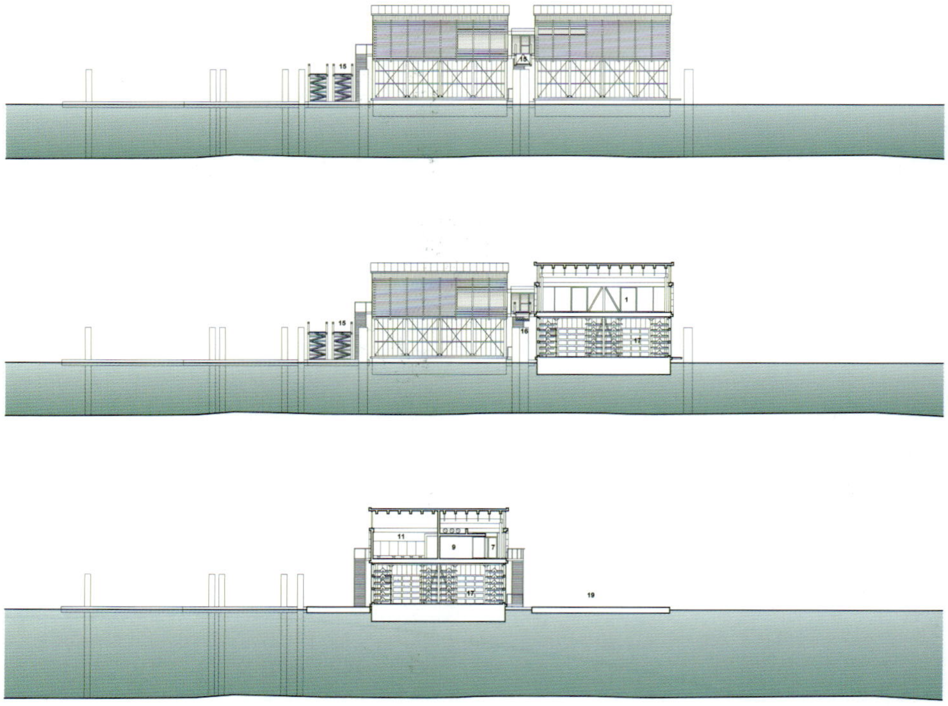

ABERDEEN CENTRE

Designed to establish a new standard for the suburban Asian mall in Canada, Aberdeen Centre is conceived as a point of visual identification for Richmond. The essential idea of the project was to create a retail and entertainment center that engages its context and displays the active life inside. This connection is made through an extensive and luminous mural of glass that wraps around the building. It is composed of a multitude of glazed glass panels that stretch the entire building and flow with the curves of the streets. The horizontal patterns of the movement are achieved by the play of light, color and transparency.

01 Colorful façade by night **02** Main entrance **03** Sections
04 Luminous glazed panels mural

Photos: Nic Lehoux

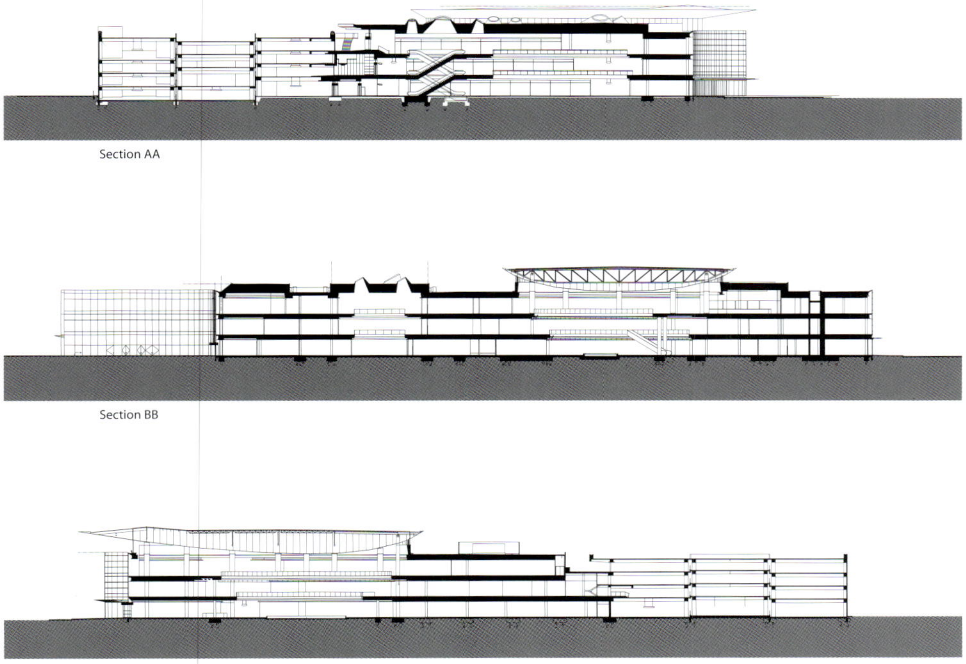

Section AA

Section BB

CITY Richmond (BC)
COUNTRY Canada
REGION North America
TYPOLOGY Retail
COMPLETION 2003
WEBSITE www.bingthomarchitects.com
ARCHITECTS Bing Thom Architects

SHALKAI

Designed as a retreat for its owners, the beautiful and peaceful site faces sloping oak meadow and sits naturally in a glorious setting. An undulating roof opens the building to the greater views and south light of the site, while a lower landscape roof unites the building with the hillside. Fine wood detailing is applied to everything from the exposed timber frame structure, wood windows and custom built furniture. The structural frame gives strength and warmth to the house, while the window system stays integral with the timber frame. The siding and the doors throughout the house are finely detailed with cedar and copper.

01 Entry garden **02** Night view from meadow **03** Floor plan **04** View from meadow

Photos: Peter Powles, Kim Smith (04)

CITY Salt Spring Island (BC)
COUNTRY Canada
REGION North America
TYPOLOGY Living
COMPLETION 2006
WEBSITE www.blueskyarchitecture.com
ARCHITECTS Helliwell+Smith.Blue Sky Architecture

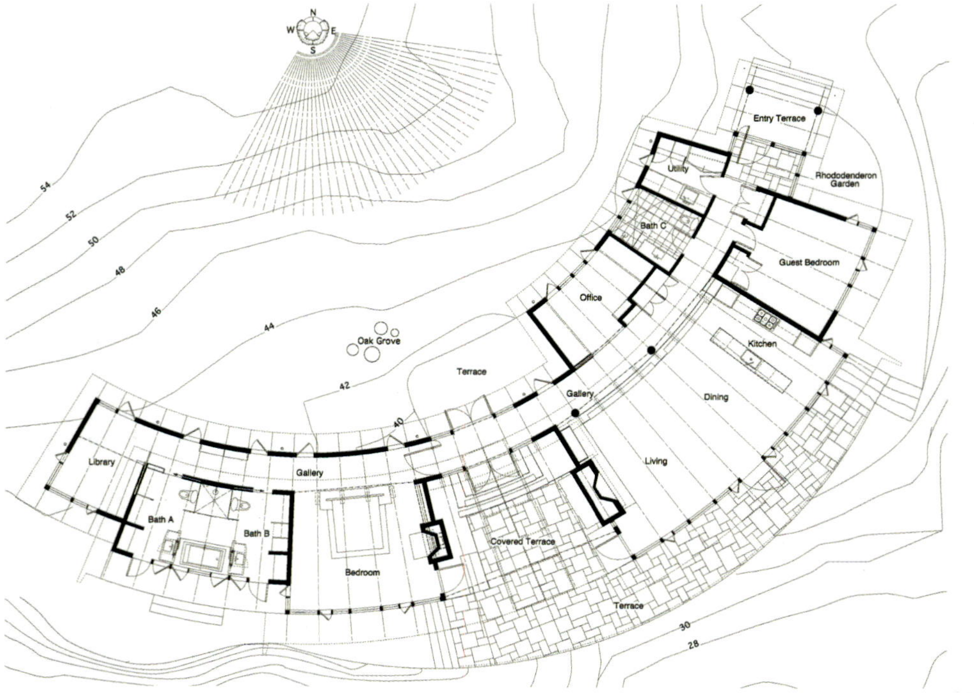

ALUMINUM TECHNOLOGY CENTRE

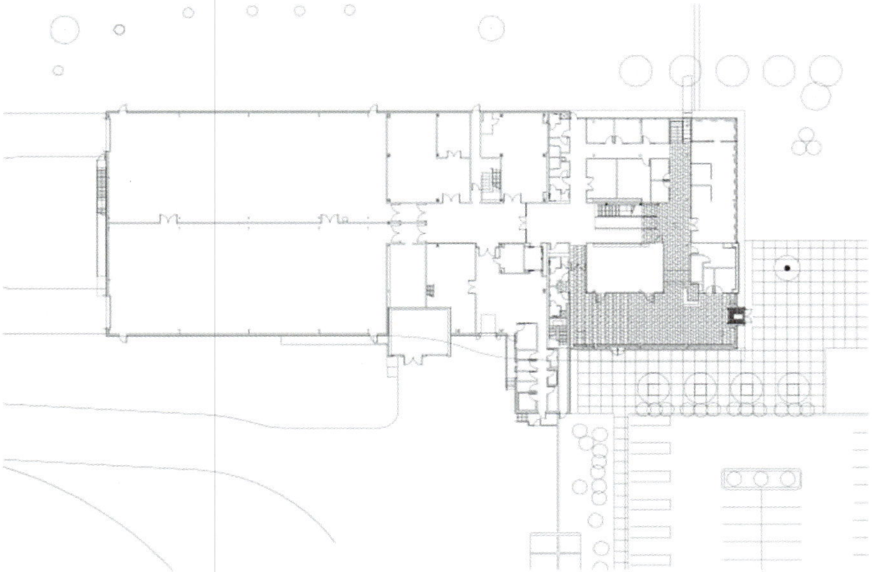

The Aluminum Technology Centre, part of the NRCC, is a 6,800 m² structure of three levels located on the campus of the Université du Québec à Chicoutimi. While compact due to buildable area constraints, the building is nevertheless spatially fluid and efficient. Raw (anodized) aluminum was used for the framework to express the metal's durability and to "open up" the main entrance to symbolize the Centre's openness to the university community and its other partners. The structure was given a slight curvature to demonstrate the transformation potential of this remarkably versatile material.

01 Anonized aluminum framework **02** Ground floor plan **03** Entrance hall **04** Slight curvature on façade

Photos: NRCC–CNRC

CITY Saguenay (QC)
COUNTRY Canada
REGION North America
TYPOLOGY Institution / Technology
COMPLETION 2004
WEBSITE www.lemay.qc.ca
ARCHITECTS Architects Lemay, Lapointe, Voyer & Associés

CITY: Surrey (BC)
COUNTRY: Canada
REGION: North America
TYPOLOGY: Culture
COMPLETION: 2003
WEBSITE: www.bingthomarchitects.com
ARCHITECTS: Bing Thom Architects

CENTRAL CITY

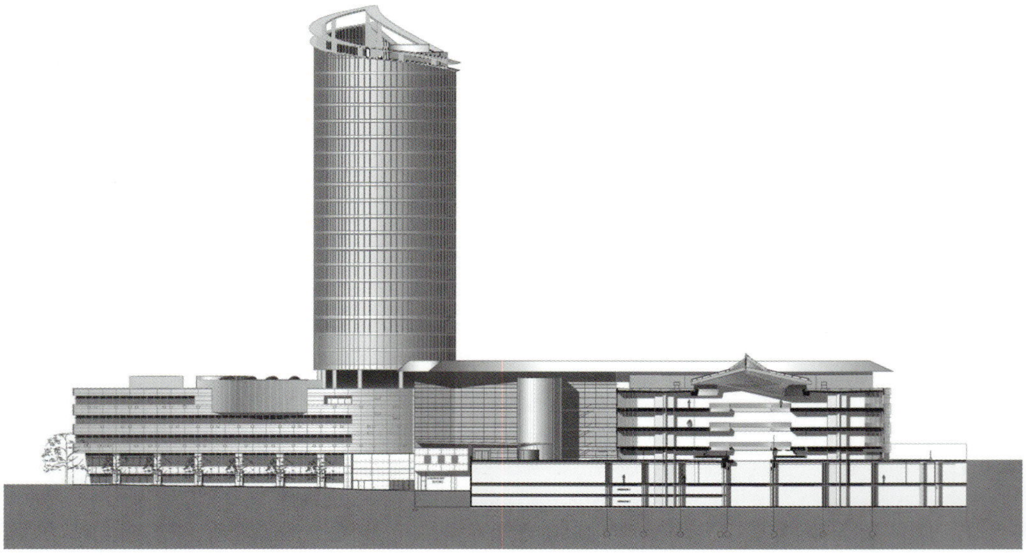

The Central City project, with its curving forms and scale alien to its area, seeks to challenge its context by reinvigorating suburban sprawl by giving a center to a place that by definition is center less. Leveraging on the existing 650,000 square feet shopping center and proximity to the transit node, the new additions to the development include a galleria, an atrium, a high-rise tower, and lastly a parkade. This hybrid complex encourages and promotes new relationships and synergies of its various users, which include the mall, university and office tenants, to become the future of urbanity.

01 Main entrance by night **02** Galleria roof **03** Section
04 New highrise tower **05** Atrium

Photos: Nic Lehoux, Ivan Hunter (02)

RESIDENCIA CANTIN COLLIN

Located on a natural site, the project's presence is clearly marked by its red color. Each stage is inter-connected and profits from the natural light coming from the higher stage. The vertical circulation acts like an element of connection between the three levels, and also as an element of progressive discovering. Two large openings make it possible to create such a vast screen, offering a connection to the external world. This private place is withdrawn in a quiet setting and presents great views, where on the last level, the main room opens to a vast terrace localized with the head of the trees.

01 Exterior view **02** Vertical circulation connecting all three levels **03** Floor plans **04** Living space **05** House in context

Photos: Croft Pelletier

CITY
Ste-Catherine-de-la-Jacques-Cartier (QC)

COUNTRY
Canada

REGION
North America

TYPOLOGY
Living

COMPLETION
2004

WEBSITE
www.croftpelletier.qc.ca

ARCHITECTS
Croft Pelletier architectes

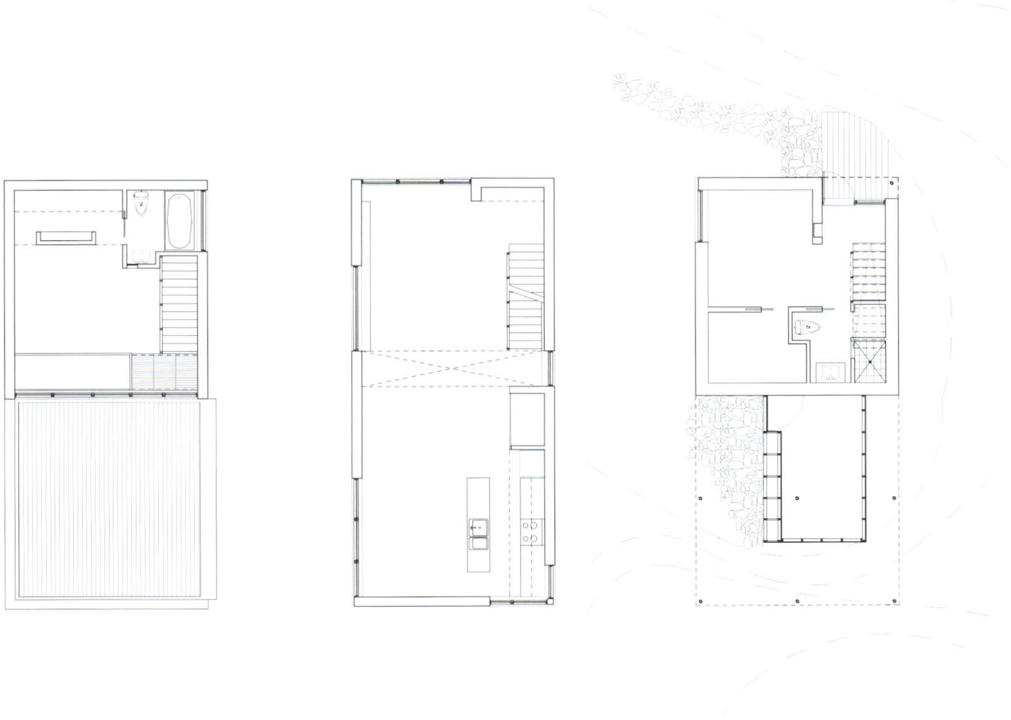

CITY
St. Williams (ON)

COUNTRY
Canada

REGION
North America

TYPOLOGY
Living

COMPLETION
2005

WEBSITE
dubbeldamarchitects.com

ARCHITECTS
Dubbeldam Design Architects

WOODSIDE HOUSE

Sheltered by a ridge of trees and situated in the corner of a large farm overlooking fields of barley, the house is conceived as a L-shaped volume defining an outdoor courtyard garden. Full-height windows look into the courtyard, creating the perception of an outdoor room that extends the interior space, allowing views across both wings of the house. Opposing clerestory windows provide privacy and excellent natural ventilation. In the manner of restrained Swiss architecture, the elevations are a repetition of elements and modular building materials intended to keep construction time and cost low.

01 Floor plan **02** View into interior from garden **03** Rear façade **04** View to garden from interior **05** Kitchen and hallway

Photos: Heather Dubbeldam

SCARBOROUGH CHINESE BAPTIST CHURCH

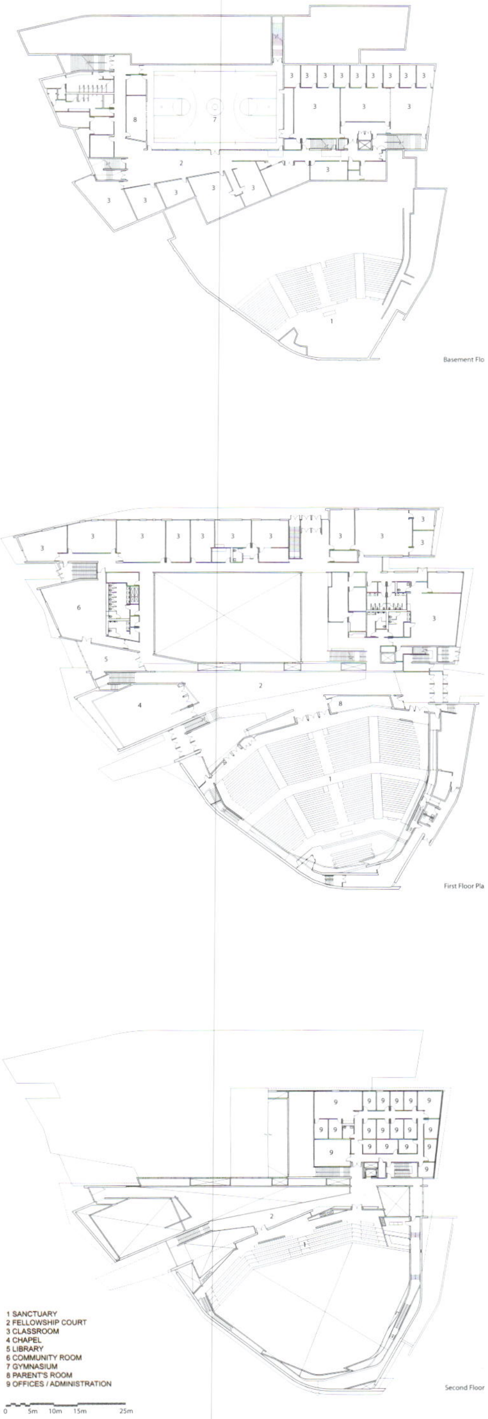

This new church and community centre has been conceived as a direct reflection of the liturgical vision of its Baptist congregation. This liturgical vision has a dual focus - fellowship, which the church characterizes as horizontal relationships between people, and spirituality, which is seen as a vertical relationship between people and God. The physical form and experience of the church directly reflect this vision. Horizontal roofs and views to the wood-lot setting characterize the community wing, while soaring vertical forms, with an emphasis on natural light from above, characterize the sanctuary.

01 Horizontal roofs and views to the wood lot **02** Floor plans **03** Main interior spacet **04** Buidling form angle bringing light into interior space

Photos: Shai Gil

1 SANCTUARY
2 FELLOWSHIP COURT
3 CLASSROOM
4 CHAPEL
5 LIBRARY
6 COMMUNITY ROOM
7 GYMNASIUM
8 PARENT'S ROOM
9 OFFICES / ADMINISTRATION

CITY Scarborough (ON)
COUNTRY Canada
REGION North America
TYPOLOGY Eclessiastical
COMPLETION 2008
WEBSITE www.teeplearch.com
ARCHITECTS Teeple Architects

CITY
Scarborough (ON)

COUNTRY
Canada

REGION
North America

TYPOLOGY
Education

COMPLETION
—

WEBSITE
www.bsnarchitects.com

ARCHITECTS
Baird Sampson Neuert Architects

THOMAS L WELLS PUBLIC SCHOOL

Commissioned by the Toronto District School Board as a model of "high performance, green design", this project integrates environmental systems with architectural design to create a terrain for students to engage in learning, society and environment. South facing rooms are grouped in "fingers" forming courtyards with a double height library at their centre. Glazed corridors overlooking the library, entry, multipurpose room and courts provide a stimulating place for a community of young learners. The first public building in a new suburban development, the school is also designed for public use and access to help forge civic community.

01 Main entrance by night **02** Interior view of double height library **03** Brick façade **04** View into library

Photos: Tom Arban Photography

THUNDER BAY REGIONAL HEALTH SCIENCES CENTRE

This Thunder Bay Centre project is a 650,000 square foot design, occupied by 375 beds, and is an acute care regional hospital that opened in February 2004. The hospital includes all acute care services, forensic mental health, a helicopter pad, and base hospital facilities to serve all of North Western Ontario. Furthermore, the complex includes the 68,000 square foot North Western Ontario Regional Cancer Centre. Embracing humanism, the complex's dramatic use of wood, and multiple-height interior spaces flooded with natural light, creates dynamic, innovative, and functional places for healing.

01 Bird´s eye view 02 Entrance area 03 First floor plan 04 Interior view

Photos: Peter Sellar, Klik Photography

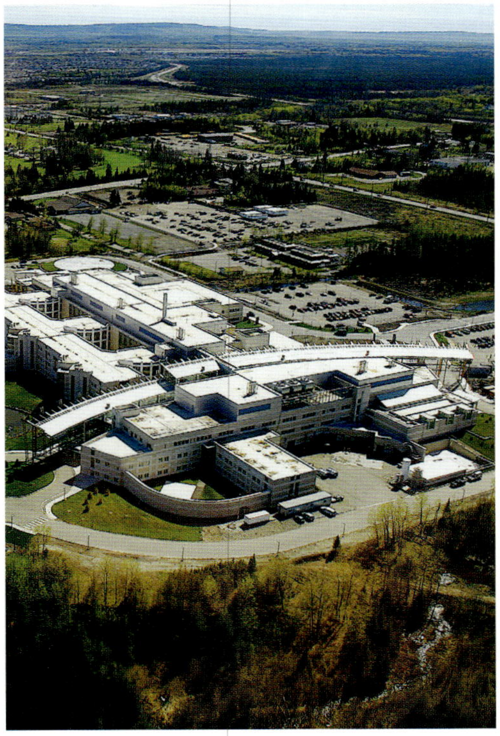

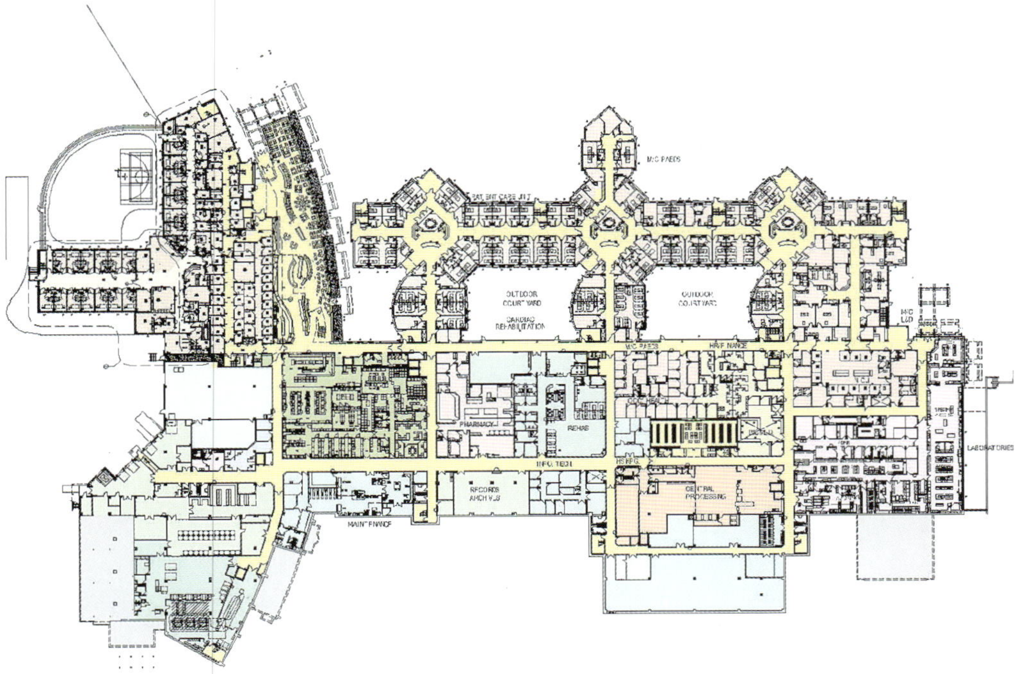

CITY Thunder Bay (ON)
COUNTRY Canada
REGION North America
TYPOLOGY Health
COMPLETION 2004
WEBSITE www.farrowpartnership.com
ARCHITECTS Farrow Partnership Architects Inc

CITY: Terrebonne (QC)
COUNTRY: Canada
REGION: North America
TYPOLOGY: Culture
COMPLETION: 2004
WEBSITE: www.ateliertag.com
ARCHITECTS: atelier T.A.G. in consortium with J.L.P.

THÉÂTRE DU VIEUX-TERREBONNE

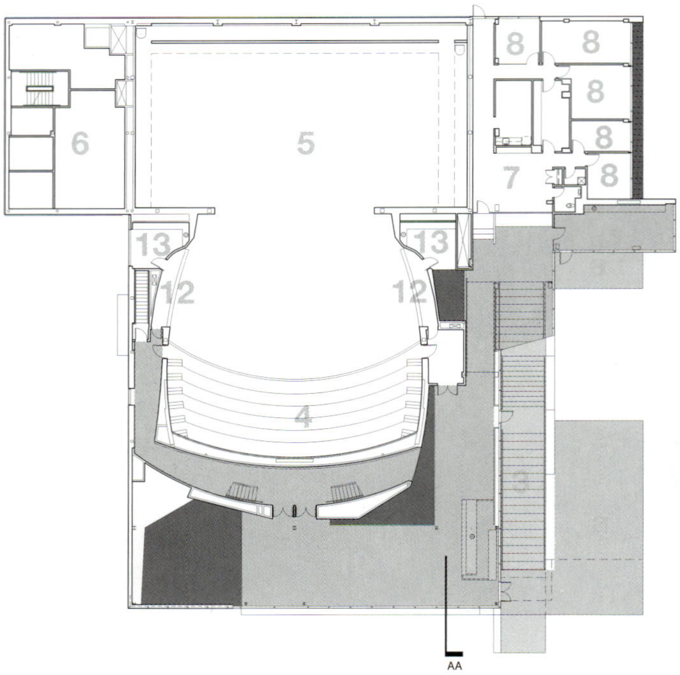

The Théâtre du Vieux-Terrebonne is an assay into the confluence and fluidity of landscape and architecture as experiential fields that provoke and inflame, on a fundamental level, the consciousness of a body in space, whereby the space is grounded in a particular place. To this end, the project develops an interconnected sequence of sectional relationships that treat the landscape and building form equally. The final result is that the performance and execution that is enticed by the architecture does not inhabit or reside entirely within the theater space, but is imbued upon all those that enter the domain of this theater.

01 V.I.P room 02 Floor plan 03 Upper foyer 04 Park façade detail

Photos: Marc Cramer

DUNN AVENUE TRIPLEX

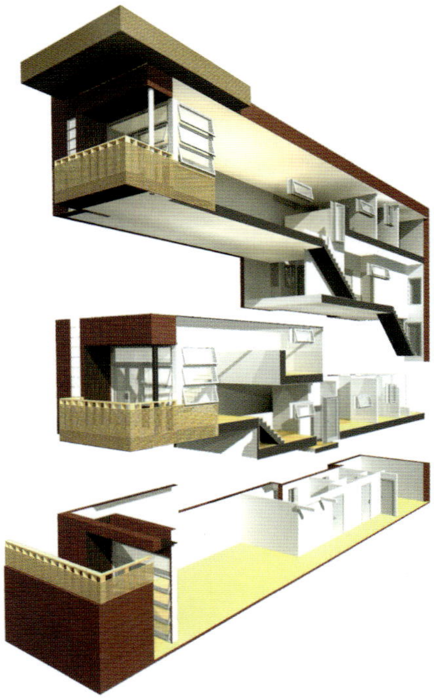

The Dunn Avenue Tripex is a new construction of a three-unit building designed by Altius Architecture in collaboration with Trevor McIvor. Concerning the features of the project, each unit is self contained with an open concept consisting of 12 ceiling living spaces, split levels, balconies, and a lower level with a walk out leading to a courtyard. The exterior resources used for the structure include day brick, cedar, and kal-wal, while for the interior such materials as cherry, slate, cork, concrete floors, drywall, birch, mahogany and stainless steel cabinetry, and mahogany detailing were all applied.

01 Brick, cedar and kal-wal façade by night **02** Exploded axonometric **03** Living space **04** View into kitchen

Photos: Jonathan Savoie

CITY: Toronto (ON)
COUNTRY: Canada
REGION: North America
TYPOLOGY: Living
COMPLETION: 2003
WEBSITE: www.altius.net
ARCHITECTS: Altius Architecture

CITY: Toronto (ON)
COUNTRY: Canada
REGION: North America
TYPOLOGY: Living
COMPLETION: 2003
WEBSITE: www.altius.net
ARCHITECTS: Altius Architecture (Trevor McIvor)

ELLIS PARK HOUSE

The Ellis Park House was conceived as a contemporary, ecological home in Toronto's vibrant Bloor West Village neighborhood. Constructed on overgrown infill site just steps from Bloor Street, the house is earth sheltered into a hillside and enjoys spectacular vistas over High Park. Passive strategies shape the design and greatly reduce the energy loads while advanced active systems efficiently address what little loads remain. The House exemplifies residential architecture that is responsive to its site, its urban context, the contemporary lifestyles of its occupants, and their desire to minimize their environmental impact.

01 Main elevation **02** Entrance hall **03** Night view **04** View to living spaces **05** Elevations

Photos: Tony Round

east elevation

south elevation

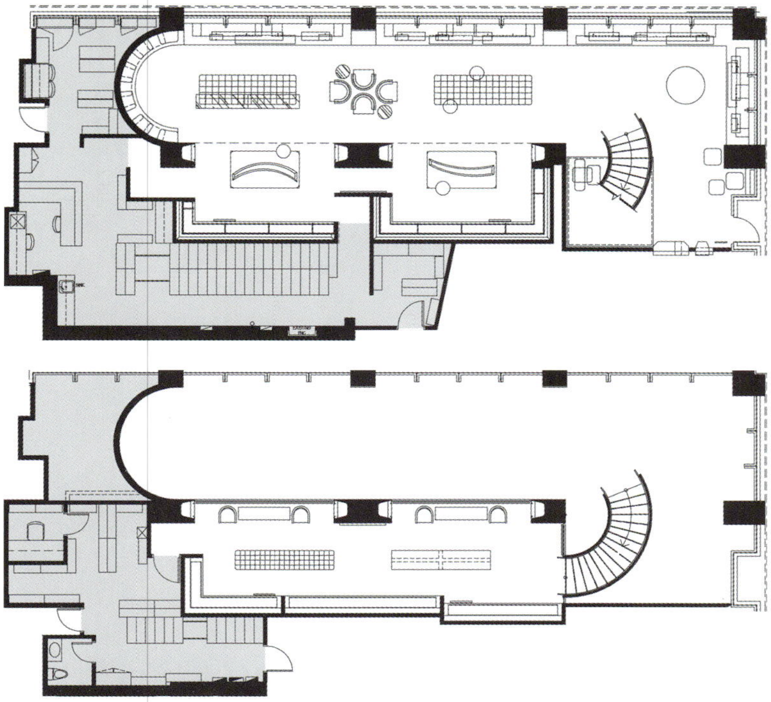

DAVIDS FLAGSHIP

The 2007 spring season brought the unveiling of the new Davids footwear flagship on Bloor Street in Toronto. Behind the revitalized new ebony façade, floor to ceiling windows expose the stunning new volume of space that glows like a pristine adornment on the street landscape. Burdifilek created an architectural language for Davids Flagship that embraces rich tones, elaborate textures and noble form to create a refined backdrop that elevates the iconic boutique and retail experience. Being progressive and modern, the open concept two-story space has women's footwear on the main floor and men's on the mezzanine level.

01 Floor plans **02** Stairs to upper floor **03** Interior wall detail **04** View into main floor and mezzanine level **05** Mezzanine level

Photos: Ben Rahn/A-Frame Inc.

CITY Toronto (ON)
COUNTRY Canada
REGION North America
TYPOLOGY Retail
COMPLETION 2007
WEBSITE www.burdifilek.com
ARCHITECTS burdifilek Interior Design

OFFICES FOR GRIP LIMITED

Located in downtown Toronto, this project is for an advertising agency recognized for their award-winning print and television ads. The design objectives for the project are three-fold; to create a space that inspires and fosters creativity for those working within the space, to evoke a spatial and notional "image" that conveys to their clients and visitors that they are first and foremost a creative agency, and that the space explore notions of play and wit. The architectural idea was the creation of a collection of formal and informal meeting spaces throughout the agency offering variegated spatial experiences.

01 Lunch / "Hot Tub" meeting area **02** Staircase and slide **03** View towards reception / waiting pod **04** Ground floor plan **05** Entrance to formal bathroom

Photos: Tom Arban Photography

CITY Toronto (ON)
COUNTRY Canada
REGION North America
TYPOLOGY Office
COMPLETION 2006
WEBSITE www.johnsonchou.com
ARCHITECTS Johnson Chou

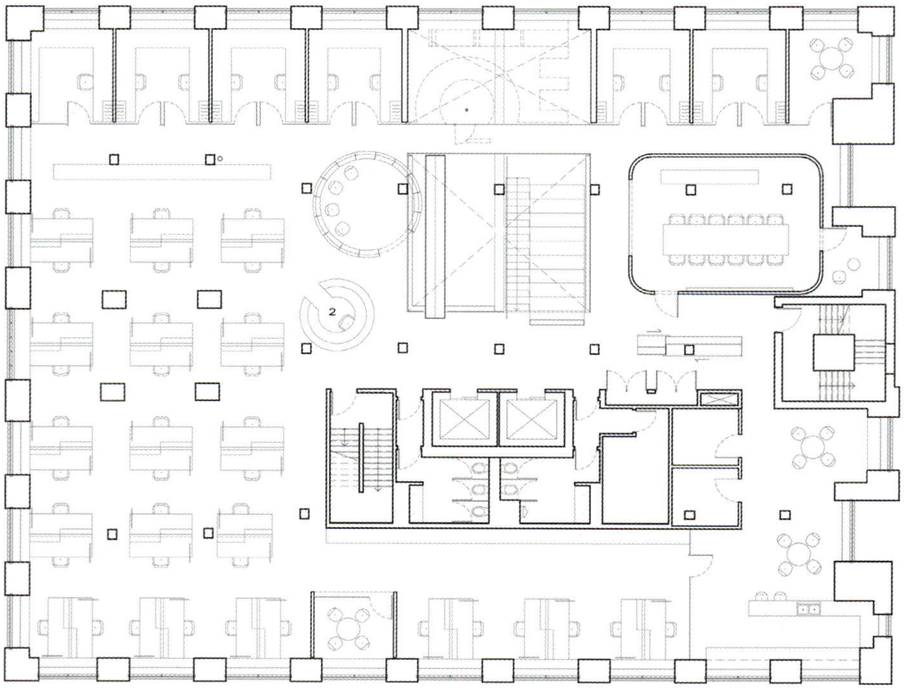

HARBOUR VIEW ESTATES SUPERCLUB

A sleek three-storey structure spanning 80 metres in length, the 30,000 square feet Harbor View Estates SuperClub features a host of amenities for both the passive and active resident including a 25-metre pool, full-size gymnasium, fitness, cardio, weight and conditioning rooms, bowling lanes, indoor golf simulator, Internet Café, winter-garden, tennis court, and several activity rooms for socializing and leisure. Panoramic views of both the spectacular cityscape and the lakefront flow into the SuperClub through oversized, floor-to-ceiling windows that form the façade of the building's gleaming glass and steel construction.

01 Building façade with floor-to-ceiling windows **02** Ground floor plan **03** Lounge and fireplace **04** Reception desk **05** Entrance

Photos: Paul Orenstein Photography

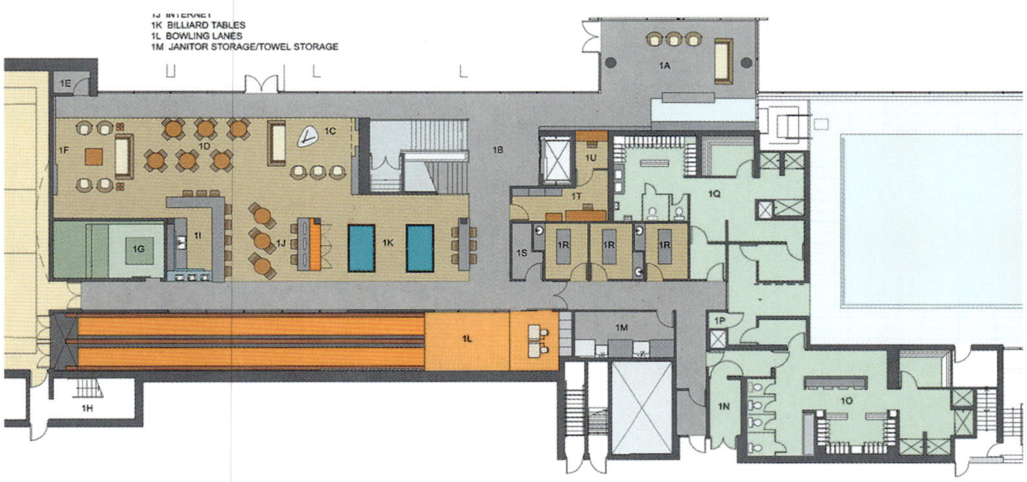

CITY Toronto (ON)
COUNTRY Canada
REGION North America
TYPOLOGY Leisure
COMPLETION 2006
WEBSITE www.corearchitects.com
ARCHITECTS Core Architects Inc

RAVINE RESIDENCE

This house is located in a private ravine setting occupying a double lot in Toronto. Its low-lying form at the front elevation drops to tower-like proportions at the back. The building is a material study using eramosa limestone throughout; the stone is either split-faced, honed, polished, sand-blasted or bush-hammered. The design intention was to blur the boundaries between the exterior and the interior and to bring the outside in. Through floor-to-ceiling windows the ravine setting can be enjoyed from any location within the house.

01 Front elevation **02** Exterior view from garden **03** Terrace **04** Site plan **05** Interior living space

Photos: Tom Arban Photography

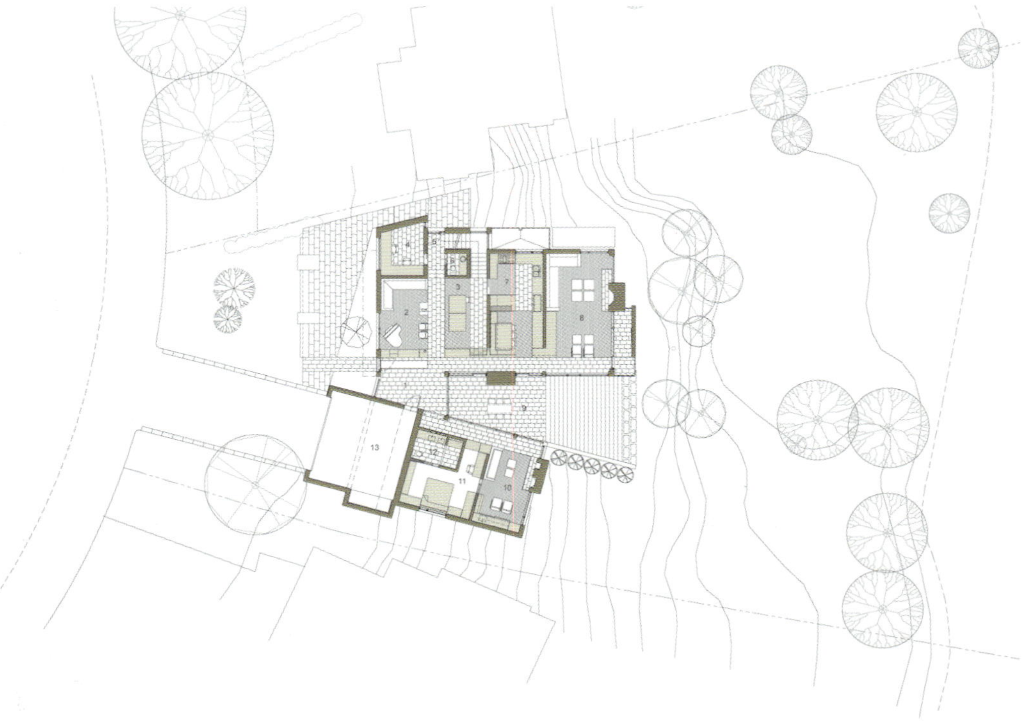

83A MARLBOROUGH AVE RESIDENCE

The single-family residential infill project occupies a mid-town Toronto lot, which was the former site of a single car garage. The project is largely determined by its constraints and access to light, and movement through space directly resolves the form of the building. Circulation spirals up and over the entrance through a series of interconnected spaces, lit with natural light from above. The project is an attempt of meaningful place making with a connection to the site from the sky, and by responding to the peculiarities of the client, the program and the neighborhood; derive the potential from this underused lot.

01 Patio by night **02** Front view **03** Floor plans **04** Exterior view from patio **05** Living space **06** Bathroom

Photos: Tom Arban Photography (01, 04), Peter A. Sellar / KLIK (02), Heather Dubbeldam / Saeed Behrouzi, Luminous Productions (05, 06)

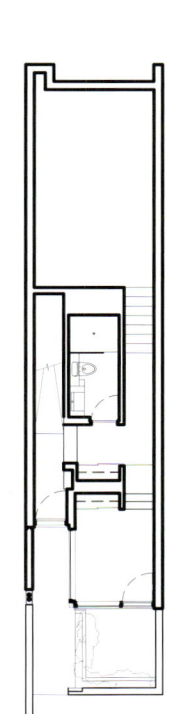

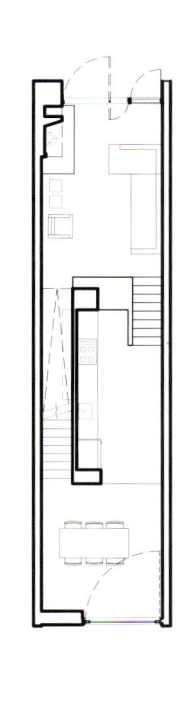

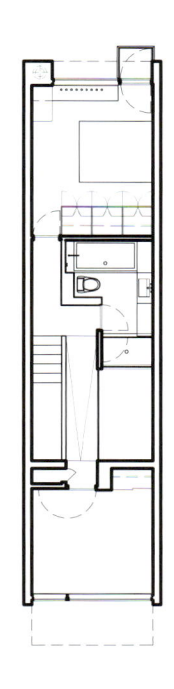

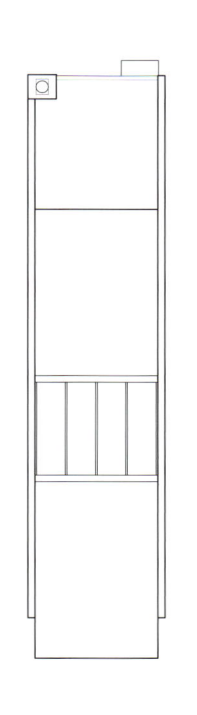

CITY Toronto (ON)
COUNTRY Canada
REGION North America
TYPOLOGY Living
COMPLETION 2007
WEBSITE www.drewmandeldesign.com
ARCHITECTS Drew Mandel Design

CITY Toronto (ON)
COUNTRY Canada
REGION North America
TYPOLOGY Living
COMPLETION 2007
WEBSITE www.drewmandeldesign.com
ARCHITECTS Drew Mandel Design

RAVINE HOUSE

The project is referred to as Ravine House, as it is mostly concerned with and oriented around its wooded ravine setting, which is Toronto's most defining, if low profile, physical characteristic. The ground floor steps down to follow the natural topography, resulting in elevated-height spaces with glass walls defining the interior and exterior. A steel structure permits rooms to be cast into the landscape, while sliding glass and mahogany walls provide direct access and a real connection to the site. Landscaping completes the residence and the occupation of the site as a coherent and integrated whole.

01 Interior with fireplace **02** Ground floor plan **03** Living room **04** View by night from wooded ravine setting **05** Entrance hall **06** Kitchen

Photos: Tom Arban Photography

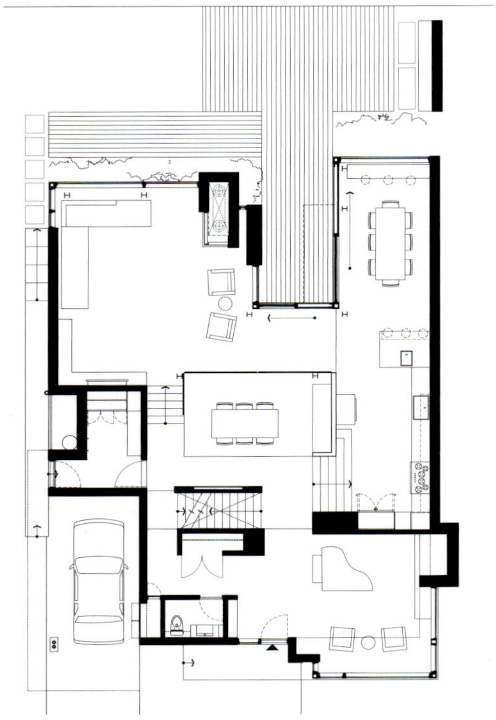

RESIDENCE AT EVERGREEN GARDENS

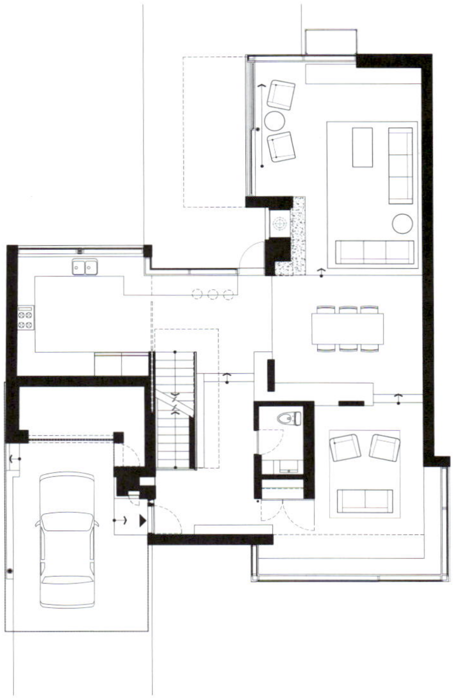

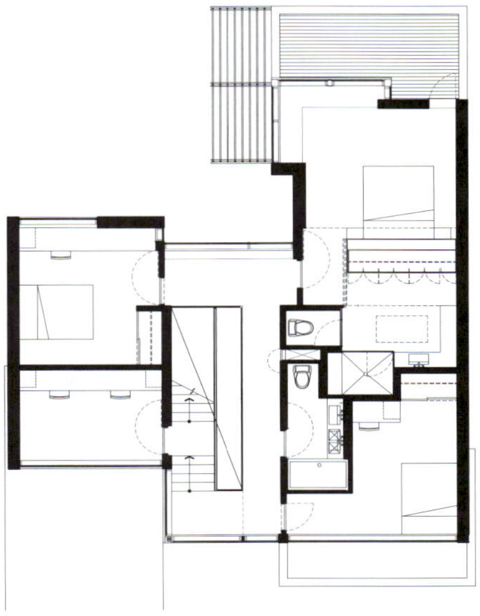

This replacement house is offered as an alternative to the McMansion developments in a transitional neighborhood, where lot values have increased to the point where they simply overwhelm the existing modest-sized homes. The more-or-less 'Z' shaped form of the proposed house is intended to embrace the site, creating a dynamic space between one area of the building and others, as well as between the house and the site. At moments, the architectural intent is also an attempt to stay out of the way, as the house endeavors to allow the owners to feel as though they are sitting under the big tree out on the front lawn.

01 Exterior view by night 02 Ground floor plan 03 Exterior view from garden 04 Second floor plan 05 Living room

Photos: Tom Arban Photography

CITY: Toronto (ON)
COUNTRY: Canada
REGION: North America
TYPOLOGY: Living
COMPLETION: 2006
WEBSITE: www.drewmandeldesign.com
ARCHITECTS: Drew Mandel Design

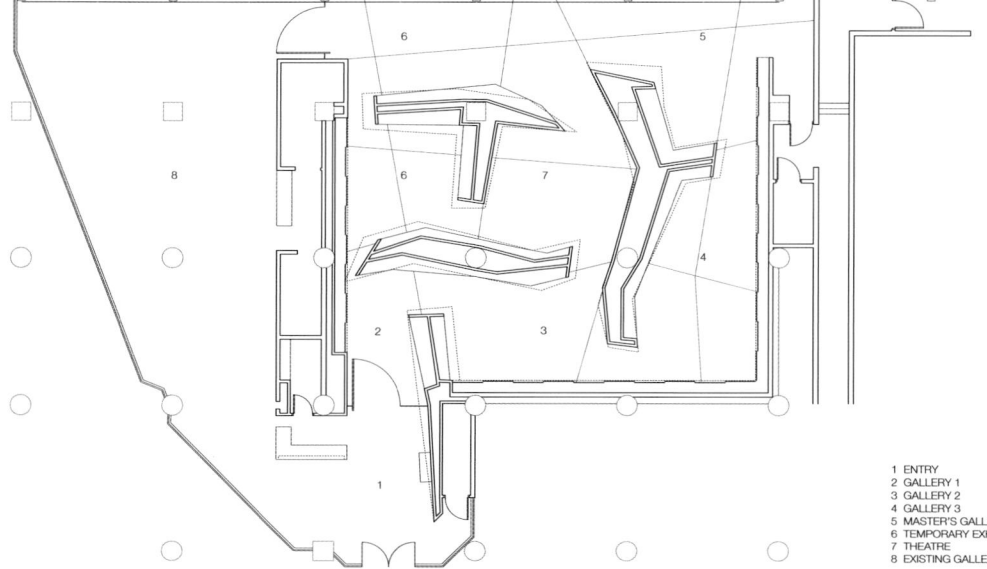

CITY: Toronto (ON)
COUNTRY: Canada
REGION: North America
TYPOLOGY: Culture
COMPLETION: 2007
WEBSITE: www.gh3.ca
ARCHITECTS: gh3

THE CANADIAN MUSEUM OF INUIT ART

Located in Queen's Quay Terminal, the new museum joins a number of other important cultural institutions on Toronto's Harborfront, but is the only museum in Canada specifically dedicated to displaying and interpreting Inuit Art. The interior of the museum is designed to remove visitors from the commercial activity in the rest of the building and place them in a more rarefied environment for viewing art. The museum is organized around 7 galleries, which are delineated by four irregularly shaped partitions. The partitions, which also hold displays, run floor-to-ceiling and are constructed of metal studs and drywall.

01 Existing gallery **02** Display of Inuit Art **03** Floor plan
04 Temporary exhibition space

Photos: Tom Arban Photography

1 ENTRY
2 GALLERY 1
3 GALLERY 2
4 GALLERY 3
5 MASTER'S GALLERY
6 TEMPORARY EXHIBITS
7 THEATRE
8 EXISTING GALLERY

RUSSELL HILL

Built during the 1970's, the house is situated overlooking one of Toronto's downtown ravines. The renovation reopened the ground floor so that it became an open loft-like space from front to back. By installing a new fully glazed wall at the rear garden side of the hose, it was possible to extend the sense of the outdoor space through the interior. Interior finishes were chosen for their neutrality and were stripped back to a more modern style, causing the house to become a neutral shell punctuated by three sculptural elements: a block of stone associated with kitchen elements, a curved stair, and a 20-inch stone bench with a fireplace wall. Each of these elements is associated with windows, skylights, and double height spaces to enhance the spatial experience.

---

01 Living room with stone bench **02** Exterior night view into interior **03** Sculpted curved stair **04** Bathtub with skylight **05** Floor plans **06** Helicoidal staircase

Photos: Tom Arban Photography

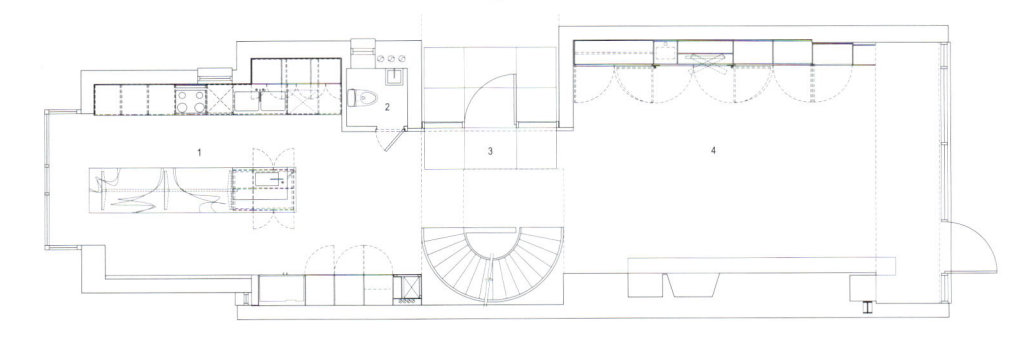

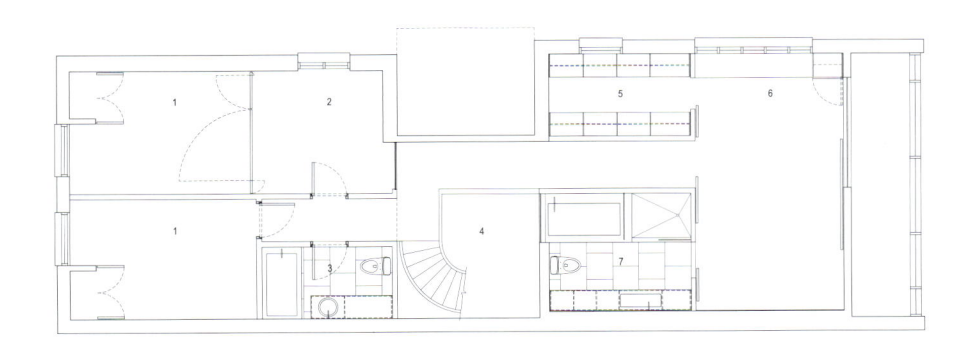

CITY
Toronto (ON)

COUNTRY
Canada

REGION
North America

TYPOLOGY
Living

COMPLETION
2006

WEBSITE
www.gh3.ca

ARCHITECTS
GH3 Architects

HUMER COLLEGE INSTITUTE OF TECHNOLOGY & ADVANCED LEARNING

This new facility at the Lakeshore Campus provides a professional level environment for production and recording. It includes a double height recording studio, a control room, an electronic classroom, and interactive workstations. Evolving out of a necessity to create interconnected volumes ideal for acoustic production, the interior is a series of folded planes, the most outstanding element being a plane of light and dark wood panels that rhythmically vary in size and depth. The exterior is expressed as a pure black box immersed into the existing single storey building, strengthening the existing court upon which it is set.

01 Exterior view **02** Recording cabin **03** Floor plan **04** Recording studio **05** Reception

Photos: Tom Arban Photography

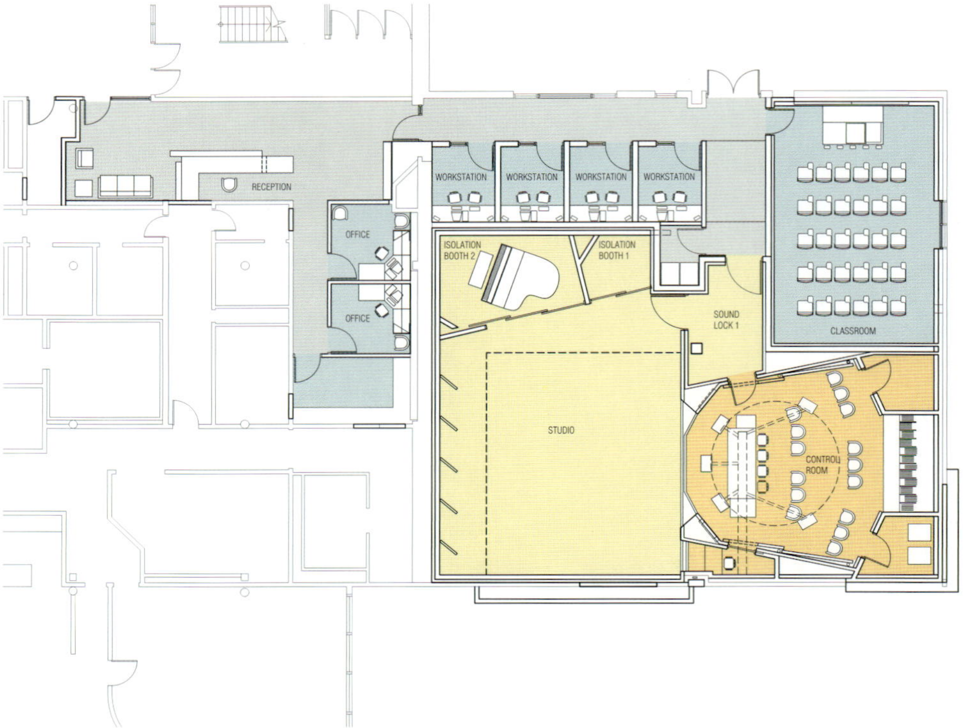

GARDINER MUSEUM

The Gardiner is Canada's only museum dedicated to ceramic arts. The renewal is one of the participating projects in Toronto's Cultural Renaissance and responds directly to the client brief to accommodate growing collections of educational and research programs. It involved the complete reorganization of the entrance and vertical circulation, and the addition of a third floor to provide column-free temporary exhibit space as well as a multipurpose space with access to south-facing terraces. The former pink granite cladding was stripped and a new, re-wrapped polished buff Indiana limestone and black granite was placed.

01 Exterior view **02** Interior **03** Main entrance **04** Exhibit **05** Cafeteria

Photos: Shai Gil (01), Eduard Hueber (02, 03, 04), Tom Arban Photography (05)

CITY Toronto (ON)
COUNTRY Canada
REGION North America
TYPOLOGY Culture
COMPLETION 2006
WEBSITE www.kpmbarchitects.com
ARCHITECTS Kuwabara Payne McKenna Blumberg Architects (KPMB)

CITY	Toronto (ON)
COUNTRY	Canada
REGION	North America
TYPOLOGY	Education
COMPLETION	2005
WEBSITE	www.kpmbarchitects.com
ARCHITECTS	Kuwabara Payne McKenna Blumberg Architects (KPMB) / Goldsmith Borgal & Company Ltd. Architects

CANADA'S NATIONAL BALLET SCHOOL PROJECT GRAND JETÉ: STAGE 1 – JARVIS STREET CAMPUS

The new training centre creates a vertical campus of three transparent elements composed around a historic residence. The concept fuses architecture, dance, and movement within a series of stacked, platforms, bringing the spectacle of dance to the city. The thoughtful refinement of all elements, from the grand volumes of the studios to the customized ballet barres, reflects the School's vision to cultivate innovation. As a model for the harmonious co-existence of heritage and contemporary architecture, the design offers a metaphorical resolution of the dilemma of contemporary ballet to both preserve and challenge its art form.

01 Lounge **02** Exterior bridge **03** Glass façade and ballerina **04** General view **05** View into studio

Photos: Tom Arban Photography, Eduard Hueber (04)

YOUNG CENTRE FOR THE PERFORMING ARTS

Located within Toronto's 19th century Gooderham and Worts Distillery District, a former industrial site transformed into an arts precinct, the Young Centre for Performing Arts occupies two historic tank houses and the space between them, has dramatically raised the district's profile as a centre for artistic life. Lauded as a new paradigm for combining a school and professional drama company in one facility, the design supports a lively culture of collaboration. The architecture creates a flexible setting to encourage vital interpretations of the theater, and to reflect a commitment to a universal art form that transcends its setting.

01 Night view from street **02** Theatre bookstore **03** Main entrance **04** Lobby

Photos: Tom Arban Photography

CITY Toronto (ON)

COUNTRY Canada

REGION North America

TYPOLOGY Education / Culture

COMPLETION 2006

WEBSITE www.kpmbarchitects.com

ARCHITECTS Kuwabara Payne McKenna Blumberg Architects (KPMB)

CITY
Toronto (ON)

COUNTRY
Canada

REGION
North America

TYPOLOGY
Institution / Technology

COMPLETION
2006

WEBSITE
www.behnisch.com
www.architectsalliance.com

ARCHITECTS
Behnisch Architekten
and architectsAlliance

TERRENCE DONNELLY CENTER FOR CELLULAR AND BIOMOLECULAR RESEARCH

Standing in contrast to neighboring brick buildings, the University of Toronto's Terrence Donnelly Center for Cellular and Biomolecular Research is a slender, elegant tower marked by a façade that is crisp, light, and colorful. In response to the narrow building site, the architects designed a rectangular structure that ascends 12 stories high. Above the atrium that connects the Center to the adjacent building, winter garden and staff lounges punctuate a system of open corridors and stairwells. The design emphasizes interdisciplinary collaboration, connections to the surrounding urban context, transparency, and community.

01 Colorful glass façade **02** Rectangular structure **03** Site plan **04** Façade transparencies **05** Winter garden and corridor

Photos: Tom Arban Photography (01, 05),
Ben Rahn/A-Frame Inc. (02, 04)

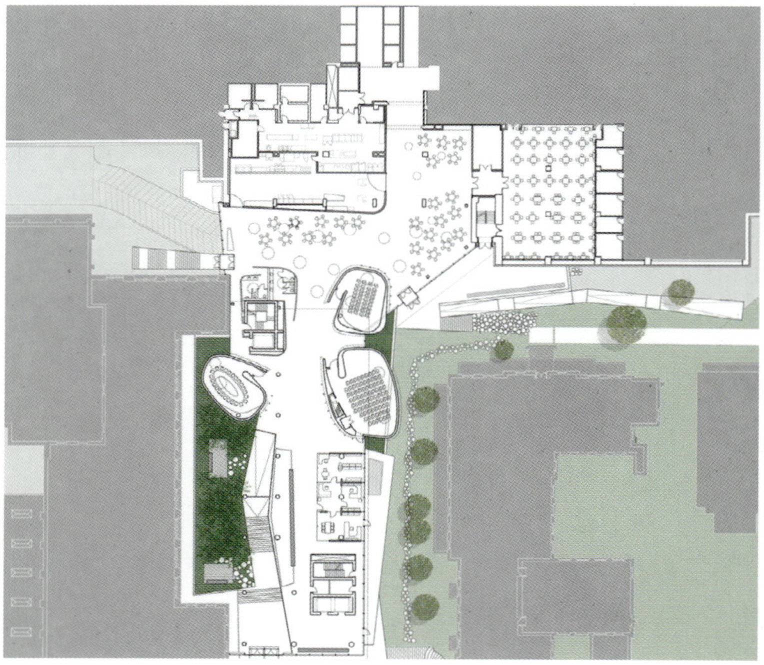

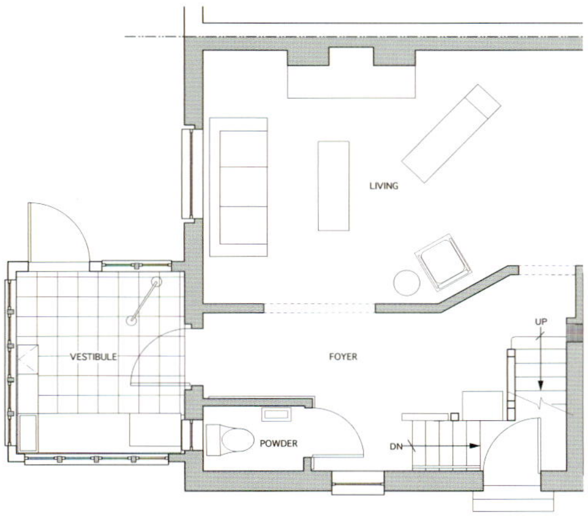

WOODLAWN RESIDENCE

The scope of this project included extensive interior renovations to a downtown three-storey house, including raising the third floor dormer roof and extensive built in millwork. The renovations focused on connecting the interior with the outside ravine while creating an exciting interconnection of interior spaces. The ground floor was almost completely rearranged to provide a layered, continuous flow of entertainment space that always has the ravine as the backdrop. Volumetric layering of the interior was achieved by using panels of frosted glass, wall slots, metal mesh curtains, lighting, and layering of shifted colours.

01 Floor plan 02 Exterior view to entrance 03 Dining room
04 Fireplace

Photos: Peter Legris Photography

CITY
Toronto (ON)

COUNTRY
Canada

REGION
North America

TYPOLOGY
Living

COMPLETION
–

WEBSITE
www.branchplant.com

ARCHITECTS
PLANT Architect Inc.

BMW TORONTO

Converted into a modernist glass-clad showroom with large vehicle display bays and a projecting, backlit billboard window, this project's original building was demolished down to its structural frame, reinforced for current earthquake standards, and new mechanical and electrical systems were installed. Two oversized freight hoists bring the automobiles up for display on five of the six floors, while substantial portions of the existing floors were removed to create double-height spaces to display the new models. The new vehicle delivery area on the fifth floor takes advantage of the panoramic view of Toronto's downtown core.

01 Glass clad showroom **02** Exterior view from highway
03 Large vehicle display bays **04** Entrance **05** Showroom
06 Ground floor plan

Photos: Robert Burley

CITY Toronto (ON)
COUNTRY Canada
REGION North America
TYPOLOGY Commercial
COMPLETION 2003
WEBSITE www.quadrangle.ca
ARCHITECTS Quadrangle Architects Limited

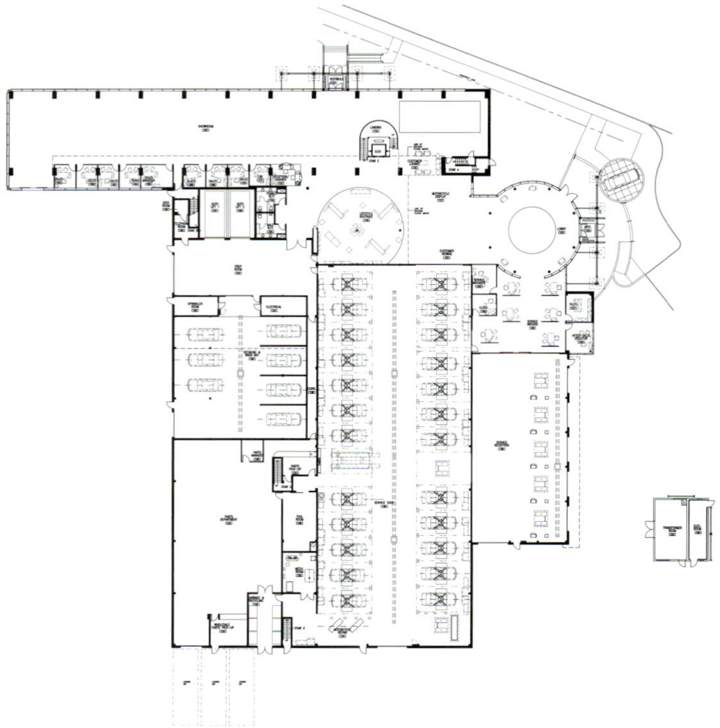

51 DIVISION POLICE STATION

Toronto's new 51 Division building projects a community friendly image while recycling a heritage building and brown field site. The design embraces the historical building as an archaeological presence, where the space captured on the public side within the historic walls and modern intervention creates a civic lobby and exhibition gallery. A generous plaza along Parliament Street is punctuated by the light-filled window of the community room. The program includes secure administration, primary and community response units, criminal & forensic investigation, detention facilities, staff support, and exhibition space.

01 Exterior view of main entrance **02, 03** Staircase **04** Detention cell **05** Reception **06** Office

Photos: Richard Johnson

CITY Toronto (ON)
COUNTRY Canada
REGION North America
TYPOLOGY Institution / Technology
COMPLETION 2004
WEBSITE www.stantec.com
ARCHITECTS Stantec Architecture Ltd., Architects (Heritage Architecture: E.R.A. Architects)

CITY Toronto (ON)
COUNTRY Canada
REGION North America
TYPOLOGY Education
COMPLETION 2006
WEBSITE www.stipartners.com
ARCHITECTS Shore Tilbe Irwin & Partners

THE HAZEL MCCALLION ACADEMIC LEARNING CENTRE

The HMALC integrates 10,000 m² of library and digital study space into a growing suburban campus. The metaphor of a Japanese puzzle box is used to create an architectural container that appears to have opened, revealing its collection and a series of public space linkages. This kinetic reading is supported by a series of unique material expressions including wood veneered phenolic panels, black granite, and glass with a graduated frit. The building features a high level of sustainability as it incorporates green roofs, daylight harvesting, and a sophisticated fuel cell technology into its design.

01 Building envelope with wood veneered phenolic panels **02** Glass façade with a graduated frit **03** General view **04** Third floor plan **05** Fourth floor plan **06** Section detail

Photos: Ben Rahn, A-Frame Studio

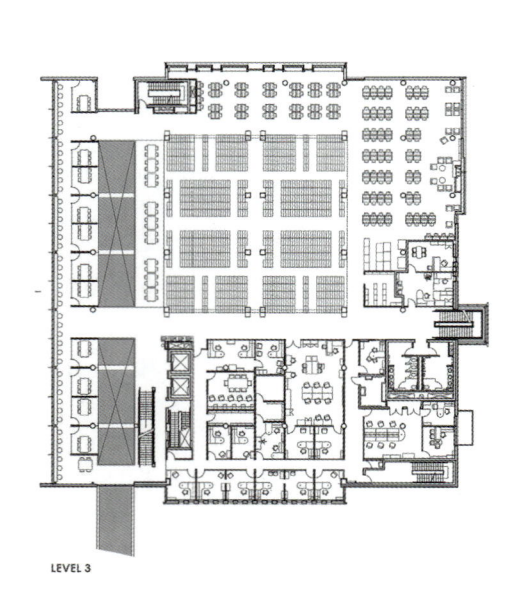

LEVEL 3

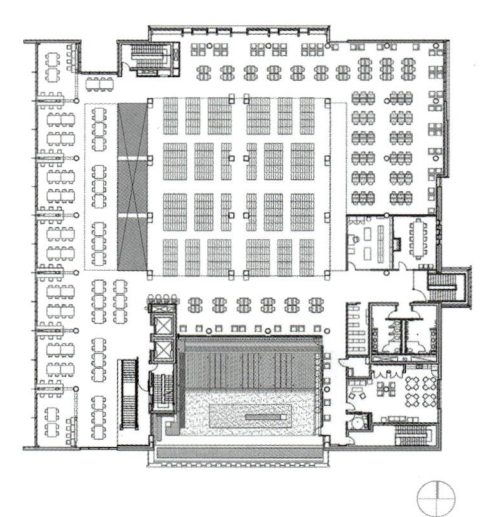

LEVEL 4

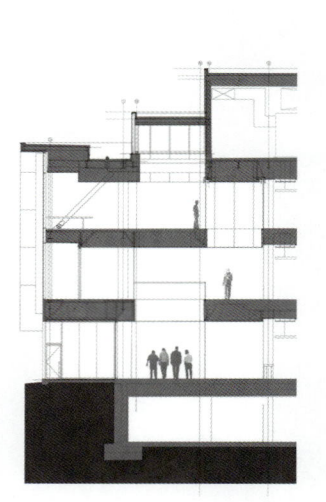

CANADIAN NATIONAL INSTITUTE FOR THE BLIND CENTRE

Originally the CNIB offered a sheltered place of work. Occupying the same site as the original building that opened in 1954, the new CNIB Centre is a state-of-the-art training facility that focuses on getting the blind and visuallay impared back into the regular work force. The new, four-storey, modernist building sets new standards of accessibility and demosntrates the principles of universal design. The robust program includes administrative areas, unique facilities for the making of Braille and Talking Books, national library. The robust program includes administrative areas, unique facilities for the making of Braille and Talking books, national library, clinics, hight-tech classrooms, an store selling techincal aids that facilitate daily activities.

01 Main entrance **02** Fragrant garden **03** Exterior view of west façade **04** Meeting room **05** Cafe

Photos: Tom Arban Photography

CITY Toronto (ON)
COUNTRY Canada
REGION North America
TYPOLOGY lEducation
COMPLETION 2004
WEBSITE www.andco.com
ARCHITECTS Sweeny Sterling Finlayson & Co Architects

CITY Toronto (ON)

COUNTRY Canada

REGION North America

TYPOLOGY Education

COMPLETION 2004

WEBSITE www.rywarch.ca

ARCHITECTS Robbie Young + Wright / IBI Group Architects

SHARP CENTRE FOR DESIGN, ONTARIO COLLEGE OF ART & DESIGN

The 125th birthday of Ontario College of Art & Design was the impetus to expanding the overcrowded home of the College in downtown Toronto. The flying, translucent rectangle vividly patterned with a colorful skin, is raised 8-storeys from the ground and houses the new Faculty of Design. The project accommodates gallery spaces, meeting and study areas, an outdoor auditorium, and a café beside the integrated new park landscape linked to Grange Park. The college satisfies its aspirations to rejuvenate a neglected area of Toronto by inviting the public to its revived café and viewing art galleries located in the building's heart.

01 New Faculty of Design **02** Atrium with exhibit **03** Exterior view by night **04** Elevation **05** Section **06** Translucent rectangle patterned with a colorful skin

Joint venture architects: Alsop Architects
Photos: Richard Johnson

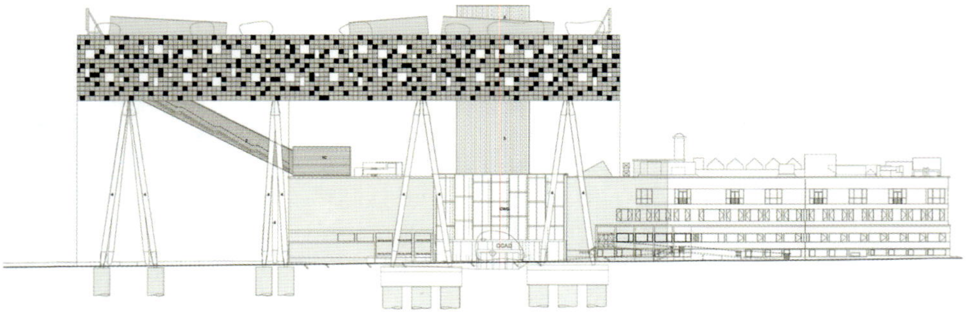

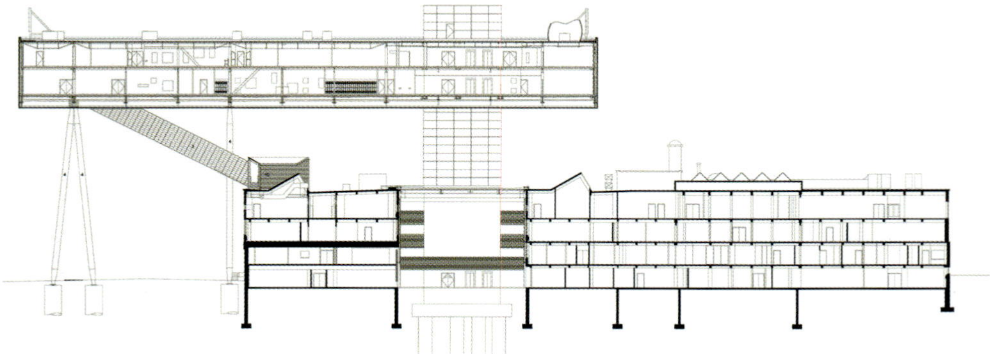

YORK UNIVERSITY GENERAL ACADEMIC AND PERFORMING ARTS BUILDING – ACCOLADE PROJECT

The new center for fine arts education offers state-of-the-art teaching, exhibition and performance facilities in two new buildings – Accolade East and Accolade West – framing the existing fine arts complex at the heart of York University's Keele campus. The buildings house the departments of music, dance and theater, the York University Art Gallery and a student-run art gallery. The project includes dozens of state-of-the-art classrooms, a 325-seat recital hall, a 325-seat proscenium theater, a 500-seat cinema, an 80-seat screening room as well as extensive support space and faculty offices.

01 Interior ribbon wall **02** Main entrance by night **03** Proscenium theater **04** Theater lobby **05** Exterior view

Photos: Tom Arban Photography

CITY Toronto (ON)
COUNTRY Canada
REGION North America
TYPOLOGY Education
COMPLETION 2006
WEBSITE www.zeidlerpartnership.com
ARCHITECTS Zeidler Partnership Architects / B+H Architects

CLAUDE WATSON SCHOOL FOR THE ARTS

Specializing in training for both Fine Arts and the Performing Arts, this project is a simple and compact form with a strong street presence while presenting an image of performance and accessibility. A 50,000 square foot program includes staff and technical facilities, conventional classrooms, music rooms, drama and art classrooms, a small gymnasium and a multi purpose space. The design takes advantage of natural lighting and boasts views over a park. Circulation spaces are wide and robust, designed to accommodate the exhibition of student work as well as the spontaneous desire to gather and perform.

01 Exterior view towards school yard **02** Gymnasium **03** School stong street presence **04** Building façade by night and basketball court **05** Sections

Photos: Tom Arban photography

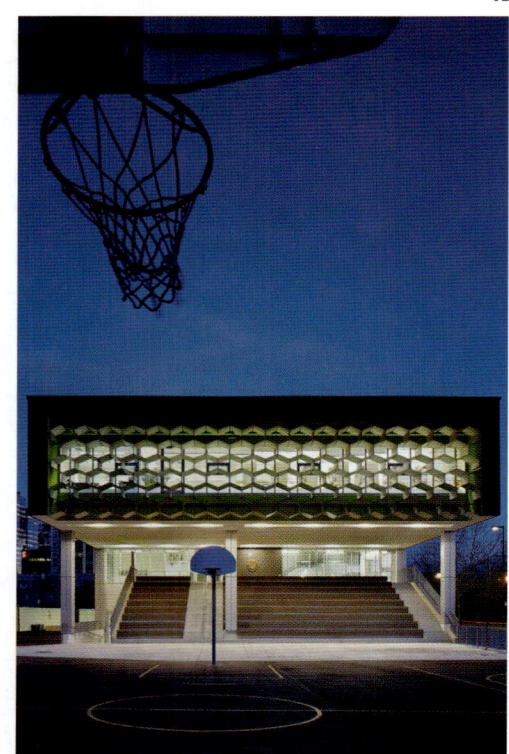

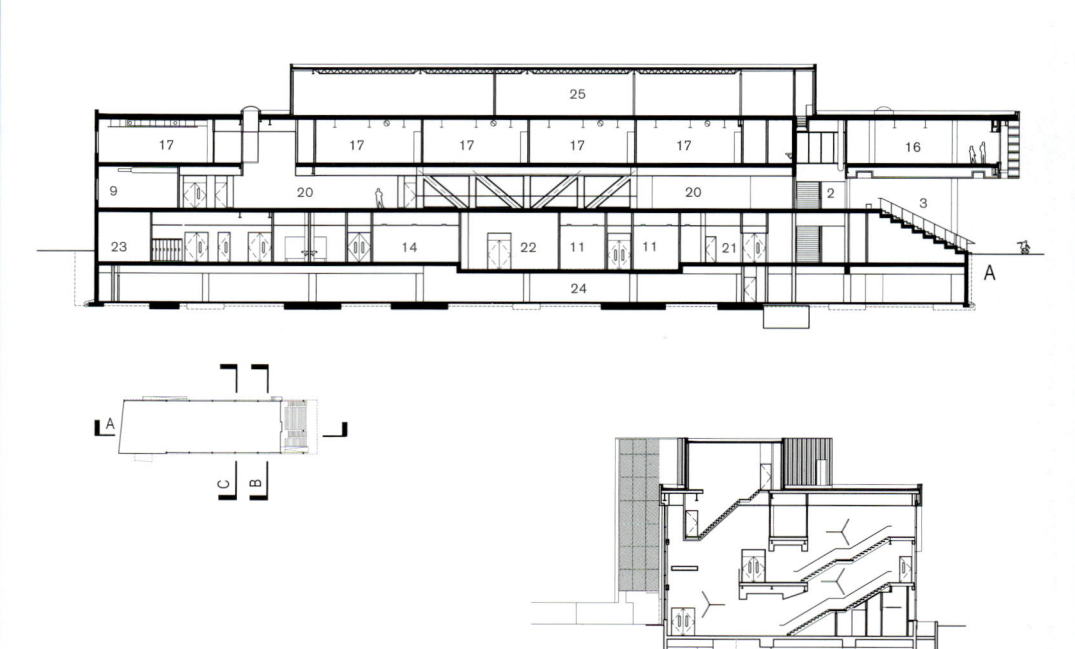

CITY Toronto (ON)
COUNTRY Canada
REGION North America
TYPOLOGY Education
COMPLETION 2008
WEBSITE www.kohnshnierarchitects.com
ARCHITECTS Kohn Shnier Architects

THE 519 CHURCH STREET COMMUNITY CENTRE

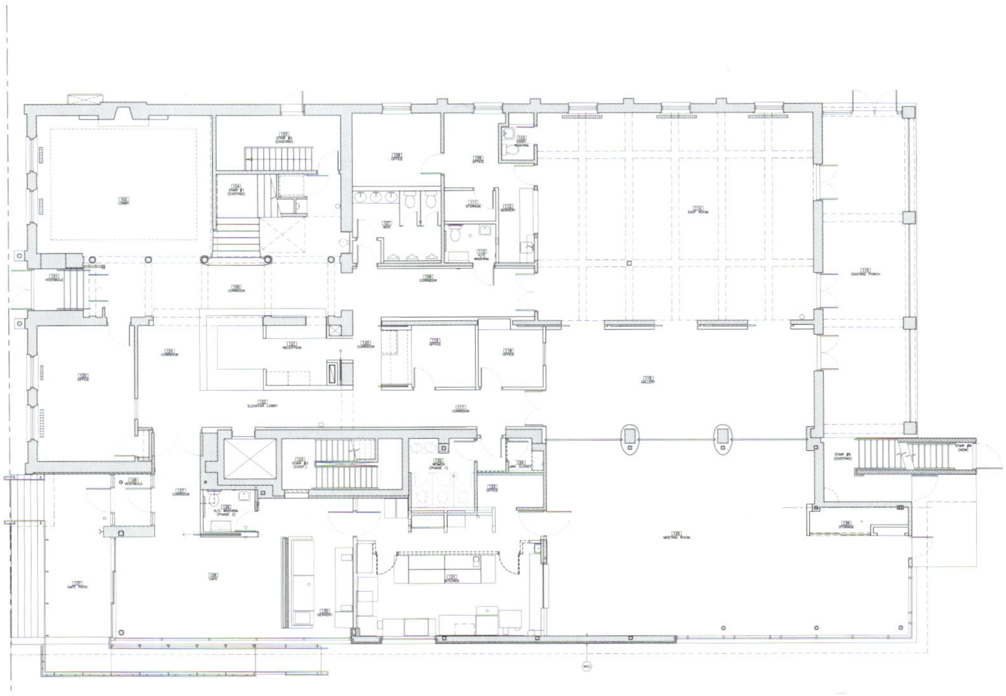

Since 1975, The 519 Church Street community Centre, which is owned by The City of Toronto and administered by a Management Board, has opened its doors to a diversity of users. The initiative to renovate recognizes a crisis point with respect to space for both programmed activities and administrative functions. A new three-storey addition is included, where the ground floor will create a new street-oriented cafe with a terrace and a stepped seating area. It will also feature a large commercial-style kitchen and new programming space on the east side. The upper floors will add program rooms, counseling and meeting rooms, and new administrative spaces.

01 Illuminated façade by night **02** Floor plan **03** Façade **04** Corner view

Photos: Tom Arban photography

CITY Toronto (ON)

COUNTRY Canada

REGION North America

TYPOLOGY Public

COMPLETION 2006 (phase 1), in progress (phase 2)

WEBSITE www.kohnshnierarchitects.com

ARCHITECTS Kohn Shnier Architects

CITY	Toronto (ON)
COUNTRY	Canada
REGION	North America
TYPOLOGY	Living
COMPLETION	2005
WEBSITE	www.kohnshnierarchitects.com
ARCHITECTS	Kohn Shnier Architects

LANEWAY HOUSE

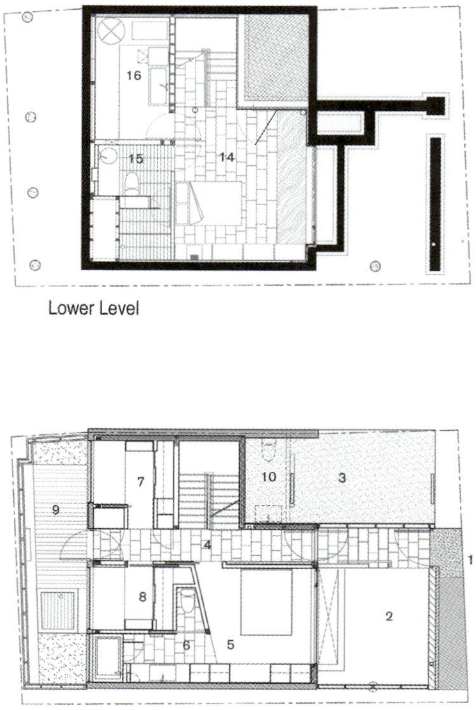

The Laneway House development inverts the conventional arrangement of a program, putting public living spaces above private sleeping spaces. Its compact 111 square meter area accommodates a family of five and their pets. Modest gardens in the front and rear offer a small oasis of amenity and relief from the dense surrounding context. The massing and material palette of the house creates an image that is immediately mysterious as well as seductive. The building appears to hover above its garage neighbours while the cut away corners offer wonderful light, while also presenting views to its inhabitants.

01 Exterior view from street **02** Front façade by night **03** Garden **04** Living room **05** Bird's eye view of oasis **06** Ground and first floor plan

Photos: Tom Arban photography

UMBRA RETAIL AND CONCEPT STORE

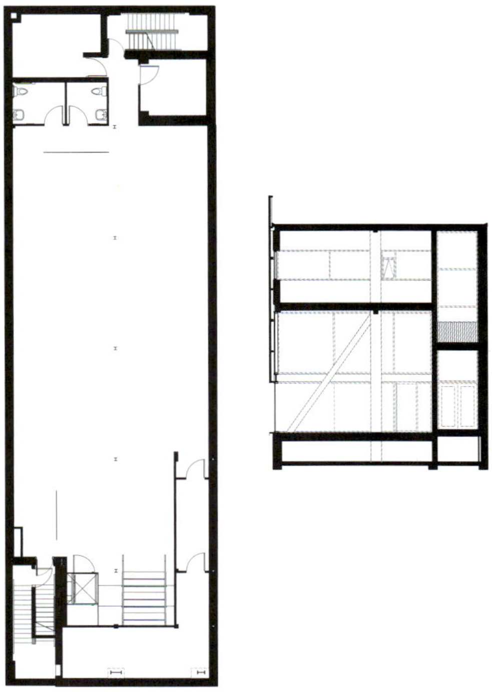

Creating an iconic approach to urban retail architecture through an adaptive reuse of an existing steel frame building, the store, fitted with an environmentally efficient envelope, has been restructured to provide a retail environment filled with natural light. Extruded pink polycarbonate panels envelop the building, ensuring that the store catches pedestrians attention. The interior, a collaboration with Figure 3 interior designers, is opened to a two storey volume by reconfiguring the floor plates and is connected by an innovative stepped ramp and stair system. At night, the alluring daytime view is transformed by ambient interior lighting and individual LED fixtures.

01 Building in context **02** Lower floor plan and section **03** Pink polycarbonate panels **04** Stepped ramp and stair system **05** Exterior view from street

Photos: Tom Arban photography

CITY Toronto (ON)

COUNTRY Canada

REGION North America

TYPOLOGY Retail

COMPLETION 2007

WEBSITE www.kohnshnierarchitects.com

ARCHITECTS Kohn Shnier Architects

CITY: Toronto (ON)
COUNTRY: Canada
REGION: North America
TYPOLOGY: Living
COMPLETION: 2006
WEBSITE: www.donaldchongstudio.com
ARCHITECTS: Donald Chong Studio

GALLEY HOUSE

Situated on a long, narrow `leftover' lot, the Galley House project occupies a once-neglected site, which was a basic lot configuration, not having matched a `desirable' architecture in the mind of the housing market. The challenge was then presented to come up with a solution for how a slender, detached urban house type in Toronto might still offer good space, natural light, and views on the inside and outside. Through an incremental urbanism, the development of the Galley House structure aims to be a new and necessary architectural and typological expression for a healthy and dense urban lifestyle.

01 Front façade **02** View into the garden **03** Stairs leading to private spaces **04** Floor plans **05** Kitchen

Photos: Bob Gundu, Steven Evans (05)

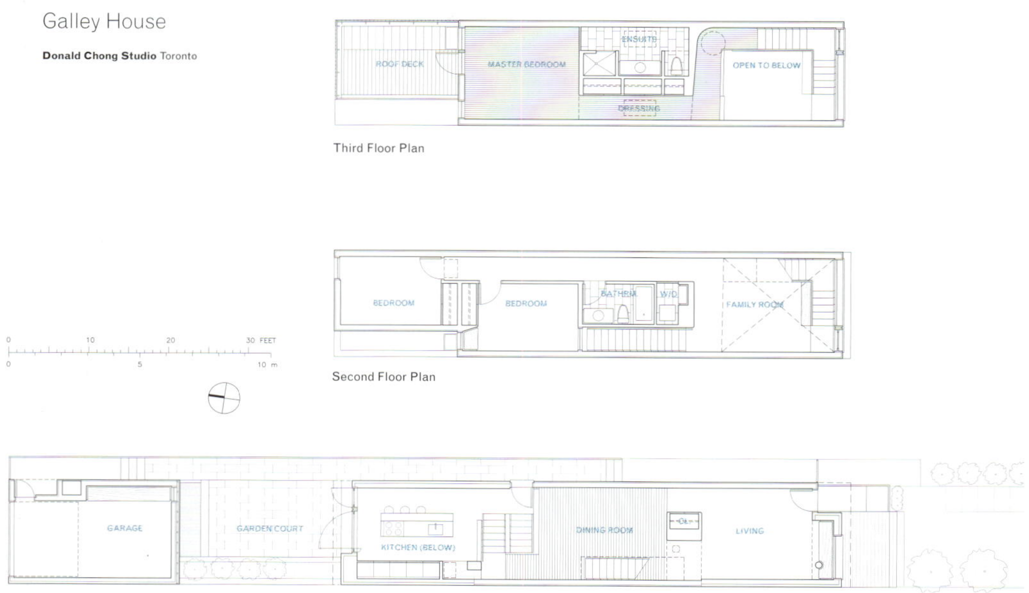

Galley House
Donald Chong Studio Toronto

COURTYARD HOUSE

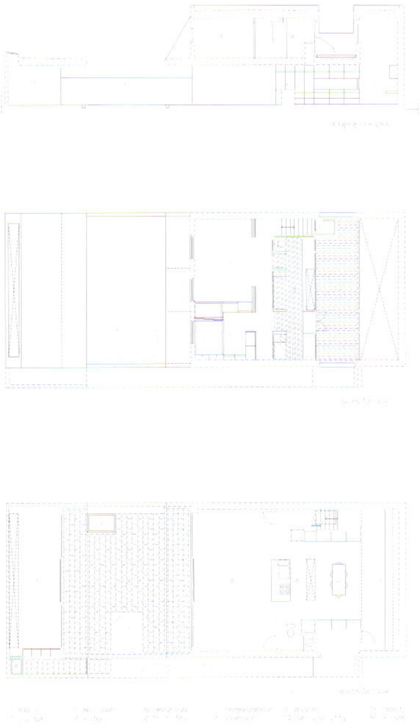

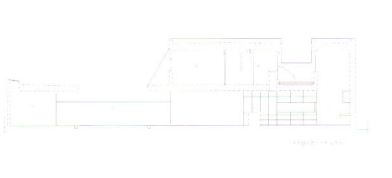

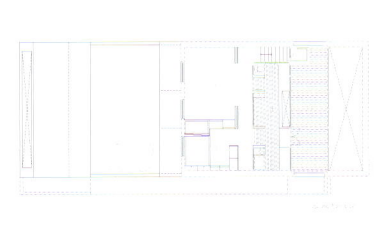

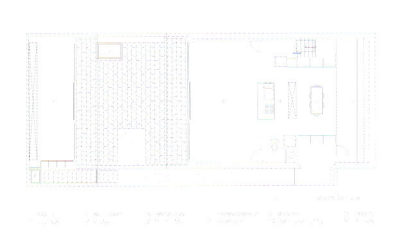

The Courtyard House was inspired by an ancient form of architecture and a desire to experiment with a new form of North American urban thinking - infill housing as an alternative urban typology. By converting a contractor warehouse in a mixed-use industrial neighborhood, the ambition was to create an affordable home and studio for a family of four - one which could successfully adapt to a mid-block situation, where there is no typical front or back. The planned design of this house is generated by an emphasis on the views and activities of the interior courtyards, where all the windows look inwards.

01 Front façade 02 Courtyard rooftop 03 Floor plans 04 Bird's eye view of courtyard rooftop 05 Hall 06 Children's bedroom

Photos: Rob Fiocca, Peter Tan (04)

CITY
Toronto (ON)

COUNTRY
Canada

REGION
North America

TYPOLOGY
Living

COMPLETION
2007

WEBSITE
www.studiojunction.ca

ARCHITECTS
Studio Junction

CITY
Toronto (ON)

COUNTRY
Canada

REGION
North America

TYPOLOGY
Commercial

COMPLETION
2007

WEBSITE
www.dialogue38.com

ARCHITECTS
dialogue38

EKO

Situated in the bustling heart of Toronto's fashionable Queen West, EKO is an established boutique carrying contemporary and unique jewelry by renowned and up and coming jewelry designers from around the world. The objectives of the renovation were to provide a retail space that reflects the creative and innovative designs of Eko's products, to increase merchandising space, and to showcase the merchandise effectively. The simple design becomes a sculptural yet neutral backdrop allowing the jewelry to color the space. The boutique embraced an unconventional idea of Hidden Treasures to entire shoppers.

01 Front façade **02** Protuding colums and recessed vertical display cases **03** Glass encased displays **04** Wall detail

Photos: Courtesy dialogue38

CABBAGETOWN RESIDENCE

Located in one of Toronto's heritage neighbourhoods, the new addition to the rear of the house is boldly modern, while the front façade is preserved. The renovation incorporates a vertical circulation spine with an open plan, allowing rooms to feel larger and more connected and improving flow in the narrow residence. A long skylight above an open riser stair draws light into the lower floors, charging them with natural light. The fully glazed rear façade has a southern orientation, maximizing solar gain in cold winter months while exploiting deciduous trees for shade and privacy during the summer.

01 Glazed rear façade **02** Bathroom **03** View into living room from vertical circulation spine **04** Longitudinal section

Photos: Shai Gil, Insite Photography

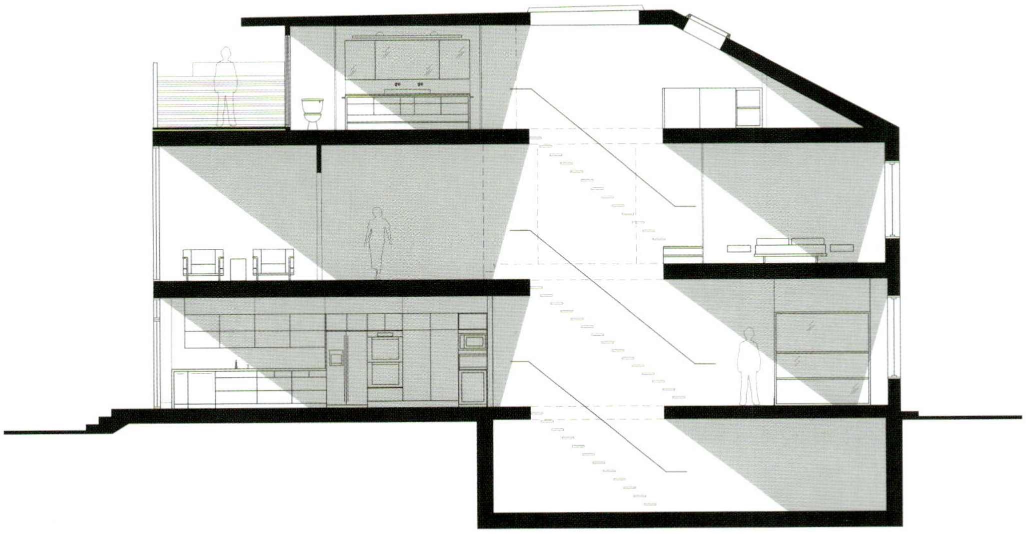

CITY Toronto (ON)
COUNTRY Canada
REGION North America
TYPOLOGY Living
COMPLETION 2007
WEBSITE dubbeldamarchitects.com
ARCHITECTS Dubbeldam Design Architects

CITY: Toronto (ON)
COUNTRY: Canada
REGION: North America
TYPOLOGY: Living
COMPLETION: 2005
WEBSITE: www.teeplearch.com
ARCHITECTS: Teeple Architects

PACHTER HOUSE, GALLERY AND STUDIO

Choosing to live, work and sell his art in one location, the Artist-Owner wanted to bring these program elements together, while keeping their architectural expression distinct. The solution came in the form of three long spatial volumes stacked on top of each other, shifted laterally and longitudinally to allow light penetration into the spaces. Each volume houses one aspect of the program; the ground floor volume is the studio, the second floor makes up the gallery, and the top floor is the residence. The clarity and directness of the concept brings dramatic expression to the sculptural form of the building.

01 Interior studio **02** Volumes stacked and shifted **03** Floor plans **04** View into gallery

Photos: Tom Arban Photography

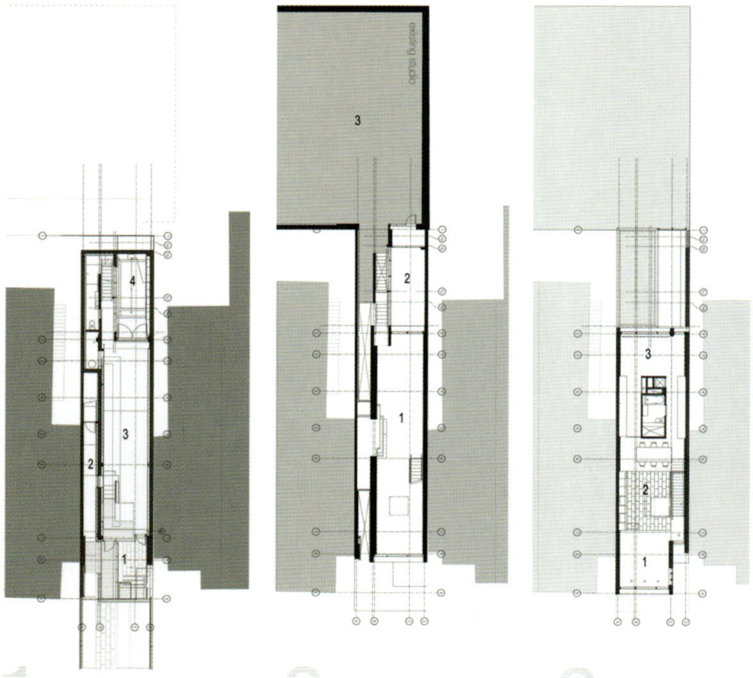

ST. GABRIEL'S PASSIONIST PARISH

St. Gabriel replaces an existing structure and provides the parish with a new legacy. The primary motivation of the Church, Canada's first LEED Silver religious space, was to establish a link between the sacredness of the gathered community of Faith and the sacredness of the Earth. In response to the client's ecological mandate, the project features passive solar heating, natural daylighting, a heat recovery wheel, a living wall, and rainwater collection. Furthermore, an unprecedented investment in the extensive green roof garden, located over the underground parking lot, reduces the building's impact on the urban heat island effect and contributes to wildlife habitat.

01 Exterior view towards glass façade **02** Nave **03** Hallway with view to nave **04** Colored skylights **05** Site plan

Photos: Steven Evans, Martin Knowles (04)

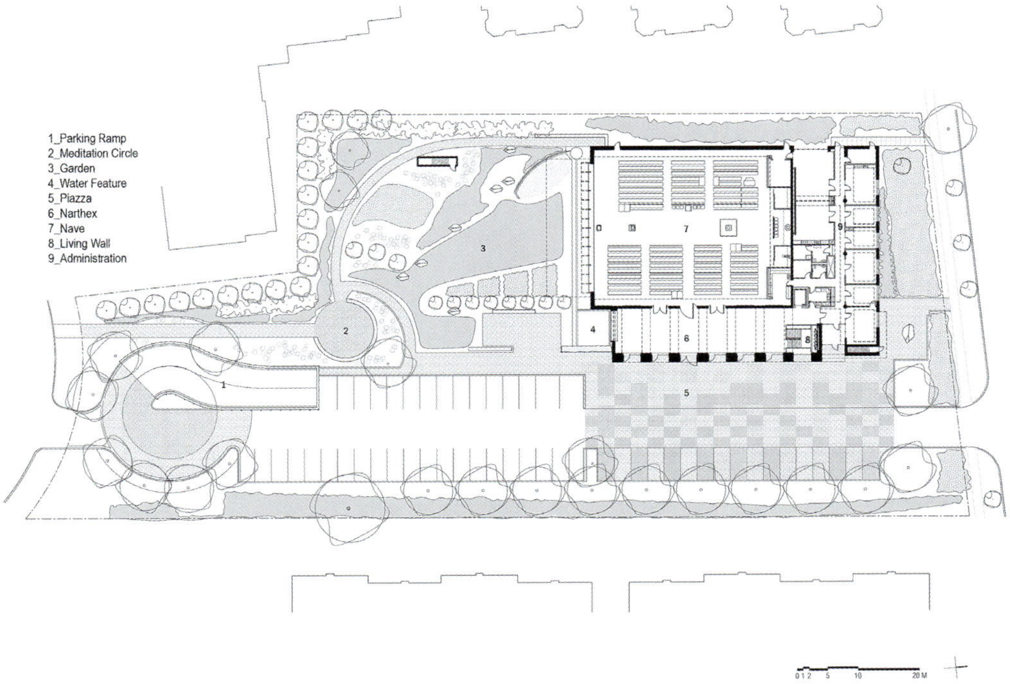

1_Parking Ramp
2_Meditation Circle
3_Garden
4_Water Feature
5_Piazza
6_Narthex
7_Nave
8_Living Wall
9_Administration

CITY: Toronto (ON)
COUNTRY: Canada
REGION: North America
TYPOLOGY: Ecclesiastical
COMPLETION: 2006
WEBSITE: www.larkinarchitect.com
ARCHITECTS: larkin architect limited

CAPEZIO FLAGSHIP

The architect's retail concept for Capezio is an experiment in progressive architecture and a departure from the formulaic and typical. Walls, ceilings and floors merge into each other as a traditional sense of space is distorted and the store becomes a sculptural installation in itself. The footwear and accessories line the perimeter of the space in avant-garde coves which merge seamlessly with the pristine white space. The floor and seating areas are rendered in the same modern Tokyo purple. The bright color offers a dramatic counterpoint to the white architectural planes of the surrounding wall and ceiling design.

01 Interior **02** Shop window, view inside **03** Floor plan **04** Interior

Photos: Ben Rahn/A-Frame Inc.

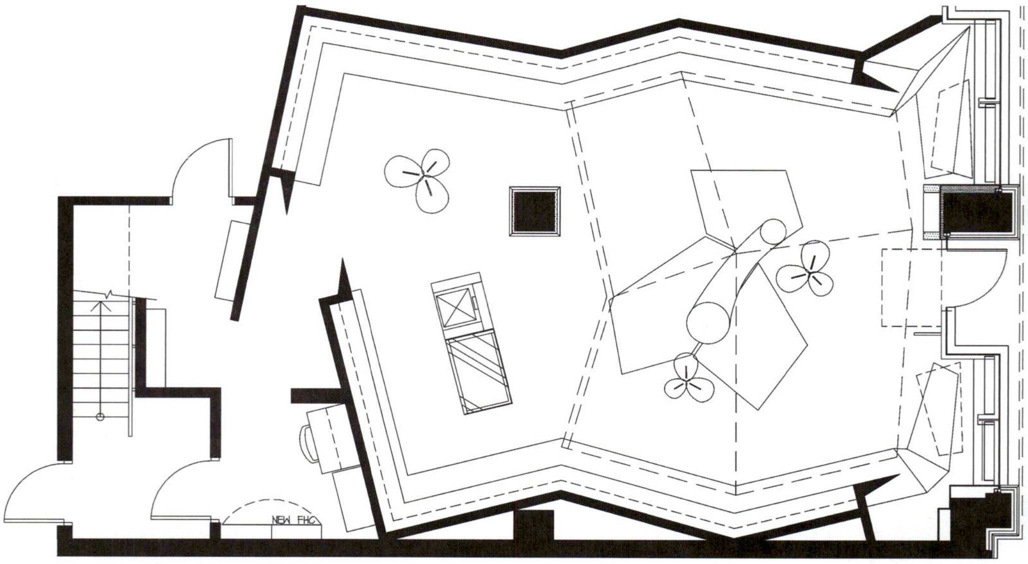

CITY Toronto (ON)
COUNTRY Canada
REGION North America
TYPOLOGY Retail
COMPLETION –
WEBSITE www.burdifilek.com
ARCHITECTS burdifilek Interior Design

IL FORNELLO

This new 100-seat restaurant in the heart of Toronto's gay village attempts to harness the spirit of its local culture into a more intimate yet dramatic experience. The rolling storefront moves approximately 18-20 feet in order to defy the limitations imposed by Toronto's climate. A patio environment can be created in the warmer season with an opportunity to recoup the space in the winter. Whether inside or outside, the patron is safely removed from the street, without compromising the rich urban connection while having the opportunity to oscillate psychologically between "back stage", "back drop" and "foreground" space.

01 Interior **02** Entry view **03** Interior **04** Floor plan **05** Detail
Photos: Courtesy Giannone Associates Architects

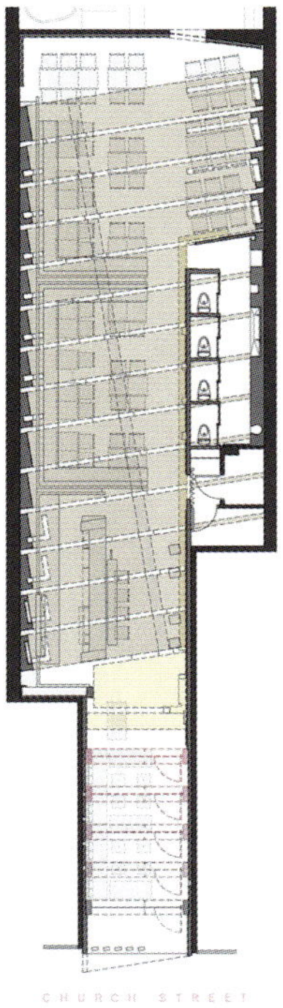

CITY Toronto (ON)
COUNTRY Canada
REGION North America
TYPOLOGY Gastronomy
COMPLETION –
WEBSITE www.giannoneassociates.com
ARCHITECTS Giannone Associates Architects

CITY: Toronto (ON)
COUNTRY: Canada
REGION: North America
TYPOLOGY: Education
COMPLETION: 2003
WEBSITE: www.kongatsarchitects.com
ARCHITECTS: Kongats Architects

CENTENNIAL COLLEGE VISUAL ARTS CENTER

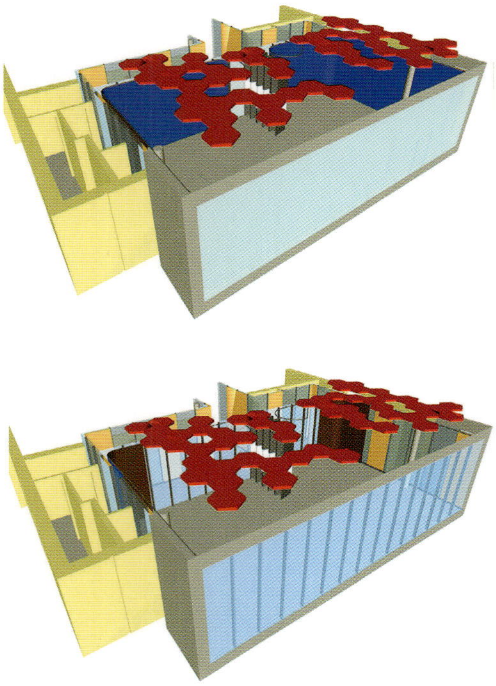

Within the volume of the construction, located in an existing auditorium at the Centre for Creative Communications, are a new interior liner shell and a second floor structure which were inserted to accommodate a mixed-use program. The program comprises of visual arts studios, class rooms, teleconferencing studio/meeting hall, student lounges, faculty offices and an electronic instruction lab. An addition on the ground level is manifested by a light box constructed of diffusible electronic glass and aluminum panels, used for projections while providing cinema graphic quality to the streetscape.

01 Exterior view by night **02** Details **03** Interior **04** Meeting space

Photos: Ben Rahn/A-Frame Inc.

ROYAL ONTARIO MUSEUM

This Royal Museum project entails renovating ten new galleries in the existing historical building and creating an extension to the museum: the Michael Lee-Chin Crystal. The new extension provides dynamic new architecture, the creation of a great public attraction, and 100,000 square feet of new exhibition space. Situated on one of the most prominent intersections in downtown Toronto, the Museum becomes a dynamic center for the city. Devoted to gallery space, the project also features a spacious new entrance and lobby, a new retail shop accessible directly from the street, and three new restaurants.

01 Exterior view by night **02** Diagonal crevices bringing light into interior gallery **03** View inside **04** View into lounge area **05** Aerial view into roof structure

Photos: Royal Ontario Museum (01, 04), Sam Javanrouh

CITY Toronto (ON)
COUNTRY Canada
REGION North America
TYPOLOGY Culture
COMPLETION –
WEBSITE www.daniel-libeskind.com
ARCHITECTS Daniel Libeskind

CITY Toronto (ON)
COUNTRY Canada
REGION North America
TYPOLOGY Culture
COMPLETION 2005
WEBSITE www.montgomerysisam.com
ARCHITECTS Montgomery Sisam Architects Inc.

GEORGE AND KATHY DEMBROSKI CENTRE FOR HORTICULTURE, TORONTO BOTANICAL GARDEN

The design intent of the addition was one of integration; new building with existing building, buildings with gardens and finally an integrated approach to issues of sustainability. The new glass pavilion is a sculptural form in the park, mute and calm during the day and taking on the more dramatic appearance of a lantern at night. Although the pavilion creates a new 'front door' to the facility, it remains deferential to the gardens. The building addition has been certified LEED® Silver, consistent with the Botanical Garden's mission of advocating stewardship of the natural environment.

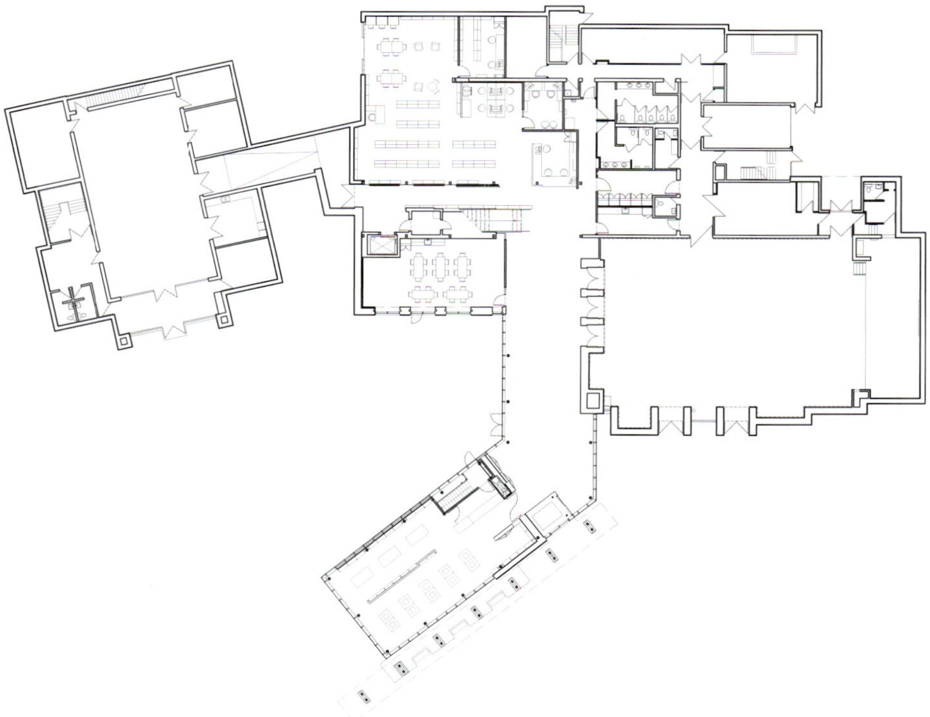

01 Entry view **02** Garden view **03** Staircase **04** Floor plan **05** Interior

Photos: Tom Arban Photography

GARDEN PAVILION

Set in a private garden, the Garden Pavilion design was inspired by Eastern philosophy of harmony with nature. It is used for sitting and dining, as well as workshops, concerts, and other activities of an Artists' Cooperative. The pavilion's lattice-like structure is made of cedar, with steel hardware and clear glazing. It allows layered views of the garden and sky, and frames the orbit of the moon. The roof structure precisely aligns to shade the sun at solstice in the hottest days of summer, but allows the sun to penetrate fully by equinox providing warmth in the cooler months of spring and fall.

01 Exterior view **02** Seating space **03** Construction **04** Detail **05** Plans

Photos: Steven Evans

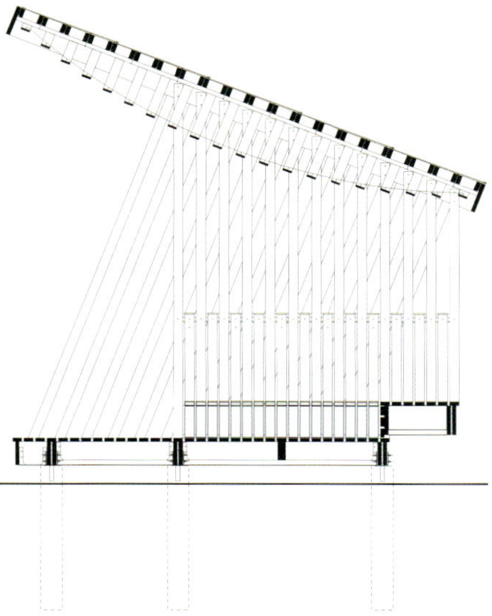

CITY: Toronto (ON)
COUNTRY: Canada
REGION: North America
TYPOLOGY: Culture
COMPLETION: 2003
WEBSITE: www.paulraffstudio.com
ARCHITECTS: Paul Raff Studio

CITY Uxbridge (ON)
COUNTRY Canada
REGION North America
TYPOLOGY Office
COMPLETION in progress
WEBSITE www.rdharch.com
ARCHITECTS Rounthwaite Dick + Hadley Architects

FIRST LEASIDE FINANCIAL OFFICE HEADQUARTERS

The project is a sustainable office development located in Ontario, Canada. Compositionally, the building form ascends in two directions: the first ascension points towards the downtown business district, while the second ascends along the length of an existing rail corridor. Environmental initiatives have been incorporated into the building including extensive and intensive roof top planting, natural ventilation, thermal chimney effect, and geothermal heating and cooling. Ecological redevelopment of the site offers an opportunity to expand an existing valley shape to incorporate a biologically active floodplain.

01 Front façade towards business district **02** Main entrance **03** Section **04** Exterior view along the length of the rail corridor **05** Exterior view with rooftop plantings

Photos: DesignStor

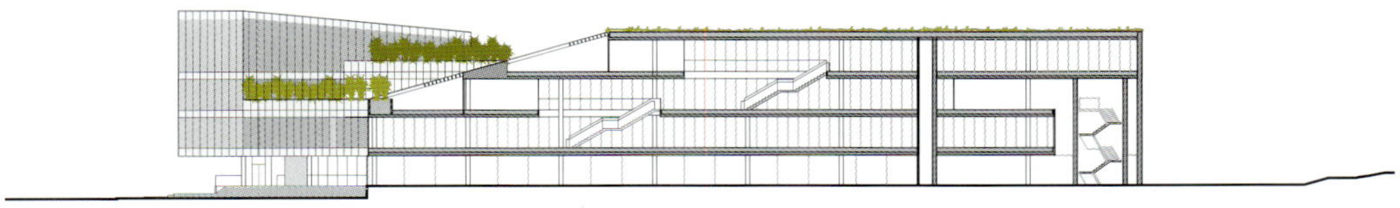

RESTORATION SERVICES CENTRE, TORONTO AND REGION CONSERVATION AUTHORITY

The Restoration Services Centre, the 1st building in Ontario to be LEED Platinum certified, supports the TRCA's mission by using simple, low-cost design solutions to drive high performance sustainable outcomes. Designed through an integrated process it reflects the best of sustainable design in both its architectural expression and internal systems. With a cost premium of less than 10%, the Centre achieves a 50% reduction in total energy costs and uses 20% of the natural gas, 70% of the electricity and 20% of the potable water of a similar structure built with conventional building practices.

01 View into interior **02** Exterior view by night **03** Interior working space **04** View along south wall

Photos: Tom Arban Photography

CITY Vaughan (ON)
COUNTRY Canada
REGION North America
TYPOLOGY Office
COMPLETION 2007
WEBSITE www.montgomerysisam.com
ARCHITECTS Montgomery Sisam Architects Inc.

MUSEE DU FJORD

Along the north shore of St. Lawrence, and stretching deep into the rugged Saguenay Fjord, the landscape leaves an indelible and inescapable sense of existing on the edge. A simple design into the elegantly detailed box plays water against land, transparency against opacity, and in doing so, introduces a subversive twist to local convention. The Musée du Fjord rests on the shores of Baie des Ha! Ha! in the hamlet of LaBaie, and the setting of this village-owned interpretive facility is intended to celebrate as well as explain this unique biodiversity and the socio-cultural history it has helped support.

01 Window with wood framing **02** Terrace with view to Baie des Ha!Ha! **03** Courtyard **04** Exterior view by night **05** Ground floor plan **06** First floor plan

Photos: Steve Montpetit

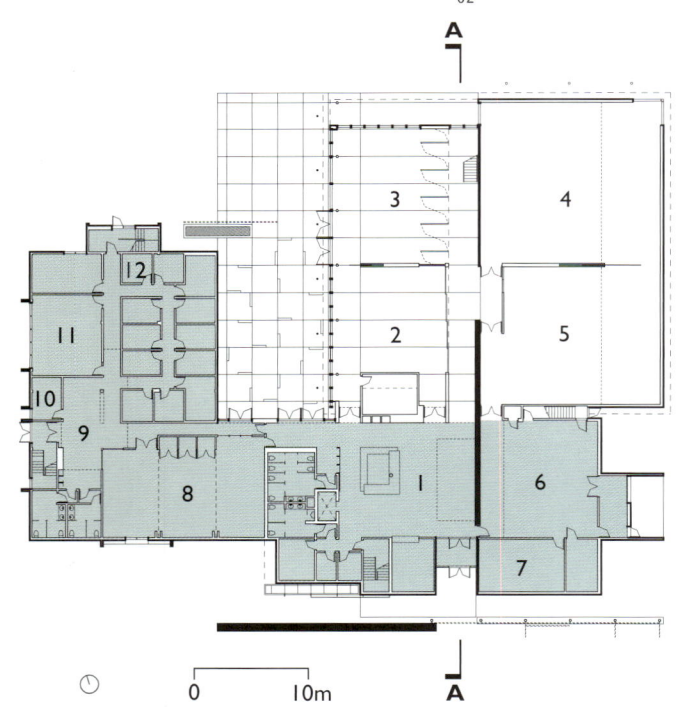

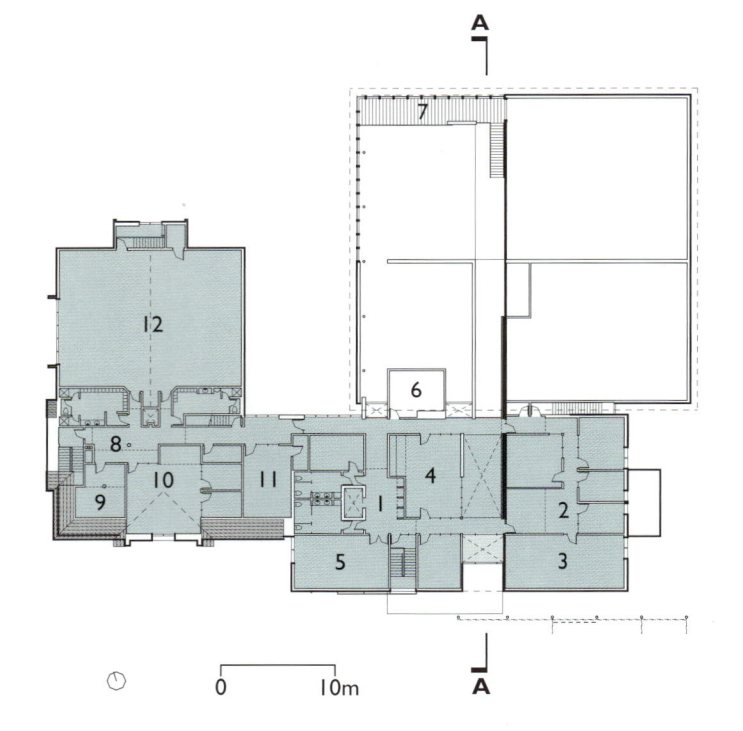

CITY Ville de La Baie (QC)
COUNTRY Canada
REGION North America
TYPOLOGY Culture
COMPLETION 2004
WEBSITE www.msdl.ca
ARCHITECTS Menkès Shooner Dagenais LeTourneux architects / BCS + M Architects (consortium)

KING DAVID HIGH SCHOOL

Being distinctly linear, the school consists of an administration wing, a classroom wing, and a large storey central gathering area that serves the purpose, symbolically and functionally, as the heart of the building. The gathering area also serves as a sanctuary, assembly hall, and student lounge. Openness to the surrounding circulation system reinforces the significance of space, strengthening the sense of connectivity and belonging of the students to their school, culture and community. The outside space furthers cultural references through a network of landscaped terraces treated as an allegorical biblical garden.

01 Exploded processional oblique **02** Main entrance **03** Exterior view **04** Multipurpose hall **05** Lounge

Photos: Martin Tessler

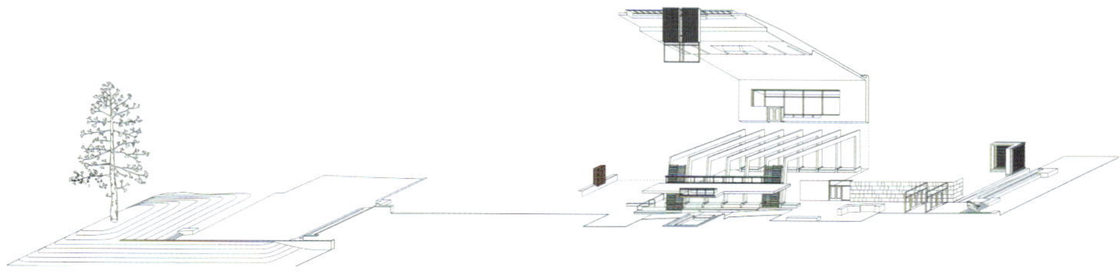

CITY Vancouver (BC)
COUNTRY Canada
REGION North America
TYPOLOGY Education
COMPLETION 2005
WEBSITE www.actonostry.ca
ARCHITECTS Acton Ostry Architects Inc

CITY Vancouver (BC)

COUNTRY Canada

REGION North America

TYPOLOGY Living

COMPLETION 2007

WEBSITE www.busbyperkinswill.ca

ARCHITECTS Busby Perkins + Will Architects Co.

SILVER SEA

The Silver Sea is a unique residential development designed to achieve a high level of architectural and urban design excellence. The design of the building incorporated advanced and progressive green building strategies that resulted in a reduction in the overall level of energy and water consumption and mitigation of the project's complete environmental impact. Concerning its site, orientation, massing, form, and material palette, the Silver Sea project provides an intimate connection to its surrounding marine and park vernacular, providing a distinct addition to the neighborhood's urban fabric.

01 Night view **02** View from pedestrian bridge **03** Panoramic view to the marine **04** Northeast elevation **05** Northwest façade

Photos: Enrico Dagostini, Nic Lehoux (03, 05)

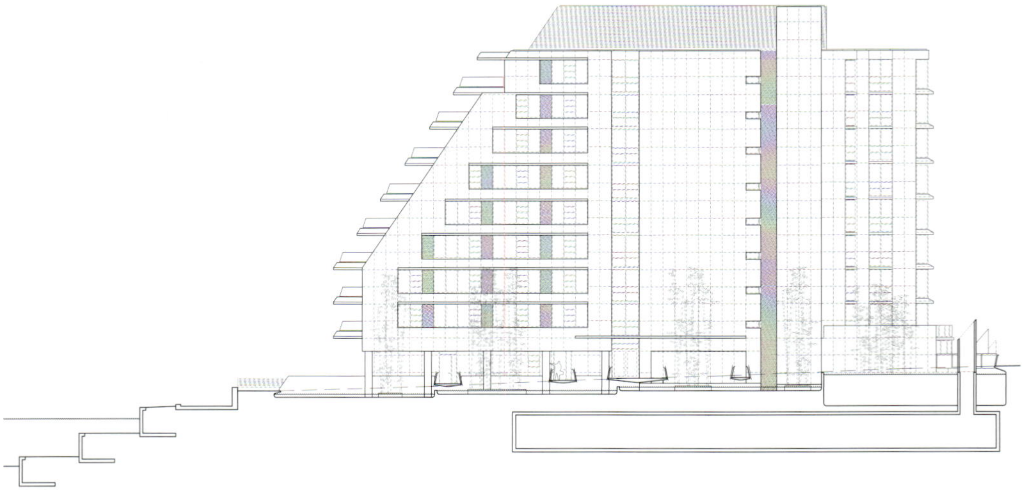

TELUS HOUSE

The Telus House project revitalizes an existing complex in a high profile location in downtown Vancouver, reinvigorating the surrounding urban area. The design 'recycled' the building, saving landfill, energy and resources and achieving a high level of environmental performance. The exterior revitalization was realized as an open, layered an sophisticated new 'sin' enveloping the old building shell. A double-glazed, fritted and frameless glazing system with operable window is suspended from the existing building creating the first double-wall/triple-skinned green building solution in Canada.

01 Lobby **02** General view **03** Structural façade detail **04** Meeting space **05** Wall diagram and elevation **06** Exterior view by night

Photos: Martin Tessler

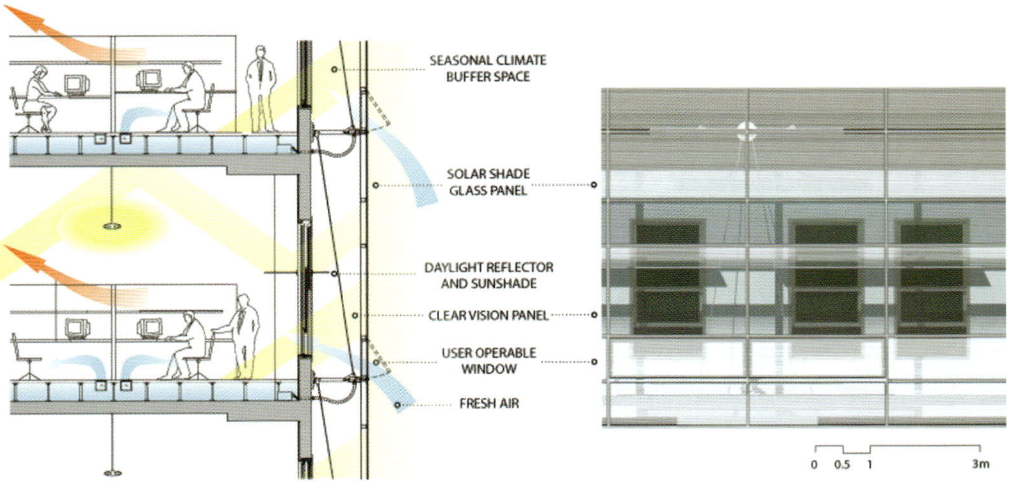

CITY Vancouver (BC)
COUNTRY Canada
REGION North America
TYPOLOGY Living
COMPLETION 2007
WEBSITE www.busbyperkinswill.ca
ARCHITECTS Busby Perkins + Will Architects Co.

CITY Vancouver (BC)
COUNTRY Canada
REGION North America
TYPOLOGY Education
COMPLETION 2007
WEBSITE www.teeplearch.com
ARCHITECTS Teeple Architects

LANGARA COLLEGE LIBRARY AND CLASSROOM BUILDING

The building was conceived as an environmental form, inflected by the natural forces acting on it, where wind and rain warp its roof. Wind towers are displaced vertically from the roof's surface, and this warped surface lifts the wind into the towers, pulling air through the building. The environmental forces create the sentient form of the building, where gardens push into its form, bringing greenery and daylight to its interior. The towers form the principle interiors while public stairs are placed under the wind towers. The building has neither air conditioning nor heating systems, but is rather naturally ventilated.

01 Exterior view by night **02** Stairs leading to classrooms **03** Exterior view into the library **04** View into wind tower and circulation **05** Floor plan

Photos: Shai Gil

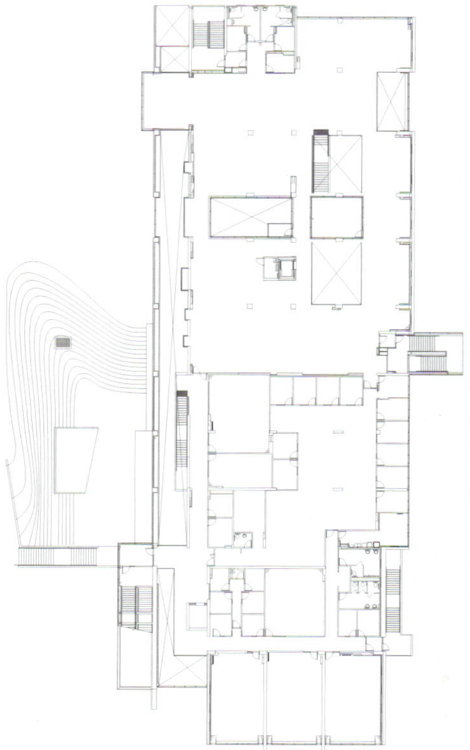

BCIT AEROSPACE TECHNOLOGY CAMPUS

The BCIT Aerospace Technology Campus acts in harmony with the natural surroundings, concedes to the flight path overhead, and caters to the needs of the students, faculty, and guests within. The 305,000 square foot, 65 million dollar facility is a series of interconnected geometric forms that flow naturally together through a central hub and massive 40,000 square foot hangar. Much more than a technical training campus, this is a facility that will revolutionize the nature of knowledge sharing in the training of students graduating into the multibillion-dollar aeronautics industry.

01 Hangar, exterio 02 Shield wall at entrance 03 Hangar interior 04 Interior walkway 05 Sketch

Photos: Nic Lehoux

CITY Vancouver (BC)
COUNTRY Canada
REGION North America
TYPOLOGY Institution / Technology
COMPLETION 2007
WEBSITE www.kasian.com
ARCHITECTS Kasian Architecture Interior Design and Planning

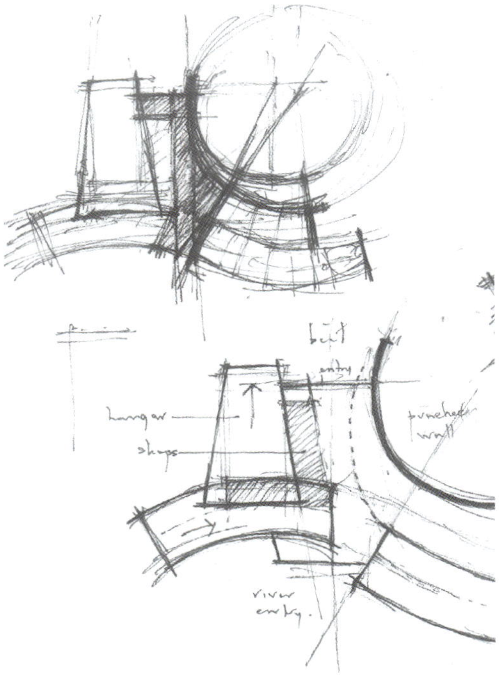

CITY Vancouver (N. Vancouver (BC))

COUNTRY Canada

REGION North America

TYPOLOGY Living

COMPLETION 2005

WEBSITE www.synthesisdesign.ca

ARCHITECTS Synthesis Design Inc.

HANNA RESIDENCE

This project's mission was to transform a non-descript 1970's home on a dramatic, steep-sloped site, and to create a welcoming entry via the use of a vertical inclined plane. A 'wedge' cuts through the heart of the front façade, forming a dramatic architectural element, which guides one down to the front door. Given the dense forest setting, emphasis was given to maximize the natural light in the new space. The upper portion of the 'wedge' fashions an open exercise room, which benefits from 360-degrees of natural light and various shadow patterns throughout the day, as well as spilling light into the heart of the house.

01 Front façade **02** Entrance **03** Side elevation **04** Entry elevation **05** Open core

Photos: Mike Wakefield

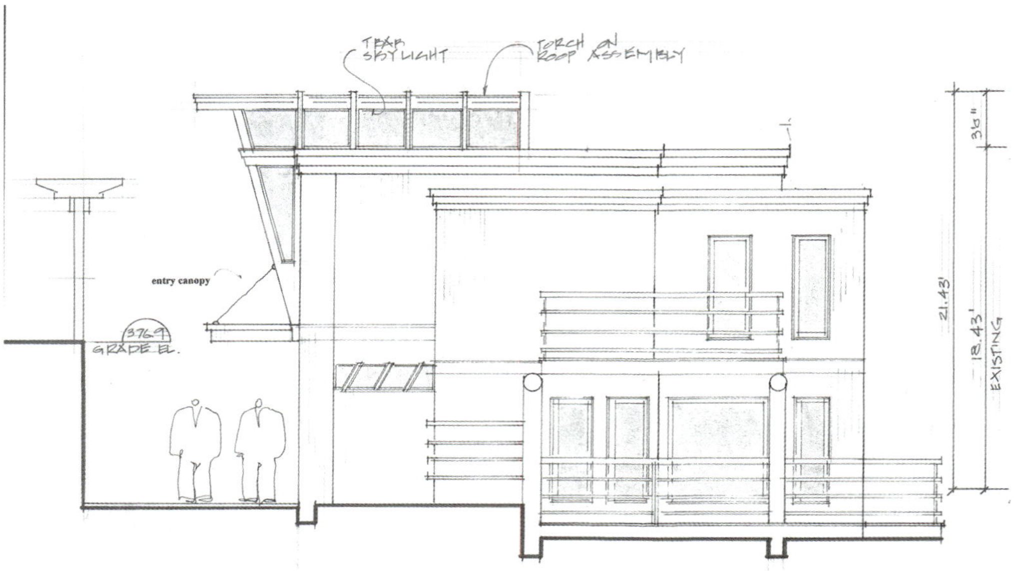

LALJI RESIDENCE

The owners requested a design that would compliment not only their lifestyle, but also their broad-mindedness and good taste. The preference of renovation over a new-build was attributed to the existing location of the house, views, landscape, greenbelt, and convenience. The proposal to open up the many rooms to a large free flowing space divided by millwork units proved rather successful as the family and friends meet regularly at the house, and this open space perfectly facilitates the entertainment needs. The clients, who have worked with FNDA for over 15 years, were delighted with the final design.

01 Exterior view by night of entrance **02** Stairs **03** Floor plan **04** Living room

Photos: Raef Grohne

CITY Vancouver (BC) (W. Vancouver)
COUNTRY Canada
REGION North America
TYPOLOGY Living
COMPLETION -
WEBSITE www.fndesign.com
ARCHITECTS Farouk Noormohamed – FNDA Architecture, Inc.

CITY Vancouver (BC) (W. Vancouver)

COUNTRY Canada

REGION North America

TYPOLOGY Living

COMPLETION 2006

WEBSITE www.frits.ca

ARCHITECTS Frits de Vries Architect Ltd

5230 SEASIDE PLACE

This four-bedroom West Vancouver waterfront home has been custom designed for a contractor's family. The entry is experienced as a series of unique features; a small waterfall descends to a pond with a bridge above, while an oversized entry door and a suspended glass canopy above beckon one into the home. In the foyer, a cantilevered open stair floats against a white wall punctuated by display niches, while glass guards reinforce the feeling of lightness and transparency. Through careful consideration in the placement of the main living rooms on the upper floor, this contemporary design maximizes panoramic ocean views.

01 Front façade **02** Oversized entry door with suspended canopy **03** Interior with view to seaside **04** Kitchen **05** First level floor plan

Photos: Frits de Vries

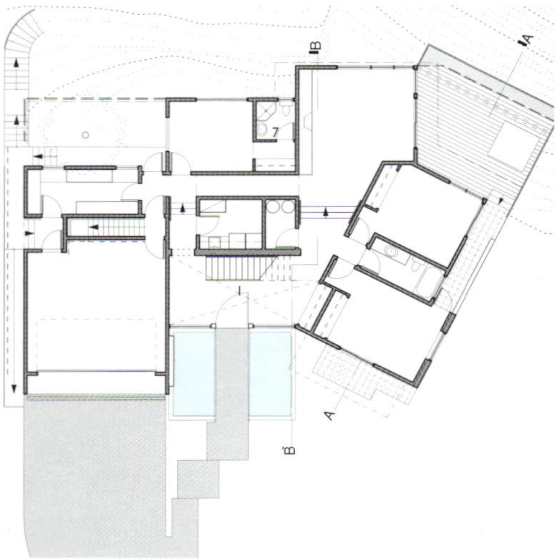

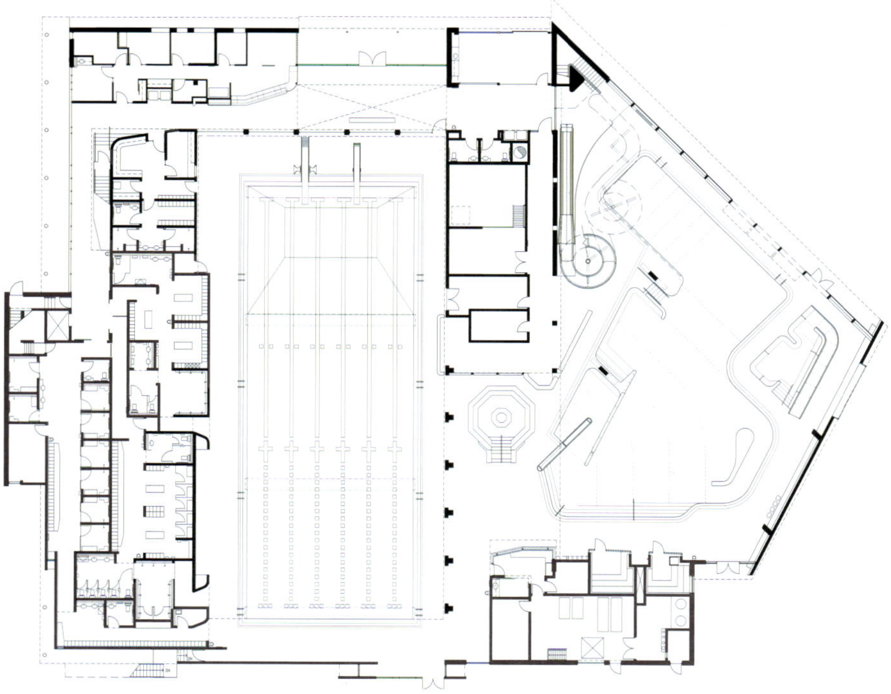

WEST VANCOUVER AQUATIC CENTRE

The West Vancouver Aquatic Centre provides the community a striking facility that speaks of wellness, accessibility and health. The facility features an accessible hot pool, sauna and steam room, sun deck, family changing rooms, multipurpose room, fitness facilities and public viewing areas. A custom glulam glazing system accommodates glazed overhead doors and a series of electrically operative solar shading devices featuring a bold public art piece. Along with natural lighting, the use of glazed overhead doors and operable vents allow fresh air to naturally ventilate through the building.

01 Main floor plan **02** Exterior view of glass façade **03** Main entrance **04** Exterior view by night **05** Wellness area

Photos: Martin Tessler, Nic Lehoux, Gray Otte

CITY Vancouver (West Vancouver) (BC)
COUNTRY Canada
REGION North America
TYPOLOGY Leisure
COMPLETION 2004
WEBSITE www.hcma.ca
ARCHITECTS Hughes Condon Marler

CITY Vancouver (W. Vancouver (BC))

COUNTRY Canada

REGION North America

TYPOLOGY Living

COMPLETION 2006

WEBSITE www.cardew.ca

ARCHITECTS Peter Cardew Architects

LEBLANC HOUSE

If judged by contemporary standards, the architecture of the recent past is often rejected as being of little worth when compared to that which is very old or very new. Although the most ubiquitous form of single family dwelling in North America since the end of World War II, the Split-Level has never achieved the iconic status that would encourage adaptation over demolition. This project not only retains architectural evidence of the most significant housing boom in Canadian history, but it also shows that this often demolished building stock can be adapted to satisfy the requirements of modern living.

01 Exterior view from the garden **02** Main entrance **03** Open iving space **04** Axonometric **05** Split-level detail **06** Stairs towards open floor

Photos: Peter Cardew (01, 02), Sarah Murray

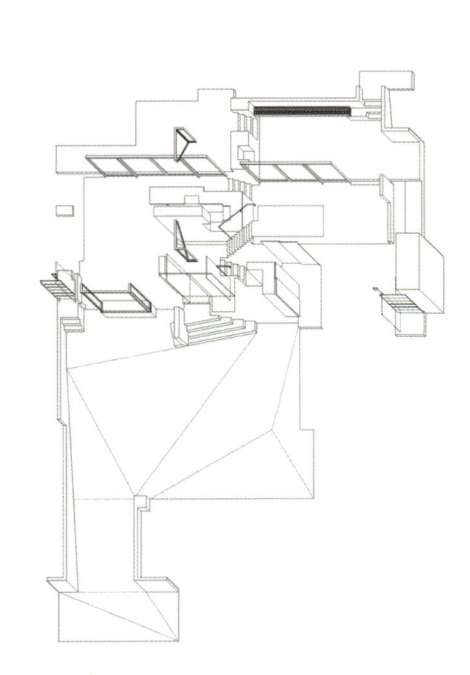

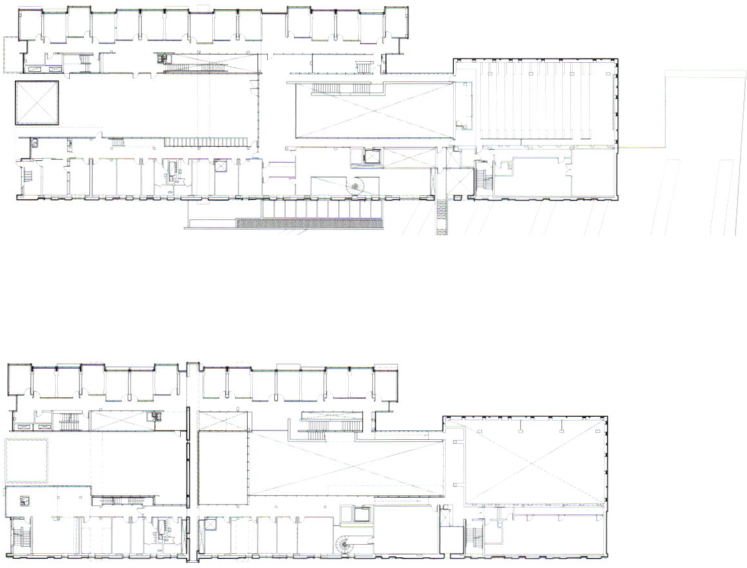

PERIMETER INSTITUTE FOR THEORETICAL PHYSICS

Riding the controversial line between public and private space, this research institute attempts to subvert the usual hard thresholds established by private enterprises in the public realm. Between city and park, the Perimeter Institute expands, inhabits, and develops the improbable space separating the two. The building defines secure zones within a series of parallel glass walls, embedded in an erupting ground plane that reveals a large reflecting pool. Bridges provide quick access to information, while facilities and research colleagues cross the space between theoretical physics and everyday life.

01 Floor plans, second and third level **02** Façade **03** Curtain wall **04** Façade detail **05** Bridges leading to information facilities

Photos: Marc Cramer

CITY Waterloo (ON)
COUNTRY Canada
REGION North America
TYPOLOGY Institution / Technology
COMPLETION 2004
WEBSITE www.saucierperrotte.com
ARCHITECTS Saucier and Perrotte Architects

CITY
Whistler (BC)

COUNTRY
Canada

REGION
North America

TYPOLOGY
Living

COMPLETION
2005

WEBSITE
www.nminusone.com

ARCHITECTS
Studio NminusOne /
Christos Marcopoulos,
Carol Moukheiber

KHYBER RIDGE HOUSE (AKA THE BOARDING HOUSE)

The Khyber Ridge House is distributed along a steep slope, developing diverse tactical relations to the landscape, the surrounding views, and the internal functions of the house. Made up of five levels, the lower level is embedded in the rock for maximum privacy, while in contrast, the main living level is a cantilevering roof with a suspended floor projecting out of the slope. The upper level bedrooms retreat back along the contours of the mountain producing discreet relationships to the surroundings. As the inhabitants navigate these volumes, they continuously weave in and out of the terrain.

01 Exterior view into living space **02** Exploded axonometric **03** House embedded in rock **04** View into living room **05** Overall view of house in site

Photos: Ari Marcopoulos

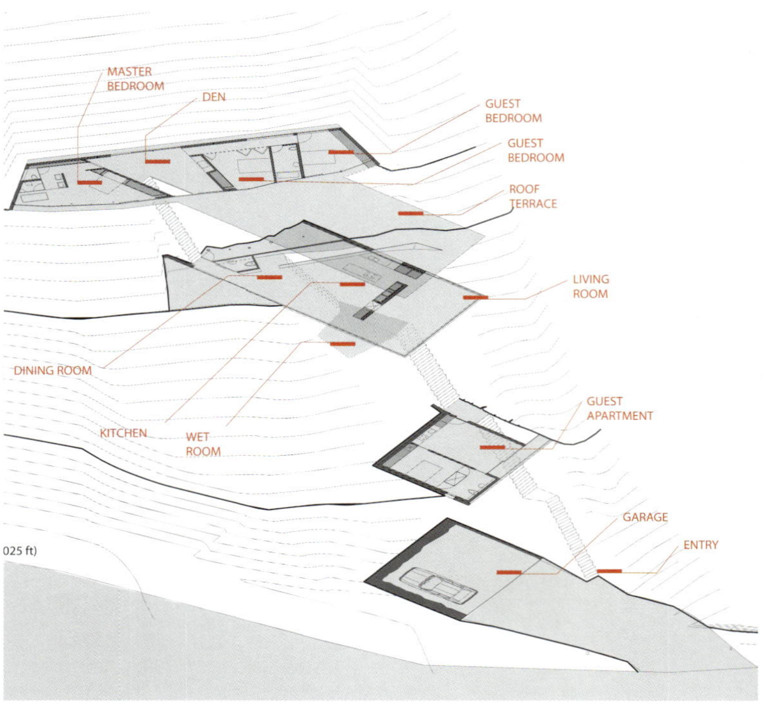

RED RIVER COLLEGE

Red River College is a business, multi-media, and information technology college accommodating about 2,000 students and 200 staff. Located in Canada's historic site of the Winnipeg Exchange District, a strong commitment is showcased to "green" architecture and conservation. The design concept was to construct an environmentally sustainable building based on the predominant warehouse typology. Conceived as a natural extension of the historic urban fabric, the campus is prominently located amongst heavy masonry warehouses and early steel frame skyscrapers, and respects the tradition of the property line.

01 Classroom **02** Brick staircase and hall **03** Campus integrated with existing warehouses **04** Sky-lit corridor **05** Main floor plan

Photos: Gerry Kopelow

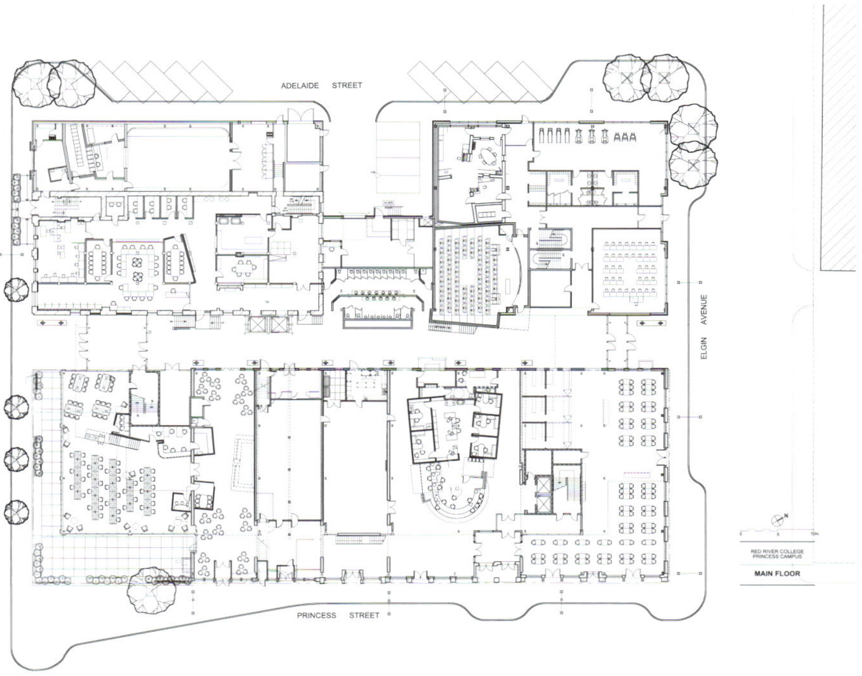

CITY Winnipeg (MB)
COUNTRY Canada
REGION North America
TYPOLOGY Education
COMPLETION 2003
WEBSITE www.cibinel.com
ARCHITECTS Corbett Cibinel Architects

CITY Yellowknife (NT)
COUNTRY Canada
REGION North America
TYPOLOGY Education
COMPLETION 2001
WEBSITE www.guyarchitects.com
ARCHITECTS Guy Architects

ECOLE ALLAIN ST-CYR

The three-story Ecole Allain St-Cyr is located on a narrow lot surrounded by sub-arctic forest. Its dramatic form and colorful interiors are inspired by the immediate environment. The connection between students and nature was the basis for designing the facility, which is one of Canada's most innovative schools. This technically sophisticated project was the first school in Canada to utilize displacement ventilation to meet the needs of hypoallergenic children.

01 Exterior view from courtyard **02** Colorful building façade **03** Activity hall **04** Terrace access

Photos: Tim Atherton

USA

CITY Allston (MA)

COUNTRY USA

REGION North America

TYPOLOGY Public

COMPLETION 2001

WEBSITE www.machado-silvetti.com

ARCHITECTS Machado and Silvetti Associates

THE HONAN-ALLSTON BRANCH OF THE BOSTON PUBLIC LIBRARY

The new Honan-Allston Branch of the Boston Public Library, constructed by Machado and Silvetti Associates, opened in June 2001. The development, which is a 20,000 square foot building, houses different elements for the purpose of study and pleasure. These different features include three reading rooms, stacks and periodicals, public computer stations, community facilities, as well as three reading gardens for enjoyment. The library's material palette includes Norwegian slate panels, Vermont slate shingles, rough sculpings, and lastly, unfinished wood cladding, all which contribute to the Library's uniqueness.

01 View of the main reading room façade **02** View of the main entrance **03** View of the front reading room **04** Ground floor plan **05** View of the children's reading room from the children's garden

Photos: Michael Moran Photography

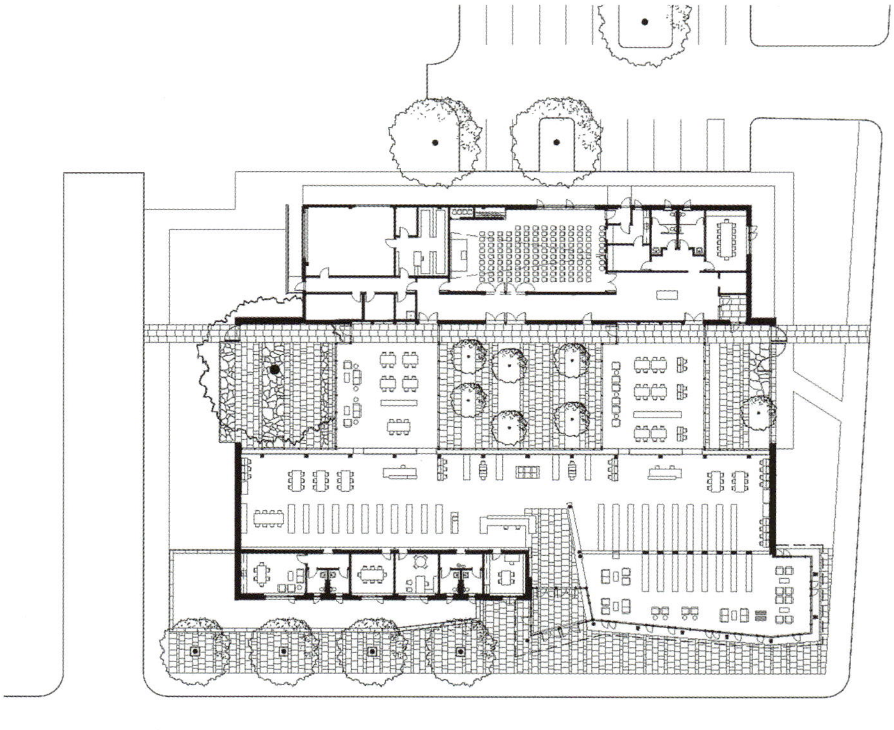

PHELPS/BURKE RESIDENCE

This long and narrow residence takes advantage of views over a nearby inlet and provides maximum sun exposure through large windows on the south and west sides. Design features of the house include a "wrap-around" deck on the upper level that functions as an extension of the living room. The north deck provides a wind-sheltered space to enjoy the Alaskan summer sunsets. The lower level features all private spaces. Large barn door shutters can be used for privacy and security. In addition to the long main body of the house two individual spaces characterize the overall volume: a home office on the lower level has a controlled view "into the indoor-outdoor garden" and an art studio, on the upper level, which provides long views over the inlet.

01 Exterior with "wrap-around" deck **02** Lower and upper level floor plans **03** Kitchen **04** Private space **05** Exterior view from north

Photos: Kevin G. Smith Photography

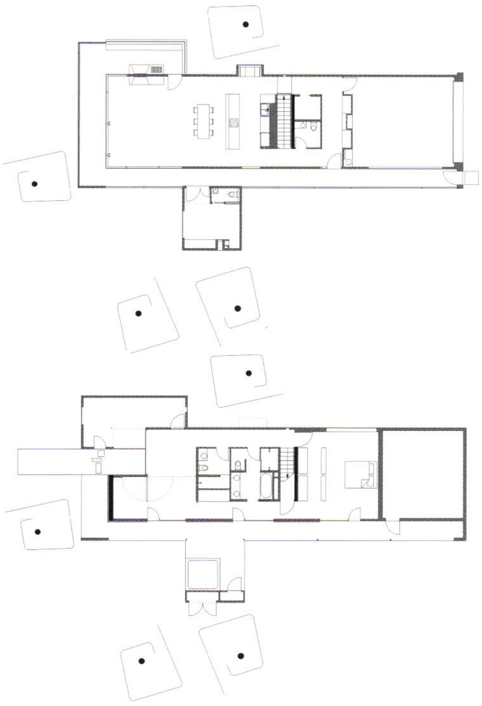

CITY Anchorage (AK)
COUNTRY USA
REGION North America
TYPOLOGY Living
COMPLETION 2004
WEBSITE www.mayersattler-smith.com
ARCHITECTS mayer sattler-smith

CITY
Ancram (NY)

COUNTRY
USA

REGION
North America

TYPOLOGY
Living

COMPLETION
2006

WEBSITE
www.levenbetts.com

ARCHITECTS
Leven Betts Studio Architects

CC01 HOUSE

The CC01 House's design begins with a reading of the landscape. Long linear grooves, formed by the dimensions of machinery – the distance between tractor wheels and the frequency of the blades of a plow – are etched into the rolling hills from years of farming. Framing the topography, these lines were developed into diagrams that inform the design of all configurations of the house, from the primary organization and form to the cladding and details of the building. Additionally, the section of the house follows the contour of the land as it steps up from east to west.

01 East view **02** Patio view **03** West view **04** Kitchen and dining area **05** Floor plans

Photos: Michael Moran Photography

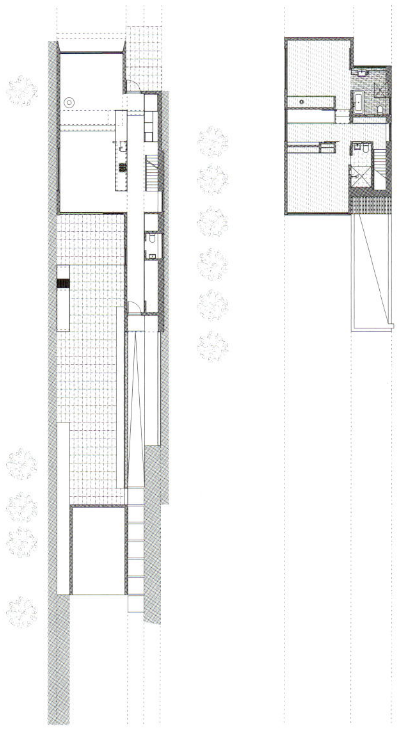

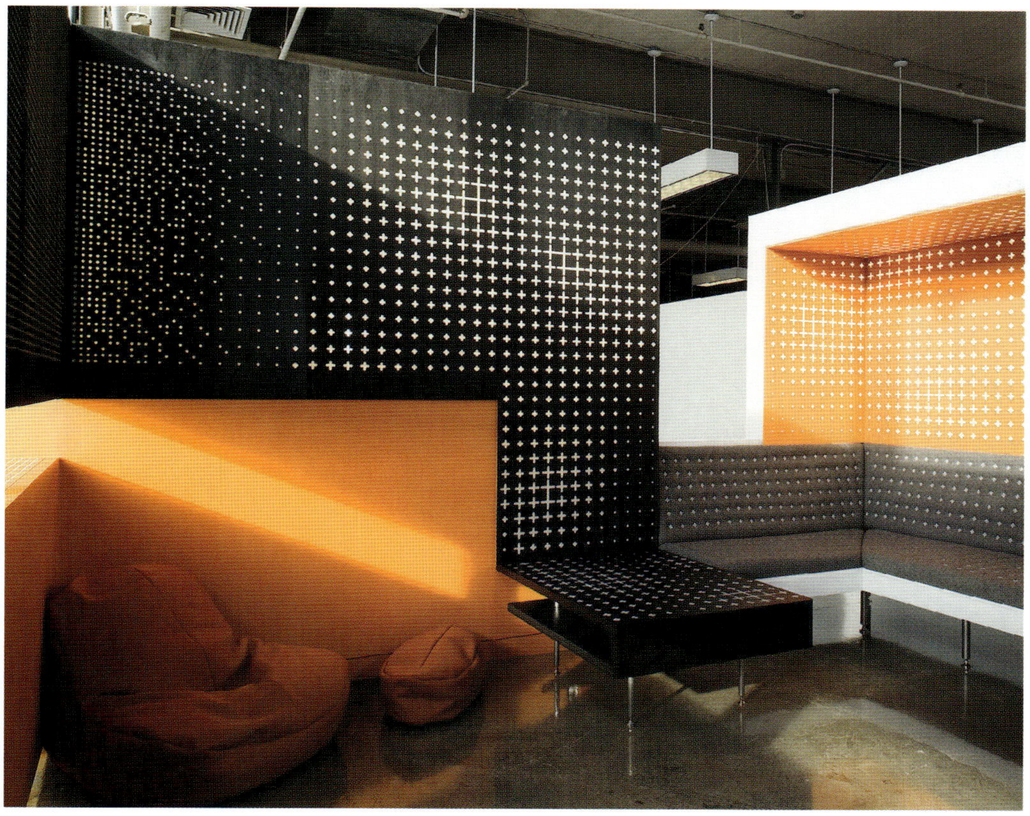

DOUBLE JEOPARDY

The commission to design and build two student lounges with student employees afforded the architects with the possibility to explore how the opposition between machine and craft could be re-negotiated through the technologies available to them. The use of a single diagrammatic strategy afforded conceptual efficiency while retaining a high degree of spatial diversity. The east space is used for small group and individual activities while the west space is used for larger meetings and social events. Rather than modulate light though depth, or three-dimensional subtractive, PEG chose to modulate the surface and artificial light through shape, or two-dimensional.

01 Custom upholstered bench and beanbag for small groups **02** Exterior view into east space **03** West space **04** East lounge plan **05** Sitting module

Photos: Beth Singer

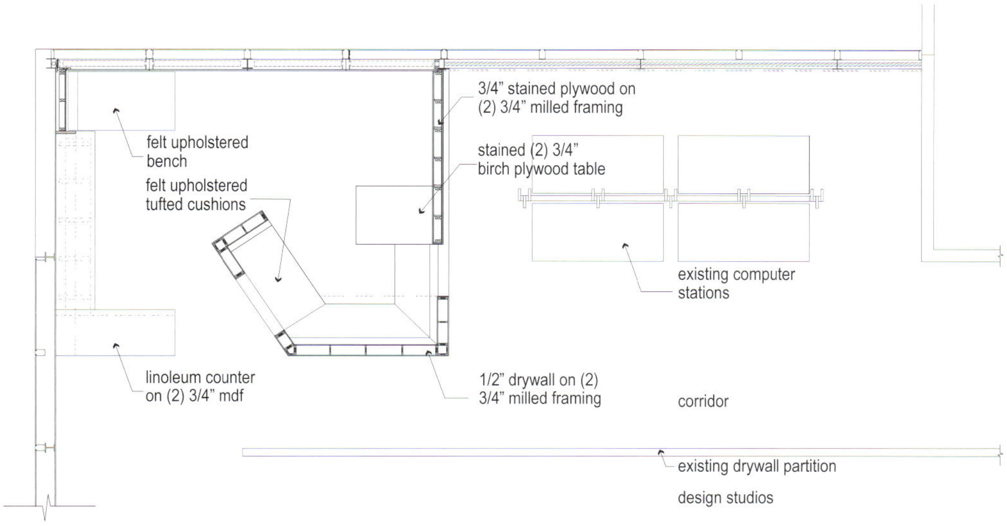

CITY Ann Arbor (MI)
COUNTRY USA
REGION North America
TYPOLOGY Education
COMPLETION 2006
WEBSITE www.peg-ola.com
ARCHITECTS PEG Office of landscape + architecture

CITY
Ann Arbor (MI)

COUNTRY
USA

REGION
North America

TYPOLOGY
Live / work

COMPLETION
2007

WEBSITE
plyarch.com

ARCHITECTS
PLY Architecture

PARK HOUSE

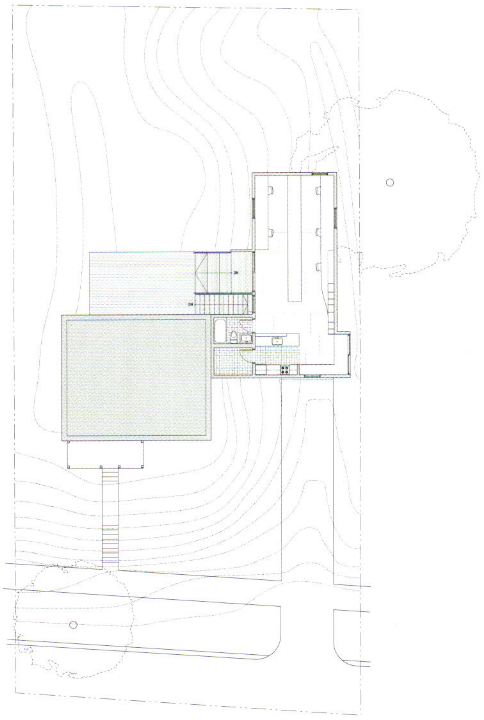

The Park House addresses generic and specific aspects of residential construction. As a generic prototypical condition, the addition exploits the local zoning to create a second residential unit that shares utilities. The project is positioned between the historic house and a city park to the North, and by deferring to the existing house, the addition pulls back from the street to create a new shared courtyard to the rear. A carport and garage/workshop are slid under the new unit as the site drops away, and one may move under the carport and up to the shared space as the building twists overhead.

01 View to historic house and addition **02** First floor plan **03** Carport **04** Living space **05** View from the courtyard

Photos: PLY Architecture

HOWARD HUGHES MEDICAL INSTITUTE JANELIA FARM RESEARCH CAMPUS

The project sits on 281 acres bounded by forest on two sides, with a sloping hillside and generous views of the Potomac River and verdant Maryland fields beyond. The 1,000-foot-long "Landscape Building" emerges from the topography in a series of three descending planted terraces, and to the northeast lie conference housing and residential village areas. Beneath the second-largest green roof in the U.S., the building's levels contain communal spaces, labs, meeting rooms, offices, and support areas. The signature green roof enhances efficiency, promotes habitat conservation, filters airborne particles, and reduces pollution.

01 Landscape Building with sunshades and trellises **02** Conference housing at night **03** Building section and site plan **04** Lobby

Photos: Brad Feinknopf - Drawings: Rafael Vinoly Architects PC

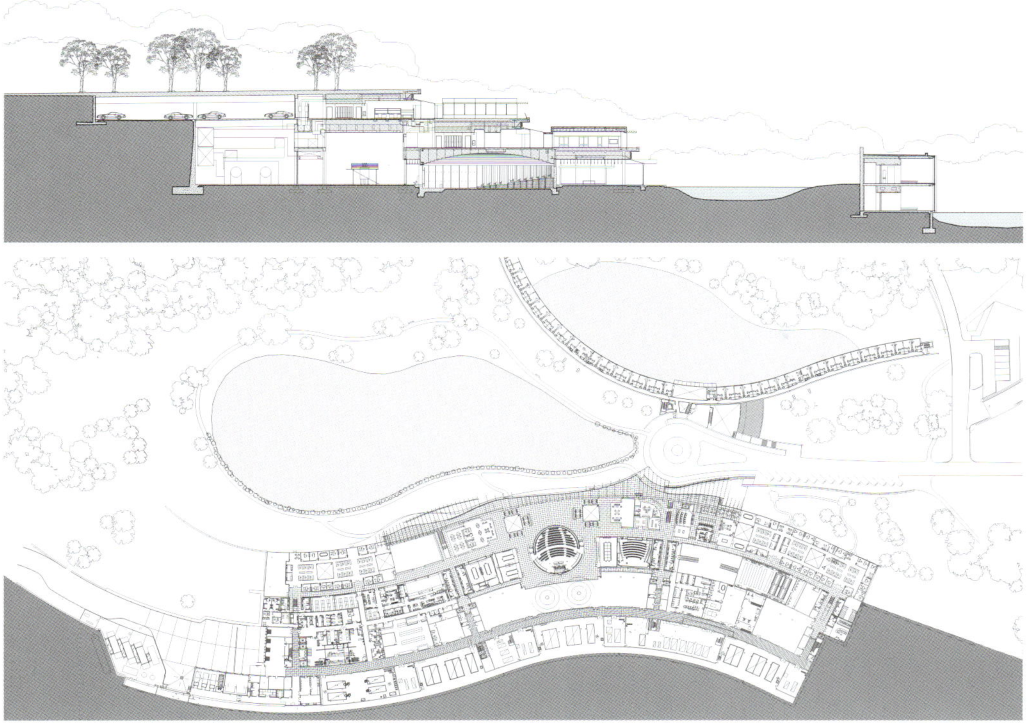

CITY
Ashburn (VA)

COUNTRY
USA

REGION
North America

TYPOLOGY
Institution

COMPLETION
2006

WEBSITE
www.rvapc.com

ARCHITECTS
Rafael Viñoly Architects

CITY
Aspen (CO)

COUNTRY
USA

REGION
North America

TYPOLOGY
Living

COMPLETION
2006

WEBSITE
www.gluckpartners.com

ARCHITECTS
Peter L. Gluck and Partners, Architects

LITTLE AJAX AFFORDABLE HOUSING

This affordable housing development transformed a formerly difficult site. Once deemed to have too steep an elevation with potential rock fall and mine waste rock nearby, the project converted the site into a multifaceted solution to the City of Aspen's overwhelming need for affordable housing. The architects acted as developer, architect and contractor in order to provide housing for 14 working families that previously could not afford to live close to their workplace. An open space parcel was created as part of the planning process, linking together the many public trails that surround the site.

01 Exterior view from street **02** Courtyard scheme **03** Second floor plan **04** Trails

Photos: Steve Mundiger

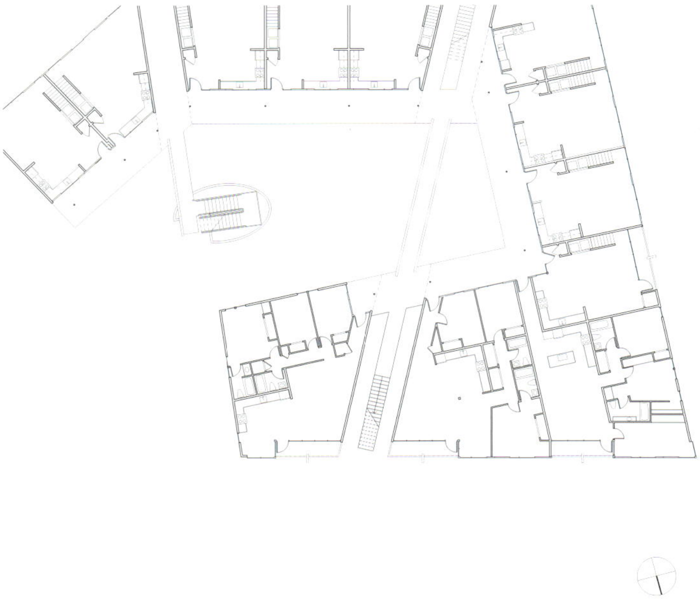

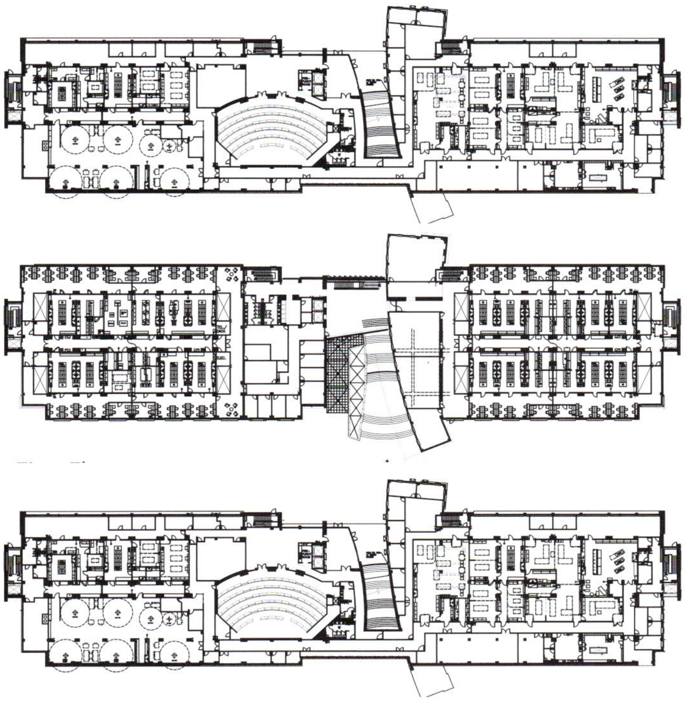

GEORGIA INSTITUTE OF TECHNOLOGY, MOLECULAR SCIENCES AND ENGINEERING BUILDING

In a radical change, the Georgia Institute of Technology has instituted a research-based organizational structure to replace the traditional discipline-based departmental facility. As the first academic institution in its class to commit to eradicating artificial and obsolete departmental divisions, it has developed a Biotechnology Campus to support these innovative methodologies. With the construction of the new Molecular Sciences and Engineering Building, the transition from departmental to interdisciplinary research is complete: a symbolically sympathetic position from which to pursue this important new science.

01 Ground, first and typical lab floor plans 02 Entry at night
03 Exterior view from cafe 04 Planted space between buildings
05 Lobby from above

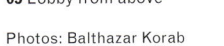

Photos: Balthazar Korab

CITY Atlanta (GA)
COUNTRY USA
REGION North America
TYPOLOGY Institution/Technology
COMPLETION 2006
WEBSITE www.cuh2a.com
ARCHITECTS CUH2A

CITY
Austerlitz, Upstate
New York (NY)

COUNTRY
USA

REGION
North America

TYPOLOGY
Living

COMPLETION
2006

WEBSITE
www.efmdesign.com

ARCHITECTS
EFM Design

AUSTERLITZ HOUSE

This second countryside home for a young family is located along the Hudson in Columbia County, upstate New York. The modulation into separate volumes responds to the topography and the program. The main and guest houses are separate units connected by a bridge. The massing maximizes exposure and views. Materials are selected based on appropriateness to the surroundings and environmentally responsible durability. Wooden paneling, large glass windows and a mirrored plinth create a formal but cheery façade with an illusion of sinking into the surrounding lush lawn. Dark jutting bays and balconies structure the exterior.

01 North façade **02** Staircase **03** Living space **04** Guesthouse **05** Ground floor plan

Photos: EFM Design

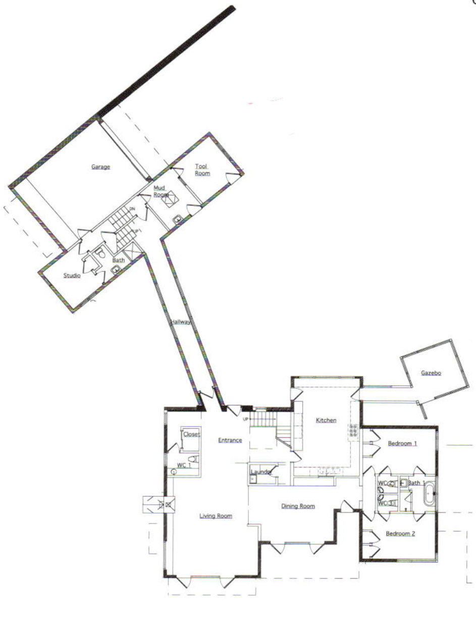

NORTHVIEW MIDDLE SCHOOL GYMNASIUM

The challenge in dealing with a building associated with obtrusive and static large boxes was met by mitigating the negative aspects of scale with a skin system that takes advantage of natural light to provide a glowing box that takes weight off the volume, bringing in natural light without glare to the interior space. The structure is a modified K-brace that is fully kinetic, and the skin is a slanted-stud system that allows for a cladding with full-length glazing strips that de-materialize the volume of the box. The inherent internalization of the program allows for the preservation of the purity of the structural solution.

01 Floor plan **02** View to main entrance **03** Façade with glazing strips **04** Gym

Photos: Yuju Yeo

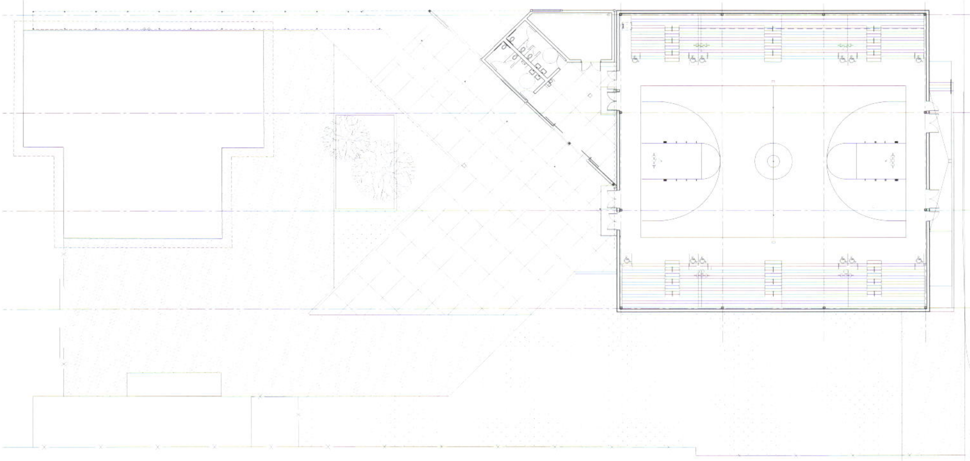

CITY: Abbotsford (BC)
COUNTRY: USA
REGION: North America
TYPOLOGY: Education
COMPLETION: 2007
WEBSITE: www.osborn320.com
ARCHITECTS: Osborn

CITY	Austin (TX)
COUNTRY	USA
REGION	North America
TYPOLOGY	Culture
COMPLETION	2009
WEBSITE	www.ltlarchitects.com
ARCHITECTS	LTL Architects

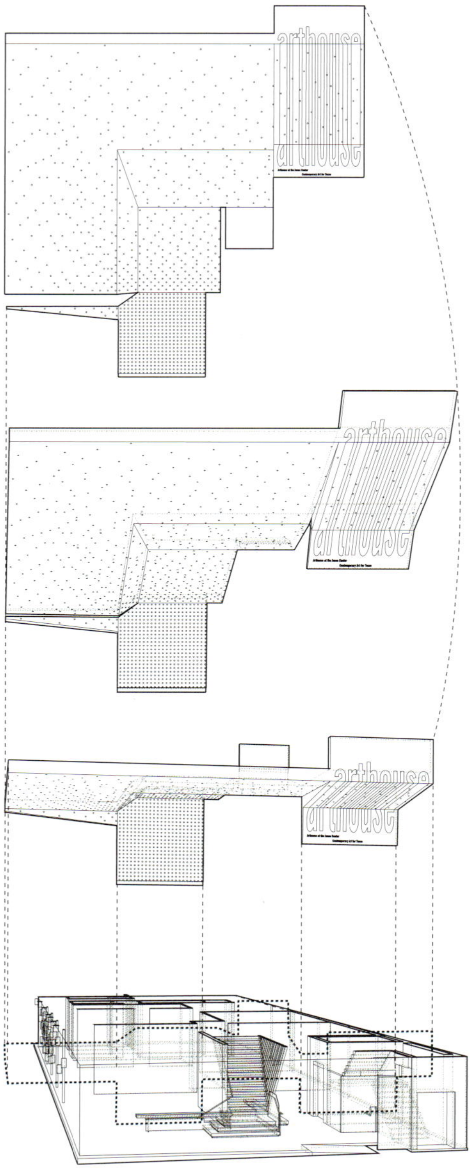

ARTHOUSE

Located in downtown Austin, Arthouse is a renovation and expansion project of an existing contemporary art space. The building currently is a rich hybrid of a turn-of-the-century theater and a 1950's department store. LTL seeks to amplify this accumulation of history by treating the design as a series of integrated tactical additions. In conjunction with the programmatic expansion of the gallery spaces, the design amplifies the visual dialog between the art and the surrounding urban environment. The project is currently in its design development phase and will be presented to the public later this year.

01 Sketches **02** View of main entrance **03** Front façade
04 Information desk

Renderings: LTL Architects

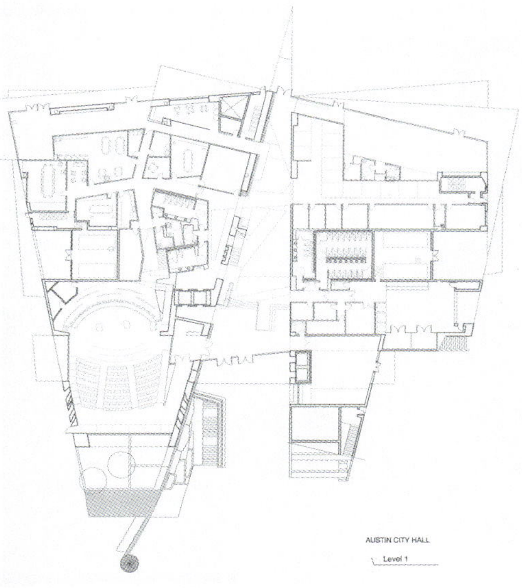

AUSTIN CITY HALL AND PUBLIC PLAZA

The new plaza graces the shores of Town Lake at the edge of the dynamic Warehouse district; an area rapidly being transformed into a tight grid of restaurants, nightspots, housing, and mid-rise office spaces. A massive arc of Lueders limestone emerges from bedrock at the lowest level of the parking garage, and metamorphosing out of this wall is a limestone base that encloses the first two stories. As the arcing wall cuts through the building, it creates an open four-story lobby transected by catwalk-like bridges at each level. A reflective bronze ceiling over the lobby reflects light from a skylight into the space below.

01 First floor plan **02** View form street **03** Limestone façade **04** Staircase to parking garage **05** Open four-story lobby

Photos: Timothy Hursley

CITY Austin (TX)
COUNTRY USA
REGION North America
TYPOLOGY Government / Public
COMPLETION 2004
WEBSITE www.predock.com
ARCHITECTS Antoine Predock Architect PC

CITY Austin (TX)

COUNTRY USA

REGION North America

TYPOLOGY Living

COMPLETION 2005

WEBSITE www.mirorivera.com

ARCHITECTS Miró Rivera Architects

GUEST HOUSE

Located on a two-acre peninsula, the Guest House is surrounded by a natural landscape that includes reed-covered wetlands, serving as a migratory stop for egrets and swans. The project utilized an analysis of the existing vegetation and wild life to implement a ten-year plan that will eliminate invasive plants, reintroduce native plants, and restore the existing wetlands. The beauty of the surroundings informs many aspects of the project beginning with the access to the peninsula from the house. To limit ecological impact, the house was conceived with a minimal footprint as a light vertical structure consisting of three floors.

01 Terrace **02** Entrance at night **03** Front entry **04** Exterior view from lake **05** Ground floor plan

Photos: Paul Finkel

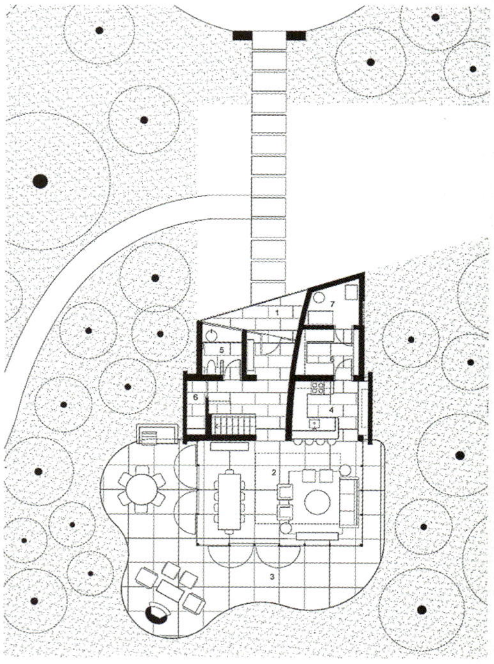

THE FLOATING BOX HOUSE

This house stands on a stunning native landscape of land-marked live oaks and frames the modern urban skyline of Austin in the distance. The forms of the house consist of a floating box, the stainless steel structure on which it sits, and the partly buried base. The guest bedrooms, media room, and service areas are located in the buried section, while an underground garage assures that the landscape remains free of automobiles and driveways. A transparent glassed enclosure gives the living room, dining room, and kitchen unobstructed views of the natural surroundings on one side and the Austin skyline on the other.

01 House in landscape **02** View into living spaces **03** Floor plans **04** Transparent glassed enclosure housing living space **05** Floating home with family bedrooms

Photos: Paul Warchol Photography

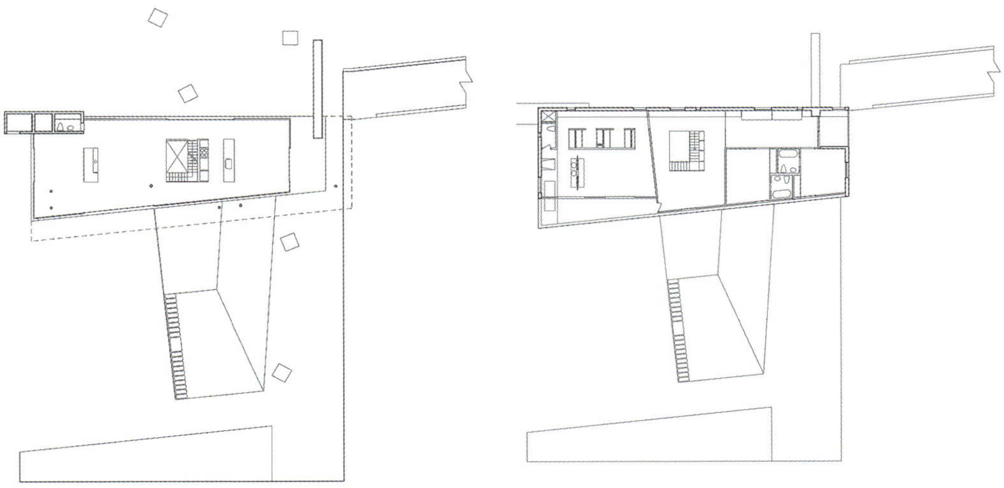

CITY Austin (TX)
COUNTRY USA
REGION North America
TYPOLOGY Living
COMPLETION 2006
WEBSITE www.gluckpartners.com
ARCHITECTS Peter L Gluck and Partners, Architects

CITY
Austin (TX)

COUNTRY
USA

REGION
North America

TYPOLOGY
Public

COMPLETION
2007

WEBSITE
www.mirorivera.com

ARCHITECTS
Miró Rivera Architects

LADY BIRD LAKE HIKE AND BIKE TRAIL RESTROOM

Conceived as a sculpture in a park, this is the first public restroom built for the park in over 30 years. It consists of forty-nine 3/4" thick vertical steel plates whose width and height vary significantly. Arranged along a spine and ranging in size, each plate is staggered in plan to control views and allow penetrating light and fresh air into the restroom. To complement the striking geometry, industrial weathering steel known-as 'Cor-ten' is the finish for the plates. The oxidation of the panels creates a protective outer layer that eliminates the maintenance associated with painting and produces a natural appearance.

01 General view **02** Entrance to restroom **03** Staggered Cor-ten steel plates **04** Site section and site plan **05** Restroom interior

Photos: Paul Finkel

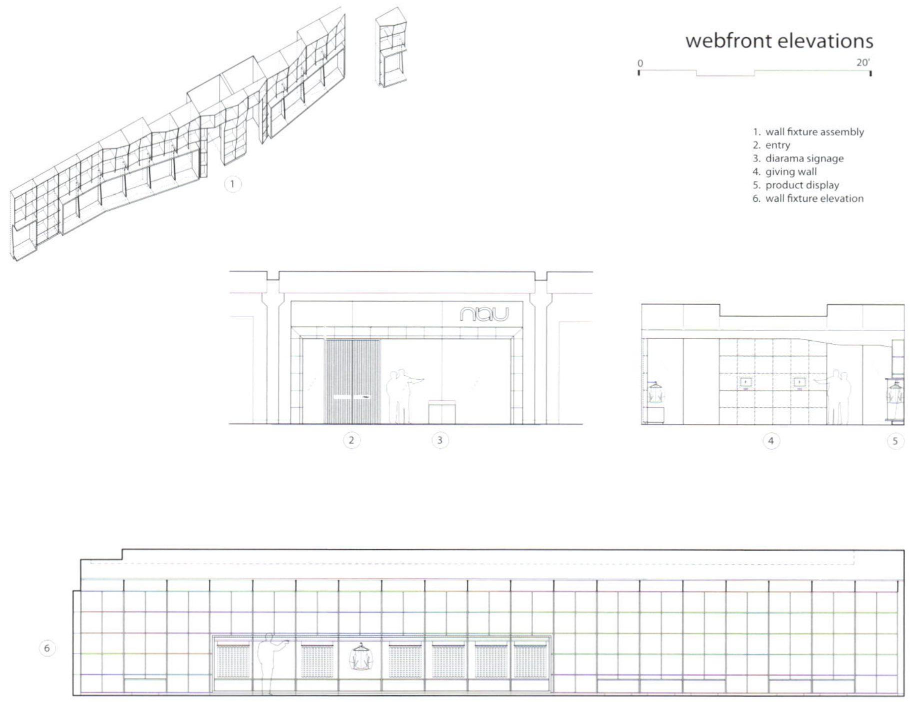

webfront elevations

0 20'

1. wall fixture assembly
2. entry
3. diarama signage
4. giving wall
5. product display
6. wall fixture elevation

NAU WEBFRONTS

NAU is an apparel company with brand principles defined by beauty, performance and sustainability. The webfronts are a three-dimensional realization of the company's primary sales channel – the Internet. The architects applied the brand principles to the design: beauty as the concept, performance as the functionality, and sustainability as the opportunity to pioneer a new type of retail environment. The concept executes as an organic landscape. The functionality is created through a small footprint. Sustainability is achieved through a prefabricated environment built of ecofriendly materials.

01 Webfront elevations **02** Product display **03** Shop window and entry **04** Showroom **05** Wall fixture

Photos: Steve Cridland

CITY Boulder (CO)
COUNTRY USA
REGION North America
TYPOLOGY Commercial
COMPLETION 2007
WEBSITE www.skylabarchitecture.com
ARCHITECTS Skylab Architecture

CITY Brentwood (CA)

COUNTRY USA

REGION North America

TYPOLOGY Living

COMPLETION 2006

WEBSITE www.tighearchitecture.com

ARCHITECTS Tighe Architecture

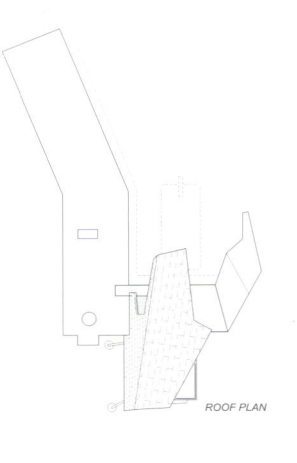

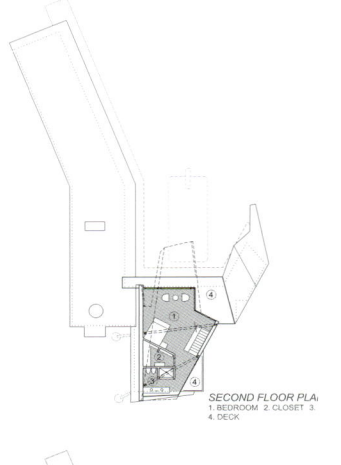

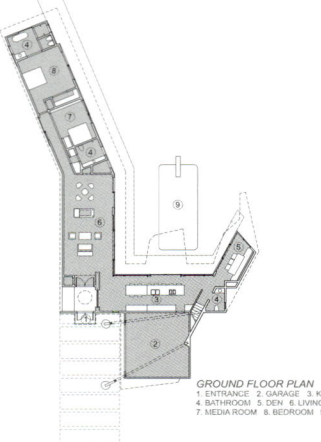

TIGERTAIL

The architecture of this 3,200 square foot residence is a result of various conditions inherent within the site and the existing building. Current building setback regulations, openings to the view and the need for solid walls for shear and privacy had an effect on the peculiar geometry of the two-story volume. Three bent steel moment frames straddle the existing one story structure, while the folded planes of the walls and roof are an extension of the rolling topography. The exterior of the folded planes is sheathed in metal whilst the interior is lined with wood blurring the distinction between wall, ceiling and floor plane.

01 View into the wood lined interior **02** Exterior view with folded planes by night **03** Floor plans **04** Exterior sheathed in metal

Photos: Art Gray

SPRING PRAIRIE RESIDENCE

This series of additions to a rambling former farmhouse sits on 75 acres approximately sixty miles north of Chicago. The project produces a comfortable retreat from the city for an extended family, and has a range of qualities that embrace animated gatherings as well as moments of solitude. It was important to open the complex to the 4 present landscape types: forest, prairie, lawn and picturesque garden. The strategy of placement for the program pieces, including bedrooms, bathrooms, sunroom, screened room, lookout tower and a modest animal barn, is akin to setting stones in a river bed to affect the flow of water.

01 Front façade **02** Exterior view by night **03** Bedroom **04** Floor plans **05** Rambling former farmhouse with additions

Photos: Nathan Kirkman, Michelle Litvin (03)

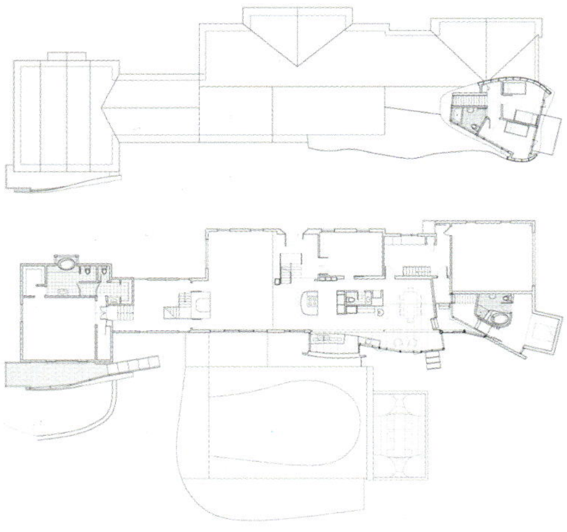

CITY Burlington (WI)
COUNTRY USA
REGION North America
TYPOLOGY Living
COMPLETION 2004
WEBSITE www.garofaloarchitects.com
ARCHITECTS Garofalo Architects

CITY Buffalo (NY)
COUNTRY USA
REGION North America
TYPOLOGY Institution
COMPLETION 2005
WEBSITE www.yazdanistudio.com
ARCHITECTS Yazdani Studio Cannon Design

HAUPTMAN-WOODWARD STRUCTURAL BIOLOGY RESEARCH CENTER

The new research center acts as the southern gateway to the Buffalo Niagara Medical Campus. The principle of scientific collaboration is the key organizing element of the building divided into two main programmatic components: research labs and offices. The two programs are housed in separate volumes linked by a glass-covered atrium that visually connects the facility to the other institutions in campus. The notion of collaboration is further enhanced by the fully glazed eastern atrium wall. The glazed lab block, rotated ten degrees west to increase visibility, exposes the inner workings of the research facility to the public.

01 Southwest façade view **02** Window detail **03** Glass covered atrium linking facilities **04** Research labs building by night **05** Central gathering space

Photos: Esto Photography

PULL HOUSE

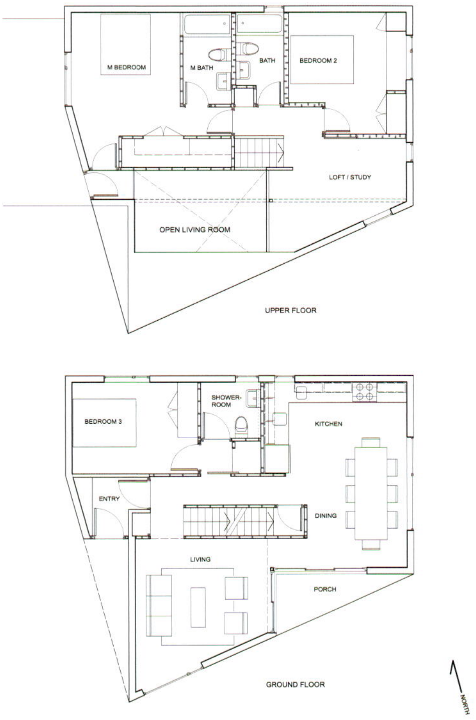

One corner of a simple pitched roof "barn" was pulled out diagonally from its rectangular locus. This has created a strong diagonal south front in contrast to the north side of the building, which appears as a vernacular "saltbox" form. The folded gable west entry façade is adorned with a strong color emphasis. The east and north façades are clad with rough timber colored to look like old weathered barn boards with random openings. Internally, the diagonal distortion generates a dramatic space with an illusion of a larger living room. Windows are positioned judiciously to extend views out to the landscape.

01 Diagonal façade with seam metal **02** Rough-colored timber façade **03** North-west façade **04** Floor plans **05** Bathroom

Photos: Fernando Rihl

CITY: Brattleboro (VT)
COUNTRY: USA
REGION: North America
TYPOLOGY: Living
COMPLETION: 2008
WEBSITE: www.procter-rihl.com
ARCHITECTS: procter-rihl architects

CITY Bayville (NY)
COUNTRY USA
REGION North America
TYPOLOGY Living
COMPLETION 2007
WEBSITE www.ethangerard.com
ARCHITECTS Ethan Gerard Architect

BOOMERANCH

The low slung boomerang shaped house has the benefit of sweeping 135 degrees views, and this appealing attribute commences from the more private, south side of the site. The Boomeranch spatial layouts are specifically applied and focused towards the water views, and are interestingly connected via a spinal circulation. The construction of the house took full advantage in using and utilizing a regional modern vocabulary. This certain element is a composition of attenuated verticals and horizontal forms, which are then reinforced by the articulation of vertical and horizontal cedar siding patterns.

01 North façade **02** Master bedroom **03** Floor plan
04 Hall leading to staircase **05** Entry

Photos: Zia O'Hara Photography

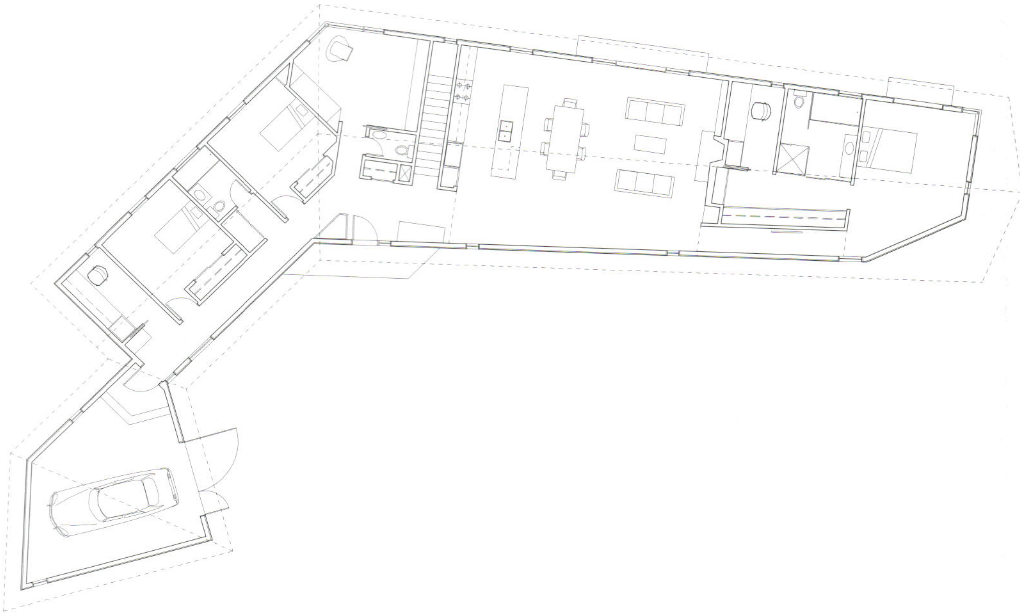

BELMONT HOUSE

In contrast to the superficial "McMansions" in the area, this project explores the fusion between two popular vernacular architecture of this region, the "mobile-trailer home" and the "Mexican pueblo" architecture. Inspired by the industrial generation of mobile homes, the upper level is a rectangular volume wrapped in metal, floating over its solid base, which is executed with heavy walls with texture and color. It hovers over the first floor as if ready to move on. This volume has large openings on both the hill and valley sides, which allow breeze to move through the house and present hillside panoramas.

01 Exterior view by night **02** Staircase **03** lounge **04** View from driveway **05** Entry door

Photos: Cesar Rubio

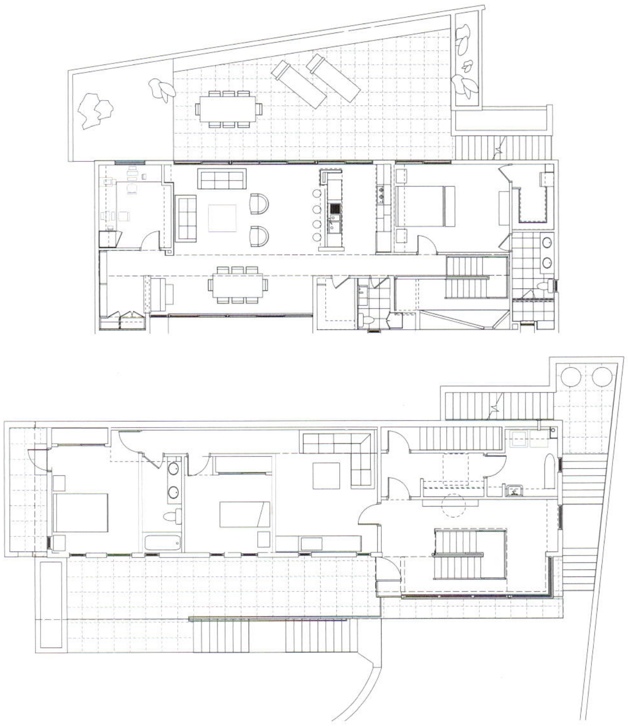

CITY Belmont (CA)
COUNTRY USA
REGION North America
TYPOLOGY Living
COMPLETION 2002
WEBSITE www.haririandhariri.com
ARCHITECTS Hariri & Hariri – Architecture

CITY: Bethlehem (PA)
COUNTRY: USA
REGION: North America
TYPOLOGY: Education / Public
COMPLETION: 2006
WEBSITE: www.bcj.com
ARCHITECTS: Bohlin Cywinski Jackson

LEHIGH UNIVERSITY
ALUMNI MEMORIAL HALL ENTRY COURT AND PARKING STRUCTURE

This 104,000-SF parking pavilion is carved into a carefully landscaped hillside, adjacent to the university's preeminent collegiate Gothic structure and principal gateway destination. An inventive structural system devised, eliminates traditional deep spandrels of pre-cast concrete parking decks. Aesthetic treatment is intrinsic to the structural system, achieving transparency and openness, human scale, color and shadow by means of an integrally cast concrete unit. At night the pavilion's translucent glass wall is an elegant backlit screen, while the cleared area in front of Alumni Memorial Hall became a generous entry court.

01 Parking pavilion's translucent glass wall **02** Detail of structural system **03** Longitudinal section and north elevation **04** Parking pavilion by night **05** Front façade

Photos: Matt Wargo (01), Nic Lehoux (02, 04, 05)

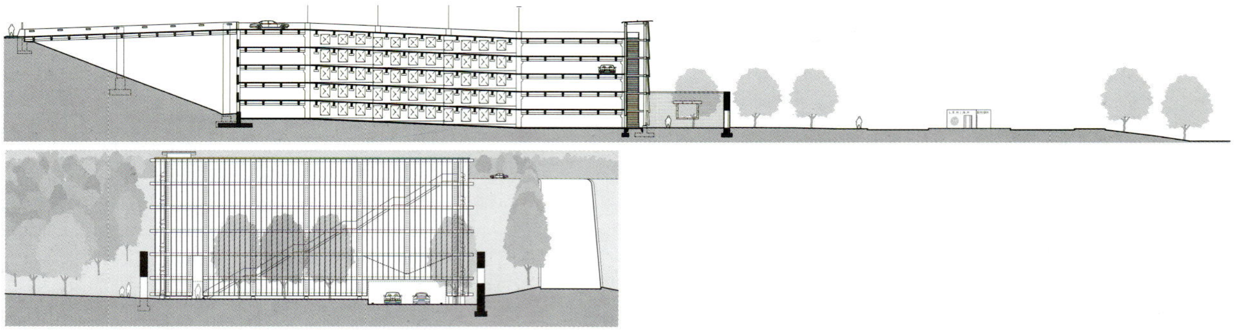

SARAH LAWRENCE COLLEGE MONICA A. AND CHARLES A. HEIMBOLD JR. VISUAL ARTS CENTER

The design for the new arts center unifies the visual arts department under one roof, housing six studio spaces for sculpture, painting and visual fundamentals. Other program elements include faculty offices, general teaching classrooms, soundstage, darkroom, printmaking facilities, visual resources library, and a 200-seat auditorium. The building is integrated into the landscape, and entrances and exits are designed to encourage students and faculty to use the building as a passageway through the campus. The use of skylights and open spaces between levels reinforces a sense of transparency, providing a view of artists at work.

01 Exterior view of north-lit painting studio **02** View of south façade, facing outdoor gathering space **03** North façade by night **04** North-south section

Photos: Richard Barnes (01, 03), Aislinn Weidele/Polshek Partnership Architects (02), Polshek Partnership Architects (04)

CITY Bronxville (NY)
COUNTRY USA
REGION North America
TYPOLOGY Education
COMPLETION 2004
WEBSITE www.polshek.com
ARCHITECTS Susan T. Rodriguez / Polshek Partnership Architects

BOWDOIN COLLEGE MUSEUM OF ART

A dramatic glass, bronze and blackened steel pavilion near the original Walker Art building provides a new entry to the expanded museum from the town to the west, and Bowdoin College quad to the east. This 600 sqf pavilion houses a gracious steel-and-stone stair and a glass elevator which both lead down to the visitor spaces and a new gallery entrance. A larger addition houses seven new galleries and a dedicated seminar room, and includes an upgraded loading facility and high capacity elevator. To support the museum's teaching mission, the design provided for a highly efficient administrative wing and archival storage spaces.

01 Glass, bronze and blackened steel pavilion **02** Gallery space **03** Walker Art building **04** Glass elevator **05** Section looking west **06** New pavilion and Walker Art Museum

Photos: Facundo de Zuviria

CITY Brunswick (ME)
COUNTRY USA
REGION North America
TYPOLOGY Culture
COMPLETION 2007
WEBSITE www.machado-silvetti.com
ARCHITECTS Machado and Silvetti Associates

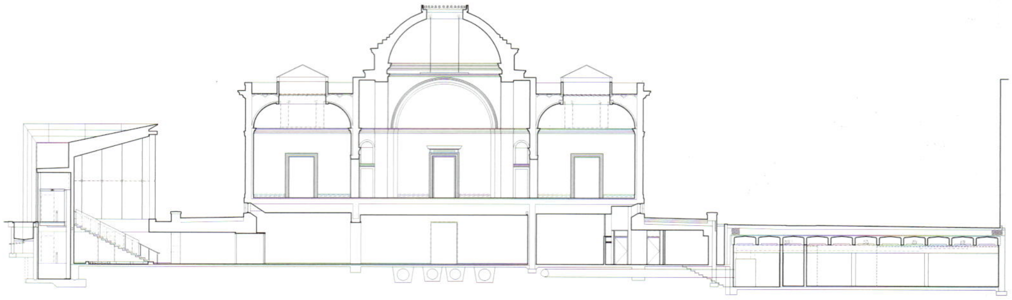

3ALITY DIGITAL

This film production facility inhabits 20,000 square feet inside two 1940's masonry warehouses, separated by a bearing wall that allowed only limited assess between the spaces. Our clients wanted a dynamic work environment to house their administrative and technical departments that include offices, meeting areas, editing rooms, equipment cage and long sight lines for camera staging. A circular conference room becomes the focal point as it straddles the central dividing wall and propels into motion a series of ripples whose trajectories penetrate and diminish the separation, while establishing auxiliary spaces for informal gathering.

01 Bearing wall **02** Circular conference room interior **03** View into circular conference room **04** Lobby **05** Floor plan

Photos: Deborah Bird

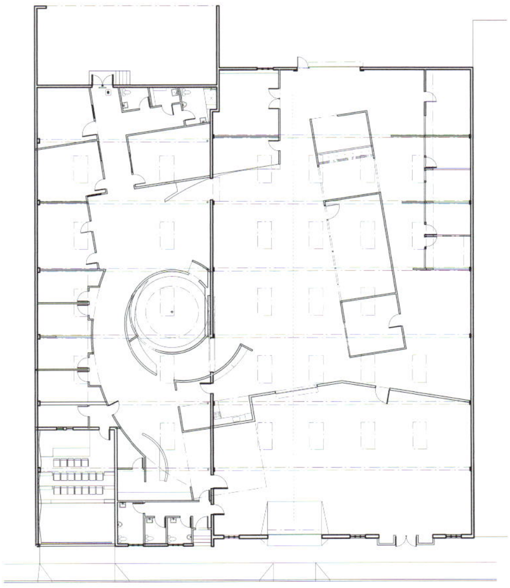

CITY Burbank (CA)
COUNTRY USA
REGION North America
TYPOLOGY Office
COMPLETION 2007
WEBSITE www.fungandblatt.com
ARCHITECTS Fung + Blatt Architects, Inc

CITY
Bronx (NY)

COUNTRY
USA

REGION
North America

TYPOLOGY
Education

COMPLETION
2004

WEBSITE
www.wystudio.com

ARCHITECTS
Weisz + Yoes Architecture

BRONX CHARTER SCHOOL FOR THE ARTS

The design of the Bronx Charter School for the Arts reflex the school´s founding principle that arts education is critical to childhood development and learning. Color, space and natural light create a direct physical connection with the content and aims of the curriculum. The budget restrictions and previous factory use required a simple but innovative approach for a healthier learning environment; the community-driven design process resulted in a unique, light-filled space. Through the adaptive re-use of the building, the school also plays a role in the transformation of Hunts Point neighborhood.

01 Color theory converted in architecture **02** Side view from the street **03** Light-filled classroom **04** Sections and front elevation

Photos: Albert Vecerka

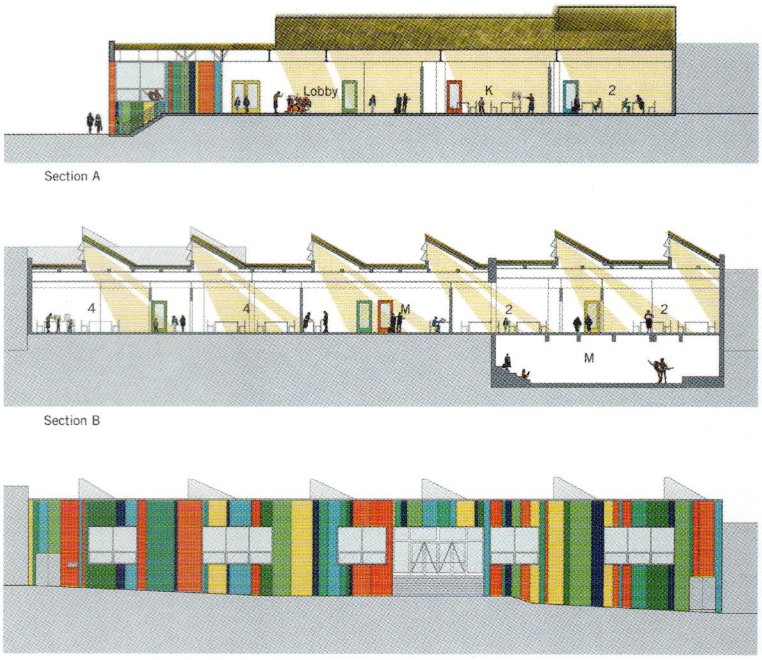

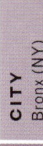

THE BRONX MUSEUM OF THE ARTS EXPANSION, NORTH WING

The three-story, 16,700 square-foot museum addition emerges from the sidewalk as an irregular folded screen made of fritted glass and metallic panels. The diagonal components emphasize the depth of the crevices, where the resulting vertical zones of metal and glass, angle and twist like an architectural origami. Pedestrians can sneak a peek into the ground floor gallery through the slivers of semitransparent glass that face them as they approach from either direction. The design dramatizes the vertical dimension of the otherwise modest structure, turning it into an unexpectedly monumental surface.

01 Circulation into exhibiton spaces **02** Fritted glass façade and metallic panels **03** Semitransparent glass slivers **04** Exhibition space

Photos: Norman McGrath Photography

CITY Bronx (NY)
COUNTRY USA
REGION North America
TYPOLOGY Culture
COMPLETION 2006
WEBSITE www.arquitectonica.com
ARCHITECTS Arquitectonica

CITY	Big Sur (CA)
COUNTRY	USA
REGION	North America
TYPOLOGY	Hospitality
COMPLETION	–
WEBSITE	www.mickeymuennig.com
ARCHITECTS	Mickey Muennig Vladimir Frank (Expansion Rooms) Janet Gay Freed (Interior Designer)

POST RANCH INN

Nestled on the cliffs of Big Sur, California, 1,200 ft above the Pacific Ocean, the inn is a luxury eco-hotel for the ultimate romantic getaway. The environmentally-sensitive 30-room 100-acre property overlooks the Pacific along and strongly supports measures to conserve resources while also helping to protect threatened flora and fauna. The free-standing structures have a curved, beamed roof covered with a soft carpet of grass and wildflowers. There are ocean views from the bed, bath, window seat and terrace. The window seat may be made into a twin bed. The glow from the two-sided fireplace may be seen from the bed and bath.

01 Restaurant overlooking the Pacific Ocean **02** View into Ocean House **03** Ocean house with ocean views **04** Bathroom with terrace

Photos: Gavin Jackson, Courtesy of Post Ranch Inn (03)

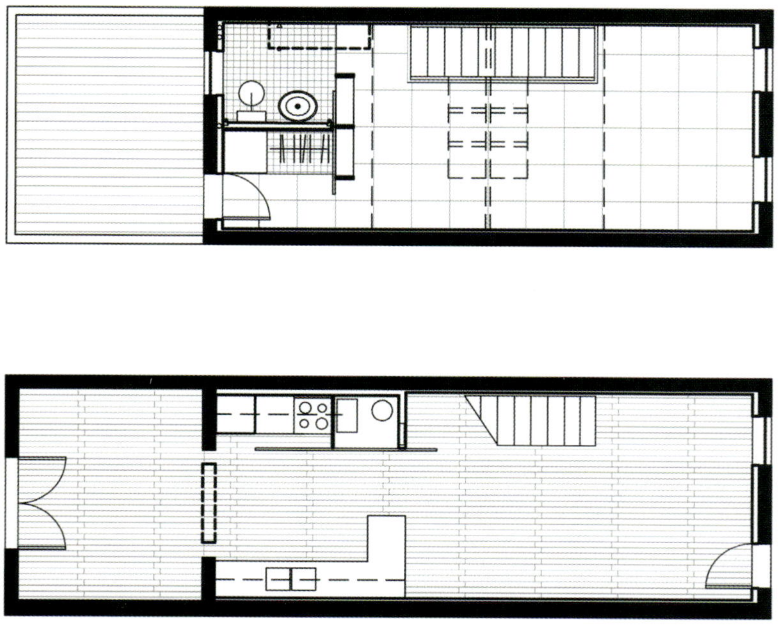

GREEN-HAB

Green-HAB is a building systems prototype for rehabbing Baltimore's row houses. The prototype reconfigures the elements of construction common to rehab projects as a structurally and materially expressive building system. Perpetual layers of joint compound and paint are abandoned in favor of exposed materials including gypsum board, metal framing, homasote, wheat board, bamboo, and concrete, which are sustainable, available, and visually compelling. The design features a central skylight, sliding walls, and an open plan with compact amenities demonstrating the spatial possibilities of even the smallest structures.

01 Floor plans **02** Upper level with central skylight **03** Exterior view of row houses **04** Open floor plan **05** Interior with exposed materials **06** Kitchen

Photos: Eric Salsbery

CITY Baltimore (MD)
COUNTRY USA
REGION North America
TYPOLOGY Living
COMPLETION 2006
WEBSITE www.kroizarch.com
ARCHITECTS Kroiz Architecture LLC

CITY
Beverly Hills (CA)

COUNTRY
USA

REGION
North America

TYPOLOGY
Living

COMPLETION
2007

WEBSITE
www.ai-architects.com

ARCHITECTS
Aleks Istanbullu Architects

LAGO VISTA GUEST HOUSE

Set atop a steep canyon, the retreat is a contemporary sculpture whose architecture engages a surprising discourse with the natural surroundings. Dividing the program into two pure volumes — a tall dominant cube that houses the retreat space an low parallel rectangle with living areas — the design maximizes use of the site and creates distinct spaces that belie the minimal floor plan. From the street, the architecture presents an uninterrupted play of painted panels that reference the color and movement of the canyon grasses. At the threshold, stone steps over a pond mediate the transition.

01 Exterior view with surrounding landscape **02** Kitchen and bedroom wing **03** Living space **04** Site plan **05** Rear view

Photos: David Lena Photography

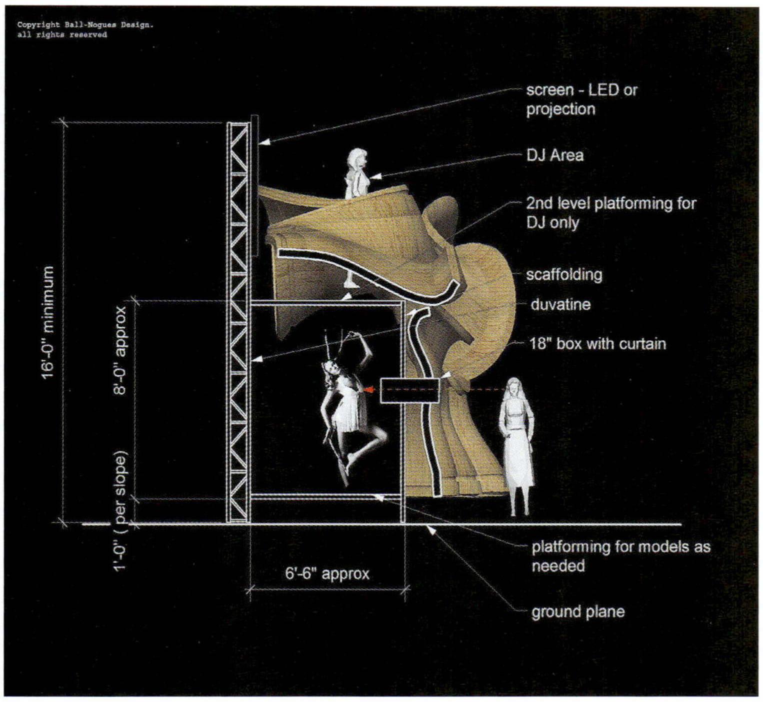

TIFFANY

This project derived from an event environment sponsored by Tiffany & Co. for Frank Gehry's gala, celebrating the launch of Gehry's signature jewelry designs. Using the material Gehry employed in his legendary "Easy Edges" furniture of the 1970's, but expanding on its forms and scale, seating elements were designed as well as a display wall with "peep show" type windows, where live nude models wore nothing but the Gehry jewelry. The project required laminating over 2,500 strips of curved, industrially cut cardboard, and to this end, Ball-Nogues created custom parametric software to study the form and facilitate fabrication.

01 Section **02** Detail of corrugated cardboard **03** Industrially cut corrugated cardboard **04** Display window **05** Display wall with "peep show" type windows

Photos: Joshua White

CITY Beverly Hills (CA)
COUNTRY USA
REGION North America
TYPOLOGY Commercial
COMPLETION 2006
WEBSITE www.ball-nogues.com
ARCHITECTS Ball-Nogues

BROSMITH RESIDENCE

This house is a sensitively sited single-family residence on a ridgeline of Mulholland Scenic Parkway, overlooking the San Fernando Valley of southern California. Following the client's objectives, the structure captures exterior space as living space, and harnesses the panoramic views of the valley below, accessible from the common areas and courtyards of the property. Separate living pods created by the layout along a central spine of the house allow different activities and interactions to occur simultaneously without mutual disruption.

01 Exterior wood panel **02** Panoramic view to valley **03** Exterior view by night **04** Living space **05** Floor plan

Photos: John Edward Linden

CITY Beverly Hills (CA)
COUNTRY USA
REGION North America
TYPOLOGY Living
COMPLETION 2004
WEBSITE www.spfa.com
ARCHITECTS SPF:architects Studio Pali Fekete architects

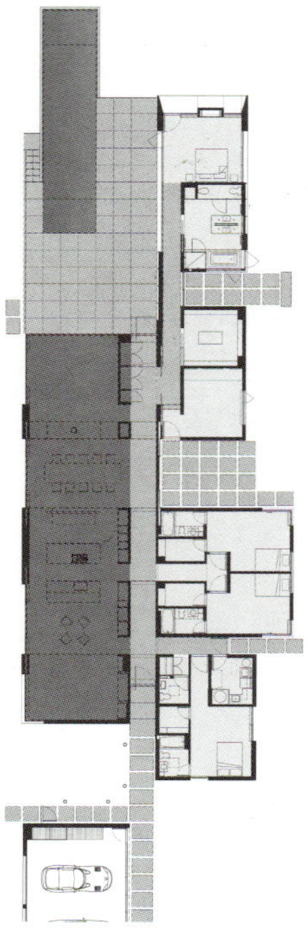

BENEDICT CANYON HOUSE

This extensive renovation featured a new folded roof element and glazed rear that opens the house up to the landscape, emphasizing the relationship between inside and outside. The ceiling is the project's main design intervention, with track lighting concealed behind a plywood panel system that is punctuated by the intersection of two sea grass resin light boxes and a skylight. The skylight reinforces internal circulation, while the light boxes emphasize motion towards the outside. The floor is a stained concrete with a resin epoxy finish that gives it a liquid feeling and a distinct, reflective quality.

01 Fully glazed façade **02** Stained concrete floor **03** Living space **04** Lighting behind plywood panels **05** Reflected ceiling plan

Photos: Benny Chan, Fotoworks

CITY Beverly Hills (CA)
COUNTRY USA
REGION North America
TYPOLOGY Living
COMPLETION 2005
WEBSITE www.griffinenrightarchitects.com
ARCHITECTS Griffin Enright Architects

CITY
Boston (MA)

COUNTRY
USA

REGION
North America

TYPOLOGY
Institutional

COMPLETION
2004

WEBSITE
www.arrowstreet.com

ARCHITECTS
Arrowstreet

ARTISTS FOR HUMANITY EPICENTER

The Boston non-profit educational group, Artists for Humanity, commissioned Arrowstreet to design a new, 22,500-square-foot headquarters and studio space on an urban site located in South Boston. The project received U.S. Green Building Council LEED certification at the Platinum level, which is the first building in Boston to be awarded this distinction. The EpiCenter was also the recipient of the AIA Committee on the Environment Award (Top Ten Sustainable U.S. Buildings), Boston Society of Architects / New York AIA Honor Award for Sustainable Design, as well as multiple other design awards.

01 View to roof with solar panels **02** Glass façade **03** Bird's eye view **04** Gallery **05** Plan mezzanine level

Photos: Peter Vanderwarker (01, 03), Richard Mandelkorn (02, 04)
Drawing: Courtesy of Arrowstreet

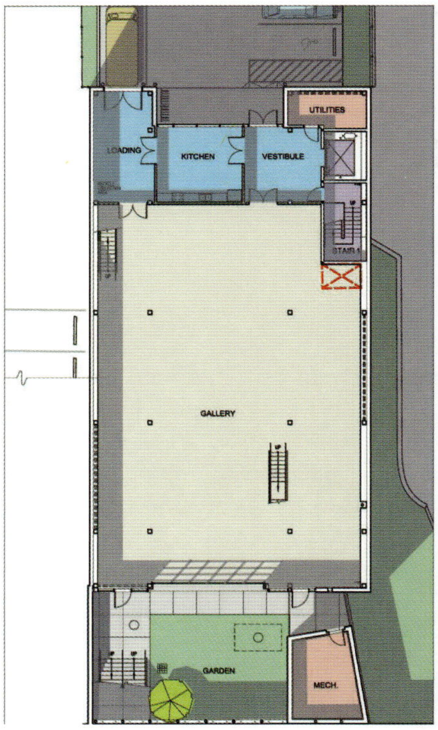

OUTSIDE-IN LOFT

By combining two 1,100 square foot loft spaces on the top floor of a Chinatown building, a unique living space was created in downtown Boston. The existing apartments were mirror images of each other, organized around a central core and partition wall. By making surgical openings in the partition wall and redistributing the bathroom spaces, the ability to unify the two into a single loft apartment was made possible. A courtyard was introduced in the place of the former bathroom, inviting the outside in, and introduces natural light into the center of the apartment, where a small garden is sometimes filled with rain and snow.

01 Shower with skylight **02** Courtyard **03** View into the courtyard **04** Floor plan and section **05** Bathtub with skylight

Photos: Höweler + Yoon Architecture

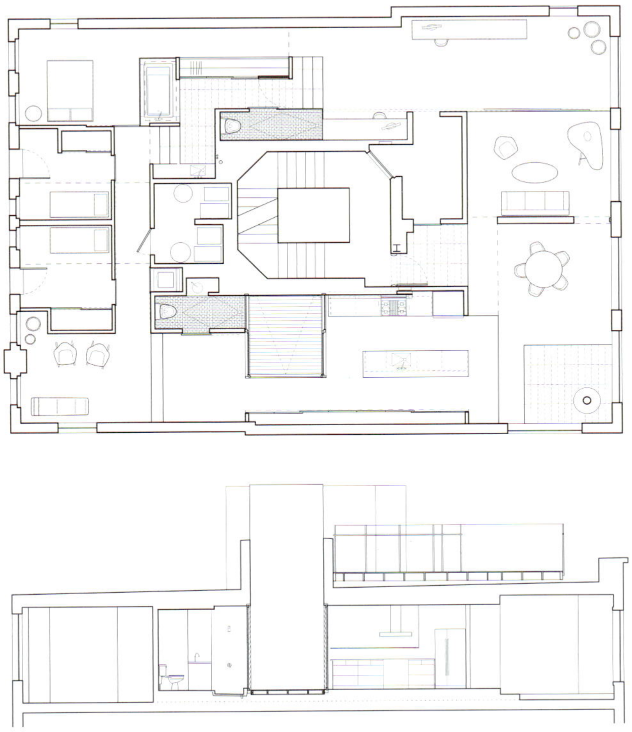

CITY Boston (MA)
COUNTRY USA
REGION North America
TYPOLOGY Living
COMPLETION 2007
WEBSITE www.hyarchitecture.com
ARCHITECTS Höweler + Yoon Architecture LLP

CITY	Boston (MA)
COUNTRY	USA
REGION	North America
TYPOLOGY	Government
COMPLETION	2007
WEBSITE	www.hyarchitecture.com
ARCHITECTS	Höweler + Yoon Architecture LLP

BOSTON CITY HALL 2.0

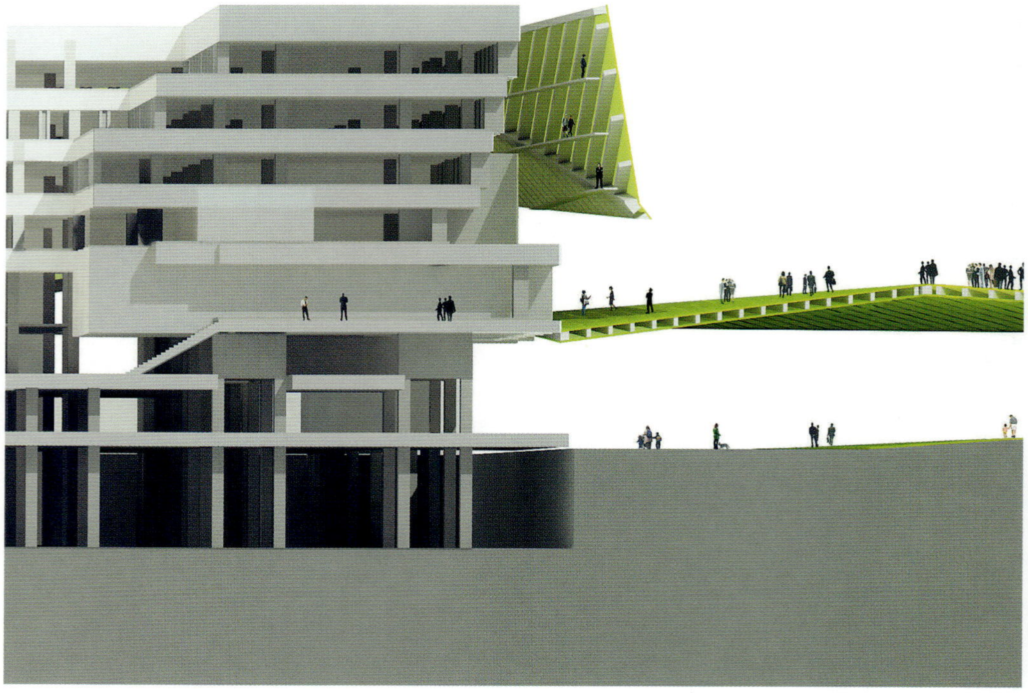

Designed to be porous and accessible to the public, City Hall stands monumental and impenetrable, with multiple entrances sealed. Focused on issues of public space and accessibility, the open menu of design proposals include strategies that outfit City Hall with public interfaces at a range of scales. Extending the original vision of City Hall as a robust scaffold for urban life, two possible combinations – "Sleeve" and "Wrap" – seek to upgrade the structure to engage contemporary public life. Wrap proposes a new ground plane that rises up to mask the existing structure.

01 New ground plane **02** Approach **03** Section **04** Entrance view

Photos: Höweler + Yoon Architecture

XSMALL

The final building for this larger residential compound, XSmall consists of three, rotated 16-by-22-foot boxes. Four-corner skylights provide natural light through minimum windows and maximum privacy, important since the design includes four houses on two lots that draw much attention. Finished in marine plywood, typically used in boat building for its broad and pronounced grain, XSmall creates the appearance of a huge piece of furniture. Each floor of XSmall has a different look and feel, including marble on the first floor and oak plywood on the second, but all are connected by a pared-down wooden staircase that threads through the space.

01 Three rotated boxes **02** Façade of marine plywood **03** Skylight **04** Wooden staircase connecting all levels **05** Bird's eye view

Photos: uni

CITY Boston (MA)
COUNTRY USA
REGION North America
TYPOLOGY Living
COMPLETION 2006
WEBSITE www.uni-a.com
ARCHITECTS uni

CITY Brooklyn (NY)

COUNTRY USA

REGION North America

TYPOLOGY Mixed-Use (culture, living, public)

COMPLETION in progress

WEBSITE www.studiomda.com / www.behnisch.com

ARCHITECTS StudioMDA / Behnisch Architects

BROOKLYN ARTS TOWER

Ashland Center is a mixed-use development program consisting of cultural, commercial, and residential spaces, and is located in the Brooklyn Academic of Music Cultural District. The goals are to provide socially, fiscally and environmentally responsible choreographic dance and living spaces. The project's design is arranged and composed of five stacked mid-rise "Sky-Communities" above a cultural plinth, where all the apartments have access to the communal gardens adjacent to shared building amenities. This development will serve as a model for future New York City sustainable, affordable housing developments.

01 Residential tower by night **02** "Sky-Community" **03** Cross section

Renderings: eskq llc

EAST NEW YORK AFFORDABLE HOUSING

The East New York Affordable Housing project acts as part of the New Foundations Program for the Department of Housing Preservation and Development, and while acting as both developer and architect, Della Valle Bernheimer coordinated the design and construction of 10 semi-detached, two-family homes in the East New York section of Brooklyn. Designed to encourage developers to create affordable housing, the 2,200 SF homes were privately developed on land owned by the HPD as part of Mayor Bloomberg's $7.5 billion affordable housing plan to create 165,000 units of affordable housing over 10 years.

01 View to semi-detached, two-family homes 02 Elevations 03 Typical front façade 04 Side window

Photos: Richard Barnes

CITY Brooklyn (NY)
COUNTRY USA
REGION North America
TYPOLOGY Living
COMPLETION 2006
WEBSITE www.dbnyc.com
ARCHITECTS Della Valle Bernheimer

CITY Cadyville (NY)

COUNTRY USA

REGION North America

TYPOLOGY Leisure

COMPLETION 1996

WEBSITE www.danhiseldesign.com

ARCHITECTS dan hisel design

CADYVILLE SAUNA

Built against a cliff, this sophisticated yet compact sauna utilizes a wall of rock to form one interior wall. A river located twenty feet below coils into a deep and powerful whirlpool, spinning reflections of sunlight against the rocks and sauna above. The sauna's intense thermal conditions work to dissolve the interior into a kind of thick space, where surface and form lose much of their traditional meaning. Both the interior and exterior spatial conditions produce a blurring of form – one where the intent is to make the body one with the sauna, and the sauna one with the world.

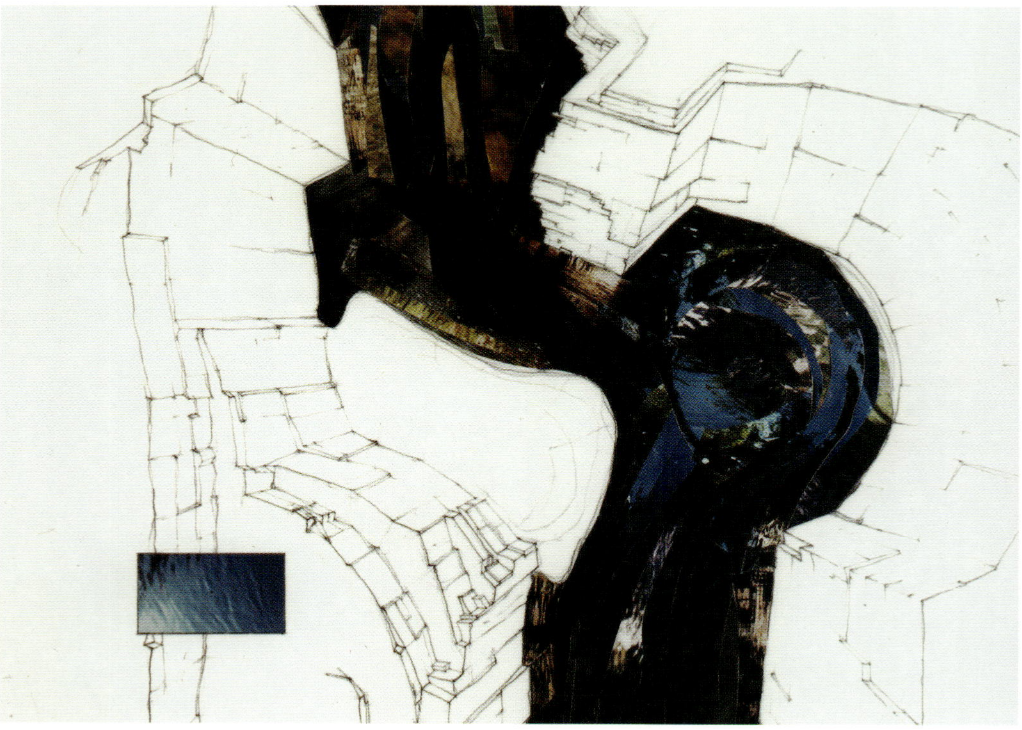

01 View into sauna **02** Mirroring the surrounding **03** Diagrammatic sketch **04** View from below

Photos: Dan Hisel

NAPA HOUSE

Set on prime wooded property in California's Napa Valley, the house in plan is an asymmetrical "H" with two parallel wings and a foyer as a connecting element. The two roofs produce a strong, horizontal graphic as the four floor levels step down with the slope of the land. The ceiling is constant and the concrete floor follows the topography, creating volumes of shifting scale throughout the house. By adapting the building to the gentle cant of the ridge, its exposure to light and views is maximized. Balancing the black steel-framed columns is a generous use of glass, with transparency being the dominant theme.

01 Exterior view **02** Rear view **03** Glass façade **04** Floor plan **05** Interior

Photos: Sharon Risedorph Photography

CITY: Calistoga (CA)
COUNTRY: USA
REGION: North America
TYPOLOGY: Living
COMPLETION: 2004
WEBSITE: www.jimjennings architecture.com
ARCHITECTS: Jim Jennings Architecture

CITY
Canajoharie (NY)

COUNTRY
USA

REGION
North America

TYPOLOGY
Culture

COMPLETION
2007

WEBSITE
www.designLABarch.com

ARCHITECTS
designLAB architects

ARKELL MUSEUM

The Arkell Arts Center explores local manufacturing, art and culture in the city of Canajoharie, New York. The building's scheme infuses the forgotten industrial site with new life through a thoughtful renovation and an engaging new program. The renovation of the old, gambrel-roofed library is blended with a contemporary gallery addition that subtly references the museum's industrial past. The sharp rectangular forms of the museum exterior are clad in white glazed brick that compliments the white, concrete frame of the factory. From the exterior, the new structure stands as a series of glowing boxes.

01 Site plan **02** View from the park **03** Interior view greathall **04** Exterior view

Renderings: designLAB architects

SULLIVAN-COWAN RESIDENCE

This house centers on the dramatic natural features of the Pacific Ocean beachfront environment. Muted, gray color architectonic forms stand in deference to the ocean front beach to the south and the wetlands and distant mountain range to the north. The ever-changing natural light accentuates the sculptural building forms creating a layered building transparency, while opaque glazing is used for circular stair treads and entry doors as translucent design elements that transmit diffused light through the spaces. Materials have been selected for their natural aesthetic beauty and suitability for the harsh coastal environment.

01 Rear façade **02** Interior **03** Bathroom with view to the ocean **04** Floor plans

Photos: Bill Zeldis Photography

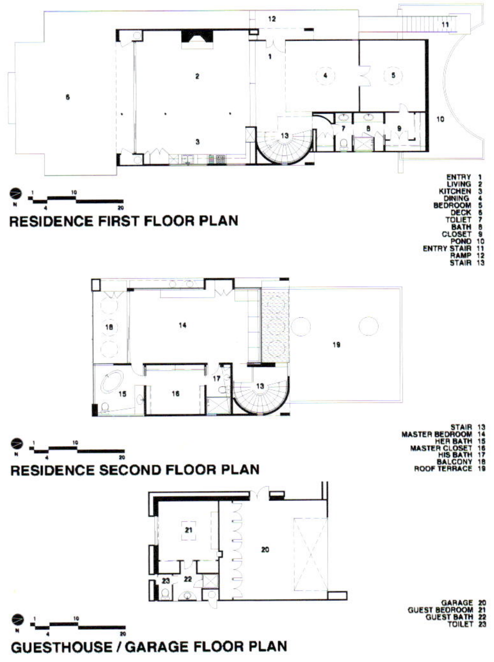

CITY Carpinteria (CA)
COUNTRY USA
REGION North America
TYPOLOGY Living
COMPLETION 2001
WEBSITE www.nmaarchitects.com
ARCHITECTS Neumann Mendro Andrulaitis Architects

CITY Casey Key (FL)

COUNTRY USA

REGION North America

TYPOLOGY Living

COMPLETION 2005

WEBSITE www.tmarch.com

ARCHITECTS Toshiko Mori Architect

ADDITION TO HOUSE ON THE GULF OF MEXICO

Built as an addition to a 1957 Paul Rudolph residence, the project consists of a kitchen and a dining area on the ground floor and a master bedroom, bath, and open terrace on the second floor. The project is linked to the older residence by a trellis that at once separates and connects the addition to Rudolph's design. An exterior stair is cast in a single piece of fiberglass by a builder of America's Cup race boats and is resistant to the severe climate of the site. The self-supporting stair is suspended from the roof by a series of fiberglass rods.

01 Staircase leading to private spaces **02** Glass façade **03** Staircase with fiberglass rods **04** Exterior night view **05** Floor plans

Photos: Paul Warchol Photography, Greg Wilson (01, 02)

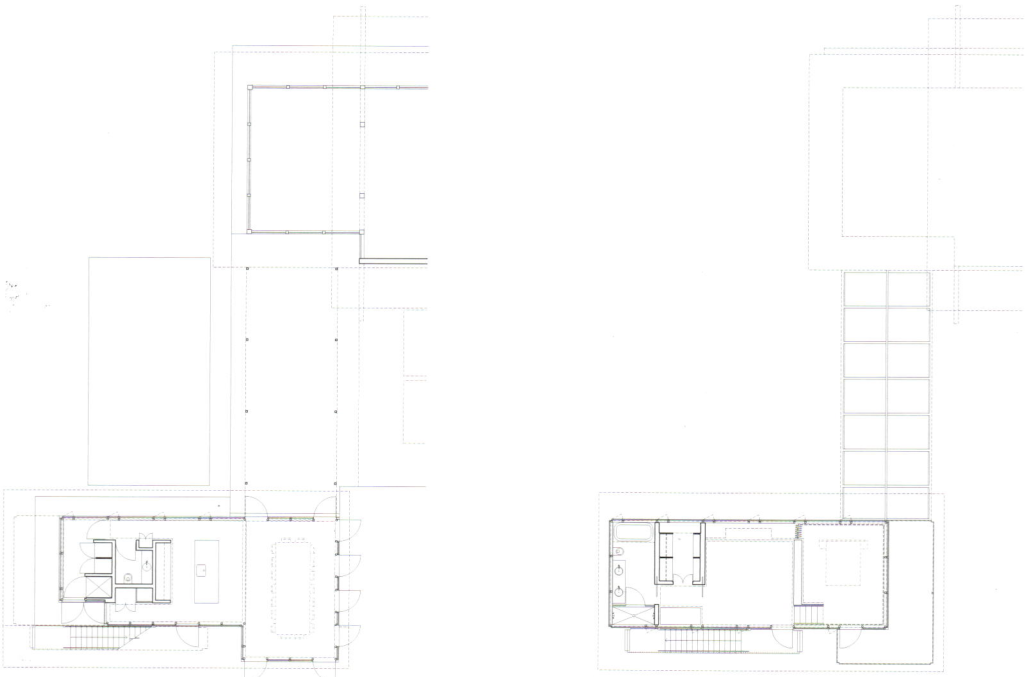

WEBB DOTTI HOUSE

Organized around an elevated terrace with views to the horizon, the house contains 2,600 square feet of interior space on an infill lot, within an established neighborhood. The street below is on axis with the land, creating an open view corridor to the horizon from within the property. The house is cleaved and sheared to define exterior landscape spaces, which include a garden terrace to the south and an automobile court on the north. The sheared organization creates two offset components; the eastern house, slid downhill, has one level and contains family living spaces, while the western house, pulled uphill, has two levels containing bedrooms and a covered car park.

01 Ground floor plan **–02** Wood panel façade **03** View of entry **04** Terrace **05** Interior staircase

Photos: John M. Hall, Gomes, Francisco Gomes (05)

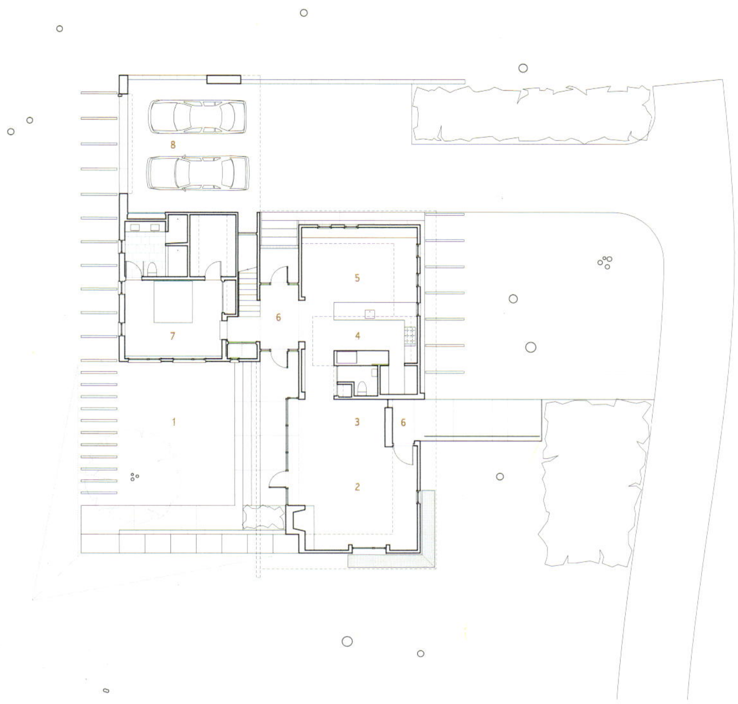

CITY Chapel Hill (NC)

COUNTRY USA

REGION North America

TYPOLOGY Living

COMPLETION 2003

WEBSITE www.gomes-staub.com

ARCHITECTS Gomes + Staub Architects

IMAGINON: THE JOE & JOAN MARTIN CENTER

The project, a partnership between the Public Library of Charlotte Mecklenburg County and the Children's Theatre of Charlotte, is designed to engage youth and offer a world of imagination and experience. Programmatic spaces include children's and teen's library spaces, 570 – and 250-seat auditoriums, a blue-screen theater, and a children's reading room with a puppet theater. Unusual spatial configurations resulting from vigorous interaction between geometric elements, each clad by unique materials, create a stimulating environment rich in textures, colors and patterns that is open to interpretation and imagination.

01 Glass façade with sunscreens **02** Blue-screen theater **03** Section **04** Exterior view by night

Photos: Kessler Photography

CITY Charlotte (NC)
COUNTRY USA
REGION North America
TYPOLOGY Public
COMPLETION 2005
WEBSITE www.holzmanmoss.com
ARCHITECTS Holzman Moss Architecture

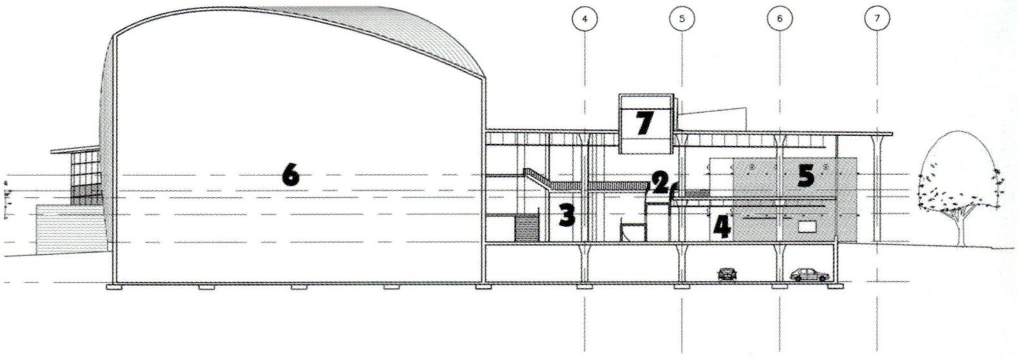

IRWIN UNION BANK

The traditionally modern and innovative building of the Irwin Union Bank is distinguished by its elegant and economic design. To maximize the budget, the design uses local materials such as brick veneer and Indiana limestone to allow for the single beautiful gesture that serves as the building's identifying moment. This bold single gesture, a glass clerestory structure akin to a "Light Box", floats above the main brick building, illuminated at night from within, becoming a floating sculpture that is visible from all directions to passing cars. The "Light Box" also functions as a canopy for the bank's drive-thru lanes.

01 View of brick façade and "Light-Box" **02** Drive-thru lanes **03** North and east section **04** Teller stations

Photos: Catherine Tighe

01 View of brick façade and "Light-Box"
02 Drive-thru lanes (section looking north) 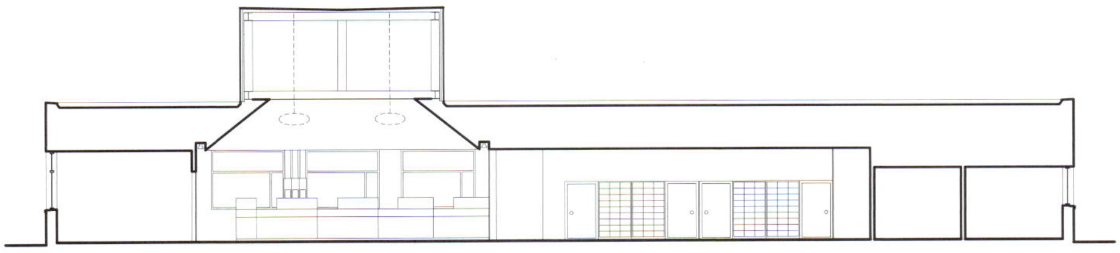
03 North and east section (section looking east)
04 Teller stations

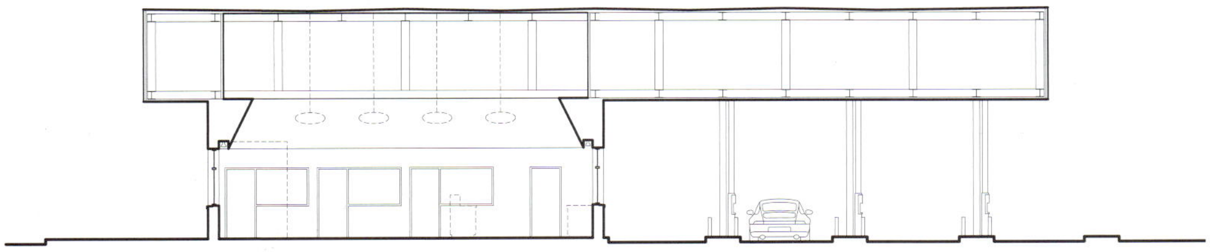

CITY Columbus (IN)
COUNTRY USA
REGION North America
TYPOLOGY Office
COMPLETION 2006
WEBSITE www.dberke.com
ARCHITECTS Deborah Berke & Partners Architects LLP

CITY Cave Creek (AZ)

COUNTRY USA

REGION North America

TYPOLOGY Public

COMPLETION 2005

WEBSITE www.richard-bauer.com

ARCHITECTS richard+bauer

DESERT BROOM PUBLIC LIBRARY

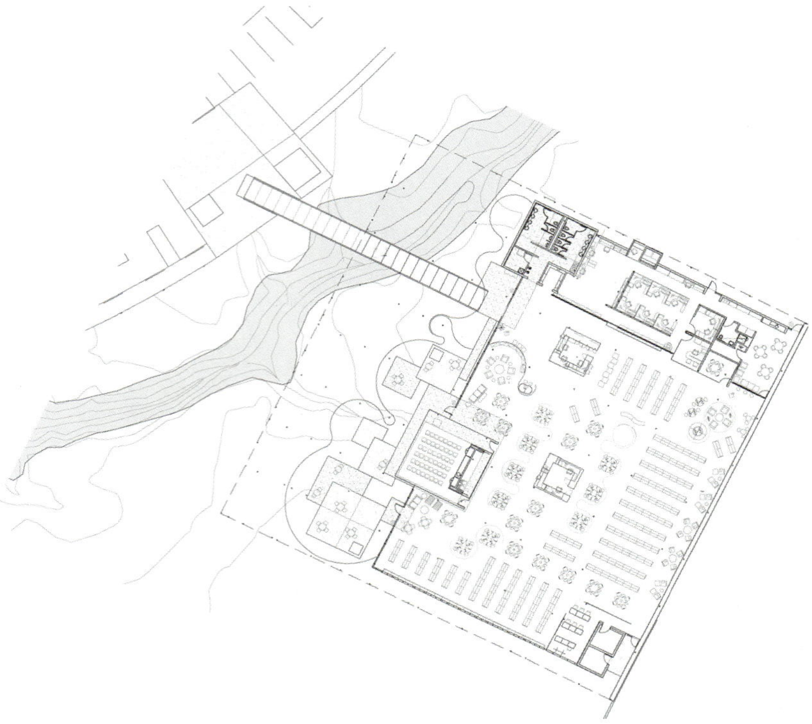

Borrowing from the symbiotic relationship of a young saguaro cacti and its nurse tree along the arroyos edge, the expansive roof of the Desert Broom Public Library creates a shaded microclimate, providing filtered daylight, shelter, and a nurturing environment for intellectual growth and development. This project's strength is in the integration of the exterior with the interior of the building. The roof form extends above an adjoining arroyo 60 feet out into the natural desert, creating indoor and outdoor transitional spaces, which provides a seamless transition into the desert.

01 Exterior view by night **02** Reading space **03** Interior space
04 General plan **05** Extended roof into desert

Photos: Bill Timmerman

ROCK BRIDGE CHRISTIAN CHURCH

The Rock Bridge Christian Church development was a program that called for a new sanctuary (3,000 square-feet), classrooms (2,000 square-feet), and a narthex as an addition of the two existing buildings. Working with the site, the project appeared as a flowing diagram against the rigidity of the existing structures. This led to the proposition of having and using two arms. On the one arm there would be the sanctuary, which would remain at the same level of the main entrance, while the second arm, the classrooms, will slope with the existing topoghaphy creating direct connections with the landscape.

01 Cooper façade **02** Main entrance **03** Interior **04** Exterior view by night **05** Floor plan

Photos: Sam Fentress, Fabian Llonch

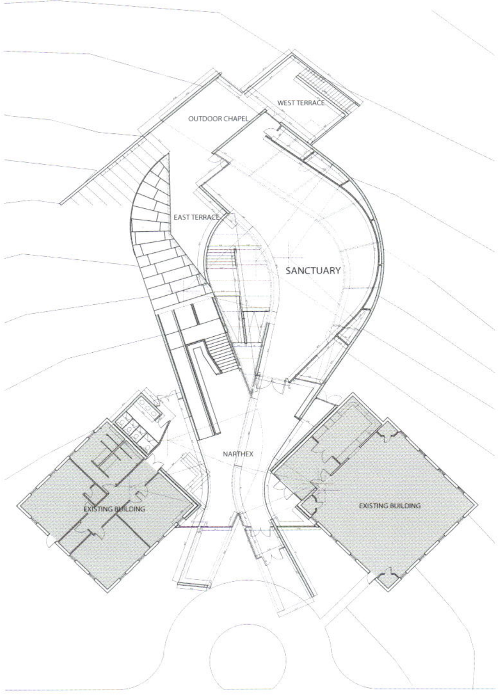

CITY Columbia (MO)
COUNTRY USA
REGION North America
TYPOLOGY Ecclesiastical
COMPLETION -
WEBSITE www.llonch-vidalle.com
ARCHITECTS llonch+vidalle Architecture

CITY	Calabasas (CA)
COUNTRY	USA
REGION	North America
TYPOLOGY	Living
COMPLETION	2003
WEBSITE	www.ai-architects.com
ARCHITECTS	Aleks Istanbullu Architects

MALIBU MEADOWS

Vertical redwood lattice negotiates the visual transition between indoor and outdoor space for this master suite addition, which rose to hover among the branches of a vast grove of California Oaks. The interestingly curved shape of the house features a reading room within the bedroom, which provides an intensifying feeling of being in the trees. Many different elements in the Malibu Meadows project come to life including the skylights, wood varieties, stone, and Venetian plaster, which all play off one another to create an open, sensuous and purposeful environment with a variety of visual experiences.

01 Wood rods façade **02** Living space **03** Exterior detail **04** Interior

Photos: Ciro Coelho Photography

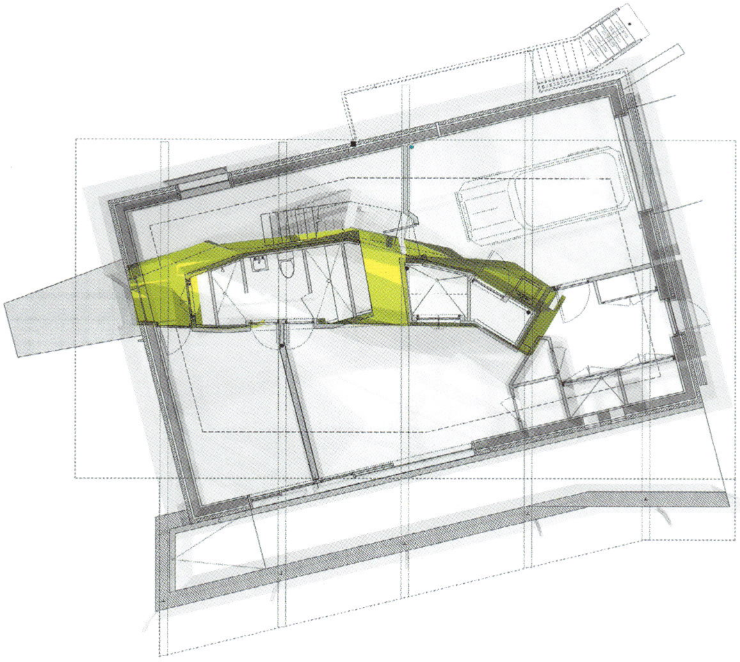

GT RESIDENCE

Archi-Tectonics studied the performance aspects of hyperactive domestic functions in the development of temporal modulations for the Arma-Ture, which is an intelligent core for the GT-Residence. The house's structural center resides in this generative core, the armature, which is a centrally located "smart structure" integrating cooking, bathing, heating and cooling systems, environmental systems, and a central music system. The development of the project emphasized that it is no longer interested in 'empty formal' aesthetics, bur rather the house embodies the anti-aesthetic, as it is designed from the inside out.

01 First floor plan **02** Section **03** Bathroom **04** Breakfast bar **05** South front **06** Staircase

Photos: Floto + Warner Studio

CITY Carmel (NY)
COUNTRY USA
REGION North America
TYPOLOGY Living
COMPLETION 2003
WEBSITE www.archi-tectonics.com
ARCHITECTS Archi-Tectonics

CITY Carmichael (CA)
COUNTRY USA
REGION North America
TYPOLOGY Living
COMPLETION Withheld
WEBSITE www.dzarchitect.com
ARCHITECTS Mark Dziewulski Architects

LAKESIDE STUDIO

The house is a combination of flexible living space, art studio and gallery. It provides a tranquil and sheltered environment from which to enjoy a rich natural landscape, making the relationship between environment and house central to the design. The sculptural form curves to take advantage of spectacular views, while uninterrupted glass walls open the room up to the landscape as the boundaries between exterior and interior are blurred. The occupant feels fully immersed in a benign landscape, while sunlight reflecting off the water dapples the ceiling with dancing patterns, constantly changing with the progress of day.

01 Exterior view **02** Fully glazed façade **03** Site plan **04** Living space with kylight

Photos: Keith Cronin

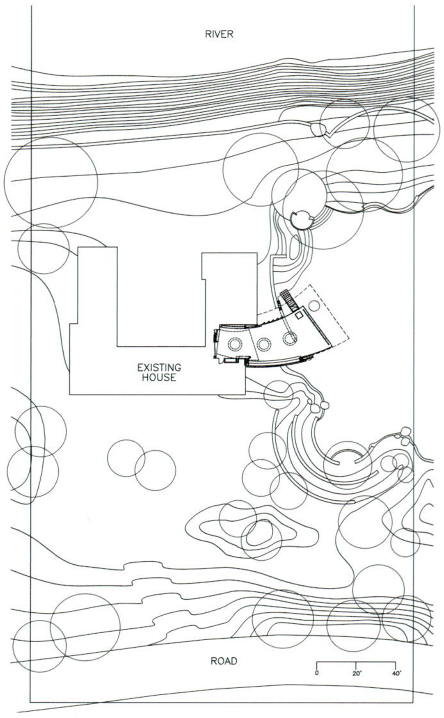

YOGA STUDIO

The idea was to create an energy efficient shape with a feeling of spaciousness and connection to nature using prefab curved SIP panels. The design maximizes the footprint at the window wall where the sun can warm the space in winter and open up to daylight and views accenting the main living space. The north side turns its back to the cold while providing limited fenestration for ventilation and balanced light. The details, materials, furniture and nature are to provide the only art expression, freeing the space of metaphysical distractions, while the morphology of the curved space inside transports all who visit.

01 South west view **02** Living space **03** View into living space from above **04** Floor plans **05** View of open floor bunks

Photos: Daniel Afzal

CITY Clarke County (VA)

COUNTRY USA

REGION North America

TYPOLOGY Living

COMPLETION 2007

WEBSITE www.carterburton.com

ARCHITECTS Carter + Burton Architecture

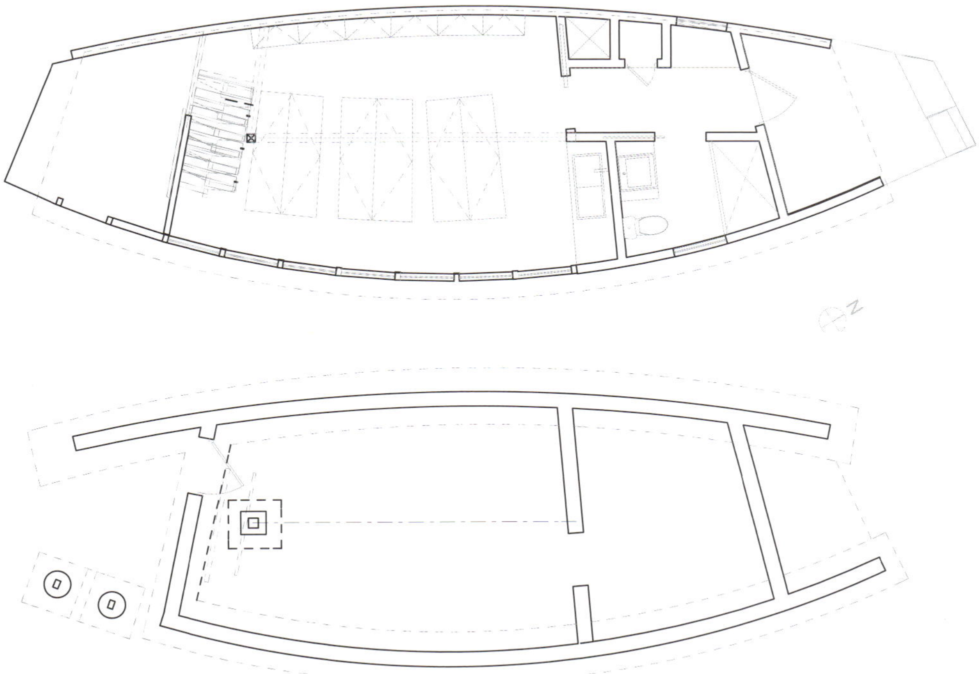

CITY Clarke County (VA)

COUNTRY USA

REGION North America

TYPOLOGY Living

COMPLETION 2007

WEBSITE www.carterburton.com

ARCHITECTS Carter + Burton Architecture

BOXHEAD

This three bedroom house has an open plan and a "boxes in boxes" design approach with an economy of scale strategy, in which each smaller box becomes more precious. The plastered insulated concrete block walls and the concrete floor provide thermal mass and a heat sink which works with the super insulation provided by the exposed structural insulated panels. These distinct materials blur the definition of inside and out. A reduction of new materials and waste is also achieved with concrete cut outs, and are recycled from a dumpster into floor and wall tile, which were specifically used for the master bathroom.

01 Exterior view by night **02** Living space **03** Exposed structure and materials **04** Floor plans

Photos: Daniel Afzal

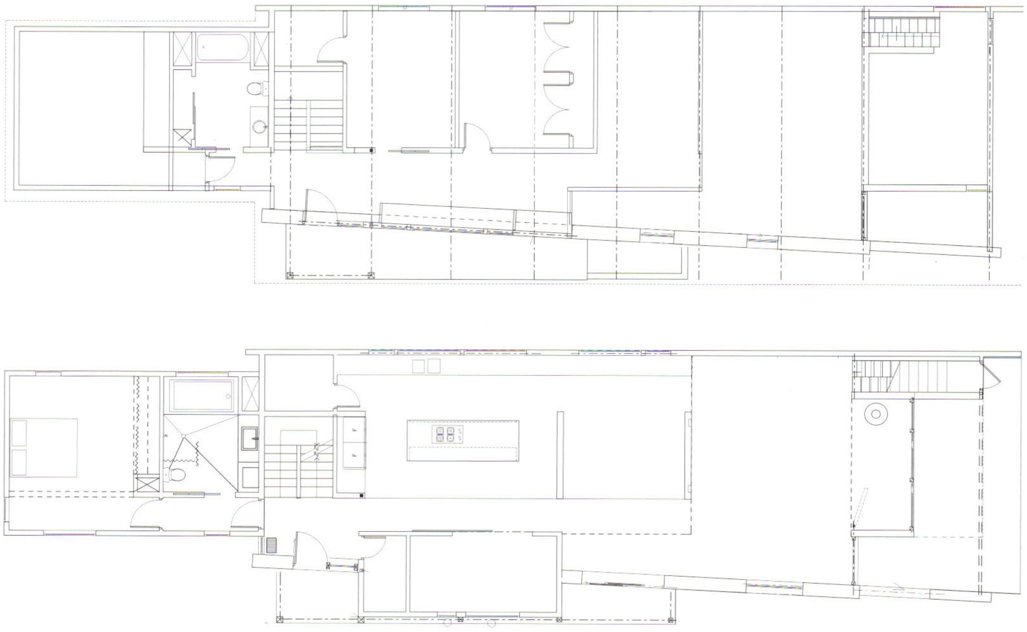

NATIONAL UNDERGROUND RAILROAD FREEDOM CENTER

The project is the centerpiece of Cincinnati's billion-dollar redevelopment of its Ohio River waterfront; the northern shores of which constituted the legal and symbolic line between the slave South and the free North. The struggle of slavery and the exuberance of freedom through winding paths and north-south free-running walls are both conveyed, while at the entrance is a stone graphic in the paving, a symbolic river and crossing. The south facing glass wall will be illuminated at night, along with an eternal flame on the south-facing roof terrace, serving as a reminder of the candles placed in the windows of 'safe houses'.

01 Travertine stone blocks and weathered copper cladding **02** Terrace cafe overlooking the Ohio River **03** Exterior by night **04** Ground floor plan **05** Lobby

Photos: Farshid Assassi, J. Miles Wolf (03)

CITY Cincinnati (OH)
COUNTRY USA
REGION North America
TYPOLOGY Culture
COMPLETION 2004
WEBSITE www.boora.com
ARCHITECTS BOORA Architects

CITY
Chicago (IL)

COUNTRY
USA

REGION
North America

TYPOLOGY
Public

COMPLETION
2007

WEBSITE
www.scb.com

ARCHITECTS
Solomon Cordwell Buenz

LOYOLA UNIVERSITY RICHARD J. KLARCHECK INFORMATION COMMONS

The Loyola Information Commons is an architectural bridge that links Loyola University's traditional past to a visionary future. By combining the latest computer technology with an open flexible design and innovative environmental systems, it is presented at the forefront of academic research facilities. The building will not only conserve significant amounts of energy, but will also create a conducive environment for study and research while ushering in a new era of campus architecture focused on resource conservation. The structure shows fore-thought and innovation by the design team and the University.

01 Fully glazed façade **02** Detail **03** Façade structure **04** Ground floor plan **05** Exterior view

Photos: Solomon Cordwell Buenz

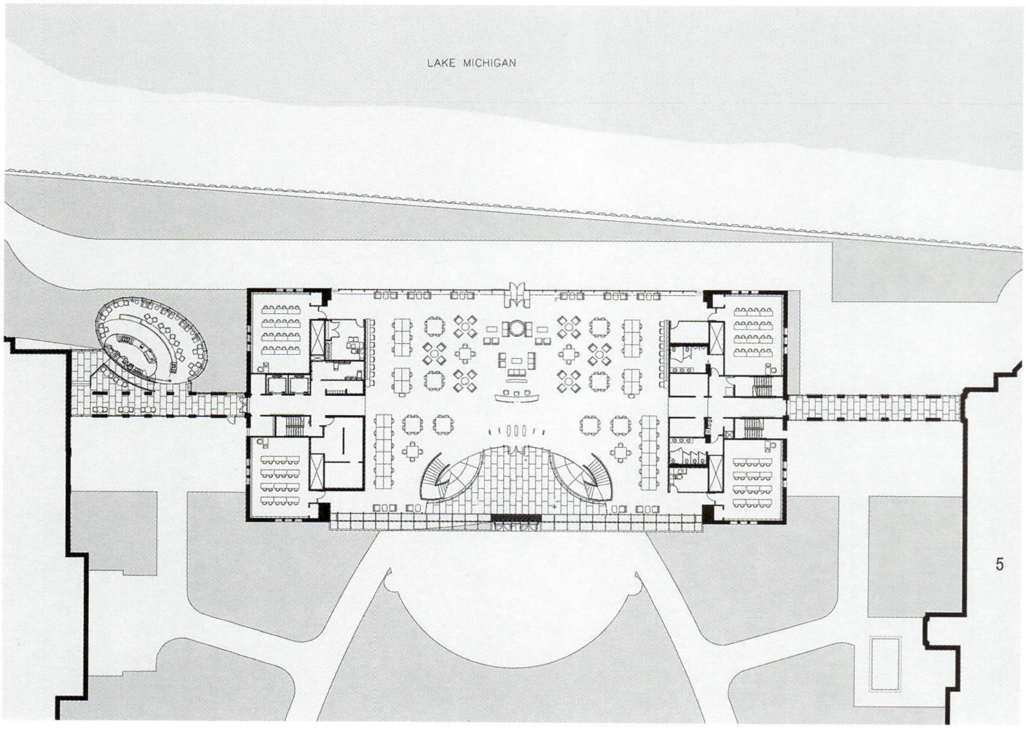

HYDE PARK ART CENTER

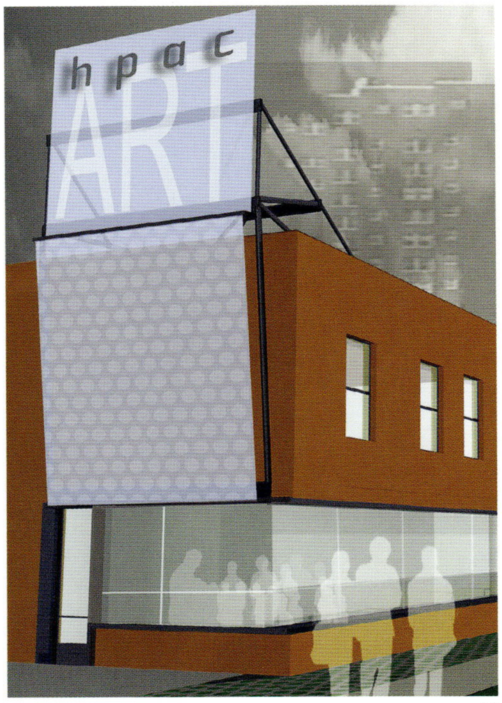

The Center has been serving the Hyde Park-Kenwood community, surrounding neighborhoods, and the metropolitan Chicago area with outstanding visual art exhibitions and education programs since its inception in 1939. The inhabitable façade and forecourt conceive to extend the center's mission by energizing the street. It is developed as an experimental electronic space, made of glass and steel, equipped with a system of digital projection screens and shades, allowing for many alternative forms of electronic art. The building becomes a device in which artists create works that are site specific and engaging with public space.

01 Inhabitable façade **02** Detail **03** Bird's eye view **04** Street side view **05** Light installation **06** Exhibit

Renderings: Courtesy Garofalo Architects

CITY Chicago (IL)
COUNTRY USA
REGION North America
TYPOLOGY Culture
COMPLETION 2006
WEBSITE www.garofaloarchitects.com
ARCHITECTS Garofalo Architects

CITY
Chicago (IL)

COUNTRY
USA

REGION
North America

TYPOLOGY
Office

COMPLETION
2005

WEBSITE
www.gpchicago.com

ARCHITECTS
Goettsch Partners

111 SOUTH WACKER

Located in downtown Chicago, 111 South Wacker is a 53-story office building and the first-ever project certified LEED-CS Gold by the U.S. Green Building Council. The building's lobby is one of its more unique features, which includes a spiraling parking ramp that defines the space. The radial pattern of the ramp is reflected in the lobby's stepped ceiling, and this pattern is further echoed in the granite and marble floor that extends beyond the enclosure. Wrapping the lobby is a cable-supported, ultra-transparent glass wall that allows inside and outside to be perceived as a single, continuous space.

01 Exterior view to spiral parking ramp **02** View into the lobby with granite and marble floor **03** Ground floor plan **04** Façade with ultra-transparent glass

Photos: James Steinkamp

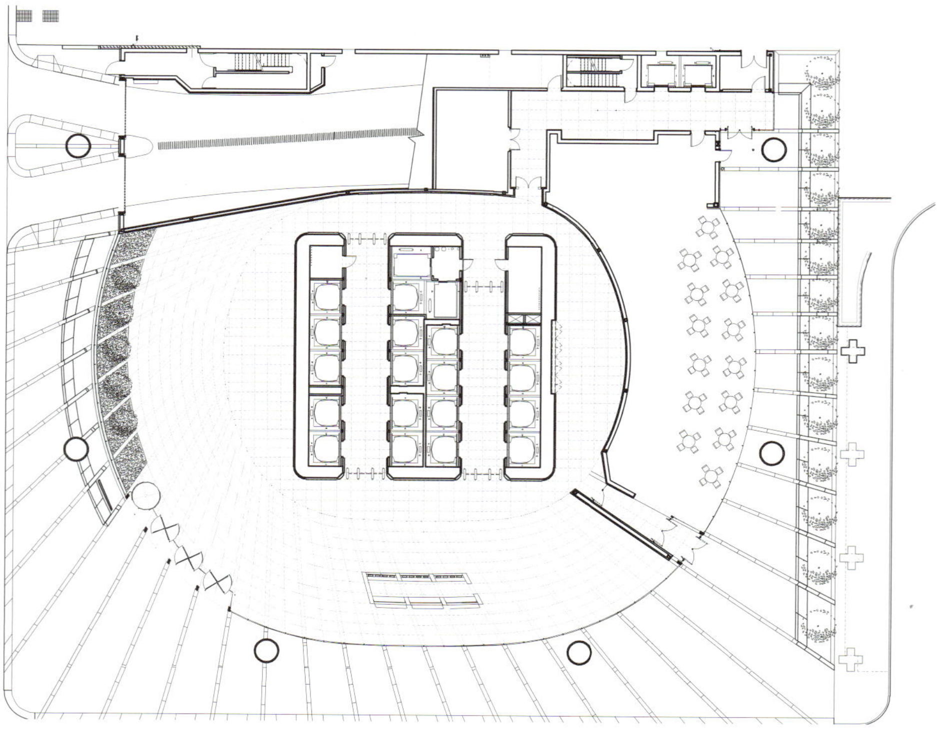

IIT STUDENT HOUSING

The project will define the East edge of the Campus Quadrangle, where forming and defending this open space as the locus of the academic campus is an essential component of a successful residential development. Six housing blocks are oriented East-west, creating three entry courts and two Sallyports to future development to the east of the El tracks. Each court is partially closed by screen walls, thereby reinstating the north-south edge required at the Quadrangle. It is intended that the courtyard will be an acoustically comfortable zone allowing students to utilize natural ventilation to a great extent.

---
01 Exterior view to one of the entry courts **02** Roof deck **03** Side elevation with grove of birch **04** Ground floor plan and west elevation **05** Bird's eye view

Photos: Doug Snower Photography

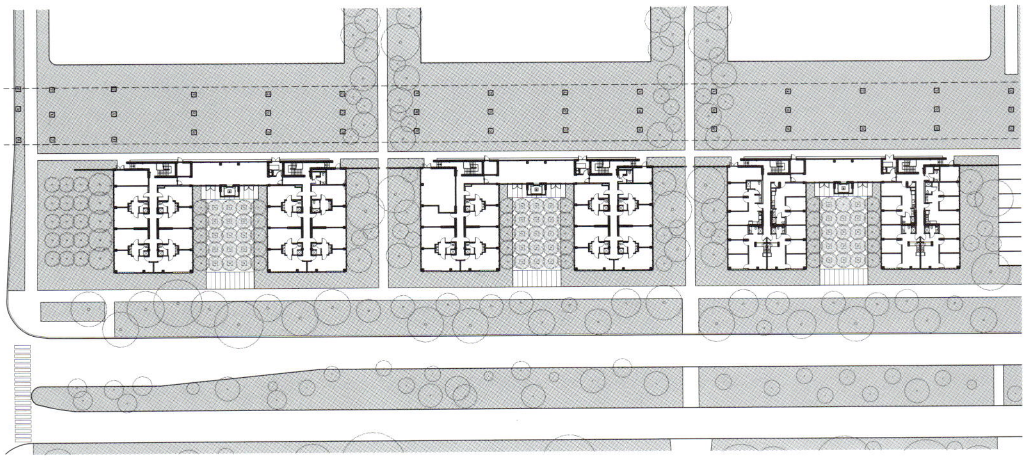

Ground Floor Plan

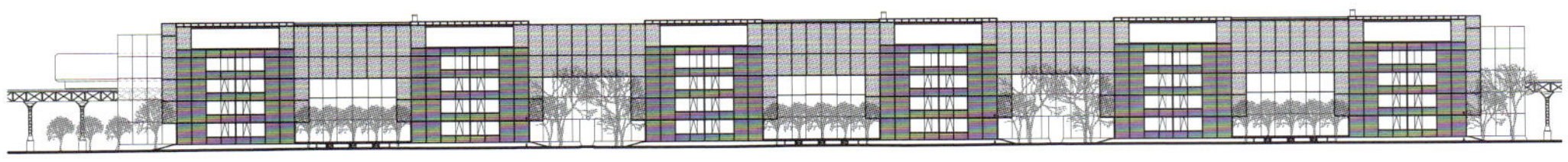

West Elevation

CITY Chicago (IL)
COUNTRY USA
REGION North America
TYPOLOGY Living
COMPLETION 2003
WEBSITE www.murphyjahn.com
ARCHITECTS Murphy/Jahn

LITTLE VILLAGE HIGH SCHOOL, CHICAGO

Little Village High School was created with numerous community groups after a thorough planning process, in which OWP/P designed a new 1,400-student community high school that integrates four, small 350-student schools into one building. Highly visible from a nearby vehicular overpass, the school serves as a beacon to the urban Little Village community. In the central commons space, a solar calendar uses the reflection of the sun to display the date, while the details of this central space symbolically commemorate the community's successful 19-day hunger strike, which was driven by the goal of providing new local school facilities.

01 Total view by night **02** Entrance at dusk **03** Solar Calendar **04** Site plan

Photos: James Steinkamp

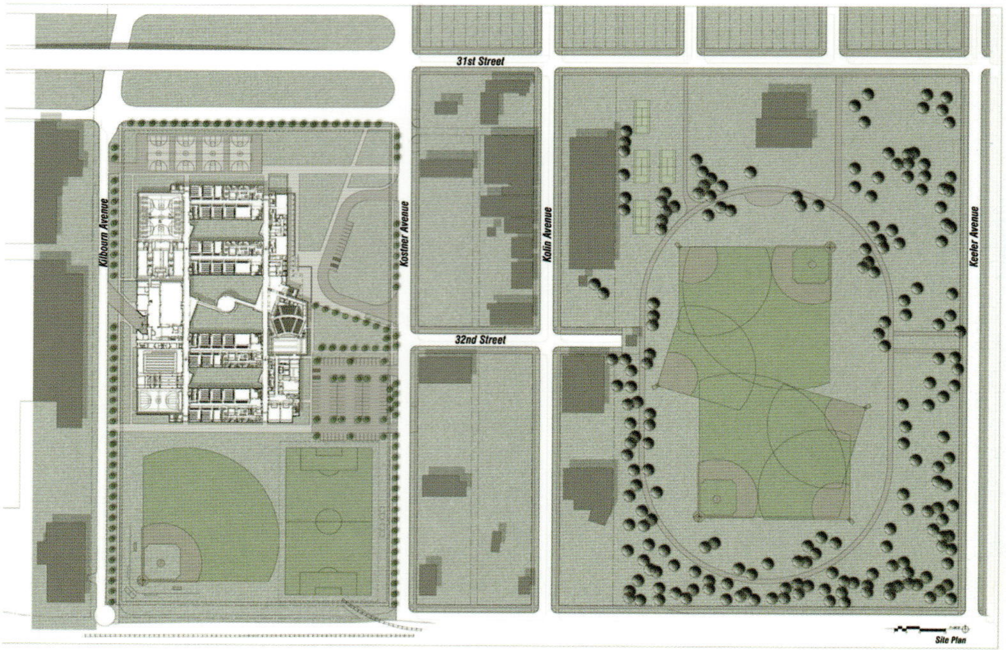

2041 W CORTLAND

This residence was created out of the basic architectural elements of light, shadow, massing, color, and transition. The design solution started with two cubes, opaque and transparent, where both are paired together to create an L-shape defining an inner courtyard. The transparent cube provides the majority of the light, allowing views from the street and home areas, while the opaque cube accommodates the more private functions of the residence. The residence blurs the boundary between exterior and interior spaces by extending exterior materials inside, creating subtle textured finishes for light to bounce off of.

01 View from the street to transparent cubes by night **02** Living space with natural daylight **03** Exterior view **04** Kitchen **05** Site plan

Photos: Marty Peters

CITY Chicago (IL)
COUNTRY USA
REGION North America
TYPOLOGY Living
COMPLETION 2006
WEBSITE www.studiodwell.com
ARCHITECTS Studio DWELL

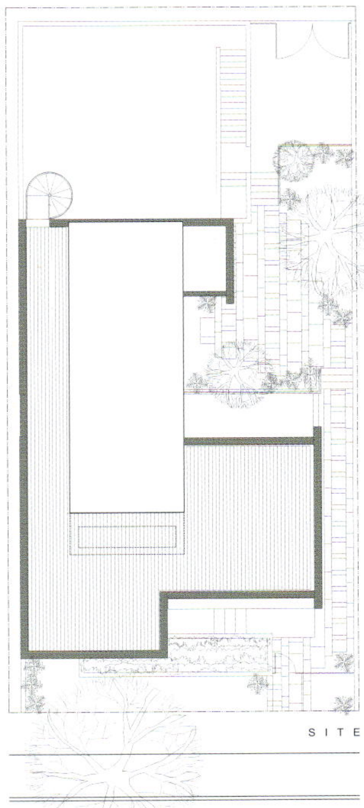

LIVE + WORK

The project is a new 3000-square-foot construction, and is a mixed-use building intended for such purposes as residency and work. The first floor is created as office space, while the second floor is solely for the purpose of providing a residential area. Prior to the construction, the site was occupied by a building that required immediate demolition for various reasons. The previous, old building was then "recycled" into a landscape mound. This proved to be a beneficial feature as the residential volume accesses the crest of the mound, giving the second floor a direct connection to the ground.

01 View to residential area on second floor 02 Living space with "fire-orb" 03 Exterior view to home and office space 04 First floor plan 05 Second floor plan

Photos: Michelle Litvin Photographer

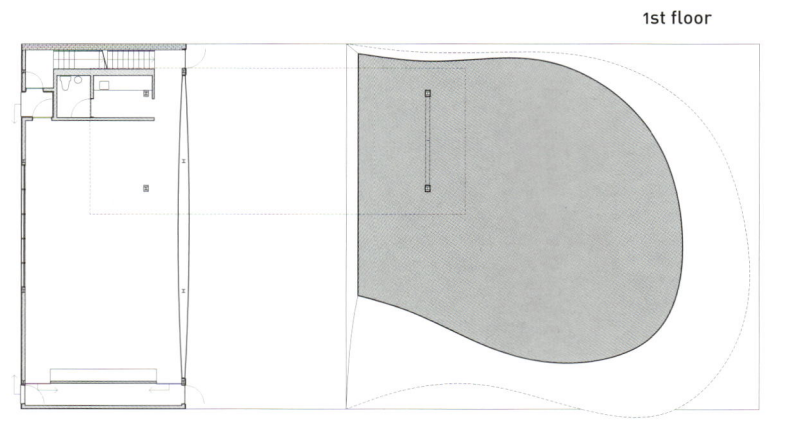

CITY Chicago (IL)
COUNTRY USA
REGION North America
TYPOLOGY Living + Office
COMPLETION 2008
WEBSITE www.urbanlab.com
ARCHITECTS urban lab

1st floor 2nd floor

UNITED NEIGHBORHOOD ORGANIZATION ARCHER HEIGHTS CHARTER SCHOOL

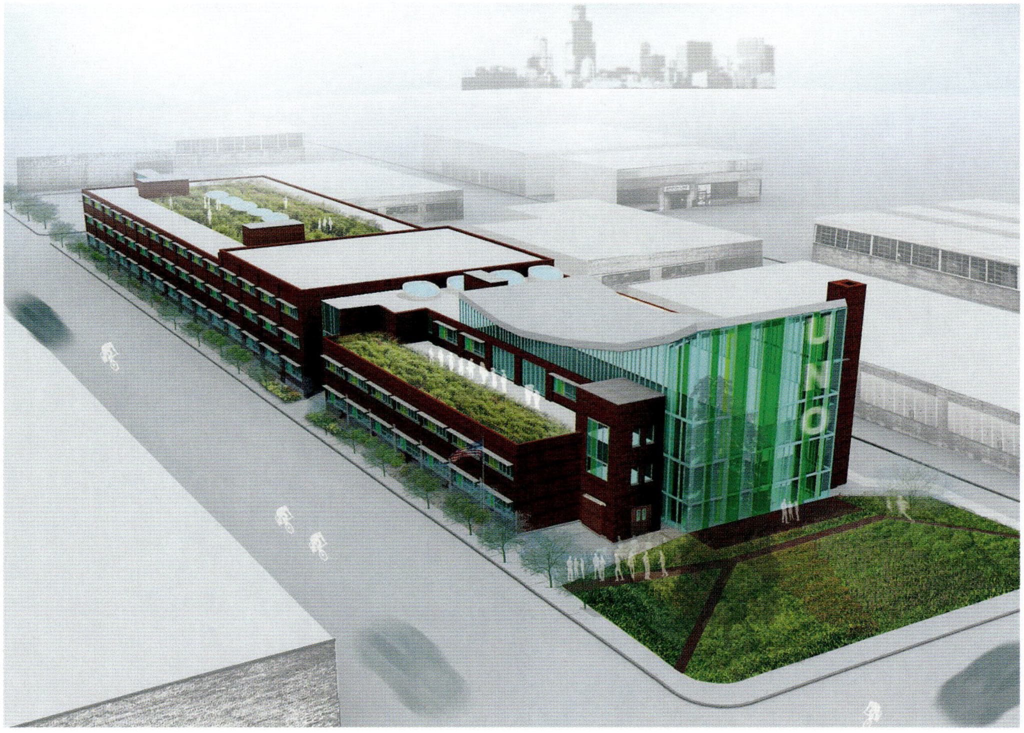

The design respected the origins of the brick manufacturing facility while inserting new dynamic communal spaces, serving the nearby community and meeting the school day needs of the students. Spatial configurations, cold, light, heat, and air quality led to a stacked school strategy, where the high school would occupy the top floor and the elementary schools would occupy the first and second floor. Common spaces, including the cafeteria, library, media resource center, and gym/auditorium would be housed in the south end of the building. Outdoor spaces were added in the form of extensive green roofs.

01 Brick façade, glass vessels 02 Roof structure providing natural light 03 Communal space 04 Bird's eye view 05 First, second and third floor plan

Renderings: Philip Schmidt, UrbanWorks Ltd.

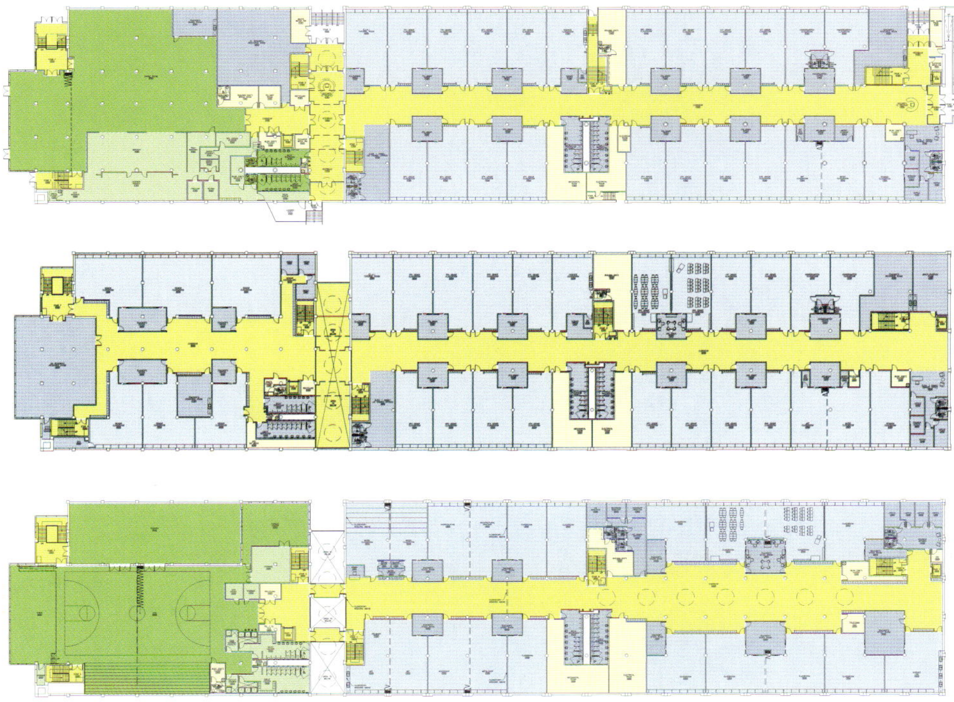

CITY Chicago (IL)
COUNTRY USA
REGION North America
TYPOLOGY Education
COMPLETION 2008
WEBSITE www.urbanworks architecture.com
ARCHITECTS Urban Works, Ltd

NEW STADIUM AT SOLDIER FIELD

This project was a joint venture of two architecture firms: Goettsch Partners, with primary responsibility for the master plan and North Burnham Park project, and Wood + Zapata, with primary responsibility for the architectural design of the Soldier Field stadium. If features a stadium with a 62,000 seat capacity, a new parkland, and underground and surface parking spaces. The country's third-largest city is moving forward with a $587 million plan for its Bears football team that preserves Soldier Field, the 1924 neoclassical structure designed by Holabird and Roche that has been the team's home since 1971.

01 View from lake **02** Grandstand detail **03** Colonnade atrium **04** Suite level three plan **05** Seating bowl

Photos: David Seide/Defined Space

CITY Chicago (IL)
COUNTRY USA
REGION North America
TYPOLOGY Sports
COMPLETION 2003
WEBSITE www.wood-zapata.com
ARCHITECTS Wood + Zapata

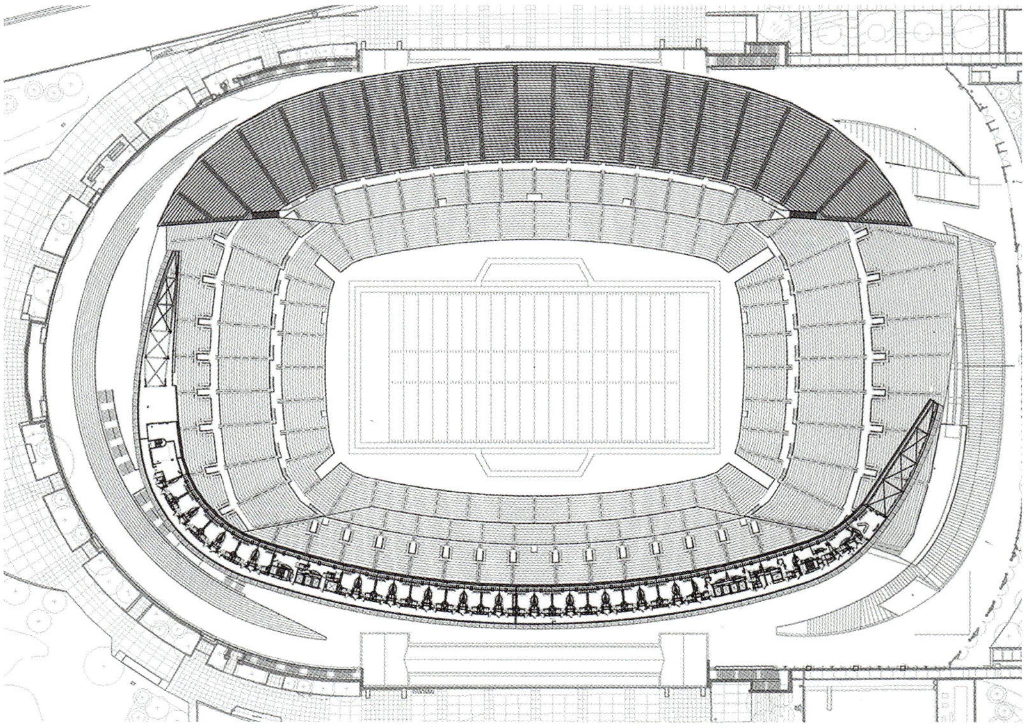

PFANNER RESIDENCE

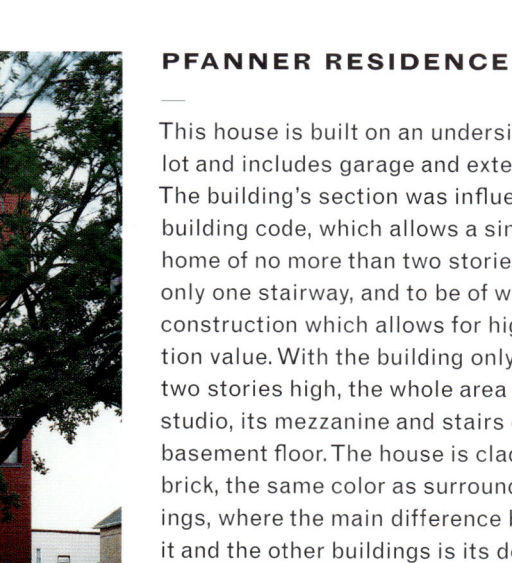

This house is built on an undersized Chicago lot and includes garage and exterior spaces. The building's section was influenced by the building code, which allows a single-family home of no more than two stories to have only one stairway, and to be of wood frame construction which allows for high insulation value. With the building only being two stories high, the whole area of garage, studio, its mezzanine and stairs count as the basement floor. The house is clad in orange brick, the same color as surrounding buildings, where the main difference between it and the other buildings is its degree of openness.

01 Brick façade **02** Interior circulation **03** Longitudinal section **04** House in context

Photos: Doug Fogelson

CITY: Chicago (IL)
COUNTRY: USA
REGION: North America
TYPOLOGY: Living
COMPLETION: 2002
WEBSITE: www.zokazola.com
ARCHITECTS: Zoka Zola architecture + urban design

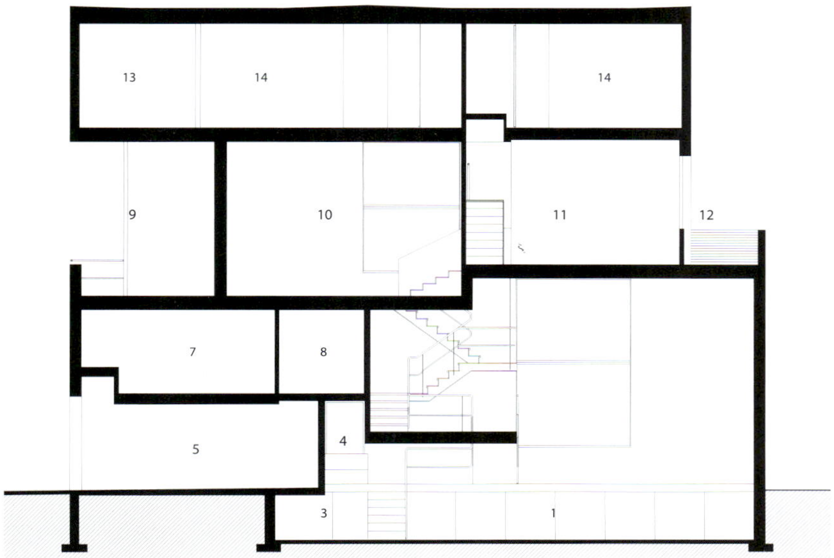

CITY
Chicago (IL)

COUNTRY
USA

REGION
North America

TYPOLOGY
Living

COMPLETION
2007

WEBSITE
www.scb.com

ARCHITECTS
Solomon Cordwell Buenz

340 ON THE PARK

340 on the Park is a predominantly glass tower that capitalizes on views overlooking Grant Park, Lake Michigan and the city of Chicago. Glass is the key element giving character to the exterior form and responding to its surrounding context. The prow-shaped profile circumvents existing views of nearby buildings and creates 360-degrees vistas around the site. The project is the first residential high rise to achieve a silver LEED rating. The design and construction approach not only make it a benchmark for green residential high-rise design, but it also promotes awareness for living in an eco-friendly environment.

01 Interior view to living space **02** Exterior view to glass façade **03** Winter garden **04** Floor plan tier two **05** Exterior north view

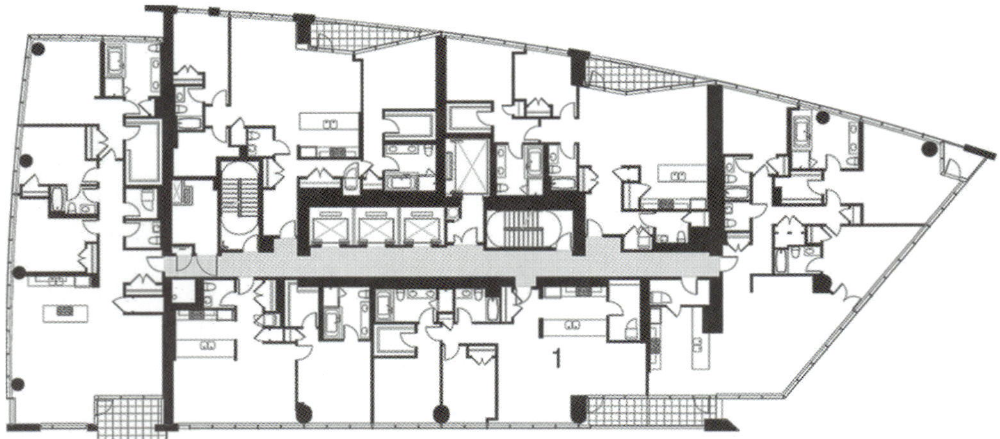

Photos: Solomon Cordwell Buenz

SOS CHILDREN'S VILLAGES LAVEZZORIO COMMUNITY CENTER

The 16,000 square foot community center in Chicago enables the international nonprofit to fulfill its mission of training foster parents and reuniting siblings into foster care families. At the entry stands a stratified wall created by layering various concrete mixes. Wavy lines, articulating each pour, preserve the physics of concrete's once fluid nature. Inside, access to daylight is maximized through orientation around a courtyard. An extra-wide stair in the lobby doubles as seating and an impromptu stage for performances.

01 Concrete façade from courtyard **02** View from street **03** First floor plan **04** Lobby

Photos: Steve Hall, Hedrich Blessing

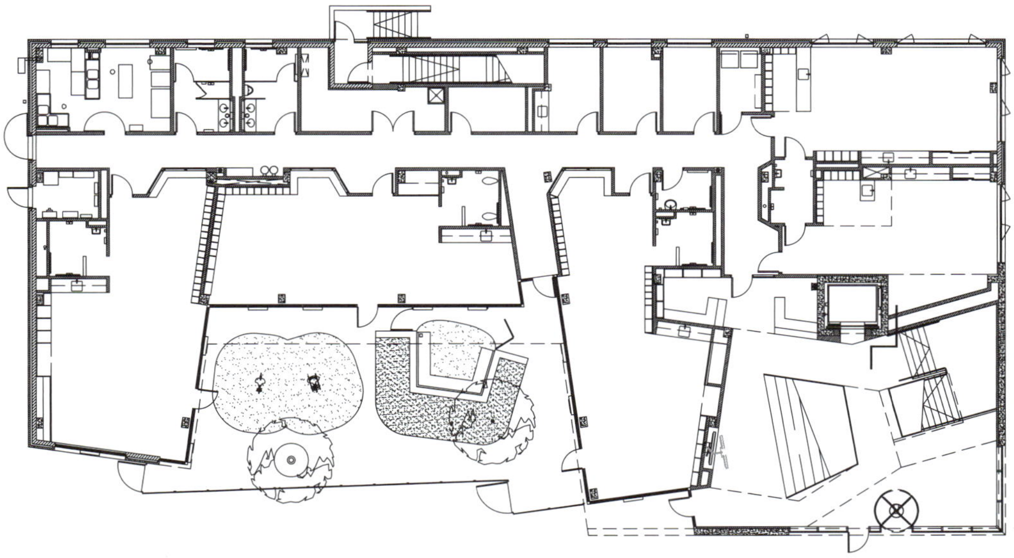

CITY Chicago (IL)
COUNTRY USA
REGION North America
TYPOLOGY Public
COMPLETION 2007
WEBSITE www.studiogang.net
ARCHITECTS Studio Gang Architects

CITY Chicago (IL)

COUNTRY USA

REGION North America

TYPOLOGY Living

COMPLETION 2004

WEBSITE www.gorlinarchitect.com

ARCHITECTS Alexander Gorlin Architect

CHICAGO TOWNHOUSE

This new townhouse is located in a residential neighborhood of traditional single-family homes. The contrast between old and new is highlighted by the dramatic cantilevered living area projected out over the front garden. On the main level, a continuous loft-like two-story space is open from front to back. The living area is placed towards the street, while the dining room is set towards the rear frames of the house. The kitchen is situated at the center, providing a space between the two other areas for family gatherings. The master bedroom and bathroom both appear to float, being suspended above this main volume.

01 Cantilievered living space **02** Open living space **03** Floor plans **04** Dining **05** Bedroom

Photos: Michael Moran

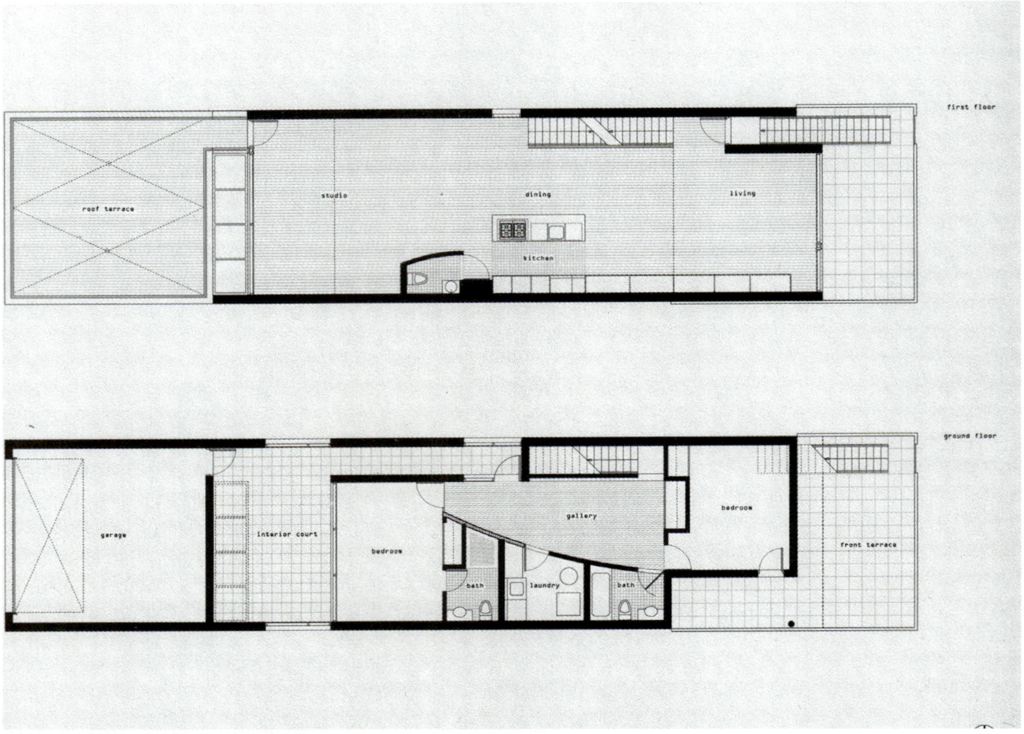

SPERTUS INSTITUTE OF JEWISH

The new facility is a mixed-use program containing exhibition galleries, library, a 400-seat multi-use auditorium, college classrooms and administrative offices. An unabashedly contemporary design, the Institute is set in a 19th Century streetscape of historic masonry buildings. The façade is composed of folded glass planes and will glow with both natural and man-made light, symbolizing the prominent role of light in Jewish religious and intellectual tradition. Modulating the scale of the building, the glass folds relate the façade to the numerous bays, windows, cornices and other projections found on the magnificent avenue.

01 Section **02** Folded glass panels façade **03** Interior
04 Street side view

Photos: William Zbaren

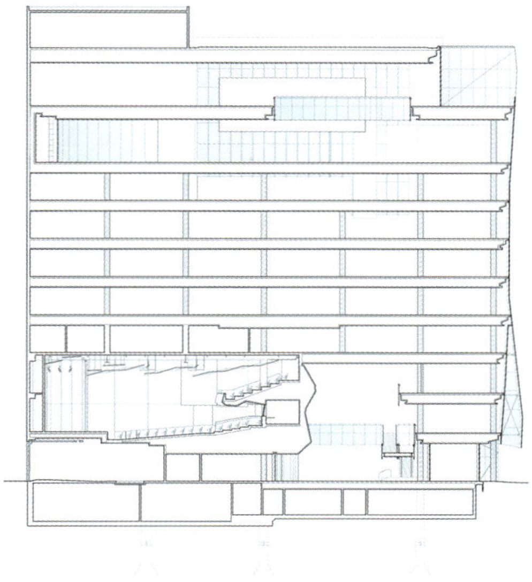

CITY
Chicago (IL)

COUNTRY
USA

REGION
North America

TYPOLOGY
Culture

COMPLETION
2007

WEBSITE
www.ksarch.com

ARCHITECTS
Krueck + Sexton Architects

CITY Chicago (IL)
COUNTRY USA
REGION North America
TYPOLOGY Living
COMPLETION 2001
WEBSITE www.landonbonebaker.com
ARCHITECTS Landon Bone Baker

ARCHER COURTS PHASE I

The project involved the rehabilitation and reuse of a late 1940's development originally built as a response to an urban renewal project which displaced thousands of Chicago residents. Options for reuse of a public housing project into a rejuvenated mixed income housing development were explored. Renovation included interior unit finishes, landscaping, addition of outdoor pavilions, new elevators and electrical systems, and the addition of a glass curtain wall to replace chain-link enclosed „galleries" with clear glass. The renovation changed the appearance of the two buildings for the benefit of their residents and the community.

01 Exterior view **02** Front court **03** Wellness Center Exterior
04 Curtainwall **05** Wellness Center Interior

Photos: Mark Ballogg Photography

VILLA_OR

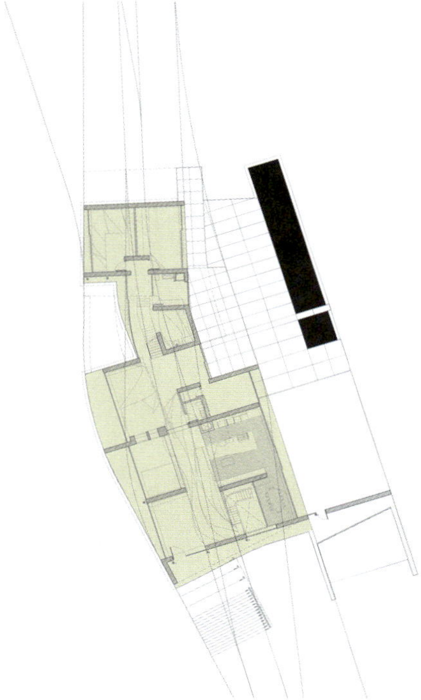

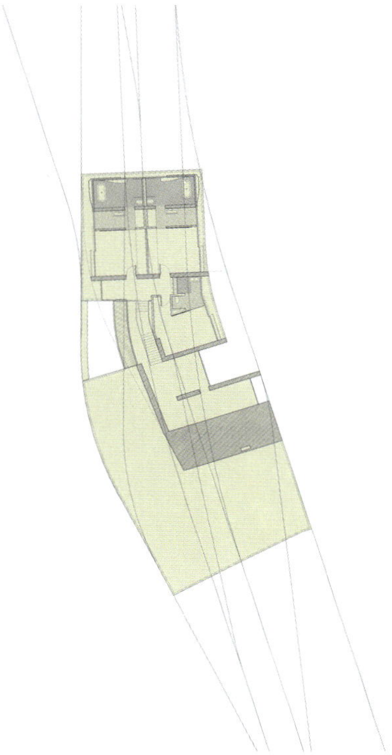

Designed for a wooded lot 50 miles west of Chicago, the project interacts with its environment to produce a new way to feel the forest. Hugging the terrain in its section, the house assembles an open living experience. Each room is conceived as a sequence of moments framed by an open exterior and disciplined by the massive bearing wall partitions on the interior. Sliding exterior glass walls further eliminate the separation between the contexts. The diminutive southern entry façade serves in direct contrast to the aggressive north terminus, resulting in a dynamic exterior choreography of nature, both constructed and existing.

01 Exterior roof **02** Ground floor plan **03** Pool **04** Upper floor plan **05** Interior

Renderings : Qua'Virarch

CITY Chicago (IL)
COUNTRY USA
REGION North America
TYPOLOGY Living
COMPLETION in progress
WEBSITE www.quavirarch.com
ARCHITECTS Qua'Virarch

CITY Culver City (CA)

COUNTRY USA

REGION North America

TYPOLOGY Living

COMPLETION 2008

WEBSITE www.sander-architects.com

ARCHITECTS Sander Architects

RESIDENCE FOR A BRIARD

Sander Architects' approach to architecture and design is in the context of a world that is increasingly eco-conscious. Designed for a board member of the Architectural Foundation of LA, this home needed to be green, world-class, with a cutting-edge, modern feel. Using a long-standing, pre-existing technology (prefab warehouse frames) in an innovative way, the challenge was to build the greenest house that had ever come out of the Sander practice. The clients also hoped to have a home where string quartets could perform, so the ramped stair allows for two chairs per tread for musicians below to be encircled by listeners.

01 Façade as tribute to Baroque and cubism **02** Façade detail **03** Interior view of glazing **04** First and second floor plan **05** Living space with high ceiling

Photos: Claudio Santini Photography

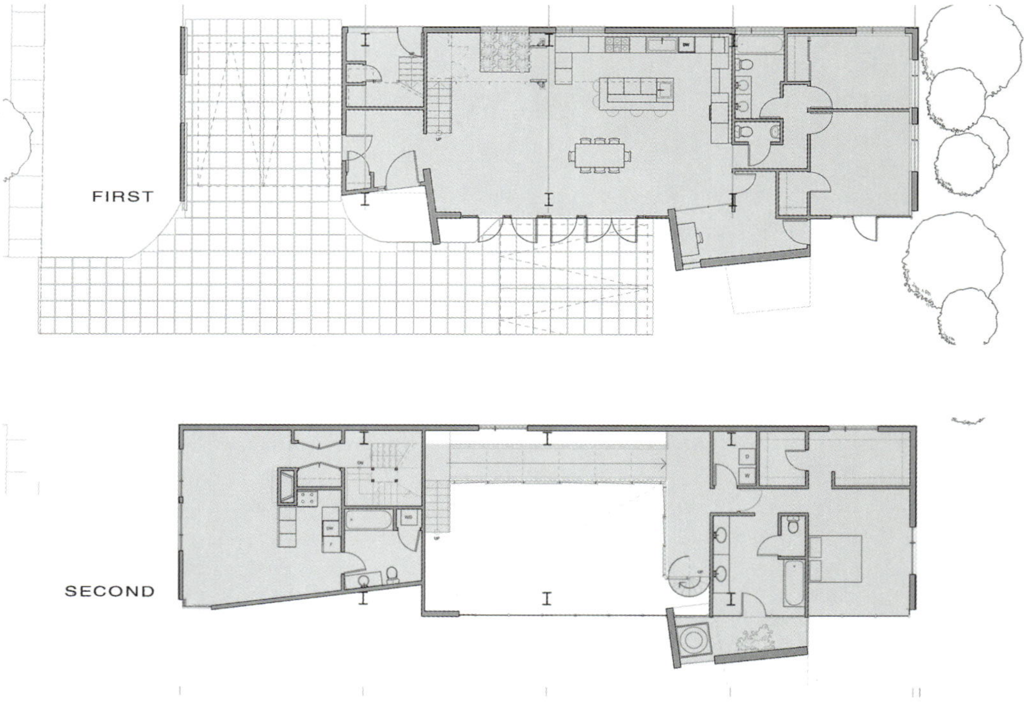

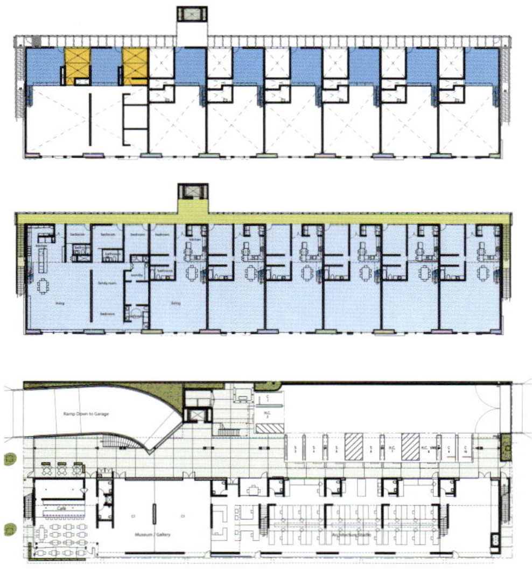

MODAA BUILDING

Seven live/work artist lofts occupy the upper floor of the MODAA building in Culver City. On the ground floor the building houses the architects' own studios, WILSON restaurant, and the Museum of Design Art & Architecture (MODAA) – a 2,000-square-foot dedicated art gallery exploring the symbiotic relationship between art and architecture. Each loft features 16-feet high ceilings, two mezzanines and two private terrace decks. Tri-panel Fleetwood sliding glass doors are used in place of windows, and the residence's exposed ceiling timbers and open floor plan represents loft living in its purest sense.

01 Loft, unit and ground level floor plan **02** Stairs to live/work artist lofts **03** Exterior view by night **04** Interior art gallery **05** Façade detail

Photos: John Edward Linden

CITY: Culver City (CA)
COUNTRY: USA
REGION: North America
TYPOLOGY: Living
COMPLETION: 2005
WEBSITE: www.spfa.com
ARCHITECTS: SPF:architects Studio Pali Fekete architects

CITY	Deal (NJ)
COUNTRY	USA
REGION	North America
TYPOLOGY	Living
COMPLETION	2008
WEBSITE	www.pfcarch.com
ARCHITECTS	Parsons + Fernandez-Casteleiro Architects

LITTMAN RESIDENCE

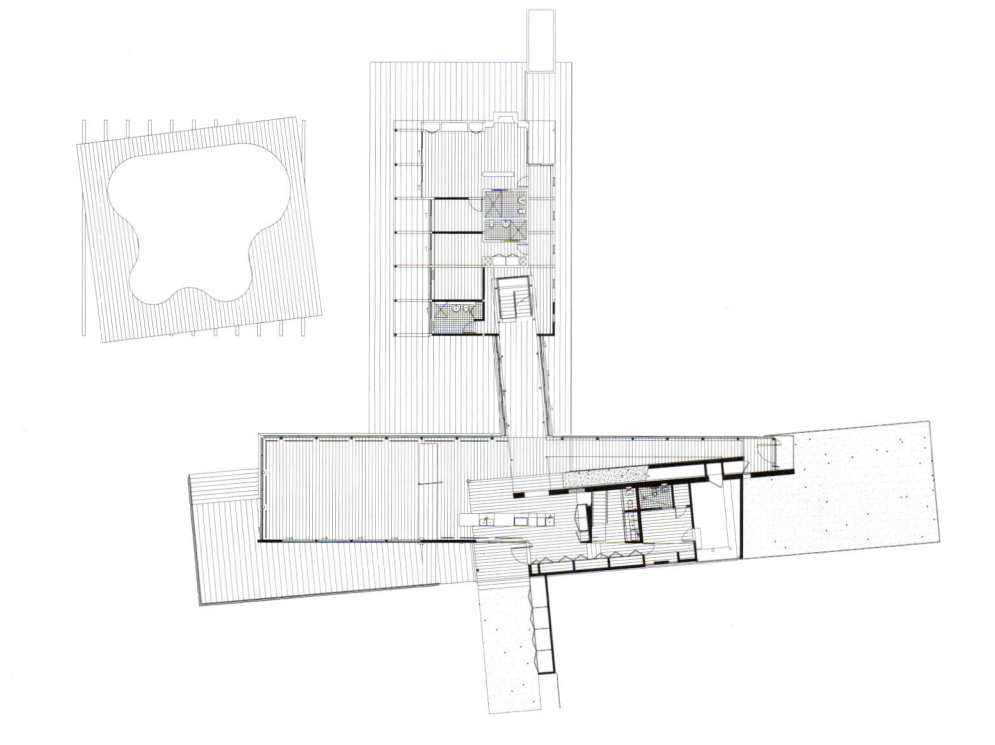

The Littman Residence project was an existing 1950s modular, redwood and glass beach house along the New Jersey shore not far from the entrance to New York Harbor. A new two-story wing was added with a bridge connecting the new wing to the remodeled existing wing. The proposed design creates an outdoor semi-enclosed court facing the ocean. Visitors enter a double ramped gallery that rises along with the ceiling to the spectacular ocean view at the end of the living room. A private balcony, suspended above the dining space, provides the master bedroom suite with impressive views of the ocean and indirect views of the pool through the living areas.

01 Exterior view to private balcony and pool **02** Double ramped entrance **03** New house wing **04** Ground floor plan

Photos: Ethel Buisson

ST. JOHN THE BAPTIST CATHOLIC CHURCH

This dramatic church evokes the sense of the sacred through the use of expressive natural light. Within, the contrasts of scale and colors and the articulation, modulation and graduation of the spaces relate to each other. Additionally, the sense of movement through patterns and repetition of elements creates visually compelling effects. The wing-like roof surmounting the nave and sanctuary suggests the dematerialized canopies of medieval churches.

01 Exterior by night **02** View into the narthex **03** Wing-like roof **04** Nave **05** Floor plan

Photos: Jon Denker, CAPS Photography courtesy of Rambush

CITY: Draper (UT)
COUNTRY: USA
REGION: North America
TYPOLOGY: Ecclesiastical
COMPLETION: 2003
WEBSITE: www.edaarch.com
ARCHITECTS: Edwards and Daniels Architects

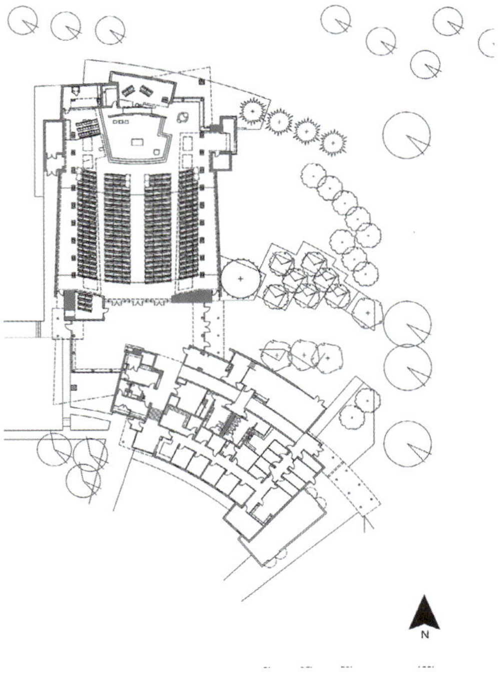

CITY	Davis (CA)
COUNTRY	USA
REGION	North America
TYPOLOGY	Education
COMPLETION	2002
WEBSITE	www.boora.com
ARCHITECTS	BOORA Architects

MONDAVI CENTER FOR THE ARTS

Indian sandstone was chosen for the design of the new Center, as it reflects the school's agricultural roots while blending with the surrounding wine land. The building not only serves as a 'front door' for a newly developed section of the campus, but also offers locals the opportunity to experience art and culture. Adding to the signature look of the new structure is the warm, golden sandstone veneer, which adorns the exterior and interior walls, and was quarried in the Gwalior region in Madhya Pradesh of central India. The Mondavi performing arts center is a 104,000 square foot construction.

01, 02, 03 Exterior view by night **04** Theater

Photos: Robert Canfield (01, 03), Jeff Goldberg/Esto (02, 04)

W DALLAS-VICTORY HOTEL & RESIDENCES

W Dallas-Vicory offers energetic ambience including a vibrant living room lobby and a signature restaurant. Luxury condominiums rise above the hotel's top floors with floor-to-ceiling commercial-grade window systems that are insulated, energy efficient and double paned. Other distinctive characteristics of the property include a full-service spa, pool and fitness facility on the 16th floor overlooking downtown, extensive meeting spaces, and the Ghost bar, which provides 33-story views of the Dallas skyline.

01 First and second level floor plans **02** Expansive terrace with pool **03** Exterior view from street **04** View to 16-story tower **05** View towards balconies

Photos: Blake Marvin - HKS, Inc.

CITY Dallas (TX)
COUNTRY USA
REGION North America
TYPOLOGY Leisure
COMPLETION 2008
WEBSITE www.hksinc.com
ARCHITECTS HKS, Inc.

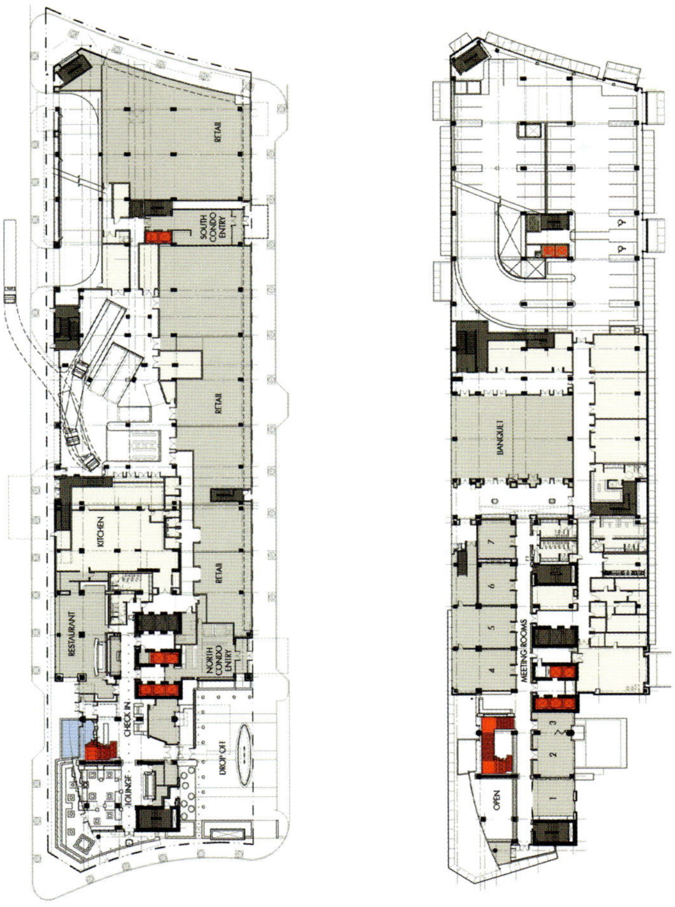

CITY Dallas (TX)
COUNTRY USA
REGION North America
TYPOLOGY Living
COMPLETION 2005
WEBSITE www.buchananarchitecture.com
ARCHITECTS Buchanan Architecture

THE ENVELOPE

A three-unit, multi-family residence located in Dallas, this dramatic building takes its name from the tightly restricted building envelope required by local zoning laws. The form of the building represents the maximum buildable volume – length by width by height plus balcony – and stands as a physical manifestation of local zoning regulations. This strict idea was developed for its clarity and became the central idea guiding the design process, thus preventing the project from becoming disjointed at a later point. The ultimate vision yielded an uncompromised solution that satisfied both the client and designers.

01 East view by night **02** West view to balcony **03** North side **04** Second and third level floor plans **05** Building envelope

Photos: Jason Franzen

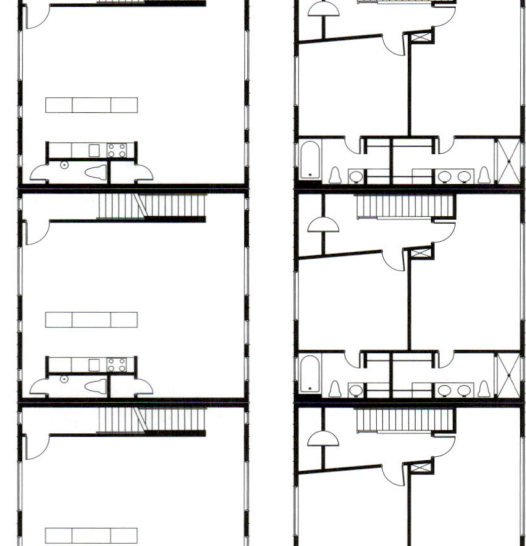

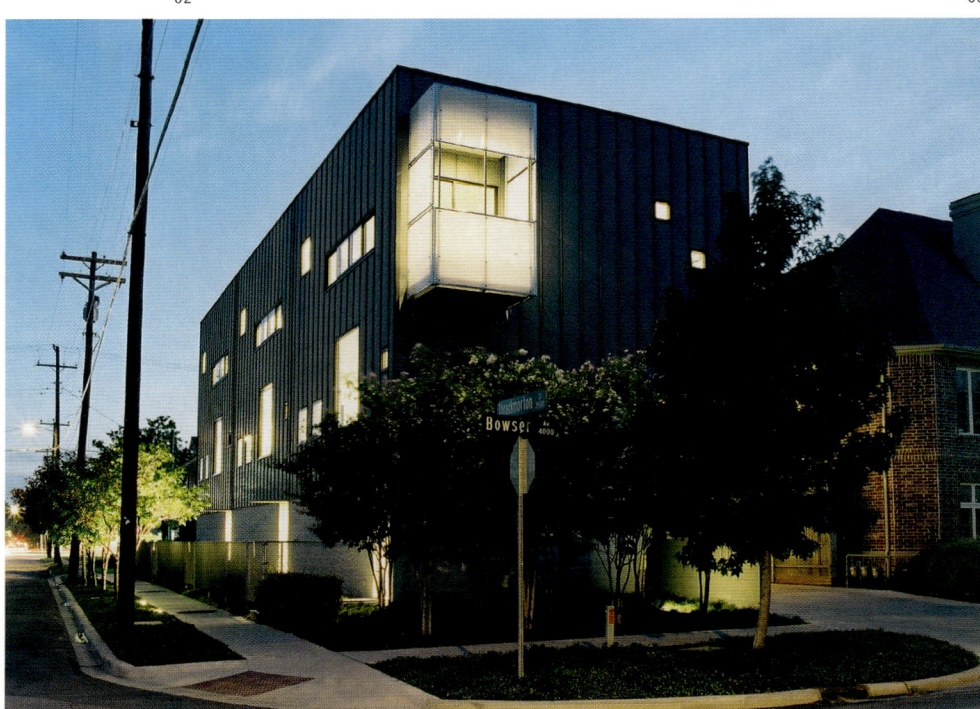

EXTENSION TO THE DENVER ART MUSEUM, FREDERIC C. HAMILTON BUILDING

The extension is an expansion of the existing museum, and is not designed as a stand alone building, but as part of a composition of public spaces, monuments and gateways in this developing part of the city, contributing to the synergy amongst neighbors, large and intimate. The materials closely relate to the existing context (local stone) as well as innovative new materials (titanium), which together form spaces that connect local Denver tradition to the 21st Century. The dialog between the boldness of construction and the romanticism of the landscape with its views of the sky and the Rocky Mountains creates a unique place.

01 Titanium façade **02** Exhibition space **03** Second and third floor plan **04** View towards interior sculptural circulation

Photos: Bitter Bredt

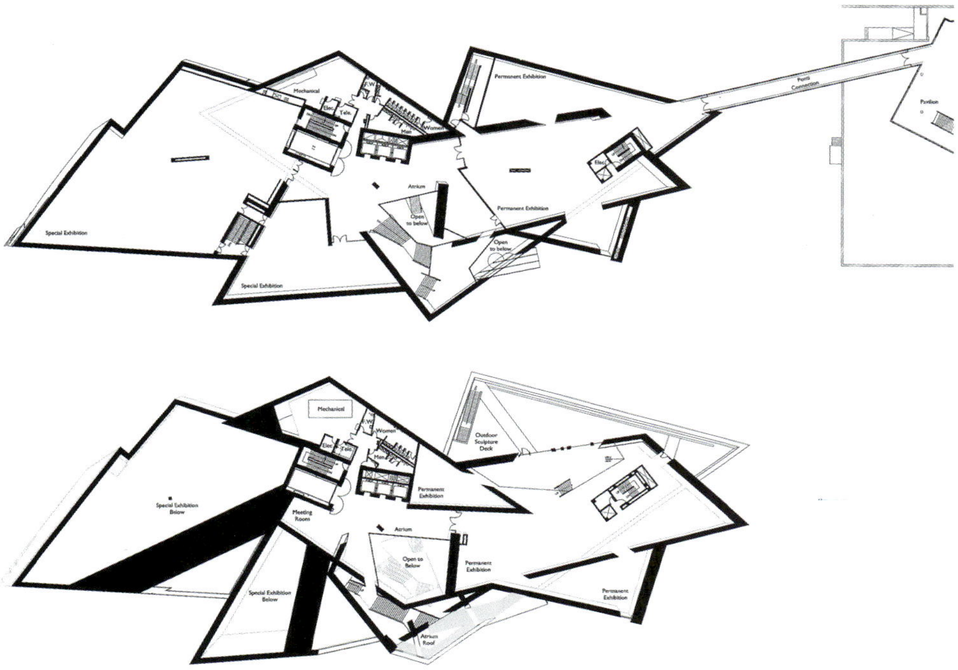

CITY Denver (CO)
COUNTRY USA
REGION North America
TYPOLOGY Culture
COMPLETION 2006
WEBSITE www.daniel-libeskind.com
ARCHITECTS Daniel Libeskind

LOWENSTEIN RETAIL AND PARKING GARAGE

In the development of the Lowenstein Retail and Parking Garage, the project's components consist of new 25,920 square feet retail space, a 203 vehicle garage. To meet the developer's desired requirements, the site needed to be built-out on all sides, while the building's height needed to be maximized to a bulk plane of 55 feet above the street. In order to resolve massing issues, small shifts were made to the garage structure, visually breaking it down into smaller pieces, while critical datums were taken from the existing historic theatre over to the new.

01 View to retail space **02** Aluminium mesh façade **03** View towards historic theater and retail development **04** Standing seam metal panels **05** Site plan

Photos: Ron Pollard Photography

CITY Denver (CO)
COUNTRY USA
REGION North America
TYPOLOGY Commercial
COMPLETION 2007
WEBSITE www.semplebrowndesign.com
ARCHITECTS Semple Brown Design

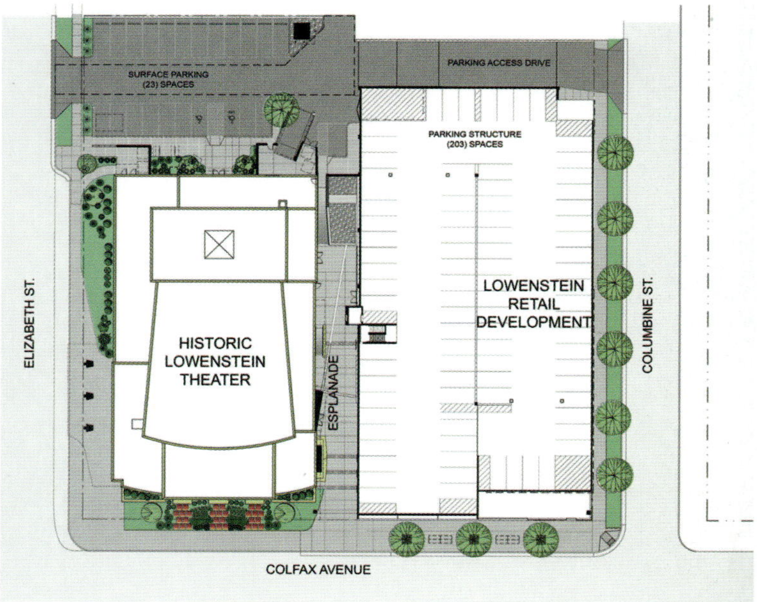

DENVER ART MUSEUM RESIDENCES

The Museum Residences make an inspiring contribution to the cultural nexus of the city and complement the neighboring extension. The soft qualities of the translucent glass skin, combined with the metal-clad geometric forms, provide an elegant partner to the titanium-clad Museum. Six of the seven floors are residential, with space on the ground floor dedicated to retail. The building wraps around two sides of a 1000-car public parking garage. Its 56 luxury units range from 800 square foot studios to 5000 square foot penthouse suites.

01 Glass skin with metal-clad geometric forms **02** Detail façade **03** View out of the window **04** Detail exterior **05** Site plan

Photos: Bitter Bredt, Ron Pollard (03)

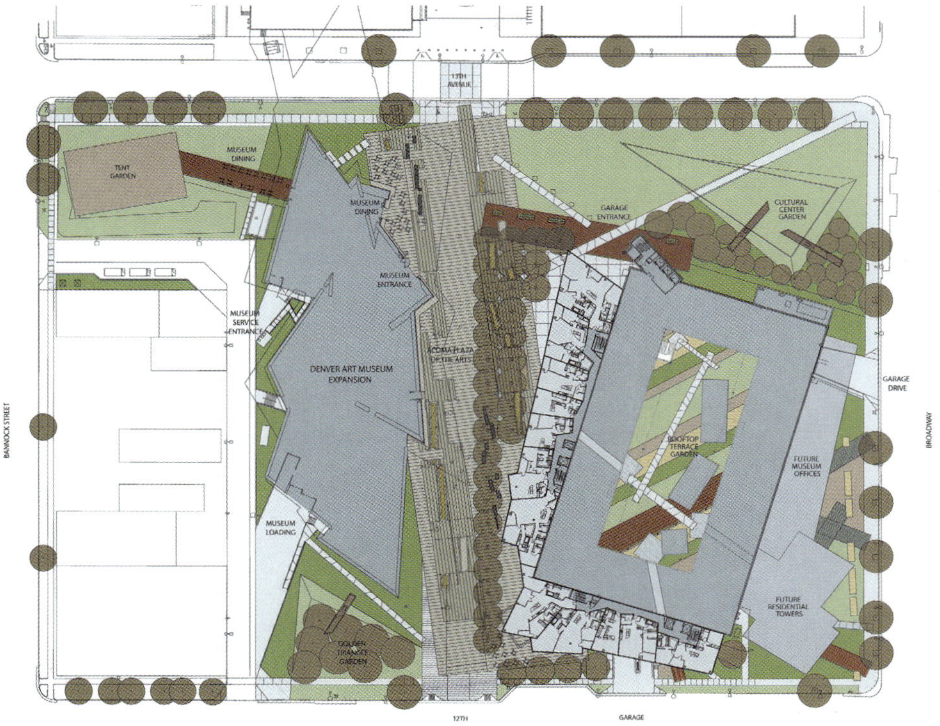

CITY Denver (CO)
COUNTRY USA
REGION North America
TYPOLOGY Living
COMPLETION 2008
WEBSITE www.daniel-libeskind.com
ARCHITECTS Daniel Libeskind

CITY: East Hampton (NY)
COUNTRY: USA
REGION: North America
TYPOLOGY: Living
COMPLETION: 2007
WEBSITE: www.reversibledestiny.org
ARCHITECTS: Architectural Body Research Foundation- "Reversible Density"

BIOSCLEAVE HOUSE

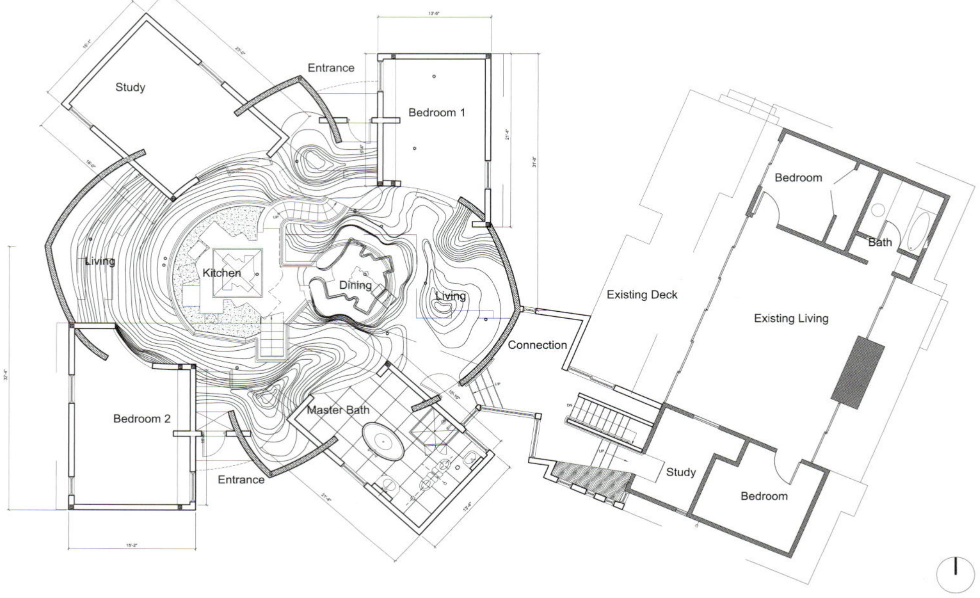

Biocleave House operates as an interactive laboratory of everyday life. According to the idea that the setting most conducive to a thoroughgoing investigation of human experience is the domestic one, the artist couple creates this house. It provides not only the means for examining human experience in our time but also important clues as to how life is likely to be lived in the future. The design features an undulating floor, walls painted in 40 different colors and windows at varying heights.

01 Building façade **02** Windows at varying heights **03** First floor plan **04** Bird's eye view

Photos: Jose Luis Perez-Griffo Viqueira, Arakawa + Gins (04)

SAGAPONAC HOUSE

Sitting on 2.7-acres of wooded land, the house is composed of two rectangular volumes forming an L-shaped plan. The center of the house is the main public space with a swimming pool, multi-level terraces, and a covered porch with a shower, taking the form of a minimalist structure placed on a platform within the untouched natural landscape. A large opening within each rectangular volume frame's the private life in the house and the pool beyond. These openings appear and disappear via a system of metal shutters mounted on the exterior walls, investigating the cultural definition of the domestic enclosure.

01 Exterior view **02** Interior view **03** First floor plan **04** Main public space with multi-level terraces and swimming pool

Photos: Paul Warchol

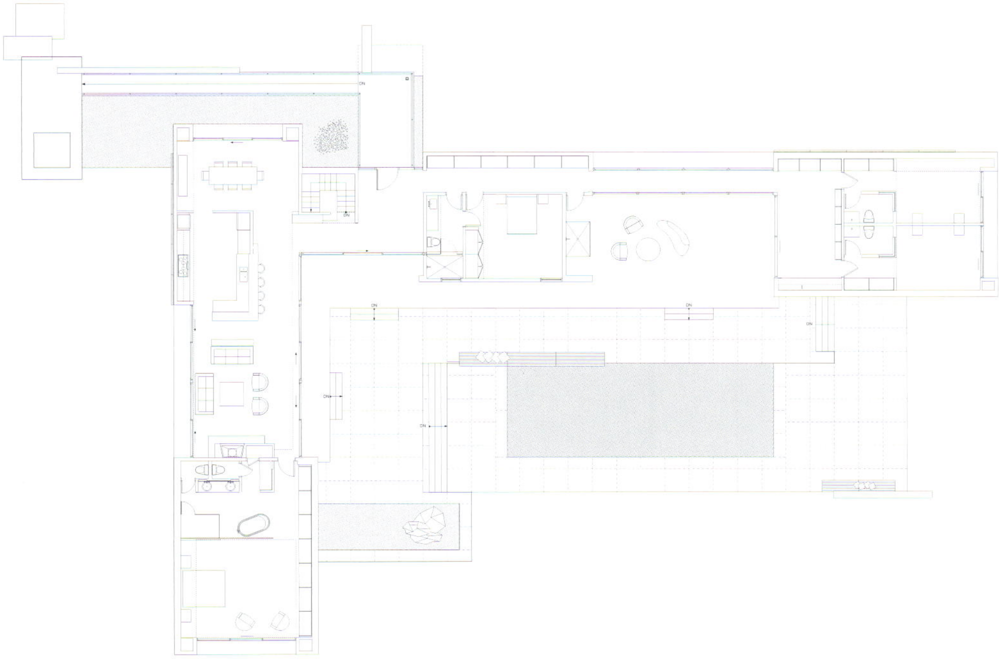

CITY East Hampton (NY)
COUNTRY USA
REGION North America
TYPOLOGY Living
COMPLETION 2005
WEBSITE www.haririandhariri.com
ARCHITECTS Hariri & Hariri – Architecture

CITY
Ellington (WI)

COUNTRY
USA

REGION
North America

TYPOLOGY
Living

COMPLETION
2004

WEBSITE
www.wendellburnette
architects.com

ARCHITECTS
Wendell Burnette Architects

FIELD HOUSE

Located in a northeast Wisconsin area dominated by crop fields and dairy farms, the site is an "altered landscape" that has been farmed for generations. The specific site is a 16-acre crop field while the house is a simple 5,000-square-foot box clad in a zinc galvanized metal skin. The site context is understood as a garden with both natural and man-made field conditions, and the rotation of crops, planted and fallow fields of corn, soybean, wheat, and oats heighten the sensation of seasonal change. From a distance the house is a stoic structure in the landscape, only revealing its purpose up close.

01 East façade **02** Transverse section **03** Screen porch **04** Roof deck with rotation cowls in distance **05** Hall and master bedroom

Photos: Bill Timmerman, Wendell Burnette Architects (02)

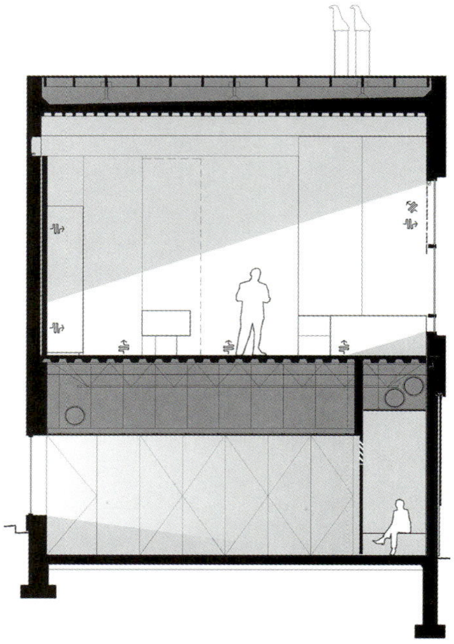

CHELSEA

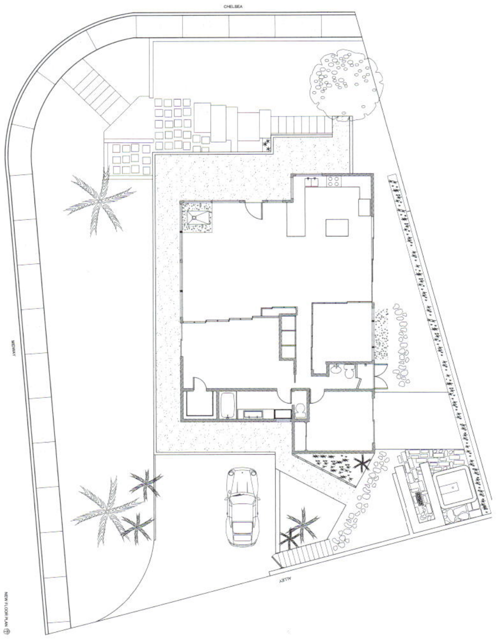

The development of 330 Neptune is a complete re-model of a residential area with a 250 square-foot addition. The intent of the project was to maximize and take complete advantage of the space through volume, and this was due to the limited building area upon which this development is sited on. The aesthetic concept was to use a dynamic set of resources, and such materials such as wood, metal and CMU block proved to be extremely vibrant and simple. These exposed features provide in giving not only a sound structure, but they also present an interesting and distinctive play of color and texture.

01 View form street **02** Floor plan **03** Interior **04** Interior detail

Photos: Steven Lombardi Architects

CITY Encinitas (CA)
COUNTRY USA
REGION North America
TYPOLOGY Living
COMPLETION 2008
WEBSITE www.stevenlombardi.com
ARCHITECTS Steven Lombardi, Architect

REGION North America
COUNTRY USA
CITY Englewood (CO)
TYPOLOGY Education
COMPLETION 2006
WEBSITE www.semplebrowndesign.com
ARCHITECTS Semple Brown Design

KENT DENVER STUDENT CENTER FOR THE ARTS

The 29,000 square foot Student Center for the Arts project fits within the campus's heritage of relatively low-intensity development, while taking advantage of the natural grades on site and pushing much of the building into the slope of a hill. The strong horizontal pre-cast concrete planes moderate the apparent scale of the building capping the lobby to align with the nearby buildings. In addition, the horizontal planes also provide shade while the vertical planes wrap and frame view corridors from specific zones within the building, giving a sense of order and hierarchy to different areas of the lobby.

01 Window detail **02** Exterior by night **03** View into main theater **04** Site plan **05** Main entry/experimental theatre

Photos: Ron Pollard Photography

FOX HOLLOW RESIDENCE

This design breaks down the conventional notion of an upscale home by separating the primary functions of the house into a series of linked pods that dance playfully along the sloped terrain. The smaller-scale structures reduce the environmental impact of the home on the site, making this home a showcase of local craft, sustainability, and efficient living. Simple shed roof forms open to the south, providing both a breathtaking view of the cascade foothills and an optimal solar orientation for passive heating. Every detail has been thoughtfully executed, from the modern steel connections to the traditional Amish wood joinery.

---

01 View to deck **02** Staircase **03** Fireplace **04** Exterior view with shed roof **05** Living space **06** Plan

Photos: Blue Rhino Studios

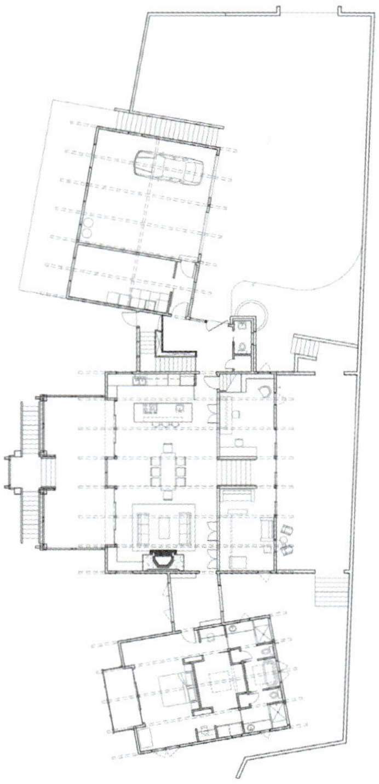

CITY: Eugene (OR)
COUNTRY: USA
REGION: North America
TYPOLOGY: Living
COMPLETION: 2007
WEBSITE: www.2-form.com
ARCHITECTS: 2fORM Architecture

UNIVERSITY OF OREGON, ATHLETIC MEDICINE CENTER

Occupying 15,000 SF, the new Center is a state-of-the-art sports therapy and training facility for more than 400 student-athletes, as well as a showcase for the University's rich athletic history. It features space for treadmills and exercise bikes, hydro-therapy tubs, a nutrition bar, custom-designed massage and taping tables, medical examination suites, a student seating area, X-ray facility, and meeting rooms. The facility is intended to apply a holistic approach to student-athlete health, with the architecture and materials infused at every corner to capture the legacy and heritage of UO athletics.

01 Interior **02** Floor plan **03** Nutrition bar **04** Therapy pools **05** Lobby

Photos: Basil Childers

CITY
Eugene (OR)

COUNTRY
USA

REGION
North America

TYPOLOGY
Education / Health

COMPLETION
2007

WEBSITE
www.zgf.com

ARCHITECTS
Zimmer Gunsul Frasca Architects LLP

FIREFLY GRILL

The Firefly Grill is a modern "roadhouse" restaurant that is built with recycled barn wood siding and a corrugated metal roof, much like the beautiful old wooden barns that dot the Midwest. Large, sliding doors provide indoor-outdoor connections at all sides of the building, while a wrap-around porch is screened and heated along the lakeside. The kitchen counter, made from maple butcher block, is part of a large exhibition kitchen that anchors the interior and acts as a hearth. High ceilings are vaulted like the inside of a barn, while the dark-stained floors are wide-plank hardwood and will wear to a patina finish.

01 Recycled barn wood siding and corrugated metal roof
02 Outdoor/lakeside dining porch **03** Exterior façade
04 Wrap around porch **05** Floor plan

Photos: Mark Ballogg Photography

CITY Effingham (IL)
COUNTRY USA
REGION North America
TYPOLOGY Gastronomy
COMPLETION 2005
WEBSITE www.ccs-architecture.com
ARCHITECTS CCS Architecture

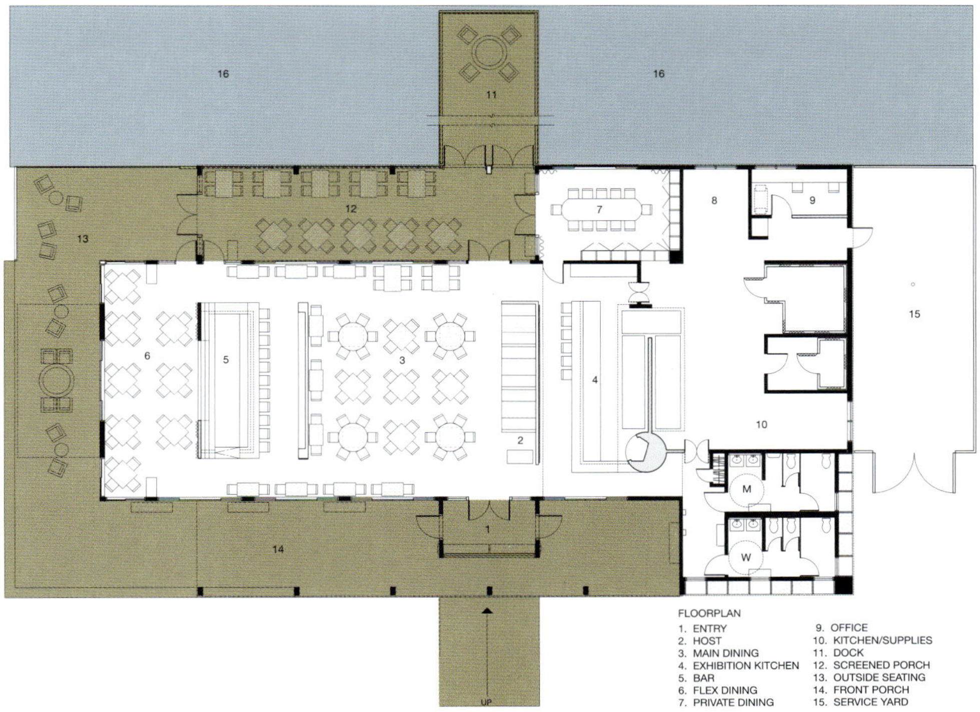

FLOORPLAN
1. ENTRY
2. HOST
3. MAIN DINING
4. EXHIBITION KITCHEN
5. BAR
6. FLEX DINING
7. PRIVATE DINING
8.
9. OFFICE
10. KITCHEN/SUPPLIES
11. DOCK
12. SCREENED PORCH
13. OUTSIDE SEATING
14. FRONT PORCH
15. SERVICE YARD

CITY
Flint (MI)

COUNTRY
USA

REGION
North America

TYPOLOGY
Education

COMPLETION
2006

WEBSITE
www.fisherpartners.net

ARCHITECTS
Frederick Fisher and Partners Architects

FLINT INSTITUTE OF ARTS

The renovation of this art school enhanced the original historic facility and called for a brand new 47,000-plus square foot addition. The new building houses galleries, art storage and administrative, basement/mechanical and public spaces. It encompasses an entrance lobby, gallery space, café, museum store and an area that the architects describe as a glass-enclosed loggia of public activity. A multi-use event space and new fixed-seat auditorium became a kind of multi-use „town square," developing a dramatic range of enfilade galleries with intuitive circulation through the existing galleries.

01 Performing art space **02** Exterior main façade **03** Rear view **04** Open-air exhibition **05** Floor plan

Photos: Christopher Lark/Lark Photography

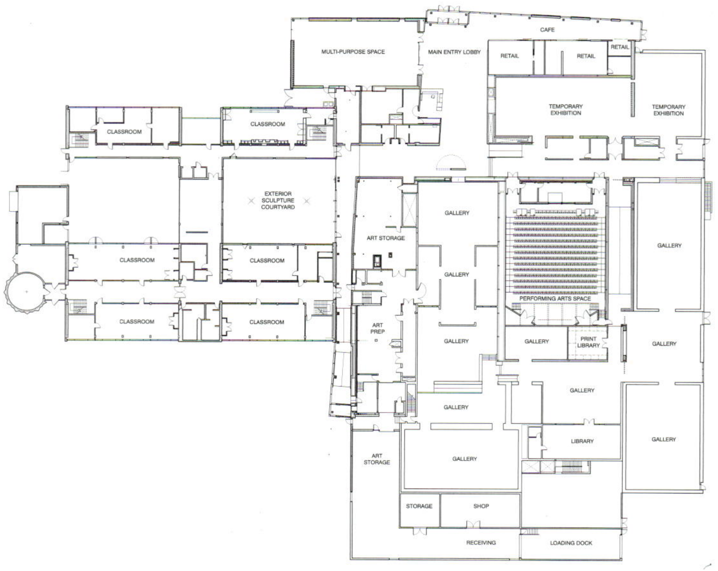

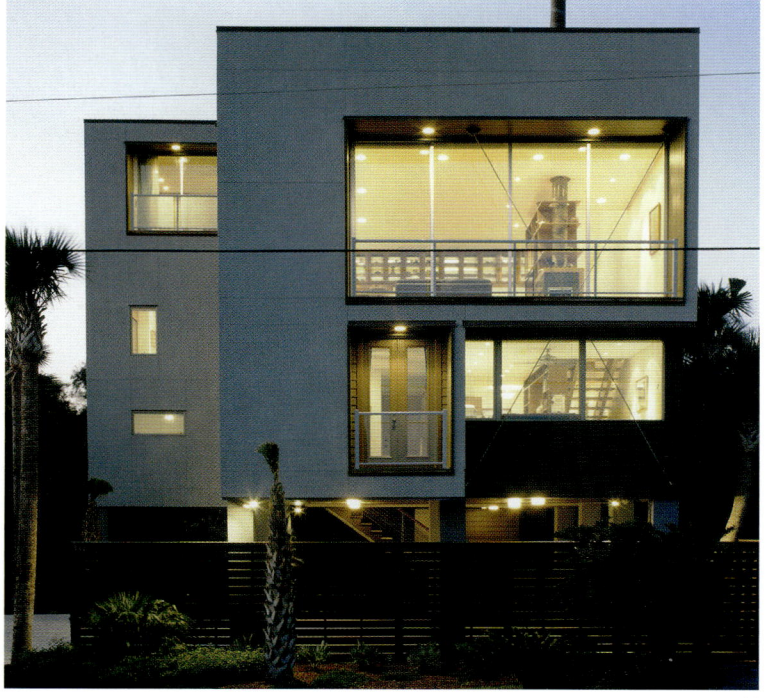

JETTY HOUSE

The house turns a second-row beach lot into oceanfront property with an elongated structure pushed to one side of the lot that captures views between two houses across the street. Inspired by the beach jetties, the linear body is used like a camera lens to foreshorten the viewing distance. The design breaks with the neighborhood's ubiquitous built-on decks and pitched roofs by treating the roof as valuable real estate, and using negative space to carve out balconies shielding the interior from the summer sun. Selectively placed windows on the east and west walls reinforce telescopic views while providing complete privacy.

01 Exterior view by night **02** View from roof deck to ocean front **03** Floor plans **04** Living space **05** East and west façade

Photos: Richard Leo Johnson

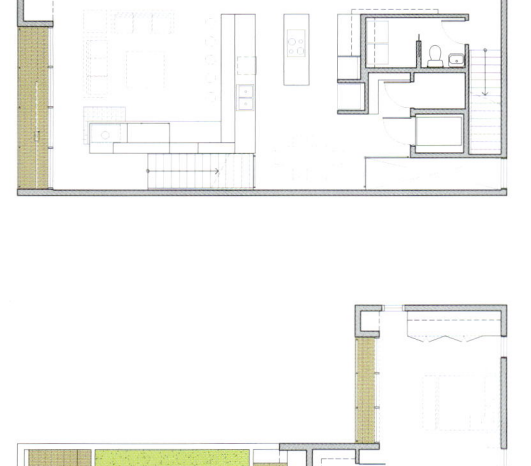

CITY Folly Beach (SC)

COUNTRY USA

REGION North America

TYPOLOGY Living

COMPLETION 2006

WEBSITE www.cubework.com

ARCHITECTS CUBE

CITY Fort Lauderdale (FL)

COUNTRY USA

REGION North America

TYPOLOGY Culture

COMPLETION 2007

WEBSITE www.glavovicstudio.com

ARCHITECTS Glavovic Studio

GIRLS' CLUB

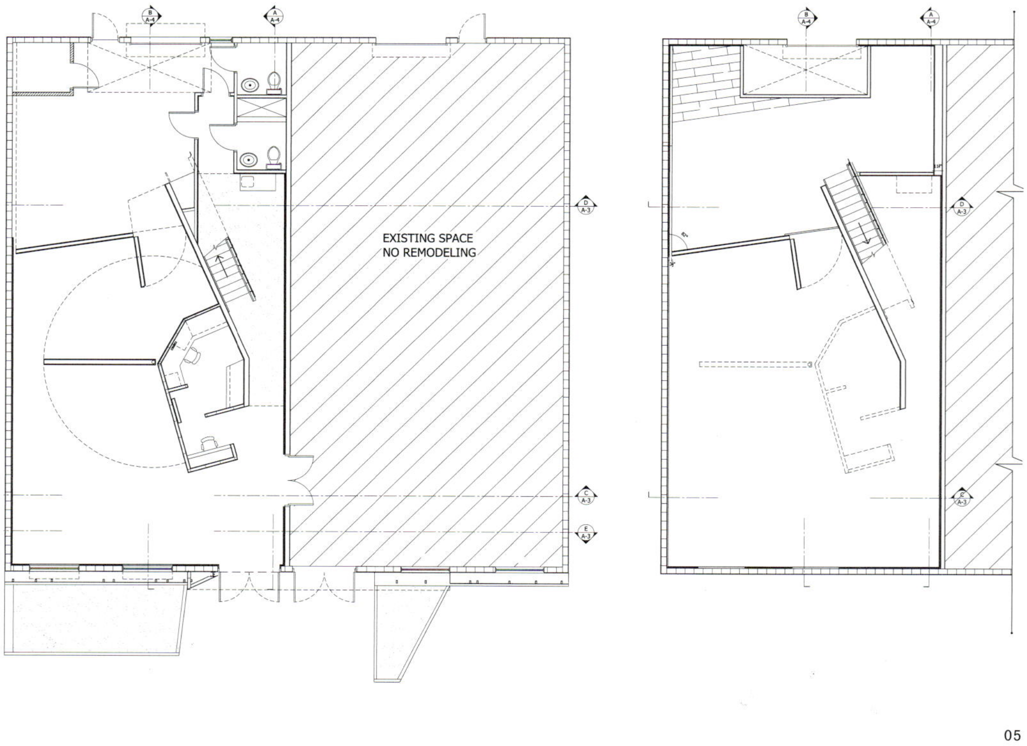

The girls' club is an interactive gallery and research center in Fort Lauderdale, Florida. Converting an existing warehouse through the layering of materials, light and movement, the architects create an art-oriented environment for the Bishop Good and Horvitz collection. The exterior façade transforms the building into a scrim and projection screen at night. The interior provides multiple zones with a central pivoting wall and raised mezzanine for interior projection. Color is used selectively to orchestrate patrons visually through different zones.

01 Stairs to mezzanine **02** Front façade **03** Gallery space
04 Art Exhibit **05** First and mezzanine floor plan

Photos: Robin Hill

FULBRIGHT BUILDING

Designed by Warren Segraves in 1962, this modernist building has been renovated to accommodate the offices of local businesses. "Ship in a bottle" is the conceptual design motive, being conscious of the way new interior partitions and 'pods' of space are resolved with the building skeleton and envelope. Brick walls at the building perimeter were replaced with a transparent and translucent glass wall that resonates with the interior interventions. The other major design intervention is the creation of a new conference space with a suspended zinc-clad acoustical shroud that also acts as a public artwork.

01 View of Addition with new stair **02** View from northeast **03** New skylight and vertical circulation space **04** New conference space **05** First floor plan **06** View into offices

Photos: Timothy Hursley

CITY Fayetteville (AR)
COUNTRY USA
REGION North America
TYPOLOGY Office
COMPLETION 2007
WEBSITE www.marlonblackwell.com
ARCHITECTS Marlon Blackwell Architect

CITY	Flushing (NY)
COUNTRY	USA
REGION	North America
TYPOLOGY	Public
COMPLETION	2008
WEBSITE	www.handelarchitects.com www.homgoldmanarch.com
ARCHITECTS	Handel Architects in association with Kevin Hom + Andrew Goldman Architects, PC

FLUSHING MEADOWS CORONA PARK NATATORIUM & ICE RINK

Located in Queens, Flushing the Meadows-Corona Park hosted the 1939 and 1964 World´s Fair celebrations. The new facilities are situated on the edge of the park, acting as a transition between the neighborhood and the open green space. By placing the pool and ice arenas in a linear relationship with a separating public lobby space, the project connects two different recreational activities under one sinuous roof. In the spirit of the World´s Fair pavilions, the building presents a vibrant silhouette from the expressway, with soaring masts supporting a long-span structure over the rink and pool, and an entry lobby that glows at night.

01 View from the south **02** Entry plaza **03** Section diagram **04** Swimming arena

Photos: David Sundberg / Esto

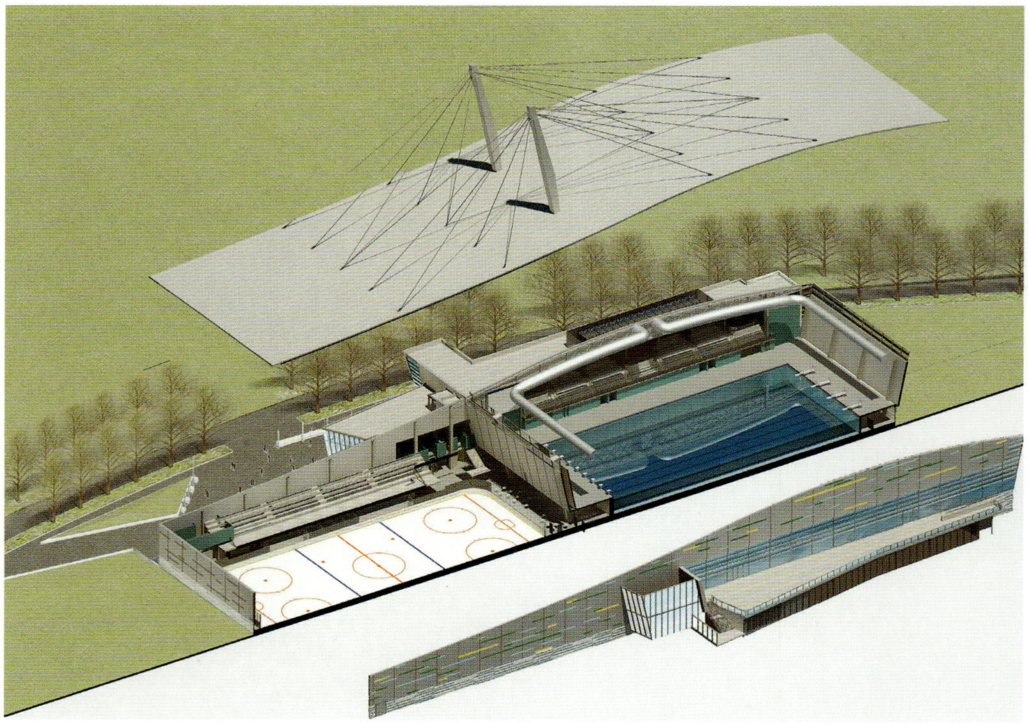

KAMPSCHROER - YOON

The Kampschroer-Yoon project is a transformation of ranch style architecture. The requirement was to add new space, making the old space more relevant and efficient, and to include a communal porch facing Lake Barcroft across the street to the south. The addition of an angled wall forms a structural valley, creating a collage of layers presented to the street frontage, giving a hybrid vigor to what was once a very staid elevation. A subtle yet noticeable complexity of spatial sequences tells the story of what was once old and new, inside and out, while giving a new richness that did not exist before.

01 South terrace façade featuring a passive solar design strategy **02** New entrance with stainless steel pivot door **03** Dual island kitchen with Nakashima stools and Ecoresin ceiling treatment **04** Main level intervention plan **05** Dining area with custom adjustable light monitor

Photos: Daniel Afzal

CITY: Falls Church (VA)
COUNTRY: USA
REGION: North America
TYPOLOGY: Living
COMPLETION: 2006
WEBSITE: www.carterburton.com
ARCHITECTS: Carter + Burton Architecture

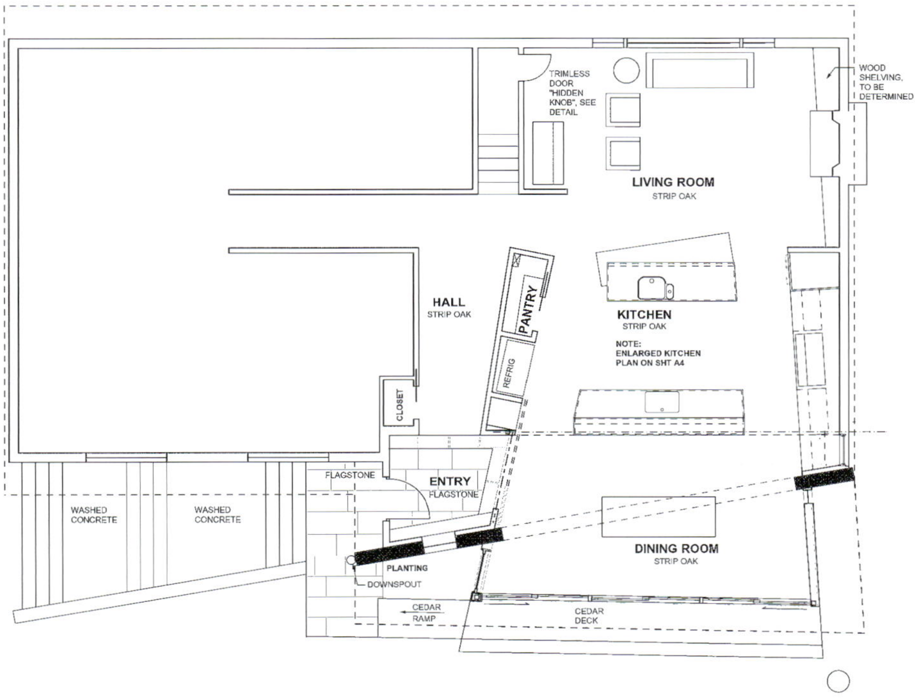

CITY Greenville (DE)

COUNTRY USA

REGION North America

TYPOLOGY Living

COMPLETION 2007

WEBSITE www.wfora.com

ARCHITECTS Workshop for Architecture

HYNANSKY HOUSE

The project is an addition / renovation to an existing split-level house on a wooded property. Because there was an existing structure, the new design became a project about expanding, removing and grafting new structures where needed. In particular the original stonework was preserved where possible and became part of a new continuous base around the house. New interior spaces have been carved out and the house was opened to new vistas and connections to the landscape. The butt-joined glass wall enclosing the living room is detailed to overlap the roof and floor structures allowing unobstructed views both in and out.

01 Butt-joined glass wall **02** Exterior view **03** Siteplan **04** Courtyard

Photos: Workshop for Architecture

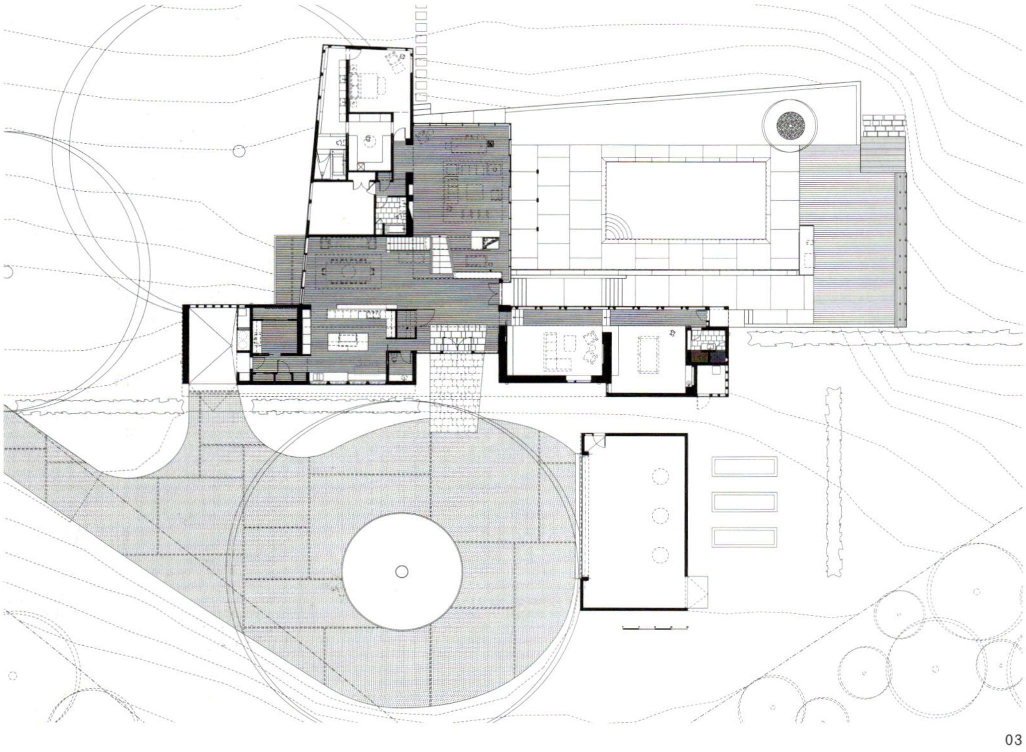

ANN HAMILTON TOWER

Built on the grounds of the Oliver Ranch in Geyserville, California, this eight-story tower is a site-specific artwork designed by artist Ann Hamilton. The concrete tower was conceived as a space for performance while the double helix stairs allow for performers on one stair and audiences on the other, letting the two intertwine as the stairs wind up the tower. Cylindrical walls, light apertures, an open ceiling and winding stairways create a unique space that instantly engages the audience. The tower was poured from more than 2,000 tons of concrete and sandblasted for an instant antiquing effect.

01 Helix stairs **02** Concrete elevation **03** Open ceiling and winding stairways **04** Section

Photos: Jensen Architects

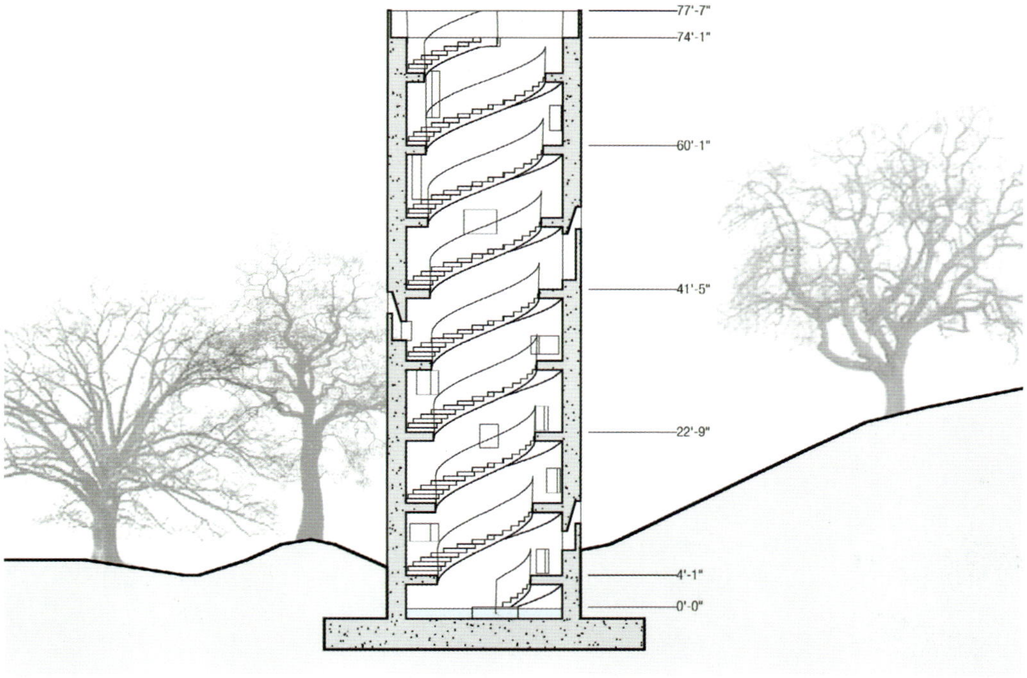

CITY Geyserville (CA)
COUNTRY USA
REGION North America
TYPOLOGY Culture
COMPLETION 2007
WEBSITE www.jensen-architects.com
ARCHITECTS Jensen Architects

CITY Glendale (CA)
COUNTRY USA
REGION North America
TYPOLOGY Commercial
COMPLETION 2008
WEBSITE www.rfa-architects.com
ARCHITECTS Ronald Frink Architects

PACIFIC BMW SHOWROOM

The intent was to create a dynamic design to showcase the luxury and quality of European automobiles in a minimal and modern showroom with optimal transparency throughout the day and evening. Located in the auto sales district of Glendale, California, the site is situated on two parcels flanking a side street in a typical low-rise auto sales context. The building exterior, with its smooth fin-like reference to contemporary auto design, is dynamically open and transparent, where the minimal design of the exterior façade integrates natural concrete, clear glass, metallic silver aluminum, white plaster, and stainless steel cables.

01 Exterior by night **02** Staircase leading to offices **03** Street front elevation and first floor plan **04** Showroom **05** Fin-like façade detail

Photos: Benny Chan, Fotoworks

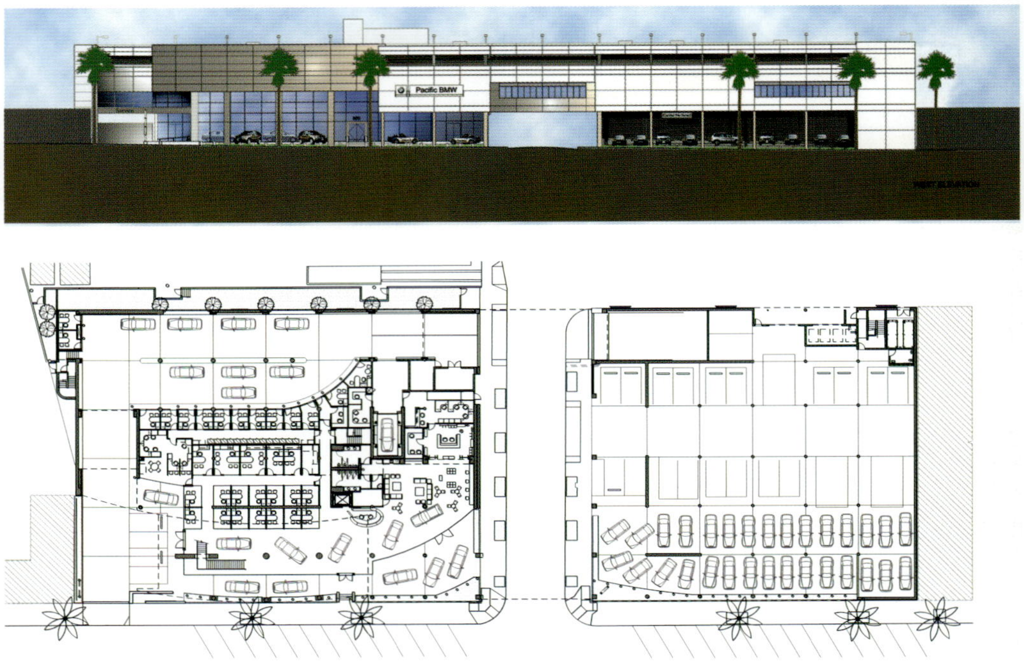

CITY	Granada Hills (CA)
COUNTRY	USA
REGION	North America
TYPOLOGY	Industry
COMPLETION	2006
WEBSITE	www.mwaarchitects.com
ARCHITECTS	Michael Willis Architects

JOSEPH JENSEN TREATMENT PLANT OZONATION BUILDING

The expansion to an existing water treatment plant in Granada Hills, California, is the largest Ozonation facility in the world and includes new ozone and oxygen generation buildings, administrative offices, a water distribution control room, laboratories, chemical storage, and a visitor center with an observation deck. The new building provides ozone disinfection, which is an improved, sustainable method of purifying drinking water. The design seeks to poetically express a thorough understanding of the rigorous requirements of industrial processes through the direct ordering of material, light, detail, texture and form.

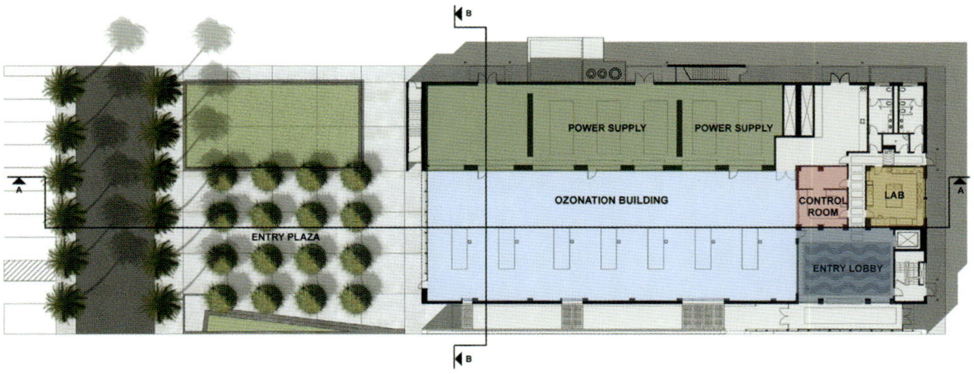

01 Entry plaza **02** Ozone generators **03** Exterior view
04 Ground floor plan

Photos: Metropolitan Water District of Southern California

CITY: Grand Rapids (MI)
COUNTRY: USA
REGION: North America
TYPOLOGY: Culture
COMPLETION: 2007
WEBSITE: www.why-architecture.com
ARCHITECTS: wHY Architecture

GRAND RAPIDS ART MUSEUM

The Grand Rapids Art Museum in Michigan is home to one of the oldest museums in the Mid-West. The new museum is designed through the integration of the arts and technology, with a mission in obtaining a high-level certification from the Leadership in Energy and Environmental Design (LEED), thus making it one of the first art museums with such recognition. The Grand Rapids Art Museum features a unique design that compliments its prominent location, in the heart of downtown, with a grand urban gesture while offering an intimate atmosphere to enjoy the arts.

01 Pocket park **02** Main entrance **03** Site plan **04** Exterior by night **05** Pocket park by night **06** Interior circulation

Photos: Grand Rapids Art Museum, wHY Architecture

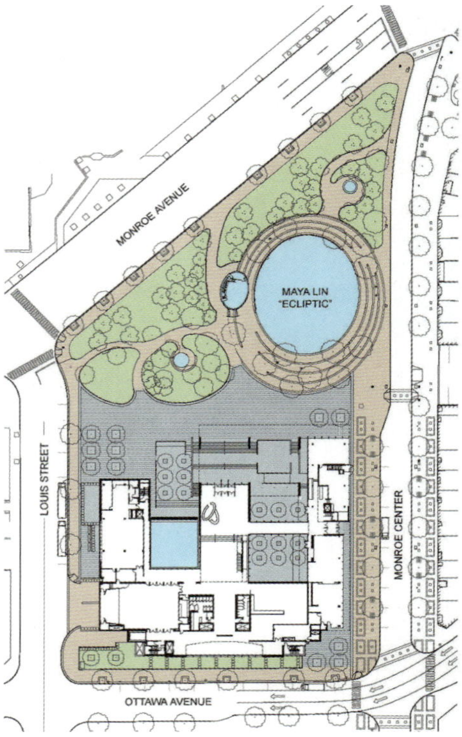

UNIVERSITY CENTER OF LAKE COUNTY

Merging degree and workforce development programs from 18 higher education institutions, the facility create a county hub for academic and professional advancement, while enhancing the client's visibility. Five "houses" surround an outdoor courtyard, with large and small gaps within and between the houses suggesting a multi-building campus. The south façade is clad in metal and glass, while a three-story glass wall fills the commons with natural light. Technology-rich spaces such as distance learning labs and tiered-lecture halls coexist with "living room" style alcoves that encourage informal gathering.

01 Building in context **02** Entry **03** Metal and glass south façade **04** Second floor plan

Photos: Timothy Hursley

CITY: Grayslake (IL)
COUNTRY: USA
REGION: North America
TYPOLOGY: Education
COMPLETION: 2005
WEBSITE: www.legat.com
ARCHITECTS: Legat Architects

CITY Gold Beach (OG)

COUNTRY USA

REGION North America

TYPOLOGY Living

COMPLETION 2000

WEBSITE www.obiebowman.com

ARCHITECTS Obie G Bowman

OREGON COAST HOUSE

Due to its location this residence can experience wind speeds of up to 100 mph. The triangular structure maintains itself with an exoskeleton of Port Orford cedar logs, inspired by the driftwood logs and debris found along the rocky shoreline. These buttresses resist all lateral loads and negate the need for shear walls. The project consists of three main parts: a house placed to capture views up and down the coastline, a free standing garage placed to help block prevailing spring and summer winds, and an over-scaled wall placed to form a courtyard while visually screening a pair of distant neighbors to the east.

01 Exterior view to triangular structure **02** Port Orford cedar buttresses **03** Living space **04** Floor plan **05** View to the Oregon coast

Photos: Tom Rider

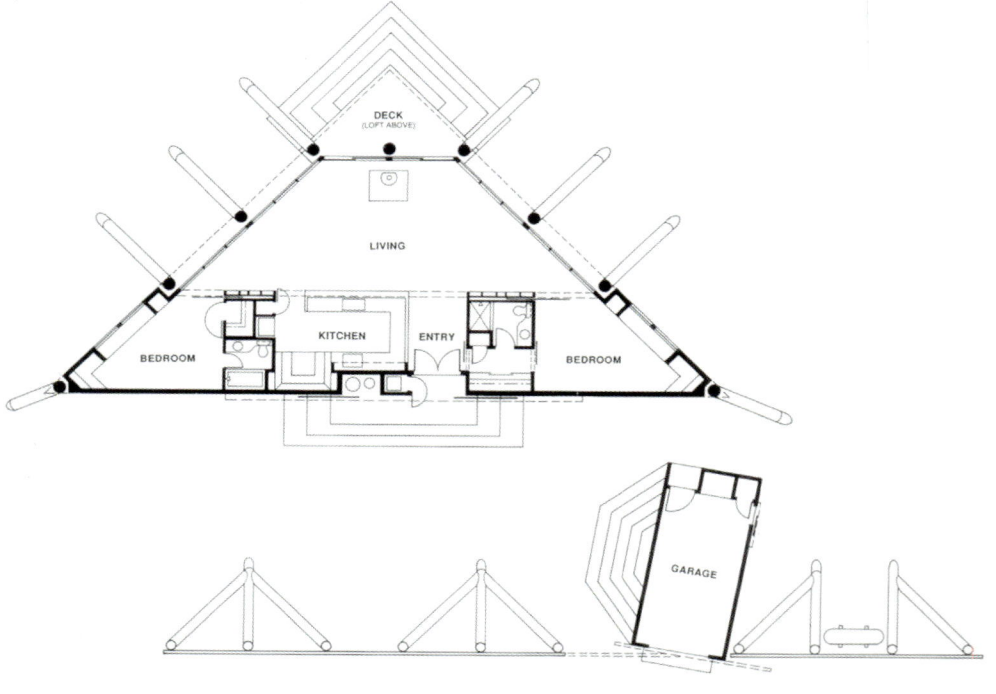

HOLLEY HOUSE

The client commissioned a second home whose program includes a master bedroom suite in a separate pavilion and an entrance pavilion with two guest bedrooms and a media room. A third pavilion houses the living and dining rooms and kitchen. Two stone walls are the main elements of the house, defining and separating the master bedroom suite from the entry area and marking the edge to the public spaces: living, dining, and kitchen. South of the house is a pool and a pool house. The house was designed to be part of its site, incorporating wood, stone, and water to create a quiet and restful retreat from New York City.

01 View from the Garden **02** Side view with extended roof **03** Entrance pavilion **04** House in context **05** Bathroom

Photos: Michael Moran, Paul Warchol (03)

CITY Garrison (NY)
COUNTRY USA
REGION North America
TYPOLOGY Living
COMPLETION 2006
WEBSITE www.hanrahanmeyers.com
ARCHITECTS hMa hanrahanMeyers architects

CITY
Garrison (NY)

COUNTRY
USA

REGION
North America

TYPOLOGY
Culture

COMPLETION
2005

WEBSITE
esedesign.com

ARCHITECTS
Ese Design
(Edward S. Eglin)

PAINTING STUDIO

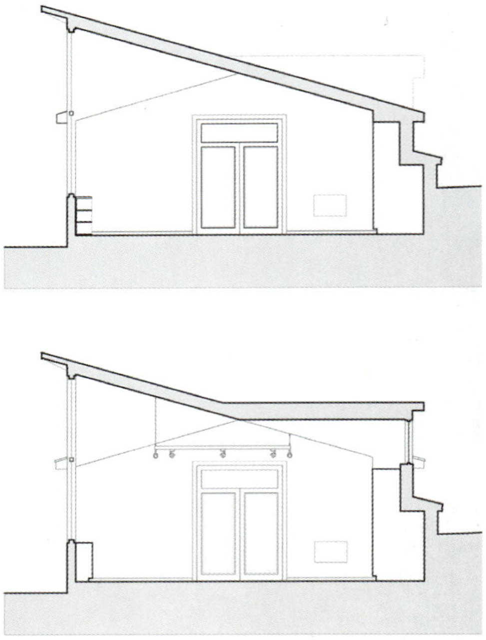

Set into a hillside along the Hudson River, this building is a retreat for a New York-based artist. The landscape serves as a source of inspiration and natural light, and a variety of apertures connect the studio to its surroundings. The large north window infuses the space with calm, steady light, while a small, deeply recessed south window provides an accent of sunlight, which traverses the floor of the studio during the day. The exterior of the studio is clad in white cedar and lead-coated copper, which will weather and soften with time, reinforcing the building's connection with the landscape.

01 Large north window **02** Sequential section through painting studio **03**, **04** Interior living space

Photos: Miko Almaleh Photography

BANNER GATEWAY MEDICAL CENTER

Gateway Medical Center is the first of Banner Health's "Franchise Model" hospitals following the award-winning prototype, Banner Estrella. At the heart of the concept is a building that enables flexibility and growth over time, allowing efficient reconfiguration while preserving innovation, safety, and clinical excellence standards. The facility combines 165 private patient rooms with obstetrics, pediatrics, general surgery, and emergency services. A regional connection to the community, along with beautifully crafted interiors and a patient-and-staff centered environment, is also incorporated.

01 Front façade 02 View into courtyard 03 Facility room
04 Interior

Photos: Frank Ooms

CITY Gilbert (AZ)
COUNTRY USA
REGION North America
TYPOLOGY Healthcare
COMPLETION 2008
WEBSITE www.nbbj.com
ARCHITECTS NBBJ

CITY
Gilbert (AZ)

COUNTRY
USA

REGION
North America

TYPOLOGY
Gastronomy / Culture

COMPLETION
2007

WEBSITE
www.debartoloarchitects.com

ARCHITECTS
De Bartolo architects

THE COMMONS

A large regional church in Arizona challenged the visionary architects to design a strategic building to facilitate the new core of the campus, and serve as the social center for all activities. As the first building of a new master-plan, the bookstore and coffee shop have positively changed and transformed the campus by becoming an inside-out building that literally opens on all sides. The transparency of the building, opened up in times of temperate weather, allows the material clarity and the overextending roof to combine and work together to successfully become the epicenter of the campus.

01 Extended roof **02** Coffee shop **03** Exterior view by night **04** Building elevation **05** Site plan

Photos: Bill Timmerman

OPENHOUSE

The house is embedded into a narrow and sharply sloping property in the Hollywood Hills. Large steel spans and double cantilevers allow the front, side and rear elevations to slide open and erase all boundaries between indoors and out, opening the architecture to gardens and terraces on two levels. The glazed open spaces are visually counterweighted by sculptural, solid elements rendered in stacked granite and dark stained oak. With the glass walls completely open, the house becomes a platform defined by an abstract roof plane, a palette of natural materials, the gardens and the views.

01 Exterior view from pool terrace **02** Interior detail of cantilevered steel and stone stair **03** Exterior view from entry drive **04** Floor plans

Photos: Art Gray

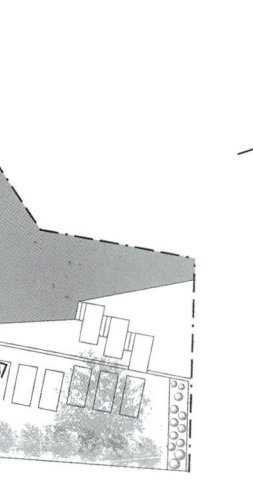

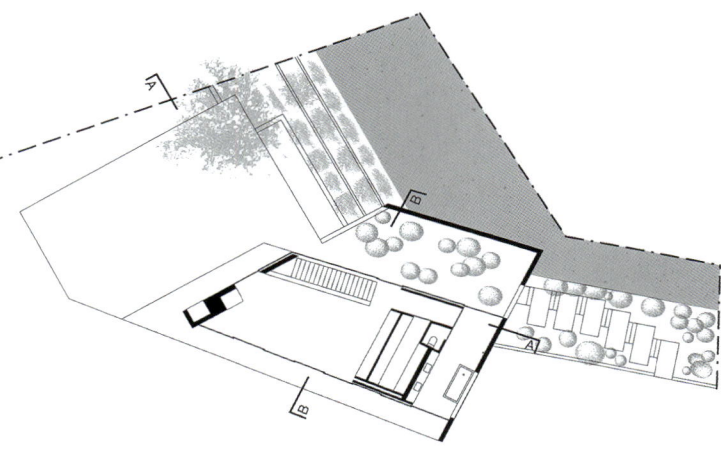

CITY Hollywood Hills (CA)
COUNTRY USA
REGION North America
TYPOLOGY Living
COMPLETION 2007
WEBSITE www.xtenarchitecture.com
ARCHITECTS XTEN Architecture

WATER + LIFE MUSEUMS AND CAMPUS

The Water + Life Museums celebrates the link between Southern California's water infrastructure and the evolution of life. A crisp, modern design concept envelops the engaging campus, whose indoor and outdoor spaces mingle within the framework of airy floor plans and endless window walls. A series of five slender steel towers blazes across each structure's façade, providing an eloquent contrast against the azure desert skyline. The buildings are examples of "living sustainability", as the building techniques are in line with the museum themes of resource conservation.

01 Slender steel towers **02** Façade **03** Courtyard **04** Exhibit

Photos: Benny Chan, Fotoworks (03), Michael B. Lehrer (04), Tom Lamb (01, 02)

CITY Hemet (CA)
COUNTRY USA
REGION North America
TYPOLOGY Culture / Education
COMPLETION 2007
WEBSITE www.lehrerarchitects.com
ARCHITECTS Lehrer + Gangi Design + Build

HERCULES PUBLIC LIBRARY

The development of the Hercules Public Library houses a circulation of approximately 800,000 books and periodicals, as well as other learning resources such as multi-use computer stations with Internet research capabilities. One feature that the Hercules Public Library is well known for is its teen homework center, which gives students the opportunity to take advantage of after-school tutoring programs. Some of the library's other highlights include the "Story Cone," meant for the purpose of children's reading events, a café, an extensive reading area with a fireside seating, as well as several meeting and study rooms.

01 Solar glazing **02** Skygarden **03** Floor plan **04** Library interior

Design architects: will bruder+PARTNERS

Photos: Bill Timmerman Photography

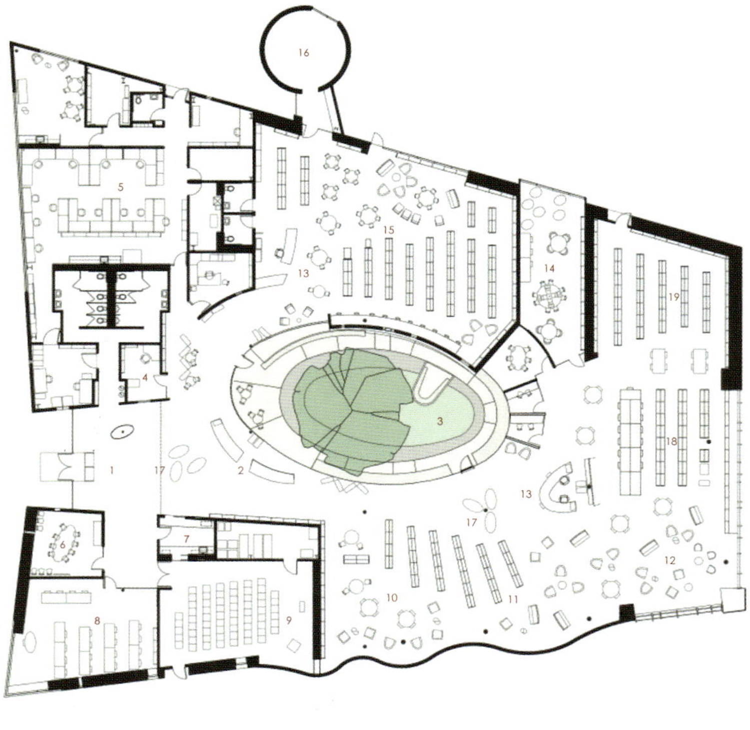

CITY Hercules (CA)

COUNTRY USA

REGION North America

TYPOLOGY Public

COMPLETION 2007

WEBSITE www.hga.com

ARCHITECTS HGA Architects and Engineers (executive architect)

STRAND RESIDENCE

Meeting the specific requirements of an active retired couple, this project's design addresses conceptual notions of merging natural light with the erosion of spatial boundaries. The result is a building that incorporates overlapping, interlocking volumes and planes, both horizontally and vertically. Spaces unite to allow for boundless ocean views or more private vistas into introspective areas without compromising privacy amidst the density. A contextual and sturdy material palette, needed in salty coastal environments, differentiates the building's massing as it cascades along the structure's primary axis.

01 Beach façade **02** Living space with ocean view **03** Main entrance from street **04** View into stairs **05** Hall with private vista **06** Floor plans

Photos: Weldon Brewster (01), Farshid Assassi

CITY Hermosa Beach (CA)
COUNTRY USA
REGION North America
TYPOLOGY Living
COMPLETION 2005
WEBSITE www.kaadesigngroup.com
ARCHITECTS KAA Design Group, Inc.

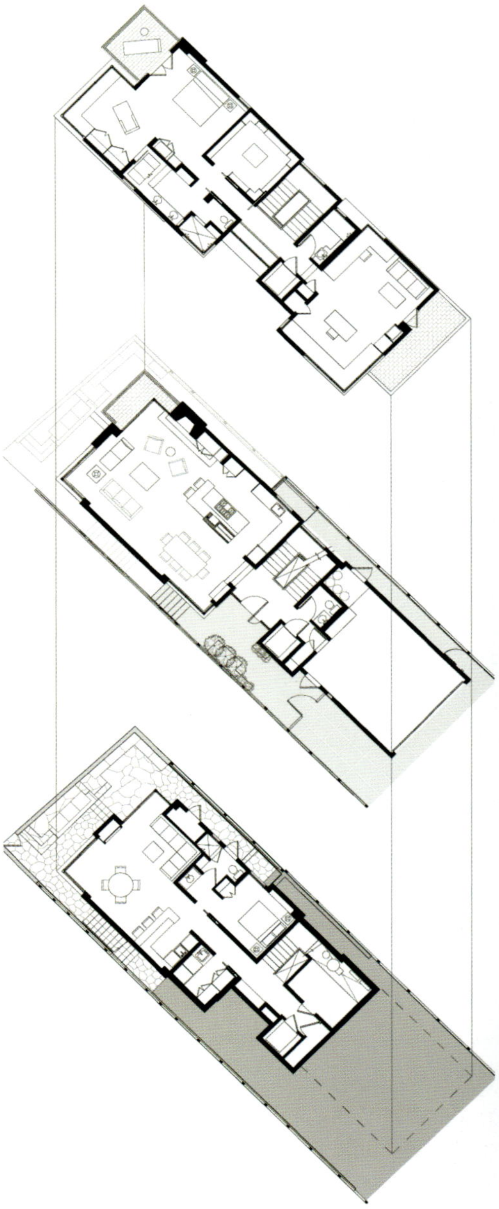

GRAHAM RESIDENCE

Upon acquiring the house, the client wanted to reconfigure its rooms and reappoint their. Working largely within the constraints of the existing structure, the architects chose to layer walls, surfaces, and steel screens to introduce dimension and texture to the monotony of the existing structure. Where the existing brick was visually overbearing, new layers of plaster were sculpted to obscure portions while permitting a reading of the underlying construction. Where the spatial volumes in the dining room and entrance were out of scale, a new system of screens made of steel and canvas was suspended from the ceiling.

01 Interior **02** Floor plan **03** Detail **04** Exterior view by night **05** Section **06** Steel construction

Photos: Greg Premru

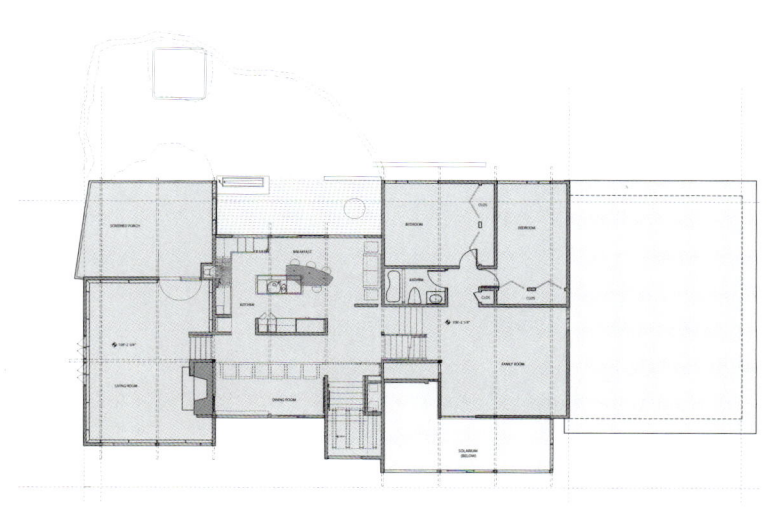

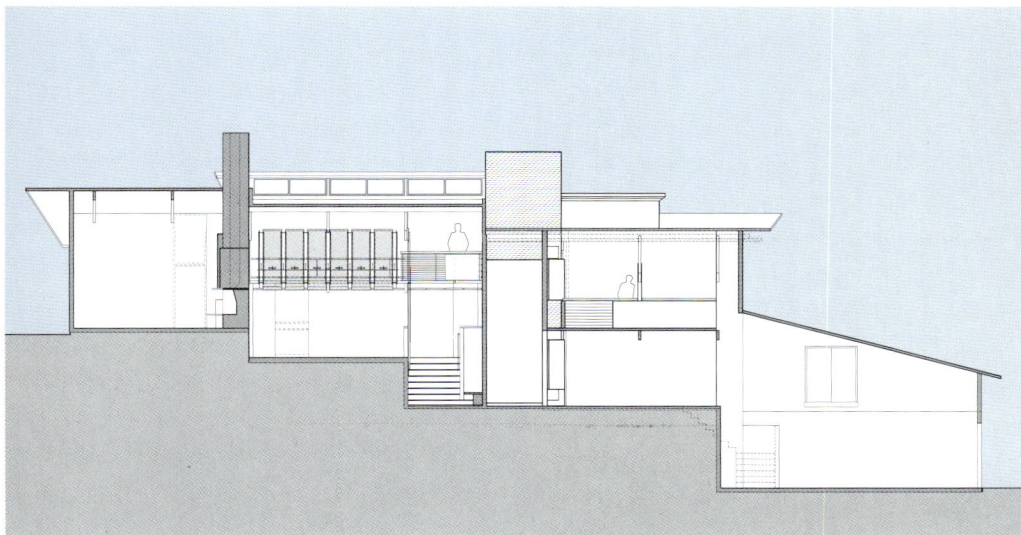

CITY Harvard (MA)
COUNTRY USA
REGION North America
TYPOLOGY Living
COMPLETION –
WEBSITE www.lukez.com
ARCHITECTS Paul Lukez Architecture

CITY: Hobe Sound (FL)
COUNTRY: USA
REGION: North America
TYPOLOGY: Education
COMPLETION: 2007
WEBSITE: www.sharc.com
ARCHITECTS: SH_Arc Scott Hughes Architects

PINE SCHOOL

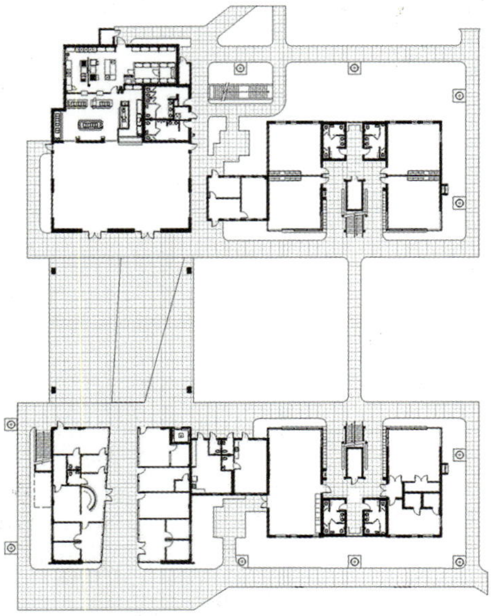

Daylight education requires an elusive dose of order and chaos, predictability and improvisation in order to succeed. The program called for classrooms, labs, a library, and places for assembly, performance, athletics and relaxation. It is an academic village where groups emerge, disband and regroup, while being a community for learning, growing and discovering. The campus design is a functional and formal response to a specific educational vision and program of both active and continuous expansion and inward change. Its structure promotes education and profoundly engages the specifics of its location.

01 Exterior view by night 02 Staircase to classrooms
03 Courtyard 04 Floor plans 05 Glazed façade

Photos: Ken Hayden

MILL CENTER FOR THE ARTS

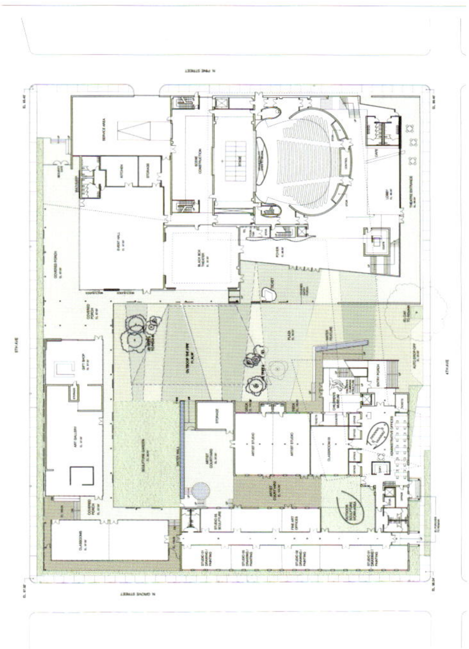

Included in this new cultural complex, located in the heart of the downtown district, is a children's museum, a 1200-seat performing arts theater, a black box theater, an event center, art galleries, classrooms, artist studios and administrative offices. Inspired by the beauty of the Carolina Mountains, the skin of the façade is composed of ionized metal panels, perforated and etched with a composite pattern of native tree varietals. The design integrates the historic existing mill building with new construction, where elements are developed to extend space and to take advantage of opportunities for outdoor activities.

01 Ionized metal panels façade 02 Floor plan 03 Above plaza
04 Exterior view by night 05 Lobby

Renderings: Pugh + Scarpa

CITY: Hendersonville (NC)
COUNTRY: USA
REGION: North America
TYPOLOGY: Culture
COMPLETION: Competition 2005
WEBSITE: www.pugh-scarpa.com
ARCHITECTS: Pugh + Scarpa (in joint venture with Eskew+Dumez+Ripple)

CITY Hendersonville (NC)

COUNTRY USA

REGION North America

TYPOLOGY Culture

COMPLETION Competition 2005

WEBSITE www.eastoncombs.com

ARCHITECTS Easton+Combs

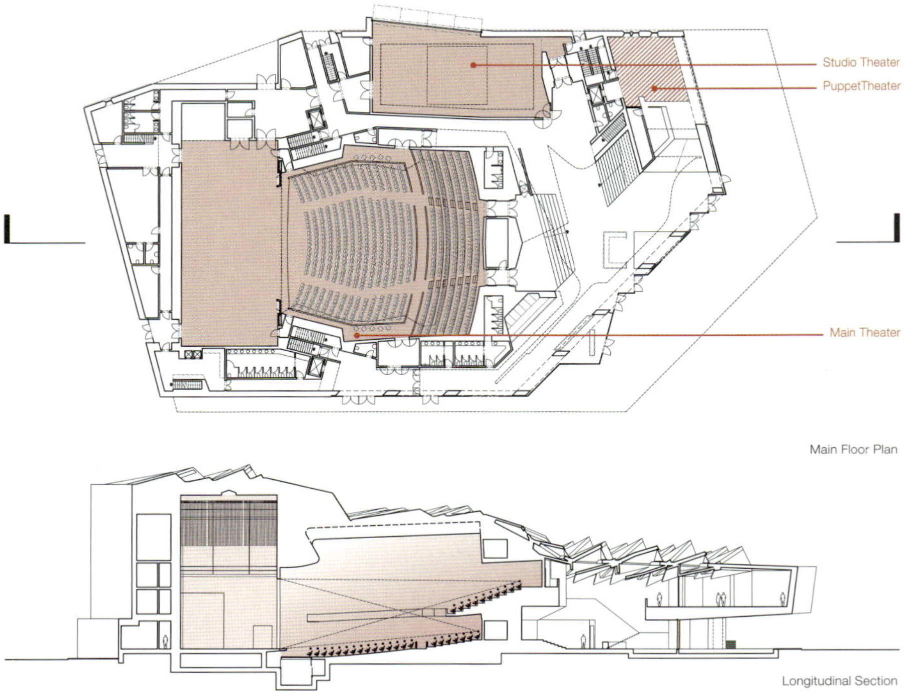

THE MILL CENTER FOR THE ARTS

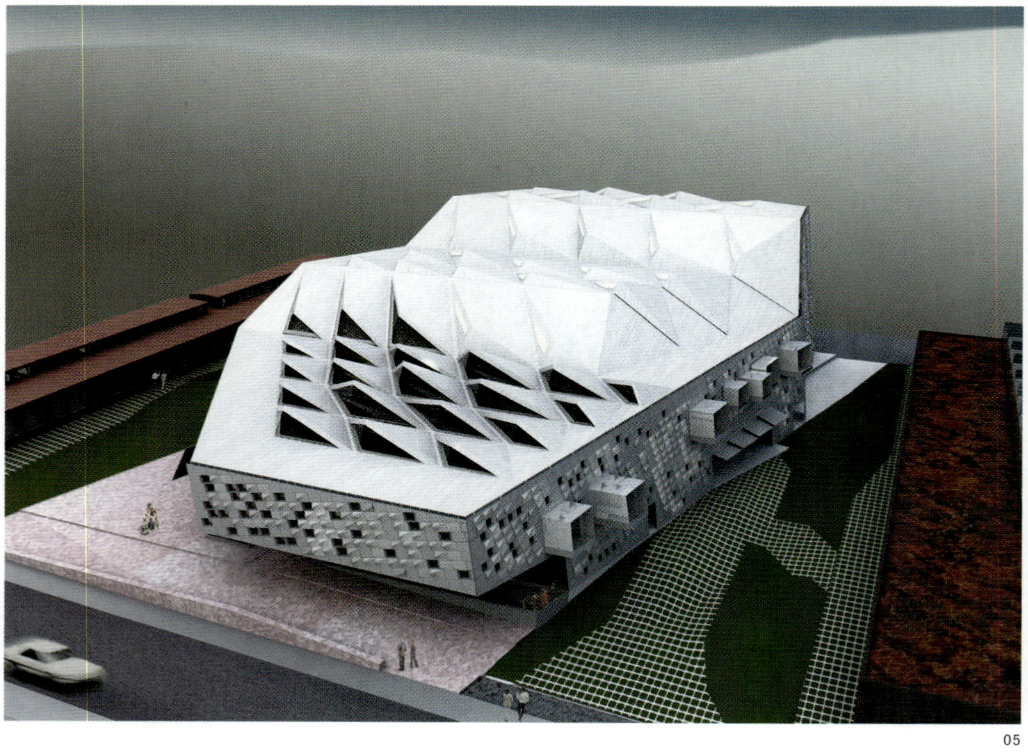

The contemporary institutions of art and performance have taken on the role of the town square as a focal point of community identity. In the Mill Center for the Arts, the idea of a performing arts venue merges with the community center to form a dynamic locus of cultural identity for the local populace and the larger region. The Mill Center design extends the topic of 'performance center' into the secondary civic role of the building as a community center. The architectural expression is a celebration of both the cultural performance of the everyday and the exceptional performance of art.

01 Main floor plan and longitudinal section **02** Detail **03** Hallway **04** Entrance **05** Bird's eye view

Renderings: Richard Sarrach

RIEGER BUILDING ADDITION

The historic Rieger Hotel Building, located near downtown Kansas City, was recently converted by a progressive couple into their own private residence. After acquiring usage of the rear portion of neighboring building for a private garage, they hired El dorado to connect the private functions of both buildings, while simultaneously adding a roof pavilion and garden. The new structure, skinned with beveled redwood slats, houses a new elevator and staircase system. The addition, appropriate for its time and new occupancy, serves as a respectful departure from the historic style of the Rieger Hotel.

01 Deck **02** Laminated fixed glazing **03** Rewood slats façade **04** Deck by night **05** Plan

Photos: Mike Sinclair

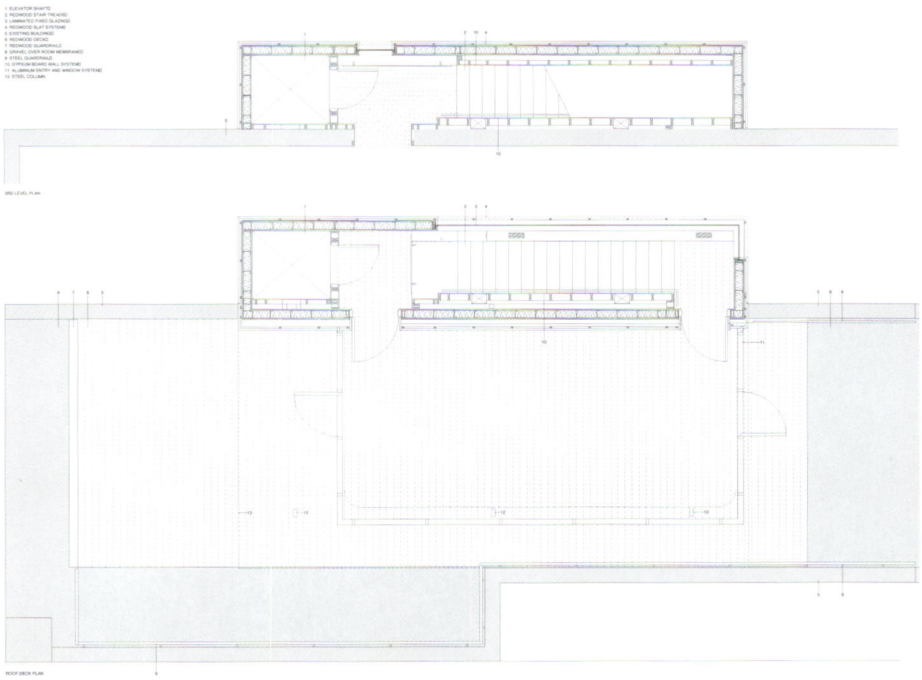

CITY Herington (KS)
COUNTRY USA
REGION North America
TYPOLOGY Living
COMPLETION 2004
WEBSITE www.eldoradoarchitects.com
ARCHITECTS El dorado Architects

CITY Herington (KS)
COUNTRY USA
REGION North America
TYPOLOGY Office
COMPLETION 2007
WEBSITE www.eldoradoarchitects.com
ARCHITECTS El dorado Architects

AN OFFICE FOR HODGDON POWDER COMPANY

Hodgdon Gun Powder Company is located in the heart of the Kansas Flint Hills, an ancient rolling prairie landscape with rich vernacular context. El dorado Architects designed a series of Quonset Huts to serve as an office facility for the plant's employees, where the development of intimate outdoor courtyard spaces created a strong connection to the subtlety of the surrounding landscape. These exterior spaces also serve to buffer and organize varying aspects of the design program. The architects also designed and fabricated all office furniture for the facility, including custom outdoor and indoor dining tables.

01 Entrance **02** Floor plan **03** Outdoor courtyard spaces **04** Covered pedestrian paths

Photos: Mike Sinclair

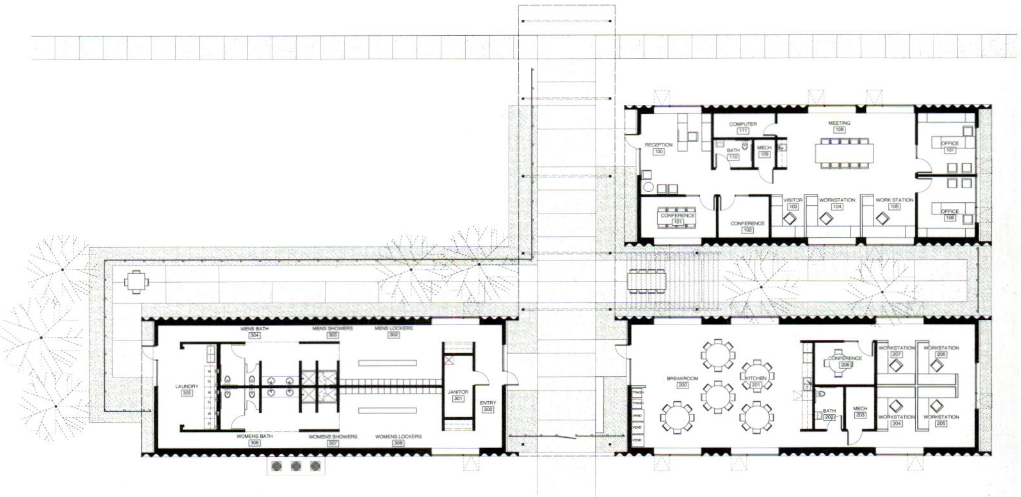

ONETWO TOWNHOUSE

This project's tectonic expression results from the needs of the program; two independent 2,500 square feet townhouses and the constraints of a small triangular lot in Houston's Montrose District. The study of turning radiuses evoked the Andy Warhol painting, "Dance Diagrams" as a planametric inspiration. Each house "steps" around the other maintaining its individuality yet at the same time is part of the greater whole within the constrained lot. The structural system is drilled concrete piers supporting grade beams with reinforced concrete masonry units, steel columns, beams and composite deck up to the height of the first floor.

01 Reinforced concrete façade **02** Exterior view **03** View of entrance **04** View of triangular lot **05** First floor plan **06** Second floor plan

Photos: Paul Warchol Photography

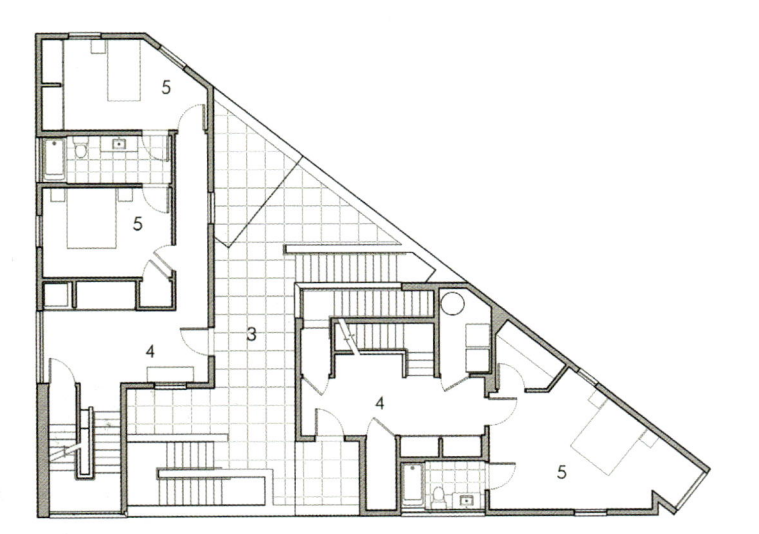

First Floor Plan

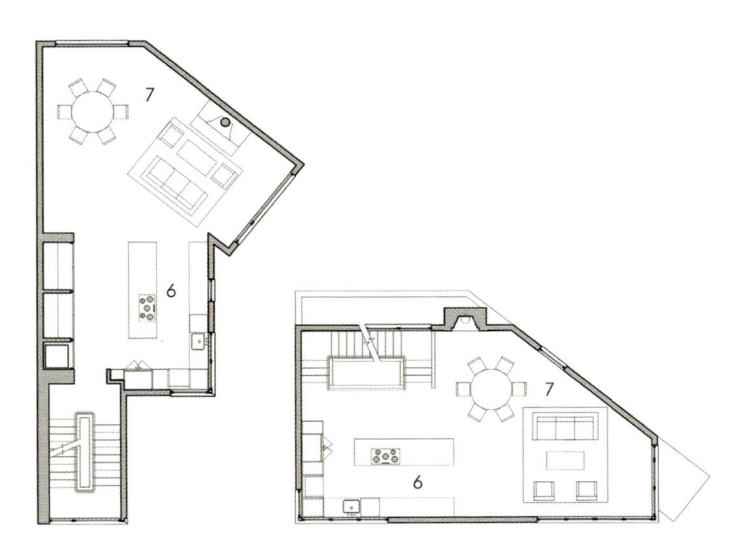

Second Floor Plan

CITY
Houston (TX)

COUNTRY
USA

REGION
North America

TYPOLOGY
Living

COMPLETION
2007

WEBSITE
www.fdmarch.com

ARCHITECTS
FdM:Arch Francois de Menil

CITY
Houston (TX)

COUNTRY
USA

REGION
North America

TYPOLOGY
Public

COMPLETION
2005

WEBSITE
www.hiepler-brunier.de

ARCHITECTS
Easton+ Combs

AIRPORT PARKING FACILITY

This parking facility project is an extension of the airport's infrastructure and functions as an intermodal link from automobile travel to the airport. Landscape and threshold express the ritual of travel in the project. The volume of program housing the automobile becomes an expression of landscape on a conceptual and figural level. The open-air structures propose an environment of over scaled waiting halls that dispatches and receives the traveler. The Gate Building forms the initial and final threshold of travel, bringing the body into a pressured relationship with the building through its linear cantilever.

01 Bird's eye view **02** View to entry **03** Section **04** Gate building

Photos: Brunier Hiepler

C-I HOUSE

Located in the historic Hudson Valley, the four-acre site is situated in southern Columbia County, bordering Duchess County to the south. Overlooking a pond, the house is surrounded by dense vegetation while commanding a vineyard view to the east, and a view of the distant Black Dome Mountain to the west. Designed as a weekend retreat, the construction consists of concrete foundation/footings, supporting a wood framed enclosure with spatial layouts based upon standard modular construction dimensions. Opening sliding glass doors give access to a sun-deck, acting as an ethereal transition between the indoors and outdoors.

01 Living space **02** Wooden staircase **03** Concrete foundation with wood framed enclosure **04** Sketch **05** Front façade

Photos: DAO-LOU ZHA

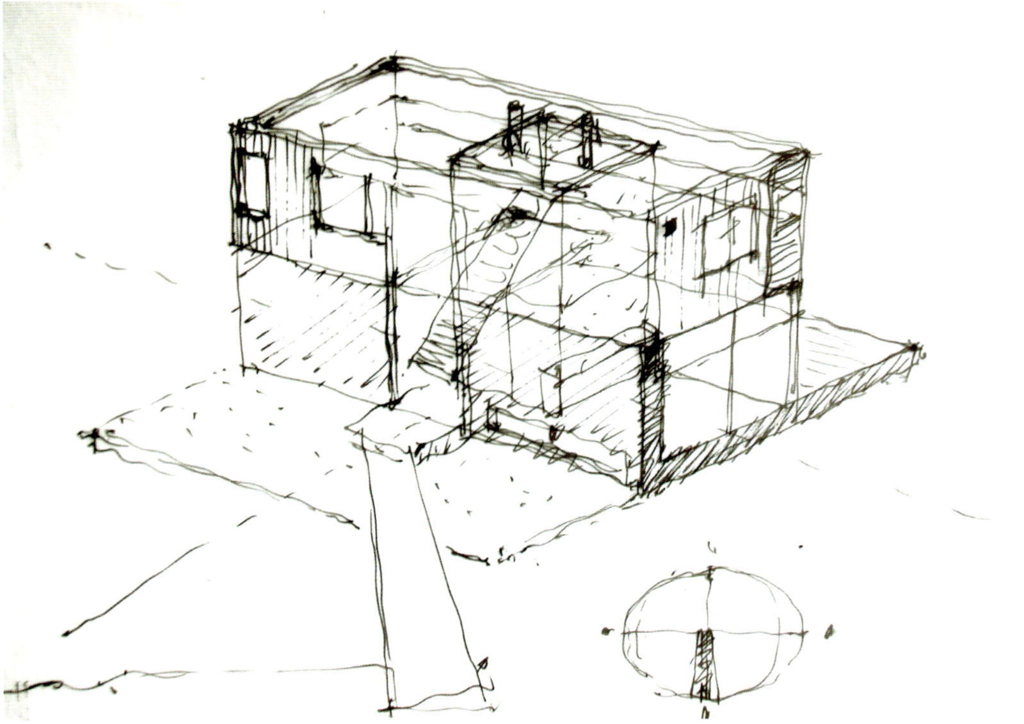

CITY Hudson Valley (NY)
COUNTRY USA
REGION North America
TYPOLOGY Living
COMPLETION -
WEBSITE www.paulchaarchitect.com
ARCHITECTS Paul Cha Architect

CITY: Hudson Valley (NY)
COUNTRY: USA
REGION: North America
TYPOLOGY: Living
COMPLETION: —
WEBSITE: www.axismundi.com
ARCHITECTS: Axis Mundi

WEEKEND RETREAT FOR A WRITER

The rehabilitation of a colonial ‚saltbox' house, an archetypal American form with a hearth located dead center, strived to create a light, simplistic interior. This involved demolishing the separating walls, including the floor, and adding an entire roof of skylights on the north wall. A side wall was completely converted into bookshelves. A sleeping loft and a work area with spectacular views of the Catskill Mountains are located on the mezzanine. The exterior is entirely clad in mirror and literally reflects the surrounding landscape, changing drastically depending on the season, weather conditions and time of day.

01 Clapboard façade **02** Book shelves for 2000 volumes **03** Open living space **04** Floor plans

Renderings: Courtesy Axis Mundi

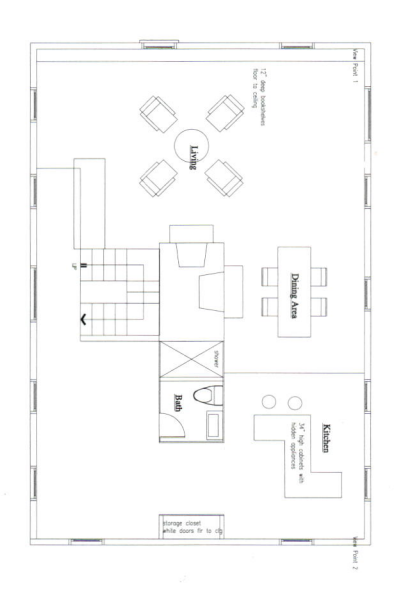

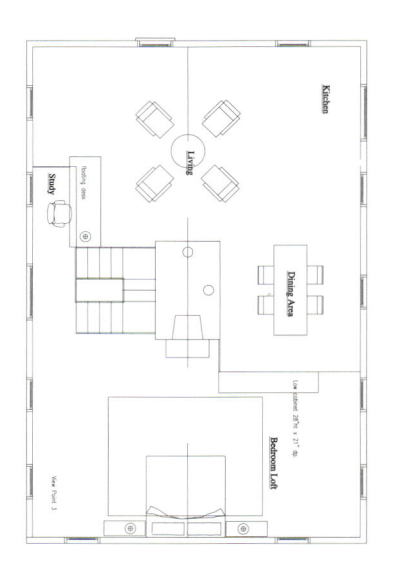

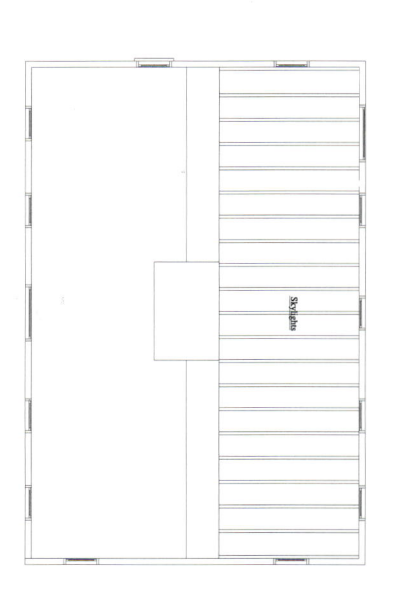

SCHOOL OF ART & ART HISTORY, UNIVERSITY OF IOWA

The site presented special conditions: an existing 1937 brick building with a central body and flanking wings located along the Iowa River, and a lagoon and connection to the organic geometry of limestone bluffs forming the edge of Iowa City's grid. The School is a hybrid instrument of open edges & open center; instead of an object, the building is a "formless" instrument. The resulting architecture is a hybrid vision of the future combining bridge and loft spaces, theory with practice, and human requirements with scientific principles, firmly positioning the University at the pinnacle of art & art history education in America.

01 Exterior view **02** Aerial view **03** Lobby **04** Floorplans

Renderings: Steven Holl Architects
Photo: Courtesy The University of Iowa (02)

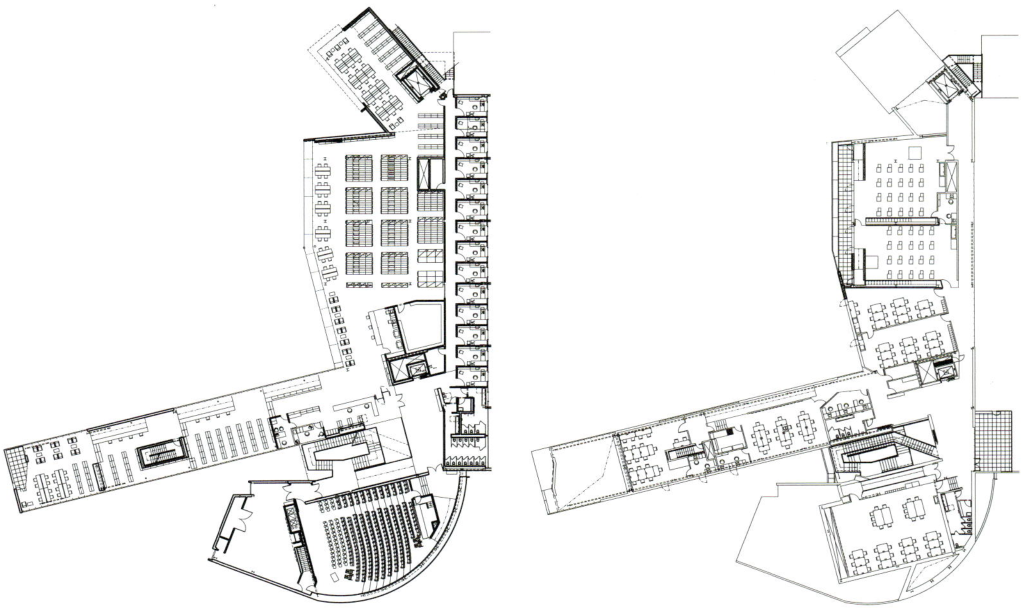

CITY Iowa City (IA)
COUNTRY USA
REGION North America
TYPOLOGY Education
COMPLETION Competition 2006
WEBSITE www.stevenholl.com
ARCHITECTS Steven Holl Architects

CITY Inverness (CA)

COUNTRY USA

REGION North America

TYPOLOGY Living

COMPLETION 2004

WEBSITE www.studiosarch.com

ARCHITECTS STUDIOS Architecture

ARCHITECT'S POINT REYES RESIDENCE

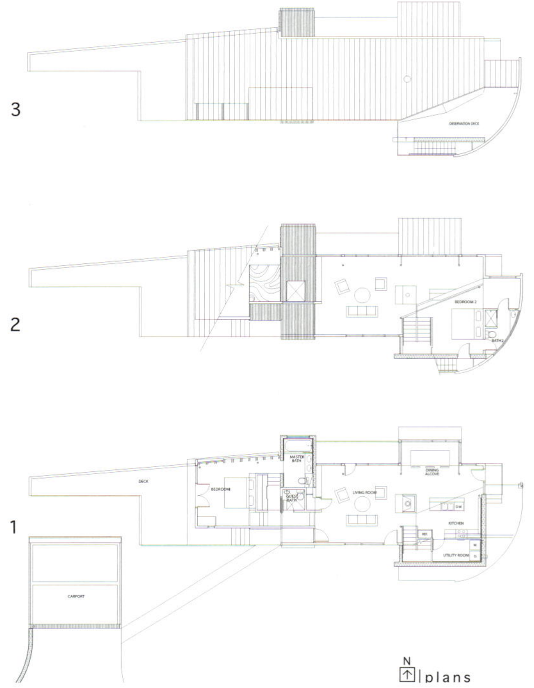

The residence is located on a steeply sloped, heavily forested site near Tomales Bay on California's Point Reyes National Seashore, an area known for its seaside woodlands and dairy farms. Wooden decks and an enclosed glass dining area thrust out from the base shed and appear to float amongst the trees. Strong, earthy materials were selected to stand up to the harsh coastal elements and to respond to the dynamics of the site. An eroded wooden shell encloses the space and positions the open-glazed steel skeleton, while an ensemble of garden walls, decks, the garage and gate house engage the site forming an outdoor compound.

01 Wooden façade **02** Enclosed glass dining area **03** Floor plans **04** Interior **05** Wooden deck

Photos: Michael O'Callahan (01, 04), Tim Griffith Photography (02, 05)

U.S. FOOD AND DRUG ADMINISTRATION. FDA AT IRVINE, PACIFIC REGIONAL LABORATORY-SOUTHWEST AND LOS ANGELES DISTRICT OFFICE

Completion of this 133,470 square foot building marked the culmination of the agency's strategic plan to consolidate aging laboratories throughout the U.S. and facilitate a changing institutional culture and new work methods to address advances in technology and science. Eliminating visual barriers between office and laboratory modules was the key to the design, as was harmonizing the building with its 10-acre undeveloped site adjacent to a freshwater marsh reserve.

01 Exterior view **02** Vertical fin **03** Second floor plan **04** Curved shaped façade

Photos: Adrian Velicescu/Standard

CITY Irvine (CA)
COUNTRY USA
REGION North America
TYPOLOGY Governement
COMPLETION 2003
WEBSITE www.zgf.com
ARCHITECTS Zimmer Gunsul Frasca Architects, LLP

CORNELL UNIVERSITY, DUFFIELD HALL

This new 150,930 square foot interdisciplinary research and instructional center within Cornell's Engineering quadrangle includes offices and laboratories to support research in the fields of electronics, optoelectronics, material synthesis and processing, microelectronics, and nanotechnology. Approximately one-third of the facility is comprised of cleanrooms. The building also has low vibration and low electromagnetic field standards and extensive central lab services requirements. The modular design can be adapted to changing functional needs without reconstruction of structural or building services.

01 Fully glazed façade **02** Front view **03** Seating space **04** First floor plan

Photos: Robert Canfield, Larry Falke Photography (03)

CITY Ithaca (NY)

COUNTRY USA

REGION North America

TYPOLOGY Education

COMPLETION 2004

WEBSITE www.zgf.com

ARCHITECTS Zimmer Gunsul Frasca Architects, LLP

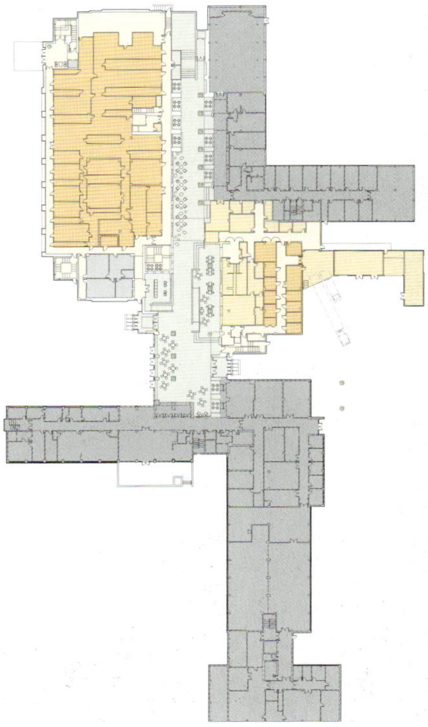

BEACH ROAD 2

The site is a long, thin strip of beachfront property on the northern coast of Jupiter Island, Florida. Beach Road 2 has ocean views to the east and south dominate the parcel, while a stone's throw to the north is a neighbor's house and directly to the west is the street. The house is made of three materials: glass, aluminum boat hull, and sand coupled to create shelter. Sand encloses the sleeping area, aluminum the entertaining space, and glass the contemplative living space. A lap pool on the roof increases landscaping on the site, shelters swimmers from the ocean breezes and through skylights living.

01 Exterior view by night **02** View into entrance **03** Floorplans **04** Kitchen **05** Terrace with pool

Photos: Ken Hayden

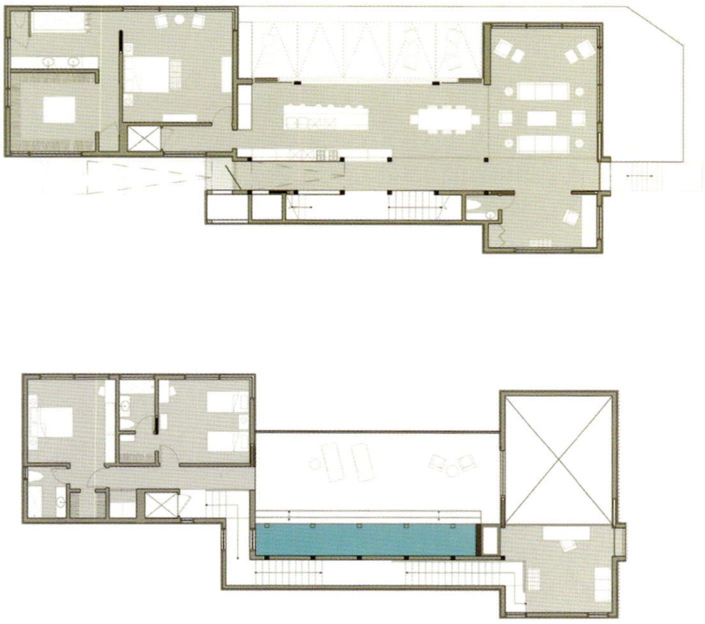

CITY
Jupiter Island (FL)

COUNTRY
USA

REGION
North America

TYPOLOGY
Living

COMPLETION
2004

WEBSITE
www.sharc.com

ARCHITECTS
SH_Arc Scott Hughes Architects

CITY Johnson (AR)

COUNTRY USA

REGION North America

TYPOLOGY Leisure / Sports

COMPLETION 2005

WEBSITE www.marlonblackwell.com

ARCHITECTS Marlon Blackwell Architect

BLESSINGS GOLF COURSE

Designed to challenge the traditional lodge commonly associated with the sport of golf, this modern clubhouse strikes a balance between function and setting, creating a unique presence in the Ozark Mountains region of Northwest Arkansas. Set at the base of the hill, the clubhouse acts as a covered bridge that creates an entry portal to the eighteen-hole green; visitors enter the building from the cool and shaded underbelly, not unlike the clefts and caves found in the nearby hills. The University of Arkansas Razorback Golf Center, located along the clubhouse's western edge, forms a larger threshold into the valley of the golf course.

01 East façade **02** Entry Portal **03** Exploded axonometric **04** Tile Corridor in wet area

Photos: Timothy Hursley

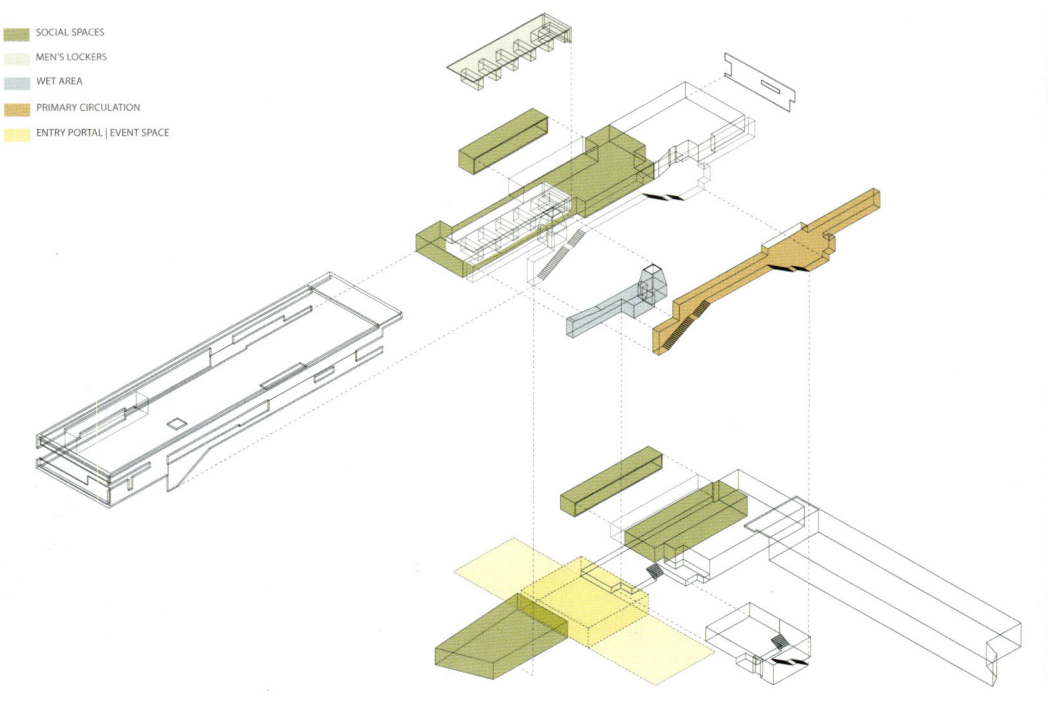

MISSISSIPPI TELECOMMUNICATIONS & CONFERENCE CENTER (MTCC)

The Center is the centerpiece in the composition of a new convention center district. The building functions as the covered arrival plaza for the new convention center and as a connector to a planned convention center hotel. From the urban design perspective, the front facade of the pavilion terminates the axis of a main street, becoming the focus and symbol of the convention district. The building is suspended above the plaza as if challenging gravity and its folding glass facade faces north towards the street. Its transparency reveals the gallery within and the meeting rooms beyond, projecting its activities to the public.

01 Folding glass façade **02** Exterior view by night **03** Gallery **04** Auditorium

Photos: Jimmy Winstead

CITY Jackson (MS)
COUNTRY USA
REGION North America
TYPOLOGY Public
COMPLETION 2006
WEBSITE www.arquitectonica.com
ARCHITECTS Arquitectonica

GRAND TETON DISCOVERY AND VISITOR CENTER

Grand Teton National Park's new visitor center is sited between a Sagebrush meadow and a Riparian forest along the Snake River, allowing visitors to be drawn into a courtyard that provides an intimate place in the vast Wyoming landscape. A colonnade of Douglas fir logs surrounds the courtyard and provides protection from the summer sun and heavy winter snowfall. The logs, beams and all structural framing timber is Forest Stewardship Council (FSC) certified, keeping with the Park's mission of sustainability. Douglas fir veneer plywood and clear heart Western red cedar are used as wall panels and casework throughout the visitor center.

01 Fir logs structure **02** Exterior view by night **03** Floor plan **04** Terrace

Photos: Nic Lehoux

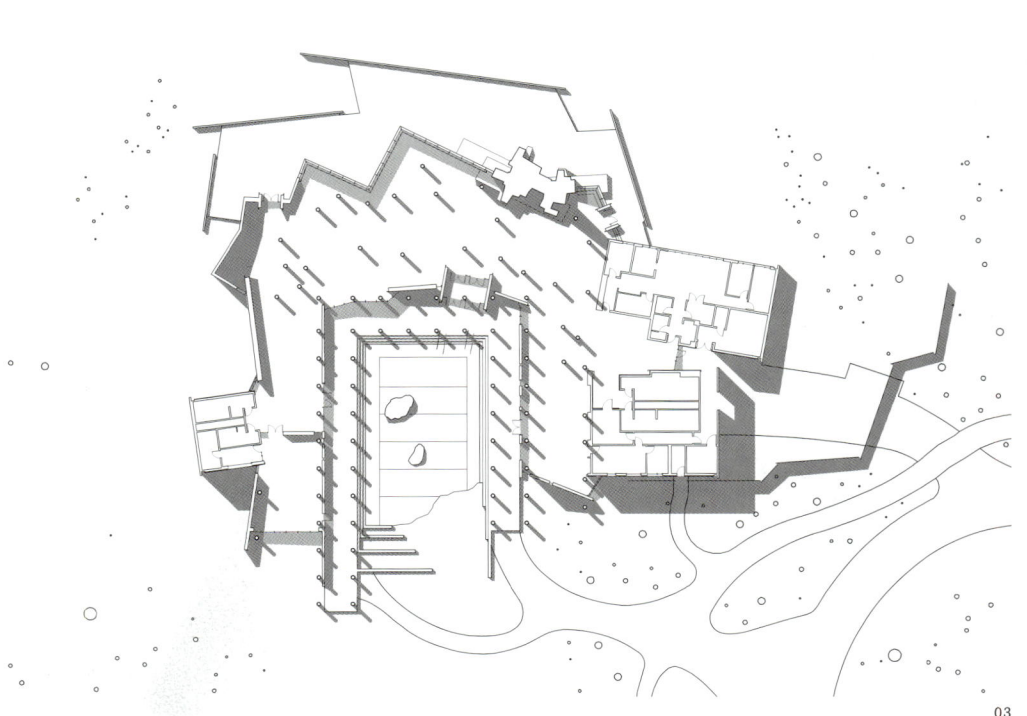

CITY Jackson (WY)
COUNTRY USA
REGION North America
TYPOLOGY Public
COMPLETION 2007
WEBSITE www.bcj.com
ARCHITECTS Bohlin Cywinski Jackson

WINE SILO

The project, a 300-square-foot Wine Silo, is designed to house the owner's private wine collection, and is connected to an existing "entertainment" building. The structure lies in the Snake River flood plain, therefore, a traditional wine cellar was out of the question. Borrowing from agrarian structures, the pure silo form is clad in oxidized steel plates to weather and blend with the existing buildings and landscape. The interior, inspired by a wine cask, is characterized by reclaimed fir woodwork and a spiral staircase which accesses carefully displayed wine bottles around its perimeter.

01 Oxidized steel plate skin **02** View from the south **03** Silo interior **04** Entertainment building and silo

Photos: Paul Warchol Photography

CITY	Jackson (WY)
COUNTRY	USA
REGION	North America
TYPOLOGY	Wine Cellar (private)
COMPLETION	2006
WEBSITE	www.carneyarchitects.com
ARCHITECTS	Carney Architects

CITY: Jackson (WY)
COUNTRY: USA
REGION: North America
TYPOLOGY: Culture
COMPLETION: 2007
WEBSITE: www.dynia.com / www.carneyarchitects.com
ARCHITECTS: Stephen Dynia Architects (Design Architect) and Carney Architects (Executive Architect)

JACKSON HOLE CENTER FOR THE ARTS PERFORMANCE HALL

The performance hall at the Jackson Hole Center for the Arts consists of a 500-seat Performing Arts Hall, a music facility, and extensive support facilities. The project design places 200 seats at the orchestra level and 300 seats at the balcony level. The balcony is accessed from the main entrance at street level while the orchestra level is accessed by descending to the lower level lobby, which is a dramatic space capped by a wood slat ceiling covering the form of the underside of the balcony above. This lobby is enclosed by a glass wall, providing a broad view of the iconic mountainscape of Jackson Hole.

01 Lobby at dusk 02 Northeast view 03 First floor plan 04 Performance hall interior

Photos: Ron Johnson

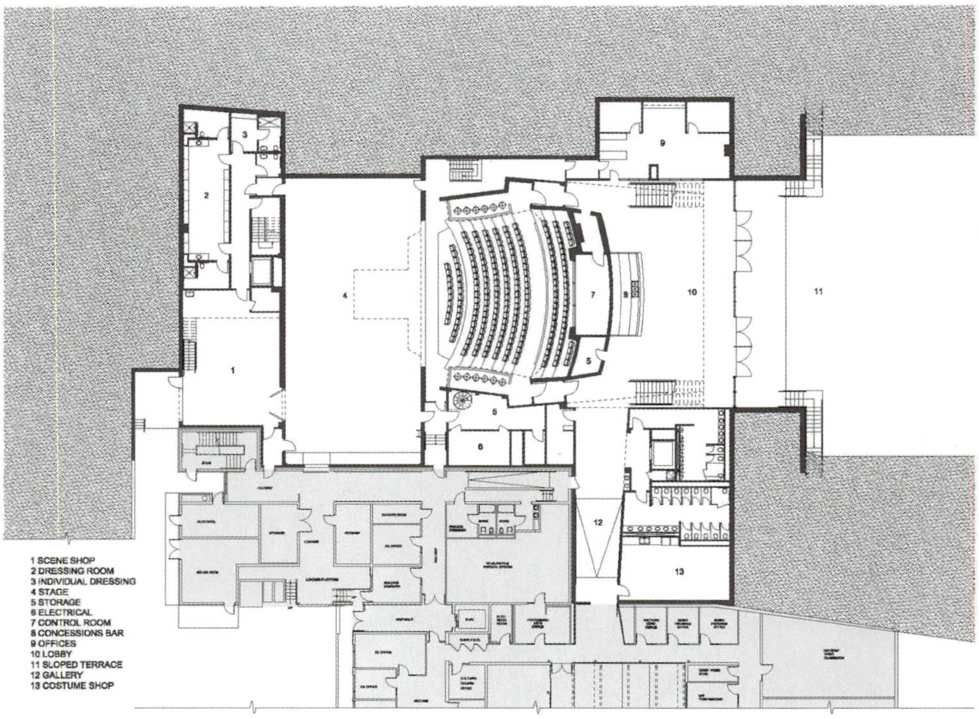

W- HOUSE

Nestled in a u-shaped, sloped terrain, the W-House's position on its site maximizes the views of the Teton Range, while at the same time utilizes the natural east-west flow of the landscape as an opportunistic moment for exchange. As the house cascades into the gully, each surface acts as a moving datum, interacting to create a new internal landscape that challenges the relationship between the geometry of the site and the surface of the building. Traditionally discernable boundaries become eroded and new spatial identities are configured. The result is one where building becomes landscape and landscape becomes space.

01 View to deck **02** Rear view **03** Stair to master loft **04** Floor plan **05** Interior

Photos: Courtesy of Ellinger / Yehia Design LLC (E/Ye Design)

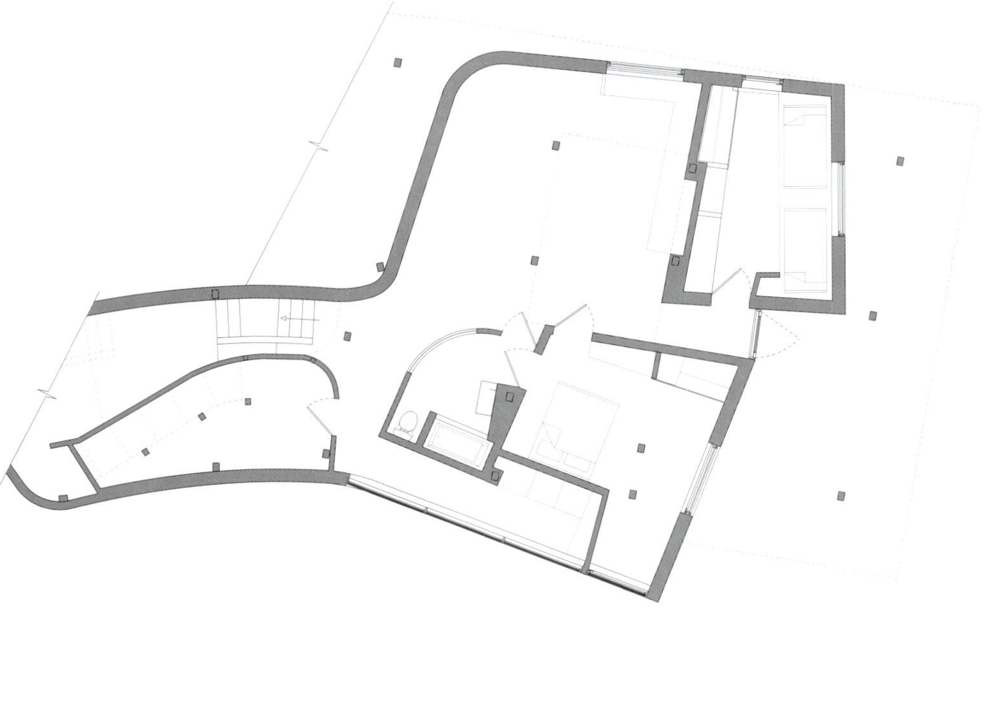

CITY Jackson (WY)
COUNTRY USA
REGION North America
TYPOLOGY Living
COMPLETION 2006
WEBSITE www.eye-des.com
ARCHITECTS E/Ye Design

CITY Kerhonkson (NY)

COUNTRY USA

REGION North America

TYPOLOGY Living

COMPLETION -

WEBSITE www.re4a.com

ARCHITECTS Resolution 4: Architecture

MOUNTAIN RETREAT

The Mountain Retreat is a prefabricated weekend home based on a system of modules of use. The project is a fusion of a 'lifted bar' and a 'two story bar'. On 1,800 square feet it includes two bedrooms and bathrooms, living and dining spaces as well as large indoor and outdoor entertaining areas. With a wrap-around deck and large sliding glass doors the house offers magnificent views of the Catskill Mountains surroundings.

01 Wrap-around deck **02** Exterior view by night **03** Sections **04** Deck with view to garden

Photos: Floto + Warner Studio

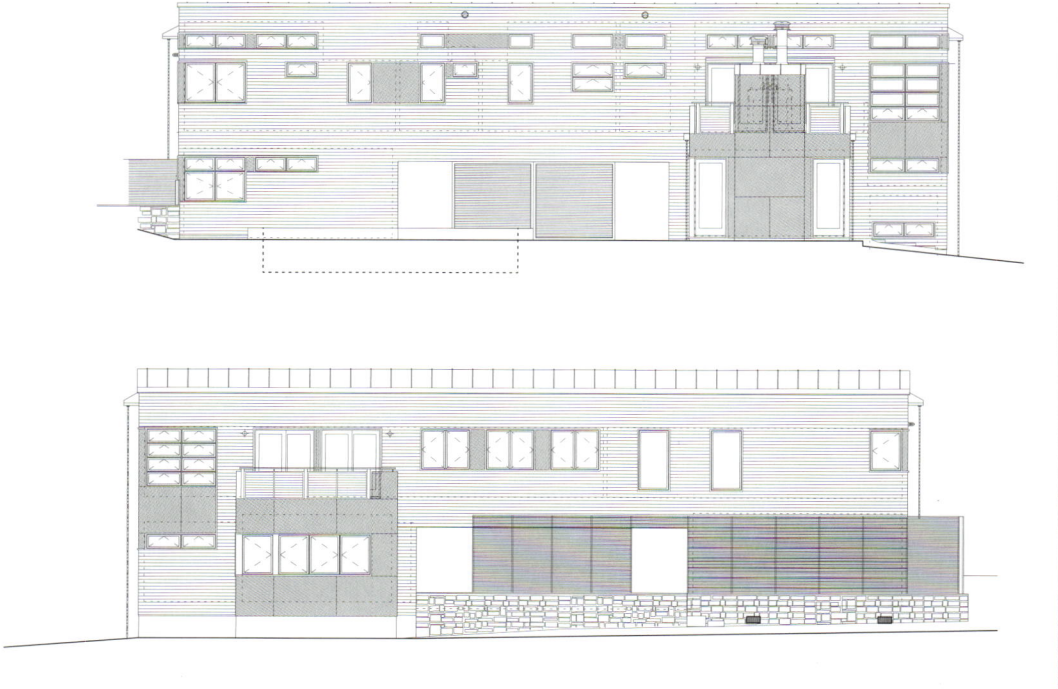

BENJAMIN FRANKLIN ELEMENTARY SCHOOL

Based on the principle that learning is all about creating connections, this school is designed to preserve and harness the environment as learning opportunity. Classroom wings reach like fingers toward the woods and visually connect students with nature. Courtyards landscaped with native plants serve as outdoor classrooms. Small learning communities are formed by clusters of classrooms around a multi-purpose activity area that faces the forest and reinforces connection between lessons and environment. Natural ventilation, windows oriented for daylighting, and low-impact materials are integrated throughout.

---

01 Exterior view **02** Site plan **03** Side view **04** Planted courtyard **05** Library

Photos: Benjamin Benschneider Photography

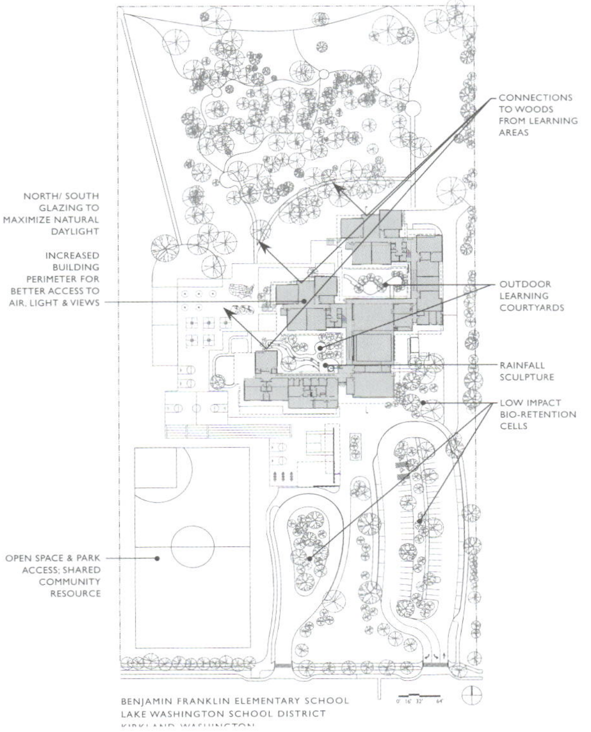

CITY Kirkland (WA)
COUNTRY USA
REGION North America
TYPOLOGY Education
COMPLETION 2005
WEBSITE www.mahlum.com
ARCHITECTS Mahlum

MODULAR 4 PROJECT

Prefabricated modular housing by nature focuses on the lifecycle of a building. By completing a majority of the construction in a warehouse, the integrity of materials are preserved, and scraps are reused which promotes less construction waste. Modular 4 features a 1500 square foot floor plan with a remarkably flexible design anchored by a core of service spaces. The project continues Studio 804's commitment towards developing responsible architecture through the means of prefabrication, materiality, and sustainability. The site consists of a once vacant brownfield lot in the heart of Kansas City.

01 Floor plans **02** West deck **03** Exterior view **04** Ramp elevation

Photos: Dan Rockhill

CITY
Kansas City (MO)

COUNTRY
USA

REGION
North America

TYPOLOGY
Living

COMPLETION
2007

WEBSITE
www.rockhillandassociates.com
www.studio804.com

ARCHITECTS
Rockhill+Associates/
Studio 804

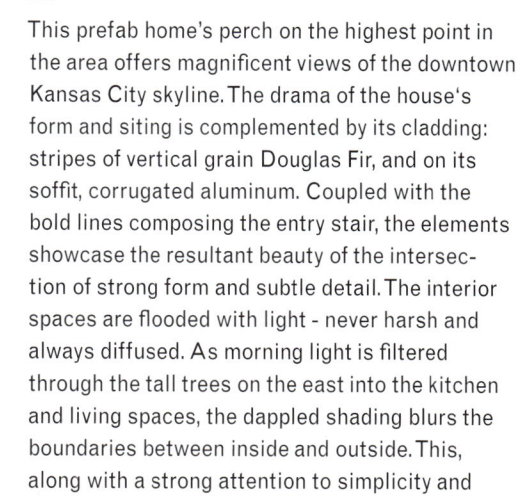

MODULAR 3 PROJECT

This prefab home's perch on the highest point in the area offers magnificent views of the downtown Kansas City skyline. The drama of the house's form and siting is complemented by its cladding: stripes of vertical grain Douglas Fir, and on its soffit, corrugated aluminum. Coupled with the bold lines composing the entry stair, the elements showcase the resultant beauty of the intersection of strong form and subtle detail. The interior spaces are flooded with light - never harsh and always diffused. As morning light is filtered through the tall trees on the east into the kitchen and living spaces, the dappled shading blurs the boundaries between inside and outside. This, along with a strong attention to simplicity and detail, displays a strong aptitude towards the customs of Modernism.

01 Kitchen **02** Side view **03** Street view **04** Vertical grain Douglas Fir façade

Photos: Dan Rockhill

CITY
Kansas City (MO)

COUNTRY
USA

REGION
North America

TYPOLOGY
Living

COMPLETION
2006

WEBSITE
www.rockhillandassociates.com
www.studio804.com

ARCHITECTS
Rockhill+Associates/
Studio 804

CITY Kansas City (MO)

COUNTRY USA

REGION North America

TYPOLOGY Public

COMPLETION 2007

WEBSITE www.hntbarchitecture.com

ARCHITECTS HNTB Architecture Inc. BNIM International Architects Atelier / Junk Architects

GRAND BALLROOM AT THE KANSAS CITY CONVENTION CENTER

The new Grand Ballroom at the Kansas City Convention Center serves as a bridge linking the city's emerging Crossroads Arts District with the convention center as part of an ongoing downtown revitalization. Among the first LEED certified U.S. convention projects, the 46,500 LEED Silver certified Ballroom features extensive daylighting, exterior sunscreens, environmentally friendly materials and construction methods, and lastly, a sophisticated lighting control system. Computer models were merged with fabrication technologies to create design motifs depicting the motion and visual character of water.

01 Main entrance 02 Entrance view 03 Section 04 Interior stack

Photos: Assassi Productions, Michael Spillers (04)

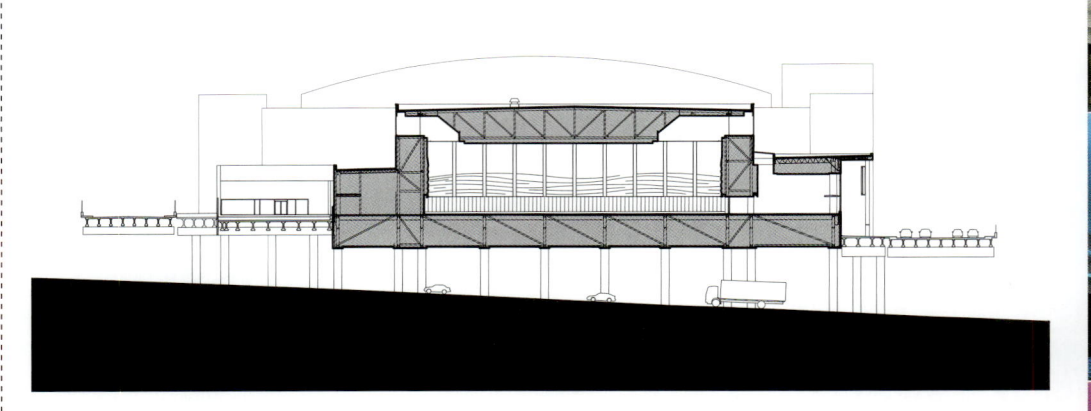

NELSON-ATKINS MUSEUM OF ART

The Bloch Building addition to the Nelson-Atkins Museum of Art fuses architecture with landscape to create a dynamic experience for visitors as they enter. Engaging the existing sculpture garden, the addition transforms the entire site and is distinguished by five glass lenses that traverse the existing building through the Sculpture Park to form new spaces and angles of vision. The innovative merging of landscape, architecture and art was executed through close collaboration with museum curators and artists to achieve a dynamic and supportive relationship between art and architecture.

---

01 Entry **02** Transparent and opaque façade **03** Glass lenses with double-glass cavities **04** Interior **05** Aerial view

Photos: Andy Ryan Photography

CITY Kansas City (MO)
COUNTRY USA
REGION North America
TYPOLOGY Culture
COMPLETION 2007
WEBSITE www.stevenholl.com
ARCHITECTS Steven Holl Architects

CITY
Lake Forest (IL)

COUNTRY
USA

REGION
North America

TYPOLOGY
Living

COMPLETION
2005

WEBSITE
www.frederickphillips.com

ARCHITECTS
Frederick Phillips and Associates

GLADE HOUSE

In a community where large, traditional houses prevail, this house is a refreshing and uplifting return to the more modest wood frame structures typical of the area before it became suburbanized. Two distinct gable structures recall, loosely, a farm-house "T" plan. Tall awning windows are proportioned and spaced with classical regularity, while a continuous band of clerestory windows separates volumes and adds light and dimension to certain interior spaces. Five species of lightwood, teak, cedar, Douglas fir, maple, and white oak provide a quiet but rich palette of interior and exterior materials.

01 Façade with tall awning windows **02** Lightwood exterior **03** Side view **04** Floor plans **05** Interior with clerestory windows

Photos: Barbara Karant

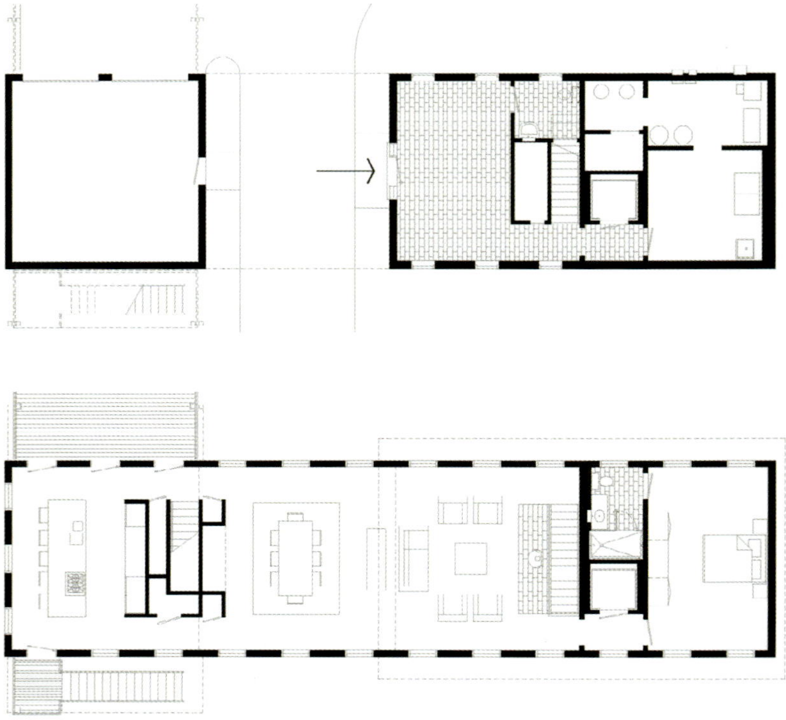

THE LAB AT BELMAR

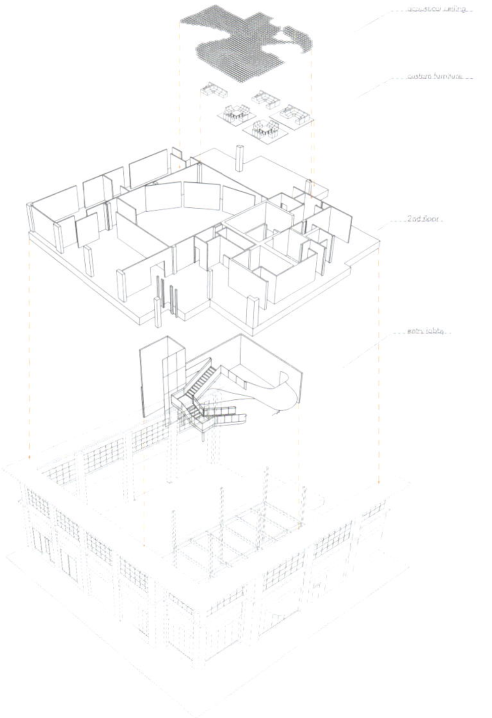

This institution, established within a development on the outskirts of Denver in the city of Lakewood, Co., is unique for its eclectic, programmatic agenda and unconventional marketing tactics. From one storefront to another, products and symbols confront the passerby through hyper-visual stimulation. A single curvilinear surface recedes to the back of the entry lobby and pushes the entry stairs toward the exterior corner of the space. The interstitial space between the curvilinear surface and the stairs twists helically from the ground floor to the second floor where the galleries and flex-function spaces are located.

01 View at night; within the existing building **02** Main entrance **03** Lobby **04** Lobby with curvilinear surface **05** Gallery **06** Axonometry

Photos: Joel Eden of Joel Eden Photography

CITY: Lakewood (CO)
COUNTRY: USA
REGION: North America
TYPOLOGY: Institution
COMPLETION: 2006
WEBSITE: www.belzbergarchitects.com
ARCHITECTS: Belzberg Architects

BIG DIG HOUSE

Boston's ongoing Central Artery Tunnel Project is one of the largest, most complex infrastructural undertakings in American urban history. In regards to the massive amount of waste that accompanies construction on such a scale, the proposed alternative was to relocate and reuse these materials. As this recycled infrastructure offers the potential to create architecture that can withstand much higher loads than conventional systems, landscape can be easily brought to the roof and upper levels of the building, increasing useable open space, controlling runoff, and bringing natural environments closer to building users.

01 Southeast façade **02** Northeast view **03** Exposed structure **04** Roofgarden **05** Bird's eye view

Photos: SINGLE speed IMAGE

CITY Lexington (MA)
COUNTRY USA
REGION North America
TYPOLOGY Living
COMPLETION 2006
WEBSITE www.ssdarchitecture.com
ARCHITECTS Single Speed Design

DRAPE ARTIST RESIDENCE AND GALLERY

Located next to the iconic Sheldon Art Gallery designed by Philip Johnson in 1963, The DRAPE responds to the inherent relationship between the two buildings. Inside, the gallery's interior space, true to its name, can be subdivided and reprogrammed by means of an operative rubber membrane. Suspended from rolling hangers, this flexible divider can be draped to form vertical partitions or pulled taut to form areas of suspended ceiling as needed. Integral service nodes containing LED light fixtures, power, and nozzle-controlled compressed air allow these services to be distributed according to the various needs of the resident artist.

01 Exterior view **02** Entry **03** Floor plan **04** Perspective **05** Façade with sunscreen **06** Bird's eye view

Renderings: Doug Jackson

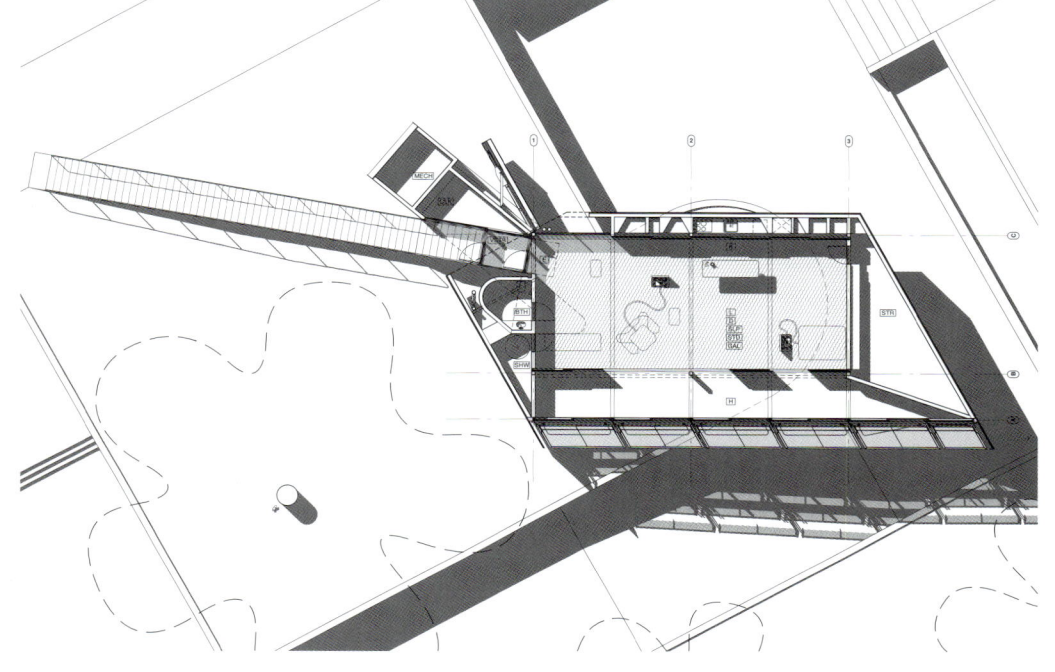

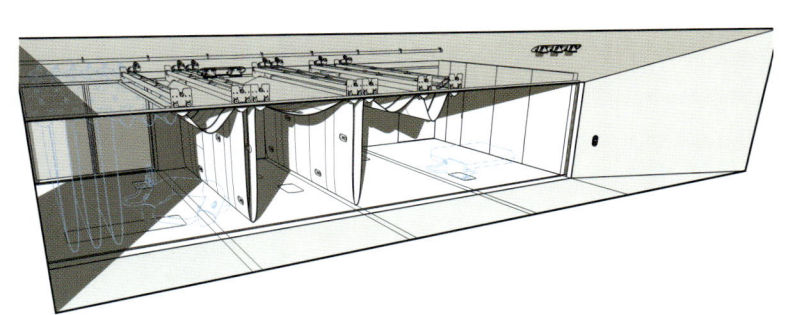

CITY Lincoln (NE)
COUNTRY USA
REGION North America
TYPOLOGY Living
COMPLETION 2007
WEBSITE www.dougjacksondesign.com
ARCHITECTS Doug Jackson Design Office

CITY
Littleton (CO)

COUNTRY
USA

REGION
North America

TYPOLOGY
Ecclesiastical

COMPLETION
2006

WEBSITE
www.semplebrowndesign.com

ARCHITECTS
Semple Brown Design

LITTLETON CHURCH OF CHRIST

The Littleton Church project is a 26,165 square foot expansion, spread out on two floors with partial basement. It includes the main entry and lobby area, 13 classrooms, 2 children's theatres, a children's library, nursery/day care, a suite of classrooms, as well as common spaces for the youth. These features were all achieved within a tight budget of $152/square foot. The stylish design breaks down the scale of the building by creating small shifts in plane, and keeping well proportioned massing changes. A steel canopy reaches out to the street and draws the eye back to the main entry.

01 Façade **02** Steel canopy **03** Main entry **04** Site plan **05** Stair

Photos: Ron Pollard Photography

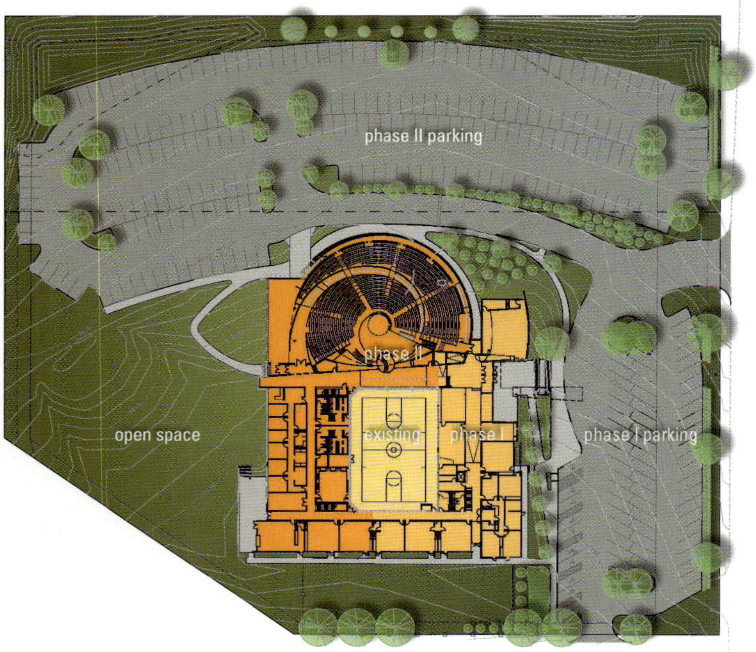

THE MANON CAINE RUSSELL AND KATHRYN CAINE WANLASS PERFORMANCE HALL

This 420-seat project is a play of geometries of both acoustical and contextual significance, featuring sculpted, geometric forms that evoke the look of the surrounding mountains. An orthogonal concrete shell with thick concrete walls enclose, the main performance space whose height, shape and materials were carefully considered for optimum sound qualities. A contrasting zinc, panel-coated entrance pavilion has origami-like folded volumes that suggest a melding of the man-made and the natural. By day, triangular skylights angle light into interior spaces and by night the pavilion faces a dramatically lit outdoor piazza.

01 Entrance to piazza 02 Triangular skylights 03 Aerial view
04 Zinc panel-coated façade 05 Concert hall

Photos: Robert Benson

CITY Logan (UT)
COUNTRY USA
REGION North America
TYPOLOGY Culture
COMPLETION 2006
WEBSITE www.sasaki.com
ARCHITECTS Sasaki Associates

CITY Los Altos Hills (CA)

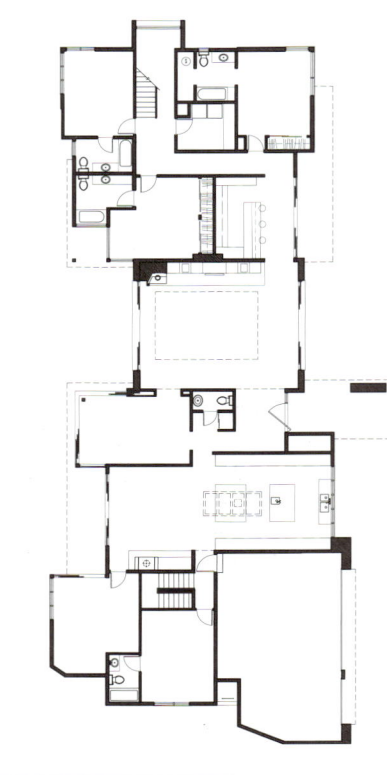

COUNTRY USA

REGION North America

TYPOLOGY Living

COMPLETION 2006

WEBSITE www.swattarchitects.com

ARCHITECTS Swatt Architects

SHIMMON RESIDENCE

This project includes a remodel and addition of the following areas: garage, kitchen, dining room, bedroom & master bedroom suite, new basement theatre, wine cellar, interior renovations of the entire building, and new hardscape and landscape. The new home now includes unified and well proportioned interior spaces and consistent exterior forms, exquisitely detailed with a minimal palette of beautiful materials. The site is an east and west facing knoll in semi-rural Los Altos Hills, in the foothills of Silicon Valley, with serene valley views, surrounded by mature landscaping, including numerous heritage oak trees.

01 Entry elevation at dusk **02** Deck and pool **03** First floor plan **04** Second floor plan **05** Living space **06** Mahagony canopy

Photos: Cesar Rubio Photography

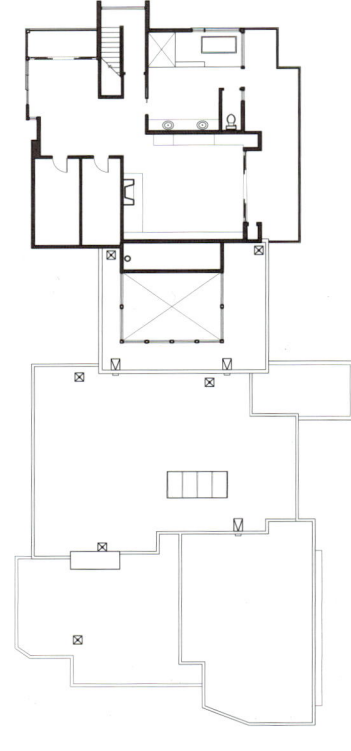

2-INNS

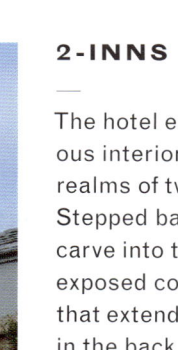

The hotel explores the qualities of a continuous interior-exterior space in the private realms of two identical adjacent houses. Stepped back from the street, the houses carve into the existing topography. The exposed concrete sub-level forms the base that extends from the front lawn to the hill in the back. Elevated from the street, the main level is enclosed by twenty five full-height glass panels, which slide away on an automated track, creating a continuous open plane that connects the back garden to the ocean views. This feature transforms the public areas into an exterior space while maintaining privacy from the street.

01 Total view **02** Side view with terrace **03** View from the garden **04** Night view of terrace with fire pit **05** View into the kitchen by night

Photos: Hisao Suzuki

CITY La Jolla (CA)
COUNTRY USA
REGION North America
TYPOLOGY Living
COMPLETION -
WEBSITE www.sebastianmariscal.com
ARCHITECTS Sebastian Mariscal Studio

CALIT2, UNIVERSITY OF CALIFORNIA SAN DIEGO

Following the launch of a state initiative to keep California at the forefront of technological advancement and innovation, the University of California envisioned a network of four institutes that would use collaboration to address large-scale societal issues. Calit2, the second of them, was established at UC San Diego, which is considered one of the nation's highest-ranked research institutions. Providing some of the most advanced facilities in the nation, the building features include clean rooms, micro-electro-mechanical labs, immersive virtual reality, and ultra-high-definition digital cinema.

01 Main building **02** Typical floor plan **03** Courtyard view **04** Exterior view from street **05** Minimized electromagnetic façade

Photos: John Durant

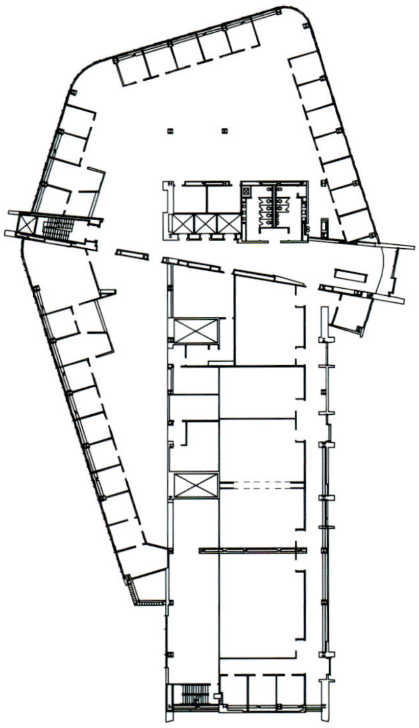

THE PROSPECT

The architect/owner used an abandoned lot to build a private, urban residence for his family with an on-site architecture studio that is fully sustainable and divorced from the grid thanks to roof-mounted electrical panels. The residence is a plaster box resting on and supported by Cor-ten steel wall planes. The main living area is surrounded by a reflecting pool on one side, and a glass floor on the opposite. In the below-grade office and recreation facilities the glass floor/ceiling liberates the space and allows ample natural light. The house is open and flowing, with boundaries dissolved and extended through sliding panels.

01 Exterior view by night **02** Living room with glass floor **03** Reflecting pool **04** Floor plan

Photos: Steve Simpson

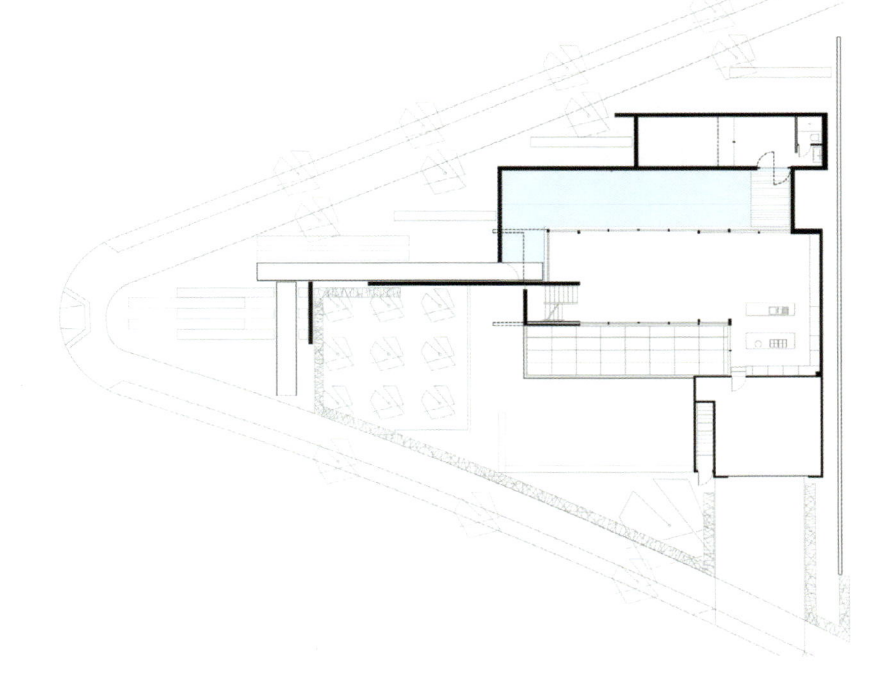

CITY La Jolla (CA)
COUNTRY USA
REGION North America
TYPOLOGY Living
COMPLETION 2004
WEBSITE www.jonathansegalarchitect.com
ARCHITECTS Jonathan Segal

CITY
Las Vegas (NV)

COUNTRY
USA

REGION
North America

TYPOLOGY
Leisure

COMPLETION
2004

WEBSITE
www.richardsonsadeki.com

ARCHITECTS
Richardson Sadeki, Designer
Klai Juba Architects, Architect of Record

BATHHOUSE SPA

The Bathhouse is a 15,000-square-foot spa for Mandalay Bay Resort in Las Vegas. The interior is defined by simple elegance, achieved by the use of slate walls and marble floors. The designing idea of the project was to oppose Las Vegas characteristics: haptic as opposed to optic, quiet as opposed to loud, intimate as opposed to distant, compressed as opposed to expansive, slow as opposed to fast. The overall space of the project subscribes to relationships of adjacencies and in doing so allows the overall experience to be implied and subjective.

01 Reception desk **02** Men's pool and lounge **03** Lobby
04 Women's pool **05, 06** Second and mezzanine floor plan

Photos: Andrew Bordwin Studio

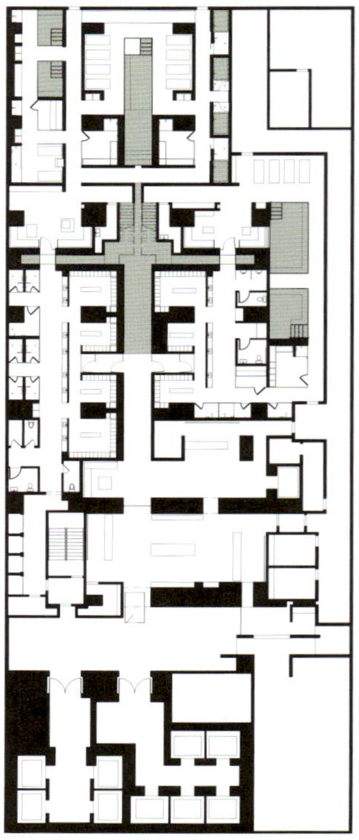

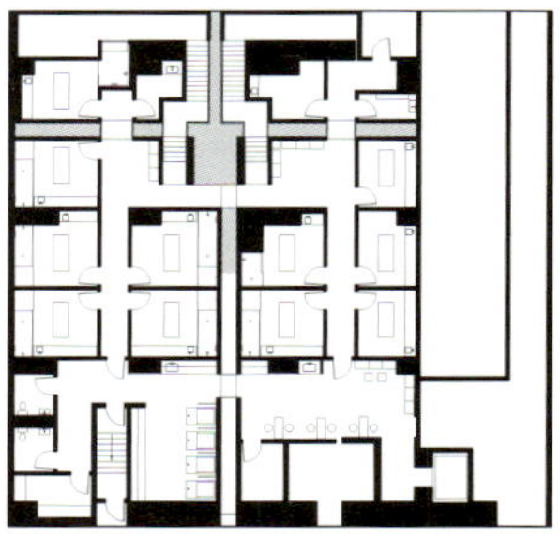

FIX

The FIX restaurant is situated inside the MGM "Bellagio" Casino in Las Vegas, Nevada. A location offering a sanctuary of impressive calmness will evolve next to the buzz of the gambling lounges as a juxtaposition to their pace and appearance. The architects designed a restaurant landscape that challenges the classic spatial canon by using an expressive topographical ceiling to structure and zone the open horizontal space. The ceiling additionally conceals all lighting fixtures and other equipment.

01 Main dining area **02** Padouk wood slats ceiling **03** Interior **04** Floor plan

Photos: Ricky Ridecos

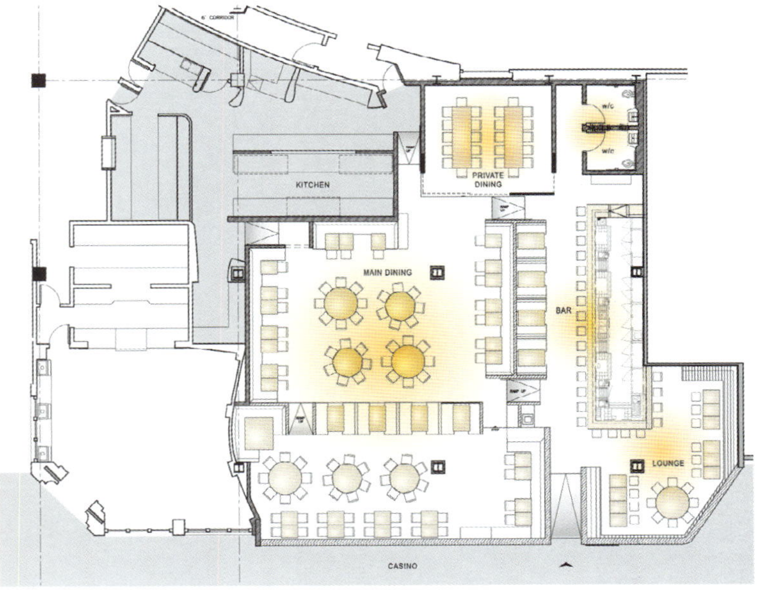

CITY
Las Vegas (NV)

COUNTRY
USA

REGION
North America

TYPOLOGY
Gastronomy

COMPLETION
—

WEBSITE
www.graftlab.com

ARCHITECTS
GRAFT

CITY
Long Island City (NY)

COUNTRY
USA

REGION
North America

TYPOLOGY
Living

COMPLETION
2004

WEBSITE
www.leroystreetstudio.com

ARCHITECTS
Leroy Street Studio

COURTYARD HOUSES

Located on a flat, twelve-acre site dotted with specimen trees and rimmed by tall evergreens, this family retreat is one block from the ocean in eastern Long Island. Responding to the need to create three separate family residences, the program for the complex is anchored around a common courtyard. Granite walls that provided internal and external spaces and a unifying texture were introduced to create a unique sense of place and to give each home ample privacy. House I's south facing entry appears solid and private, while its north side, facing the agricultural reserve, is expansively glazed. House II is entered at its narrowest point, through a glazed hall opening to a raised court of bamboo, extending up through an opening in the long, low roof plane.

01 Glazed hall **02** Exterior view **03** Dry-stack granite walls **04** Interior **05** Site plan

Photos: Paul Warchol Photography

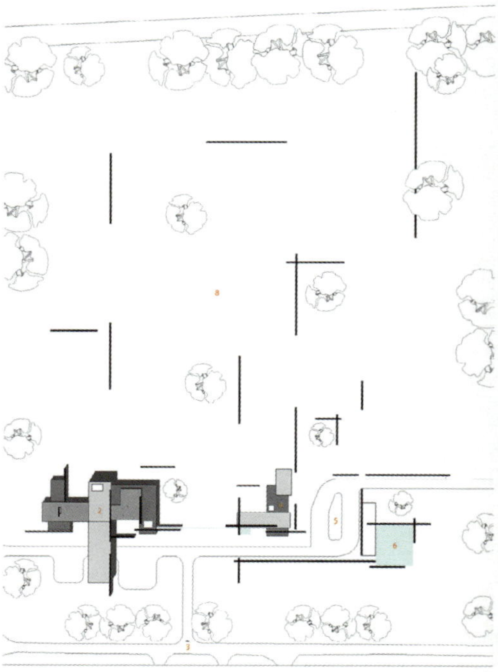

PS1/MOMA

The romance of the aquatic world becomes a reality, and the white glare of direct sun blurs into a glimmering, golden, luminescent glow. In the courtyard of PS1, that experience and sensation of submersion and immersion, basking and bathing is felt. Echoing the languid sways of kelp, sixteen modular structures of carbon steel tubing curve high above. Under their undulating twists and soft contours, expanded metal mesh and light metal sheets beckoning with glints of flash and hints of form provide a shelter. Sunny by day, glittering by night, small LED's are bunched like sparkling fruit in the canopies above.

01 Interior courtyard **02** Model **03** Main courtyard **04** Overall by night **05** Plan of shadows

Renderings: Gage/Clemenceau

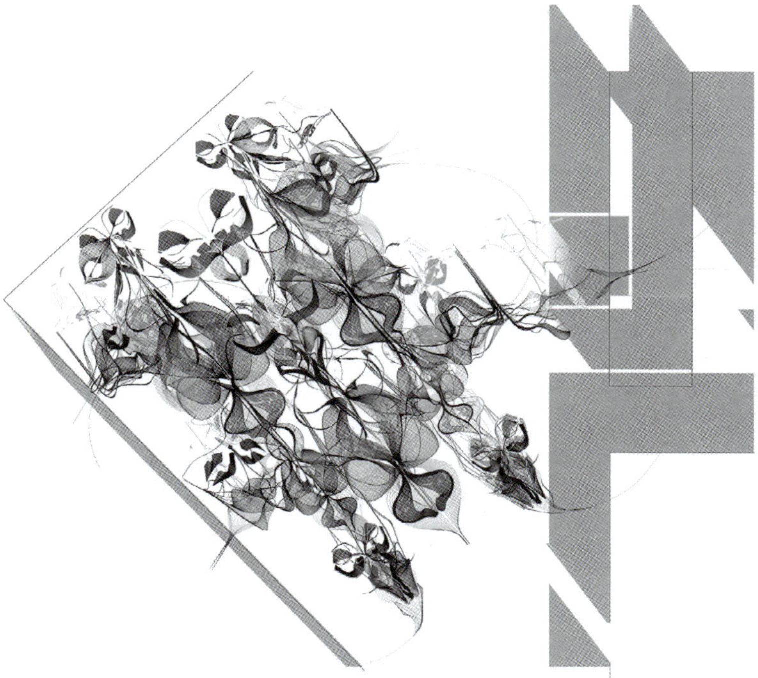

CITY Long Island City (NY)
COUNTRY USA
REGION North America
TYPOLOGY Culture
COMPLETION Unbuilt
WEBSITE www.gageclemenceau.com
ARCHITECTS Gage/Clemenceau Architects

CITY Long Island City (NY)
COUNTRY USA
REGION North America
TYPOLOGY Education
COMPLETION 2004
WEBSITE www.goldnerarchitects.com
ARCHITECTS Daniel Goldner Architects

IRONWORKERS TRAINING FACILITY (II)

The new facility project for New York City's Local Union serves the union's apprenticeship program. Set within a low-rise industrial district, the main two-storey building was combined with an adjacent setback one-storey building to form the open-plan welding and erection shops. Classrooms occupy the basement level of the main building, with the second-floor space set aside for a commercial tenant. The use of 14 different metal types demanded unusual craftsmanship, providing both inspiration and a practical learning experience for the apprentices. The glass section of floor in the lobby allows daylight into the lower level.

01 Metal façade **02** Exterior façade **03** Front façade **04** First floor plan

Photos: Courtesy of Daniel Goldner Architects

MONTAUK RESIDENCE GUESTHOUSE

Modeled on a motel, this guesthouse, part of a pair of ocean front houses situated on adjacent lots in Montauk, NY, is nearly entirely airborne. The design creates a series of covered spaces and processional gateways that lead to the main house. The guesthouse is the second floor of the low-slung main house, dislocated to the entry side of the site where it can participate in defining the large landscaped courtyard hovering 75 feet above the ocean. Access to the rooms is off a continuous balcony facing the courtyard, while the louvered side of the house preserves the ocean views, while concealing the neighboring house.

01 Exterior view by night **02** Spiral stairs **03** Interior with ocean views **04** Plan **05** Hallway

Photos: Peter Mauss/Esto

CITY Long Island (NY)
COUNTRY USA
REGION North America
TYPOLOGY Living
COMPLETION –
WEBSITE www.pentagram.com
ARCHITECTS Pentagram

RIDGEWOOD RESIDENCE

The Ridgewood Residence development boldly establishes itself as a stamp of a new generation of California modernism. The Ridgewood House captures the full advantage of the Southern California climate by attempting to blur the boundary between indoor and outdoor. Large walls of glass slide past solid walls to allow the interior spaces of the home to seamlessly transition to the exterior spaces. Due to the sloped lot, it was possible to build an expansive wood rooftop deck over a semi-subterranean garage, spilling into the yard, setting up a dynamic relationship between the house and its landscape.

01 Exterior view **02** Floor plan **03** Wooden roof top balcony **04** Sliding glass door **05** Deck

Photos: Michael Weschler

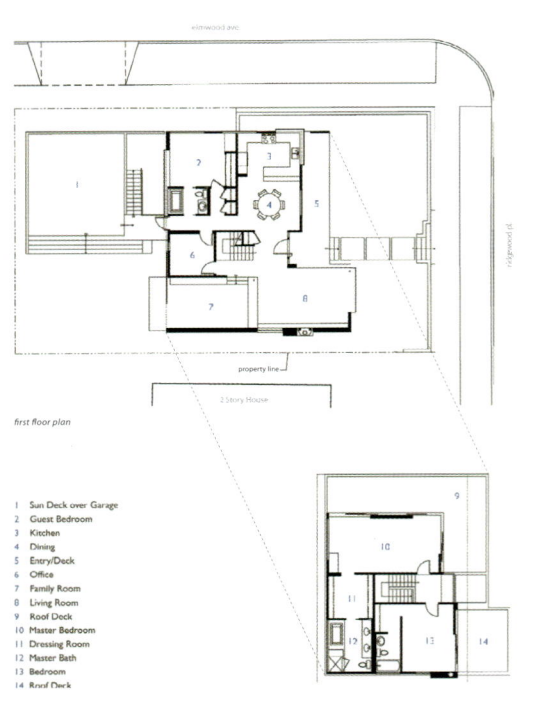

CITY Los Angeles (CA)

COUNTRY USA

REGION North America

TYPOLOGY Living

COMPLETION 2006

WEBSITE www.assembledge.com

ARCHITECTS assembledge+

BARSKY RESIDENCE

This small addition attaches itself to the rear of a quaint Spanish-style house in the Melrose area of Los Angeles, California. The modernist character of the addition creates a harmonious and elegant connection between old and new, where the architects designed a cantilevered foundation so that the box would appear to float off the ground. On a very limited budget, the project tried to make use of rather simple materials and formulate their uniqueness. The standard material of Stucco was translated into a lively material by creating a vertically combed finish that allows for a dynamic play of light and shadow throughout the day.

01 - Floor plan 02 Sliding glass door 03 Vertically combed façade 04 Pool view

Photos: Michael Weschler

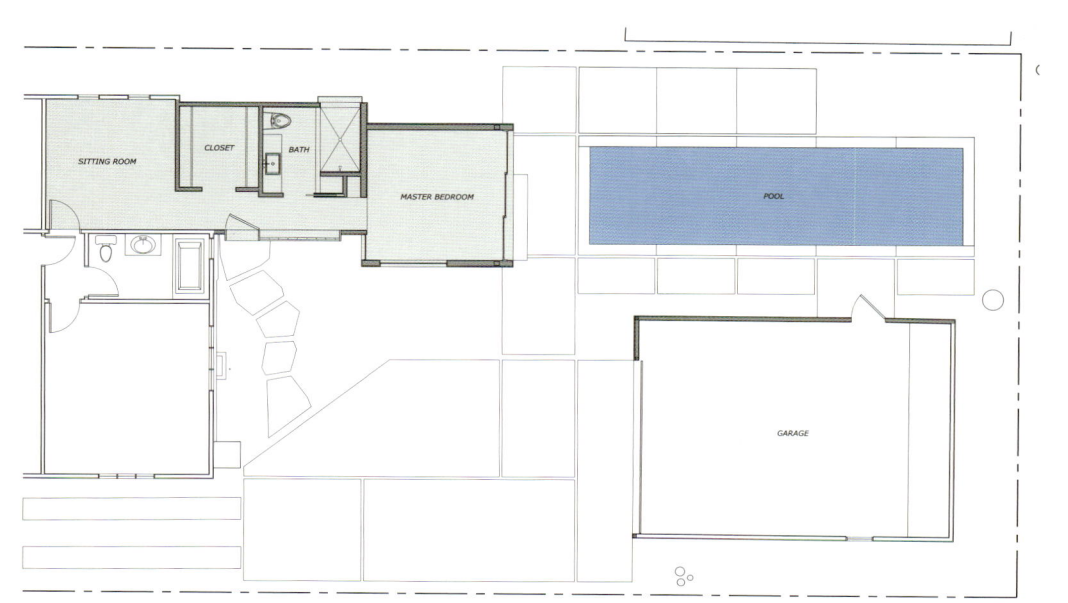

CITY Los Angeles (CA)

COUNTRY USA

REGION North America

TYPOLOGY Living

COMPLETION 2005

WEBSITE www.assembledge.com

ARCHITECTS assembledge+

CITY Los Angeles (CA)

COUNTRY USA

REGION North America

TYPOLOGY Living

COMPLETION 2007

WEBSITE www.belzbergarchitects.com

ARCHITECTS Belzberg Architects

SKYLINE RESIDENCE

Perched atop a ridgeline in the Hollywood hills, the Skyline Residence has been transformed into a modern home with spectacular views of downtown Los Angeles, Laurel Canyon, and the San Fernando Valley. The ambitions of the project were to use the prominence of the location as the impetus for the design, resulting in an architecture that is gracefully complimented by its surroundings. The linear nature of the site encouraged a layout in which each room was defined by at least one fully glazed wall. The infinity-edge pool brings the valley to the edge of the pool enhancing the vastness and immediacy of the city below.

01 Roof detail at front entrance **02** Movie projection onto guest house with the city below **03** View from entry drive **04** View from living room **05** Front entrance

Photos: Belzberg Architects

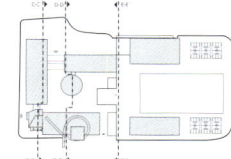

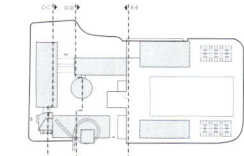

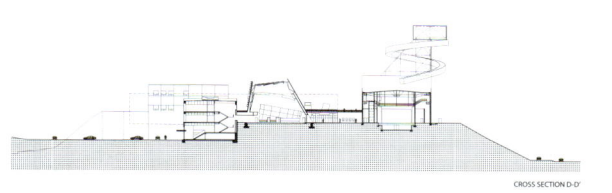

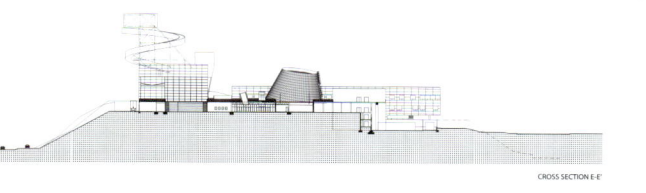

CENTRAL LOS ANGELES AREA HIGH SCHOOL #9 FOR THE VISUAL AND PERFORMING ARTS

Labelled "A School for the Future," this dramatic high school project developed for the Los Angeles Unified School District is located in the same downtown corridor as the Disney Concert Hall, the Museum of Contemporary Art and the Cathedral of Our Lady of Angels. A flagship high school focused on the arts, the school campus will include education in music, dance, theater and visual arts. The design's prominent tower symbolizes the importance of the arts to the city and is fitted with a spiral ramp in the form of the number nine. The adjacent billboards will act as both signage and an information interface for the school.

01 Cross sections **02** Façade **03** Interior **04** Front view
05 Spiral ramp by night

Photos: COOP HIMMELB(L)AU, ISOCHROM.com (02)

CITY Los Angeles (CA)
COUNTRY USA
REGION North America
TYPOLOGY Education
COMPLETION 2008
WEBSITE www.coop-himmelblau.at
ARCHITECTS COOP HIMMELB(L)AU

CITY: Los Angeles (CA)
COUNTRY: USA
REGION: North America
TYPOLOGY: Living
COMPLETION: 2006
WEBSITE: www.emergent architecture.com
ARCHITECTS: EMERGENT Tom Wiscombe

CELL HOUSE

The Cell House's design is organized around the principles of cellular tectonics and structural performance rather than program or function. The residence's walls do not divide space and resolve loads in favor of a multidirectional system of forces and behaviors. Rather, throughout the residence, the floor plates, structural frame and building envelope create a three-dimensional cellular pattern, one that evolves toward performance-based conditions that don't break the design's logic.

01 Three dimensional cellular pattern **02** Upper floor plan **03** Downstairs **04** Exterior view

Photos: EMERGENT

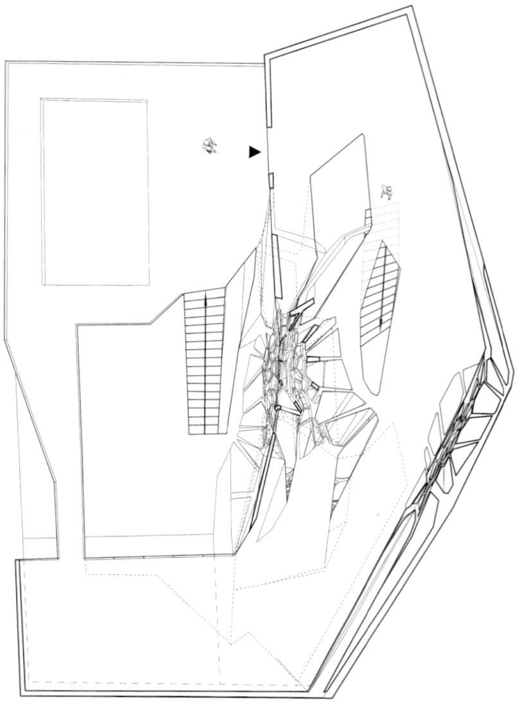

NOONAN RESIDENCE

Accommodating diverse living arrangements, the Noonan Residence's cubic form offers multiple levels that open to views of the city and relate one interior space to another. The second level houses the main living areas, as well as the master bedroom and a future elevator that provides for single-level living should accessibility issues become necessary later. The first level houses a suite, which, with its own exterior entry, can function as a caretaker's apartment or additional workspace. Carved into the third level is a roof terrace that allows southern light to penetrate the living space below.

01 Front façade **02** Front door **03** Roof terrace **04** Section **05** Roof top detail

Photos: Josh Perrin

CITY: Los Angeles (CA)
COUNTRY: USA
REGION: North America
TYPOLOGY: Living
COMPLETION: 2006
WEBSITE: www.fungandblatt.com
ARCHITECTS: Fung + Blatt Architects, Inc

290

CITY Los Angeles (CA)
COUNTRY USA
REGION North America
TYPOLOGY Living
COMPLETION 2004
WEBSITE www.xtenarchitecture.com
ARCHITECTS XTEN Architecture

VHOUSE

The residence is a small courtyard pavilion set in a wooded canyon site. The detailing and materiality of the house is minimal yet indivisibly bound to the architectural concept. Four bearing walls are set perpendicular to the hillside and wrapped in redwood planks that continue inside the house to define three program zones. Glass doors, minimal shear walls and ribbon windows at the interior corners comprise the secondary façades. The folds of the roof geometry are articulated to respond to specific site conditions, shielding the house from the street and opening it elsewhere to nature.

01 Wall of redwood planks and entrance **02** Terrace with fire pit **03** View from the garden showing three program zones **04** Living room **05** Interior view showing roof geometry **06** Floor plan

Photos: Art Gray

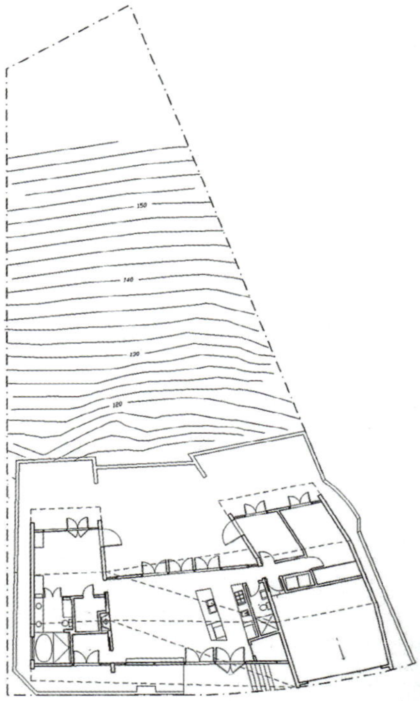

HOLLYWOOD BOWL

The architects reinterpreted the Hollywood Bowl's trademark creamy-white curvilinear shell while infusing advanced technologies to provide world-class acoustics. The design includes a re-conception of the arch, an expansive stage, and state-of-the-art engineering features. A highlight of the digital sound system is a grand acoustic canopy, which floats as an elliptical ring above the stage and reflects sound waves to all parts of the stage. The Bowl features a functional, flexible space that is adaptable to future technologies and endeavors while maintaining the glamour of this timeless venue.

01 Acustic canopy **02** Expansive stage **03** Creamy-white curvilinear shell **04** Canopy detail

Photos: Hodgetts + Fung Design and Architecture

CITY Los Angeles (CA)
COUNTRY USA
REGION North America
TYPOLOGY Culture
COMPLETION 2004
WEBSITE www.hplusf.com
ARCHITECTS Hodgetts + Fung Design and Architecture

CITY Los Angeles (CA)
COUNTRY USA
REGION North America
TYPOLOGY Gastronomy
COMPLETION 2006
WEBSITE www.jfak.net
ARCHITECTS John Friedman Alice Kimm Architects

LUCKY DEVILS

The project, a new 2,000 square foot restaurant located in an existing storefront building on Hollywood Boulevard, contributes to the resurgence of the historic district. The target patrons are business people, families, tourists, and late night clubhoppers who want high quality "fast" food in a setting that is dynamic, warm, and authentic. The project utilizes a simple layout that includes a main eating area on one side of a central banquette and a high eating & drinking counter on the other. The contrasting materials and color include terrazzo, concrete, walnut, vinyl, wallpaper, stainless steel, aluminum, acrylic, glass, and mirror.

01 View from entrance **02** Dining area **03** Sections **04** Entrance

Photos: Benny Chan, Fotoworks

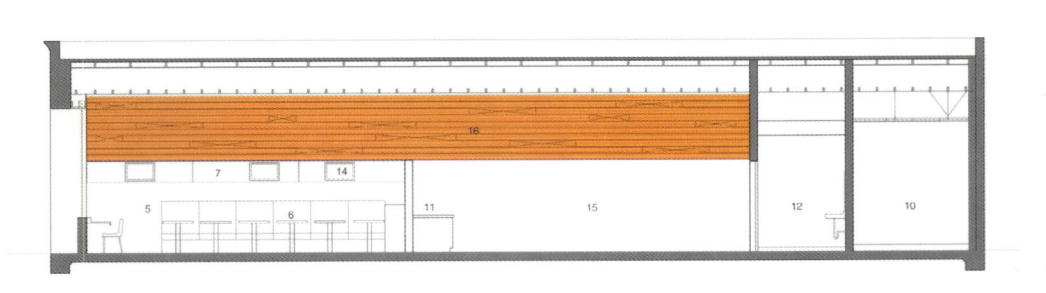

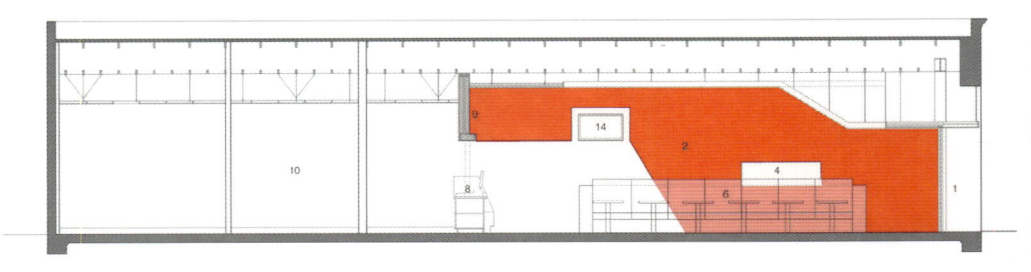

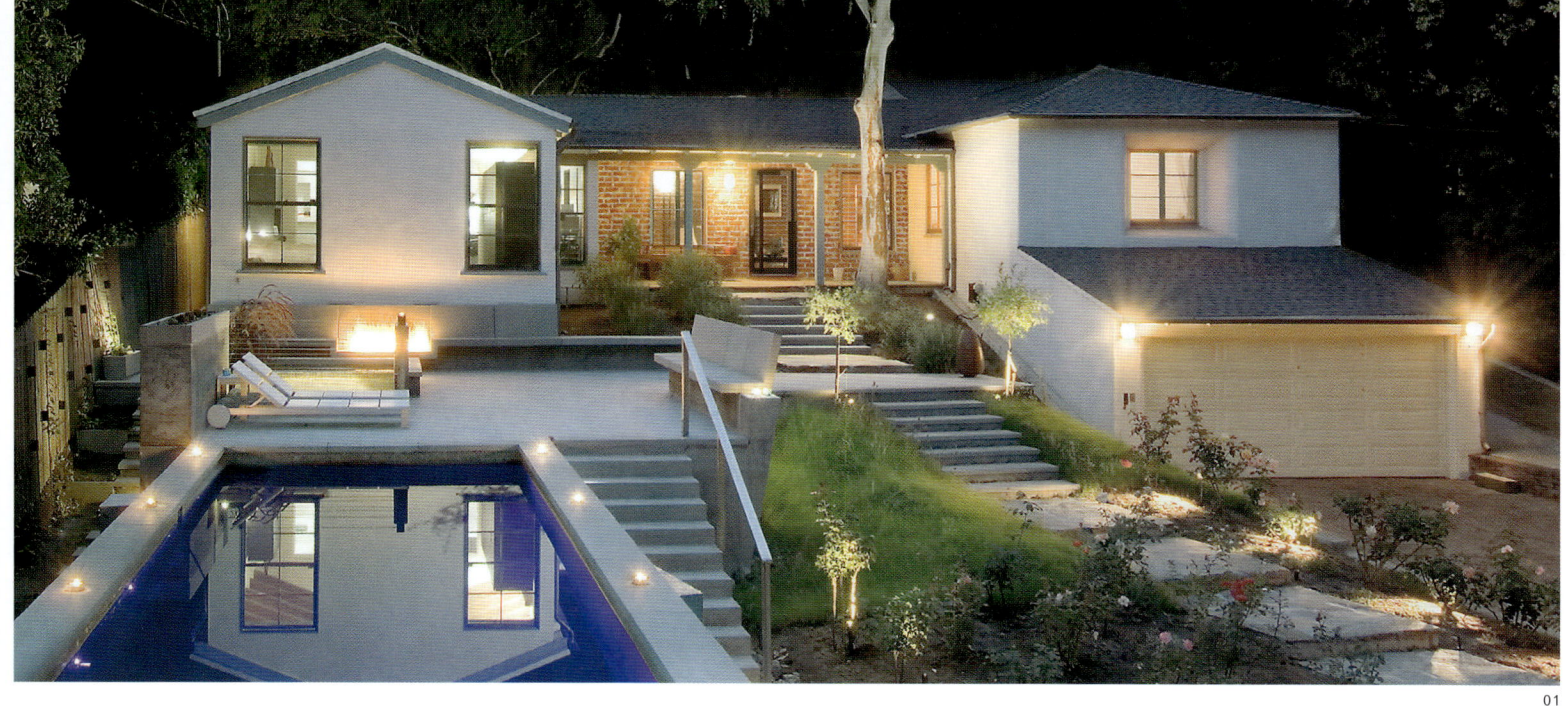

KAZOVSKY RENOVATION

Alla Kazovsky desired a home that would expertly marry new with existing elements to bring out the warmth she sensed from the house. In addition, she set out to create a design laboratory of her own where she could prototype, test, and showcase new ideas and products. Kazovsky completely renovated the house's interiors, opening the kitchen, creating a dining room and powder room, and expanding the bathrooms. The home features artwork by her daughters, demonstrating the collaboration between parent and children. The home represents a merging of old and new – in building, design, and attitude.

01 Exterior view **02** Deck and pool **03** Floor plan **04** Living room

Photos: Josh Perrin

CITY Los Angeles (CA)
COUNTRY USA
REGION North America
TYPOLOGY Living
COMPLETION 2007
WEBSITE www.designedrealestate.com
ARCHITECTS Alla Kazovsky (Designed Real Estate)

294

CITY
Los Angeles (CA)

COUNTRY
USA

REGION
North America

TYPOLOGY
Institution / Technology

COMPLETION
2007

WEBSITE
www.lblarch.com

ARCHITECTS
Lee Burkhart Liu Architects

HNRT

The Harlyne J. Norris Research Tower, part of the Norris Cancer Center at USC, centers on a light-filled ten-story circulation core that unites disparate buildings. The tower is a square concrete structure expressed in curves at the south side, with glass-and-steel side articulations that are angled on the west and orthogonal on the east. Consisting of flexible, transitional laboratories, providing wet, dry, and shared core labs, the biomedical research facility includes a 200-seat conference center, administrative offices, double-height lounge areas and meditation garden.

01 Fully glazed façade **02** Ground floor plan **03** Tower view **04** Bird's eye view of courtyard

Photos: Benny Chan, Fotoworks

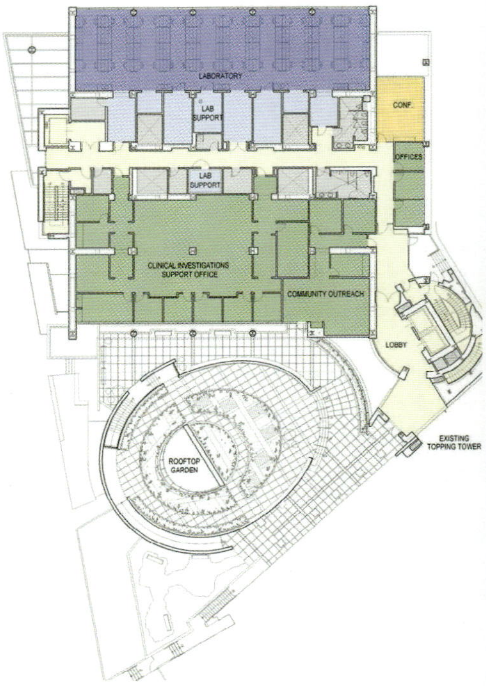

VIENNA WAY

This 4,100 square foot residence is located on a large lot that divides into thirds. The two main structures exist on the outer edges of the property and maximize the interaction between the indoor-outdoor space as well as the available land. A kitchen spans the two structures and is covered by a green roof. The northern wing contains the private living quarters that run from the rear of the property and end in an outdoor living space with a fireplace. The southern wing contains the formal, public spaces that begin in the front of the property and conclude in an outdoor dining area.

01 View of courtyard **02** Exterior view by night **03** Glazed sliding door **04** Living space **05** Kitchen

Photos: Joe Fletcher

CITY Los Angeles (CA)
COUNTRY USA
REGION North America
TYPOLOGY Living
COMPLETION 2007
WEBSITE www.marmol-radziner.com
ARCHITECTS Marmol Radziner and Associates

WARD RESIDENCE

Located in Rustic Canyon, the 4,000 square-foot residence is divided into two masses that are integrated within the hillside. The public space includes the kitchen, living room and dining areas, while the private space contains the bedrooms. Dividing the program into public and private spaces, the two main masses connected by a glass enclosed walkway, maximizes the space on the hillside, while minimizing the impact of the structures on the property. With filtering in the landscape, the site introduces a skewed procession that leads up to the pavilions and looks beyond to the additional structures.

01 View from street **02** Pool and courtyard **03** Fully glazed upper floor **04** Walkway

Photos: Benny Chan, Fotoworks

CITY: Los Angeles (CA)
COUNTRY: USA
REGION: North America
TYPOLOGY: Living
COMPLETION: 2003
WEBSITE: www.marmol-radziner.com
ARCHITECTS: Marmol Radziner and Associates

GREENFIELD RESIDENCE

This development is a simplistic, eco-conscious design that is focused on functionality and creating a breathing family environment, with an effort in using materials in their most organic form. Maximum use of natural light cuts down electrical cost, and a heated patio for outdoor dining maximizes outdoor/indoor living. Floor material connected in an unobtrusive manner increases the floor plan flow and space. The design and use of color inspired by a dramatic landscape creates a contrasting stimulating interior, while the kitchen island creates a multi-functional gathering point in the heart of the house.

01 Outdoor dining deck **02** Structural detail **03** Outdoor sleeping area **04** Eames wood lounge and stair case representing waterfall **05** First and second floor plan

Photos: Ralf Seeburger, Torfi Agnarsson (04)

CITY Los Angeles (CA)
COUNTRY USA
REGION North America
TYPOLOGY Living
COMPLETION 2007
WEBSITE www.minarc.com
ARCHITECTS Minarc

CITY Los Angeles (CA)
COUNTRY USA
REGION North America
TYPOLOGY Living
COMPLETION in progress
WEBSITE nocturnaldesignlab.com
ARCHITECTS n:dL [nocturnal design Lab]

AEROFORM – SUBSIDIZED URBAN LIVING MODULE

Aeroform is a prototype that explores the dimensionality of the urban billboard and creates a subsidized living module that would allow people with limited means to own a home. This fusion of the billboard and the house creates an opportunity for homeowners to generate income from the billboard. The prefabricated, lightweight unit is constructed off-site, shipped to the site, and grafted to the existing billboard structure. The outer shell is made of structural insulated panels covered with a layer of carbon fiber in order to reduce the weight of the structure and minimize any structural reinforcement to the existing billboard.

01 Module installation **02** Carbon fiber shell **03** Enclosure assembly **04** Plans **05** Billboard façade

Renderings: n:dL [nocturnal design Lab]

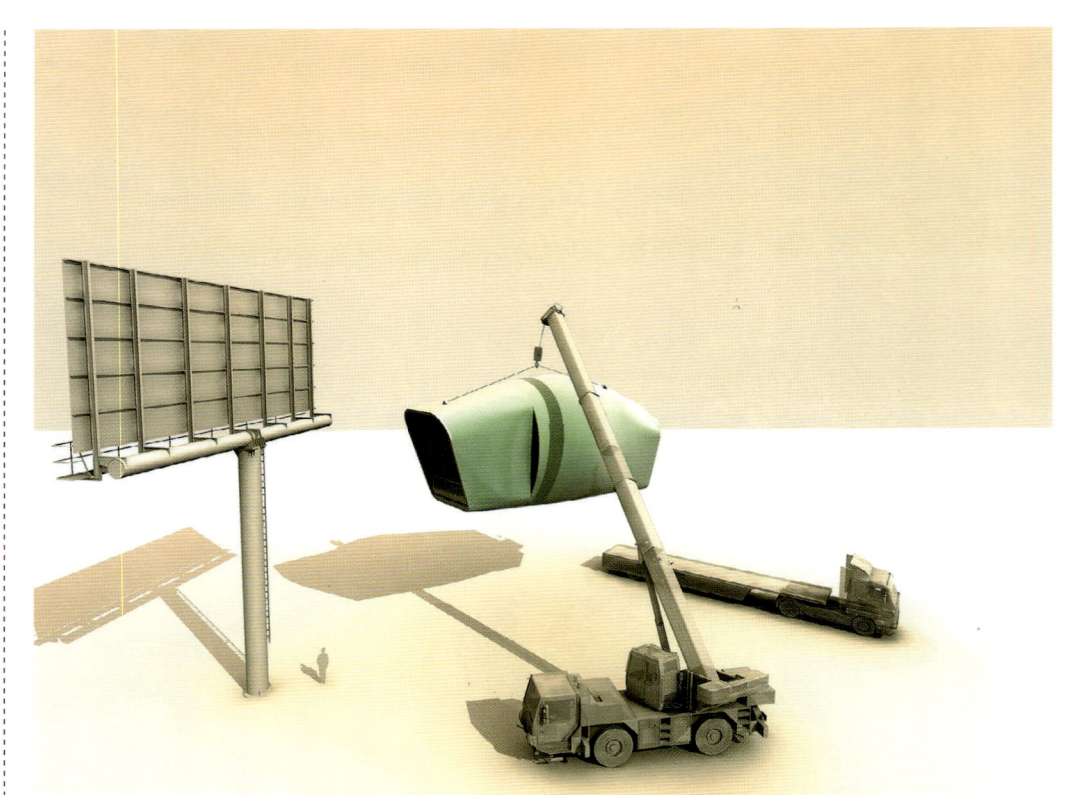

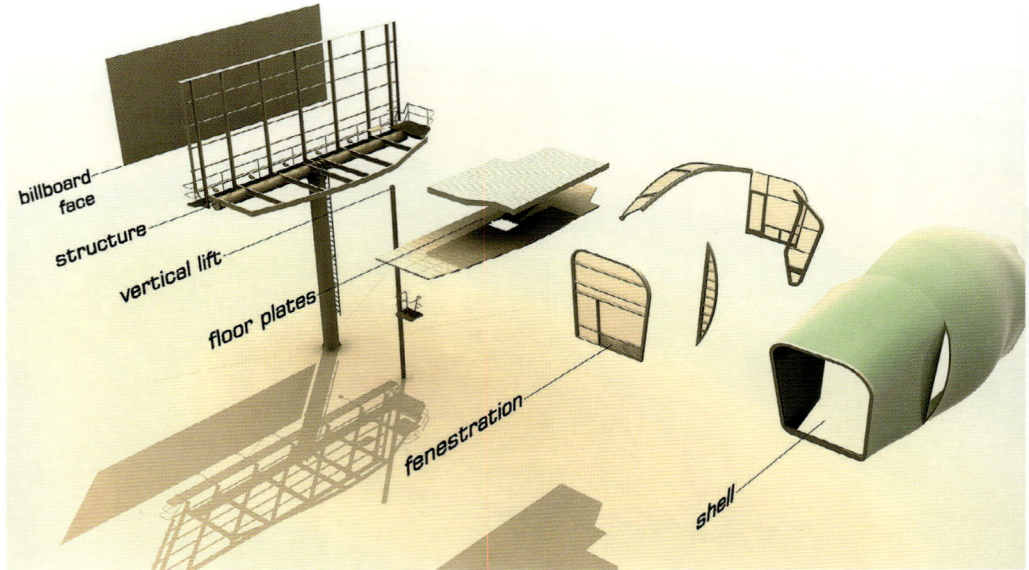

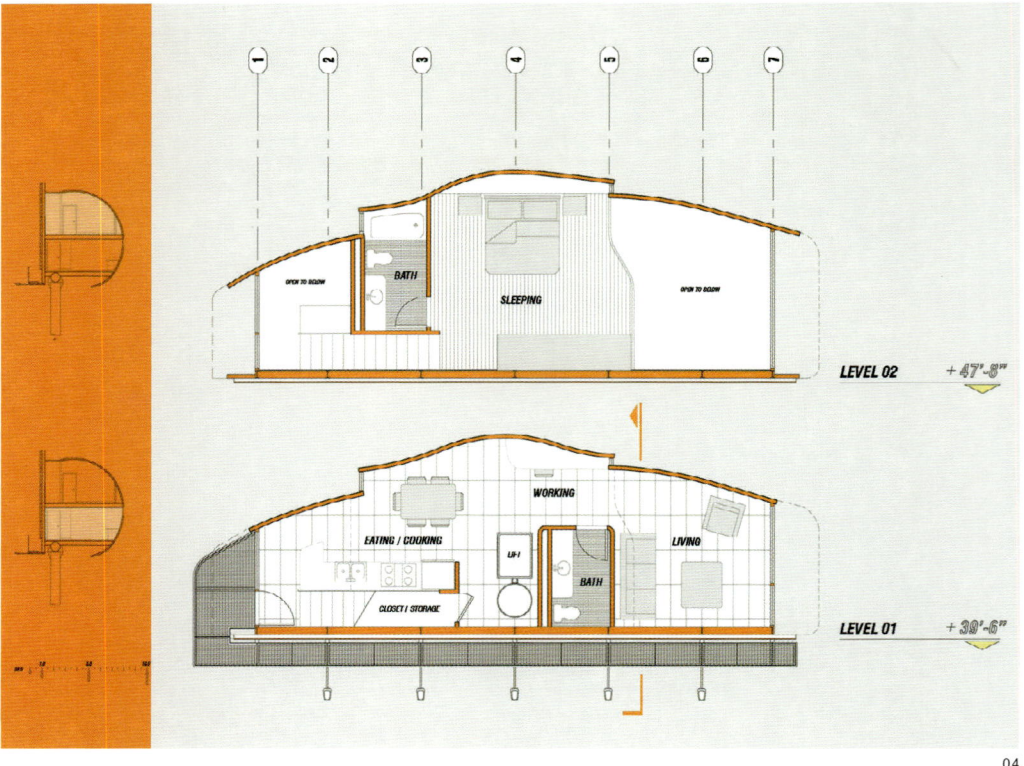

BROUGHTON STUDIO

Designed for a composer and located in the Bel Air area, this building is a simple two-story 1000- square-foot structure. The main purpose of the building is to provide the client with a private and serene workspace. The building is accessed via a descending ramp, which leads to the main space located on the upper floor, and contains a single open space that acts as the heart of the studio. The building is located in a heavily wooded ravine and conceived as a landscape object. Inspiration came from a rusty old tin can protruding from the wet mulch; an object which is artificial and foreign, yet friendly and unobtrusive.

01 Descending ramp into main entrance **02** Window detail **03** South view **04** Sketch **05** Outdoor space

Renderings: Alejandro Ortiz Architects

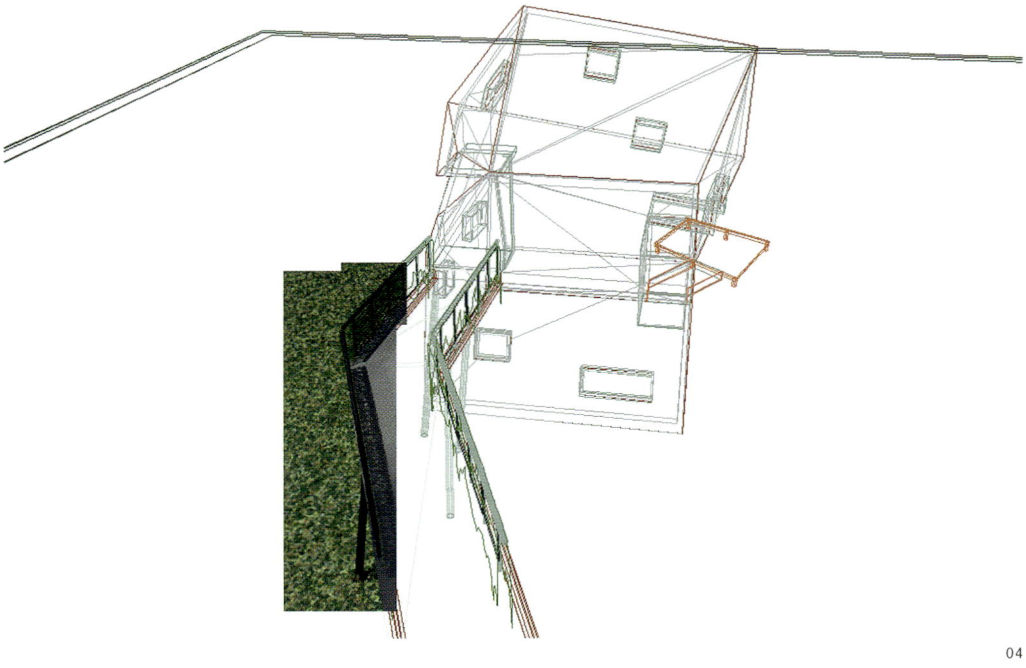

CITY Los Angeles (CA)

COUNTRY USA

REGION North America

TYPOLOGY Office

COMPLETION unbuilt

WEBSITE www.ortizarchitects.com

ARCHITECTS Alejandro Ortiz Architects

CITY Los Angeles (CA)

COUNTRY USA

REGION North America

TYPOLOGY Public

COMPLETION 2007

WEBSITE www.oylerwu.com

ARCHITECTS oyler wu collaborative

DENSITY FIELDS

The project is an investigation into the spatial qualities resulting from the strategic and site-specific buildup of material densities. This "extreme cantilever" built of aluminum and polypropylene rope, hovers over a courtyard in Silver Lake, Los Angeles. Defying classification as either sculpture or architecture, the piece flexes with a gesture that extends imaginary lines beyond the small courtyard, seeming to pierce buildings and features in the neighborhood. The goal was in balancing a set of structural ideas, the programmatic needs of space, and a desire to use basic geometries to create a rich spatial experience.

01 Interior view **02** View of luminum and polypropylene rope **03** Structure **04** Courtyard

Photos: Art Gray

CENTER OF COMMUNITIES OF FAITH

Seeking to educate, support and inspire harmonious work and dialogue among various faiths, this building's final design was inspired by clergy of numerous faiths. The architecture incorporates the use of sacred geometry and numeric principles. The golden ratio and other principles were frequently used in determining the dimensions of a floor plan, garden layout or even the dimensions of the towering beams that encircle the chapel. The layout of the chapel, with its attached amphitheater, is based on the "vesica piscis," which commonly symbolizes a sense of unity, God's eye and common ground.

01 Public plaza **02** View towards center **03** View up from chapel **04** Plan chapel and plaza paravant

Renderings: Paravant

CITY: Los Angeles (CA)
COUNTRY: USA
REGION: North America
TYPOLOGY: Public
COMPLETION: in progress
WEBSITE: www.paravant.org
ARCHITECTS: Paravant

OFF-USE

This live/work residence occupies a previously undeveloped corner lot. By fitting tightly to the site boundaries, the house is able to reclaim and regularize a maximal 25 x 100 foot landscape band. Comprised of three systems: a long galvanized metal wall folds over to serve as the roof and carport; a series of material samples separated by glass forms the envelope; and an exposed concrete slab on grade contains radiant heat, plumbing, electrical and up-lighting. This economy of means with regard to figural massing as well as building systems and materials allows off-use to address the two scales or speeds of the context: the major thoroughfare of Olympic Boulevard to the south, and the domestic neighborhood to the west and north.

01 Pool **02** Elevation from Olympic Boulevard **03** Site plan **04** Galvanized metal envelope

Photos: Deborah Bird, Brad Wheeler

CITY Los Angeles (CA)
COUNTRY USA
REGION North America
TYPOLOGY Living
COMPLETION 2004
WEBSITE www.pxsarchitecture.com
ARCHITECTS P XS (Linda Polari, Robert Somol)

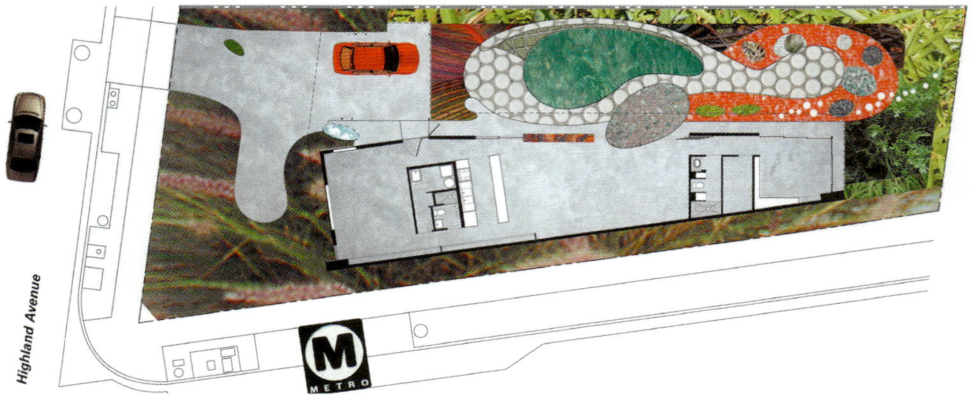

THE CALIFORNIA ENDOWMENT

The interdisciplinary design firm of Rios Clementi Hale Studios created the building and landscape design as a bold, colorful centerpiece that visually connects the area's disparate ethnic communities, honors the surrounding urban context, and espouses the tenets of transparency, openness, and health. The building is light, crisp, accented with lively colors, and is generously nurtured with green plantings and connections to the outdoors. Instead of a single, monolithic edifice, the facility is organized into three connecting volumes that reflect the varying scales of the area's built environment.

01 Outdoor area **02** Courtyard **03** Aerial view **04** Section **05** Planted courtyard

Photos: Tom Bonner Photography, Lisa Romerien (05)

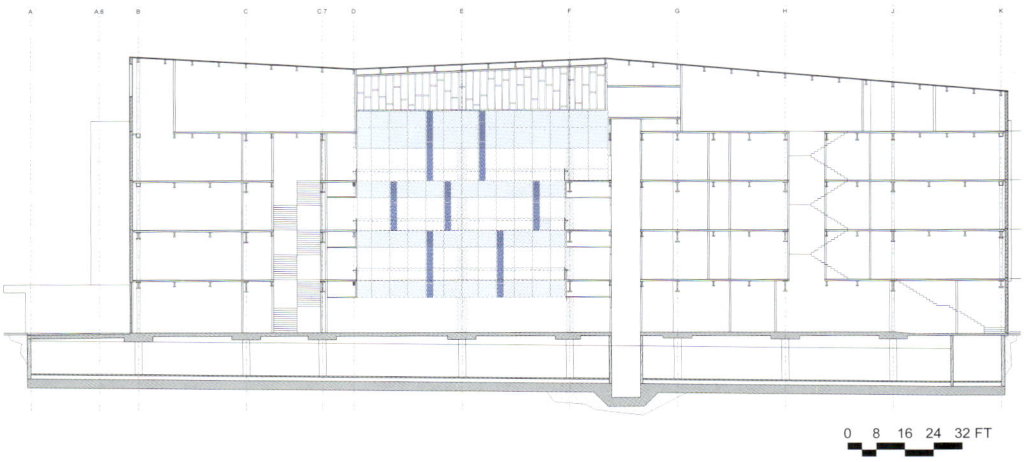

CITY: Los Angeles (CA)
COUNTRY: USA
REGION: North America
TYPOLOGY: Institution
COMPLETION: 2006
WEBSITE: rchstudios.com
ARCHITECTS: Rios Clementi Hale Studios

CITY Los Angeles (CA)
COUNTRY USA
REGION North America
TYPOLOGY Living
COMPLETION 2006
WEBSITE www.ripplesite.com
ARCHITECTS Ripple Design

COURTYARD HOUSE

This residence straddles the seemingly desperate notions of urbanity and privacy. The defining courtyard reveals itself as a kind of plaza on a micro-urban scale ideal for relaxing or entertaining. Many of the materials are sustainably forested, long-lasting and break down easily in landfills. The ultimate choice is to improve the quality of life in order to reduce the perceived need — especially in a city like Los Angeles — to wander so frequently from home. Utilizing passive strategies of climatic control reduced ecological footprint to the greater community, it also folds in a premium quality of life for its inhabitants. Just one example of this is the courtyard doors. When opened, the outside becomes the inside of the house.

01 Exterior view by night **02** View into courtyard **03** Indoor-outdoor space **04** Ground floor plan

Photos: Marla Aufmuth Photographer

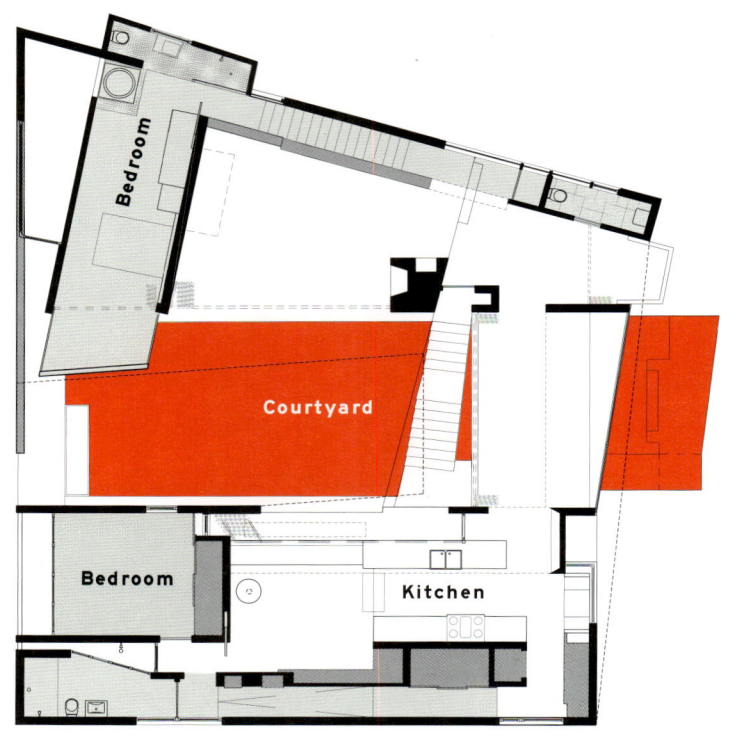

BEUTH RESIDENCE

Perched on a steep, nearly 45-degree grade, the structure provides four levels of panoramic vistas of the Los Angeles basin below. The residence features a crisp concrete plinth base of two levels, housing a full suite of entertaining components, including parking garages, living areas, a screening room, billiards room, gymnasium, wine cellar, disco lounge and weight room. Teak panels clad the upper level of the house, floating as if on air, above an all-glass main level. Jutting off the master bedroom, a Miesian sitting room steals 180-degree views of the city.

01 Swimming pool **02** Concrete plinth base and teak panles façade **03** Elevation **04** Interior

Photos: John Edward Linden Photography

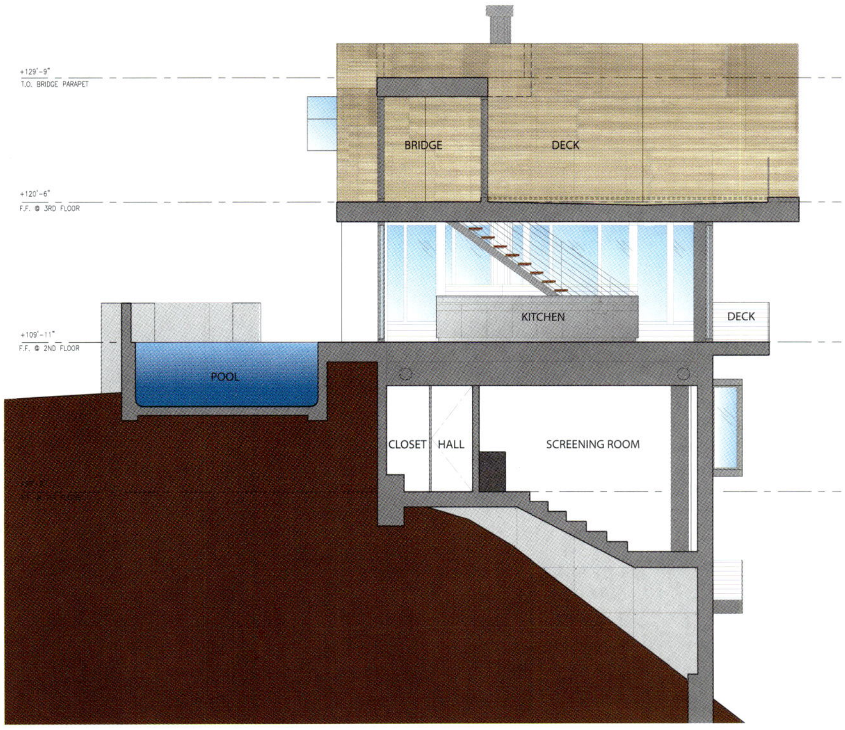

CITY
Los Angeles (CA)

COUNTRY
USA

REGION
North America

TYPOLOGY
Living

COMPLETION
2005

WEBSITE
www.spfa.com

ARCHITECTS
SPFarchitects Studio
Pali Fekete architects

CITY Los Angeles (CA)
COUNTRY USA
REGION North America
TYPOLOGY Living
COMPLETION 2002
WEBSITE www.spfa.com
ARCHITECTS SPF:architects Studio Pali Fekete architects

SOMIS HAY BARN

The design concept is inspired by the use of hay as barn cladding. When hay is stacked along the outer storage shelves in the winter, it is green; as the season unfolds, the hay turns yellow, and the caretaker removes it from the shelves as it is used for feed. Both factors keep the façade in a constant state of evolution. The building is a metaphor for life, death and birth, common seasonal themes in an agrarian society. The bales of hay animate the visual experience of the barn and simultaneously provide insulation. The building has ample natural ventilation a roof overhang to protect the cladding from rain.

01 Breezeway **02** Hay façade **03** Steel structure **04** Floor plan

Photos: John Edward Linden Photography

ANIMO FILM AND THEATRE ARTS HIGH SCHOOL

The Animo Film and Theatre Arts High School involves the adaptive re-use of an existing industrial building and its conversion into a carbon-neutral high school for inner-city students in Central Los Angeles. In the process of redesigning Studio Shift in collaboration with Arup Engineers merged seamlessly progressive architecture with the latest research in sustainable building strategies. The result is a didactic structure with a harmonious blend of nature and technology where students have the ability to reconfigure internal spaces to suit daily learning needs.

01 Vines growing over façade **02** Overall view **03** Clerestoy windows **04** Solar energy canopy

Renderings: Studio Shift

CITY Los Angeles (CA)
COUNTRY USA
REGION North America
TYPOLOGY Education
COMPLETION unrealized
WEBSITE www.studioshift.com
ARCHITECTS Studio Shift

EL CENTRO DEL PUEBLO

El Centro Del Pueblo is a community-based, nonprofit social service agency in the Echo Park area of Los Angeles, serving at-risk and gang-involved youth, as well as court-referred offenders and their families. A run-down office building reborn as a vibrant youth recreation center, the program includes boxing and weights studio, a dance and martial arts studio, a youth drop-in center and lounge, a library/computer-lab, classrooms, and bathroom facilities. An opening between the first and second level creates a two-story reception/entry space, connecting the two visually while allowing light to penetrate into the hallways.

01 Section **02** Hallway **03** Exterior view **04** Front façade
05 Windows for natural light

Photos: Courtesy Fernando Vasquez Studio

CITY Los Angeles (CA)
COUNTRY USA
REGION North America
TYPOLOGY Education
COMPLETION 2003
WEBSITE www.studiofv.com
ARCHITECTS Fernando Vazquez Studio

ALAN-VOO FAMILY HOUSE

The goal of this renovation and extension project was the addition of 1,000-square-foot of space to the existing 1,000-square-foot house. The scheme leaves half of the house for the daughter's bedrooms and incorporates the other half plus new extensions in front and back into a public zone and a private bedroom for the parents. This strategy amounts to a new 16-foot wide linear house being inserted into the existing house. Multitoned, bright colors accentuate the new pieces, which suggests a graphic expression representative of the family's interests.

01 New house insertion into existing **02** Interior structural detail **03** Kitchen **04** Exterior view by night **05** Overall view

Photos: Benny Chan, Fotoworks

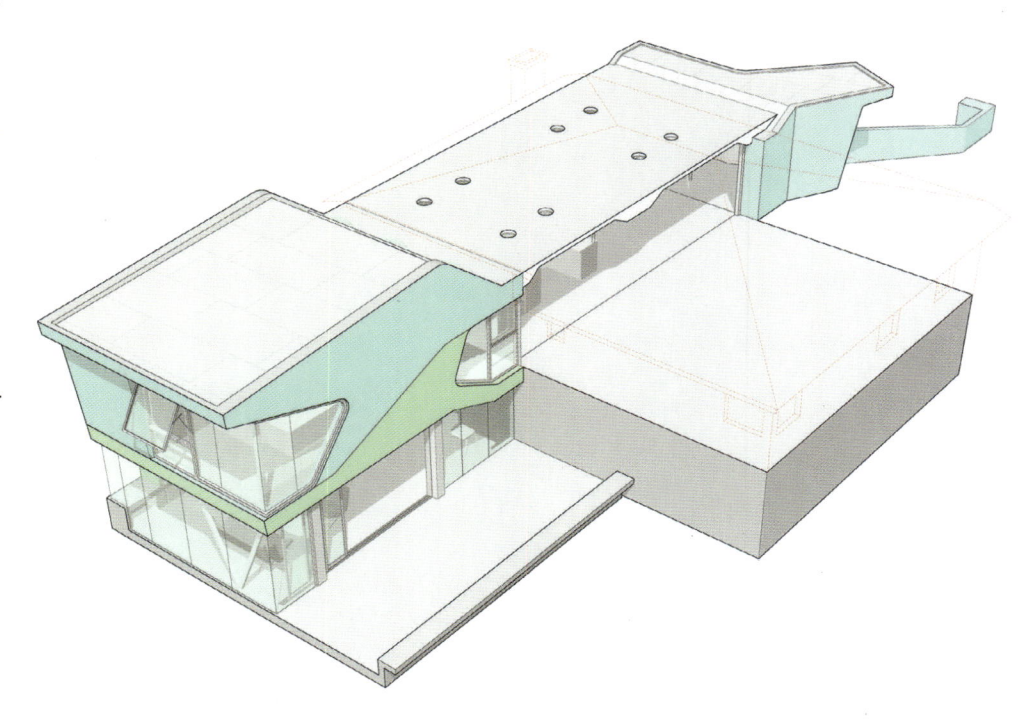

CITY Los Angeles (CA)
COUNTRY USA
REGION North America
TYPOLOGY Living
COMPLETION 2007
WEBSITE www.nmda-inc.com
ARCHITECTS Neil M. Denari Architects, Inc.

CITY: Los Angeles (CA), South Central
COUNTRY: USA
REGION: North America
TYPOLOGY: –
COMPLETION: 2004
WEBSITE: www.null-lab.com
ARCHITECTS: Arshia+Reza [null:lab]

BOBCO METALS

Bobco Metals is a metal distribution and fabrication company located in the South Central district of LA, initiated by the idea to improve the existing warehouse structure to accommodate for new offices and a showroom. Situated along the Alameda corridor, the harsh urban vibe bestowed a kind of dramatic merit on a landscape covered by deteriorated concrete and littered with graffiti. The remix of steel and hardware represents the structure of a "desire machine", while the de-gravitating metallic particles and forms themselves, shape a „crystalline narration" in response to the strange and disturbed nature of its milieu.

01 Interior **02** Remix of steel and hardware **03** Façade
04 Exploded isonometric

Photos: Tara Wujcik + Barbara Runcie (01, 02),
Benny Chan, Fotoworks (03)

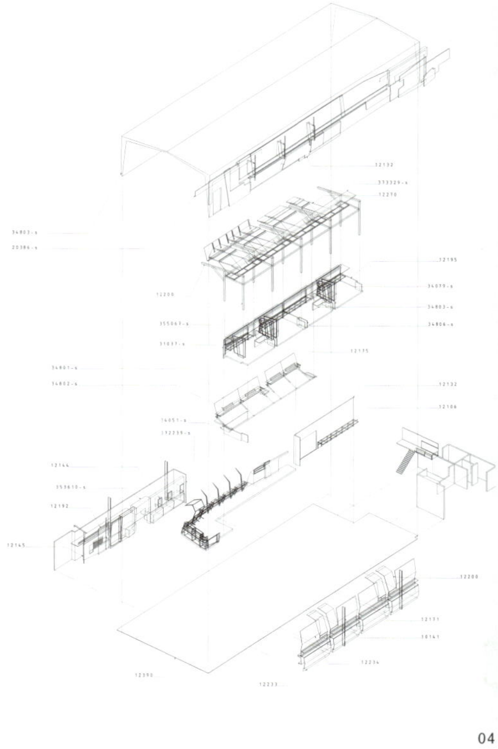

SOUND CITY

Sound City is an urban development study for downtown Los Angeles that explores the use of sound as an architectural design tool. The programmatic outline was to add a variety of public spaces to the site in combination with mixed use development. The design concept was to generate a master plan in which building envelopes and massing are determined not only by zoning regulations, sightlines and the city grid, but are shaped by sound clouds recorded on the site and transformed into a three dimensional Gestalt. This became the starting point for a series of spatial prototypes that occupy the existing grid structure and envelope.

01 Mixed-use tower façade **02** Siteplan **03** Flex shelter
04 Mixed-use tower **05** Interior **06** Model

Renderings, photos: B+U, LLP

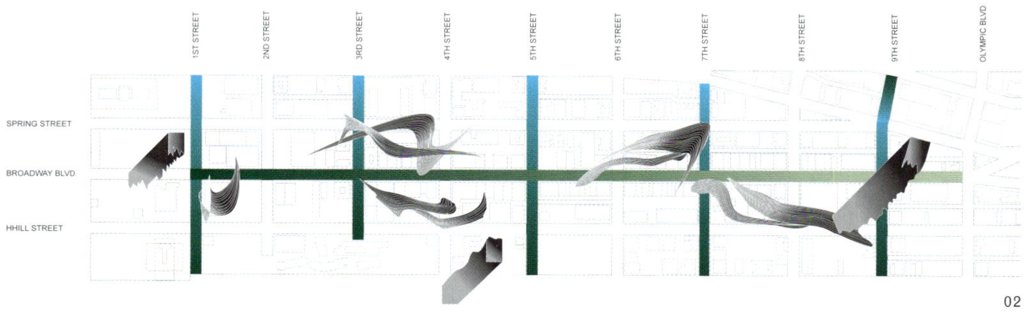

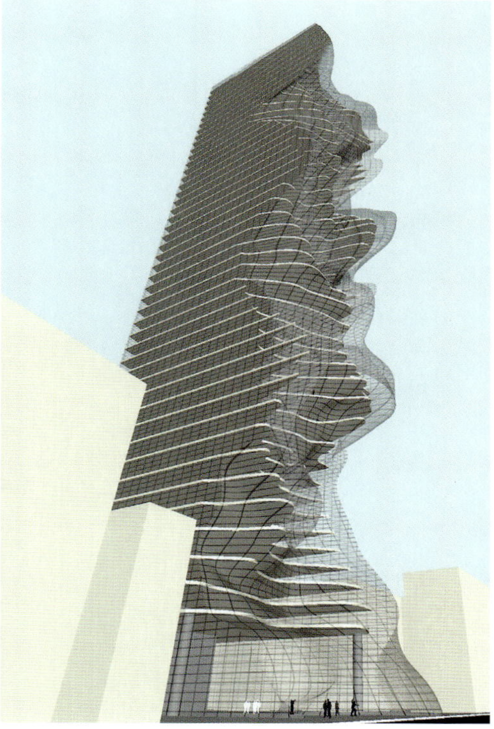

CITY
Los Angeles (CA)

COUNTRY
USA

REGION
North America

TYPOLOGY
Urban Development

COMPLETION
unbuilt

WEBSITE
www.bplusu.com

ARCHITECTS
B+U, LLP Baumgartner & Uriu

CITY Los Angeles (CA)
COUNTRY USA
REGION North America
TYPOLOGY Culture
COMPLETION unrealized
WEBSITE www.coalabs.com
ARCHITECTS COA: Central Office of Architecture

(N)QMA: NEW QUEENS MUSEUM OF ART

The conceptual approach to the Museum constructs a set of scenarios that engage the immediate future of the institution as well as provide a provisional long view. By conceptualizing the museum as a place determined by the interplay between the past and an ongoing present, the (N)QMA will move from an identity based on static exhibition to one based on change and interaction. The driving strategic concept stacks a densely programmed local campus floor over a fast global public floor. The mat organization produces a spectrum of different conditions including mutable programs, multiple events and catalytic combinations.

01 Entry ramp **02** Three distinly different floors **03** Roof garden with sculpture gallery **04** Diagrammatic layers

Renderings: COA: Central Office of Architecture

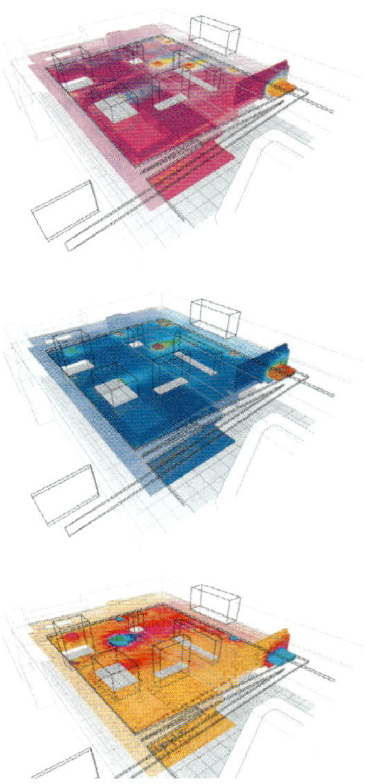

SNAKE COMING OUT OF A METAL CAGE

Located almost at the top of the hill, this project's design concept is based on a metal box (the cage) that includes most living spaces, and in its shape, pays homage to the late bungalow and a 8-inch thick flesh colored stucco ribbon (the snake) that creeps in and out of the box generating all the miscellaneous events in the front and rear façade, which includes an entry canopy, balcony, roof deck, office and storage room. To improve the view compromised by wonderfully overgrown eucalyptus trees and development, a third floor studio was added with a roof deck providing an updated version of the "lookout".

01 Rear balcony **02** Office and roof deck **03** Front entrance **04** Night view

Photos: Alex Vasilescu

CITY Los Angeles (CA)
COUNTRY USA
REGION North America
TYPOLOGY Living
COMPLETION 2006
WEBSITE www.vergaraarchitects.com
ARCHITECTS Daniel Vergara Architecture

CITY Los Angeles (CA)
COUNTRY USA
REGION North America
TYPOLOGY Institution
COMPLETION 2005
WEBSITE www.hplusf.com
ARCHITECTS Hodgetts + Fung Design and Architecture

HYDE PARK MIRIAM MATTHEWS BRANCH LIBRARY

The architects designed Hyde Park Library to reflect the exuberance of the neighboring community. The vibrant culture and history of South Los Angeles informed much of the building's design, which is marked by a vigorous layering of materials and angled forms. The exterior's linear presence—a pleated layer of moss-colored cement board and copper-tinted steel—gives way to the dynamic interface of glass, metal grating, cement board, and copper-tinted steel that converges and pivots. Elements that diverge in various directions and orientations lend a vibrant texture to the open interior space.

01 Moss-colored cement board **02** Cooper-tinted steel structure **03** Site plan **04** Support detail

Photos: Benny Chan, Fotoworks,
Hodgetts + Fung Design and Architecture (01)

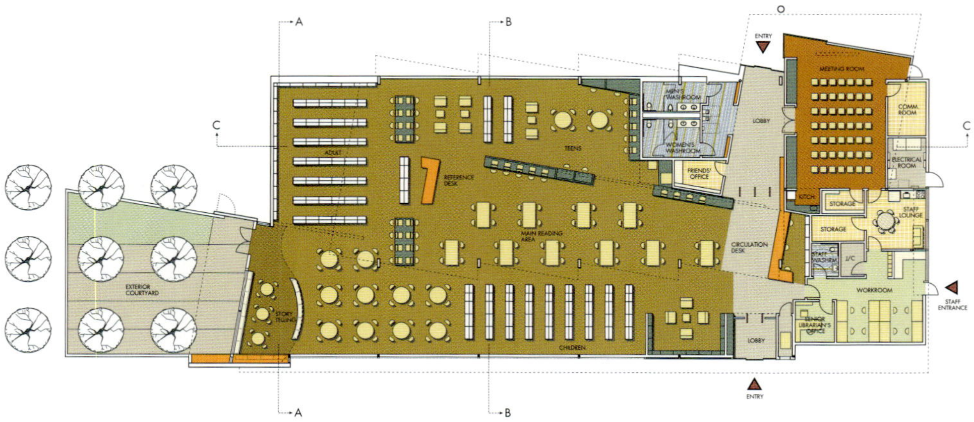

FUNG+BLATT RESIDENCE

This residence is an environment that evolves with the occupant's changing needs. Accessible via a garden, the living space culminates in north-facing clerestories that provide even light and passive cooling throughout the day. A central open stair organizes public spaces into living and service functions, and links a study to the private spaces above. Around the exterior, a living terrace bridges to a dining patio leading to the upper garden, from which one can re-enter the house. The design presents a circularity of movement that pleasantly challenges our perception of where we stand and of where a path begins and ends.

01 Exterior view by night **02** Staircase **03** Section **04** Fireplace **05** Living space

Photos: Deborah Bird, David Lauridsen

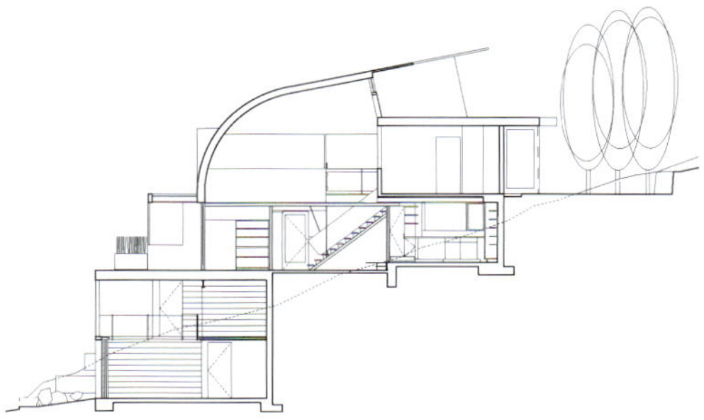

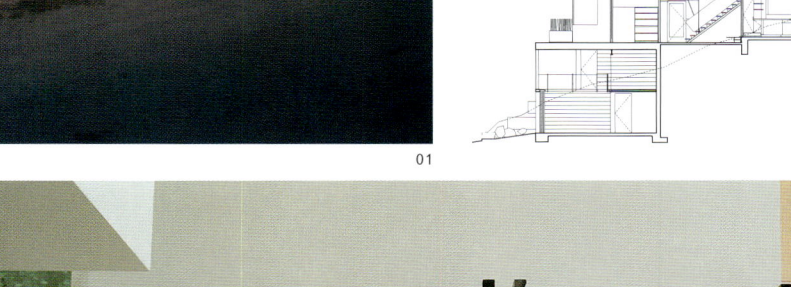

CITY Los Angeles (CA)
COUNTRY USA
REGION North America
TYPOLOGY Living
COMPLETION 2003
WEBSITE www.fungandblatt.com
ARCHITECTS Fung + Blatt Architects, Inc

MIYOSHI RESIDENCE

This 1,500 square foot house perches lightly on a ridge and projects outward to command a panoramic view. An internal open stairwell with a suspended stair connects a mezzanine study, the daytime functions at mid-level, and the nighttime functions below. Three levels of inverted gable trusses diminish the apparent weight, allowing the building to appear to float. The combination of wood elements and reflective metal cladding creates a state of suspension between the open sky and the wooded surroundings, while the rectangular and wide-angled shapes infuse a dynamic character into the structure.

01 Rear view **02** Exterior view by night from ridge **03** Lower floor plan **04** Balcony **05** Section

Photos: Deborah Bird, Alice Fung

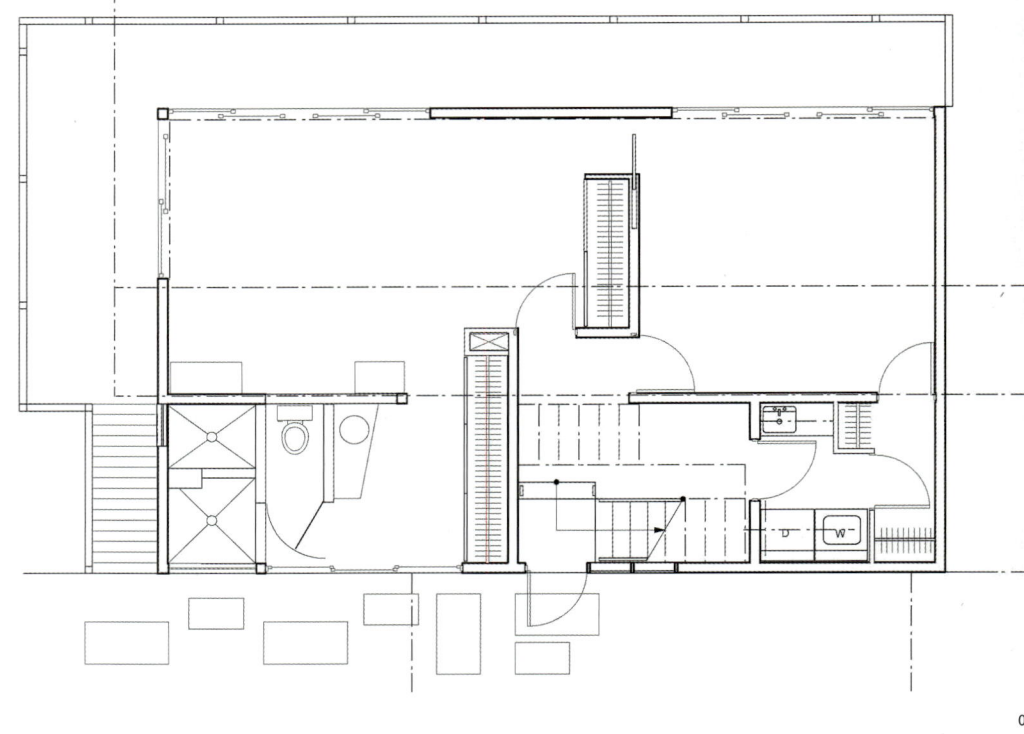

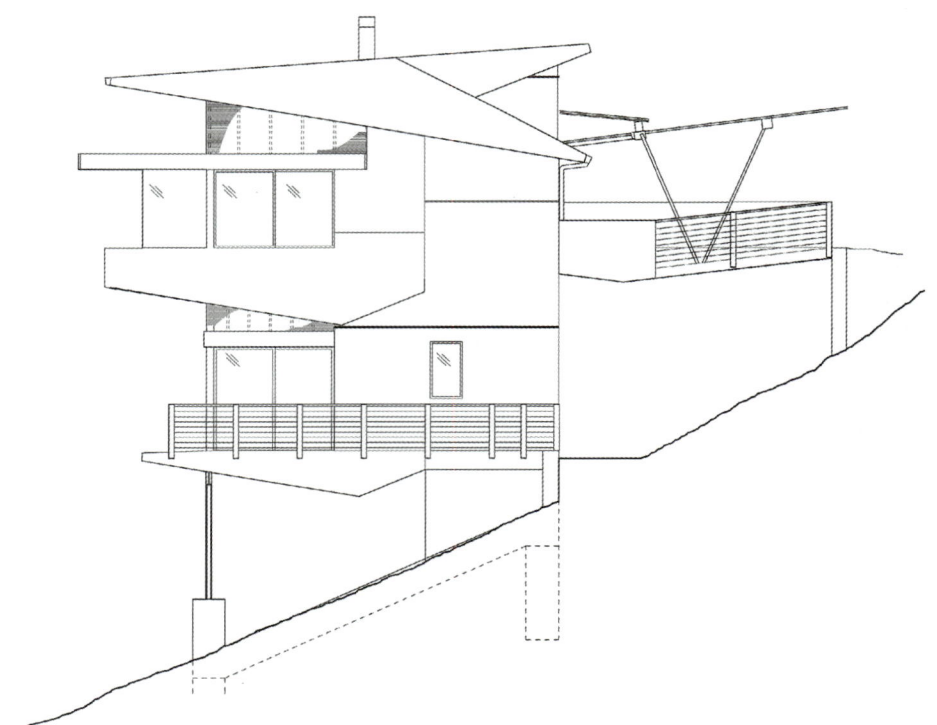

CITY Los Angeles (CA)
COUNTRY USA
REGION North America
TYPOLOGY Living
COMPLETION 2004
WEBSITE www.fungandblatt.com
ARCHITECTS Fung + Blatt Architects, Inc

LA LOFT

The loft is located in an existing warehouse in downtown L.A., and is designed as a live-work environment for a creative professional. The angular geometry of the faceted stone monolith initiates a dialog with the harmoniously shaped elliptical room. Technology is used to control the environment as well as to design and create space. The building materials were chosen for their light reflecting properties. Raised flooring transforms into lounge seating and a desk. A spa area features a stylized garden and a floating fireplace. Undulating curved walls create a womb-like kitchen enclosure.

01 Interior view **02** Working space **03** Interior **04** Kitchen **05** Floor plan

Photos: Art Gray

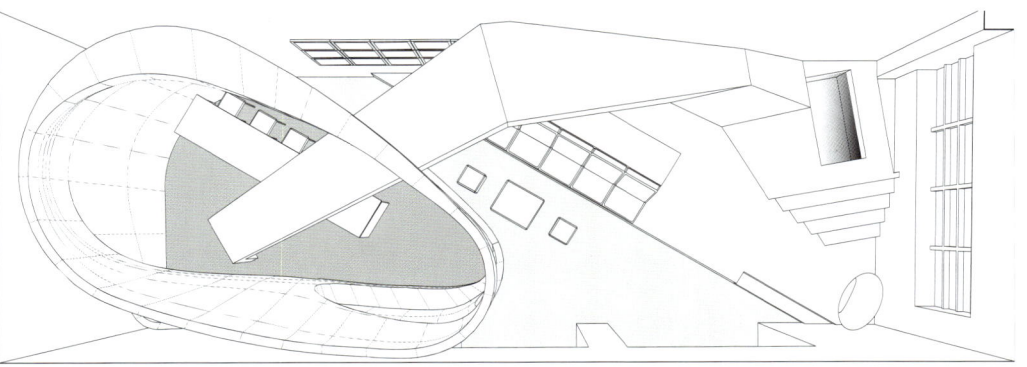

CITY
Los Angeles (CA)

COUNTRY
USA

REGION
North America

TYPOLOGY
Living

COMPLETION
2007

WEBSITE
www.tighearchitecture.com

ARCHITECTS
Tighe Architecture

CITY Los Angeles (CA)

COUNTRY USA

REGION North America

TYPOLOGY Education

COMPLETION 2003

WEBSITE www.cxcarch.com

ARCHITECTS Cigolle X Coleman, Architects

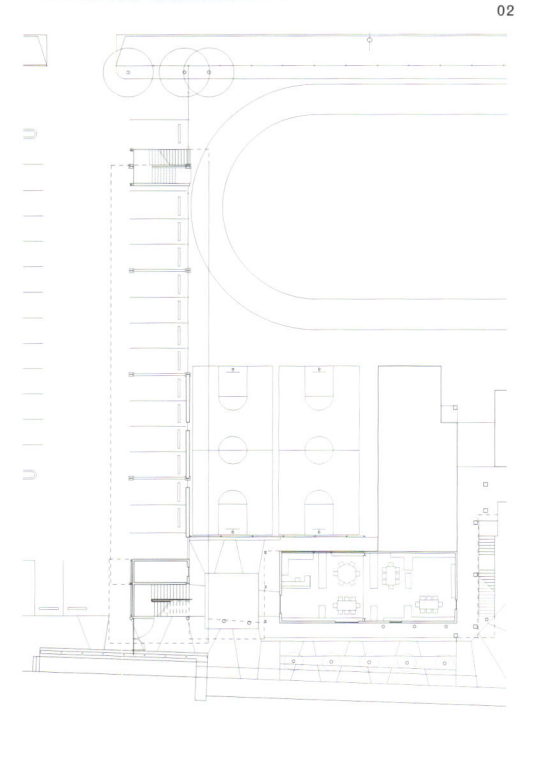

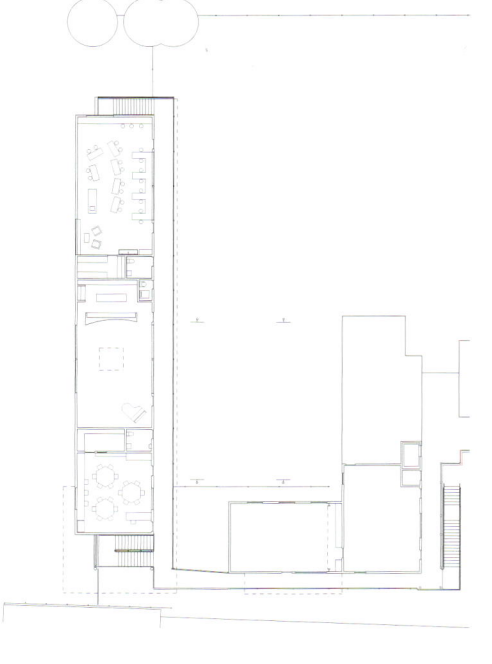

BUILDING 9, WILDWOOD ELEMENTARY SCHOOL, LOS ANGELES

Wildwood Elementary School by Cigolle X Coleman inhabits an aggregation of nine separate buildings. Among these buildings is the newest structure, known as Building 9, which hovers over the edge of the parking lot. The site strategy preserves the existing buildings in a couple ways. The first of these revolving around its capability to save as much positive outdoor open space as possible, and the second of these strategies allowing the construction to occur without disrupting the functioning of the campus. The new construction both complements the aggregation and provides a frame to complete the campus.

01 Building over parking lot **02** Structural detail **03** Galvanized metal façade **04** Floor plans

Photos: Cigolle X Coleman

ELYSIAN PARK RESIDENCE

The clients purchased a site located in the hills overlooking Los Angeles to the west and bordering Dodger Stadium. The desire was to maintain certain open, borderless conditions of the public programs, while at the same time recognize the more domestic need for sequestered, private spaces for guests and a future family. The building envelope stratifies into two floors, where complementary trays of space are connected by a single stair. While the lower floor is methodically deployed as a series of cells or units of privacy, the upper floor is continuous and transparent, vaporizing like a cloud hovering above the land.

01 Rear façade **02** Interior living space **03** Elevations **04** Outdoor space

Photos: Courtesy of COA: Central Office of Architecture

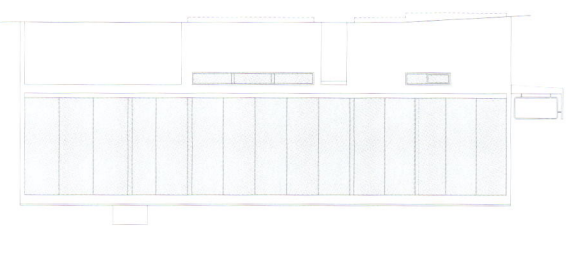

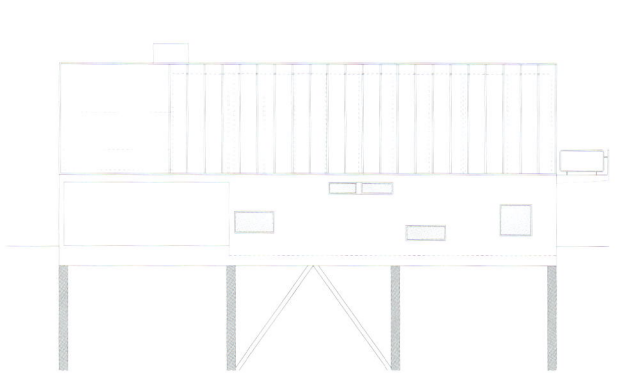

CITY
Los Angeles (CA)

COUNTRY
USA

REGION
North America

TYPOLOGY
Living

COMPLETION
2003

WEBSITE
www.coalabs.com

ARCHITECTS
COA: Central Office of Architecture

CITY Los Angeles (CA)

COUNTRY USA

REGION North America

TYPOLOGY Gastronomy

COMPLETION in progress

WEBSITE www.darosaward.com

ARCHITECTS dRW-build

PIZZA RIO

The da Rosa Ward design firm concept was to create a pizzeria in the Culver City area of Los Angeles County. Because this area is highly saturated with a number of Brazilian restaurants, the firm incorporated the rich history of Brazil's famed Corcovado Mountain, which is located in Rio de Janeiro, dubbing this project "Pizza Rio". This merged the familiarity of one of Brazil's largest cities with a small, yet superb, Brazilian restaurant. The logo and design symbolically incorporate the eye-catching curves of the Corcovado's two little mountains, creating an exciting experience for restaurant goers.

01 Curved wooden slats interior **02** Outdoor seating area **03** Ordering counter and kitchen area **04** View of exterior by night

Renderings: dRW-design lab

BROAD CAFE @ SCI_ARC / INTERSTITIAL SENSATIONS

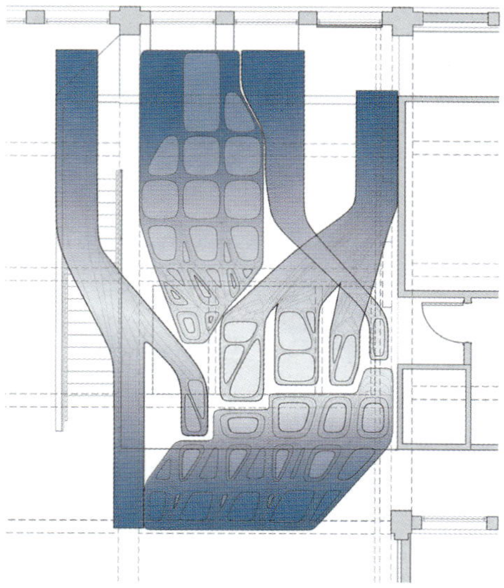

Located adjacent to the Santa Fe entry, the project creates an intensive atmosphere of light, color and material, inducing social exchange and enhancing body sensations. The ground level is dedicated to the Café and preparation kitchen, while the Student Lounge on the upper level is organized as a free plan with modulating lighting effects. Continuity through the two levels is achieved through a ceiling funnel system, redirecting natural light coming from the windows and skylight on the existing building. A gradient finish of bluish grey indexes the transition between natural and artificial light.

01 Student lounge **02** Ceiling plan **03** Cafe and preparation kitchen **04** Front view **05** Lower level floor plan

Photos: P.A.T.T.E.R.N.S.

CITY Los Angeles (CA)
COUNTRY USA
REGION North America
TYPOLOGY Gastronomy
COMPLETION 2008
WEBSITE www.p-a-t-t-e-r-n-s.net
ARCHITECTS P.A.T.T.E.R.N.S. Marcelo Spina

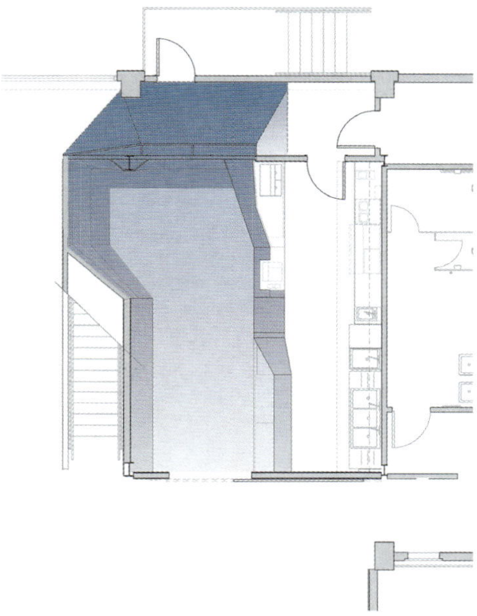

CITY Los Angeles (CA)
COUNTRY USA
REGION North America
TYPOLOGY Education
COMPLETION 2005
WEBSITE www.jfak.net
ARCHITECTS John Friedman Alice Kimm Architects

ARAGON AVENUE ELEMENTARY SCHOOL CLASSROOM BUILDING AND LUNCH SHELTER

Located in the Cypress Park neighborhood of Los Angeles, this addition to an existing elementary school contributes to the extensive rebuilding program undertaken by the Unified School District. Composed of three different structures, the largest is a 3 story building that provides parking for the school's staff as well as sixteen classrooms. The siting of the new structures creates a coherent campus plan. Adding a wing to the existing L-shaped structure, the new classroom bar completes the street edge and defines a central courtyard. Within this courtyard, the new kitchen and lunch shelter creates a series of outdoor rooms

01 Floor plan **02** Exterior view from the courtyard **03** Entrance area **04** Courtyard with benches

Photos: Benny Chan, Fotoworks

L.A. DESIGN CENTER

The L.A. Design Center renovated two run-down warehouses to result in 80,000 sq.ft. of furniture showrooms and tenant space. The project also transformed the parking lot between the warehouses into a hybridized motor court and event space – the social heart of the project. The buildings are layered with a textured, heterogeneous palette of materials and screens that seem permanent and impermanent at the same time. By turns hiding, revealing, and filtering aspects of the original buildings and the surrounding environment, they animate what is original while also enriching the public event space as an outdoor foyer for the complex.

01 Billboard and fence 02 Public event space 03 Floor plan
04 Detail entrance area

Photos: Benny Chan, Fotoworks

CITY: Los Angeles (CA)
COUNTRY: USA
REGION: North America
TYPOLOGY: Commercial
COMPLETION: 2004
WEBSITE: www.jfak.net
ARCHITECTS: John Friedman
Alice Kimm Architects

CITY	Los Angeles (CA)
COUNTRY	USA
REGION	North America
TYPOLOGY	Leisure
COMPLETION	2008
WEBSITE	www.xtenarchitecture.com
ARCHITECTS	XTEN Architecture

SAPPHIRE

Sapphire is a gallery addition that displays a growing art collection while allowing for glass façades and views of the surrounding hills. The building geometry is articulated as a large tapered double cantilever, allowing for three separate galleries and a minimal building footprint. The south façade and inclined roof are clad in solar cells customized into a diamond array, a pattern that continues on the other façades in perforated aluminum. A ceramic frit gradient applied to the insulated glass and specialized façade shutters further modulate the natural daylight and protect the artworks.

01 Total view **02** Detail view from outside **03** Detail view from inside **04** Interior: gallery space

Renderings: XTEN Architecture

PRIVATE RESIDENCE

Situated on a wooded, four-acre property in a residential community in Southern California, this residence is reachable only by passing through a gate, traveling down a long curving driveway and crossing over a natural stream. The primary concept for the residence was to design a home that incorporated modernist philosophy while being well adapted to today's contemporary lifestyle. Paul Goldberger, a noted architecture critic for the New Yorker magazine, calls the home "an essay in modernism...particularly sumptuous, with a dignity and a precision of detail."

01 Main view by night **02** Deck and pool area **03** Floor plans **04** Interior view

Photos: Erhard Pfeiffer

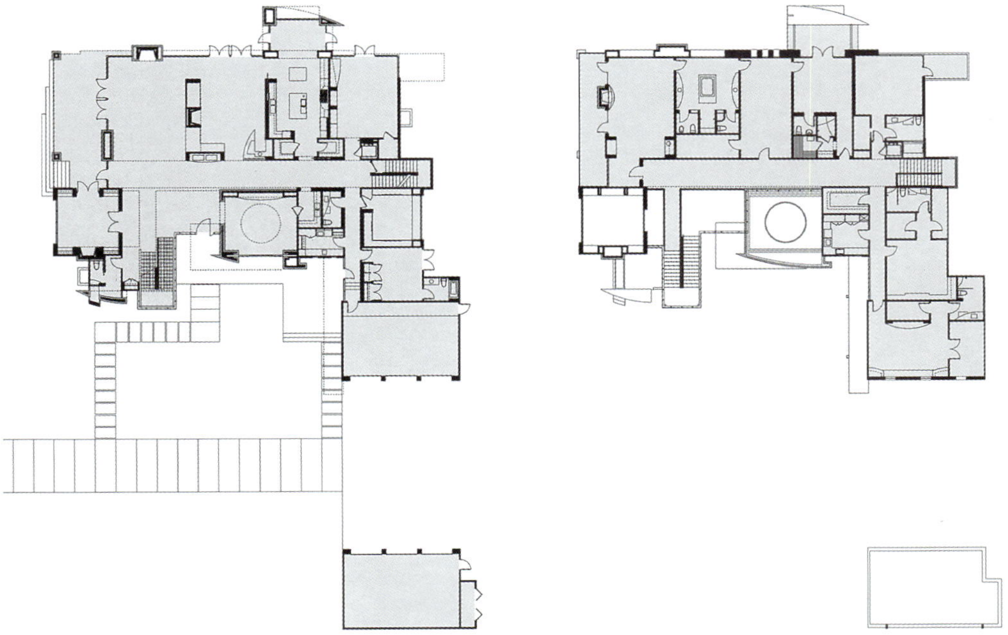

CITY Los Angeles (CA)
COUNTRY USA
REGION North America
TYPOLOGY Living
COMPLETION 2006
WEBSITE www.landrydesigngroup.com
ARCHITECTS Landry Design Group

CITY
Louisville (KY)

COUNTRY
USA

REGION
North America

TYPOLOGY
Office

COMPLETION
in progress

WEBSITE
www.quavirarch.com

ARCHITECTS
Qua'Virarch

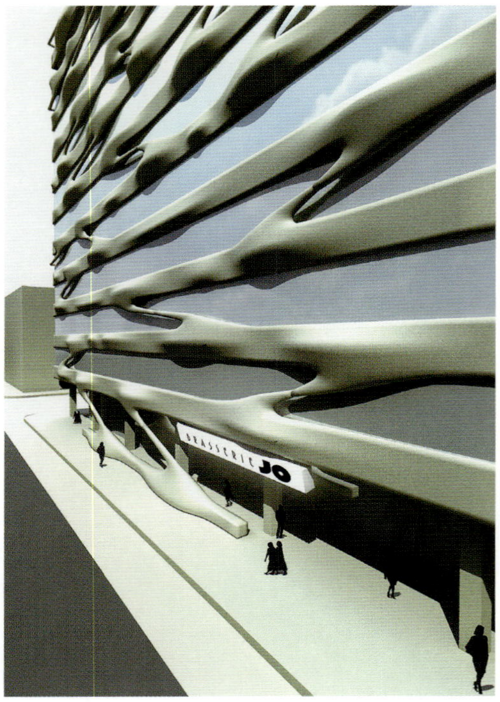

300MAIN

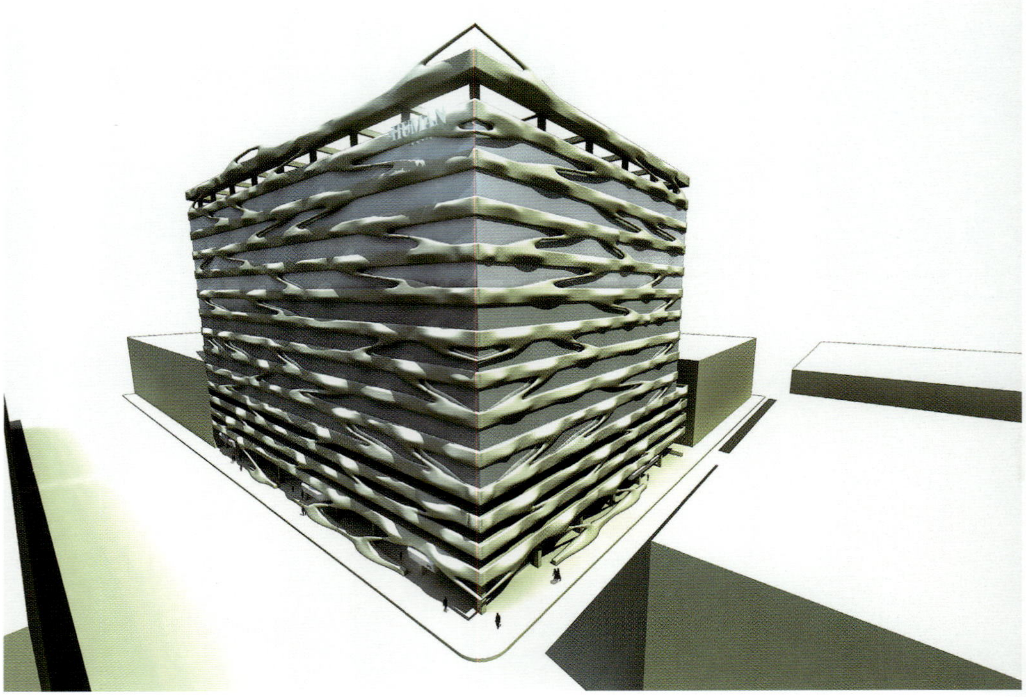

Designed for a downtown parcel in Louisville, Kentucky, 300MAIN develops the exterior personality of the office template to present a new model of civic interaction with its surrounding. Normalized in its plan, with the retail base receding from the street, the project organizes a sidewalk environment to create a new region of civic culture within Kentucky. The pre-cast concrete spandrels allow for an alien exterior that effortlessly welcomes attention in distraction. Ribbon windows slip behind the concrete tendrils that diagonally migrate up and down the façade. The project provides a contemporary approach towards office exteriors within a metropolitan environment.

01 Entrance area **02** Exterior view **03** Detail façade **04** Elevation **05** Pre-cast concrete spandrels

Renderings: Qua'Virarch

YEW DELL GARDENS

The new learning and resource center is the first component of a multi-phase program to facilitate public use and enjoyment of the arboretum and themed gardens, and seeks to provide a collection of flexible activity spaces through the rehabilitation of a historic bank barn and the construction of a new pavilion. The 4,800-square-foot program includes a multi-use hall, various event/activity outdoor terraces, workshop, catering kitchen, and restrooms. Through a dialogue between the two primary components of barn and pavilion, shifting visual alignments and spatial experiences reinforces a continuum of garden paths.

01 Exterior view, pavilion **02** Façade detail **03** Passage barn / pavilion **04** Site plan with floor plan **05** Outdoor terrace

Photos: De Leon & Primmer Architecture

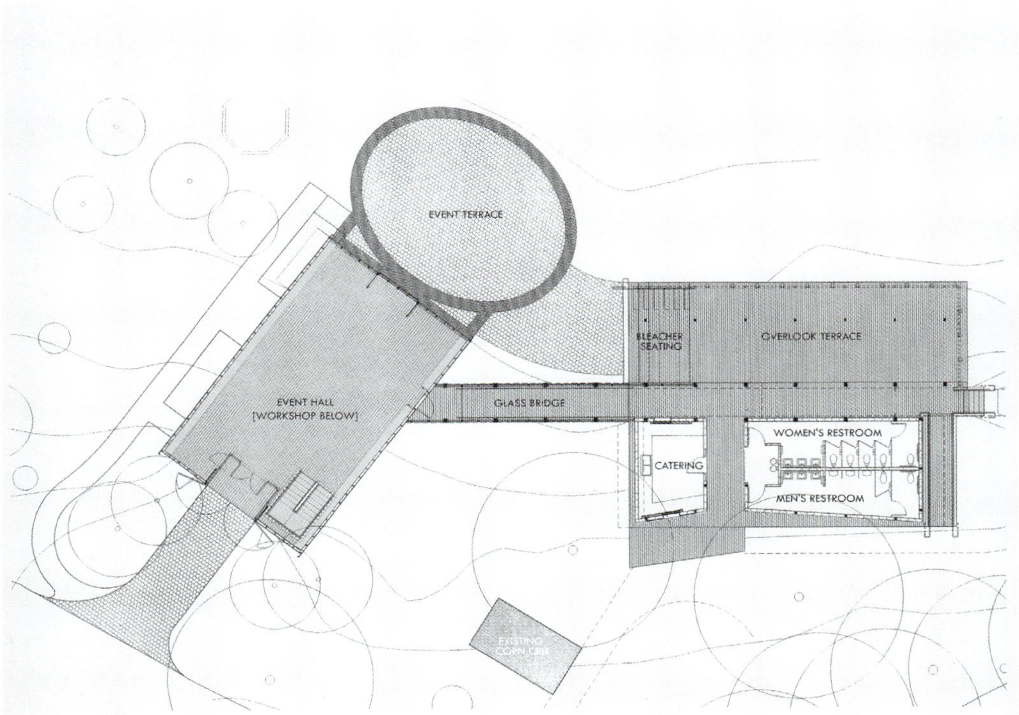

CITY Louisville (KY)
COUNTRY USA
REGION North America
TYPOLOGY Education
COMPLETION 2006
WEBSITE www.deleon-primmer.com
ARCHITECTS De Leon + Primmer Architecture

FULLER RESIDENCE

Perched above a pedestrian street in an historic beach community, the house occupies a narrow seaside lot. Recalling nearby lifeguard towers and beach bungalows, the house takes its place among a lively landscape of building scales and housing styles, which has evolved over the last century. The lower floor of the house consists of social spaces—a ground floor family room and guest space opens directly onto the street across a small courtyard, participating in the life of the street. The main living spaces occupy the second level and are linked to their surroundings by large sliding pocket doors, letting in the ocean breeze.

01 Outdoor space **02** Front façade **03** Interior view **04** Living space with ocean views

Photos: Benny Chan, Fotoworks

CITY: Manhattan Beach (CA)
COUNTRY: USA
REGION: North America
TYPOLOGY: Living
COMPLETION: 2006
WEBSITE: www.designarc.com
ARCHITECTS: DesignARC

EQUINOX HOUSE

The Equinox House is more of an evolution than a renovation. The sturdy existing house was transformed into a leaner, more flexible frame for its expansive views of San Francisco Bay. The house is named after the vernal and autumnal equinoxes, as the sun and moon are visible from rise to setting along the interior arc of its main living room and outdoor terraces. The interior space was extended to the outside to establish loop circulation wherever possible, while the exchange of materials and finishes for more durable surfaces was part of the transformation of the house from a suburban mansion into a museum of views.

01 Interior view, detail of living room **02** Main entrance view
03 South elevation **04** Deck view **05** Balcony with bay views
06 Detail main façade

Photos: Matthew Millman Photography

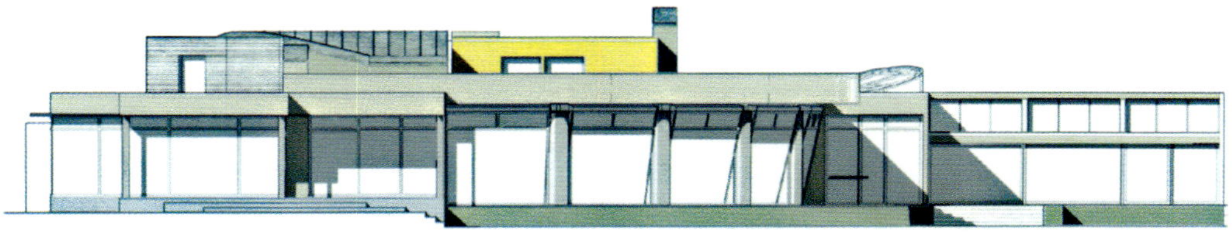

CITY Marin County (CA)
COUNTRY USA
REGION North America
TYPOLOGY Living
COMPLETION 2005
WEBSITE www.bantadesign.com
ARCHITECTS Philip Banta & Associates

CITY McLean (VA)

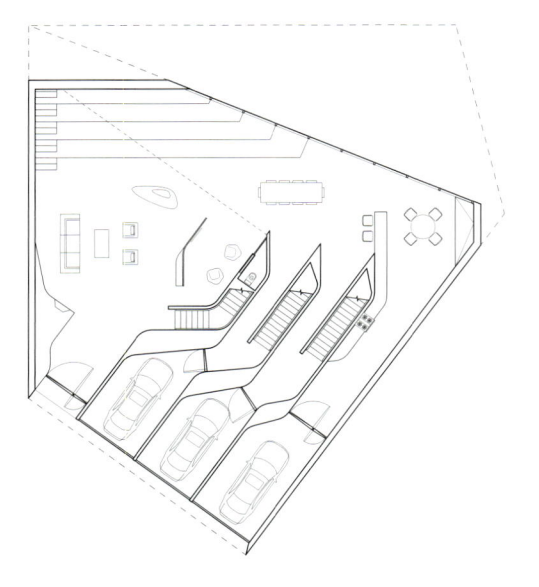

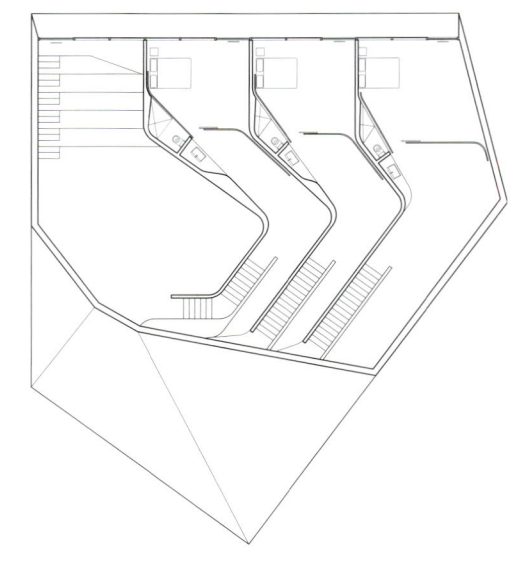

COUNTRY USA

REGION North America

TYPOLOGY Living

COMPLETION 2008

WEBSITE www.hyarchitecture.com

ARCHITECTS Höweler + Yoon Architecture LLP

TRIPLE HOUSE

The house shares with its suburban neighbors many of the traits of the quintessential single family suburban house, however, while its appearance is similar, it does not operate like one. The clients' ambition is to design a house in order to bring the family back together, putting three generations under one roof, where the house, being a post-nuclear home, re-examines issues of private and public within the extended family. The brief calls for a three car garage and three bedrooms, located on the upper level. A three car garage port on the ground floor is its input and three bedrooms with a view of the ravine are its output.

01 Exterior view **02** Interior view **03** Ground floor plan
04 Main floor plan

Photos: Squared Design

MARLBORO COLLEGE SERKIN CENTER

The Marlboro College Serkin Center is an 11,000-square-foot performing arts center, which respects the mountainous landscape and the white farmhouse buildings that make up the Marlboro College campus. The building's silver-colored standing seam metal roof, which is a common feature in the area, and its simple white-painted wood siding, make a home for the arts that is built with elements of the local architectural language. The building includes all the functions for the two academic programs of music and dance, including classroom and office spaces, rehearsal rooms, digital recording studio, and a 135-seat recital hall.

01 Floor plan **02** Detail metal roof and wood siding **03** Exterior view **04** Performance hall **05** Dance studio

Photos: Victoria Sambunaris

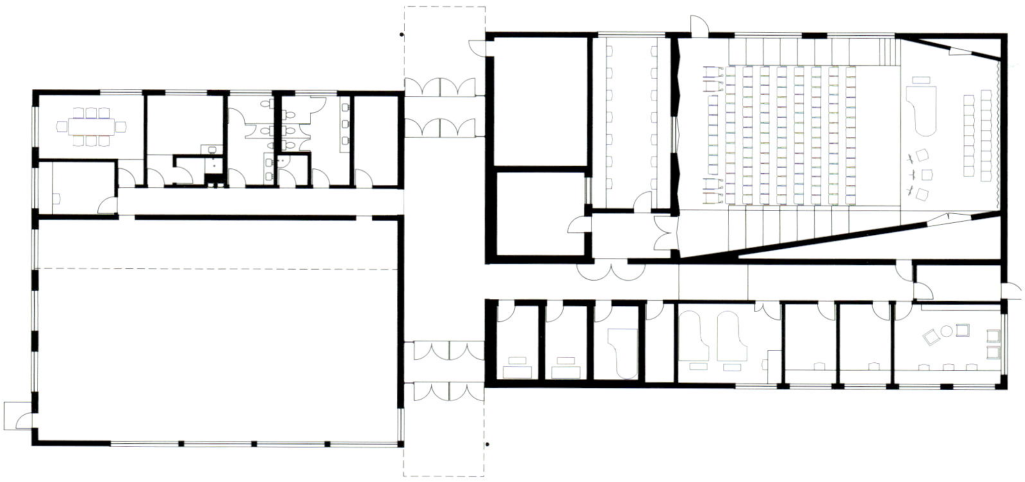

CITY
Marlboro (VT)

COUNTRY
USA

REGION
North America

TYPOLOGY
Education

COMPLETION
2005

WEBSITE
www.dberke.com

ARCHITECTS
Deborah Berke & Partners Architects LLP

MASSAPEQUA-BAR HARBOR PUBLIC LIBRARY

The Bar-Harbor Branch of the Massapequa Public Library was an addition and renovation project completed in 2000. The original library building, which was completed during the period of the 1950's, was not only doubled in size, but was also rendered accessible to the handicap by means of a ramped entry and a new internal elevator. The bold forms of the addition mimic the simple geometries of the existing new-Colonial style structure without stylistic copying. On the interior, large penetrations between floors coupled with expanses of exterior glass insure that the building is light-filled and airy.

01 Exterior view 02 Entrance area 03 Interior view, detail
04 Floor plan 05 Interior view, reading room

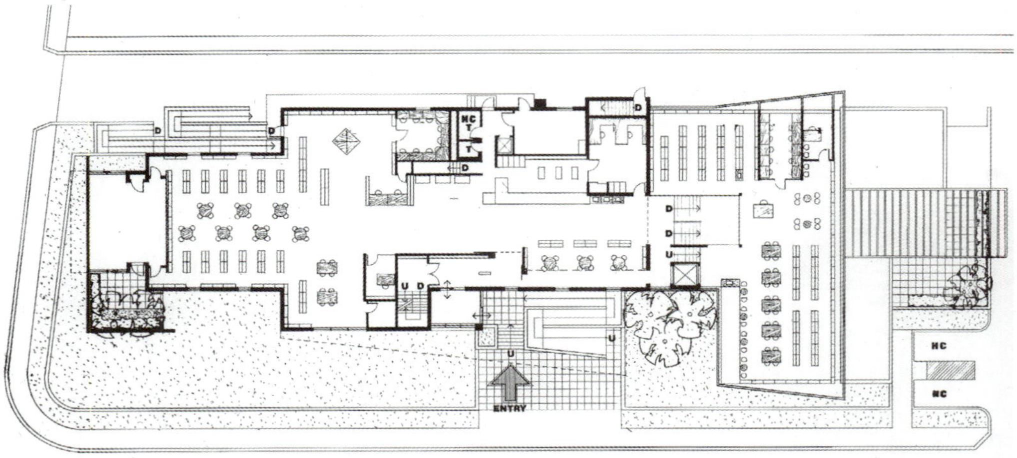

Photos: ArcPhotoInc/Eduard Hueber

MESA ARTS CENTER

The project in Mesa, Arizona, represents a radical discontinuity in the development patterns that have rendered this community a sleepy suburb of Phoenix, despite being the 38th largest city in the US. The Center offers a shared venue supportive of local, regional, national, and international artists alike. In the desert climate of Arizona's Valley of the Sun, it provides an oasis with contextual building forms sheltering a richly planted, sun-tempering landscape called the Shadow Walk. The activities that take place in the complex's four theaters, studio education spaces, and contemporary art gallery activate this landscape.

01 Dance studio **02** Lobby view **03** Performance hall
04 View of the shadow walk

Photos: Timothy Hursley

CITY Mesa (AZ)
COUNTRY USA
REGION North America
TYPOLOGY Culture
COMPLETION 2005
WEBSITE www.boora.com
ARCHITECTS BOORA Architects

MINNESOTA GATEWAY LANDMARK

Within the monument focused at the day chamber, an inversion of the day's light into stellar constellations is presented. The sun rays, cast upon the overhead Cor-Ten plane, are focused through perforations and form points of light that reproduce and refract the day sky as it appeared on the founding date of the University. As day becomes night, the exterior Cor-Ten planes project the night sky using lighting from within the structure. The West and East Blades juxtapose the night sky of the founding date with the present sky, acknowledging the University's inception and continuing vitality as an institution of learning.

01 Principal view to entry **02** Site plan **03** Cor-Ten planes by night **04** View from east

Photos: Courtesy of Antoine Predock

CITY Minneapolis (MN)

COUNTRY USA

REGION North America

TYPOLOGY Public

COMPLETION 2005

WEBSITE www.predock.com

ARCHITECTS Sculptor Constance DeJong in collaboration with Antoine Predock Architect PC

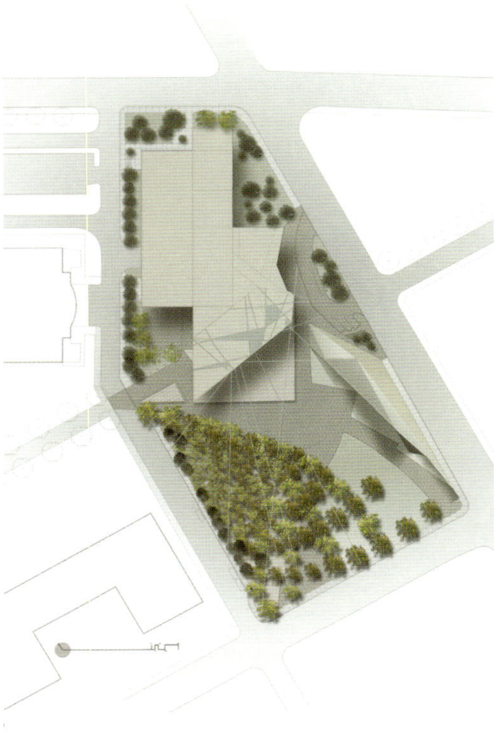

LAURANCE S. ROCKEFELLER PRESERVE, GRAND TETON NATIONAL PARK, WYOMING

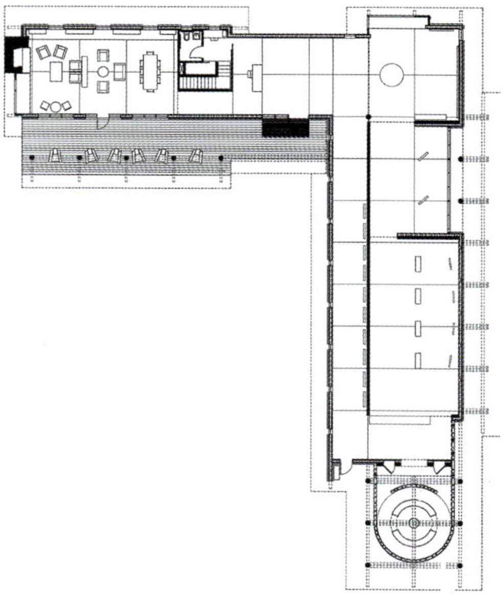

This 7,000-square-foot USGBC LEED Platinum Certified Interpretive Center, and its related trails, represents a gift of 1,100-acres from the Rockefeller family to the National Park Service. The building is self-guiding, with the goal of awakening the senses so that visitors may gain a heightened appreciation of the landscape. More like a chapel than a visitors center, the L-shaped, rectilinear order of the building curves to an apse-like form at its south end. Vertical wood slats reminiscent of old barns, bring narrow slits of light into the chapel-like space, suggesting the spiritual power of nature.

01 Exterior view **02** Main floor plan **03** View from north **04** Porch detail **05** Interior view

Photos: David Swift

CITY: Moose (WY)
COUNTRY: USA
REGION: North America
TYPOLOGY: Public
COMPLETION: 2007
WEBSITE: www.carneyarchitects.com
ARCHITECTS: Carney Architects

CITY Mountain View (CA)

COUNTRY USA

REGION North America

TYPOLOGY Education

COMPLETION 2004

WEBSITE www.cavagnero.com

ARCHITECTS Mark Cavagnero Associates

COMMUNITY SCHOOL OF MUSIC AND ARTS

This building is the first permanent home of the Community School of Music and Arts, which is a 35-year-old non-profit organization located in Mountain View, California. The project was built to be a state-of-the-art education facility, and includes features that typify what the school and its community represent and work towards achieving. Two of the main space components of the building comprise of music classrooms and private music studios, which provide an opportunity for growth. In addition to that, the building provides visual arts studios, an administration space, a recital hall, and an outdoor performance space.

01 Recital hall **02** Entrance court **03** Longitudinal section **04** North elevation **05** Front east elevation

Photos: Tim Griffith

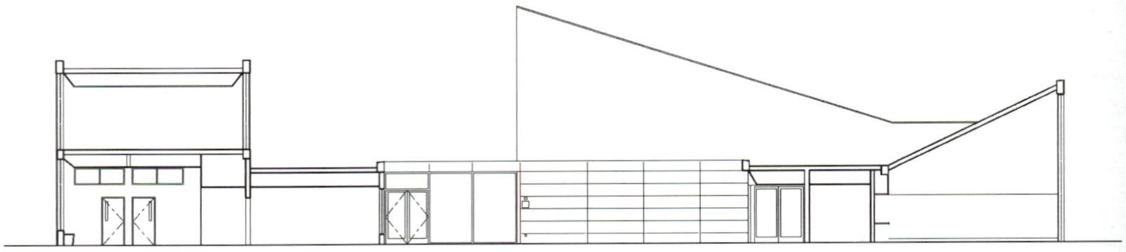

WHEELER RESIDENCE

Integrating high-end modern design and a commitment to green building, this new house makes use of an existing foundation to create dramatic living spaces that flow into the landscape. The material palette includes Cor-ten steel, stained concrete mixed with fly-ash and Fin-Ply panels. Passive ventilation, radiant floors, solar hot water and photovoltaic power dramatically reduce energy use. Ground floor open-plan living and kitchen areas can become continuous with the poolside garden thanks to retractable glass walls.

01 Interior view, bathroom **02** Exterior view **03** Rear façade **04** Floor plan **05** Detail façade

Photos: Lucas Fladzinski

CITY Menlo Park (CA)
COUNTRY USA
REGION North America
TYPOLOGY Living
COMPLETION 2007
WEBSITE www.wdarch.com
ARCHITECTS William Duff Architects

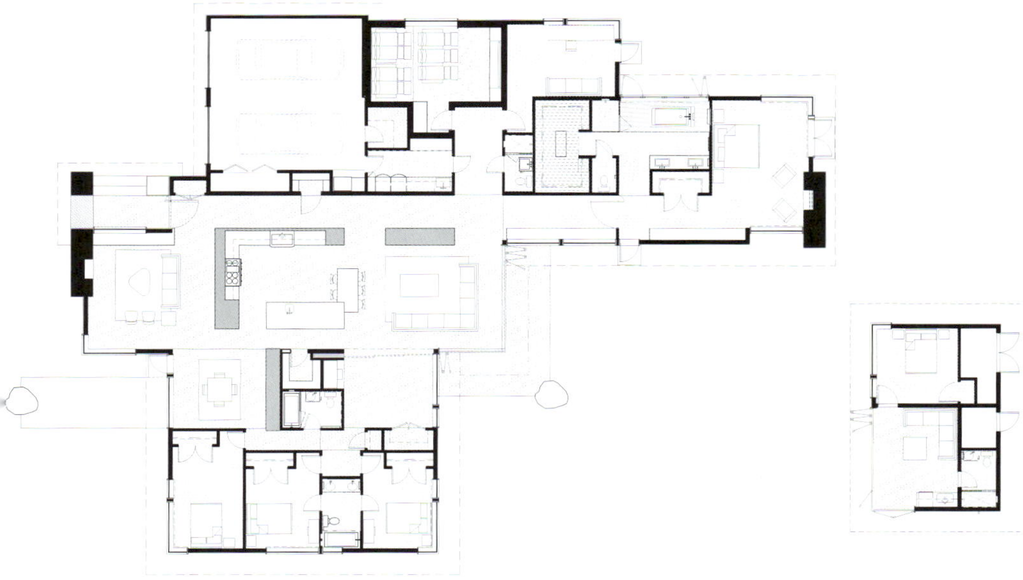

CITY
Milwaukee (WI)

COUNTRY
USA

REGION
North America

TYPOLOGY
Public

COMPLETION
2006

WEBSITE
www.ladallman.com

ARCHITECTS
LA DALLMAN

GREAT LAKES FUTURE, DISCOVERY WORLD

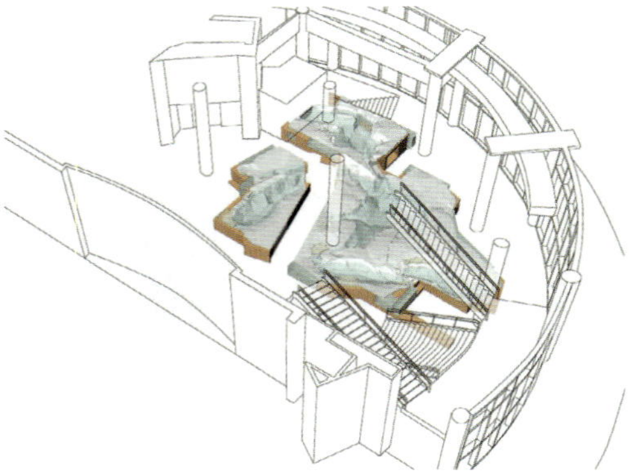

The 3,600-square-foot permanent exhibit of Great Lakes Future integrates highly technical life support systems for aquatic and amphibious life including digital imagery, interactive displays, cartography, fossils, and live-fed atmospheric data. The exhibit design reveals opportunities to explore and discover the intersection between man-made and natural systems, illuminating the primordial relationship between earth and sky. The design mediates between the organic and man-made, the physical and atmospheric, neutral existing space and the flexible, complex insertion, and finally, the grounded and celestial.

01 View from occulus embedded in skycanopy **02** Axon of terrain **03** View of occulus within skycanopy **04** View of exhibit through window at Discovery World

Photos: LA DALLMAN Jim Brozek (04)

ATWATER COMMONS, MIDDLEBURY COLLEGE

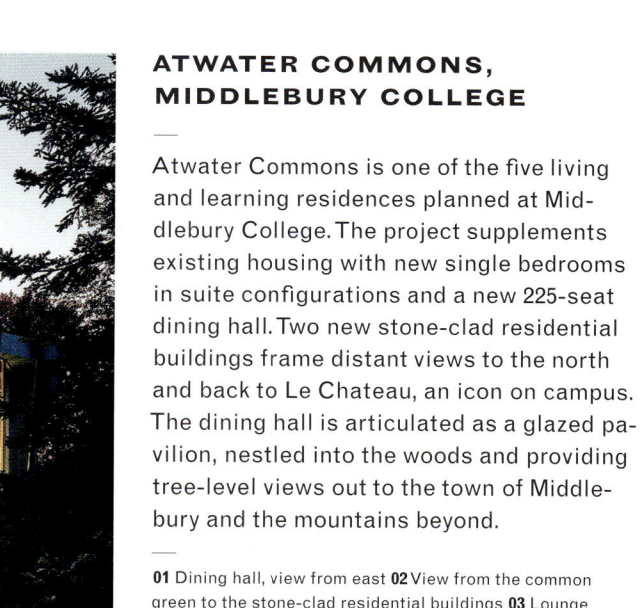

Atwater Commons is one of the five living and learning residences planned at Middlebury College. The project supplements existing housing with new single bedrooms in suite configurations and a new 225-seat dining hall. Two new stone-clad residential buildings frame distant views to the north and back to Le Chateau, an icon on campus. The dining hall is articulated as a glazed pavilion, nestled into the woods and providing tree-level views out to the town of Middlebury and the mountains beyond.

01 Dining hall, view from east **02** View from the common green to the stone-clad residential buildings **03** Lounge **04** Glass façade detail **05** Floor plan

Photos: Halkin Photography LLC

CITY Middlebury (VT)

COUNTRY USA

REGION North America

TYPOLOGY Education

COMPLETION 2004

WEBSITE www.kierantimberlake.com

ARCHITECTS KieranTimberlake Associates

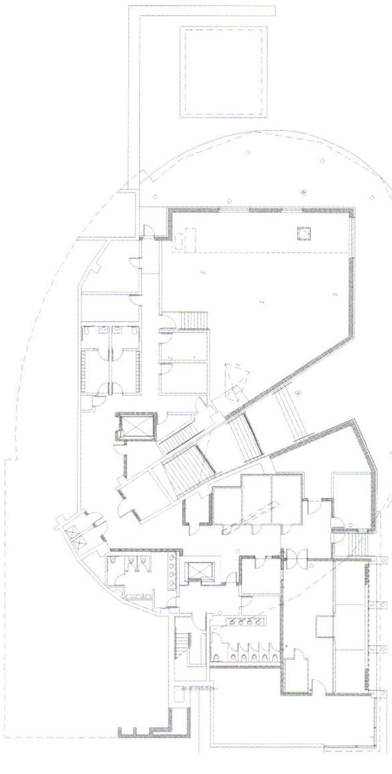

U.S. BORDER PATROL STATION

This station is used by agents of the U.S. Border Patrol who are investigating reports of illegal immigration. The station responds to the arid climate of the region by receding into the earth, presenting to the public a "garden wall" that conceals the activities of the facility and creates a secure environment. The resulting shadowed areas on the west in combination with operable louvers on the east allow passive ventilation and cooling. Additional sustainability features include the optimization of natural sky light through cuts in the building, and the management of water runoff through sub-surface retention gardens.

01 Courtyard **02** Hallway filled with natural light **03** Exterior view of agents' entrance **04** Sustainability diagrams **05** Muster room

Photos: Benny Chan, Fotoworks

CITY: Murrieta (CA)
COUNTRY: USA
REGION: North America
TYPOLOGY: Government
COMPLETION: 2006
WEBSITE: www.garrisonarchitects.com
ARCHITECTS: Garrison Architects

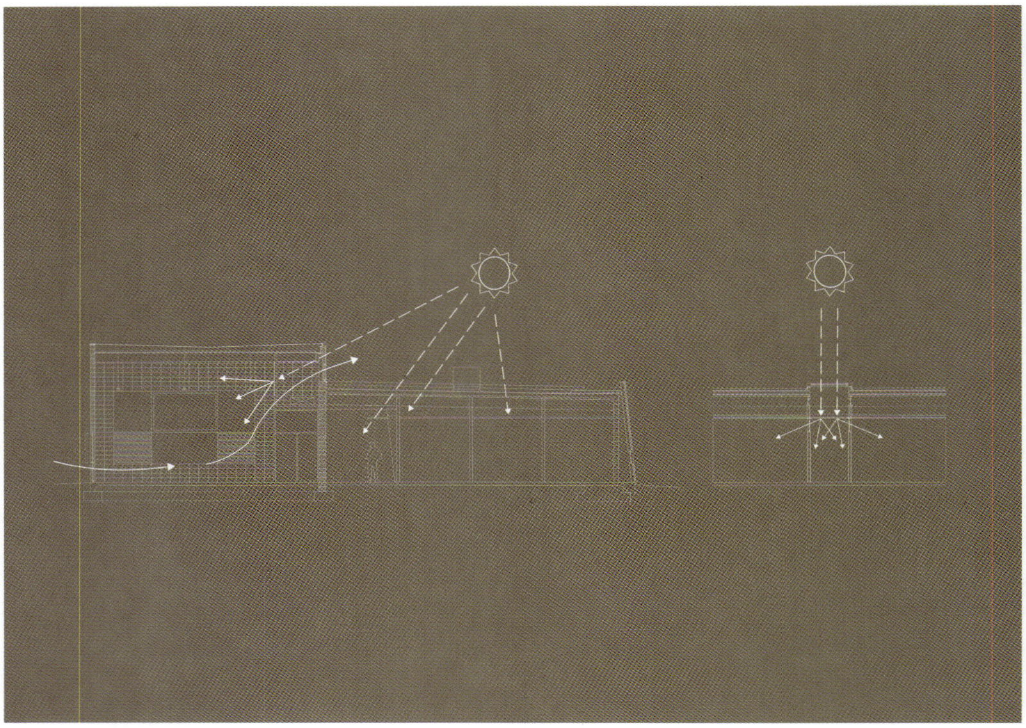

CHRIST COMMUNITY CLINIC BOARD STREET

Christ Community Clinic is a new medical facility for a non-profit group in an economically depressed neighborhood. The building, organized by a long blue wall, is a simple box form that utilizes concrete masonry and corrugated metal siding in response to its context. The clinic's design expresses the client's desire to improve the surrounding neighborhood with an inviting and healing image. Strong geometrical shapes and a restricted palette work to create a light but introspective building.

01 Exterior view **02** Entrance view by night **03** Side view of entrance area **04** Hallway **05** Interior view, working spaces

Photos: Jeffrey Jacobs Photography

CITY Memphis (TN)
COUNTRY USA
REGION North America
TYPOLOGY Health
COMPLETION -
WEBSITE www.archimania.com
ARCHITECTS archimania

GE 5 CONDOS

GE5 is a multi-family infill project consisting of five modern town homes located in a former parking lot on the edge of an historic district. The three-storied town homes are designed as live-work units, offering a variety of user options. The design, comprised of concrete masonry punctuated by galvanized metal bays, is a careful and deliberate flirtation between modern and historic architecture. The buildings are unmistakably modern, but respectful of the site offering views of Memphis city center.

01 Floor plan **02** Detail entrance area **03** Exterior view of all five townhouses **04** Rear view **05** Interior view, residential floor

Photos: Jeffrey Jacobs Photography

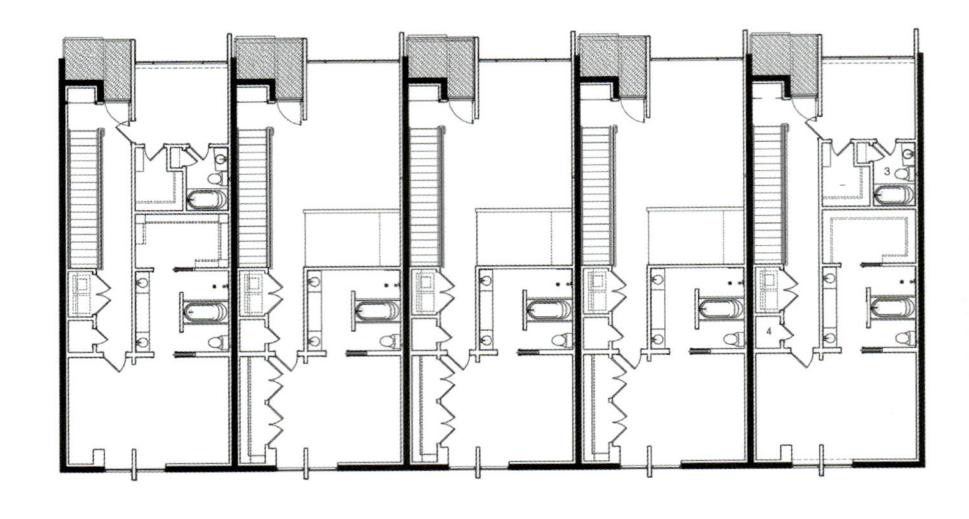

CUBE TOWER

This project represents the next frontier in urban multifamily high-rise housing. A dramatic steel infrastructure allows ultimate volumetric flexibility, letting the homeowner customize spatial prerogatives. Rising 22 stories, the building encourages occupants to design their own domain by connecting multiple cube modules vertically, horizontally, and diagonally in addition to creating double height volumes, garden voids and cantilevered living environments. Generated by desire and need rather than architectural assumption, the volumetric play of the building creates intriguing arrangements of solid and void.

01 Sky terrace **02** Cantilevered units **03** Pool deck **04** East elevation **05** North elevation

Renderings: DBOX

CITY: Miami (FL)
COUNTRY: USA
REGION: North America
TYPOLOGY: Mixed-use
COMPLETION: unbuilt
WEBSITE: www.oppenoffice.com
ARCHITECTS: Oppenheim

CITY
Miami (FL)

COUNTRY
USA

REGION
North America

TYPOLOGY
Culture

COMPLETION
2001

WEBSITE
www.oppenoffice.com

ARCHITECTS
Oppenheim

TEN MUSEUM PARK

TEN MUSEUM PARK is an exploration of the hedonistic possibilities of architecture in a futuristic tropical playground of urban sophistication. This project represents the rare opportunity when imagination and reality fuse to create new luxuries and experiences beyond fantasy. A crisp, well proportioned exoskeleton engages a pure crystalline volume soaring 50 stories above the bay – a dynamic beacon for the majestic cruise ships as they return from their voyages around the globe. Framing fragments of water, city and sky, every personal and communal space within the complex was designed to serve as a backdrop for life in its most beautiful form.

01 Front façade **02** View of tower at dusk **03** View from the bay **04** Pool deck and garden **05** North elevation

Renderings: Robin Hill (01), Totus Photography (02, 03), Digitart (04)

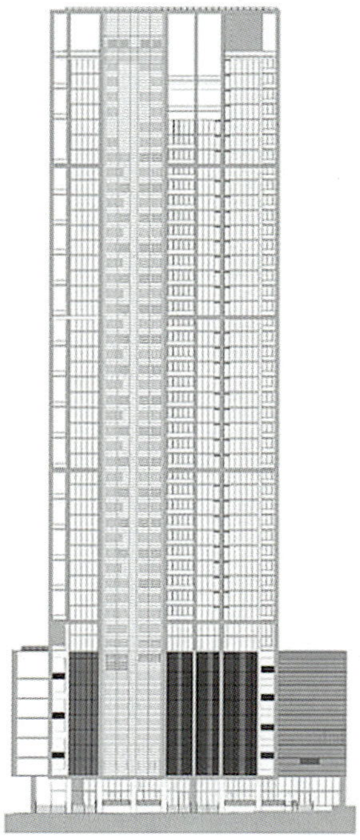

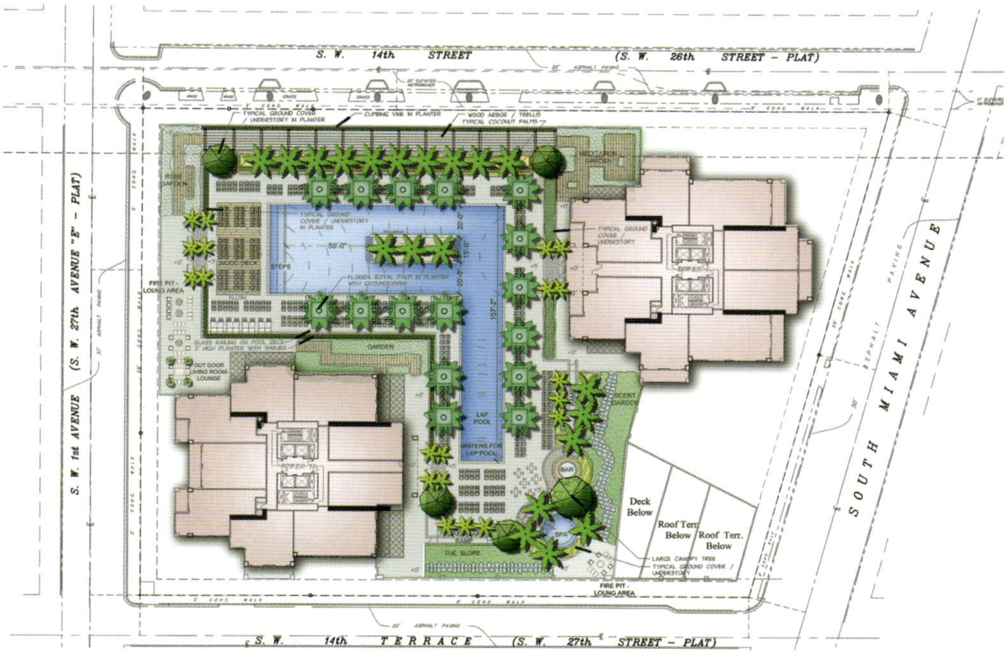

CAPITAL AT BRICKELL

Miami's downtown is a developing metropolis, approaching the importance of NY and San Francisco. The elements that make up an important urban core are housed in striking statements of architecutre that define the streets and skyline. Given the opportunity to add to the composition, the challenge was to design a city block that would suport a mixed use development to include retail, office, and residential uses. The Capital at Brickell building captures the essence of urban living, paying tribute to the historically significant icons of The Chrysler and the Empire State Building, from which it was inspired.

01 Landscape plan 02 Entrance view by night 03 Exterior view
04 Creating a skyline for Miami 05 Detail lofts and penthouse

Renderings: Spine 3D

CITY
Miami (FL)

COUNTRY
USA

REGION
North America

TYPOLOGY
Mixed-use

COMPLETION
2008

WEBSITE
www.fdarchitects.com

ARCHITECTS
Fullerton Diaz Architects

CITY Miami (FL)
COUNTRY USA
REGION North America
TYPOLOGY Living
COMPLETION 2006
WEBSITE www.oppenoffice.com
ARCHITECTS Oppenheim

COR

This residential project is nestled among important city buildings including the Miami City Ballet, the Bass Museum, and the Miami Beach Library. Because of its position, the form of the townhouse project acts as a gateway to Miami Beach and contributes to the future growth of this upcoming area. The program of the project consists of two luxury town homes with enclosed parking spaces and private rooftop pools. Each owner has a private entry garden along with mid-level spacious verandas. The intention of the project is to limit its impact on the neighborhood by creating 2 high-end residences as opposed to 20 smaller units.

01 Rooftop garden **02** Ground level entry and retail **03** Elevation: use of photovoltaic cells on façade and wind turbines on parapet wall **04** Typical residential floor plan

Renderings: DBOX

PARK LANE

Three multi-dimensional crystalline volumes create garden, residential, amenity, parking, office, and commercial spaces aimed to maximize the area's value. Pure in form and its materiality, the project establishes an optimum abstraction within the skyscape while maintaining contextual sensitivity at the street level. A large rooftop sky garden provides ample room for recreation. The tripartite configuration around a shared central core generates optimum efficiency and offers dynamic views, corner exposures, private elevator access, expansive terraces, and full floor units for all residents as the building ascends.

01 View into untis **02** View of tower from accross the bay
03 Pool deck **04** Interior living space with bay views

Photos: DBOX

CITY Miami (FL.)
COUNTRY USA
REGION North America
TYPOLOGY Mixed-use
COMPLETION unbuilt
WEBSITE www.oppenoffice.com
ARCHITECTS Oppenheim

CITY
Miami (FL)

COUNTRY
USA

REGION
North America

TYPOLOGY
Living

COMPLETION
2004

WEBSITE
www.oppenoffice.com

ARCHITECTS
Oppenheim

VILLA ALLEGRA

Multiple rooms, both interior and exterior, have been added to a nondescript, one-story home. While the effect is striking, minimal alterations were made to the existing structure. The house is entered through a 20x30x30-foot volume where a reflecting pool and oculus align to activate the space with reflection and luminance. A large room organizes the house into private and public realms. Tremendous spaces with oversized windows overlook the pool and canal. A large circular column contains an outdoor shower open to the sky. The second floor contains a secluded courtyard garden, off the master bedroom, for private activities.

01 Front entry view **02** Rear façade **03** Interior **04** Pool

Photos: Oppenheim

SUGAR BOWL RESIDENCE

A new home on a site accessible only by foot in the winter takes its cues from the surrounding Sierra Nevada Mountains. A stone base of Sierra White granite holds a strongly profiled natural cedar wood exterior above the normal twelve foot snow line. The house is capped with a simple planar zinc roof in order to shed the heavy snowfall. Structural interior "trees" carry roof snow loads to allow the south facing wall to open to views and to passive solar gain. A three-story atrium allows light to enter the lower level to provide illumination for a twenty-four foot climbing wall for exercise on off days.

01 Detail rear façade **02** Exterior view **03** Section **04** Floor plans **05** Living room with fireplace

Photos: Mark Horton

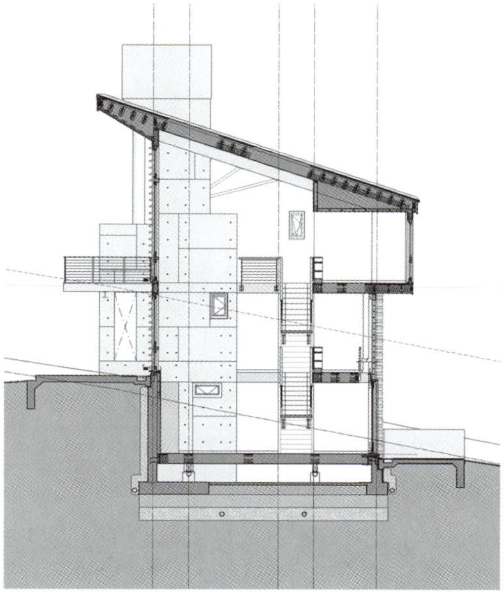

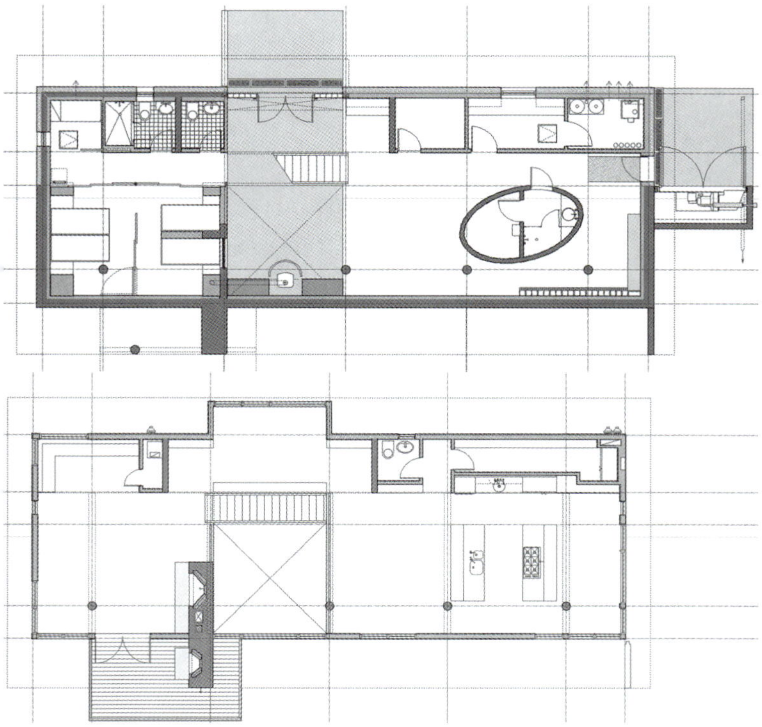

CITY: Norden (CA)
COUNTRY: USA
REGION: North America
TYPOLOGY: Living
COMPLETION: 2004
WEBSITE: www.mh-a.com
ARCHITECTS: Mark Horton/Architecture

CITY	Nashville (TN)
COUNTRY	USA
REGION	North America
TYPOLOGY	Living
COMPLETION	2003
WEBSITE	www.ericrosen.com
ARCHITECTS	Eric Rosen Architects

FAIRWAYS RESIDENCE

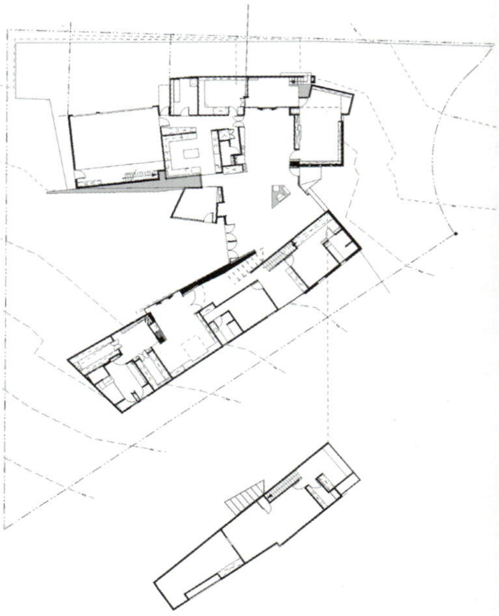

Exploring the nature of boundaries was the basis for the design for the Fairways Residence in Nashville, Tennessee. As evident in both the city and the site, the boundary between the order of the city and the order of nature must continually respond to the changing urban fabric and the way in which it is inhabited. The house, with its fortress-like street façade and otherwise more transparent courtyard façade, becomes a new threshold between the community and the inner sanctum of the private courtyard. The project attempts to exist as a new boundary between the order of the city and the order of nature.

01 Courtyard from above **02** Front view **03** Floor plans
04 Gallery skylight by night **05** Detail entry area

Photos: Erich Koyama

BIGELOW CHAPEL AT UNITED THEOLOGICAL SEMINARY

The project of Bigelow Chapel realizes the United Theological Seminary's request for a timeless, spiritually uplifting, ecumenical worship space. The design for the 5,300-square-foot building includes a processional, narthex, chapel and bell tower. The designers conveyed warmth and light through a variety of design innovations, including thin maple veneers sandwiched between sheets of clear, non-reflective acrylic that filter and modulate light coming through a glass wall. The sanctuary succeeds by creating a chapel both beautiful and unique, with a tranquil and serene environment for worship and prayer.

01 Exterior view by night **02** Interior view, maple veneers **03** View into the chapel **04** Floor plan

Photos: Paul Warchol Photography

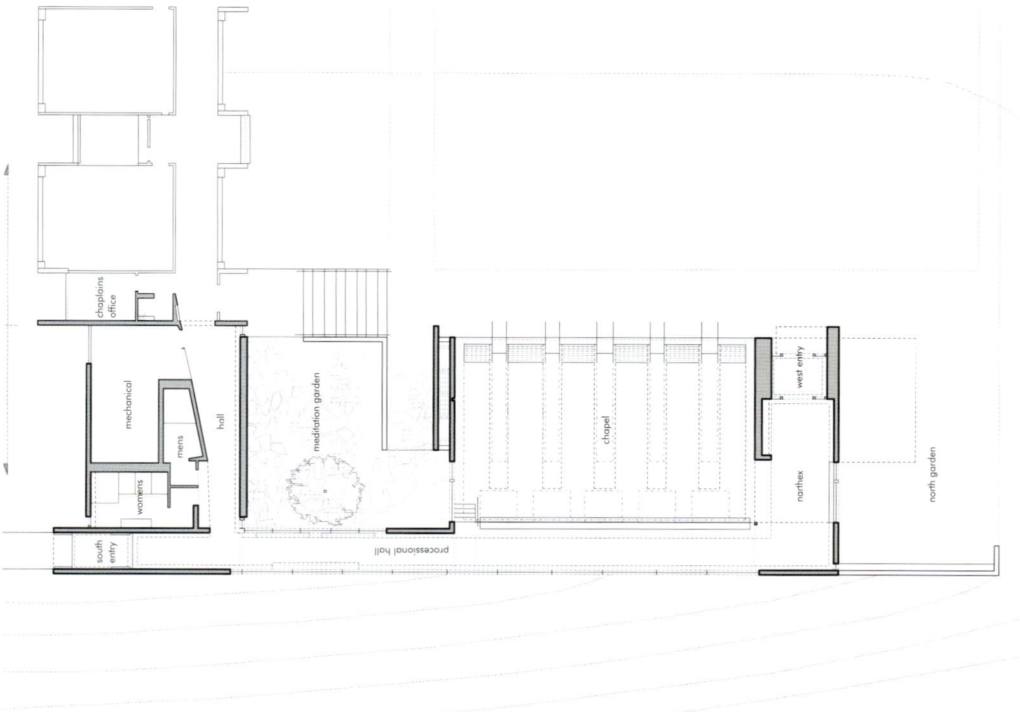

CITY: New Brighton (MN)
COUNTRY: USA
REGION: North America
TYPOLOGY: Ecclesiastical
COMPLETION: 2004
WEBSITE: www.hga.com
ARCHITECTS: HGA Architects and Engineers

CITY Norman (OK)
COUNTRY USA
REGION North America
TYPOLOGY –
COMPLETION 2004
WEBSITE www.hughjacobsen.com
ARCHITECTS Hugh Newell Jacobsen

THE MARY AND HOWARD LESTER WING, UNIVERSITY OF OKLAHOMA

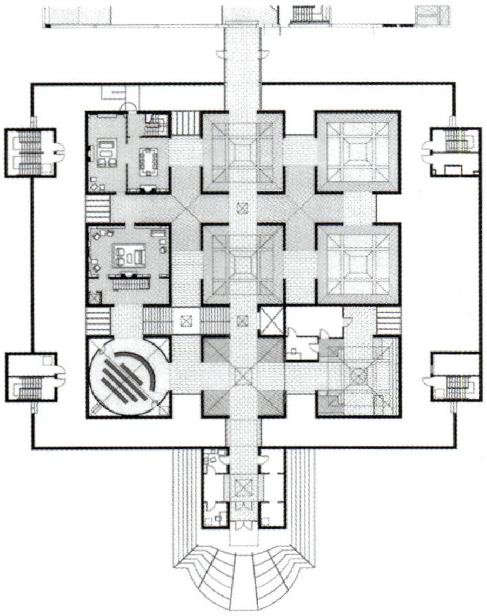

The focus on this project was the recent addition of a new wing, built to house the large collection of Impressionist and Post-Impressionist paintings, generously donated by an alumna. The new wing consists of 14 individual limestone pavilions, each with a slate pyramidal roof, topped with a pyramidal skylight. The main level consists of Weitzenhoffer historic "rooms" and galleries including an entry pavilion, main lobby, Orientation Theater, and the museum store. Ten-foot ceilings provide a residential scale throughout the wing, while soaring skylights pull a grander scale into each pavilion.

01 Hallway **02** Exterior view by night **03** Main level floor plan **04** Limestone pavilions with pyramidal roof **05** Gallery

Photos: Courtesy of Hugh Newell Jacobsen

JOE'S SALON + SPA

Encompassing a gut renovation of the 3,000-square-foot, two-story building in the sleepy town of New Milford, Connecticut, the new design adds a forward-thinking façade to a traditional streetscape and creates a dramatic change in the building's character. The storefront, opened up with large panels of glass, reveals a series of layered spaces within the ground level hair salon and an orange glow emanating from the interior of the spa. The design not only speaks to its contemporary internal needs, but also addresses the typical preservation problem of how to integrate an "of the moment" design into a long-established urban setting.

01 Exterior elevation **02** Workstation **03** Interior salon
04 Ground and second floor plan **05** Cashwrap desk

Photos: Michael Moran

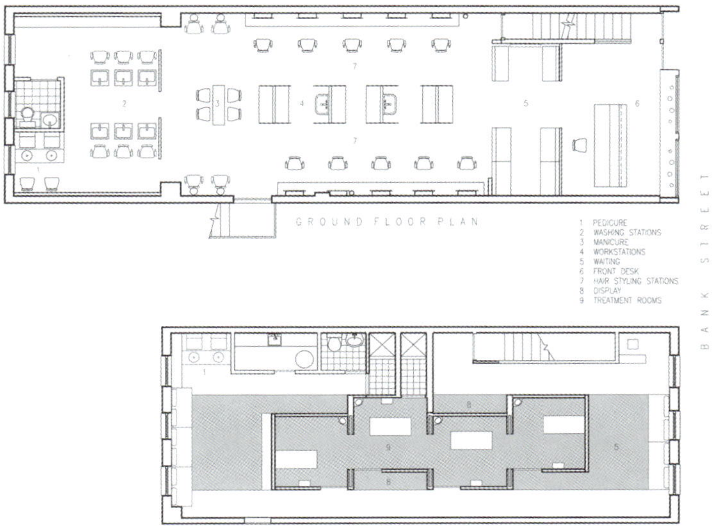

CITY
New Milford (CT)

COUNTRY
USA

REGION
North America

TYPOLOGY
Leisure

COMPLETION
–

WEBSITE
–

ARCHITECTS
Louise Braverman

NEIMAN MARCUS AT NATICK COLLECTION

The specialty store in Natick, Massachusetts is the most unusual and unique store for a company whose business plan and corporate image requires that it create environments specifically tailored to each business location. The design represents the style and sophistication of the Neiman Marcus product line, while also emphasizing its New England location. The undulating patterned stainless steel exterior is evocative of a silk scarf, or sophisticated fabrics from the Neiman couture line, billowing in the coastal breezes. The surrounding landscape recalls the sea grass of tidal marshes and traditional stone walls of the region.

01 Undulating patterned stainless steel façade **02** Entrance area by night **03** Exterior view **04** Section at entry

Photos: Bruce T. Martin

CITY Natick (MA)

COUNTRY USA

REGION North America

TYPOLOGY Retail

COMPLETION 2007

WEBSITE www.elkus-manfredi.com

ARCHITECTS Elkus Manfredi Architects

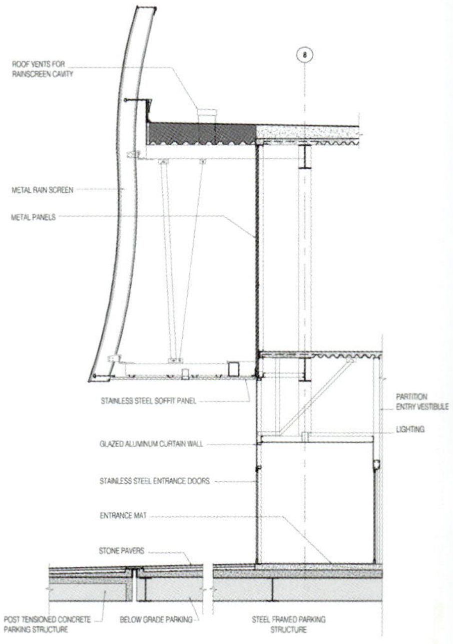

CHAMELEON HOUSE

The house explores the use of SIPs panels as cost-effective solutions of building structures from standardized components to accommodate a variety of sites. The small building footprint and foundation reduces the cost of the area of the house and allows the foundation to step up the site together with the slope of the hill. The small house has nine different living levels, including a residential roof deck. Although the SIPs panels are used as structural elements throughout, the addition of a two-story prefabricated steel frame allows for a double-height window wall and open loft-like spaces in the main living area.

01 Detail wall of SIPs panels **02** Front façade **03** Exterior view **04** Detail panoramic window **05** Interior view

Photos: Anthony Vizzari and James Yochum

CITY Northport (MI)
COUNTRY USA
REGION North America
TYPOLOGY Living
COMPLETION 2002
WEBSITE www.andersonanderson.com
ARCHITECTS Anderson Anderson Architecture

FIREHOUSE 12 RECORDING STUDIO

The goal was to seek out potential public spaces within a tightly programmed building and connect them back to the streetscape. The challenge was to design the dual purpose "live room" to accommodate conflicting acoustical requirements. For recording, space needed to be acoustically dead, while for performance; the reverberant character of the room was crucial. A continuous plywood shell was developed that transforms along its surface to create necessary acoustic conditions. At the back of the stage, the shell splits and distorts to act as a diffuser, while above the recording area, it undulates to refract high frequency sound.

01 "Live room" with plywood shell **02** Entrance area **03** Section **04** Detail bar **05** Firehouse bar

Photos: Robert Benson Photography

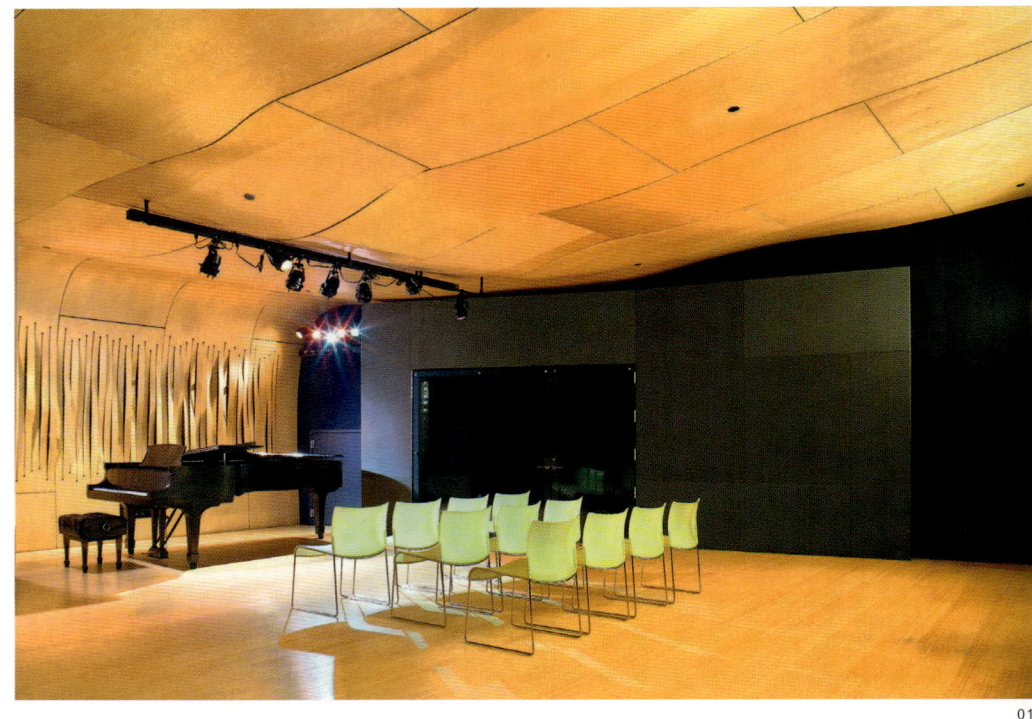

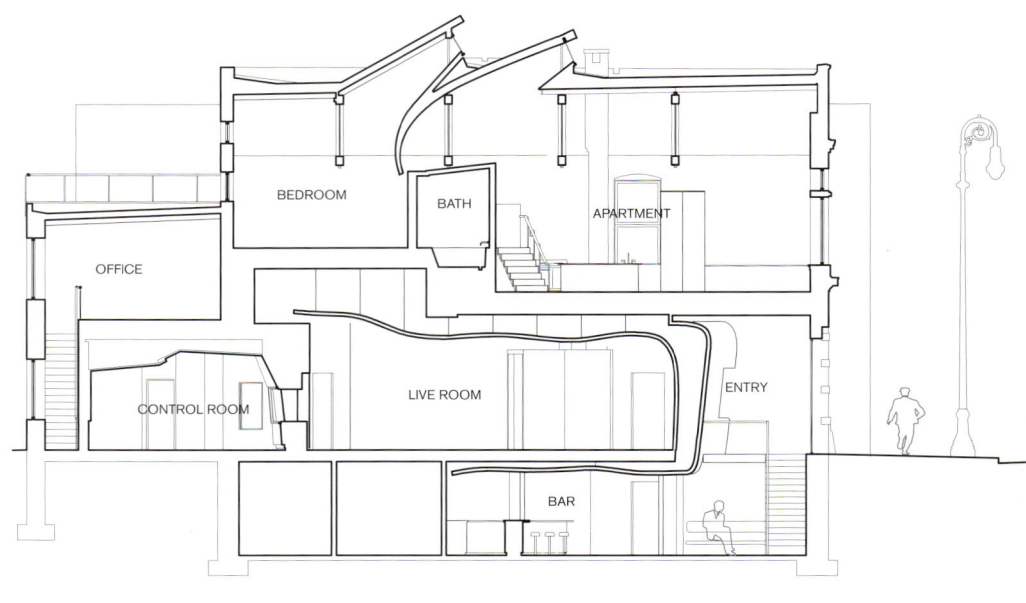

CITY New Haven (CT)
COUNTRY USA
REGION North America
TYPOLOGY Mixed-use (culture, leisure and living)
COMPLETION 2005
WEBSITE www.grayorganschi.com
ARCHITECTS Gray Organschi Architecture

MOD SET: FROM TRANSIENCE TO PERMANENCE

A topographic roof structure warps up from Chartres St. to make a continuous storefront and access to the parking, retail, and institutional space it covers. Planted, it becomes a public park to serve the neighborhood and a landscaped setting for four double-loaded slab structures containing apartments. The landscape spans the railroad right-of-way and the levee, folding down to augment a planned riverside promenade. Workshop plans prefabricated modular construction to economically build units that step around a central circulation "chimney" that aids natural ventilation, offering sun-dappled views to the river.

01 Interior view **02** Front façade **03** Plan **04** Living area

Photos: Studio 2A

CITY New Orleans (LA)
COUNTRY USA
REGION North America
TYPOLOGY Living / Public
COMPLETION in progress
WEBSITE www.workshopapd.com
ARCHITECTS workshop/apd

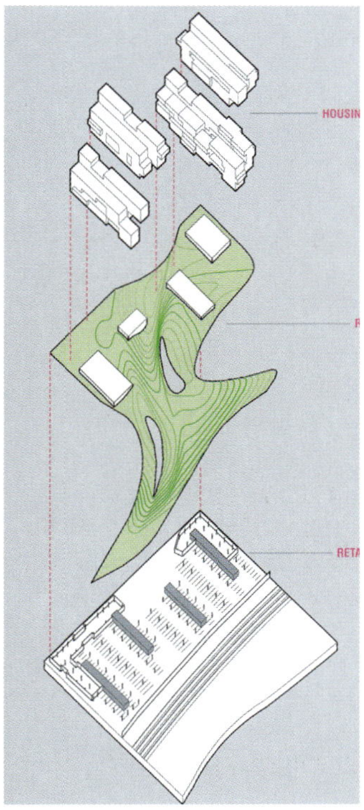

CITY New Orleans (LA)
COUNTRY USA
REGION North America
TYPOLOGY Living
COMPLETION –
WEBSITE www.graftlab.com
ARCHITECTS GRAFT

PINK – MAKE IT RIGHT

The Lower Ninth Ward, a rich cultural community long known for its high proportion of resident ownership, was left devastated and with widespread homelessness in the wake of Hurricane Katrina. To date, initiatives to rebuild this once vibrant area have unfortunately fallen short. Pink does not dwell on the past but rather empowers the future, attempting to do so through the immediate potency of the spectacle, aided by local and global media. The project aids the victims of Hurricane Katrina in New Orleans by raising awareness and empowering global humanitarian actions, bringing people that had been forgotten back home.

01 Interior **02** Exterior view **03** Detail pink house **04** View of 150 placeholders for real homes **05** Model of a future house

Renderings: GRAFT
Photos: Ricky Ridecos (03, 04)

REPAIRS AND RENOVATIONS TO THE LOUISIANA SUPERDOME

When the iconic Louisiana Superdome was devastated in the aftermath of Hurricane Katrina, Billes Architecture, LLC was successfully teamed with Trahan Architects and Sizeler Thompson Brown Architects to design and manage the $125 million repair project and the additional $41 million renovation. Though the project required a fast-track delivery, it was essential that extensive documentation of damage, assessment, design and coordination with numerous oversight agencies including the State of Louisiana, FEMA, insurance underwriters, and consultants around the United States occur. The firm's stunning new additions include a 100-foot band of windows that allow for greater transparency and a more direct connection to the city.

01 Superdome **02** Horizontal view **03** Lounge bar **04** Hallway
Photos: Billes Architecture

CITY New Orleans (LA)
COUNTRY USA
REGION North America
TYPOLOGY Leisure / Sports
COMPLETION in progress
WEBSITE www.billesarchitecture.com
ARCHITECTS Billes Architecture

CITY
New York (NY)

COUNTRY
USA

REGION
North America

TYPOLOGY
Office

COMPLETION
2006

WEBSITE
www.212box.com

ARCHITECTS
212box

THE WONDERFACTORY

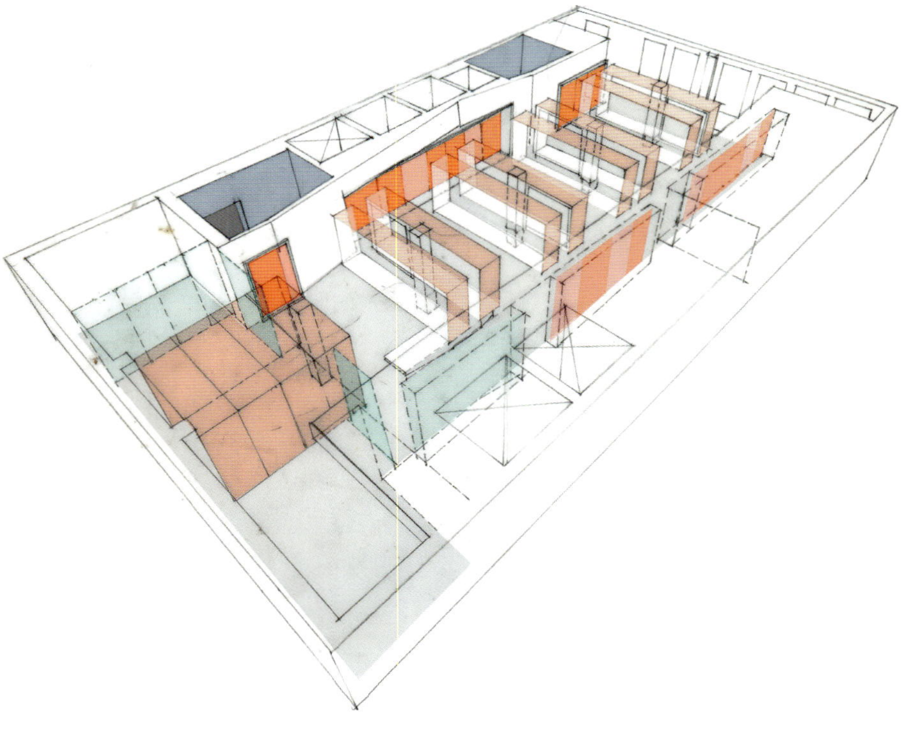

When David Link and Joe McCambley established The Wonderfactory, they hired 212box to design a space that would reflect the intense creativity and sense of wonder that defines their branding work. With the idea that creativity is contagious, 212box conceived a 4,000 square foot space for up to 36 employees that encourages communication, inspires ideas, and fuels the imagination. Beginning as the desks of the partners, this surface penetrates windows, and changes form and materials but is never broken. Two kinked walls along the east side undulate to contain all the office's storage needs, punctuated by signature orange frames.

01 Interior long view **02** Library and desks **03** Waiting room **04** View to working area **05** Bird's eye view

Photos: Jody Kivort (01), Jim Cooper

AUSTRIAN CULTURAL FORUM

The new tower in midtown Manhattan provides a state-of-the art home for an institution devoted to international cultural exchange. The building is the first major US project for Austrian-born New York architect Raimund Abraham, whose design was selected in an open competition hosted by the Republic of Austria in 1992. Facilities of the tower include exhibition galleries, a flexible theater for performances, screenings and lectures; a library, a loft-like presentation area and seminar rooms, reception space, staff offices, a multi-level residence for the Forum's director; and an open-air loggia at the tower's pinnacle.

01 Library **02** Exterior view **03** Hallway **04** Detail staircase

Photos: Raimund Abraham

CITY New York (NY)
COUNTRY USA
REGION North America
TYPOLOGY Culture
COMPLETION 2002
WEBSITE –
ARCHITECTS Raimund Abraham

GREENWICH PROJECT

The GW497/8B Loft project is an open-plan, 3,200-square-foot loft designed for an artist. The wide-open development is generated by a central spine-like structure, which arranges the different spaces adjacent to its organic folds. The spine is attached and configured of a thin black metal frame with bogwood, veneered plywood panels, while a lowered ceiling plane contains air conditioning and recessed lighting. The loft has a generous living/dining space as well as a large roof terrace overlooking the Hudson River. The loft was the 2006 Smart Environment Award Winner from IIDA + Metropolis Magazine.

01 Exterior view **02** Façade with balconies **03** Detail glass façade **04** Cross section

Photos: Floto + Warner Studio
Renderings: Archi-Tectonics

CITY New York (NY)
COUNTRY USA
REGION North America
TYPOLOGY Living
COMPLETION 2006
WEBSITE www.archi-tectonics.com
ARCHITECTS Archi-Tectonics

UPSIDE DOWN SKYSCRAPER

The design approach is to observe the landscape as a random network of pure trajectories, generated by people and their social behaviors, whose occasional collisions suggest a possible topography, creating flows and path, determining the principal directions, and consequently the space. The design strategy consisted on reversing the idea of the classic skyscraper with the public areas on the ground floor. An inter-connecting lobby with adjacent offices spaces is located on the top of the entire complex. Bridge gardens on different levels double functions as green areas for the residents, the hotel and the public as well as circulations.

01 Total view with garden levels **02** View from street **03** South elevation **04** Exterior view by night

Renderings: ARCHI[TE]NSIONS

CITY New York (NY)
COUNTRY USA
REGION North America
TYPOLOGY Mixed-Use (residential, offices, public)
COMPLETION unbuilt
WEBSITE www.architensions.com
ARCHITECTS Alessandro Orsini/ARCHI[TE]NSIONS

CITY
New York (NY)

COUNTRY
USA

REGION
North America

TYPOLOGY
Living

COMPLETION
2009

WEBSITE
www.asymptote.net

ARCHITECTS
Asymptote

166 PERRY STREET / LUXURY CONDOMINIUMS

A collection of newly designed buildings are redefining the western edge of the West Village on the Hudson River, a trend kick started by Richard Meier's glass and steel towers. This project adjoins the first of Meier's three towers and is simultaneously an antidotal design and a formal and tectonic play off of his buildings. The intimate and elegant approach emerged from a search for an apropos musical assembly of glass and geometry whereby a play of reflections, atmosphere and surface produce an envelope of effects that weld the disparities of brick, ornament and stoops with glass, smoothness and constant plays of space.

01 Detail glass façade **02** Front view **03** Hallway **04** Entrance area

Renderings: Asymptote: Hani Rashid + Lise Anne Couture, © ArchPartners 2007

GREENE STREET LOFT

The Greene Street Loft was designed to allow the existing industrial loft construction to remain along the periphery, while creating a highly crafted contemporary interior. The distinction between old and new is dissolved when the large translucent glass folding walls are collapsed and the space becomes unified. A new steel and glass stair enclosure, which combines elements from both the existing industrial loft and the more refined intervention, provides access to a landscaped terrace.

01 View into the bathroom **02** Steel stair to the terrace **03** Roof terrace by night **04** Stairway **05** Kitchen and living room

Photos: Tony Hamboussi

CITY: New York (NY)
COUNTRY: USA
REGION: North America
TYPOLOGY: Living
COMPLETION: 2005
WEBSITE: www.brharchitect.com
ARCHITECTS: Ben Hansen Architect

CITY: New York (NY)
COUNTRY: USA
REGION: North America
TYPOLOGY: Gastronomy
COMPLETION: 2005
WEBSITE: www.bentelandbentel.com
ARCHITECTS: Bentel & Bentel, Architects

THE MODERN

The restaurant distinguishes itself by manipulating the scale of the spaces it occupies and by intensifying the presence of the materials that define it. The insertion of a system of sinuous lighted glass walls both bind the restaurant spaces that straddle different building areas as well as separate the various program areas of the informal bar room, and the formal and private dining rooms. These gauze-like veils of luminous glass reiterate, along with other significant design elements such as the brushed marble bar and the custom-designed seating, the desire to create a spare yet warm series of interior dining environments.

01 Exterior view, glass façade **02** Restaurant **03** Bar **04** View of bar room **05** Floor plan

Photos: ArchPhotoInc / Eduard Hueber

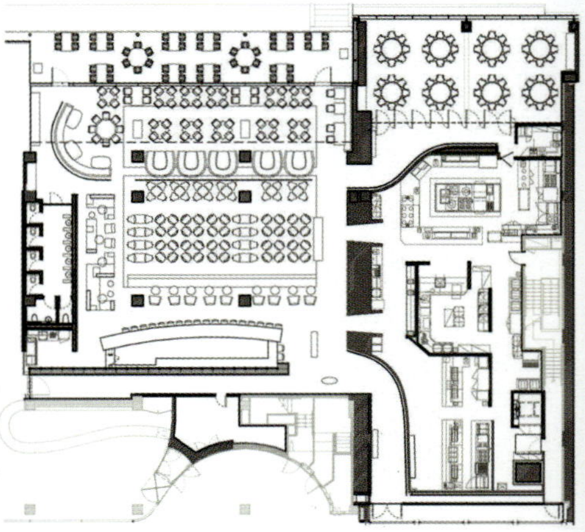

WEST MIDTOWN FERRY TERMINAL

WNB+A was selected by the New York City Economic Development Corporation from a short list of New York's top architectural firms to design the new West Midtown Intermodal Ferry Terminal on Pier 79 located at West 39th Street. This new terminal will be a municipally owned multi-user facility, providing ferry service including short haul commuters, water taxis, and high-speed long distance services from midtown Manhattan to points along the Hudson River. Plans call for a new state-of-the-art Terminal as well as six new boat slips. The project is planned to be part of the larger Hudson River Park development.

01 Glass façade **02** Interior view, entrance **03** Panoramic view **04** Interior view, hallway

Photos: Jim Roof, ©Christine Bodouva

CITY New York (NY)
COUNTRY USA
REGION North America
TYPOLOGY Transportation
COMPLETION 2005
WEBSITE www.bodouva.com
ARCHITECTS William Nicholas Bodouva & Associates

CITY
New York (NY)

COUNTRY
USA

REGION
North America

TYPOLOGY
Office

COMPLETION
2007

WEBSITE
www.jcdainc.com

ARCHITECTS
James Carpenter Design
Associates Inc.

PODIUM LIGHT WALL

Located on two façades of the new 7 World Trade Center, the Podium Light Wall use a double layer of prismatic stainless steel wire with integrated LEDs to create a dynamic and rhythmic interplay of light that appears to emerge from the building day and night... At dawn and dusk the wall transforms itself into a blue volume before gradually returning its blue and white color. By integrating the functional aspects of street lighting and mechanical ventilation for the building, this unique wall system creates a dynamic streetscape environment that artfully merges reflection and illumination.

01 Total view **02** Detail prismatic steel façade **03** Detail façade by night **04** Vertical bars of blue light

Photos: David Sundberg (01, 04), Andreas Keller (02, 03)

VERSADOME MODULAR BUILDING SYSTEM

This modular building system's smooth forms and clean details emulate the organic shapes of rigid structural shells found in nature. Uniquely designed for easy and affordable transportation, assembly and expansion, the system's energy efficient and low-maintenance units can be stacked and transported in one standard shipping container. Designed for ultimate adaptability and flexibility, the system creates limitless possibilities for a wide range of multi-purpose usages, meeting the needs of anyone in search of lightweight and open plan solutions.

01 Usage: penthouse **02** Swimming pool with canopy **03** Rain system **04** Shell section **05** Usage: huts

Renderings: D.A.R.E.design+architecture

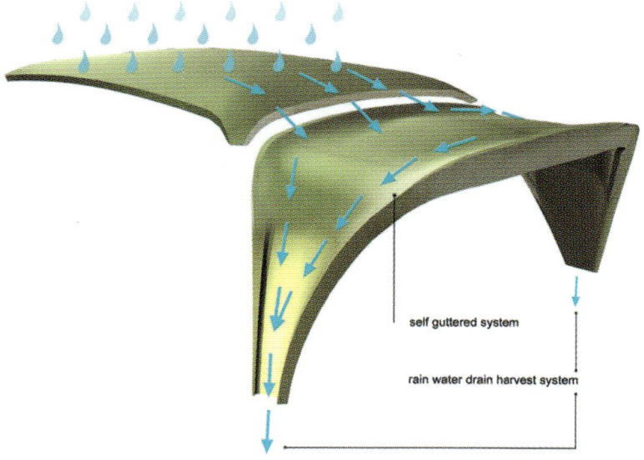

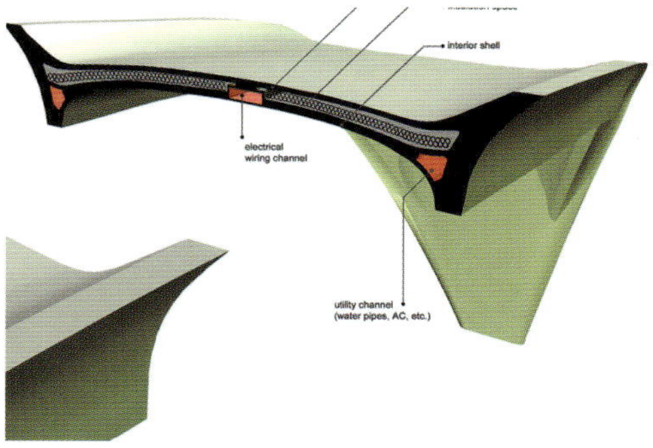

CITY New York (NY)
COUNTRY USA
REGION North America
TYPOLOGY Living
COMPLETION in progress
WEBSITE www.versadome.com
ARCHITECTS Deger Cengiz

CITY New York (NY)

COUNTRY USA

REGION North America

TYPOLOGY Residential

COMPLETION 2008

WEBSITE www.dbnyc.com

ARCHITECTS Della Valle Bernheimer

245 TENTH

This project looked to the natural context as inspiration for the design of this 11-story residential condominium located in Manhattan's West Chelsea gallery district. Its shape and surface is inspired by the beauty of the transient forms of clouds and in nostalgic reference to trains that once frequented the adjacent High Line. A unique cladding of expansive glass and stainless steel panels animates the building as it reflects the ever-changing play of light and vibrant surroundings. As light migrates across the building's skin, passers-by may view a structure that appears to change in a display of mutable perspective.

01 North elevation **02** Living area **03** View to deck **04** Seventh floor plan

Renderings: Encore

ALICE TULLY HALL, LINCOLN CENTER

Lincoln Center is a valued icon inextricably linked with NYC and will undergo a large-scale makeover. The new architectural features include a floating hyperbolic parabolic lawn that roofs over a 250-seat restaurant on the North Plaza, an architectural strip-tease that exposes theaters and activities buried behind opaque travertine-clad street walls, a 45,000-square-foot cantilevered expansion of Juilliard's top three stories whose underside creates a sloped canopy framing Alice Tully Hall's expanded lobby, and the integration of smart technologies with traditional building materials to deliver information throughout the campus.t

01 North elevation **02** Entrance area **03** Ground floor plan **04** View of Juilliard's expansion and lobby Alice Tully Hall

Renderings: Diller Scofidio + Renfro

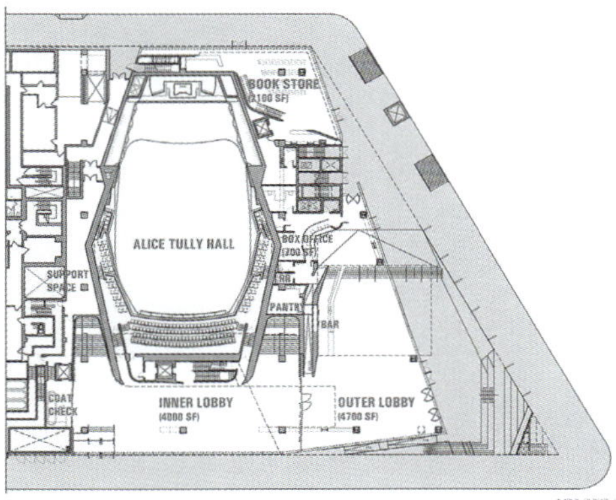

CITY New York (NY)
COUNTRY USA
REGION North America
TYPOLOGY Education
COMPLETION 2008
WEBSITE www.dillerscofidio.com
ARCHITECTS Diller Scofidio + Renfro, FXFowle Architects PC

CITY
New York (NY)

COUNTRY
USA

REGION
North America

TYPOLOGY
Retail

COMPLETION
2006

WEBSITE
www.eightinc.com

ARCHITECTS
Eight Inc.

NOKIA, NEW YORK FLAGSHIP STORE

The Nokia, New York Flagship Store provides a dynamic new retail channel for the company and establishes a global brand presence with the ability to achieve local relevance. The interior of the store features a perimeter of LCD multimedia screens set into low-iron glass walls backed by color-shifting LED lighting. Each live handset navigates the consumer through the given product's features and benefits in an interactive, hands-on Nokia product tutorial. The flexibility of the visual content allows for unique visual merchandising opportunities on global and local levels.

01 Longitudinal section **02** Exterior view **03** Glass walls with LED lighting: blue **04** Illuminated mezzanine **05** Glass walls with LED lighting: red

Photos: Erhard Pfeiffer, Grey Crawford, Julius Shulman & Juergen Nogai

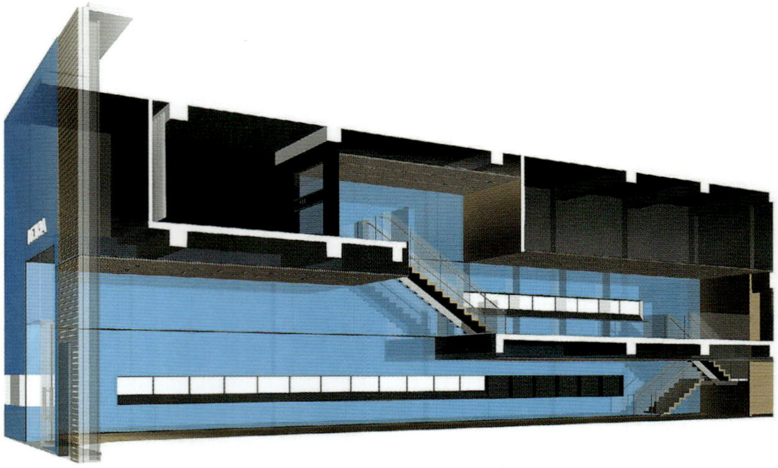

SIXTY USA: HEAD OFFICE AND SHOWROOM

Within the large floor plate of a former printing building in Greenwich Village, the client sought a lofty and kinetic space to reflect the youth and dynamism of their clothing lines. The challenge was to maintain a distinction between public and private spaces, while satisfying the seemingly competing requirements of openness and privacy. The solution responds with a neutral backdrop of polished concrete floors and sandblasted brick walls, into which is inserted a single sculptural element to define areas and circulation. This assembly is perceived as a continuous band of wood that begins as wall and finishes as seating.

01 Reception **02** Detail polished concrete floor **03** Showroom **04** Plan and section **05** Detail band of wood

Photos: Atelier FABRIQ

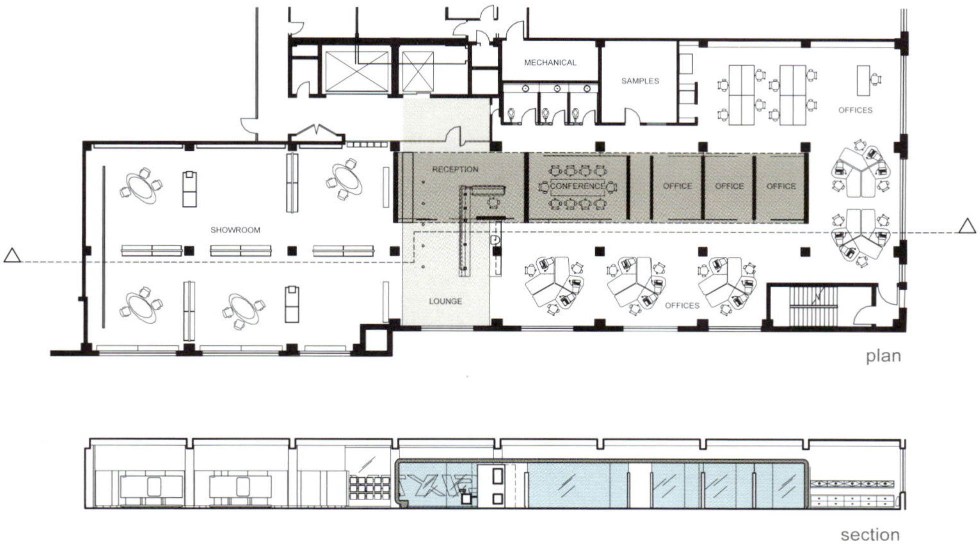

CITY
New York (NY)

COUNTRY
USA

REGION
North America

TYPOLOGY
Office

COMPLETION
2003

WEBSITE
www.fabriq.com

ARCHITECTS
Atelier FABRIQ (Peart Bertrand Koch architectes)

NYC TOWNHOUSE

The renovation of this historic 1913 townhouse required restoring its historic front façades and creating a modern interior. Large glazed openings at the first and second levels were inserted in the new rear façade and the garden was enlarged. A steel balcony and stair connected the garden to the second kitchen level. Light was brought inside through both the vertical circulation core that contains the stair and elevator, and through a light well that was inserted into the middle of the house. A glazed opening in the second floor ceiling brought additional daylight to the dinning area.

01 View of bedroom from hallway **02** Library at interior light well **03** Staircase **04** Bedroom **05** Elevation **06** Exterior view, garden façade

Photos: Paul Warchol Photography

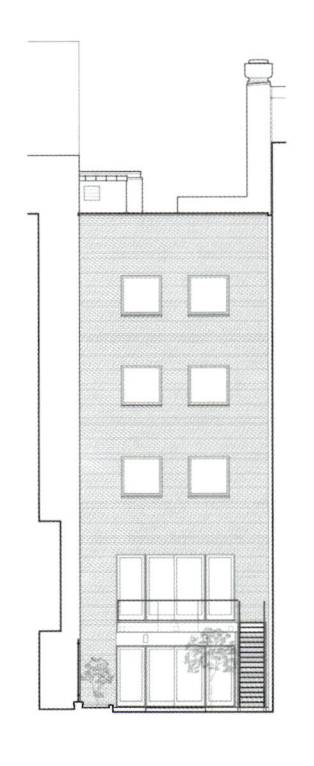

CITY New York (NY)
COUNTRY USA
REGION North America
TYPOLOGY Living
COMPLETION 2005
WEBSITE www.fdmarch.com
ARCHITECTS FdM: Arch Froncois de Menil

MEGACHURCH

MEGAchurch, a proposed design for a 200,000-square-foot worship space in New York City, adapts the MEGAchurch typology that is traditionally suburban and car-centered, to fit an urban and pedestrian-centered environment. The project morphs the horizontal, mall-like space of a typical MEGAchurch into a vertical tower. It responds to the surrounding religious institutions, pedestrian and vehicular conditions, as well as to the prescribed volumetric and zoning constraints. A gradated perforated skin encloses the complex, and the tower features a giant elevator that transports 3,600 people to a chapel in the sky.

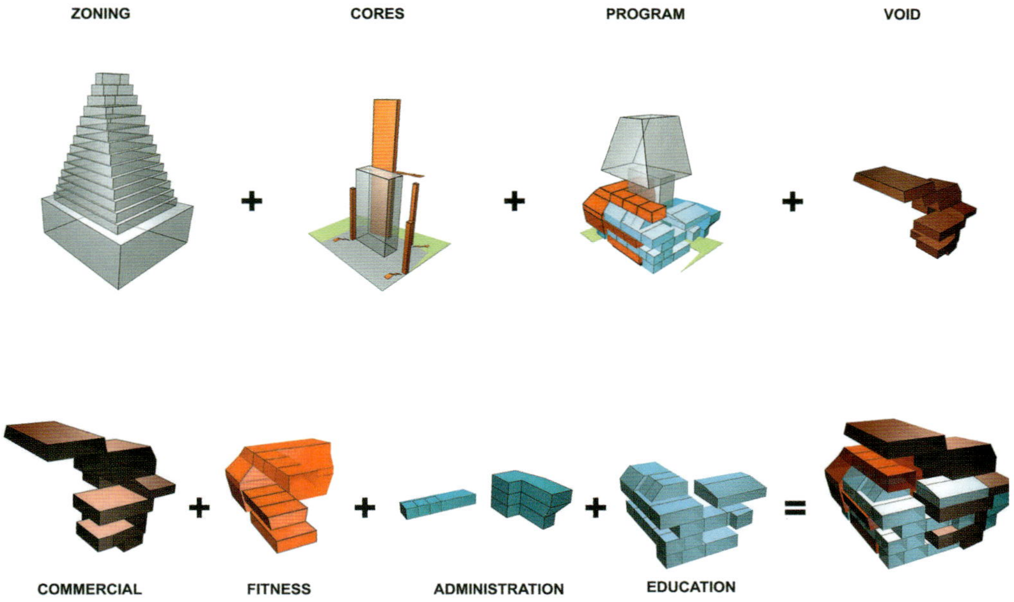

01 Southern view of the tower **02** View from the street
03 Interior view of sky chapel **04** Concept

Renderings: © William Feuerman

CITY: New York (NY)
COUNTRY: USA
REGION: North America
TYPOLOGY: Ecclesiastical
COMPLETION: 2006, speculative
WEBSITE: www.officefeuerman.com
ARCHITECTS: Office Feuerman

CITY New York (NY)

COUNTRY USA

REGION North America

TYPOLOGY Ecclesiastical

COMPLETION unrealized

WEBSITE www.fgca.com

ARCHITECTS Franke, Gottsegen, Cox Architects

WEST-PARK PRESBYTERIAN CHURCH

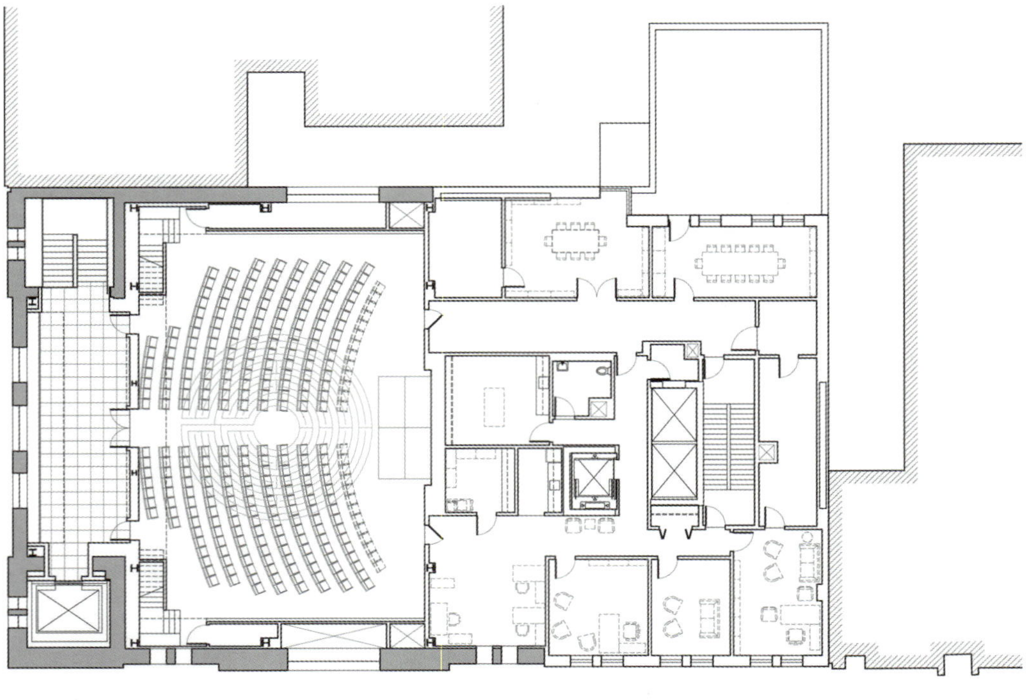

The proposal to build a new 21-story apartment building makes it possible for the church to remain on the corner of 86th Street and Amsterdam Ave on the upper west side of Manhattan, where it has been for more than 125 years. The modernist design of the church interior is a reflection of the congregation's desire to express their forward thinking mission for the 21st Century, while maintaining historical continuity by preserving the exterior, viewed as a significant landmark by the neighboring community. With this in mind, the apartment building would fit into the neighborhood context of early 20th Century masonry buildings.

01 Exterior view, apartment building **02** Rendering **03** Interior view, sanctuary **04** Floor plan sanctuary

Photos: Chuck Choi
Renderings: Jon Seagull

THE HIGH LINE

The master plan for this elevated railroad spur stretching 1.45 miles along Manhattan's Westside, is inspired by the melancholic beauty of the ruin today, where nature has reclaimed a once vital piece of urban infrastructure. The team retools this industrial conveyance into a postindustrial instrument of leisure reflection about the very categories of "nature" and "culture". By changing the rules of engagement between plant life and pedestrians, the strategy of "agri-tecture" combines organic and building materials into a blend of changing proportions that accommodate the wild, cultivated, intimate, and the hyper-social.

01 Bird's eye view **02** View from the street **03** Strategy of "agri-tecture" **04** Staircase **05** Exterior view by night

Renderings: FO - Field Operations; Diller Scofidio + Renfro

CITY
New York (NY)

COUNTRY
USA

REGION
North America

TYPOLOGY
Transportation

COMPLETION
2008

WEBSITE
www.fieldoperations.net;
www.dillerscofidio.com

ARCHITECTS
FO - Field Operations;
Diller Scofidio + Renfro

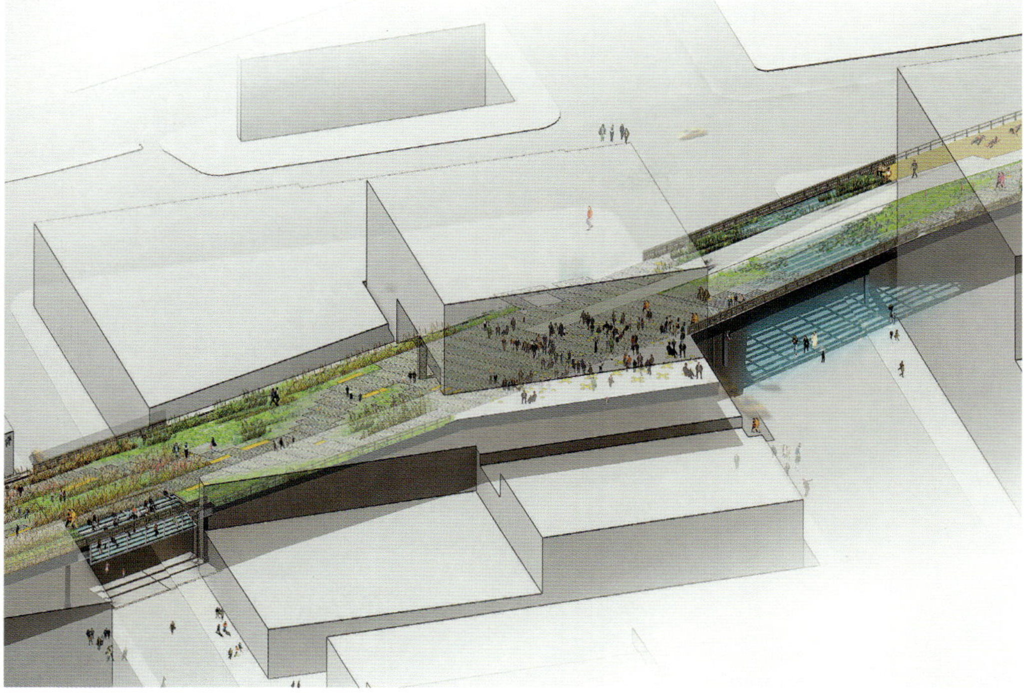

CITY
New York (NY)

COUNTRY
USA

REGION
North America

TYPOLOGY
Living

COMPLETION
2006

WEBSITE
www.gluckmanmayner.com

ARCHITECTS
Gluckman Mayner Architects

ONE KENMARE SQUARE

Located at the east end of Delancey St., the main thoroughfare leading from the Williamsburg Bridge into Manhattan, this mixed-use residential building acts as the terminus of the view corridor from the Bridge. Sited on a flag-shaped lot, the project consists of two buildings; an 11-story building on Lafayette St., and a 6-story building on Crosby St. 73 residential apartments are accommodated on the upper floors, while retail space is provided on the ground level. Derived from the banded masonry façades of early 20th-century warehouse construction, the undulating façade animates the continuous street wall along Lafayette St.

01 Detail undulating façad **02** View from Lafayette St
03 Glass detail of façade

Photos: Gavin Jackson

NEW YORK TOWNHOUSE

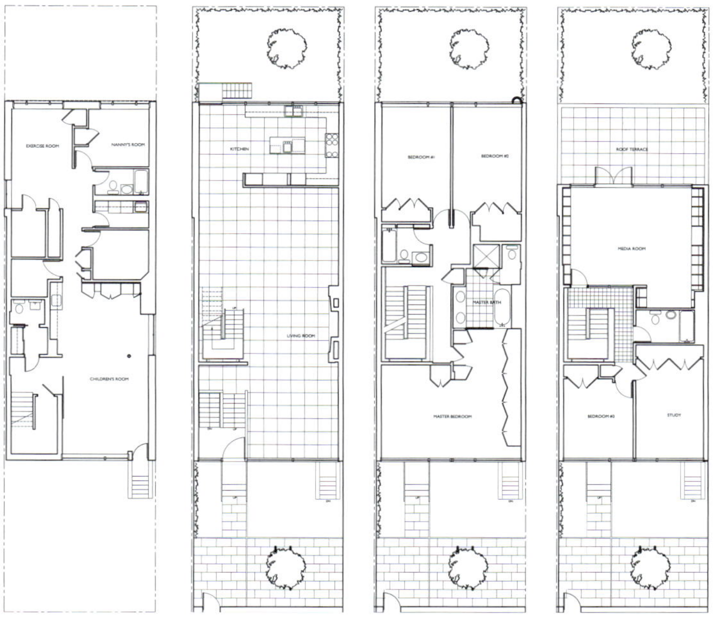

This project involved the renovation and expansion of a 1958 town house. A floor was added to the two-story building, extending the facade vertically while respecting the vocabulary of the original structure. The interior was gutted, with the exception of the main floor where original finishes were maintained. The central stair was restored and brought up to the third level, adding an interesting space element to the development. A large skylight floods the atrium with light, illuminating the main level through translucent glass block floors, giving this New York Townhouse a bright elemental feature.

01 Interior view, fireplace 02 Detail kitchen 03 Exterior view
04 Interior view, media room 05 Floor plans

Photos: Peter Aaron/Esto

CITY
New York (NY)

COUNTRY
USA

REGION
North America

TYPOLOGY
Living

COMPLETION
—

WEBSITE
www.gorlinarchitect.com

ARCHITECTS
Alexander Gorlin Architect

NORFOLK STREET RESIDENCES

The Norfolk Street Residences, an architectural structure creatively designed by the company of Grzywinski Pons Architects, is a development where such expressions of simplicity, lucidity, and clarity transmit a certain transparency that really seems to work and triumph at these residential complexes, which are located on the Lower East Side. Different characteristics such as the façade's curtain wall, reveals an interesting interior assemblage and combination of materials and massing, resulting in such features as the culmination of a roof-deck, where you can also find an appealing swimming pool.

01 Roof-deck with swimming pool **02** Exterior view curtain wall **03** Sketch **04** View through the façade

Renderings: Grzywinski Pons Architects

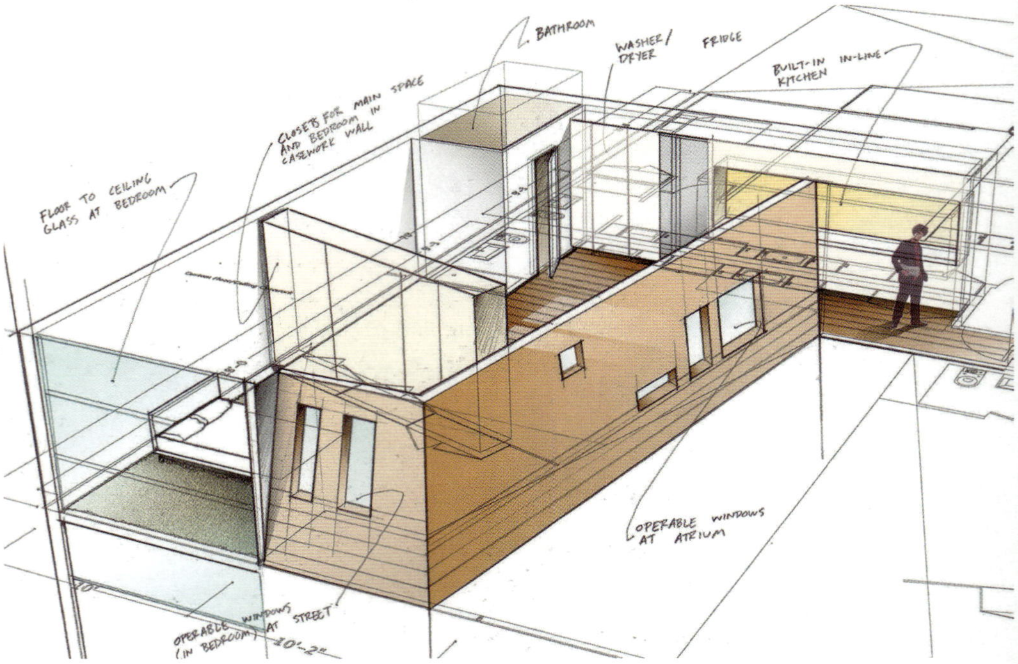

MIYAKE MADISON

The design for Issey Miyake's Madison Avenue store consisted of an interior renovation and a new façade on the historic shopping street. Breaking the threshold between the sidewalk and the world of Issey Miyake, the transparent façade creates a seamless barrier from which the volume of the shop is extruded. To further multiply this effect, an electronic mirror allows customers to see themselves from all perspectives and in turn extends the space through electronic means. In effect, the entire shop becomes a giant store window with mannequins dispersed throughout the entire depth of the space.

01 Floor and ceiling plan **02** Exterior view, transparent façade **03** Display desk **04** Interior view

Renderings: Mikiko Kikuyama

CITY: New York (NY)
COUNTRY: USA
REGION: North America
TYPOLOGY: Retail
COMPLETION: 2006
WEBSITE: www.gtects.com
ARCHITECTS: Gordon Kipping (GTECTS)

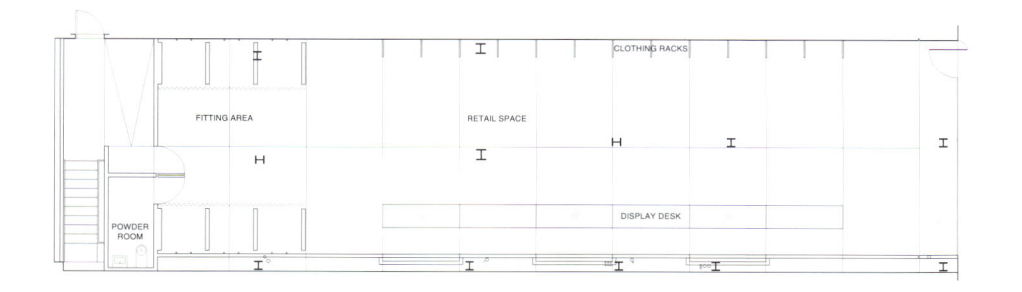

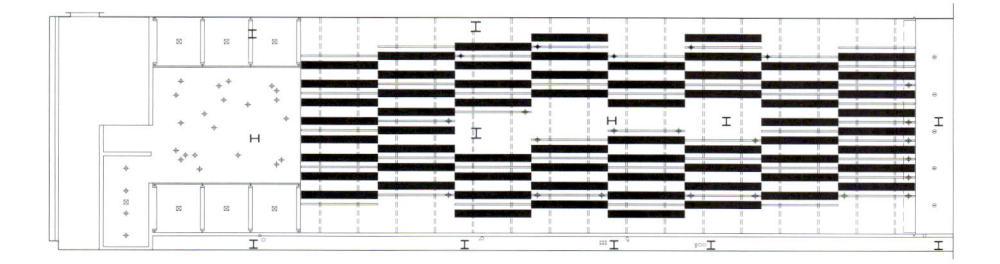

NATIONAL SEPTEMBER 11TH MEMORIAL AT THE WORLD TRADE CENTER

The project's elegant simplicity conceals an incredible complexity of architectural design and engineering. The fourteen-acre WTC site will contain, in addition to the memorial and the museum, a visitor center, a new train station, a subway station, an underground retail concourse, an underground road network with security screening areas, five new office towers, and an arts center. Most of these projects interlock physically and programmatically with the eight-acre Memorial site. The project presents creative design responses that are specific to the Memorial project yet address concerns ranging from sustainability to security.

01 Memorial plaza at night **02** South pool **03** Site plan **04** Aerial view

Renderings: Handel Architects

CITY
New York (NY)

COUNTRY
USA

REGION
North America

TYPOLOGY
Public

COMPLETION
2011

WEBSITE
www.handelarchitects.com

ARCHITECTS
Michael Arad, AIA /
Handel Architects, LLP

JULIANA CURRAN TERIAN PRATT PAVILLION

Showcasing work from the Institute's various arts programs, the project is a new focal point for the Pratt Institute campus in Brooklyn, New York. Clad with stainless steel and suspended between two existing industrial loft buildings, the project includes a glass entry area for the Pavilion and its neighbors, Steuben Hall and Pratt Studios. The overall new construction for the Pavilion and its auxiliary areas including the glass entrance and a new circulation bridge to the south, comprise of 10,000 square feet. Behind the Pavilion, a new courtyard makes an outdoor room for informal meetings and classes in warm weather.

01 Detail stainless steel façade **02** Floor plan **03** Interior view, gallery **04** Glass entry area

Photos: Paul Warchol Photography

CITY New York (NY)
COUNTRY USA
REGION North America
TYPOLOGY Culture
COMPLETION 2006
WEBSITE www.hanrahanmeyers.com
ARCHITECTS hMa hanrahanMeyers architects

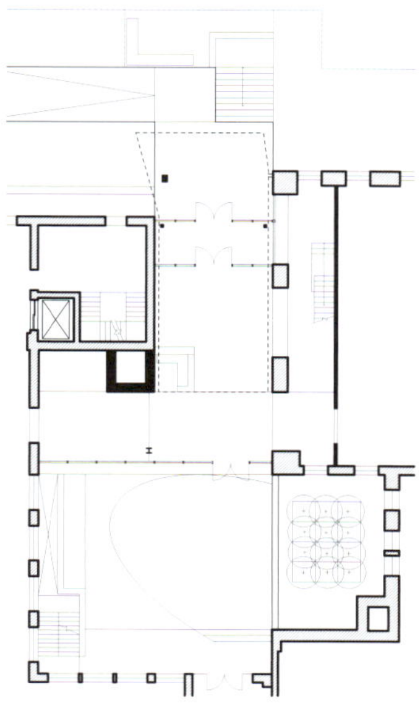

CITY New York (NY)

COUNTRY USA

REGION North America

TYPOLOGY Culture

COMPLETION 2007

WEBSITE www.hanrahanmeyers.com

ARCHITECTS hMa hanrahanMeyers architects

WAVELINE

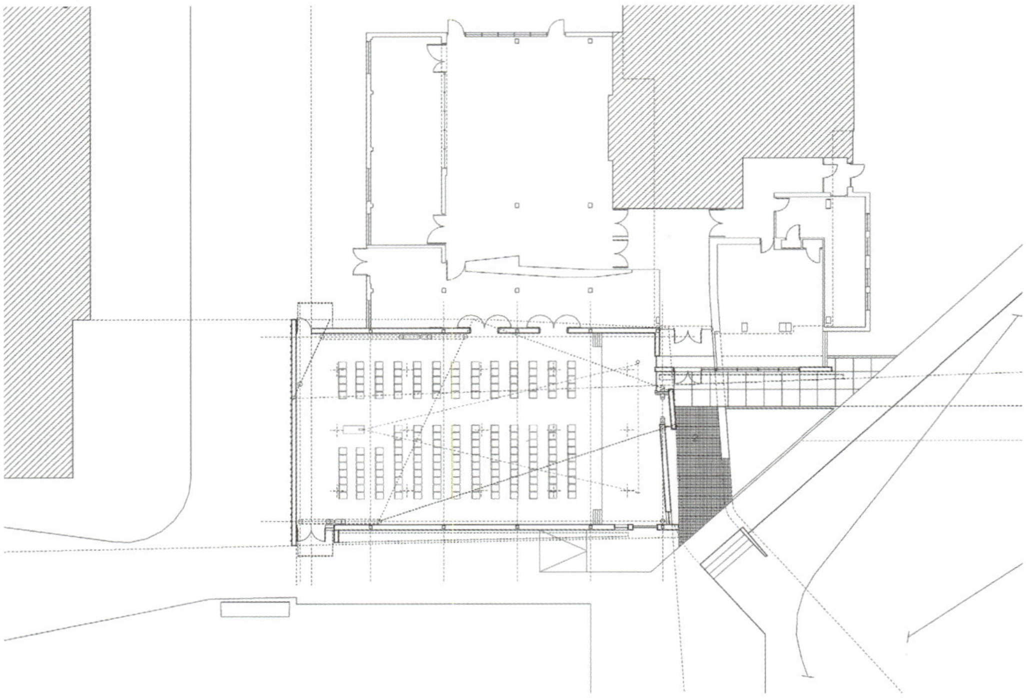

Waveline is a 5,000-square-foot multi-purpose theater adjacent to an existing community center in Queens, New York. Within a 90-foot by 50-foot site footprint the structure is as large as possible to accommodate theatrical productions. The roof, the principal design feature of the new building, is a bent plane running east west and resting on columns. It was designed as a sculptural shape with standing seam stainless steel cladding. The roof shape is also a direct response to acoustic studies, developing optimal sound projections for theatrical productions in the space.

01 Exterior view of waveline with focus on stainless steel cladding **02** Entrance plaza **03** Interior view **04** Main floor plan

Photos: Michael Moran Photography

DIANE VON FÜRSTENBERG STUDIO'S NEW HEADQUARTERS

This building in New York City's Meatpacking district serves as the new headquarters for Diane von Furstenberg Studio, a fashion design company. The building houses the company's New York store, a 5,000 SF showroom, design and administrative offices and an executive suite. The project's diverse program is unified through a singular iconic gesture: a stairway that collects and distributes light from the roof through to the deepest interior parts of the building. The guardrail will be created from vertical cables, between which will be strung glass crystals provided by Swarovski. A heliostat mirror will track the sun throughout the day and focus light on the crystals, spreading natural light across the ceiling of each floor.

01 Interior view **02** Aerial view by night **03** Interior view

Photos: Elizabeth Felicella Photography

CITY New York (NY)
COUNTRY USA
REGION North America
TYPOLOGY Mixed-use
COMPLETION 2007
WEBSITE www.work.ac
ARCHITECTS Work Architecture Company

ALVIN AILEY AMERICAN DANCE FOUNDATION

Being the largest facility dedicated exclusively to dance in the US, the building links projects to a mix of both vibrant and eclectic cultural and entertainment venues in the Times Square area. Features include 12 dance studios, a 5,000-square-foot black box theater with flexible seating, adjacent green room and concession stand/boutique, dressing rooms and warm-up areas, archive and library facilities, costume shop, physical therapy facilities, lounges, and administrative offices. In addition to these spaces, the building features long-distance learning capabilities in various studios as well as a performance theater.

01 View from the street **02** Exterior view from east **03** Detail glass façade **04** Ground floor plan

Photos: Arch Photo Inc.

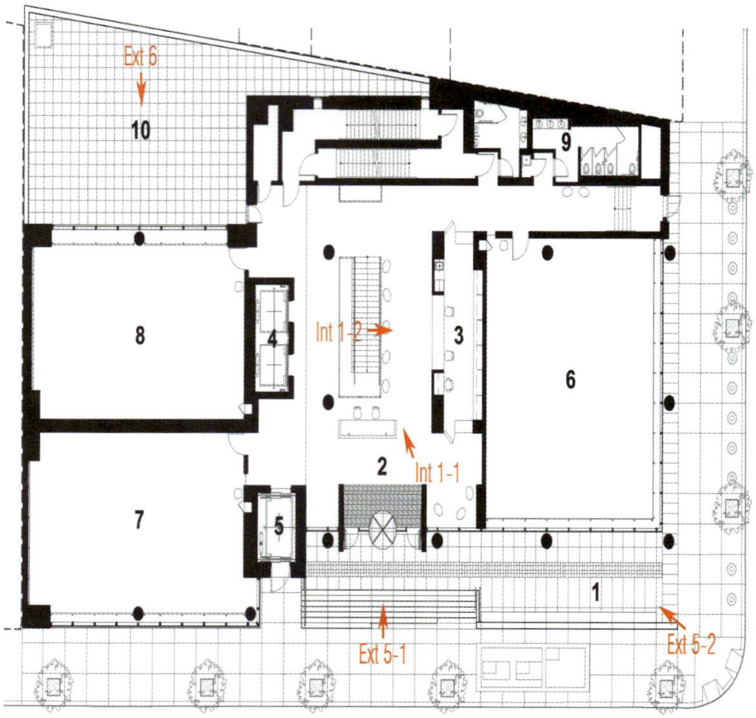

ONISHI GALLERY / GALLERY MEMORIA

Onishi Gallery / Gallery Memoria located in the heart of Manhattan's Chelsea neighborhood was conceived as a mediating space. The space is designed to enhance the moment for contemplation, differentiated for contemplation of art and contemplation of traditionally crafted altars from Japan. The definition of space is determined by moments of transition between the different surfaces, exposing the perceptual continuity of the gallery.

01 Interior view, gallery as mediating space **02** Detail interior
03 Surfaces in transition **04** Exterior view from the street
05 Interior view

Photos: Seong Kwon Photography

CITY New York (NY)
COUNTRY USA
REGION North America
TYPOLOGY Culture
COMPLETION 2007
WEBSITE www.knobsdesign.com
ARCHITECTS José Salinas / KNOBSDesign

CITY
New York (NY)

COUNTRY
USA

REGION
North America

TYPOLOGY
Culture

COMPLETION
2005

WEBSITE
www.kpf.com

ARCHITECTS
Kohn Pedersen Fox Associates (in collaboration / joint venture with: Taniguchi Associates)

MUSEUM OF MODERN ART

The 630,000 - square-foot Museum is twice the size of the former facility, offering dramatically expanded and redesigned spaces for exhibitions, public programming, educational outreach, and scholarly research. The primary objective is to create an ideal environment for the interaction of people and art, with the first floor consisting mainly of public spaces, while the galleries all begin on the second level. A book & design store, and restaurant entrances are all deployed along the street side, at ground level. Curatorial departments & skylit conservation areas are collectively located above the new expansion-site galleries.

01 Bird's eye view of the garden and museum by nigh **02** Rockefeller building **03** Atrium view **04** View of the sculpture garden by day

Photos: Timothy Hursley

FLOWER HOUSE

The Flower house is a design project brought to an architectural scale, challenging prefabrication and mobility. Playful in nature, it is an experimental design aimed at broadening our social conditioning of modern living. Although portable architecture is not new, the defining 'new' element here is the way to look at it and the way to design it. Current architectural attempts at temporary living space reduce the idea of "mobility" to transportable boxes (containers turned into living spaces). The Flower House is about temporary living "outside of the box", enhancing the perception of the space inside and out.

01 Main view house in Arizona **02** Interior view **03** Section **04** Living room

Renderings: LADESIGN New York

CITY New York (NY)
COUNTRY USA
REGION North America
TYPOLOGY Living
COMPLETION unbuilt
WEBSITE www.l-a-design.com
ARCHITECTS leonardo Annecca / LADESIGN New York

CITY
New York (NY)

COUNTRY
USA

REGION
North America

TYPOLOGY
Culture

COMPLETION
2001

WEBSITE
www.leeser.com

ARCHITECTS
Leeser Architecture

EYEBEAM ATELIER, MUSEUM OF ART & TECHNOLOGY

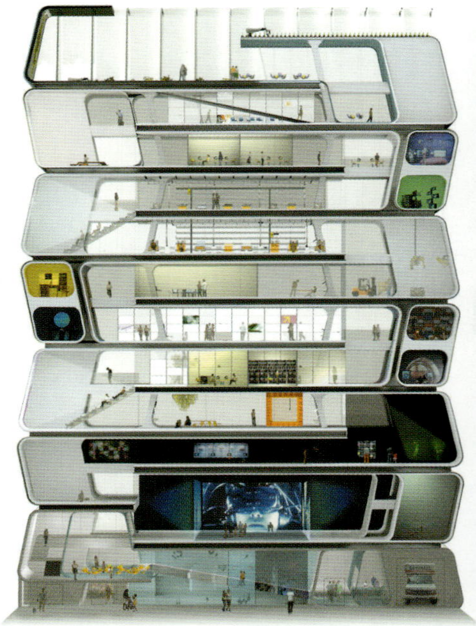

The design concept is rooted in the context of Chelsea as a transforming industrial neighborhood. The contextual scale of two-storey warehouses and garages serves as the organizational structure for the new museum, with the garage being an incomplete, ever changing, but perfect space. Stacking and interlocking this model produces an assembly of high-tech new media shops, blurring the traditional boundaries of production and exhibition, visitor and visited, curator and artist, observer and observed. The notion of the museum as an incomplete instrument to be used, altered and explored renders this building timeless.

01 Rear view **02** Exterior view, front façade **03, 04** Lobby **05** Section **06** Detail roof

Renderings: Leeser Architecture

MIXED GREENS GALLERY

The space the client secured for the gallery, located in the Chelsea Art District of Manhattan, had an irregular structural condition: a series of large wood columns and beams running variably down the middle of the space. Initially seen as an impediment to the organization, exhibition layout, and clean mechanical runs, this wiggly line of structure became the generator of all patterns. The features evolving from this 'line' of the project include two separate exhibition spaces, gallery offices, storage, and a lounge space for browsing the gallery's online collection or simply for hanging out during opening receptions.

01 Interior view, gallery office **02** Detail **03** Entrance area **04** Exterior view from the street **05** Floor plan

Photos: Michael Moran Photography

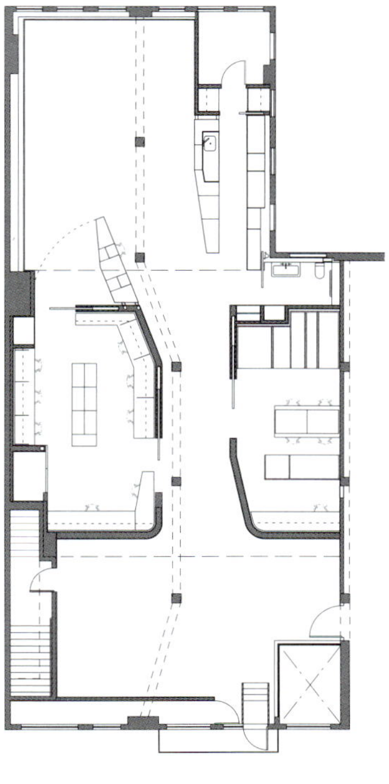

CITY New York (NY)
COUNTRY USA
REGION North America
TYPOLOGY Culture
COMPLETION 2005
WEBSITE www.levenbetts.com
ARCHITECTS Leven Betts Studio Architects

MEMORY FOUNDATIONS / WORLD TRADE CENTER DESIGN STUDY

The design study was selected in February 2003 as the master site plan for the rebuilding of the World Trade Center Site. In addition to a towering spire of 1,776 feet, the plan proposed a complex program which called for the construction of a memorial with waterfalls, an underground museum, a visitor center, retail space, a special transit hub and four office towers spiraling to the height of the Freedom Tower. In addition to the the Freedom Tower, a world-class transportation hub designed by Santiago Calatrava, are four more towers and an awe-inspiring memorial currently under construction in Lower Manhattan.

01 Site plan **02** Four office towers and the Freedom Tower **03** East elevation **04** Exterior view Freedom Tower

Renderings: Silverstein Properties (02, 03), Foster and Partners (01), Studio Daniel Libeskind (04)

CITY: New York (NY)
COUNTRY: USA
REGION: North America
TYPOLOGY: Public
COMPLETION: 2010
WEBSITE: www.daniel-libeskind.com
ARCHITECTS: Daniel Libeskind

SHEILA C JOHNSON DESIGN CENTER / THE NEW SCHOOL

The Center is a comprehensive urban renovation that unites the street-level lobbies of four adjacent pre-1917 buildings, creating new common space and identity for Parsons The New School for Design. The facility houses a series of public programs including a new West 13th Street entry, a renovated 5th Avenue entry, an auditorium, conservation quality art galleries and archives, a future design store, a sky-lit "urban quad," an orientation center, and two new seminar rooms. These expanded programs represent a significant opportunity to raise the visibility, quality and functionality of academic and public program spaces.

01, 02 Interior view, united street level lobbies **03** Lobby critique zone **04** Building sections

Photos: Michael Moran
Renderings: Lyn Rice Architects

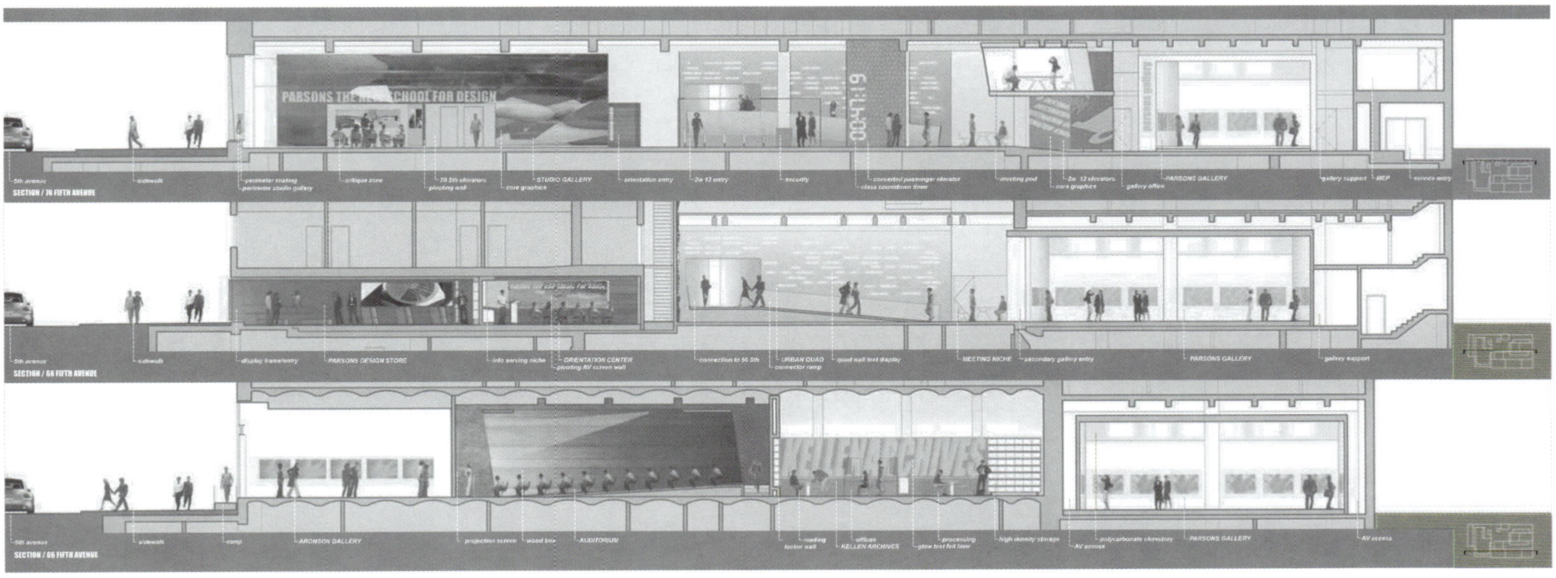

CITY New York (NY)
COUNTRY USA
REGION North America
TYPOLOGY Education
COMPLETION 2008
WEBSITE www.lrany.com
ARCHITECTS Lyn Rice Architects

NIKE ID DESIGN STUDIO

The project is an interactive showroom where guests can create their own sneakers, aided by in-house design assistants. In detailing the interior, the architect was guided by the inherent contradiction between luxury, which is sedentary, comfortable, and elite, and athleticism, seen as active, strenuous, and egalitarian. An implied sense of movement suffuses every surface and finish, injecting a sense of restlessness into the otherwise stolid space. Flocked wallpaper, which at first resembles a stuffy Victorian floral pattern, reveals on closer examination tiny images of sneakers, basketballs, and the patterns of sneaker soles.

01 Exterior view **02** Floor plan **03** Studio **04** Reception

Photos: Paul Warchol Photography

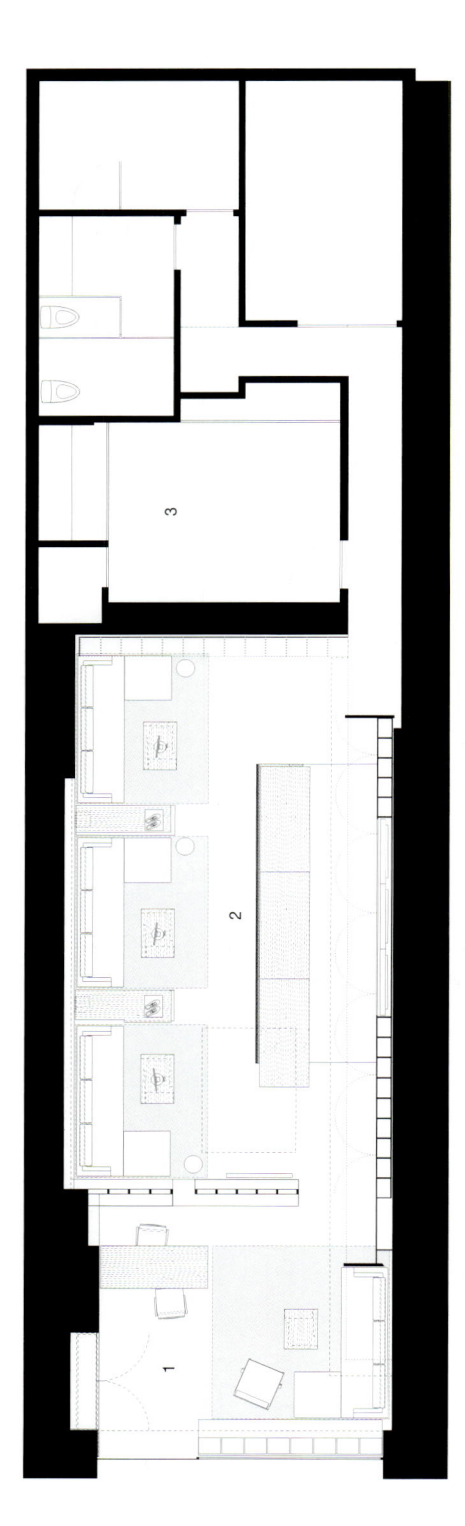

CITY New York (NY)
COUNTRY USA
REGION North America
TYPOLOGY Retail
COMPLETION 2005
WEBSITE www.lyncheisingerdesign.com
ARCHITECTS Lynch / Eisinger Design

LARCHMONT RESIDENCE

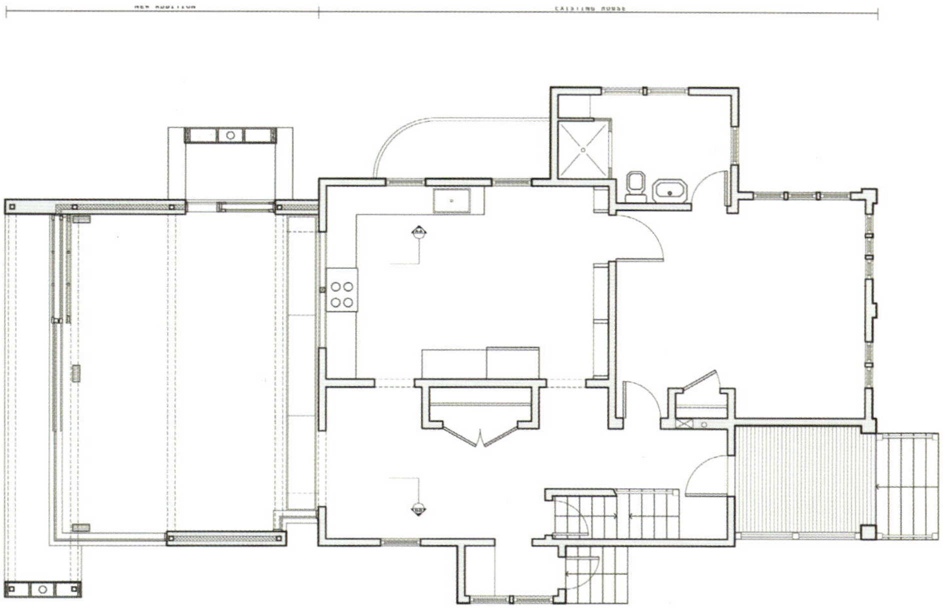

Located in the small suburban village of Larchmont just north of NYC, this typical suburban neighborhood is known for its tree-lined streets and traditional houses. The rear portion of the house faces directly south in order for floor-to-ceiling glass to maximize the views and sun penetration during winter. A developed method to manually screen glass walls by creating a series of sliding panels were hung from the ceiling. A glass floor and linear skylight separate the new addition from the old and provide natural light.

01 View from south, glass opening **02** Interior view **03** Side view addition and old house **04** Floor plan

Photos: Wade Zimmerman

CITY New York (NY)
COUNTRY USA
REGION North America
TYPOLOGY Living
COMPLETION 2007
WEBSITE www.mccrumarchitects.com
ARCHITECTS mccrumarchitects

CITY New York (NY)
COUNTRY USA
REGION North America
TYPOLOGY Living
COMPLETION 2003
WEBSITE www.mesh-arc.com
ARCHITECTS MESH Architectures

DOWNTOWN DUPLEX

Starting from the concept of a loft as a microcosmic urban space, this duplex became a dynamic setting for exploration and concentration by creating loosely connected zones with varied environments. A fiberglass wall runs along the length of the two-storey space and contains loft infrastructure including plumbing, air conditioning, electrical, and lighting. LCD screens embedded in walls, furniture, and cabinetry, provide access to the Home Operating System; a web-based home control and communication system. The exterior-viewless home is an inward-focused sanctuary and an active site for mediated connection to the outside world.

01 Upper floor with glass fireplace **02** Glass bridge over old timber structure **03** Fiberglass bathroom **04** Kitchen **05** Floor plans **06** Stair with programmed LED floor and wall

Photos: Andrew Bordwin

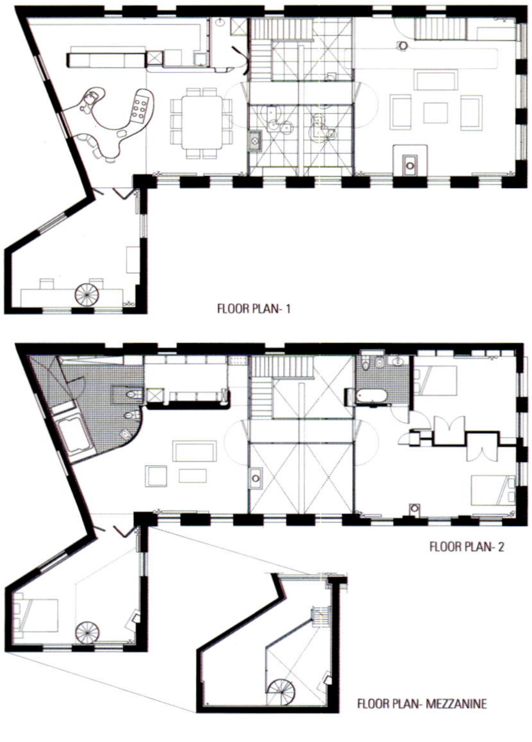

NEW ACADEMIC BUILDING FOR THE COOPER UNION FOR THE ADVANCEMENT OF SCIENCE AND ART

The facility is conceived as a stacked vertical piazza, contained within a semitransparent envelope, articulating the classroom and laboratory spaces. Organized around a central atrium, a connective volume, spanned by sky bridges, opens up view corridors across Third Avenue to the Foundation Building. Many of the public functions, including retail space and a lobby exhibition gallery, are located at ground level, while a second gallery and a 200-seat auditorium are easily accessible from the street. The interior space configuration encourages interconnection between the school's Engineering, Art, and Architecture departments.

01 Detail atrium and sky bridges **02** Exterior view from the street **03** Atrium silk screen **04** Section

Renderings: Morphosis

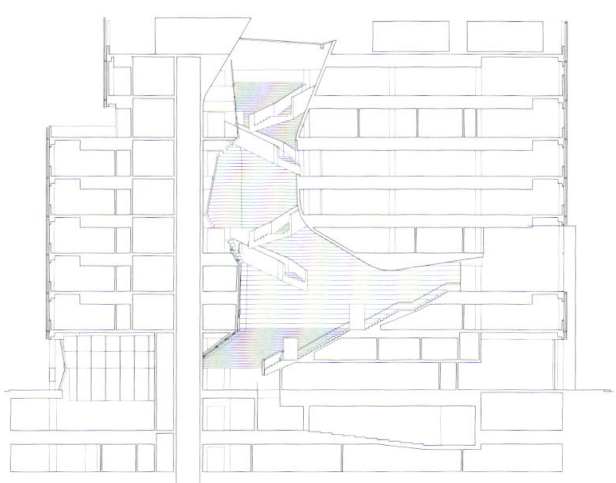

CITY New York (NY)
COUNTRY USA
REGION North America
TYPOLOGY Culture / Education
COMPLETION 2008
WEBSITE www.morphosis.net
ARCHITECTS Morphosis / Thom Mayne

CITY New York (NY)

COUNTRY USA

REGION North America

TYPOLOGY Living / Culture

COMPLETION 2007

WEBSITE www.narchitects.com

ARCHITECTS nARCHITECTS

SWITCH BUILDING

Switch Building is a 7-story apartment and art gallery building in Manhattan's Lower East Side. The project's design emerges not only from a creative interpretation of some of the narrow constraints imposed by zoning, but also in regards to the developer's needs. While the apartment plans are identical, the `switching` of bay windows and balconies allow each unit to be unique in providing light qualities and views to the city. The gallery introduces a larger scale into the Lower East Side's burgeoning art scene, which has been primarily inserting cultural programs into former tenement buildings.

01 View from the street **02** Detail bay windows **03** Lobby
04 Interior view, staircase **05** Floors plans

Photos: Frank Oudeman

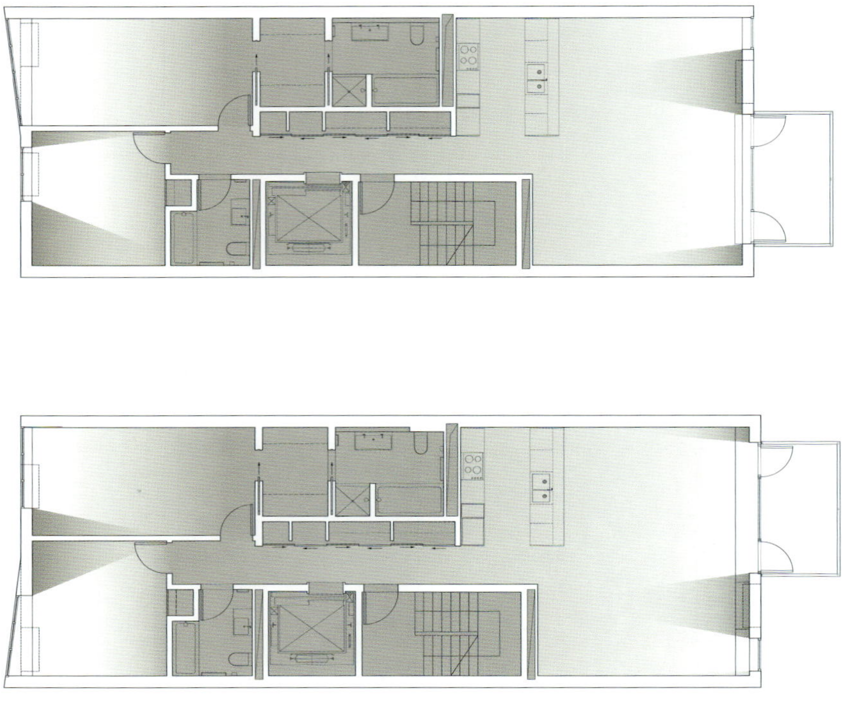

THE MOUNTAIN HUT

The roof, wall and floor surfaces are designed with consideration of environmental criteria for harnessing sunlight energy, water, and natural ventilation. The layout was generated using software which charted gravity-pulled particles flowing towards four distributed nodes optimized for structural load and rain-water collection. The roof is perforated with the "zipper", and the "eyelid" systems of openings. Whereas the "zippers" are manually opened vents, the "eyelids", contain photo and heat-sensitive gels that passively react to heat or direct sunlight by changing phase states to provide shade and insulate the interior.

01 Detail roofing membrane with embedded thin-film photovoltaic material **02** Exterior view **03** Roof diagrams **04** Section

Renderings: Seong Kwon

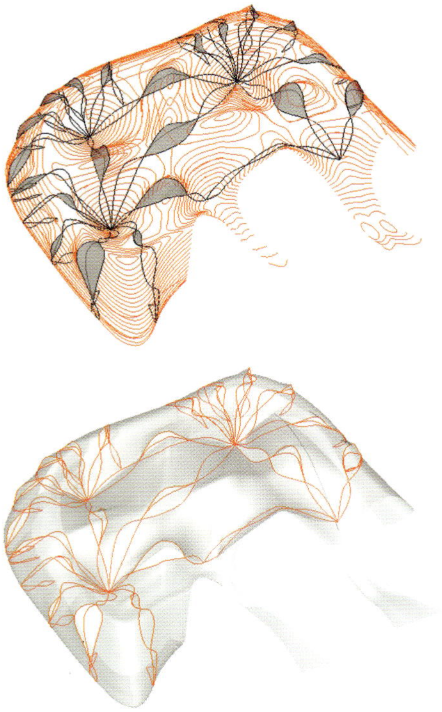

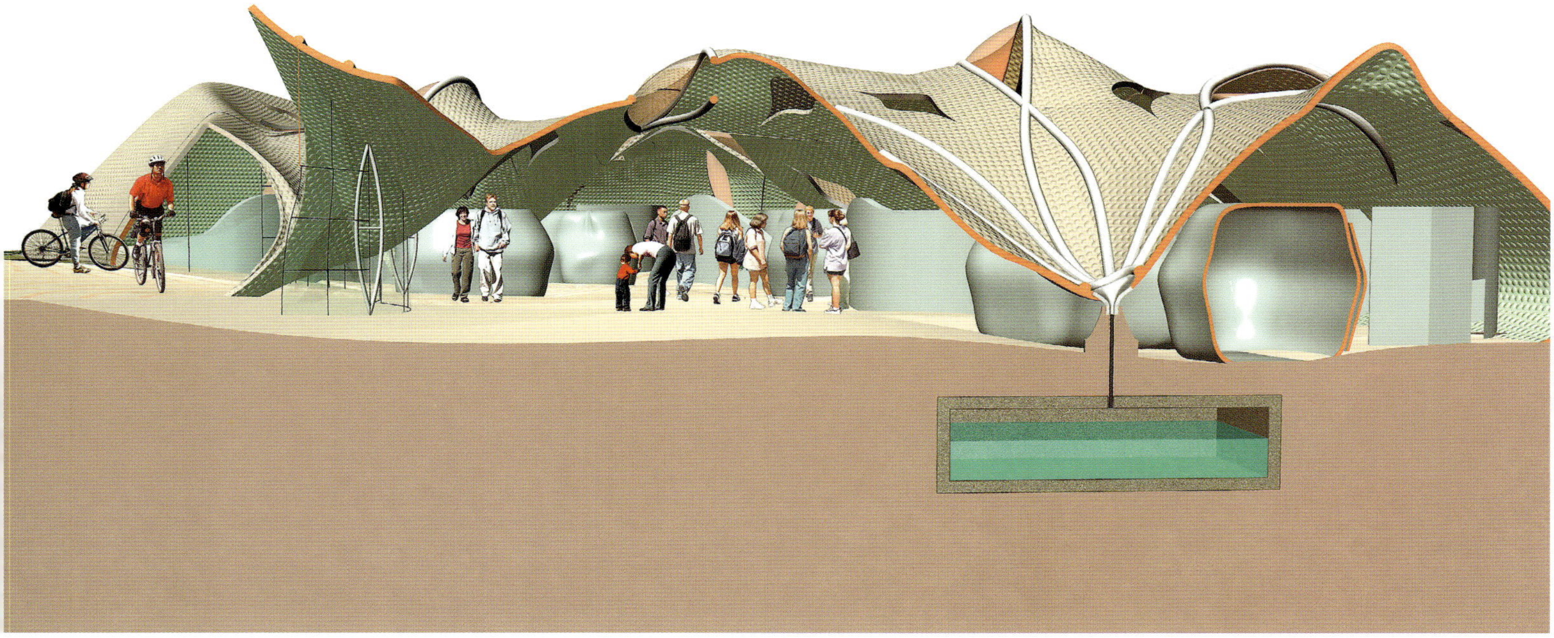

CITY: New York (NY)
COUNTRY: USA
REGION: North America
TYPOLOGY: Leisure
COMPLETION: unbuilt
WEBSITE: www.oceand.com
ARCHITECTS: Ocean D

CITY New York (NY)
COUNTRY USA
REGION North America
TYPOLOGY Living
COMPLETION 2007
WEBSITE www.openshopstudio.com
ARCHITECTS Openshop|Studio

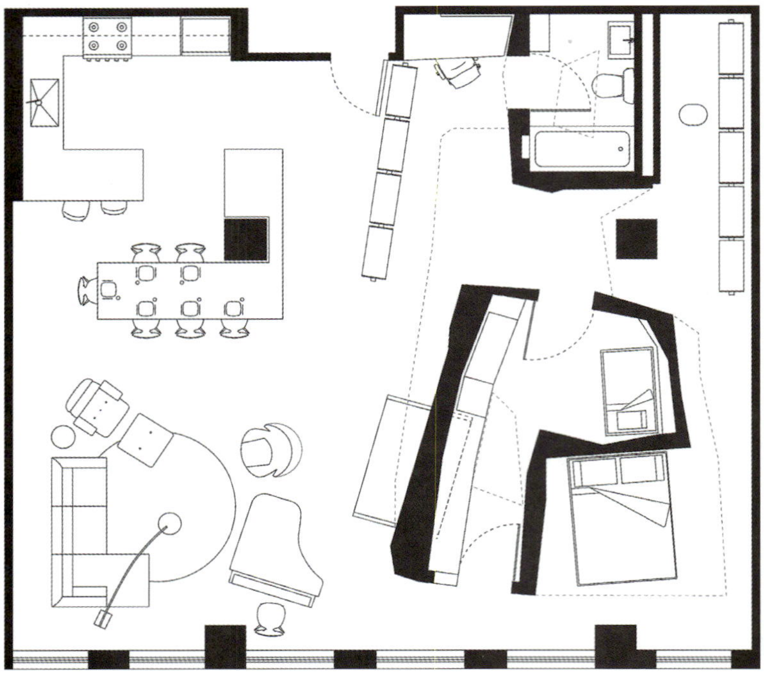

HIVE LOFT

The existing shell of the space in the former Ex-Lax factory was excavated from years of additions, unearthing massive, starkly beautiful concrete columns, smooth concrete floor slabs, and simple, pristine white walls. Working with the client's single request for openness, the enclosed spaces were detached from the surrounding walls and ceiling, creating a freestanding volume that would allow for light and air to be circulated freely. Continually shifting canted surfaces allow the form to fluctuate between a solid, rooted object and one that floats in the space in an apparent defiance of gravity.

01 Floor plan **02** Kids room **03** View from living room to form **04** View from the kitchen **05** Furnished kids room

Photos: Courtesy of Openshop|Studio

TIMES SQUARE RECRUITING CENTER

The Times Square Military Lifestyle Center mines a cache of new military technologies with a domestic agenda – bringing it back to the public in the form of entertainment, sport, and a pioneering new-military-lifestyle. The Pentagon is transplanted to Times Square as an icon from which a new image of the military can be constructed. The military lifestyle center provides many familiar amenities including health & fitness, space for socializing, and a theater. Yet these spaces are uniquely enabled by demilitarized technologies, made available to the public as a gesture towards a more unified domestic and military way of living.

01 Exterior view, façade of sky reflecting EFTE pillows
02 Bird's eye view **03** Plan **04** Section

Renderings: Para-Project

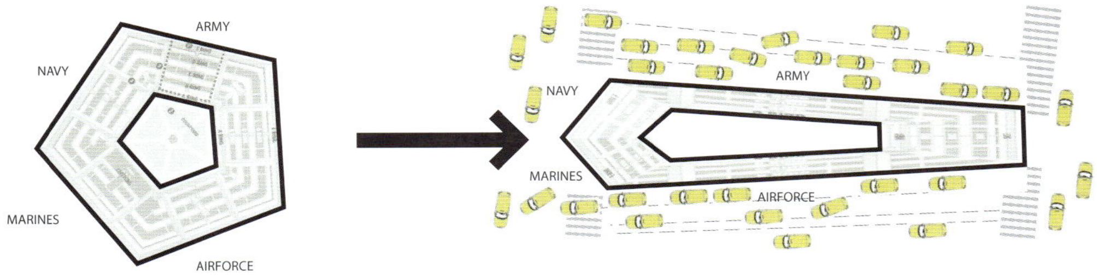

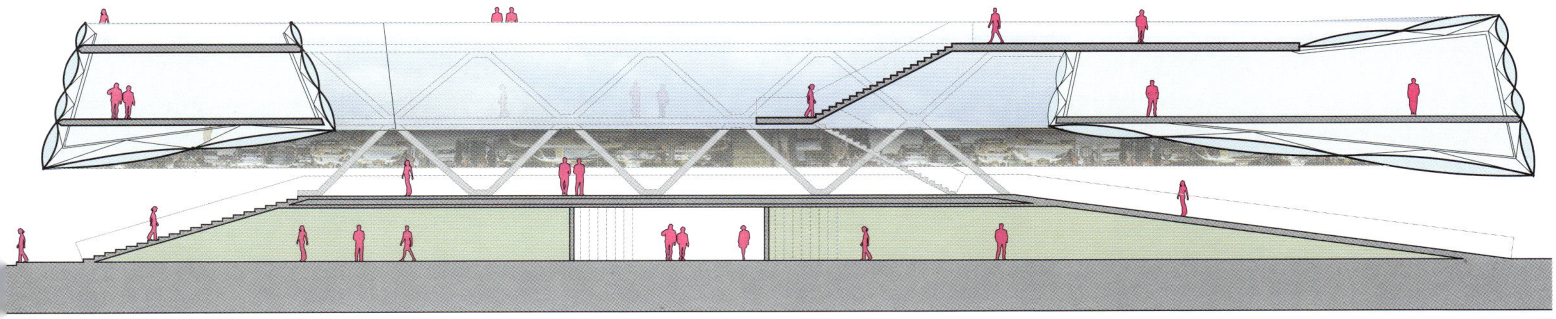

CITY: New York (NY)
COUNTRY: USA
REGION: North America
TYPOLOGY: Institution
COMPLETION: –
WEBSITE: www.para-project.org
ARCHITECTS: PARA

QUEENS HOSPITAL CENTER AMBULATORY CARE PAVILION

The six-story, 144,000-square-foot building is composed of pre-cast concrete and a glass curtain wall. It provides a complement to a recently completed inpatient building and is connected by two pedestrian bridges. A glazed public concourse along the southern perimeter, which provides the central way finding organizing principle, connects to each floor plate's system of waiting rooms, exam rooms, and private staff spaces arranged in a hierarchy of the main spine. The refined interior finishes and use of natural light and clerestory windows reinforces the complex's modern aesthetic.

01 Exterior view with pedestrian bridge to inpatient building **02** Side view **03** Front elevation of pre-cast concrete and glass curtain wall **04** Interior view **05** Entrance area

Photos: Paúl Rivera/ArchPhoto

SUNSHINE CINEMA

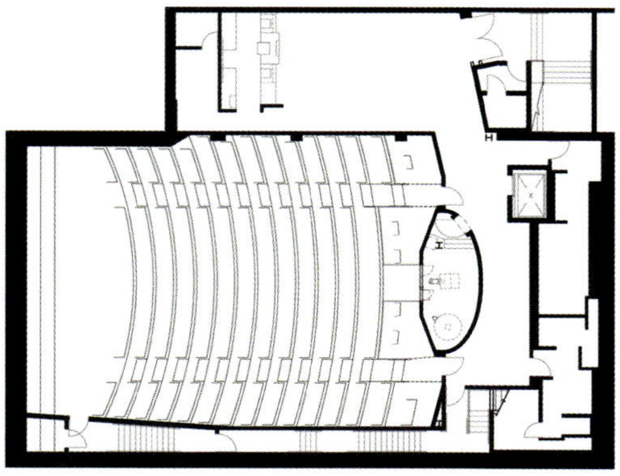

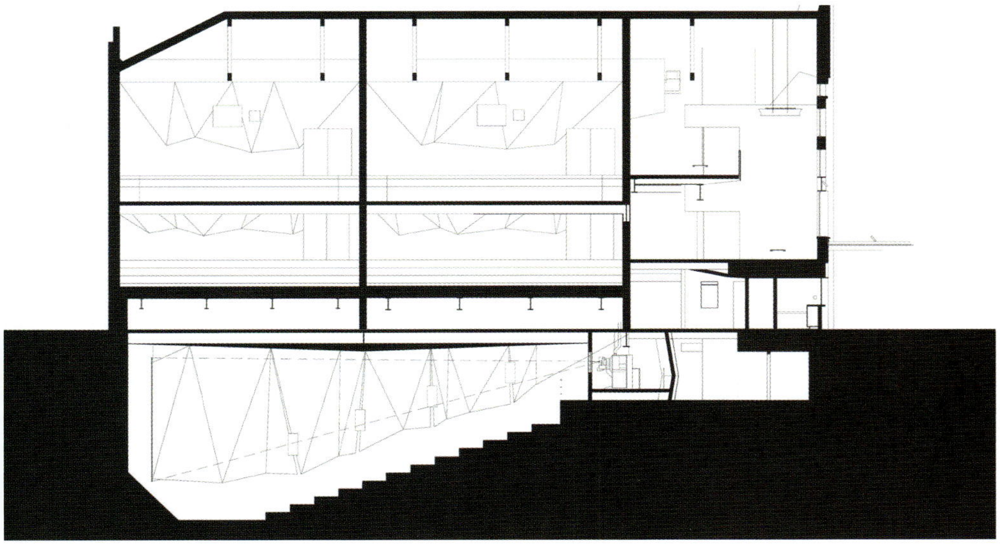

The Sunshine Cinema represents a complete restoration and addition to a century-old theater on the Lower East side of Manhattan to create a new 5-screen, 27,550-square-foot cinema dedicated to first-run Independent and Foreign film for Landmark Theaters. The theaters are housed in the pre-existing structure, and the newly built annex, utilizing a contemporary language of simplicity and transparency, accommodates circulation, concessions and access into the five theaters. The designs deliberate use opposing architectural language strenghtens the relationship between the structures.

01 Detail façade **02** Lower level floor plan **03** Third floor plan **04** Front façade by night **05** Stairway to upper lobby **06** Longitudinal section thru auditoriums

Photos: Whitney Cox, PleskowRael

CITY: New York (NY)
COUNTRY: USA
REGION: North America
TYPOLOGY: Culture
COMPLETION: –
WEBSITE: www.pleskowrael.com
ARCHITECTS: PleskowRael Architecture(s)

408

CITY	New York (NY)
COUNTRY	USA
REGION	North America
TYPOLOGY	Gastronomy
COMPLETION	2005
WEBSITE	www.karimrashid.com
ARCHITECTS	Karim Rashid

NOOCH

Nooch New York is a contemporary noodle restaurant design to interact with the city through its openness and graphical nature. The entrance greeting is a "billboard" of a Pan-Asian model that reflects the nature of the food served and the attitude of the restaurant. The back wall is a large format version of one of Megan Lang's paintings that emphasize the energy of the city and global technical reach of today's culture. The entire restaurant is open through the full-length wrap around glass façade. The city is welcomed in and the diners have the energy of the streets as their backdrop.

01 Front view with "billboard" **02** Interior view, bar **03** Floor plan **04** Interior view, bathroom

Photos: Brian Park

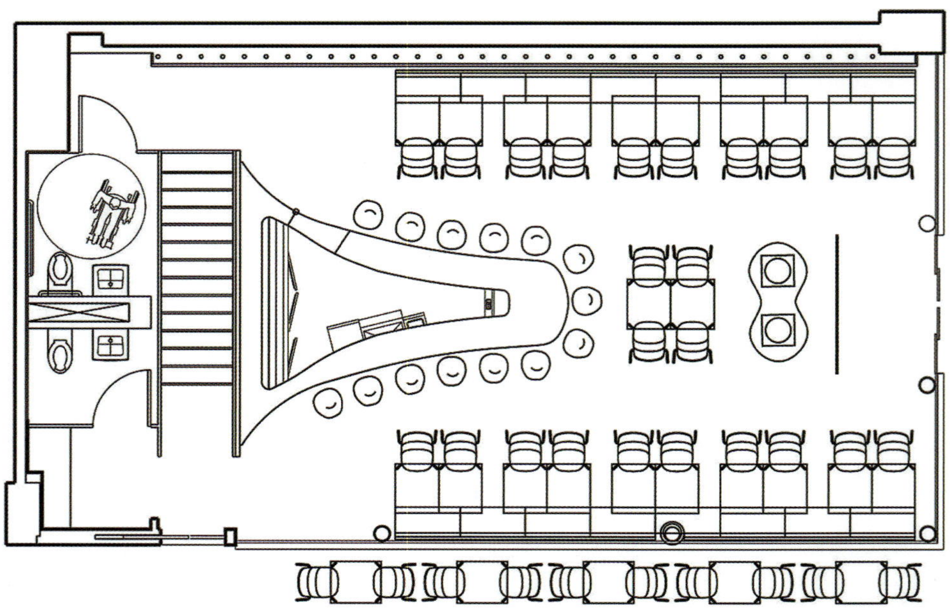

CHOCOLATE BAR

Inspired by the need to meld the hip, "down-town" look of Chocolate Bar with the luxe "uptown" feel of Henri Bendel's, the space faces the atrium in Bendel's, with its landmark Lalique windows, and artfully juxtaposes retail elements and café areas with bronze glass tables and lush banquettes, where the space is designed like a great piece of chocolate to be fun and luxurious. A bronze glass bar offers to-go service set off against a blue backdrop with silver and gold patterns inspired by the Lalique windows. Mirrors and vintage lighting and pared down Victorian pieces contrast the clean lines of the retail displays.

01 View from Bendel's atrium **02** Floor plan **03** Seating and retail display **04** Entrance from the atrium cafe **05** Detail bronze glass bar

Photos: Fabian Birgfeld - photoTECTONICS

CITY
New York (NY)

COUNTRY
USA

REGION
North America

TYPOLOGY
Gastronomy

COMPLETION
2007

WEBSITE
www.reddymadedesign.com

ARCHITECTS
reddymade design

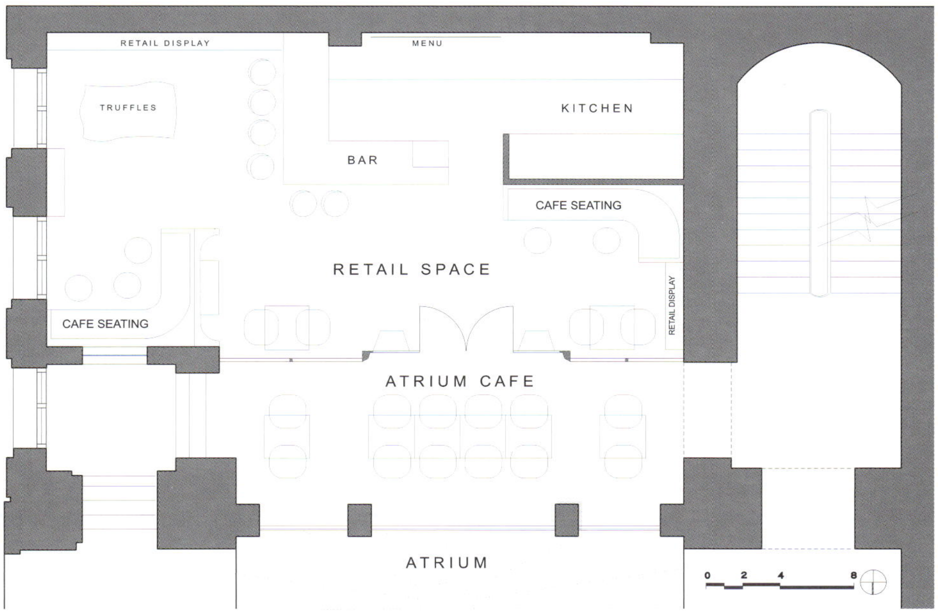

55 WATER STREET PLAZA

55 Water Street Plaza (done in collaboration with landscape architect Ken Smith) seeks to uncover the essential characteristics of a site, creating a new design vocabulary informed by nuances of specific place and audience. In this way, the "elevated acre" responds to its dense urban environment by drawing inspiration from the richly layered context of the city. New escalators, elevators plantings, terraces and a lit beacon bring the park down to the street level, and encourage those on the street to enter the park.

01 Vantage points **02** Exterior view by night **03** Escalator from street level to park

Photos: Nathan Sayers

CITY New York (NY)
COUNTRY USA
REGION North America
TYPOLOGY Public
COMPLETION 2005
WEBSITE www.rogersmarvel.com
ARCHITECTS Rogers Marvel Architects

325 FIFTH AVENUE

Conceived as a classic urban skyscraper, the new 41-story luxury condominium is situated across the Empire State Building, and is a new landmark in the Manhattan skyline. The glass curtain wall assembly incorporates opaque and transparent glass panels, programmed by interior function. The building has 250 bedroom apartments, where one of the floors is devoted to amenities such as a lounge, screening room, children's playroom, outdoor terrace, a fitness center, sauna, and indoor pool. The light-washed lobby welcomes residents with a bamboo forest, waterfall, and a landscaped courtyard garden.

01 Bird's eye view **02** West elevation **03** Interior view, apartment **04** First floor plan

Photos: Christopher Lovi

CITY
New York (NY)

COUNTRY
USA

REGION
North America

TYPOLOGY
Living

COMPLETION
2005

WEBSITE
www.sbjgroup.com

ARCHITECTS
Stephen B. Jacobs Group

412

CITY
New York (NY)

COUNTRY
USA

REGION
North America

TYPOLOGY
Transportation

COMPLETION
2005

WEBSITE
www.schwartzarch.com

ARCHITECTS
Frederic Schwartz Architects

STATEN ISLAND FERRY TERMINAL

The Staten Island Ferry Terminal is located at one of the most spectacular sites in the world: the very tip of Manhattan with the historic New York Harbor as foreground and the picture-postcard Manhattan skyline as the background. This dramatic location sets the project's symbolic role as a gateway to the city. Its function as a significant intermodal transportation node demanded that the new building be imbued with a strong sense of civic presence for the 70,000 commuters and tourists coming through each day, connecting the ferries with a new subway station, four subway lines, three bus lines and taxis.

01 Water view with Manhattan skyline **02** View from plaza to entrance **03** View from east

Photos: Frederic Schwartz Architects

NOMADIC MUSEUM (NEW YORK)

Built in New York last year and ending up near the Santa Monica Pier in Los Angeles this year, photographer Gregory Colbert's Nomadic Museum is a logical system of a traveling museum moving from one city to another. As the main structure of the museum consists of 20-foot long shipping containers, only a small part of the construction materials need to be transported. The transporting of materials was easy, but issues such as increasing the floor area for a bookstore and cinemas of varying sizes had to be overcome. The Museum is scheduled to travel to Tokyo among other Asian countries beginning next year, and afterwards to Europe.

01 View of the historic waterfront pie **02** Interior view, hallway **03** Detail exhibition space **04** Site plan **05** Exterior view

Photos: Michael Moran

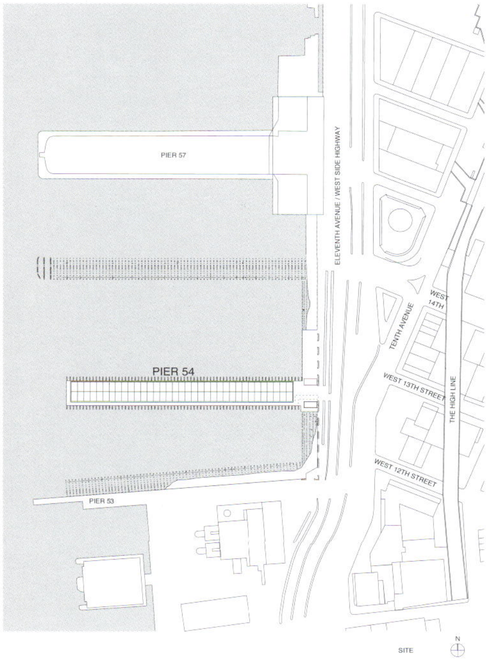

CITY New York (NY)
COUNTRY USA
REGION North America
TYPOLOGY Culture
COMPLETION 2005
WEBSITE www.shigerubanarchitects.com
ARCHITECTS Shigeru Ban Architects (Associate Architect: Dean Maltz Architect)

CITY New York (NY)

COUNTRY USA

REGION North America

TYPOLOGY Living

COMPLETION 2003

WEBSITE www.shoparc.com

ARCHITECTS SHoP Architects

THE PORTER HOUSE

Located in Manhattan's Meatpacking District, the Porter House consists of the renovation and the conversion of a six-story, 30,000-square-foot warehouse to residential condominium use. A new, 15,000-square-foot addition adds four stories to the structure, which cantilever over the lower neighboring buildings to the south. The development produced 22 residences ranging in size from 900 to 3,400-square-feet. The façade uses a custom fabricated metal panel system and floor to ceiling windows that accentuate both the verticality of the structure and the unique interface between the original renaissance revival façade and the new addition.

01 Total view **02** Detail metal panel façade **03** Exterior view by night **04** Seventh floor plan

Photos: Seong Kwon

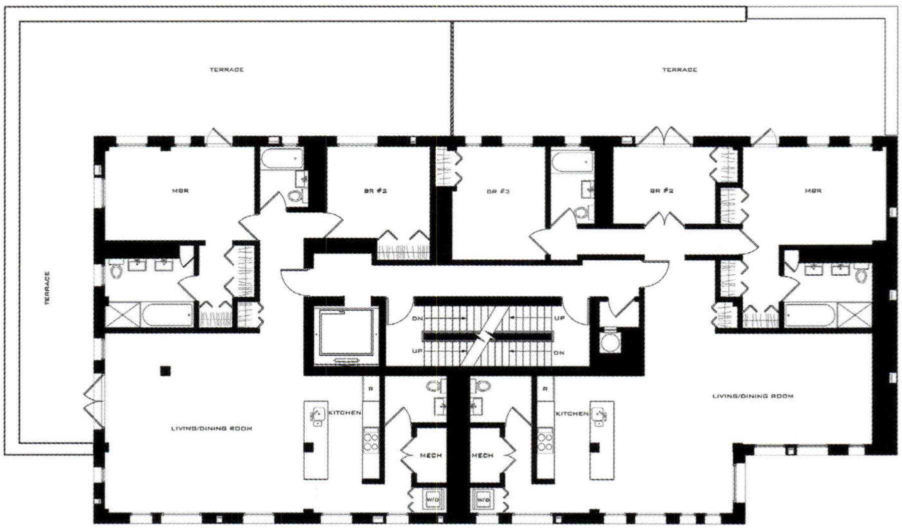

ART GALLERIE & ARCHITECTS' STUDIO

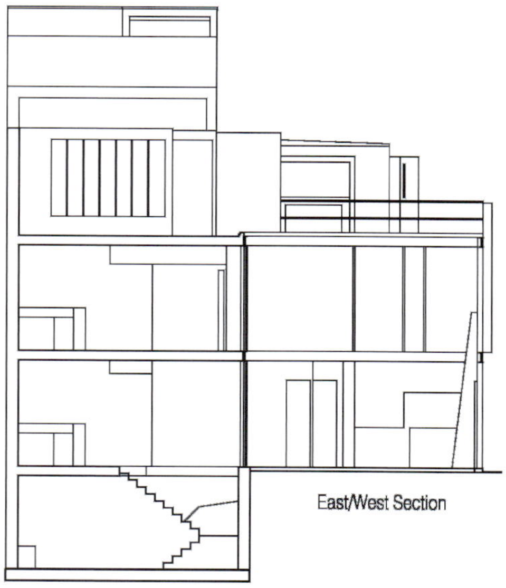

On the outside the character of the oversized steel plates refer to the local industrial and railroad bridges, but on the inside these same plates offers a serene courtyard that makes you forget you're in the middle of Manhattan. Once inside the large sheets of windows and the natural way that the different spaces flow into one another exhibit just how well the architects' understand the fragile symbiosis between natural daylight and interior experience. Subtle visual access between spaces and the elegant way of detailing makes this project a perfectly balanced urban landmark on a corner that became more than just a corner.

01 Courtyard **02** East-west section **03** Living area **04** Corner 23rd Street, detail façade made of steel plates **05** Interior view

Photos: Michael Moran

CITY New York (NY)
COUNTRY USA
REGION North America
TYPOLOGY Culture / Office
COMPLETION 2004
WEBSITE www.smithandthompsonarchitects.com
ARCHITECTS Smith & Thompson Architects

GREENWICH VILLAGE TOWNHOUSE

The renovation of the Greenwich Village Townhouse began with extensive demolition for structural reasons. As a starting point for this project, the townhouse was completely gutted and re-oriented toward the rear garden. The internal space, which was left open at every floor, has clearly defined volumes at the center. These polished plaster boxes containing discrete functions of bathrooms and closets, set the edges of living spaces. Large panels, both solid and translucent, slide or pivot to close off or open up the malleable programmatic arrangements, allowing for either privacy or connection.

01 Rear view, detail façade **02** Floor plans **03** Interior view, detail panel **04** Hallway

Photos: Langdon Clay & Andrew Garn

CITY New York (NY)

COUNTRY USA

REGION North America

TYPOLOGY Living

COMPLETION 2006

WEBSITE www.spgarchitects.com

ARCHITECTS SPG Architects

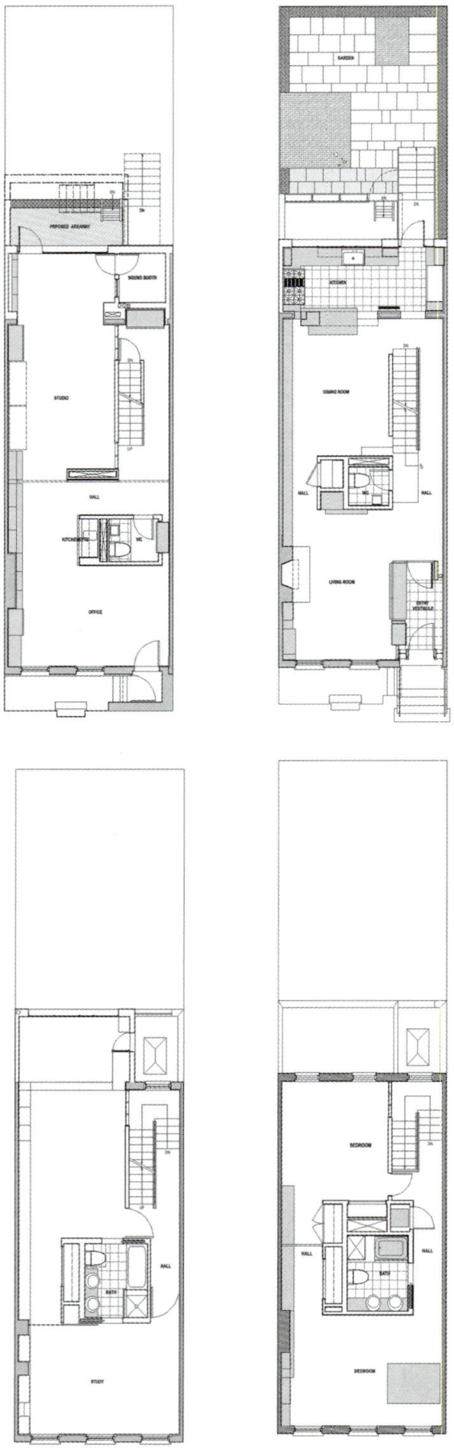

EAST SIDE DUPLEX

This renovation combined two small apartments into a functional duplex home. The new plan for the lower level is an open loft-like living space that includes a kitchen, living room and dining room. On the upper level there are three bedrooms and a new, minimalist stair connection the two levels. The stair is composed of simple wood treads and a delicate steel handrail. A conscious decision was made to limit the palate of materials so the unique beauty of each material would stand out and provide the client with a sumptuous, yet visually understandable, interior space.

01 Living room **02** Steel stair railing with wood treads **03** Kitchen **04** Floor plan, lower level **05** Floor plan, upper level

Photos: Bilyana Dimitrova

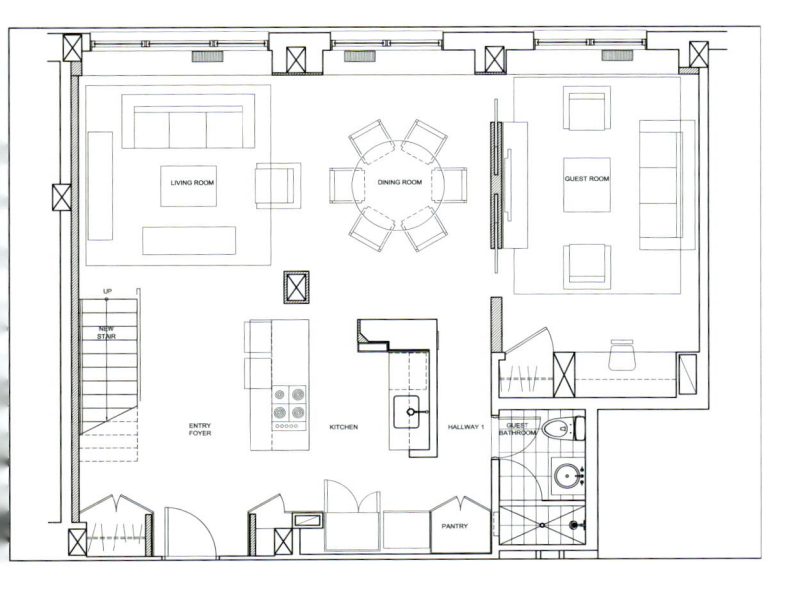

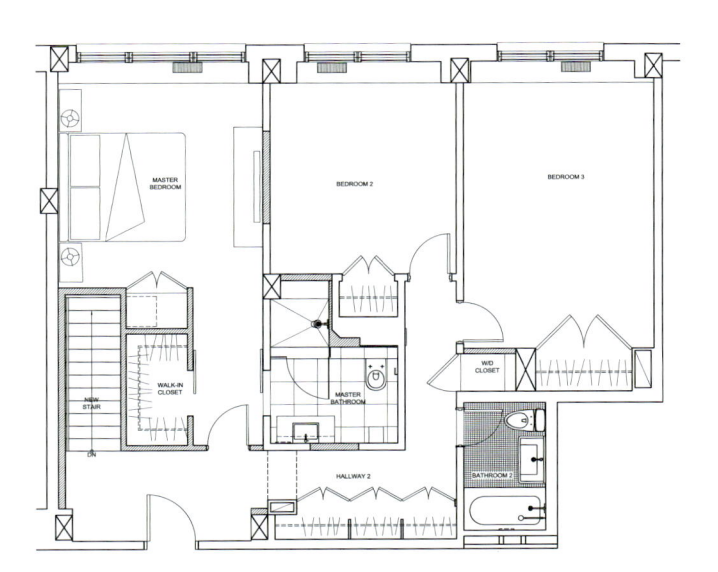

CITY: New York (NY)
COUNTRY: USA
REGION: North America
TYPOLOGY: Living
COMPLETION: 2006
WEBSITE: www.studio-st.com
ARCHITECTS: Esther Sperber / Studio ST Architects

CITY New York (NY)

COUNTRY USA

REGION North America

TYPOLOGY Office

COMPLETION 2004

WEBSITE www.shca.com

ARCHITECTS Swanke Hayden Connell Architects

ATLANTIC TERMINAL

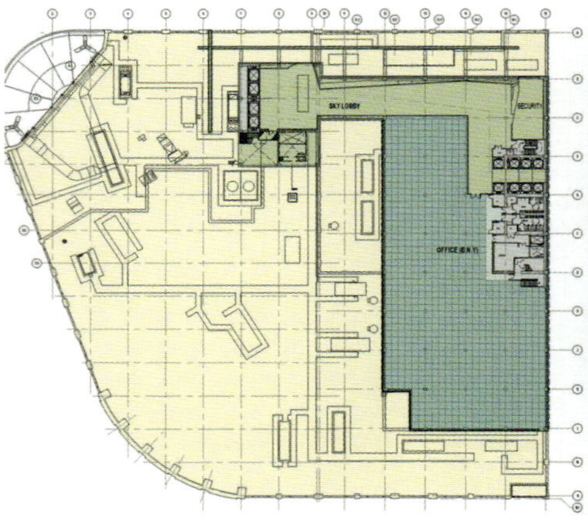

This 400,000-square-foot, 10-story office building is the first terra cotta clad high-rise curtain wall building in New York City. Sitting above a four-story retail podium, the design challenge included handling the offset location of the tower due to the complex transit system under the site and the tower's regulated bulk limiting the width. A band of glass at the sky lobby "lifts" the tower above the retail base allowing distinct architectural expressions while creating unity. Overall, the design addresses three primary relationships: the retail base, the Williamsburg Bank and the surrounding residential neighborhood.

01 Northwest elevation **02** Detail terra cotta clad curtain wall **03** Fifth floor plan **04** Exterior view of the office tower

Photos: Elliott Kaufman

LADY M CAKE BOUTIQUE

A refrigerated frosty-white display case resembling a crepe cake is the centerpiece of Lady M Cake Boutique, a 600 square feet cafe in New York. The 24-foot long case is fronted with quartz agglomerate and inlaid with onyx strips, all resting on two-inch diameter steel legs through which run its power line. The table legs and the entrance door's stainless-steel handle are the lone weighty elements among cream-painted walls and a limestone floor.

01 Exterior view **02** Frosty-white display case **03** Interior view **04** Floor plan

Photos: Paul Warchol

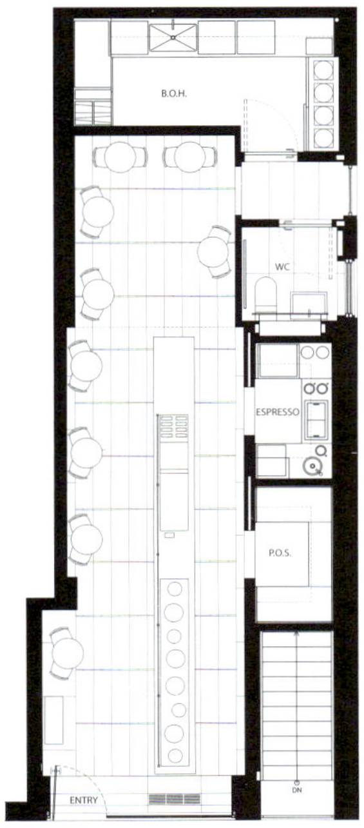

CITY New York (NY)
COUNTRY USA
REGION North America
TYPOLOGY Gastronomy
COMPLETION 2004
WEBSITE www.samtrimble.com
ARCHITECTS Sam Trimble Design

BLUE

This residential mid-rise in New York's Lower East Side occupies a lot zoned for residential use and cantilevers over an existing building designated for commercial use. The slightly angled walls artfully negotiate the varying setback rules, crossing the line between the commercial and residential zoning districts. The building consists of 32 residences ranging from one and two-bedroom units, to full-floor units with large terraces, and finally crowned by a duplex penthouse. The apartments are fitted out with sustainable materials, including bamboo floors and wall panels, palm flooring, and river-pebble bathroom tiles.

01 Exterior view **02** Interior view, penthouse **03** North-south section **04** Characteristic: slightly angled walls

Photos: Bernard Tschumi Architects

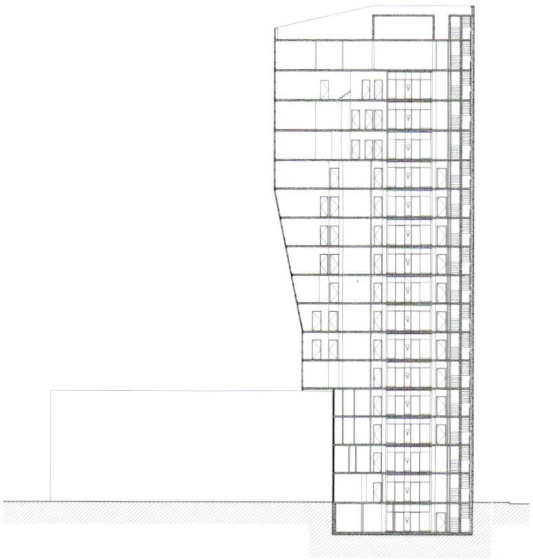

EAST 61ST STREET RESIDENCE/NYC, NY

TCA transformed the interior of this 19th century townhouse into a light-filled space, while retaining the original brownstone detail on the front of the building. In the process of redesigning the scheme, the interior and back walls were removed, reconstructed, and modernized. A refreshingly airy skylight illuminates the open staircase in the midsection of the house, and the direct and immediate result from this is that it provides natural light into every room. TCA selected natural materials that reinforce and highlight the design's simplicity, where stone, travertine, and sisal are used throughout.

01 Front view **02** Rear view, modernized back wall **03** Open staircase **04** Section **05** Interior view **06** Bedroom

Photos: Paul Warchol

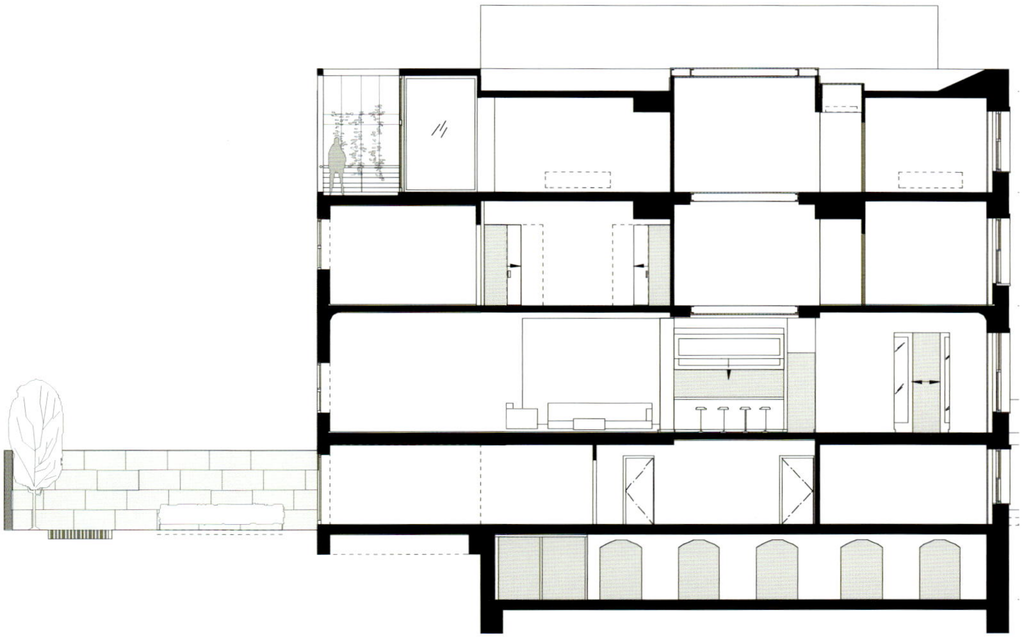

CITY New York (NY)

COUNTRY USA

REGION North America

TYPOLOGY Living

COMPLETION 2005

WEBSITE www.turettarch.com

ARCHITECTS Turett Collaborative Architects

CITY New York (NY)
COUNTRY USA
REGION North America
TYPOLOGY Office
COMPLETION 2007
WEBSITE www.umproject.com
ARCHITECTS UM + Two Ton

THE STATION

UM designed and built The Station, a new animation and production studio in New York City, in collaboration with architectural firm Two Ton Inc. The client provided specific programmatic requirements for a multifunctional space including reception, lounge, editing suites, filming area, screening room, production areas, and offices. That foundation helped develop the floor plan and the overall flow of the space, relying on sensuous, curves and clean lines. The design was carried over seamlessly throughout the space and the custom furniture, creating an open, bright and free-flowing environment.

01 Exterior view **02** Reception **03** Editing suite **04** Lounge **05** Floor plan

Photos: Francis Dzikowski/Esto

GROVE STREET TOWNHOUSE

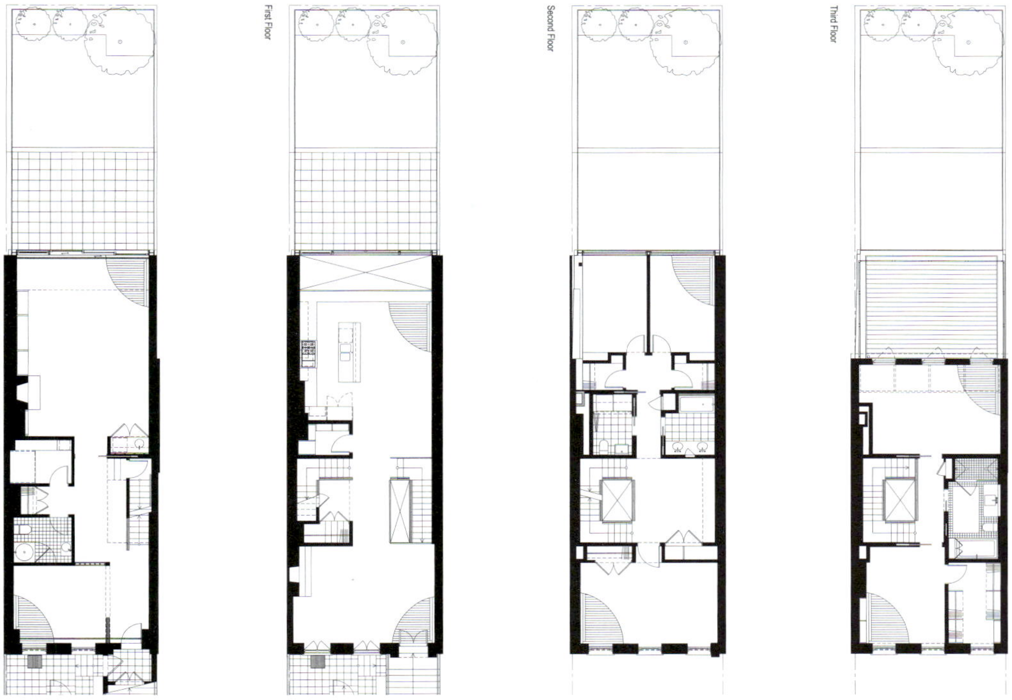

During the planning process the architects orientated to the owners wish designing this townhouse complimentary to their collection of mid-century modern furniture, lighting and decorative objects. They removed a ramshackle greenhouse appendage at the rear of the house and created a new façade of exposed structural steel and large custom wood windows. These windows bring now light and warmth into the kitchen and family room, which face the rear garden.

01 Detail interior **02** Floor plans **03** Rear view by night **04** Rear view, façade of structural steel and wood windows **05** Interior view

Photos: Tom Rider

CITY	New York (NY)
COUNTRY	USA
REGION	North America
TYPOLOGY	Living
COMPLETION	2001
WEBSITE	www.oda-ny.com
ARCHITECTS	Ogawa Depardon Architects

CITY
New York (NY)

COUNTRY
USA

REGION
North America

TYPOLOGY
Public

COMPLETION
in progress

WEBSITE
www.rzaps.com

ARCHITECTS
Zurita Architecture

COMFORT STATIONS

As the smallest structure designed for the master plan of Randall's Island Park, the comfort stations act as bold visual landmarks. Each is a multidirectional object clad entirely in a uniform, brightly colored ribbed metal. From a distance the buildings are perceived as monolithic forms. When approached, the doorways appear as the subtle results of the folding in of wall panels. Clearstories appear as splits between exterior panels and windows as shuttered openings that disappear when the building is closed. The omni-directional form and singular color give each building a focal presence in its respective surroundings. As a collective each serves to remind the visitors of the continuity of parkland.

01 View of a station with information window **02** View of toilet entrance **03** Basic unit plan **04** Folded panels

Renderings: Zurita Architects

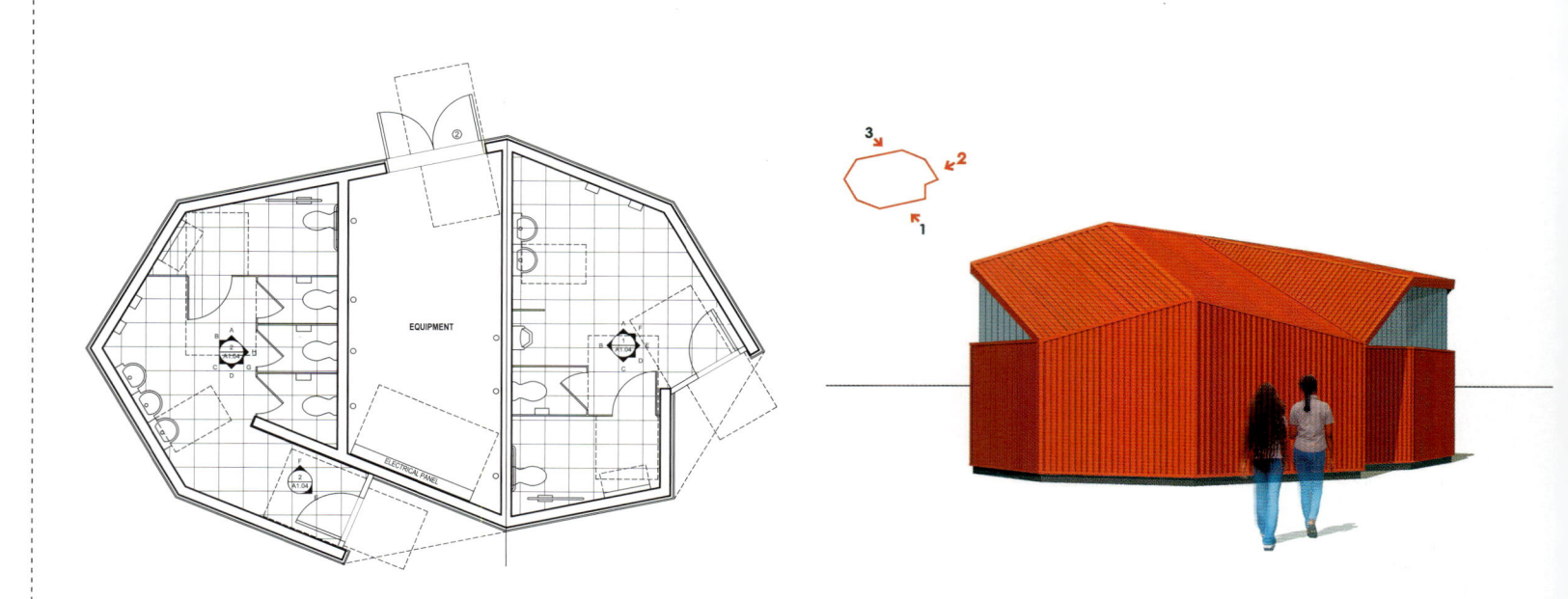

PS1 MOMA BEATFUSE! YOUNG ARCHITECTS PROGRAM 2006 WINNER

The design was a winning project of the 2006 Young Architects Program, where the space is partially covered with 10 concertina shells manufactured in a workshop and later deployed on site. Digitally modeled using a CNC router to achieve their dynamic curved form, the concertinas are covered with a skin of polypropylene mesh scales, which allow wind and rain to move through them without excessively taxing the structure with lateral or lifting loads. Each concertina shell is unique and fuses into each other, creating a realm that spans the entire courtyard, and producing multiple places of distinctive mood and atmosphere.

01 Courtyard and concertina shells **02** Thermae plan **03, 04, 05** Detail ahells: skin of polypropylene mesh scales

Photos: Ocean D

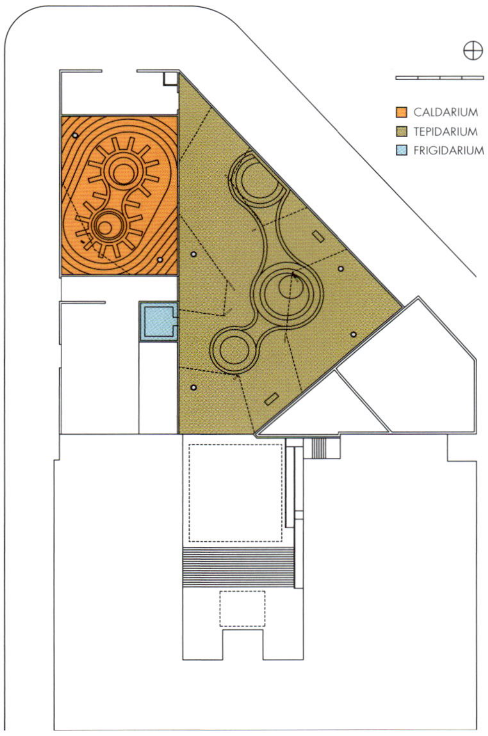

CITY New York (NY)
COUNTRY USA
REGION North America
TYPOLOGY Culture
COMPLETION 2006
WEBSITE www.obraarchitects.com
ARCHITECTS OBRA Architects

426

CITY
New York (NY)

COUNTRY
USA

REGION
North America

TYPOLOGY
Living

COMPLETION
2008

WEBSITE
www.axismundi.com

ARCHITECTS
Axis Mundi

CHATHAM HOUSE

The house in the heart of Shaker County provides living accommodations for a small family, and is home to a private art gallery for contemporary art and design objects. The building is raised on a low concrete dais; access is via a gently inclined ramp sprouting grass. The architectural gesture is composed of two shifted rectangular volumes bisected by a 16ft high, light-filled entrance gallery, which separates the main living space from the guest rooms. A detached studio clad in Cor-ten steel shingles is separated from the main block, yet the entire composition is neatly held together under one continuous roof sheathed in copper.

01 Dining room **02** Exterior view, detail low concrete dais
03 Elevation and floor plan **04** Entrance gallery

Photos: Reinhold & Co.

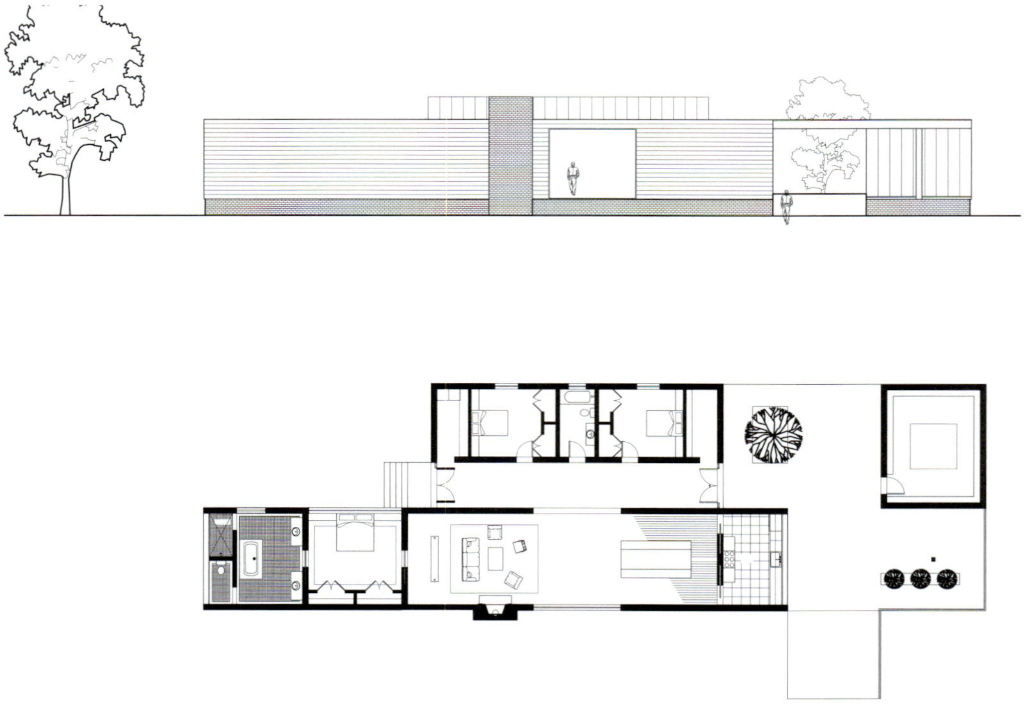

EATON RESIDENCE

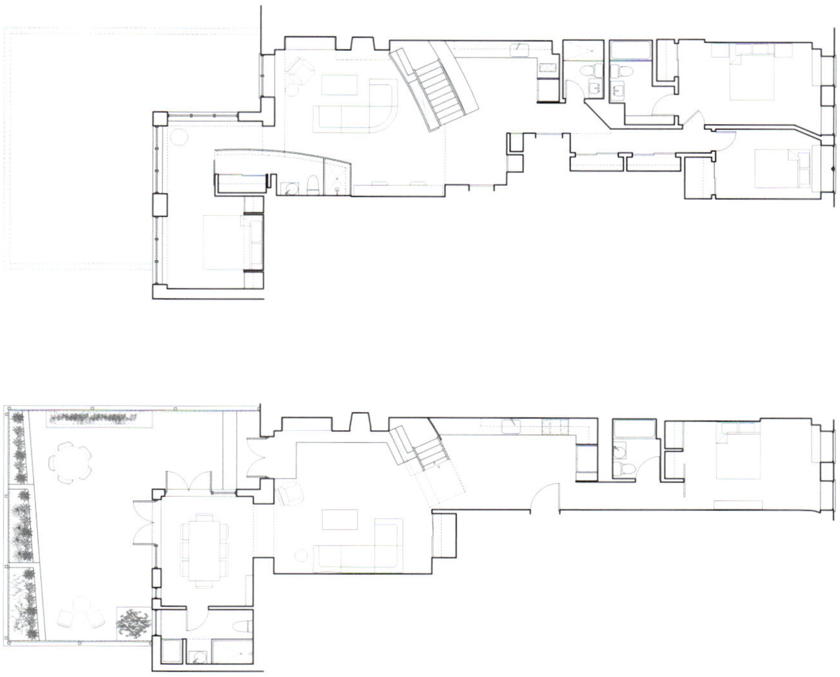

This private residence is a duplex garden apartment in a multi-family brownstone. The downstairs consists of the entry, family room, kitchen, living room, dining room, stair, two bathrooms, and garden. The upper floor consists of the master bedroom and bathroom, sitting room and pantry, and an extra 2 bedrooms and bathrooms. The project is a renovation requiring an entirely new two-story rear façade, new exterior garden with a connection from the inside, and two reconfigured floors interconnected by a new stair. The goal was to create an industrial modern space with both Western and Asian influences.

01 Upper floor with fireplace 02 Interior view upper floor 03 View to the garden 04 Floor plans 05 Stair, connecting two floors

Photos: Chuck Choi

CITY
New York (NY)

COUNTRY
USA

REGION
North America

TYPOLOGY
Living

COMPLETION
2007

WEBSITE
www.dma-ny.com

ARCHITECTS
Dean Maltz Architect

CITY New York (NY)
COUNTRY USA
REGION North America
TYPOLOGY Living
COMPLETION 2006
WEBSITE www.lot-ek.com
ARCHITECTS LOT-EK

LOT-EK (CHK)

CHK (Container Home Kit) uses the huge world surplus of ISO cargo containers to create sustainable homes, while exploiting the natural strength, durability and transportability of ISO containers. It enhances the beauty of these containers by creating exciting, affordable and modern homes. CHK is easily shipped and installed in any location, while being fully insulated for every climate. The project includes fully furnished and accessorized kitchen and bathrooms, as well as built-in closets in each of the bedrooms. Coming in a variety of sizes, CHK features a ground floor porch and a second floor terrace.

01 Exterior view with ground floor porch **02** Exterior view, CHK in smaller size **03** Detail ISO cargo container **04** Interior view

Renderings: LOT-EK

FAB TREE HAB

This whimsically named design takes its cue from the complexity of tree trunks. The load-bearing structure weaves together branch 'studs' that support a thermal clay and straw-based infill system. The resulting single-family home's plan encompasses three bedrooms, a bathroom, and an open living, dining and kitchen area placed on the southern façade in accordance with passive solar principles.

01 Floor plan and solar path **02** 100 % living grafted tree home **03** Growing habitat fabricated with reusable CNC scaffolding **04** Case studies of grafted trees **05** Rapid prototype model

Renderings: Mitchel Joachim (01, 02, 03, 05), Graham Murdoch (02), Axel Erlandson (04), Richard Reames (04), Edward Ward (05)

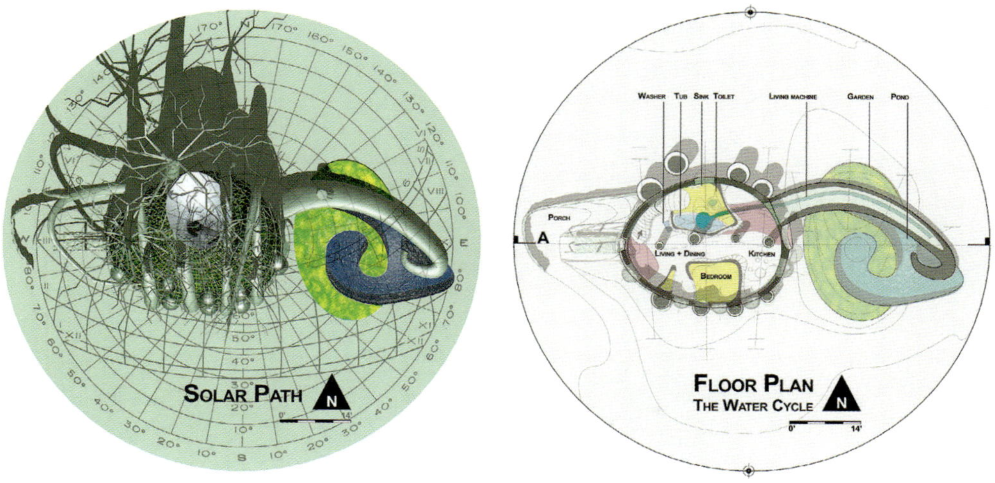

CITY New York (NY), variable
COUNTRY USA
REGION North America
TYPOLOGY Living
COMPLETION in progress
WEBSITE www.terreform.org, www.archinode.com
ARCHITECTS Mitchell Joachim, Terreform 1, Javier Arbona, Lara Greden

SCHEIN LOFT

Located on the edge of Soho, NYC, a former six-story warehouse is renovated with a new 11 story 'smart loft' building wrapping up and over it. The introduction of a modern glass and concrete building creates a strong contrast with the existing structure, allowing for great views over the Hudson River. The loft has a generous living and dining space with an open kitchen, a 7-foot long fireplace, as well as a large roof terrace. Along the spine of the loft, a large master bedroom with an adjacent bathroom and walk-in closet can be found, while a music room and a guest bathroom are also features of the project.

01 Living and dining space **02** Hallway **03** Bedroom **04** Section and floor plan **05** Detail spine veneered with bogwood

Photos: Floto and Warner

471 WASHINGTON STREET

The 471 Washington Street development project is 9 stories tall, with one apartment per floor, where irregular site geometries informed the overall building composition. The structure is poured in place concrete, with curtain walls of glass and perforated stainless steel, and large structural transfers give the building a muscular profile. Thinly profiled mullions and railings appear to stretch the glass skin taut over the concrete structure, while heating and cooling of the building employs three 1,500 foot deep geothermal wells. Extensive green walls and sedum terraces retain rainwater on site.

01 Exterior view, façade of concrete, glass and steel **02** Bird's eye view **03** Roof-decks **04** View from kitchen to living room **05** Floor plan

Renderings: Ben Hansen Architect

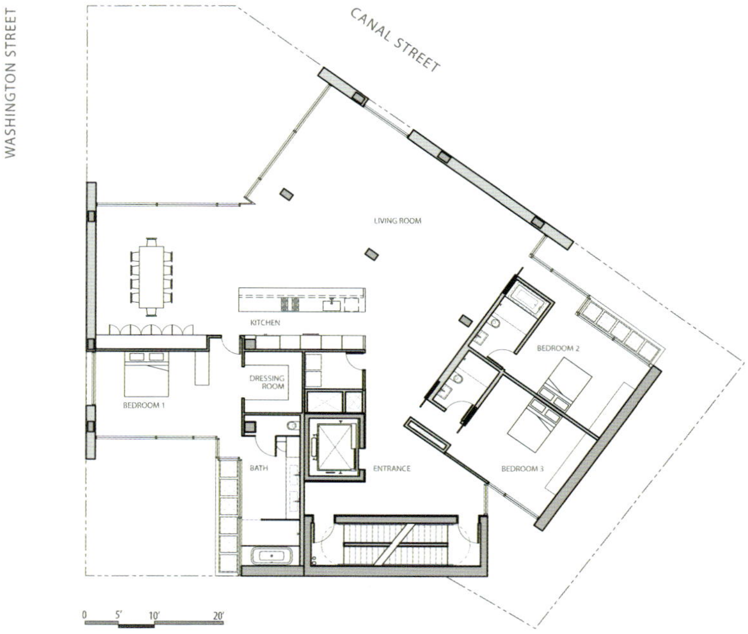

CITY New York (NY)

COUNTRY USA

REGION North America

TYPOLOGY Living

COMPLETION in progress

WEBSITE www.brharchitect.com

ARCHITECTS Ben Hansen Architect

627 GREENWICH STREET

Ben Hansen Architect carefully grafted new architectural components onto the existing building. Continuous, cantilevered balconies with faceted steel plate enclosures extend upwards to the communal roof deck. These generous south facing balconies provide excellent exterior space for breakfast or evening cocktails. Large masonry openings were cut into the façade to accommodate folding glass doors that extend the interior space outward. In conjunction with the balconies, the upper floors are constructed with a combination of dark stucco walls and full height glass, which provide both privacy and expansive views.

01 Dark stucco walls and full height glass 02 Floor plan 03 Communal roof-deck 04 Exterior view 05 Cantilevered balconies with steel plate enclosures

Renderings: Ben Hansen Architect

CITY
New York (NY)

COUNTRY
USA

REGION
North America

TYPOLOGY
Living

COMPLETION
in progress

WEBSITE
www.brharchitect.com

ARCHITECTS
Ben Hansen Architect

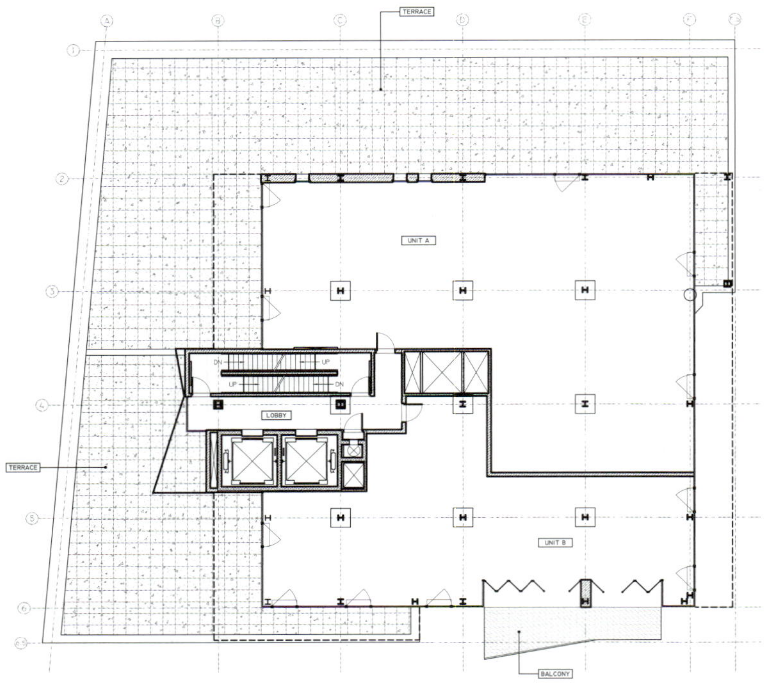

CATALYST

The main goals of the project were to provide a destination for recreation during the summer and to catalyze interactions and cultural exchanges between local visitors and tourists and the center. Using information from the study of leisure activities and climatic needs, the architects designed areas that have the most potential to catalyze interactions between people by designing an expressive canopy through the site. The fantastical canopy catalyzes qualities of light, moods and interactions with its shadows cast upon the seductive material interplay of jelly marine-tinted cushions, hard and wet surfaces on the landscape below.

01 Model 02 Side view 03 Detail 04 View inside

Renderings: Contemporary Architecture Practice

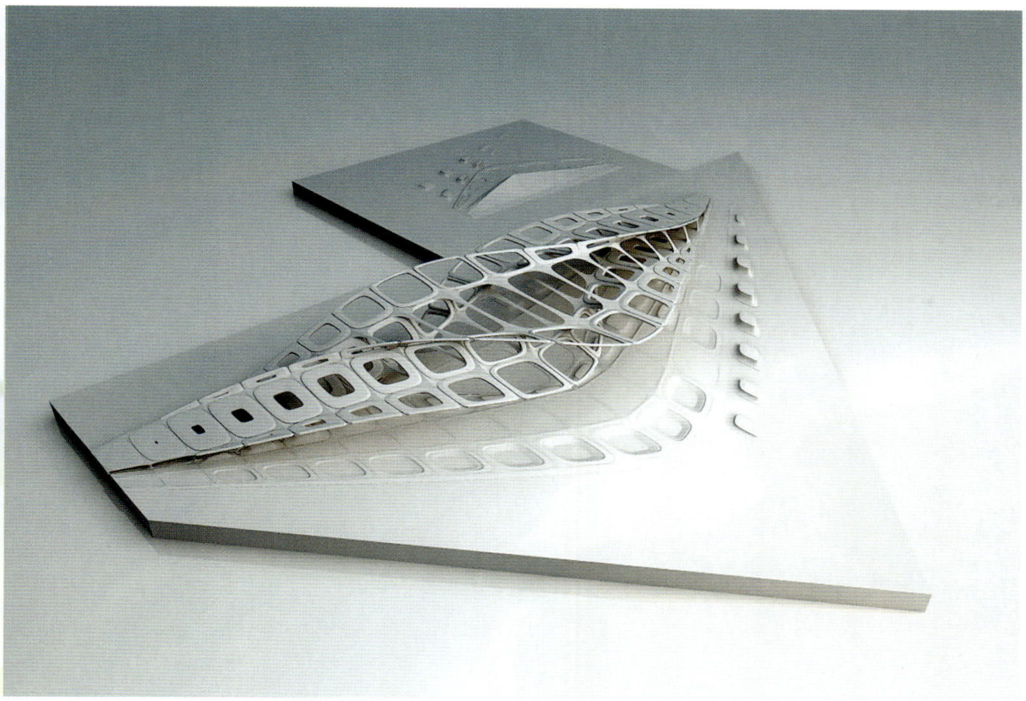

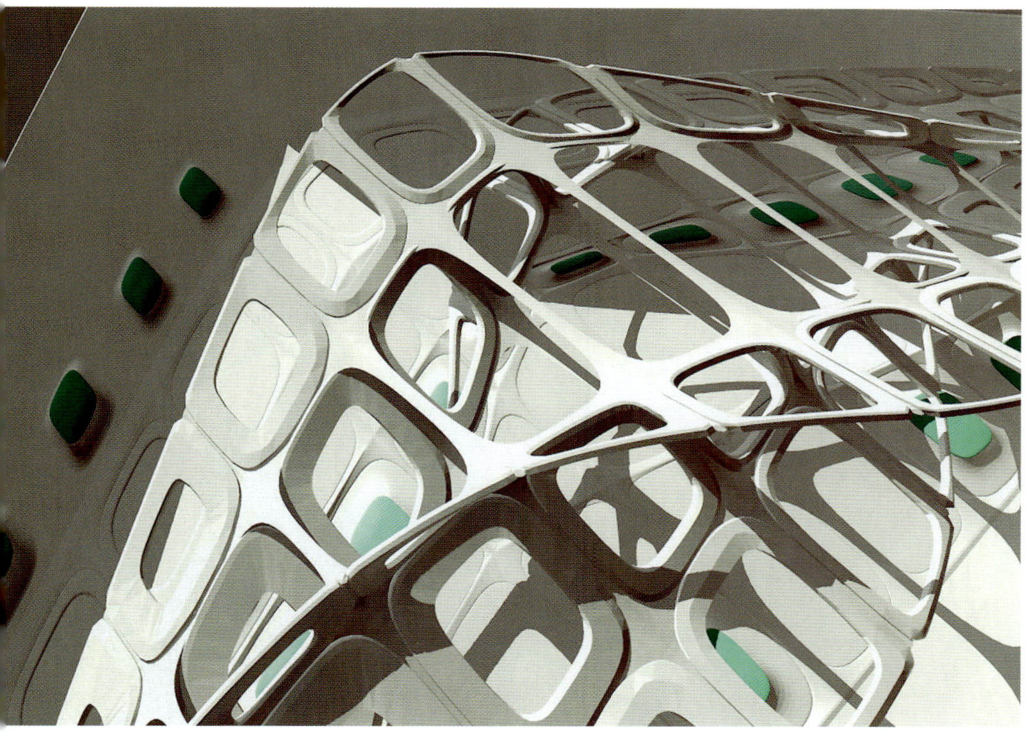

CITY New York (NY)
COUNTRY USA
REGION North America
TYPOLOGY Public
COMPLETION –
WEBSITE www.c-a-p.net
ARCHITECTS Contemporary Architecture Practice

59E59 THEATERS

59E59 Theaters is a new 8,000-square-foot facility, which retains elements of an existing building's shell. It houses a 199-seat theater, a 96-seat theater, and a small black box performance space. It has an impressively dramatic four-story glass facade, which makes the theater lobbies and stairs visible from the street. As associate architect to uRED Architecture, Franke, Gottsegen, Cox Architects assisted in everything from the design development, the preparation and coordination of all architectural contract documents, as well as providing all construction phase services throughout the building process.

01 Detail four-story glass façade **02** Exterior view **03** Lobby with stairway **04** Floor plan **05** Detail stairway

Photos: Leo Modrcin

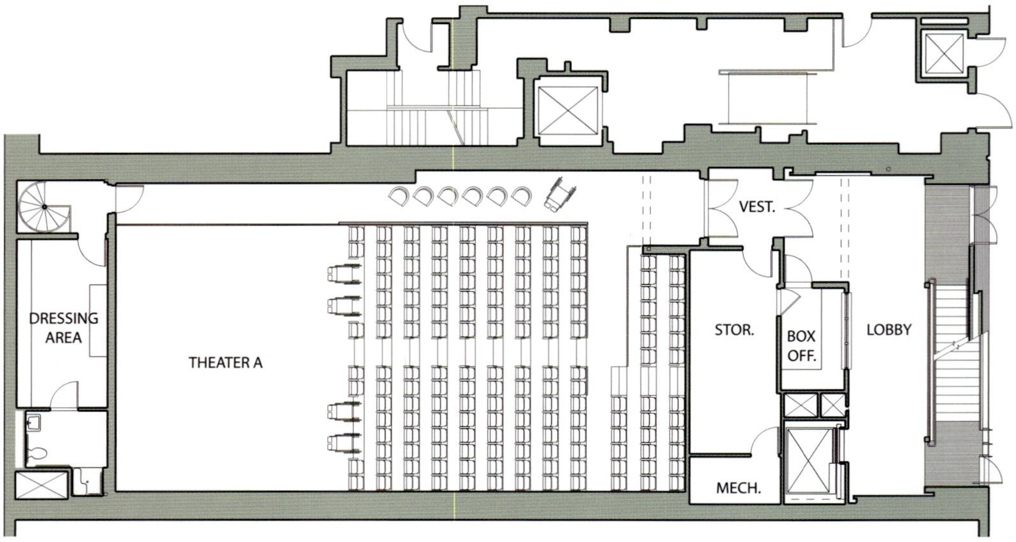

THE ARS NOVA BUILDING

This new four-story building, named The Ars Nova, provides offices and performance space for an entertainment company. The ground floor houses a 100-seat cabaret performance space, while the upper floors provide offices for the business as well as a large open space with features such as catering facilities for receptions and group entertainment. The facade is composed of Roman brick and black steel, which are materials similar to nearby nineteenth-century buildings. Owner Jenny Wiener Steingart's close participation in the design was a tribute to the memory of her brother, who initiated the project.

01 Façade made of Roman brick and black steel 02 Side view 03 Stairway 04 Theater

Photos: Jonathan (01, 02), Ofer Wolberger (03, 04)

CITY	New York (NY)
COUNTRY	USA
REGION	North America
TYPOLOGY	Culture
COMPLETION	2003
WEBSITE	www.fgca.com
ARCHITECTS	Franke, Gottsegen, Cox Architects

CITY
New York (NY)

COUNTRY
USA

REGION
North America

TYPOLOGY
Living / Education

COMPLETION
–

WEBSITE
www.garrisonarchitects.com

ARCHITECTS
Garrison Architects

ARTISTS IN RESIDENCE: STUDENT HOUSING FOR PRATT INSTITUTE

This project was developed for a modular housing competition at Pratt Institute. The challenge was maximizing the number of units within a relatively constrained site and restrictive zoning guidelines. The solution combined the density of a double-loaded corridor with the openness and environmental benefits of a single-loaded corridor by creating an atrium in the center of the building that lets in sunlight and air. Tectonic shifts in the buildings modular form create a network of porches and walkways within this atrium, which encourage collaboration and exchange. A gallery, theater and lounges provide collective spaces.

01 Exterior view by night **02** Atrium **03** Hallway and atrium **04** Plan **05** Interior view

Renderings: Garrison Architects

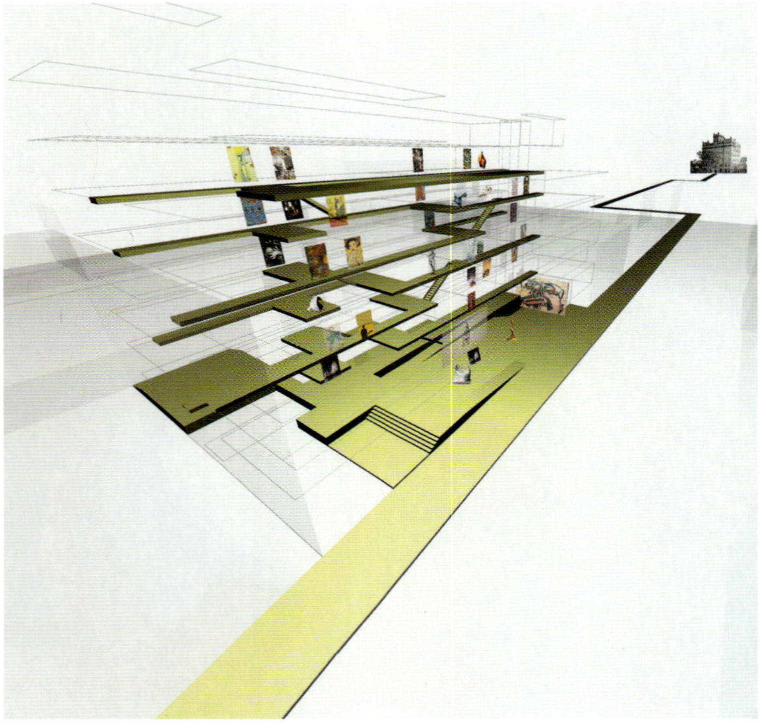

MCKINLEY HOUSES COMMUNITY CENTER

The McKinley Houses Community Center was completed as part of a citywide modernization program, and in this new community center such features include office and administrative facilities, classrooms, games and activity rooms, along with a multi-purpose auditorium and theater space. The architectural forms and materials used in the project provide a contrast to the dark mass of the adjoining brick apartment buildings. Providing such elements of transparency and brightness, the community center is an inviting and welcoming space for its users, which creates a new focal point for the community.

01 Detail transparent façade **02** Detail ceiling **03** Exterior view from the street **04** Floor plan **05** Interior view

Photos: Michael Moran

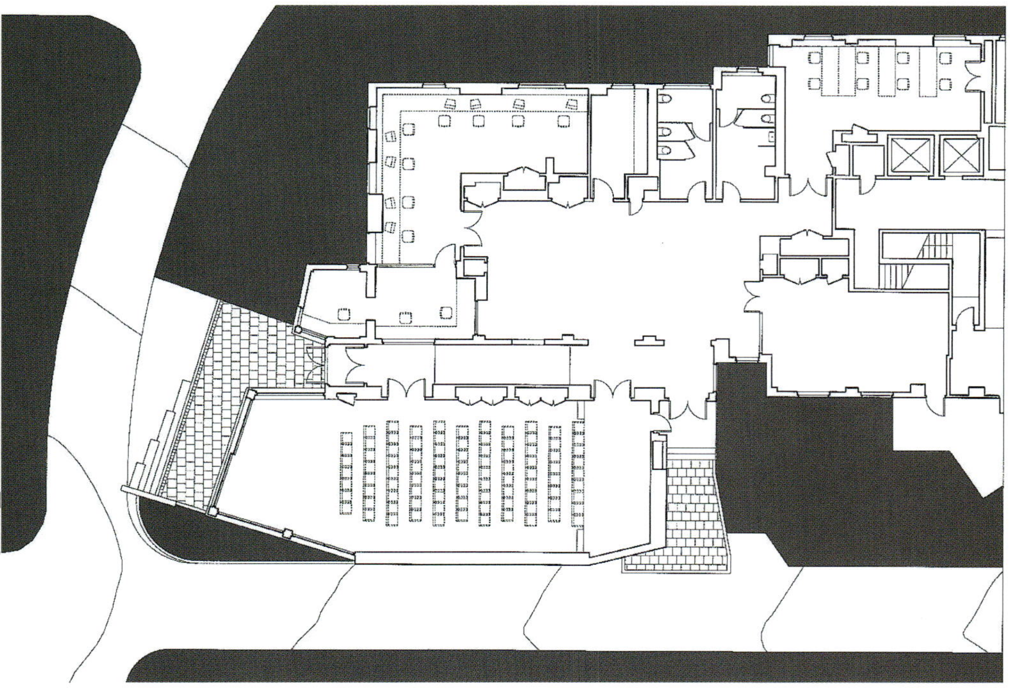

CITY New York (NY)
COUNTRY USA
REGION North America
TYPOLOGY Public
COMPLETION 2005
WEBSITE www.gorlinarchitect.com
ARCHITECTS Alexander Gorlin Architect

CITY
New York (NY)

COUNTRY
USA

REGION
North America

TYPOLOGY
Public

COMPLETION
unbuilt

WEBSITE
www.studiomda.com

ARCHITECTS
studioMDA

GOVERNORS ISLAND TOWER

Governors Island Tower takes clues from an existing historic island and implements contemporary ideas to create a place that represents the future identity of New York City. This is a future that is self-sustaining, a future that combines technology and nature. It is a future that creates an active setting conscious of its environment, beckoning tourists and inhabitants alike. The proposed Tower will accommodate the necessary development floor area for a hotel, while maintaining a maximum of green park area.

01 Exterior view to Manhattan **02** Exterior view **03** Sketch **04** Site plan

Renderings: studioMDA

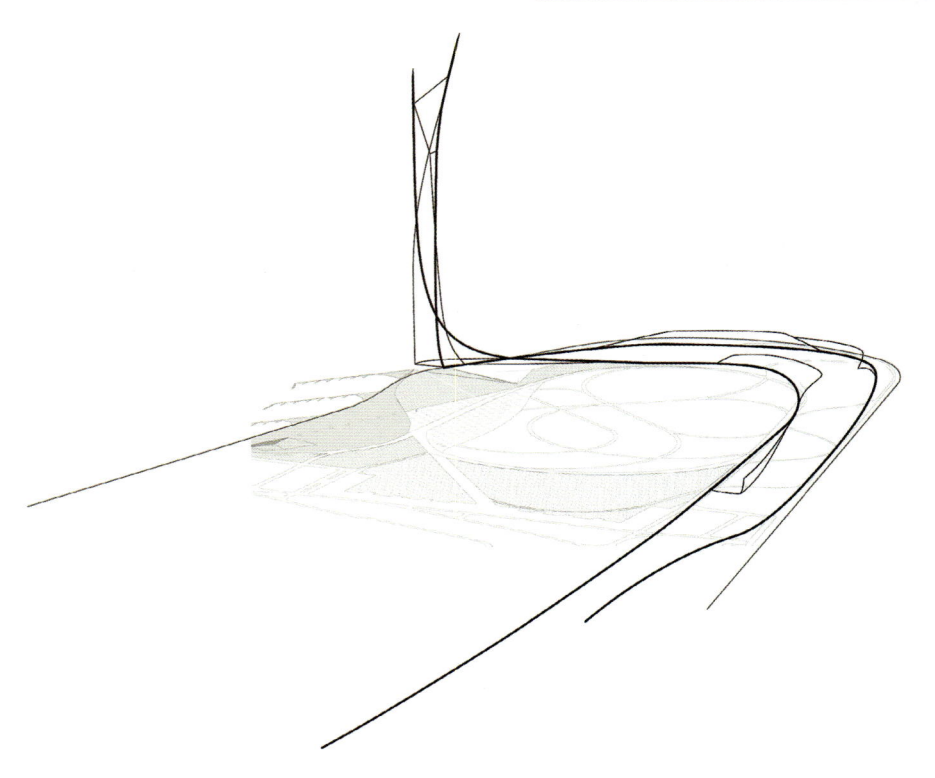

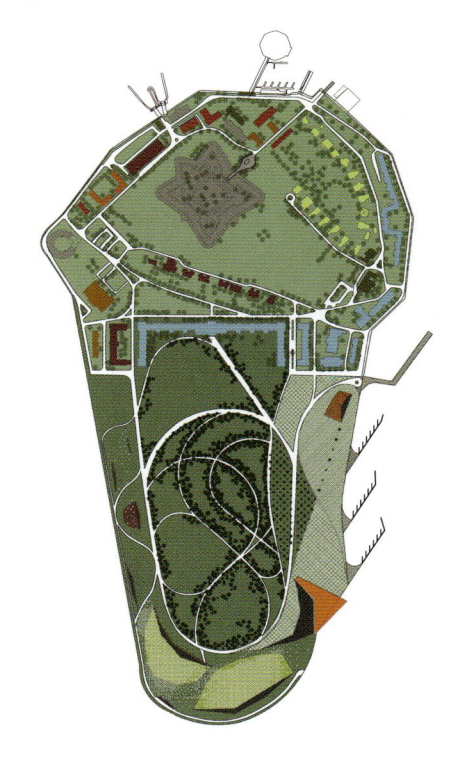

HARRISON STREET RESIDENCE

The owners of this 3,000-square-foot historic landmark building in Tribeca wished to maximize the interior space while restoring the original glazed terracotta façade. Construction of the penthouse involved lowering the existing roof to accommodate a warped, luminescent crown. Although the penthouse roof is completely level, walls of high-strength laminated compound-curved glass create a dynamic plan as well as a distorted reflection of the adjacent streetscape. Natural light penetrates and illuminates the core through cantilevered glass stairs joined with a floor-to-ceiling sculptural bronze banister.

01 Exterior view **02**, **03** Interior view, living room with working space **04** Floor plans **05** Stairway

Photos: Michael Moran Photography, Inc.

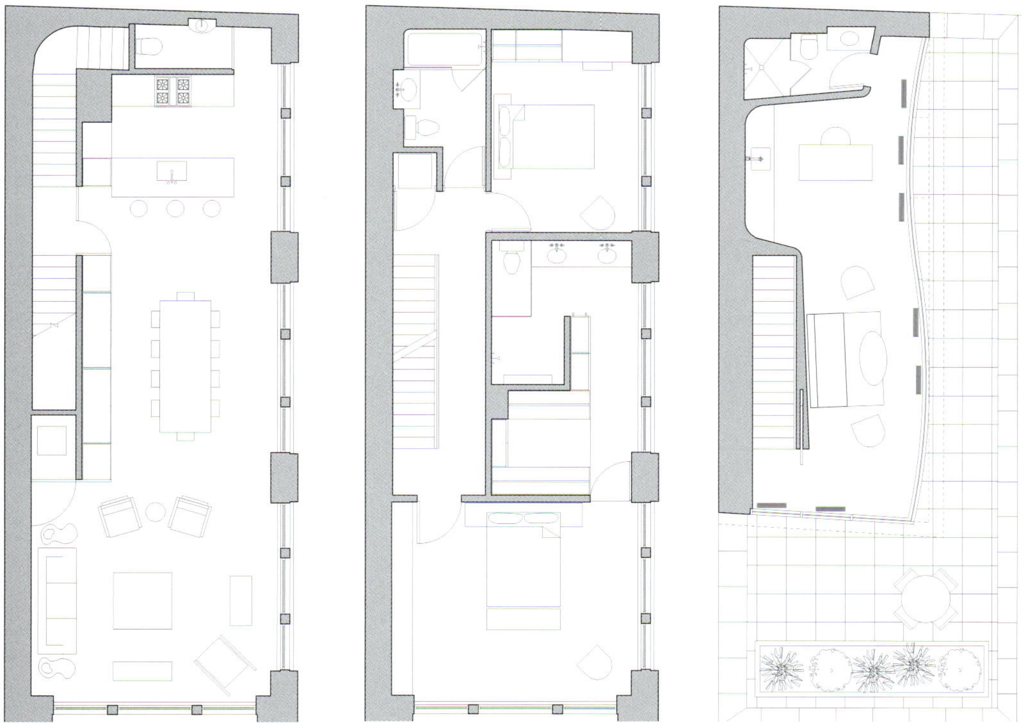

CITY New York (NY)
COUNTRY USA
REGION North America
TYPOLOGY Living
COMPLETION 2005
WEBSITE www.1100architect.com
ARCHITECTS 1100: Architect

CITY: New York (NY)
COUNTRY: USA
REGION: North America
TYPOLOGY: Public
COMPLETION: 2005
WEBSITE: www.gabellinisheppard.com
ARCHITECTS: Gabellini Sheppard Associates

TOP OF THE ROCK OBSERVATION DECK AT ROCKEFELLER PLAZA

The project went beyond renovating the existing viewing decks to create new entry and exhibition spaces within a three-level area. The new entrance features a helical spiral stairway that introduces the idea of ascent. The elliptically shaped space encourages visitors to stroll past graphic and text panels, archival images, and video screens that illustrate the history of Rockefeller Center. A cocoon-shaped theater is the last stop on the mezzanine before one takes a dramatic elevator ride up to the Top of the Rock. The double layers of UV-shielding glass serve as a wind barrier, offering virtually unhindered viewing.

01 67th floor grand viewing room **02** Exterior view **03, 04** Grand atrium stair

Photos: Peter Murdock

GREENWICH VILLAGE TOWNHOUSE

The project rehabilitates an 1840's landmark townhouse competed in the Greek revival style, respecting the charms and scale of the original without mimicking its period details. The resulting home had to create a suitable context for the client's collection of XXe century artwork. The interior is decidedly modernist in its attention to details, most of which were specially designed – from the marble mosaics in the bathrooms, to the millwork and shutters in the kitchen. A sculptural bronze-and-mirror screen creates an entrance foyer and uses cast glass that was salvaged from Gio Ponti's Alitalia showroom on Fifth Avenue.

01 Exterior view **02** Living room **03** Detail bronze-and-mirror screen with cast glass **04** Kitchen with millwork and shutters **05** Floor plans

Photos: Andrew GARN

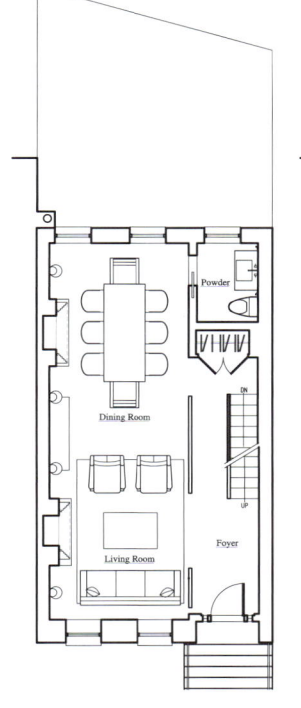

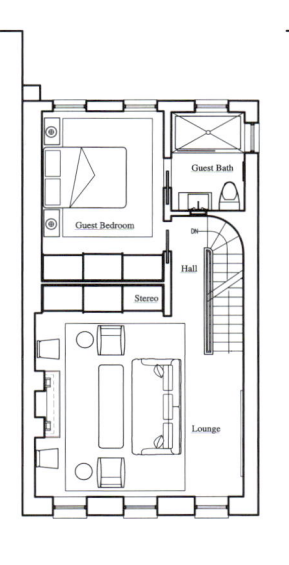

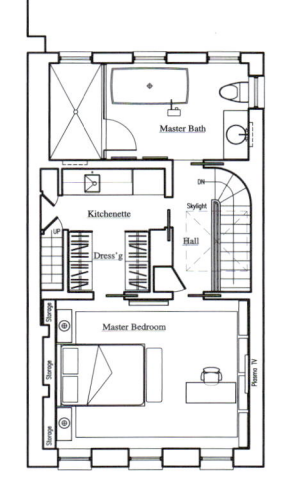

CITY New York (NY)
COUNTRY USA
REGION North America
TYPOLOGY Living
COMPLETION 2007
WEBSITE www.axismundi.com
ARCHITECTS Axis Mundi

PENTHOUSE 360

The apartment was primarily purchasd as semi-raw condo space in a new building, and is a 3600-square-foot duplex penthouse, with one of its striking features being a 1300-square-foot L-shaped terrace. The apartment, which came to be known as Penthouse 360, has an open, modern, and rather minimal feel, though with somewhat eclectic furnishings it must be said. The penthouse has remarkable and extensive urban views, and this feature provides a quintessential New York feel. This "feel" is particularly seductive in the evening hours, when the spectacular apartment lighting comes into full play.

01 Floor plans **02** Staircase **03** Deck **04** Living space with ceiling-high window **05** Kitchen

Photos: Georg Muller-Nicholson/ baufoto.com

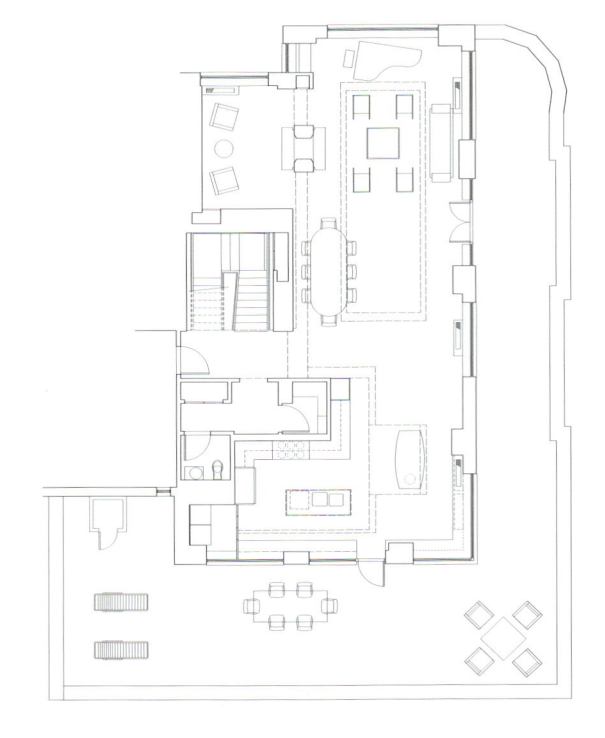

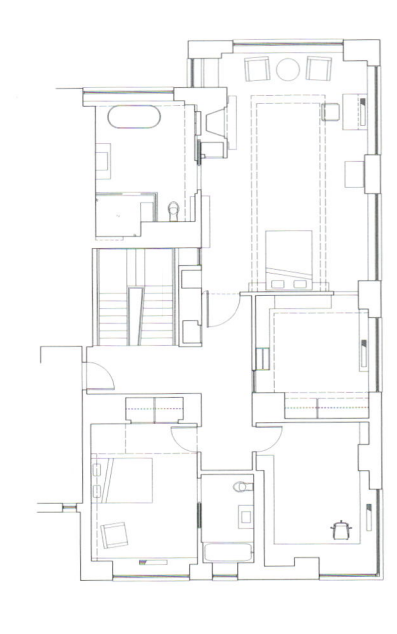

CITY New York (NY)
COUNTRY USA
REGION North America
TYPOLOGY Living
COMPLETION 2006
WEBSITE www.ethangerard.com
ARCHITECTS Ethan Gerard Architect

BAYSIDE RESIDENCE

This 3,000-square-foot residence located in the Bayside neighborhood of Queens, New York was completed at the end of 2007. The triplex home disguises its mass by shuffling the proportions of its fenestration and features an inclined outdoor space at the rear that is contiguous with the indoor space. Minimalist forms and white-walled interiors result in an open, airy atmosphere which contrasts with the compact appearance of the façade. Wood and concrete surfaces are featured throughout the design.

01 Exterior view **02** Rear view inside **03** Living space with fire place **04** View to pool **05** Exterior hallway

Photos: Floto + Warner

CITY New York (NY)
COUNTRY USA
REGION North America
TYPOLOGY Living
COMPLETION 2007
WEBSITE www.gp-arch.com
ARCHITECTS Grzywinski Pons Architects

444

CITY
New York (NY)

COUNTRY
USA

REGION
North America

TYPOLOGY
Public

COMPLETION
Prototype Phase

WEBSITE
www.xefirotarch.com

ARCHITECTS
Xefirotarch – Hernán Díaz Alonso

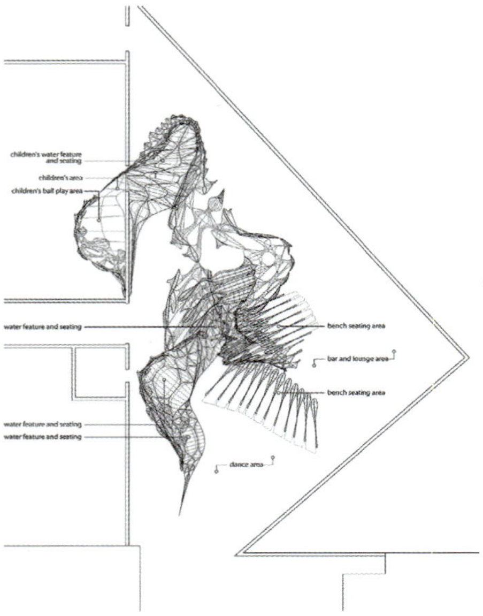

PS1 MOMA / WARM UP / "SUR"

With the flair of a circus and the ambience of a playground, this project activates affects and sensations. Playful distraction and absorption are created as familiar spatial cues are stimulated by unfamiliar figures with emerging aesthetics that define a grotesque and horrific affect. Artfully flamboyant, the space is intensified by means of contortion and exuberance. It is dense and textured, the light is filtered but bright, and the atmosphere is not loud but disturbing. The project functions as a cinematic game, where there is no narrative, only active affects, and emergent grotesque aesthetics are in constant actualization.

01 View to the constuction **02** Detail **03** Floor plan **04, 05** Bird's eye view

Photos: Xefirotarch

MARIANNE BOESKY GALLERY

Located in West Chelsea, the new 10,000-square-foot building for the Marianne Boesky Gallery features two floors of gallery space, art preparation, administration spaces, as well as a caretaker's apartment. The gallery is adjacent to the High Line, an abandoned elevated railroad that will soon become the city's newest public greenway. The exterior's glazed white brick is supplemented by materials that are at home among the old warehouses, garages, and the elevated railroad that lend the neighborhood its industrial character, but are not nostalgic or unauthentic in any manner to the new structure.

01 Exterior view, glazed white brick façade **02** Gallery space **03** Floor plan **04** View to gallery space **05** View to administration space

Photos: Catherine Tighe, Eduard Hueber/archphoto (02)

CITY: New York (NY)
COUNTRY: USA
REGION: North America
TYPOLOGY: Culture
COMPLETION: 2006
WEBSITE: www.dberke.com
ARCHITECTS: Deborah Berke & Partners Architects LLP

CITY
New York (NY)

COUNTRY
USA

REGION
North America

TYPOLOGY
Education

COMPLETION
2007

WEBSITE
www.stevenholl.com

ARCHITECTS
Steven Holl Architects

NYU DEPARTMENT OF PHILOSOPHY

The interior renovation of an 1890 corner building at 5 Washington Place will be used by the NYU Department of Philosophy. Here it isn't only a metaphor of light to learning, but practical space of interaction between students and professors who can meet casually on the large landings. A new stair shaft below a new skylight joins the 6-level building vertically with a shifting porosity of light and shadow that change seasonally. The ground level contains a new curvilinear wooden auditorium on a cork floor, while the upper level contains Faculty Offices and Seminar Rooms, done in different shades and textures of black & white.

01 Wooden auditorium on cork floor **02** Detail stair shaft below skylight **03** Floor plans **04** Exterior view of the 1890 corner building

Photos: Andy Ryan

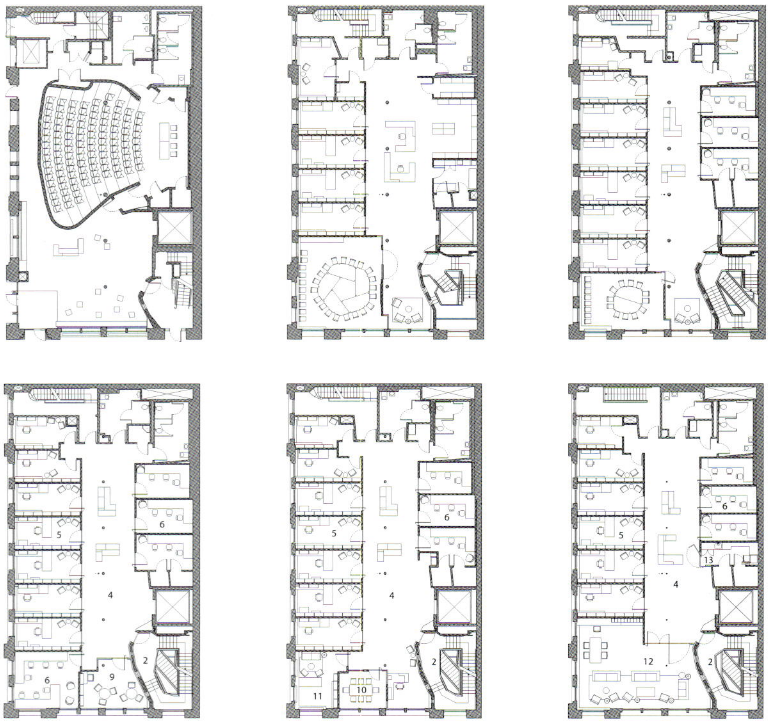

THE NEW YORK TIMES BUILDING

The 52-story project is sheathed entirely in layers of clear glass, in which this transparency, revealing the activity within, embodies the paper's mission of transmitting an unclouded, lucid report of the news to its public. The most innovative feature of the curtainwall design is an exterior veil of ceramic tubing that functions as an aesthetic device and provides critical sunshading. Aesthetically, the tubing serves as a canvas for the environmental conditions, changing color with the sun and weather. The New York Times space incorporates the largest whole-building underfloor air distribution system in New York City.

01 Staircase leading towards meeting space **02** Exterior view of tower by night **03** Elevation **04** Newsroom

Photos: Nic Lehoux, David Sundberg/Esto (02)

CITY
New York (NY)

COUNTRY
USA

REGION
North America

TYPOLOGY
Office

COMPLETION
2007

WEBSITE
www.rpbw.com
www.fxfowle.com

ARCHITECTS
Renzo Piano Building Workshop in association with FXFOWLE Architects

CITY
Ogden (UT)

COUNTRY
USA

REGION
North America

TYPOLOGY
Mixed-Use

COMPLETION
2007

WEBSITE
www.ffkr.com

ARCHITECTS
FFKR Architects

MEGAPLEX 13

Taking its clue from the original complex, the MegaPlex 13 Ogden is a high-tech response to contemporary cultural fascinations. The curved façades transparent and translucent glass walls, combined with the curved steel beams, create an organic and vibrant new destination that visually connects the food court and the lobby with the streetscape. Visitors can stroll along the beautifully illuminated façade, ascending and descending pathways along and across the street. The digital/synthetic environments within offer "lifestyle experiences" that create a dynamic visual impact as visitors approach from multiple directions.

01 Curved glass and steel façade 02 Front view by night 03 Food court 04 Floor plan, level 1

Photos: Mustafa Kanishka, AIA, Douglas Haven, Digital Knight Photography, 2007 (02)

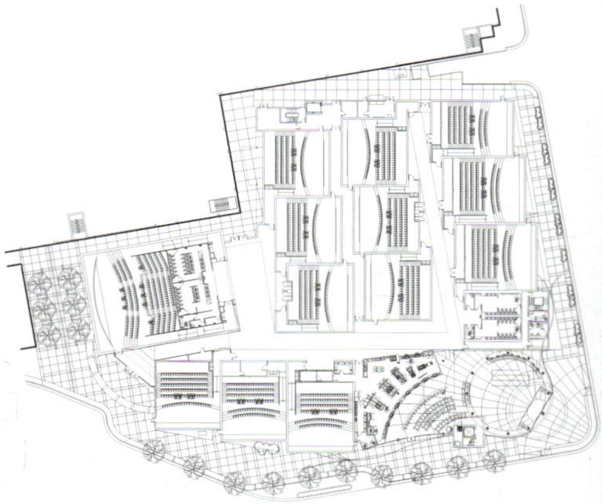

THACHER ARTS BUILDING

Set between a mountain range and coastal valley, the hillside campus of this 115-year-old boarding school is an academic community of 235 students, 40 faculty members, and 140 horses. Insertion of the Arts Building into its historic core prompted an evaluation of the existing campus layout and the extraordinary power of the surrounding terrain. One of the goals was to demonstrate the new buildings' ability to maximize usefulness of the adjoining outdoor spaces and to enhance the campus experience. As a multi-use performing arts theatre, the building promotes increased student participation in arts programs.

01 North elevation **02** Arts court with new view corridor **03** Operable wall panels **04** New view corridor to upper school **05** Site plan

Photos: Benny Chan, Fotoworks

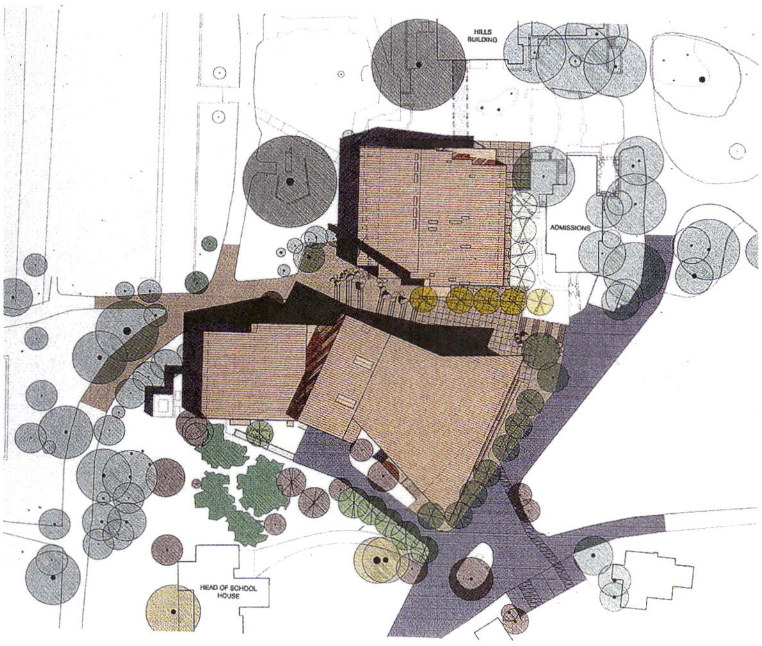

CITY Ojai (CA)
COUNTRY USA
REGION North America
TYPOLOGY Education
COMPLETION –
WEBSITE www.bpala.com
ARCHITECTS Barton Phelps & Associates

CITY Oldsmar (FL)

COUNTRY USA

REGION North America

TYPOLOGY Leisure

COMPLETION 2005

WEBSITE www.wjarc.com

ARCHITECTS Wannemacher Jensen Architects

CYPRESS FOREST PARK RECREATION CENTER

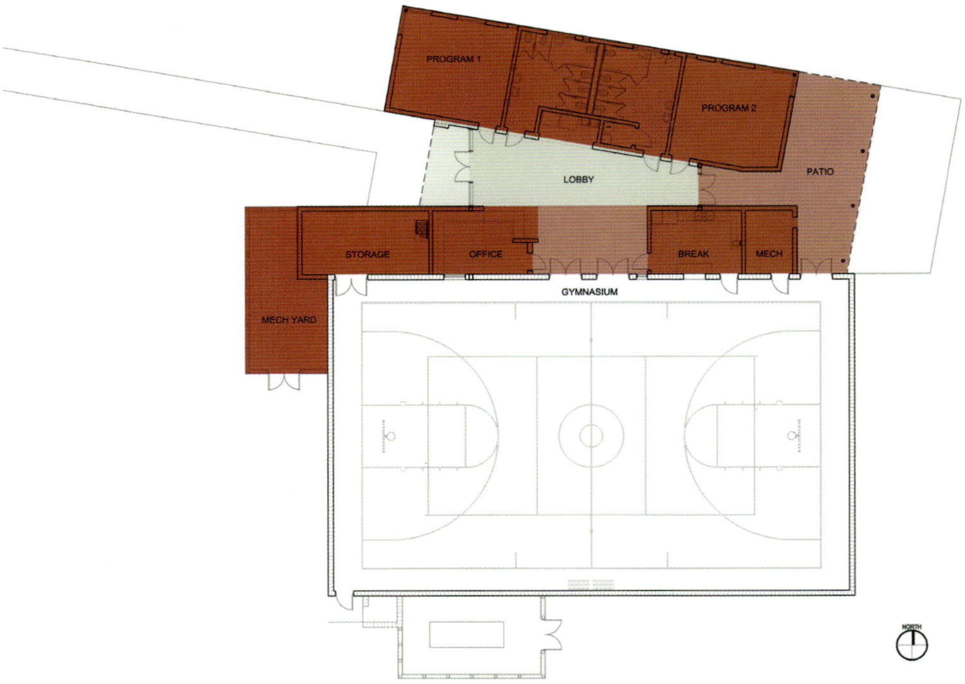

Located just outside a suburban context, this building is located within 70-acres of cypress forest and wetlands, and was able to uniquely respond to its environment. The wood clad volumes unravel into the landscape, opening views to the forest and concealing the scale of the adjacent gymnasium. The program includes a computer lab, multi-purpose room, offices and a warming kitchen, where circulation was consolidated within a double height open lobby defined by a monolithic folding plane. Cedar siding, split faced masonry, and metal wall panels combine to create a warm composition of the program elements inside.

01 Interior view, reception **02** Main entry, west elevation **03** Lobby **04** North elevation **05** Ground floor plan

Photos: James Borchuck

SINQUEFIELD HOUSE

This venture is part study center, part family compound, part working farm, with a complexity of initiative and landscape change, and are all themes of the house overlooking the Osage River in the Missouri Ozarks. Major spaces relate outside views to inside moods, with bedroom suites cantilevering above the forest floor that frame a niche in the larger landscape, creating a gathering place inspired by Rosellino's Piazza in Pienza. A central portal affords a view of the river, where smaller entryways meet paths to natural wonders scattered over 1000 acres. The public wing drops off the bluff to enclose an indoor pool below.

01 Exterior view by night **02** Bird's eye view **03** Main floor plan **04** Living area **05** West entry

Photos: Courtesy of Barton Phelps & Associates

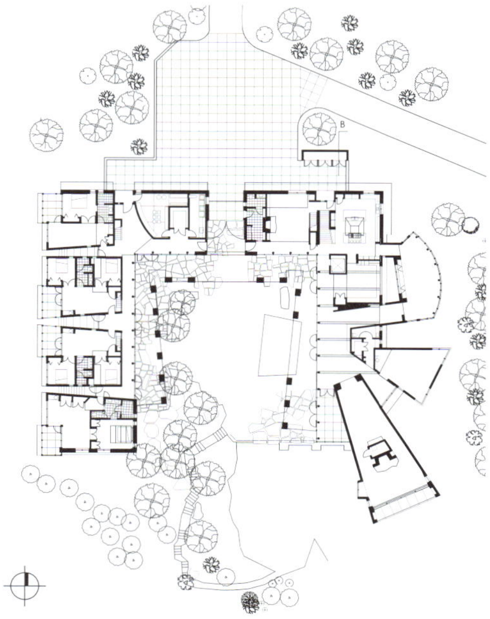

CITY Osage County (MO)
COUNTRY USA
REGION North America
TYPOLOGY Living
COMPLETION 2003
WEBSITE www.bpala.com
ARCHITECTS Barton Phelps & Associates

452

CITY Overland Park (KS)

COUNTRY USA

REGION North America

TYPOLOGY Culture

COMPLETION 2007

WEBSITE www.kswa.com

ARCHITECTS Kyu Sung Woo Architects

NERMAN MUSEUM OF CONTEMPORARY ART

The Nerman Museum is a landmark for the College, marking the campus entry from adjacent, well travelled regional roads. This distinction is solidified by a 1.5 acre sculpture garden stretching from the Museum to the knolls at the edge of the campus. The site immediate to the Museum is organized around campus circulation and spatial extension into the landscape. A 22' cantilever of the main gallery space, and long, rough cut stone walls extend from the building into the landscape reinforcing the connection between the two, while providing definition of exterior terraces, sculpture gardens and circulation.

01 Exterior view by night **02** Entrance hall **03** Gallery space **04** Floor plan

Photos: Timothy Hursley

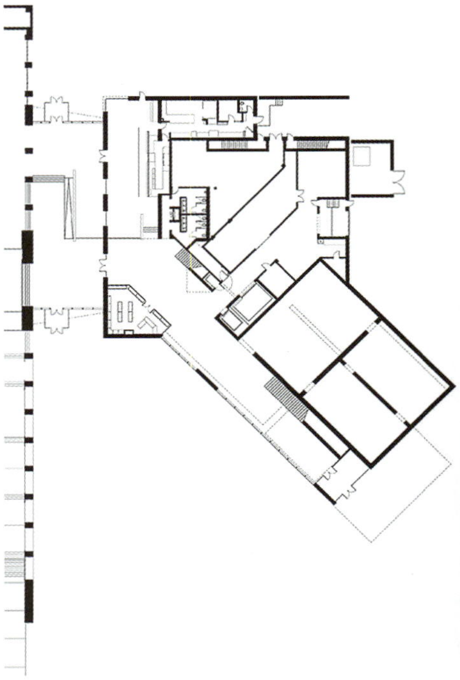

RESIDENTIAL REMODEL

The plan and energy problems addressed are the reflections of the Owners' vision, leading to such features as a remarkable entry with a memorable experience inside, walking past the sculptural stair into the heart of the home, as quality of light and color continuously change. Lifting the entry roof created a breathtaking 19-foot high interior space with daylight filtered through colored art glass in a wall lined with eucalyptus. Every remodeled room maximized daylight, views and energy efficiency. All new windows and skylights contain low-emission insulated glass, while radiant heat was installed and exterior shading was provided.

01 Stair overlook at entry **02** Front view in the evening **03** Working space **04** Cross section

Photos: Mark Luthringer

CITY: Orinda (CA)
COUNTRY: USA
REGION: North America
TYPOLOGY: Living
COMPLETION: 2006
WEBSITE: www.pmotzkinaia.com
ARCHITECTS: Patricia Motzkin Architecture

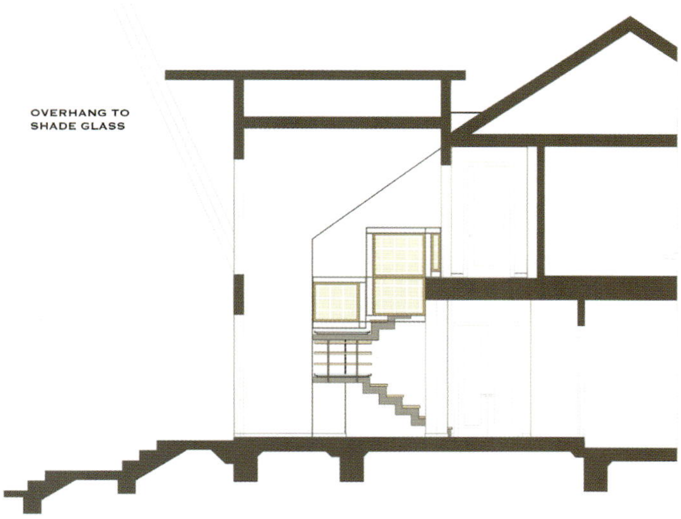

OVERHANG TO SHADE GLASS

454

CITY Olive Bridge (NY)

COUNTRY USA

REGION North America

TYPOLOGY Education

COMPLETION 2004

WEBSITE www.gluckpartners.com

ARCHITECTS Peter L. Gluck and Partners, Architects

SCHOLAR'S LIBRARY

In addition to the library, the family retreat features a restored farmhouse and a guest dormitory, which sleeps twenty-five. The library is a free-standing building containing a study space above and a 10,000 volume library below. The building is a cube with twenty-foot sides, with books stored in a windowless space on the first floor. The tightly packed stacks preserve the books and minimize the cost of heating them in the winter. The upper floor contains a workspace and has continuous glass on all four sides. The entire study can be turned into an open area by sliding open large glass panels.

01 Section **02** View from forest **03** Façade **04** Reading room with unobstructed views to forest

Photos: Paul Warchol Photography

CCA DORMITORY

Responding to an acute need for affordable housing for its students, CCAC constructed its first dedicated dormitory. Adjacent to the idyllic Oakland campus, the new building acts as a hard edge as well as a transitional element between the commercial and institutional fabric to the west and the residential condition to the east around the campus. The 14,000 square feet parcel is built with a two-story concrete podium housing a 38-car parking structure and the building lobby. A three-story wood structure above houses 124 beds in 64 bedrooms. Lounges and kitchens are located in an attached building.

01 Exterior view by night **02** Detail concrete podium **03** Exterior view **04** Interior view **05** Floor plans

Photos: Ethan Kaplan

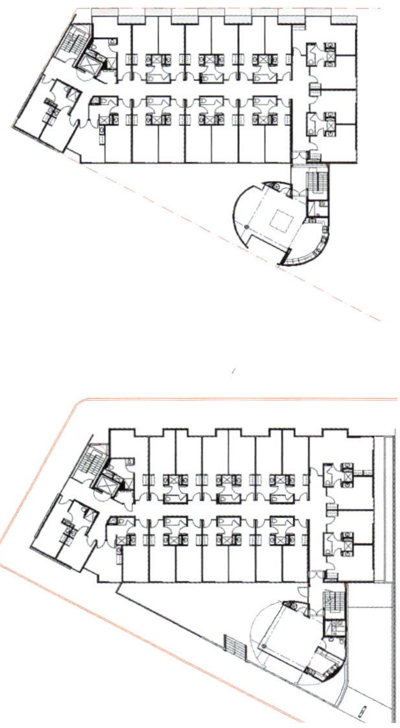

CITY	Oakland (CA)
COUNTRY	USA
REGION	North America
TYPOLOGY	Education
COMPLETION	2003
WEBSITE	www.mh-a.com
ARCHITECTS	Mark Horton/Architecture

CITY
Oakland (CA)

COUNTRY
USA

REGION
North America

TYPOLOGY
Public

COMPLETION
2000

WEBSITE
www.fisherfriedman.com

ARCHITECTS
Fisher Friedman Associates
Design Architects

CHABOT OBSERVATORY

The Chabot Observatory Center was designed as a replacement for a historic observatory built in the 1920's. The purpose of this multi-building complex, in addition to providing celestial observation capabilities, is to provide teacher training in the sciences-educational facilities for primary and secondary education students, and also to provide educational facilities for the general public. Facilities include a Physics and Chemistry Lab, a Bio-Lab, a Discovery Lab, an EnviroLab, a Computer Lab, a Planetarium, a domed Science Theater, among many other educational resources that offer proficient scientific environments.

01 Bird's eye view **02** Exterior view of the domes by night **03** Detail façade **04** Site plan and floor plans **05** Corridor

Photos: Charles Callister Jr., Steve Proehl (1), Richard Barnes (2)

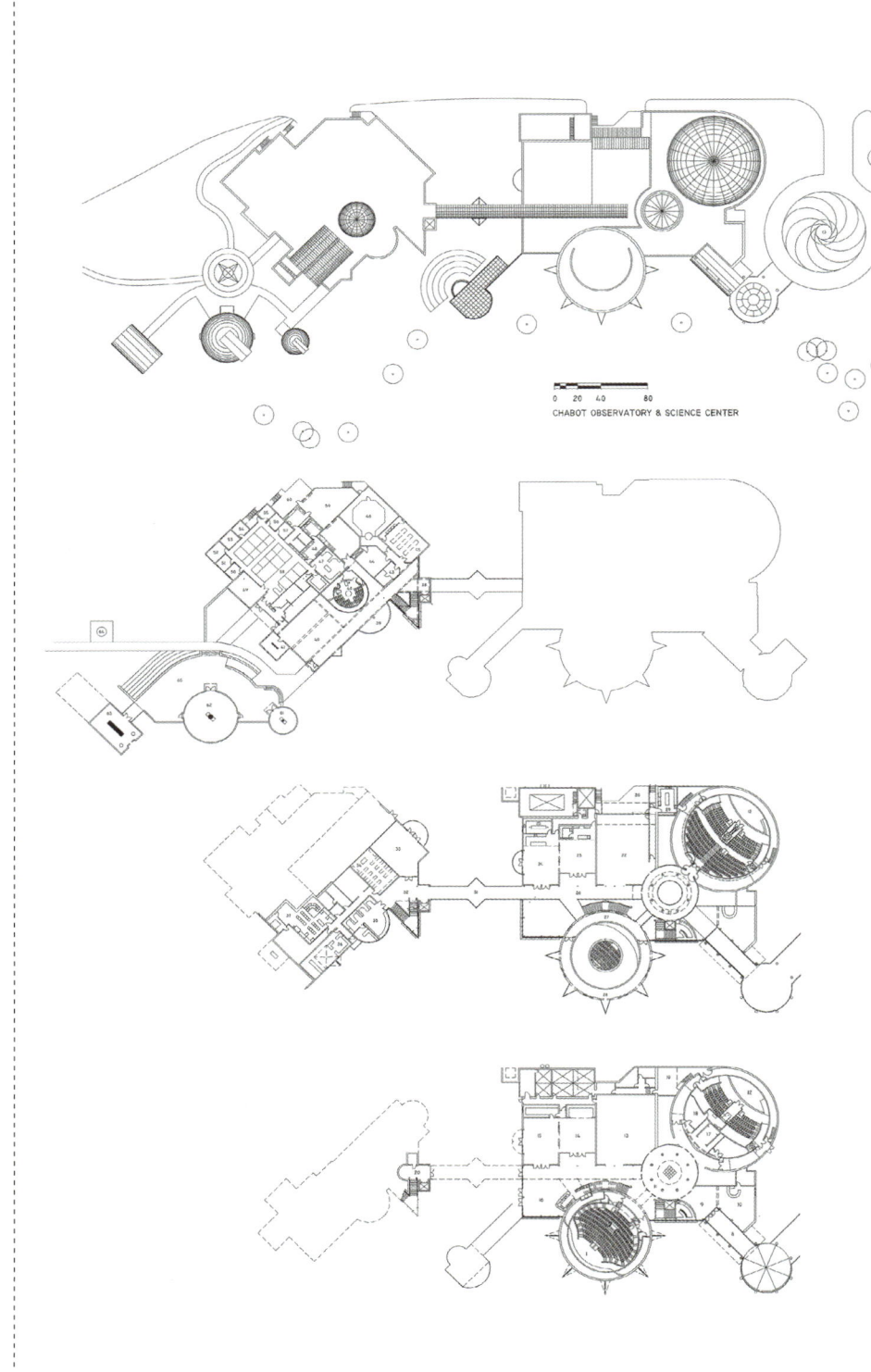

BIZARRE

This 1,400-square-foot space is being designed for an upscale paper store, experimenting with new ways of maximizing space, creating continuity between store fixtures and interior surfaces, and to design a fluid space to display paper art objects. The space plan proposes a series of pods in which to organize the different merchandise, where the pods are constructed with clear glass and plastic, with the purpose of achieving as much transparency as possible, so that the merchandise appears to float in the space. The interior space idea developed from experiments with the folding and cutting of a piece of paper to create dynamic space.

01 Overall view **02** Cash wrap **03** Entry **04** Detail pods made of glass and plastic

Photos: Farshid Assassi

CITY	Omaha (NE)
COUNTRY	USA
REGION	North America
TYPOLOGY	Retail
COMPLETION	–
WEBSITE	www.randybrownarchitects.com
ARCHITECTS	Randy Brown Architects design / build

CITY Omaha (NE)
COUNTRY USA
REGION North America
TYPOLOGY Retail
COMPLETION 2004
WEBSITE www.randybrownarchitects.com
ARCHITECTS Randy Brown Architects design / build

VILLAGE POINTE EAST

The L-shaped mall, built into a slope, takes advantage of the terrain to maximize square footage. Among the other tenants are a doctor's office, a salon, a Subway, a Hertz, and, directly above the daycare center, a martini bar. "Day care with a bar above – that is what I call mixed use!" A ribbon of copper panels winds from the trash pen at the bottom of the hill (a Randy Brown signature is the care he takes to tidy away dumpsters), up a beacon that announces the center to passing cars on Dodge Street, and around the front of the building, which is also composed of sandy brick and aluminum storefront doors and windows.

01 View from the courtyard **02** Exterior view **03** Pedestrian entrance with signage **04** Detail exterior cladding: copper flat seam panels

Photos: Farshid Assassi

LABORATORY

Developed as a laboratory for architectural experiments, the aptly named 'Laboratory' is a design-build collaboration between the architecture firm and college architecture students who assisted with design and construction each summer. The entire residence's core elements, including the five staircase designs, panelized wall systems, custom hurricane clips and hybrid wood and steel wall structures, were custom-designed and built on site. The residence incorporates various sustainable features, including passive solar strategies, natural ventilation, insulated concrete forms, radiant flooring and a green roof system.

01 Exterior view by night **02** Hybrid wood and steel wall **03** Living room **04** Floor plan **05** View to the bedroom, separated through wooden volume

Photos: Farshid Assassi

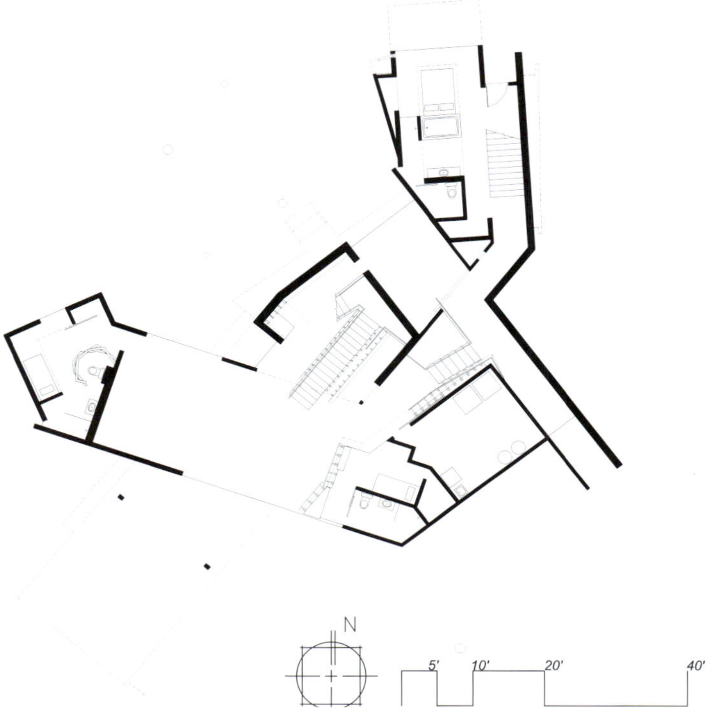

CITY: Omaha (NE)
COUNTRY: USA
REGION: North America
TYPOLOGY: Living
COMPLETION: in progress, addition completed in 2007
WEBSITE: www.randybrownarchitects.com
ARCHITECTS: Randy Brown Architects design / build

CITY	Palos Verdes (CA)
COUNTRY	USA
REGION	North America
TYPOLOGY	Mixed-Use
COMPLETION	2006
WEBSITE	www.xtenarchitecture.com
ARCHITECTS	XTEN Architecture

SILVERSPUR

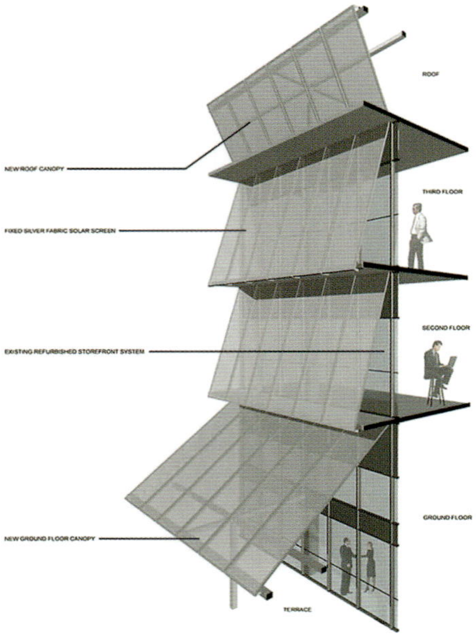

Silverspur is a 30,000-square-foot renovation to a modernist office building located on the Palos Verdes peninsula in Southern California. Small offices were removed from the interior to create large, open loft interiors, while sustainable design elements were introduced to the building. On the exterior, a new façade was developed to both increase the energy efficiency of the building and create a transformative new building envelope. New high-efficiency equipment, recycled carpeting, and tile were added throughout the building, while full height vision glass maximizes daylight and reduces the need for artificial light.

01 Detail of the silver façade **02** Main floors section **03** Front view **04** View from the street

Photos: Art Gray

PEORIA CENTER FOR THE PERFORMING ARTS

This new multi-theater performing arts center is located in the Old Town section of Peoria, Arizona. A striking feature of the design is the irregular, patinated copper roof, echoing the distant mountain ranges. It provides visual impact to the complex, which is constructed of concrete block in colors that are complementary to the natural landscape. The complex features a 250-seat theater with support spaces, and an 80-seat 'black box' performance space, as well as exhibition and educational spaces.

01 North elevation **02** Exterior view with focus on the entrance **03** Interior view **04** Site plan

Photos: Bill Timmerman

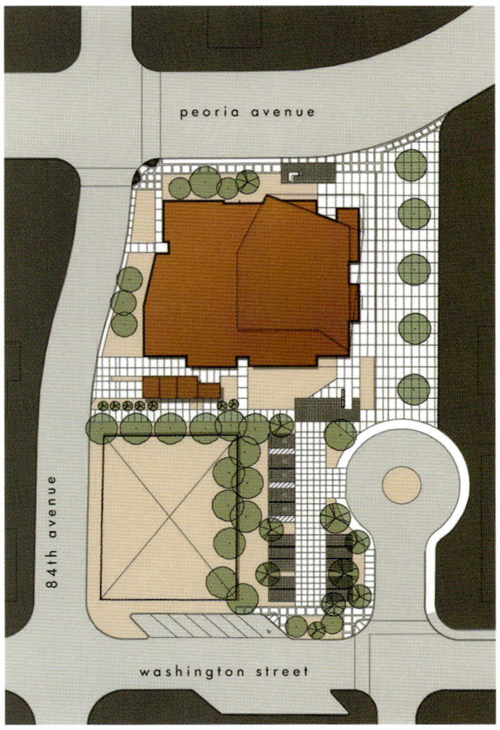

CITY Peoria (AZ)
COUNTRY USA
REGION North America
TYPOLOGY Culture
COMPLETION 2007
WEBSITE www.wrldesign.com
ARCHITECTS Westlake Reed Leskosky

CITY Pullman (WA)

COUNTRY USA

REGION North America

TYPOLOGY Education

COMPLETION 2004

WEBSITE www.barnstone.com

ARCHITECTS Robert Barnstone

WOOD MATERIALS ENGINEERING LABORATORIES, ANNEX BUILDING

This building's interaction between aesthetic interests and inventive material exploration, experiments with the potentials of wood plastic composite (WPC), materials that use ultraviolet (UV) light inhibitors and color additives to WPC blends, and unique profiles for envelope and rain-screen applications. The structure is fabricated from complex box beams made entirely from engineered wood products. Frank Lloyd Wright's use of box beams in his later Usonian homes was the inspiration, in which WPC can be more durable than traditional wood products and can be extruded to a desired length and molded into a range of shapes.

01 Exterior view **02** North wall **03** Section **04** East window and detail wall

Photos: Robert Barnstone

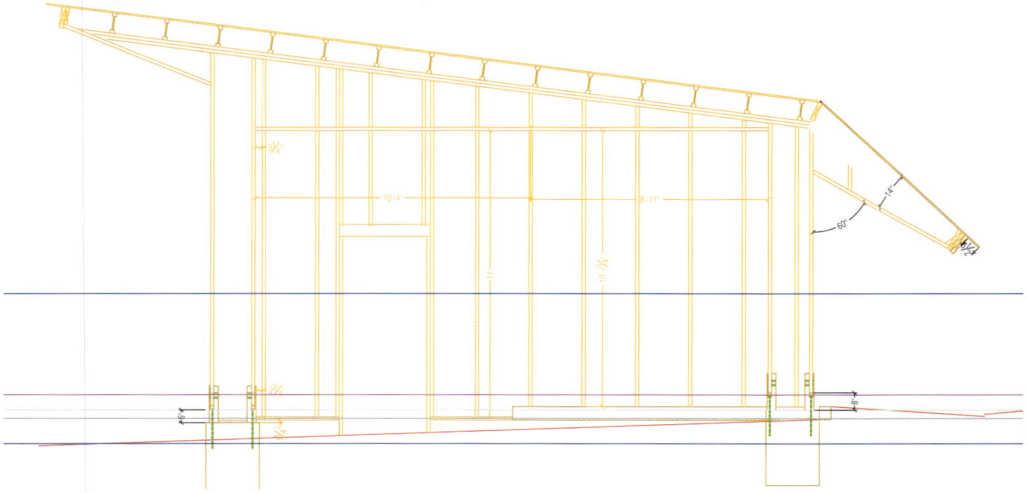

PSYC AT THE PARKER PALM SPRINGS

The Parker Palm Springs is situated on thirteen acres of landscaped gardens surrounded by the desert and mountains. The Yacht Club offers a full range of massage and body treatments, private men's and women's indoor swimming pools, Jacuzzis, steam and sauna rooms, and a 24-hour exercise facility. Discovered by Hollywood stars during the 1930s to 1970s, Palm Springs remains a major cultural hub with iconic architecture and stimulating artistic venues. The guest rooms and private villas reflect the hotel's unique topography in one of the world's most scenic deserts.

01 Courtyard garden **02** Interior viiew **03** Lounge area **04** Eastern view of the front

Photos: Gavin Jackson

POOLHOUSE

The site is a one-acre hillside lot in Palo Alto, adjoining open space with views to the south and west. The project involves the total reworking of the rear yard, which includes a home built in the 1970's. The new Poolhouse consists of a series of interlocking spaces organized within a uniformly repeated structure of Douglas-fir posts and beams. Closest to and most visible from the main house is the screened porch, evoking a summer cabin, while a small kitchen is strategically located between terrace, porch and main living area. A Douglas-fir butterfly roof opens the room to sunlight, revealing views and a steep landscape.

01 View of northwest corner of living area and cedar clad sauna volume **02** Interior view, kitchen **03** View of maple AV cabinet **04** View of cedar-clad mechanical sauna volume

Photos: Todd Hido

WALDFOGEL

An 8,000-square-foot house on a flat, half-acre site a mile from Stanford University takes its cues from the urbanity of the community and the sophistication of its owners, who wanted a home suitable for displaying their contemporary art collection. The house opens itself on all sides through a pinwheel plan that forms four distinct courtyards. Taut horizontal planes that extend beyond the building envelope and are clad in gray Rhinezinc connect two two-story volumes. An axial wall of poured-in-place concrete, which continues indoor to become the north-south circulation spine of the house, flanks the entrance.

01 View from courtyard with swimming pool and deck **02** Front view **03** First floor plan **04** Interior view, detail

Photos: Sharon Risedorph

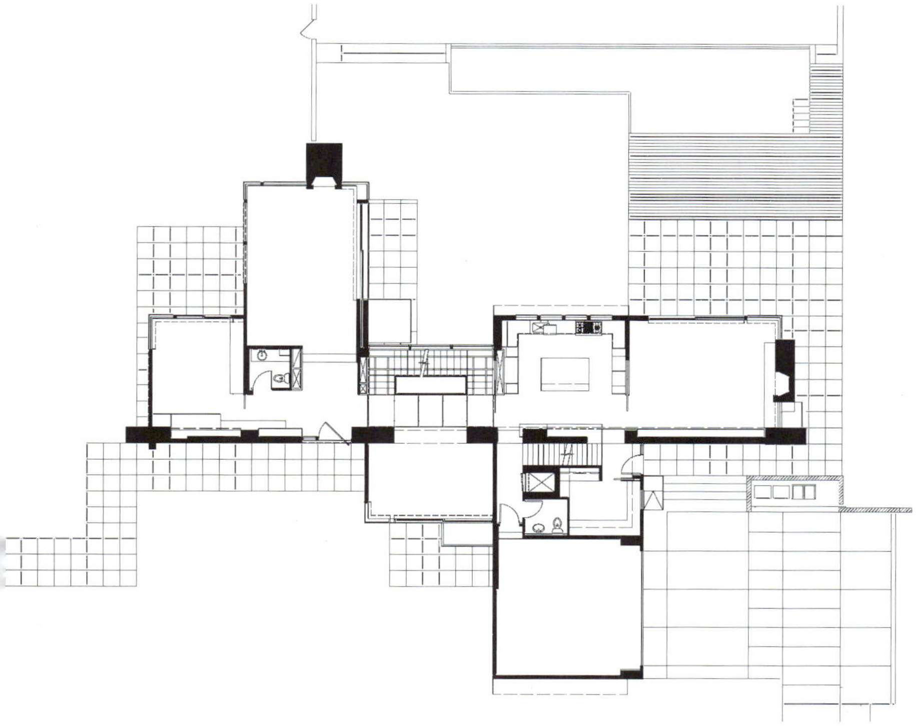

CITY Palo Alto (CA)
COUNTRY USA
REGION North America
TYPOLOGY Living
COMPLETION 2006
WEBSITE www.s-ehrlich.com
ARCHITECTS Steven Ehrlich Architects

DWELL HOME

The winning entry of the Dwell Home Design Invitational, this popular prefab home is comprised of five prefabricated modules that equal 2,042-squaree-feet. Regarded as the leader in superior, prefabricated building technology, the Dwell Home's compact and efficient quarters offer large open living spaces with a master bedroom at one end of the volume, and two bathrooms and an office that run along the same axis. Since approximately 80% of the house was built in a factory, the construction process leveraged the efficiency of wood framed modules, and the time required of crews on-site was significantly diminished. This, in turn, minimized the environment impact on the local ecosystems.

01 Sun deck 02 View to roof terrace 03 Kitchen 04 Rear view 05 Front view

Photos: Courtesy of Resolution 4: Architecture

CITY: Pittsboro (NC)
COUNTRY: USA
REGION: North America
TYPOLOGY: Living
COMPLETION: –
WEBSITE: www.re4a.com
ARCHITECTS: Resolution 4: Architecture

TR-1 HOUSE AND STUDIO

The project development of the TR-1 House and Studio by Cigolle X Coleman is conceived as a laboratory to test the ideas concerning the certain elements of light, space, and material. The sloping site has extensive views of the Santa Monica Bay to the east, while the Santa Monica Mountains to the north can also be seen. The elements of the project are divided into two typologies: the first of these typologies is the habitable walls that completely define the site, while the second is volumes that define hierarchically important spaces, which are positioned at places that consist of a special advantage.

01 View from the garden **02** Exterior view of habitable walls **03** Living room **04** Floor plan, lower level

Photos: Erhard Pfeiffer

CITY: Pacific Palisades (CA)
COUNTRY: USA
REGION: North America
TYPOLOGY: Living
COMPLETION: 2003
WEBSITE: www.cxcarch.com
ARCHITECTS: Cigolle X Coleman, Architects

CITY: Pacific Palisades (CA)
COUNTRY: USA
REGION: North America
TYPOLOGY: Living
COMPLETION: –
WEBSITE: www.kannerarch.com
ARCHITECTS: Kanner Architects

511 HOUSE

The 3,500-square-foot two-story home is designed to take full advantage of the bright light and cool Southern California breezes of the Pacific Palisades. The top design objective was blurring the line between inside and outside. The glass-clad main body was pushed to the north side of a lot the size of a tennis court (60 feet by 120 feet). A wide patio used extensively for dining and extends to the south off of the lower level. This generous setback allows natural light to penetrate the house from the south.

01 Glass-clad main body **02** Stairwell, light-flooded **03** Total view by night **04** Floor plans **05** Patio

Photos: John Edward Linden

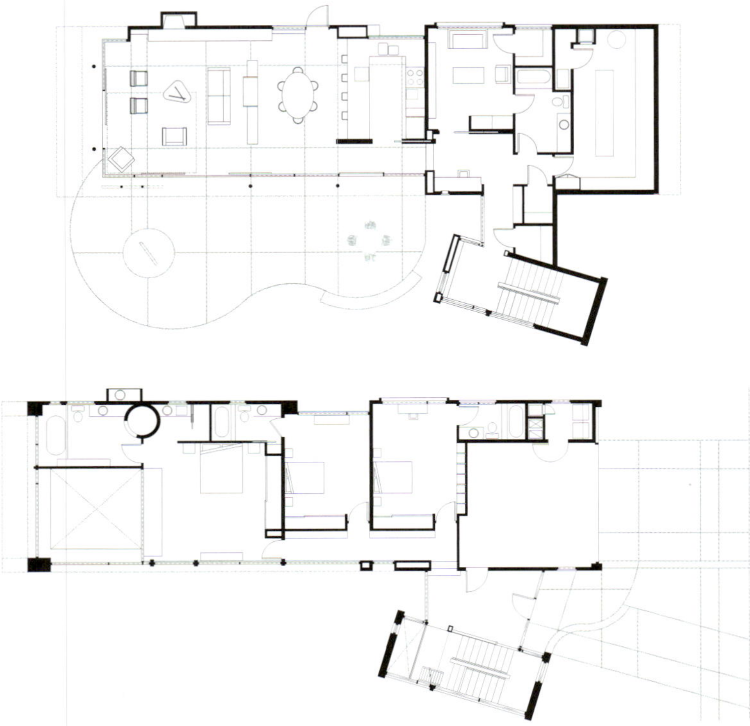

RUSTIC CANYON RESIDENCE

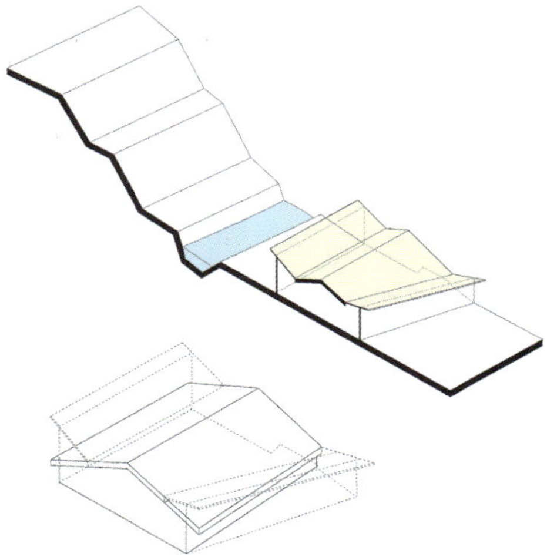

The residence represents a shift in the conventions for designing a single family dwelling by reconfiguring an existing ranch style home to open up a previously compartmentalized floor plan. The new expansive living area is under an undulating roof which is derived from the sloped hillside beyond. In the main space, an active ceiling line is perforated by natural light, filling the interior spaces with an atmosphere found in the tree-filled garden, while at night the uplit ceiling floats amid a soft ambiance. The living, dining and kitchen areas become a single interactive loft-like space, creating an informal atmosphere.

01 Front view 02 Exterior view, library 03 Dining area 04 View from garden to sliding glass doors 05 Diagram 06 Living area under the undulating roof

Photos: Art Gray

CITY: Pacific Palisades (CA)
COUNTRY: USA
REGION: North America
TYPOLOGY: Living
COMPLETION: 2003
WEBSITE: www.griffinenright architects.com
ARCHITECTS: Griffin Enright Architects

CITY
Palm Desert (CA)

COUNTRY
USA

REGION
North America

TYPOLOGY
Living

COMPLETION
2007

WEBSITE
www.patelarchitecture.com

ARCHITECTS
Patel Architecture

DIAMOND RESIDENCE

In this signature streamlined modern desert home, architect Narendra Patel created a delicate pavilion, overlooking a golf course, valley, and mountains. The home's defining element is a daring inverted shell roof that lifts up towards the exterior, bringing light into airy interiors. The main living spaces including the great room, dining & family room, kitchen, and the master suite are located facing the pool as the primary choice view, while sheltered by the hovering roof. Circulation to the bedrooms is separate from the public areas, giving each bedroom its own access to private patios and views, while maximizing privacy.

01 Wall and window detail **02** Exterior pathways **03** View into bathroom **04** Front façade **05** Exterior with pool by night

Photos: Arthur Coleman

FRITZ RESIDENCE

To achieve a feeling of simplicity, the house reflects a strategy of enclosure and openness focused toward the main outdoor space. Two wings are connected together at the main living, dining, and kitchen space to define a corner with one wing containing the guest bedrooms and the other the master suite. Designed in the Modern idiom to reflect the Palm Springs location, the house is open, flowing, and bathed in natural light. All rooms access the outdoor pool/courtyard space through large sliding glass walls.

01 Exterior view with focus on the terrace and swimming pool **02** Interior view **03** Floorplan **04** Hallway

Photos: Ciro Coelho

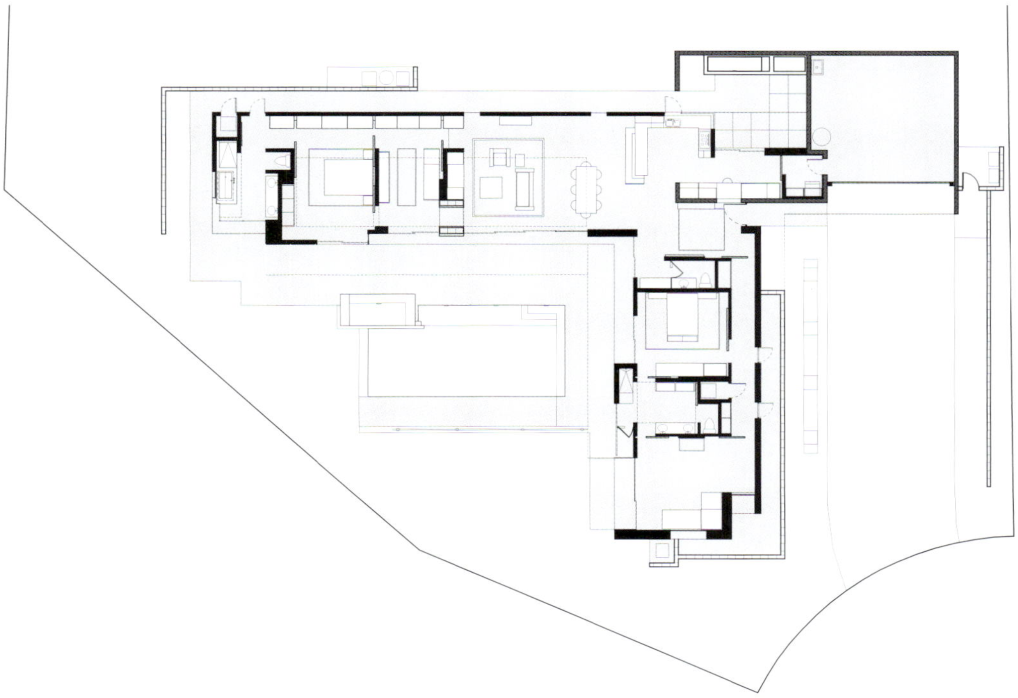

CITY Palm Desert (CA)
COUNTRY USA
REGION North America
TYPOLOGY Living
COMPLETION 2004
WEBSITE www.ojmrarchitects.net
ARCHITECTS OJMR Architects

THE CHILDREN'S CENTER AT CALTECH'S OUTDOOR SCIENCE LABORATORY

The Children's Center is an education and care facility for preschool children. The design of the outdoor science laboratory accurately reflects the identity and philosophy of the Center, the culture and heritage of Caltech, and actively supports its mission. The goal was to create significant architecture that both adds value to the school and contributes to the greater community.

01 Front view **02** Workspaces on the deck **03** Floor plan, strategy **04** View from the garden

Photos: David Lena

MARIPOSA RESIDENCE

Commissioned by the Brophy Jesuit Community to design a new home for ten Jesuit Priests, the scheme draws inspiration from the two existing white-flowering oleander hedges along the east and west margins of the site. The program for the residence called for a public zone of the house including the kitchen, living room, study, library, chapel, and a private zone, including the ten individual dwellings. Based on simple principles of light, shade, orientation, scale and proportion, the house is shaped and sculpted by climate and function where many of the spaces have a singular relationship to light.

01 View from the deck **02** Detail meditation chapel wrapped in channel glass **03** Garden view **04** Public zone: living room **05** Floor plans

Photos: Bill Timmerman

CITY Phoenix (AZ)
COUNTRY USA
REGION North America
TYPOLOGY Living
COMPLETION 2003
WEBSITE www.debartoloarchitects.com
ARCHITECTS DeBartolo architects

CITY Phoenix (AZ)

COUNTRY USA

REGION North America

TYPOLOGY Public

COMPLETION 2006

WEBSITE www.gouldevans.com, www.wendellburnettarchitects.com/

ARCHITECTS Gould Evans (in collaboration with Wendell Burnette Architects)

THE PALO VERDE LIBRARY & MARYVALE COMMUNITY CENTER

The new library and community center is a mixed-use project on the west side of Phoenix. The complex comprises the library collection, a sports hall, a large public collection area and a 150-seat auditorium. Two similarly scaled volumes clad in stainless steel hover upon a long horizontal 8-foot high glass base. The design provides a mixture of balanced glare-free natural light with the warmth of recycled wood used on the walls and floors of the respective interiors.

01 Building components: steel hover and glass base **02** Sports hall **03** Library **04** First floor plan **05** Learning area

Photos: Bill Timmerman

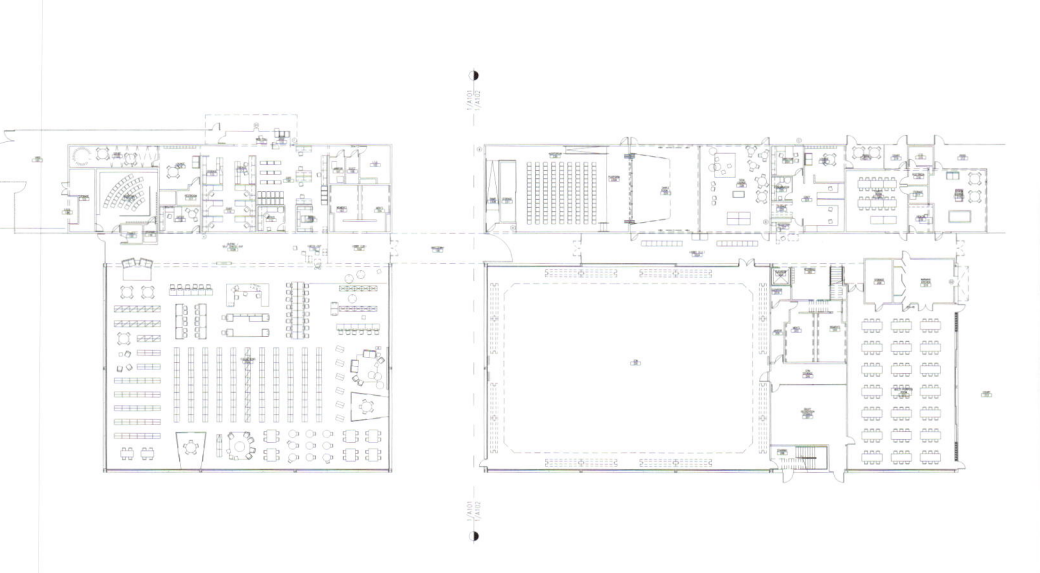

NEIGHBORHOOD RESOURCE CENTER

The Neighborhood Resource Center includes a police station, neighborhood services offices, and public areas. Despite the modest scale of the building the architectural character creates a dramatic and ambitious "presence" surpassing its size while still retaining an open, community-friendly atmosphere. The resulting building is both striking and welcoming, a powerful symbol of neighborhood change. Key components include offices for command, administrative staff and motoring officers, secured parking and lighting for 50 vehicles, interview rooms, briefing room for 30 persons, and property/evidence rooms.

01 View from northwest **02** North entry **03** Lobby **04** Floor plan

Photos: Bill Timmerman

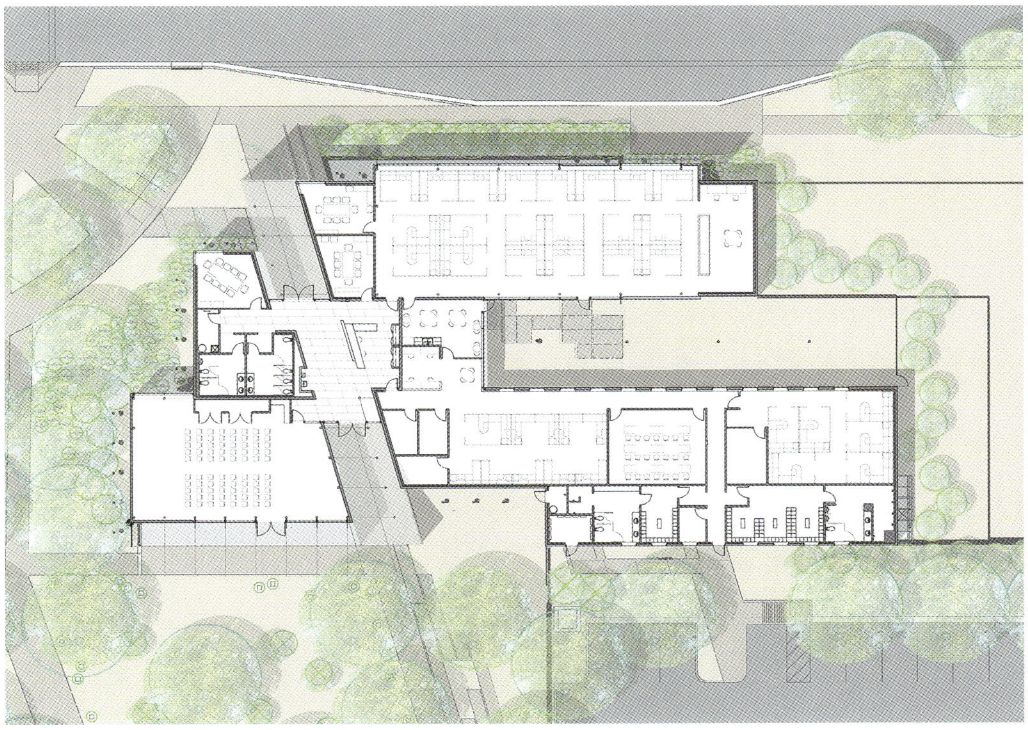

CITY Phoenix (AZ)
COUNTRY USA
REGION North America
TYPOLOGY Public
COMPLETION 2006
WEBSITE www.imirzian-architects.com
ARCHITECTS Marlene Imirzian & Associates Architects

CITY
Phoenix (AZ)

COUNTRY
USA

REGION
North America

TYPOLOGY
Living

COMPLETION
2003

WEBSITE
www.jonesstudioinc.com

ARCHITECTS
Jones Studio

HOUSE OF 5 DREAMS

This 30,000 square foot residence and private museum was designed for a pair of prolific art and artifact collectors. The clients asked that their residence and artwork be separated into distinct areas. Knowing that much of their collection has been excavated from the ground, the decision was made to place exhibition space underground. Above the gallery, a floating residential pavilion was designed to evoke their existing home, which is an entire floor of a high rise. A large hole was dug, and the four-foot thick walls of the gallery were built with rammed earth.

01 Exterior view by night **02** Detail façade **03** Glass stairway to gallery **04** Entrance area **05** Interior view, residential pavilion

Photos: Courtesy of Jones Studio

CESAR CHAVEZ LIBRARY

Located adjacent to an existing lake in a public park, the 25,000-square-foot library is designed to serve a projected 40,000 visitors per month within one of the fastest growing areas of Phoenix. Conceived as a "Living Room" for the expanding community, the Library provides natural daylight, minimizing the use of conventional fixtures and offering occupants connection to the surrounding outdoors. Earth berms quietly integrate the Library into the public parkscape, providing thermal mass against the building and a barrier from noise. Rainwater is harvested from the roof and stored in the adjacent lake for use in irrigation.

01 North elevation **02** Light interior **03** Window towards the lake **04** Ground floor plan

Photos: Bill Timmerman

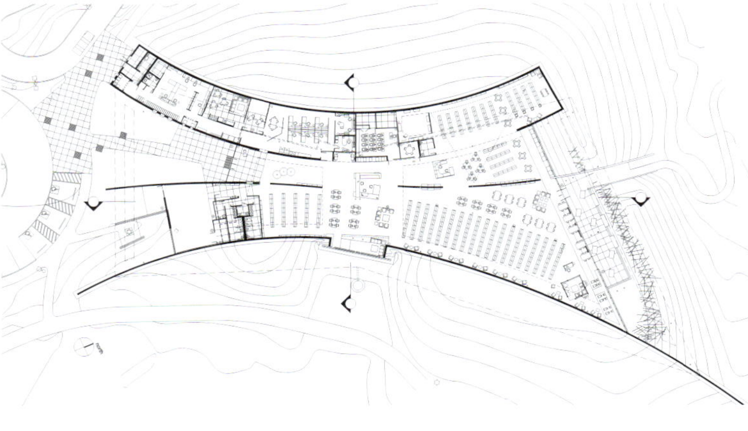

CITY: Phoenix (AZ)
COUNTRY: USA
REGION: North America
TYPOLOGY: Public
COMPLETION: 2007
WEBSITE: www.lineandspace.com
ARCHITECTS: Line and Space, LLC

CITY
Phoenix (AZ)

COUNTRY
USA

REGION
North America

TYPOLOGY
Living

COMPLETION
2007

WEBSITE
www.merzproject.com

ARCHITECTS
[merz]project

HOOVER HOUSE

This urban-infill project located in the Ashland Historic District near downtown Phoenix is an addition and remodel of an existing bungalow originally constructed in 1924. The cellular character of the original floor plan was dissolved in the old house, opening it up to large multi-use indoor/outdoor rooms, blurring a traditional boundary between indoors and outdoors. The existing brick bungalow is complemented by a zinc-clad rectangular addition whose boundaries define new garden areas and is situated in the existing backyard. By utilizing similar structural systems and proportions, but clearly different materials, the resulting zinc-clad structure possesses a pre-patina that provides aged appearance that contrasts with the older structure.

01 Exterior view **02** View from master bedroom to living room **03** Ground floor plan **04** Kitchen

Photos: Matt Winquist

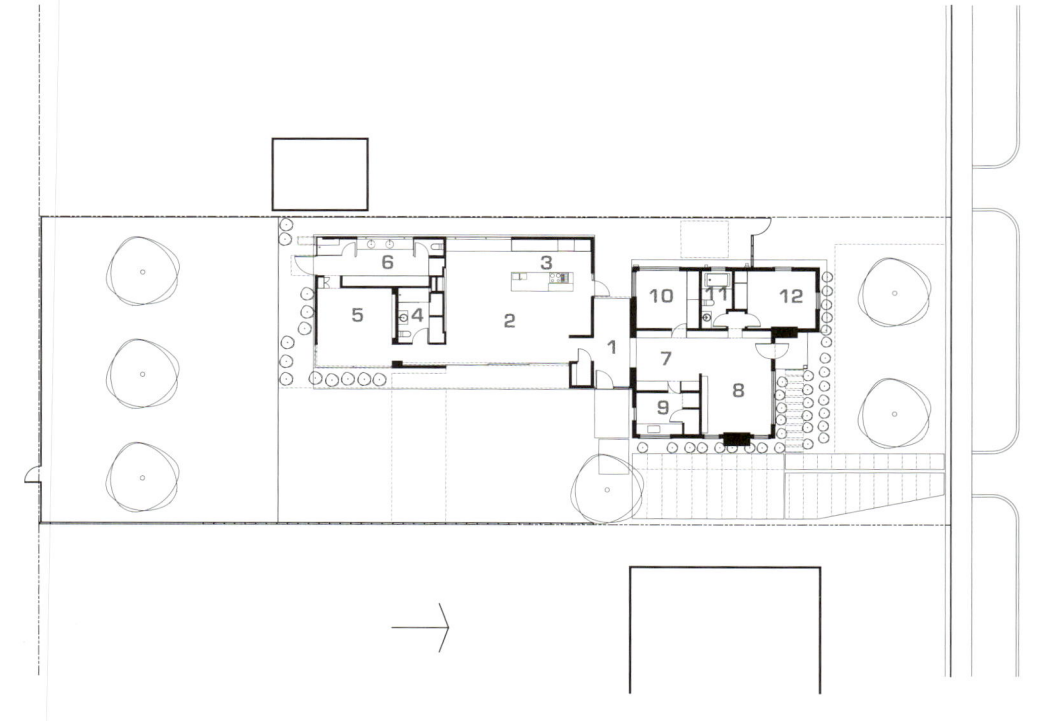

DUPLEX RESIDENCE

The Duplex Residence is a project that combines two units being built on a single city lot, and is intended for a couple and their best friend. An important feature that made this possible was a spatial joint, which was developed in the overlap of entrances and the roof access. The L-shaped complex is a double bar scheme that is divided into served and service areas. This division allows all functions including cooking, bathing, washing, etc., to be built-in as furniture, for example an inhabitable loaded core wall. The house also provides relief from the desert sun with a lap pool for all residences.

01 Courtyard **02** Exterior view **03** Lap pool **04** Detail overlap entrances

Photos: Terry Surjan

CITY	Phoenix (AZ)
COUNTRY	USA
REGION	North America
TYPOLOGY	Living
COMPLETION	2006
WEBSITE	www.plusminusstudio.com http://web.mac.com/surjan/site/C_U_P.html
ARCHITECTS	Plus Minus Studio + C U P

PHOENIX ART MUSEUM EXPANSION

The expansion of the Phoenix Art Museum is a composite of several buildings constructed and developed over a period of 50 years. In 1996, construction was completed for a renovation which saw the addition of two large galleries and a new entrance. In response to the success that the museum was generating, the same architects were chosen in 2001 to rethink and strategize the growth of the museum site. Completed in late 2006, this addition provides a new 10,000 square foot indoor/outdoor entrance oriented towards a new entry court, and over 30,000 square foot of galleries in the new south wing of the museum.

01 New gallery exterior façade **02** Indoor/outdoor entrance
03, 04 Gallery interior views **05** Site plan

Photos: Bill Timmerman

CITY
Phoenix (AZ)

COUNTRY
USA

REGION
North America

TYPOLOGY
Culture

COMPLETION
2006

WEBSITE
www.twbta.com

ARCHITECTS
Tod Williams Billie Tsien Architects

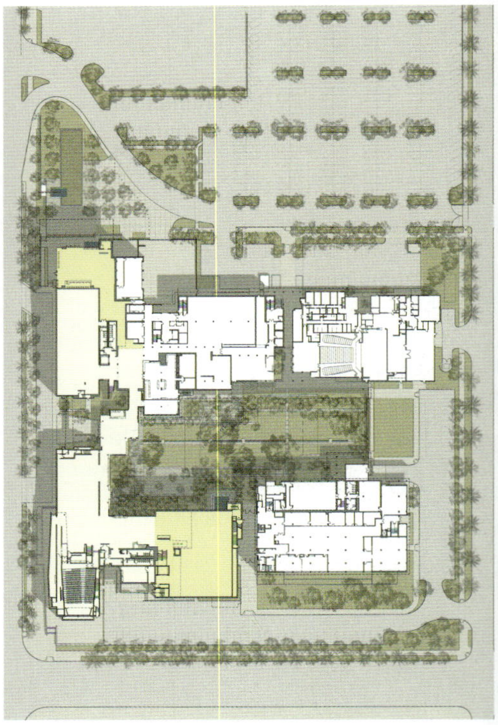

XEROS RESIDENCE

Located within a 1950's era development, where the urban city grid is overtaken by the organic landforms of a mountain preserve, the Xeros Residence creates a dramatic presence. The live-work design accommodates a design studio on the lower level and a single-story residence on the upper level accessible only by an external stair. The primary building material is exposed steel that will weather naturally and meld with the color of the surrounding hills. The residence is dubbed 'Xeros' to serve as a reminder that all design solutions should be in direct response to the environment.

01 Main view at dawn **02** Sections **03** Interior view, design studio **04** Detail external stair to upper level residence **05** Color meld: steel façade and environment

Photos: Bill Timmerman

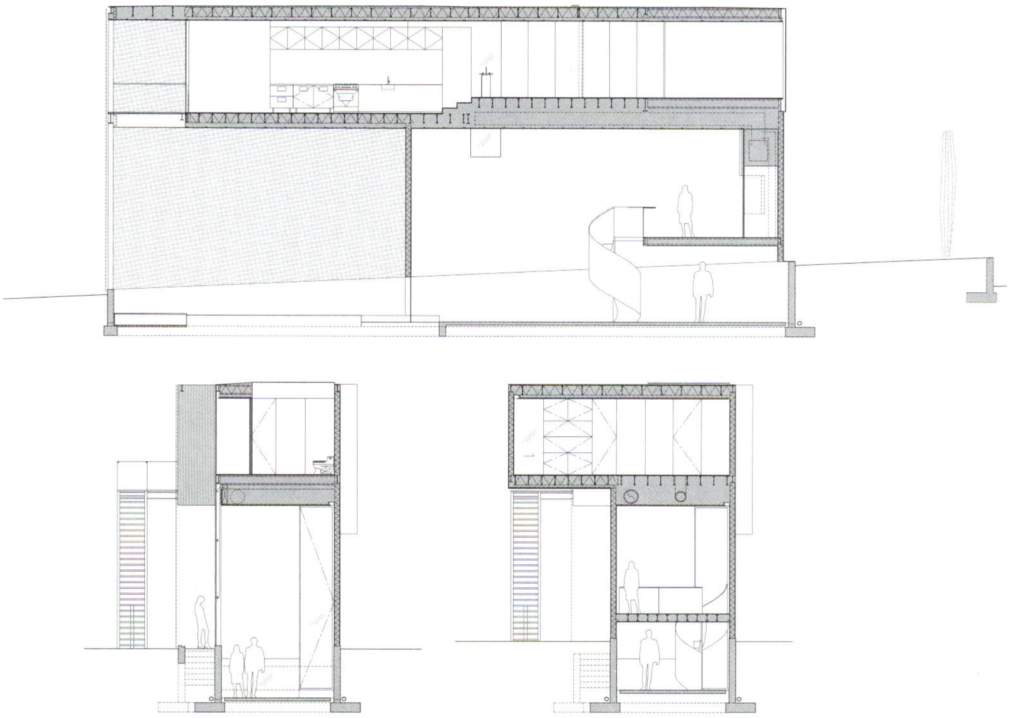

CITY: Phoenix (AZ)
COUNTRY: USA
REGION: North America
TYPOLOGY: Living
COMPLETION: 2006
WEBSITE: www.blankspaces.net
ARCHITECTS: blank studio

CITY: Portland (OR)
COUNTRY: USA
REGION: North America
TYPOLOGY: Transportation
COMPLETION: 2007
WEBSITE: www.agps.ch
ARCHITECTS: agps architecture

PORTLAND AERIAL TRAM

An aerial tram was determined to be the most effective system to connect the sites of a historic neighborhood, a protected park, and major traffic arteries, while also reducing congestion and air pollution. The tram is designed as a minimal intervention with light and open structures that dematerialize transportation infrastructure. The building elements include an upper and lower station, an intermediate support tower, and two tram cars, which operate in a jig-back configuration. The upper station is an open-air covered platform supported by braced steel legs balancing on a steep site, wedged between hospital buildings.

01 View of lower station 02 East elevation, upper station 03 Detail, steel legs 04 Rear view upper station

Photos: Eric Staudenmaier

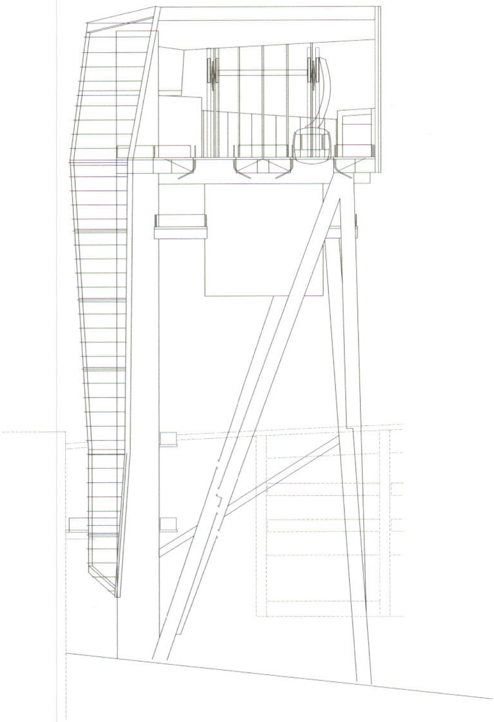

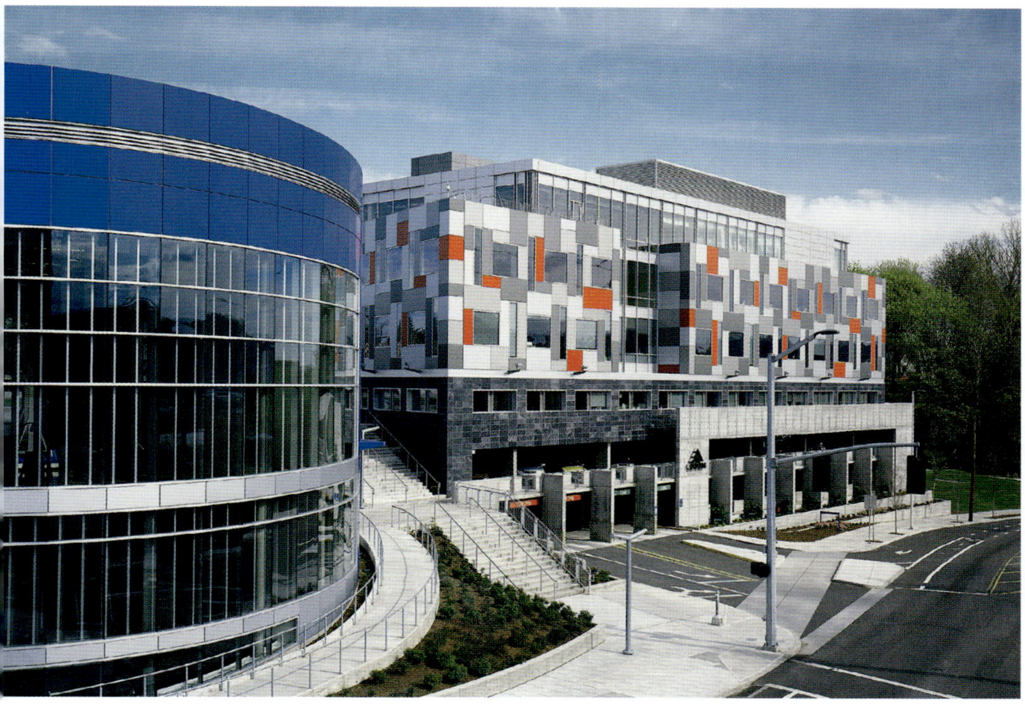

ADIDAS AMERICA HEADQUARTERS

This project is an adaptive reuse of a former hospital complex, where the site was developed as a unified whole, renovating existing structures and linking them to new buildings and sport facilities using public plazas. The site is divided by a street and has an elevation difference of thirty-five feet. The stairs on each side of the sports building, the bridge, and the pedestrian crossing visually connect both sides. Existing and new buildings share similar scale and massing. The new "active skin" that wraps most of the new construction is also applied to existing buildings wherever original cladding had to be altered.

01 Exterior view of building E and F **02** Detail of "active skin" façade **03** Pedestrian bridge crossing Greeley Avenue **04** Exterior view building B **05** Basketball court

Photos: David Papazian

CITY Portland (OR)
COUNTRY USA
REGION North America
TYPOLOGY Office
COMPLETION 2003
WEBSITE www.boora.com
ARCHITECTS BOORA Architects

CITY Portland (OR)
COUNTRY USA
REGION North America
TYPOLOGY Living
COMPLETION 2005
WEBSITE www.krownlab.com
ARCHITECTS Stefan Andren / Krown Lab

SKYBOX

Perched atop a steep hillside surrounded by green space, Skybox is designed to encompass more loft-like qualities than those of a traditional house. Decks and terraces are created within the dwelling itself, leaving its surroundings untouched and allowing it to better blend in with the natural environment. The house has an open, flowing floor plan, which allows one space to stream into the next, creating a flexible and space efficient dwelling. Rather than the use of walls and doors, shifts in ceiling heights and floor levels are used to emphasize division of space.

01, **02** Exterior view **03** Living room **04** Kitchen **05** Top and main floor plan **06** View from sleeping room to deck

Photos: Stefan Andren / Krown Lab

FENNELL RESIDENCE

The Fennell Residence, a floating house on the Willamette River, just outside Portland, Oregon, presents a unique opportunity for design. Curved glue lam beams of Douglas fir seem to ebb and flow over the structure in sympathy with the ripples along the river's surface, bringing a sense of fluidity throughout the home. The loft style residence with the master suite on the second floor and the living areas below is punctuated at its western end by an expansive glass wall that allows sweeping views of the river and a physical connection to the water via a sliding door and a wooden deck.

01 Exterior view 02 Interior view, living area 03 Exterior view from the deck to the glass wall 04 Floor plans 05 Interior view, master suite

Photos: Cameron Neilson

CITY Portland (OR)
COUNTRY USA
REGION North America
TYPOLOGY Living
COMPLETION 2005
WEBSITE www.oshatz.com
ARCHITECTS Robert Harvey Oshatz Architect

CITY Portland (OR)
COUNTRY USA
REGION North America
TYPOLOGY Living
COMPLETION 2004
WEBSITE www.oshatz.com
ARCHITECTS Robert Harvey Oshatz Architect

WILKINSON RESIDENCE

The flag lot and a fast sloping grade provided the opportunity to bring the main level of the house into the tree canopy to evoke the feeling of being in a tree house. This house evades the mechanics of the camera, which makes it difficult to grasp the spaces as they flow inside and out. One has to actually stroll through the house to capture its complexities and its connection to the exterior. Being part of the landscape, a natural wood ceiling floating on curving laminated wood beams passes through a generous glass wall, which wraps around the main living room.

01 Exterior view of wood beams and pivotal glass entry door 02 Interior view 03 Floor plans 04 Rear view

Photos: Cameron Neilson

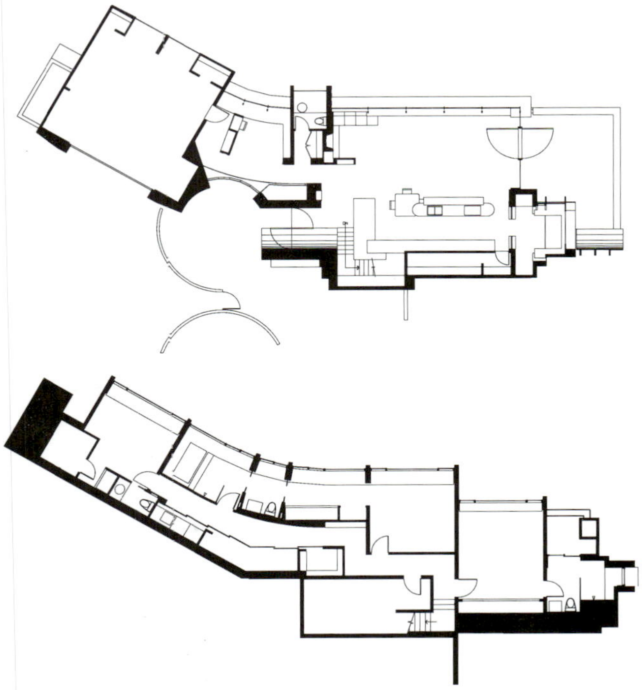

GLENSTONE RESIDENCE

Located on 125 acres of landscaped lawns, meadows and woods in Potomac, Maryland, this residence contains an assemblage of buildings and outdoor sculpture for a private client. The property has two parts, a farm side and a residential side, accessed by separate entry gates and drives. The new buildings, all located on the residential side, are comprised of a main residence, guest house, pool house and museum.

01 View of main residence from southwest **02** Main residence living room **03** Exterior view of the ensemble **04** Main stair at lower level **05** Section looking west through master bedroom

Photos: Scott Frances – 2006

CITY
Potomac (MD)

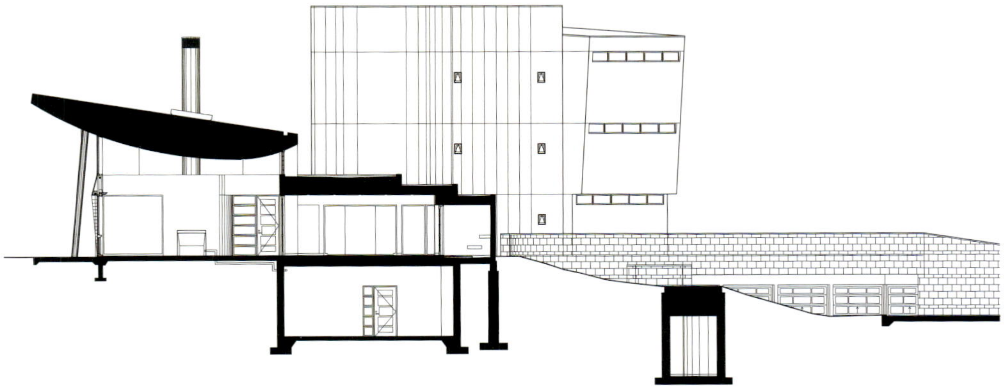

COUNTRY
USA

REGION
North America

TYPOLOGY
Living

COMPLETION
2006

WEBSITE
www.gwathmey-siegel.com

ARCHITECTS
Gwathmey Siegel & Associates Architects

BAY EDUCATIONAL CENTER

2030 targets to move the US away from oil dependence are dramatically bested by this small, super-performance education center. The integrated photovoltaic, high-performance envelope, high efficiency lighting and controls, and gas-fired heater/chiller mechanical system reduce the peak electricity load by 73% and produce 67% less NOx and SOx. CO^2 emissions are reduced by 51% and potential ozone depletion by 100%. The building opens to the south as well as east for light and views, while the north is bermed into the earth, resulting in a fully day-lit building in which all occupied spaces have a view to the Bay.

01 Exterior view, photovoltaic envelope **02** Lobby **03** Rear view, detail **04** Entrance **05** Plan and elevations

Photos: Ruggero Vanni

CITY: Providence (RI)
COUNTRY: USA
REGION: North America
TYPOLOGY: Education
COMPLETION: 2005
WEBSITE: www.croxtonarc.com
ARCHITECTS: Croxton Collaborative Architects PC

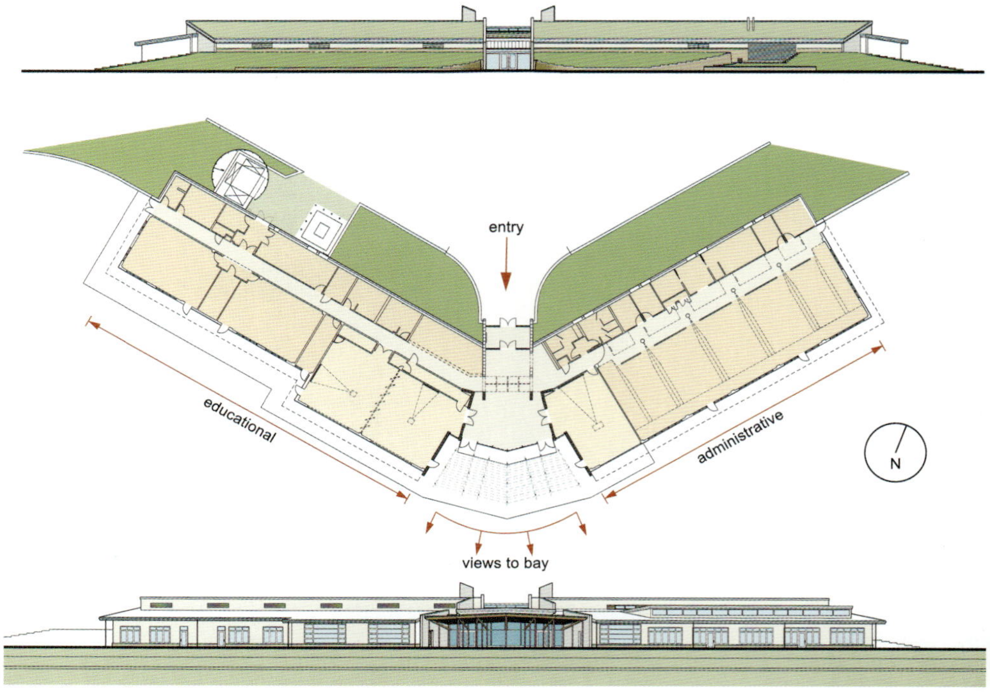

RENOVATIONS TO GRANT HALL, BROWN UNIVERSITY

Grant Recital Hall is placed within the masonry shell of a small existing carriage house on Brown University's campus in Providence, Rhode Island. With just 135 seats, it is an intimate venue for the department's presentation of chamber music, electronic music, and smaller jazz combos. Exposing the entire volume of the carriage house and inserting two distinct wall systems enhanced the acoustic performance of the space. The sidewalls of the hall were shaped with a plaster and wood scrim to prevent the buildup of 'flutter' within the space and a perforated bamboo screen envelopes the stage itself.

01 Auditorium **02** Interior, detail stair at entry **03** Detail pivot door **04** First floor plan **05** Detail window

Photos: John Horner Photography, Silvia Illia

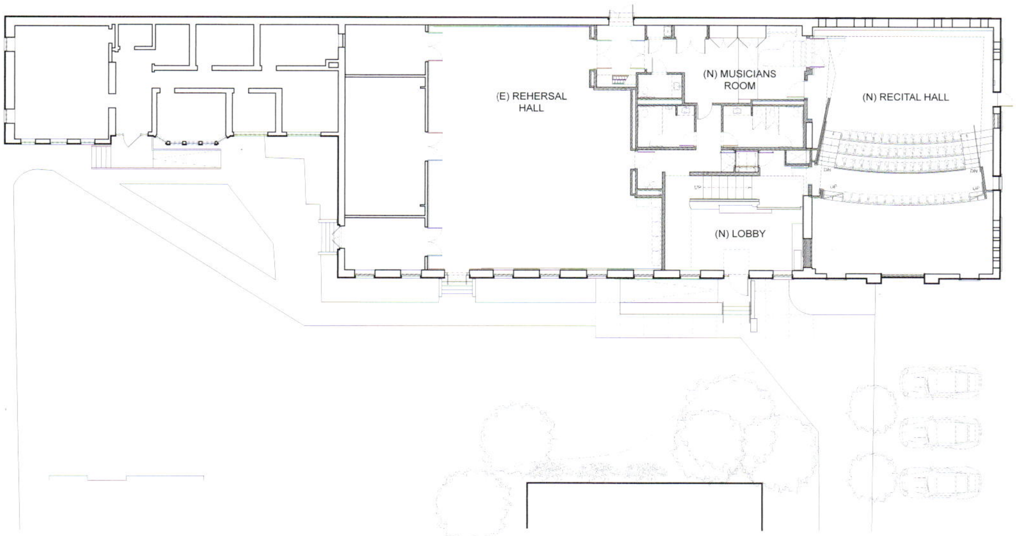

CITY Providence (RI)
COUNTRY USA
REGION North America
TYPOLOGY Education
COMPLETION 2007
WEBSITE www.brianhealyarchitects.com
ARCHITECTS Brian Healy Architects

CITY: Queens (NY)
COUNTRY: USA
REGION: North America
TYPOLOGY: Public
COMPLETION: in progress
WEBSITE: www.marblefairbanks.com
ARCHITECTS: Marble Fairbanks

GLEN OAKS BRANCH LIBRARY

Awarded by the Department of Design and Construction, the mandate for this project is to replace an existing one-story facility with a new high performance, LEED certified building. The program includes adult and children's reading areas and collections, periodicals, a cyber-center, and community meeting rooms along with staff workspaces. The building's surfaces join with the landscape to modulate light, privacy, views, and information content in various degrees. A double-height space acts as a large skylight and connects the ground floor to the lower level, with three strip skylights in the plaza allowing for further light.

01 Interior view **02** View from the street **03** Bird's eye view
04 South elevation, cement board with reflective fasteners
05 Floor plan with landscape

Photos: Marble Fairbanks

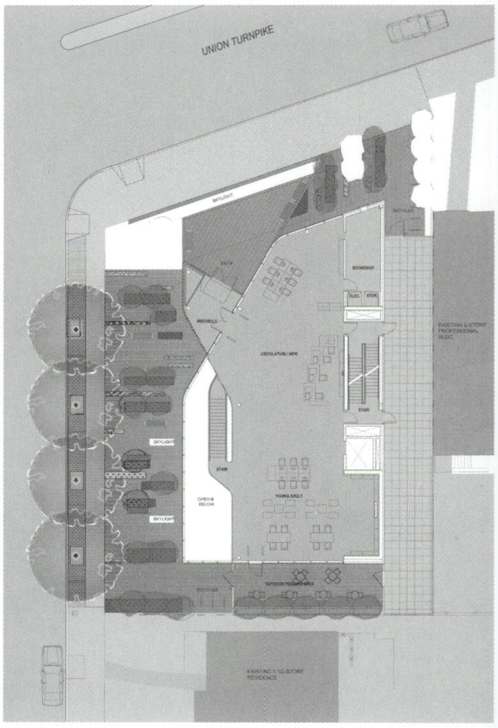

HIGH SCHOOL FOR CONSTRUCTION TRADES, ENGINEERING AND ARCHITECTURE

The project is a 155,000 square feet high school for 900 students with a 300-seat the-ater, double-height lobby, and specialized labs for material technologies, mechanical drafting, model building and computer drafting. The concept was to express large programmatic elements and specialized spaces in different colors and cladding materials. The auditorium is in pre-cast concrete panels punctured by a series of dynamic, narrow-paned window slats and topped by a canary-yellow extrusion; the cafeteria and art room in corrugated metal; the gym in glass block; the library in colored porcelain panels; and the classrooms in bright red brick.

01 Detail pre-cast concrete auditorium **02** Entrance area **03** L-shaped brick portion **04** First floor plan **05** Lobby

Photos: Norman McGrath

CITY Queens (NY)
COUNTRY USA
REGION North America
TYPOLOGY Education
COMPLETION 2006
WEBSITE www.arquitectonica.com
ARCHITECTS Arquitectonica

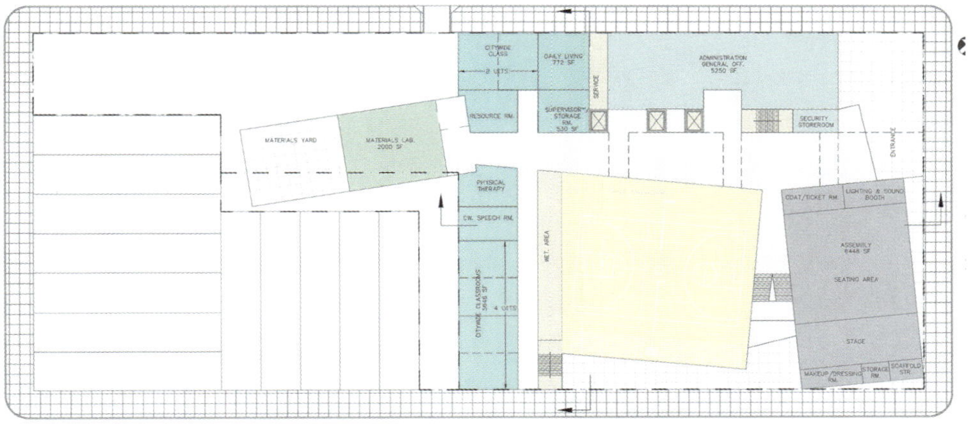

CITY
Red Mesa Chapter, Navajo Nation (UT)

COUNTRY
USA

REGION
North America

TYPOLOGY
Living

COMPLETION
2004

WEBSITE
www.designbuildbluff.com

ARCHITECTS
DesignBuildBLUFF

ROSIE JOE HOUSE

Designed and built by eight students for a single mother working three jobs to support her Navajo family, this house provided several design challenges and a crash course for students in rural self-sufficiency. The location provided a rich cultural experience for all involved, where the immersion into a community monetarily impoverished but humanly vibrant, provided a learning experience at the very heart of architecture. The development's features include a rammed earth Trombe wall for thermal mass, rainwater collecting roof, PV electricity, and recycled and reclaimed materials including wood pallets and highway signs.

01 Side view **02** Detail rainwater collecting roof and deck **03** Total view **04** Interior view, hallway

Photos: Courtesy of DesignBuildBLUFF

HOUSE ON THE HILL

The site is an open meadow exposed to sun and breezes, surrounded on three sides by a new growth forest that ensures privacy. The building is conceived as a simple industrial shed that evokes the numerous farm buildings of the area. An auxiliary wing is set perpendicular to the main volume to form an "L" configuration, which together with the forest boundary and old stonewall, creates an intimate private garden at the rear of the house. The main façade faces south, taking full advantage of solar orientation and spectacular views. The ground floor is set into the hilltop and appears to be a natural extension of the landscape.

01 Double-height living room **02** View of dining area from loft **03** Ground and second floor plan **04** Industrial look of the exterior **05** South elevation

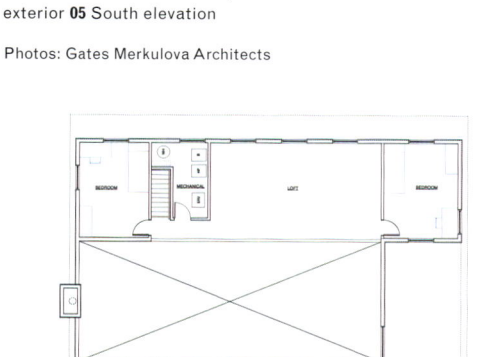

Photos: Gates Merkulova Architects

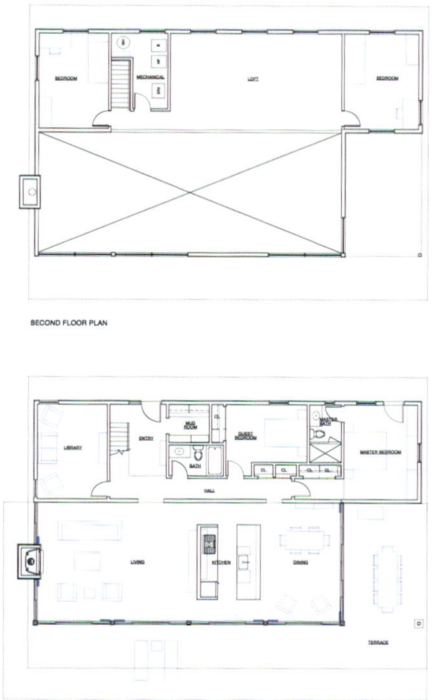

CITY Red Rock (NY)
COUNTRY USA
REGION North America
TYPOLOGY Living
COMPLETION 2007
WEBSITE www.gmarch.com
ARCHITECTS Gates Merkulova Architects

CITY: Redondo Beach (CA)
COUNTRY: USA
REGION: North America
TYPOLOGY: Living
COMPLETION: 2007
WEBSITE: www.demariadesign.com
ARCHITECTS: DeMaria Design

REDONDO BEACH CONTAINER HOUSE

The building structure is a family residence employing recycled cargo containers. Combined with technologies from the aerospace industry, these components have been brought together with traditional stick frame construction to create a "hybrid" home that is environmentally conscious and affordable. The use of materials and methods from other industries, non-related to residential construction, is part of the architect's philosophical approach. Features include airplane hangar doors, denim insulation, polyurethane insulated roof panels, tank less hot water heaters, greenhouse acrylic panels, and Formaldehyde-free plywood.

01 Detail recycled cargo container **02** View from the garden to decks **03** Exterior view **04** First floor plan **05** Interior view

Photos: Andre Movsesyan

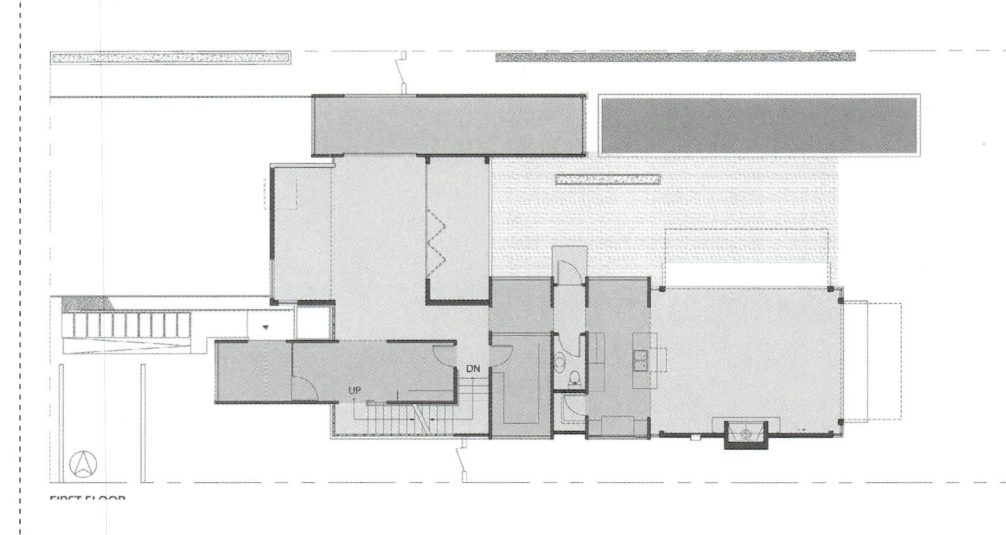

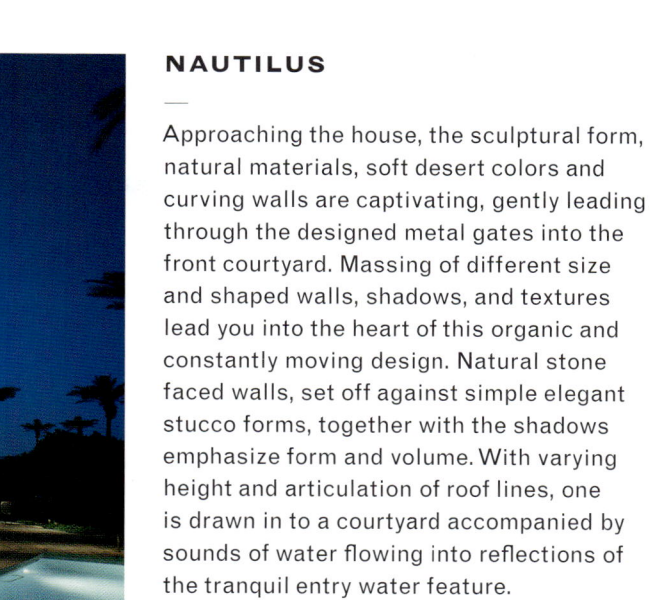

NAUTILUS

Approaching the house, the sculptural form, natural materials, soft desert colors and curving walls are captivating, gently leading through the designed metal gates into the front courtyard. Massing of different size and shaped walls, shadows, and textures lead you into the heart of this organic and constantly moving design. Natural stone faced walls, set off against simple elegant stucco forms, together with the shadows emphasize form and volume. With varying height and articulation of roof lines, one is drawn in to a courtyard accompanied by sounds of water flowing into reflections of the tranquil entry water feature.

01 Front courtyard with pool **02** View to living room with natural stone faced wall **03** Bathroom **04** View from living room to deck **05** Detail bathroom

Photos: Arthur Coleman

CITY Rancho Mirage (CA)
COUNTRY USA
REGION North America
TYPOLOGY Living
COMPLETION 2006
WEBSITE www.patelarchitecture.com
ARCHITECTS Patel Architecture, Narendra Patel AIA

CITY Sylmar (CA)
COUNTRY USA
REGION North America
TYPOLOGY Institution
COMPLETION 2004
WEBSITE www.hplusf.com
ARCHITECTS Hodgetts + Fung Design and Architecture

SYLMAR LIBRARY

The architects sought to reflect the design idioms of the neighborhood by uncovering and revealing the underlying themes of Sylmar. Sylmar Library's palette is taken from the surroundings, and its structural system is manipulated to emulate the posture of the "attitude" prevalent in the area. A jagged roof system, with peaks and valleys, echoes the rhythm of the mountain range. Rendered in deep-deck structural steel, painted in alternating colors drawn directly from the surrounding environment, the structure is both a civic symbol and a reaffirmation of the neighborhood reality.

01 View from the street 02 Detail concrete and glass façade 03 Plans 04 Interior view

Photos: Marvin Rand

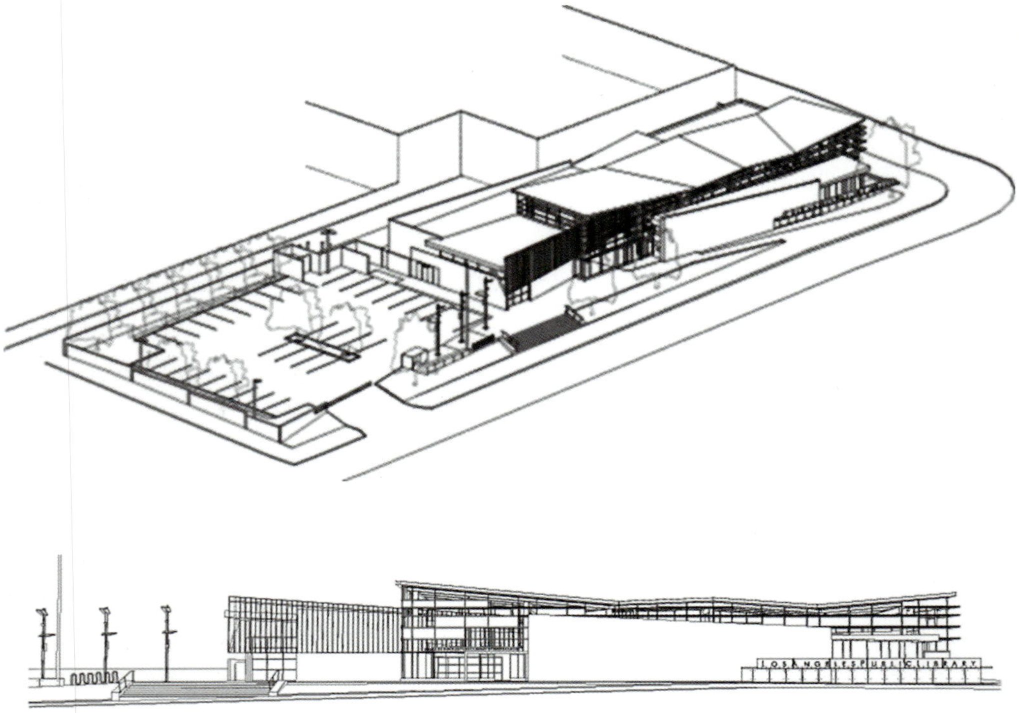

PEACH HOUSE PROJECT

The project, located in a commercial center at the corner of Valley Boulevard and New Avenue in San Gabriel, was an opportunity to inject a simple architectural move in a small space in the form of repetitive ribs that punctuate at the customer counter with vibrant color. When entering the frozen yogurt shop, the customer encounters high gloss white repetitive "rings" that define the spatial extent of the walls and ceiling. Where tables/seating and the customer counter occurs, these rings take a more sinuous form, peeling away from the wall to provide flat usable surfaces while maintaining the overall aesthetic.

01 Overall view 02 Detail high gloss white table "ring" 03 White wall 04 Floor plan 05 Interior view from the customer counter to entry

Photos: John Edward Linden

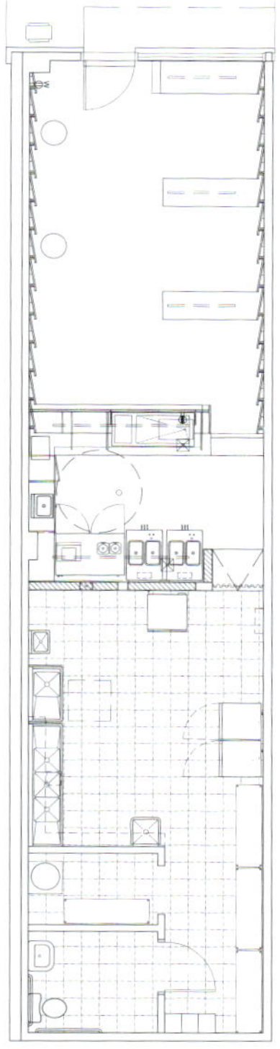

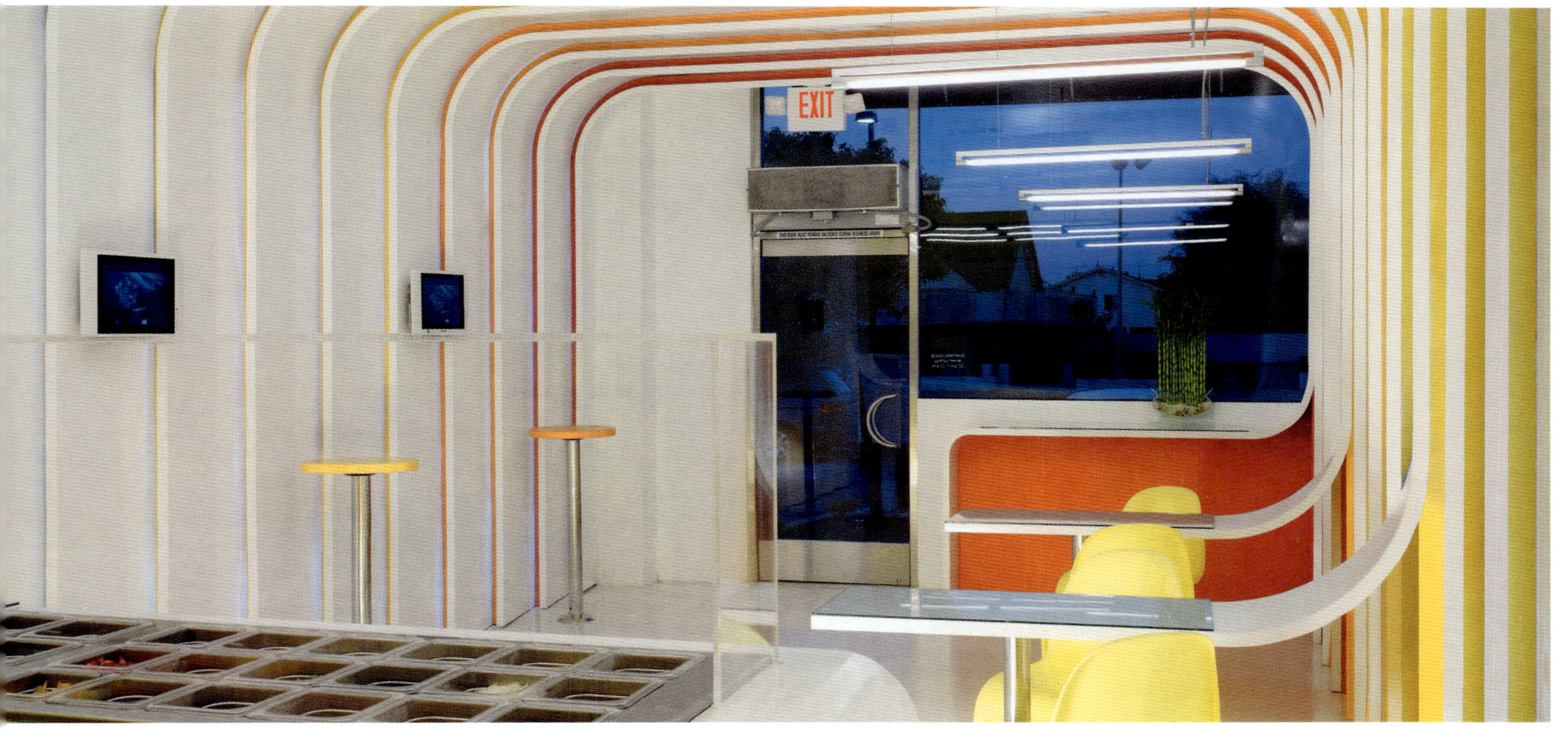

CITY: San Gabriel (CA)
COUNTRY: USA
REGION: North America
TYPOLOGY: Living
COMPLETION: 2007
WEBSITE: www.makearch.com
ARCHITECTS: Make Architecture

CITY Santa Clara (CA)
COUNTRY USA
REGION North America
TYPOLOGY Office
COMPLETION 2003
WEBSITE www.form4inc.com
ARCHITECTS Form4 Architecture

NVIDIA

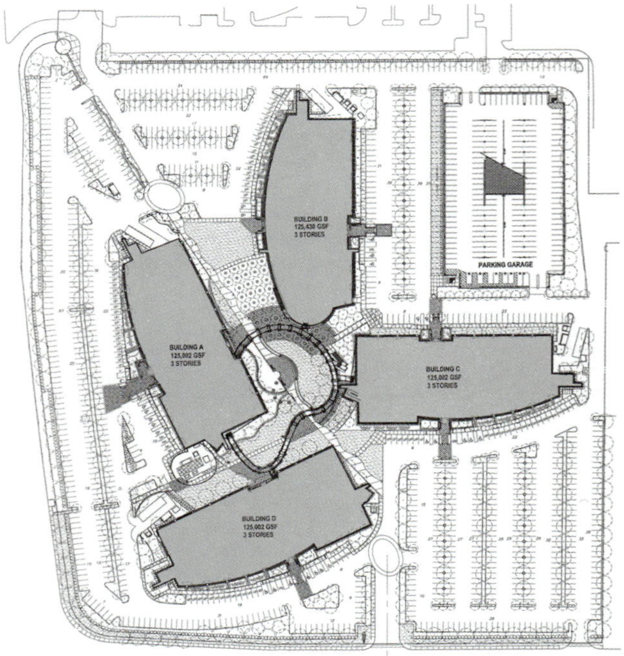

One of nVidia's goals as they scaled up to a multi-building campus, was to maintain a sense of community and interaction. Form4 helped them realize that specific objective by designing space and forms that flow together both literally and poetically. Generous use of clear glass allows people to see activity on all three levels, while a curving walkway extends the design out into the landscape, connecting the buildings and interacting with the usefully programmed outdoor spaces. The combination of light and layered architecture together with an urbane organization of space creates an energizing experience.

01 Rear view **02** Site plan **03** Exterior view of garden and walkway **04** View from the street by night

Photos: JD Peterson

THE JEPSON CENTER FOR THE ARTS AT THE TELFAIR MUSEUM OF ART

In the heart of the Savannah Historic District, a contemporary structure, harmonious with Savannah's urban fabric, respects the traditional grid of the area. The museum's foyer is framed by the glazed wall facing the square and a curved stonewall, through which a grand stair rises toward the two upper levels. The second floor contains a 200-seat auditorium, museum offices, library, and educational galleries, while the top floor is devoted to exhibition galleries, Southern and African-American art, and photography. The building's exterior and major interior walls are clad with light-colored Portuguese limestone.

01 Foyer, framed by curved stonewall on the one side **02** Detail grand stair **03** Exterior view from square to glazed wall **04** Floor plan, lower level **05** View to foyer

Photos: Timothy Hursley

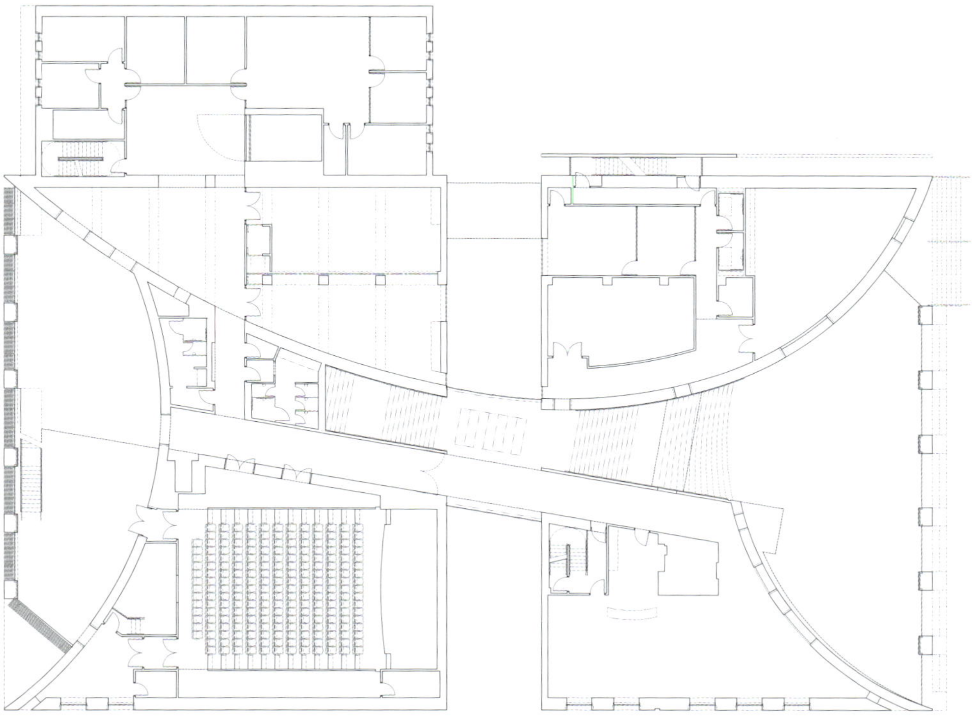

CITY Savannah (GA)
COUNTRY USA
REGION North America
TYPOLOGY Culture
COMPLETION 2006
WEBSITE www.msafdie.com
ARCHITECTS Moshe Safdie
Associate Architect: Hansen Architects, P. C.

VERTICAL HOUSE

The vertical house offers urban living on a rural site. The concept of a townhouse transposed to the country offers a unique solution to a difficult topology, and affords spectacular views. A long and dramatic bridge provides entry to a viewing platform from which one ascends a staircase into the house. The kitchen and dining areas are located on the first level, the living area is on the second level, and the master bedroom is on the third level. An open air garden is situated on the roof. The intention is that over time the house will be covered with vines descending from the roof, in effect making it into a modern ruin.

01 Sections **02** Entry bridge to viewing platform **03** Exterior view, hillside **04** Model **05** Floor plans

Photos: Reinhold & Co.

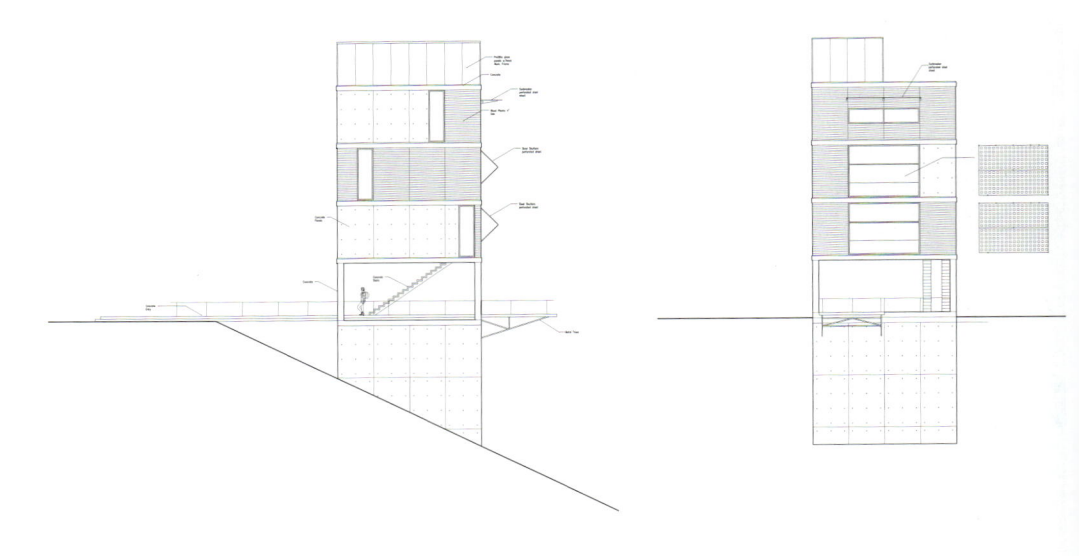

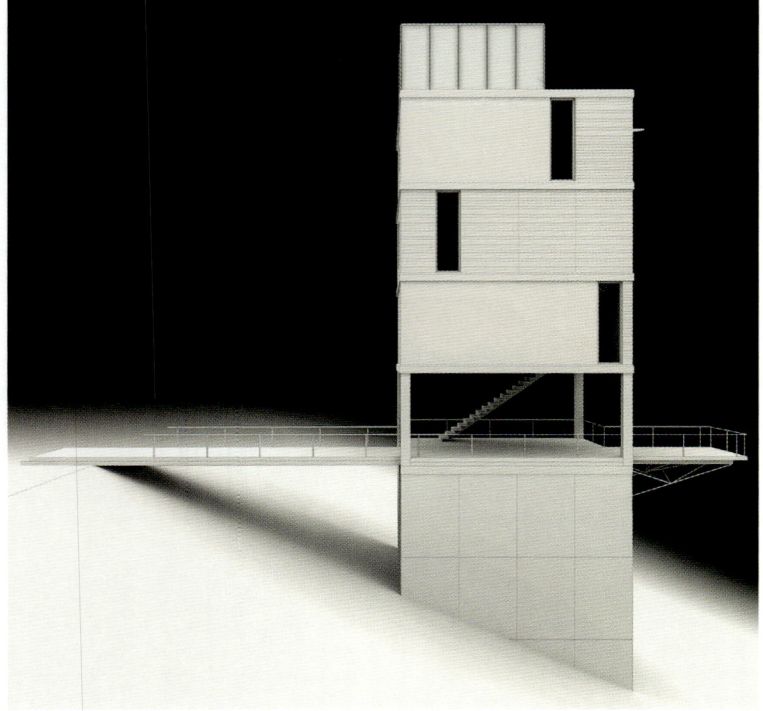

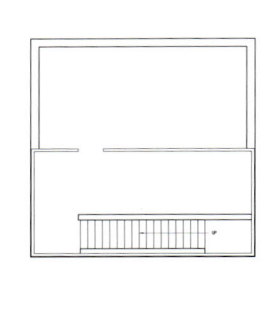

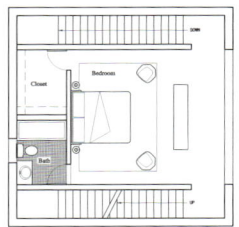

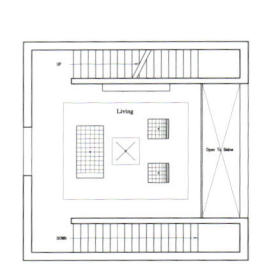

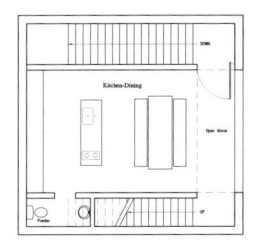

VILLAGE STREET LOFT

The structure from a 19th century bronze foundry provided the starting point for this live-work complex on a tight urban site in Somerville, Massachusetts. The enclosed building was renovated with a new second level to create a living space, while a small steel-framed mezzanine was hung from the existing gantry crane structure. A studio was created at the opposite end of the site, where a new curved roof and glass wall enclosed the space formed by three existing brick walls. A new glazed conservatory on the south side creates an all-weather garden, where fruit-trees fill the ruins of the old foundry between the two spaces.

01 Exterior view, glass façade studio **02** Interior view, from mezzanine to ground floor **03** Ground and mezzanine floor plan **04** Detail, studio

Photos: Eric Oxendorf

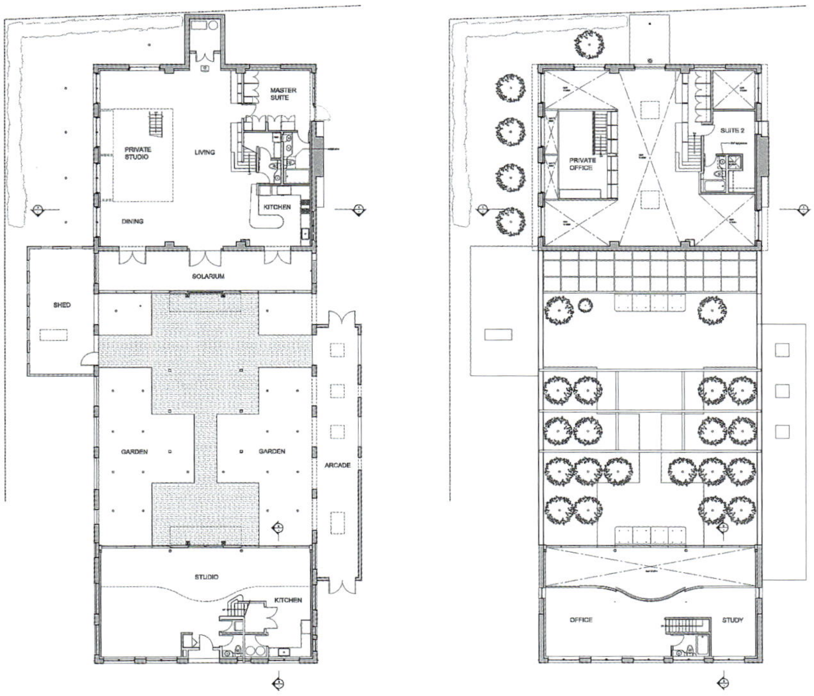

CITY
Somerville (MA)

COUNTRY
USA

REGION
North America

TYPOLOGY
Live-Work

COMPLETION
2006

WEBSITE
www.santosprescott.com

ARCHITECTS
Santos Prescott and Associates

CITY Sonoma (CA)
COUNTRY USA
REGION North America
TYPOLOGY Living
COMPLETION 2005
WEBSITE www.aidlindarlingdesign.com
ARCHITECTS Aidlin Darling Design

SONOMA VINEYARD RESIDENCE

Nestled into the forest's edge, with expansive views over the vineyard and valley beyond, this monastic stone structure serves as private residence, environment for art, and mapping device for its site. The design quietly mediates the complexities of site and program, and enhances the relationship of indoor and outdoor space. Living spaces and daily rituals are organized along a north/south reflecting pool. As one moves through the building, a series of sequentially measured and choreographed experiences unfolds cinematically, each contributing to a mnemonic mapping of place.

01 Exterior view of monastic stone strucure **02** Detail north/south reflecting pool **03** Bird's eye view **04** Section looking north **05** Interior view

Photos: Patrick Belanger, John Sutton, Matthew Millman

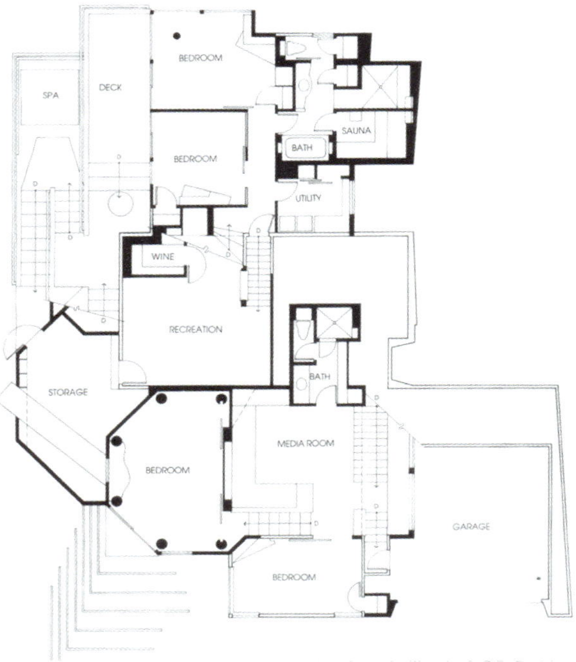

SONOMA COAST HOUSE

This is a complete makeover of an existing 3,800 square foot residence which was remodeled over time into a conglomeration of level changes, multiple stairways, and dark, awkward rooms. The site, part of a subdivision on the Sonoma County coast, is a wonderful bluff top overlooking a small cove below. The new construction opens up the interior spaces to one another, as well as to the surrounding light and trees. One now approaches the house from the east via a new meandering stone path, passes beneath the boughs of a magnificent old Monterey Pine, and arrives at a massive redwood and concrete trellis designed to support Giant Honeysuckles.

01 Lower levels floor plan **02** View to ventilation chimneys **03** Exterior view of deck by night **04** Earthquake resisting braced frame **05** Interior

Photos: Tom Rider

CITY	Sonoma (CA)
COUNTRY	USA
REGION	North America
TYPOLOGY	Living
COMPLETION	2001
WEBSITE	www.obiebowman.com
ARCHITECTS	Obie G Bowman

CITY Spring Prairie (WI)

COUNTRY USA

REGION North America

TYPOLOGY Living

COMPLETION 2007

WEBSITE www.johnsenschmaling.com

ARCHITECTS Johnsen Schmaling Architects

FERROUS HOUSE

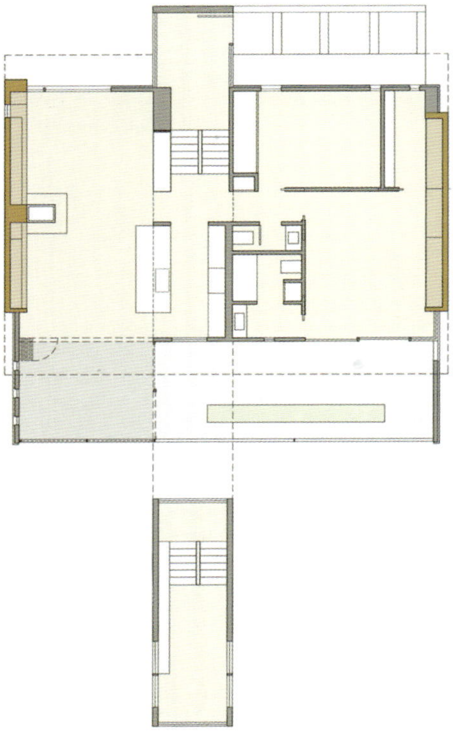

Sitting on top of an existing foundation, the rectangular volume of the house is wrapped on three sides with a suspended curtain of weathering steel panels, protecting the inside of the house from the scrutiny of suspicious neighbors and the elements, and extending beyond the building's back where it shelters the sides of a linear south-facing terrace. Linear storage boxes penetrate the steel curtain and cantilever over the edge of the building. The long northern clerestory radiates its warm light into the night, echoing the iconic glow of the dairy barns that once dotted the area.

01 Exterior view **02** Floor plan **03** View from stairway to upper level **04** Detail steel façade and storage box. **05** Living room with fireplace

Photos: Doug Edmunds Studios

HOLY ROSARY CHURCH COMPLEX

The commission, an honest exploration of form, function, natural light and materials, provides a profound study in sacred space. The oratory is the focal point of its rural Roman Catholic campus, predominant by its unique placement, floating within a courtyard space. Design of the oratory stems from the concept of identifying a pure, comfortable, sacred space every human has experienced – the womb. Since the womb has no orientation of up or down, all sides are treated equally, thus evoking a strong sense of mystery. All six sides of the oratory cube are the same size, color and texture, creating this same lack of orientation.

01 Exterior view chapel **02** Open ceiling **03** Exterior view pavilion and chapel **04** Interior view chapel **05** Floor plan

Photos: Timothy Hursley

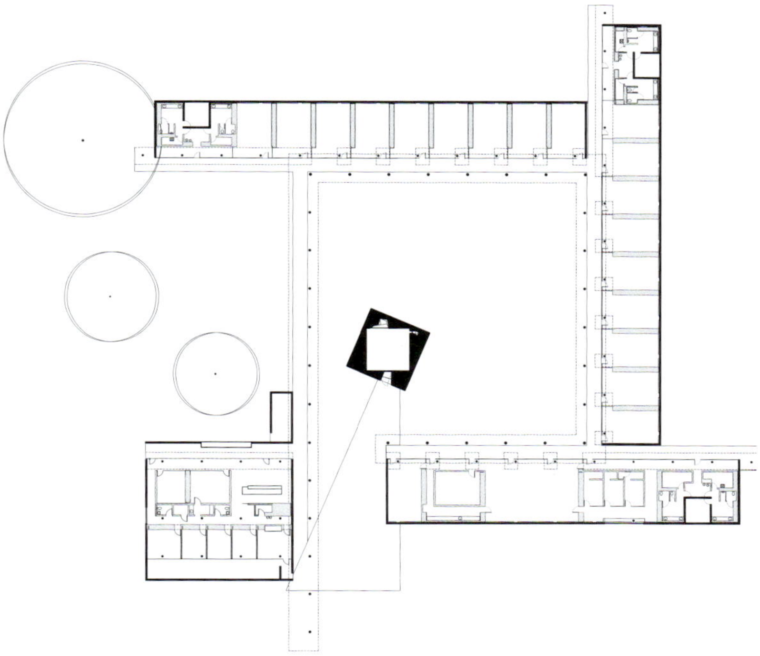

CITY: St. Amant (LA)
COUNTRY: USA
REGION: North America
TYPOLOGY: Ecclesiastical
COMPLETION: 2004
WEBSITE: www.trahanarchitects.com
ARCHITECTS: Trahan Architects

CITY
Sagaponack (NY)

COUNTRY
USA

REGION
North America

TYPOLOGY
Living

COMPLETION
2006

WEBSITE
www.shigerubanarchitects.com

ARCHITECTS
Shigeru Ban Architects
(Associate Architect: Dean Maltz Architect)

SAGAPONAC HOUSE

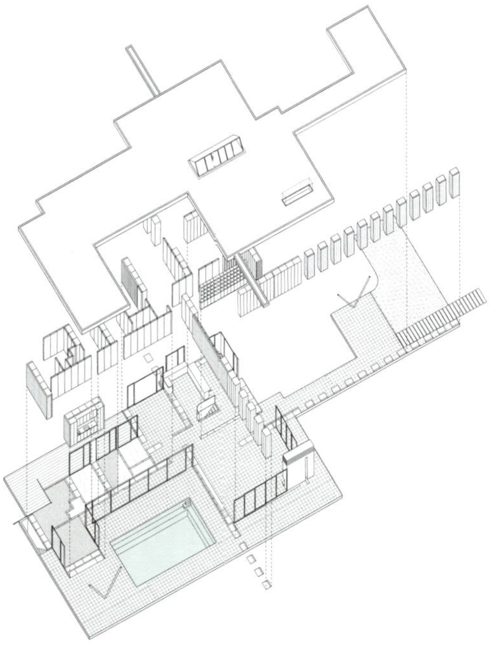

Sitting on 2.7-acres of wooded land, the house is composed of two rectangular volumes forming an L-shaped plan. The center of the house is the main public space with a swimming pool, multi-level terraces, and a covered porch with a shower, taking the form of a minimalist structure placed on a platform within the untouched natural landscape. A large opening within each rectangular volume frame's the private life in the house and the pool beyond. These openings appear and disappear via a system of metal shutters mounted on the exterior walls, investigating the cultural definition of the domestic enclosure.

01 Detail large opening **02** Axonometric **03** Main public space with swimming pool, terraces and porch **04** Interior view

Photos: Michael Moran

ARADO WEEHOUSE®

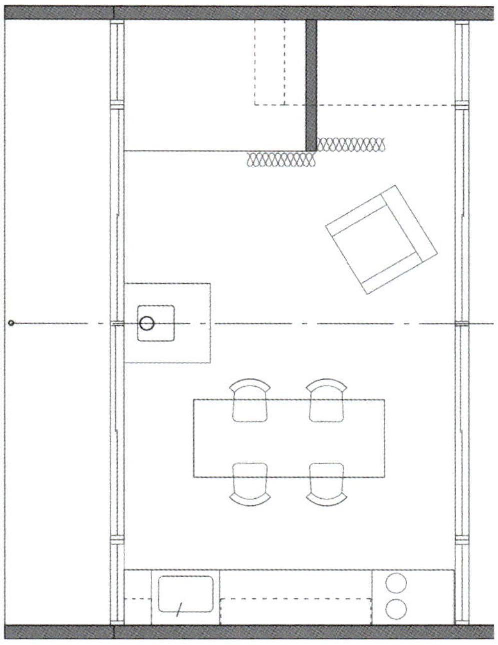

The architectural office develops modular housing units measuring 14 by 10 feet, which can be used to create studio, 2 or 3 bedroom dwellings according to custom design. The modules are industrial and factory-fabricated, which significantly reduces the finished house's environmental impact and construction costs. The measurements of the modules make them transport-ready. Tall energy-efficient windows and included kitchen cabinetry makes the houses design-conscious and ready for use. The exterior of the Arado house is painted with oxidizing paint and the interior is wrapped in Douglas fir.

01 Exterior view **02** Floor plan **03** Detail rust color façade
04 Interior view, sleep / storage area

Photos: Geoffrey Warner, Alchemy LLC

CITY	St. Paul (MN)
COUNTRY	USA
REGION	North America
TYPOLOGY	Living
COMPLETION	2005
WEBSITE	www.weehouses.com
ARCHITECTS	Alchemy Architects

CITY St. Petersburg (FL)
COUNTRY USA
REGION North America
TYPOLOGY Leisure
COMPLETION 2006
WEBSITE www.wjarc.com
ARCHITECTS Wannemacher Jensen Architects

NORTH SHORE POOL

The canopy slices through the sky like the edge of a swimmers hand through water. That surprising sense of lightness is achieved by utilizing the unique properties of the material, where concrete allows structure, volume, and shelter to be defined within one thin dimension. Only 700 square feet of program space was allocated to North Shore Pool's new entry building, serving as the pool complex's main entrance. A folding concrete canopy and a perforated sculpture enclosure were used to define an exterior room and direct entry, while the structures edges are focused on the pool center as a focal point.

01 Exterior new entry building **02** Detail concrete canopy **03** Site plan **04** Detail canopy and perforated sculpture

Photos: James Borchuck

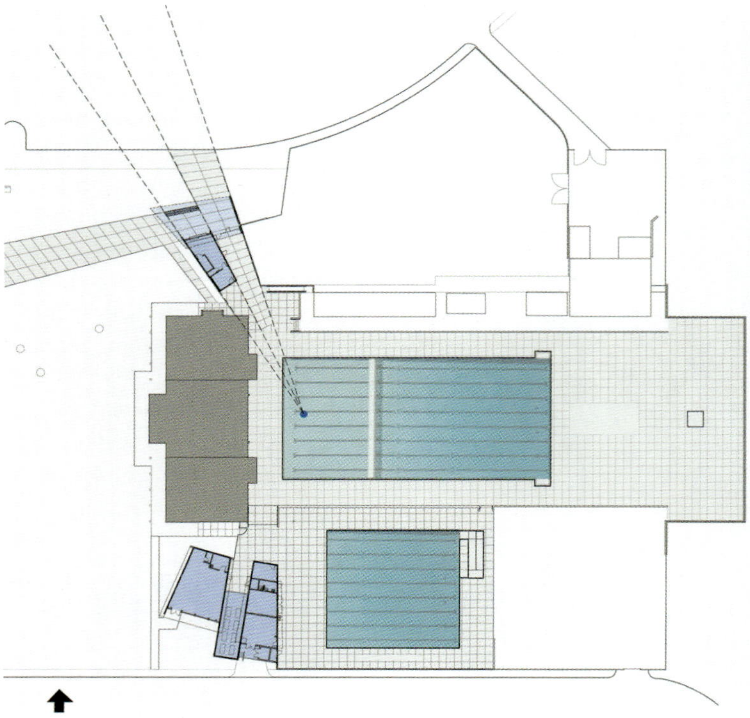

THE CHILDREN'S SCHOOL

Conceived of as a "one room schoolhouse," this school's uninterrupted classroom space allows the children to move freely and visit different disciplines. The inner spaces are linked by a diagonal view through the overlapping spaces of the classrooms, and divided by the structural lines of the beams overhead and the variegated exterior wall condition. The younger children occupy the east-facing wing as they are only in school in the morning; the older children occupy the west wing to take advantage of afternoon light. The entry area hosts quiet activities that calm the child upon arrival, acting as a space of mediation between the two wings.

01 West wing 02 Entrance 03 Open interior 04 Floor plan
05 Overlapping classroom

Photos: Chuck Choi

CITY Stamford (CT)
COUNTRY USA
REGION North America
TYPOLOGY Education
COMPLETION 2007
WEBSITE www.maryannthompson.com
ARCHITECTS Maryann Thompson Architects

CITY Stockbridge (MA)

COUNTRY USA

REGION North America

TYPOLOGY Leisure

COMPLETION in progress

WEBSITE www.roseguggenheimer.com

ARCHITECTS Rose + Guggenheimer Studio

KRIPALU CENTER HOUSING TOWER

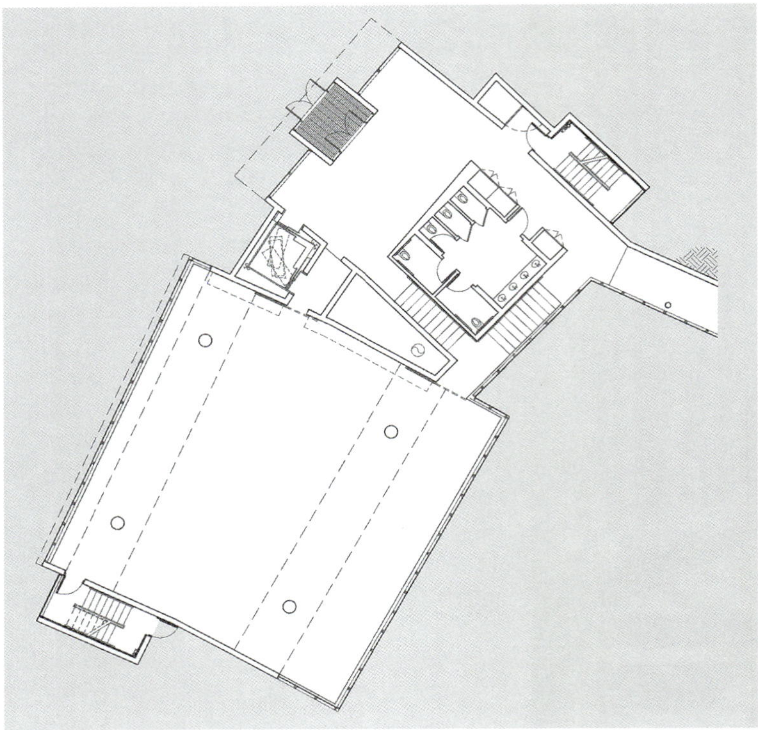

The Kripalu Center Housing Tower is a residential dormitory, and is also the first and primary stage of a multi-phase master plan for the 40-year-old wellness center. The five-story building will contain 80 guest rooms with private baths, as well as a multipurpose room located on the ground floor. Though it will be a freestanding building, it will connect to the campus's main building by way of an enclosed passage. The building is intended to exist in harmony with its surroundings both aesthetically and ecologically. The construction of the project is scheduled for completion in the spring of 2008.

01 Interior view, ground floor **02** Ground floor plan **03** Detail passage **04** Guest room

Photos: Rose + Guggenheimer Studio

U.S. CENSUS BUREAU HEADQUARTERS

SOM's goal in designing this new headquarters complex was to bring the latest and very best of corporate workplace design to a government agency. The 2.5-million-square-foot complex was designed to minimize the real and perceived impact to its site, adopt sustainable principles, and explore an architectural expression that celebrates this relationship. In addition to the rigorous sustainability measures SOM applied to achieve a Silver LEED rating, the buildings' shape, massing, and cladding strategies create a new language for "green" architecture.

01 Exterior view **02** Auditorium pod and façade **03** Ground floor plan **04** Interior view

Photos: Eduard Hueber | archphoto.com, SOM (02)

CITY Suitland (MD)
COUNTRY USA
REGION North America
TYPOLOGY Institution
COMPLETION 2007
WEBSITE www.som.com
ARCHITECTS Skidmore, Owings & Merrill LLP

CITY Superior (AZ)
COUNTRY USA
REGION North America
TYPOLOGY Mixed-Use
COMPLETION 2007
WEBSITE www.blankspaces.net
ARCHITECTS blank studio

SOCIAL CONDENSER FOR SUPERIOR

The Social Condenser is a mixed-use building located at the base of the Superstition Mountain Range. The project is a renovation and expansion of an existing two-story building, as well as an addition of an exterior dining terrace, and was informed by the concept of the "public house". Classically an obscured, introverted diagram, the Social Condenser aims to balance concealment with exuberant exposure of the internal activities. The project is envisioned to be the living room of the community in order to serve as a place to congregate, view work of local artists, and enjoy the landscape that envelops the region.

01 Entrance area **02** Sections **03** Façade detail **04** Exterior dining terrace at dusk **05** Detail interior dining area

Photos: Bill Timmerman

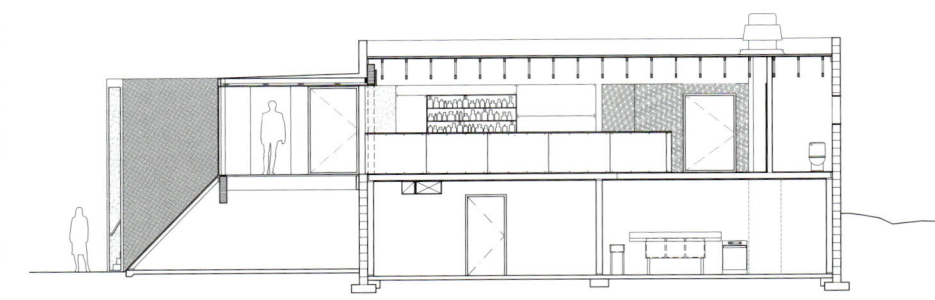

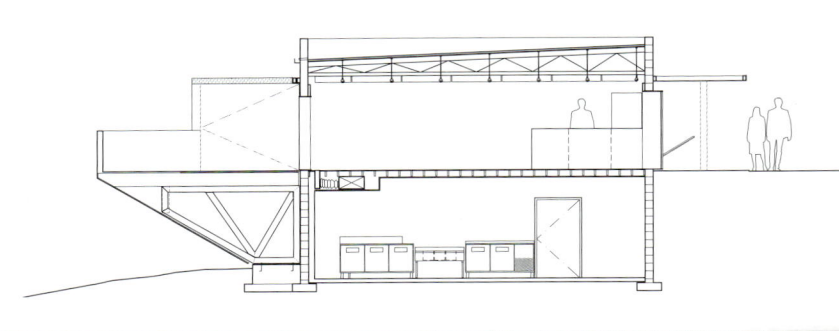

HOUSE FOR A BUTCHER AND AN ART MAVEN

The residents of this lush, three-acre land wanted their empty nest to better suit their active lifestyles. The existing house had two wings – a 70's "ranch-burger" and an 80's rear yard pavilion. Today, the re-configured guest wing sutures an entirely new public wing that celebrates a collection of young contemporary artists as well as a four-car garage, specifically for sports cars. The house defers to the landscape in every direction, which was returned to a more native, sustainable condition. The solution was ostensibly a teardown, marrying new to old by three moves – a cut, a fold, and a stitch.

01 Detail stairway **02** Side view from east courtyard **03** Exterior view by night **04** Interior view **05** Concept

Photos: Tom Powel

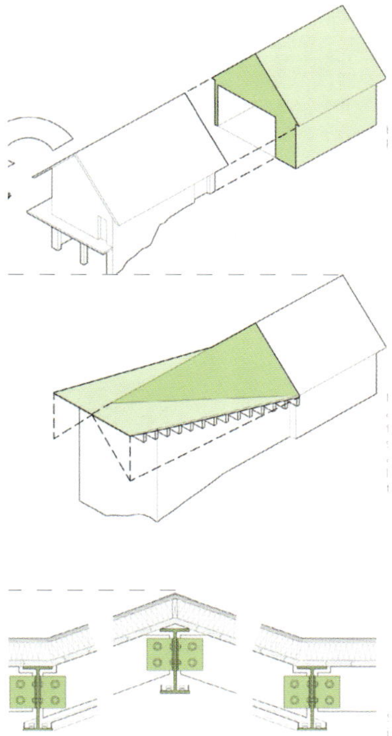

CITY Syosset (NY)
COUNTRY USA
REGION North America
TYPOLOGY Living
COMPLETION 2006
WEBSITE www.architecture-if.com
ARCHITECTS Architecture in Formation, PC

CITY
Stinson Beach (CA)

COUNTRY
USA

REGION
North America

TYPOLOGY
Living

COMPLETION
2007

WEBSITE
www.ccs-architecture.com

ARCHITECTS
CCS Architecture

SEADRIFT RESIDENCE

CCS Architecture designed this sustainable, 1900-square-foot beach house in Stinson Beach, CA, as a second home for a three-generation San Francisco family. Located in Seadrift, a gated vacation community that originated in the 1950's, the design follows a rigorous sustainability program, achieving the Marin Planning Department's highest rating for resource efficiency. All the home's systems – hot water, HVAC, and radiant heating – are integrated, electric-based, and powered by the PV panels on the roof. The only use of natural gas is at the cooking range, which draws from a 50-gallon propane tank.

01 Exterior view of Lagoon side deck **02** Entry **03** Living room and fire orb at dusk **04** Exterior façade **05** Floor plan **06** Detail of rotating fire orb and skylights

Photos: Matthew Millman

MUSEO ALAMEDA DEL SMITHSONIAN

Museo Alameda del Smithsonian was designed by a group of international Latino scholars from across the country including Amalia Mesa Baines, Tomas Ybama Frausto and Henry R. Muñoz III. Rather than create an abstract expression of technology or sculptural form related to current architectural fashion, the community goal was to create a museum that was approachable by the community and unpretentious in a nature that related to American Latino culture. The central design goal developed was to express the concept of "mestizaje" using an American story of blending of cultures in the United States.

01 View from street **02** Ground floor plan **03** Gallery space **04** Façade detail

Photos: Eric Gay

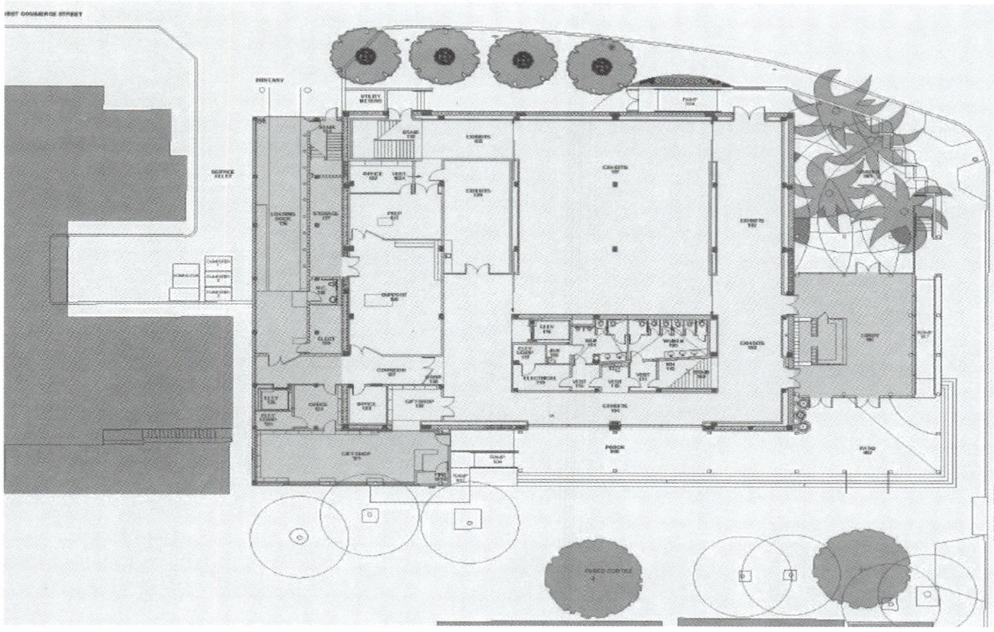

CITY San Antonio (TX)

COUNTRY USA

REGION North America

TYPOLOGY Culture

COMPLETION 2007

WEBSITE www.jacksonryan.com

ARCHITECTS Jackson & Ryan Architects of Record

CITY
San Pedro (CA)

COUNTRY
USA

REGION
North America

TYPOLOGY
Public

COMPLETION
2004

WEBSITE
www.bpala.com

ARCHITECTS
Barton Phelps & Associates

CABRILLO MARINE AQUARIUM

This project is a one-story teaching facility, which wraps exhibits, auditorium, and labs around a chain-link volume, while a realigned entry drive approached confusingly from the rear. The expansion frames the original core but recasts it as one of three courtyards. The new library cantilevers protectively over new life-support systems to announce the facility and views connection to the ocean, while a fiberglass screen leads the eye to the original entry now visually reinforced by the walls of a new access ramp. Interiors continue the rough post and beam / exposed conduit texture of the existing structure.

01 Detail façade **02** Exterior view **03** Laboratory **04** Site plan **05** Detail exterior

Photos: Benny Chan, Fotoworks

THAI STYLE HOUSE

Nature provided extraordinary vistas for this house in Southampton, which is built on a narrow strip of land bounded by Shinnecock Bay to the north and the Atlantic Ocean to the south. The client was intent on building a house with a distinctly Asian flavor, styled after houses seen in Thailand and Japan. Built on wood pilings and exteriorly finished in mahogany siding, the house provides views of the ocean and bay, and features three spacious bed-bath suites. A central stair tower is intricately detailed in glossy mahogany, while the gunite pool features a vanishing edge, easily camouflaged in the encroaching marsh.

01 Detail interior **02** Front view **03** Cross section **04** Bed-bath suite **05** Detail glossy mahogany stair tower

Photos: Catherine Tighe

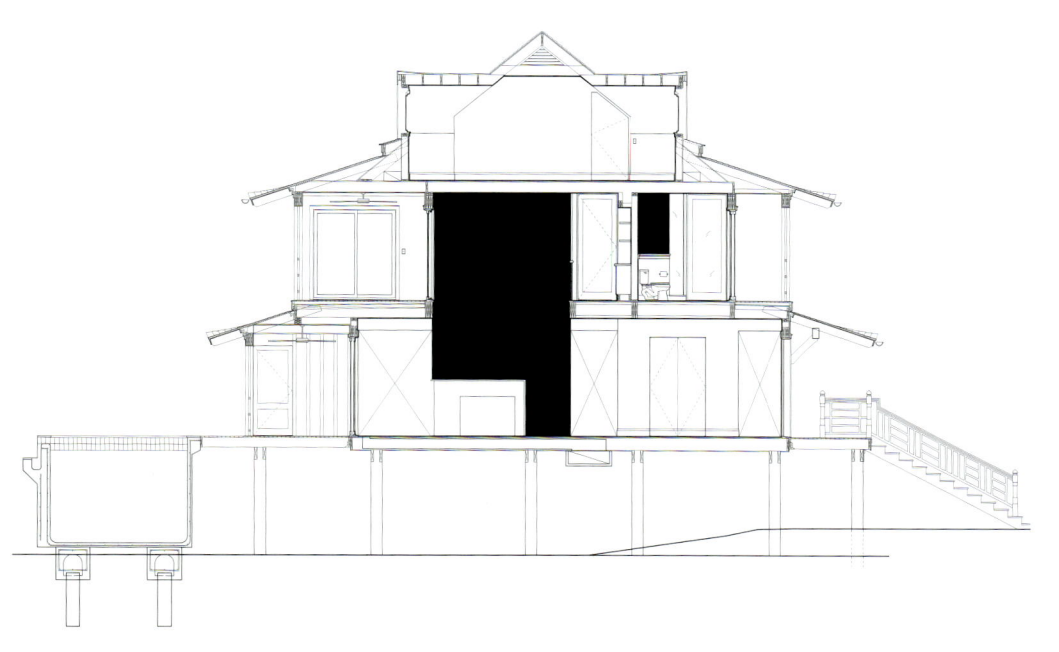

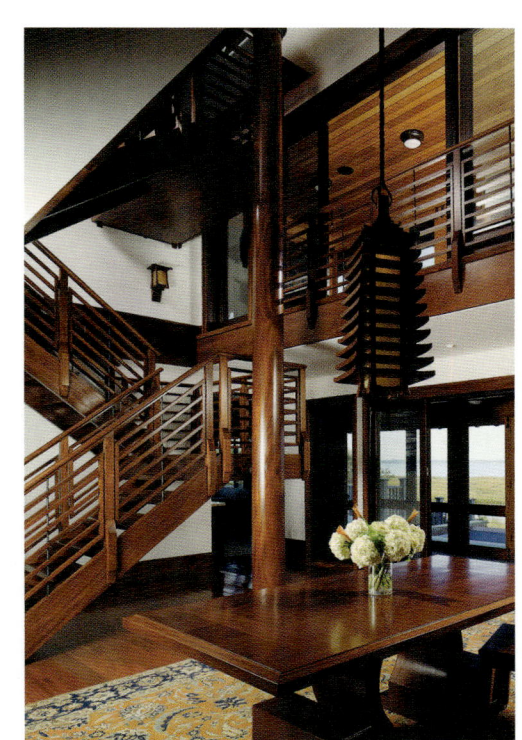

CITY Southhamton (NY)
COUNTRY USA
REGION North America
TYPOLOGY Living
COMPLETION –
WEBSITE www.coburnarchitecture.com
ARCHITECTS Coburn Architecture

CITY Stanford (CA)
COUNTRY USA
REGION North America
TYPOLOGY Institution / Research
COMPLETION 2003
WEBSITE www.ehdd.com
ARCHITECTS EHDD Architecture

DEPARTMENT OF GLOBAL ECOLOGY, CARNEGIE INSTITUTION FOR SCIENCE

The Carnegie Institution for Science studies interactions among the earth's ecosystems; its research center demanded lofty sustainability goals. While lab buildings typically use four times the energy of most campus buildings, the building reduces greenhouse gas emissions to an absolute minimum. A night sky cooling system sprays a thin film of water on the roof, which radiates heat to the cold, deep space sky, producing chilled water. This water is stored and circulated through the slab to cool the space. A high wind catcher and misters cool the indoor/outdoor lobby, lowering the temperature of air cascading into the space.

01 View to front façade with solar chimney **02** Hallway
03 Laboratory with ventilation **04** Interior working space
05 View into the solar chimney

Photos: Doug Snower Photography

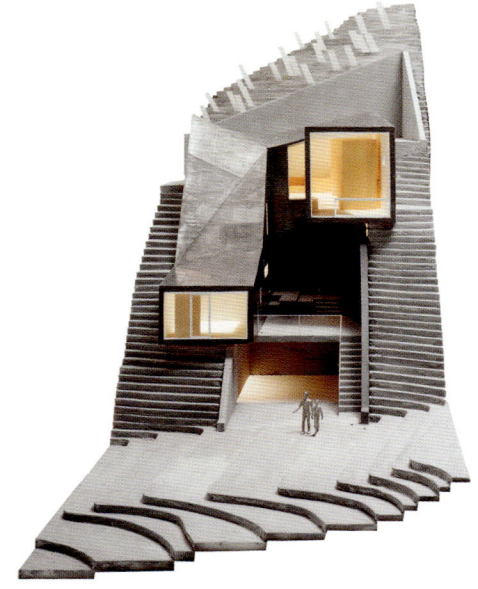

VAIL GRANT HOUSE

The building volume is created by a simple extrusion of a square, a neutral elongated twisted box that is projected into the site and sculpted along its contours. The building's movement on the site describes a spiral that begins at a lower point closest to the street, travels up the hill, and then turns back towards the street and the lake, overlooking itself and creating an enclosed court in the center. Structural Concrete Insulated Panels (SCIP) made by Green Sandwich Technologies were chosen for their structural and insulating properties, as well as sustainability: they are made from 100% recycled and post consumer foam and have a 50% fly-ash content in the concrete.

01 Front façade **02** Model **03** Elevation **04** Section **05** Exploded isonometric **06** Interior

Renderings: Pugh + Scarpa

CITY Silver Lake (CA) (Los Angeles)
COUNTRY USA
REGION North America
TYPOLOGY Living
COMPLETION 2004
WEBSITE www.pugh-scarpa.com
ARCHITECTS Pugh + Scarpa

CITY Sacramento (CA)

COUNTRY USA

REGION North America

TYPOLOGY Mixed-Use

COMPLETION 2005

WEBSITE www.dzarchitect.com

ARCHITECTS Mark Dziewulski Architects

F65 CENTER TRANSIT VILLAGE

The design for this mixed-use project focused around a public transit system. As a whole, the project aimed to be a catalyst for renewal in the surrounding area. The modern dynamic forms of the buildings reflect their role as an urban transit hub as well as their history within the context of the industrial area. The project additionally creates a recognizable urban environment, with a level of detail and complexity that provides a pedestrian scale at the street level.

01 Exterior view **02, 05** Interior view **03** Exterior view by night **04** Site plan

Photos: Keith Cronin

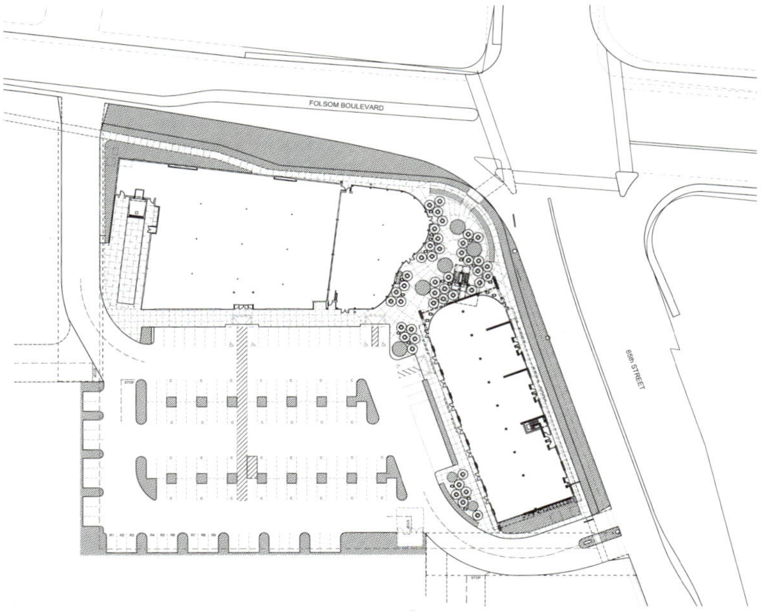

RIVER HOUSE

The form of the River House is a response to the natural context; a gently rolling and wooded slope overlooking a river and State Park on the opposite bank. The plan frames views of the river and park, opening up to the setting with a continuous wall of glass, protected beneath extended cantilevered overhangs. The project also creates a dynamic and sculptural form floating above the bluff. The design described the journey from public realm to a private sanctuary: from street to entry court, over a bridge and into the private inner world, which opens up to the spectacular natural context beyond.

01 Detail glass façade **02** Pond with bridge **03** Role model nature: house form **04** Interior view, open rooms **05** Living room

Photos: Keith Cronin

CITY Sacramento (CA)
COUNTRY USA
REGION North America
TYPOLOGY Living
COMPLETION 2003
WEBSITE www.dzarchitect.com
ARCHITECTS Mark Dziewulski Architects

CITY
San Diego (CA)

COUNTRY
USA

REGION
North America

TYPOLOGY
Culture

COMPLETION
2007

WEBSITE
www.gluckmanmayner.com

ARCHITECTS
Gluckman Mayner Architects

MUSEUM OF CONTEMPORARY ART SAN DIEGO

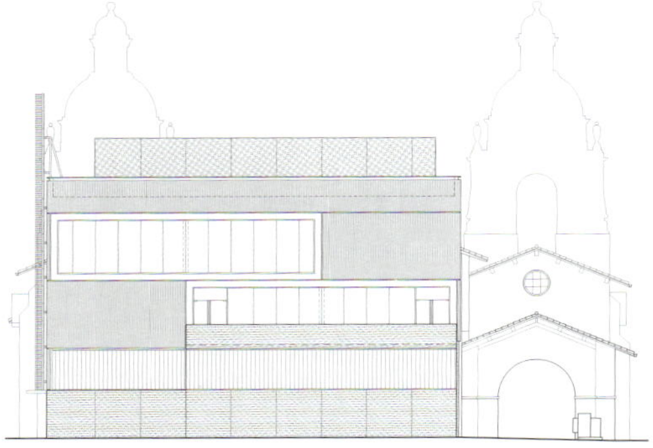

The Museum has expanded its current downtown campus by creating new exhibition spaces in the Baggage Building of the historic Santa Fe Depot, and by adding a new, adjacent three-story structure on the site of the former Railway Express Agency Building. The new addition was designed as a contemporary response to the surrounding historic structures, while converting the Baggage Building into a Kunsthalle-type exhibition venue. The new facilities will complement the curatorial programs of the museum's primary site in La Jolla, while expanding and connecting with the museum's existing downtown venue across the street.

01 Exterior view by night **02** North elevation **03** Street site view **04** Exhibit

Photos: David Heald (01), Philipp Scholz Ritterman)02), Pablo Mason (03), courtesy of MACASD

TOWER 23

Tower 23 is an urban resort on a 23,000 square feet coastal site right on the ocean-front boardwalk of Pacific Beach in San Diego. The 45,000 square feet, three-story building encompasses 44 designer rooms and suites, an 10,000 square feet JRDN restaurant, expansive decks and patios. The design represents a bold infusion of pared-down, contemporary minimalism with clean, streamlined design apparent in simple compositions of positive and negative forms. Interior and exterior spaces are integrated to capitalize on the most appealing qualities of California style coastal living.

01 Beach side **02** Exterior façade **03** Private beach deck view **04** JRDN dining room/bar **05** JRDN Sushi bar

Photos: Gray Payne

CITY San Diego (CA)
COUNTRY USA
REGION North America
TYPOLOGY Hospitality
COMPLETION 2005
WEBSITE www.grahamdownes.com
ARCHITECTS Graham Downes Architecture

CITY San Diego (CA)

COUNTRY USA

REGION North America

TYPOLOGY Living

COMPLETION 2007

WEBSITE www.macyarchitecture.com

ARCHITECTS Macy Architecture

POINT LOMA RESIDENCE

This residence was designed to be low-maintenance and incorporate a variety of energy and resource-conserving features. The living, dining, kitchen and master bedroom are located on the upper level and oriented to capture views of the surrounding area. The form of the house is simple and compact with a very efficient exterior surface area to volume ratio. In addition to the thermal benefits, this compact form requires less exterior finish work and shorter electrical and plumbing runs. In addition to employing passive solar and natural ventilation strategies, the design incorporates net-metering photovoltaics and rainwater recovery system for irrigation purposes.

01 Entry patio **02** View from street **03** View from deck to living room **04** First floor plan **05** Second floor plan **06** Atrium

Photos: Scot Conti

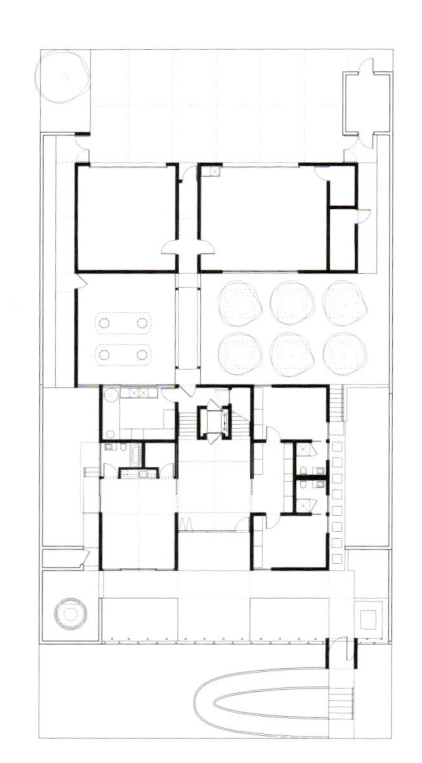

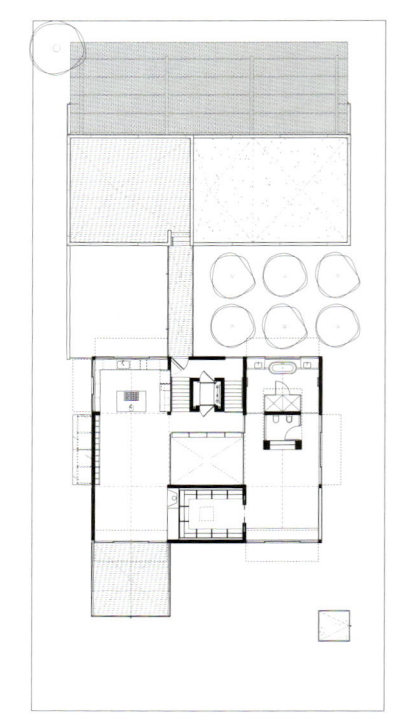

THE UNION

During the 1970's San Diego had a flourishing textile business and strong union membership. The Golden Hill area directly adjacent to the San Diego Freeway and Downtown became the home for the textile manufactures union hall. Subsequently the union and textile manufacturing industry moved away and the site fell in disarray. Rather than demolishing the nondescript 1970's slump block building, the architect took a sustainable approach and acting as owner/developer/contractor brought this building to present day standards with sustainable elements that include a photovoltaic system, cross ventilation and drought tolerant landscaping.

01 Street site view **02** Entry view **03** Fully glazed façade **04** Detail photovoltaic system **05** Patio

Photos: Paul Body Photo

CITY: San Diego (CA)
COUNTRY: USA
REGION: North America
TYPOLOGY: Living
COMPLETION: 2007
WEBSITE: www.jonathansegalarchitect.com
ARCHITECTS: Jonathan Segal

ONE SPACE (HOUSE/APARTMENT)

The temporary presence of the client made this space a rental, and considered the needs and desires of future tenants. Components were designed with this terminal condition in mind. Each piece built required varying amounts of physical energy to construct, therefore the future use and potential destiny of each component was speculated. If an element could be designed and fabricated in a generic fashion, then the material qualities and dimensional aspects were chosen in consideration of a future use. If an element was deemed unique to this space, then an inexpensive material with a determinate life span was chosen.

01 Wardrobe **02** Book shelves **03** Living space **04** Kitchen **05** Floor plan

Photos: Brighton Knowing

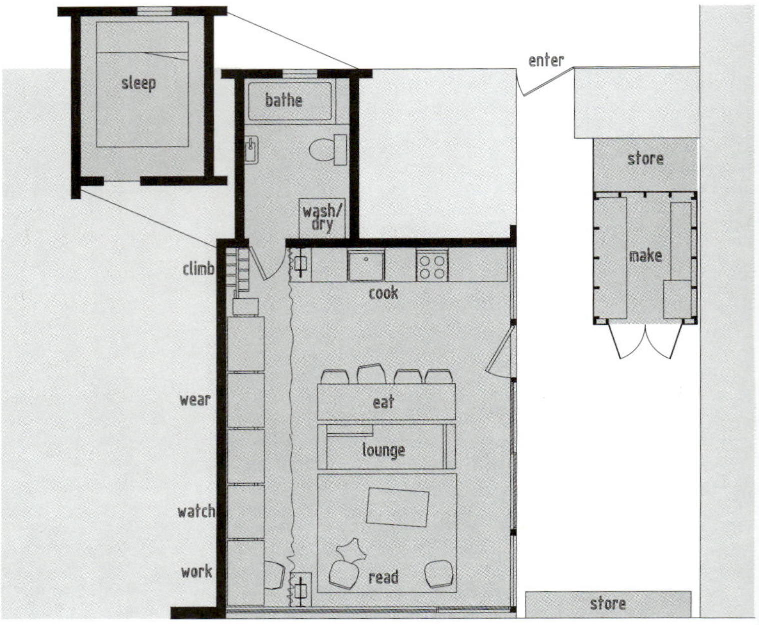

R3 TRIANGLE BUILDING

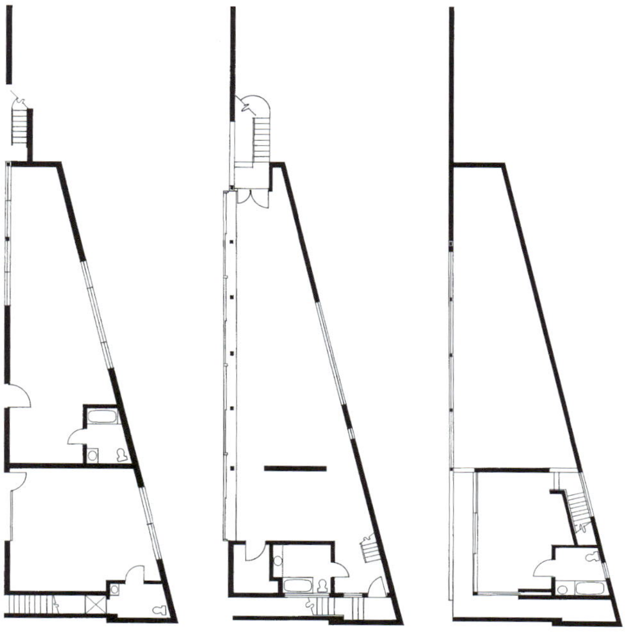

The R3 Building is an infill development of a prominent but small triangular lot. It is constrained by geometry, noise, and geological conditions. A flexible program responds to current and future economic realities while making an iconic building that expresses the handmade yet modern construction techniques that define the neighborhood and the region. The structure achieves minimizing street noise with a closed façade, which nonetheless offers stretching views of the cityscape. The back of the house opens up on a lushly greened hillside.

01 Street site view **02** Floor plans **03** CMU façade from freeway **04** Living space

Photos: Dave Harrison

CITY San Diego (CA)
COUNTRY USA
REGION North America
TYPOLOGY Mixed-Use
COMPLETION 2006
WEBSITE www.lloyd-russell.com
ARCHITECTS Lloyd Russell

CITY: San Diego (CA)
COUNTRY: USA
REGION: North America
TYPOLOGY: Living
COMPLETION: 2006
WEBSITE: www.jonathansegal-architect.com
ARCHITECTS: Jonathan Segal

K LOFTS

K LOFTS is a collection of simplistic architectural forms collaged to create a nine-unit loft building on an urban property in downtown San Diego. An existing convenience store and gas station was saved and integrated into the new design to make adaptive reuse of the existing building. The modern building integrates urban living environments, creating a mixture of low-income and market rate rental units, each containing large private outdoor spaces and oversize glazing. The sustainable project provides 50% renewable electricity. The architect worked closely with the community to ensure a positive reception.

01 Oversize glazing **02** Exterior view by night **03** Façade

Photos: Paul Body Photo

ON GRAPE

The approach for this urban infill project was to subdivide the land for two single-family residences, which maximizes the enclosed, narrow space. The design focused on planes of space, achieved by constructing continuous horizontal spaces between the properties and keeping the interior void open to the sky. The wood frame structure receives a floating exterior skin of engineered stone and CorTen steel with an internal air chamber, providing thermal and acoustic insulation. Spatially, the residences offer a quiet respite within the city. Materially, dark stone, steel and Ipe wood accentuate San Diego's diverse urban fabric.

01 Front view in context **02** Detail façade and view into interior **03** Bridge connecting the two spaces **04** Interior garden

Photos: Hisao Suzuki

CITY: San Diego (CA)
COUNTRY: USA
REGION: North America
TYPOLOGY: Living
COMPLETION: –
WEBSITE: www.sebastian-mariscal.com
ARCHITECTS: Sebastian Mariscal Studio

CITY San Francisco (CA)

COUNTRY USA

REGION North America

TYPOLOGY Living

COMPLETION 2007

WEBSITE www.cbstudio.com

ARCHITECTS Cary Bernstein Architect

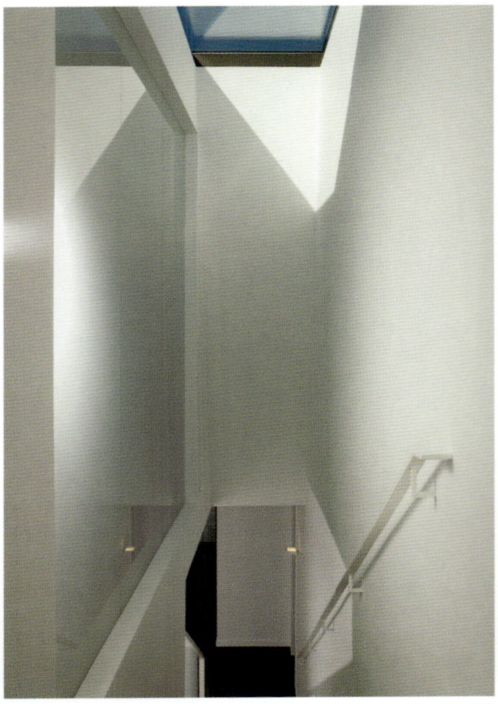

LIBERTY STREET RESIDENCE

This project completely transformed the character of a dark, 1950's, ranch-style house into a modern and minimalist home. The new, upward pitch of the central roof invites the spectacular view and broad sky into the central living area. Multiple skylights and acid-etched glass panels infuse the building with diurnal patterns. The lower level was excavated and rebuilt to house a media room, guest suite and patio. Custom interior lighting was designed to compliment the abstraction of the architectural language.

01 Stair **02** Entry view **03** Skylight for natural light **04** First floor plan **05** Ground floor plan **06** Fireplace

Photos: David Duncan Livingston

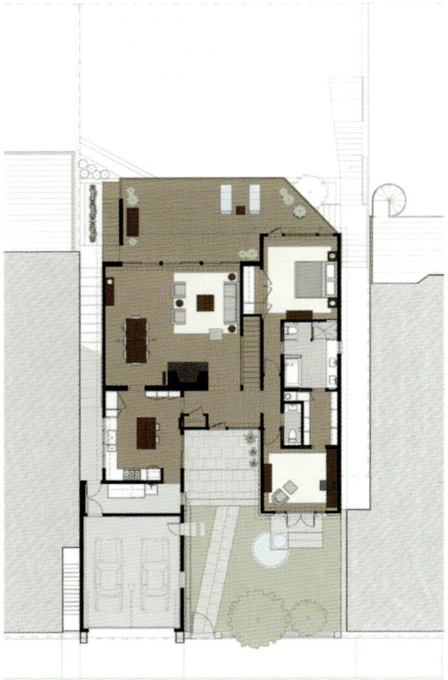

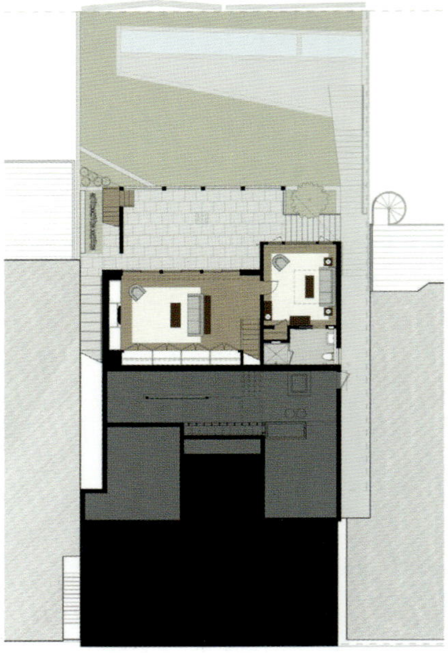

NEW SUSTAINABLE CALIFORNIA ACADEMY OF SCIENCES

Designed to receive a "Platinum" LEED rating, the new California Academy of Sciences in San Francisco proves that innovative and sustainable design can achieve outcomes that are both beautiful and functional. Renzo Piano's design was inspired by the natural world, reflecting its beauty and interdependence, and works in harmony with the landscape surrounding the museum. A close collaboration between the architects and engineers yielded innovative strategies that help preserve the natural integrity of the park, conserve water and energy, reduce pollution, maximize natural ventilation and light, and use environmentally friendly building materials.

01 Bird's eye view **02** Entry view **03** Glass dome **04** Interior

Photos: Courtesy Holcimfoundation

CITY: San Francisco (CA)
COUNTRY: USA
REGION: North America
TYPOLOGY: Culture / Public
COMPLETION: 2005
WEBSITE: www.chongpartners.com
ARCHITECTS: Chong Partners Architecture

CITY San Francisco (CA)
COUNTRY USA
REGION North America
TYPOLOGY Retail
COMPLETION 2006
WEBSITE www.wdarch.com
ARCHITECTS William Duff Architects

TIMBUK2

Timbuk2's first flagship store in the Hayes Valley district of San Francisco was designed to act as an anchor for the company's retail identity. The store interior emphasizes the rugged, urban, but design-oriented culture of the company. The display shelving provides a clean but neutral backdrop to highlight the multi-colored messenger bags the company is famous for. The concept of the 800-square-foot space was also inspired by the idea to complement the urban aesthetic of San Francisco featuring refined elements against the rough, weathered concrete and steel that form the backbone of the city.

01 Shop window **02** Sales floor **03** Floor plan **04** Messenger bags

Photos: Jo Peterson

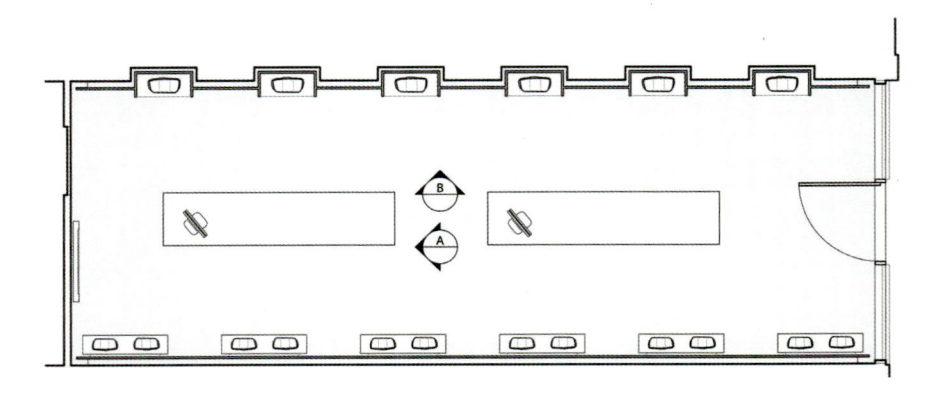

MERCEDES-BENZ OF SAN FRANCISCO

Located in the South of Market district of San Francisco, this new Mercedes-Benz showroom had once been a television production studio. In addition to the existing 50,000-square-foot facility the architects designed showroom floors, sales offices and a vehicle maintenance center. With its visibility to the streetscape, the former storefront was transformed into an expansive showroom by removing the second floor and widening the original fenestration. The windows feature a low-iron glass, which provides maximum transparency and reveals the true paint color of the cars on display.

01 Atrium roof **02** Atrium wall **03** Fully glazed façade **04** Floor plan **05** Lounge

Photos: David Wakely Photography

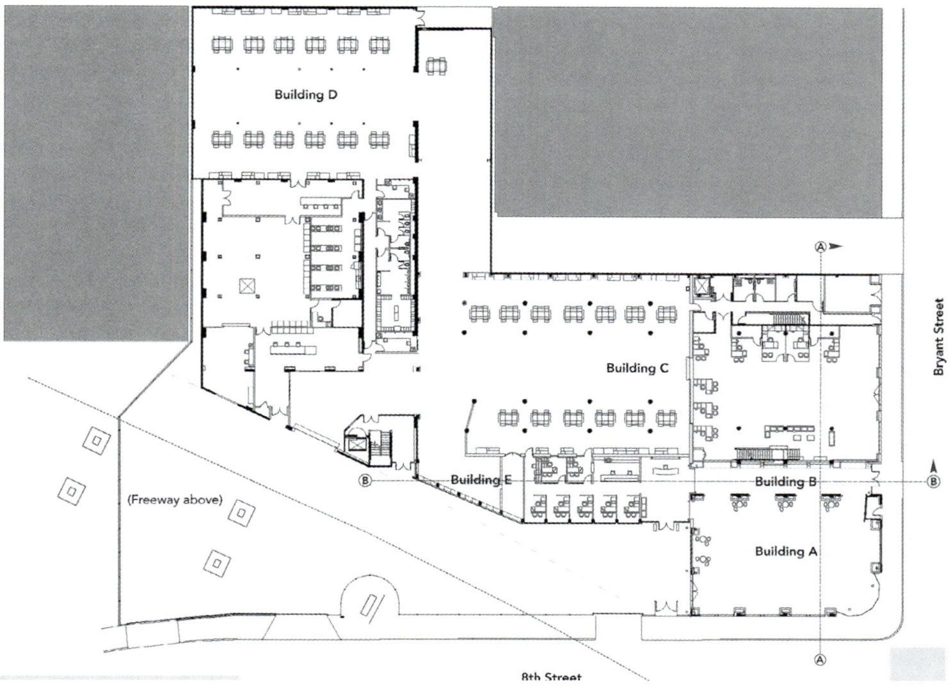

CITY: San Francisco (CA)
COUNTRY: USA
REGION: North America
TYPOLOGY: Retail
COMPLETION: 2006
WEBSITE: www.huntsmanag.com
ARCHITECTS: Huntsman Architectural Group

CITY
San Francisco (CA)

COUNTRY
USA

REGION
North America

TYPOLOGY
Living

COMPLETION
2006, unbuilt

WEBSITE
www.iwamotoscott.com

ARCHITECTS
IwamotoScott Architecture

JELLYFISH HOUSE (EXHIBITION)

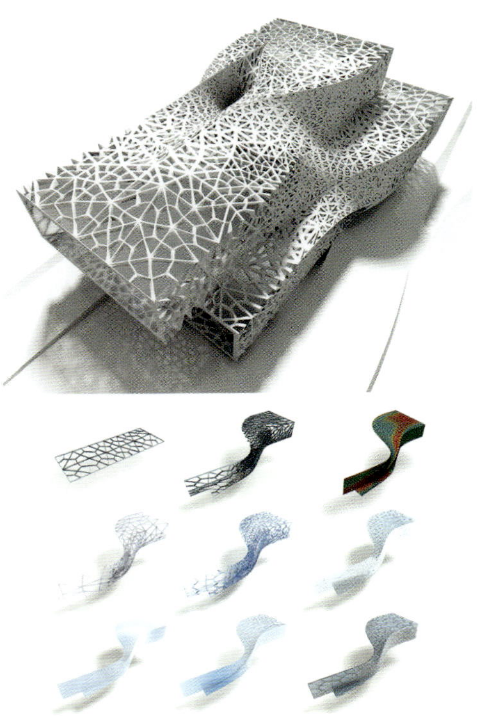

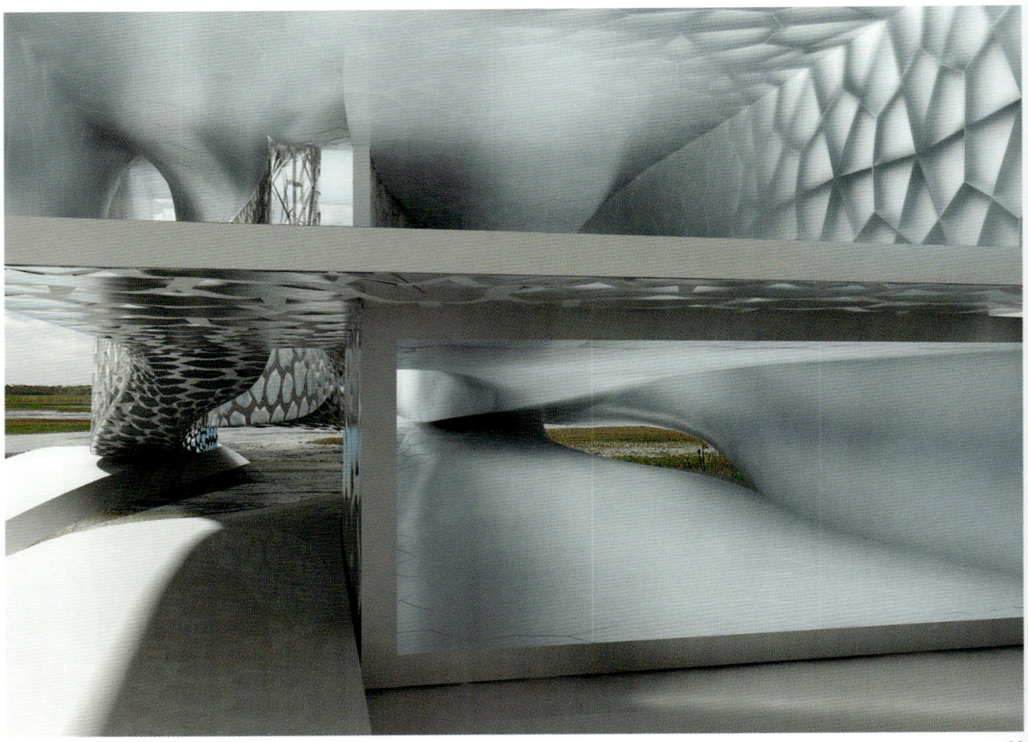

This project was designed for the exhibition "OPEN HOUSE: Architecture and Technology for Intelligent Living" that speculates on emerging technologies for homes of the near future. Jellyfish House is modeled on the idea that, like the sea creature, it coexists with its environment as a set of distributed, networked senses and responses. It incorporates emerging material and digital technologies in a reflexive, environmentally contingent manner. The house is a transformative prototype for reclaimed land, sited on Treasure Island which has recently been decommissioned by the military, and is currently being redeveloped.

01 Exterior view **02** Structure and skin diagram **03** Interior view **04** Structure detail

Photos: IwamotoScott Architecture

THE STARFISH HOUSE

At three stories tall on a hillside site, this house has commanding views of the Bay, Golden Gate Bridge and downtown San Francisco. A repair project became a major renovation when a completely new façade changed the floor plan and inspired the owners to reconsider their way of living. A small third-story addition created a generous south-and-east-facing kitchen and deck. The second floor master suite and adjacent bedroom were expanded by the façade changes. Throughout the house the use of natural materials and minimalist detailing provide a sense of peace within.

01 Kitchen **02** Exterior view **03** Master bedroom **04** Floor plans **05** Wooden panels

Photos: Stephen Barker

CITY
San Francisco (CA)

COUNTRY
USA

REGION
North America

TYPOLOGY
Living

COMPLETION
2007

WEBSITE
www.kpad.com

ARCHITECTS
Karin Payson architecture + design

CITY
San Francisco (CA)

COUNTRY
USA

REGION
North America

TYPOLOGY
Living

COMPLETION
2003

WEBSITE
www.kuthranieri.com

ARCHITECTS
Kuth/Ranieri Architects

PARK PRESIDIO RESIDENCE

This residence is sited in a dense urban residential area adjacent to San Francisco's Park Presidio, capturing sweeping views of the park's open space with distant views of the Golden Gate Bridge and Pacific Ocean beyond. The 6,500-square-foot domestic program is intertwined with gallery exhibition for the client's extensive large-format collection of contemporary photography. The introduction of a 75-foot long gallery links the front entry court with the primary living zones and rear garden. The program called for the house to be fully self-sufficient in its energy production, operating off grid as needed.

01 Front façade **02** Stair **03** Interior **04** Dining area

Photos: Sharon Risedorph (01), Cesar Rubio (02), Kuth/Ranieri Architects (03, 04)

SPROULE-ROWEN RESIDENCE

The design of this third-floor addition is deceptively simple, consisting of a living space and master bedroom, separated by a service core containing a bathroom and closet. A new concrete staircase with a custom aluminum-grating guardrail connects the addition to the existing lower floor. Ten-foot ceilings and corner windows enhance the expansive feel of the house. The palette of materials is subtle, yet refined – white walls with terrazzo floors, steel and aluminum elements, and a rich slate blue accent – providing an elegant backdrop to the owner's museum-quality photography collection.

01 Exterior view **02** Floor plans **03** Living space **04** Hallway **05** Built-in tub

Photos: Sharon Risedorph

CITY San Francisco (CA)
COUNTRY USA
REGION North America
TYPOLOGY Living
COMPLETION –
WEBSITE www.johnlumarchitecture.com
ARCHITECTS John Lum Architecture

CITY
San Francisco (CA)

COUNTRY
USA

REGION
North America

TYPOLOGY
Education

COMPLETION
2003

WEBSITE
www.pfauarchitecture.com

ARCHITECTS
Pfau Architecture

LICK-WILMERDING HIGH SCHOOL

The architects' scheme maintains the current campus' open vista to the east while creating a central focus to the Lick-Wilmerding campus. Program elements include the insertion of the new Technology and Design Center into the heart of the school's existing field, an expansion of an existing theater to 425-seat capacity and the creation of a new student center and cafeteria. Sustainable elements of the design include the building's siting strategies, use of natural ventilation and recycled materials, photovoltaic and wind generated power elements.

01 Fully glazed façade **02** Deck **03** Courtyard **04** Solar panel **05** Floor plan

Photos: Tim Griffith

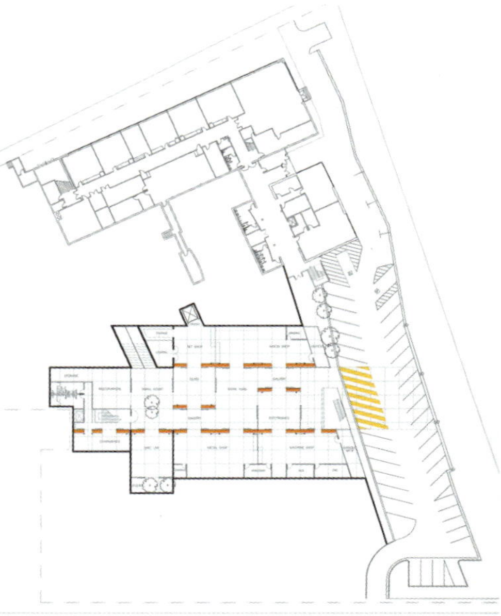

SAGAN PIECHOTA ARCHITECTURE OFFICE

The renovation of this 1920's bakery warehouse called for the creation of a retail space, an architecture office with shop space, and a city residence for the owner of the building. The goals for the architecture studio were to create flexible, naturally lit space that would inspire and encourage the creative process. The concept was to pull light into the middle of the building through the introduction of a third story. This created a soaring, double high space with flanking mezzanines connected by a bridge. Additionally, by pulling the third story back from the façade, it was possible to create outdoor garden areas that are further linked to the adjacent indoor areas through the use of expansive sliding glass doors.

01 Loft **02** Office **03** Façade **04** Floor plans **05** Entry view

Photos: Sharon Risedorph Photography

CITY: San Francisco (CA)
COUNTRY: USA
REGION: North America
TYPOLOGY: Office
COMPLETION: —
WEBSITE: www.sp-architecture.com
ARCHITECTS: Sagan Piechota Architecture

CITY
San Francisco (CA)

COUNTRY
USA

REGION
North America

TYPOLOGY
Living

COMPLETION
2003

WEBSITE
www.saitowitz.com

ARCHITECTS
Stanley Saitowitz/Natoma Architects Inc.

SHAW RESIDENCE

The Shaw Residence strips and rebuilds a 1960's house at the top of Russian Hill, retaining the zoning envelope but revising materials and openings. The base is a stucco wall with perforated stainless apertures, while the bay above, glazed with channel glass, becomes a singular defining element. An existing elevator and a reconfigured stair, which floats away from the walls, link the floors. On the top of the house is the living room with a panorama window and the terrace. The terrace railing is etched glass, which screens the rooftops in the foreground and reflects the water beyond.

01 Opaque glazed stair **02** Stainless apertures **03** Living space **04** Stair

Photos: Tim Griffith

1028 + 1022 NATOMA STREET

This pair of San Francisco infill sites is characterized by a similar design, although the projects were built 14 years apart from each other. The front façades have a bay-window-silhouette constructed of horizontal aluminum bar grating, which provides standing for the southern exposure. One thickened party wall of 1028 Natoma Street provides vertical access and a light court; the other acts as a service zone, condensing kitchens, bathrooms, laundry, and storage behind sliding glass doors. Floating walls divide the free space in the center, which is finished with a variety of materials all in different shades of white.

01 Horizontal aluminum bar grating **02** Spiral stair **03** Working space **04** Exterior view

Photos: Tim Griffith (01), Richard Barnes

CITY San Francisco (CA)
COUNTRY USA
REGION North America
TYPOLOGY Living
COMPLETION 1991 + 2005
WEBSITE www.saitowitz.com
ARCHITECTS Stanley Saitowitz/Natoma Architects Inc.

NOE VALLEY RESIDENCE

The owners' desire was to have a contemporary interior and a traditional façade fit into the urban streetscape. The down sloping site contains a street-access garage, where a family room with an opening to the garden sits just behind it. Orientation and detailing of the staircase were carefully considered, as it constitutes first impression, along with the sky-lit stair hall, which leads to the main living level. A built-in dining booth fits into the façade's bay window, while a balcony overhangs and emphasizes the entrance below. Above the living area is the master suite which sits atop the building like an urban penthouse.

01 Rear view 02 Street view 03 Interior 04 Section

Photos: David King (01), Sharon Risedorph

CITY: San Francisco (CA)
COUNTRY: USA
REGION: North America
TYPOLOGY: Living
COMPLETION: 2004
WEBSITE: www.veverka.com
ARCHITECTS: Veverka Architects

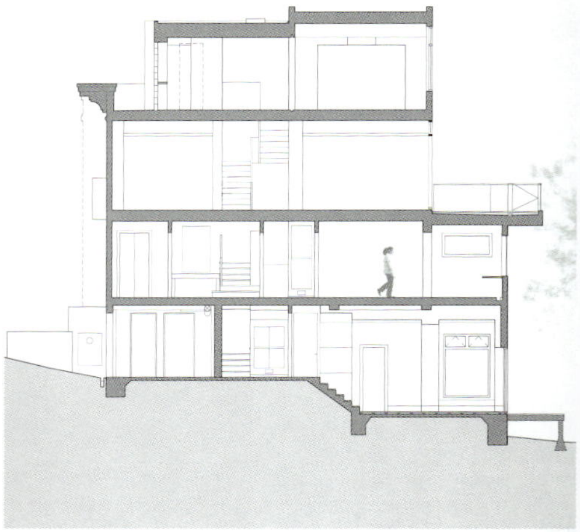

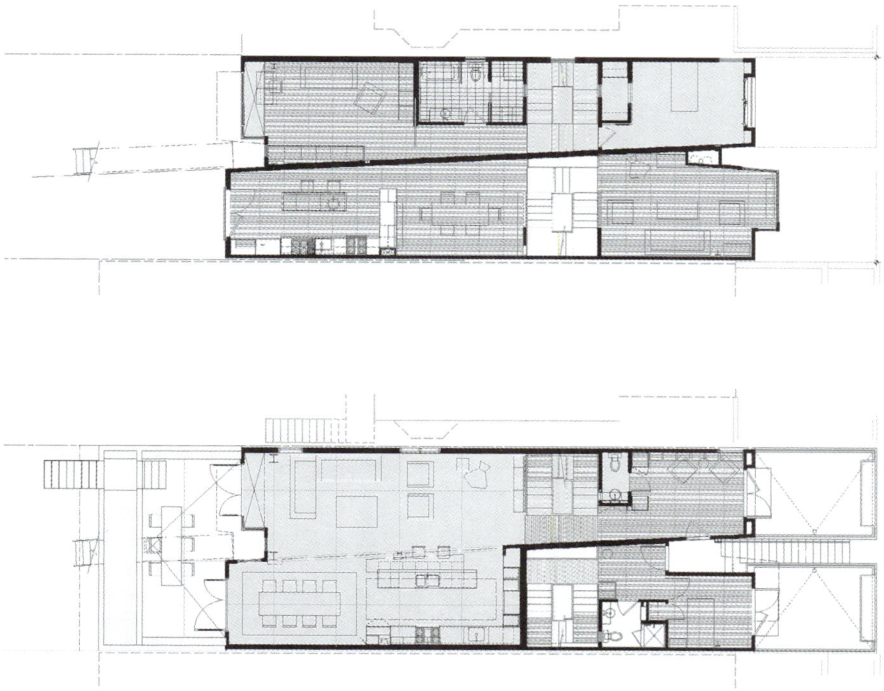

CHATTANOOGA RESIDENCE

The three primary goals for the project were: to design a distinctly modern building sensitive to the predominantly Victorian character of the neighborhood, second to design two units that had equal access to the natural amenities of the site – light, air and views, and finally, taking advantage of the design/build approach to the project, be expressive in the use of materials, detail and craft. The program included two side-by-side townhouses, each with three floors of living over a basement and tandem garage. The main living levels have an open plan, connected to the other floors by a dramatic, light filled central stair.

01 Floor plans **02** Interior **03** Two car tandem garage, front deck **04** Central stair connecting all levels

Photos: Massimiliano Bolzonella

CITY	San Francisco (CA)
COUNTRY	USA
REGION	North America
TYPOLOGY	Living
COMPLETION	2004
WEBSITE	www.zackdevito.com
ARCHITECTS	Zack / de Vito Architecture

CITY: San Francisco (CA)
COUNTRY: USA
REGION: North America
TYPOLOGY: Living
COMPLETION: 2005 proposal
WEBSITE: www.beigedesign.com
ARCHITECTS: Thom Faulders Architecture

CHROMOGENIC DWELLING

A strategy was invented for situating large buildings that maximize real-estate potentials into smaller neighborhoods through utilizing an electronic version of camouflage. To create its Disruptive Patterning System camouflage (DPS) skin, larger forms dissolve into a broad visual noise of indefinable geometries. The Chromogenic Dwelling uses Electrochromic glass to create a real-time changing texture of visible solids and voids. In response to climate, light effects, and privacy requirements, the building's occupants electronically switch the thermal glass into an opaque, transparent, or translucent exterior surface.

01, 03, 05 Electrochromic glass switched into opaque, transparent or translucent 02 Section, floor plans front view 04 Section, floor plans rear view

Renderings: Thom Faulders Archtiecture

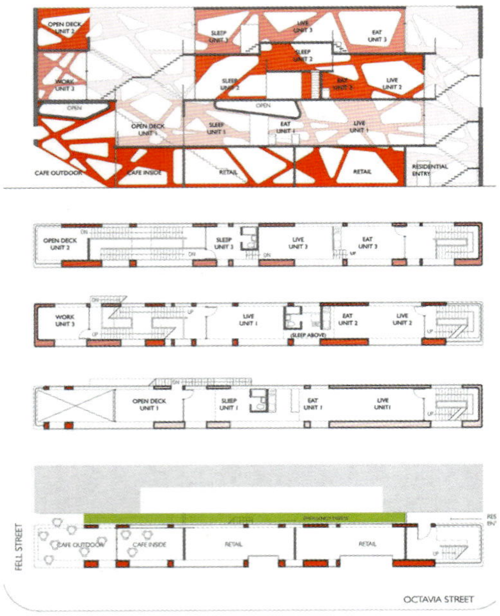

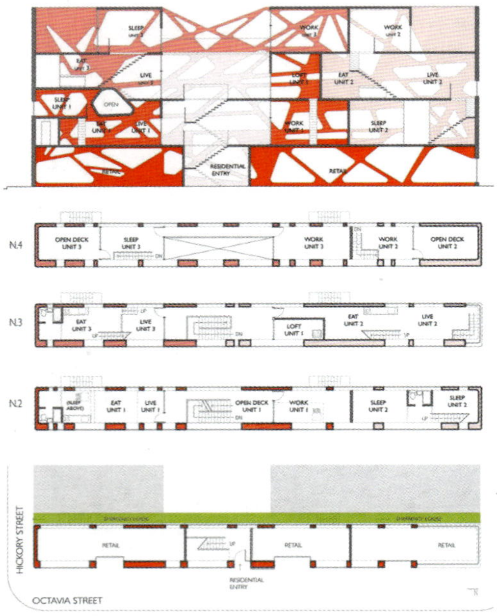

CONTEMPORARY JEWISH MUSEUM

With the opening of its new building, the Contemporary Jewish Museum will usher in a new chapter in its 20-plus year history of engaging audiences and artists in exploring contemporary perspectives on Jewish culture, history, art and ideas. The site of the CJM is an abandoned turn-of-the-century power station which provides a complex urban locus and the necessary pressure for the emergence of a unique form and energy. The building will provide access to new spaces through the imposing Polk façade of the substation which will be incorporated within the old structure and will articulate a close relationship to the new Millennium Tower and the pedestrian connector.

01 Façade by night 02 Stainless steel façade 03 Interior
04 Ground floor plan 05 Bird's eye view

Photos: Bruce Damonte, Mark Darley (02, 03)

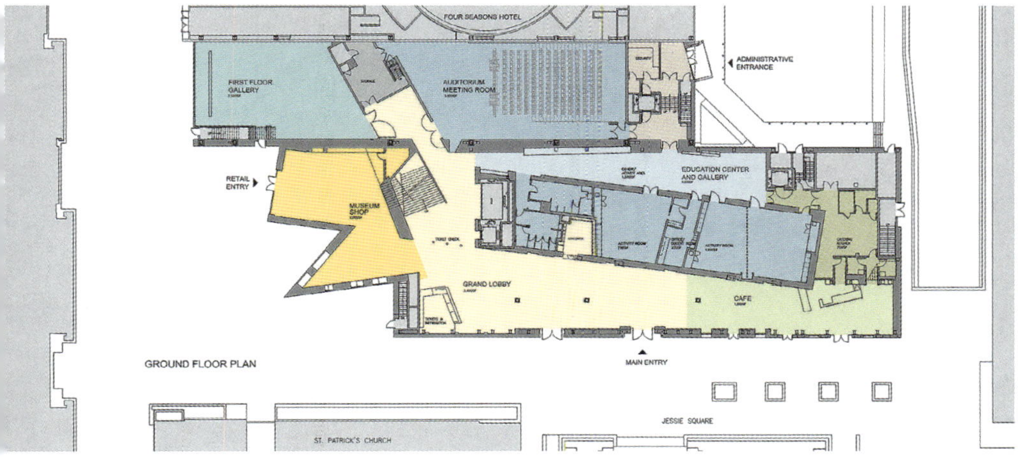

CITY San Francisco (CA)
COUNTRY USA
REGION North America
TYPOLOGY Culture
COMPLETION 2008
WEBSITE www.daniel-libeskind.com
ARCHITECTS Daniel Libeskind

CITY San Francisco (CA)
COUNTRY USA
REGION North America
TYPOLOGY Living
COMPLETION 2007
WEBSITE www.aidlindarlingdesign.com
ARCHITECTS Aidlin Darling Design

OCEAN BEACH RESIDENCE

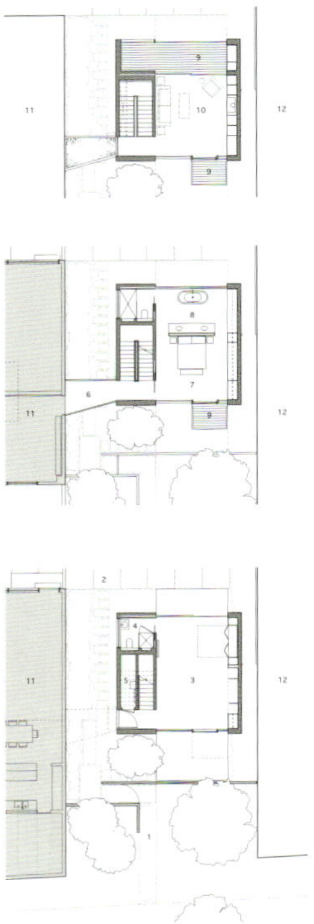

The client needed an addition to an existing mid-century modern house without compromising the existing home in any way. A three-story pavilion 10 feet away from the main house is connected to it through an incision in the side of the second floor, where a translucent glass bridge connects the two structures. The pavilion is divided into two masses flanking a central void. The northern mass is dedicated to bathing and vertical circulation, and the southern mass articulates a three-story Douglas fir storage cabinet that houses the adjacent program's contents. Cor-Ten steel siding was selected to endure the abrasive coastal climate.

01 Exterior view **02** Floor plan **03** Rear view **04** Masterbath

Photos: Sharon Risedorph Photography

351 11TH STREET

This mixed-use commercial building, created by Aidlin Darling Design, is a sustainably designed renovation of a historic industrial structure, with one of its main intents being to achieve LEED GOLD status. A new performative skin of perforated metal unifies functional, perceptual, and historic criteria, which is one of the elements that allow the building to go on and attain the LEED GOLD status. This diaphanous zinc scrim creates a dynamic façade of shifting and dissolving boundaries, referencing the original building's corrugated siding during the day, while unveiling its reclaimed interior at night.

01 West street by dusk **02** Sketches **03, 04** West street façade

Renderings: Aidlin Darling Design

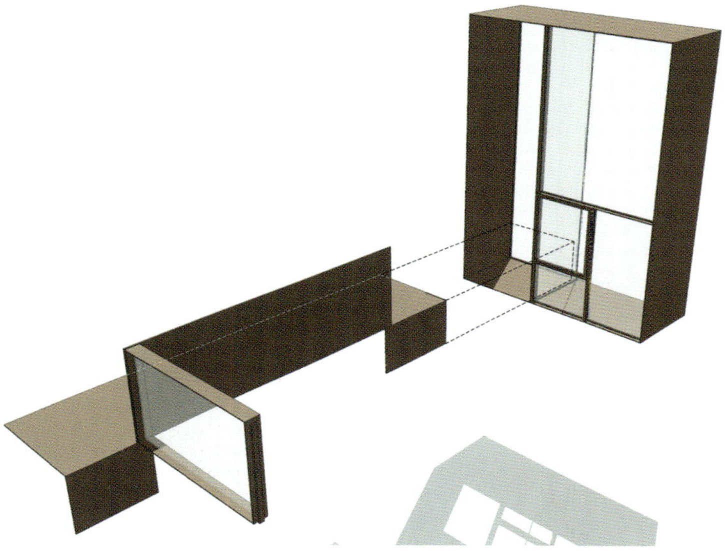

CITY San Francisco (CA)
COUNTRY USA
REGION North America
TYPOLOGY Mixed-Use
COMPLETION –
WEBSITE www.aidlindarlingdesign.com
ARCHITECTS Aidlin Darling Design

548

CITY San Francisco (CA)
COUNTRY USA
REGION North America
TYPOLOGY Mixed-use
COMPLETION –
WEBSITE www.archengine.com
ARCHITECTS Office of Charles F. Bloszies

ULTRA-SUSTAINABLE SKYSCRAPER

Comprised of 3 photovoltaic clad sections separated by wind turbines, the building form is a consequence of rotating a simple floor plan 5 degrees at each successive level. The resulting helical shape sheds the full force of the wind, in which a planar façade must resist while capturing enough to drive the turbines. Its skin is comprised of transparent photovoltaic panels, and while the structure may be located on any site with enough solar and wind exposure providing sufficient "fuel" to satisfy energy demands, the goal of the design is to integrate advanced energy generating technologies in an aesthetically sustainable manner.

01 Exterior view **02** Helical shape **03** Photovoltaic façade separated by wind turbines **04** Detail photovoltaic panels **05** Floor plan

Photos and renderings: Office of Charles F. Bloszies

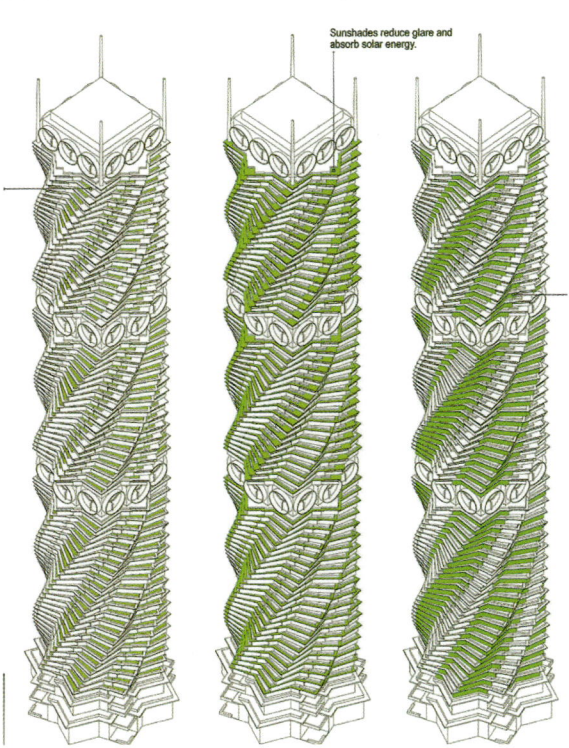

THE LESBIAN GAY BISEXUAL TRANSGENDER COMMUNITY CENTER

The project is sited at a prominent mid-Market Street location bridging many lesbian, gay, bisexual and transgender neighborhoods, and the community center itself houses 20 meeting rooms, two large assembly spaces, a computer lab and classrooms for City College, a café, and non-profit offices. The Community Center's design foregrounds relationships between interior and exterior, as well as between the perception of façade and the experience of space. The interplay of transparency and opacity is used throughout the 40,000-square-foot building to speak about relationships and associations between sexuality and identity.

01 Corner view **02** Atrium by night **03** Floor plan **04** Roof deck **05** Interior

Photos: Livia Corona, Tim Griffith (CEE-02, CEE-03)

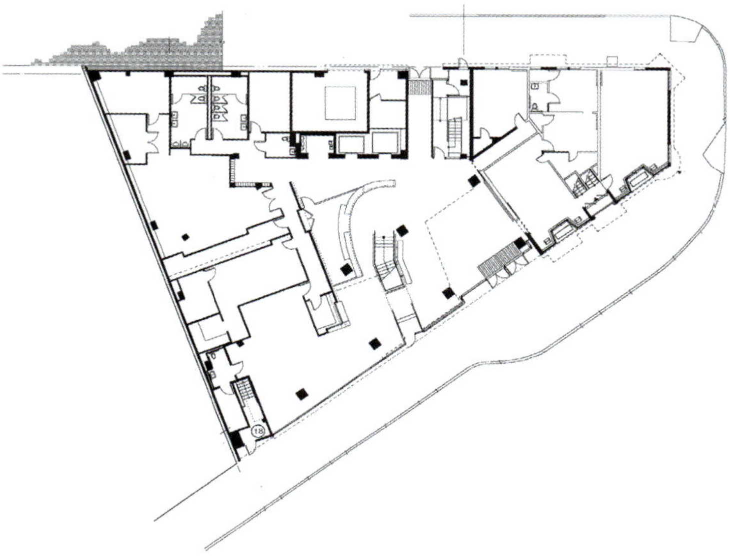

CITY: San Francisco (CA)
COUNTRY: USA
REGION: North America
TYPOLOGY: Institution
COMPLETION: 2002
WEBSITE: www.ceearchitects.com
ARCHITECTS: Cee Architects (in collaboration with Pfau Architecture)

550

CITY
San Francisco (CA)

COUNTRY
USA

REGION
North America

TYPOLOGY
Office

COMPLETION
2007

WEBSITE
www.jensen-architects.com

ARCHITECTS
Jensen Architects

TURNER DUCKWORTH OFFICES

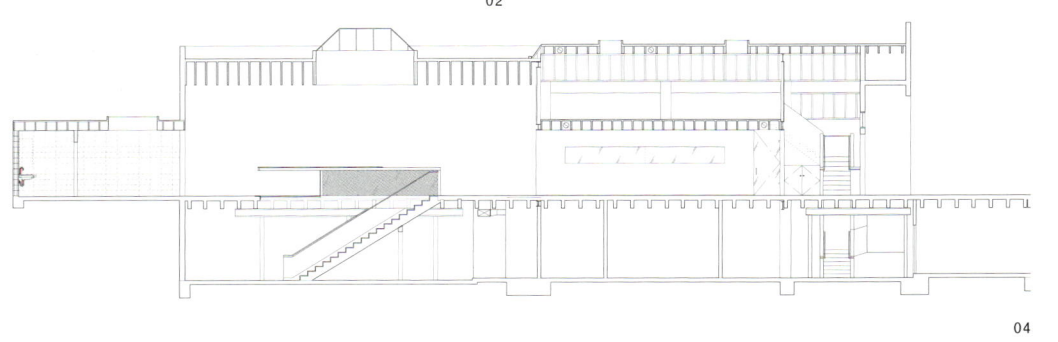

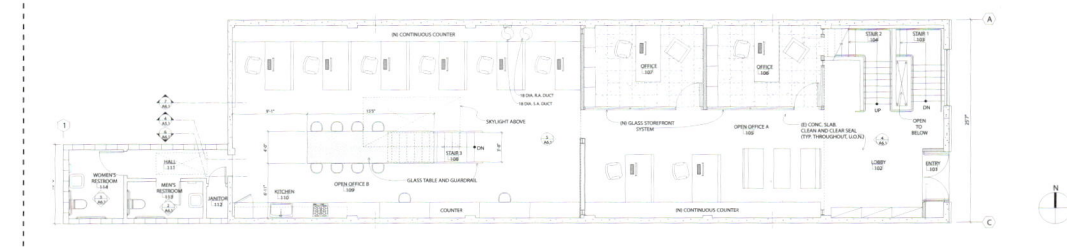

This office for a graphic design firm occupies a two-story warehouse building in a historic district. The warehouse's existing concrete shell and wood-framed roof were stripped clean, left exposed, and painted a uniform off-white. Bright, translucent red punctuates this luminous space in a series of dramatic, glass-clad rooms and structural details. The project's focal point is a cantilevered glass meeting table that floats over a glass floor, letting light into the basement below. Finally, the existing brick front façade was painted black and white, referencing the storefronts of London where this firm has a satellite office.

01 Brick façade **02** Stair **03** Working space **04** Section **05** Floor plan **06** Glass meeting table, glass floor

Photos: Sharon Risedorph

SUNSET MAGAZINE IDEA HOME

The client's concern for the natural environment inspired the remodel and reorganization of the existing two-story structure that became a showcase of new design ideas set in an urban context. This home features innovative building systems including photovoltaic electrical generation, a wind turbine, gray-water system, living roofs and ecological materials, yielding a self-sustaining house with zero-net energy usage. Welcoming the outside in, the house opens to landscaped areas on the ground floor and to a roof terrace at the third story addition, while clerestory windows that top the three-story glass stairwell permit natural light to penetrate deep into the interior.

01 Additional third floor **02** Exterior **03** Kitchen **04** Street façade **05** Steel and glass tread staircase

Photos: Sharon Risedorph (01, 04), Richard Barnes

CITY	San Francisco (CA)
COUNTRY	USA
REGION	North America
TYPOLOGY	Living
COMPLETION	2007
WEBSITE	www.johnlumarchitecture.com
ARCHITECTS	John Lum Architecture

LAKE STREET RESIDENCE

This project was charged with transforming a poorly-lit 5 bedroom Victorian house into a cohesive, light-filled modern home for two. The previous arrangement that separated rooms into south and north-facing spaces created underutilized spaces with imbalanced light. Skylights, widows and wall openings created a new interior, where space flows from front to back and left to right. The staircase was transformed into a dramatic, luminescent two-story focal point at the center of the layout. The renovation demonstrates how appreciation for design and contemporary lifestyle can be satisfied in the context of traditional home.

01 Shower detail 02 Master bath 03 Entry 04 Kitchen
05 Floor plan

Photos: Joe Fletcher Photography

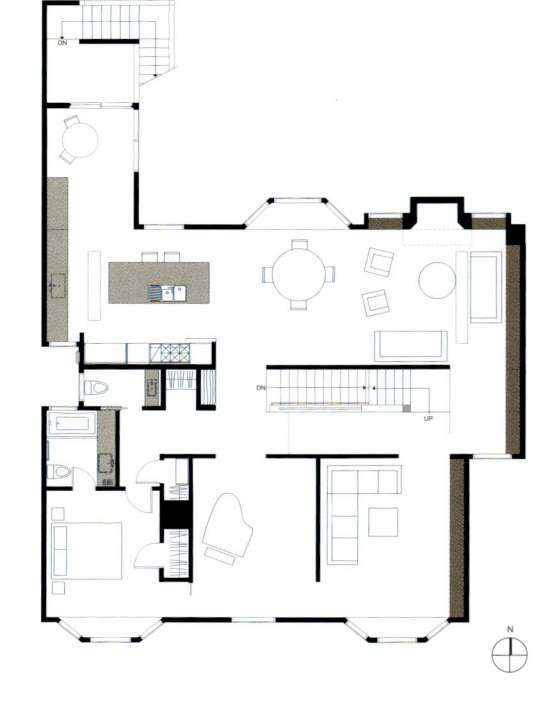

CITY San Francisco (CA)
COUNTRY USA
REGION North America
TYPOLOGY Living
COMPLETION 2006
WEBSITE www.ccs-architecture.com
ARCHITECTS CCS Architecture

HAUS MARTIN

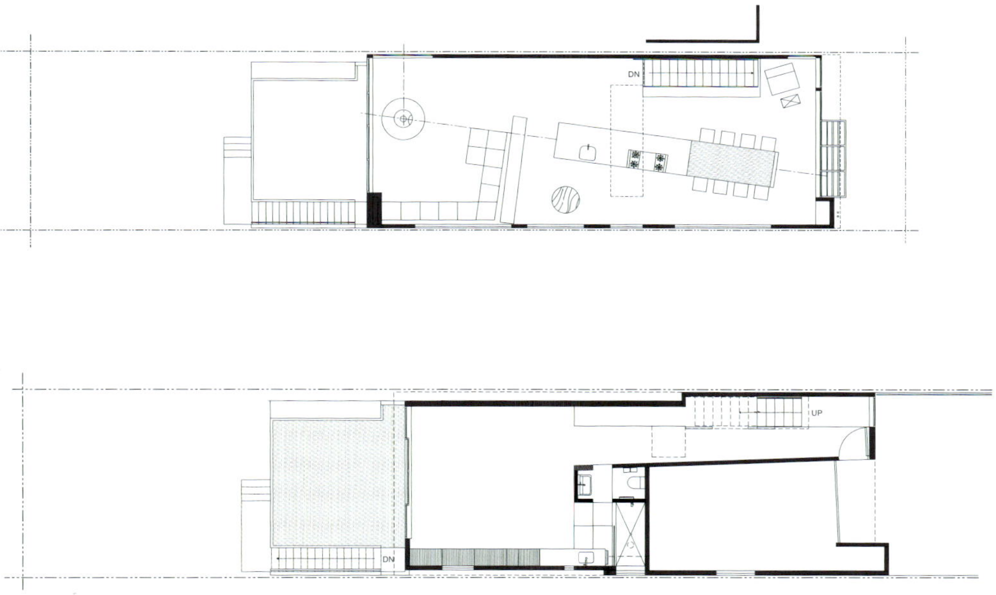

This new 1,800 square foot, single-family house in the Buena Vista Park District replaces an existing home with the same footprint and number of stories. Aside from the client's program, the house is designed to respond to two contextual influences: the excellent views of the park to the east and of the ocean to the west, plus the richly ornate façades of the adjacent neighbors. The intent was to create a façade that would equate to the adjacent façades in intensity, materiality, and interest, yet be purely modern. This goal was merged with maximizing the width of windows to create a horizontal pan of the dramatic views.

01 Wooden façade **02** East view **03** Kitchen **04** Floor plans **05** Stair

Photos: Tim Griffith

CITY San Francisco (CA)
COUNTRY USA
REGION North America
TYPOLOGY Living
COMPLETION 2004
WEBSITE www.ccs-architecture.com
ARCHITECTS CCS Architecture

CITY
San Francisco (CA)

COUNTRY
USA

REGION
North America

TYPOLOGY
Education

COMPLETION
–

WEBSITE
www.jensen-architects.com

ARCHITECTS
Jensen Architects

CALIFORNIA COLLEGE OF THE ARTS GRADUATE CENTER

The fencing is the façade for this expansion to the Graduate Studies Campus at the California College of the Arts. Aluminum expanded metal mesh forms an open scrim-like wall at the street's edge. Behind the mesh skin are two pre-engineered steel buildings that house sixty-eight individual artist studios, classrooms, administrative offices and exhibit spaces. The open space between the buildings forms a courtyard with shade trees and outdoor workshops. This project is connected to the previously completed Graduate Center project by Jensen Architects and creates a 50,000 square foot graduate studies campus.

01 Detail aluminum metal mesh skin **02** Courtyard **03** Exterior view **04** Ground floor plan **05** Interior view

Photos: Mark Luthringer, Jensen Architects

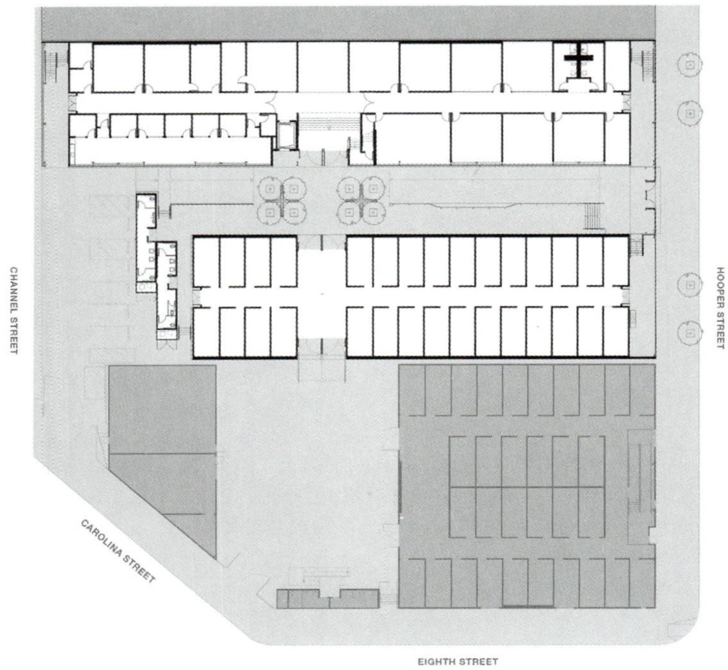

SCHEY RESIDENCE

Positioned at the foot of a 100 foot wooded canyon, this house utilizes its topology to create an outdoor living room sculpted by the landform that borders it. In fact, the house is a microcosm of California; the outdoor area is bordered by an indoor living space that is completely opened to the outside in myriad different ways. The garden is delimited by a sloping retaining wall lined with a fireplace, a grill, waterfalls and an ochre plastered fence wall with randomly placed openings through which passersby can peek in. The rear border is a wooded hillside with winding landscaped pathways.

01 Rear view **02** Garage and entry **03** Rear patio **04** Master bedroom

Photos: Courtesy of GRAYmatter Architecture

CITY Santa Monica (CA)
COUNTRY USA
REGION North America
TYPOLOGY Living
COMPLETION 2004
WEBSITE www.graymatter architecture.com
ARCHITECTS GRAYmatter Architecture

CITY: Santa Monica (CA)
COUNTRY: USA
REGION: North America
TYPOLOGY: Living
COMPLETION: –
WEBSITE: www.jfak.net
ARCHITECTS: John Friedman Alice Kimm Architects

EHRLICH RESIDENCE

Proving that it is not necessary to sacrifice beauty for sustainability, this residence incorporates a number of passive and active green strategies, as well as a number of recycled and sustainably harvested materials. Its openness provides the sense of continuous space and connection to the garden that the client desired, while allowing sunlight and ocean breezes to warm and cool the house naturally. The koi pond cools the air before it enters the house; the concrete floor absorbs the sun's heat, saving it to be released at night. Motorized skylights over the stair atrium draw warm air out of the house and also provide museum-quality lighting for the client's art collection.

01 Exterior view **02** Street view **03** Koi pond **04** Rear view **05** Concrete floor

Photos: Benny Chan, Fotoworks

LIVINGHOMES MODEL 1.0

The firm produces factory production homes integrating great design and extremely high environmental ratings. The company's first home was the first residential building to receive a LEED for Homes Platinum rating. The dwellings are custom-built and expand with the needs of the client. All modules have standard and optional sustainable features like LED lighting, gray water recycling and ecological materials, and extra rooms can be added at a later date. The homes are calculated to be more affordable than a 'regular' single-family home and are expected to serve their owners longer due to their high levels of flexibility.

01 Living room **02** View from above into living spaces **03** Exterior view by night **04** Interior structural detail **05** Elevations

Photos: CJ Berg Photographics/Sunshine Divis

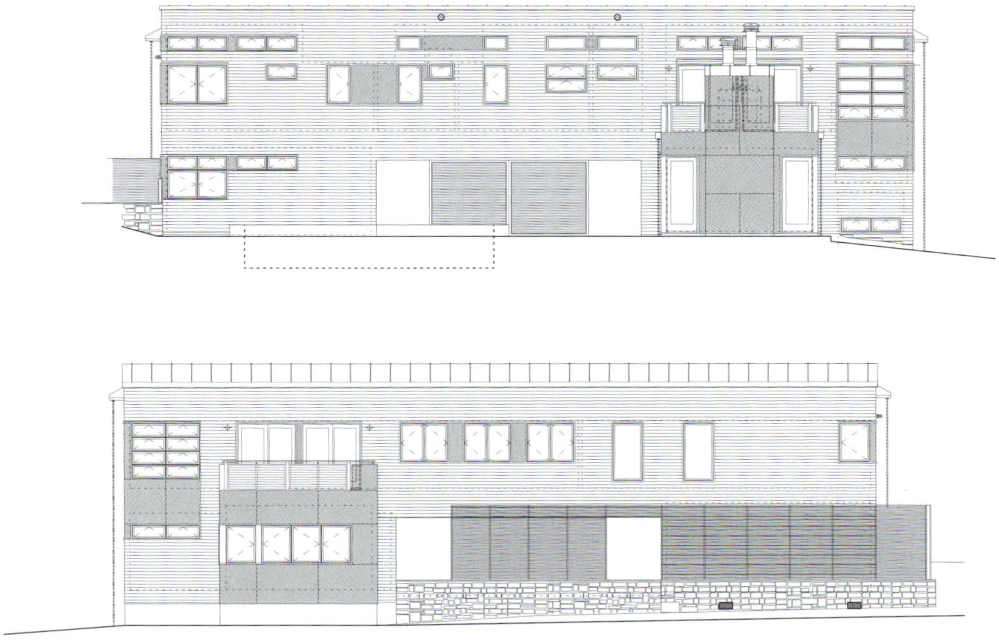

CITY: Santa Monica (CA)
COUNTRY: USA
REGION: North America
TYPOLOGY: Living
COMPLETION: –
WEBSITE: www1.livinghomes.net
ARCHITECTS: Ray Kappe

BROADWAY HOUSING

Broadway Housing consists of 41 units of family affordable housing with two levels of subterranean parking; community spaces and courtyard with play area. The building skin is partially clad with recycled aluminum cans formed into building blocks about twice the size of concrete blocks. These are joined by a perforated metal screen on the façade, which acts as sun and privacy screen. East-facing walls swell with asymmetrical pleats and folds that lend unexpected visual depth. Enhancing the structure's geometric texture, the irregular array of windows variably project and recede from the building's surface.

01 External staircase **02** Typical floor plan **03** Irregular array of windows **04** Perforated metal screen **05** Street façade

Photos: Marvin Rand

CITY Santa Monica (CA)

COUNTRY USA

REGION North America

TYPOLOGY Living

COMPLETION 2006

WEBSITE www.pugh-scarpa.com

ARCHITECTS Pugh + Scarpa

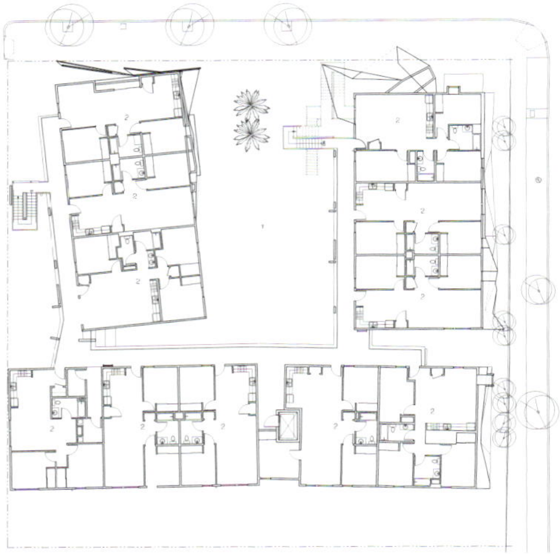

26TH STREET LOW-INCOME HOUSING

The product of an exhaustive community outreach mission, this affordable housing development was designed with considerable input from the city of Santa Monica and community at large. The final design incorporates the region's mild climate, historical precedents of Southern California Modernist architecture, and the human scale of residents and pedestrians. Comprised of 44 units, the development includes a community room, a courtyard designed to encourage family and community interaction and 81 parking spaces. Drywells were dug beneath the project to collect and disperse storm water runoff and minimize the project's impact on the city's storm sewer system.

01 Exterior view by night **02** Courtyard **03** Interior **04** Floor plan **05** External staircase

Photos: John Edward Linden Photography

CITY Santa Monica (CA)
COUNTRY USA
REGION North America
TYPOLOGY Living
COMPLETION 2006
WEBSITE www.kannerarch.com
ARCHITECTS Kanner Architects

HYDRAULX

The architecture of Hydraulx expresses the operation of the machine. The material truth of exposed structure and raw industrial materials, joined with exposed details forced to perform with the precision of furniture, define the palette employed to create the workspace. Touches of Douglas fir soften the space. The rooms were built for multi-purpose use and flexibility to keep up with the constant changes in the post-production industry, and the space planning was crucial to providing the right environment for clients and artists – spaces that were private and could accommodate collaborative group efforts.

01 Steel construction 02 Meeting space 03 Working space
04 Floor plans

Photos: Tom Bonner Photography

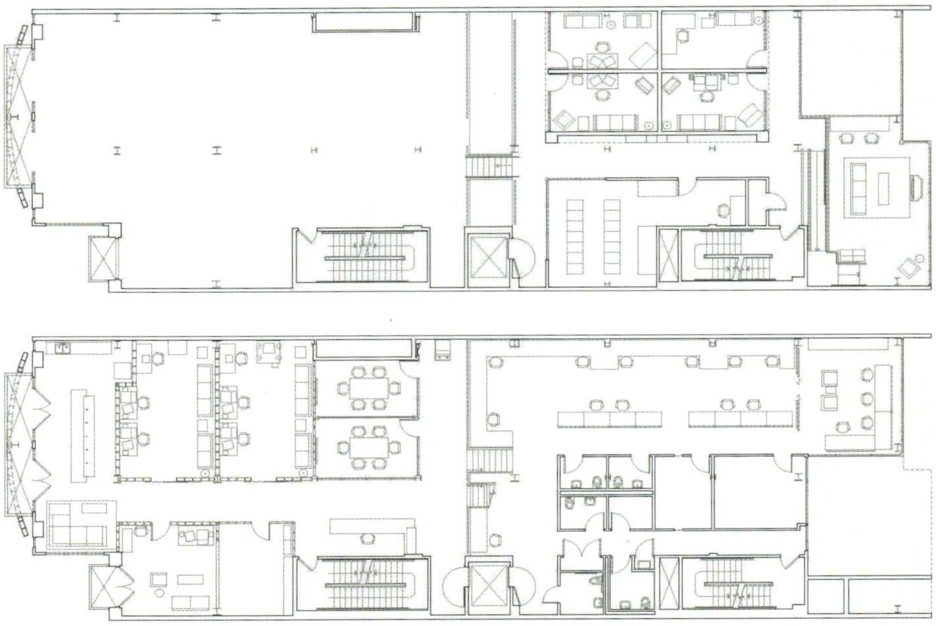

CONCRETE PANEL HOUSE

The goal of the design was to create a simple, contemporary house using prefabricated elements and green building guidelines. The house has a box-like shape and a private inner courtyard. The openings on all sides are the same size. The structure of the house consists of steel frames, metal joists and prefabricated concrete panels. To facilitate the speed and ease of construction, all walls were made the same size and shape, and were prefabricated on site. This project demonstrated the feasibility of creating beautiful, efficient, simple architecture that is cost effective and yet superior to conventionally built homes.

01 Concrete façade **02** Roof deck **03** Inner courtyard **04** Reading room, upstairs

Photos: Robert Gregory, Roger Kurath (01)

CITY: Santa Monica (CA)
COUNTRY: USA
REGION: North America
TYPOLOGY: Living
COMPLETION: 2007
WEBSITE: www.goDesign21.com
ARCHITECTS: Roger Kurath / Design*21

CITY Scottsdale (AZ)
COUNTRY USA
REGION North America
TYPOLOGY Hospitality
COMPLETION 2005
WEBSITE www.allenphilp.com
ARCHITECTS Allen + Philp Architects/Interiors

HOTEL VALLEY HO

Preservation, reuse and celebration are the design themes used in renovating and adding on to this historic hotel in Scottsdale, Arizona. Noted for its organic architectural style with a "southwestern" character that bridged modern and western detailing, new retro-contemporary elements are featured including a perfectly circular pool defining the space, with private cabanas, a new bar and grill area, a dramatic fire and fountain feature, and translucent bathroom walls. The most dramatic addition to the property is a seven-story tower that contains a spa and fitness center and five levels of condominium residences.

01 Pool at night **02** Site plan **03** Exterior guest rooms **04** Front façade **05** Courtyard

Photos: Bill Timmerman Photography, Mark Boisclair (01,04)

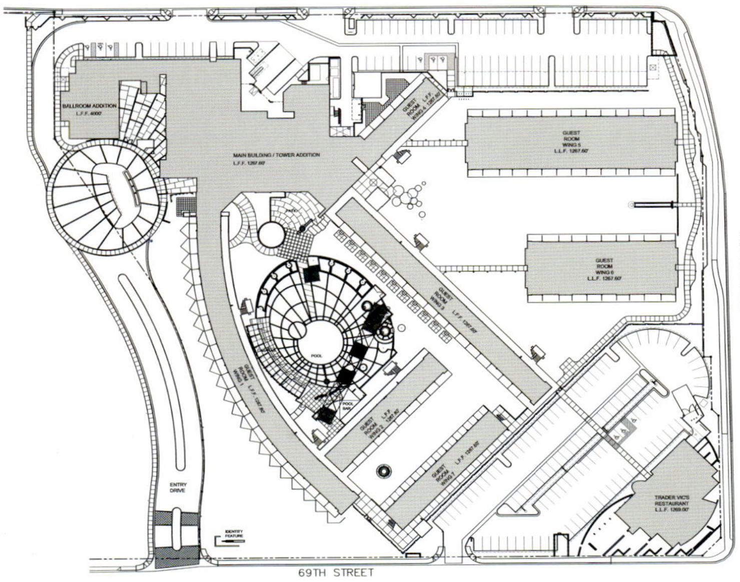

THE DUKE

The Duke is an urban desert, multi-family residential environment consisting of eight attached town homes; three stories high, each with a one-car garage. The modern, pure building cuts a clean sharp edge through the randomly built environment of the surrounding area. Compact and efficient, emphasis was placed on sustainable design through successfully participating in Scottsdale's Residential Green Building Program. The Duke's intent is to express individuality as a singular building with eight individual homeowners, while promoting community through architectural transparency on the second floor.

01 Street view **02** Façade detail **03** Section **04** Exterior view **05** Kitchen

Photos: Rieser Photography

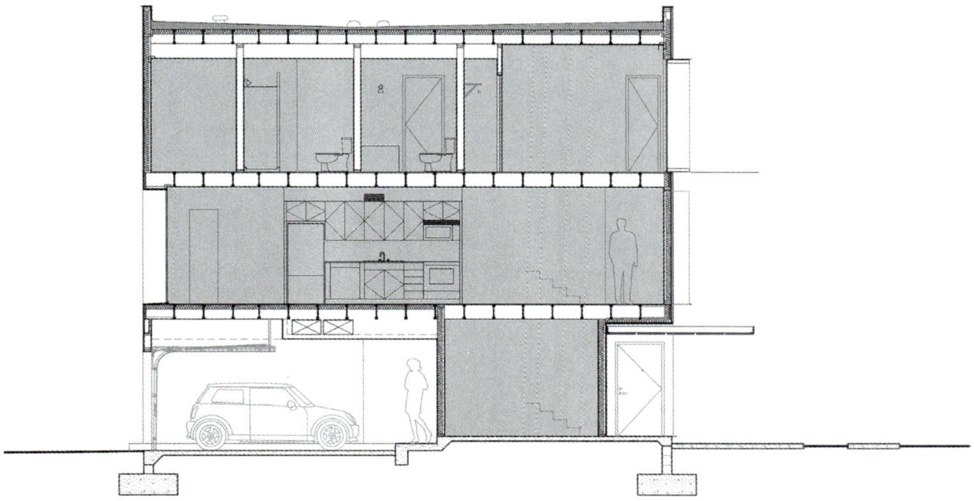

CITY Scottsdale (AZ)
COUNTRY USA
REGION North America
TYPOLOGY Living
COMPLETION 2006
WEBSITE www.circlewest.net
ARCHITECTS Circle West

SCOTTSDALE FIRST ASSEMBLY

This masonry structure in the desert is a regional church in North Scottsdale accommodating 1000 per service, along with administration and classroom spaces. It represents the first phase of a long range architectural plan composed of masonry planes, weathered metal and glass. From the entry plaza the various programs pivot from the central lobby and worship space, where the linear arrangement of offices and classrooms foreshadow the future growth of the campus. The structures are organized around an existing natural wash, diagonally bisecting the site and aligned to views of the nearby Pinnacle Peak.

01 Courtyard 02 Exterior 03 Weathered metal and glass façade 04 Garden 05 Upper level floor plan

Photos: Bill Timmerman Photography

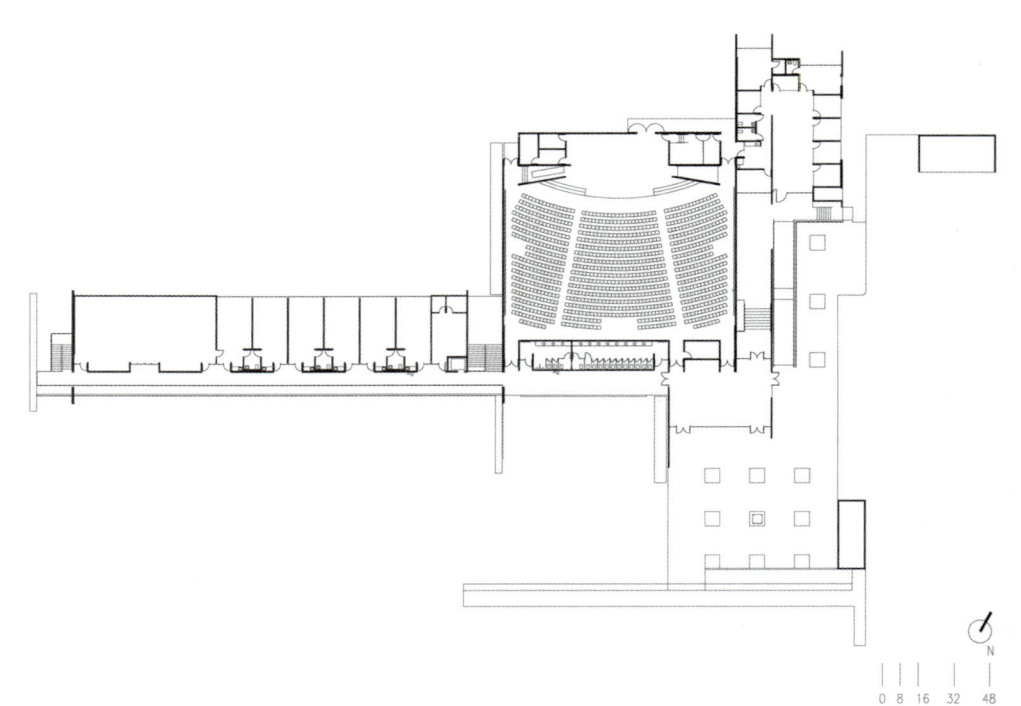

CITY Scottsdale (AZ)
COUNTRY USA
REGION North America
TYPOLOGY Culture
COMPLETION 2005
WEBSITE www.debartoloarchitects.com
ARCHITECTS DeBartolo architects

LAKE UNION FLOATING HOME

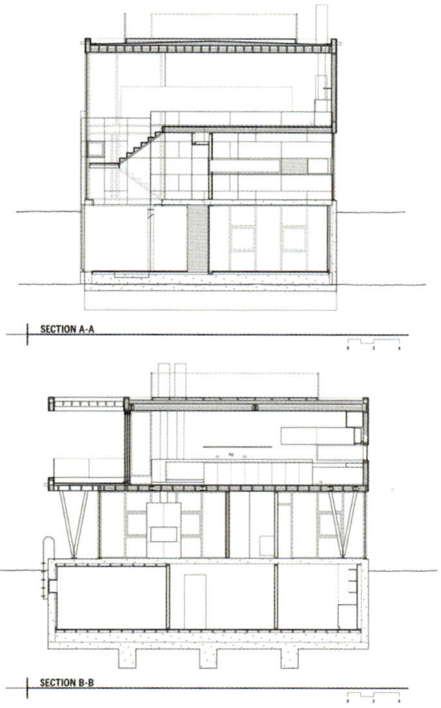

Defined by the constraints and limitations of the zoning envelope, this floating home investigates the idea of coding the internal program as a means to articulate a box. Entertaining functions are coded in Ochre Slatescape panels, while service areas are clad by gray aluminum panels. The main living spaces are located on the top level, adjacent to a large terrace and rooftop deck, while the bedrooms are located on the float level, and other service areas being located below in the basement. Natural light, views and cross ventilation were all carefully considered while going about the design of this project.

01 Northeast view from shore 02 Spiral stair to second floor terrace 03 Sections 04 Southwest view from water 05 Interior view, living space at top level

Photos: Benjamin Benschneider

CITY Seattle (WA)
COUNTRY USA
REGION North America
TYPOLOGY Living
COMPLETION 2007
WEBSITE www.vc-arch.com
ARCHITECTS Vandeventer+Carlander Architects

SOMA HOUSE

An expressive residence that stands in contrast to the modest structures in the neighborhood, the Soma House playfully experiments with the concepts of solid and void. Through an exploration of the ways in which they are interlocked to actively shape a broad range of experiences, the house is made up of three distinct boxes. The boxes are shifted, offset and stacked to create five distinct exterior spaces, including a Wet Terrace, Grass Room, Dry Terrace, Activity Court and Extreme Ledge. Voids are then interspersed around and under the solid boxes offering light, space and selected views to the street as well as adjacent properties.

01 Street site view **02** Upper deck and lower terrace **03** Garden view **04** Kitchen **05** First floor plan

Photos: Paul Warchol Photography

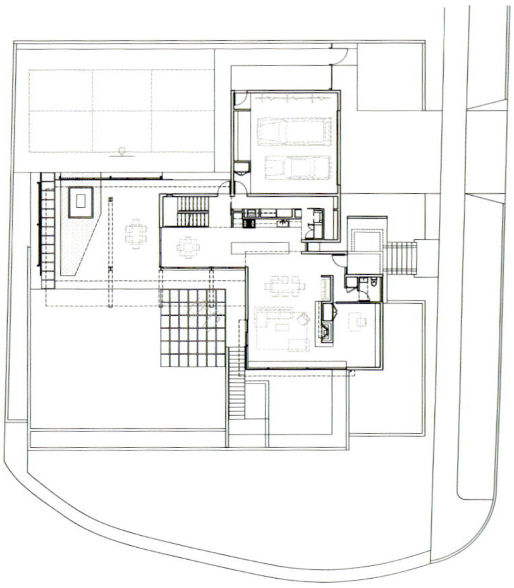

FAUNTLEROY RESIDENCE

The residence stands out as an instance of masterful design and an achievement of international stature. Seattle's climate, mild, sometimes wet or dry, is welcomed with deep overhanging eaves, while the patient sequencing of rooms are alternately open and enclosed, covered and uncovered. The site's history is evident in two original structures; small beachside cabins, and the use of the prior residence's foundation and porch as a transition between the new structure and the old. A continuous stream engages the house along its northern edge, narrowing and then pooling in the way that people, flow or pause, and then gather.

01 Dining terrace **02** Entry courtyard **03** Outdoor living space **04** Floor plan **05** Pond

Photos: Paul Warchol (01–03), Suyama Peterson Deguchi (04), Lara Swimmer (05)

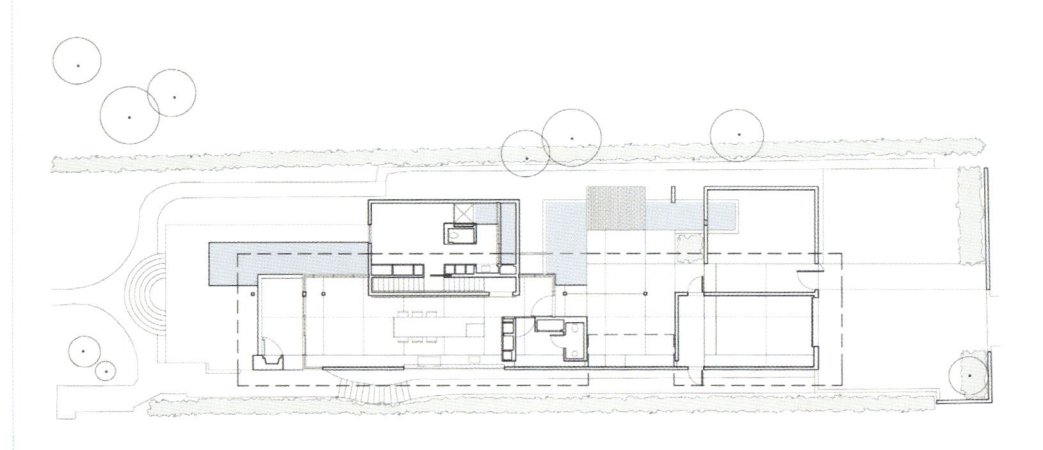

CITY Seattle (WA)
COUNTRY USA
REGION North America
TYPOLOGY Living
COMPLETION 2003
WEBSITE www.s-pd.com
ARCHITECTS Suyama Peterson Deguchi

MAD PARK

Located on a steep slope corner lot, the existing site conditions establish the vertical datum to which the new design responds. The concept of served and service spaces is the organizing tool used in plan. Thus the parallel bars separated by the glazed gallery. Whereas the house is organized vertically by activity – children on the ground floor, public on the main floor, and private family functions above. Public spaces are defined by extensive glazing on three sides, and structurally by a series of steel moment frames, allowing maximum flexibility for entertaining and display. Fundamental to the concept of the house is a linear, light filled gallery.

01 Exterior view, entry elevation **02** Exterior view, south elevation **03** Southwest view from side yard **04** Level one floor plan **05** Gallery

Photos: Benjamin Benschneider

CITY Seattle (WA)
COUNTRY USA
REGION North America
TYPOLOGY Living
COMPLETION –
WEBSITE www.vc-arch.com
ARCHITECTS Vandeventer+Carlander Architects

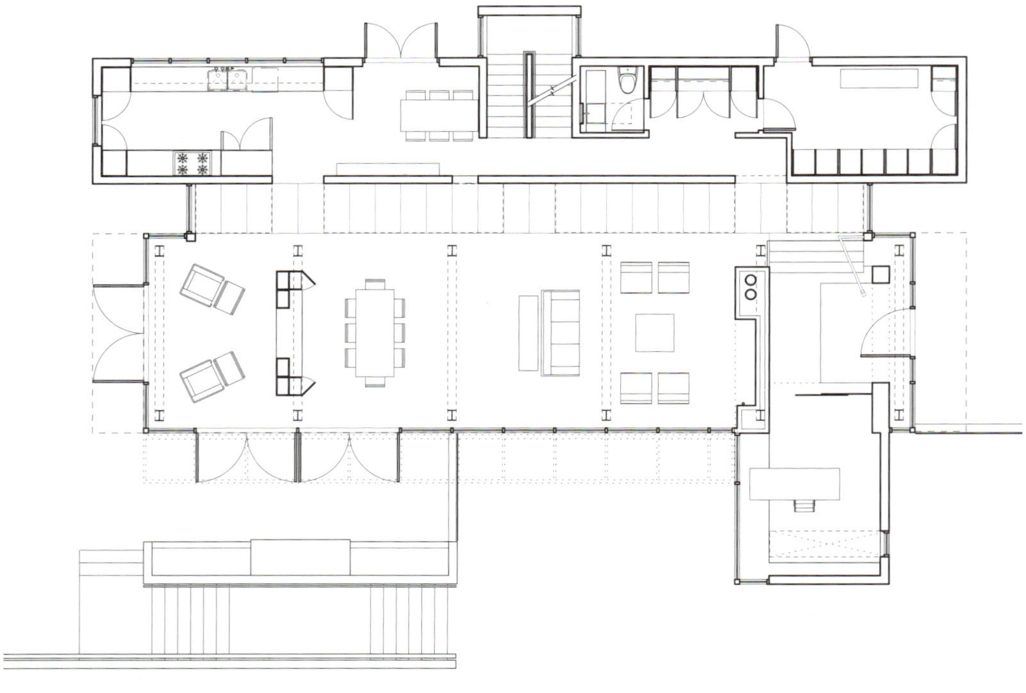

OLYMPIC SCULPTURE PARK

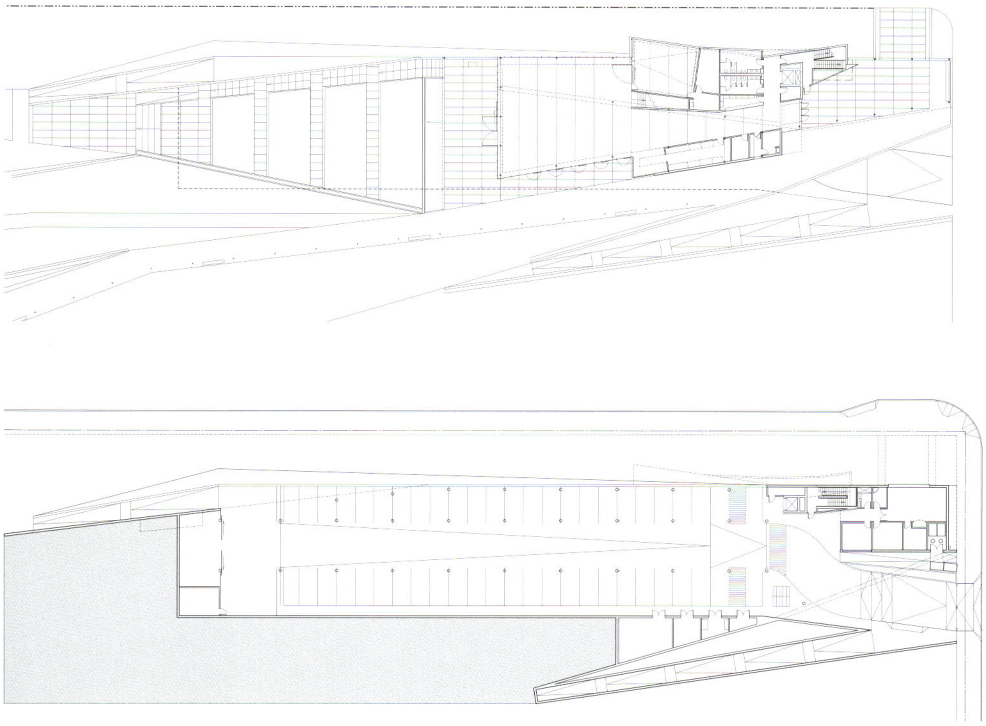

The Olympic Sculpture Park transforms a 9-acre industrial site into open and vibrant green space for art. Reconnecting the urban core to the revitalized waterfront, the park gives Seattle residents and visitors the opportunity to experience a variety of sculpture in an outdoor setting, while enjoying the views of the Olympic Mountains and Puget Sound. The idea was to bring sculpture outside of the museum walls and the park itself into the landscape of the city. The design forms a Z-shaped path that leads from a steel-and-glass pavilion to the water. It provides space for art, performances and educational programming.

01 Aerial view of park 02 Plans 03 Pavilion interior 04 View of pavilion from the valley

Photos: Paul Warchol Photography (01), Benjamin Benschneider

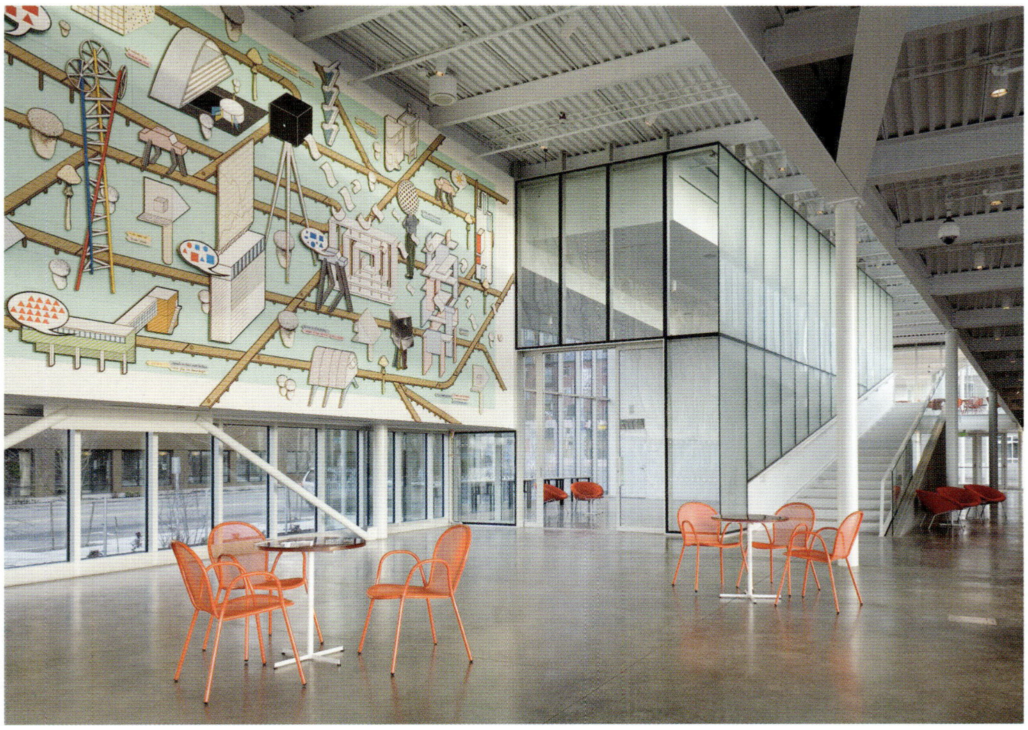

CITY: Seattle (WA)
COUNTRY: USA
REGION: North America
TYPOLOGY: Public
COMPLETION: 2007
WEBSITE: www.weissmanfredi.com
ARCHITECTS: Weiss/Manfredi

FIRE STATION 10

Located on a full city block in downtown Seattle, just south of the Civic Center, the lot slopes almost 50-feet from high-to-low points, and is bounded on the north by an elevated roadway. This new 69,000-square foot public safety complex was built to essential facility standards and provides for 72-hour standalone operation. The facility co-locates Seattle's Emergency Operations Center – the seat of government in an emergency, the Fire Alarm Center, the 24/7 911 medical and fire dispatch, and Fire Station 10, the City's primary hazardous materials response unit. The building is pursuing a LEED™ Silver rating.

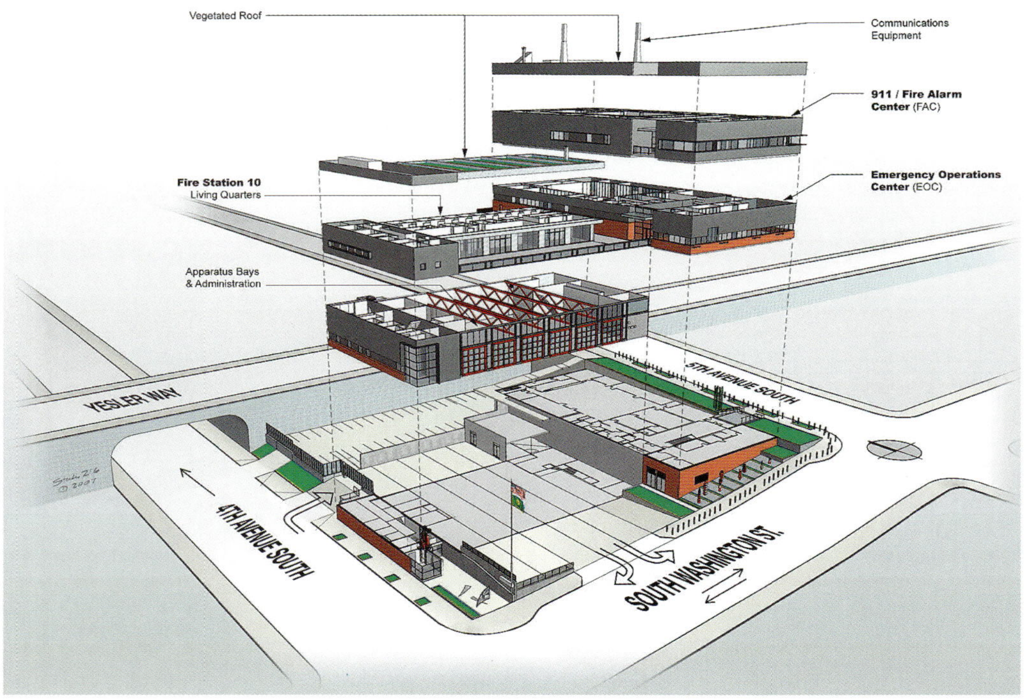

01 Apparatus Bay **02** Exterior view looking north **03** Emergency Operations Center **04** Exterior looking northwest **05** Organizational diagram

Photos: Michael Burns

DOUGLASS-TRUTH BRANCH OF THE SEATTLE PUBLIC LIBRARY

To preserve the historic character of the landmark building, the bulk of the addition is located below grade. The green to the west of the library and views of the library's most prominent façades have been preserved. The historic main entry continues to provide access to the expanded library. The new, lower level reading room is covered by a copper clad light monitor that brings generous amounts of daylight into the new structure and frames views looking back to the historic building. The wall of the addition facing the historic library is glazed, reflecting the color and details of the landmark building by day and allowing light inside the addition to spill out at night.

01 Front view by night **02** Exterior by night **03** Interior view towards staircase **04** Floor plan **05** Interior View

Photos: Michael Jensen

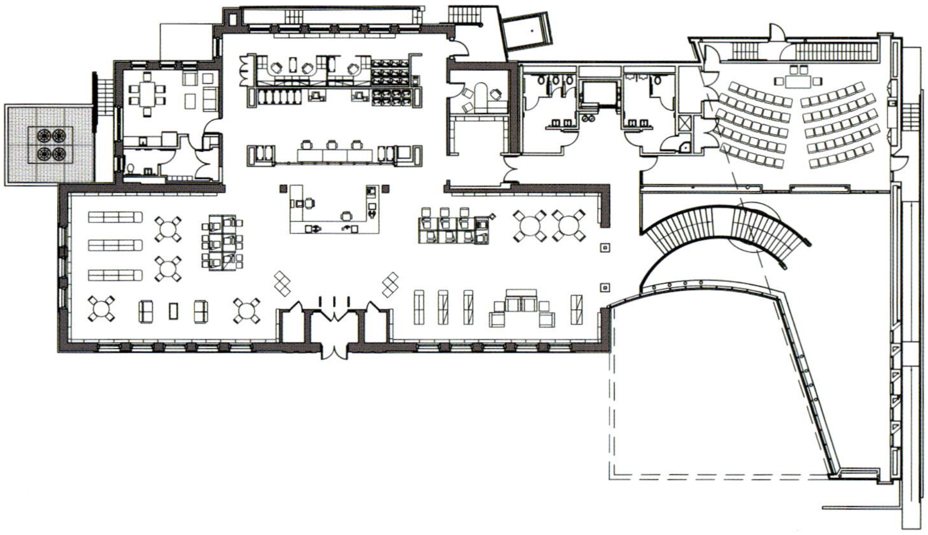

CITY Seattle (WA)
COUNTRY USA
REGION North America
TYPOLOGY Public
COMPLETION 2006
WEBSITE www.saarch.com
ARCHITECTS Schacht Aslani Architects

CITY Seattle (WA)

COUNTRY USA

REGION North America

TYPOLOGY Living

COMPLETION 2004

WEBSITE www.vc-arch.com

ARCHITECTS Vandeventer+Carlander Architects

MADRONA HOUSE

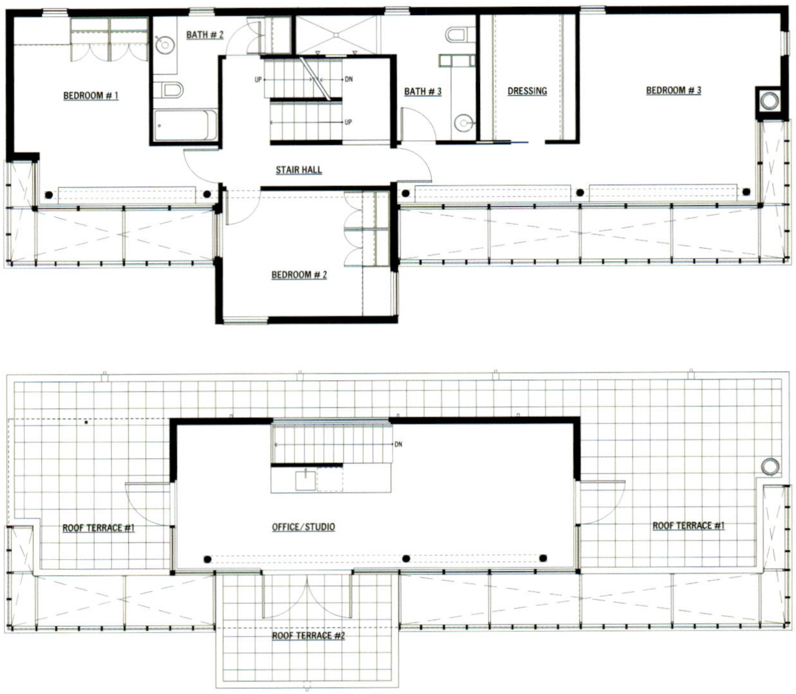

The Madrona House development, designed by Vandeventer & Carlander Architects, is located on a small urban lot, taking full advantage of its southern exposure to bathe the interior in natural light. The program is dispersed over three floors and a basement, in which public spaces are located on the ground floor, private spaces found on the second floor, while offices and roof terraces are featured on the third. Cedar siding was utilized in a number of different configurations to code the home's internal organization. In addition, a cedar screen completes the composition providing for sun control and privacy.

01 Living room **02** Exterior view from the street **03** Detail cedar screen **04** Second and third floor plan **05** South elevation at rear yard **06** Interior view from entry

Photos: Michael Moore

CITY	Seattle (WA)
COUNTRY	USA
REGION	North America
TYPOLOGY	Living
COMPLETION	2006
WEBSITE	www.bcj.com
ARCHITECTS	Bohlin Cywinski Jackson

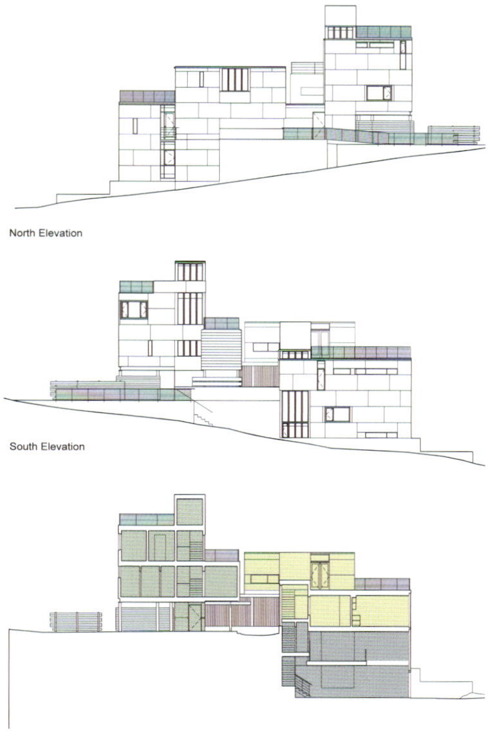

ENVELOPE SUMMER

Designed under new Seattle building regulations, this small multi-unit structure fits neatly onto its narrow urban site. The program was to develop three living units, which would maximize the investment potential of this long held property. Two articulated volumes cascade down the sloping site and shape an elevated central courtyard. Flanked by reading pods and two transparent stair volumes, the courtyard becomes a vertical garden. Small bay windows push outward like saddlebags to capture the magnificent views of Lake Union and the Seattle skyline, while casually screening neighboring properties.

01 View from central courtyard to transparent stair volume **02** Exterior view by night **03** Elevations and section **04** Detail reading pod

Photos: Nic Lehoux

SEATTLE CENTRAL LIBRARY

The ambition is to redefine the library as an information store where all potent forms of media are presented equally and legibly. A project emerges that is sensitive, the geometry providing shade or unusual quantities of daylight where desirable; contextual, each side reacting differently to specific urban conditions; and iconic. The Book Spiral liberates the librarians from the burden of managing ever-increasing masses of material, while the Mixing Chamber is an area of maximum librarian-patron interaction; a trading floor for information orchestrated to fulfill an essential need for expert interdisciplinary help.

01 Program distribution and stability diagram **02** Exterior view by night **03** Lighting as orientation aid **04** Detail platforms

Photos: Pragnesh Parikh photography, OMA / LMN Architects

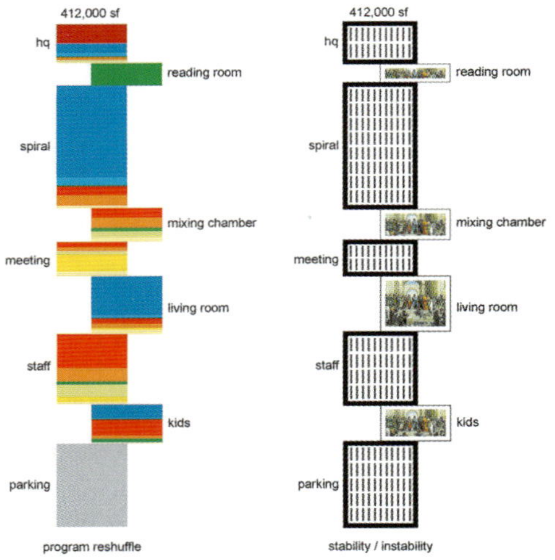

CITY Seattle (WA)
COUNTRY USA
REGION North America
TYPOLOGY Culture
COMPLETION 2004
WEBSITE www.oma.com
ARCHITECTS Office for Metropolitan Architecture (OMA), Rem Koolhaas, Ole Scheeren (in joint venture with LMN Architects)

ORCHARD HOUSE

The house is a low, single story, wheelchair accessible single family home. Sited within an apple orchard in Sonoma County, it is built using a limited set of repeated, modular concrete formwork producing a dense pattern of mass and empty space which mimics the planting pattern of its surrounding orchard. This a highly site-specific, cast concrete construction, rationally pre-fabricated through the use of formwork, and standardized SIPS sandwich panel and pre-fabricated truss framing components. This approach allows a high degree of adaptability to the landscape, while keeping construction costs to a minimum.

01 Interior living room with fireplace **02** Hallway **03** Floor plan **04** Exterior view **05** Outdoor space

Photos: Anthony Vizzari

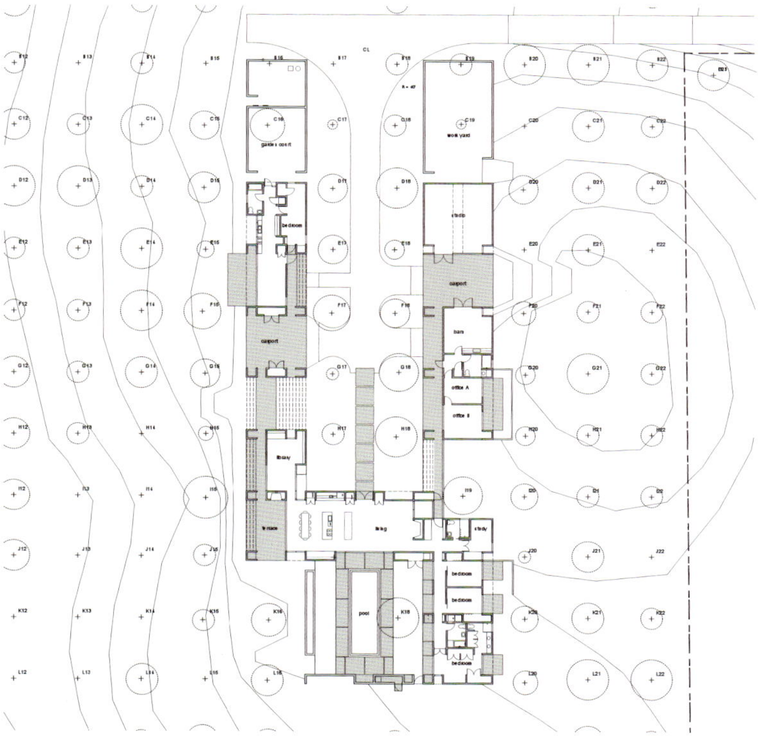

CITY Sebastopol (CA)
COUNTRY USA
REGION North America
TYPOLOGY Living
COMPLETION 2005
WEBSITE www.anderson-anderson.com
ARCHITECTS Anderson Anderson Architecture

SEBASTOPOL WINE BARN

This small structure used in the production of wine acts as an object in the landscape and an architectural boundary at one end of a parcel of land. With a single-family house at the other end it creates a landscaped precinct between the two structures. As an object, the building expresses itself in a very formalistic way through the manipulation of volume, material, and form.

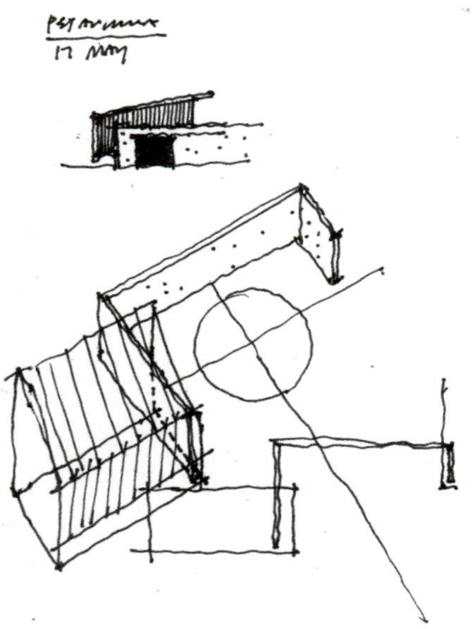

01 Rear façade **02** Façade detail **03** Outdoor dining area **04** Sketch **05** Side entrance

Photos: Matthew Millman

COR JESU ACADEMY

Cor Jesu Academy is a Catholic college preparatory high school for young women in St. Louis, Missouri. In 2005 the most recent phase of expansion was completed with a new front entrance and courtyard, and a new building, which is called Clelian Hall. Last year during 2007, the school entered into an agreement to purchase the land bordering its campus from Grant's Farm Manor owner, Andy Busch. This element and acquisition will allow Cor Jesu to not only double the size of its campus, but also allow the school to potentially expand classroom and athletic facilities.

01 Exterior view **02** Ensemble by night **03** Detail façade
04 Interior view **05** Ground and second floor plan

Photos: ArchPhotoInc/Eduard Hueber

CITY St. Louis (MO)
COUNTRY USA
REGION North America
TYPOLOGY Insitution
COMPLETION 2005
WEBSITE www.bentelandbentel.com
ARCHITECTS Bentel & Bentel, Architects

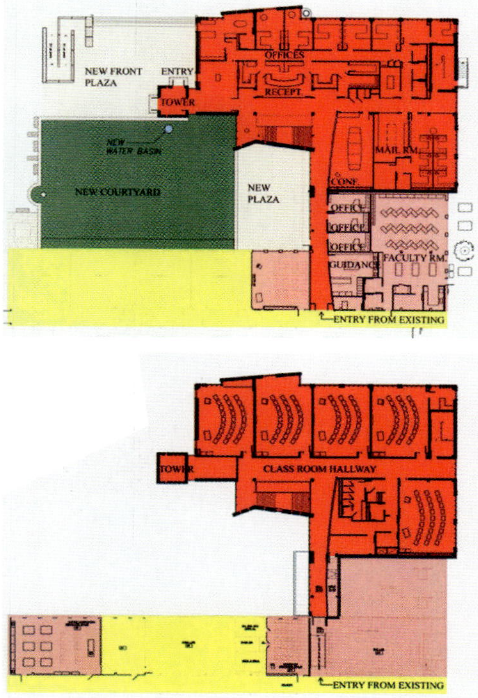

CITY
St. Louis (MO)

COUNTRY
USA

REGION
North America

TYPOLOGY
Office

COMPLETION
2006

WEBSITE
www.thelawrencegroup.com/ny

ARCHITECTS
The Lawrence Group

MOMENTUM WORLDWIDE HEADQUARTERS ST. LOUIS

The fundamental and essential idea by the planners of the Lawrence Group was to attempt at depicting and showcasing the progressively innovative Momentum brand through a sensually vivid spatial experience. The interior is designed to inspiringly stimulate creativity while continuously playing with spatial images, visual illustrations, and material interactions. The supporting element in the office's proficiently designed scheme is an amorphous and fluid band, which leads employees and guests alike throughout the workplace, creating a uniquely different environment for all those passing through.

01 Hallway **02** Lobby **03** Divided workspace **04** Detail band throughout office

Photos: Frank Oudeman Unit Photography

CONTEMPORARY ART MUSEUM SAINT LOUIS

The museum encompasses 27,000 square feet of space for exhibition, performance and education, and includes curatorial workrooms, administrative offices and public amenities. The design balances the need to provide flexible and durable spaces for exhibitions and programs with the desire to achieve maximum transparency at ground level and offer passersby views through the building. Straight-edged concrete blocks alternate with strips of glazing to create evenly lit, intimate yet inviting spaces.

01 Entrance area by night **02** Exterior view of façade **03** Floor plan **04** Open exhibition space

Photos: Helene Binet

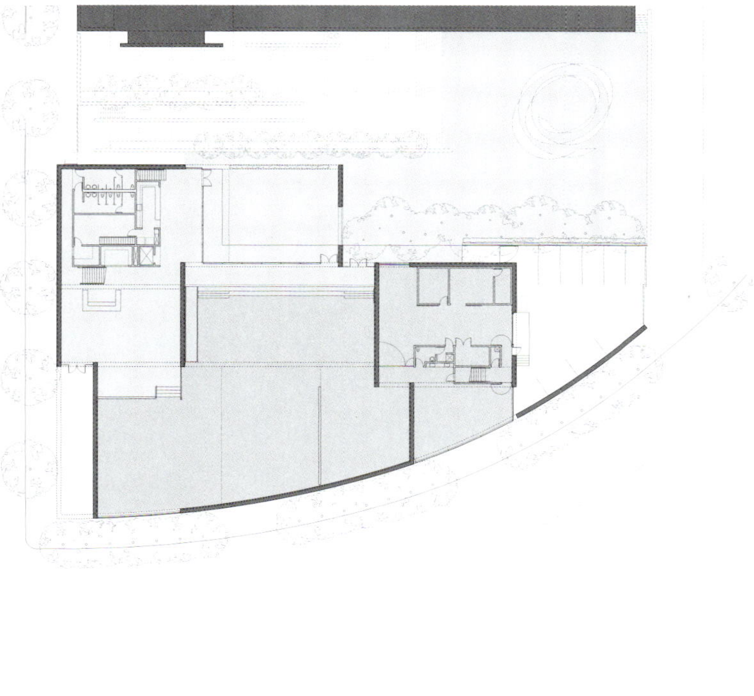

CITY St. Louis (MO)
COUNTRY USA
REGION North America
TYPOLOGY Culture
COMPLETION 2007
WEBSITE www.alliedworks.com
ARCHITECTS Allied Works Architecture

CITY Topeka (KS)

COUNTRY USA

REGION North America

TYPOLOGY Industry

COMPLETION 2007

WEBSITE www.eldoradoarchitects.com

ARCHITECTS El dorado Architects

A NEW DISTRIBUTION CENTER FOR COX COMMUNICATIONS

When asked to design a new Distribution Center for Cox Communications in Topeka, Kansas, El dorado developed straight-forward, yet elegant strategies, elevating basic warehouse construction to innovative, sustainable design. A large roof overhang protects the south facing corrugated galvalume skin from the hot Kansas summer sun, while linear operable vents activate a convection cooling system allowing cooler air to enter at floor level, forcing hot air to exit the building through large roof vents. Integrated fluorescent lighting provides the interior and exterior with soft, efficient ambient lighting.

01 West elevation **02** View from the street **03** Detail corrugated façade **04** View from southwest

Photos: Mike Sinclair

ROBBINS ELEMENTARY SCHOOL

The Robbins Elementary School project articulates itself around the existing historic school building, as it extends towards a new green space positioned on the south edge of the proposed site. This space is seen as an outdoor resource for the school, as well as a potential fragment within a system of small parks in the neighborhood. The presence of this operable open space strengthens the role of the Elementary School as a primary hub for the local community. Our proposal envisions an open-campus composed by a system of 5 finger-like and 3 discreet buildings, which extend to the proposed Garden.

01 The 5 finger-like new buildings **02** Passage historic building/extension **03** View of ensemble **04** Courtyard
Photos: Courtesy Urban Office Architecture

CITY: Trenton (NJ)
COUNTRY: USA
REGION: North America
TYPOLOGY: Education
COMPLETION: unbuilt
WEBSITE: www.uoa-architecture.com
ARCHITECTS: Urban Office Architecture

CITY
Tribeca (NY)

COUNTRY
USA

REGION
North America

TYPOLOGY
Living

COMPLETION
2002

WEBSITE
www.samtrimble.com

ARCHITECTS
Sam Trimble Design

ROBERT'S RESIDENCE

An urban cave inspired by descriptions of the geological phenomenon of tectonic caves is the thought for this project. Originally designed as a gallery for a minimalist art collection, the owner decided to make the space itself a statement with almost no art installed. The space consists of a penthouse with skylights and terraces, while walls and floors in honed limestone slabs are polished on plaster ceiling. All air conditioning, lighting controls, and electrical receptacles are integrated and invisible. A 1000 pound vanity has a custom waterfall faucet with gradual temperature gradiant from cold to hot across the waterfall.

01 View from dining room to gallery **02** Upper level study area **03** Bedroom **04** View from bathroom towards dressing room **05** Floor plan

Photos: Paul Warchol Photography

TAMPA

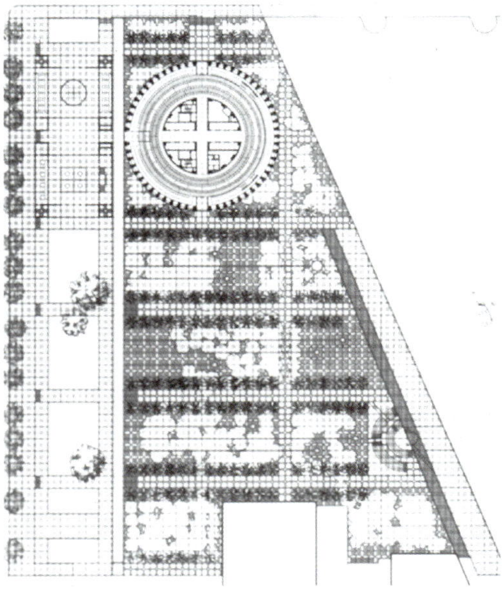

This 660,000-square-foot, 33-story tall office structure includes 12,000 square feet of public space banking halls, a three-acre public park, and a 225-car garage. The client's principal concern was to create an iconic structure to convey the significance of a major bank corporate headquarters, within the budgetary constraints and functional efficiencies of an investment office building. The office tower, located at a pivotal point in the fabric of the city, takes the form of a cylinder – the archetypal tower – evoking the metaphors of lighthouse and citadel tower guarding the entrance to the city.

01 Tower ensemble **02** Lobby **03** Site plan **04** Bird's eye view of roof and environment **05** Bird's eye view of lobby

Photos: R. Alexander (01), Eric Oxendorf (02), C. Robinson (04, 05)

CITY	Tampa (FL)
COUNTRY	USA
REGION	North America
TYPOLOGY	Office
COMPLETION	-
WEBSITE	www.wolfarc.com
ARCHITECTS	Wolf Architecture

TOPANGA RANCH

Located in the hot and dry landscape of Southern California's coastal canyons, the Topanga Ranch investigates alternative approaches of living in relation to the land. Out of the site's hillside topography, a series of narrow contours and wider plateaus emerge, articulated as the generating lines for the project. The house's lower zone, constructed of concrete, is conceived as being of the earth, covered by a planted roof, making its extend ambiguously beneath the ground. In contrast to the earth level, the residence sits lightly above the land, conceived as a device for viewing and engaging the landscape.

01 Wrapped in terra-cotta colored roofing membrane **02** Floor plans **03** View from southwest **04** Living and dining room **05** Embedded in the landscape

Photos: Eric Staudenmaier Photography

CITY: Topanga (CA)
COUNTRY: USA
REGION: North America
TYPOLOGY: Living
COMPLETION: 2006
WEBSITE: www.agps.ch
ARCHITECTS: agps architecture

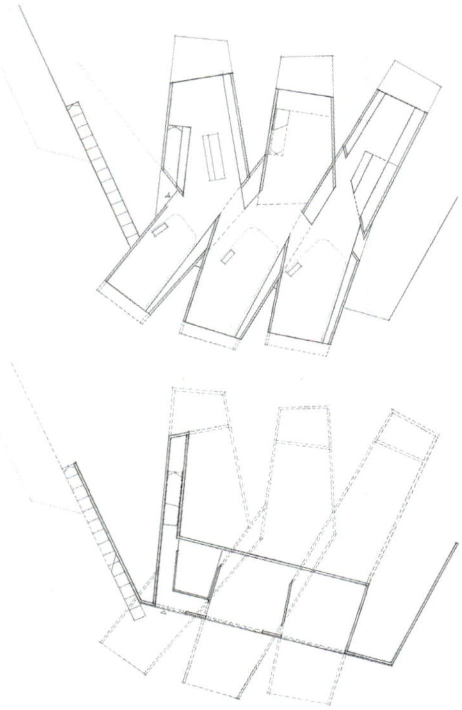

CHIHULY BRIDGE OF GLASS

The project is a 500-foot-long pedestrian bridge linking downtown Tacoma, Washington, to the city's waterfront; the Thea Foss Waterway. Conceived by Dale Chihuly, artist and native of Tacoma, the bridge is a display of color and form soaring 70 feet into the air. Commissioned by the Museum of Glass, International Center for Contemporary Art, the bridge was a gift from the museum to the city of Tacoma. It crosses Interstate 705, linking the Washington State History Museum with the Museum of Glass. The collaboration between artist and architect evolved, as did their thinking of the size and character of the bridge installations.

01 Bridge with art and wall displays **02** Detail **03** Side view
04 Bridge display

Photos: Timothy Hursley

CITY Tacoma (WA)
COUNTRY USA
REGION North America
TYPOLOGY Culture
COMPLETION 2003
WEBSITE www.anderssonwise.com
ARCHITECTS Andersson·Wise Architects, in collaboration with artist Dale Chihuly

CITY: Town of Hillsdale (NY)
COUNTRY: USA
REGION: North America
TYPOLOGY: Living
COMPLETION: 2007
WEBSITE: www.dbnyc.com
ARCHITECTS: Della Valle Bernheimer

COPPER HOUSE

Clad almost entirely in corrugated copper siding and copper roofing, the skin of the house will age and develop a patina that reflects time through material change. The three-bedroom house features distinctive, sculpted south-facing skylights that allow light into various public and private spaces. The ground floor contains two bedrooms, living room, dining room, kitchen and a home office. A 30-ft bookshelf runs the length of the ground floor, delineating the rooms while retaining visual connections across the various spaces. The 2nd floor master bedroom, playroom and attic have windows that overlook the skylights.

01 Corrugated copper façade **02** Exterior view **03** Dining room **04** Living space **05** Floor plans

Photos: Richard Barnes

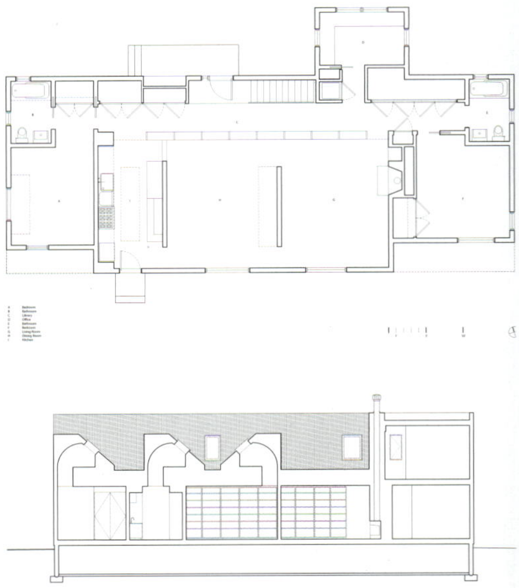

THE BIODESIGN INSTITUTE AT ARIZONA STATE UNIVERSITY, BUILDING B

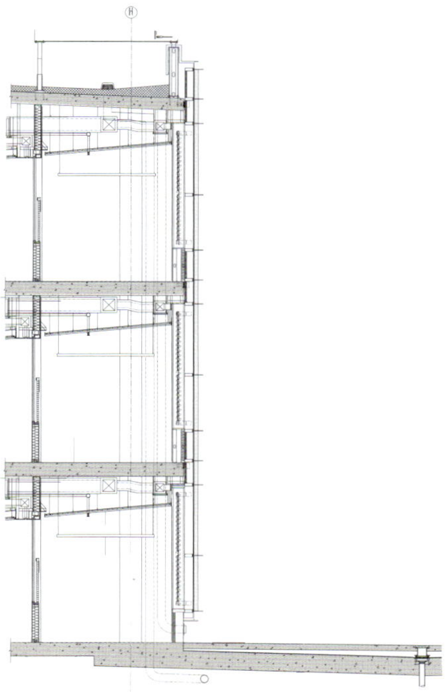

The project is a state-of-the-art research facility that houses the vanguard of contemporary science, bridging across discip s of industry, government and academia. Envisioned as a world-class demonstration of ecological laboratory design, interdisciplinary research is at the heart of the Institute's strategy and serves as inspiration for the building design to enhance the Institute's value, mission and culture. Green design features range from site and urban planning to interior finishes, in which Building "A" received LEED Gold Certification, while Building "B" became the first LEED Platinum building in Arizona.

01 Exterior view from north **02** Interior view, atrium **03** Section east façade **04** Exterior view from northeast

Photos: Mark Boisclair

CITY Tempe (AZ)
COUNTRY USA
REGION North America
TYPOLOGY Institution
COMPLETION 2004 / 2005
WEBSITE www.gouldevans.com, www.lordaecksargent.com
ARCHITECTS Gould Evans (in collaboration with Lord Aeck Sargent)

CITY
Tempe (AZ)

COUNTRY
USA

REGION
North America

TYPOLOGY
Education

COMPLETION
2003

WEBSITE
www.architekton.com

ARCHITECTS
Architekton
chandler-gilbert

CHANDLER-GILBERT COMMUNITY COLLEGE STUDENT CENTER

The new Student Center, located at the intersection of major pedestrian malls, has become the "new heart" of student activity accommodating a broad range of uses. Architectural detailing and dramatic lighting of the pavilion-like form create a lantern, shining in the night, further enhancing the facility as the social hub of campus activity and life.

01 Shade louvers become colorful lanterns at night **02** Porch reaches out to engage campus **03** Solar shade veil protects student pavilion below **04** Pavilion interior

Photos: Timmermann Photography, Michael T. Masengarb (04)

TEMPE CENTER FOR THE ARTS, TEMPE, ARIZONA

The Tempe Center for the Arts is an 88,000-square-foot performing and visual arts center, including a 600-seat main theater, 200-seat flexible theater, gallery and multi-purpose room, café and arts park. The Center's design draws upon significant historic, climatic, and contextual traditions for inspiration; meanwhile, it utilizes modern technology to create outstanding performance and exhibition spaces. On the exterior, a curved concrete wall serves to enclose and unify the main building, while a sculptural shed roof provides necessary acoustical and solar protection.

01 Front façade **02** Exterior view by night **03** Main floor plan **04** Theater

Photos: Michael Masengarb, John Edward Linden (01)

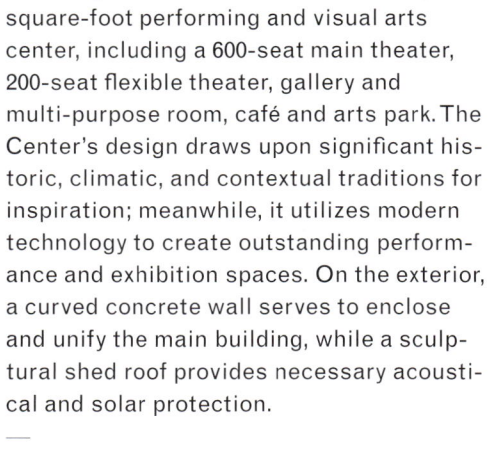

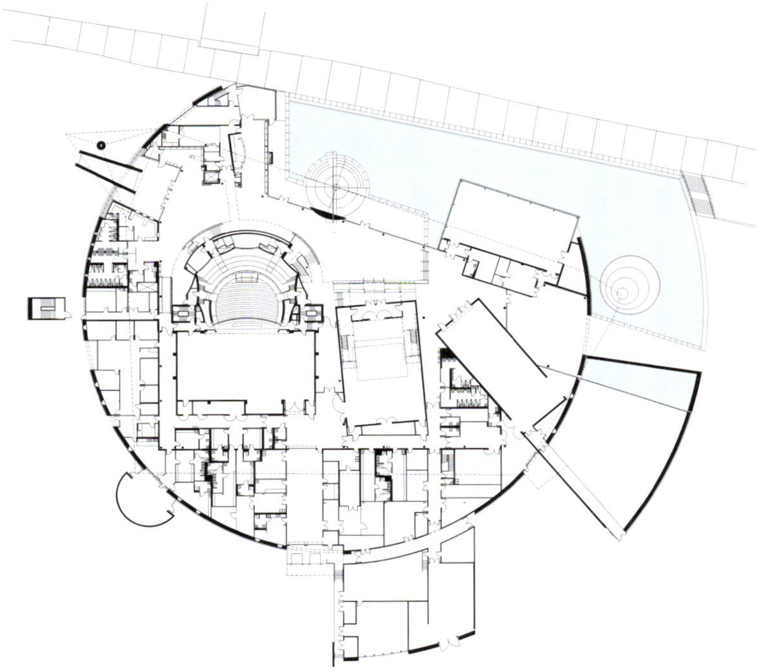

CITY Tempe (AZ)
COUNTRY USA
REGION North America
TYPOLOGY Culture
COMPLETION 2007
WEBSITE www.bartonmyers.com
ARCHITECTS Barton Myers Associates Inc. + Architekton

CITY Tempe (AZ)
COUNTRY USA
REGION North America
TYPOLOGY Living
COMPLETION unbuilt
WEBSITE www.circlewest.net
ARCHITECTS Circle West

LANDSOURCE TEMPE

The basis of the building design was to develop a vertically integrated neighborhood, with an emphasis on identity, connectivity to neighbors, and gathering spaces. A prominent, articulated entry and lobby at ground level highlights the transparency to the street, while live/work environments reinforce the vertically integrated neighborhood. The "green roof" over the three story parking deck, is utilized as an amenities deck, providing a community gathering space that includes appropriate desert landscaping, shade, and a swimming pool.

01 Lobby **02** Exterior view by night **03** Community space: swimming pool **04** Detail living unit

Renderings: Circle West

INTERDISCIPLINARY SCIENCE + TECHNOLOGY BUILDING 2 – ARIZONA STATE UNIVERSITY

Reflecting its purpose as an engineering and research facility, the Interdisciplinary Science & Tech primary building systems are exposed within the centralized courtyard flanked by open flexible loft lab spaces. This configuration minimizes penetrations and fixed elements in the lab plan maximizing flexibility and adaptability. In response to the harsh desert climate and the need for material movement to the labs, the building's linear shaded courtyard, 280 feet in length and over 60 feet in height, is enclosed by perforated corten steel panels, providing a balance of natural daylight and filtered shade.

01 Front façade **02** Staircase and circulation ways **03** Interior view, between the labs **04** Central court **05** Section

Photos: Bill Timmerman Photography

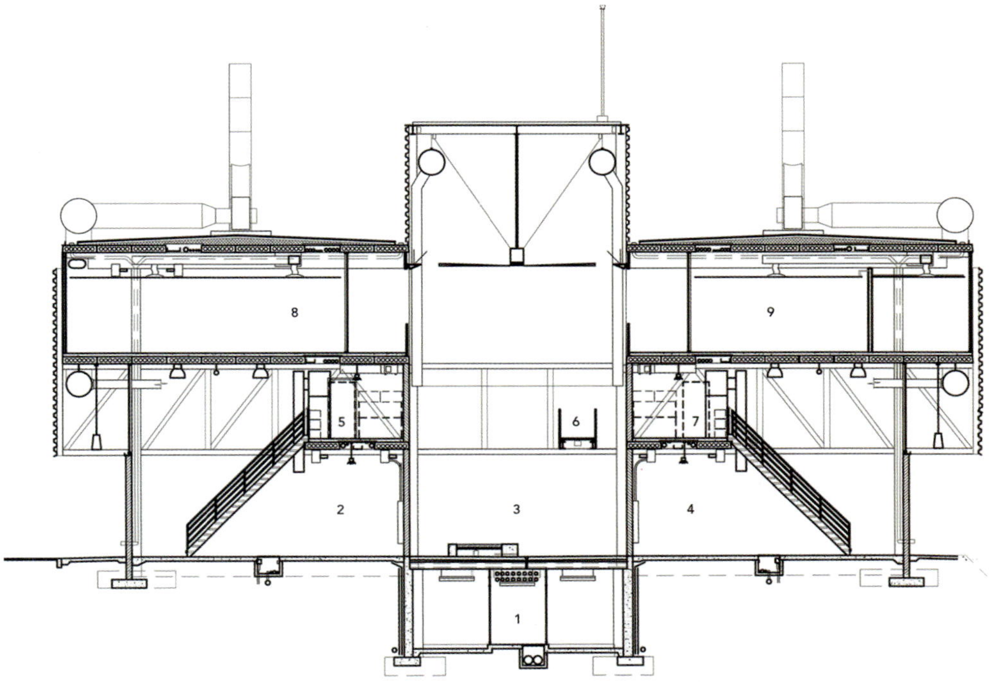

CITY Tempe (AZ)
COUNTRY USA
REGION North America
TYPOLOGY Education
COMPLETION 2004
WEBSITE www.richard+bauer.com
ARCHITECTS richärd+bauer

CITY: Tucson (AZ)
COUNTRY: USA
REGION: North America
TYPOLOGY: Public
COMPLETION: 2002
WEBSITE: www.architekton.com
ARCHITECTS: Architekton + GLHN

PATRICK K. HARDESTY MIDTOWN MULTICENTER-SERVICE CENTER

The dramatic form of the City of Tucson's highly visible new police substation is intended to invoke imagery of nearby desert rock formations, while responding to the site's location within 100-year floodplain. The wall serves as both figural and literal separation between public functions and secured police activities and is penetrated by the form of the public meeting room. With vertical and horizontal shading elements to the south and east the design was basically influenced by the desert climate.

01 Flag balcony **02** Accessible ramp integrated in rusted metal façade **03** Public meeting room **04** Main level floor plan **05** Exterior view by night

Photos: Timmermann Photography

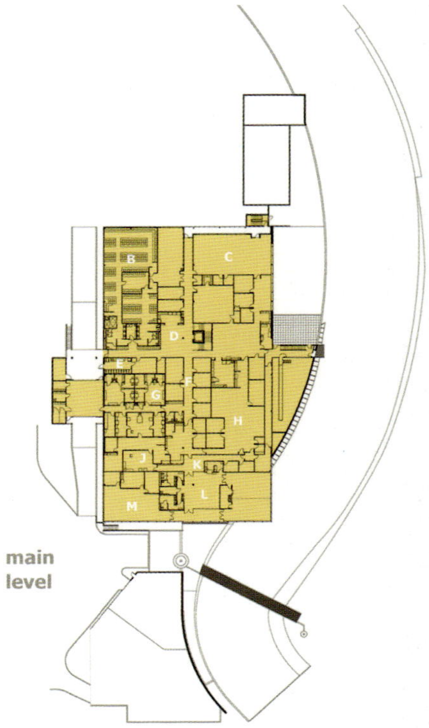

WINTER RESIDENCE

The owners of the Winter Residence wanted to transform their dark, circulation-dominated 1940's brick residence into a luminous space reminiscent of the boutique hotels and spas they had visited. Using the metaphor of a cloud resting gently on a hill, Ibarra Rosano Design Architects took an approach of simplification and reduction. The key to liberating the plan, improving flow and introducing daylight was to remove the bulky fireplace that bisected the living spaces. The interior is now reintegrated with the exterior through courtyards that provide privacy, shelter and frame distant views.

01 Outdoor space with pool and fireplace **02** Entry view **03** Floor plan **04** Living space with skylight

Photos: Bill Timmerman

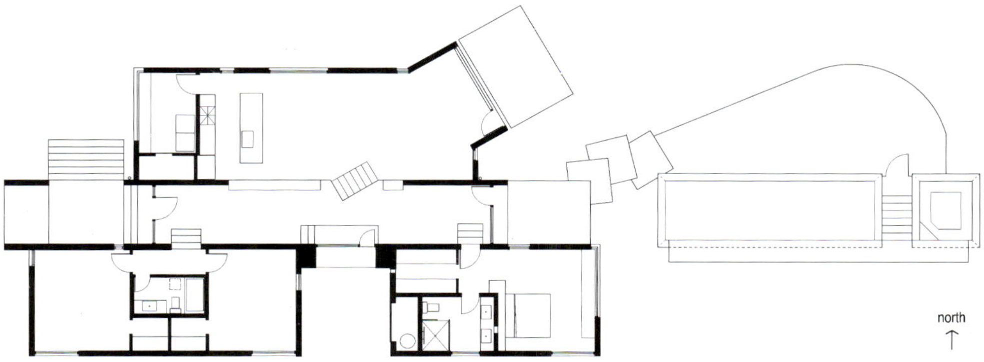

CITY Tucson (AZ)
COUNTRY USA
REGION North America
TYPOLOGY Living
COMPLETION 2005
WEBSITE www.ibarrarosano.com
ARCHITECTS Ibarra Rosano Design Architects

CITY Tucson (AZ)

COUNTRY USA

REGION North America

TYPOLOGY Living

COMPLETION 2007

WEBSITE www.robpaulus.com

ARCHITECTS Rob Paulus Architects

INDIGO MODERN

IndigoMODERN is an eleven-unit infill project that emphasizes simple form with "responsible density". A maximized unit count, per local zoning, separates vehicle from residence, organizing a sustainable community along a central circulation axis. Native landscaped in-between spaces, irrigated by harvested rain, become habitable slot canyons, which is a welcome reprieve in the desert climate. Highly insulated enclosures of recyclable materials, combined with efficient glazing and mechanical systems, have achieved that units be up to 51% more energy efficient than the national average.

01 Metal framing **02** Detail **03** Interior staircase **04** Section

Photos: Ross Cooperthwaite – Cooperthwaite Photography

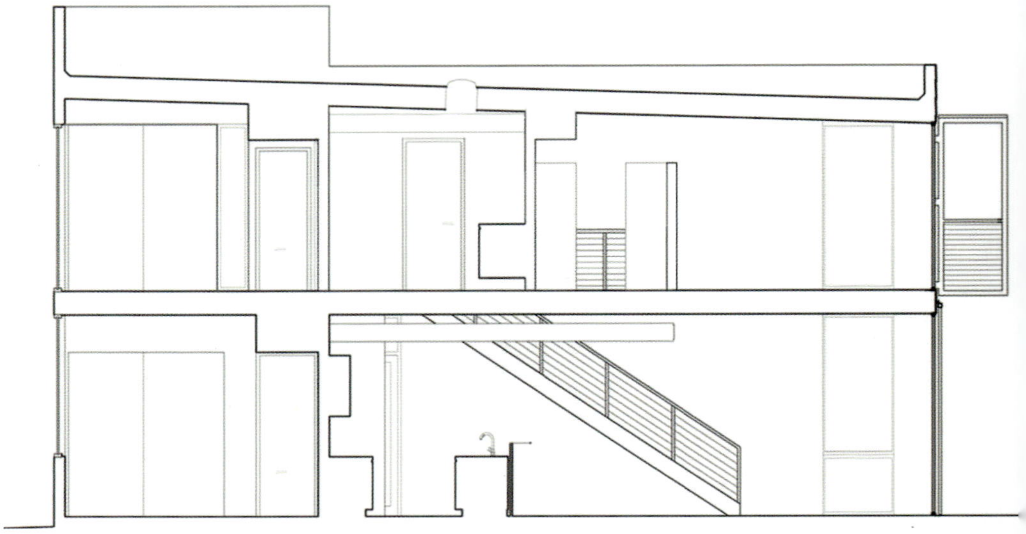

MEINEL OPTICAL SCIENCES BUILDING - UNIVERSITY OF ARIZONA

The Meinel Building is a study of light, where it's form is conceived from the Camera Obscura. The design demonstrates the power that light possesses in illuminating the experience inside of the building. Within the simple volume, daylight is introduced through a series of apertures, interacting and modulating the spaces within. Three vertical light shafts penetrate the building and terminate in a series of 2-story interaction spaces. Each shaft features a specific optical effect rendered in a white veneer plaster, allowing natural daylight to actively integrate into the daily activities of the building.

01 Fully glazed façade **02** View into interior **03** Atrium **04** Copper façade

Photos: Bill Timmerman Photography

CITY: Tucson (AZ)
COUNTRY: USA
REGION: North America
TYPOLOGY: Education
COMPLETION: 2007
WEBSITE: www.richard-bauer.com
ARCHITECTS: richard+bauer

CITY
Tucson (AZ)

COUNTRY
USA

REGION
North America

TYPOLOGY
Living

COMPLETION
2007

WEBSITE
www.ibarrarosano.com

ARCHITECTS
Ibarra Rosano Design Architects for Dreamspace, LLC

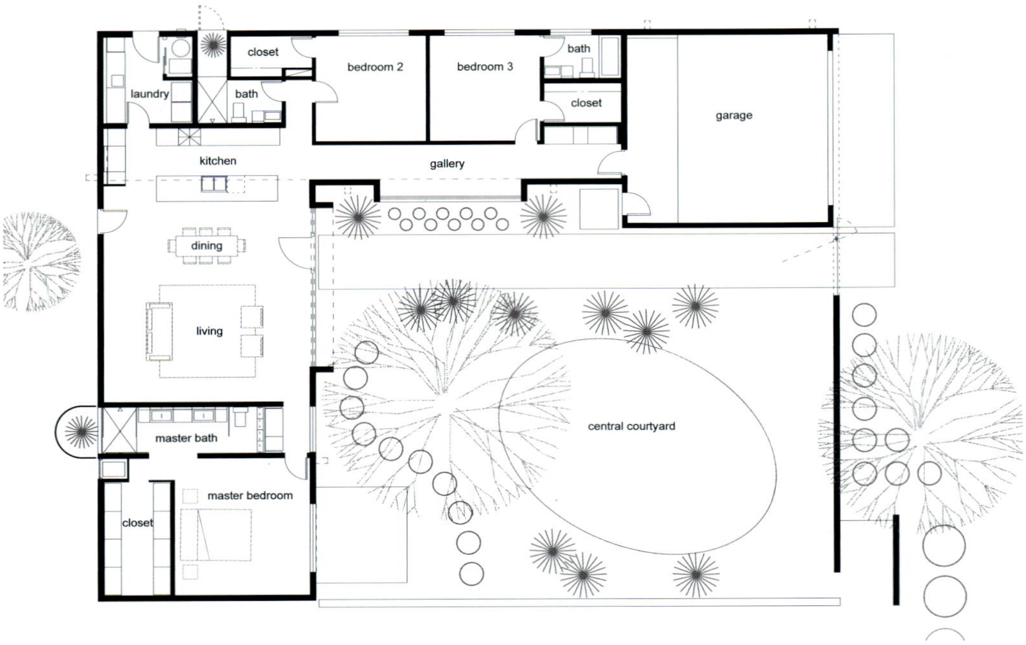

THE SIX

The Six is an urban infill project comprised of six courtyard houses. Each house's primary living spaces open onto a central courtyard, while the more intimate bathing areas extend into landscaped light wells inviting the interior spaces to expand into private ones and secure exterior enclosures, blurring the line between inside and out. While the Six takes cues from Tucson's architectural past and the neighboring historic adobe house with its central courtyard, plastered masonry walls, and minimal western exposure, it is also an emphatic expression of our time and place in future history.

01 Floor plan **02** Living space **03** Exterior view **04** View from street into courtyard **05** Dining room

Photos: Bill Timmerman

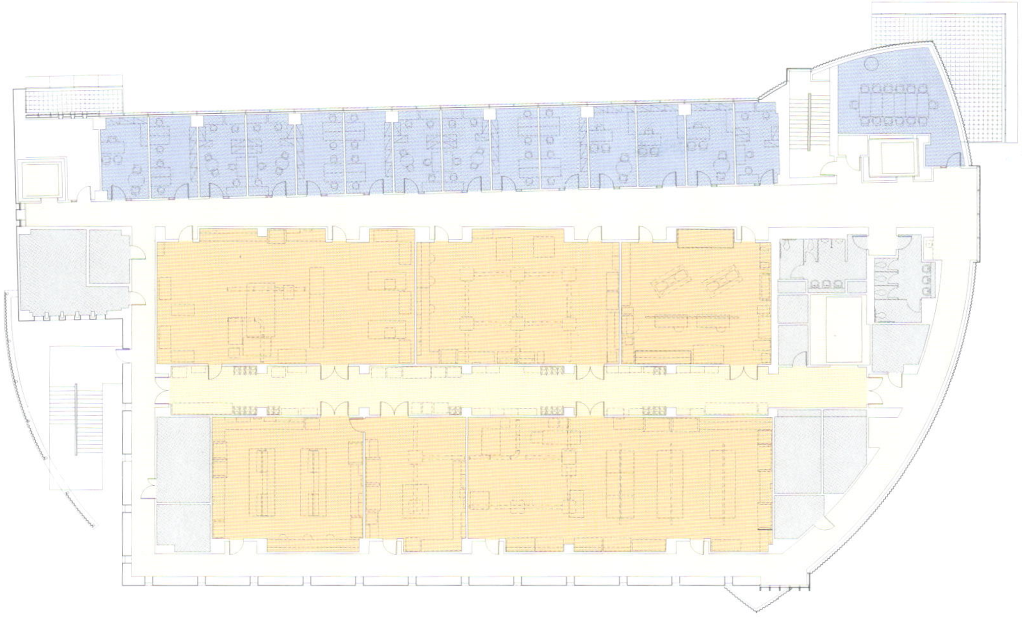

THE UNIVERSITY OF ARIZONA, CHEMICAL SCIENCES BUILDING

ZGF programmed and designed a new 85,661 sq ft laboratory building to house the Department of Chemistry. Program areas include organic, inorganic, analytical and physical chemistry research laboratories and supporting spaces, a class 1000 cleanroom, instrument laboratories, faculty and student offices, and administrative support spaces. Brick, a traditional building material on campus, was used primarily, updated with glass and copper. Conference room and corridor windows are covered by a copper skin, which is perforated to provide sun protection while allowing natural daylight into the spaces.

01 Floor plan 02 Brick and perforated copper façade 03 Garden 04 Courtyard 05 Laboratory 06 Conference room

Photos: Robert Canfield

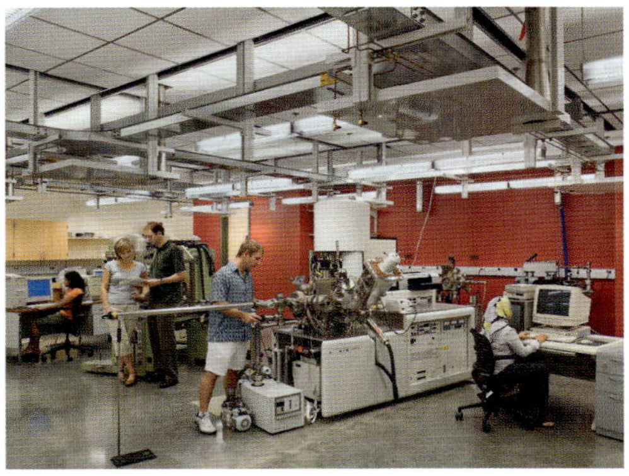

CITY: Tucson (AZ)
COUNTRY: USA
REGION: North America
TYPOLOGY: Education
COMPLETION: 2006
WEBSITE: www.zgf.com
ARCHITECTS: Zimmer Gunsul Frasca Architects LLP

CITY
Tucson (AZ)

COUNTRY
USA

REGION
North America

TYPOLOGY
Living

COMPLETION
2001 (house), 2003 (pool)

WEBSITE
www.ibarrarosano.com

ARCHITECTS
Ibarra Rosano Design Architects

GARCIA RESIDENCE

The site is a north-facing slope in the foothills of the Tucson Mountains with views of city lights and the surrounding mountains. The challenge was to design a structure that would appear to grow out of the rocky desert hillside without dominating the landscape. The house is set on an axis parallel with the site contours, creating three narrow bays that terrace up the hill, allowing excavation to be kept to a minimum. The terracing platforms contain the three zones of the house: living, circulating and sleeping. The entry "gallery" in the middle bay functions as both, circulation and as an extension of the living spaces.

01 Infinity pool 02 Exterior view by night 03 View to the Tucson mountains 04 Interior 05 Floor plan 06 Sections

Photos: Bill Timmerman

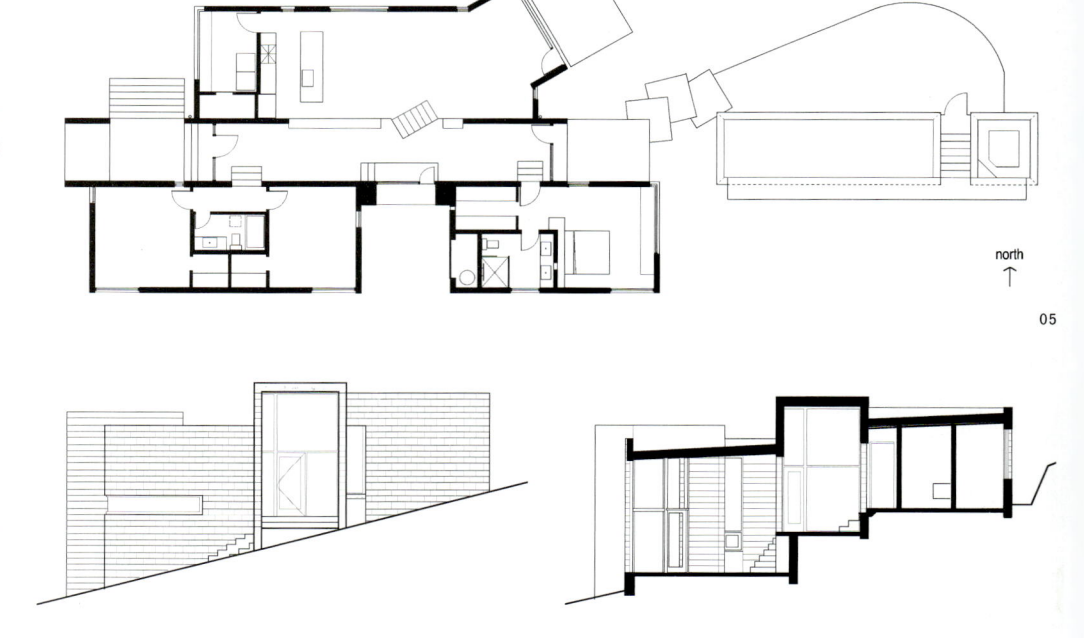

DOWNING RESIDENCE

The Downing Residence is a carefully nested desert dwelling on a hillside west of Tucson organized between existing saguaros. The 3,500-square-foot design splits the floor plan into three smaller pavilion-like footprints in order to rest more gently between areas of dense vegetation. From a distance, the Downing Residence is barely discernable from its east-facing mountainside backdrop. The structure blends with the surrounding rock outcroppings as each of its three volumes sits reverently within a grove of saguaro that dot the hillside.

01 Exterior view **02** Infinity pool with view to mountains **03** Kichen **04** Living space **05** Bathroom

Photos: Bill Timmerman

CITY Tucson (AZ)
COUNTRY USA
REGION North America
TYPOLOGY Living
COMPLETION 2003
WEBSITE www.ibarrarosano.com
ARCHITECTS Ibarra Rosano Design Architects

NEWFIELD HOUSE

The Newfield House project is located on 14-acres of dense forestry in upstate New York, where a residence for a couple is carefully positioned and thoroughly situated in the landscape to take full and complete advantage of extensive views, sunlight, and the nature that engulfs the home. Concluding with the construction of a garage at one end, while an outdoor terrace can be seen on the other, the house is organized in such a way forming a long rectangular bar. The spaces are set up and deployed within an open plan arrangement using such features as the cabinetry and bathroom cores in order to define separation.

01 Interior view, living room **02** Detail façade **03** Exterior view **04** Floor plan and elevation

Photos: Jon Reis Photo + Design

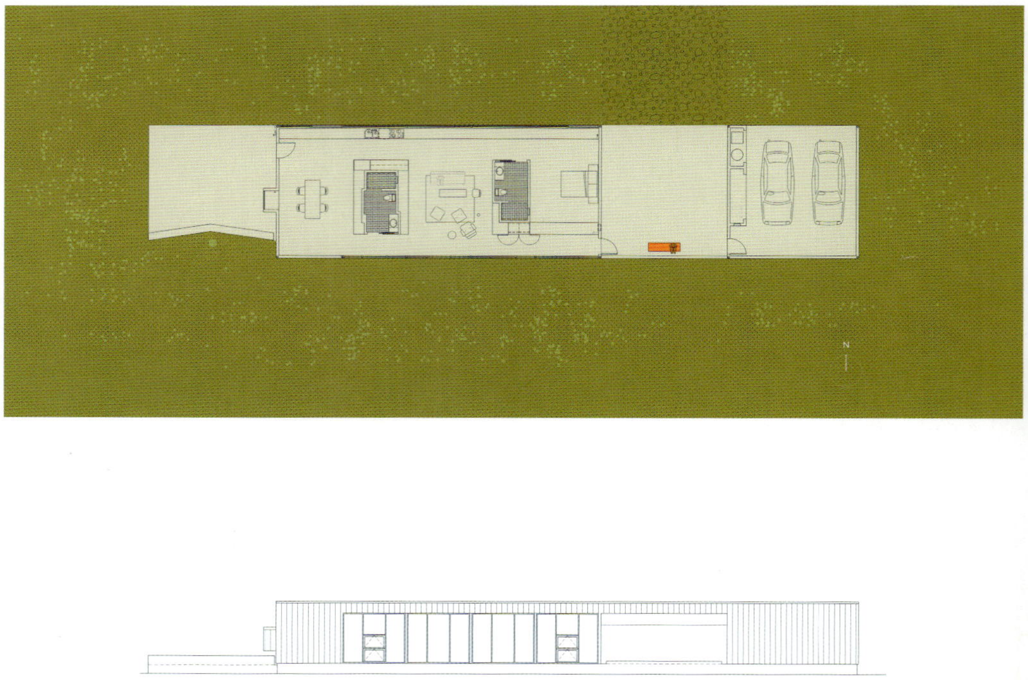

HOUSE IN UPSTATE NEW YORK

Nestled on a ten-acre site in Upstate New York, this weekend residence takes advance of the surrounding landscape as it cantilevers into the treetops and towards the view. The only way to approach the home is through the woods on foot. The main entrance is the open courtyard, which leads from beneath the cantilever directly up into the core of the house and to the roof deck. The open plan design calls for living room walls that dematerialize and become transparent, further framing the view and bringing the outdoors in. Its poetry is in the age-old dialogue between nature and architecture, and in the delicate balance where the two meet.

01 Exterior view 02 Entrance from open courtyard 03 Ground and first floor plan 04 Living room 05 Interior view

Photos: Focus Photography, Seth Boyd Photography

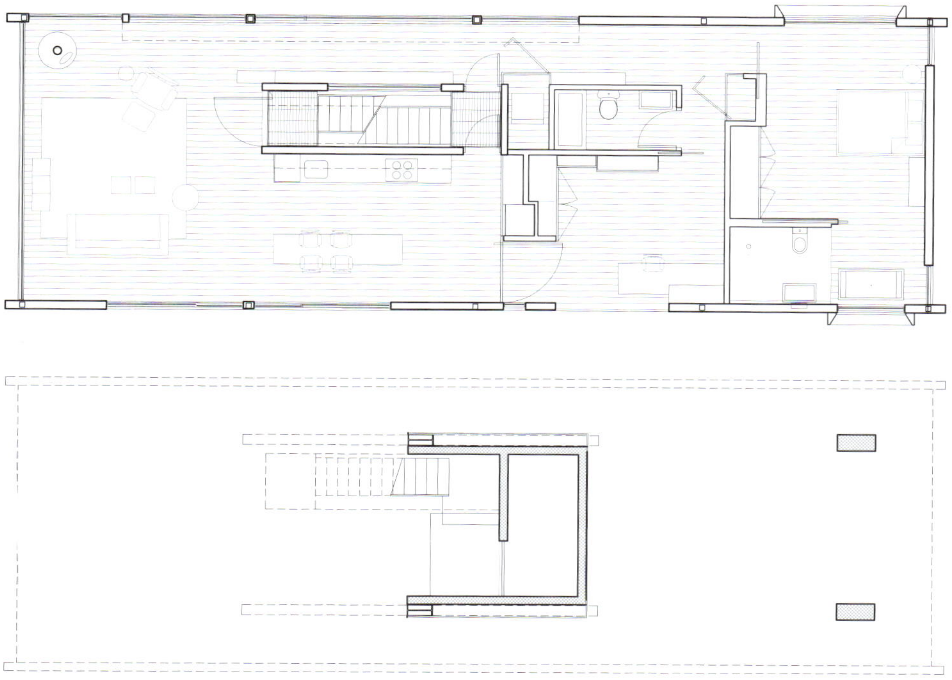

CITY
Upstate New York (NY)

COUNTRY
USA

REGION
North America

TYPOLOGY
Living

COMPLETION
2005

WEBSITE
www.guardiaarchitects.com

ARCHITECTS
guardia architects

CITY
Ventura (CA)

COUNTRY
USA

REGION
North America

TYPOLOGY
Living

COMPLETION
2005

WEBSITE
www.designarc.com

ARCHITECTS
DesignARC

MUSSEL SHOALS HOUSE

Located at a critical juncture of the California coastline between Los Angeles and Santa Barbara, the project responds to the significant constraints of a paucity of budget and a requirement to secure the house against storm and absence. The result is a confident and self-effacing home that defers to the repose and tranquility of the sea while providing a place of quiet respite for the client. The introduction of rolling sunshades and storm doors complete the house's protective layering, fending off the depredations of sun, salt air, and rogue surfers, while allowing variability in living space based on weather conditions.

01 Rear façade with sunshades and storm doors **02** View from street **03** Living room **04** Bathroom

Photos: Benny Chan, Fotoworks

VICTORVILLE CITY HALL

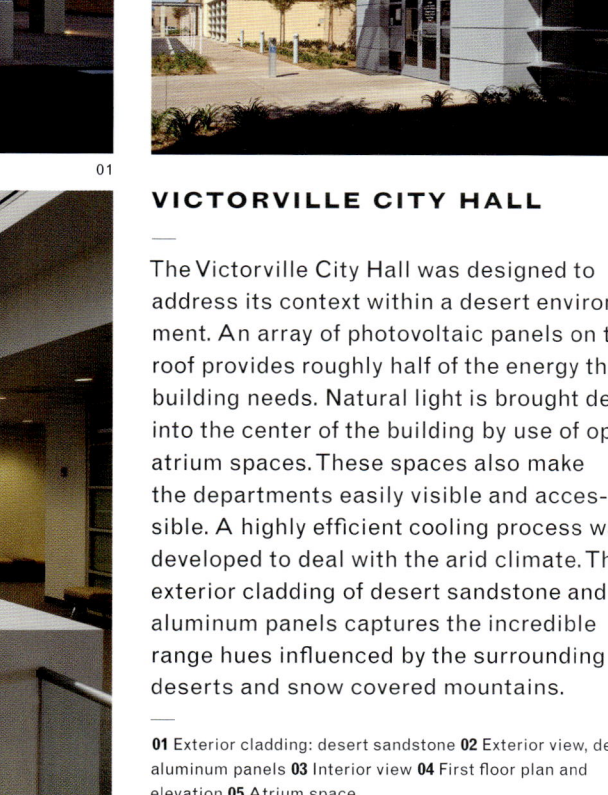

The Victorville City Hall was designed to address its context within a desert environment. An array of photovoltaic panels on the roof provides roughly half of the energy the building needs. Natural light is brought deep into the center of the building by use of open atrium spaces. These spaces also make the departments easily visible and accessible. A highly efficient cooling process was developed to deal with the arid climate. The exterior cladding of desert sandstone and aluminum panels captures the incredible range hues influenced by the surrounding deserts and snow covered mountains.

01 Exterior cladding: desert sandstone **02** Exterior view, detail aluminum panels **03** Interior view **04** First floor plan and elevation **05** Atrium space

Photos: Tom Bonner Photography

CITY
Victorville (CA)

COUNTRY
USA

REGION
North America

TYPOLOGY
Institution

COMPLETION
2007

WEBSITE
www.tagarch.net
www.rachlinarchitects.com

ARCHITECTS
Albert+Rachlin Architects

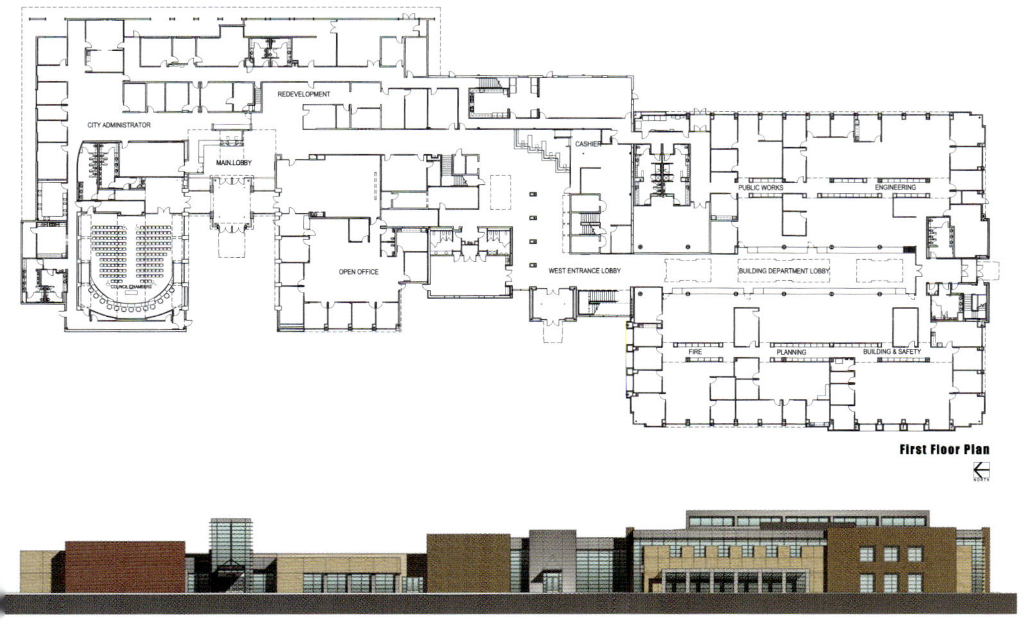

CITY Venice (CA)

COUNTRY USA

REGION North America

TYPOLOGY Living

COMPLETION 2004

WEBSITE www.s-ehrlich.com

ARCHITECTS Steven Ehrlich Architects

700 PALMS

The lively bohemian spirit of Venice, California, is expressed within urban residential constraints in this project. The design maximizes volume, light, and privacy on a narrow lot sensitive to the scale of its eclectic neighborhood of beach bungalows a half mile from the Pacific Ocean. Raw, honest materials fit the grittiness of the environment; the maintenance-free exterior of Corten steel, Trex, copper, and stucco weathers naturally, while interior surfaces are left unpainted. The wood-and-steel frame structure is outlined by a steel exoskeleton, while the juxtaposition of confined and monumental rooms animates the design.

01 East view **02** Living space **03** Cor-ten steel façade and pool view **04** Elevations and sections **05** Glazed wall

Photos: 700 Palms: Erhard Pfeiffer, Grey Crawford (03, 05)

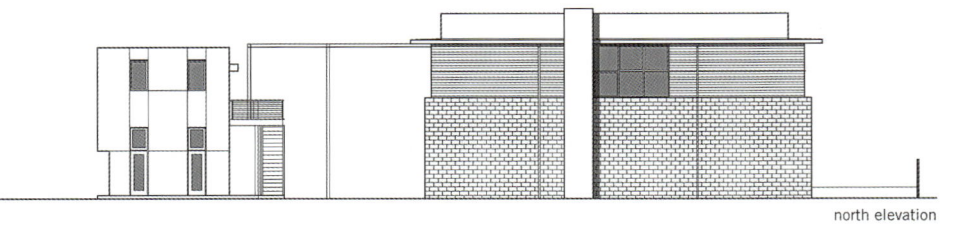

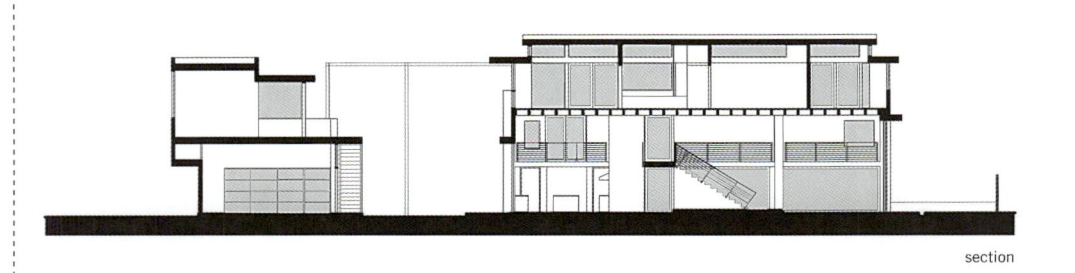

7TEN PROJECT

7ten Project is a sustainable spec house and the first non-prefab LEED house in California. The approach to the design was to express its sustainability boldly and honestly. The second floor volume tilts (in its entirety) toward the southerly solar orientation to charge roof top solar panels, which provide complete independence from the grid for electricity and hot water. Framing and stairs are made with recycled wood, as are stair treads and the kitchen island eating bar. Skylights run along the center of the house for light and ventilation, and are on sensors that allow them to open when the temperature requires it.

01 Floor plans **02** Interior view **03** Front façade **04** Recycled wood stair **05** Section and elevation

Photos: Courtesy of GRAYmatter Architecture

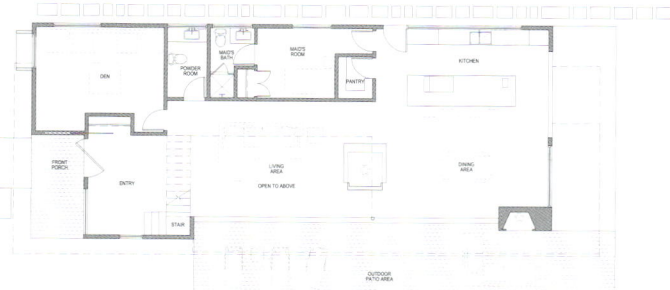

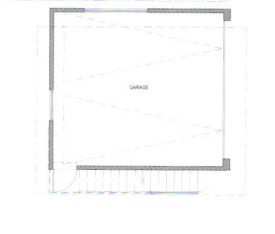

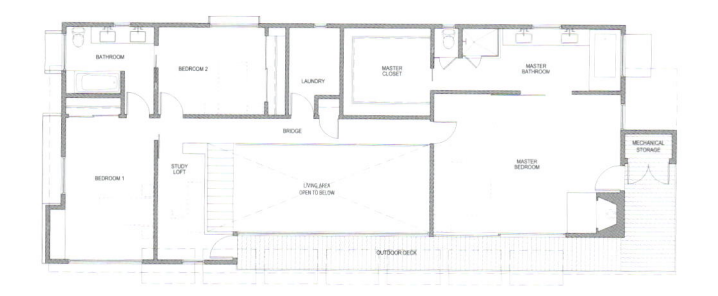

CITY Venice (CA)
COUNTRY USA
REGION North America
TYPOLOGY Living
COMPLETION —
WEBSITE www.graymatterarchitecture.com
ARCHITECTS GRAYmatter Architecture

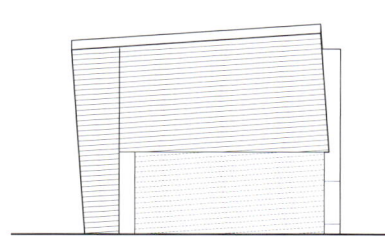

CITY Venice (CA)
COUNTRY USA
REGION North America
TYPOLOGY Office
COMPLETION 2005
WEBSITE www.montalbaarchitects.com
ARCHITECTS Montalba Architects, Inc.

VENICE PROPERTIES

Supportive of a busy workplace, ideas of light, volume, and precise proportion come together in the design of the open office environment. The design celebrates a collective workspace by merging volumes of public and private space to create a cohesive area where different activities can take place. A two-story gallery, quiet loft, and vibrant kitchen/conference area are spatially defined by custom millwork and steel components. In the main office area, material surfaces with varying levels of texture and transparency work together to create illusions of contrast and depth.

01 Interior structural detail **02** Exterior view **03** Kitchen **04** Entry and two-story gallery **05** Upper level floor plan

Photos: Marvin Rand

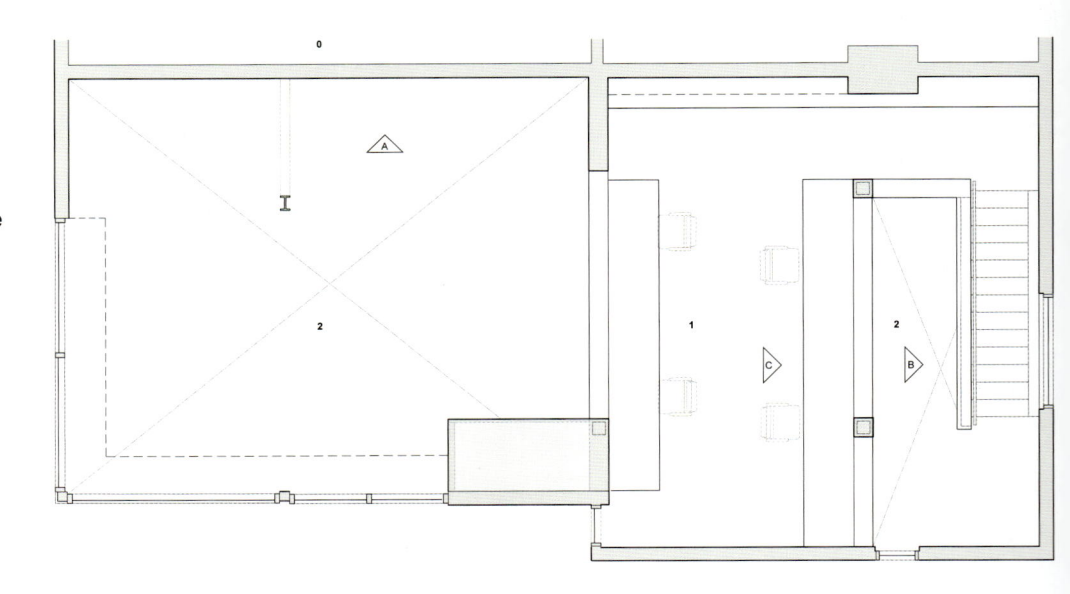

AK LIVE/WORK

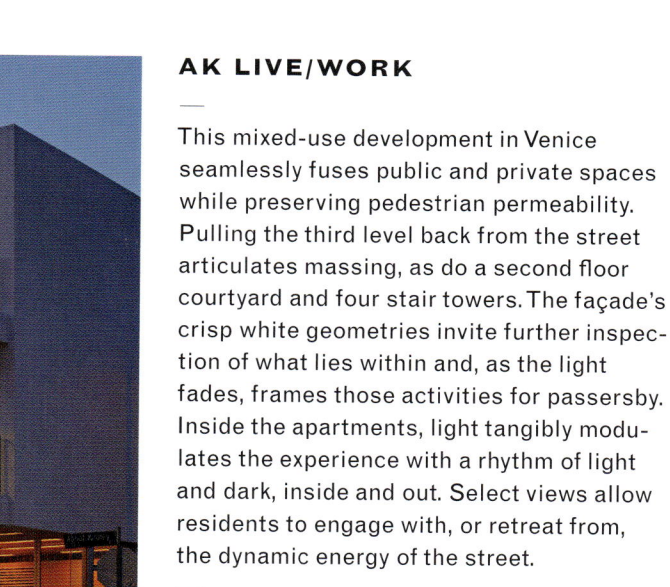

This mixed-use development in Venice seamlessly fuses public and private spaces while preserving pedestrian permeability. Pulling the third level back from the street articulates massing, as do a second floor courtyard and four stair towers. The façade's crisp white geometries invite further inspection of what lies within and, as the light fades, frames those activities for passersby. Inside the apartments, light tangibly modulates the experience with a rhythm of light and dark, inside and out. Select views allow residents to engage with, or retreat from, the dynamic energy of the street.

01 Exterior view by night **02** Interior **03** Section **04** Side view **05** Staircase

Photos: John Edward Linden

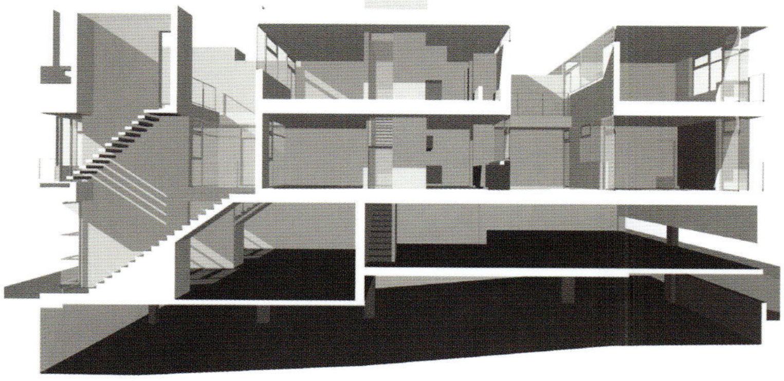

CITY
Venice (CA)

COUNTRY
USA

REGION
North America

TYPOLOGY
Living / Office

COMPLETION
–

WEBSITE
www.santarchitects.com

ARCHITECTS
Sant Architects Inc.

ONE WINDOW HOUSE

As housing prices soar in Los Angeles due to a low inventory of available housing, urban neighborhoods are becoming increasingly dense by Los Angeles standards. By going up instead of out, this 1,500-square-foot house has views of the city and mountains and proposes a new model for meeting zoning requirements while leaving plenty of open space on the tight urban lot. The house is "zoned" by level and creates a seamless flow from front to back yards through the ground level living space. The volume is clad with corrugated, galvanized metal; other materials include cellular plastic glazing and sanded OSB.

01 Street view **02** Corrugated, galvanized metal façade **03** Living space **04** Closet space **05** Sections

Photos: Benny Chan, Fotoworks

CITY
Venice (CA)

COUNTRY
USA

REGION
North America

TYPOLOGY
Living

COMPLETION
2006

WEBSITE
www.touraine-richmond.com

ARCHITECTS
Touraine Richmond Architects

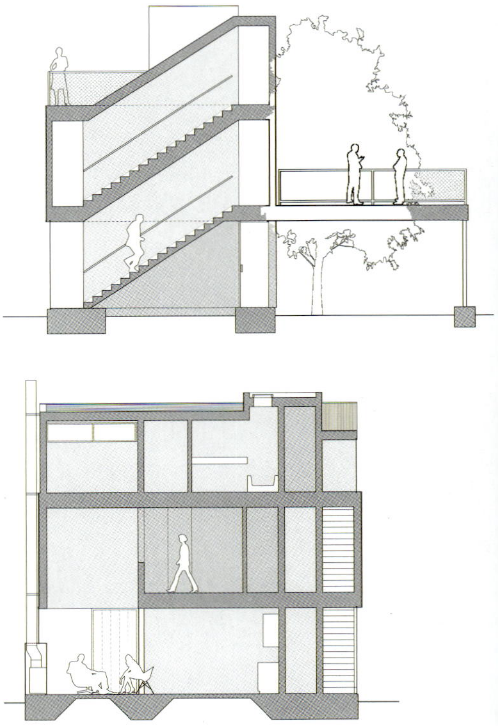

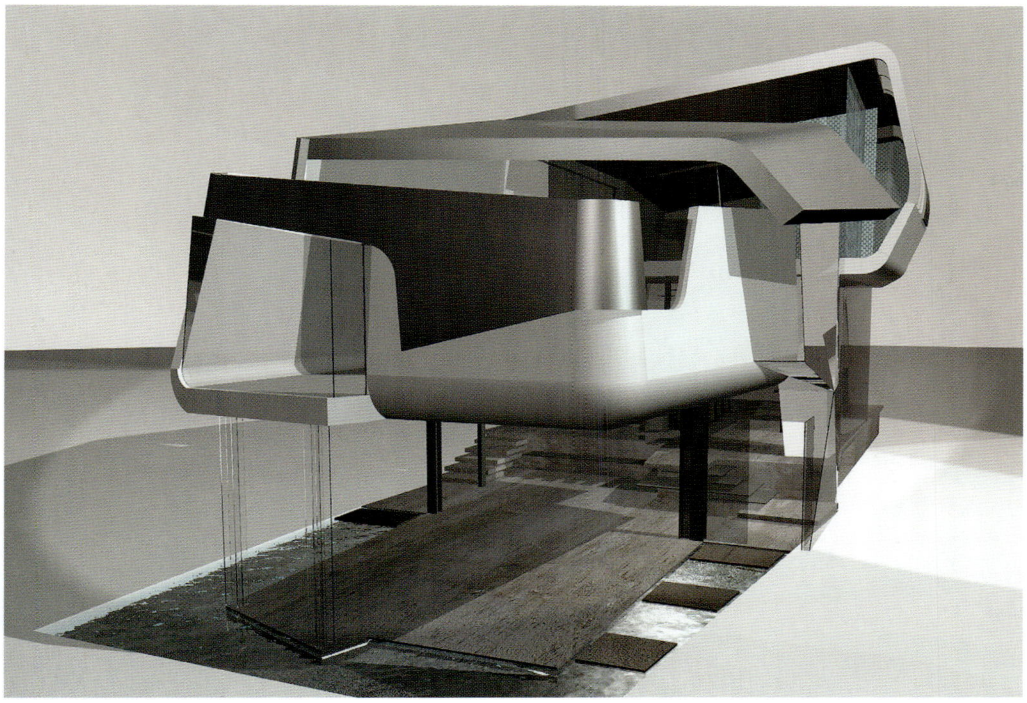

747 HOUSE

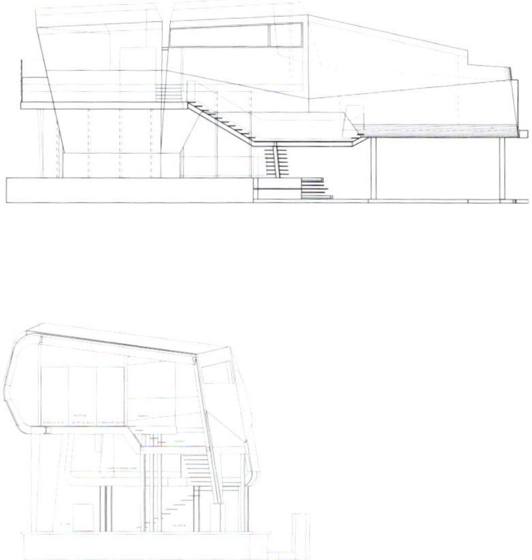

Inspired by the concept of origami as a method to produce fluid folded space, this residence's sculptural form was taken from a single articulated plane that contorts itself to produce volume with differing spatial sections. The architectonic concept of the house redefines traditional notions of roof, wall and floor while simultaneously blurring boundaries between interior spaces. To build the house, a steel detailer worked hand in hand with a computer software company to fabricate the steel structure with the correct position geometries required. The resulting prototype will be used to inform future client projects.

01 Front view **02** Sections **03** Interior **04** East elevation

Renderings: Coscia Day Architecture & Design

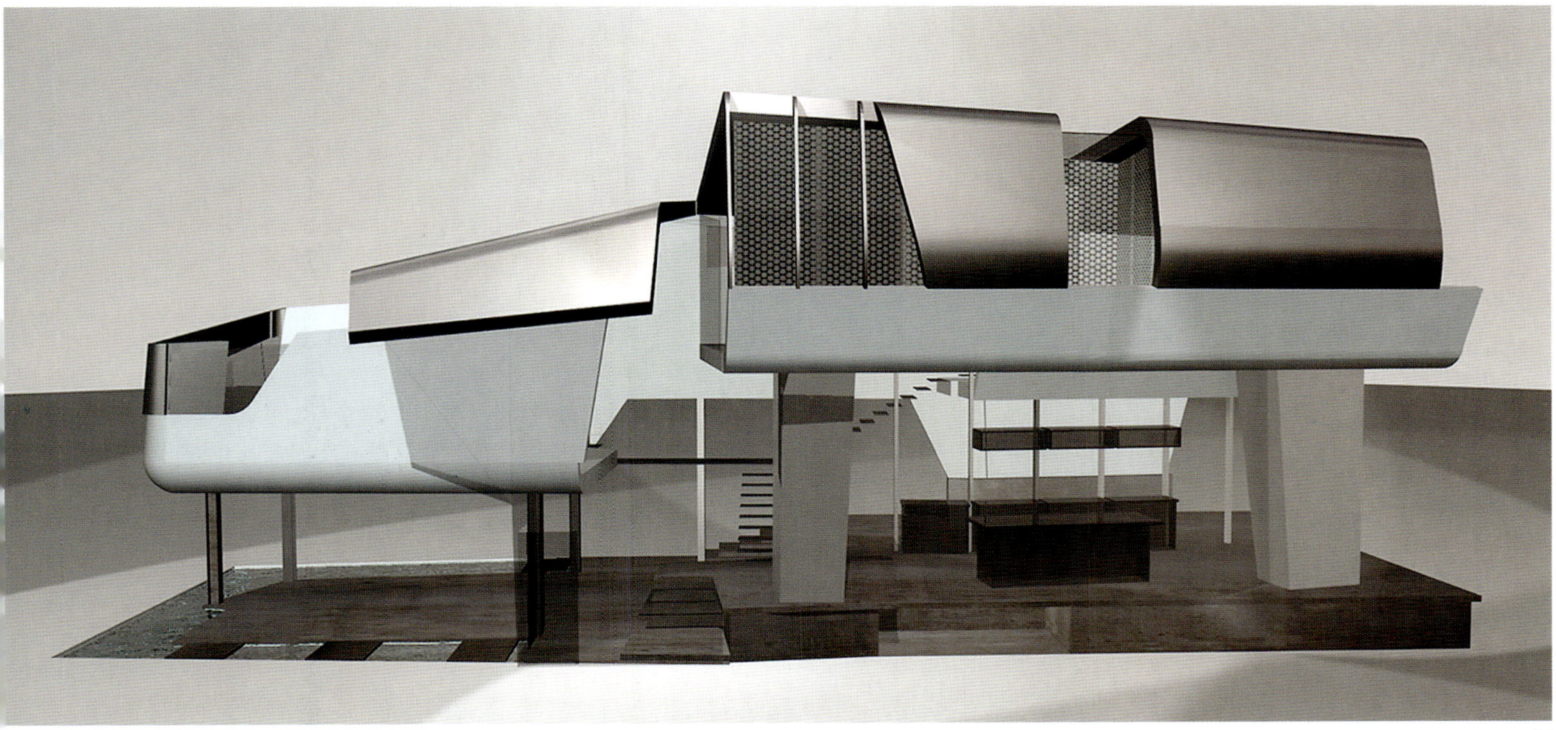

CITY Venice Beach (CA)
COUNTRY USA
REGION North America
TYPOLOGY Living
COMPLETION 2008
WEBSITE www.cosciaday.com
ARCHITECTS Coscia Day Architecture & Design

CITY
Venice (CA)

COUNTRY
USA

REGION
North America

TYPOLOGY
Living

COMPLETION
2006

WEBSITE
www.designmobile.com

ARCHITECTS
Office for Mobile Design (OMD) / Jennifer Siegal

SHOWHOUSE

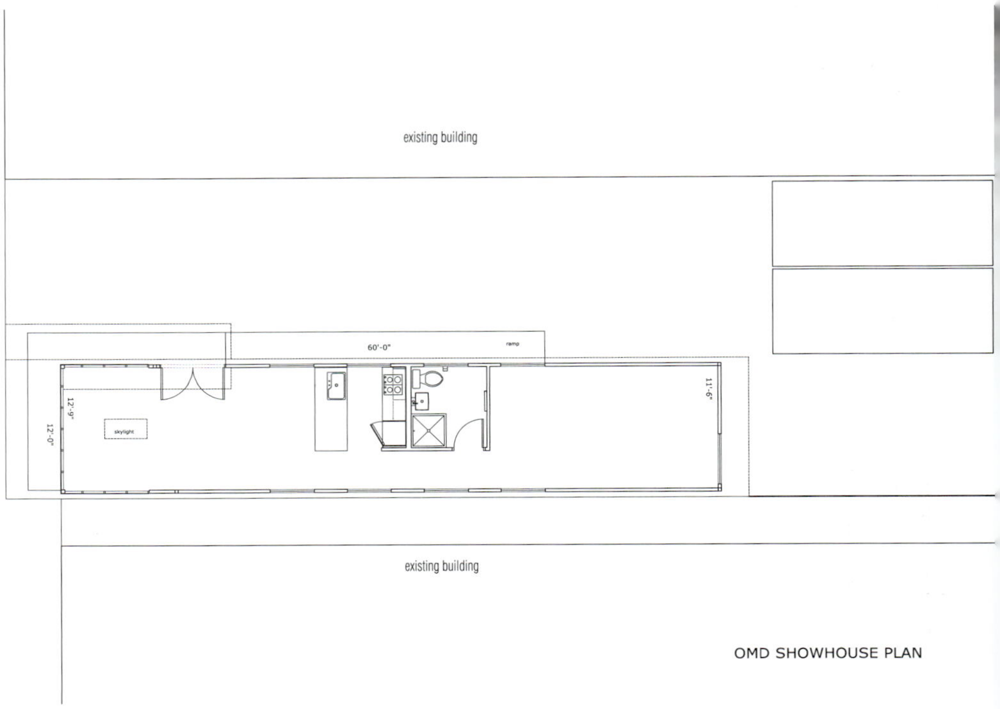

OMD's Prefab ShowHouse, a development of the Portable House, exhibits the ideas of prefabrication, flexibility, portability and compact spaciousness. Its central kitchen/bath core divides and separates the sleeping space from the eating/living space in a compact assemblage of form and function. The steel frame structure was trucked to its site and set on a temporary foundation. Its exterior is clad with metal siding and translucent polycarbonate panels, while its interior features a high sloping ceiling, a small Boffi kitchen, flowing ventilation, radiant heat panels, and a variety of floor and ceiling materials.

01 Steel frame structure **02** Metal siding and translucent polycarbonate panels cladded exterior **03** Living space **04** Floor plan **05** Kitchen

Photos: Benny Chan, Fotoworks

CANAL HOUSE

The Canal House is composed of three cubes: one raised at the street as a studio, and two together at the canalside as the residence. In its concept and execution, the house is informed by two ideas, one embracing the possibility of the poetic, the other a more specific kind of material formation. The house sets up an opposition between studio and residence: work/live, sky/earth, idea/body. The studio is a raised, pure space, marked by horizontal steel fins providing indirect light through three transparent walls, while the residence might be considered solidly grounded, mostly opaque, and somewhat inward.

01 Exterior view by night **02** Floor plans **03** Skylight **04** Acrylic panels wrap atrium beneath skylight **05** Steel construction

Photos: Sharon Risedorph Photography

CITY Venice (CA)
COUNTRY USA
REGION North America
TYPOLOGY Living
COMPLETION 2004
WEBSITE www.sander-architects.com
ARCHITECTS Sander Architects

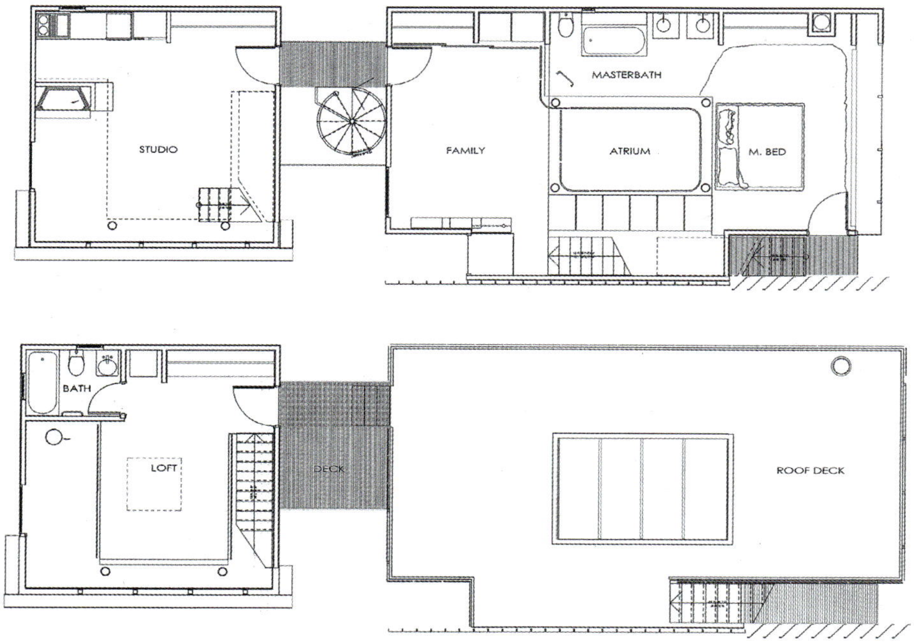

CITY Venice (CA)
COUNTRY USA
REGION North America
TYPOLOGY Hospitality
COMPLETION unbuilt
WEBSITE www.belzbergarchitects.com
ARCHITECTS Belzberg Architects

HOTEL RAY

This 57-room green hotel stands on the site of the original Eames studio, introducing a new paradigm of ecotourism to the already diverse Venice tourist culture. While 'green' is typically associated with engineering feats of new hybrid materials, energy generation and carbon reduction, Belzberg Architects took their cue from the research and production methodologies of the Eames' and capitalized their interest in digital design techniques, combining with the affordances of new hybrid materials to generate novel effects. Subterranean cogeneration plants and cooling systems free the roof for multiple activities and amenity.

01 Hotel in context **02** View from street **03** Subterranean cogeneration plants and cooling systems on roof **04** Structural and widow detail

Renderings: Belzberg Architects

SHENANDOAH RETREAT TEASER

Located on the North Fork of Virginia's Shenandoah River, this 24-acre property stretches from a steeply wooded mountainside, north to a grassy flood plain, bordering the river to the south. The Main House site is located in a small clearing in the woods, allowing full southern exposure and panoramic views of the Blue Ridge Mountains. The Guest House is sited at a lower elevation with views of the flood plain. A concrete bridge leads one into the entry hall where the stair tower emerges as the central element, separating the house's private master bedroom wing from the open kitchen, living and dining areas of the Great Room.

01 Retreat front daytime 02 Retreat living room 03 Retreat west deck at dusk 04 Lower level plan (above) and main level plan (below)

Photos: Daniel Afzal

CITY Warren County (VA)
COUNTRY USA
REGION North America
TYPOLOGY Living
COMPLETION 2007
WEBSITE www.carterburton.com
ARCHITECTS Carter + Burton Architecture

MARCONI COMMUNICATIONS CORPORATE CAMPUS

The design for this six-building campus needed to evoke a sense of community since employees typically remain on the grounds throughout the workday. Easy access to amenities such as dining and fitness facilities was important. Additionally, the design emphasizes circulation and incorporates interior and exterior common areas to encourage interaction between employees. Open stair lobbies create visual connections between floors, and enclosed pedestrian spine encourages travel between buildings. The new complex features office, research and development facilities, a light assembly space, a large, multi-purpose dining facility and parking for 1,000 employees.

01 Copper coated roof/wall assembly of building 5 **02** Exterior view **03** Detail steel shell **04** Site plan **05** Side view
Photos: Edward Massery Photography

CITY Warrendale (PA)
COUNTRY USA
REGION North America
TYPOLOGY Office
COMPLETION 2003
WEBSITE www.studiosarch.com
ARCHITECTS STUDIOS Architecture

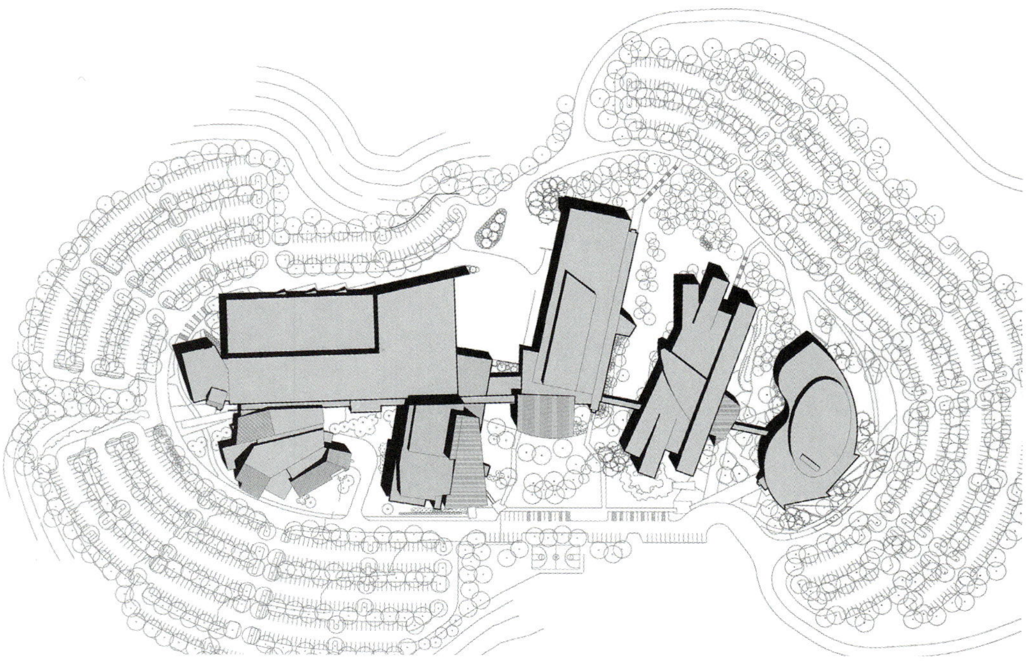

WESTCHESTER/LOYOLA VILLAGE BRANCH LIBRARY

The project, located at the present site of the Loyola Village Branch Library and adjacent to the Municipal Hall, combines two branch libraries and serve 12 elementary schools, 4 junior high and high schools, and a large local population. Sustainable technologies including solar collectors and storm water retainage systems were incorporated into the design strategy. The site strategy was to create a large urban park, preserving existing mature trees, linking the new community with the existing Hall. The main hall forms the central core of the library and accommodates the circulation desk and children's reading areas.

01 Exterior view **02** Circulation desk **03** Detail ceiling

Photos: Tom Bonner

CITY	Westchester (CA)
COUNTRY	USA
REGION	North America
TYPOLOGY	Public
COMPLETION	2004
WEBSITE	www.ai-architects.com
ARCHITECTS	Aleks Istanbullu Architects

CITY Wilmington (DE)

COUNTRY USA

REGION North America

TYPOLOGY Living

COMPLETION 2006

WEBSITE www.sander-architects.com

ARCHITECTS Sander Architects

SANDER TREE HOUSE

The Tree House sits in a residential subdivision surrounded by century-old trees and a seasonal stream. The vertical form allows the house to sit in the trees and to have marvelous views of the canopy from the two upper floors. Horizontal windows provide select views into the landscape, while a large window in the living room provides dramatic views into the deep woods. The exterior entrance stair, cantilevered away from the façade, enters through a trio of trees and provides a view of the stream as one rises to enter the house. A spiral stair leads from the ground to the roof, where the tree canopy sits close overhead.

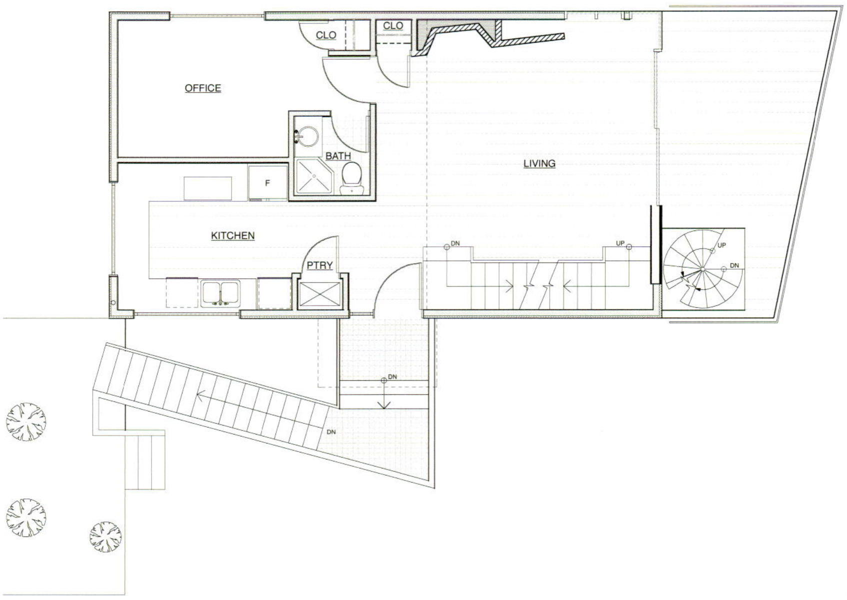

01 Exterior view at dusk **02** Entrance stair **03** View from east
04 First floor plan

Photos: Sharon Risedorph Photography

INDIAN PAINTBRUSH RESIDENCE

This 2400-square-foot house sits in an aspen grove at the base of the Teton Mountain Range. The parameters included a building with a better connection to its beautiful site, a building less derived from the traditional western vernacular, and one that could be built on a budget of $160 USD per square-foot. The small build-able area required that the building have a small footprint. This constraint, combined with the requirements of the owners' program, pushed the living areas of the house to an upper floor and into the canopy of the trees, creating an upside-down version of a traditional house diagram.

01 Exterior view **02** Detail glass façade **03** Living area on the upper floor **04** Stairway behind glass façade **05** Upper level plan

Photos: Paul Warchol Photography

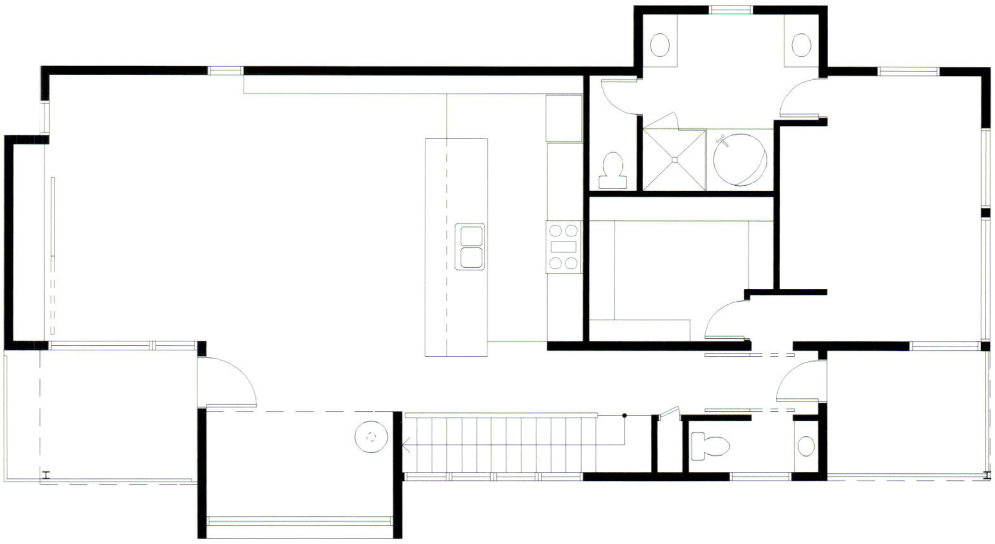

CITY Wilson (WY)
COUNTRY USA
REGION North America
TYPOLOGY Living
COMPLETION 2004
WEBSITE www.carneyarchitects.com
ARCHITECTS Eric Logan

MODERN BARN

The Modern Barn is a renovation of a 4,500-square-foot dairy barn and silo dating from the 1870's. Mindful of the rural and historical context, the architects chose to restore the exterior of the gambrel barn while completely reconfiguring the interior spaces. The private spaces (master suite and private studies) are housed in the elevated volume, allowing the ground floor to be completely open for more public functions and creating a loft-like space. Framed views and material continuity create a powerful connection to the outside garden and meadow.

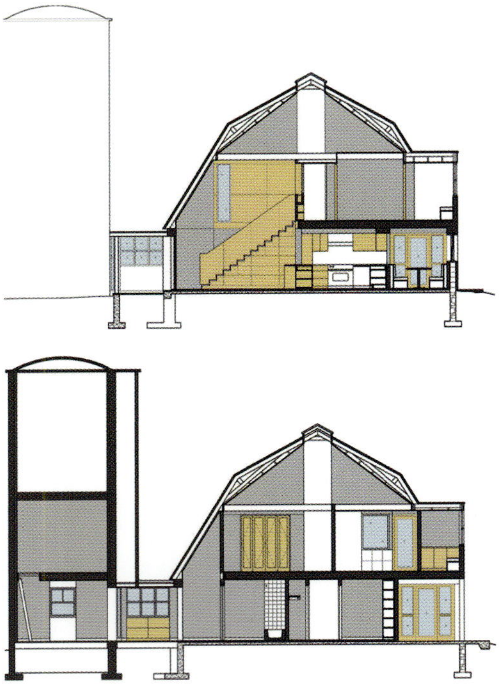

01 Sections 02 Fireplace in the open dining and living room
03 Dining room 04 Bedroom 05 Bathroom 06 Exterior view

Photos: Michael Moran

EARL'S SILO

The charge was to design a house that is both cozy in scale and yet comfortable for weekend guests. Two linked corrugated metal grain silos are the structural basis for this building. They are so arranged as to allow the most proximate visual and aural access to the adjacent Provo River. The metal grating provides shading during the summer month, while the southern exposure ensures passive solar heat gain during the winter. An electric mesh is embedded into the slabs of the lower floor as a first auxiliary heat source, and a propane-burning stove provides the back up.

01 Detail metal façade **02** First floor plan **03** Sleeping room **04** Rear view

Photos: Scott Zimmerman

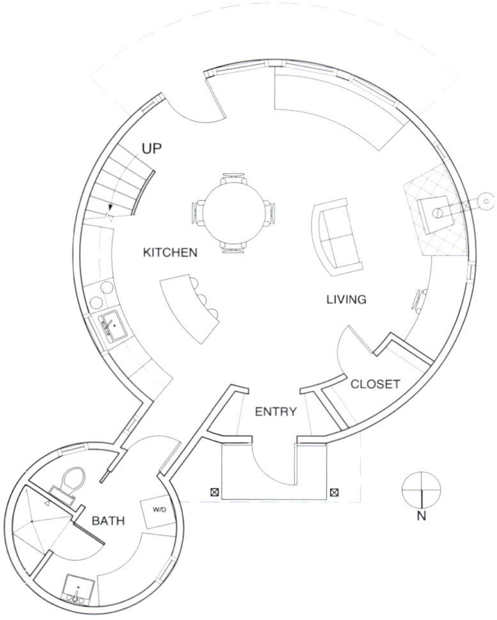

CITY Woodland (UT)
COUNTRY USA
REGION North America
TYPOLOGY Living
COMPLETION 2006
WEBSITE www.gigaplexdesign.com
ARCHITECTS Gigaplex

CITY Westport (MA)
COUNTRY USA
REGION North America
TYPOLOGY —
COMPLETION —
WEBSITE www.maryannthompson.com
ARCHITECTS Maryann Thompson Architects

MEADOW HOUSE

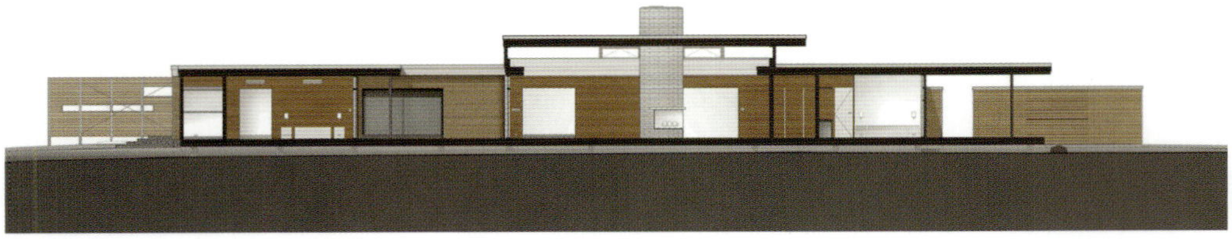

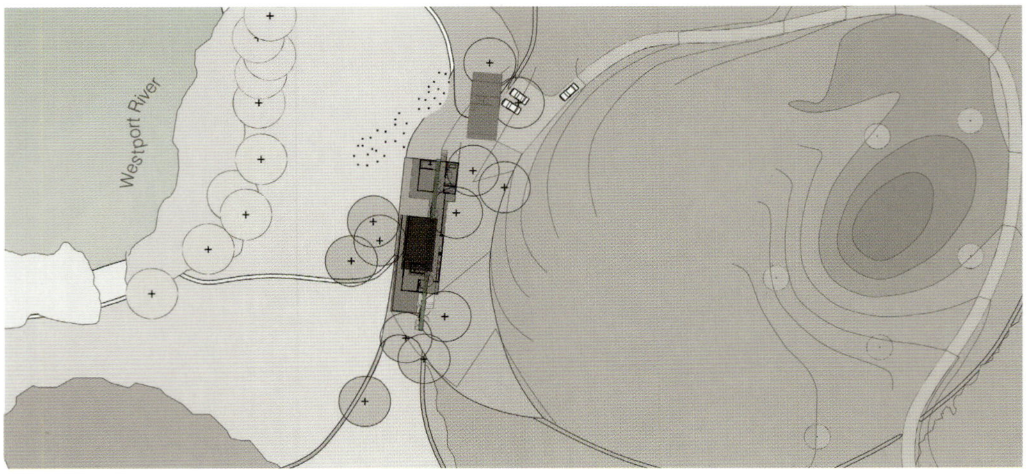

This one-story house nestles into a forty-acre meadow and is conceived as an "indoor/outdoor" space which is firmly rooted to its site. A large deck stretches along the western elevation and perforates the plan at the entry. Enclosed by the living room and master bedroom, this space becomes an "interiorized" outdoor room and a threshold between public and private spaces. Floor and ceiling planes in the living room and bedrooms continue onto the decks, further blending inside and outside space. Light passes through the four-sided clerestory in the living room, illuminating the volume with changing patterns through the day.

01 Total view **02** View through and out of the living room
03 Reading rooms both as interior and exterior spaces
04 Section **05** Siteplan

Photos: Chuck Choi

THE LINNEAN FAMILY

Inspired by the trees and rock outcroppings located on its site, this residence appears as an abstracted tree. As though suspended from the branches of the giant oaks that surround it, the design attempts to blend into the park through the use of matching natural colors and glass that reflectively display the preserved trees surrounding it. The design metaphor is taken from the abundance of trees that split the rocks within a park streambed that runs through this section of Washington, DC.

01 Exterior view **02** Floor plan **03** Detail new glass cube on the roof **04** Interior view, glass cube **05** Detail stairway

Photos: Kenneth M. Wyner

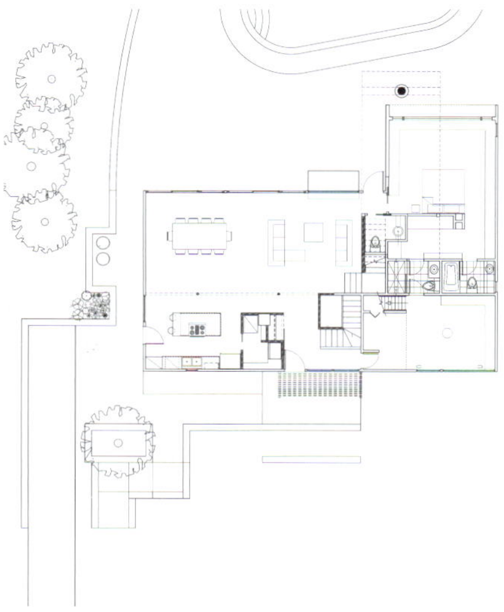

CITY Washington (DC)
COUNTRY USA
REGION North America
TYPOLOGY Living
COMPLETION 2007
WEBSITE www.travispricearchitects.com
ARCHITECTS Travis Price Architects

CITY	Washington (DC)
COUNTRY	USA
REGION	North America
TYPOLOGY	Living
COMPLETION	2004
WEBSITE	www.travispricearchitects.com
ARCHITECTS	Travis Price Architects

PRICE RESIDENCE

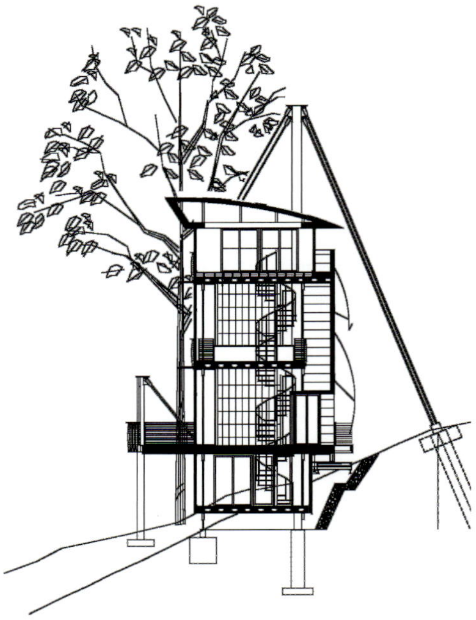

The Price Residence project is a creative design inspired by the simple and natural virtues of the site's trees and rock outcroppings, where an abundance of trees splitting rocks near a stream bed are the essence of the Park running through the center of Washington, DC. The home is seen as an abstracted tree at the cliff's edge hung by steel cables, while seeming to appear to be suspended from the branches of the giant oaks that surround it. The design desires to blend into the park by its matching natural colors, as well as its use of glass, which reflectively display the preserved trees surrounding it.

01 Exterior view by night **02** Exterior view, top of the building **03** Rear façade **04** Interior view **05** Section

Photos: Kenneth M. Wyner

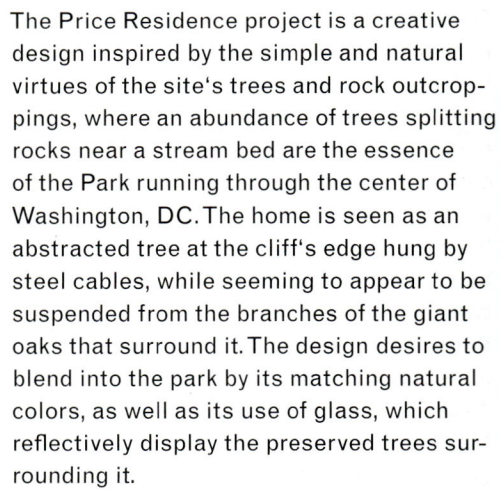

WATERMILL HOUSE

The central volume of the house contains kitchen, dining and living, where opposing 16-foot-wide glass doors pocket into the exterior walls and open the house to the pool and grounds. A butterfly roof a-top a clerestory provides a sense of cover, rather than enclosure, and a broad view of the sky from the inside. The family quarters are located at the east end of the house in the two stories of the original structure, while a three-story "tower" rising from the opposite flank provides a panoramic ocean view from its 30-foot high terrace. The lower floors of the "tower" hold the children's art room, guest suite, and study.

01 View from the garden **02** Main living spaces **03** View from yard through the open glass doors **04** Ground floor plan

Photos: Jeff Heatley

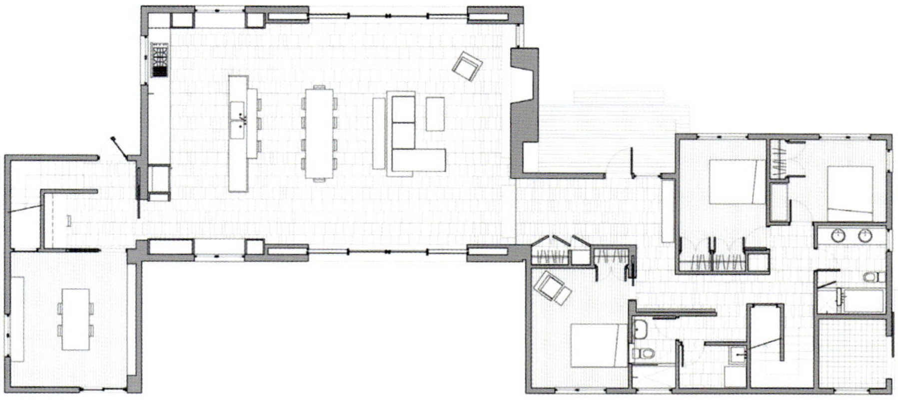

CITY Watermill (NY)
COUNTRY USA
REGION North America
TYPOLOGY living
COMPLETION 2006
WEBSITE www.hs2architecture.com
ARCHITECTS HS2 Architecture

WATERMILL HOUSES

The design of this private family complex is deferential to the fifteen wooded acres of land upon which it is situated. Each building is an unobtrusive, rational form that rests quietly within the trees and responds to the sloping of the terrain. The main house functions as a sophisticated tree house, with a shielded bottom floor for sleeping and an open, transparent second floor for living. Both the glass walls and the central court that leads up to the roof terrace embody a philosophy of transparency, allowing the architecture to encompass a wider realm of experience than the immediate interior.

01 Exterior view by night, main house 02 Guest House 03 Exterior view, main house 04 Bunk house 05 Living area, main house 06 Section, main house

Photos: Peter Aaron/Esto

CITY Watermill (NY)
COUNTRY USA
REGION North America
TYPOLOGY Living
COMPLETION 2003
WEBSITE www.1100architect.com
ARCHITECTS 1100: Architect

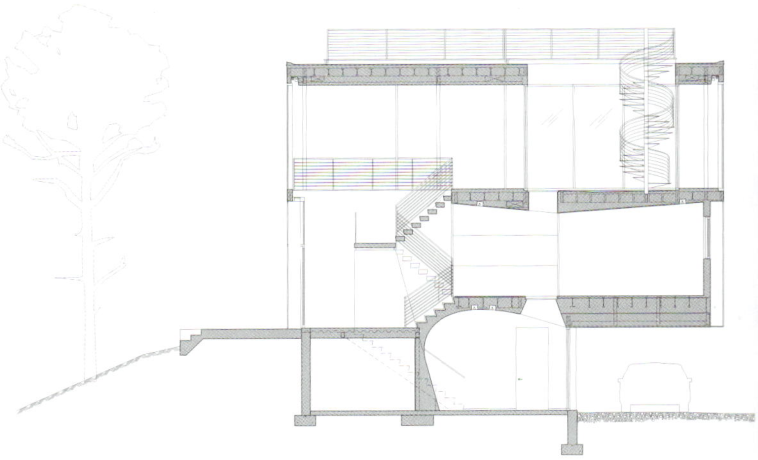

FAKE PLASTIC TREE

The project is an attempt to investigate the formal, spatial and atmospheric potential of a vertically sustainable garden in sync with the most advanced technology for plant growth. The new proposal accepts the existing conditions of the site without trying to resolve the prevailing conflict between a historic architectural masterpiece and a new building development. The garden is composed of a branching circuitry network made of plastic PVC tubes that distribute water and nutrient solution. Depending on the section of tubes, their capacity to carry more or less water, different scale of plants can grow from and within them.

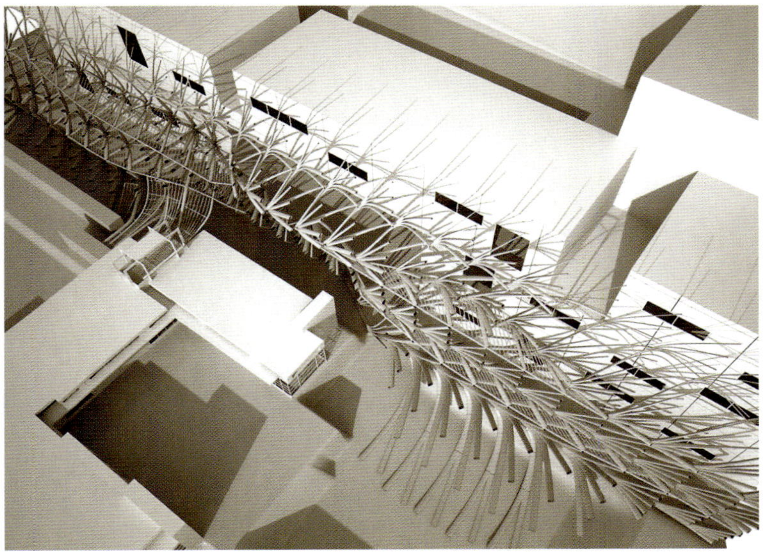

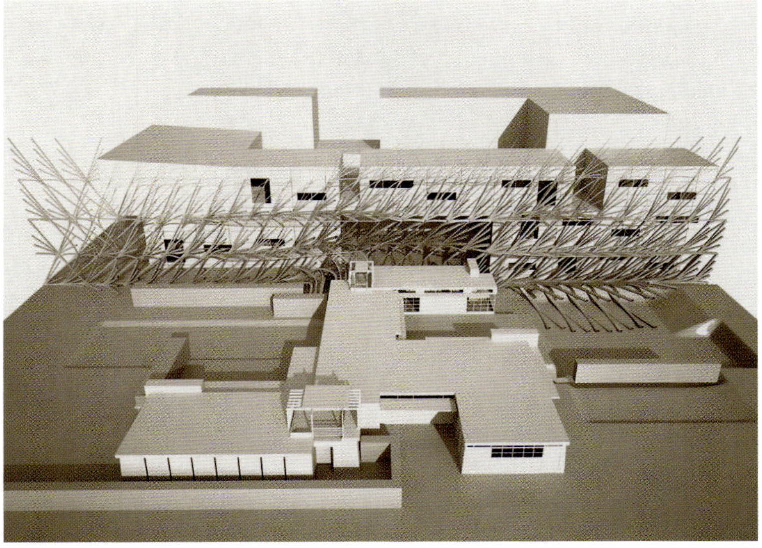

01 Garden with branching network **02** Aerial view **03** Model **04** Branching detail

Renderings: P.A.T.T.E.R.N.S.

CITY West Hollywood (CA)
COUNTRY USA
REGION North America
TYPOLOGY Culture
COMPLETION 2003
WEBSITE www.p-a-t-t-e-r-n-s.net
ARCHITECTS P.A.T.T.E.R.N.S. Marcelo Spina

CITY West Hollywood (CA)
COUNTRY USA
REGION North America
TYPOLOGY Living
COMPLETION 2003
WEBSITE www.lehrerarchitects.com
ARCHITECTS Lehrer Architects

NORTON TOWERS-ON-THE-COURT

Norton Towers-On-The-Court, a six-unit condominium project on a narrow lot in West Hollywood, is the first prototype successfully realizing the city's courtyard standards. This urban courtyard community of townhouses maximizes light and space while offering a sense of privacy, intimacy and grandeur. Bathed in light and air, each unit contains its own four-story glass tower, allowing for daylight to penetrate deep into the interior. The west-facing aluminum enlivens the facade and controls natural light and ventilation, while bold colors accentuate the exterior, giving a sense of richness and luxury.

01 Side view **02** Front façade **03** Interior space **04** Aerial rendering

Photos: Tom Bonner

GARDNER 1050

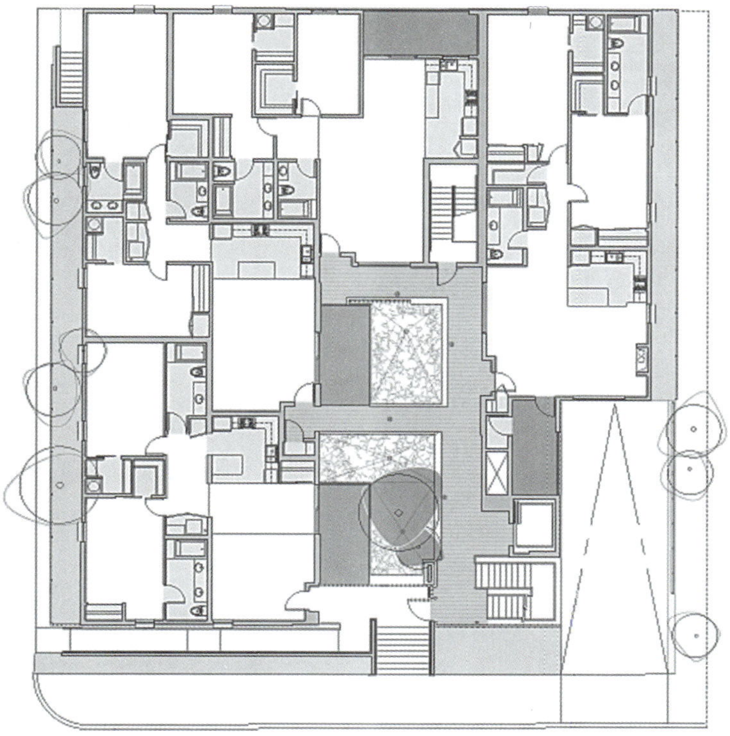

Located in the city of West Hollywood, California, Gardner 1050 is the result of a series of studies into how various housing typologies can be re-invigorated to create new opportunities for living within the extremely tight economic and spatial parameters of the speculative housing market. As a model of courtyard housing developments, the project utilizes a variety of design strategies to elevate it above the mundane infill developments typical of speculative housing.

01 Exterior view from street **02** Front façade detail **03** First floor plan **04** Bridges connecting units **05** Dining area

Photos: Lawrence Anderson Photography

CITY West Hollywood (CA)
COUNTRY USA
REGION North America
TYPOLOGY Living
COMPLETION 2006
WEBSITE www.loharchitects.com
ARCHITECTS LOHA (Lorcan O'Herlihy Architects)

CITY
West Hollywood (CA)

COUNTRY
USA

REGION
North America

TYPOLOGY
Commercial

COMPLETION
2008

WEBSITE
www.p-a-t-t-e-r-n-s.net

ARCHITECTS
P.A.T.T.E.R.N.S.
Marcelo Spina

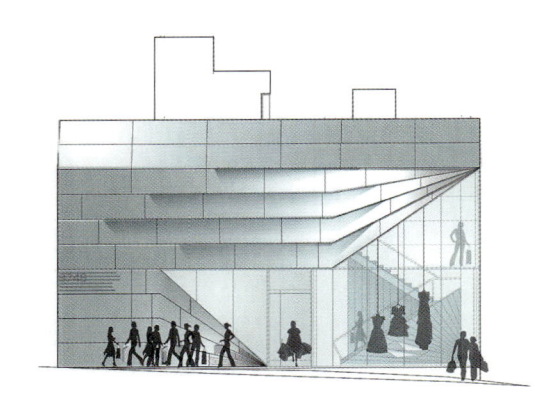

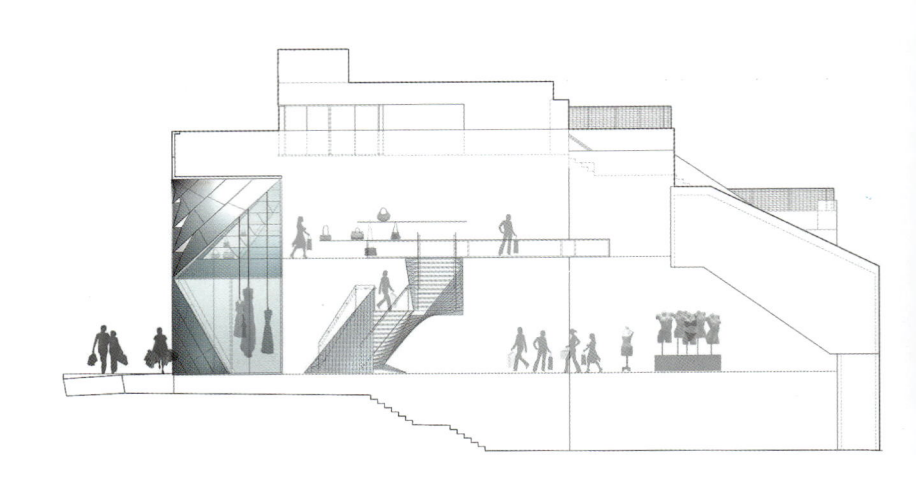

8746 SUNSET BOUTIQUE
PLASTIC SENSATION

Based on a radical geometric contextualism, the façade attempts to produce an architecture of subtle sensations by inducing a physical and optical dynamism that both challenge and enhance the movement of the body. Mounted on a support structure, the materiality of the façade is based on 3/8" composite resin-based extruded polycarbonate panels. The bluish grey color and its degree of translucency are entirely customized so the façade can perform in an elusive plastic way; extremely lustrous with an almost metallic gloss at daylight, softly glowing and refractive when backlight at night.

01 Elevations 02 Main entrance 03 Front façade 04 View from Sunset Boulevard

Renderings: P.A.T.T.E.R.N.S.

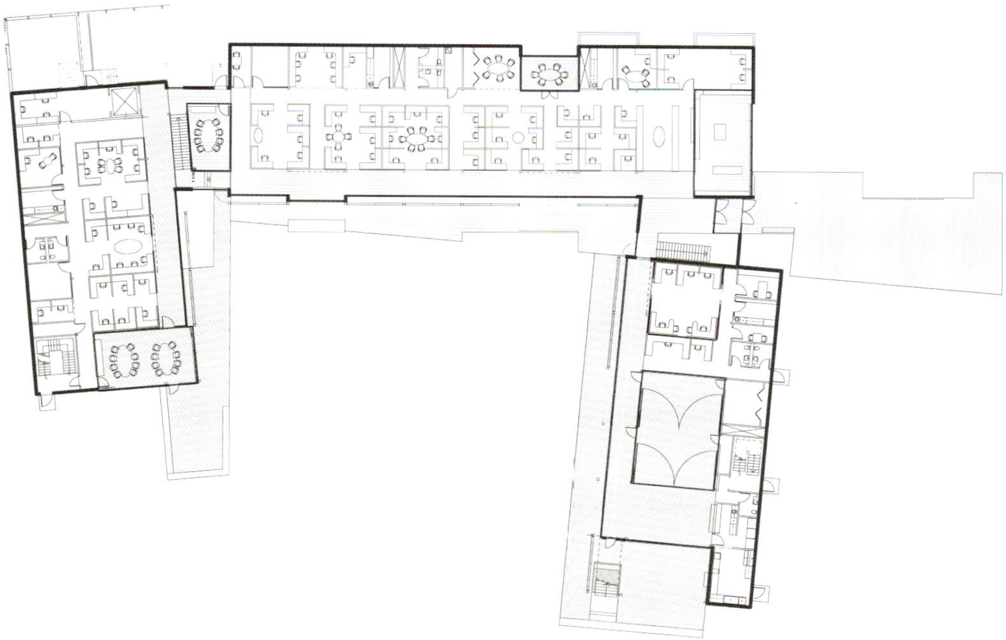

WORLD HEADQUARTERS FOR THE INTERNATIONAL FUND FOR ANIMAL WELFARE

The World Headquarters for the International Fund for Animal Welfare is the new 54,000 square-foot sustainable home for this influential and dynamic global organization based out of Cape Cod. The building, striving for LEED Gold certification, maximizes the organization's global advocacy, strategic planning and communications, while consolidating their 165 local employees into one centralized location. Created by designLAB architects, the building is designed to facilitate open communication, collaboration and interaction, while promoting IFAW's global mission "to provide a better world for animals and people."

01 First floor plan **02** Façade detail **03** View of exterior courtyard **04** View of lobby

Photos: Peter Vanderwarke

CITY: Yarmouth Porth (MA)
COUNTRY: USA
REGION: North America
TYPOLOGY: Office
COMPLETION: 2008
WEBSITE: www.designLABarch.com
ARCHITECTS: designLAB architects

CITY Yellow Springs (OH)

COUNTRY USA

REGION North America

TYPOLOGY Living

COMPLETION 2007

WEBSITE www.mitnickroddierhicks.com

ARCHITECTS Mitnick Roddier Hicks

LL HOUSE

Sitting on a small lot at the heart of Yellow Springs, Ohio, the original front façade, with its classic pilasters and entablature, lines the interior space of the new and largely exposed interior space, while the interior volume of the original brick house has been transformed into an entry courtyard with a large square aperture in the roof that allows for the movement of sunlight to be traced across its asphalt-paved floor. The procession of the visit thus begins at the center of the site, and spirals outwards from there. Moving through the house, one experiences a rich sequencing of visual screens and spatial drifts.

01 Floor plans **02** Entry courtyard with asphalt-paved floor
03 Hallway **04** Living room **05** Interior view, detail

Photos: Mitnick Roddier Hicks

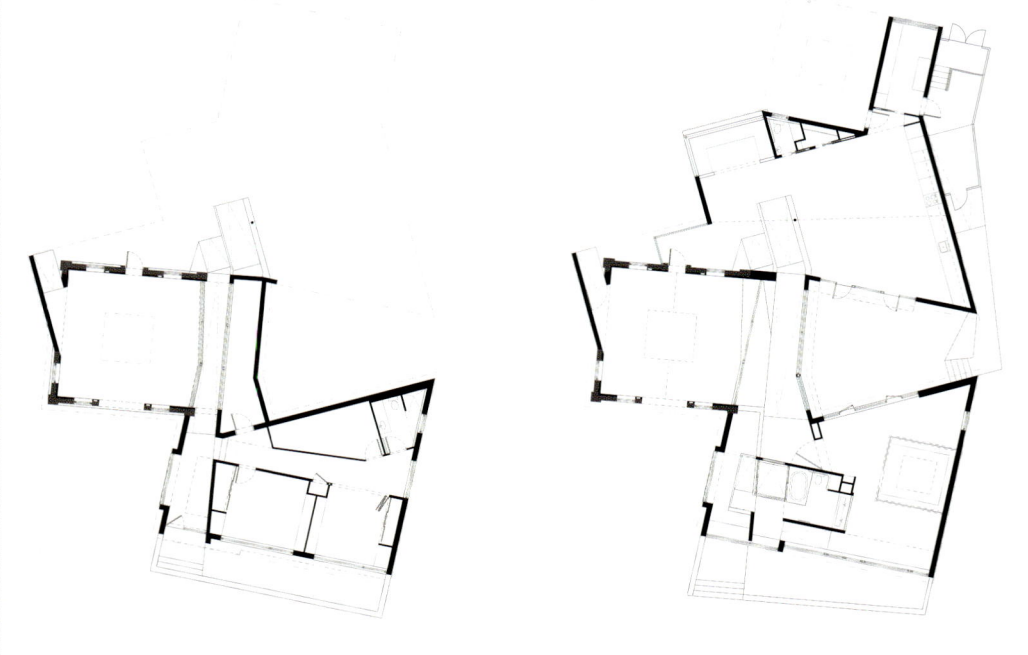

STONE RIDGE CHURCH

In 1999, a small Baptist Church commissioned DeBartolo architects to create a master plan for their 23-acre desert campus. The site, clearly visible from the interstate, is highly covered with blowing sand and scrub-bush. This exciting yet different feature prompted the owners into challenging the architects to go ahead and try to conceive an 'oasis' in the desert. This was no easy task, however phase one began and it went on to include such features like a worship center (a future youth space), classrooms, and finally a courtyard where a canopy of trees and grass surround an outdoor baptismal pool.

01 Exterior view by night **02** Courtyard **03** Floor plan **04** Interior view

Photos: Bill Timmerman Photography

CITY Yuma (AZ)
COUNTRY USA
REGION North America
TYPOLOGY Culture
COMPLETION 2005
WEBSITE www.debartoloarchitects.com
ARCHITECTS DeBartolo architects

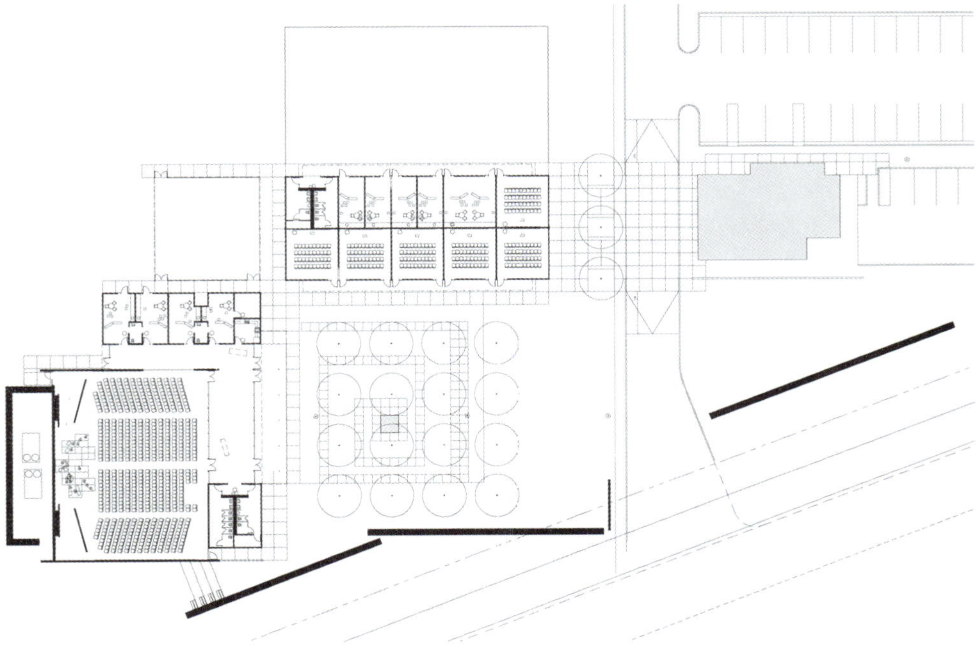

139x
CENTRAL AMERICA

0634 **BELIZE**

0635 **COSTA RICA**

0640 **GUATEMALA**

0641 **HONDURAS**

0642 **MEXICO**
0651 **GUADALAJARA**
0661 **MERIDA**
0667 **MEXICO CITY**
0740 **MONTERREY**
0750 **PLAYA DEL CARMEN**
0753 **QUERETARO**
0765 **ZAPOPAN**

0768 **PANAMA**

TURTLE INN

The original beach resort was wiped out by a hurricane in 2001, and the owner hired the Balinese-based designer to create the current resort, which combines the strong Balinese embrace of nature with an Italian slant on style. The nineteen thatched guest villas and cottages rise on stilts above the beach. A large screened-in porch with a carved wooden day bed leads to a living area and bedrooms. Elaborately carved doorways imported from Bali separate the rooms, where the furnishings are set on polished wood floors. There are no phones, air-conditioning or Internet access, letting the guest unwind and take in the views and quiet.

01 Outdoor pool **02** Exterior view, thatched roof **03** View from the beach **04** Interior, bedroom

Photos: Courtesy of Made Wijaya

PERGOLA BUILDING

The challenge during this project was to produce a US$ 400/m² building with finished public areas and designed façades, while the rest was left in basic structural works. In order to attain such a difficult objective, a prefabricated 10 x 10 m concrete structure was designed, covered with a specially designed curtain wall façade. Since this type of solution generates very high radiation levels and, consequently, high temperatures in the structure's interior, the frontage was covered in surrounding foliage aimed at refreshing the walls, to keep them in the shade, thereby reducing the heat load.

01 Entrance **02** Surrounding foliage **03** Interior view on entrance area **04** Detail façade **05** Façade with surrounding foliage

Photos: Alegre Saporta

CITY: Heredia
COUNTRY: Costa Rica
REGION: Central America
TYPOLOGY: –
COMPLETION: 2004
WEBSITE: www.brunostagno.info
ARCHITECTS: Bruno Stagno

CASA WILLIAMSON

The house is located on the southern Pacific coast. The modern tropical design has a strong relationship to the location. Extremely long eaves and overhangs offer abundant protection from the sun; the interiors are naturally ventilated by wind currents. The overall elongated plan takes advantage of the fantastic ocean views.

01 General view **02** Outdoor pool **03** View on bay **04** Cross section **05** Longitudinal section **06** Entrance

Photos: Rodrigo Montoya Grupo Nación

CITY Puntaneras
COUNTRY Costa Rica
REGION Central America
TYPOLOGY Living
COMPLETION 2003
WEBSITE -
ARCHITECTS Sylvia Fournier

HOLCIM

A large industrial complex, devastated and rocky, is transforming from a desert into a pleasant industrial estate. To achieve these objectives, the architects designed the landscaping and the different buildings that make up this spatial unit on an enjoyable scale, surrounded by patios. A variety of novel options were designed that reflect sophisticated applications of rustic materials, while also including lightweight elements to regulate solar radiation and lower the heat load of the building, which is devoid of air conditioning. An advantage used was of the rock-strewn nature of the terrain, incorporating boulders and trees.

01 General view **02** Façade Detail **03** Detail front façade **04** Detail fontains **05** Floor plan

Photos: Alegre Saporta

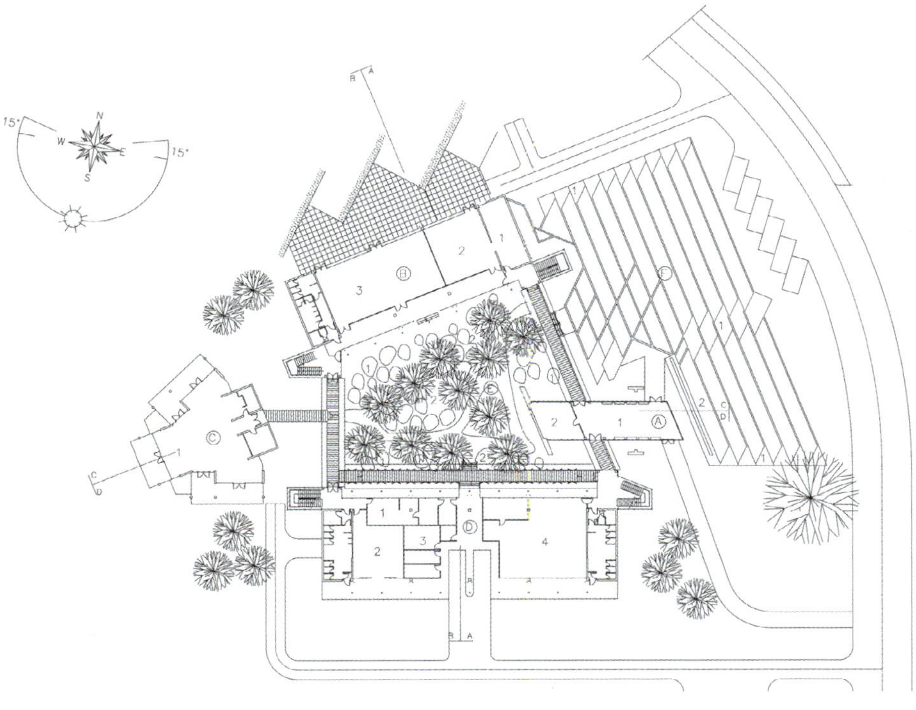

CITY San José
COUNTRY Costa Rica
REGION Central America
TYPOLOGY Culture
COMPLETION 2004
WEBSITE www.brunostagno.info
ARCHITECTS Bruno Stagno

EDIFICIO VAN DER LAAT & JIMENEZ

The program of the building demanded new office headquarters for V & J, one of Costa Rica's oldest and most important construction firms. A new 3-story addition and the remodeling of an existing 2-story building were undertaken by the architects. The exterior is executed using concrete tiles and pre-patinated copper sheathing on structural reinforced concrete and features enameled painted steel-plate windows. Enclosed parking occupies the ground level, while the upper levels are office space.

01 Interior, circular stairs **02** Exterior view **03** Clerestory **04** Cross section and longitudinal section **05** Interior view

Photos: Rodrigo Montoya

CITY San José
COUNTRY Costa Rica
REGION Central America
TYPOLOGY Office
COMPLETION 2005
WEBSITE www.foroarq.net
ARCHITECTS Alvaro Rojas/FoRo Arquitectos

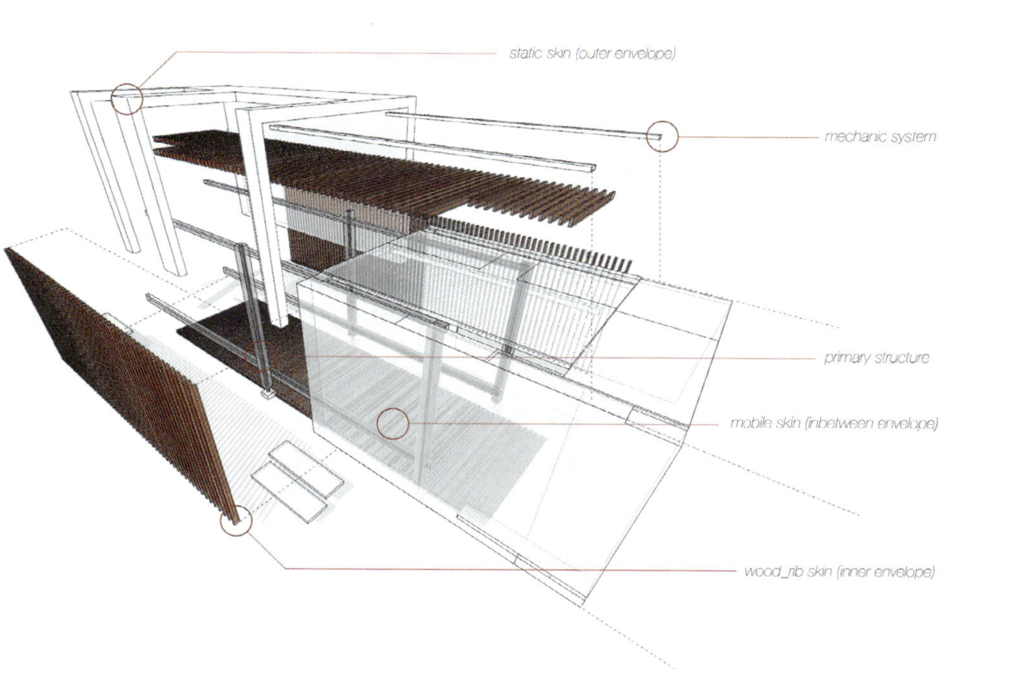

PAVILION FOR THE DESIGN EXHIBITION SU CASA EN VIVO, BARRIO AMON

The 3 by 10-meter pavilion was built as a temporary structure for the SU CASA EN VIVO event held in Barrio Amon, one of the oldest neighborhoods in San Jose. The proposal is developed within the former walls of an abandoned house, where an existing window frame dictated the box's height and width. The floating white box encloses a warmer interior space, a series of shifting skins alter circulation, light filtration and space configuration. As the outer skin shifts, it opens up an entrance, a way out, transforming the box into a pathway, a bridge... by shifting again, the exit disappears and the box can become a space for dwelling.

01 Exploded axonometric **02** Exterior view by night **03** Integrated window frame of abandoned house **04** Pathway **05** Interior of pavilion

Photos: Rodrigo Montaya

CITY San José
COUNTRY Costa Rica
REGION Central America
TYPOLOGY –
COMPLETION Culture
WEBSITE www.sanjosereves.com
ARCHITECTS Diego van der Laat, sanjosereves

CITY
Lake Peten Itza, Tikal

COUNTRY
Guatemala

REGION
Central America

TYPOLOGY
Hospitality

COMPLETION
2003

WEBSITE
–

ARCHITECTS
–

LA LANCHA

Opened in 2004, the lodge is owned by movie director Francis Ford Coppola and is located a thirty minutes away from the Mayan site of Tikal. The lodge offers secluded guest casitas decorated with native art furnishings and featuring two rooms, queen-size beds, decks with hammocks and private bathrooms. Six Rainforest Casitas are nestled in the forest with a partial view of the lake and four Lake View Casitas with a large deck and chairs that provide a comfortable setting for views of the lake and rainforest. Lakeview casitas also offer large marble tile bathrooms.

01 Thatched roof 02 Swimming pool 03 View into courtyard 04 Bedroom 05 Living space

Photos: Courtesy of Hotel La Lancha

PANORAMA

Seemingly lighting up the night sky, these twin juxtaposed residential towers in San Pedro Sula, Honduras have been created and designed to imply motion. Inspired by a pinwheel concept, the development of the plan provides a central and compact core from which all units radiate, while providing panoramic views. These terraces which are shaped to reinforce the pinwheel silhouette, provide expansive views and cross ventilation. The Panorama project, designed by Fullerton Diaz Architects, is further enhanced by four pools arranged to compliment the tropical oasis that defines the local environment.

01 General view **02** Entrance view **03** Relaxing space with pool **04** Bird's eye view **05** Kitchen **06** Perspective, roof deck

Renderings: Fullerton Diaz Architects

CITY San Pedro
COUNTRY Honduras
REGION Central America
TYPOLOGY Living
COMPLETION -
WEBSITE www.fdarchitects.com
ARCHITECTS Fullerton Diaz Architects

CITY	Acapulco
COUNTRY	Mexico
REGION	Central America
TYPOLOGY	Living
COMPLETION	2005
WEBSITE	www.gutierrez-alonso.com
ARCHITECTS	Gutiérrez-Alonso Arquitectura

CASA JADE

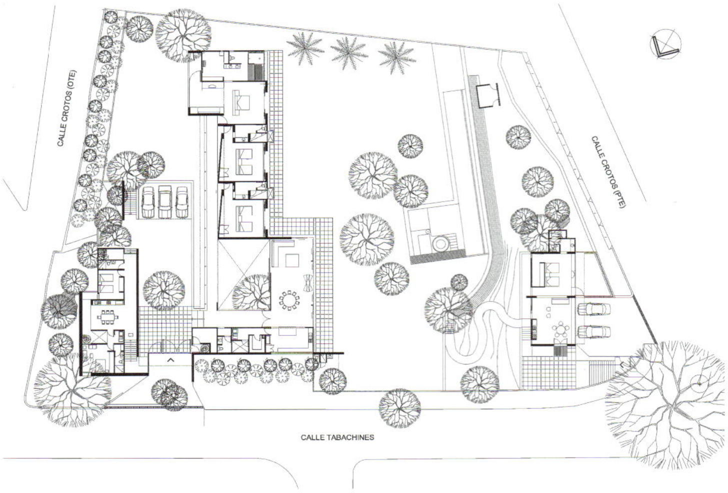

This house is located in the heights of Acapulco Bay, on a land with great trees and abundant tropical vegetation. The construction offers the enjoyment of the ebullient surroundings and the view, composed from some prisms and planes ready around a patio, is a synthesis of its spirit of serenity. Two routes articulate the spaces: the outside set by a plane pergolado throughout the gardens, the pond and the rooms, while the interior offers to its inhabitants the abstract experience of the corridor that is overflowed in the relation that it looks for to establish with the climate of this latitude of the Mexican Pacific.

01 Exterior view **02** Detail glass façade **03** Floor plan **04** Hallway **05** Courtyard

Photos: Alberto Moreno

NATHAI NATURAL HISTORY MUSEUM

The proposal for the museum uses the promenade along the park to lure pedestrians to the museum and under the building itself. There, they are presented with several options: visiting the museum, continuing on to the cafeteria or the restaurant, exploring the temporary galleries and the small auditorium or continuing along glass bridges, which strongly emphasize visitors´ movement to the park. The project is composed of two volumes – one is a majestic glass box facing the river, while the south building is built as an enclosed space which contains a massive curved concrete wall that holds three levels.

01 Exterior view from the pedestrian bridge **02** Used materials: glass and concrete **03** Side view **04** Open air theater

Photos: Courtesy Marván Arquitectos

CITY: Celaya
COUNTRY: Mexico
REGION: Central America
TYPOLOGY: Culture
COMPLETION: –
WEBSITE: www.marvanarquitectos.com
ARCHITECTS: Marván Arquitectos

MUSEO DE HISTORIA NATURAL TAMUX

The formality of the Museum, which is known as the Museum of Natural History and constructed by Marvan Arquitectos, uproots all the way from a cylindrical volume to the way of an encounter place, where such elements as the light, the materials and the game of circulations all act as part of the route of the space, while also becoming somewhat jumbled but in a sensible form. Here, taking the main and sensible route through its five located rooms comes off in a way as being descendent ordinate, and taking the visitor again to converge in the great cylinder equipped with a visual space towards the city.

01 Exterior stairway **02** Interior view, mezzanine floor **03** General view **04** Interior view, hall **05** Ground floor plan

Photos: Francisco J. Marván, Rodrigo Marván C., Eric Wuotto

CITY Ciudad Victoria
COUNTRY Mexico
REGION Central America
TYPOLOGY Culture
COMPLETION 2004
WEBSITE www.marvanarquitectos.com
ARCHITECTS Marván Arquitectos

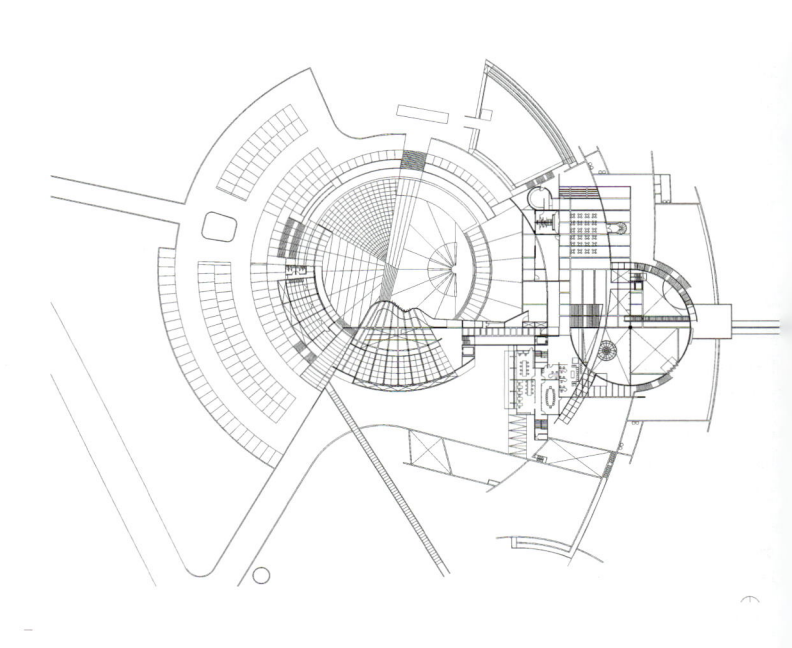

CAFÉ CINCO

Café Cinco is a coffee shop built on a rural zone in Morelos, in front of a Montessori school, making it useful during the day. The café was built under the concept of an ecological site in order to instruct the young students, while respecting the landscape that surrounds it, allowing for great views of La Sierra del Tepozteco. It is a space closed by recycled steel panels that work by using a pulley system and flexible wheels. The project is constantly being painted by the children that work on mobile chalkboard panels, and provides an awareness of ecological consciouseness to the kids; an aim set out by the café.

01 Exterior view **02** Entrance area **03** Detail façade **04** Rough landscape **05** Elevation **06** Rear view

Photos: Claudia Leon, T3ARC

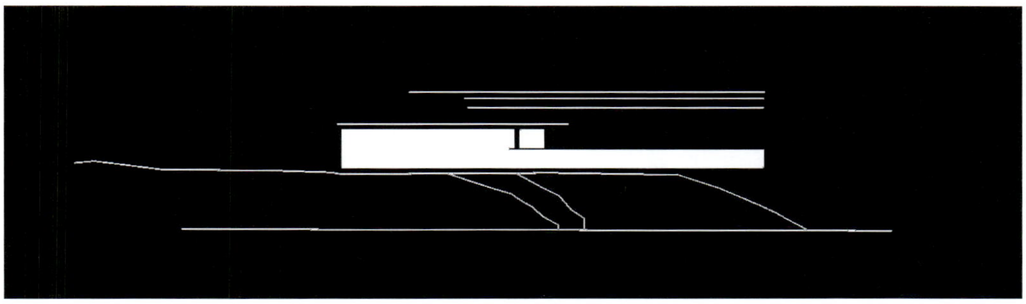

CITY Cuernavaca
COUNTRY Mexico
REGION Central America
TYPOLOGY Gastronomy
COMPLETION 2007
WEBSITE www.t3arc.com
ARCHITECTS T3ARC Taller de Arte y Arquitectura / Alfredo Raymundo Cano Briceño

CITY
Cuernavaca

COUNTRY
Mexico

REGION
Central America

TYPOLOGY
Ecclesiastical

COMPLETION
2007

WEBSITE
www.bunkerarquitectura.com

ARCHITECTS
Bunker Arquitectura

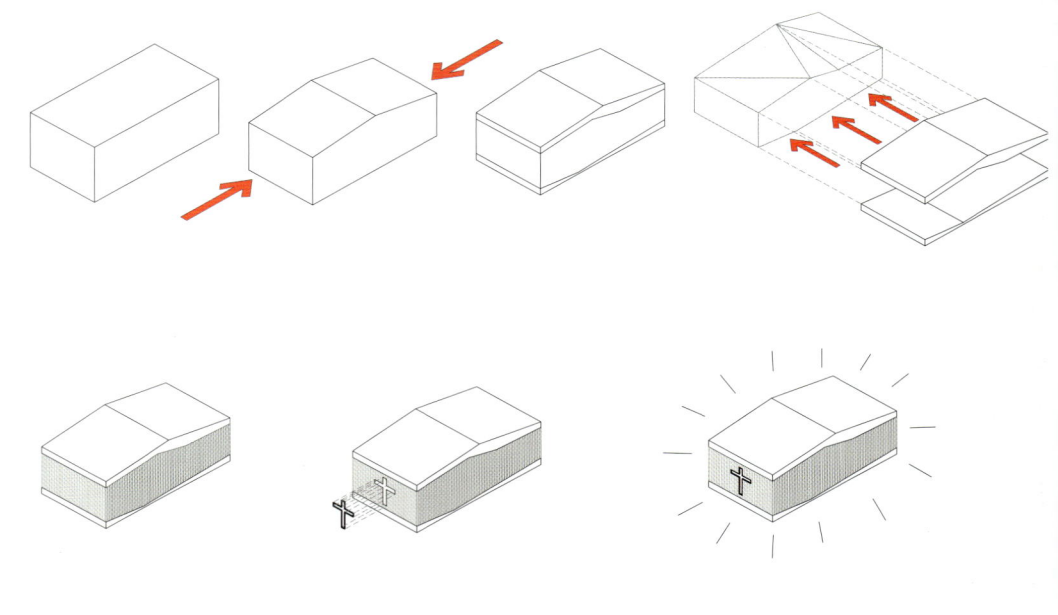

CHAPEL IN A GARDEN

Located in the town of Cuernavaca, a popular destination for couples, the chapel was planned for a beautiful Mexican colonial garden that caters to weddings. A modern chapel was designed to contrast with the surroundings and is presented like a sculpture in the garden. A glass façade acts as lattice walls, creating a cross-ventilated space, while the exuberant vegetation and tall jacaranda trees permeate through the walls, creating a graceful and rhythmical dialogue between the interior and exterior space. The original floor design was conceived in white polished concrete.

01 Detail façade, cut out cross **02** Exterior view by night, lattice glass façade **03** Interior view to altar **04** Diagrams **05** South elevation

Photos: Megs Inniss, Sebastian Suárez

ORIGAMI

Considering prevailing climatic aspects at Cuernavaca City, a geometric diagram was proposed which has playful character. The design builds up by unfolding itself to generate a clear space, avoiding scale's prominence, exalting up visual changes and causing in the observer an inevitable game to create the constructive metamorphosis of the principal section: one extended structure which responds to solar effect, allowing for crossed ventilation. The form and volumetric condition reflect a clear influence of functional architecture taken away to the edge, with working like the Glass house by Philip Johnson.

01 Bird's eye view **02** Glass façade **03** Ground floor plan
04 Interior view, floor windows to underground garden

Photos: Rec Arquitectura

CITY	Cuernavaca
COUNTRY	Mexico
REGION	Central America
TYPOLOGY	Commercial (Showroom)
COMPLETION	2007
WEBSITE	www.recarquitectura.com
ARCHITECTS	Rec Arquitectura / Gerardo Recoder

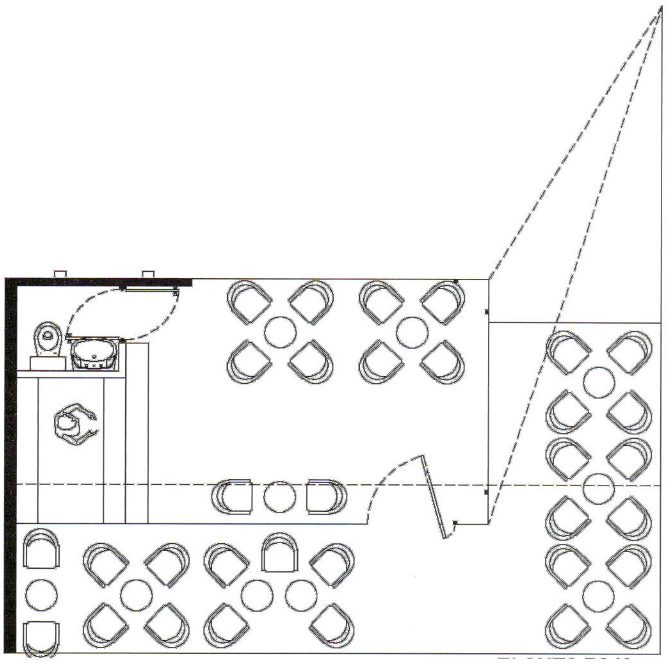

PETATGLASS

A binary space was generated in the Petatglass development, involving tradition with a creative language in this geometric orthogonal building, which is discreet and respectful toward the environment, where combination is used in each of the creative phases from the conception to the pragmatic construction. A reinterpretation of palapa creates the skin of the façade which has the biggest solar exposition while generating a unique visual mimicry accentuating its presence with a new language. The façade offers a new form of seeing the straw or palapa, which is commonly used for the roof in horizontal elements.

01 Section **02** New box and existent house **03, 04** Detail façade: dried and woven palm-tree leaves alternate with glass

Photos: Rec Arquitectura

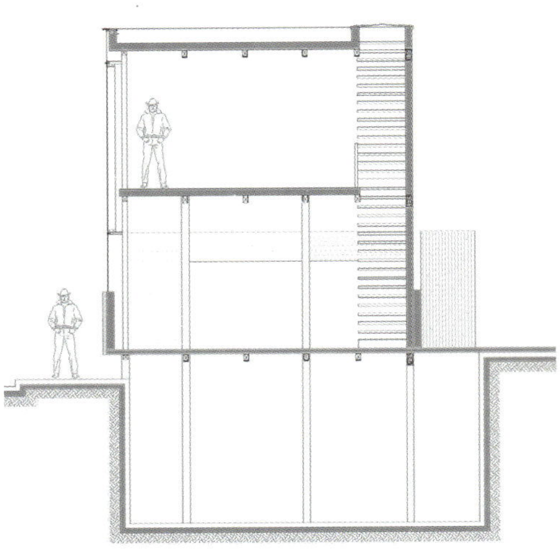

CITY
Cuernavaca

COUNTRY
Mexico

REGION
Central America

TYPOLOGY
Commercial

COMPLETION
2006

WEBSITE
www.recarquitectura.com

ARCHITECTS
Rec Arquitectura / Gerardo Recoder

HOUSE IN SAN MIGUEL DE ALLENDE

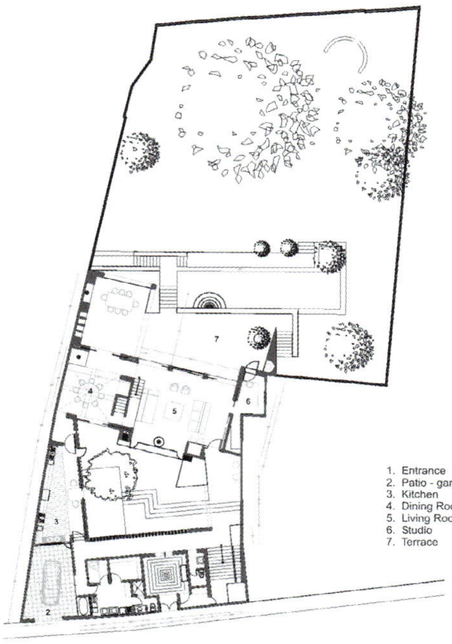

The façade design facing Aldama St. took into consideration the strict rules of the National Institute of Anthropology and History. The main concern was not to break the general milieu of the city center, conserving the proportions of windows, heights and colors. The project was developed around an existing tree, creating a courtyard as the focal point of the house, which is surrounded by the access corridor, kitchen, living & dining room. The access corridor takes the form of a pathway around the courtyard, surrounded by lattice windows with vertical elements that let one discreetly view the garden, terrace, and pool.

01 Garden view **02** Ground floor plan **03** Courtyard with red onix outdoor table **04** Stairway to the second floor, next to water ramp **05** View from upstairs corridor to dining room

Photos: Lourdes Legorreta

CITY Guanajuato
COUNTRY Mexico
REGION Central America
TYPOLOGY Living
COMPLETION 2005
WEBSITE www.legorretalegorreta.com
ARCHITECTS Legorreta + Legorreta

LINDA VISTA HOUSE

This old residential zone of Guadalupe México provided possibilities to experiment with a pragmatic solution to its surroundings. Responding to factors such as traffic, noise and graffiti, the house is designed like a shell protecting the inner life. An L-shaped plan adjusts to the street sides of the site, allowing the program towards the interior. Facing the street are openings that provide little light and a subtle blending with the exterior, while each room, with its own privacy, faces the patio where social activities take place. A simple system of concrete walls and steel columns are the main house structure.

01 Exterior view **02** Staircase **03** Floor plans **04** Entrance area **05** Interior view

Photos: Vicente San Martin

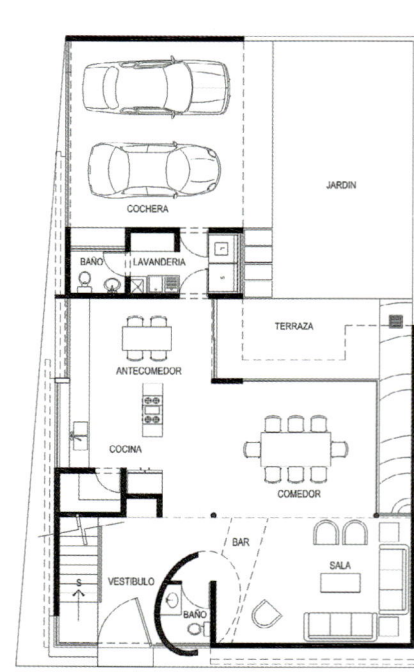

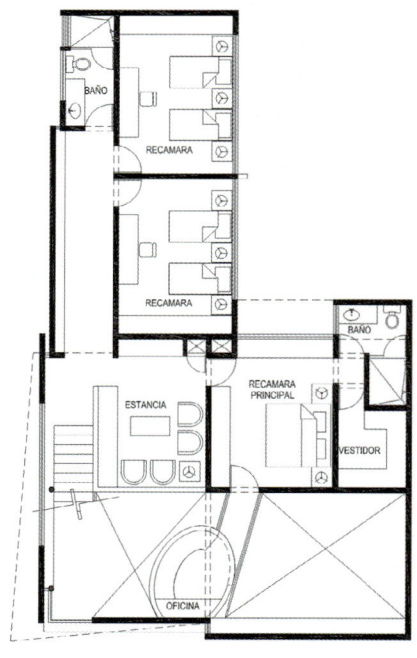

GDL1 HOUSE

The project, located in the suburbs of Guadalajara, has fantastic views of the city. The house is composed by two rectangular prisms, one over the other with a perpendicular orientation between them, where the bottom prism contains private areas and the vestibule. This parallelogram cuts the lot creating a private courtyard of white gravel in the highest part of the site, and a garden, terrace and pool in the lowest. The second volume, running parallel to the street, houses public activities and floats over the place in a cantilever. A double-height vestibule area with a skylight and reflective pond is also featured.

01 Terrace and pool **02** Exterior view from east **03** View into intersection of prisms **04** Longitudinal sections **05** Vestibule area with pond and skylight

Photos: Jaime Navarro

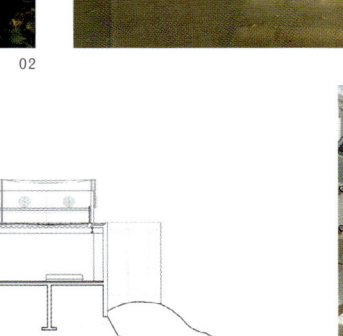

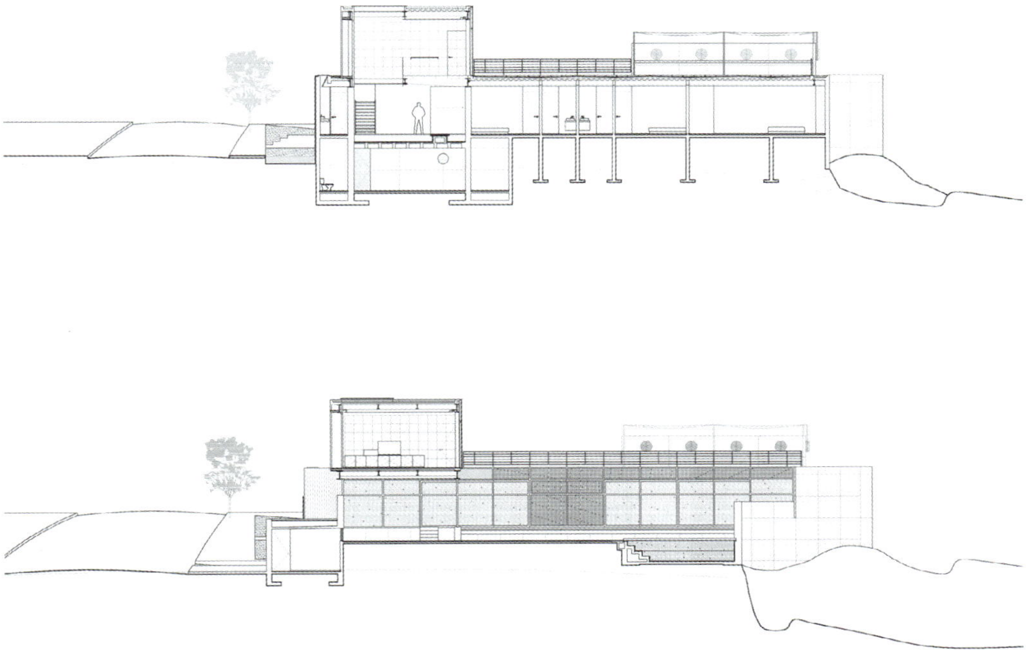

CITY Guadalajara
COUNTRY Mexico
REGION Central America
TYPOLOGY Living
COMPLETION 2005
WEBSITE www.bgp.com.mx
ARCHITECTS bgp arquitectura

CITY Guadalajara
COUNTRY Mexico
REGION Central America
TYPOLOGY Office
COMPLETION 2007
WEBSITE www.ad11.com.mx
ARCHITECTS AD 11, Salvador Macias, Francisco Gutierrez

ADVERTISING AGENCY

The project consists of two buildings with different functions. One of them contains the administrative and creative offices, and the other one, the printing and production complex. The project's goal was to open up the façade in order to show what the company represents: a merchandising brand, and serve as an advertising billboard. The staircase acts as the communications articulator, maintaining the dialogue between the two buildings. To bring natural light into the working spaces was a fundamental part of the project, thus skylights were carefully placed to infuse the entire buildings with it.

01 Building 2, north façade **02** Interior view building 1, lobby **03** Building 1, north façade **04** First floor plan **05** Building 2, west façade

Photos: Mito Covarrubias

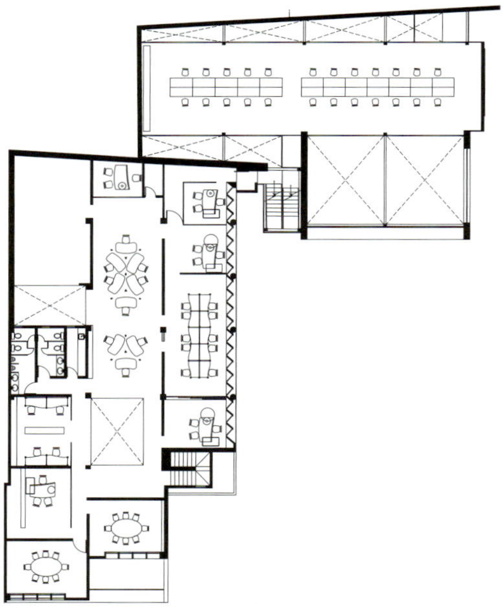

CIME

This building of a singular nature is inserted into a traditional urban context. The architectonic proposal for these offices is to avoid simulation and, keeping in accord with our present time, to contribute a modern style to the location. The frontage reflects the tension of past and present. On the one hand, it respects the neighborhood through its introverted character, its moderate height and the harmony of its horizontal lines and neutral colors. On the other hand, it affirms its contemporary character by means of its solemn expression, the severity of its geometry and by its discreetly apparent structure.

01 Courtyard, entry ground floor **02** Courtyard, first floor
03 Ground and first floor plan **04** Exterior view from the street
05 Courtyard, backside ground floor

Photos: Mito Covarrubias

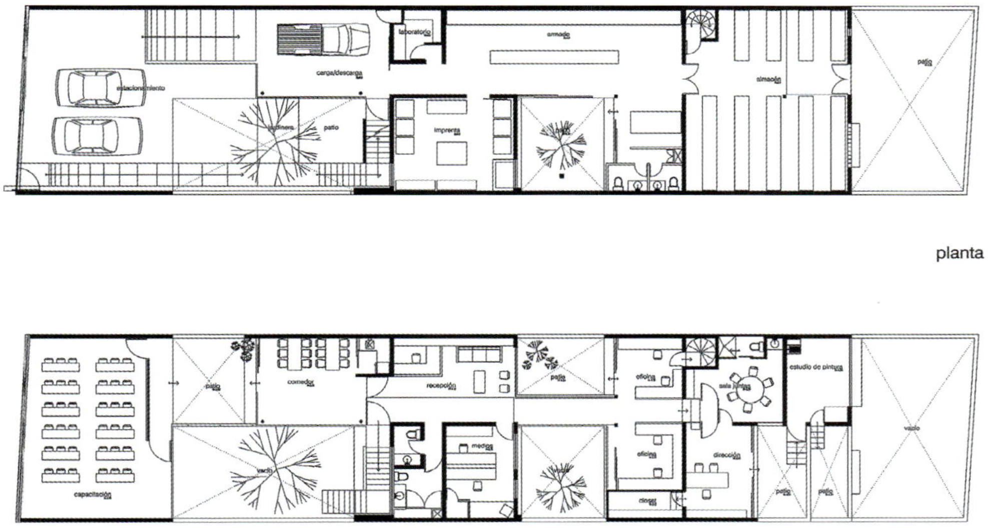

planta baja

CITY
Guadalajara

COUNTRY
Mexico

REGION
Central America

TYPOLOGY
Office

COMPLETION
2007

WEBSITE
www.ad11.com.mx

ARCHITECTS
AD 11
Salvador Macías
Francisco Gutiérrez

CITY
Guadalajara

COUNTRY
Mexico

REGION
Central America

TYPOLOGY
Public

COMPLETION
2007

WEBSITE
www.ad11.com.mx

ARCHITECTS
AD 11
Salvador Macias
Francisco Gutierrez

ARIA PAVILLION

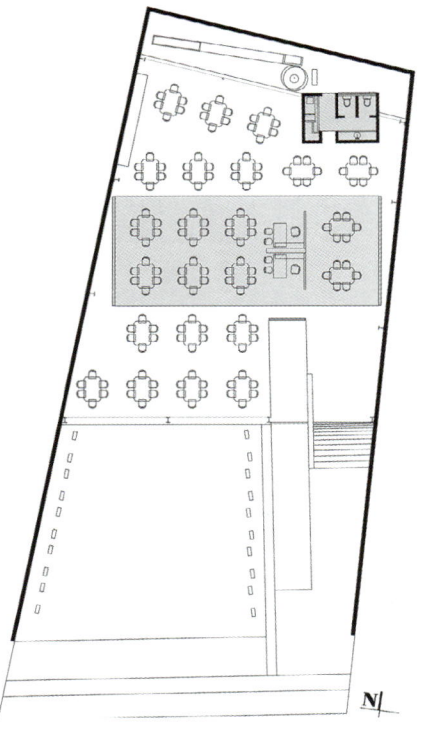

The Aria Pavillion project is being placed inside an industrial warehouse conditioned by its existing structure and boundaries. It consists of two inner pavilions within the existing shed that serve as a showroom for the exhibition and sale of catalog furniture. Among the limit of the ephemeral, the house also finds the lavatory areas as a useful space. In order to gain a back patio which would allow and provide light and ventilation for the interior, the shed detaches itself from the back boundary. The last element is a curtain wall of glass, that encloses the shed at the front and back façades.

01 Front view **02** Floor plan **03** Interior view, entrance area **04** Interior view

Photos: Francisco Gutierrez

ATENAS 354

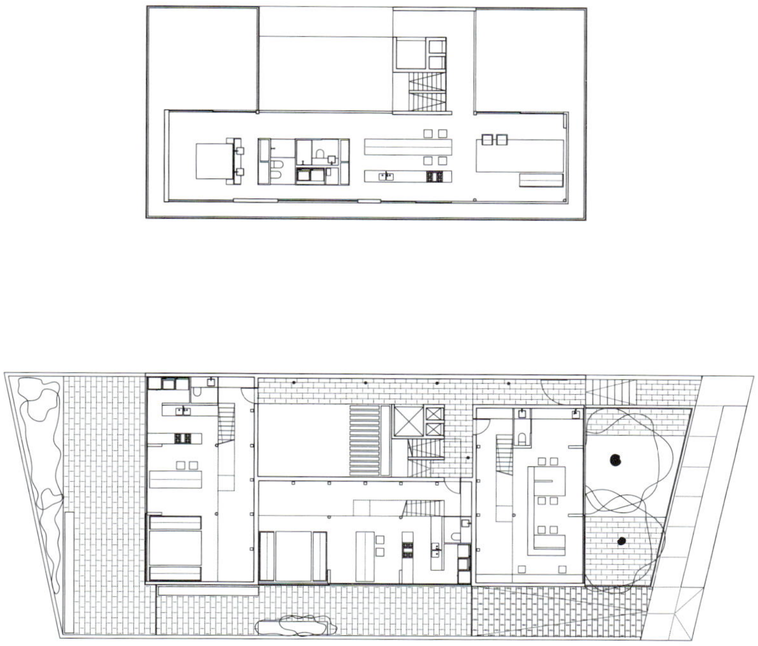

The project known as Atenas 354 consists of a building for 6 lofts and a penthouse. The lofts are formed by means of a free plant of 6 by 12 meters, while the mezzanine of 4 by 12 meters conforms the second plant leaving one double height that crosses the entire loft and contains stairs that dress the space. The penthouse consists of a space of 20 by 5 meters where a project in free plant with panoramic views is developed on the American colony. The facades of the building are satisfied by means of the structure of concrete, with the particularity of which it pigments completely with black color.

01 View from deck to penthouse **02** Exterior view, concrete façade **03** Interior view, loft **04** Floor plans **05** Courtyard

Photos: Antonieta Rojas

CITY: Guadalajara
COUNTRY: Mexico
REGION: Central America
TYPOLOGY: Living
COMPLETION: 2007
WEBSITE: www.hipogeo.com
ARCHITECTS: Hipogeo

CITY
Huixquilucan

COUNTRY
Mexico

REGION
Central America

TYPOLOGY
Education

COMPLETION
2006

WEBSITE
www.cuarto.com.mx

ARCHITECTS
Cuarto Arquitectura Y Diseño

COLEGIO EL ROBLE

The project was born next to the academic project, when a group of compromised people gathered together with the common objective to improve education in Mexico, and initiated in 2004 the creation of the School. The idea came about from the excellent results obtained by Descubre, an institution focused on helping people with ADD. Located west of Mexico City, in Interlomas, the design contemplates to be built in different phases, as the increment of school grades demand it. Today, Kindergarten and Elementary are in operation, with a gymnasium, Middle School, High School and a complementary parking lot still to be built.

01 Side view **02** Rear view, cast-in-situ concrete façade **03** Interior view **04** Floor plans **05** Exterior stairway

Photos: Diego García

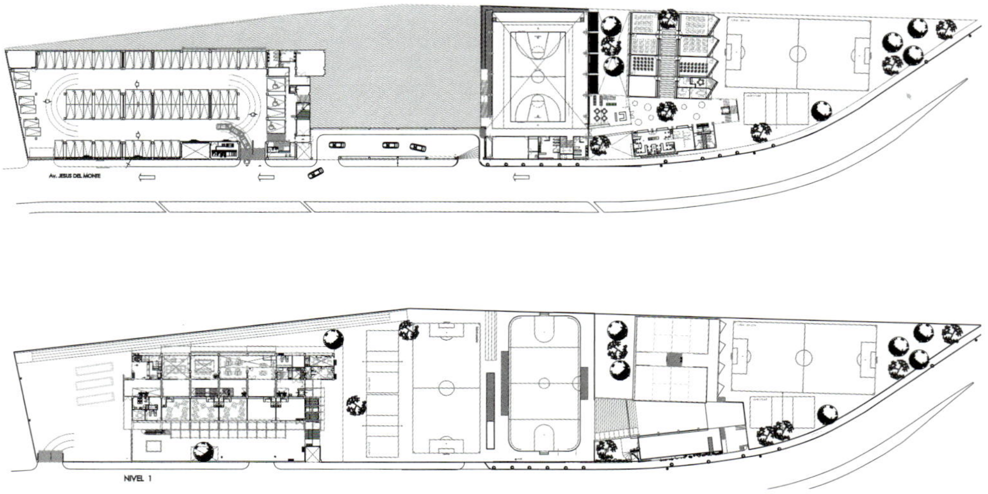

CA HOUSE

Camino a Barra de Potosí Lote # 39, Col. Agrícola Playa Blanca, Municipio de José Azueta, Ixtapa, Guerrero is where this development project is situated. The single-family house is located on a 8,200 square foot lot with an 80 feet beach front facing the Pacific Ocean. The land is practically plain and is located on a low urbanized area. The structure is made of reinforced concrete walls and waffle flat slabs, finished in exposed concrete mixed with local sand as an aggregate. The main level is located on the second floor in order to provide the best views to the ocean with all living spaces arranged along a central gardened patio.

01 Exterior view from the beach side 02 Extended terrace resting on landscape 03 Rear façade 04 Bird's eye view 05 Front façade

Renderings: Eliud Aguirre / Iñaki Echeverria Taller de Arquitecture

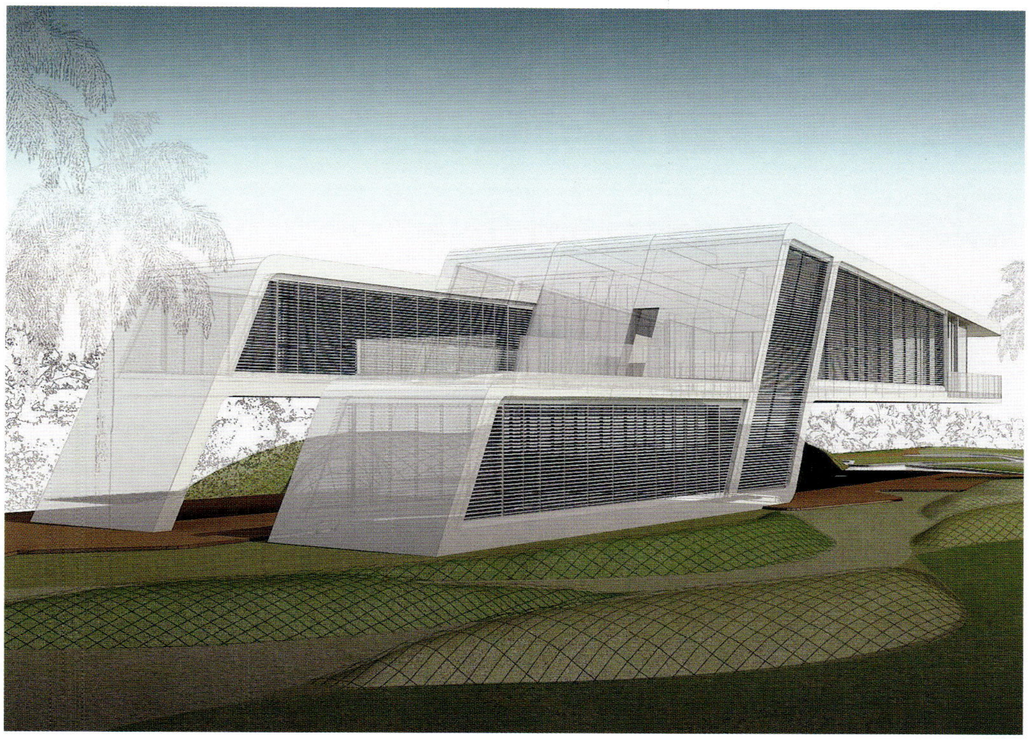

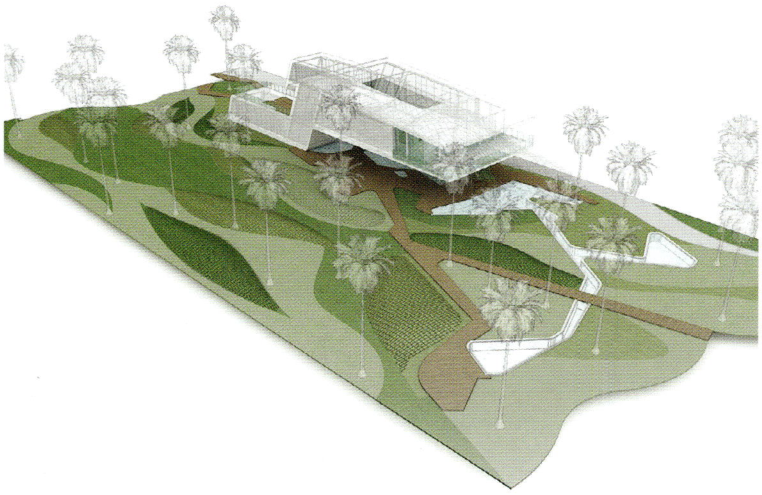

CITY: Ixtapa
COUNTRY: Mexico
REGION: Central America
TYPOLOGY: Living
COMPLETION: unbuilt
WEBSITE: www.inakiecheverria.com
ARCHITECTS: Iñaki Echeverria

CITY Los Cabos
COUNTRY Mexico
REGION Central America
TYPOLOGY Hospitality
COMPLETION 2002
WEBSITE www.archetonic.com.mx
ARCHITECTS Archetonic, Arq. Jacobo Micha Mizrahi

HOTEL MARQUIS LOS CABOS

The Hotel Marquis Los Cabos by Jacobo Micha Mizrahi consists of 204 junior suites, 5 Marquis suites, 1 presidential suite, 28 small houses, 3 open level gyms of 500 m², spa of 1,000 m² with massage areas, outer and inner Jacuzzis, snack bar, restaurant of different and various specialties, 39 deprived ponds, a VIP pond, 2 infiniti ponds with Jacuzzis that warm up gradually, integrated and modern dance halls, a future casino that is currently in the works, a business center, lobby, group lobby, and finally an area of administration and control. All in all, this Resort screams the word 'fun'.

01 Main lobby **02** Spa access and lobby **03** Detail waterfall platforms **04** Floor plan **05** Lobby

Photos: Paúl Czitrom

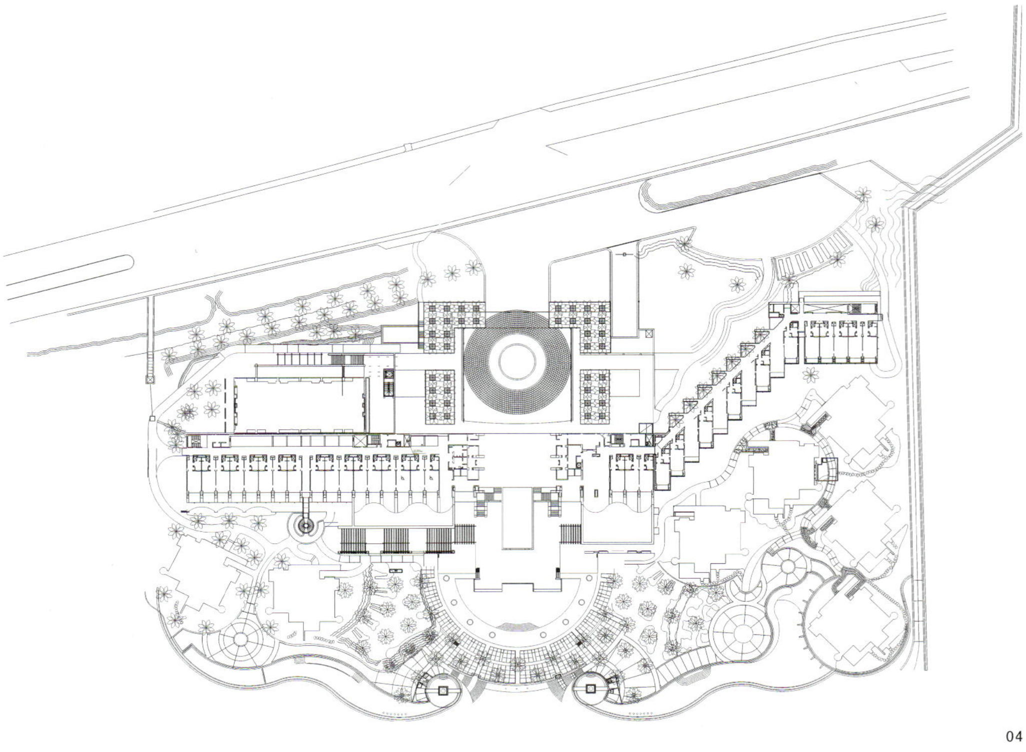

CASA LOS AMATES

Located in a tourist resort in Morelos, Mexico, the factors of the design included vegetation, warm climate, and the customer's needs. A light stone platform separates the house from the ground, where on the first level, light vertical reinforcements and a glass curtain create space for the dining room area. A detailed wooden lattice makes it possible to communicate the guest's bedroom with all the other services of the house while providing warmness and texture. An outdoor corridor serves as a mirador and link to communicate with each space on this level, while the swimming pool merges with its natural surroundings.

01 Exterior view house sitting on stone platform **02** Detail outdoor corridor and wooden lattice **03** View from the street **04** Floor plans **05** View from living room to platform with swimming pool

Photos: Paúl Czitrom

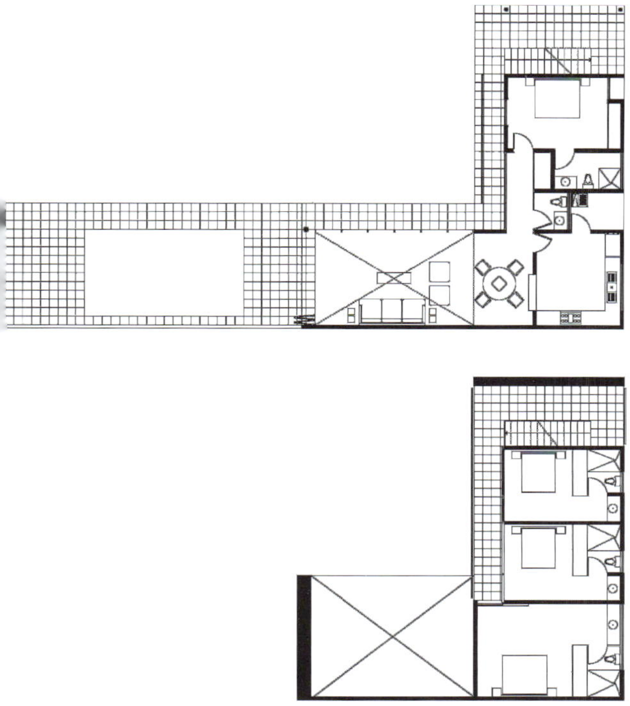

CITY Morelos
COUNTRY Mexico
REGION Central America
TYPOLOGY Living
COMPLETION 2005
WEBSITE www.hernandezdelagarza.com
ARCHITECTS JHG Jorge Hernández de la Garza

CORPORATIVO FREXPORT

Using the architectonic program, an attempt was made to produce form rhetoric of the promenades in the countryside. The gardens became the soul of the project, while also introducing the landscape. The green palette of vegetation and the force of natural stone were the elements that marked the design, leaving in its steps all the crops that constitute the company's line of production. The corporate offices were considered to be open-built, taking down the dividing walls to become part of the contiguous gardens. Three-stories were formed by lightweight concrete parallelepipeds, conceived to absorb.

01 Detail garden: mix of plants and stone **02** Detail staircase **03** Linking passage **04** Ground floor plan **05** Front view

Photos: Luis Gordoa

CITY Michoacan
COUNTRY Mexico
REGION Central America
TYPOLOGY Office
COMPLETION 2007
WEBSITE www.ccarquitectos.com.mx
ARCHITECTS CC Arquitectos

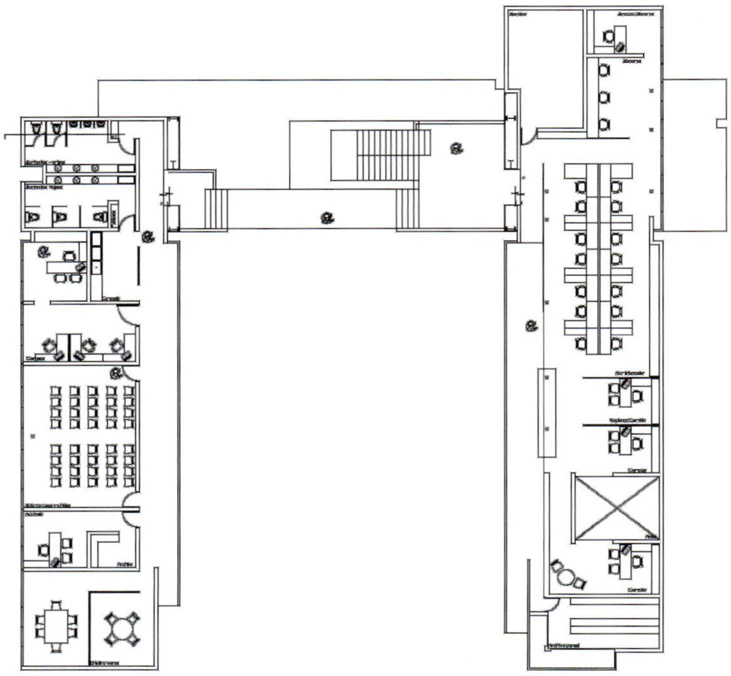

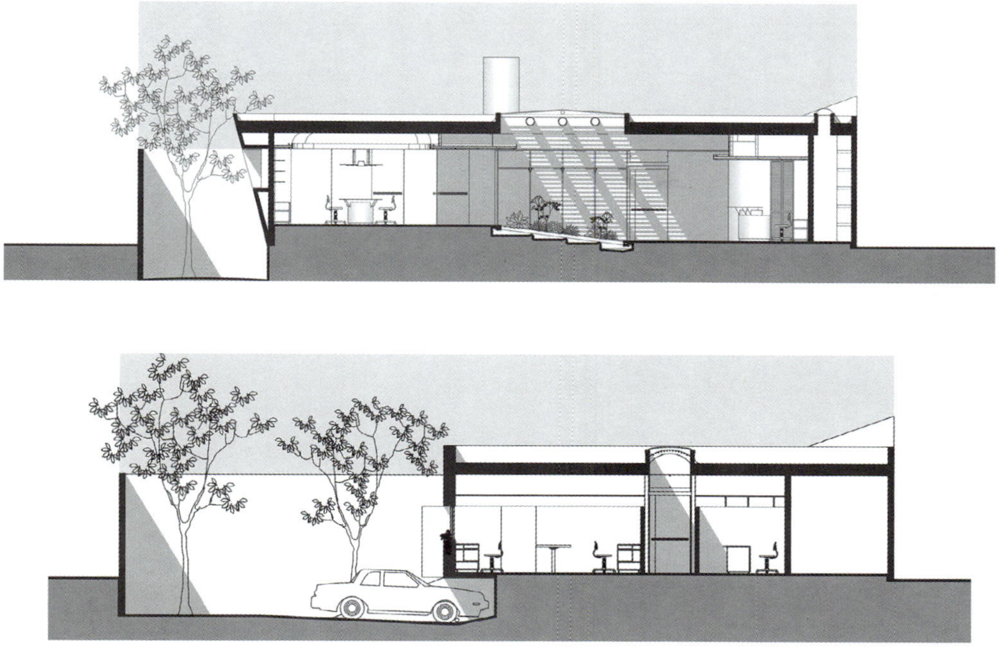

OFICINAS CORPORATIVAS CONSTRUCTORA PROSER

The simplicity of design in this project comes together as two volumes – one in the form of an L-shaped prism and another one with a triangular profile – embrace each other to produce the access space that receives visitors. The triangular forms accentuate the horizontal depth of the space reflecting their contemporary nature and at the same time, they reference the forms of Mayan architecture. The product of a careful study of function, the building is divided into four main areas: reception, managerial, administration, articulated by means of a central circulation that links all parts, obtaining simplicity and space savings.

01 Longitudinal section **02** Interior courtyard **03** Main façade **04** Exterior view by night **05** Interior courtyard

Photos: Roberto Ancona Riestra, Roberto Cárdenas

CITY	Mérida
COUNTRY	Mexico
REGION	Central America
TYPOLOGY	Office
COMPLETION	2005
WEBSITE	–
ARCHITECTS	Roberto Ancona Riestra

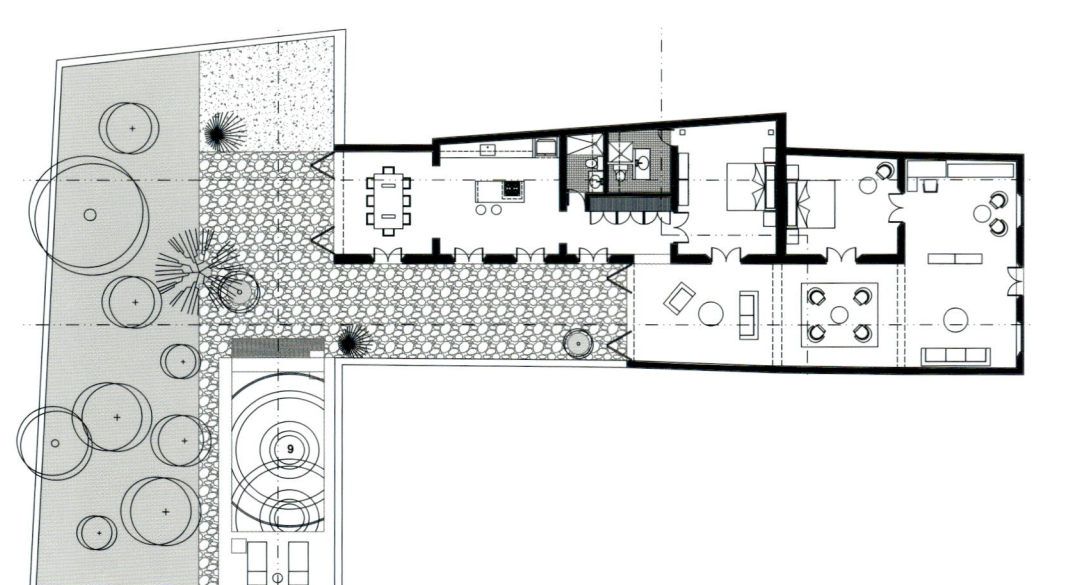

CITY Mérida
COUNTRY Mexico
REGION Central America
TYPOLOGY Living
COMPLETION 2007
WEBSITE www.estiloyucatan.com
ARCHITECTS Victor Cruz, Atahualpa Hernandez, Luis Estrada, Silvia Cuitun / Estilo Yucatan

CL53 HOUSE

The CL53 House attempts at Preserving integrity within its context, reusing the existing spaces, and reorganizing according to the new needs by maximizing the architectural virtues and aesthetic qualities of materials, clean lines and extraordinary resources. The project maintained one of its greatest space virtues of the old homes; "introverted life, a wide interior-exterior relationship, and a rich culture integration and respect for the past." The result is a space created about one century ago, completely renovated, that utilizes its rich space and aesthetic, adding value with its cultural heritage.

01 View from deck to kitchen **02** Swimming pool by night **03** View into hall **04** Floor plan

Photos: Roberto Cárdenas Cabello

LW49 HOUSE

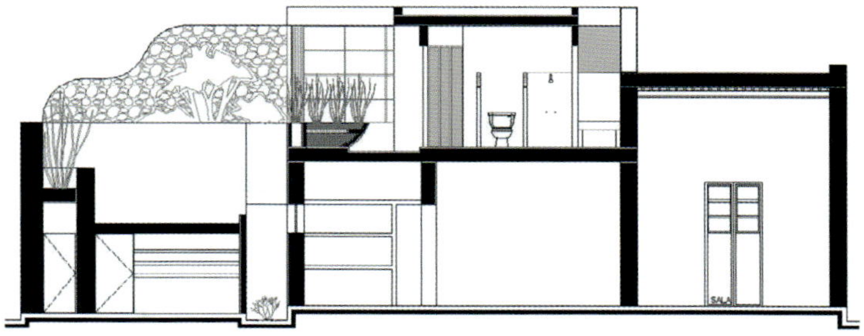

A large house built during different periods of the 20th Century has been adapted to current functional and aesthetic needs without neglecting its historical and architectural value. Original architectural elements of this house were restored and in some cases re-evaluated adding modern day materials like glass and concrete. It is hard to imagine life in these big mansions without the central courtyard, around which life revolves. It was evident this was the important relationship between the indoors and the outdoors. The house maintains this communication between the old and the new without either one overbearing the other.

01 View through glass doors into living room **02** Section **03** Backyard **04** Detail staircase **05** Upper floor, view to bedroom

Photos: Roberto Cárdenas Cabello, Alberto Caceres Centeno

CITY Mérida
COUNTRY Mexico
REGION Central America
TYPOLOGY Living
COMPLETION 2007
WEBSITE www.estiloyucatan.com
ARCHITECTS Victor Cruz, Atahualpa Hernandez, Luis Estrada, Silvia Cuitun / Estilo Yucatan

BIBLIOTECA DE CIENCIAS SOCIALES

Located at the center of a new campus, the Library of Social Sciences will amount to the most important collection about Mayan culture in the area. One of the two contrasting forms is "C" shaped and embraces a central courtyard that links the exterior gardens with the reading areas. The list of spaces includes the main hall, media center, different reading areas for group or individual work and balconies and terraces on the upper levels. A central dome provides sunlight and shadow variations to the main hall used as a cultural center and exhibition area. Angled planes, platforms and simple forms create a well-integrated complex.

01 Backside view **02** Exterior view **03** Interior isonometric **04** Informal reading area

Photos: Roberto Ancona Riestra

CITY: Mérida
COUNTRY: Mexico
REGION: Central America
TYPOLOGY: Culture
COMPLETION: 2007
WEBSITE: –
ARCHITECTS: Roberto José Ancona Riestra

HOSPITAL REGIONAL DE ALTA ESPECIALIDAD

Based on the investigations of Roger S. Ulrich, Ph. D., and his proposals on comprehensive design, this project incorporated aspects that are of privilege to the patients of the mechanical operation. Constant interaction with exteriors was allowed, and since the inhabitants are more familiarized with the exterior, the project resorted to profuse native vegetation, besides conserving the existing trees, and to promote shade, while improve airflow naturally. Privacy is obtained with porches restricting the view of interior spaces, while suppressing corridor and doctors offices to allow lines of vision to the outside.

01 View to entrance plaza **02** Exterior view, detail passage **03** Different volumes **04** Sections **05** Operating room

Photos: Roberto Cárdenas Cabello

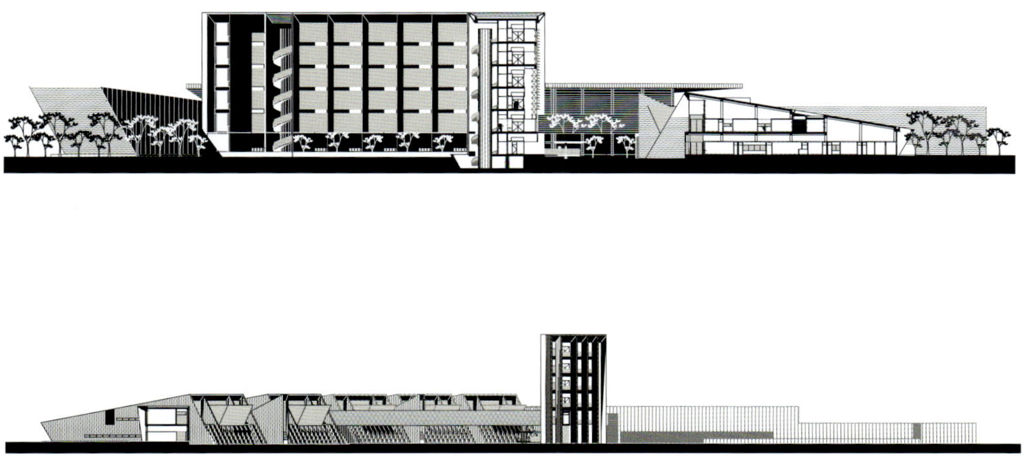

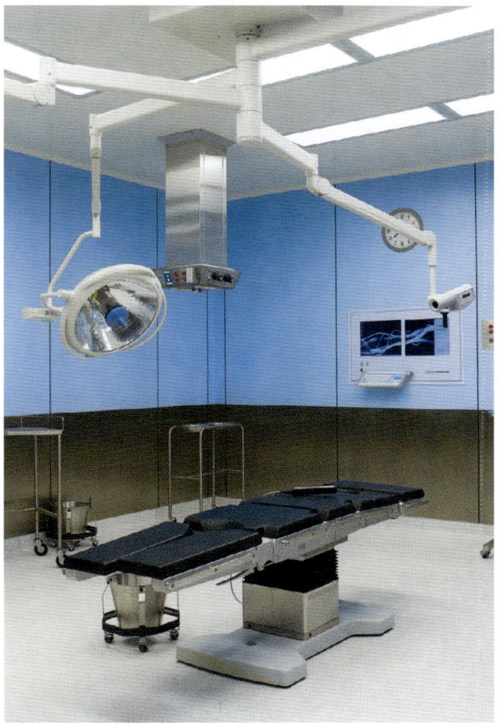

CITY: Mérida
COUNTRY: Mexico
REGION: Central America
TYPOLOGY: Health
COMPLETION: 2007
WEBSITE: www.duarteaznar.com
ARCHITECTS: Duarte Aznar Arquitectos, S.C.P

PROCURADURÍA GENERAL DE JUSTICIA DEL ESTADO DE YUCATÁN

Located in the peripheral ring of the city of Merida, this project allowed to propose a scheme of linear configuration that catches the kindness of the north, while providing a correct climatic operation of the building. In order to avoid long-hauls, the access in the intermediate point set out where the user could go towards a desired section. A roof is put on by a great slab where the general offices of the Solicitor and other services are located. This slab assembles with a tower of cubical configuration that contains the circulations, the services, and the departments of administration and computer science space.

01 Exterior view by night **02** Detail exterior **03** Sections and elevations **04** Assembly group, bathhouses **05** Interior view, staircase

Photos: Roberto Cárdenas Cabello

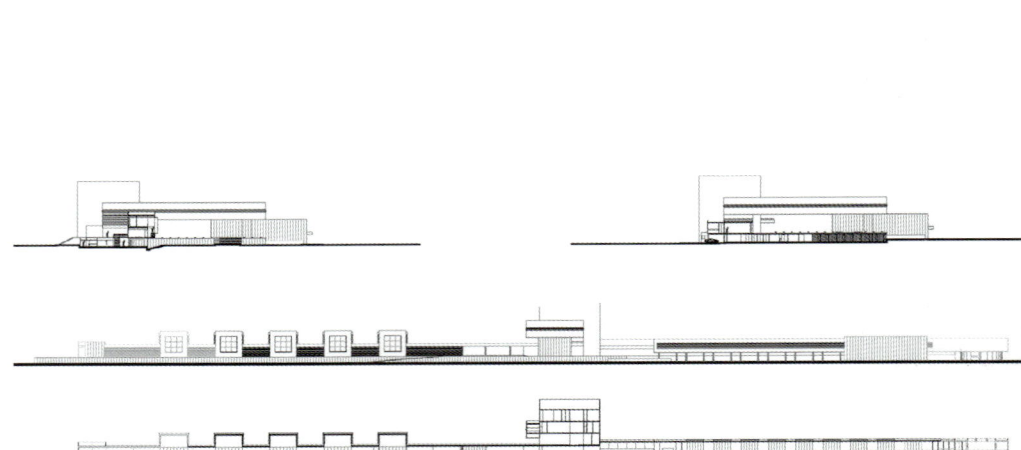

CITY Mérida
COUNTRY Mexico
REGION Central America
TYPOLOGY Institution
COMPLETION 2005
WEBSITE www.munozarquitectos.com
ARCHITECTS Muñoz Arquitectos Asociados S.C.P.

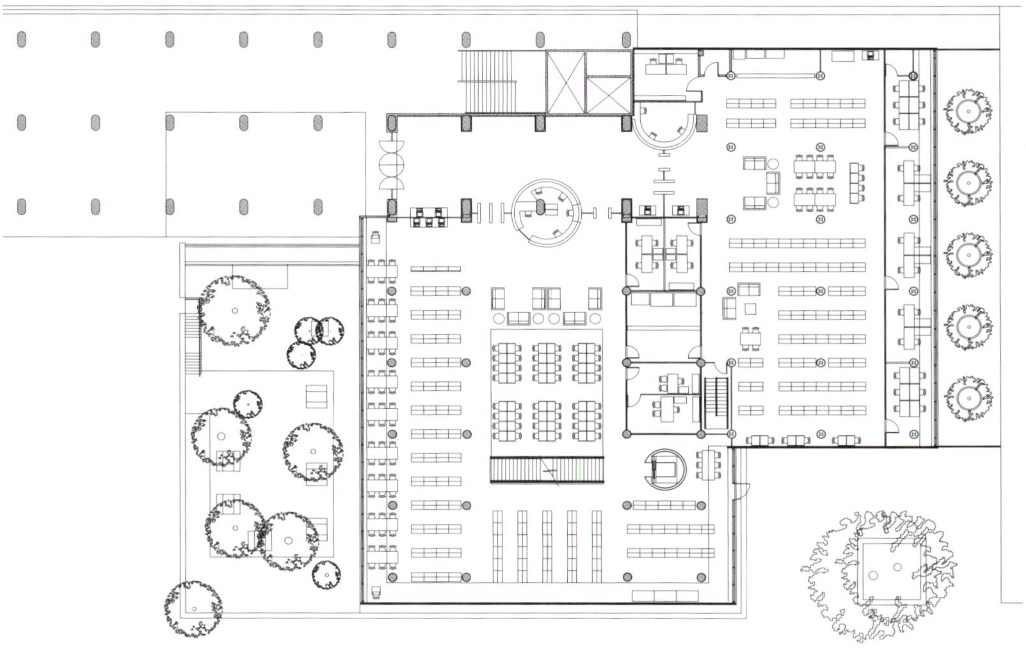

BIBLIOTECA DE LA FACULTAD DE MEDICINA CIUDAD UNIVERSITARIA, UNAM

The museum, along with a library, a school of arts and a theatre is part of a cultural center, and occupies an important city corner. In order to identify the importance of the place and to incorporate the city into to the center, a terrace with the access was placed on the corner. The terrace extends towards the interior of the museum and becomes the main lobby, continuing to the bottom of the building, ending in a garden. This great space of double height has the same ceiling, with a plafond of wood and several skylights that bathe the enclosure in light. From the lobby one can access the cafeteria and other support spaces.

01 Ground floor plan **02** Main façade **03** Exterior view **04** View double-height interior **05** Rear façade

Photos: Gerardo Villanueva

CITY Mexico City
COUNTRY Mexico
REGION Central America
TYPOLOGY Education
COMPLETION 2006
WEBSITE –
ARCHITECTS Nuño, Mac Gregor y de Buen Arquitectos, S.C.

CITY Mexico City
COUNTRY Mexico
REGION Central America
TYPOLOGY Living
COMPLETION 2008
WEBSITE www.alejandroaptilon.com
ARCHITECTS Alejandro Aptilon Arquitectos

ETC. BUILDING

The 750 m² six-story building is located on a narrow lot in the Condesa neighborhood. It consists of three apartments that interlock in a complex configuration designed to maximize space quality and quantity, reflecting each individual client's specific requirements. The building is inspired by the popular use of industrialized materials in its surroundings, which creates a spontaneous language of diverse shapes and volumes. While the final product represents a juxtaposition of three distinct dwelling configurations, it also reflects various layers of the local urban landscape, collapsed in a single integral structure.

01 Comic image 02 Front view 03 Side view from the street 04 Interior view, apartment

Photos: Gabriel Ramírez / Alejandro Aptilon Arquitectos

FLOW HOUSE

The 400 m² single-family house is located on a narrow lot with a steep slope and beautiful views. The layout of each level of the house determines its zoning, with the lowest floor designated for play and entertainment, the middle for private areas, the ground floor for social areas, and the top for services. This combination of zoning and band configuration allows interaction between artificial and natural landscapes. Inserted within a series of disparate single-family houses that is typical of Mexico City's suburbia, this project aims to make sense of the chaos with which it coexists rather than attempt to organize the existing context.

01 Exterior view by night **02** Detail façade **03** View from deck **04** Isonometric **05** Living area on the ground floor

Photos: Jorge del Olmo

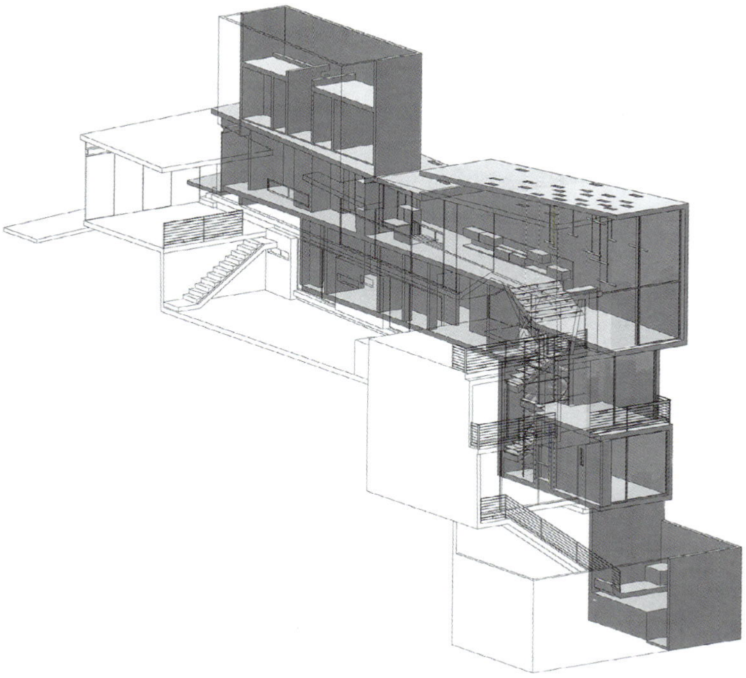

CITY Mexico City
COUNTRY Mexico
REGION Central America
TYPOLOGY Living
COMPLETION 2005
WEBSITE www.alejandroaptilon.com
ARCHITECTS Alejandro Aptilon Arquitectos / Ricardo Nurko

CITY Mexico City

COUNTRY Mexico

REGION Central America

TYPOLOGY Living

COMPLETION 2004

WEBSITE www.archetonic.com.mx

ARCHITECTS Archetonic, Arq. Jacobo Micha Mizrahi

PARRAL 67

This development contemplated to go ahead with the project in the estate located on the street indicated with number 67 within the Colony Countess, with a total surface of 219,00 m². The design is defined by two modules divided symmetrically by a composition axis; these modules where the departments are located are united by a unit of stairs that act as a central axis and that allow to transfer horizontally and vertically within the set. These modules to which reference is made of will be integrated virtually thanks to the fact that in both they were used as the same type of materials and distinguishing elements.

01 View from the street **02** Detail façade, courtyard **03** Front view **04** Floor plans

Photos: Paúl Czitrom

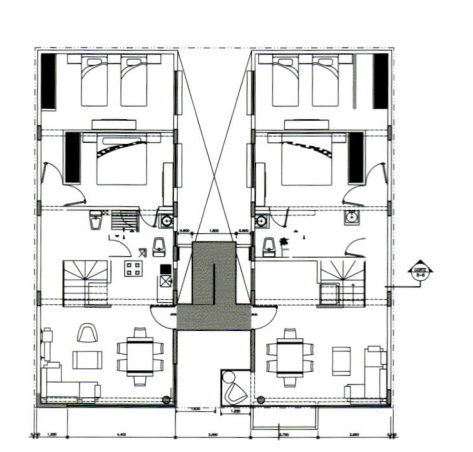

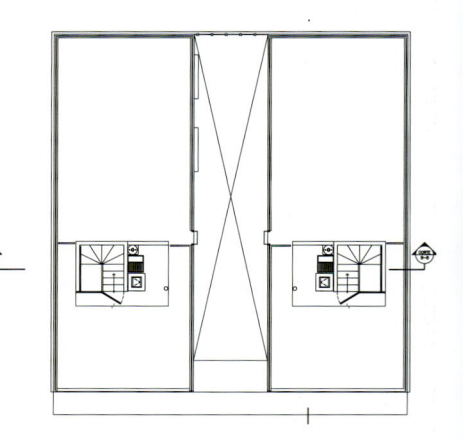

CORPORATIVO BANORTE

The decision to generate strong and simultaneously effective spaces provided results where the user is the center of attention. It is a corporative building dedicated to offer the most advanced concept to world-wide level in spaces of corporative type, integrating maximum efficiency, functionality, security, and bringing back ecological consciousness to technology of end with the use of materials of the highest quality. It consists of a tower with 14 levels of offices, mezzanine for private offices or diverse commerce of public attention, a main lobby, 7.5 levels for underground parking, and a neli-puerto on the roof.

01 Detail façade **02** Exterior view main façade **03** Entrance area **04** Floor plan **05** Deck

Photos: Paúl Czitrom

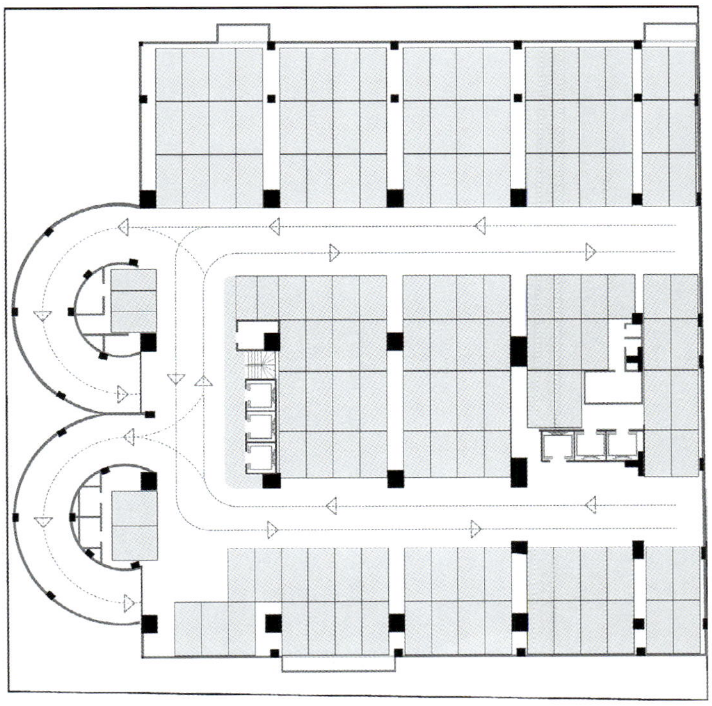

CITY: Mexico City
COUNTRY: Mexico
REGION: Central America
TYPOLOGY: Office
COMPLETION: 2006
WEBSITE: www.ardittiarquitectos.com
ARCHITECTS: Arditti+RDT arquitectos

CITY Mexico City
COUNTRY Mexico
REGION Central America
TYPOLOGY Living
COMPLETION 2000
WEBSITE www.armeestudio.com
ARCHITECTS armE_Studio, Pablo Velazquez, Manuel Moreno

CASA TLALPUENTE

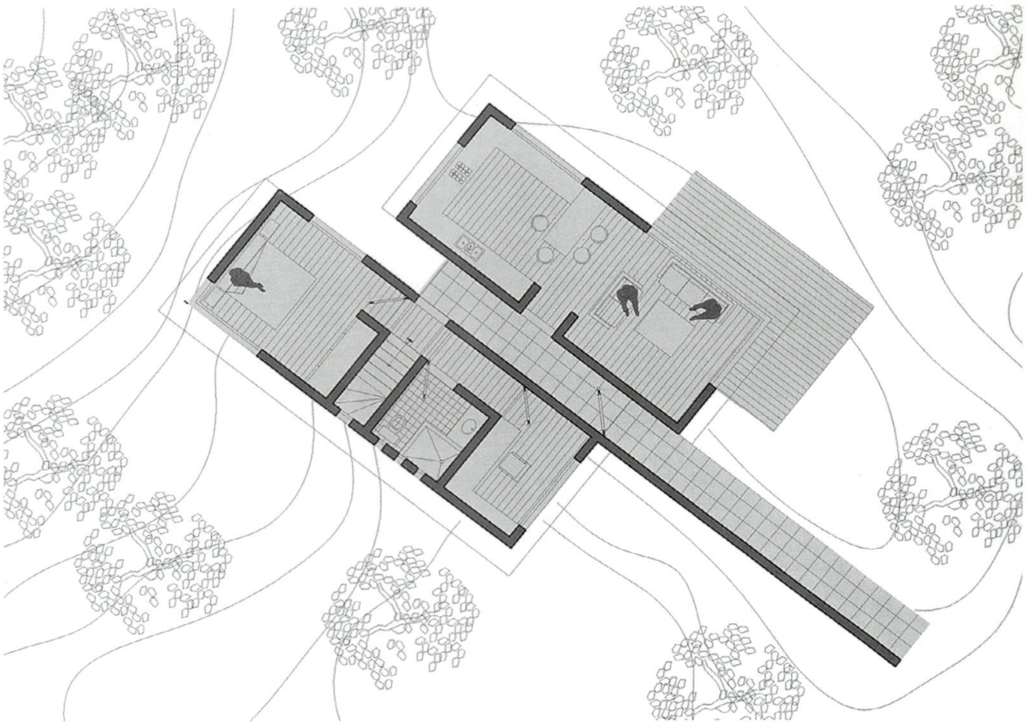

A simple detached house lies in a forested landscape, integrating a mixed program of housing and a recording studio. The house has been segmented horizontally and vertically in program and tectonics. The topography of the site allows different views of the house to exist – a one-leveled house from the entry point, and a two-storied volume from the lowest point of the site. One of the two volumes opens onto a terrace that links the interior with the exterior. On the ground, a solid base of volcanic rock connects the house to the landscape. Local materials and specialized handicrafts were used for wall finishings and window mullions.

01 West elevation **02** View from garden to main entry axis and deck **03** Ground floor plan **04** View from north

Photos: Pablo Velazquez

GM1607

The client is an architect, who envisioned an 8-unit building on this 12.5 by 25 meter plot. The apartments are arranged two per floor in a longitudinal orientation that is interrupted by three voids. The central void contains functional spaces, while the two lateral ones are terraces that act as separators between private and public spaces. The main entrance is framed by a sculptural pink front, whose facetted surface contrasts with the black-dyed concrete façade poured in wooden molds. Random perforations appear every 60 to 90 centimeters, creating a 40% open front. Each unit has 2–3 bedrooms, garage parking and a roof garden.

01 Exterior view by night **02** Detail entry, pastel glossy pink Boolean **03** Elevation, section and ground floor plan **04** View from apartment to staircase

Photos: Fito Pardo

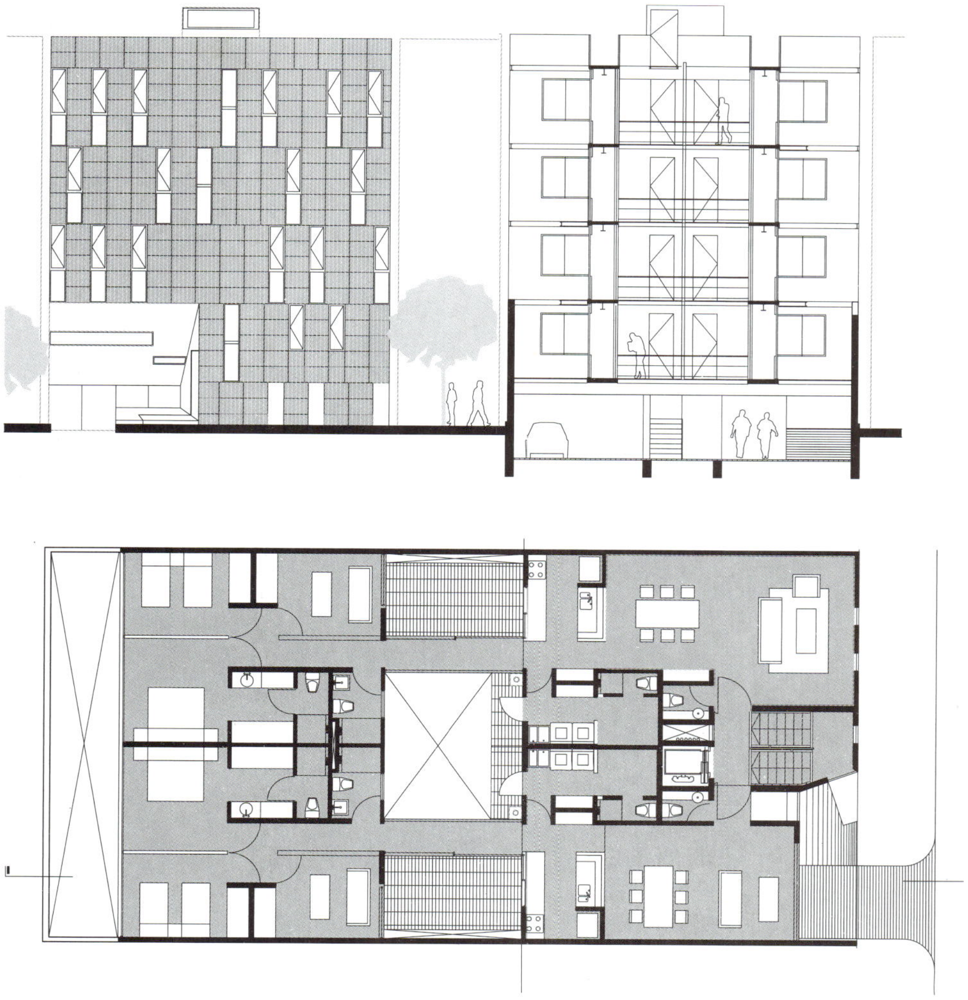

CITY Mexico City
COUNTRY Mexico
REGION Central America
TYPOLOGY Living
COMPLETION 2005
WEBSITE www.at103.net
ARCHITECTS at103 Julio Amezcua + Francisco Pardo

CITY Mexico City
COUNTRY Mexico
REGION Central America
TYPOLOGY Office
COMPLETION 2002
WEBSITE www.beckerarquitectos.com
ARCHITECTS Becker Arquitectos

CENTRO CORPORATIVO DIARQ

The building was projected as having a departure point, necessary to create a discreet presence, but at the same time staying elegant and solid. Its urban implantation respond with its outer porch and its column of double height, with the principle place depth in the curve describing the avenue and the lines of vision towards both flanks of the lot in which it is located. Under the mass level, it causes a grazing line of vision on the ample green area of the camels and gardens of the properties that border this avenue, at the same time this unevenness contributes to fulfill the regulation of heights of this zone.

01 Entrance area **02** Illuminated staircase **03** Outdoor hallway **04** Underground parking **05** Lobby

Photos: Fernando Cordero

ZACATECAS

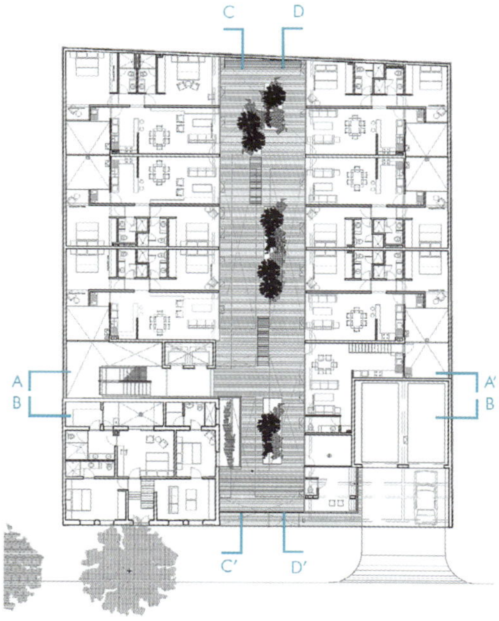

This apartment building is located in Mexico City's the Roma neighborhood founded in the 1920's. The integration of an existing listed house at the edge of the property was an important issue considered in the proposal. This house serves to define the project's main axes and create a central pedestrian throughway that will enhance the neighbors' encounters and coexistence. The road will become a street of lights through the use of glazed surfaces with different levels of transparency and translucency to reflect sunlight. The project creates 32 apartments on 4 levels in addition to the existing house to be restored.

01 View from the street **02** Ground floor plan **03** Detail throughway, ground floor **04, 05** Pedestrian throughway **06** Detail glazed surfaces

Photos: Rafael Gamo

CITY
Mexico City

COUNTRY
Mexico

REGION
Central America

TYPOLOGY
Living

COMPLETION
2006

WEBSITE
www.bgp.com.mx

ARCHITECTS
bgp arquitectura

CITY
Mexico City

COUNTRY
Mexico

REGION
Central America

TYPOLOGY
Public

COMPLETION
2006

WEBSITE
www.bgp.com.mx

ARCHITECTS
at 103 / bgp arquitectura

AVE FENIX FIRE STATION

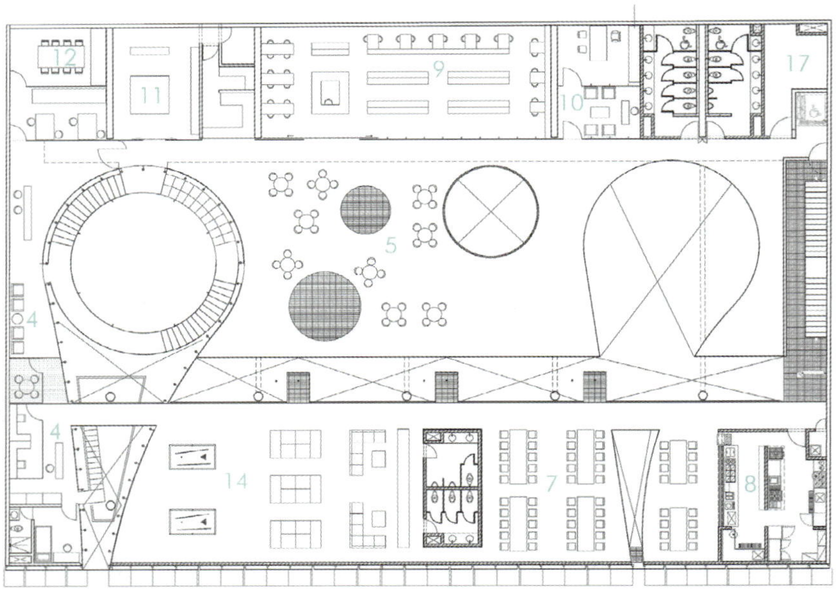

In addition to the Fireman Station, the program includes a space of consultation and a training center which is open to the public. The design chosen for the station appears on the outside like a simple high box that almost disappears after a facade plays with the context in a game of reflections, floating on the patio. This space extends towards the street or, in inverse reading, incorporates the urban space. Within the chromed box, both uses are alternated and complemented, organized by planes with holes in different sizes and shapes that allows natural lighting, while communicating between the different levels.

01 Exterior view chromed box **02** Ground floor parking
03 Interior view, double stair **04** Multible use courtyard
05 First floor plan

Photos: Jaime Navarro

BLACK HOUSE

A fireplace, a kitchen bar and a marble platform 20 meters long laid as a free floor plan for public areas and garage, on top of a solid block which houses the rest of the program, namely services, three bedrooms and a family room. The covered roof garden becomes the most important part of the house, where one-half-huse is then one-half-terrace, protected from the exterior conditions when needed by means of four meter tall sliding glass panels towards the landscape, and a wall as high as the garage doors towards the street, is always detached from the concrete canopy to turn it into a fence more than a wall.

01 Exterior view **02** Open kitchen bar **03** Staircase **04** Floor plans **05** One-half-terrace with closed glass panels

Photos: Rafael Gamo

CITY
Mexico City

COUNTRY
Mexico

REGION
Central America

TYPOLOGY
Living

COMPLETION
2007

WEBSITE
www.bgp.com.mx

ARCHITECTS
bgp arquitectura

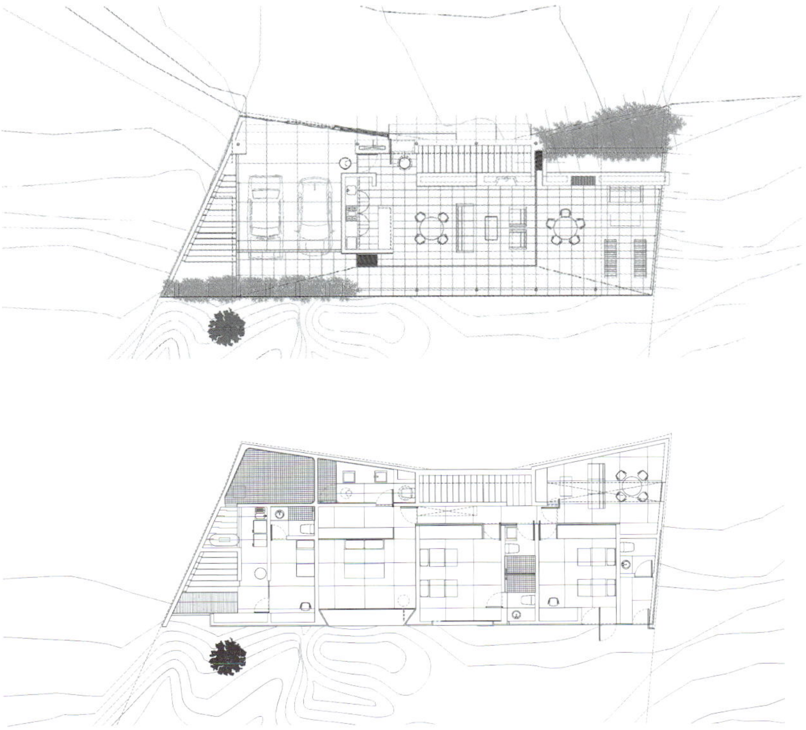

AMATEPEC

The project, a single-family house built over a ravine in Mexico City, responds to the need for adaptation on a rough topography. The rough landscape caused for the use of a reinforced concrete structure of three levels of height, where space had to be adapted to the architectonic program. The program required two premises: the residence and a space to accommodate a collection of contemporary art. The concept was then to create a house that causes generous passages while receiving art and visuals, while also creating peaceful atmospheres by incorporating the green color of the plants and the black color from water mirrors.

01 Entry **02** Courtyard with pond **03** Detail stair to mezzanine **04** Living room **05** View from interior to pond

Photos: Luis Gordoa

EUGENIO SUE

The design was born from restriction, and while seeking for light, the façade became a great crystal box inserted in a limestone monolith resting on the ground in a dense neighborhood in Mexico City. Sober materials, and of neutral appearance, create interior spaces that aim to distract the daily routine of the city, making the foliage of trees the main view. Natural light in every room is demanded in the layout, obtaining within an urban profile, a design of interior spaces towards the exterior, where privacy requires all attention. The interior space is the main architectonic proposal of a basic and simple aesthetic design.

01 Exterior view by night **02** Front view **03** Courtyard **04** Detail façade

Photos: Luis Gordoa

CITY Mexico City
COUNTRY Mexico
REGION Central America
TYPOLOGY Living
COMPLETION 2006
WEBSITE www.ccarquitectos.com.mx
ARCHITECTS CC Arquitectos

CITY	Mexico City
COUNTRY	Mexico
REGION	Central America
TYPOLOGY	Culture
COMPLETION	2006
WEBSITE	–
ARCHITECTS	Jorge Hernández de la Garza, Gabriel Covarrubias, Gerardo Broissin

CENTRO CULTURAL VLADIMIR KASPE

Punctual elements include a stony solid anchor with art work erected above it and a visible structure materializing itself in columns for reasons of equilibrium and function, express the strength of the edified object posing on the land. The lightness and transparency of the wrap emphasizes the swelled crystal plane that marks the pavilion's main entrance and limits it from the immediate environment. An exterior ramp with an ascending feel avoids the eternal human wish to unravel the immemorial knowledge of life, while the last level features a delicate box of glass shelter donated by Vladimir Kaspe.

01 Detail ramp and crystal plane **02** View from courtyard **03** Interior view, hallway **04** Exterior view main entrance, swelled crystal plane

Photos: Paúl Czitrom

DUMAS + HORACIO

This building of departments is located in a strategically important point of the city, against one of the extensive public squares of the street of Horacio in the Polanco colony. The project is formed by thirteen departments, distributed in two towers of four levels each, and one more level for parking. These towers are united; in the first one can find the first six departments, while the remaining seven are in the second. The pedestrian access is located on Alexander Dumas Street, where a lobby and stairs uproot from the parking level to the second floor, while the access to carry is located on Horacio Avenue.

01 Exterior view **02** Detail façade, glass cubes **03** View from the street **04** Side view

Photos: Louis Gordoa

CITY Mexico City
COUNTRY Mexico
REGION Central America
TYPOLOGY Living
COMPLETION 2005
WEBSITE www.centraldearquitectura.com
ARCHITECTS Central de Arquitectura

CITY Mexico City
COUNTRY Mexico
REGION Central America
TYPOLOGY Living
COMPLETION 2003
WEBSITE www.dellekamparq.com
ARCHITECTS Dellekamp Architects

AR58

In the avenue of Alfonso Kings, arriving at one from the edges of the colony Countess, this land with three fronts is exhibited unequal with resisted atmospheres. The extended front agrees with the hoisted ridge of the avenue, staying chaotic, while the other two streets are small and much less journeyed. The views and the noise change radically on the side that moves away of Patriotism, while the south direction, suggested like a departure point, creates an exhibited inner patio to the north in which all the services are grouped. Each level is crossed with emptiness that go from the street to the inner patio.

01 West elevation **02** View from deck to living room **03** Interior view, living and dining space **04** Section **05** Detail façade **06** Detail deck

Photos: Oscar Necoechea

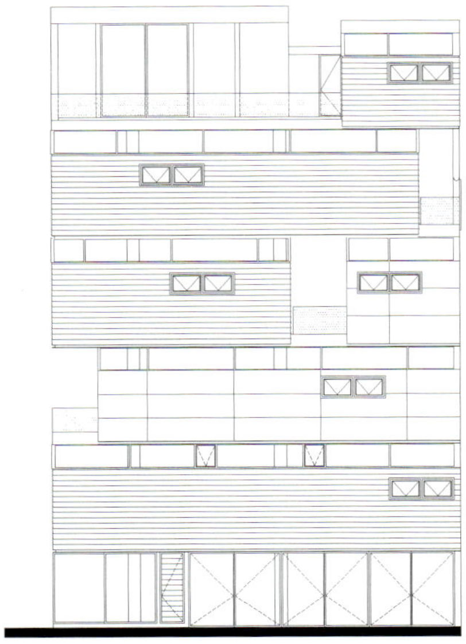

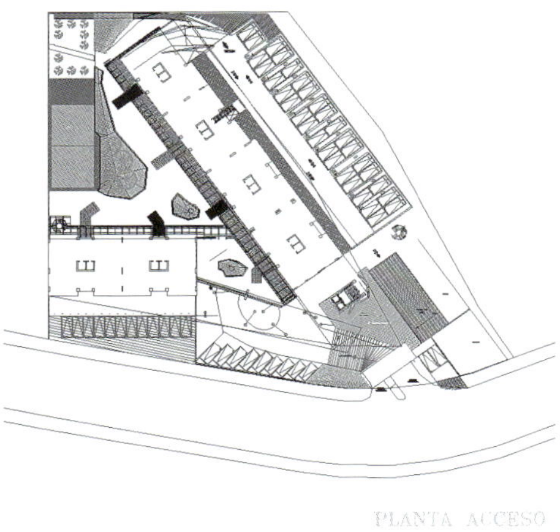

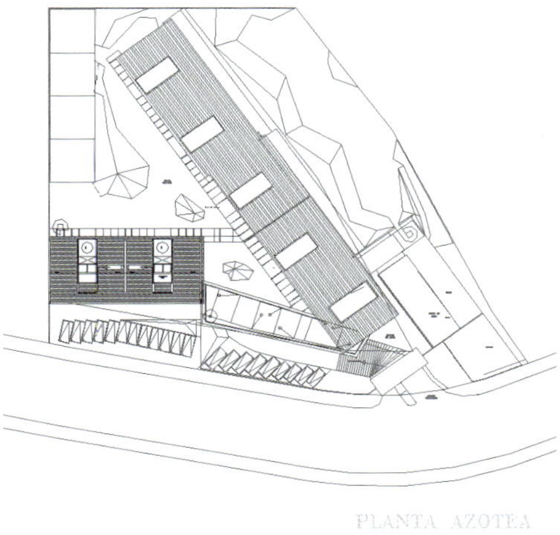

L' ATELIER

The development consists of two buildings articulated by two common spaces: the pond area and the gymnasium. The scheme followed for the design responds to three concepts: the urban plan, the views and to the form of the estate. The towers are oriented with respect to the two avenues, with one of them lateral to the highway, which delimit the estate. This way, each tower offers western panoramas. The generated open space spanning both buildings functions as the center. Both buildings are articulated by the house club, a volume maintained by diagonal steel columns and which contains the development's common areas.

01 Detail façade **02** Side view **03** Exterior view **04** Detail entrance area **05** Top and ground floor plan

Photos: Marisol Paredes, Luis Gordoa

CITY: Mexico City
COUNTRY: Mexico
REGION: Central America
TYPOLOGY: Living
COMPLETION: 2004
WEBSITE: www.diametroarquitectos.com
ARCHITECTS: Diametro Arquitectos / Vidarq

CITY
Mexico City

COUNTRY
Mexico

REGION
Central America

TYPOLOGY
Living

COMPLETION
2004

WEBSITE
www.diametroarquitectos.com

ARCHITECTS
Diametro Arquitectos

PUNTA DEL PARQUE

In a land of 3000 m², two towers of 31 levels uproot, where each tower is the result of a composition between two elements; the first rectangular and pure but fractured in its façade, and the other irregular but very horizontal. The use of the development is residential and is complemented with several other spaces, giving particularity to the project. The area of the gymnasium on floor 18 is generated from a crystal bridge that breaks the building and connects with the other tower, ending in the area of the covered pond which occurs with a space quadruple the height and breaks the monotony of a very horizontal façade.

01 Lounge **02** Detail lounge with panoramic view **03** Detail façade **04** Lobby with spa and gym **05** Total view

Photos: Luis Gordoa

RANCHO EL ORTIGO

Within a densely forested site, a massive ranch house centered on horse keeping was built in an open valley. Conceived as an extending line stretching 120 meter, the house is set on an inclined platform overlooking the majestic views of the valley and the stables below. The most important element of the project was always the preservation of the horses on the ranch. This helped the development of a design based on the different horizontal planes that are required for horses to thrive: stables, corrals, feeding pastures, open fields, training and riding fields, etc.

01 Detail house on inclined platform **02** View of horizontal planes up to house **03** Detail façade **04** Site plan **05** Exterior view by night

Photos: Paúl Czitrom

CITY
Mexico City (Valle de Bravo)

COUNTRY
Mexico

REGION
Central America

TYPOLOGY
Living

COMPLETION
2006

WEBSITE
www.grupoarquitectura.com

ARCHITECTS
GA Grupo Arquitectura, Daniel Alvarez

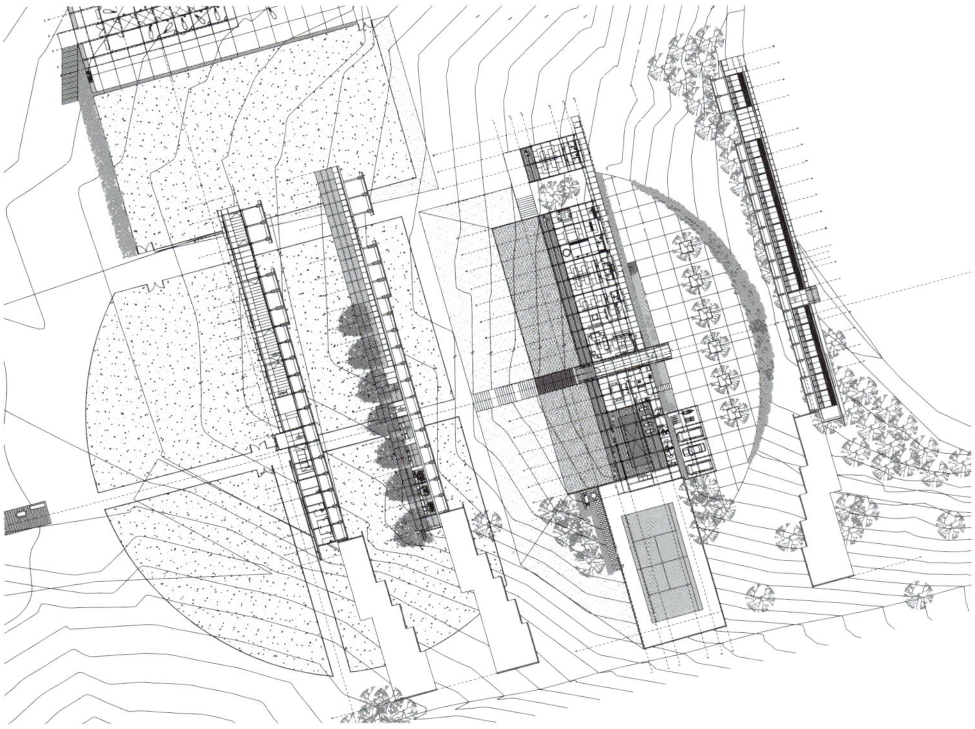

CITY
Mexico City

COUNTRY
Mexico

REGION
Central America

TYPOLOGY
Living

COMPLETION
2004

WEBSITE
www.gardunoarquitectos.com

ARCHITECTS
Garduño Arquitectos

LA LOMA II HOUSE

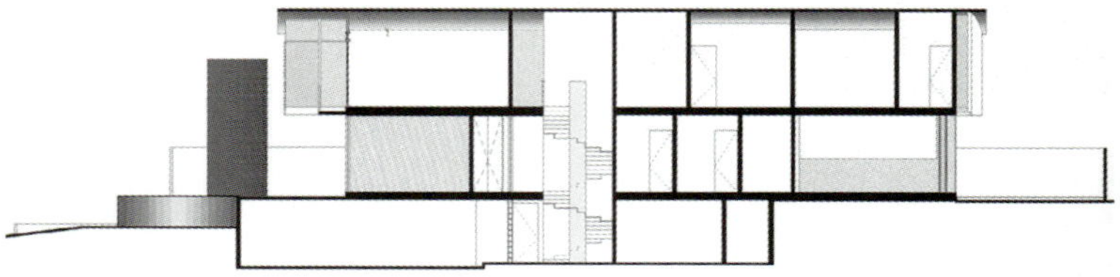

The project includes natural elements like water and wood, being the protagonists of the access area that is surrounding the house. The water is used as an ornamental element in a cylindrical form contained by steel walls. A tropical wood lattice window acts like a protective skin isolating the house from the outside. The additional areas of the house are developed in a "L" shape of 705 m2 that integrates the garden. As a means of the separation of two volumes that uproot the construction in different angles, a lobby of double height forms and a tunnel of crystal floating to the center unites both bodies of the construction.

01 Detail north wing dining room contained by glass **02** Interior view, living room **03** View from deck **04** Interior view **05** Longitudinal section **06** Entrance area by night

Photos: Paúl Czitrom

V-3 HOUSE

The site, a 700 m² single-family lot with a 60 degree slope angle accessible only from the street, was an interesting challenge. An incision was made at the intermediate level of the slope, in order to provide south orientation with optimal sun exposure, taking advantage of the terrain while providing openness with security. The adobe colored concrete wall was pre-impregnated with the color of the soil obtained from the terrain, emerging as a central wall. Street and house are connected by a circular staircase and an auxiliary elevator, while the central atrium provides integration and connectedness throughout.

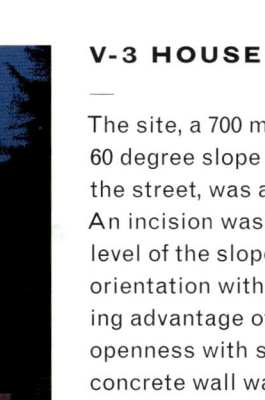

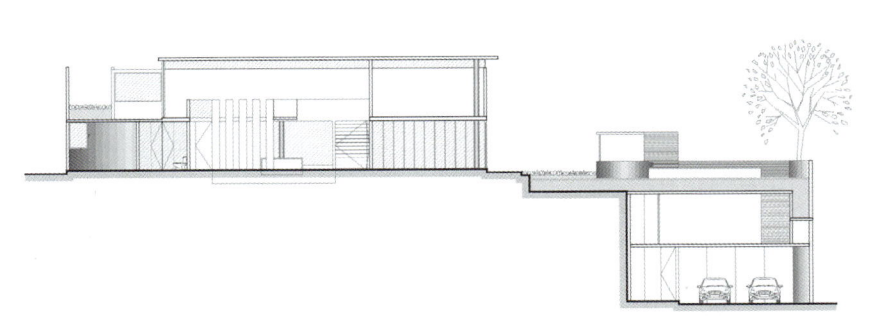

01 Exterior view from west **02** View from pond to living room **03** Living room **04** Master bedroom **05** Section **06** Detail

Photos: Paúl Czitrom

CITY Mexico City
COUNTRY Mexico
REGION Central America
TYPOLOGY Living
COMPLETION 2007
WEBSITE www.gardunoarquitectos.com
ARCHITECTS Garduño Arquitectos

CITY Mexico City
COUNTRY Mexico
REGION Central America
TYPOLOGY Office
COMPLETION 2000
WEBSITE www.gdu.com.mx
ARCHITECTS Grupo de Diseño Urbano, Mario Schjetnan / José Luis Pérez

TORRE SIGLUM

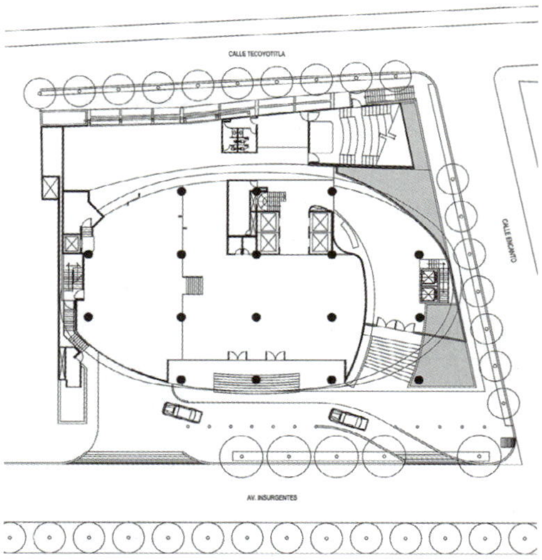

This multi-storied office building is located on Insurgentes Avenue, one of Mexico City's most important arteries. Its striking modern form has helped it to instantly become one of the architectural landmarks of the southern part of the city. The elliptical plan provides continuous views onto the surrounding landscape and interesting vistas of the busy avenue below.

01 Lobby showing urban landscape integration **02** Ground floor plan **03** Night view with lighting of tower **04** Abstracted mural-sculpture by Brad Howe and reception niche

Photos: Pedro Hiriart

CENTRO COMUNITARIO CIUDAD DE MÉXICO

The Centro Comunitario is a multifunctional building of great complexity, and is thought to maintain diverse activities at the same time as being communitarian. It is a collection of interconnected spaces, in which each takes a different characteristic of congruent light and materiality to each other. The building is a construction squad that surrounds an enormous garden, where all the spaces are within that constructed mass and express their logic through the facade. The temple, the most important piece of all in the form of a great crystal cylinder, comes off the building and flies over the garden, which head the composition.

01 Exterior view of Centro Comunitario **02** Central patio, Colegio Atid **03** Hallway **04** Synagogue

Photos: Paúl Czitrom

CITY Mexico City
COUNTRY Mexico
REGION Central America
TYPOLOGY Public
COMPLETION 2003
WEBSITE www.gfa.com.mx
ARCHITECTS GFa Grupo Inmobiliario (in collaboration with HOK)

CITY
Mexico City

COUNTRY
Mexico

REGION
Central America

TYPOLOGY
Living

COMPLETION
2005

WEBSITE
www.gomezcrespoarquitectos.com

ARCHITECTS
Gomez Crespo Arquitectos

ADOLFO PRIETO 1369

The project consists of 22 departments with very flexible distribution in the interior, with which the users have several features to indulge in including a chamber, a closed kitchen, or an abierta with a bar towards the entrance. The heart of this project occupies a central patio at which all the departments watch. To the center of this patio are the vertical circulations of the building such as the elevator and stairs, sculpturally designed in steel and marble, playing a fundamental paper in the life project. The access to all the departments is by means of a bridge that crosses the patio and unites the vertical circulations.

01 Exterior view **02** Detail elevator clad with stone **03** Courtyard **04** Stairway **05** Typical floor plan

Photos: Alfonso de Béjar

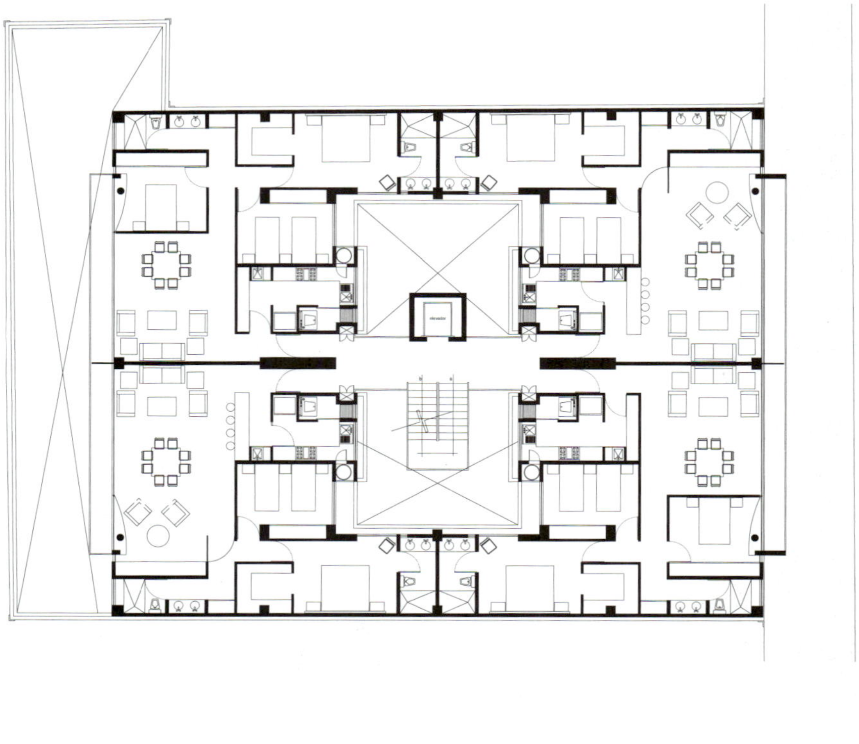

TORRE REFORMA 115

The building, the Torre Reforma 115, will be destined to be used as administrative offices deprived of diverse nature in a condominium triple "A" category. The building counts on places of access, the lobby motor, ground floor, main lobby reception and services, Mezzanine 1 and 2, and 23 levels for use of private offices and 10 levels for parking, to really display the unique features of this project. The access, framed by a great crystal vestibule of two leaves of 11 meters of height, ends only at the great lobby, which is a multi-colored visual as it contrasts to the great sobriety of the rest of the space.

01 Ground floor plan **02** Exterior view **03** Entrance area **04** Detail façade, entry underground parking

Photos: Paúl Czitrom

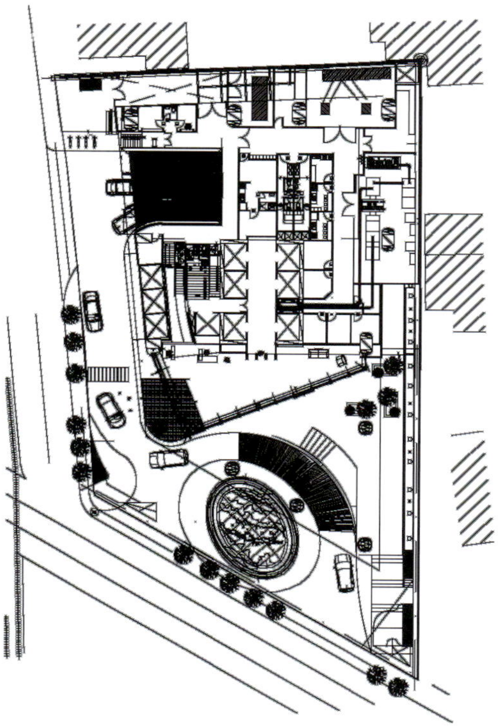

CITY
Mexico City

COUNTRY
Mexico

REGION
Central America

TYPOLOGY
Office

COMPLETION
2005

WEBSITE
www.inmobiliariabrom.com

ARCHITECTS
Inmobiliaria Brom (Arquitectos Brom Asociados)

CITY Mexico City
COUNTRY Mexico
REGION Central America
TYPOLOGY Living
COMPLETION 2004
WEBSITE www.jsadd.com
ARCHITECTS JS² (formerly Higuera + Sánchez)

13 DE SEPTIEMBRE

The project recycles an old trade union warehouse, converting it into small, 56 m² double height dwellings. The intervention into the building is made in the central patio. The floor slabs of the original structure were cut and stairs inserted. This circulation center offers access to the apartments located on different levels by means of bridges and stairways. It is in this communal space that the dimensions of the original structure can be read. Walls facing into this circulation cut-in are covered in white polycarbonate paneling.

01 Detail interior façade **02** View top floor from patio bridges **03** Patio **04** Exterior view

Photos: Luis Gordoa

AMSTERDAM 315

The public area of the complex is located in the building facing the street, while the private spaces are in the building facing the rear patio. Both areas are connected by a glass-covered bridge which serves both as an access and a link. Some apartments have access through the top floor, and others are entered from the lower floor, with the bridge on the middle level. The idea was to have only a vertical elevator system and stairs to provide access to all the apartments. The intermittent layout of the interior bridges creates a disordered space as a result of the diverse typologies of the custom-built apartments.

01 View from Amsterdam Avenue **02** Detail staircase **03** Detail glass covered bridge **04** Fourth floor plan **05** Connecting private and public area

Photos: Luis Gordoa, Paúl Rivera – Archphoto

CITY	Mexico City
COUNTRY	Mexico
REGION	Central America
TYPOLOGY	Living
COMPLETION	2005
WEBSITE	www.jsadd.com
ARCHITECTS	JS² (formerly Higuera + Sanchez)

TEMÍSTOCLES 12

The building is on a rectangular-shaped property, similar to many others in Polanco. A cube providing lighting and ventilation in the center is used for stairs that go up the five levels, reaching the eight apartments and the pent-house on the top level. Four concrete walls go through the building, becoming thinner toward the street, and form two volumes which make up the façade. All the apartments have an irregular terrace to the front, accentuating the verticality of the walls and the depth of the facade. In addition to the range of materials, a large tree covers the west facade, resulting in a building with character.

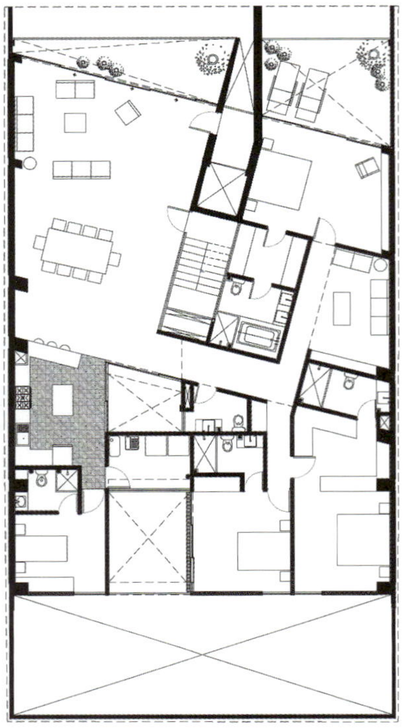

01 Penthouse floor plan **02** Exterior view from the street **03** Detail balcony **04** Interior view **05** View from apartment to balcony

Photos: Paúl Rivera – Archphoto, Mariana Ugalde

UCSJ CENTER FOR GRADUATE AND CONTINUOUS EDUCATION STUDIES

The program includes 16 classrooms and four kitchens intended for graduate courses. Gastronomy, Biology, among other majors are taught, in which the Universidad del Claustro de Sor Juana is well-renowned for. The patio was 'mirrored' from the Spanish Viceroyalty period, while creating a second one in the building meant for remodeling. The effect of both patios emphasizes the importance of the space within the layout of the cloister, further achieving better integration of the students. The materials employed are for rough usage, all in black and gray shades, in addition to the "Viceroyalty" red.

01 Exterior view **02** View into the patios **03** Detail façade **04** Hallways around patios **05** Cross section

Photos: Jaime Navarro

CITY
Mexico City

COUNTRY
Mexico

REGION
Central America

TYPOLOGY
Education

COMPLETION
2006

WEBSITE
www.jsadd.com

ARCHITECTS
JS¹ (formerly Higuera + Sanchez)

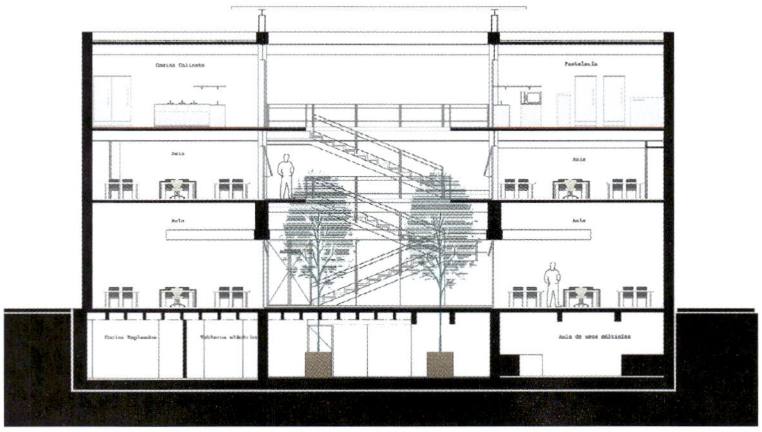

SOUMAYA MUSEUM

The challenge of this visionary project is in becoming the first Art Museum in Mexico City with such an avant garde form, breaking all the paradigms in the country, while creating a state-of-the-art facility to house and display artwork that meet the standards of International Art Institutions. Features include an auditorium, library, offices, restaurant and a gathering lounge, in which intermediate levels are open to each other in a continuous volume, but partially separated by enclosed areas. The subterranean structure will have four underground levels of parking below two underground levels of storage and restoration labs.

01 Interior view, hall **02** Exterior view **03** Open intermediate levels **04** Detail exhibition space

Renderings: LAR / Fernando Romero

CITY Mexico City
COUNTRY Mexico
REGION Central America
TYPOLOGY Culture
COMPLETION 2009
WEBSITE www.laboratoryofarchitecture.com
ARCHITECTS LAR / Fernando Romero

CHILDREN'S ROOM

A beautiful 1950's villa in a suburban area of Mexico City needed an extension. A continuous unlimited space was proposed, where the scheme is that of a snail shell, providing an intimate interior space for the children, and a ramp that connects the existing villa to the garden. The building consists of a metal structure covered with polyurethane foam, where the polyurethane surface was later equalized and treated with a polymer coating. The result became an interesting confrontation between two historical moments: a modernist Mexican house from the 1950's and a continuous skin out of contemporary materials.

01 Interior view **02** Interior view, staircase **03** Floor plan
04 Exterior view of snail shell and ramp to garden

Photos: Luís Gordoa

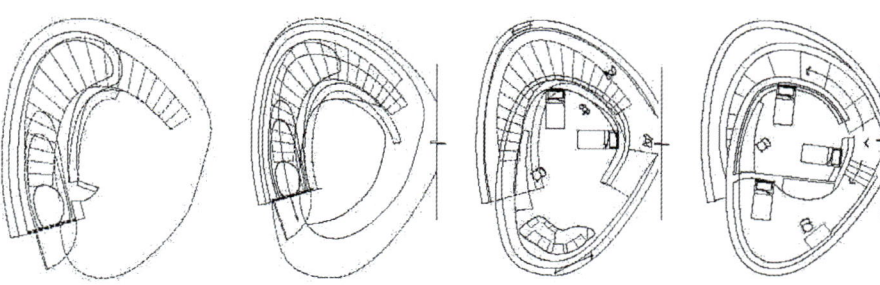

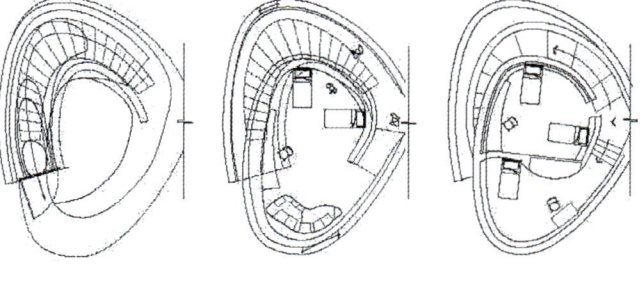

CITY Mexico City
COUNTRY Mexico
REGION Central America
TYPOLOGY Living
COMPLETION 2001
WEBSITE www.laboratoryofarchitecture.com
ARCHITECTS LCM / Fernando Romero

CITY Mexico City
COUNTRY Mexico
REGION Central America
TYPOLOGY Sport
COMPLETION 2005
WEBSITE www.migdal.com.mx
ARCHITECTS Jaime Varon, Abraham Metta, Alex Metta / Migdal Arquitectos

SALÓN DE USOS MÚLTIPLES TARBUT

The Tarbut School is located in the western zone of Mexico City. The project needed a multipurpose building where sport activities could be developed as a cultural tradition, since climatic conditions demand more of this. The building element known as a "staple" leans but is also reconciled to the building, taking in the topography from the land, thus generating circulation and services. Back-to-back volumes are featured to the east and west with great variety of colors, thus interacting with the set as with the ravine. Features include a gym, cellar, multimedia classroom, artistic activity area, and a projection room.

01 View from the courtyard **02** Side view **03** Staircase **04** Solid and translucent surfaces

Photos: Paúl Czitrom

CORPORATE HEADQUARTERS AUTOFIN

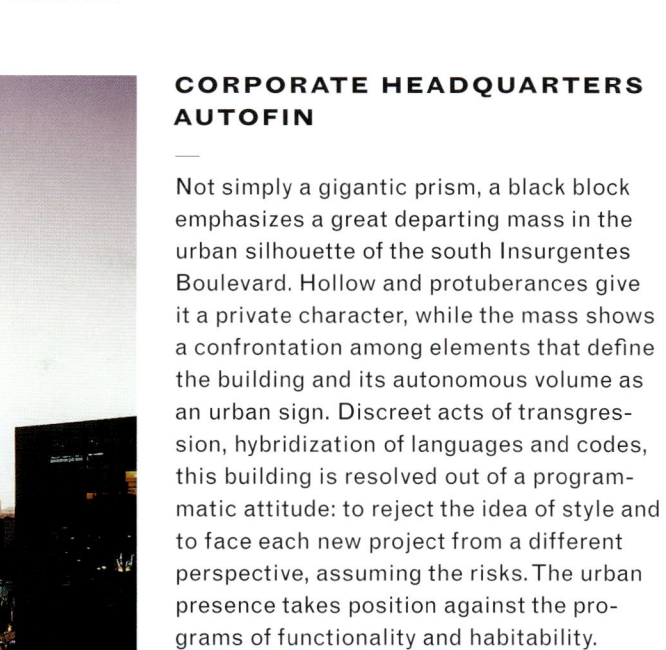

Not simply a gigantic prism, a black block emphasizes a great departing mass in the urban silhouette of the south Insurgentes Boulevard. Hollow and protuberances give it a private character, while the mass shows a confrontation among elements that define the building and its autonomous volume as an urban sign. Discreet acts of transgression, hybridization of languages and codes, this building is resolved out of a programmatic attitude: to reject the idea of style and to face each new project from a different perspective, assuming the risks. The urban presence takes position against the programs of functionality and habitability.

01 Exterior view **02** Section **03** Interior view **04** Detail black box **05** Hallway

Photos: Fernando Cordero

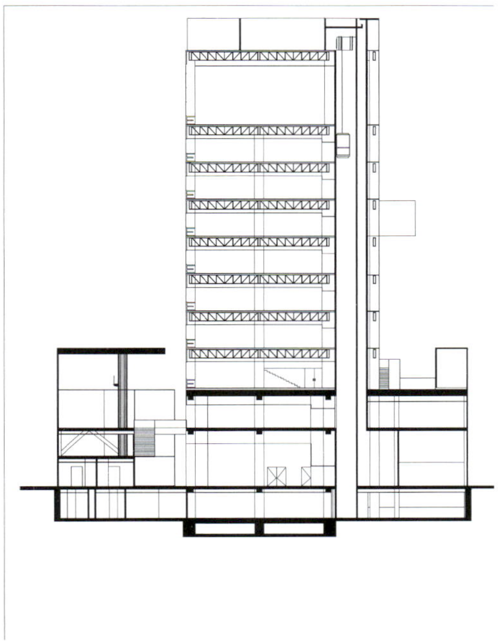

CITY Mexico City
COUNTRY Mexico
REGION Central America
TYPOLOGY Office
COMPLETION 2003
WEBSITE www.lmetal.com.mx
ARCHITECTS Lucio Muniain et al Arquitectura & Urbanismo

700

CITY Mexico City
COUNTRY Mexico
REGION Central America
TYPOLOGY Ecclesiastical
COMPLETION 2006
WEBSITE www.pascalarquitectos.com
ARCHITECTS Pascal Arquitectos

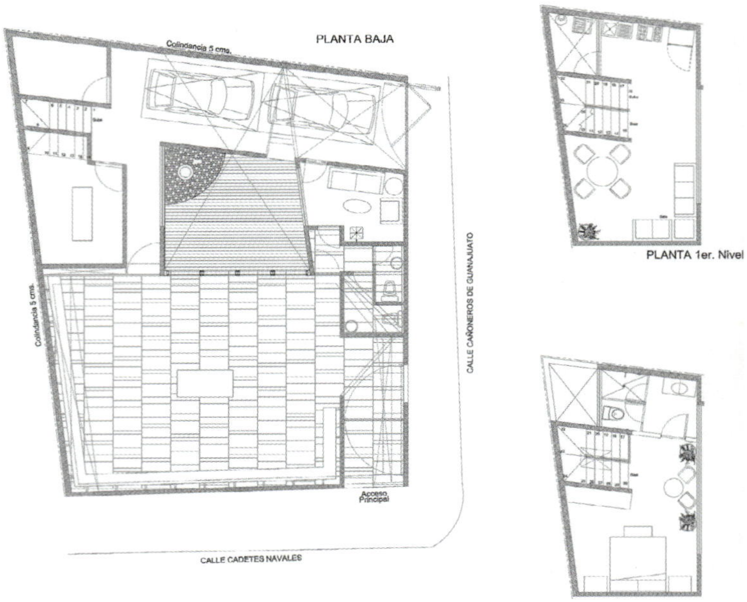

MEDITATION HOUSE

This project was crafted with exceedingly strong emotional implications. While having to understand and grasp the mood of the user, the attempt was to create a space with the correct spiritual mood, while designing a structure that is of ancient origin, such as what the Egyptians and the Mayan people produced. The building welcomes the visitor with a vast, triangular, wooden shaped door, leading to an access tunnel much of the same shape. This entrance leads to a hallway that opens to a large granite hall illuminated by the northern light coming from the indoor courtyard, and placed in the center of it is a tall Dracaena.

01 Wooden door **02** Ground, first and second floor plan **03** Interior view, double height granite hall **04** Indoor courtyard **05** Detail Grissal flamed granite façade

Photos: Victor Benitez

PEDREGAL SHOPPING CENTER

This project comes to set a new architectural statement in the Pedregal area of Mexico City; an area neglected in the past. The project consists of two commercial levels, a roof garden, and two underground parking levels. Mobility impaired individuals have access to areas through ramps, special parking spaces, and elevators, while numerous garden areas and a car delivery zone are also featured. This is a sustainable and intelligent development with a control system that contemplates passive and active energy saving resources including lighting and extraction control, air conditioning, and security access, just to name a few.

01 Exterior view **02** Interior view **03** Detail façade, zinc plates with irregular perforations and yellow and translucent glass sections **04** Floor plan

Renderings: Antonio Scheffler

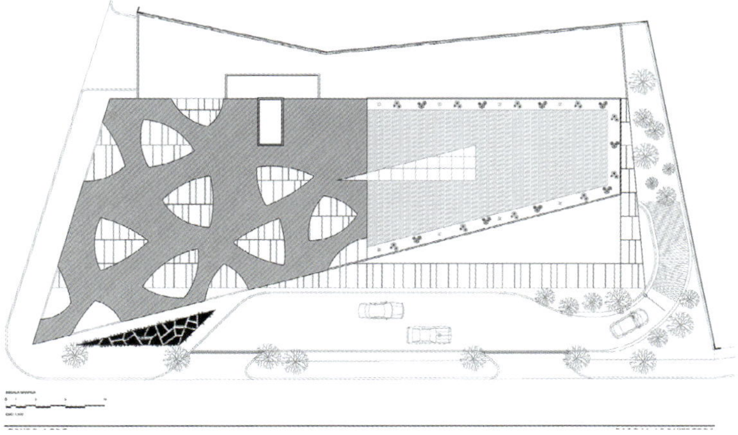

CITY: Mexico City
COUNTRY: Mexico
REGION: Central America
TYPOLOGY: Retail
COMPLETION: 2008
WEBSITE: www.pascalarquitectos.com
ARCHITECTS: Pascal Arquitectos

CITY Mexico City
COUNTRY Mexico
REGION Central America
TYPOLOGY Living
COMPLETION 2006
WEBSITE www.productora-df.com.mx
ARCHITECTS PRODUCTORA (in association with FRENTE arquitectura / Juan Pablo Maza)

CASA MIXCOAC

Located in the Mixcoac neighborhood, the façade of the existing building is kept intact while a new construction is erected on the small plot of land behind it. A spacious effect was desired in this project due to the limited area, so the ground floor plan was divided lengthwise into a living area, allowing the garden to extend along the plot. At the ground level the small house features a kitchen, studio, living area, bathroom, and a bedroom, while the upper floor includes the master bedroom, walk-in closet, bathroom and a terrace. The upper floor consists of a turned volume breaking the orthogonality of the scheme.

01 Exterior view upper floor **02** Detail ground floor **03** Floor plans **04** Stairway

Photos: Paúl Czitrom, Juan Pablo Maza (04)

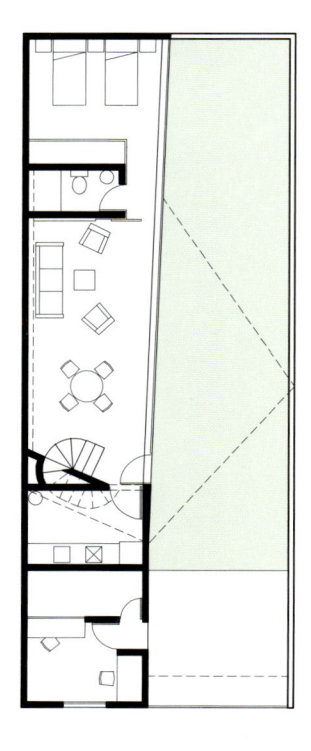

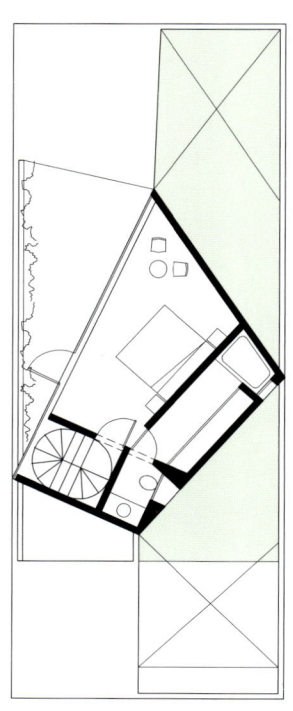

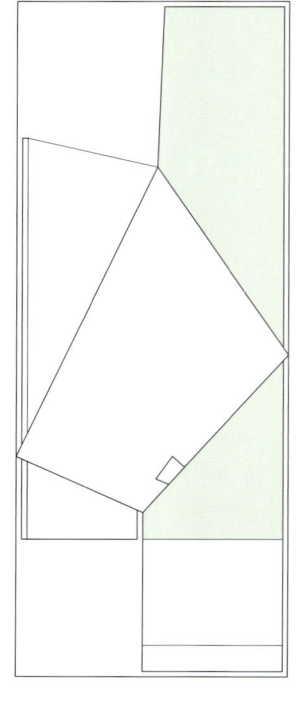

GALILEO 211

This project involved adapting a new six-storey apartment building to a lot intended for a house. The volume is oriented to the south-east while weather-proof, environment-friendly curtains are employed on the façade to filter sunlight. These colorful membranes, controlled independently, lend a sense of movement to the facade. The design has a clear division between common and private spaces, achieved by two core elements united by internal bridges crossing the interior patio, which provides natural light and ventilation in all the spaces. The structure is exposed everywhere, allowing for an easy reading of the functions.

01 Exterior view **02** Inner courtyard **03** Entrance area **04** Interior view, hall **05** Detail flexible façade of moving panels

Photos: Diego Valez

CITY Mexico City
COUNTRY Mexico
REGION Central America
TYPOLOGY Living
COMPLETION —
WEBSITE www.puukarquitectos.com
ARCHITECTS puuk arquitectos

CITY
Mexico City

COUNTRY
Mexico

REGION
Central America

TYPOLOGY
Living

COMPLETION
2007

WEBSITE
www.recursostudio.com

ARCHITECTS
ReCURSO studio

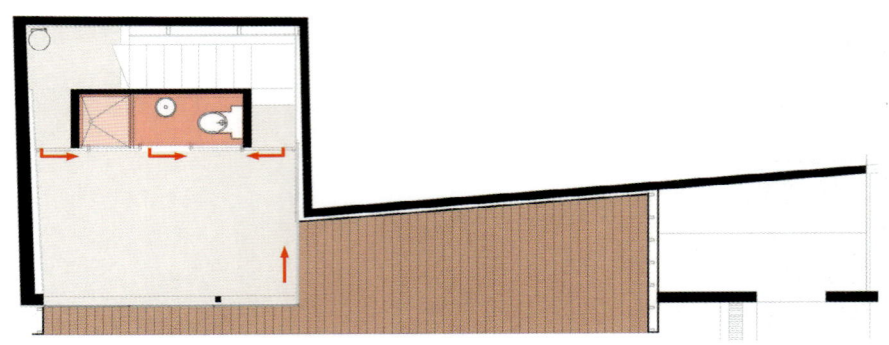

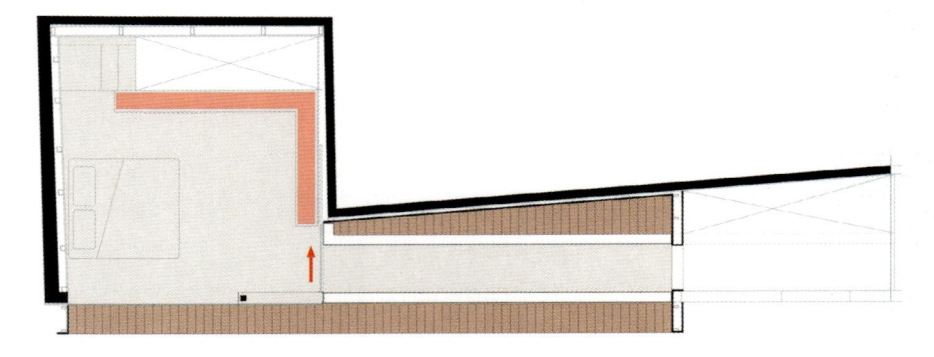

EL HUACAL

The project's name refers to a typical wooden basket used to transport fruit at Mexican markets. The small-scale intervention is an effort to add quality of life to the existing conditions in a poorly designed backyard and a dark studio apartment. The space was reused to create a single square element that acts to divide two sunny room sections, a bathroom, a storage space and a new outside terrace. The original structure is linked for a long bridge to the new space. All materials used were manufactured using 'cradle to cradle' production techniques.

01 Exterior view **02** Detail outdoor hallway **03** Outdoor hallway between residence and annex **04** First and second floor plan **05** Exterior view

Photos: ReCURSO studio

FALCON HEADQUARTERS

Dedicated to instruments and medical equipment, Corporativo Falcon required a new headquarters building in Mexico City. The premise was to offer the building a radical change of image, where the center of sales would become a precinct of work, while being represented as a high-tech business. A property in an undisturbed street was acquired, near the San Angel district, in which three groups of construction existed. Beginning from the quality of the main construction of having a structure of big clear gaps, the interior distribution was liberated and the project was conceptualized as a crystal box floating in the garden.

01 Detail orange glass façade **02** Crystal box and garden
03 Interior view, working area **04** Floor plan

Photos: Jaime Navarro

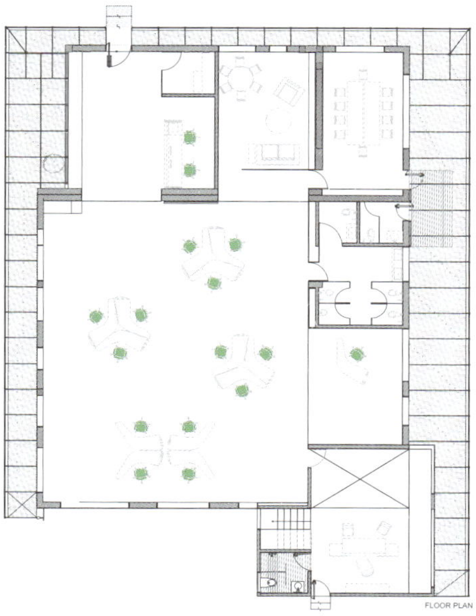

CITY	Mexico City
COUNTRY	Mexico
REGION	Central America
TYPOLOGY	Office
COMPLETION	2004
WEBSITE	www.rojkindarquitectos.com
ARCHITECTS	Rojkind Arquitectos

CITY
Mexico City

COUNTRY
Mexico

REGION
Central America

TYPOLOGY
Retail

COMPLETION
2007

WEBSITE
www.arielrojo.com

ARCHITECTS
Ariel Rojo Design Studio

BOUTIQUE DE CLUB MED EN LA CIUDAD DE MÉXICO

The project is divided mainly into 3 zones; the facade, the store and the offices. The facade is an original idea of Red deriving from the present situation of the city which was reviewed along with the commercial avenues. An enormous weave of enredaderas covers the part superior to the facade, generating a full spectacular marquee of texture, capturing the attention of passers-by, inviting them to discover the name of the Club that floats over the leaves. Main elements of the interior are the counter, a waiting room, and the zone of attention, satisfied by three tables surrounded by a thread curtain.

01 Interior view, detail illuminated curtain of strings **02** Entrance view, wooden path **03** Section **04** Exterior view to canopy clad in ivy

Photos: Jorge Rojo

CORPORATIVO SANTA ROSALIA

The design is based on the intersection of two main volumes: a curved, blue crystal with particles that run throughout the façade and another in the form of an inverted "L" made up of crystal grinding with an aluminum blind that lodges to the area of vertical circulations. From the lateral façade, a volume of crystal grinding gives status between the other levels when lodging into the boardroom. The building counts on five levels: two cellars of parking acceded by means of a freight elevator, and three levels of offices, the last one with a terrace and a partial roof, located in the point of the main directorate.

01 + 04 Detail glass façade **02 + 05** Detail staircase and atrium **03** Exterior view **06** First and second floor plan

Photos: Josefina Barroso Álvarez

CITY	Mexico City
COUNTRY	Mexico
REGION	Central America
TYPOLOGY	Office
COMPLETION	2005
WEBSITE	www.rrarquitectos.com
ARCHITECTS	R+R arquitectura – Reinoso & Rodriguez

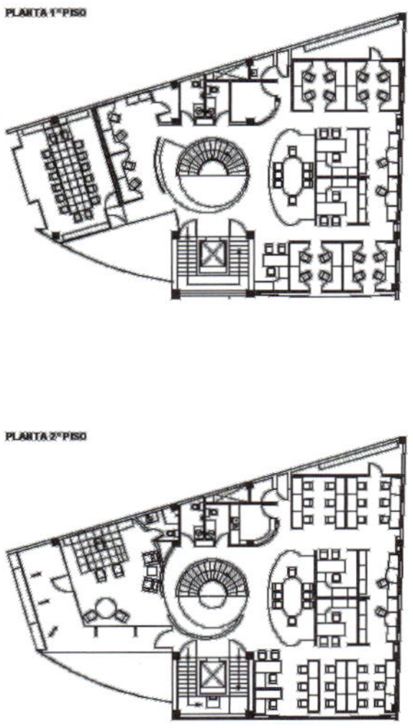

TORRE DE INGENIERÍA UNAM

The opportunity to design a space inside the National Autonomic University of Mexico (UNAM) campus in Mexico City represented a privilege and a professional challenge. Surrounded by the work of great exponents from the Modern movement in Mexico, a dialogue was established with the original idea of the campus while exploring a new expression, signifying the changes in architecture over the past 50 years. The building was designed with exposed concrete, with the dominant theme being a visible steel structure. Installations travel through the interior of the building seeking construction economy and functionality.

01 Detail façade made of exposed concrete and steel **02** Interior view, hall **03** Exterior view **04** Ground floor plan

Photos: Gustavo López Padilla

CITY Mexico City
COUNTRY Mexico
REGION Central America
TYPOLOGY Education
COMPLETION 2005
WEBSITE www.sanchezarquitectos.com
ARCHITECTS Sánchez Arquitectos y Asociados

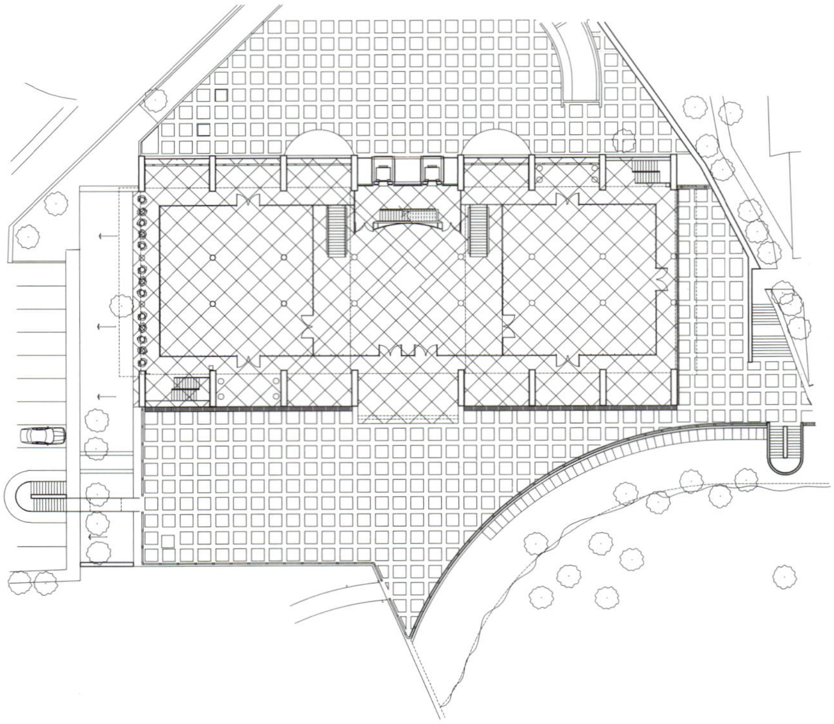

HOUSE GG

The "Duplex" house is built in Las Lomas de Chapultepec, one of the most important districts in Mexico City. The house was projected according to spaces and art pieces already selected, and had a very specific program. It is composed on the basis of a central axis dividing the two houses into similar parts. On the axis, the house welcomes one with Zuñiga's sculpture, while the area of service is used as a transition point to enter the house, communicating with a patio and trees that existed on the original plot. Each house has independent access, with corner spaces showcasing designed sculptures, paintings, lamps and antiques.

01 Exterior view **02** Wrapped by concrete volume **03** Presenting art pieces **04** Section

Photos: Luis Gordoa

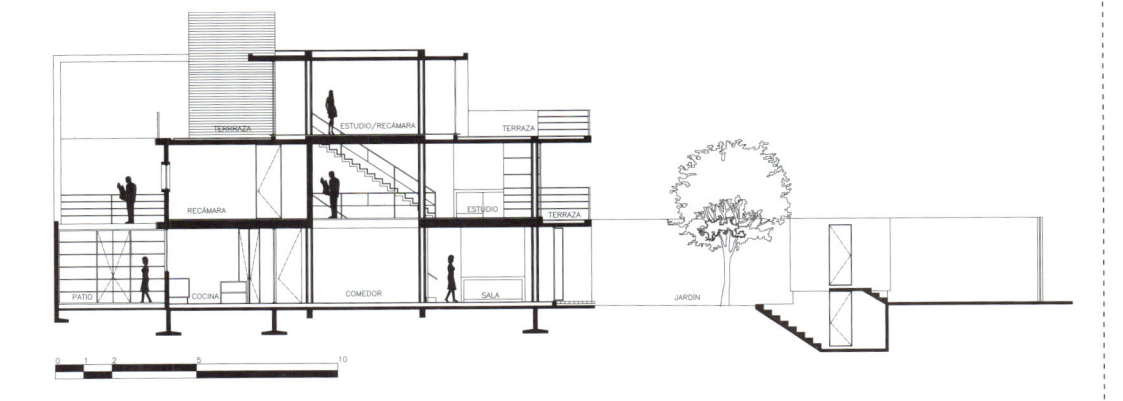

CITY Mexico City
COUNTRY Mexico
REGION Central America
TYPOLOGY Living
COMPLETION 2005
WEBSITE www.scap-arquitectura.com
ARCHITECTS SCAP (Juan Carlos Alvear / Homero Hernández)

CASA ORGANICA

The organic house was born with the idea to create a space adapted for man, according to its environmental needs, physical and psychological. In agreement with the terrain, the essential postulates of the work, the embryonic idea of the project took its resemblance from a peanut rind: two ample oval spaces with much light, united by a low and close space, in penumbrae. This idea arose in base with the requirements of the functions of the man; a space to sleep, with vestidor and bath, to be, eat and cook. One reached the conclusion that the house would have only two great spaces, one diurnal and another nocturne.

01 Interior view, living room **02** Exterior view of the two oval spaces, integrated in the landscape **03** Plan, form like peanut shell **04** Interior view

Photos: Jaime Jacott

AMSTERDAM 253

This housing project in Mexico City is located in the hip and central Hipódromo Condesa neighborhood. In this six-storey building with a rooftop terrace and underground parking, are 25 living units and a single floor unit. Plants grow on a structure made out of steel and wires throughout the whole back façade, while in the central courtyard are the lifts and a cantilevered stairway. The rooftop terrace features Jacuzzis, a fabric tension structure, wooden decks and furnishings for the enjoyment of open-air, urban dwelling and great views of the city. High importance was given to all the vegetation and lighting design.

01 Exterior view, common deck with jacuzzis **02** Interior view **03** Central courtyard **04** Fourth floor plan **05** Detail wooden deck bridge

Photos: Marisol Paredes

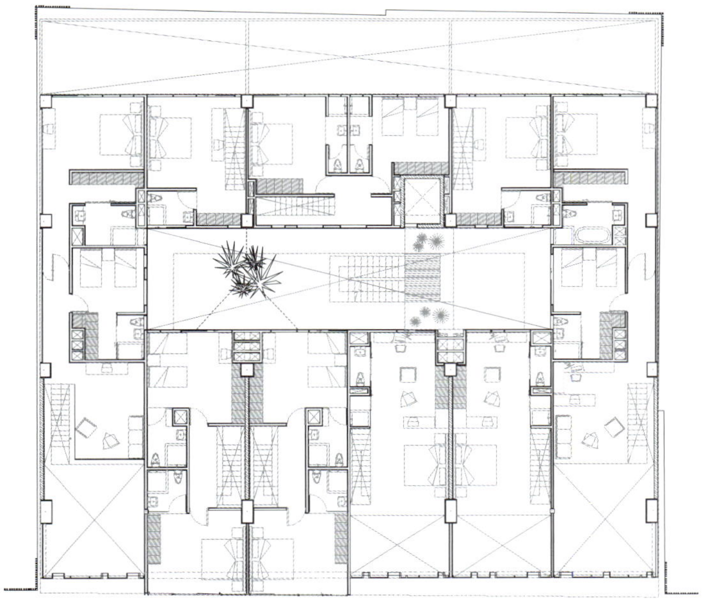

CITY Mexico City
COUNTRY Mexico
REGION Central America
TYPOLOGY Living
COMPLETION 2006
WEBSITE www.taller13.com
ARCHITECTS Taller 13 Arquitectos [elias cattan + patricio guerrero]

CITY Mexico City

COUNTRY Mexico

REGION Central America

TYPOLOGY Retail

COMPLETION 2004

WEBSITE www.tallerdearquitectura.com.mx

ARCHITECTS Taller De Arquitectura – Mauricio Rocha

MERCADO SAN PABLO OZTOTEPEC

The market of San Pablo Oztotepec is located in High Milpa, one of the poorest zones in the Mexico City, just a few meters from the Zapatista Quarter, a historical site in Mexico. Several factors were determining in this project such as the limited budget and the time of delivery. A decision was taken in response to the extreme topography of the zone, to the limits with the untouchable existing facades, operating this way the fifth façade, while also looking to simulate the canvases, which allowed for good illumination and ventilation from the markets. The materials were practical and easy to clean and maintain.

01 Detail roof made of corrugated steel **02** Interior view **03** Exterior view from above **04** Floor plan

Photos: Luis Gordoa, Mauricio Rocha (03)

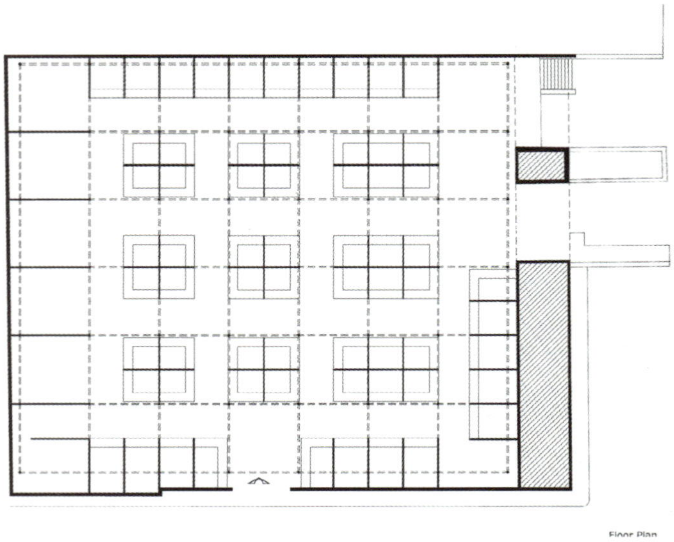

CHOPO MUSEUM

The original building was built during the 19th Century in Germany, before being imported to Mexico City. While the pavilion-like structure lent itself to various uses, the museum proposed expansion and improvment, particularly concerning environmental controls. The solution is an inserted volume with suitable mechanical systems which leaves the original pavilion untouched. The addition is entirely autonomous, producing a series of ramped gallery spaces that fill the old builidng, yet barely seem to touch the ground. The expansion also includes auditoriums in a below-grade excavation and a library near the roof.

01 Interior view **02** View to main entrance **03** Interior view of inserted volume **04** Section **05** Floor plan

Photos: TEN Arquitectos

CITY Mexico City
COUNTRY Mexico
REGION Central America
TYPOLOGY Culture
COMPLETION 2003
WEBSITE www.ten-arquitectos.com
ARCHITECTS Taller de Enrique Norten Arquitectos, SC (TEN Arquitectos)

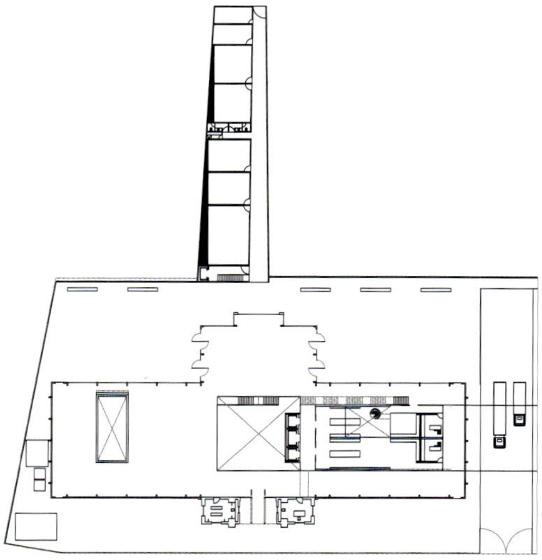

CITY
Mexico City

COUNTRY
Mexico

REGION
Central America

TYPOLOGY
Living

COMPLETION
2006

WEBSITE
www.zda.com.mx

ARCHITECTS
Yuri Zagorin and Erik Carranza / ZD+A

CERVANTES

Built on a former semi-industrial area in Mexico City, this building accommodates 11 different apartment configurations ranging from a 70 m² studio to a 160 m² penthouse. On top of four parking levels, the building consists of 10 stories topped by a jogging track and a roof garden. A corner commercial space is proposed as a way to achieve a positive urban interaction. The rear site restriction and the central vertical circulation ensure that all units have maximum exterior exposure. The rational concrete structure, equally spaced on a 5.8-meter grid, generates a module traversed by aluminum composite panel-clad balconies.

01 Interior view **02** Detail façade **03** Open stairway **04** Exterior view **05** Elevation

Photos: Alberto Moreno Guzmán

LIBRERIA PORRUA

Formally, this project answers with a unique gesture to the different conditions, including Insurgentes Avenue's noise, the tallness of the neighboring buildings, and the relationship between the property with streets and pedestrians. The project adds new programs – a small auditorium for presentations, a space for children, a cafeteria, a roof terrace and a series of spaces for private meetings. Divided into two volumes with an outdoors central area between them, the architectural program is developed throughout the entire space. Through their dimensions and double heights, the volumes offer different spaces to the visitor.

01 Exterior view 02 Side view with entrance 03 Floor plan
04 Exterior view

Renderings: Arquitectura 911SC

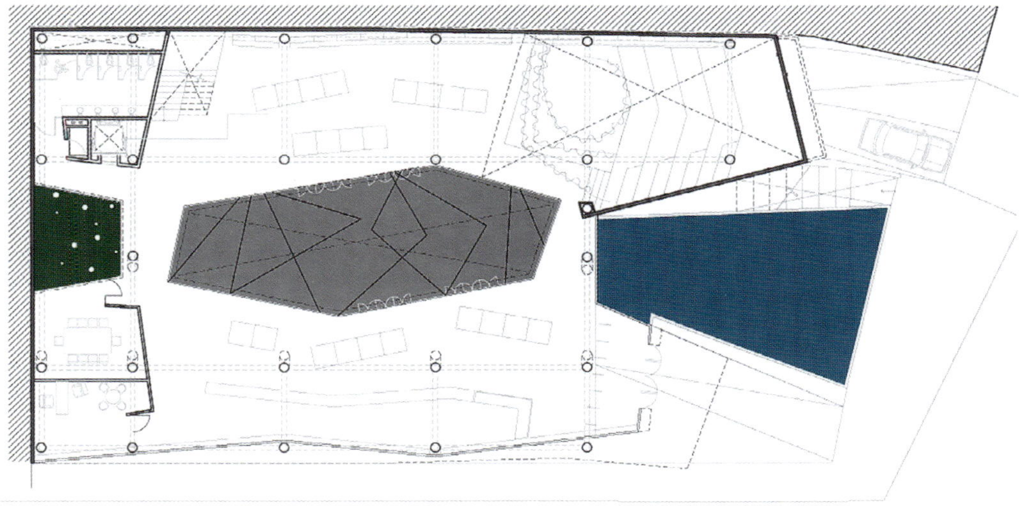

CITY: Mexico City
COUNTRY: Mexico
REGION: Central America
TYPOLOGY: Commercial
COMPLETION: -
WEBSITE: www.arquitectura911sc.com
ARCHITECTS: Arquitectura 911SC

CITY: Mexico City
COUNTRY: Mexico
REGION: Central America
TYPOLOGY: Office
COMPLETION: 2000
WEBSITE: www.beckerarquitectos.com
ARCHITECTS: Becker Arquitectos

CORPORATIVO IMAGEN

This project consists of five free plants for corporative offices, with air conditioning, security systems, telephone systems with structural wiring, and optical fiber systems. Two elevators of luxury, pressurized stairs, a sanitary, services of facilities, finished of luxury on floors, walls and plafones, and four baths on each level completely equipped are all features of this development. Three average levels of underground parking, with one hundred independent drawers, electrical substation, emergency unit, an engine room in the roof, a control center, and warehouses with individualized cellars are also presented.

01 Detail façade 02 Detail courtyard 03 Exterior view by night 04 Exterior view

Photos: Fernando Cordero

CASA TAANAH SAK

The orientation of the ground defined the disposition of the house, where a dome covers the entire end, making it possible to light the halls and circulations, including public and private spaces facing the garden. The entrance level is made up of an axis parallel to the South frontage that gives access and includes the services of the party room and swimming pool. These two services face the garden, having six columns and a translucent crystal curtain. A water mirror marks the continuity of the dome, giving evidence to its sculptural purpose, which together with a masterpiece, makes sense of the triple height and terrace.

01 Exterior view first floor with deck and pond **02** View from the garden to entrance level **03** Interior view, living/dining room **04** Staircase **05** Section and elevation

Photos: Paúl Czitrom

CITY Mexico City
COUNTRY Mexico
REGION Central America
TYPOLOGY Living
COMPLETION 2006
WEBSITE –
ARCHITECTS Gerardo Broissin

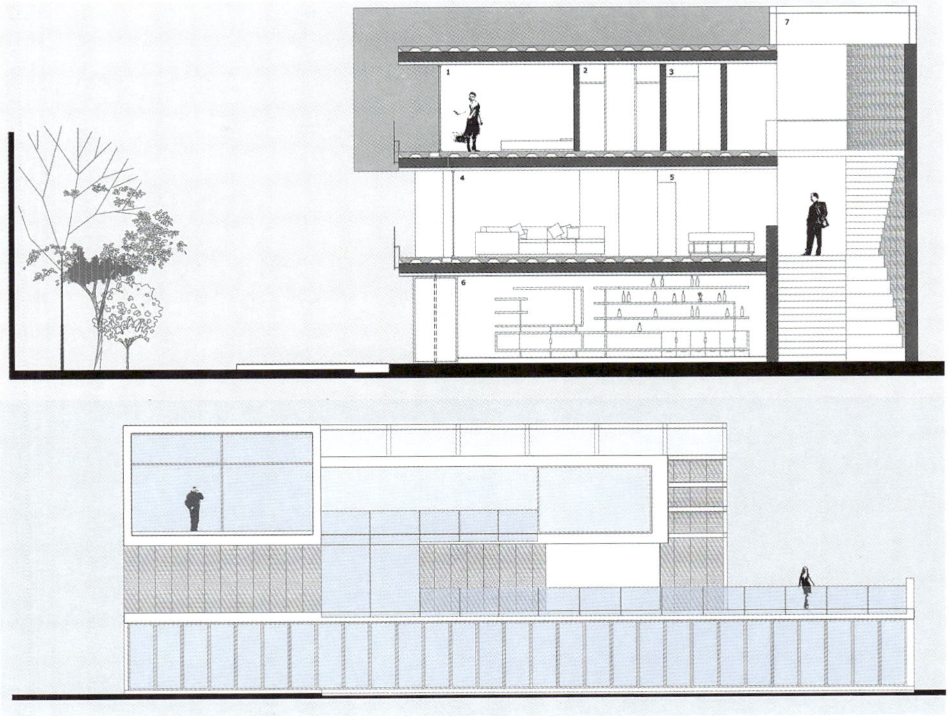

CITY	Mexico City
COUNTRY	Mexico
REGION	Central America
TYPOLOGY	Health
COMPLETION	2004
WEBSITE	www.fabric.com.mx
ARCHITECTS	Fabric arquitectura

JIVA

Located to the south of the city of Mexico in the colony of San Angel, the Jiva project development, constructed by Fabric Arquitectura, is a center of corporal work, and is composed of two pavilions that feature yoga and meditation. In addition to this, a set of three cabins for the purpose of relaxation and massage is also presented, while baths and vestidores can also be found. The project really attempted to be based on the movement of elements as well as lightness and air into the set, trying to invite in all spaces of tranquility and an encounter with this same kind of serenity and stillness.

01 Front view **02** Side view **03** Hallway **04** Interior view

Photos: Luis Gordoa

ANEXO A EL ECO

The proposed building grants the ECO the privileged condition of a corner, through the incorporation of a patio that continues Goeritz's own patio but offers a duality. The original building stands as closed, while the new is completely open towards the street, complying with multiple functions such as becoming a foyer or vestibule for press conferences. It also becomes a packing and loading area, an auxiliary zone for the workshop, and a parking space. The private upper area includes offices and recreational zones that face the patio, while its roofs incorporate windows that guarantee natural ventilation.

01 Exterior view by night **02** Exterior view, detail patios
03 Floor plans

Renderings: LAR / Fernando Romero

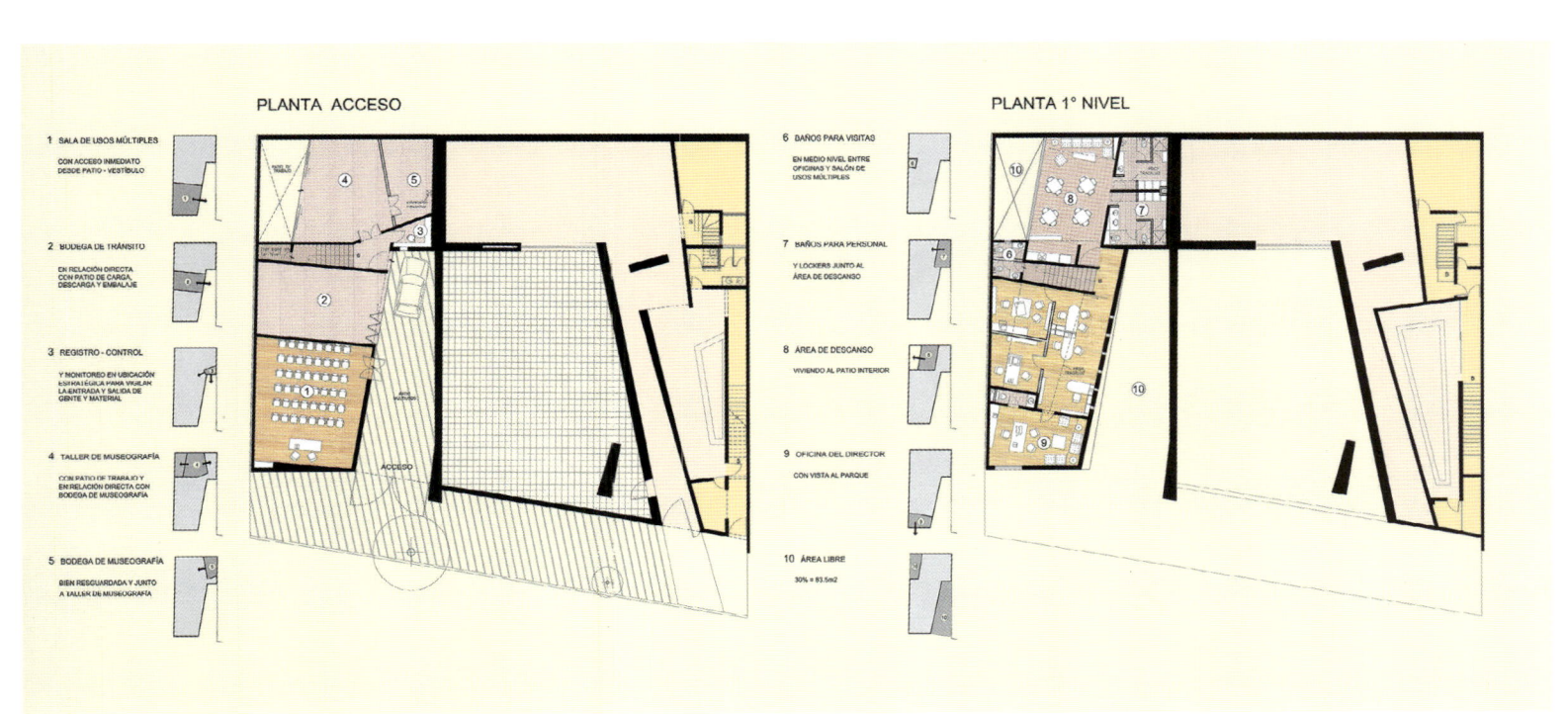

CITY Mexico City
COUNTRY Mexico
REGION Central America
TYPOLOGY Culture
COMPLETION unbuilt
WEBSITE www.frentearq.com
ARCHITECTS LAR / Fernando Romero, FRENTE arquitectura / Juan Pablo Maza

CITY Mexico City
COUNTRY Mexico
REGION Central America
TYPOLOGY Culture
COMPLETION –
WEBSITE –
ARCHITECTS Teodoro González de León

CENTRO CULTURAL BELLA ÉPOCA Y LIBRERÍA

The Cine Lido development of the 1940's is now the biggest bookshop in Mexico with over 250,000 books on display. This certain feature has grown throughout the years allowing for education and literacy to be on the rise in this certain area, giving young kids the opportunity to develop their skills in this part of Mexico. Other features in this project development include a large cinema and an art gallery displaying the many different and unique artworks. This large modern space filled with light is characterized by the work of Jan Hendrix, in which a panel with 256 sheets of glass simulates bamboo branches.

01 Interior view, library upper level **02** Passage book shop and library **03** Library, reading room **04** Ground floor plan **05** Exterior view

Photos: Martin Nicholas Kunz, Michelle Galindo (01)

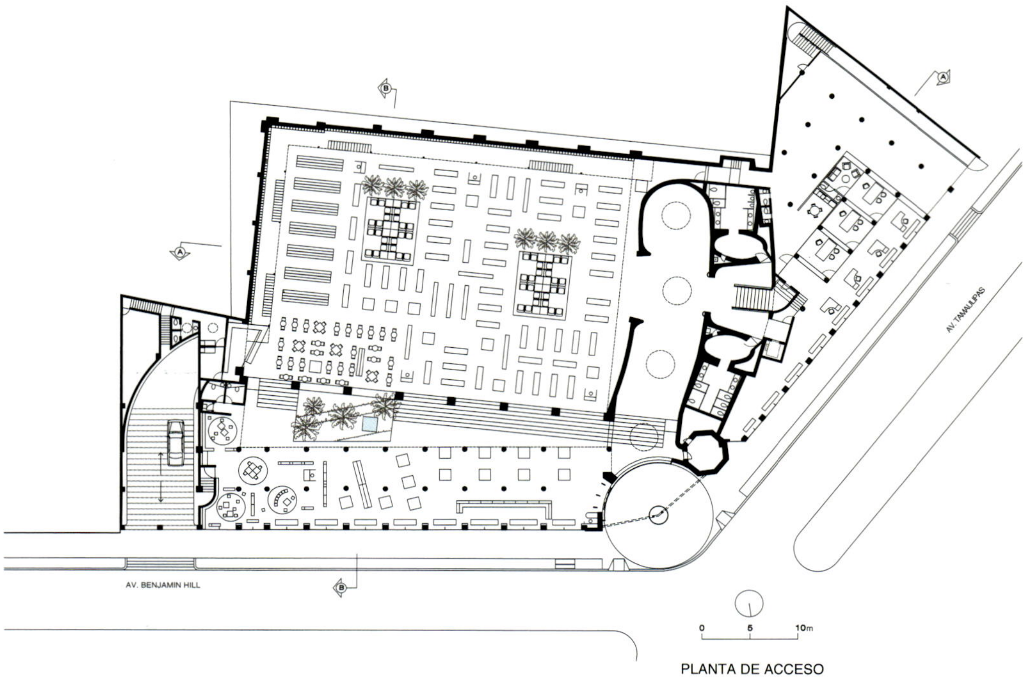

MUSEO DE ARTE POPULAR

The old headquarters of the Firefighters and Police Station now houses an area for the exhibition, diffusion and research of the Mexican craft work. In its intervention, contemporary elements were incorporated, such as a helicoidal staircase in the tower and a large glass dome in the central courtyard. The museum counts on four permanent rooms and one temporary one whose collection is made up of a set of comodatos with public and deprived Institutions of particular collections. The MAP is a Public Trust created by the Federal Government and coordinated through the Secretariat of Culture of the DF.

01 Atrium with elevator **02** Glazed skylights **03** Exhibition space with skylight **04** Exterior view

Photos: Martin Nicholas Kunz, Pedro Hiriart (01)

CITY Mexico City
COUNTRY Mexico
REGION Central America
TYPOLOGY Culture
COMPLETION 2006
WEBSITE –
ARCHITECTS Teodoro González de León

CITY Mexico City
COUNTRY Mexico
REGION Central America
TYPOLOGY Office
COMPLETION 2002
WEBSITE www.inmobiliariabrom.com
ARCHITECTS Inmobiliaria Brom (Arquitectos Brom Asociados)

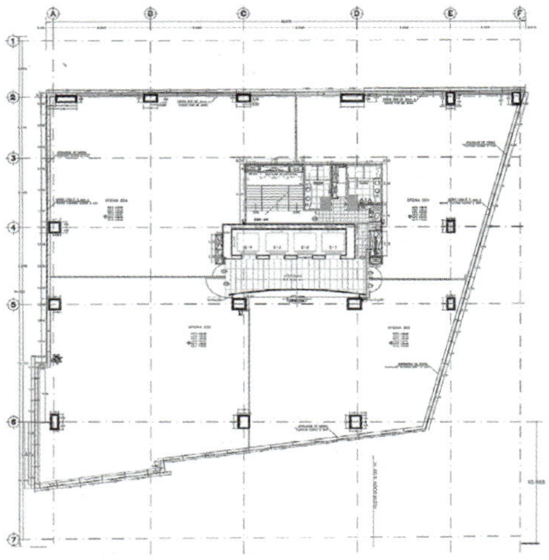

TORRE OPTIMA 3

A state of the art office and commerce building, Optima 3 is located in the prestigious Lomas de Chapultepec area in Mexico City. The tower includes space for luxurious offices on twelve floors, where two are for mixed commercial use and eight for underground parking for over 550 vehicles. The objective was to create a building that can integrate itself with the city's life while becoming a virtual lighthouse of actual and metaphorical light, movement and activity. The use of materials such as laminated glass allow efficiency in energy saving and low maintenance, and turn Optima 3 into a veritable center of light.

01 Typical floor plan **02** Side view **03** Exterior view by night, center of light **04** Lobby, polished granite floors and walls

Photos: Paúl Czitrom

REFORMA 222

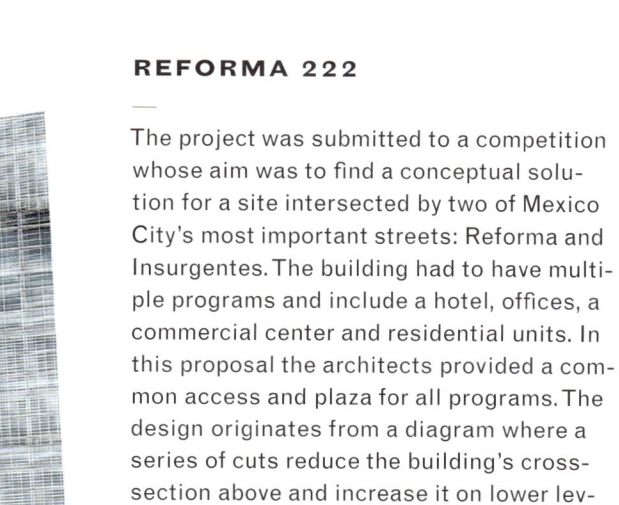

The project was submitted to a competition whose aim was to find a conceptual solution for a site intersected by two of Mexico City's most important streets: Reforma and Insurgentes. The building had to have multiple programs and include a hotel, offices, a commercial center and residential units. In this proposal the architects provided a common access and plaza for all programs. The design originates from a diagram where a series of cuts reduce the building's cross-section above and increase it on lower levels. This improves the structure's seismic durability and adds public areas such as commercial and common spaces.

01 Detail façade **02** Ground floor plan **03** Fourth floor plan
04 Exterior view, plaza and access area

Renderings: LAR / Fernando Romero

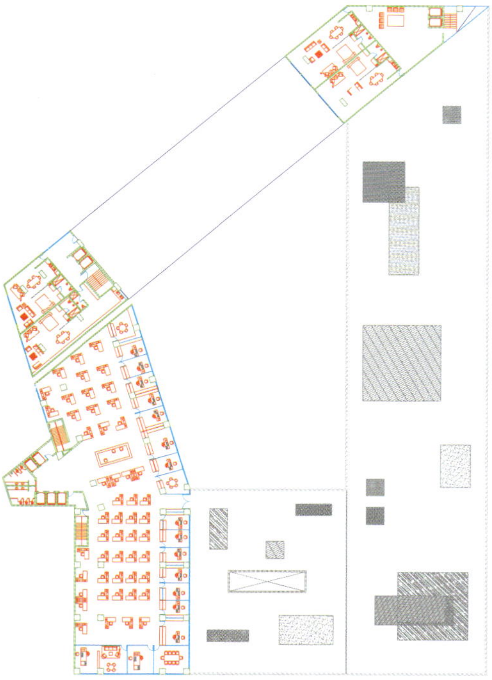

CITY Mexico City
COUNTRY Mexico
REGION Central America
TYPOLOGY Mixed-use
COMPLETION 2001 (design), unbuilt
WEBSITE www.laboratoryofarchitecture.com
ARCHITECTS LAR / Fernando Romero

CITY
Mexico City

COUNTRY
Mexico

REGION
Central America

TYPOLOGY
Living

COMPLETION
2006

WEBSITE
www.migdal.com.mx

ARCHITECTS
Jaime Varon, Abraham Metta, Alex Metta / Migdal Arquitectos

PLAZA RESIDENCES

Its base is formed by stony materials, which gives continuity to the urban plan, granting presence to the first levels that lodge commercial and common services areas. The main volume of Plaza Residences by Migdal Arquitectos which incorporates the architects Jaime Varon, Abraham Metta, and Alex Metta, is developed from an outline in a horseshoe form that surrounds the Public square of Columbus, while a sequence of volumes is opened towards Paseo de la Reforma conforming its facades.

01 Front view, horseshoe-shaped main volume **02** Rear view **03** Ground floor plan **04** Exterior view to Columbus square

Photos: Courtesy Migdal Arquitectos

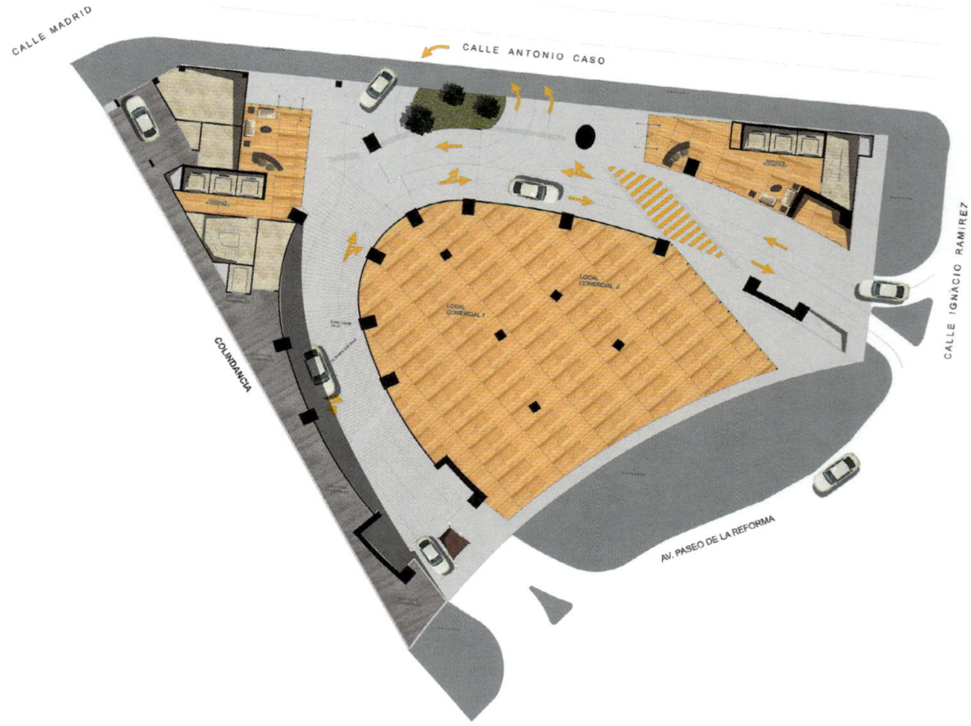

SHAKESPEARE'S DWELLINGS

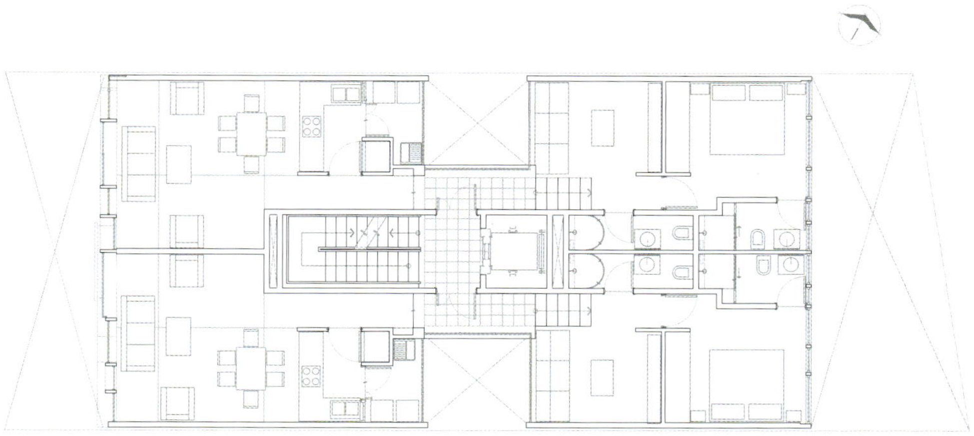

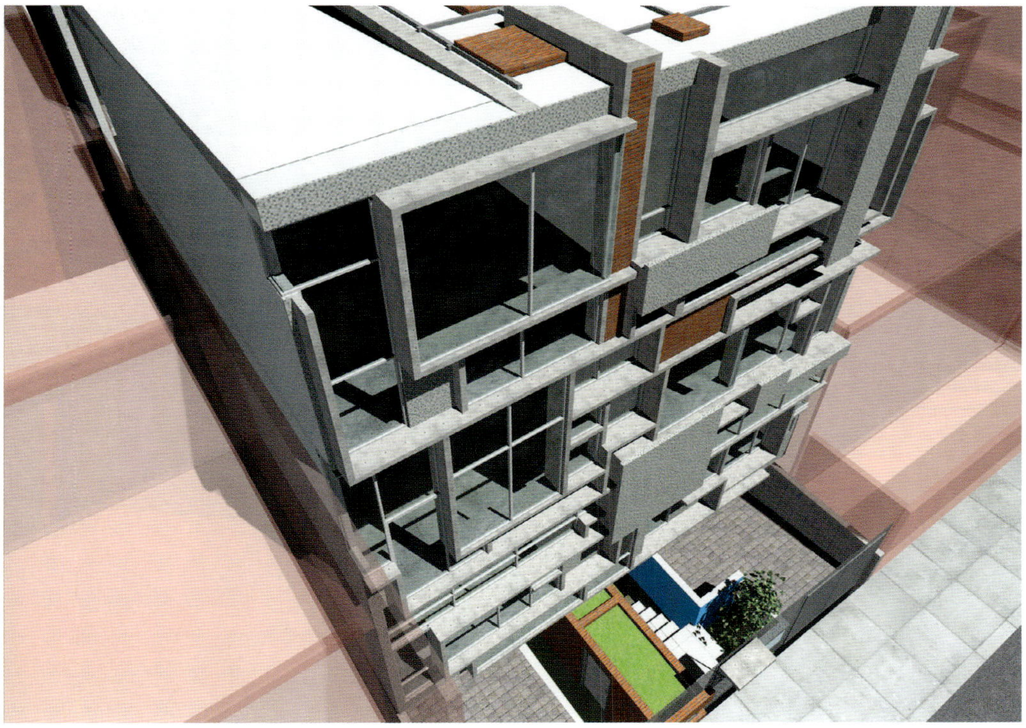

Located on Shakespeare Street in the Anzures neighborhood, a residential area located on the centric zone of Mexico City, is a house with an opportunity of recycling the former residence and creating five new apartments. One apartment and the ground floor of the second are located on the first level. On the second level is the third apartment with the second's upper level, while the fourth and fifth housings are lodged on the third level. One of the project's primacies is achieving privacy in the interiors' sights that are exposed to the street through the main façade, and this was done by creating visual filters.

01 Exterior view from the street **02** Detail façade **03** Interior view, window assembly **04** Third floor plan **05** Bird's eye view

Renderings: nurko arquitectos

CITY: Mexico City
COUNTRY: Mexico
REGION: Central America
TYPOLOGY: Living
COMPLETION: in progress
WEBSITE: www.aptilonnurko.com
ARCHITECTS: nurko arquitectos

SHERATON CENTRO HISTORICO

The Sheraton project is the first built effort in Mexico's Centro Historic since the 1985 eathquakes. Its modern design integrates the latest technologies with the possibility to adapt to the subsequent ones, and at the same time it intentionally breaks up with the context giving space to new mis-en-scenes, and at the same time creating added real estate value. This development in the historic center is in many ways a rebirth of the commercial, cultural, and social activities of Mexico in the fifties, a time when hotels were considered a must meeting point, such as it was with the Hotel Del Prado.

01, 02 Interior view, lobby 03 Interior view, service areas
04 Detail façade

Photos: Michelle Galindo, Martin Nicholas Kunz (01, 04)

CITY Mexico City
COUNTRY Mexico
REGION Central America
TYPOLOGY Hospitality
COMPLETION 2007
WEBSITE www.pascalarquitectos.com
ARCHITECTS Pascal Arquitectos

ANTARA POLANCO

The dream was to construct a church and museum, and today it is on the verge of seeing the first stage concluded, and in addition it has the order of the project of the Mariana Place. The construction stores Iron Palace in Monterrey as well as in Guadalajara, in which the Mariana Place includes a museum and a center of evangelization, as well as a cattle ranch of Xajay, considered some of the best in the country, with a main target being to think about something useful to offer to the city. It is located in the crossing of the avenues Army National and Molière de Polanco, in the estate that lodged the plant of General Motors.

01 Public area **02** Detail roof **03** Cloister at the pond by night **04** Detail façade

Photos: Martin Nicholas Kunz

CITY: Mexico City
COUNTRY: Mexico
REGION: Central America
TYPOLOGY: Retail
COMPLETION: 2006
WEBSITE: www.sma.com.mx
ARCHITECTS: Sordo Madaleno Arquitectos

CITY Mexico City

COUNTRY Mexico

REGION Central America

TYPOLOGY Hospitality

COMPLETION 2005

WEBSITE www.jsadd.com

ARCHITECTS JS⁴ (formerly Higuera + Sanchez)

CONDESA DF

Tucked away on a tree-lined avenue in Mexico City is a cool Condesa neighborhood, upon which the new Condesa df Hotel imaginatively fuses the name and spirit of its environment with interior designer India Mahdavi's inventive and playful simplicity. Mahdavi's design offers functional originality from rooms to rooftop, incorporating a range of local materials in elements including custom-made furniture and stone tile flooring. The Condesa df's ground-floor restaurant exemplifies this ideal, with its indoor/outdoor feel flowing through a series of privacy-optional rooms, ringing a vivid, flora-filled courtyard.

01 View to rooftop **02** Interior view, restaurant "The Condesa" **03** Detail façade **04** Interior view, room with private deck

Photos: Undine Pröhl, courtesy Condesa df (03)

EDIFICIO PARQUE ESPAÑA 23

The space complexity must be studied in such form that it is allowed to control the decision making of the design in real terms; understanding the environment like space systems, analyzing the configuration and trying to demonstrate the landlords. Without a theoretical approach at this level, any application would be within the dominion of the empiricist, and therefore, to be subject of bad interpretations. The buildings are physical organizations, although its intrinsic roll is to generate the spaces and interconnections that in fact were used, where the effect of each physical intervention creates these space landlords.

01 Detail façade **02** Exterior view by night **03** Courtyard

Photos: Oliver Llaneza

CITY Mexico City
COUNTRY Mexico
REGION Central America
TYPOLOGY Living
COMPLETION 2007
WEBSITE www.slvk.com
ARCHITECTS SLVK / Gustavo Slovik

CITY: Mexico City
COUNTRY: Mexico
REGION: Central America
TYPOLOGY: Living
COMPLETION: -
WEBSITE: www.slvk.com
ARCHITECTS: SLVK / Gustavo Slovik

EDIFICIO MANANTIALES POLANCO

The building located in a regeneration zone of Mexico City that is growing in popularity houses 47 apartments, 55 m² each. The building has a green rooftop that stands in contrast with the gray surroundings. The structure is "u" shaped, with all the apartments having views both on the inside and out. The windows on the outside where designed as a reference to barcodes used to tag commercial products. The inside windows bring light and movement together. The architecture of the building reflects a very dynamic expression which contrasts the regular form of the plan.

01 Courtyard **02** Exterior view from the street **03** Detail façade **04** Detail staircase

Photos: Courtesy SLVK / Gustavo Slovik

FIREFLY

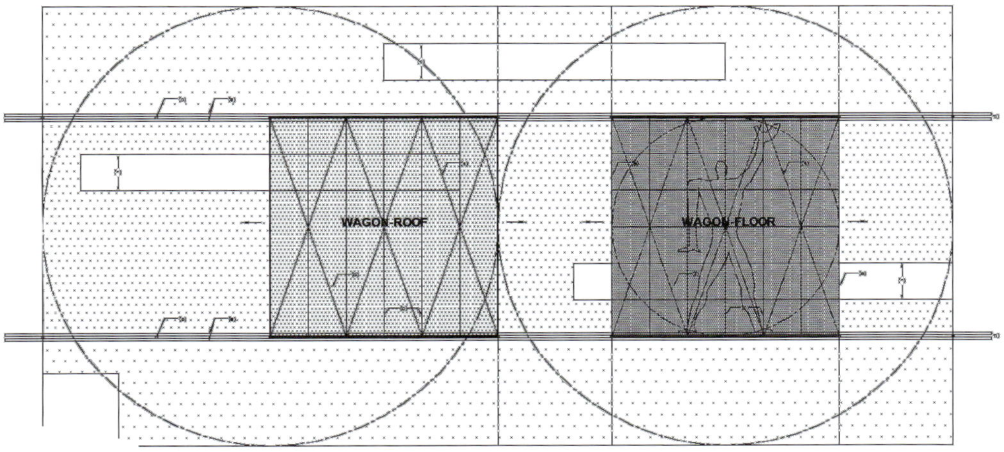

The design strategy takes courtyards or "patios" of downtown Mexico City, and incorporates additions such as cafeterias or spaces for social and cultural interaction, where the characteristics of the additions directly relate to the specific site, generating interconnected floating urban corridors. The proposal is materialized in a light and classical structure accessible to developing countries, borrowing basic structural systems found in NYC subways and railroads. The idea is that these collections will become glowing objects at night, art display boxes during the day, and as light sources or fireflies in constant movement.

01 Glowing object at night **02** Model: patio **03** Plan **04** Art display boxes during day

Photos: Rec Arquitectura

CITY Mexico City
COUNTRY Mexico
REGION Central America
TYPOLOGY Commercial (showroom)
COMPLETION 2008 (design), unbuilt
WEBSITE www.recarquitectura.com
ARCHITECTS Rec Arquitectura / Gerardo Recoder

CITY
Mexico City

COUNTRY
Mexico

REGION
Central America

TYPOLOGY
Public

COMPLETION
2006

WEBSITE
www.kalach.com

ARCHITECTS
Taller de Arquitectura X /
Alberto Kalach

BIBLIOTECA VASCONCELOS

This mega-project does not just involve the expansion of the old Library of Mexico, but also creates a new concept that embraces different services on its five levels: auditorium, foreign language center, museum and bookshop, all surrounded by a botanical garden. The project essentially transforms the old library into a modern one. The construction had three main goals: To constitute an axis of integration, technical support and development of new information services for the National Network libraries; To create a new paradigm of the public library with the most advanced systems; To extend access to the services.

01 Interior view **02** Detail façade **03** Embedded in gardens and an industrial park **04** Concrete volume

Photos: Martin Nicholas Kunz, Michelle Galindo (01)

W MEXICO CITY

This is the first W hotel in Latin America, and it differs from all others because of its passionate and youthful style. The use of native Mexican materials, Koi ponds in the interior, a terrace with fireplaces and vibrant colors give it a relaxing and seductive ambiance. All rooms offer high speed internet access, office facilities, in-room CD and DVD libraries, luxurious jet-stream showers and maid service. Split-level loft suits have terraces offering spectacular views, dining areas for up to 8 persons and Bose surround sound systems.

01 Lounge **02** Restaurant **03** Lobby **04** Spa area **05** Lounge

Photos: Ilan Waisbrod

CITY Mexico City
COUNTRY Mexico
REGION Central America
TYPOLOGY Hospitality
COMPLETION 2003
WEBSITE www.studiogaia.com
ARCHITECTS Studio Gaia / Ilan Waisbrod

CITY Mexico City
COUNTRY Mexico
REGION Central America
TYPOLOGY Living
COMPLETION 2005
WEBSITE www.gutierrez-alonso.com
ARCHITECTS Gutierrez-Alonso Arquitectura

CASA ECHEGARAY

The project of Casa Echegaray by Gutierrez – Alonso Arquitectura contains four blocks which are superposed in terraces, and adapt to a land with a slope which is very pronounced, distinct, and well-defined. In the superior block, a descendent route made by a sequence of spaces of diverse qualities begins. A series of retaining walls of stone at the site as well as a surrounding one of concrete pretend to constitute the space, while the concrete bays are of apparent magnitude, where one defines the inner-outer relation, and frame pleasing views of limits to the west of the metropolitan zone of Mexico City.

01 Exterior view **02** Detail **03** Concrete façade **04** Longitudinal section **05** Floor plan, living area

Photos: Alberto Moreno

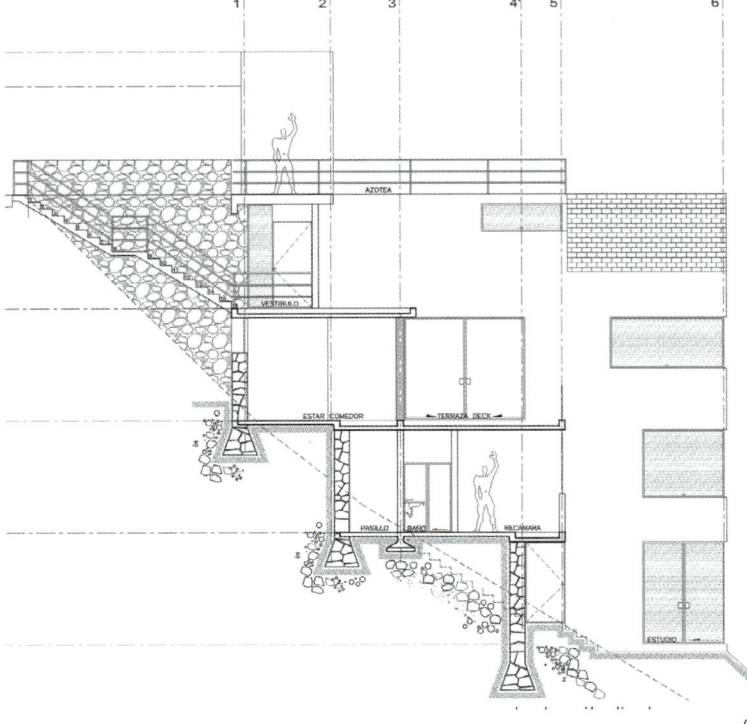

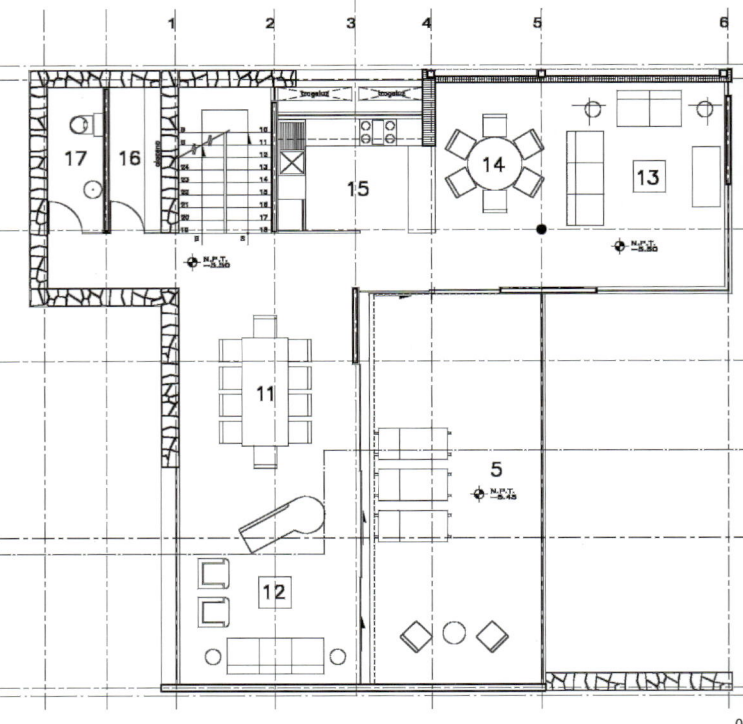

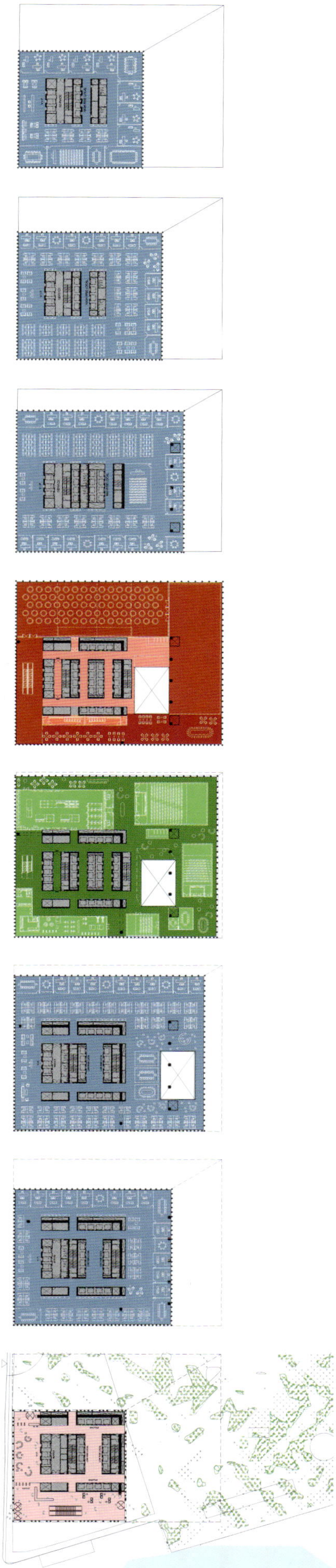

TORRE BICENTENARIO

Poised to harness the economic and symbolic potential of the Bicentennial, Mexico City will celebrate a historic moment with the emergence of a new skyscraper: Torre Bicentenario. The site lies at the northeast corner of Chapultepec Park, and will provide much needed class AAA office space for Mexico City, together with public amenities – a sky lobby, convention center, shops and restaurants – for the surrounding communities and visitors to the Park. A void cuts through the building's widest point, providing access to light and natural ventilation, while creating a relationship between the floors within.

01 Floor plans **02** Exterior view by night **03** Emergence of a new skyscraper **04** Detail structural curtain wall

Photos: Frans Parthesius

CITY: Mexico City
COUNTRY: Mexico
REGION: Central America
TYPOLOGY: Mixed-Use
COMPLETION: discontinued
WEBSITE: www.oma.com
ARCHITECTS: Office for Metropolitan Architecture (OMA), Rem Koolhaas, Ole Scheeren

LOPE DE VEGA 324

This low-rise apartment building has 19 housing units with different typologies, with a subterranean parking level that occupies the entire lot. On the top of the parking level two different five-level volumes are built, one on the west side facing the street and the other on the east side on the back of the lot. Both bodies are divided by a gardened patio where apartment's access paths and stairways are located. These pathways and stairways are made of light structure in order to allow natural light and ventilation into the space. This traditionally service space is reconsidered and becomes the principal trait of the building.

01 Floor plan, inner courtyard level **02** Exterior view **03** Lobby **04** Staircase leading to upper units **05** Inner courtyard with garden

Photos: Luis Gordoa

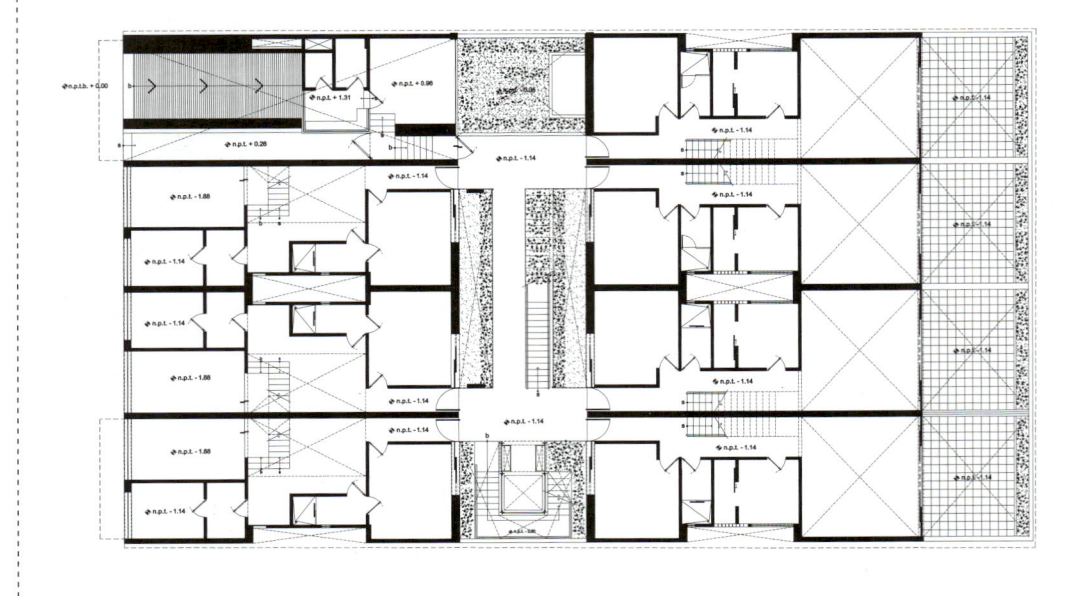

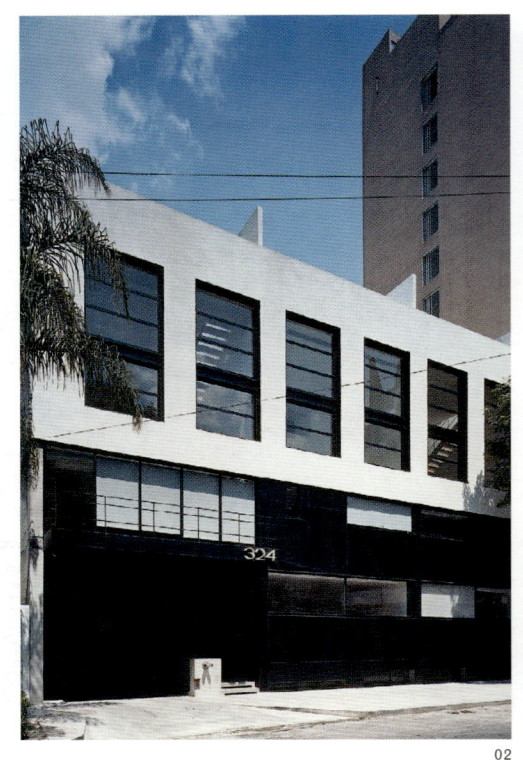

CITY Mexico City
COUNTRY Mexico
REGION Central America
TYPOLOGY Living
COMPLETION 2003
WEBSITE www.volvox.tv
ARCHITECTS Iñaki Echeverria

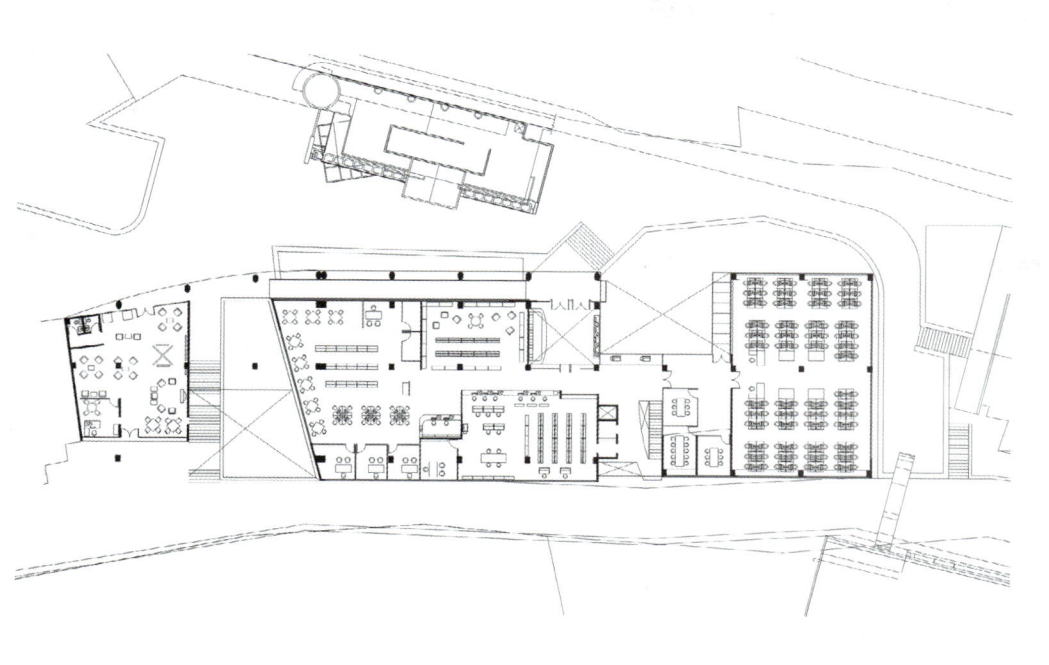

CENTRO DE INFORMACION Y BIBLIOTECA C.I.D.E.

The building, The Central Library of Investigation, done by RDZ + LARA Arquitectura, is approximately 4500 meters squared, distributed among six levels, in which three of them are used for heap and the rest divided for cataloguing, lessons, rooms of work and conferences. The outer volumes are grouped by means of staples in "Ls" of concrete pretends that limit and surround each one of the bodies. In order to prevent the direct incidence of the sun to the interior, horizontal lines and a facade set out a vertical jealousy. On the last level, a light cover that remembers the natural arrangement of an open book is featured.

01 Floor plan **02** Detail façade **03** Night view **04** View towards façade **05** Stairs

Photos: Alberto Moreno Guzman

CITY
Mexico City

COUNTRY
Mexico

REGION
Central America

TYPOLOGY
Culture / Education

COMPLETION
2007

WEBSITE
www.rdz-lara.com

ARCHITECTS
RDZ + LARA arquitectura / Miguel Angel Navarro Robles

EBC CAMPUS TLALNEPANTLA

City life is enriched with mixed land uses, and the setting of La Roma is no different. This neighborhood is seen as a lively sector of the city, where many school facilities are in place. Sánchez Arquitectos was asked to continue with this trend, and develop and design a dynamic and functional school. The theme design of the project was to create a reunion place, and this gave rise to the idea of a skylight patio where passersby create the feeling of a community. The building responds to the west with a louver façade and to the north with a high tech façade, while the school itself is done in a steel structure.

01 West elevation, louver façade **02** Patio **03** Interior view **04** Floor plans **05** Detail skylight patio

Photos: Ricardo Castro

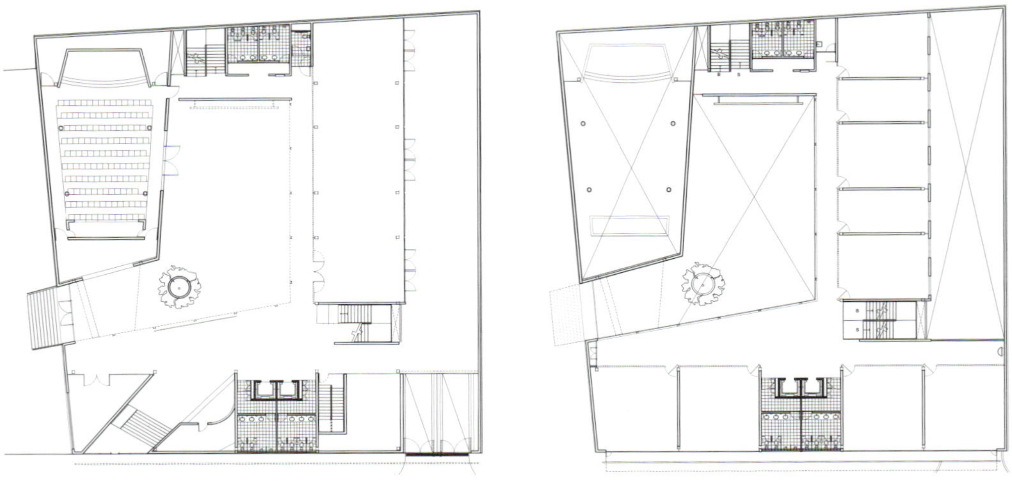

NAUTILUS

Harmonic space in three dimensions where the continuos dynamics of the Nautilus house. The fourth dimension when journeying in spiral is perceived on the flight of steps, with the sensation to float on the vegetation. Promoting the flight of steps in spiral, it continues through the lobby and passes by the living room, sheltered by the belly of the crustacea, and climbing by the snail stairs the user gets to the study from where a glimpse of the mountainous landscape is appreciated it.

01 Interior **02** Living room **03** Wall detail **04** Section **05** Curved wall with sink

Photos: Jaime Jacott

CITY	Mexico City (Naucalpan)
COUNTRY	Mexico
REGION	Central America
TYPOLOGY	Living
COMPLETION	2006
WEBSITE	www.arquitecturaorganica.com
ARCHITECTS	Arquitectura Organica - Javier Senosiain

CITY Monterrey
COUNTRY Mexico
REGION Central America
TYPOLOGY Living
COMPLETION 2004
WEBSITE www.fernandacanales.com
ARCHITECTS Fernanda Canales

CASAS M

In adjacent lots of 250m², each house adapted to the variants that the slopes of the land and the views raised. The programs and solutions are different in each case, but the general logic and the use of materials cause the four houses to be part of a same perceived sequence. The project is located in the East Colony Valley, a zone of development that tries to stretch the Colony of the Valley towards the Hill of the Chair. The project has a double façade, one towards the south that gives the interior a tightened division, and another towards the Avenue Founders to the north, while forming access to the houses.

01 Exterior view, ensemble **02** Interior view **03** Rear view, detail **04** Ground floor plan

Photos: Luis Gordoa, Jorge Taboada

MIRAVALLE TOWER

This is a multifamily housing project consisting of 84 high-level apartments plus four luxury two-leveled penthouses. The site, with a spectacular vegetation density for the area, including pecan trees reaching 80 feet in height, had suggested the high-rise solution in order to preserve the views and respect the greenery. The building has a layout accommodating four apartments on each floor with an integrated central core vertical circulation. The final solution is a 26-storey tower with three levels of underground parking and storage. The project also includes a swimming pool with a party pavilion in the existing gardens.

01 Exterior view by night **02** Section **03** Interior view, lobby with social area **04** View from the garden, detail façade

Photos: Jorge Taboada, Alejandro Rodriguez

CITY Monterrey
COUNTRY Mexico
REGION Central America
TYPOLOGY Living
COMPLETION 2006
WEBSITE www.gilbertolrodriguez.com
ARCHITECTS Gilberto L. Rodriguez / GLR architects

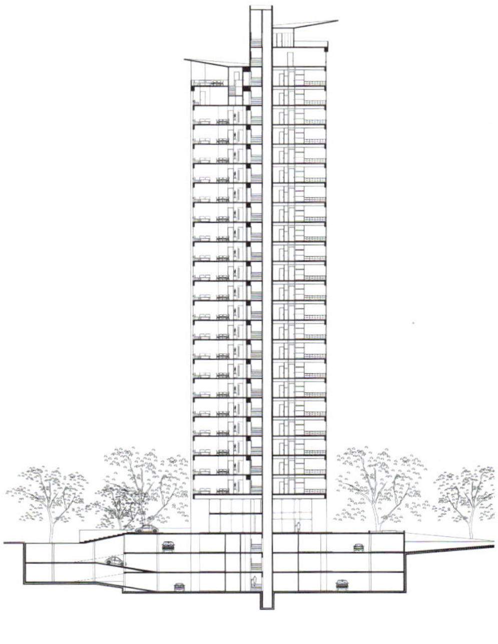

CITY: Monterrey
COUNTRY: Mexico
REGION: Central America
TYPOLOGY: Education
COMPLETION: 2006
WEBSITE: www.landaarquitectos.com
ARCHITECTS: Landa Arquitectos

ESCUELA DE MEDICINA ITESM

The building is contiguous to a preexisting hospitable complex, the San Jose Hospital. It lodges a medicine school in fast growth with respective classrooms, spaces of investigation, library, cafeteria and laboratories equipped with biomedical instruments and of robotics. Additionally, the building includes Annexes to the cardiology hospital - clinical ambulatory, oncology, and a parking with capacity for 200 automobiles. The Technological Institute and Studies Superiors of Monterrey (ITESM) made important investments in recent years, oriented to make of its school a medicine center of competitive technological development.

01 South elevation **02** Detail ramp **03** Courtyard **04** Interior view, auditorium **05** Interior view, detail entry auditorium

Photos: Javier Orozco

MUSEO DEL ACERO

In summer of 2005, Grimshaw was commissioned to design the Museo del Acero (Museum of Steel) in and around Horno Alto #3, a decommissioned Blast Furnace from the late 1960s. Marking a return for Grimshaw to the industrial city of Monterrey, the design converts the 70-meter-high furnace structure into a series of habitable volumes, adding 9,000 m² of indoor and outdoor museum space. Intended to host an exposition of steel, the museum is being created partially as an adaptive re-use of the furnace, its platforms, tanks and control rooms, and partially as a new extension adjacent to the existing complex.

01 Exterior view 02 Detail helical steel stair with lift 03 Detail blast furnace and re-cladded cast hall 04 Ground floor plan

Photos: Courtesy Grimshaw

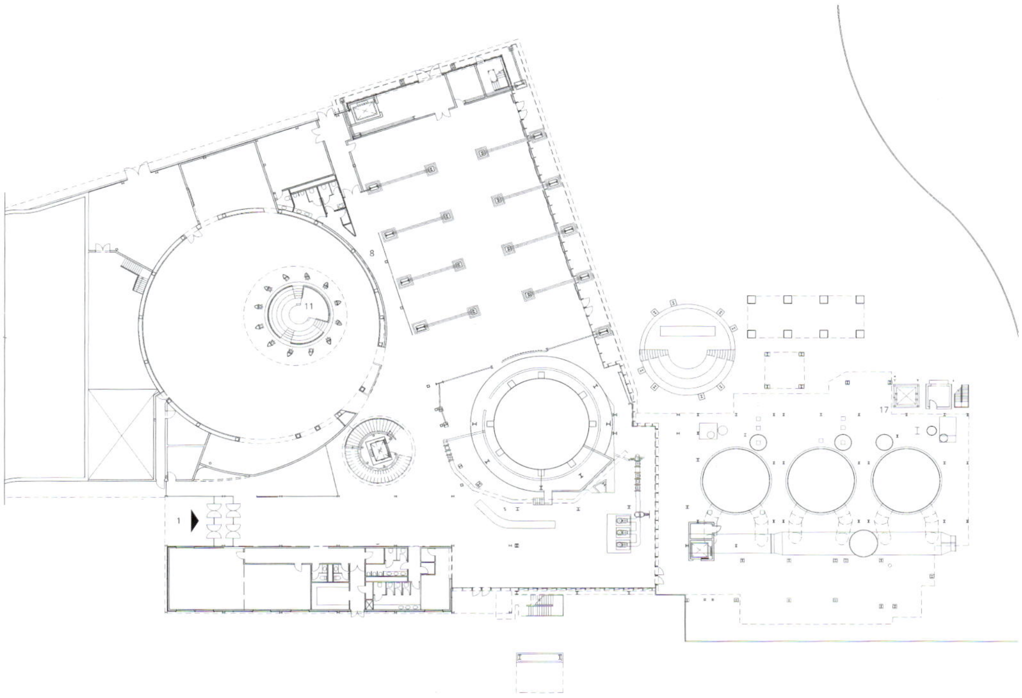

CITY: Monterrey
COUNTRY: Mexico
REGION: Central America
TYPOLOGY: Culture
COMPLETION: 2007
WEBSITE: www.grimshaw-architects.com
ARCHITECTS: Grimshaw

CITY
Monterrey

COUNTRY
Mexico

REGION
Central America

TYPOLOGY
Living

COMPLETION
2007

WEBSITE
www.vidalarquitectos.com

ARCHITECTS
Vidal Arquitectos

CONDOMINOS LA DIANA

This project development, the Condominios La Diana, created by Vidal, consists of two towers of departments, and attempts to obtain an urban dialogue among them through the inclination of its facades that simulate the hills that they are surrounded by. Between the two towers a duality exists, and these include the elements of solid versus emptiness, and material versus crystal. From the beginning of this construction, the aim of the project was set out and was marked by the two covers of concrete at the end of each tower, while the necessity of each tower with the other determines the existence of both.

01 Bird's eye view **02** Side view **03** Interior view, dining and living room **04** Interior view, lobby **05** Lateral elevation

Photos: Jorge Taboada
Renderings: ARKIMEDIA

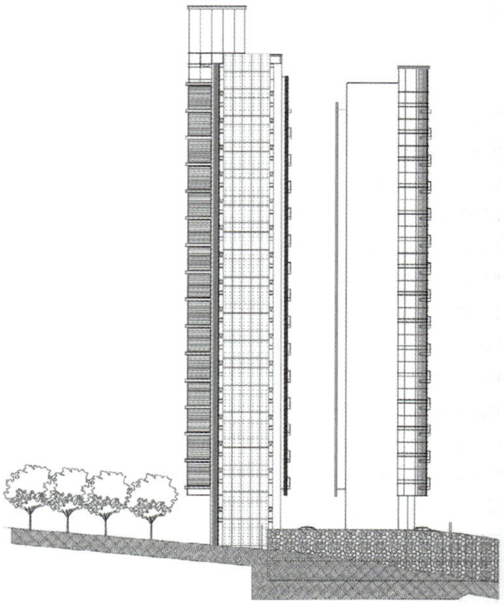

SMOOTH BUILDING FOR CORPONET

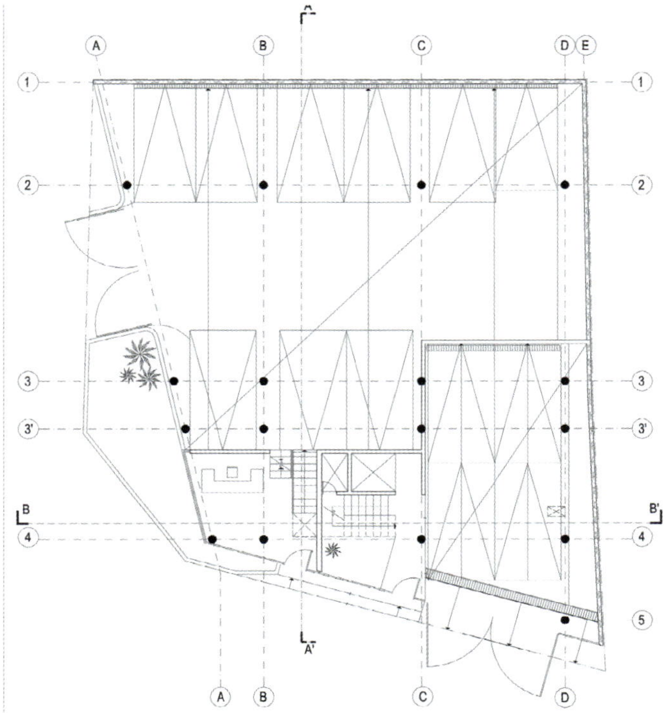

The building is located on a south-oriented lot in a residential area in San Pedro Garza Garcia, Nuevo Leon. This project's design challenge was to combine residences and offices within the maximum allotted space. To achieve this objective, it was necessary to mix the spaces and uses in the allowed four stories' height. The structure responds to the topography and the unforgiving hot temperatures of the site, using only 70% of the lot. The shape optimally places every space inside a curved continuous skin using different materials that respond and open to the immediate context in order to obtain the best conditions and views.

01 View from the street **02** Exterior view with focus on office space on the first floor **03** Exterior view by night **04** Ground floor plan **05** Interior view, private space

Renderings: JHG

CITY Nuevo León
COUNTRY Mexico
REGION Central America
TYPOLOGY Office
COMPLETION 2007
WEBSITE www.hernandezdelagarza.com
ARCHITECTS JHG Jorge Hernández de la Garza

CITY
Ocotlán

COUNTRY
Mexico

REGION
Central America

TYPOLOGY
Public

COMPLETION
2007

WEBSITE
www.leap.com.mx

ARCHITECTS
LeAP Laboratorio en Arquitectura Progresiva S. C.

LIBRARY AND MEDIA CENTER FERNANDO DEL PASO

On 2007 the new Library and Media Center for the State University in the city of Ocotlán, Jalisco, Mexico, was finally opened to the public. This building pioneers the implementation of standardized norms for accessibility for people with disabilities, featuring a set of ramps and aisles specially designed to make it 100% accessible. It will house a collection of 120,000 books, DVDs and videos on a total area of 5,346 m², making it the biggest public library in western Mexico, and the second in size after the recently opened Central Library Jose Vasconcelos in Mexico.

01 Exterior view of media library **02** Detail glazed staircase media library **03** Detail ramp **04** Floor plans **05** Sections and elevation

Photos: Heriberto Hernandez Ochoa

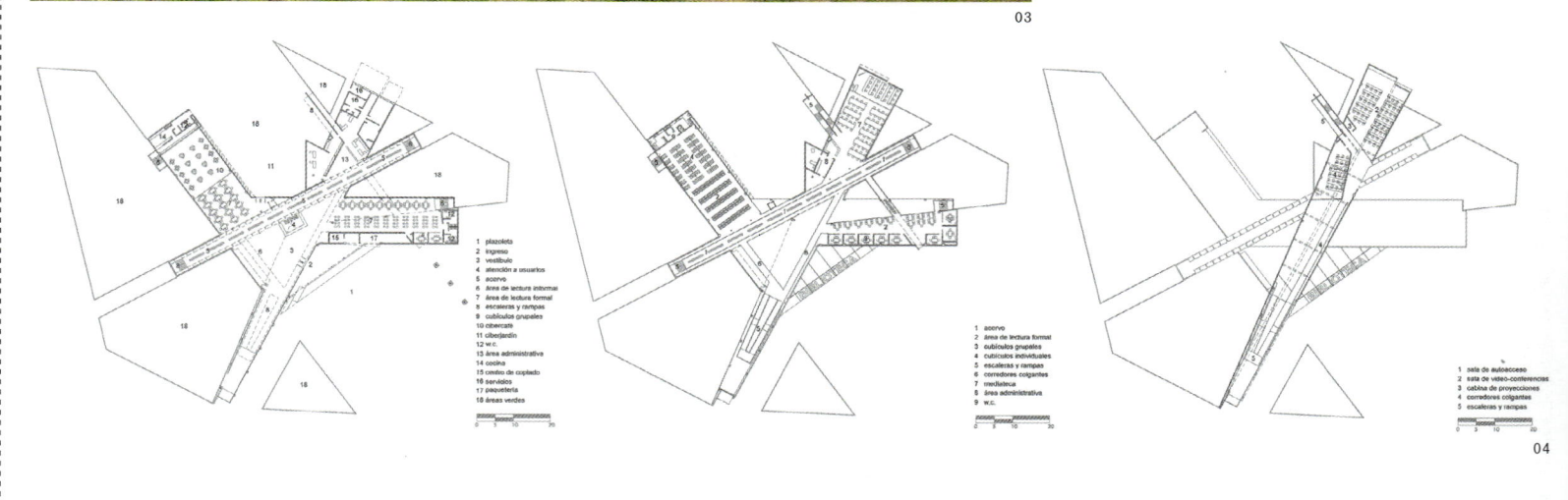

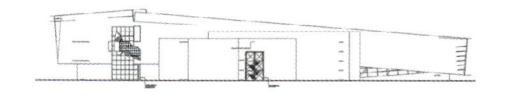

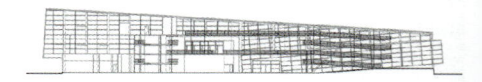

HOTEL BASICO

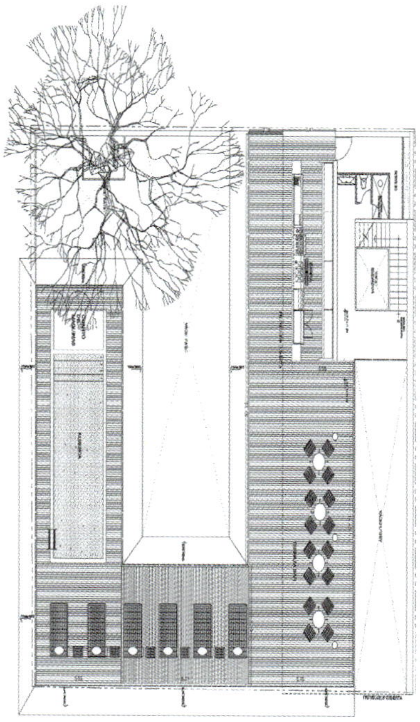

Playful cultural references populate this small Mexican hotel, where interior designer Héctor Galvan writes of Básico; a 15-room hotel located one block from the beach in Quintana Roo, Mexico, is a work that allows one to approach and interpret culture under a new light, getting rid of the habitual stigmas about Mexicans and the way in which they work and do things, while taking advantage of natural talent for improvisation and guilt. The intention was to design and to achieve comfort and sophistication without pretension, while recalling the great spirit of Mexican beaches thirty or forty years ago.

01 Exterior view by night **02** Third floor plan **03** Roof with pools **04** Detail room **05** Detail

Photos: Undine Prohl

CITY Playa del Carmen
COUNTRY Mexico
REGION Central America
TYPOLOGY Hospitality
COMPLETION -
WEBSITE www.ccarquitectos.com.mx
ARCHITECTS Central de Arquitectura

ESENCIA

Esencia is a 50-acre private estate, with an awe-inspiring beachfront, two swimming pools, day spa, gourmet restaurant, and an indulgent atmosphere becoming of royalty. Located along a two-mile empty stretch of Mexico's best beach, this is a quiet sea side refuge. Guest quarters are simple and elegant, featuring native hardwood furnishings, crisp white walls and floors, twelve-foot high ceilings, mahogany louvered doors and large windows that frame tropical garden and sea views. Nestled in a private area within the estate's tropical gardens, two-story cottages feature large living rooms and outside terraces with dining areas.

01 View of pool and pool bar **02** Exterior view **03–04** Detail room **05** Courtyard

Photos: Martin Nicholas Kunz, Michelle Galindo (02, 03)

CITY Playa del Carmen
COUNTRY Mexico
REGION Central America
TYPOLOGY Hospitality
COMPLETION 2007
WEBSITE –
ARCHITECTS –

AMPLIACION DE OFICINAS CORPORATIVAS

In addition to equipping the building with a character that's in agreement with the company, which is dedicated to the manufacture of lights of high design, the growth of the existing facilities was required to transfer the corporative one in an Industrial zone of the city. The approach of the project, Ampliacion Oficinia, is based on a system of slight and simple construction, contemplating a crystal facade that is well lit during the night. The form of the facade corresponds to a smoothly curved element that ends at the volume of the main directorate, which has been extended towards the front.

01 Detail metal curtain wall **02** Between curtain wall and building **03** Side view **04** Section, detail façade

Photos: Zoom Colors

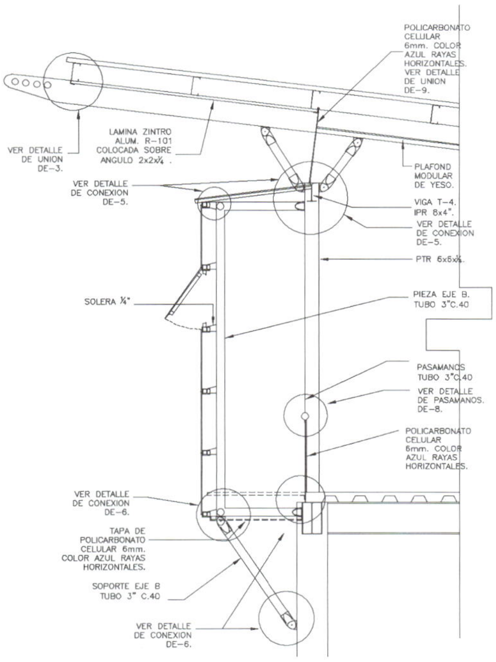

CITY Querétaro
COUNTRY Mexico
REGION Central America
TYPOLOGY Office
COMPLETION 2004
WEBSITE www.intelarq.com.mx
ARCHITECTS Intel-Arq

CITY Queretaro
COUNTRY Mexico
REGION Central America
TYPOLOGY Living
COMPLETION 2006
WEBSITE www.at103.net
ARCHITECTS at103 Julio Amezcua + Francisco Pardo

CASA ROMERO

The design is developed on an existing foundation, on which it was necessary to clearly define the volumes that would constitute the house with a program for a 4-member family in two 'boxes.' The stone box is hermetic; it contains the main bathroom and services areas such as storage, maid's room and garage. The wooden box contains the living room, dining room, studio, bar, kitchen, TV room and children's rooms. Access is laid through the void generated in between the two, connecting to the living room and creating a double-height space where the main stairs and the bridge between the boxes are located.

01 Exterior view of boxes **02** Interior view **03** Floor plans **04** Detail stone box **05** Detail wooden box and linking bridge

Photos: Rafael Gamo

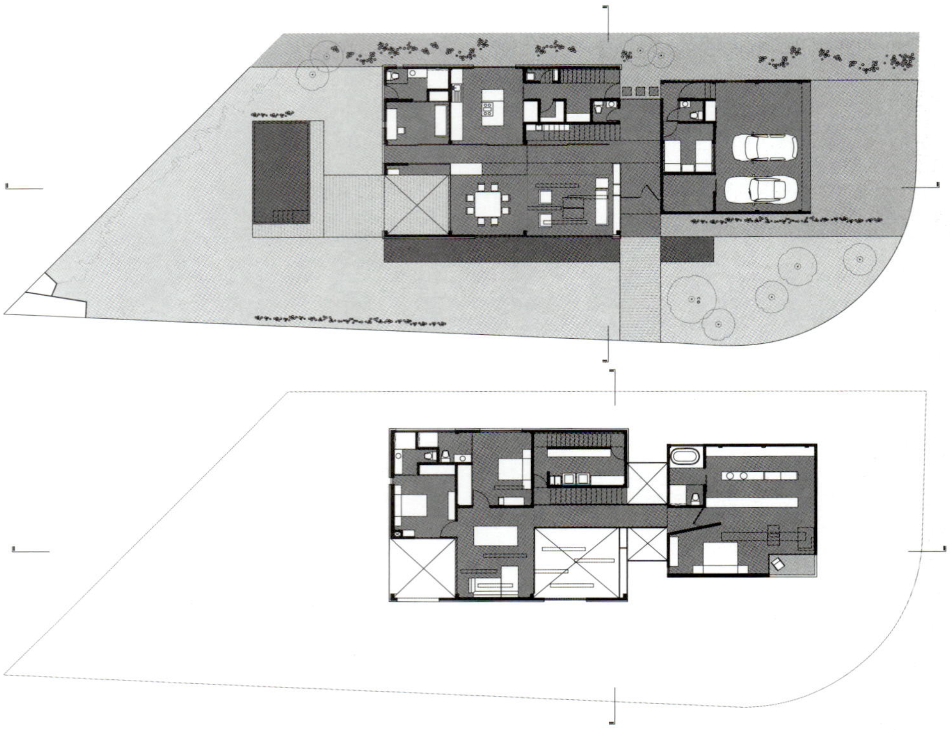

MESA DE LA CORONA

An injured irregular land with privileged views to the Mountain Range Mother, lodges this residence. The composition of this responds to an organization of the program and as it takes advantage of the views and surroundings. A closed, massive and heavy volume visually contains the firing chambers in the highest part of the land while the social areas are divided into three levels: it is acceded by the part from above the main room, dining room and kitchen, with the low part being a covered terrace and a level set as an entertainment area for games. The social program tours the garage exhibiting a collection of cars.

01 Exterior view from the street **02** Detail entrance area
03 Cellar and ground floor plan **04** Section

Photos: José Borrani, Alejandro Treviño

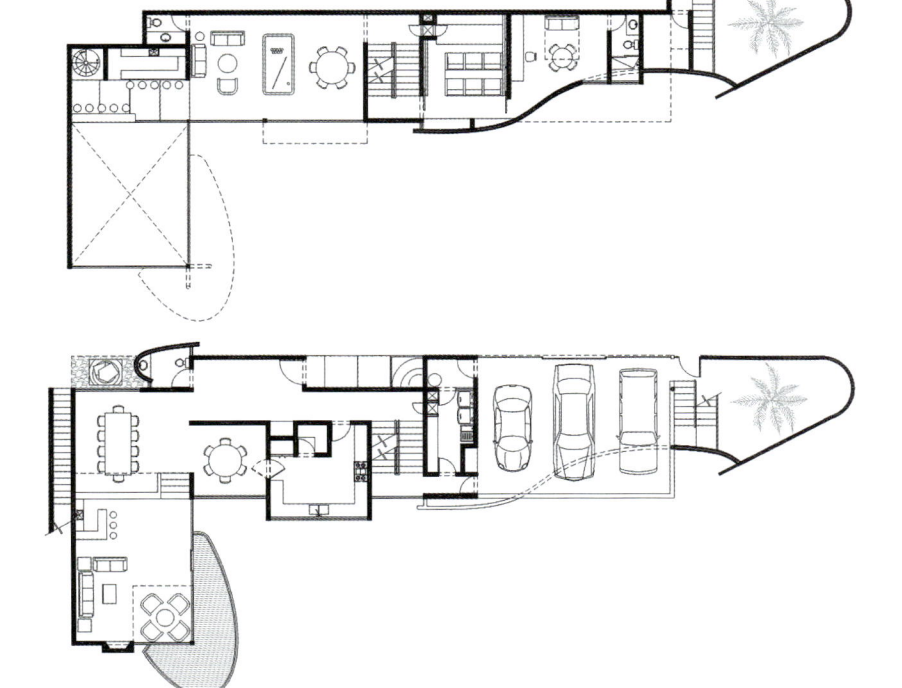

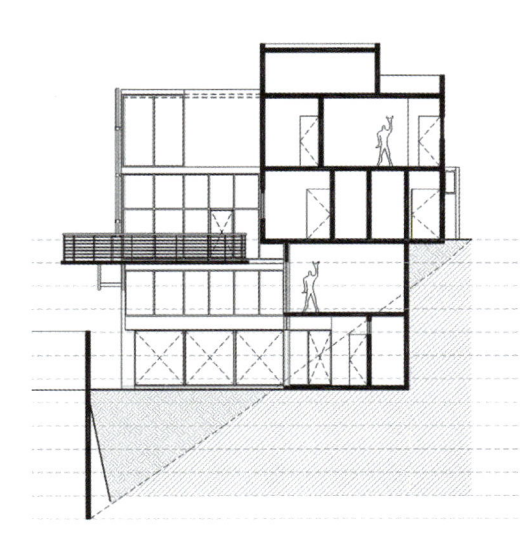

CITY San Pedro
COUNTRY Mexico
REGION Central America
TYPOLOGY Living
COMPLETION in progress
WEBSITE www.7xa.com.mx
ARCHITECTS 7xa arquitectura / Ángel López, Carlos Ortiz

CITY Santiago de Querétaro

COUNTRY Mexico

REGION Central America

TYPOLOGY Living

COMPLETION 2007

WEBSITE www.microarq.com

ARCHITECTS Herman Bottle H. + Mercedes Castro W / micro.arq

CASA ESTUDIO BC

With the idea of constructing a small home studio as part of a later expansion, the project, a livable and flexible "micro home", was undertaken as a case study. By integrating the concepts of sustainability, simplicity, and modular low-cost building, the final space proved to be a coherent proposal, easy to live in, with low energy consumption. Materials such as OSB, apparent brick, MDF and prefab concrete panels were installed in an aesthetic way generating changes of texture and planes on an otherwise block like volume. A movable, usable wall unit was implemented to separate private and public areas.

01 View from the garden **02, 03** Detail deck **04** Floor plan **05** Detail

Photos: Mercedes Castro

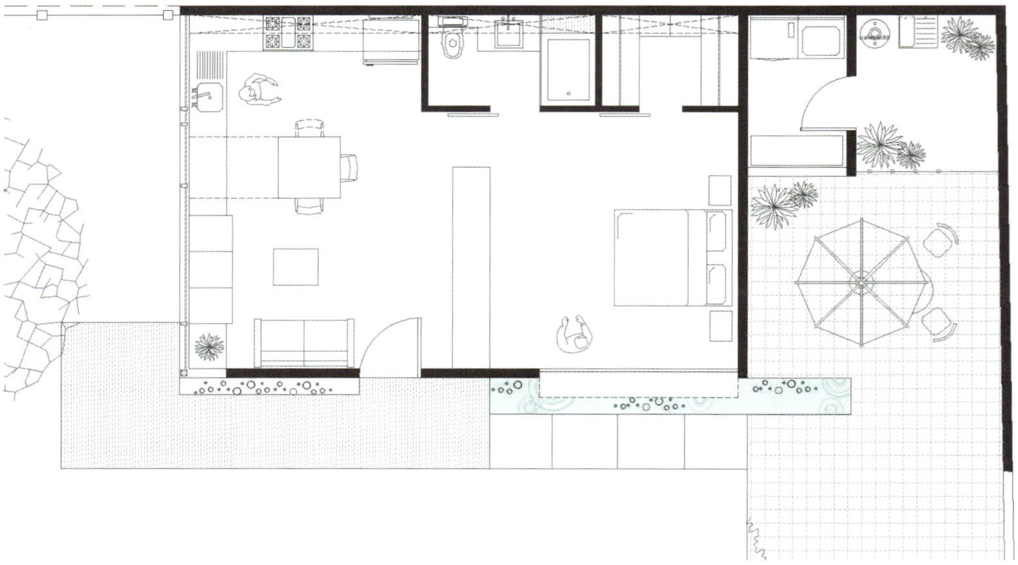

SMO HOUSE

Santa Maria del Oro Lake is a landscape built filling a volcano with water. The result is a topographical concavity, a circular shaped slope that ends down in the water. The project's lot is located at the water's edge on a small bay. The client camped on the terrain for years; therefore the house was to be built with a deep relationship to the lake, weather and views in order for the inhabitants to feel as if they were camping. The house is composed of three pieces: a long pavilion on pilots, transparent and facing the lake, a smaller pavilion behind with bedrooms for the kids, and an open platform.

01 Long pavilion on piles **02** View to the lake **03** View from the garden **04** Floor plan **05** Detail transparent façade long pavilion

Photos: Alejandro Guerrero Gutiérrez

CITY Santa Maria del Oro
COUNTRY Mexico
REGION Central America
TYPOLOGY Living
COMPLETION 2005
WEBSITE www.atelierars.com
ARCHITECTS Ars atelier de arquitecturas

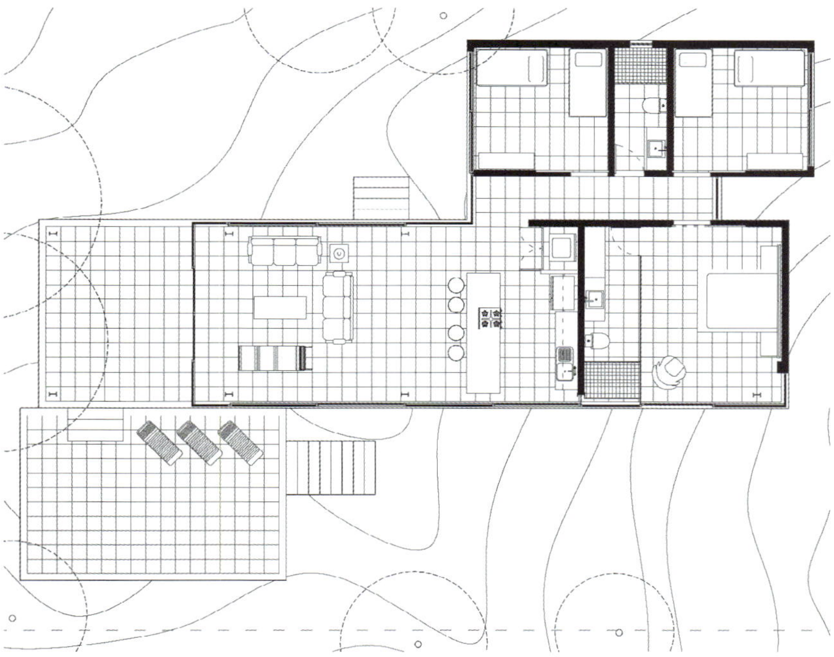

CITY
Santa Catarina

COUNTRY
Mexico

REGION
Central America

TYPOLOGY
Living

COMPLETION
in progress

WEBSITE
www.7xa.com.mx

ARCHITECTS
7xa arquitectura / Ángel López, Carlos Ortiz

OL-411 HOUSE

The house, CASA OL-411, is placed in a residential division to the foot of the tube of the Huasteca in Santa Catarina, N.L. The main kindness of that land is indeed its visual relation with this natural icon of the city. One is made up of two levels in two bodies, the inferior opaque and light is totally abierto towards the street and the later garden, while the superior is solid and stony, of polished cement, with precise openings towards where the view must go. The ground floor lodges an open social space that is related to the street by means of a complex lattice window with ovals of golden color.

01 View from the garden **02** Roof floor plan **03** Front view **04** First floor plan **05** Interior view, living room **06** Ground floor plan

Photos: José Fernando Cerecer

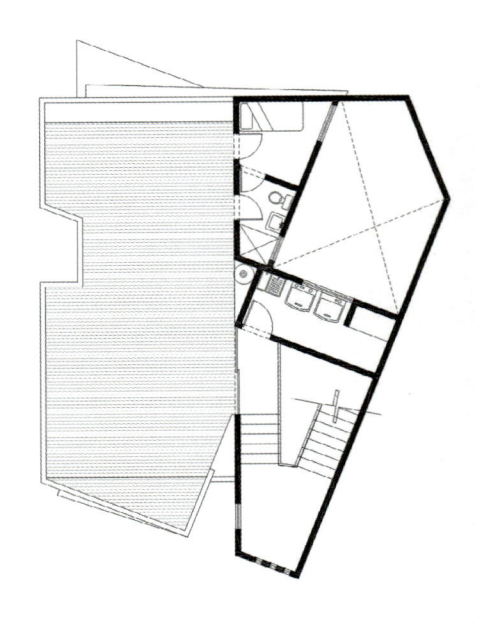

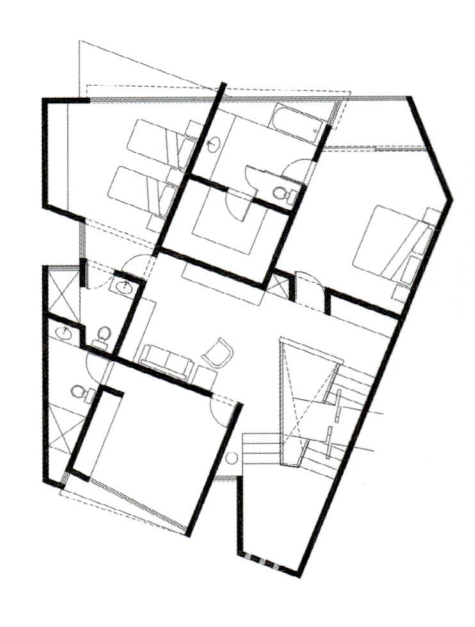

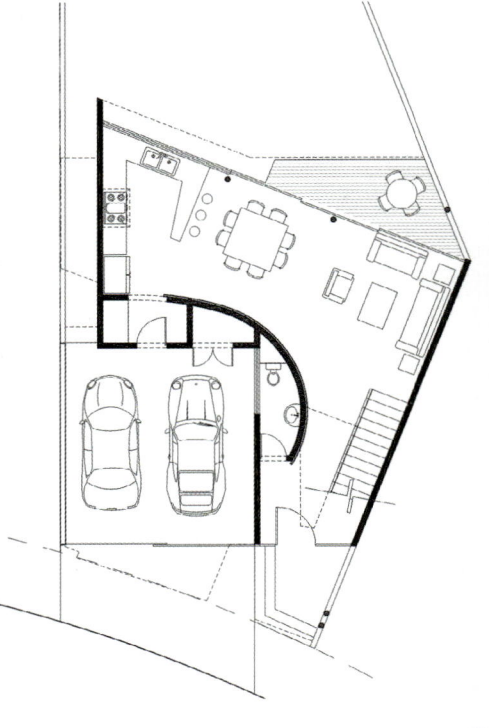

CASA BRAVO

Situated in the Valley of San Pedro, the house is organized in two concrete bodies that are articulated through a double-height vestibule, which serves as the access and transition between its social and private areas. Surrounding it are diverse gardens varying in size and proportion according to the characteristics of interior space to which they respond. The façades were designed in relation to orientation; the north-south orientation of the site permits the house to open its façade towards the north, while towards south-west it opens through discreet openings that capture views of the Sierra Madre.

01 View from the pool **02** View from the street **03** Exterior view by night **04** Garden view **05** Interior view, stairway to first floor

Photos: Javier Orozco, Francisco Rodarte

CITY San Pedro Garza García
COUNTRY Mexico
REGION Central America
TYPOLOGY Living
COMPLETION 2006
WEBSITE www.taltaller.com
ARCHITECTS TAL (Taller de Agustín Landa R) / Agustín Landa and Rolando Martínez

CASA GA

This original prefabricated house from the architects consists of two counterbalancing structures connected by a central stairway. The differing siding of the two units – dark redwood and white polycarbonate panels – and their striking wrapping skin sparks a dialog between the two volumes and the surrounding dense fabric of Tijuana. The modular construction results in sleek and often surprising resolution of space (recessed garden around a glazed ground floor) and lighting (corner-wrapping windows). The partially cantilevered structure provides great views of the town below.

01 Interior view **02** Exterior view from the street **03** Interior view, bedroom **04** Courtyard

Photos: Pablo Mason (01, 02), Eduardo de Regules (03, 04)

CITY Tijuana
COUNTRY Mexico
REGION Central America
TYPOLOGY Living
COMPLETION 2004
WEBSITE www.graciastudio.com
ARCHITECTS Gracia Studio / Jorge Gracia

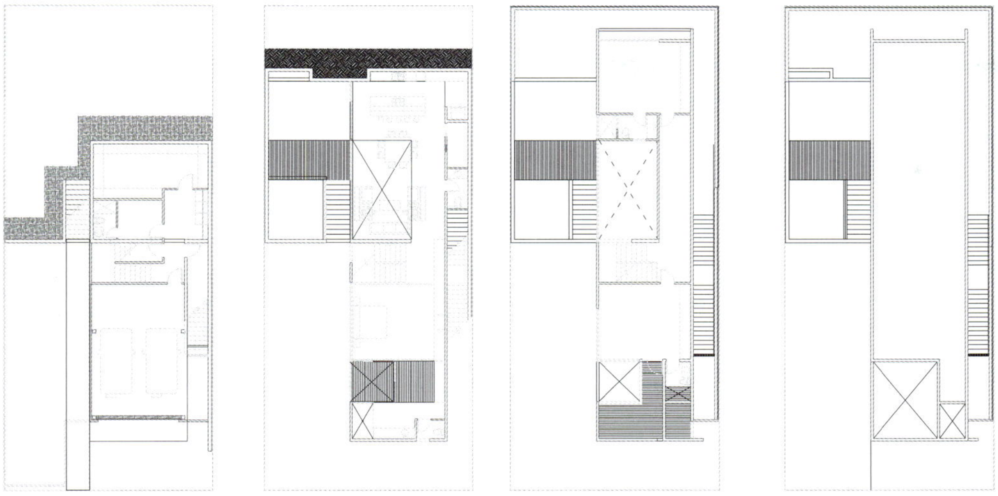

CASA BECERRIL

Gracia Studio designed this house project after primarily building a residence for the client's daughter. The Casa Becerril development is created to be a design for the purpose of being versatile and as a resourceful space for the family's numerous members, as well as its many pets around the home. This objective went forward and was thouroughly met by creating not only open, common areas for the purpose in which to spend quality time together as a family, but also on a more individual level, it features areas to enjoy and experience a more private space, including for both indoors and outdoors.

01 Floor plans **02** View from the street **03** Exterior view, detail pool and deck **04** Courtyardi **05** Interior view, bedroom **06** Interior view, kitchen

Photos: Michelle Galindo

CITY Tijuana
COUNTRY Mexico
REGION Central America
TYPOLOGY Living
COMPLETION 2007
WEBSITE www.graciastudio.com
ARCHITECTS Gracia Studio / Jorge Gracia

CITY Uaymitún, Yucatán
COUNTRY Mexico
REGION Central America
TYPOLOGY Living
COMPLETION 2004
WEBSITE www.augustoquijano.com
ARCHITECTS Augusto Quijano Arquitectos, S.C.P.

CASA PA´LMAR

This house is located in the coast of Yucatan and responds to the needs of one's own space and to the activities of summer vacations. The architectonic concept part to generate a strong fluidity of all the spaces, faces towards the beach, and therefore, created a freedom and opening. The house is developed by way of a great suspended box, generating a series of public spaces, obtaining an opening to the sea, while consuming the prevailing winds that cross through the aligned spaces. A house of guests accompanies, in longitudinal sense to the main house, generating the same concept of openness.

01 Exterior view **02** Exterior view from the beach **03** Floor plans **04** Interior view, ground floor

Photos: Roberto Cárdenas Cabello

HOTEL AZUCAR

The founders of ultra-hip Mexican hotels have created Hotel Azucar, named for the sugar cane grown in the Gulf state of Veracruz, where their latest hideaway is located. The resort focuses on effortless elegance and a fusion with nature. Step in and step back in time to a place of breathtaking natural beauty as you saunter through the 20 low-lying whitewashed palapas, (bungalows) each topped with a thatched roof and having a private, intimate terrace overlooking the stunning Gulf of Mexico. Just one look at the blues of sky and sea, and guests are overcome by an atmosphere that is airy, breezy and easy.

01 Exterior view, bungalow park **02** Detail white washed bungalow **03** Detail shower doors made of fiberglass **04** Library, wicker chairs and pink pillows under jug lamps **05** Private deck

Photos: Undine Pröhl

CITY Veracruz
COUNTRY Mexico
REGION Central America
TYPOLOGY Hospitality
COMPLETION 2005
WEBSITE –
ARCHITECTS Grupo Taller de Arquitectura SC (José Robredo y Elías Adam)

CITY Victoria
COUNTRY Mexico
REGION Central America
TYPOLOGY Living
COMPLETION 2005
WEBSITE -
ARCHITECTS Rodríguez + Guerra Arquitectos

SAN ANGEL HOUSE

In this project, the architects wanted to exhibit an air of modernity and style. Neutral colors, use of natural and industrial materials as well as wood for doorframes and furniture elements, exposed concrete walls, use of large crystals facing the interior that help integrate gardens and reservoirs, all serve this goal. The use of double height ceilings achieves unique family and social spaces. Dichroic light and projectors were used to resolve illumination, providing a comfortable and elegant atmosphere.

01 View from garden **02** Detail entrance **03** Interior view, glass façade towards garden **04** Exterior view from the street

Photos: Courtesy Rodríguez + Guerra Arquitectos

ML HOUSE

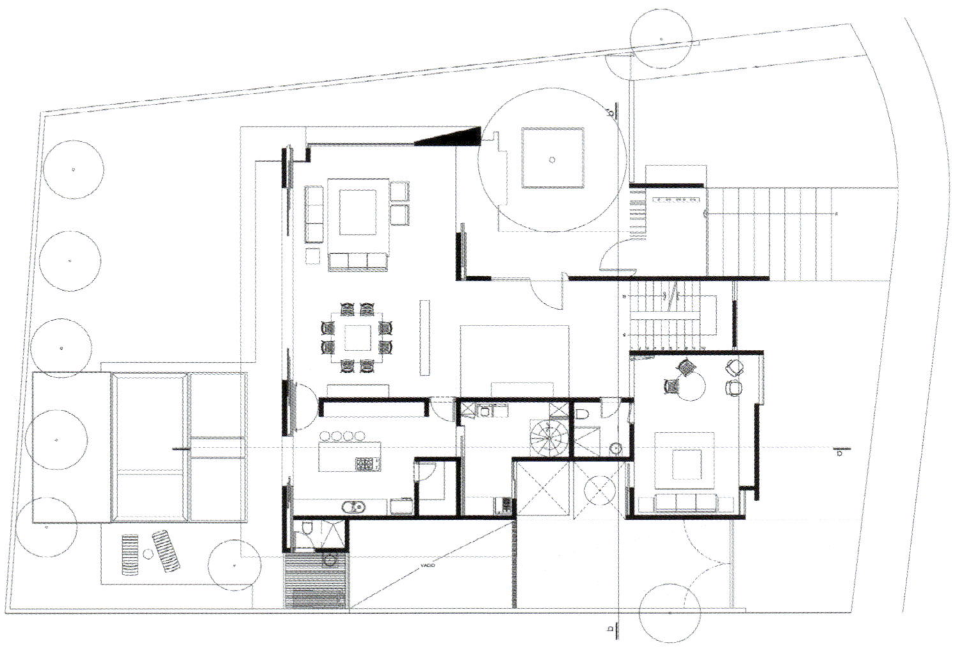

The house was conceived as architecture that can contain and display the spirit of each member of the family. The project proposes the dissolution between urban and residential boundaries; the street transforms into a plaza and the interior is a garden. Space configuration becomes a variable resulting from the interplay of light and shadow. Natural light permeates the double height ceiling through a wooden skylight and transforms sun rays into seasonal patterns, becoming an ornament that transforms light into an ever-changing play of surface and texture. Vertical circulation is a continuous spine that emerges from below.

01 Exterior view **02** Interior view, stairway **03** Detail skylight
04 Ground floor plan **05** Interior view, dining area

Photos: Mito Covarrubias

CITY Zapopan
COUNTRY Mexico
REGION Central America
TYPOLOGY Living
COMPLETION 2007
WEBSITE www.agrazarquitectos.com
ARCHITECTS AGRAZ ARQUITECTOS / DI VECE ARQUITECTOS

PAVILION + TWO PATIOS HOUSE

The project was to build a mid-high standing house in a triangular shaped terrain with interesting views to a little garden. The initiated design guidelines included a living program relating to contemporary Guadalajara citizens and a specific lot geometry. The floor plan contains kitchen, dining/living room, and a lobby with staircase. The main space is placed between sequences of open spaces including the backyard, patio and frontal garden. The elevated condition responds to the idea of liberating the views for the floor plan, while the patio guaranties intimacy for the pavilion, and light and fresh air to the floor plan.

01 View to staircase **02** Detail pavilion on pilots containing master bedroom **03** Front view, patio entrance **04** Entrance area

Photos: Francisco Gutiérrez Peregrina

CITY Zapopan
COUNTRY Mexico
REGION Central America
TYPOLOGY Living
COMPLETION 2008
WEBSITE www.atelierars.com
ARCHITECTS Ars atelier de arquitecturas

CASA BS

The project development is located in the later part of the division Pine of the Sale, the same part that is contiguous to the south with the Forest of the Spring. The house is uprooted on a circular platform, allowing focused views of the forest without any obstruction. The structure was oriented to compass a way to obtain an exact adjustment of the longitudinal axes to the magnetic north. The integral outline of the project is made up by orthogonal axes that in their three dimensions were designed using the golden section. The roof is without doubt the element of the program with the best view of the landscape.

01 Exterior view from helical access road **02** Rear view **03** Jacuzzi on the roof deck **04** Detail deck and master bedroom **05** Ground and first floor plan

Photos: José Martínez Verea

CITY Zapopan

COUNTRY Mexico

REGION Central America

TYPOLOGY Living

COMPLETION 2005

WEBSITE www.jcname.com

ARCHITECTS JCNAME Arquitectos

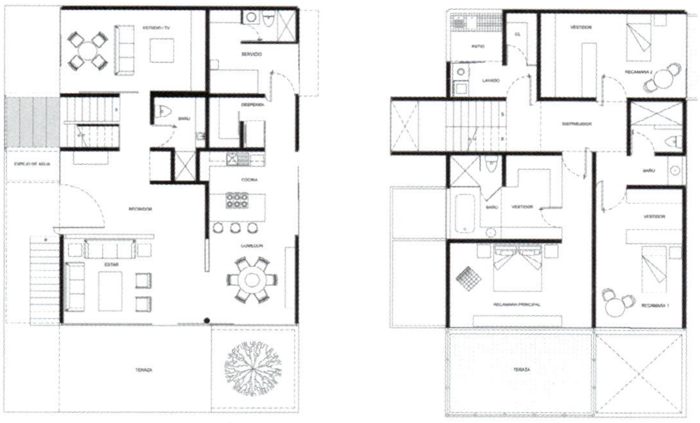

CITY: Chiriqui
COUNTRY: Panama
REGION: Central America
TYPOLOGY: Public
COMPLETION: in progress
WEBSITE: www.bt.com.pa
ARCHITECTS: Bettis Tarazi Arquitectos (David M. Bettis, Teofilo Tarazi)

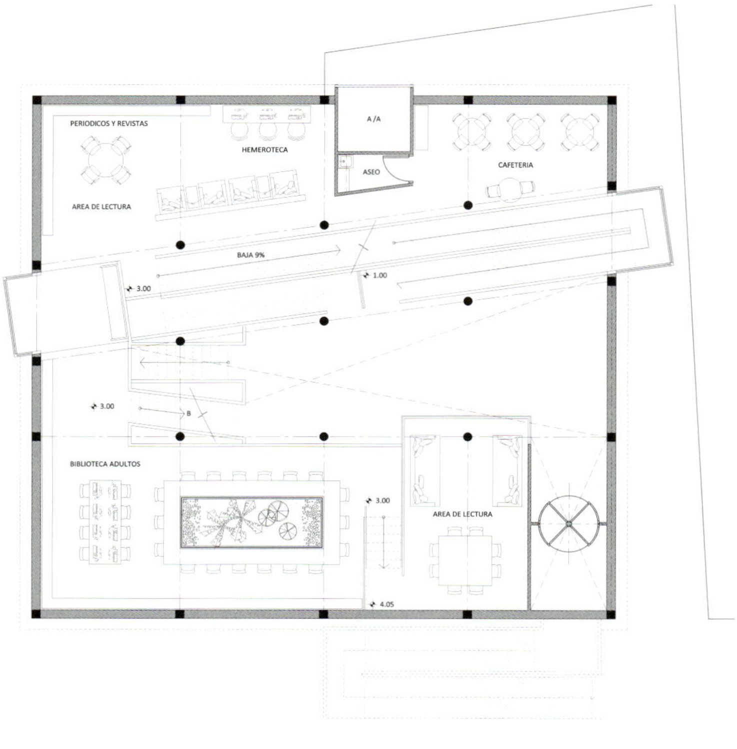

BIBLIOTECA BOQUETE

The library is intended to evoke the quite ambience in which it is located, while the wooden exterior finish with native woods evokes the history of wooden constructions in the area. The program includes another library for children, a cyber café, newspaper library, a small cafeteria and a public garden with rich selection of vegetation. The vertical circulation is contained under a glass skylight that delivers soft light to the complex and creates an ambience for peaceful reading. The hermetic characteristic of the construction is intended to create a micro-environment to take advantage of the weather in order to save energy.

01 Exterior street side view **02** Glass and wooden façade
03 Interior with skylight **04** Floor plan

Photos: Pixel Arquitectura

CENTRAL PARK PANAMA

Central Park Panamá is the largest and most important development in Panama City. This project is located in the middle of the banking and financial quarter, just in front of the most important avenue in Panamá. Central park is just minutes from banks, residential buildings, two shopping malls, hospital, and is very near to Panama's night life district. The program includes three office buildings, a five star hotel, convention center and a multi story shopping mall. The three towers offer 200,000 m² of sale space for commercial offices, in which the 400 room hotel includes restaurants, swimming pool, gym and spa.

01 General view **02** Façade planting **03** Pathway between buildings **04** Roofed path **05** Bird's eye view

Photos: Pixel Arquitectura

CITY: Panama City
COUNTRY: Panama
REGION: Central America
TYPOLOGY: Mixed-use
COMPLETION: in progress
WEBSITE: www.bt.com.pa
ARCHITECTS: Bettis Tarazi Arquitectos (BT Arquitectos, David M. Bettis)

CITY
Panama City

COUNTRY
Panama

REGION
Central America

TYPOLOGY
Living

COMPLETION
in progress

WEBSITE
www.bt.com.pa

ARCHITECTS
Bettis Tarazi Arquitectos
(BT Arquitectos, David M.
Bettis, al3 arquitectos)

Q TOWER

Q TOWER is an oceanfront masterpiece, created especially for those who look for luxury, comfort, and exclusivity. All of its units have astonishing ocean views, high floor-to-ceiling height, and the best quality finishes. The Punta Pacifica location, Panama's prime neighborhood, will let you enjoy a central location offering everything you need within a walking distance.

01 General view **02** Deck with swimming-pool **03** Living space **04** Typical floor plan

Photos: Pixel Arquitectura

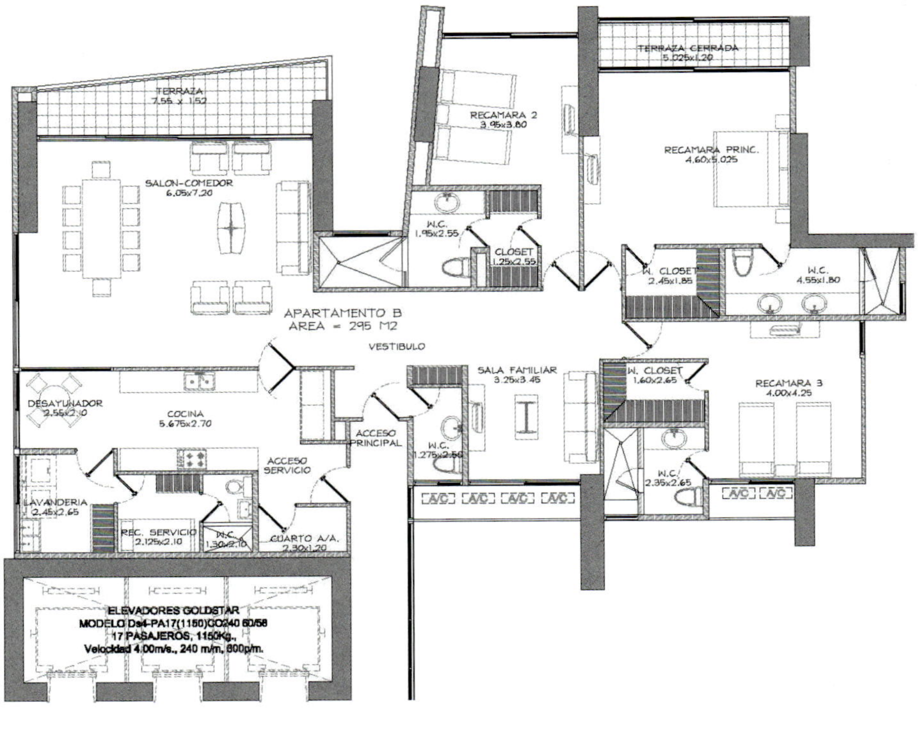

TELEFONICA FLAGSHIP STORE

The Telefonica project is a design instigated by Bettis Tarazi Arquitectos, with David Bettis and Teofilo Tarazi at the forefront. Recently, Telefonica inaugurated their first flagship store worldwide in the exclusive Costa del Este Business Park, which is situated in Panama City. Following the brand's image, an ideal space was then created for them to offer their products and services while acquiring a contemporary touch. A quick background note concerning the development of Telefonica claims that BT Arquitectos received this project after being invited to and participating in an international contest.

01 Working space **02** Ceiling area lighting **03** Customer service space **04** Ceiling, showroom **05** Interior view

Photos: Fernando Bocanegra

CITY Panama City
COUNTRY Panama
REGION Central America
TYPOLOGY Commercial
COMPLETION 2006
WEBSITE www.bt.com.pa
ARCHITECTS Bettis Tarazi Arquitectos (BT Arquitectos, Teofilo Tarazi)

CITY
Panama City

COUNTRY
Panama

REGION
Central America

TYPOLOGY
Living

COMPLETION
in progress

WEBSITE
www.bt.com.pa

ARCHITECTS
Bettis Tarazi Arquitectos
(BT Arquitectos, David M. Bettis)

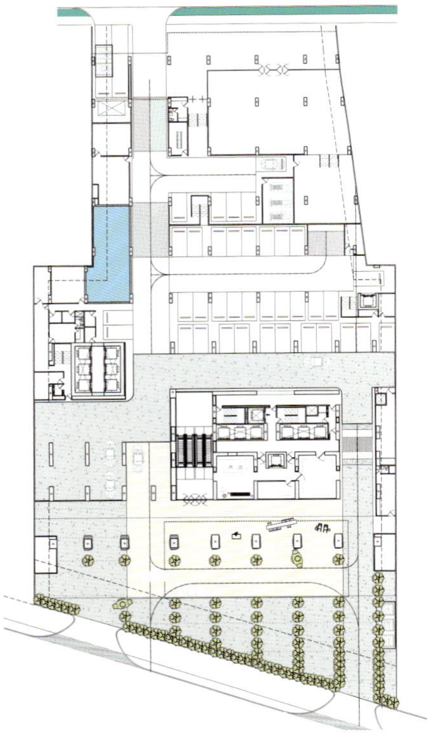

ARTS TOWER

ARTS is an astonishing top of the art project located in the heart of the Balboa Avenue. This one-of-a-kind tower will offer one or two bedroom units, with penthouse options available. ARTS will delight you with an eternal ocean front! In addition, the beautiful common areas were conceptualized by Philippe Starck.

01 Site plan **02** Exterior view by night **03** Library and reading space/ lobby **04** Pool deck

Photos: Pixel Arquitectura

CARIBBEAN

6x CARIBBEAN

6x ARCHITECTURE OF THE AMERICAS IN THE CARIBBEAN

0776 **BARBADOS**

0777 **JAMAICA**

0778 **PUERTO RICO**

0780 **TRINIDAD & TOBAGO**

CITY Gibbs Beach

COUNTRY Barbados

REGION Caribbean

TYPOLOGY Living

COMPLETION 2007

WEBSITE www.architectscubed.com

ARCHITECTS Architects Cubed Inc

SHOESTRING

Located on the West Coast of the Caribbean island of Barbados, the conceptual simplicity and the architectural language characterizing "Shoestring" are an unmistakable response to historically prevalent local typological circumstances. Set against a backdrop of towering trees and aquamarine sea, the composition of this single-family beach house celebrates Barbados' vernacular wooden Chattel house by placing it on an elevated masonry ground plane while preserving the layers of privacy, typical in this iconic typology.

01 Rear view of building 02 Front view, entrance 03 Interior
04 Floor plans, ground floor & first floor

Photos: Bob Kiss

GOLDENEYE

Goldeneye is nestled among tropical forests and lush gardens on a seaside bluff overlooking the Caribbean. Twelve airy cottages, designed by Ann Hodges, cluster beside the Caribbean's only Aveda Concept Spa, located at the resort. Wood-shingled and gracious, the architecture reflects the original nineteenth-century buildings that once stood here with cooling louvers, ceiling fans, fretwork and gables. Hammocks and rockers stand on the verandahs. Hardwood floors and mahogany furniture – handcrafted on the premises – complete the genteel ambiance.

01 Exterior view of cottage **02** Detail of façade **03** Loggia
04 Detail bathroom **05** Outdoor bathroom
Photos: Courtesy Hodges + Hulanicki

CITY Oracabessa
COUNTRY Jamaica
REGION Caribbean
TYPOLOGY Hospitality
COMPLETION –
WEBSITE –
ARCHITECTS Anne Hodges, Barbara Hulanicki

CITY San Juan
COUNTRY Puerto Rico
REGION Caribbean
TYPOLOGY Living
COMPLETION 2006
WEBSITE www.fusterpartners.com
ARCHITECTS Nataniel Fúster / Fúster + Partners, Architects, PSC

CASA DELPIN

Casa Delpín is the product of the renovation and addition to an existing single-family structure located on a small lot on the Miramar sector in San Juan, Puerto Rico. The design objective was to create a spatially rich living experience and provide a greater capacity for passive lighting and cooling, while also allowing mechanical cooling when needed. The perforated glass reinforced concrete (GRC) panels help to redefine and reorient exterior public patios and interstitial spaces towards the interior. This strategy of absorbing the remnant exterior areas of the lot, allows the house to open-up, while also providing greater privacy.

01 Entrance 02 Interior, cylindrical skylights 03 Section 04 Indoor pool

Photos: Nataniel Fúster

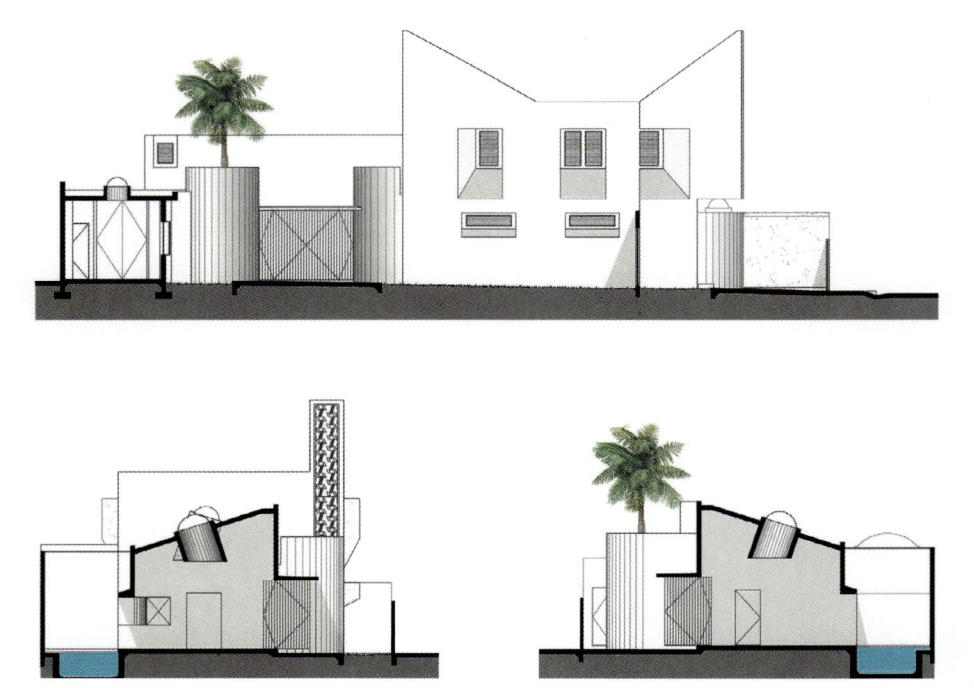

LA CASONA

"La Casona" is a Carribean retreat that strives to provide the ultimate peaceful escape in harmony with the elements, while offering a venue to entertain large groups of guests. The house is constructed using indigenous materials (blocks of cement and stucco) and methods (Wabi-Sabi), and is hurricane, earthquake and fireproof. Energy efficiency is ensured by unglazed windows that allow breathtaking vistas and are strategically placed to let trade winds provide natural air circulation, and by the use of solar panels for water heating and electricity. As a whole, the house appears as a modernist sculpture absorbed by the landscape.

01 Floor plan 02 Entrance 03 Courtyard 04 Courtyard by night, outdoor pool 05 Interior view

Photos: Courtesy John Hix

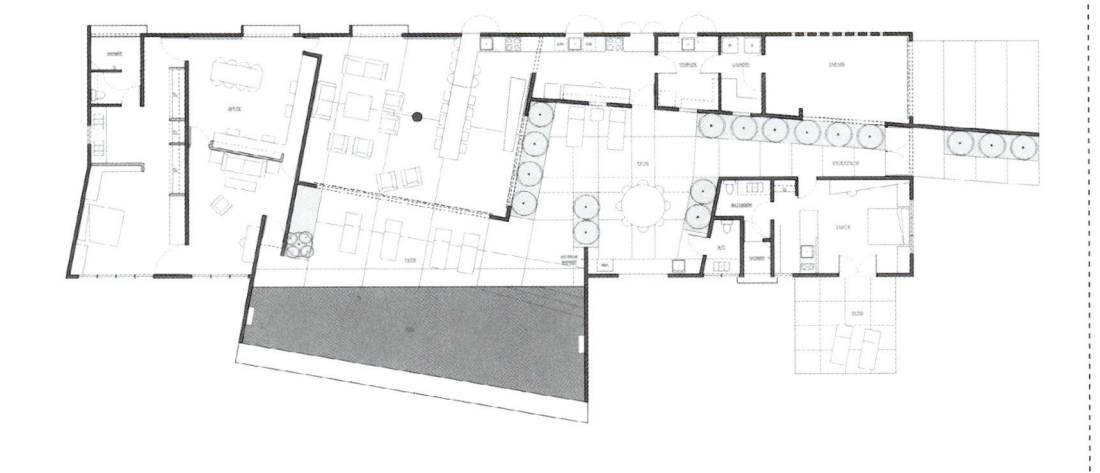

CITY: Vieques
COUNTRY: Puerto Rico
REGION: Carribbean
TYPOLOGY: Living
COMPLETION: 2005
WEBSITE: –
ARCHITECTS: John Hix

CITY Champs Fleurs
COUNTRY Trinidad & Tobago
REGION Caribbean
TYPOLOGY Education
COMPLETION 2005
WEBSITE www.gillespiesteeltt.com
ARCHITECTS Gillespie & Steel Limited

ARTHUR LOK JACK GRADUATE SCHOOL OF BUSINESS

The initial phase of the development provides accommodation for academic spaces, administrative offices, and common user facilities. Site planning allows for future growth of individual buildings, a projected conference centre and parking facilities. The concept is comparable to the structure of a growing village community, allowing for the individual grouping of elements interspersed with landscaped open areas. Academic, administrative and support services are organized along a circulation spine, while the academic unit is arrayed around an atrium - the village square - and becomes the natural focus of the composition.

01 Main entrance by night **02** Outside pond **03** Courtyard
04 Staircase to first floor **05** Atrium

Photos: Marlon Rouse

UNIVERSITY OF THE WEST INDIES LECTURE THEATER & CLASSROOM BUILDING

The building comprises of three clearly programmatic, and consequently volumetric, elements: the 450-seat lecture hall, the classroom and the entrance loggia. To maximize its space efficiency, the hall is expressed as a mere volumetric necessity – a box. The smaller classroom volume, tucked in below the upward sloping lecture hall, creates a foil to the larger lecture hall by virtue of its curving walls. Entry to the building is achieved through an open-air loggia. This element allows the building to readily engage its surroundings while providing a covered space in harmony with the scale and grandeur of the adjacent mature trees.

01 Exterior loggia **02** Western façade **03** Auditorium **04** Detail staircase

Photos: Stephen Jameson, Stephan Homer

CITY St. Augustine
COUNTRY Trinidad & Tobago
REGION Caribbean
TYPOLOGY Education
COMPLETION 2008
WEBSITE www.gillespiesteeltt.com
ARCHITECTS Gillespie & Steel

234x
SOUTH AMERICA

234x ARCHITECTURE OF THE AMERICAS IN SOUTH AMERICA

782

0784	**ARGENTINA**	0988	**COLOMBIA**
0785	**BUENOS AIRES**	0988	**BOGOTA**
0801	**ROSARIO**	0991	**MEDELLIN**
0805	**BRAZIL**	0993	**ECUADOR**
0815	**BRASILIA**	0995	**QUITO**
0831	**GUARUJÁ**		
0848	**PORTO ALEGRE**	1002	**PERU**
0857	**RIO DE JANEIRO**	1004	**LIMA**
0879	**SÃO PAULO**		
		1016	**URUGUAY**
0921	**CHILE**		
0940	**PUERTO NATALES**	1017	**VENEZUELA**
0946	**SANTIAGO**		

HOUSE IN PATAGONIA

The house is developed in a wooded terrain with a severe south-oriented slope with a lake view. The roof is designed using irregularly formed strips which break, superimposing over each other, leaving a space that allows the north sun to come in. A metallic frame is covered with an asphalt plate with 4 inch lenga wood ceilings that curve following the superimposed breaks. To take advantage of the slope and the views, the floor plan was inverted, placing the living room, main bedroom, terrace, kitchen and service room on the upper level, while the children's bedrooms, a small wine cave and the barbecue are below.

01 Exterior view **02** Entrance in winter **03** Exterior view on living room **04** Section **05** Snow covered valley

Photos: Joaquin Adot

CITY Bariloche
COUNTRY Argentina
REGION South America
TYPOLOGY Leisure
COMPLETION 2002
WEBSITE www.alricgalindez.com.ar
ARCHITECTS Alric Galindez Arquitectos

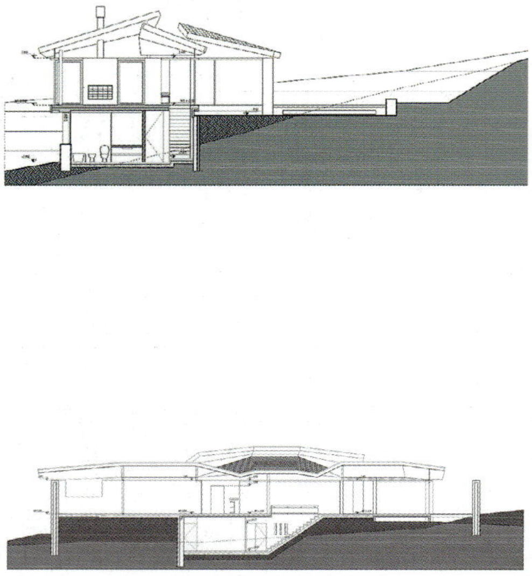

PUMACAHUA HOUSING

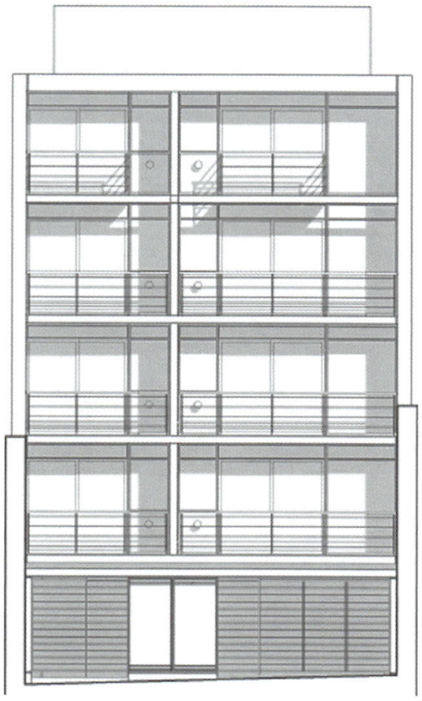

The building is constructed as an overlapping stratum between two dividing planes. Every level shelters four units, except the last one. The whole volume is recessed from the front line in order to obtain the maximum height permitted. In front, an access volume moves back to re-compose this line. Each level is composed of four units and a central core linking them. This organization around a court obtains ideal lighting both in the departments and in the access hall. The vertical core finishes off in a metallic structure composed by a bridge and a battery of stairs that forms an ad hoc structure providing access to the terraces.

01 Front elevation **02** Front View **03** Night view towards the units **04** Detail Façade

Photos: Alejandro Simik

CITY Buenos Aires
COUNTRY Argentina
REGION South America
TYPOLOGY Living
COMPLETION 2003
WEBSITE www.cgu.com.ar
ARCHITECTS Canda Gazaneo Ungar arquitectos

CITY Buenos Aires

COUNTRY Argentina

REGION South America

TYPOLOGY Living

COMPLETION 2007

WEBSITE www.adamo-faiden.com.ar

ARCHITECTS adamo-faiden

CASAS LAGO

The houses are situated in a mixed residential and industrial area. A family managing a small footwear company wanted to build a house on the grounds for each of their 2 sons without disrupting production. Each house is organized as a whole space that foresees its future subdivision when each one of the sons starts its own family. Steel diamond-shaped netting guarantees security, at the same time finalizing a light façade and copying the silhouette of the neighboring house in an ethereal way. Other decisions correspond to an adjusted budget and a will to simplify and intensify contemporary living.

01 Outdoor stairs **02** Entrance **03** Exterior view **04** Floor plan

Photos: Francisco Berreteaga

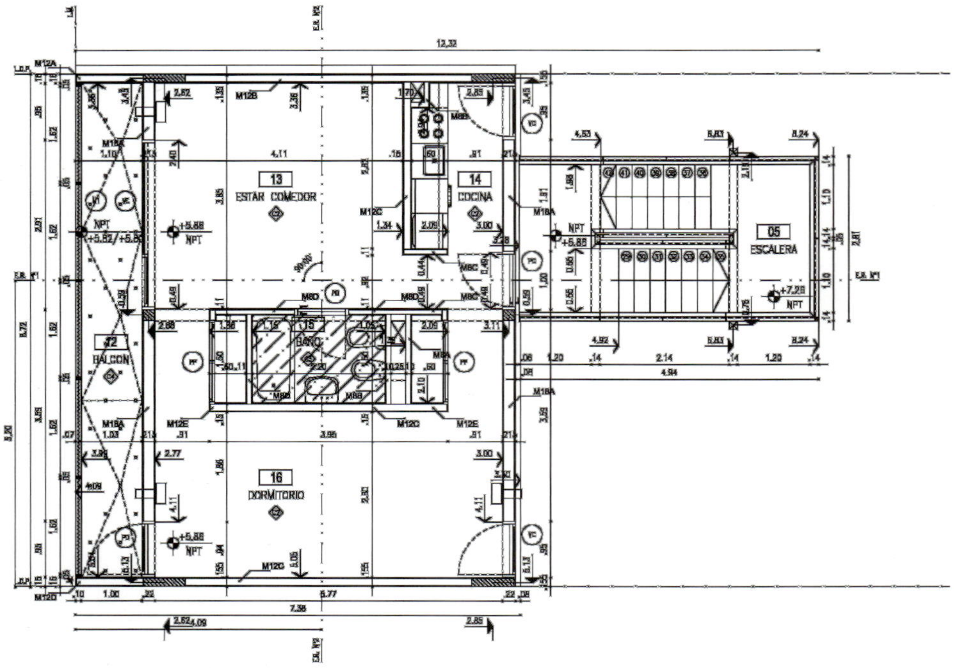

CONDE 3234

The set presents 8 typologies of residences: 2 houses on the ground floor with a garden, 4 semi-floors to the front with ample terraces, and 2 penthouses. In the building to the front, departments of 2 or 3 dormitories, with the particularity of having width with great large windows of floor to ceiling, fold in similar style to that of a book. The 2 houses occupy a special insertion on the set, with architecture that is closed towards the patio, while opening towards the gardens. They are in a condominium, but simultaneously, they are independent houses in a calm district of the city of Buenos Aires.

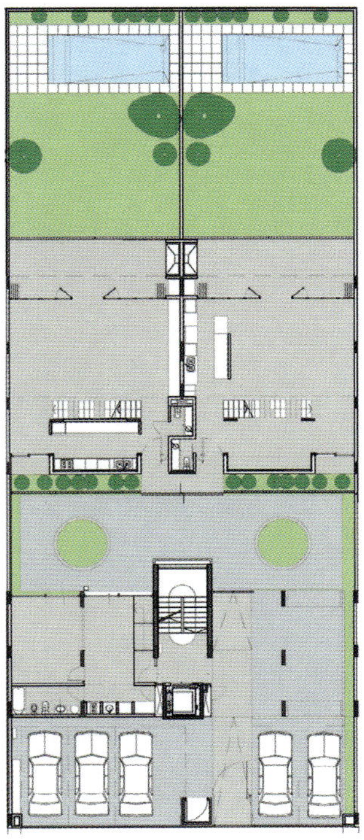

01 Rear view from garden **02** Front view, entrance **03** View on terrace **04** Interior view **05** Stairs **06** Floor plan

Photos: Albano Garcia

CITY: Buenos Aires
COUNTRY: Argentina
REGION: South America
TYPOLOGY: Living
COMPLETION: 2007
WEBSITE: www.barq.com.ar
ARCHITECTS: Barq Julian Berdichevsky, Joaquin Sanchez Gomez

CITY Buenos Aires

COUNTRY Argentina

REGION South America

TYPOLOGY Public

COMPLETION unbuilt

WEBSITE –

ARCHITECTS Santiago Bozzola

MARKET SQUARE

Though a series of diagrams the proposal is organized as a system that accommodates diverse activities and ensures the free flow of rainwater though them. Three areas are differentiated according to the land elevation degree. The programmatic zones are the highest ones, where leisure activities take place. Circulation areas, made up of a walkway net, run around the perimeter of the former ones. Illumination and water drainage areas form the lower parts of the project, where benches, lighting fittings and water drainage sources made of glass collect the water and ensures the utility of the illumination system.

01 Detail pavilion **02** General view **03** Parking level

Renderings: Santiago Bozzola

CASA MA - ESTANCIA ABRIL

Located on the outskirts, on a very well oriented lot but of an irregular geometry, this project remembered to be a house of monumental character but of strong contemporary language. Considering these particularities of the lot and the requirements of the clients, one thought about a party of two strong volumes, related by a great central space. The house is solved towards the front with a facade introvert, and another abierta towards the garden where the glass predominates on the wall. Access is emphasized with a central space of double height, where the light invades the heart of the house.

01 Rear view from garden **02** Interior view on garden **03** Living room **04** Front view **05** Ground floor plan

Photos: Tejo Ediciones

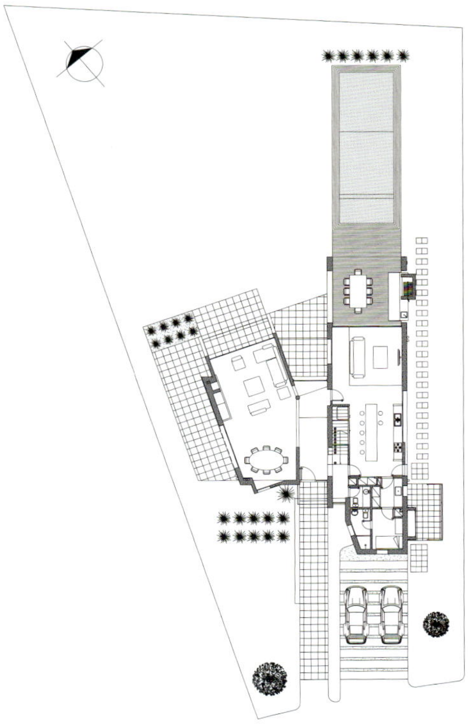

CITY Buenos Aires
COUNTRY Argentina
REGION South America
TYPOLOGY Living
COMPLETION 2006
WEBSITE www.dejdureguisalas.com.ar
ARCHITECTS De Jauregui Salas

CITY Buenos Aires
COUNTRY Argentina
REGION South America
TYPOLOGY Living
COMPLETION 2006
WEBSITE www.dvsaa.com.ar
ARCHITECTS DVS, AA Diaz Varela Sartor, Arquitectos

GRECIA 3191

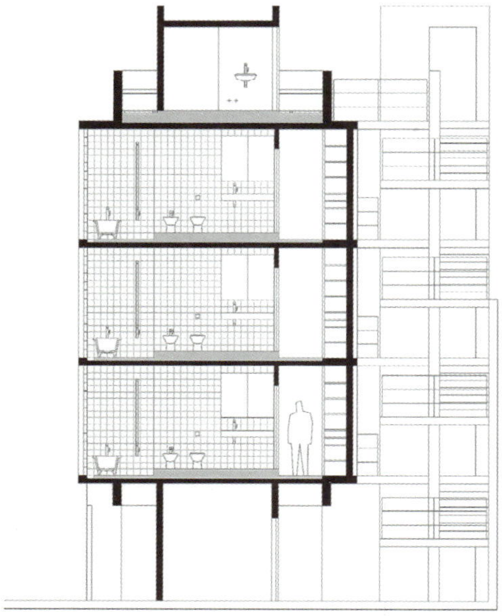

This project is a three-story, multi-family residential building. Each floor consists of a 328-square-foot apartment with a large space where different functions are clustered without curtailing continuity. The module is the underlying criterion that provides order: it organizes and relates the various elements, giving a sense of harmony to the relationship between the parts and the whole. The structure defines the building; the different structural elements of reinforced concrete resolve the structural demands by means of the construction and at the same time, define the space as a whole.

01 View on façade **02** Inner courtyard **03** Section **04** Interior view **05** Interior with views towards street

Photos: Gustavo Sosa Pinilla

CASA EN LAS GLORIETAS

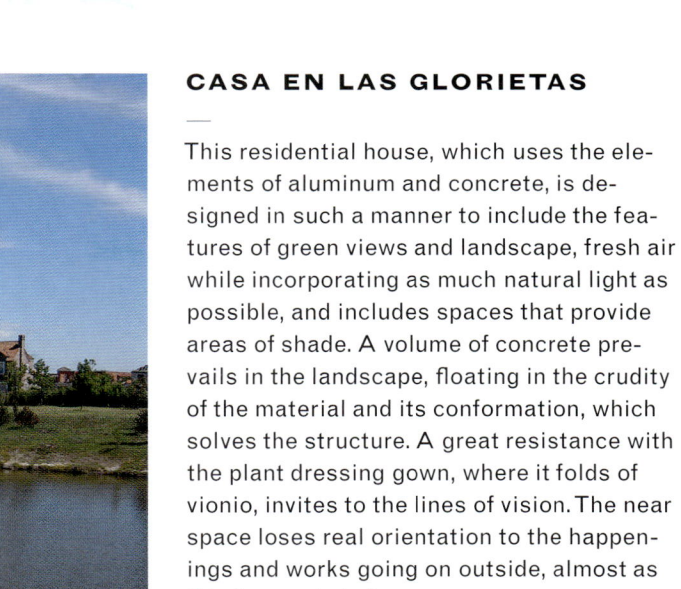

This residential house, which uses the elements of aluminum and concrete, is designed in such a manner to include the features of green views and landscape, fresh air while incorporating as much natural light as possible, and includes spaces that provide areas of shade. A volume of concrete prevails in the landscape, floating in the crudity of the material and its conformation, which solves the structure. A great resistance with the plant dressing gown, where it folds of vionio, invites to the lines of vision. The near space loses real orientation to the happenings and works going on outside, almost as if being secluded.

01 View on outdoor pool **02** View from the street **03** Interior **04** Floorplan

Photos: Eugenio Valentini

CITY Buenos Aires
COUNTRY Argentina
REGION South America
TYPOLOGY Living
COMPLETION 2005
WEBSITE www.grupoabv.com.ar
ARCHITECTS GrupoABV-Amsel-Boruchowicz-Vilamowski Arquitectos

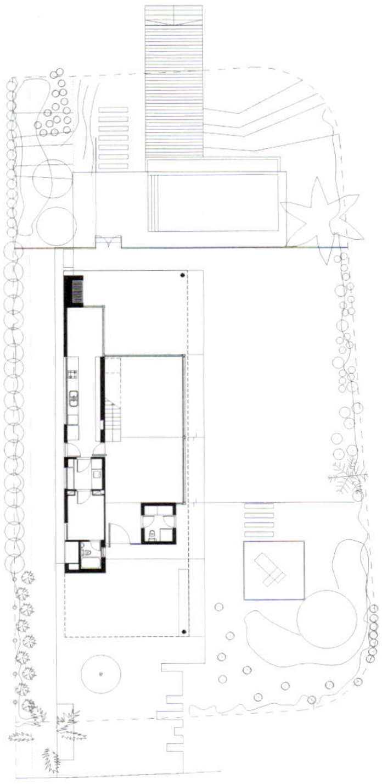

CITY Buenos Aires
COUNTRY Argentina
REGION South America
TYPOLOGY Office
COMPLETION 2006
WEBSITE www.mathiasklotz.com
ARCHITECTS Mathias Klotz, Edgardo Minond

TURNER INTERNATIONAL STUDIOS

The project is a restoration of a patrimonial building that originally hosted a printing office, in a traditional area of Buenos Aires. The assignment was to distribute and design working spaces, offices, meeting and conference rooms, an interior space with perimeter windows, and a big skylight in the centre. Part of the proposal is to invert the traditional office layout, locate meeting rooms and auditoriums in the centre of the building, while surrounding an interior garden that is illuminated by the skylight. The garden duplicates its perception through a huge mirror that covers the elevator's hall.

01 Interior **02** Translucent roof **03** Section **04** Offices and conference rooms **05** Public area

Photos: Claudio Manzoni

LOFT 34

Located in an industrial building, Loft 34 is mainly occupied with theater workshops, artists, designers and architects, but also includes a residential area on its wing. The renewal prompted a slight intervention, as a mezzanine was the built-in addition in order to duplicate the area. The ground floor is used as one big space for cooking, eating, and relaxing, and also consists of a bathroom. The upper floor features a workspace and a bedroom, where you can also find access to the patio and a roof of the existing construction, displaying panoramic view to the roofs of the old electrical plant.

01 Roof terrace **02** Interior view **03** Bedroom **04** Living room **05** Dining

Photos: Csaba Herke

CITY Buenos Aires

COUNTRY Argentina

REGION South America

TYPOLOGY Living

COMPLETION 2005

WEBSITE www.n-o-a.net

ARCHITECTS [NOA] Najmias Oficina de Arquitectura

CITY Buenos Aires
COUNTRY Argentina
REGION South America
TYPOLOGY Living
COMPLETION 2007
WEBSITE www.danielventura.com.ar
ARCHITECTS Daniel Ventura Arquitecto

EDIFICIO ARGERICH

The five houses building is situated over a lot on the neighborhood of Villa del Parque in Buenos Aires, in which four of them are three-story flats while the fifth is a ground floor; the latter incorporating two patios on its surface. The construction and structural logics are part of a material work, which organizes both the shape and the space. The building is composed by two blocks of 12-meters, separated by a patio of 6-meters which functions as the common trajectory of all of the houses. The esthetic structure of the compositive elements is synthesized to see the various formal, functional and semantic answers.

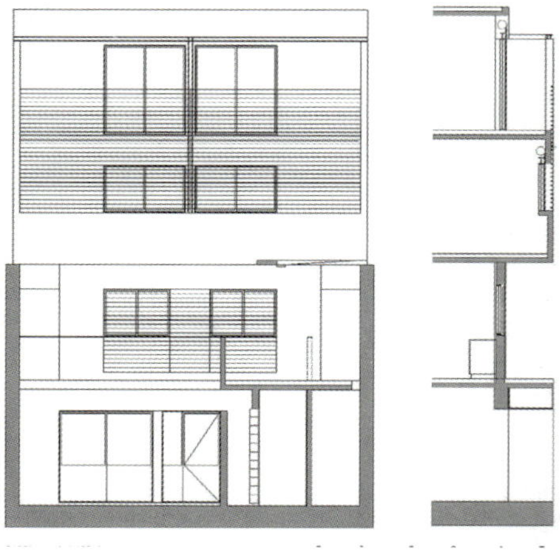

01 Patio **02** Detail patio **03** Façade **04** Living room **05** Section

Photos: Ramiro Lotti

VIVIENDA UNIFAMIIAR EN KENTUCKY CLUB DE CAMPO

This house is implanted on the edge of a golf course, with two volumes of concrete and glass, articulated by an inner patio. The two glances, one towards the inner patio on the ground floor where dormitories and spa are located, and the other towards the golf course are presented. Two opposed situations coexist in this project; the exhibition, to be able to visualize the golf course, and the repairs, the privacy, to count on a protected place. There are two possibilities of access, where one takes place crossing a winding way through a small forest, while the pedestrian access leads through the main plant entrance.

01 Side view **02** View on patio **03** General view, entrance **04** Terrace **05** Floor plan

Photos: Gustavo Frittegotto

CITY	Funes
COUNTRY	Argentina
REGION	South America
TYPOLOGY	Living
COMPLETION	2008
WEBSITE	-
ARCHITECTS	Mariel Suárez

IBLR HOUSE

Located in the estate of the "Kentucky Field Club", this lot is of trapezoidal form placed in the intersection of the Ibira Pita and the Aromitos streets. The program suggested a house of three dormitories, one of which is a suite. The clients required that all would be developed on the ground floor, and in addition, each one of the premises would have to be oriented towards the North. In the implantation strategy, the project is developed from the priorities of demand of the programmatic disposition with respect to the best directions not only to the lines of vision and privacy, but also to the direction of the sun.

01 View from garden **02** Garden entrance **03** Floor plan
04 View from secondary entrance

Photos: Guillermo Banchini

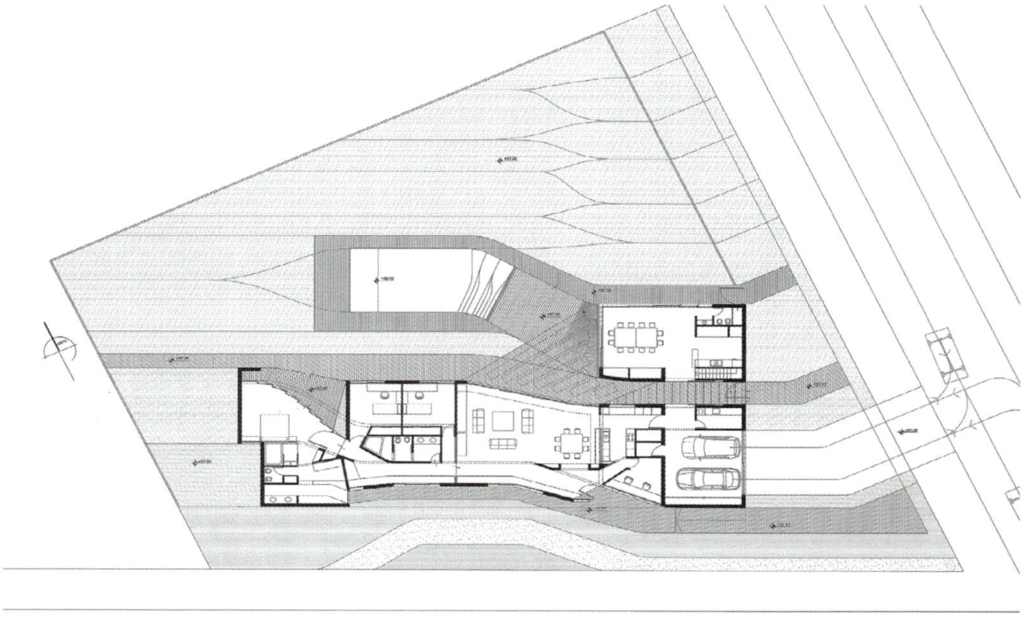

CITY
Funes

COUNTRY
Argentina

REGION
South America

TYPOLOGY
Living

COMPLETION
2007

WEBSITE
www.banchiniarquitectos.com

ARCHITECTS
Guillermo Banchini

CASA DE HORMIGÓN

Mar Azul is a seaside town south of Buenos Aires, characterized for its large dune beach and leafy coniferous forest. The owners chose a field in the forest with a challenging topography, away from the sea and dense zones, in order to construct a cottage without losing the important presence of the landscape. Located on a flat surface in the terrain with a strong diagonal slope, the house was solved like a concrete prism of extended proportions and minimum height. The house does not contain a main entrance, but is rather a flexible construction with entry from anyone of the rooms, assuring natural light throughout.

01 Outside view **02** Detail façade **03** Interior **04** Floorplan **05** Bedroom

Photos: Daniela Mac Adden

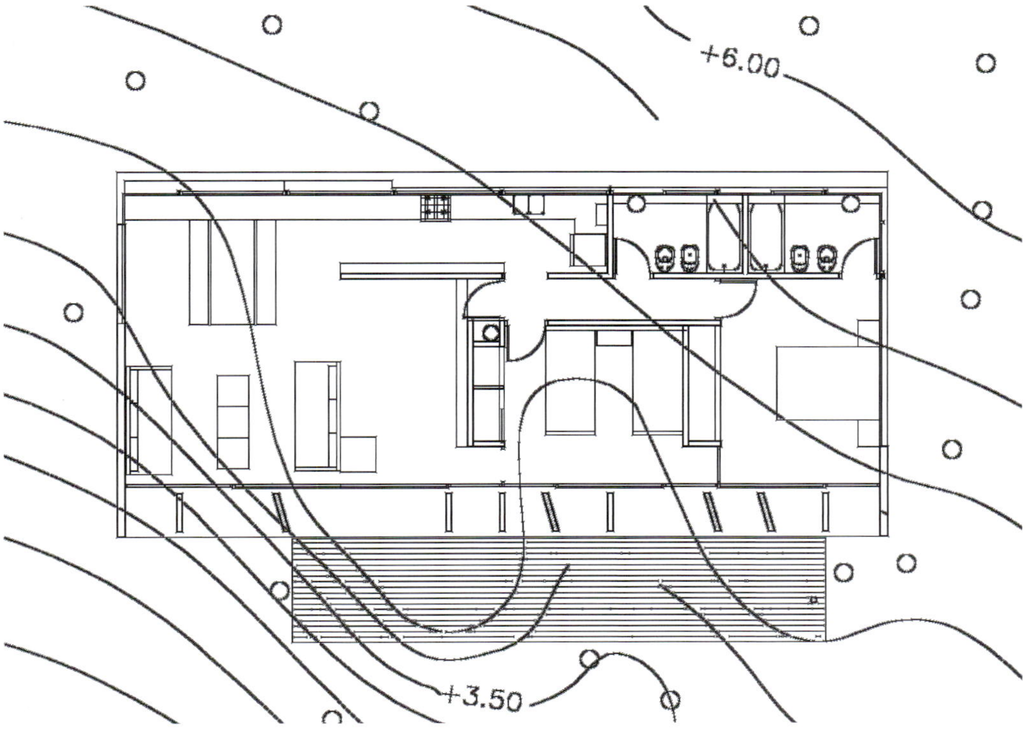

CITY Mar Azul
COUNTRY Argentina
REGION South America
TYPOLOGY Living
COMPLETION 2007
WEBSITE www.bakarquitectos.com.ar
ARCHITECTS besonias almeida kruk arquitectos

CITY
Mendoza

COUNTRY
Argentina

REGION
South America

TYPOLOGY
Living

COMPLETION
2007

WEBSITE
www.brunzini.com

ARCHITECTS
Brunzini Arquitectos
& Asociados

EDIFICIO DA VINCI

The Building is a 76-meter high massive concrete seismic resistant structure, and is the tallest building in the west-Argentina region. The building's sculptural sensibility of curving walls is related to the natural shape of the mountains and also breaks the monotony of a crowded and aging urban environment, creating a memorable and easily recognized landmark. Two emeralds mirror as crystal curtains, reflecting the gorgeous context of the green Plaza Italia, the unique deep indigo Mendoza sky, and the infinity of the Andes Mountains. The use of natural light and external views played a key component in the design.

01 General view by night **02** Detail waiting area in lobby
03 Floorplan **04** Top floor, outdoor pool

Photos: Carlos Alejandro Calise (01, 02, 04), Gonzalez Mena

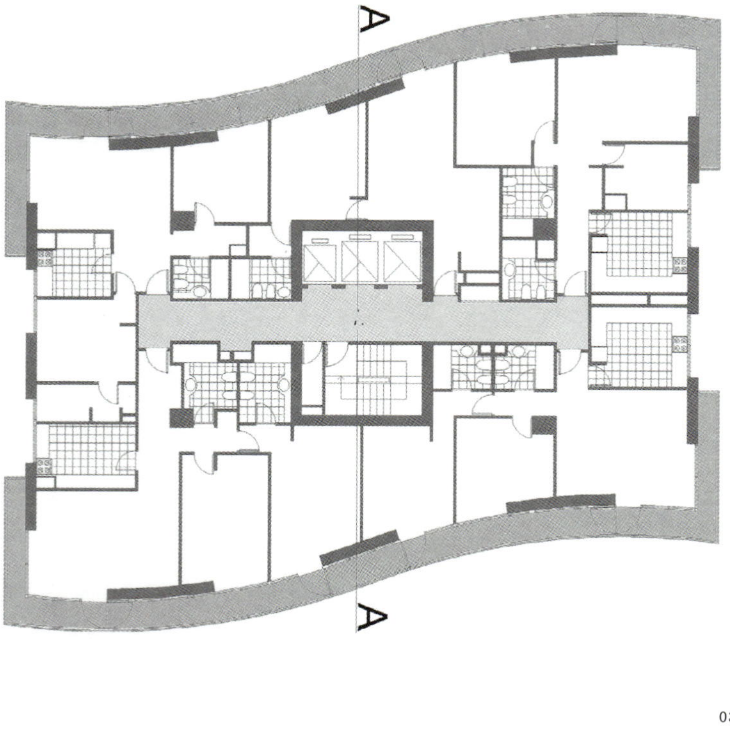

CASA CH

With a complex game of fit volumes, the house development of Casa de la Cascada by Andres Remy Arquitectos, takes to its maximum and highest expression the fusion between the two components of architecture and water. The water surrounds the main space by nearly double the height of the first level, while lowering the temperature of the atmosphere. This same space overflows, which goes on to form a cascade that breaks in the sink of the ground floor. The infinite edges of the same space again have the same effect on the two plants, while the water mirrors and the lagoon are left completely based.

01 Front view **02** Detail façade **03** Water cascade **04** Surrounding outdoor pool **05** Livingroom **06** Floor plan, ground floor & first floor

Photos: Juan Raña, Facundo Santana

CITY Nordelta, Tigre
COUNTRY Argentina
REGION South America
TYPOLOGY Living
COMPLETION 2004
WEBSITE www.andresremy.com
ARCHITECTS Andres Remy Arquitectos

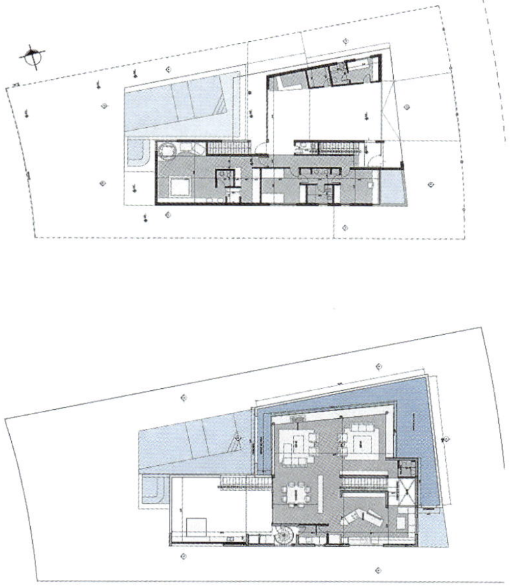

HOTEL TERRITORIO

The design of this small luxury hotel surrounded by exceptional ocean landscape reflects the history of the architecture in this whaling town. Waved sheet metal was chosen for the two volumes to unite memories of past immigration with the latest technology. One volume houses social activities and the other contains the guestrooms, both offering ocean views. The volumes' form is reminiscent of the shape of the wave, allowing all the rooms to enjoy the view. In the spacious rooms and lounge areas one finds ancient zinc combined with limestone, reflecting a once-used style of construction.

01 Curved façade **02** Exterior view **03** Floorplan **04** Wellness area

Photos: Gustavo Sosa Pinilla

CITY Puerto Madryn
COUNTRY Argentina
REGION South America
TYPOLOGY Hospitality
COMPLETION 2006
WEBSITE www.ajaespilcobelo.com
ARCHITECTS Aja Aspil Cobelo Arqs S.A

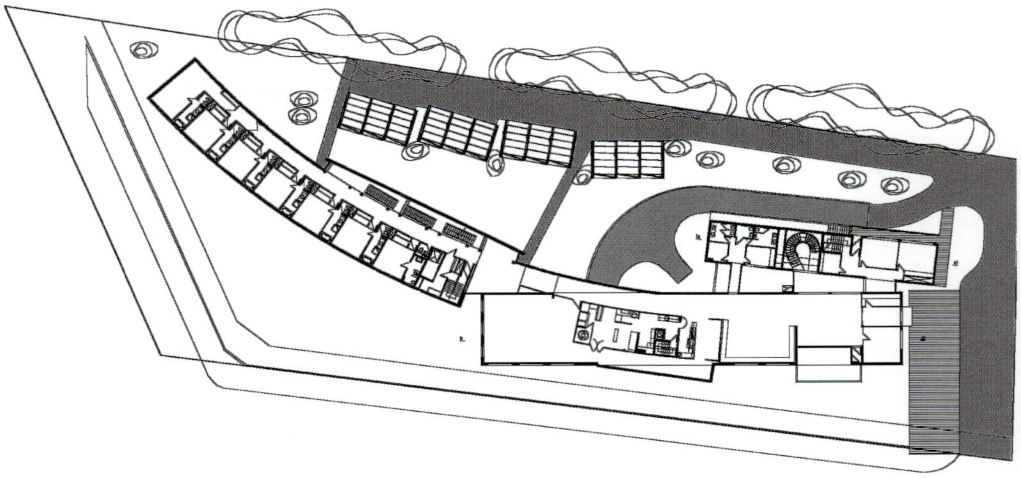

FYF RESIDENCE

The FYF Residence is located in the outskirts of Rosario, the second largest city in Argentina approximately 300 km north of Buenos Aires. The small house, rox. 200 m², is being built on a new residential development adjacent to a traditional neighborhood. FYF Residence can be described as an attempt to deal with the generic and undifferentiated flatness of the pampas landscape. The project was conceived as a monolithic solid, a monochrome form only punctuated by subtle inflections that establish a complex physical relationship among the different spaces while maintaining a sense of identity and privacy between them.

01, 02, 03 Exterior view **04** Interior view with glass-encased garden **05** Elevations

Renderings: P.A.T.T.E.R.N.S.

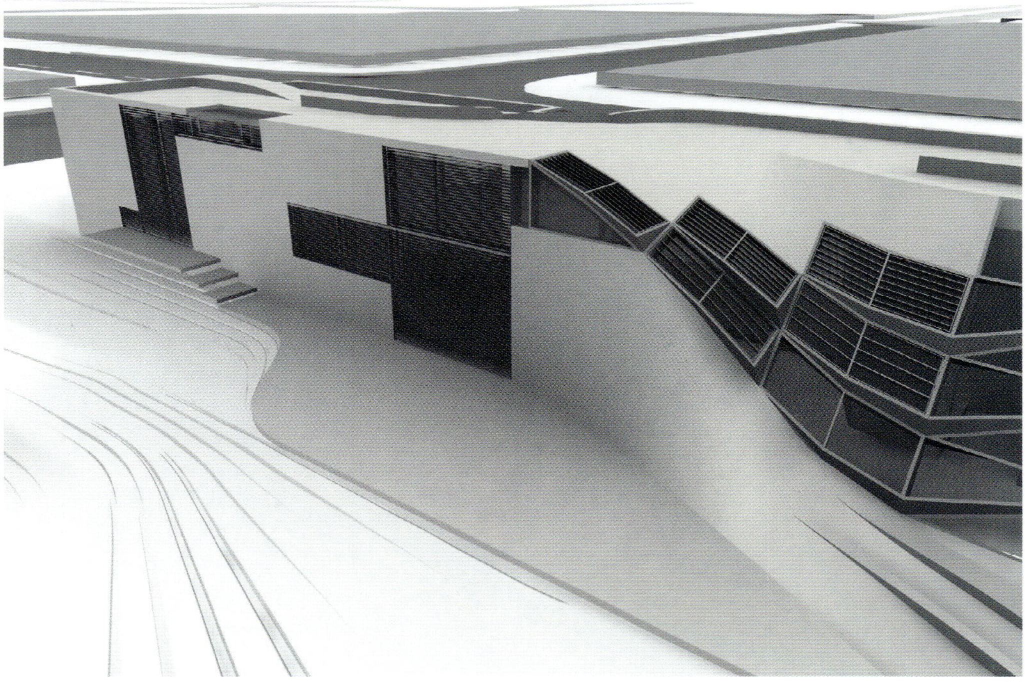

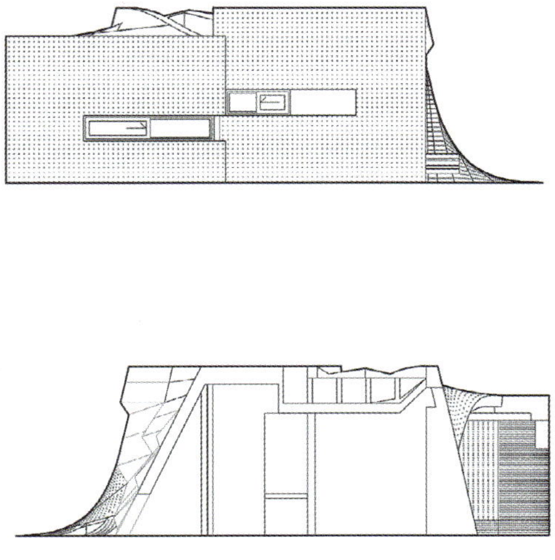

CITY Rosario
COUNTRY Argentina
REGION South America
TYPOLOGY Living
COMPLETION 2008
WEBSITE www.p-a-t-t-e-r-n-s.net
ARCHITECTS P.A.T.T.E.R.N.S. Marcelo Spina

CITY
Rosario

COUNTRY
Argentina

REGION
South America

TYPOLOGY
Living

COMPLETION
2006

WEBSITE
www.gerardocaballero.com

ARCHITECTS
Gerardo Caballero
Maite Fernández

EDIFICIO BROWN

The project is located in the North zone district in the city of Rosary, which has acquired interest due to a series of public interventions, equipping it with new spaces of services. At first glance, the place does not offer much attractiveness but the project has been stimulated by the possibility of establishing visual bonds with the landscape of the river and islands. This encouraged the idea to develop plants in the form of visual cones, eloquent from the interior of the houses, framing the horizon of the landscape. A building of 18 units, 9 located in each one of the 2 towers, features a swimming pool and gymnasium.

01 Detail of the façade **02** Exterior view **03** Interior view
04 Detail inner courtyard **05** Floor plans

Photos: Gustavo Frittegotto

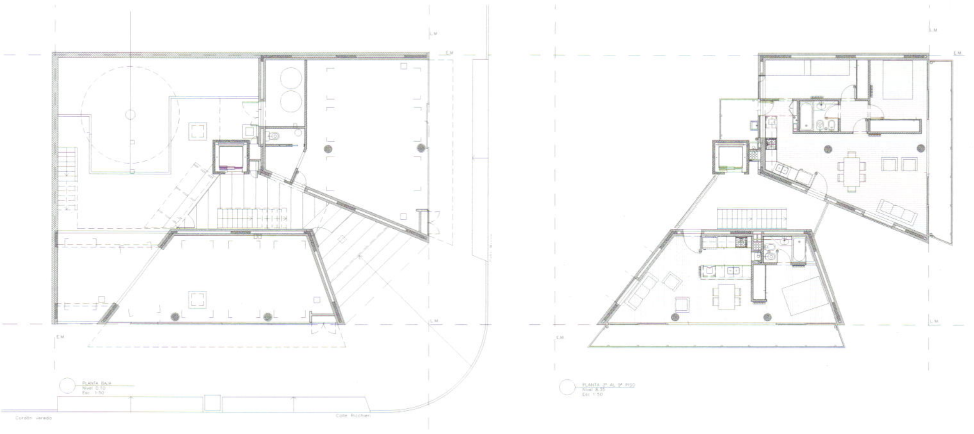

ALTAMIRA APARTMENT BUILDING

This building, the Altamira Apartment, arises from the repetition of an element; a beam which was organized following a logical sequence. Generally, in these projects, taking part is kept to a minimum, while mostly relying on the raised law, which claims that "what there is to do is not interrupted with opinions, since these change with time and depend on humor." What was done was in the form of integration. This way one enters or leaves, although it is not necessarily a door of what it is understood by "the door". In many ways, an architect is not one who projects or constructs, but who identifies.

01 View from building **02** Exterior view from street **03** Detail façade **04** Entrance area **05** Floor plan

Photos: Gustavo Frittegotto

CITY Rosario
COUNTRY Argentina
REGION South America
TYPOLOGY Living
COMPLETION 2007
WEBSITE www.rafaeliglesia.com.ar
ARCHITECTS Rafael Iglesia

CITY San Vicente
COUNTRY Argentina
REGION South America
TYPOLOGY Living
COMPLETION -
WEBSITE -
ARCHITECTS Guillermo Di Renzo (interior design: Gustavo y Malena Castaing)

DON ENRIQUE LODGE

The inn is in the heart of a thick ravine on the bank of the Paraíso River. It consists of four bungalows with comfortable decks to relax and enjoy, with all elements built using wood from the area. The house is designed as a common space and is decorated in a simple, rustic fashion with lots of sofas, hammocks and pillows. The rooms have a warm inviting atmosphere, with the freshness of the forest coming in through the windows. This nature symphony invites you to rest in one of the hammocks on the cabin's porch. Another fine attraction is enjoying the sun on the deck a few meters away from the transparent river waters.

01 Loggia **02** Detail loggia **03** Living room **04** Bathroom

Photos: Courtesy Don Enrique Lodge

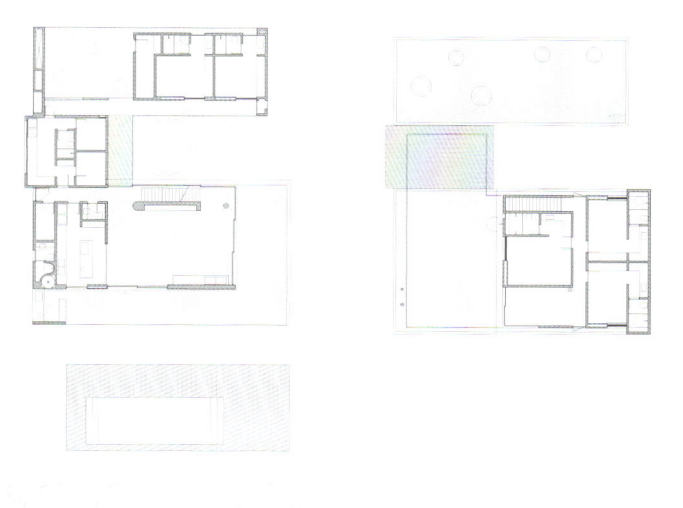

CASA EN ARAÇOIABA

The proprietors searched for a rest place, and found a land that was as deep as a golf field. They had become entranced for the controlled landscape, which was marked for vegetation that if transformed throughout the year, would be able to provide certain features that the city of São Paulo does not have. Bands are organized in direction to the golf and are configured as different places, while keeping its proper relation with the green. From this, the axles of circulation of the house are structuralized, providing passages in the parallel direction, while legalizing the spaces that have been broken of the image of a ribbon.

01 Floor plan **02** Side view **03** Exterior view by night **04** Front view by night

Photos: Nelson Kon

CITY Araçoiaba
COUNTRY Brazil
REGION South America
TYPOLOGY Living
COMPLETION 2004
WEBSITE –
ARCHITECTS Flavia Cancian + Renata Furlanetto

CITY Aldaia da Serra
COUNTRY Brazil
REGION South America
TYPOLOGY Living
COMPLETION 2005
WEBSITE www.a1arquitetura.com.br
ARCHITECTS A1 Arquitetura - Alessandra Pires e Carla Barranco

ALDEIA DA SERRA HOUSE

The party of the project is to come back toward the integration, visualizing it to such an extensive manner that it becomes physical. The visual amplitude happens through the preponderant presence of openings and glasses. The physical integration is made possible by the generous and continuous circulation, where the façade is presented more closed and imposing. The Aldeia da Serra House (Village of the Mountain Range) was projected for a family who decided to change the metropolis for a condominium in the city. The development is done in such a way that a transition made possible, tranquila and prazeirosa, in the way of life of the family.

01 Exterior view **02** View to outdoor pool **03** View to valley **04** Floor plan **05** Side view

Photos: Courtesy A1 Arquitetura

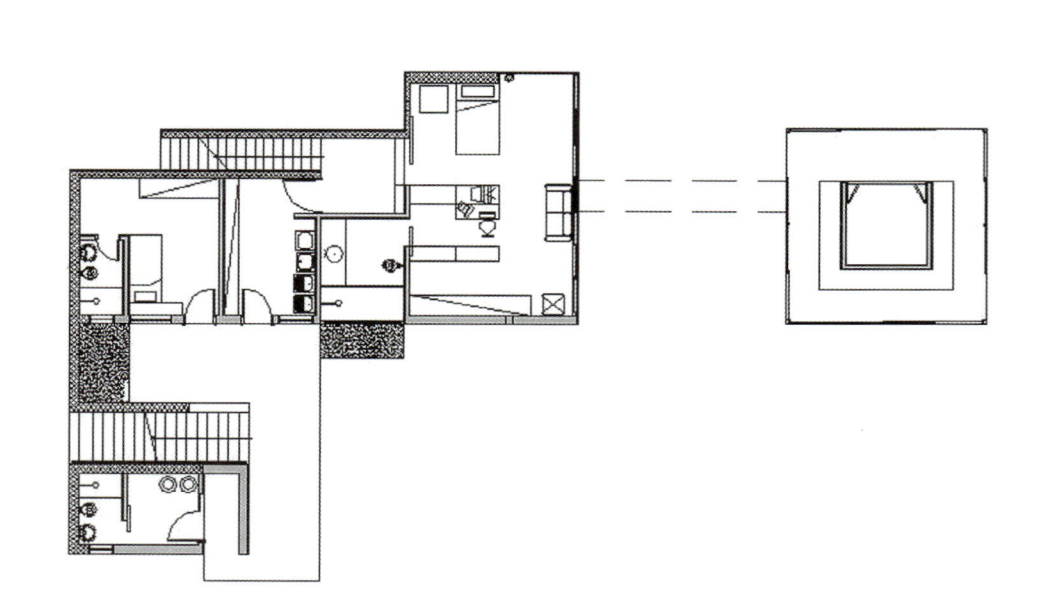

CASA FOLHA

This house was inspired by Brazil's indian architecture, developed over the centuries for the hot and humid climate where it stands. The roof, acting as a big leaf protects all the enclosed and in-between spaces of the house from the sun while allowing trade winds from the sea to provide passive cooling and natural ventilation. The architecture here, is understood as a device to enhance the interaction between man and nature, never to separate them. There are no corridors, only open spaces under the leaf to provide circulation and nature, as landscape, to pass trough the house. All of the rich roof structure was constructed with laminated reflorestation wood. The central steel column collects rain from the roof.

01 General view **02** Roof construction **03** Detail façade
04 View into veranda and outdoor pool

Photos: Leonardo Finotti

CITY Angra dos Reis
COUNTRY Brazil
REGION South America
TYPOLOGY Living
COMPLETION –
WEBSITE www.mareines-patalano.com.br
ARCHITECTS mareines+patalano

HOUSE AM

The interior design of the MPM advertising agency, distributed on 3 double floors with mezzanines, is the embodiment of what the customer represents: dynamism, integration and objectivity. While the space is ethereal and has integrated forms, freijó wood panels separate the space, protecting the privacy necessary for each activity. In a minimalist way, the synthesis of finishings and standardization and modulation confer the dimension idea generation to the environment. The utility of the abstractly-formed furniture, also in freijó wood, is disclosed from the relation between itself and the user.

01 Exterior view **02** Terrace **03** View on the bay **04** Interior view

Photos: Leonardo Finotti

CITY Angra dos Reis
COUNTRY Brazil
REGION South America
TYPOLOGY Living
COMPLETION 2006
WEBSITE www.bjaweb.com.br
ARCHITECTS Bernardes + Jacobsen Arquitetura

MEDICAL LABORATORY DR. PAULO AZEVEDO

Positioned on the intersection of two busy avenues, the project had to act as a visual landmark. The form and colors make the building visible from all directions. The design consists of two intersecting blocks. The completely transparent, elevated volume houses public functions; the other building contains the labs and service spaces and is set directly on the ground level. The transparency creates interior spaces with diffused light throughout the day, creating a comfortable ambience and optimizing energy resources. The architecture reflects the company's corporate identity.

01 Façade, glass panels **02** Exterior view **03** Interior view **04** Floor plan **05** Detail of the façade

Photos: Otávio Cardoso

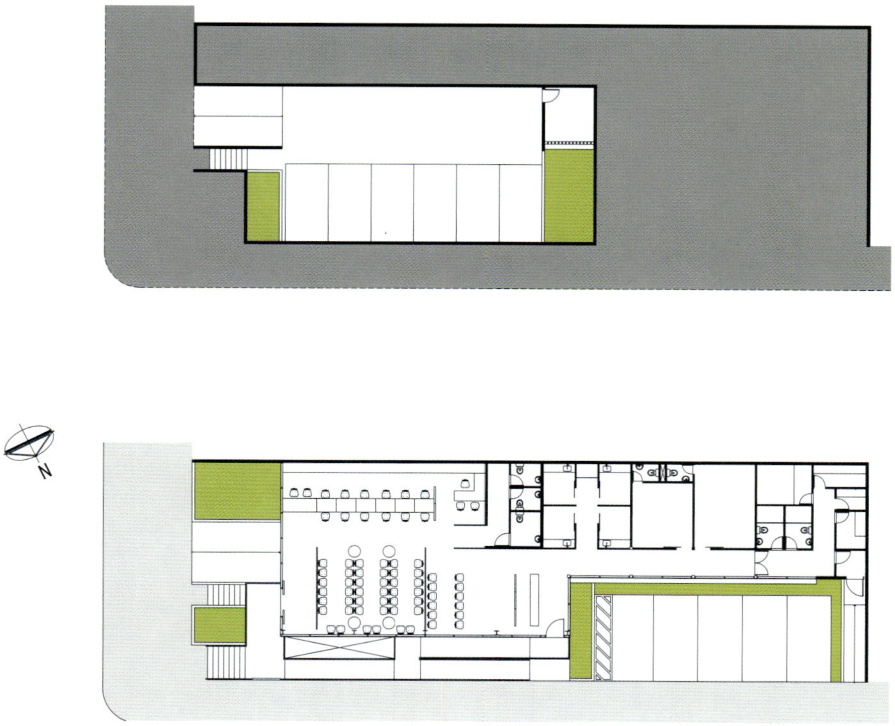

CITY Belém
COUNTRY Brazil
REGION South America
TYPOLOGY Health
COMPLETION 2005
WEBSITE –
ARCHITECTS m2p arquitetura - Aurélio Meira, Joaquim Meira, Marci Pereira e Silvana Meira

CITY
Belo Horizonte

COUNTRY
Brazil

REGION
South America

TYPOLOGY
Culture

COMPLETION
2004

WEBSITE
www.gustavopenna.com.br

ARCHITECTS
Gustavo Penna Arquiteto & Associados

EXPOMINAS

GPA and A's project, present in Gameleira since 1997, was concluded almost two years ago. In addition to the circular and square pavilions, two new pavilions are already being used, in which those initial structures were finished in the primary phase of the development. The four pavilions together offer fairgoers an extensive area of 22,000 square meters and may house up to 50,000 visitors. Such features as the food court, security offices, and communications and conference sectors will all be located in the building, a section known as Parallel Events, in the main hall of the Expominas center.

01 EXPOMINAS Gate **02** Exterior view by night **03** General view **04** Interior

Photos: Leonardo Finotti

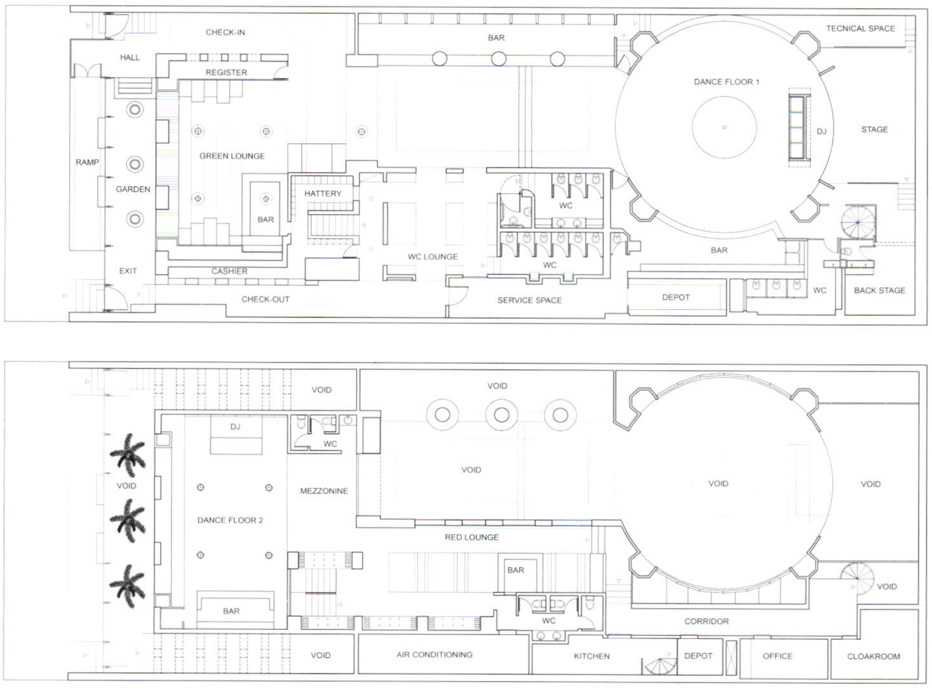

CLUB ROXY

Located at Savassi, the most bohemian neighborhood in Belo Horizonte, ROXY's main goal is to fill a gap in the city: the lack of high attendance and technology-pattern nightclubs. A special illumination is spread all over the club through a system called "Change Color", which is the structural basis of the project, allowing the constant shift along its interior. The circular shaped dance floor has an acoustic coating along the walls and high-definition screens allow for amazing graphic effects. The façade, as a gift to the urban chaos, is minimalist, composed by a mirrored glass sheet covered by a pierced white pellicle.

01 Ground and first floor plan 02 Bar 03 Main access ramp
04 Integrated seats 05 Lounge illuminated in red

Photos: Jomar Bragança

CITY Belo Horizonte
COUNTRY Brazil
REGION South America
TYPOLOGY Commercial
COMPLETION 2007
WEBSITE www.fredmafra.com.br
ARCHITECTS Fred Mafra

S401 HOUSE

The material, decoration and layout of House S401, located in the countryside of São Paulo, are a commentary about Brazilian architecture. The elements and organized reflections stimulate dialogue among the colonial, popular and modern. Organized around a central patio, the house articulates daily living through large window-door openings, forming fluid spaces. The windows of the living room open to the patio and, by means of an open circulation, give access to the bedrooms. At night, the spatial arrangement creates new situations, while the lighting from the rooms, filtered through soft curtains, light-up the central garden.

01 Front view, terrace **02** View of terrace by night **03** Floor plan **04** Interior view, fireplace

Photos: Nelson Kon

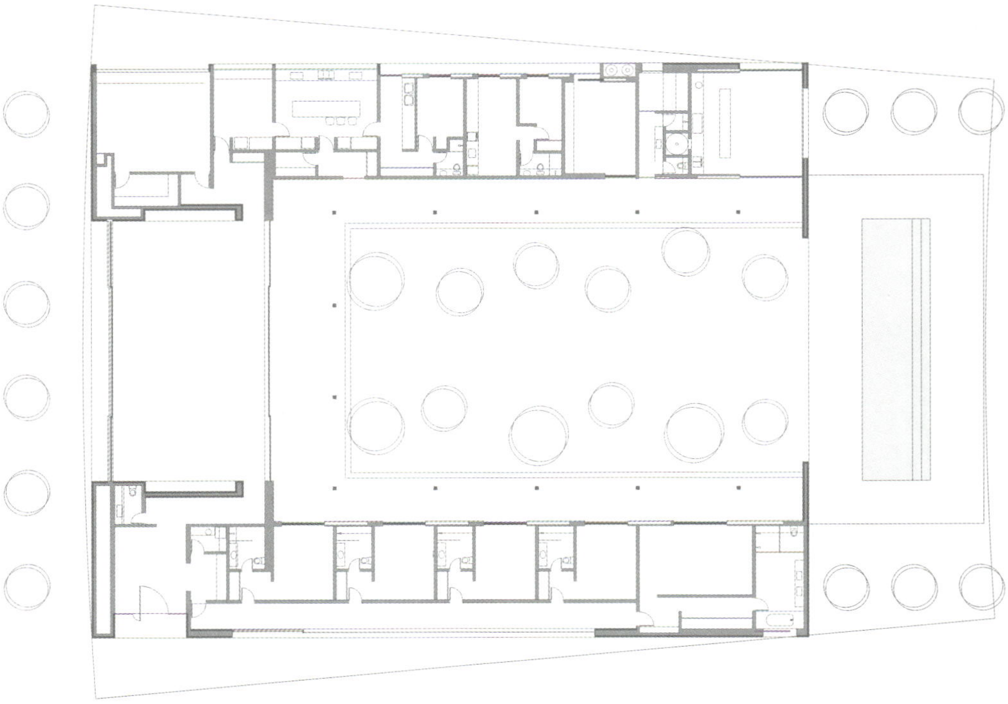

CITY Bragança Paulista
COUNTRY Brazil
REGION South America
TYPOLOGY Living
COMPLETION 2006
WEBSITE www.marciokogan.com.br
ARCHITECTS Marcio Kogan

GLASS HOUSE

This holiday residence is a rectangular volume distributed on two levels which follows the rising slope of its plot. The architects explored contrasting building techniques as a method of defining space function. Light iron walls and glass were used in the public areas and around the porch. Traditional load-bearing walls were implemented for the private and service areas, and the circulation executed using a ramp and a corridor brings the two types of structure together into a whole. The open and light structure as well as its use of glass creates a strong relationship between the exterior environment and the interior space.

01 Exterior view by night **02** View to outdoor pool
03 Veranda **04** Floorplan

Photos: Nelson Kon

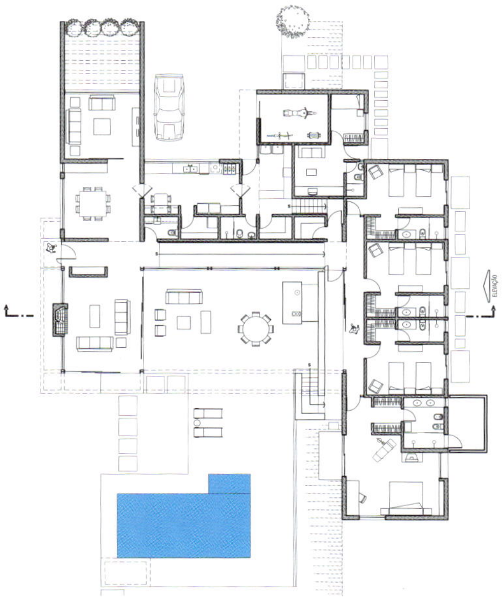

CITY Bragança Paulista
COUNTRY Brazil
REGION South America
TYPOLOGY Living
COMPLETION 2004
WEBSITE www.rmaa.com.br
ARCHITECTS Henrique Reinach e Maurício Mendonça

RED HOUSE

The Casa Vermelha, translated as the Red House, is a Country House which is built nearly 100 kilometers away from São Paulo. The project is intended for a family who enjoy spending time together and being with one another during the weekends. Most of the featured spaces and elements of the house are located on the ground floor, while the only room provided upstairs is the main bedroom. An underground space is also provided, in which one can find a sauna meant for relaxation and a small music room, which is also included. The main place of the house is the Veranda, which is situated by the pool.

01 Exterior view by night **02** View to swimming pool
03, 04 Exterior view, veranda

Photos: Leonardo Finnotti

CITY
Bragança Paulista

COUNTRY
Brazil

REGION
South America

TYPOLOGY
Living

COMPLETION
2003

WEBSITE
www.rmaa.com.br

ARCHITECTS
Henrique Reinach e
Maurício Mendonça

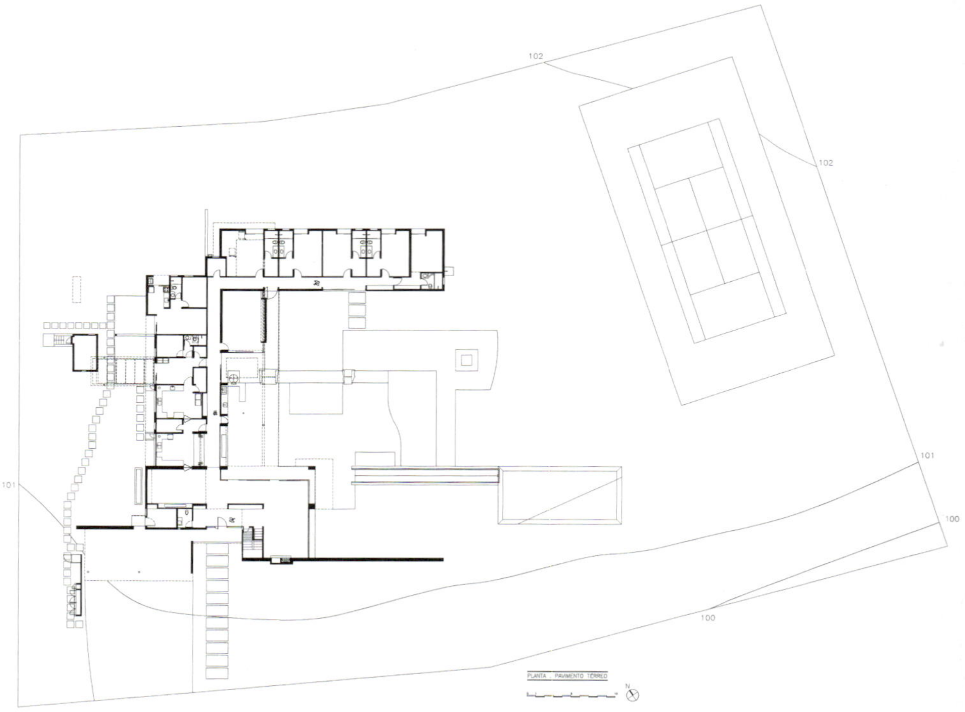

MUSEU NACIONAL HONESTINO GUIMARÃES

The museum is constructed as a great cupola with a 90-meter diameter and a 28-meter height. The scale and the pureness of the new building contrast with the cathedral, which is situated at its side, partially affects the calm reading of the church. The museum possesses an extremely simple internal arrangement. There are two auditoriums as well as administrative and sanitation areas on the ground floor. The upper level has a separate access along two arching ramps offering fantastic views. Above it is a mezzanine level, housing additional exhibitions; this level is also accessed by two external ramps.

01 Gallery space **02** Exterior view **03** Curved ramp **04** Front façade

Photos: Leonardo Finotti

CITY Brasilia
COUNTRY Brazil
REGION South America
TYPOLOGY Culture
COMPLETION 2006
WEBSITE -
ARCHITECTS Oscar Niemeyer

CITY Brasilia

COUNTRY Brazil

REGION South America

TYPOLOGY Living

COMPLETION 2003

WEBSITE www.danilo.arq.br

ARCHITECTS Danilo Matoso Macedo e Paulo Menicucci

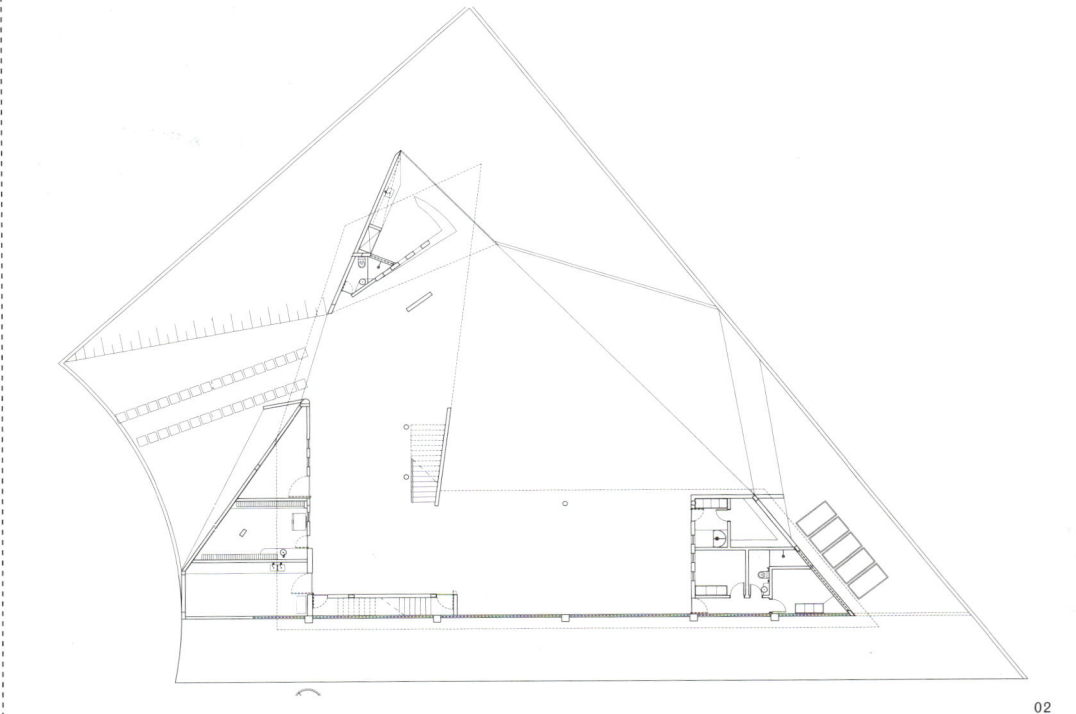

HOUSE IN NOVA LIMA

The project of House in Nova Lima is placed in the suburb of Belo Horizonte, which is the capital of the State of Minas Gerais. The open location of Minas Gerais is a place where urban codes and security conditions allow full public and private continuity, making the process of this project uniquely different. The development is L-shaped and is leveled by the upper part of the lot, and this is done in order so that the natural slope allows the desired fluidity and the necessary intimacy. The inner glazed façades open and expose the hilly natural landscape to all the rooms throughout the house.

01 Exterior view **02** Floor plan **03** Terrace **04** Entrance area

Photos: Daniel Mansur

MERCADO DESIGN

The Mercado Design project is born from the understanding of the building using a number of concepts: a single flat volume with considerable permeability that is able to provoke the effect of surprise. At first glance, it presents more of a challenge than an explicit revelation. It is not intended to sell material goods, but rather discuss motivations that lead people to search for bigger values, to desire a better quality of life. The design hopes to aim at something that is not limited to palpable issues, but can rather suggest a wider perception.

01 Front view **02** Showroom **03** Front façade detail **04** Interior **05** Sileston stairs **06** Ground and first floor plan

Photos: TAO Arqitetura, Telmo Ximensi (02)

CITY Brasilia
COUNTRY Brazil
REGION South America
TYPOLOGY Office
COMPLETION 2007
WEBSITE www.pauloheriqueparanhos.com
ARCHITECTS Paulo Henrique Paranhos (tao arquitectura)

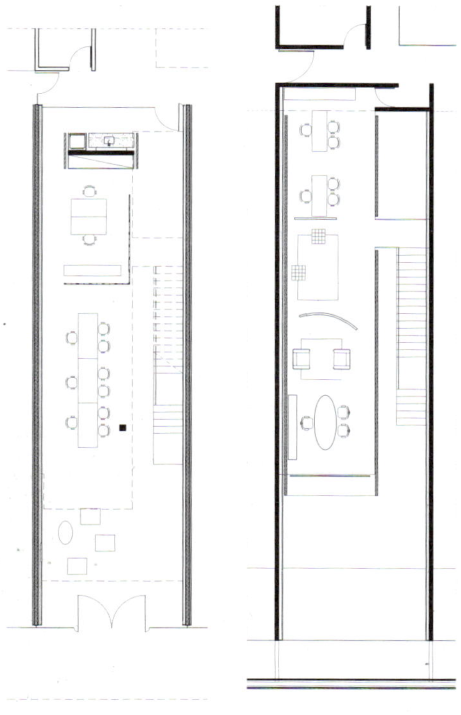

ANTAQ BUILDING

The building's design aims to integrate interior space with the surrounding city. The five storey-high atrium is a continuation of the street, its shops alternating with vistas of the landscape below. From the outside, the building appears as an orthogonal box with its two main façades protected by continuous panels of trellised woodwork, which controls luminosity and shields from direct sun. On all four-office floors, access to individual units takes place via winding terraced corridors overlooking the atrium, converting the circulation scheme into a formal element of design and a life-enhancing factor for the building.

01 Façade 02 Front view 03 Curved floors 04 Interior

Photos: Leonardo Finotti

CASA BRASILIA

The house is organized into two levels – ground floor (entertaining and service areas) and first floor (bedrooms). On the ground floor, the social areas feature double-height ceilings, and the service areas are regular-height, thus making the space to "fit" in an intermediate level. The region's climate conditions encouraged a high level of integration between the indoors and the outdoors. Several outdoors areas were created, such as the inner court, the terrace next to the living room, the long raised deck and a dining area fitted with a firewood stove and grill. Likewise, the bedrooms open onto a common balcony.

01 Loggia by night **02** General View **03** View on inner courtyard **04** Detail façade

Photos: Leonardo Finotti

CITY Brasilia
COUNTRY Brazil
REGION South America
TYPOLOGY Living
COMPLETION –
WEBSITE www.isayweinfeld.com
ARCHITECTS Isay Weinfeld Arquitetura

CITY	Corumbau
COUNTRY	Brazil
REGION	South America
TYPOLOGY	Hospitality
COMPLETION	2005
WEBSITE	www.tauana.com
ARCHITECTS	Ana Catarina Ferreira da Silva

TAUANA HOTEL

Tauana Hotel is located in a very exclusive beach in Corumbau, Bahia, between two National Parks and in front of beautiful coral reefs. A place born out of nature and setting itself apart by the location, architecture, detail, and concept, the nine perfectly integrated "cabanas", each 130-m² and only a few meters from a wild beach, are surrounded by coconut trees and the Atlantic forest. The hotel has been built using traditional building techniques and materials of local earthen construction such as Adobe and wattle and daub walls, as well as wooden tiles and "piaçava" (a local palm tree) thatched roofs.

01 View to "cabanas" **02** "Cabanas" surrounded with cocunut trees **03** Lounge **04** Thatched "piaçava" roof construction

Photos: Jomar Braganca (01, 04), Nelson Kon

CEPEMA ENVIRONMENT EDUCATION AND RESEARCH CENTER (TORRES EN ALTURA)

The CEPEMA – Environment Education and Research Center, built and supported by Petrobás (Brazilian oil) for a five-year management provided by Universidade de São Paulo, shall act in the research-promoting field and in the conception of innovative solutions. Donated to the University by Petrobrás, the center will rely on two large laboratories, chemistry and biochemistry, where six classrooms, an auditorium, a documentation center, storeroom, support area, accommodation for researchers, administrative sector, nursery, and wild fauna classification and rehabilitation services will all be provided.

01 Internal view, staircase **02** General view of the building **03** External view of the laboratory **04** Floor Plan **05** Ceiling detail auditorium

Photos: José Moscadi Jr.

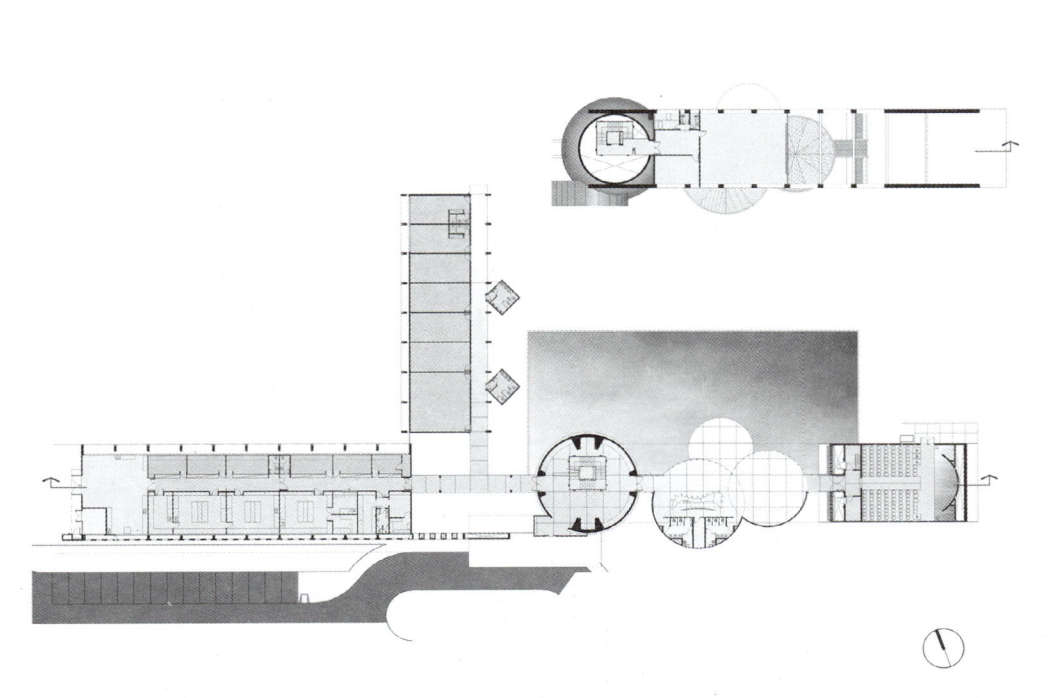

CITY Cubatão
COUNTRY Brazil
REGION South America
TYPOLOGY Institution
COMPLETION 2007
WEBSITE www.bratke.com.br
ARCHITECTS Carlos Bratke Ateliê de Arquitetura

CITY
Cumbuco

COUNTRY
Brazil

REGION
South America

TYPOLOGY
Living

COMPLETION
2004

WEBSITE
www.gersoncastelobranco.com.br

ARCHITECTS
Gerson Castelo Branco

CASA DO CUMBUCO

Located on a 6,400m² site, the house was designed in three modules – the main one with three floors houses the living room, kitchen and bath on the lower floor and two suites on the second and third floors; the master suite, balcony and mezzanine are on the fourth story. The second module is to receive the area with a large pool, bathrooms, sauna, and a bar / kitchen deposit. There is still room for a garage and an employee home. The structure was finished completely in autoclaved eucalyptus and has resulted in a constructed area of 750m².

01 Exterior view **02** Detail cocktailbar **03** General view on the buildings **04** Interior living space

Photos: João Ribeiro

SCHOOL IN CAMPINAS

The School integrates a pilot program of the São Paulo state government for the construction of schools using structural systems of pre-moulded concrete, as an alternative to the present low quality system of standard schools. Situated in a housing complex, destitute of any urbanity or architectonic quality, the site was an essential component to determine the compact and vertical plan. The indoor sports court was incorporated to the volume on the top of the building, allowing for the almost totality of the ground floor to be liberated for aspects such as the gardens and entertainment facilities.

01 Exterior view by night **02** Interior view of gymnasium **03** Floor Plan **04** Detail staircase

Photos: Nelson Kon

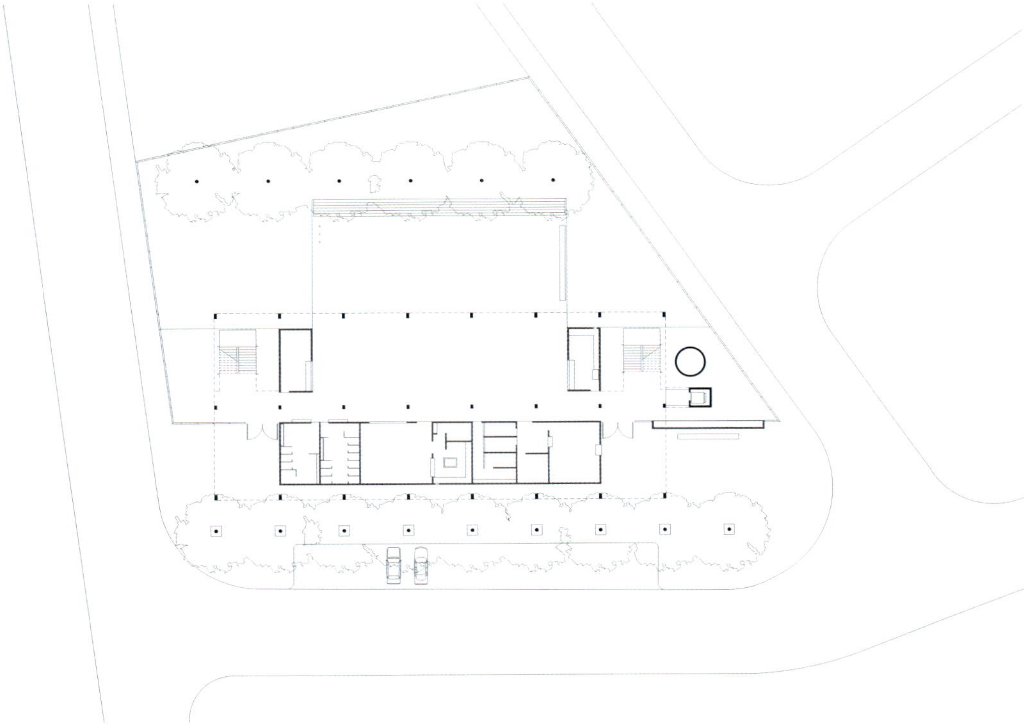

CITY Campinas
COUNTRY Brazil
REGION South America
TYPOLOGY Education
COMPLETION 2004
WEBSITE www.unaarquitetos.com.br
ARCHITECTS una arquitetos

CITY
Campinas

COUNTRY
Brazil

REGION
South America

TYPOLOGY
Education

COMPLETION
2005

WEBSITE
www.piratininga.com.br

ARCHITECTS
Piratininga Arquitetos Associados

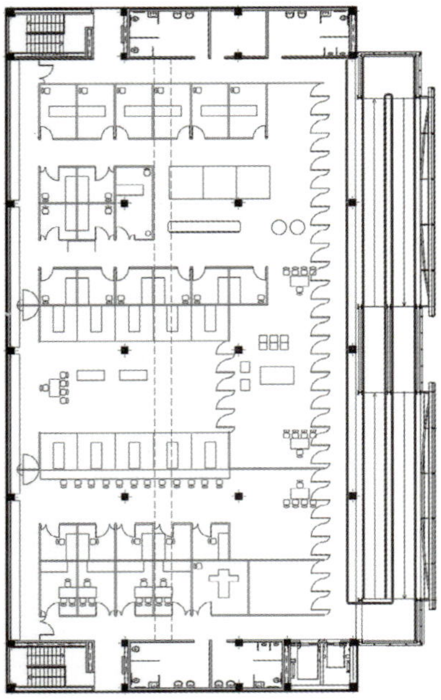

BIBLIOTECA Y AMBULATÓRIO DE FISIOTERAPIA

The project set out to establish an implantation level that is common to the buildings proposed, intensifying the spatial relations with the surrounding buildings and characterizing an esplanade; a plaza connecting the new buildings to the dynamics of the university campus. In the library, the central space of the floors is used for consultation and reading, integrated by a void receiving indirect lighting, while natural ventilation system allows for fresh air. The building offers physiotherapy rehabilitation services, with the ground floor enclosing a hydrotherapy department with a swimming pool and equipment.

01 Second floor plan **02** Library interior **03** Library south façade **04** Esplanade **05** View from the south

Photos: Bebete Viégas

MAIN LIBRARY – CENTRO UNIVERSITARIO POSITIVO/ UNICENP

Considered by the board of directors of UNICENP (Centro Universitário Positivo) as the most important building on Campus, the Library represents both the conversion and diffusion of education and knowledge. The importance of this building is signified by its prestigious location; a site where the building opens itself to a large lake surrounded by luscious greenery. A massive volume made out of concrete can be noticed from both inside and outside, holding the collection of administrative and support departments. Study and reading areas are located in narrow metallic mezzanines from where visitors can gaze upon panoramic views.

01 Exterior view by night **02** Interior into library **03** Front view **04** Floor plan **05** Curtain wall

Photos: Sérgio Sade, Pedro Paulo Coelho

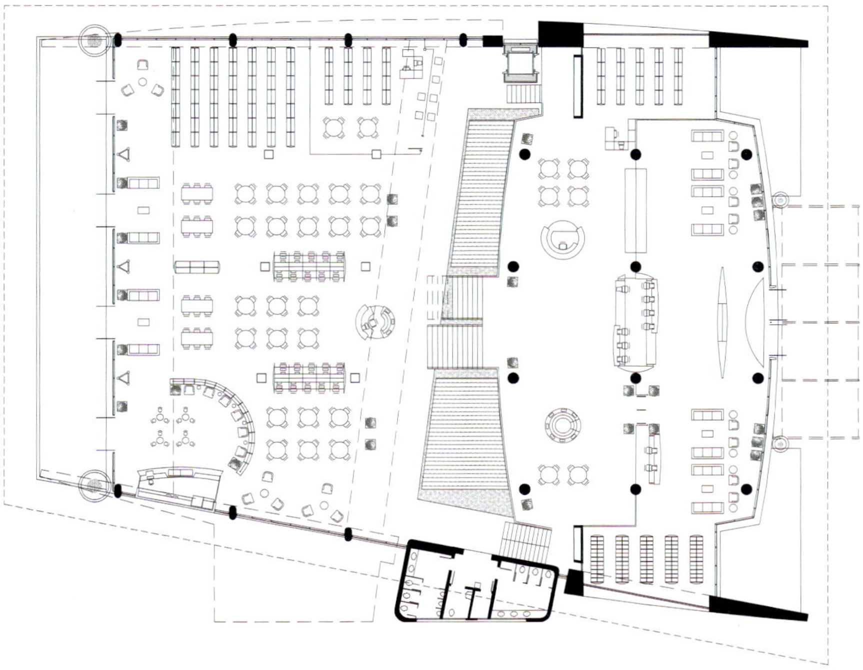

CITY Curitiba
COUNTRY Brazil
REGION South America
TYPOLOGY Education
COMPLETION 2004
WEBSITE www.mcacoelho.com.br
ARCHITECTS MCA Manoel Coelho Arquitetura & Design

CITY Curitiba

COUNTRY Brazil

REGION South America

TYPOLOGY Living

COMPLETION 2003

WEBSITE –

ARCHITECTS Marcos Bertoldi/Studio Bertoldi

CASA CASAGRANDE BERTOLDI

The house is divided into two parts: one for the service and support areas set under the street level and second containing the daily family activities area. The first one – totally coated with black slate – was organically installed in the lot, in a friendly integration with the site and the second one – suspended on stilts – in a white cubic volume. All the main rooms of the house are headed north over viewing the nearby Tingui Park; the spaces are set linearly providing long horizontal perspectives.

01 View by night **02** Rear façade with extended views **03** Longitudinal section **04** Pond and pathways **05** View into interior

Photos: Ricardo Almeida

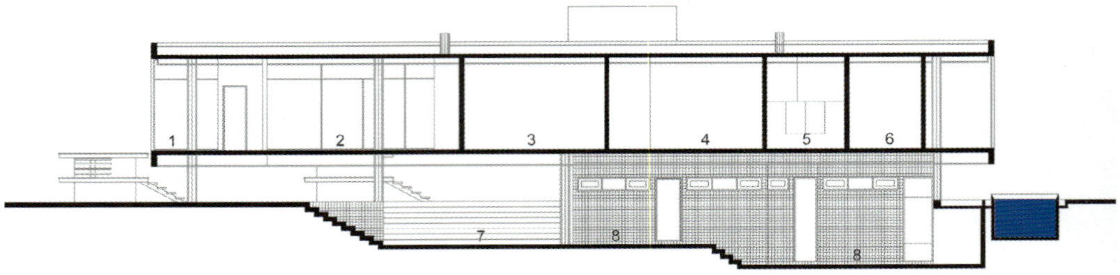

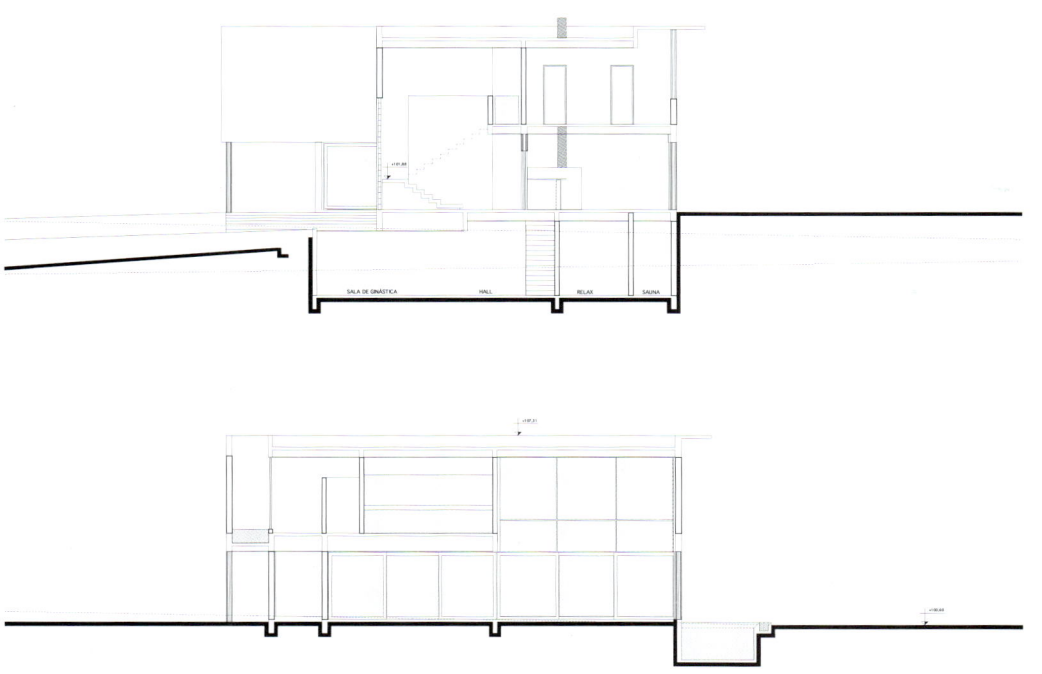

CASA ROVEDA CARVALHO

The house is made up of three levels where the lower floor is coated with black slate and serves as a base for the upper white volumes which contain the ground and first floor. In the front façades, the few openings and the proportions of the volumes turned to the co-op give it the expected character. In the back façades, the walls are interrupted, providing large openings to the garden and pool. The internal area is intentionally dynamic, creating vertical perspectives through double headrooms. Several internal open gardens balance the lack of openings of some walls, bringing natural light and vegetation into the rooms.

01 Sections 02 Main entrance 03 Exterior and interior view by night 04 Stais leading towards main entrance

Photos: Ricardo Almeida

CITY Curitiba
COUNTRY Brazil
REGION South America
TYPOLOGY Living
COMPLETION 2005
WEBSITE Living
ARCHITECTS Marcos Bertoldi/Studio Bertoldi

828

CITY Fortim
COUNTRY Brazil
REGION South America
TYPOLOGY Living
COMPLETION 2001
WEBSITE www.gersoncastelobranco.com.br
ARCHITECTS Gerson Castelo Branco

CASA DO FORTIM

Located in an exuberant landscape at the mouth of Rio Jaguaribe, the building is deployed to 8 meters above the river. Its structure is made of autoclaved eucalyptus, with three floors and two modules with an area of approximately 1,000 meters. The access courtyard has a reflection pool and a garage. From any area anywhere in the house one can enjoy views of the river and the sea.

01 Exterior view with bridge connecting spaces **02** House with extended roof and swimming pool **03** Interior **04** Structural detail **05** Terrace

Photos: João Ribeiro

CENTRO CULTURAL OSCAR NIEMEYER

The center will be situated on an artificial island, next to the town's industrial area. Over 17,000 m² are planned for the construction. The initial design is simple: four distinct volumes with different forms (a spiral, a pyramid, a suspended cylinder and a pavilion) and uses (theater, memorial, museum and library) are placed on a rectangular esplanade. The theater is located to the right of the memorial, has a minimalist form with a recessed entrance, and is surrounded by a reflection pool. The memorial is a curious building of red and white elements shaped as a concrete pyramid 75 meter in height and hollow on the inside.

01 General view **02** Central building **03** Auditorium **04** View from plaza

Photos: Leonardo Finotti

CITY Goiânia
COUNTRY Brazil
REGION South America
TYPOLOGY Cultural
COMPLETION 2006
WEBSITE –
ARCHITECTS Oscar Niemeyer

AUTO SHOPPING CIDADE EMPRESARIAL

This building dedicated to vehicle trade is equipped with support and services to provide maximum comfort and convenience. The infrastructure was inserted to accomodate the flow of vehicles and to produce minimal urban impact. The fronts of 32 shops present goods and serve as green areas. The complex is composed of two major buildings with metal arches, united by a central covered terrace. This system was chosen because of flexibility and versatility of steel, associated with multiple design possibilities. Another important detail is the standardization and industrialization of building components, helping to streamline construction.

01 Interior, central view **02** Exterior view, detail **03** Total view

Renderings: Giusepe Branquinho, Renata Caiaffo, Carolina Guarita

CITY: Goiânia
COUNTRY: Brazil
REGION: South America
TYPOLOGY: Commercial
COMPLETION: 2007
WEBSITE: www.oliveirajr.com
ARCHITECTS: Oliveira Jr. Arquiteto

RESIDÊNCIA PK

The project was built as a vacation house for a couple with two children, and was brought to life during the visit to the land. The house includes such features as suites, living rooms, balcony and a swimming pool, which is backed toward the spectacular sight of the Guaruja Sea. Landscape and vegetation were preserved, with the structural platform becoming the base of the new area for development of the project. The client's desire for an external area where his children could play was integrated into the house, and the house itself is structuralized in steel, while the closings are all done in glass and wood.

01 Exterior view by night **02** Detail terrace **03** Façade and pool **04** Living room

Photos: Leonardo Finotti

CITY
Guarujá

COUNTRY
Brazil

REGION
South America

TYPOLOGY
Living

COMPLETION
-

WEBSITE
www.arthurcasas.com.br

ARCHITECTS
Studio Arthur Casas

CITY
Guarujá

COUNTRY
Brazil

REGION
South America

TYPOLOGY
Living

COMPLETION
2005

WEBSITE
www.marcosacayaba.arq.br

ARCHITECTS
Marcos Acayaba

ACAYABA HOUSE

This house located 150 meters away from the beach is a prototype for occupation of sloping sites in concern to nature preservation. Only three pillars fitted between existing trees suspend the house, preserving the site's vegetation and soil. The triangular structure that expands like a tree was assembled with industrialized elements: wooden pillars and beams, steel cables and connections. Roof and floors consist of triangular plaques, pre-cast in lightweight concrete. Walls and parapets are industrialized plywood panels. Using these components, 4 workers completed the dwelling in 4 months with minimal impact on the environment.

01 Detail of bridge **02** Façade detail **03** Interior **04** Structural detail

Photos: Leonardo Finotti

GUARUJÁ HOUSE

The project was built as a vacation house for a couple with two children, and was brought to life during the visit to the land. The house includes such features as suites, living rooms, balcony and a swimming pool, which is backed toward the spectacular sight of the Guaruja Sea. Landscape and vegetation were preserved, with the structural platform becoming the base of the new area for development of the project. The client's desire for an external area where his children could play was integrated into the house, and the house itself is structuralized in steel, while the closings are all done in glass and wood.

01 Exterior view **02** Terraced levels **03** Terrace with lap pool **04** Ground and first floor plan **05** Total view from distance

Photos: Leonardo Finotti

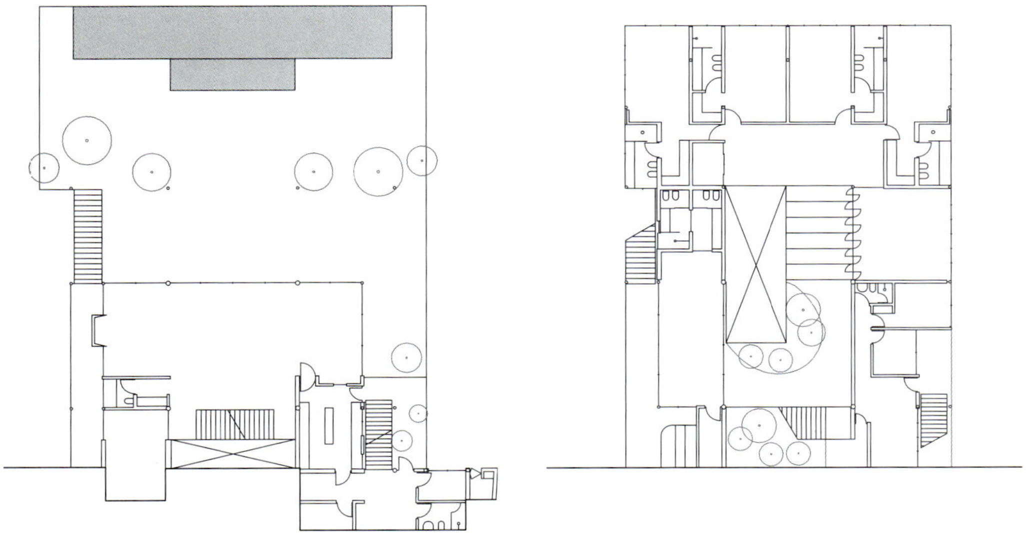

CITY Guarujá
COUNTRY Brazil
REGION South America
TYPOLOGY Living
COMPLETION 2007
WEBSITE www.bjaweb.com.br
ARCHITECTS Bernardes + Jacobsen Arquitetura

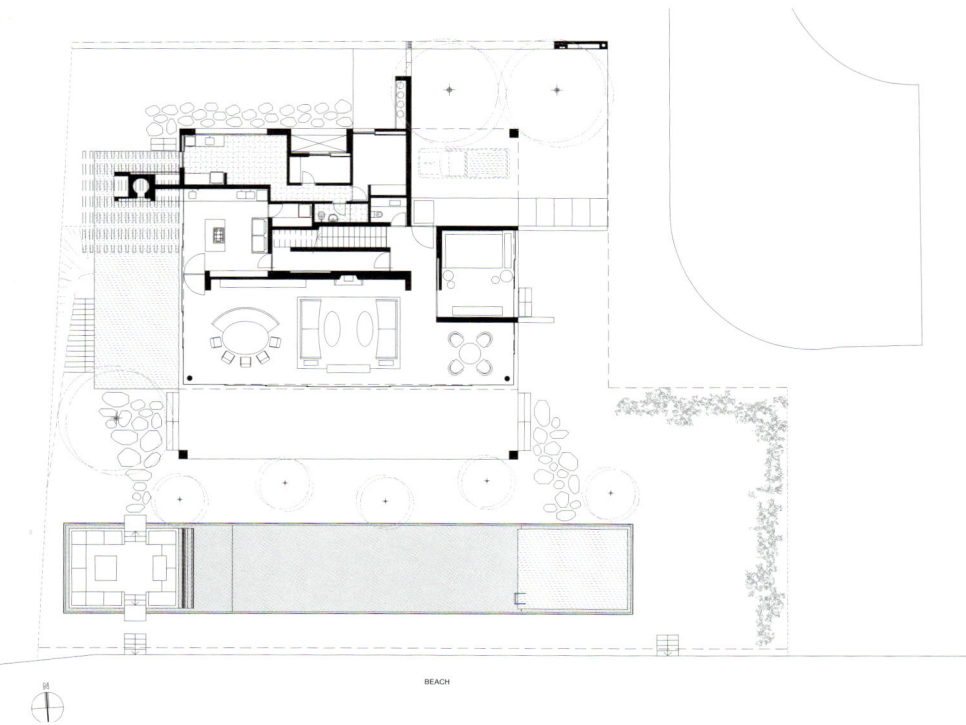

CITY	Guarujá
COUNTRY	Brazil
REGION	South America
TYPOLOGY	Living
COMPLETION	2006
WEBSITE	www.isayweinfeld.com
ARCHITECTS	Isay Weinfeld Arquitetura (in collaboration with Domingos Pascali)

IPORANGA HOUSE

Located in Iporanga, a retreat for summerhouses on São Paulo's coast, this condo is situated in a well-preserved area of the original Atlantic Rainforest. The exuberance of the forest demanded that the house occupy minimum space, while still allowing for comfort and openness. Splitting the program into 3 levels, five suites were built with features such as dining and living rooms, kitchen, and swimming pool. The aluminum frame volume is the "private" part of the house, with the street side enclosed by opaque boards and glass panels, while on the forest side, aluminum sliding doors open the master bedroom to a common veranda.

01 View on ocean **02** Exterior view by night **03** Extended living space and pool **04** Floor plan

Photos: Nelson Kon

IPORANGA BEACH HOUSE I

Located in Iporanga, a retreat for summerhouses on São Paulo's coast, this condo is situated in a well-preserved area of the original Atlantic Rainforest. The exuberance of the forest demanded that the house occupy minimum space, while still allowing for comfort and openness. Splitting the program into 3 levels, five suites were built with features such as dining and living rooms, kitchen, and swimming pool. The wood frame volume is the "private" part of the house, with the street side enclosed by opaque boards and glass panels, while on the forest side, aluminum sliding doors open the rooms to a common veranda.

01 Exterior view by night **02** Fully glazed façade **03** Detail façade **04** Interior with forest views **05** Detail staircase by night

Photos: Nelson Kon

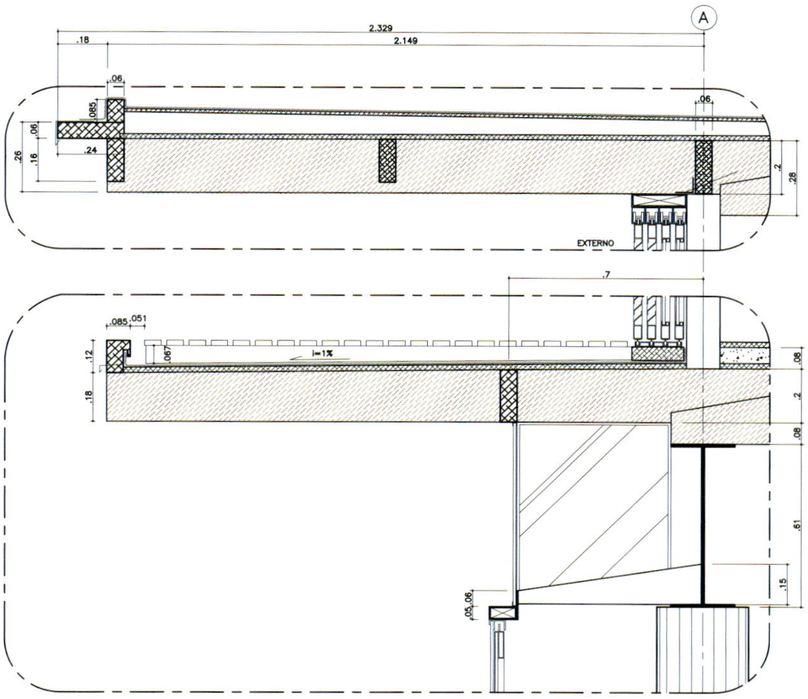

CITY Guarujá
COUNTRY Brazil
REGION South America
TYPOLOGY Living
COMPLETION 2006
WEBSITE –
ARCHITECTS Nitsche Asociados

IPORANGA HOUSE

This beach house, located in São Paulo at the top of a forest-covered hill, boasts ocean views and quiet surroundings. The house has four floors, where high ceilings and ample glass covered surfaces are used to unite indoor and outdoor areas, highlighting magnificent views. Pure lines and white surfaces are the defining characteristics, while a slender roof and extensive glass surfaces provide airiness to the house. The garage is suspended above the service area by a metallic grill, allowing natural light and proper ventilation. The lower floor is for social events, while a pool, sauna, suites, and terraces are all featured.

01 Front façade by night **02** Side view **03** Swimming pool with forest views **04** Interior living space **05** Side and front elevation

Photos: Leonardo Finotti

CITY Guarujá
COUNTRY Brazil
REGION South America
TYPOLOGY Living
COMPLETION 2005
WEBSITE www.ximenesleite.com.br
ARCHITECTS André Leite / Bruna Ximenes / Mario Biselli

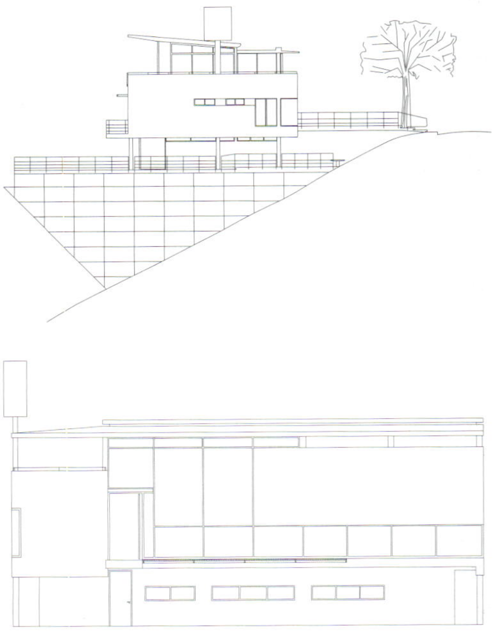

RESIDÊNCIA ACAPULCO

The residence presents the 'implantation' of two blocks; a great pavilion on the front, and a smaller at the back of the site, where three elements define the residence: the white volume on the lower level, the wooden panel on the upper floor, and the covering frame. Located at the front side of the volume are the service areas, at the back the social areas and a covered terrace; while on the upper floor are the suites' terraces. The swimming pool area and a metallic covering, sheltering an open leisure area, connect the two blocks, configuring the great internal patio, while a closed leisure area is also featured.

01 Exterior view from street **02** Double-height living room **03** View from garden **04** General view by night

Photos: J.R. Basiches / Graziela Widman

CITY Guarujá
COUNTRY Brazil
REGION South America
TYPOLOGY Living
COMPLETION 2005
WEBSITE www.josericard-basiches.com.br
ARCHITECTS José Ricardo Basiches

VALEO VSS PLANT – GUARULHOS

The design of the new industrial plant for the French car part multinational Valeo emphasizes environmental efficiency and complies with international quality standards, for example, optimally using available natural light. The round and elegant form of the building is a reference to modern Brazilian architecture; it eliminates gutters and guarantees complete rainwater drainage from the roof. The best level location was chosen in order to minimize groundwork. Transparent elements such as glass separate different activities inside the building. All structural elements are steel, enabling fast, low cost construction.

01 View from highway by night **02** Main on entrance
03 Longitudinal sections **04** Interior, structural detail

Photos: Nelson Kon, Kiko Coelho (02)

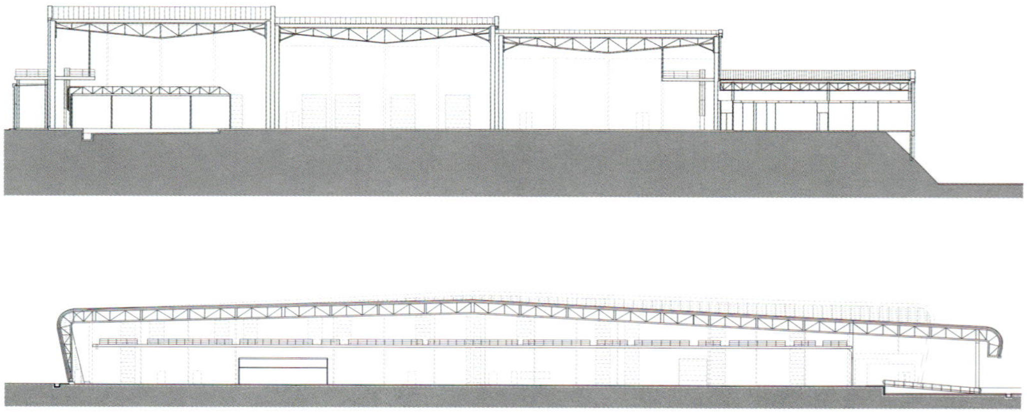

FDE SCHOOL – JARDIM ANGÉLICA III

The premise of this project is a single, compact unit closed to the outside, except for the public entrances and skylights. The accentuated topography of the slender plot organizes the various entry points and distinguishes clearly between the functional blocks of the program. The building is divided into four blocks: two standard (containing classrooms) and two special (with communal spaces and the administration). The entry points are located on three different levels of the plot and connect with the surrounding city via two bridges and a flight of steps.

01 Total view from distance **02** Exterior view by night
03 Hallway with city views **04** Site plan

Photos: Nelson Kon

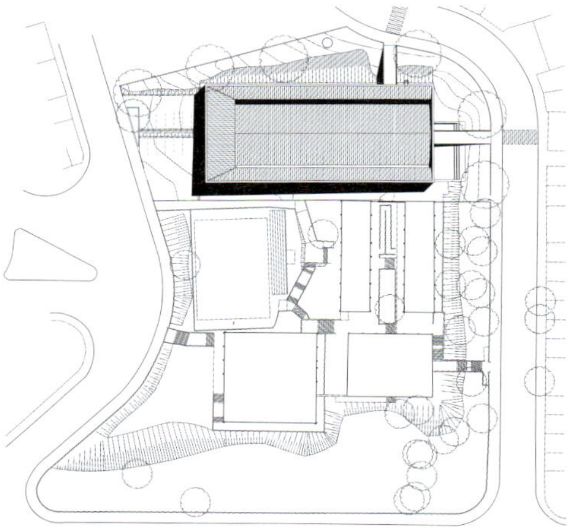

CITY	Guarulhos
COUNTRY	Brazil
REGION	South America
TYPOLOGY	Education
COMPLETION	2006
WEBSITE	–
ARCHITECTS	Núcleo de Arquitetura

CITY Itamambuca

COUNTRY Brazil

REGION South America

TYPOLOGY Living

COMPLETION 2007

WEBSITE www.andrademorettin.com.br

ARCHITECTS Vinicius Andrade and Marcelo Morettin

HOUSE RR

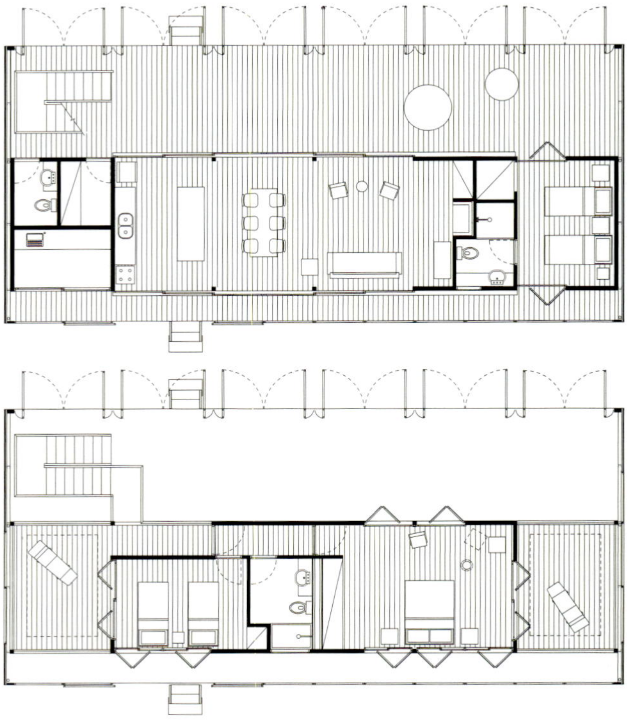

This summerhouse is situated a few meters distance from the sea on the north coast of the State of São Paulo; a place with exuberant vegetation and a hot humid climate. The project began with the idea of a big shelter, a "shell", making it possible to locate the program, and protect it from the intense sun and the frequent rains, without blocking the permanent natural cross ventilation. The roof was built using a prefabricated timber structure with galvanized steel joints, and this adoptive constructive system assured a dry construction site, with little generation of waste and low environmental impact.

---

01 Exterior view **02** Extended covered terrace **03** Kitchen with extended terrace **04** Floor plans **05** View into interior space with exposed materials

Photos: Nelson Kon

ITU HOUSE

The main idea behind the design on this weekend house, located on a lot privileged by a beautiful sunset view, was to orient it towards the vista and to protect it from the sun. The total volume is divided into blocks in order to connect all rooms to the exterior, creating diffuse, fresh illumination. A large concrete volume with high walls acts as the connecting articulator between the single blocks. A ramp leads to the bedrooms on the upper floor or to the living room and service areas below. The living areas are protected from the strong rays of the setting sun by a concrete wall, while a small opening in it frames the landscape for viewing from the ground floor.

01 Exterior view by night **02** Ramped hallways **03** Detail entrance **04** Floor plan **05** View from pool

Photos: Nelson Kon

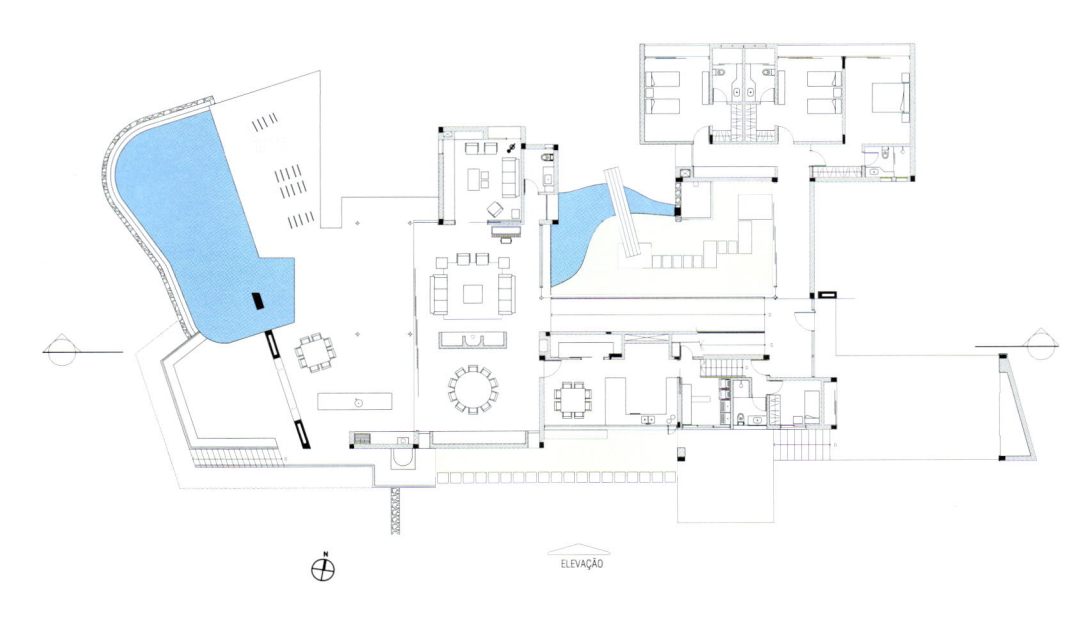

CITY Itu
COUNTRY Brazil
REGION South America
TYPOLOGY Living
COMPLETION 2006
WEBSITE www.rmaa.com.br
ARCHITECTS Henrique Reinach e Maurício Mendonça

LM HOUSE

The house occupies a sloping corner site, which led to an L-shaped implementation around a central inner court with pool and leisure areas. The living and dining areas located on the intermediate floor exist in a spatial continuum with the court. The bedrooms are relegated to an upper, more enclosed volume, which shelters them from the surrounding streets. The typology of the residence seeks to reinterpret the modern vocabulary, exploring the free structure and open plans to create a dramatic volumetric composition that is reinforced by the use of various natural Brazilian materials like Bege Bahia stone and Cumaru wood panels.

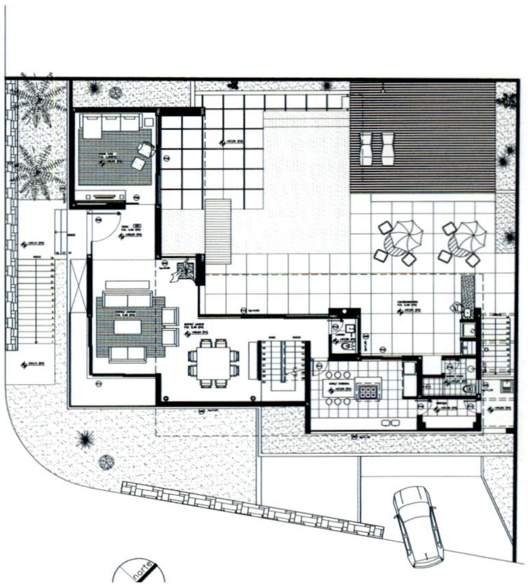

01 Outdoor spaces **02** Floor plan **03** Exterior view by night **04** Swimming pool **05** Living room, view to pool

Photos: Márcio Brigatto

CITY Juiz de Fora
COUNTRY Brazil
REGION South America
TYPOLOGY Living
COMPLETION 2005
WEBSITE www.lourencosarmento.com.br
ARCHITECTS Lourenço Sarmento Arquitetos

UNIQUE GARDEN

It is the details that make the difference in this luxury hotel – everything here has its personality. The main volume is clad in pre-oxidized copper plates, resulting in a green tint. Conceived as an upside-down arc, it houses 95 apartments of varying size and a presidential suite on its six floors. Each unit has views of the city and can alternate between air conditioning and natural ventilation using movable windows. The hotel is surrounded by an exotic rock garden with sculpted swimming pools and reflecting water pools, as well as a gourmet restaurant.

01 General view **02** Exterior by night **03** Organic shaped swimming pool **04** Bungalow

Photos: Leonardo Finotti

CITY Mairiporã
COUNTRY Brazil
REGION South America
TYPOLOGY Hospitality
COMPLETION 2002
WEBSITE www.ruyohtake.com.br
ARCHITECTS Ruy Ohtake

CITY Nova Lima
COUNTRY Brazil
REGION South America
TYPOLOGY Living
COMPLETION 2003
WEBSITE www.vazio.com.br
ARCHITECTS Carlos M. Teixeira – Vazio S/A Arquitetura

VILA DEL REY HOUSE

This is a residence built with mixed materials: laminated eucalyptus beams in the center, and reinforced concrete on the perimeter. The two structures are mixed and create a certain excess of pillars throughout the house. The central element is a 9 meters-high stairway that connects all four levels, whereas the rooms are located about the void. In a country where the majority of timber comes from illegal producers in the Amazon, the project is also a way to disseminate Eucalyptus as an alternative type of wood on Brazil's domestic market.

01 Rear view **02** Façade by night **03** Interior **04** Entrance and stairs **05** Façade detail

Photos: Jomar Bragança, Eduardo Eckenfels

CASA ALPHAVILLE

The master line for the Alphaville project intended to construct a home for a middle aged lady who has married and divorced sons with numerous grandchildren, with the purpose being to create a house that features elements of of pleasure and entertaininment for family and friends. The house is fully integrated, rather than being compartmentalized with wide spaces, and is never obsolete. Extensive transparency enhancing the landscape is visibly included, while an enormous automatic glass door is provided integrating the garden and the living room to the project, giving the home a special personality.

01 General view **02** Detail entrance by night **03** Rear view by night **04** Interior **05** Façade by night

Photos: Leonardo Finotti

CITY Nova Lima
COUNTRY Brazil
REGION South America
TYPOLOGY Living
COMPLETION 2006
WEBSITE www.gustavopenna.com.br
ARCHITECTS Gustavo Penna Arquiteto & Associados

CITY Olinda
COUNTRY Brazil
REGION South America
TYPOLOGY Culture
COMPLETION 2006
WEBSITE –
ARCHITECTS Borsoi Arquitetura

ESPAÇO CIÊNCIA

The Science Museum was developed in an open space situated on a long empty urban plot along a road between Recife and Olinda. The project is inserted into the landscape and interacts with its environment. The architects aimed to change the paradigm of contemporary architecture of Brazil. The load-carrying elements and round columns, conceptual elements as formulated by Corbusier, are technological resources of the building that are distributed on its periphery. The museum is noted for its interactive nature and social inclusiveness.

01 Front view **02** Interior **03** Rear view **04** Elevations

Photos: Leonardo Finotti

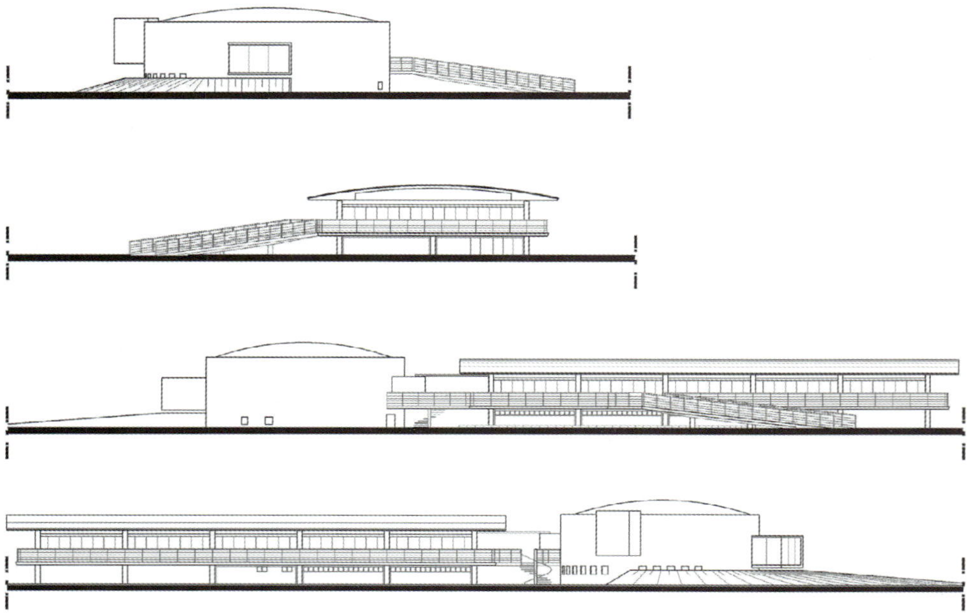

PETROPOLIS HOUSE

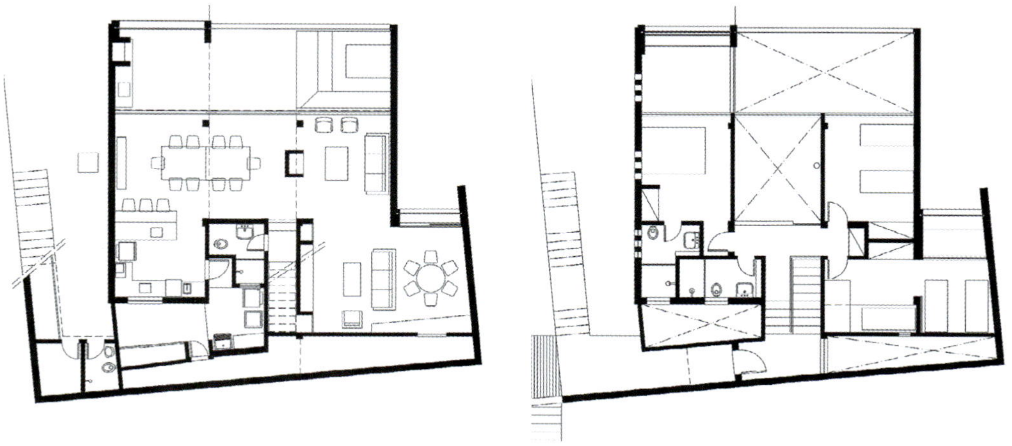

This holiday house is located on a sloped site on the mountains near the city of Rio de Janeiro. A 10 x 10 meter cubic volume aligned with the upper edge of the site was used as the starting point to respond to the main requirements: security when the object is not occupied; protection of land humidity; flat areas for child recreation. A bright green retaining wall linking an existing rock to the upper site limit directs the dwelling entrance while separating the house from the terrain, the rainy winds and neighbors' views.

01 Total view by night **02** Detail terrace **03** View from the pool **04** Floor plan ground floor and first floor **05** Rear view

Photos: Nelson Kon

CITY: Petropolis
COUNTRY: Brazil
REGION: South America
TYPOLOGY: Living
COMPLETION: 2004
WEBSITE: www.prourb.fau.ufrj.br/jkos.htm
ARCHITECTS: José Kós

CITY
Porto Alegre

COUNTRY
Brazil

REGION
South America

TYPOLOGY
Sports

COMPLETION
in progress

WEBSITE
hypestudio.com.br

ARCHITECTS
Hype Studio

BEIRA-RIO STADIUM RENOVATION AND URBAN MASTER PLAN

Beira-Rio Stadium has been home to the Internacional Sport Club since 1969 and had witnessed great moments of the club's history. In order to bring the nearly 60,000-seat stadium up to the new safety and comfort standards and FIFA requirements, Hype Studio has developed a comprehensive renovation plan which includes new seating tiers, new services and a new roof, which will also modify the stadium's façade. An urban master plan for the currently underused neighboring areas is also being proposed. New facilities will include hotels, offices, parking garages, bars, restaurants and a convention center.

01 Visualisation of the stadium **02** View from the harbour **03** Inside the stadium **04** Site plan

Photos: Hype Studio

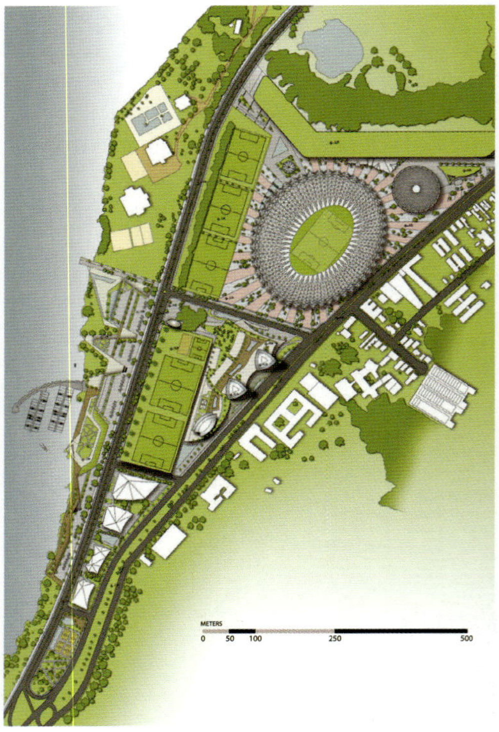

E-BOX PARKING

This project allowed the architects to explore the language of contrasts. Without much of a plot, but with a need to create a local office, a full functioning office is created on a parking lot. In essence, simply a box, the building contains an administrative office, a check in/out and a bathroom, all in a space no larger than an area of a parking occupancy. The distribution seeks to establish the best area utilization, exploring the site's complete functionality. The choice of cladding materials means to provide harmony and crosstalk in the relationship between the box and the parking lot.

01 Exterior view by night **02** Detail entrance **03** Ground and first floor plan **04** Façade from street **05** Office interior

Photos: Mathias Cramer

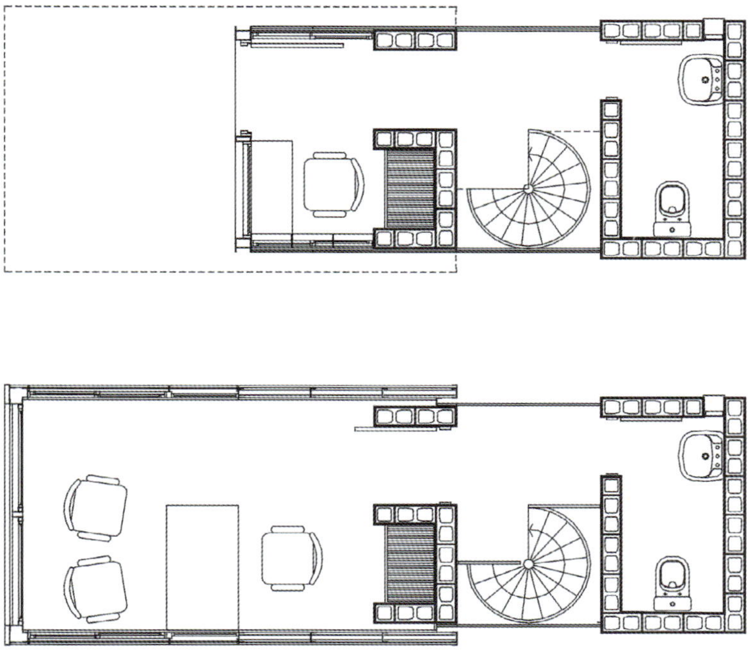

CITY Porto Alegre
COUNTRY Brazil
REGION South America
TYPOLOGY Commercial
COMPLETION 2003
WEBSITE www.studioparalelo.com.bt
ARCHITECTS Luciano Andrades + Rochelle Castro + Gabriel Gallina / Studio Paralelo

SLICE HOUSE

The project was selected to represent Brazil in the IV Latin American Architecture Biennale. The house makes a series of references to modern Brazilian architecture, adding new elements regarding its complex prismatic geometry, which generates spatial illusions in the interior spaces. A hybrid of Brazilian and British concerns, the building makes reference to Brazilian modernist architecture, but takes a more contemporary European interest in asymmetrical complexity. The insertion of a courtyard extends the living space, balances daylight levels, optimises cross ventilation and creates privacy in a dense urban environment.

01 Bird`s eye view **02** Façade at night **03** Interior view **04** View to outdoor plunge pool

Photos: Leonardo Finotti

ADVOCACIA FONTANA LAWYERS OFFICE

The project has a rectangular layout, delineated by three façades and divided into three strips. One section is for service spaces, the second for collective work spaces and the third contains individual offices. A mesh regulator measuring 1.2 x 1.175 meters and corresponding to the façade's vertical mountings defines the position of the elements. The walls that separate the lawyer's offices from the central space are coated with wood. Inside the collective zone, subdivisions of aluminum and glass accentuate the flow of space. At the plan's center is a chart that defines circulation and space usage.

01 Reception area **02** Entrance **03** Office space **04** Kitchen **05** Floor plan **06** Interior view, corridor

Photos: Eduardo Liotti

CITY Porto Alegre
COUNTRY Brazil
REGION South America
TYPOLOGY Office
COMPLETION 2006
WEBSITE –
ARCHITECTS Nicolás Sica Palermo/Claudia Titton & Tais Lagranha

CITY Porto Alegre
COUNTRY Brazil
REGION South America
TYPOLOGY Culture
COMPLETION 2006
WEBSITE –
ARCHITECTS Alvaro Siza

IBERÊ CAMARGO MUSEUM

The white concrete building rises immaculately from the ground; opacity and massing react to the technical requirements of the museum, and define the western orientation and reduction of the noise from the promenade. The openings appear small from the outside, and extend inward in a telescopic way. They frame views over the greened hills and the adjacent city center together with the river and the sky. The atrium curves toward the road, held together by a system of double ramps. Below the main volume is a basement housing stockrooms, administrative offices, library, lecture-room and workshops as well as an underground parking.

01 Exterior view from street **02** Detail entrance area **03** View upwards from entrance area **04** Interior ramps **05** Gallery spaces at different levels

Photos: Leonardo Finotti

CENTRO DE ENSINO CICERO DIAS

The principal needs for this school project had to do with principles of modulation and the use of traditional techniques of construction. The site is flat, and according to the program and physical relations to the site, it was a natural thing to do to divide the school into five different blocks: administration, classrooms and laboratories, restaurant and service areas, library and computer's room, and a media theatre. These volumes are connected by metallic structures and surround an internal playground. This organization takes advantage of natural ilumination, ventilation and stimulates external, elective activities.

01 Colourful windows on façade **02** Internal playground **03** Detail façade **04** Site plan **05** Corridor

Photos: Carlos Cajueiro

CITY	Recife
COUNTRY	Brazil
REGION	South America
TYPOLOGY	Education
COMPLETION	2006
WEBSITE	www.oficina.arq.br
ARCHITECTS	Oficina de Arquitetos

CITY Recife

COUNTRY Brazil

REGION South America

TYPOLOGY Leisure

COMPLETION 2006

WEBSITE www.metro.arq.br

ARCHITECTS Metro Arquitetura

CLUB NOX

Club Nox was conceived as the new standard for dance clubs in Brazil. Light is at the heart of this building. From the street, a box of Cor-ten steel wraps a glass prism that radiates at night in different colors as an urban chandelier. Inside, a transparent skin of fiberglass covering the ceiling and walls flows in parallel and perpendicular continuous stripes that create a matrix around the dance floor. Sparks of light penetrate this membrane coming from a DMX system based on 256 sets of RGB LEDs. That allows infinite possibilities of color and movement effects involving both people and the space.

01 Exterior view by night **02** Entrance **03** Illuminated fiberglass on walls and ceiling **04** Interior view to bar **05** Sections

Photos: Leonardo Finotti

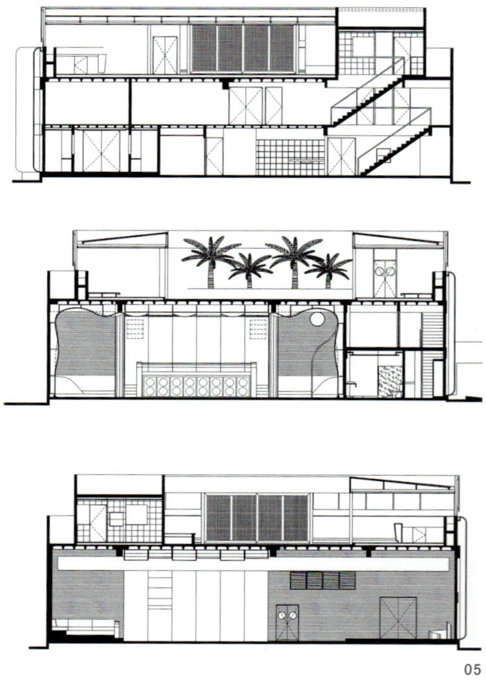

BRENNAND CHAPEL

This chapel is located on the grounds of a ceramics factory nestled in an exuberant Atlantic Forest reserve on the banks of the Capibaribe River. The project transformed an old 19th Century masonry and tile ruin that was a part of the ancient factory, into a modern chapel. The new roof, a flat pre-stressed concrete slab, rests upon two columns on the longitudinal axis of the nave and stretches above the area enclosed by the old walls, now restored. The entire internal perimeter is cased by a crystal wall that provides transparencies, reflections and refractions in a game of light.

01 External view by night **02** Restored old walls **03** Nave **04** External view **05** Internal view, chorus

Photos: Leonardo Finotti

CITY Recife
COUNTRY Brazil
REGION South America
TYPOLOGY Ecclesiastical
COMPLETION 2005
WEBSITE -
ARCHITECTS Paulo Mendes da Rocha

RESIDÊNCIA DERBY

This project is a design for a dismountable residential house consisting of two primary materials, concrete (kitchen and bathrooms) and wood (bedrooms and living room). The wooden volume is raised over the concrete base on beams, and is constructed of perpendicularly layered wooden elements, creating semi-opaque walls for the upstairs spaces which shield the house from sunlight. Space underneath the upper level can be used as a terrace or a parking space.

01 Façade by night **02** Kitchen **03** Interior view **04** Floor plans **05** Front view **06** Rear view

Photos: Leonardo Finotti

CITY Recife
COUNTRY Brazil
REGION South America
TYPOLOGY Living
COMPLETION 2004
WEBSITE www.onorte.arq.br
ARCHITECTS O Norte Oficina de Criação - Bruno Lima, Chico Rocha e Lula Marcondes

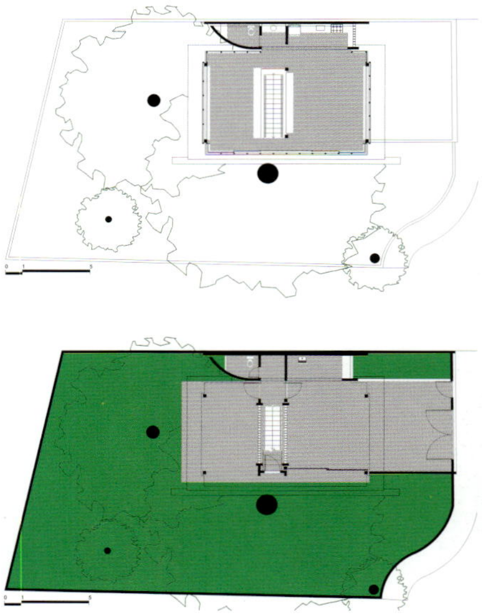

ENCOSTA DO CORCOVADO

This architectural project, known as the Encosta do Corcovado, had a very determining element, the magnificent views which became a strong component during the design. These views are ones that capture the Lagoon Rodrigo de sea Freitas and have a definite impact on the development of this project. The symmetry and rigidity is due to the natural results of a metallic structure that co-challenges the defined or divided the architectural structure. With ample spaces, the details are clearly seen while the technical architectural element of the project considers value and pure concepts, giving order, functionality and beauty.

01 Exterior view **02** Terrace **03** Balcony **04** Floor plan **05** View from garden

Photos: Tiago Muraes, Tuca Reinés

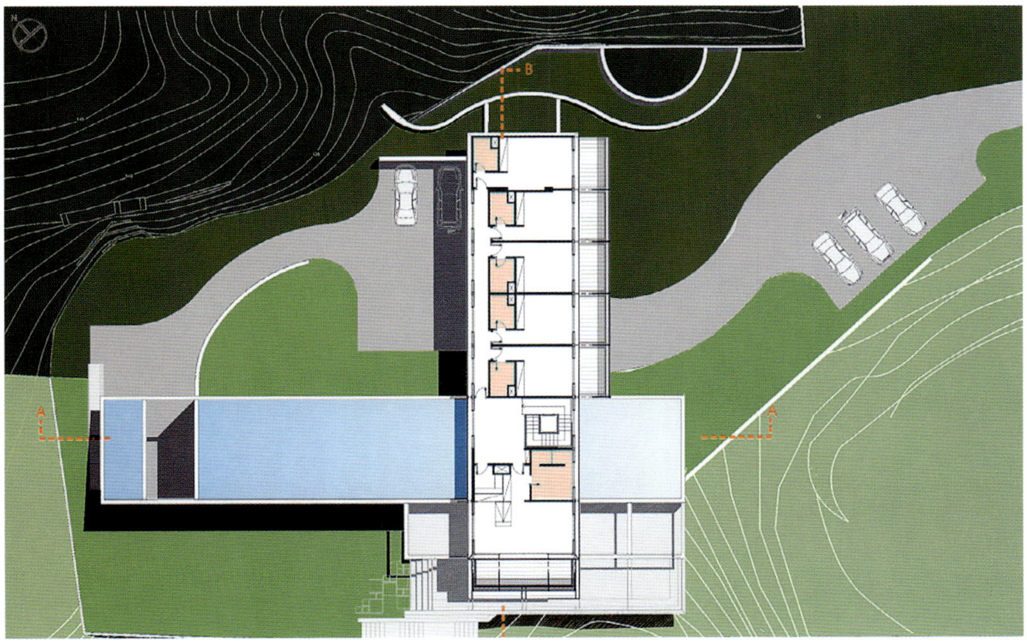

CITY Rio de Janeiro
COUNTRY Brazil
REGION South America
TYPOLOGY Living
COMPLETION –
WEBSITE www.indiodacosta.com
ARCHITECTS Indio da Costa Arquitetura e Design

CITY Rio de Janeiro
COUNTRY Brazil
REGION South America
TYPOLOGY Public / Sports
COMPLETION 2006
WEBSITE www.bcmfarquitetos.com
ARCHITECTS BCMF Arquitetos / Bruno Campos, Marcelo Fontes e Silvio Todeschi

BRAZILIAN NATIONAL SHOOTING CENTER, PAN AMERICAN GAMES RIO 2007

Strong horizontal lines predominate in this concrete sports complex located on a roughly rectangular plot in a breathtaking valley surrounded by mountain peaks. The complex has indoor and outdoor facilities such as training halls and grandstands, and features parking and service areas. The night-time periodical pattern of lighting along the peripheral wall and on the right-angled overhead structures produces an otherworldly effect of floating in the dark valley against the backdrop of a slowly setting sun.

01 Entrance by night **02** Aerial photography **03** Detail entrance area **04** Interior view

Photos: Kaká Ramalho, Bruno Carvalho (02)

BAZZAR RESTAURANT

To make the best of this 200 m² area the architects decided to apply a vertical design using traditional materials. Large glass walls and a gable of concrete and brick characterize the exterior. A marquee and the typical brise-soleil in wood protect the façade from the sun. The interior is a mixture of wall planes, small patios and natural vegetation like palms that grow vertically in the interior open gardens.

01 Front façade 02 Interior view from above 03 Interior
04 Sections

Photos: Hector Etchebaster

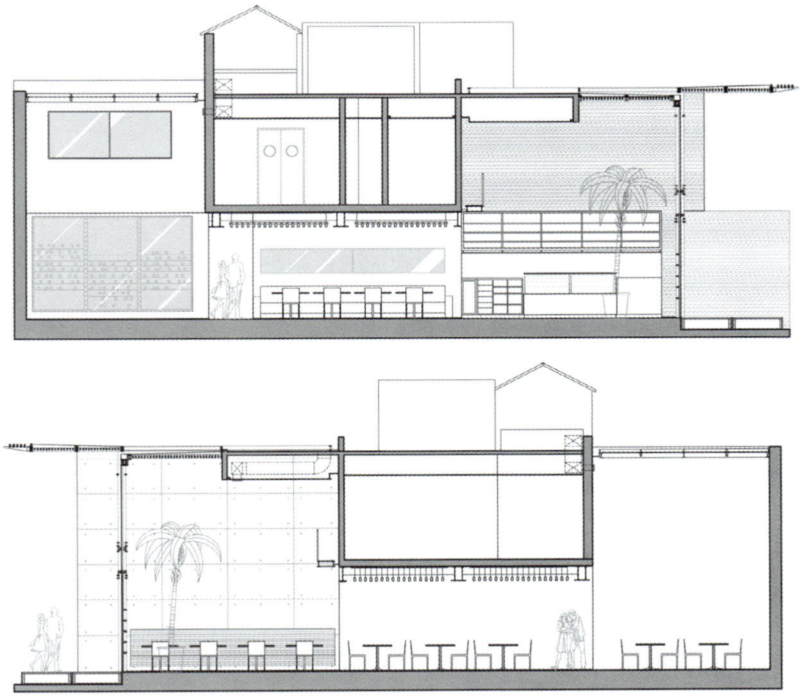

CITY
Rio de Janeiro

COUNTRY
Brazil

REGION
South America

TYPOLOGY
Gastronomy

COMPLETION
—

WEBSITE
www.belbob.com.br

ARCHITECTS
Bel Lobo & Bob Neri Arquitetos

CITY
Rio de Janeiro

COUNTRY
Brazil

REGION
South America

TYPOLOGY
Public

COMPLETION
2006

WEBSITE
www.blac.com.br

ARCHITECTS
BLAC - Backheuser e Leonídio Arquitetura e Cidade (João Pedro Backheuser)

RIO DAS OSTRAS BRIDGE

This cable-stayed bridge is made up of metal tray and concrete masts. With a total span of 66-meters made of 268 tons of steel and 1,753 m³ of reinforced concrete it has four traffic lanes and sidewalks on both sides (22-meters wide board). The characteristic features are the two 35-meters high concrete masts with inserts of galvanized steel tubes. In addition to meet technical and functional demands the architects also intended to establish a new urban landmark for the city.

01 Bridge by night **02** Detail pillars **03** General view **04** Suspension cables

Photos: Mário Grisoli

MASSIMO – HOUSE IN RIO DE JANEIRO II

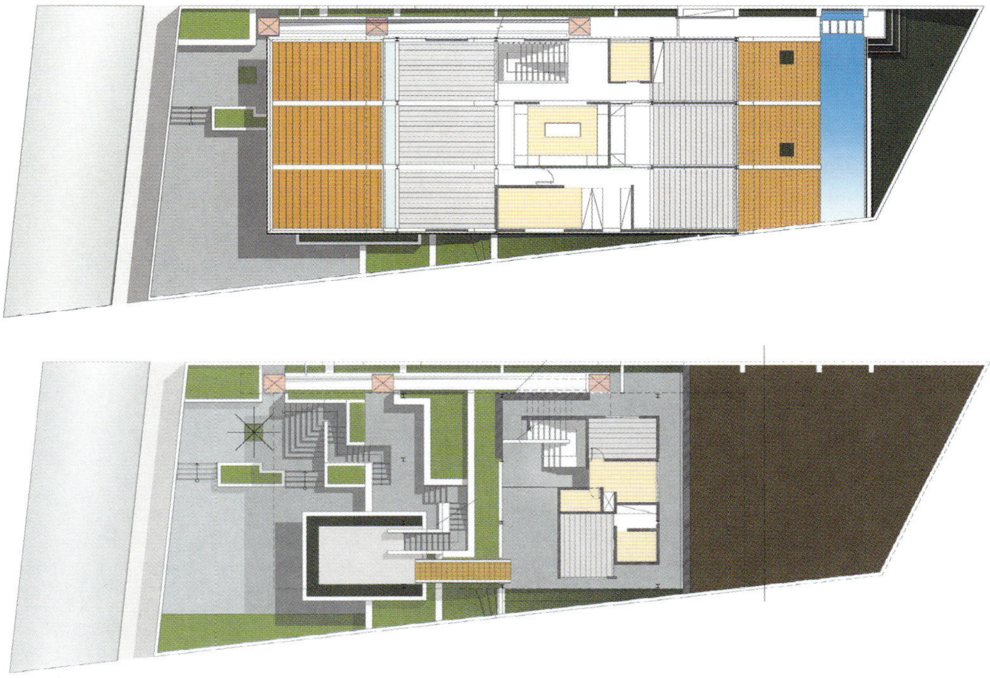

The main idea of the proposal was to create an architectural piece that should be both, rational and organic. The principles that guided the project were rationalism and structural lightness, comfort and versatility. To achieve structural lightness the architects used welded steel SAC beams with proper modulation and audacious cantilevers. Comfort was reached through an inclined lift that connects the different levels without the potential visual pollution and versatility through an automatically sliding awning on the roof that allows having an open or covered sky observation deck.

01 Interior view 02 Terrace 03 Detail terrace 04 Floor plans 05 Entrance

Photos: Courtesy Indio da Costa Arquitetura e Design

CITY	Rio de Janeiro
COUNTRY	Brazil
REGION	South America
TYPOLOGY	Living
COMPLETION	2003
WEBSITE	www.indiodacosta.com
ARCHITECTS	Indio da Costa Arquitetura e Design

CIRCO VOADOR

The proposal for the new Circo Voador focuses on creating dynamic forms and spaces with a strong identity without losing the casual atmosphere that was the original venue's trademark. Permeability of the space was sought after in every aspect of the building, allowing one to follow the movement of people through the ramps, gardens and terrace. The architectural elements rise above the floor, generating a versatile ground level. The internal and external environments melt together in an affirmation of the new Circo Voador's democratic character.

01 Entrance by night **02** Interior **03** Rear view **04** Front view **05** Floor plan

Photos: DDG Arquitetura

CITY Rio de Janeiro
COUNTRY Brazil
REGION South America
TYPOLOGY Culture
COMPLETION 2004
WEBSITE www.ddgarquitetura.com.br
ARCHITECTS DDG Arquitetura

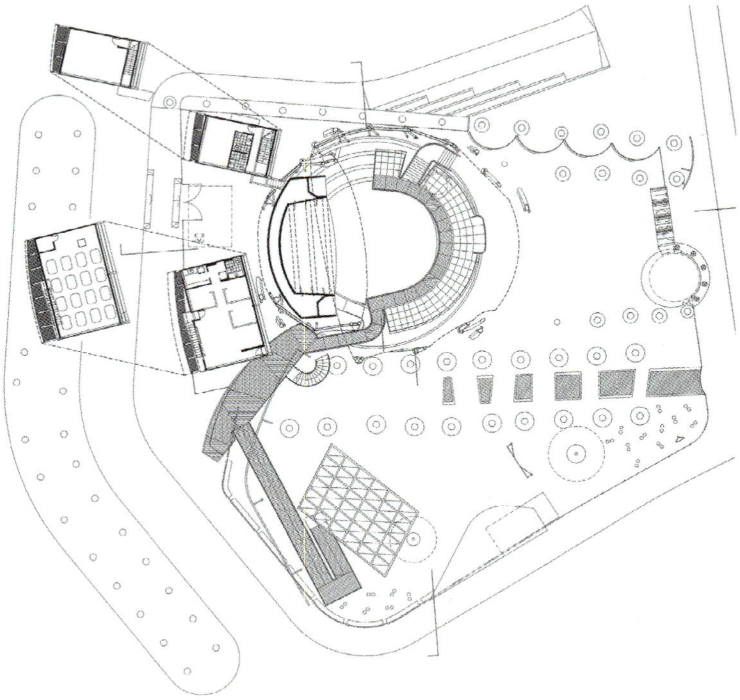

HOUSE JARDIM BOTANICO

Located in the southern part of the city, with great views of the beach, the ;agoon and the green, this house allows the outside to enter the spaces in spite of its closed form. The terrace with its green roof provides thermal comfort and creates the impression that the house has been grown from the site. The illumination of the interior comes through a large skylight in the middle of the plan, above the stairs. In a quiet neighborhood, all the rooms inside are marked by the dissolution of interior and exterior boundaries, with large movable doors, where nature is the scene.

01 View from the pool **02** Stairs **03** Interior view **04** Living room **05** Section **02** View from second floor

Photos: Andre Nazareth

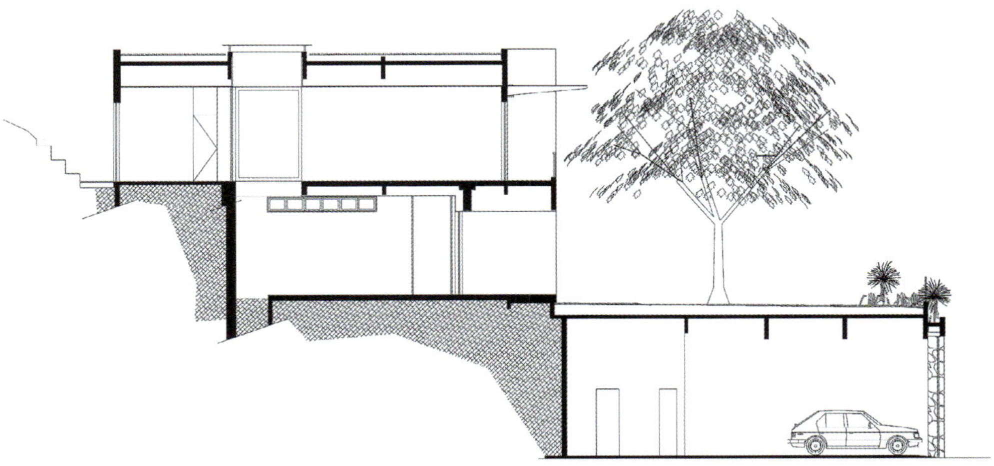

CITY Rio de Janeiro
COUNTRY Brazil
REGION South America
TYPOLOGY Living
COMPLETION 2006
WEBSITE www.desenhobrasileiro.com
ARCHITECTS Washington Fajardo + Patricia Fendt / DeBR Desenho Brasileiro

CITY: Rio de Janeiro
COUNTRY: Brazil
REGION: South America
TYPOLOGY: Living
COMPLETION: 2006
WEBSITE: www.desenhobrasileiro.com
ARCHITECTS: Washington Fajardo + Patricia Fendt / DeBR Desenho Brasileiro

HOUSE CAMBOINHAS

This house follows the precedent of simple forms found in its planned urban area while breaking with that tradition to a more contemporary living situation. The central patio is the main living space, and the three floors with their terraces are linked by enlarged doors. The swimming pool is at the center and composes the axis from the main entrance to the end of the patio. From the inside, openings frame the changing landscape. The mix of concrete, wood and iron is geometrically harmonic and articulates the structural concept of the house. All structural walls are of concrete, and others are made of brick; the doors are of wood.

01 View from courtyard **02** View from terrace **03** Entrance by night **04** Floor plan **05** Interior view

Photos: Andre Nazareth

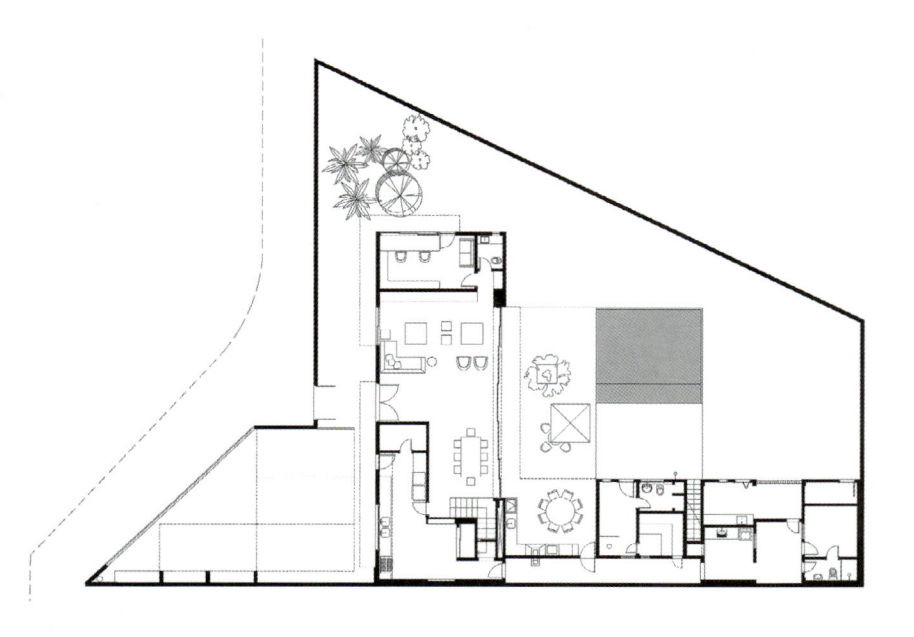

LA MAISON

The environment of the house combines elegance, a dream-like atmosphere, and the refinement of the "French touch". This is a haven of luxury and pleasure 10 minutes away from the beach of Ipanema and its commercial streets. In an environment dominated by the tropical vegetation, the house located in a private street provides exoticism, calm and safety to its guests. Each room is painted a different shade – acid green, poppy pink, lavender and saffron – with a deluxe bathroom clad in matching marble. All have private terraces with sea views. There's a small plunge pool, two cabanas, and an infinity pool on the way.

01 Lounge **02** Outdoor pool **03** Guestroom **04** Detail bathroom sink **05** View to garden from bedroom **06** Dining area

Photos: Rodrigo Harold

CITY Rio de Janeiro
COUNTRY Brazil
REGION South America
TYPOLOGY Hospitality
COMPLETION 2004
WEBSITE www.lamaisonario.com
ARCHITECTS Francois-Xavier Dussol

CITY Rio de Janeiro

COUNTRY Brazil

REGION South America

TYPOLOGY Living

COMPLETION 2005/2007

WEBSITE -

ARCHITECTS Carla Juaçaba

CASA VARANDA

The metal structure with glass façades is suspended from the ground, and from the conceptual point of view, is a reminder of Mies van der Rohe's Farnsworth House. Located in the middle of the Mata Atlântica, in Rio de Janeiro's Barra da Tijuca, the building has a rectangle-shaped symmetric plan. The bedrooms are located in the rectangle's extremities. The living room is placed in the middle, and its layout and transparency give it a feel of a veranda, from which the building gets its name: Casa Varanda. A skylight stretches lengthwise through the entire house, illuminating all its spaces.

01 Interior **02** General view **03** Detail bathroom **04** Kitchen **05** View from garden **06** Floor plan

Photos: Fran Parente

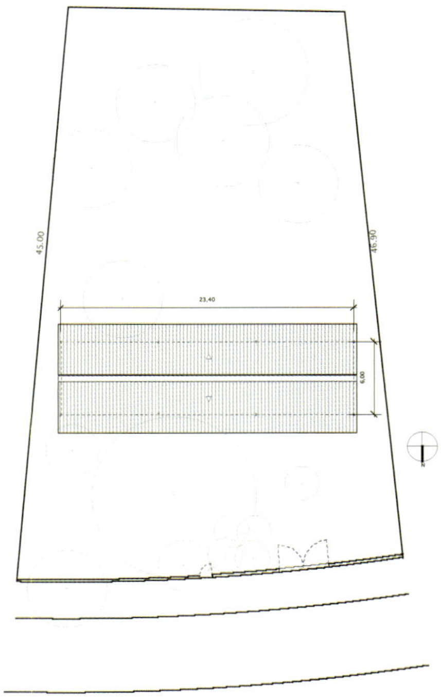

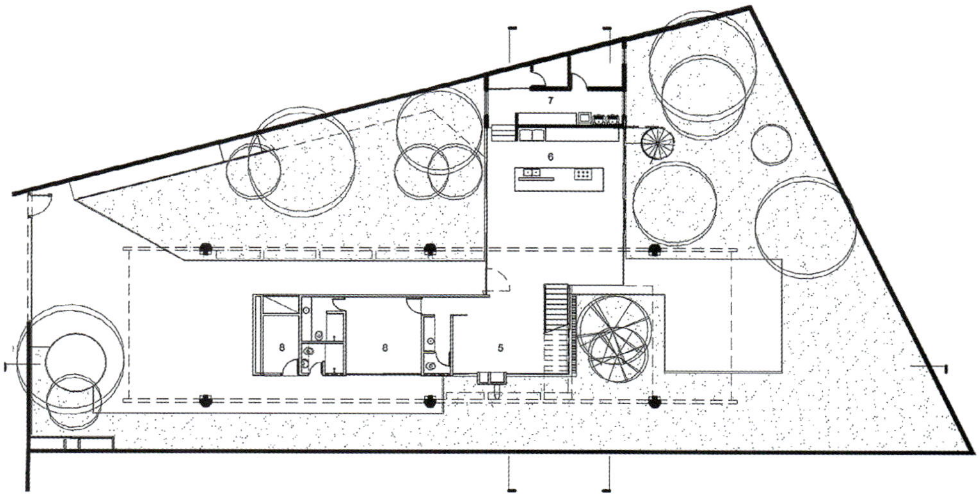

ITANHANGA HOUSE

The project of the residence in Itanhangá, a suburb of Rio de Janeiro and a city which boasts a hot and humid climate, considered the particularity of a land of 800 m² with the presence of considerable trees of significant ages. The solution adopted in the project left with the intention to implant the house in the land with the minimum of possible impact to the existing trees. The trees are of great importance as one may chose to marry in the pantry of the trees, as seen in the past, and so the development is organized in order to coexist an exuberant nature in the tropical climate harmoniously.

01 Floor plan **02** Backyard façade **03** Intersecting volumes **04** View to façade from garden **05** Courtyard **06** Entrance

Photos: Celso Brando

CITY Rio de Janeiro
COUNTRY Brazil
REGION South America
TYPOLOGY Living
COMPLETION 2003
WEBSITE www.piratininga.com.br
ARCHITECTS Piratininga Arquitetos Associados

868

CITY
Rio de Janeiro

COUNTRY
Brazil

REGION
South America

TYPOLOGY
Living

COMPLETION
—

WEBSITE
www.bjaweb.com.br

ARCHITECTS
Bernardes + Jacobsen Arquitetura

HOUSE CG

The narrow site is between two built-up plots, which required that the house have adequate openings to provide light to the interiors. The plan is distributed on three levels with the floor service area floor as a half level, and the main floor (living room and two bedrooms) above the entry; the first floor is one-and-a-half levels above the ground level. Big white panels articulate large spaces. A minimum number of supports create transparency in the level of the living room, integrating the exterior and the interior. The building defines an entrance garden, and the other the main inner private garden contained by its volumes.

01 Exterior view on kitchen **02** Interior view **03** Corridor **04** Façade

Photos: Leonardo Finotti

FORNERIA I RIO

The restaurant's informal atmosphere is totally in tune with the 'carioca' relaxed spirit and way of living. A large rolling door in the front keeps the place widely open onto the street and looking inviting to passers-by, just like an extension of the sidewalk. In the front section, a wood pergola creates a transition area between the hot exterior and the cooled interior, a few tables in a shadowed yet bright space. The long rectangular salon is divided lengthwise by an L-shaped counter, tables to one side and an open kitchen to the other. The menu features a long list of Italian favorites and a classic rock music selection at night.

01 Detail bar **02** Interior **03** View on the bar **04** Front full glazed faade

Photos: Leonardo Finotti

CITY
São Paulo

COUNTRY
Brazil

REGION
South America

TYPOLOGY
Gastronomy

COMPLETION
2001

WEBSITE
www.isayweinfeld.com

ARCHITECTS
Isay Weinfeld Arquitetura

CITY
Rio de Janeiro

COUNTRY
Brazil

REGION
South America

TYPOLOGY
Culture

COMPLETION
—

WEBSITE
—

ARCHITECTS
Oscar Niemeyer

POPULAR THEATER

Constructed in reinforced concrete, the theater is an arched covering that originates in the projections of the building's base. The 3,500 m² structure is distributed on two floors. Audience of up to 400 gathers in the foyer; a helical slope leads visitors up into to the hall. The façades of the building received different solutions – in the area of the foyer, a great glass cloth was adopted; the northwestern façade facing the bay has double brise soleils, while the façade opposite it is finished in yellow tile decorated with the architect's drawings. The space accommodates large and small audiences equally well.

01 Exterior view **02** Rear façade **03** Detail curved wall with mural on titles **04** Interior theater

Photos: Leonardo Finotti

HOTEL FASANO

This design-conscious beachfront hotel creates an orthogonal, regular façade whose height is in accordance of Rio de Janeiro's shade laws. The ordered front offers spectacular views for each unit from glass balconies and ensures their autonomy. Room design in playful but uses a limited palette of materials and color. Rich dark wood tones of native Brazilian wood predominates walls and floors, while mirrors open up the space that would have otherwise been too dark. Round columns support the volume on the ground floor, creating a continuum with the beach and a pleasant shaded atmosphere.

01 Front view by night **02** View to the beach **03** Guest room terrace with beach views **04** Interior guest room

Photos: Leonardo Finnotti

CITY: Rio de Janeiro
COUNTRY: Brazil
REGION: South America
TYPOLOGY: Hospitality
COMPLETION: 2007
WEBSITE: www.philippe-starck.com
ARCHITECTS: Phillip Starck

CITY
Salvador

COUNTRY
Brazil

REGION
South America

TYPOLOGY
Culture

COMPLETION
2006

WEBSITE
www.brasilarquitetura.com

ARCHITECTS
Brasil Arquitectura - Francisco Fanucci and Marcelo Ferraz

RODIN MUSEUM

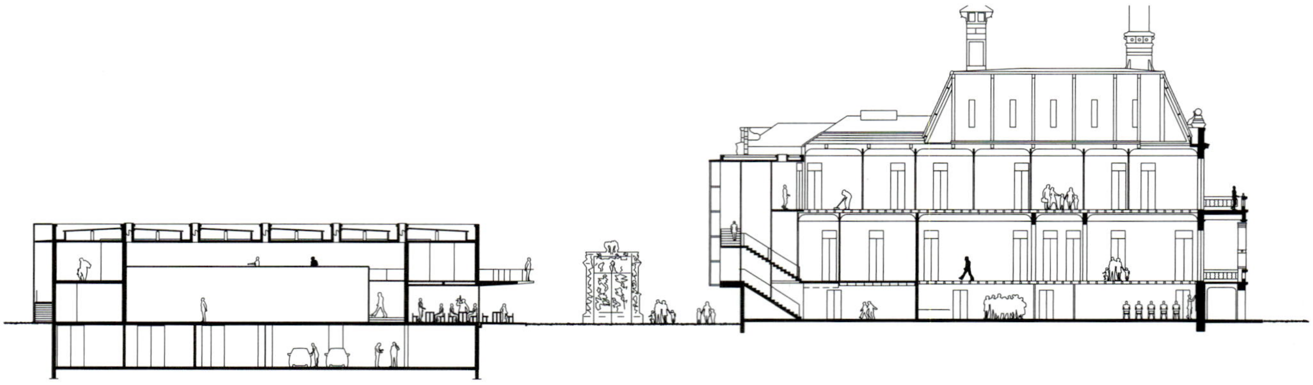

The objective of both projects – the restoration of the existing building and the new interventions – was to provide the necessary infrastructure, adapting the spaces to the activities of the museum. Two buildings, two historical moments that engage the inner garden in a dialogue define a cultural space intended as a meeting point, a place for social interaction that adds value and life to the urban environment.

01 Detail façade, front view **02** Detail façade, rear view
03 Section **04** Connecting bridge

Photos: Nelson Kon

HOUSE IN SÃO PEDRO

The house is set on the rural at the top of the 'Serra de São Pedro'. Its footprint suggests the letter Y, in which two arms form the main body of the house and follow the profile of the terrain. The third element meanwhile, at the lower level, projects itself towards the edge of the rock face embracing the only tree in this area, which was constantly used for pasture. The house converges to a central space where all these three volumes meet – a double height veranda acts as the core of the house, and this certain feature is used as both a living and outdoor eating space.

01 Façade by night **02** View on valley **03** Exterior view **04** Interior **05** Floor plans

Photos: Leonardo Finotti

CITY: São Pedro
COUNTRY: Brazil
REGION: South America
TYPOLOGY: Living
COMPLETION: 2005
WEBSITE: www.oliveirarosa.com
ARCHITECTS: Eduardo de Oliveira Rosa

CITY Sorocaba
COUNTRY Brazil
REGION South America
TYPOLOGY Living
COMPLETION 2004
WEBSITE www.gersoncastelobranco.com.br
ARCHITECTS Gerson Castelo Branco

SOROCABA'S HOUSE

This spacious, light house with a total area of over 1,000 m² on two floors has a captivating modern structure. An iron framework creates cavernous spaces under a sloping roof that is additionally supported by outlying pillars. The first floor has a large living room with other social areas, kitchen, garage and servants' quarters. Four bedrooms with their own baths and terraces occupy the top floor. Interior and exterior walls are white and have a simple geometrical pattern that adds to the sophistication of the design.

01 Front view by night **02** Interior, circular stair **03** Rear view, outdoor pool **04** Floor plan **05** Interior view

Photos: João Ribeiro

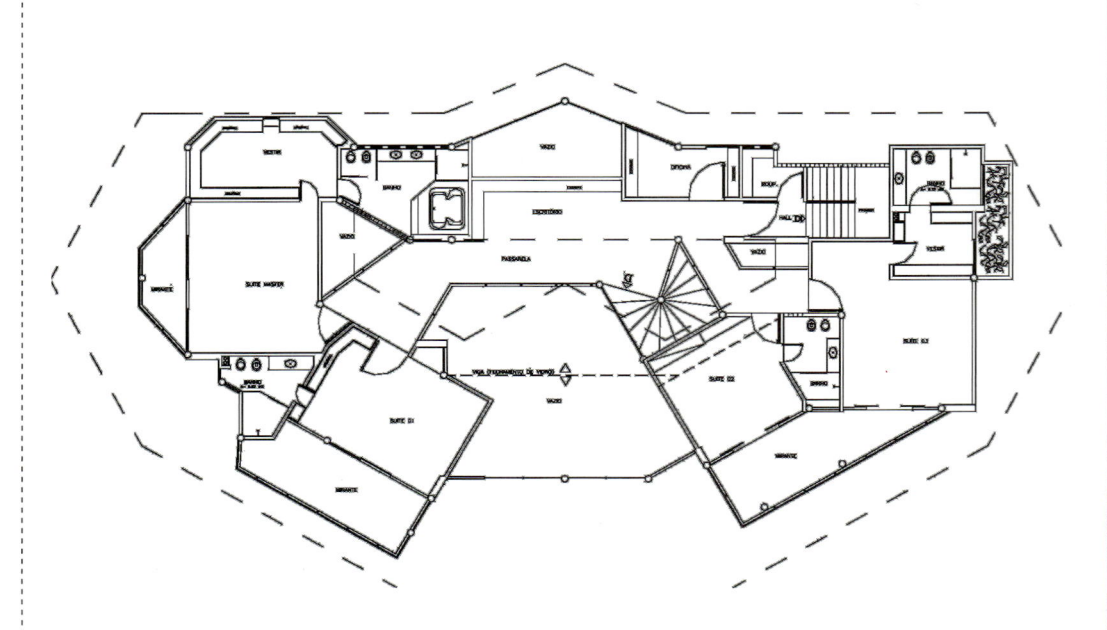

FARM BUIDLING

This 170 m² building is designed for an organic farm in the mountains. On the lower level, the transected long red volume houses a cheese laboratory, the manager's apartment, and a general office, complemented by a dressing room and sauna for guests. In the back, a large space roofed with transparent polycarbonate can accommodate different programs like garage, product processing, meetings, etc. Upstairs, an apartment with a terrific roof terrace with an astonishing view was furnished to accommodate professional and weekend visitors. Simple local materials were chosen to preserve the rural atmosphere.

01 Exterior view **02** Floor plan **03** Entrance **04** Interior view **05** Bedroom

Photos: Francisco Zelesnikar

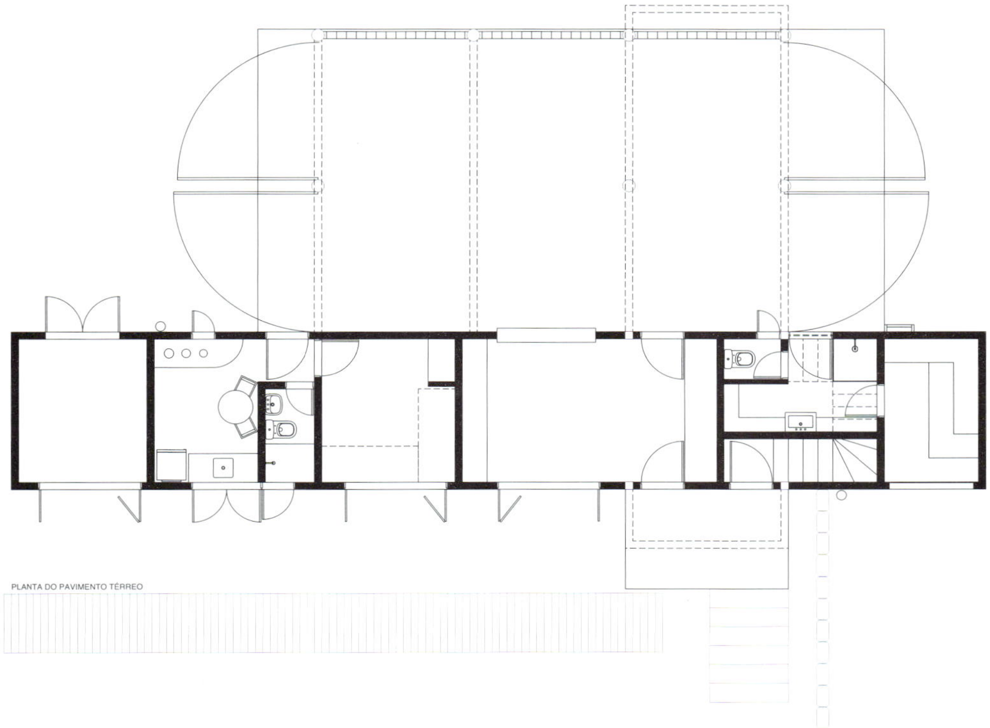

CITY: Sapucaí Mirim
COUNTRY: Brazil
REGION: South America
TYPOLOGY: Hospitality
COMPLETION: 2005
WEBSITE: www.arqdonini.com.br
ARCHITECTS: Donini Arquitetos Associados (ARQDONINI 10x10, Marco Donini / Francisco Zelesnikar)

CITY: Sete Lagoas
COUNTRY: Brazil
REGION: South America
TYPOLOGY: Living
COMPLETION: 2006
WEBSITE: www.arquitetosassociados.arq.br
ARCHITECTS: Arquitetos Associados do Brasil

EC HOUSE

The house is organized around an internal court with an oval swimming pool. All social spaces open out onto the court, and explore the extensive view of the city through a concrete brise-soleil that ensures the pool's privacy by eliminating side views from the street and form a nearby club. The personal spaces, on the other hand, are in communication with a closed garden which reinforces their privacy. All service areas are located on the lower level, beside the public entrance and the garage, taking part of the variation of topography in order to reinforce the elevated pure prism of the main level.

01 Exterior view **02** Interior view on inner court pool **03** Inner courtyard, outdoor pool **05** Entrance area by night

Photos: Courtesy Arquitetos Associados do Brasil

WP HOUSE

This project promotes the integration between built and free open areas through the elimination of residual spaces, assuring total use of the small urban lot, located in front of a small lake. A tripartite linear block built along one of the edges of the site occupies half the land, treating the other half as an extension of the internal spaces. These extensions define the gardens, garage, terrace and patio, with subtle degrees of privacy assured by light variations on topography. This strategy allowed to implant the garage slightly lowered in relation to the main social spaces of the house, and over it, a terrace.

01 Exterior view **02** Entrance **03** Residential building by night **04** Floor plans **05** Detail façade

Photos: Eduardo Eckenfels

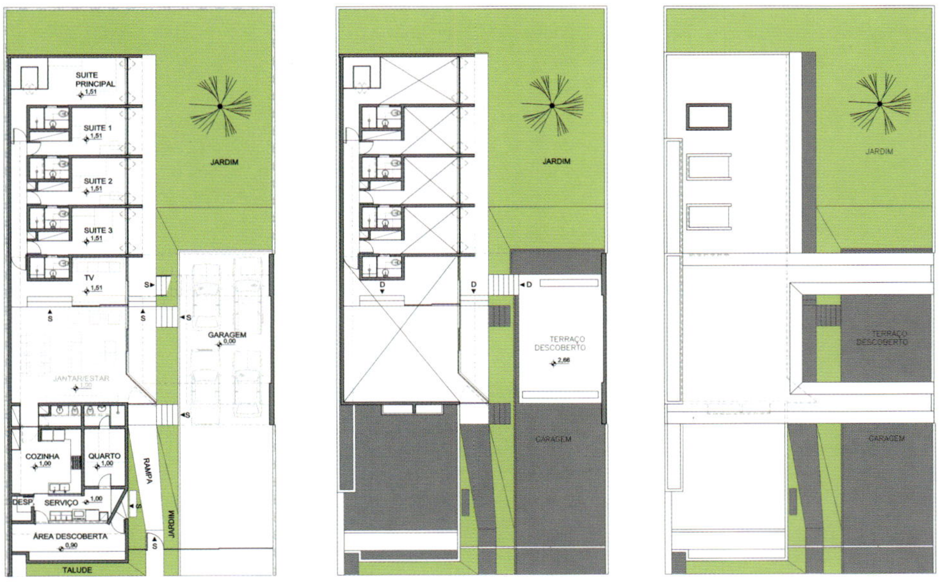

CITY: Sete Lagoas
COUNTRY: Brazil
REGION: South America
TYPOLOGY: Living
COMPLETION: 2007
WEBSITE: www.arquitetosasociados.arq.br
ARCHITECTS: Arquitetos Associados / Alexandre Brasil / Carlos Alberto Maciel

SABINA SCHOOL PARK OF ARTS AND SCIENCE

This project was proposed by Santo André City Hall for the installation of a science museum for children, affiliated with the public schools network. The great pavilion allows other activities, related with art exhibitions and a rich program of other events related to educational diversity. The building lies close to the limits of the perimeter of a large park in way to avoid disturbing the park's other activities. The entire ensemble is situated in a poor neighborhood and means to transform the urban relationship of this site.

01 Exterior view **02** Exterior view by night **03** Interior view **04** Interior with ramps

Photos: Leonardo Finotti

CITY: Santo André
COUNTRY: Brazil
REGION: South America
TYPOLOGY: Education
COMPLETION: 2003
WEBSITE: –
ARCHITECTS: Paulo Mendes da Rocha

EMILIANO (HOTEL)

Emiliano is located on Rua Oscar Friere, the center of Jardins. It was built in the effort to bring a new concept of hospitality to São Paulo, offering guests a pleasant and contemporary ambience. Emiliano is known for its spa: It has 3 cabins equipped for massage programs and a bathing room with a landscape view of the city.

01 Entrance by night **02** Exterior view by night **03** Spa **04** Restaurant

Photos: Gavin Jackson

CITY São Paulo
COUNTRY Brazil
REGION South America
TYPOLOGY 2003
COMPLETION 2003
WEBSITE www.ruyohtake.com.br
ARCHITECTS Ruy Ohtake

CITY São Paulo

COUNTRY Brazil

REGION South America

TYPOLOGY Office

COMPLETION 2005

WEBSITE www.aflaloegasperini.com.br

ARCHITECTS Aflalo & Gasperini Arquitetos

E TOWER

The E-Tower project is an office building with 32 floors, situated among big avenues in São Paulo, Brazil. It was projected as a slender building 148-meters high, becoming the third tallest building of Sao Paulo, and consists of varying floor sizes for the purpose and comfort of attending organizations in the real-estate market. The finishings most used were granites, marbles, curtain walls of anodized aluminum, high performance glasses, and other coverings such as aluminum and wood. Separated by 3 volumes, the tallest has 14 floors with 550 m² finalized with a remarkable crown and helipad.

01 Façade by night **02** General view **03** Floor plan **04** Interior, corridor

Photos: Gal Oppido

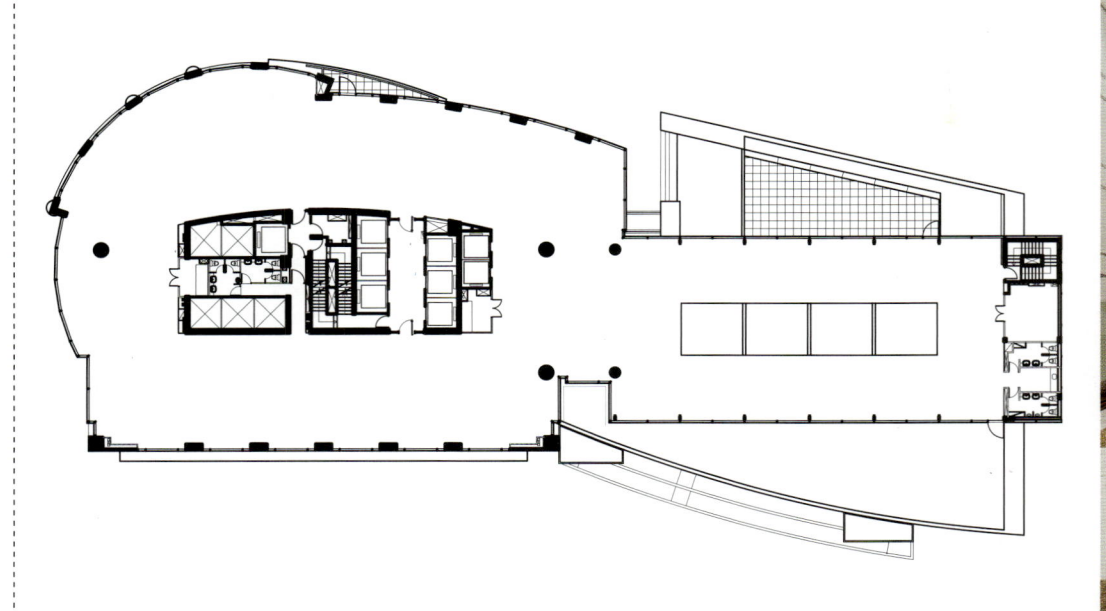

STATIONS FOR THE TRANSPORT OF SÃO PAULO

The design of the project was the subject of an idea competition won by architects Marcelo Barbosa and Jupira Corbucci for the Integrated Transport System of São Paulo in the 2001–2004 administration. Due to the project's constraints, it was proposed that the stations should not include a façade and interference to the neighborhood reduced to a minimum. The portico is designed with two curves in its extremities, creating continuity between floor and roof, and defining the concept of a closed and aerodynamic object. The ceiling is made of metallic plates and received a ceramic basis painting for thermal protection.

01 Curved structure **02** Bus stop **03** View to bus stop **04** Front view **05** Aerial view by night

Photos: Nelson Kon

CITY
São Paulo

COUNTRY
Brazil

REGION
South America

TYPOLOGY
Transportation

COMPLETION
2004

WEBSITE
www.bacco.com.br

ARCHITECTS
Barbosa & Corbucci Arquitetos Associados

CITY São Paulo
COUNTRY Brazil
REGION South America
TYPOLOGY Education
COMPLETION 2005
WEBSITE www.bkweb.com.br
ARCHITECTS biselli + katchborian arquitetos associados

CÁRITAS SCHOOL

This school complex consists of three five-story buildings arranged in a triangle defining the volume and an inner courtyard covered by a translucent roof. With a capacity for 1000 students the school offers 40 classrooms, a library and an auditorium. The variety of the program allows different ceiling heights and a framework composition shown in the façades. The continuous curved slab connects the block of classroom, auditorium and chapel by a marquee. The horizontal connections and the vertical circulation are placed on the vertices of the triangular floor plan.

01 Façade by night **02** Side view **03** Front view **04** Floor plan **05** Interior, translucid roof

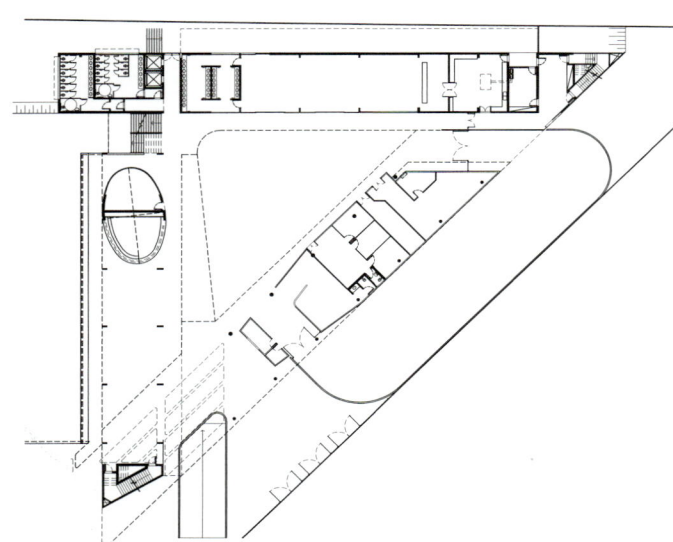

Photos: Nelson Kon

HOUSE IN IPORANGA

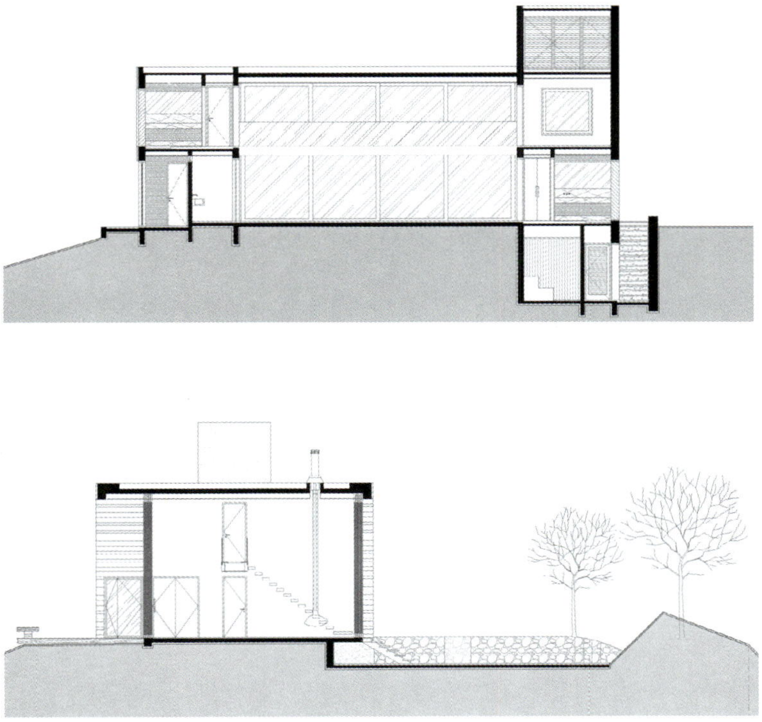

The minimalist house is the architect's residence deep in the forest outside Sao Paolo. Cumaru wood is used as the only color element, and is featured as façade paneling and flooring, contrasting against stark white interior walls. Two cubes are connected by retractable 36-foot glass walls that frame the dining and living area flanked by outdoor terraces. The north cube contains the kitchen and service area along with a separate bedroom and bathroom; the second cube contains the studio and another bedroom and bath. The design aims to create an escape into the Brazilian forest, effortlessly blending the house into its surroundings.

01 Exterior view, terrace 02 Interior view 03 Façade
04 Section 05 Living room, view on garden

Photos: Tuca Reinés

CITY São Paulo
COUNTRY Brazil
REGION South America
TYPOLOGY Living
COMPLETION 2007
WEBSITE www.arthurcasas.com.br
ARCHITECTS Studio Arthur Casas

CITY
São Paulo

COUNTRY
Brazil

REGION
South America

TYPOLOGY
Living

COMPLETION
2005

WEBSITE
www.arthurcasas.com.br

ARCHITECTS
Studio Arthur Casas

W. K. PRIVATE RESIDENCE
ALPHAVILLE

The master line for the Alphaville project intended to construct a home for a middle aged lady who has married and divorced sons with numerous grandchildren, with the purpose being to create a house that features elements of of pleasure and entertaininment for family and friends. The house is fully integrated, rather than being compartmentalized with wide spaces, and is never obsolete. Extensive transparency enhancing the landscape is visibly included, while an enormous automatic glass door is provided integrating the garden and the living room to the project, giving the home a special personality.

01 Interior view **02** Front elevation **03** Stairs **04** Outdoor dining space

Photos: Leonardo Finotti

RESTORING AND RENOVATION PROJECT OF IBIRAPUERA´S PLANETARIUM

The restoring and renovation works in 2004 of the planetary in Ibirapuera Park in São Paulo, BR, was part of the celebration of the 450th anniversary of the city of São Paulo, as well as the 50th anniversary of the Park. Ibirapuera Park and its buildings were built in the beginning of the 50's and are considered a landmark of Brazilian Modern Architecture in São Paulo. The building and its synthetic lines fit perfectly to the concepts of Ibirapuera Park, which is part of the Astrophysics School. The mezzanine was designed for exhibitions and events, while service and administration facilities are located on the ground floor.

01 General view 02 Interior 03 Joined situation, intervention 04 Entrance 05 Mezzanine

Photos: Nelson Toledo

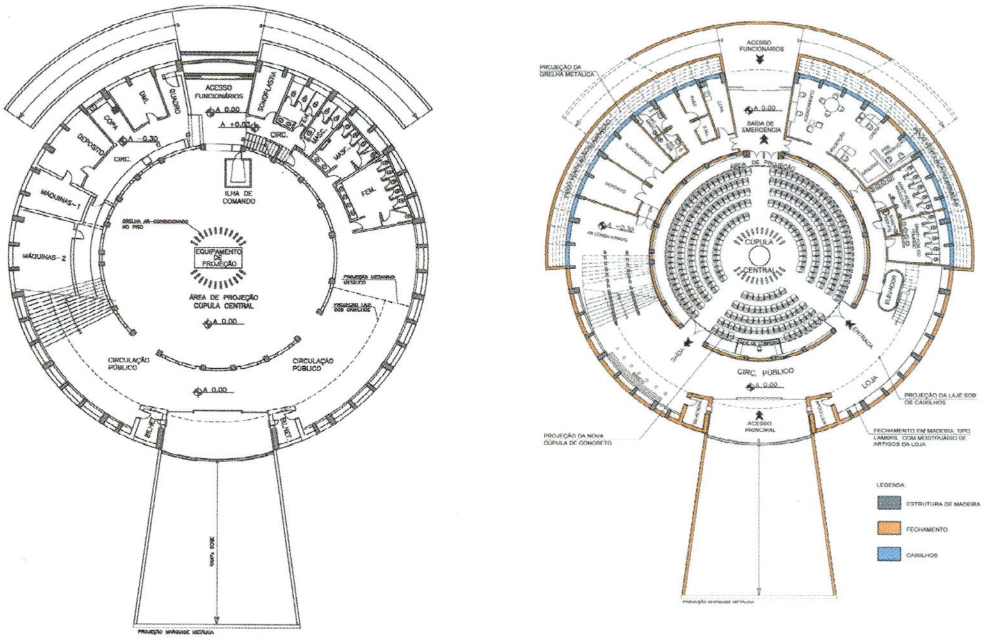

CITY São Paulo
COUNTRY Brazil
REGION South America
TYPOLOGY Culture
COMPLETION 2006
WEBSITE www.pparquitetura.com.br
ARCHITECTS Paulo Faccio, Pedro Dias, Luis Magnani

886

CITY
São Paulo

COUNTRY
Brazil

REGION
South America

TYPOLOGY
Office

COMPLETION
2003

WEBSITE
www.fgmf.com.br

ARCHITECTS
Forte, Gimenes & Marcondes Ferraz

KAZE MOOCA

This two-story building takes advantage of constant natural lighting and has an efficient natural cooling system. Facing north, which is equivalent to southern orientation in the northern hemisphere, the façade receives constant Brazilian sun. For this reason, the building is 'dressed' in continuous steel crating which provides shade to a strip of garden that separates the crating from the glass curtain façade. Trapped in the interstitial space, this plant-cooled air eliminates the need for air conditioning. The Cor-ten steel structure is supported by only one pair of pillars on one side, which frees up space for underground parking.

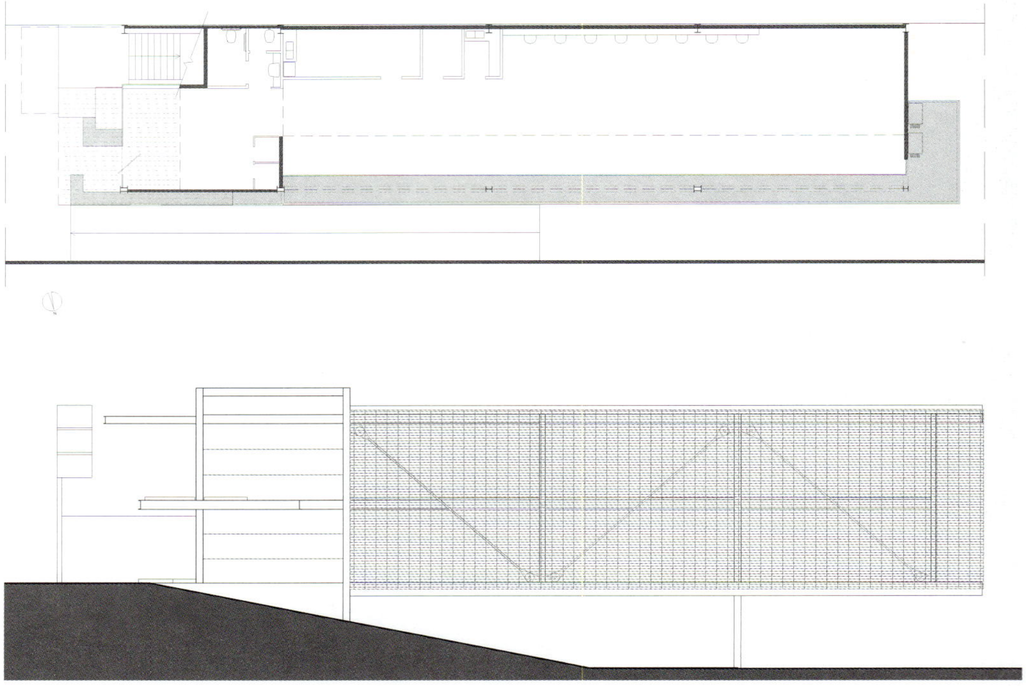

01 Entrance **02** Interior **03** Detail staircase **04** Detail façade
05 Floor plan and elevation

Photos: Marcelo Scandarolli

LLUSSÁ MARCENARIA

Located in a traditional neighborhood, the new store effectively stands out in contrast to the old two-storey houses that flank it. The design of the wooden furniture showroom wanted to counterpoint the objects' material with their setting. The light-flooded store features glass, steel, prefab slabs, polished concrete floors and industrial panels; the interior is dominated by the exhibited compact wooden objects. Two levels of displays are connected by a flight of stairs. The upper level is shaped like a glass box that protrudes to the front, and is suspended from a cantilever in an eye-catching way.

01 Front elevation by night **02** Interior view **03** General view **04** Detail façade

Photos: Nelson Kon

CITY
São Paulo

COUNTRY
Brazil

REGION
South America

TYPOLOGY
Retail

COMPLETION
2003

WEBSITE
www.frentes.com.br
www.llussa.com.br

ARCHITECTS
José Alves (Frentes Arquitetura) and Julianaa Llussa (Llussá Marcenaria)

CITY São Paulo

COUNTRY Brazil

REGION South America

TYPOLOGY Commercial

COMPLETION 2007

WEBSITE www.isayweinfeld.com

ARCHITECTS Isay Weinfeld Arquitetura

LIVRARIA DA VILA

The inventive and well-thought-out design has made the new Livraria da Vila bookshop in the Jardins district one of the most popular relaxation spots in São Paulo. The interconnected three-storey interior is designed entirely around the books, with each floor devoted to a different genre. Low-ceilinged spaces, dark tones, soft lighting, vintage furniture and, most importantly, row upon row of full-height shelves create a warm and inviting atmosphere. The store features an unexpected surprise – custom-designed revolving doors with glass bookshelves, which are sure to get the attention of passers-by.

01 View from the street **02** Front elevation **03** Interior view, stairs **04** Floor plans

Photos: Leonardo Finotti

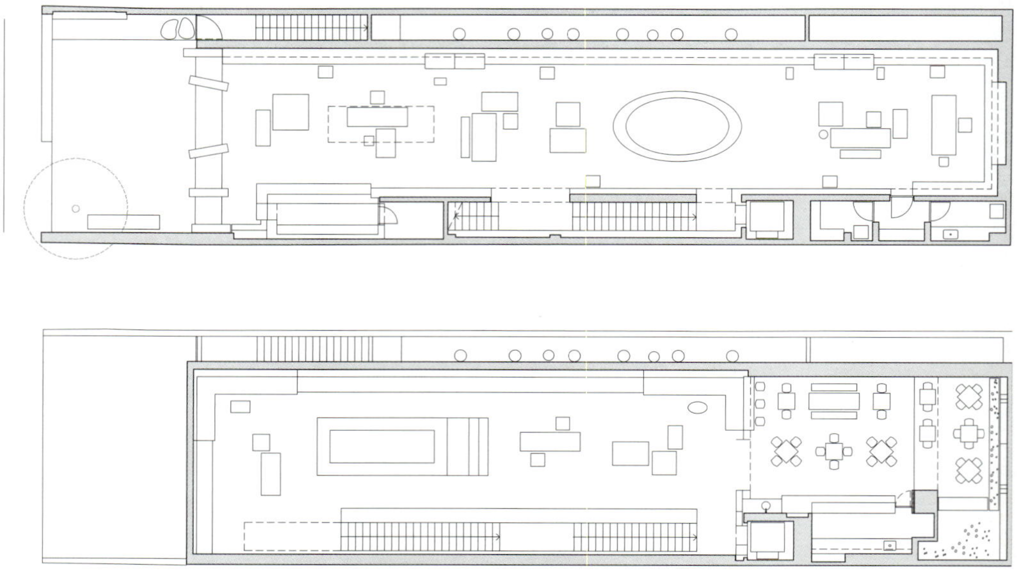

MIRINDIBA'S HOUSE

The house is the alignment of design, of exhaustingly elaborated details, and of execution. Cleanliness and organization of the project are evident in its completion, where the workmanship, meticulous, handicraft labor, gives weight, form and color to the project. At the entrance, a small atrium links the spaces together with a path to the dining room and kitchen. On the top floor, two large wooden lathe doors open onto a deck displaying a beautiful view of the city on one side and the garden on the other. A wooden floor, a reflecting pool and minimalist vegetation structure the garden.

01 Exterior view by night **02** Dining room **03** Detail window **04** Sections

Photos: Nelson Kon

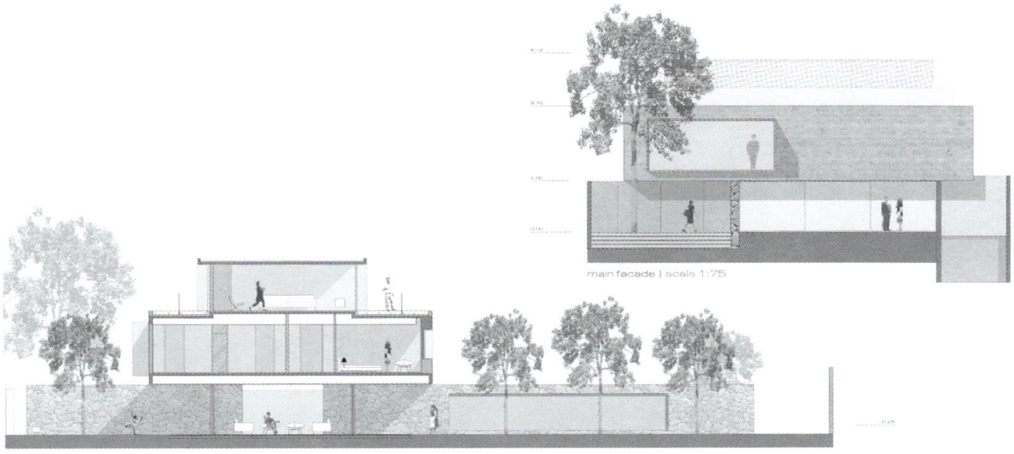

CITY
São Paulo

COUNTRY
Brazil

REGION
South America

TYPOLOGY
Living

COMPLETION
2006

WEBSITE
www.marciokogan.com.br

ARCHITECTS
Marcio Kogan

BERÇÁRIO PRIMETIME

The project aims to incorporate the specifics of a nursery program while seeking creative space solutions. Circulation is achieved using ramps and child-friendly materials such as soft flooring, and focuses on operational ergonometry to create a safe and comfortable environment. The technical team followed the same orientation, offering optimal solutions for the best air and water quality, floor heating and balanced lighting. The landscaping was equally conceived to guarantee safe interaction among children. In addition to using natural materials, colors yellow, orange and red were selected to create a stimulating atmosphere.

01 General view by night **02** Façade **03** Front view by night **04** Facade detail by night **05** Elevations

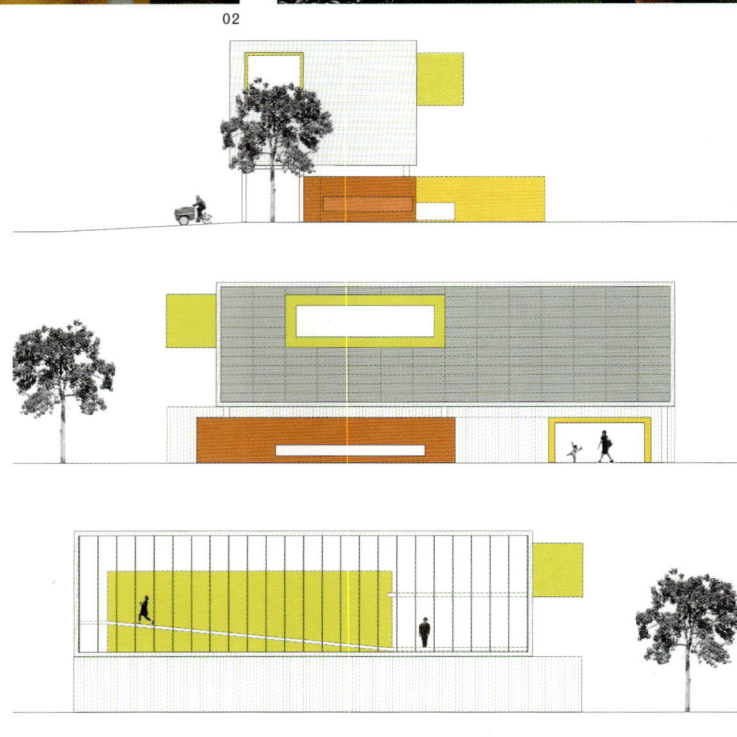

Photos: Nelson Kon

CITY São Paulo
COUNTRY Brazil
REGION South America
TYPOLOGY Education
COMPLETION 2007
WEBSITE www.marciokogan.com.br
ARCHITECTS Marcio Kogan + Lair Reis

CASA BOLA

This is an 8:10 scale mock-up of an LHS (Longo Housing System) built on top of the architect's former house/studio. A spherical plug-in module is attached to the tall mega-structures, or the buildings formed by free-standing apartments. A second full-scale mock-up was built also in Sao Paulo, although no LHS building was raised up to now.

01 Aerial view 02 Entrance 03 Dining room 04 Resting place 05 Section

Photos: Leonardo Finotti

CITY	São Paulo
COUNTRY	Brazil
REGION	South America
TYPOLOGY	Living
COMPLETION	2005
WEBSITE	www.eduardolongo.com
ARCHITECTS	Eduardo Longo

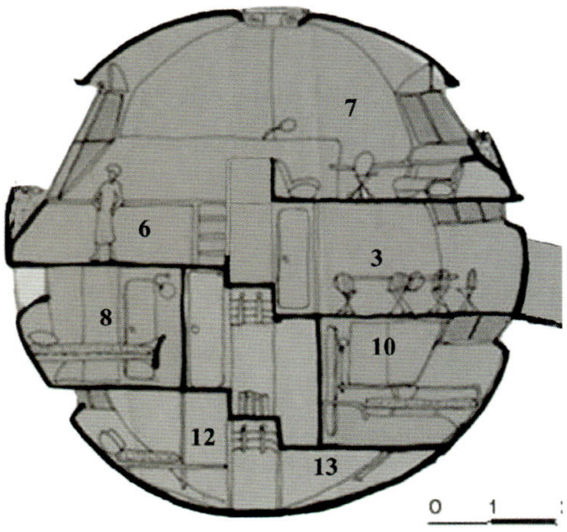

CITY
São Paulo

COUNTRY
Brazil

REGION
South America

TYPOLOGY
Living

COMPLETION
2005

WEBSITE
www.simonemantovani.com.br

ARCHITECTS
architect Simone Mantovani/
Simone Mantovani Arquitetura

FKL HOUSE

The project has been developed from a large internal garden with decks and a swimming pool 25-meters long, integrated to the house blocks through glass and aluminum panels, providing interior light, and favoring the union between interior end exterior. The façade has the same minimalist concept as the whole house, in overlapped blocks, with different finishing materials and textures with monumental dimensions, without any visible openings, providing privacy to the house interior. The contrast between black and white, light and shadow, is very evident and gives more value to the external garden.

01 Exterior view by night **02** Hallway **03** First Floor, working space **04** View from garden **05** Detail façade

Photos: Tuca Reines

ESTUDIO LEME

The Studio Leme is conformed by coverings closing its extremities. These closings are the only additions to the old locksmith shop that existed in the place beyond the spiraled stairs. For the association of two types of wavy panels, one in white poly-carbon and another one in perforated metallic plate, it was possible to get a luminous interior, protected for these membranes. The remains of the intervention summarize the withdrawal of all elements, with the rearrangement of beams and roofing tiles that already existed there. The Studio lodges visiting artists in residence and serves as a production space as well.

01 Translucent façade **02** Exterior view by night **03** Interior, spiral stair **04** Front view

Photos: Leonardo Finotti

CITY São Paulo
COUNTRY Brazil
REGION South America
TYPOLOGY Office / Studio
COMPLETION 2006
WEBSITE www.metroo.com.br
ARCHITECTS metro arquitetos associados

VILA ROMANA RESIDENCE

The design of the Vila Romana Residence is derived from the twin imperatives of topography and usage. It is situated on a corner plot with views of the town's principal valley with a drop of 10 meters; the building houses not only the residence but also the working studio of the artist owner. The strategy adopted was to divide the building into two autonomous blocks. The studio is in contact with the terrain, partly embedded in the hill. Suspended above the terrain is the residence itself, open to the views that surround it. A large veranda has been created between the two volumes and the roof was defined as an unexpected sky deck.

01 View from southeast 02 Longitudinal and cross section 03 Interior view 04 South view of the building 05 View on valley from roof terrace

Photos: Nelson Kon

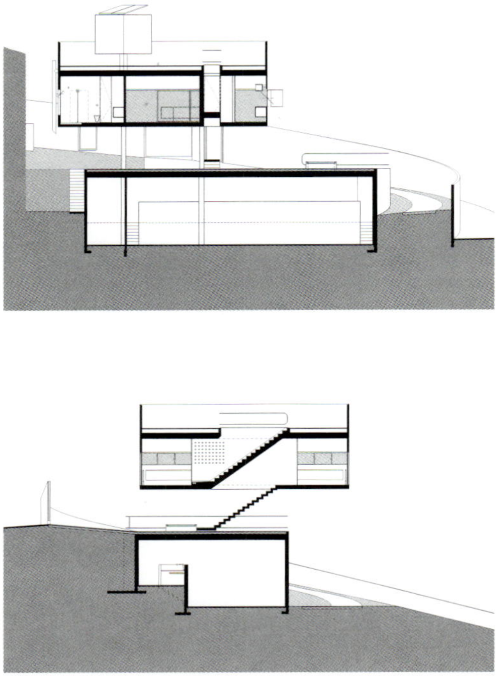

CITY
São Paulo

COUNTRY
Brazil

REGION
South America

TYPOLOGY
Living

COMPLETION
2006

WEBSITE
www.mmbb.com.br

ARCHITECTS
MMBB

HOUSE AT VILA ZELINA

Built in Vila Zelina, a residential district in east São Paulo, this project had been commissioned by a young couple with two small kids. The clients required the creation of a veranda opening to the garden, used for entertaining guests and as a space for kids to play. The long and narrow plot led to a linear distribution of the program, with its openings facing north in order to provide better lighting and ventilation for every room. The top floor includes intimate features such as bedrooms, bathrooms and a studio. The staircase is lit and ventilated from above, flooding the house with natural light and fresh air.

01 Detail façade 02 Entrance 03 Interior view 04 View on veranda 05 Floor plans

Photos: Nelson Kon

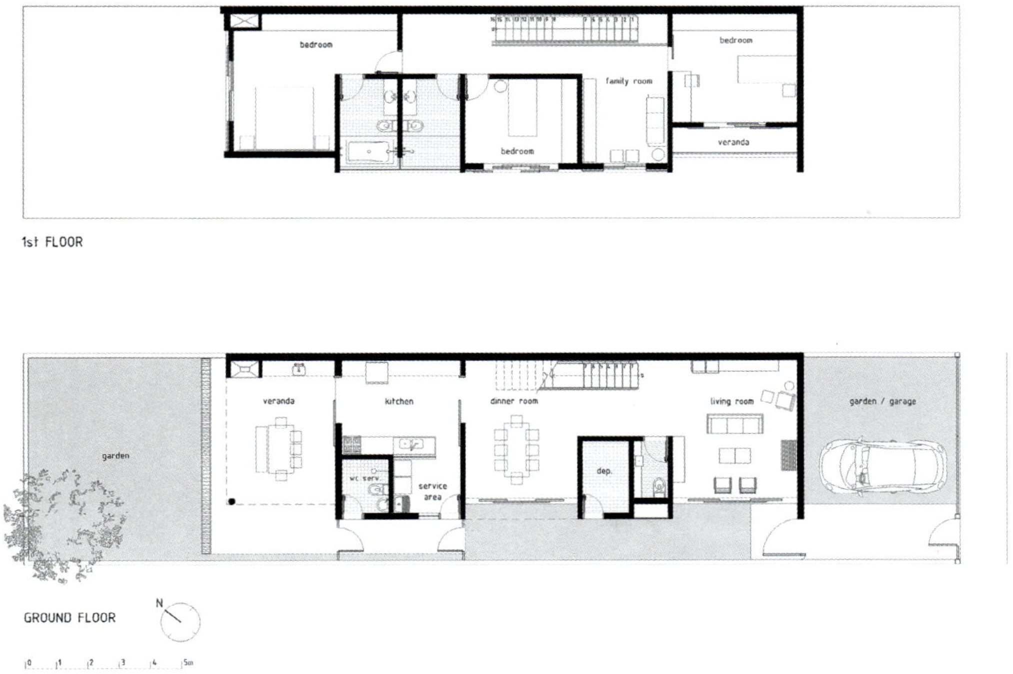

CITY
São Paulo

COUNTRY
Brazil

REGION
South America

TYPOLOGY
Living

COMPLETION
2005

WEBSITE
www.nave.arq.br

ARCHITECTS
Nave Arquitetos Associados

CITY São Paulo

COUNTRY Brazil

REGION South America

TYPOLOGY Culture

COMPLETION –

WEBSITE –

ARCHITECTS Oscar Niemeyer

IBIRAPUERA AUDITORIUM

The auditorium's stand-out form and resolution of mass set it apart from other concert venues. Resolved as a single block with a trapezoidal plan and a triangular section, the building is executed in white reinforced concrete, similarly to other work by the architect. The foyer, audience and stage are arranged as three consecutive sections. A marquee of red-colored metal extends over the main entrance, giving the building an unmistakable identity, setting it apart from other buildings in the surrounding Ibirapuera park. This feature of the building also acts as its logo, branding the auditorium Lebareda, Portuguese for 'flame.'

01 Front façade **02** Elevation **03** Interior view, foyer

Photos: Leonardo Finotti, Nelson Kon (01)

YOUNG & RUBICAM

In a region undergoing great transformation, an abandoned building was invaded and looted. The architects freed selected structural lines of the building with the strategy to clean and reveal. The introduction of translucent, colorful glass volumes placed inside and on the terrace and interconnected vertically through a central slit lights up the interior. Glass volumes cross the building vertically and bring natural light into the central square, allowing the integration of all floors. A red volume crosses the building, creating a 12 meter-high space that accommodates the central square for public activities.

01 General view **02** Interior view **03** View on the ground floor **04** First floor plan **05** Ground floor, detail

Photos: Nelson Kon

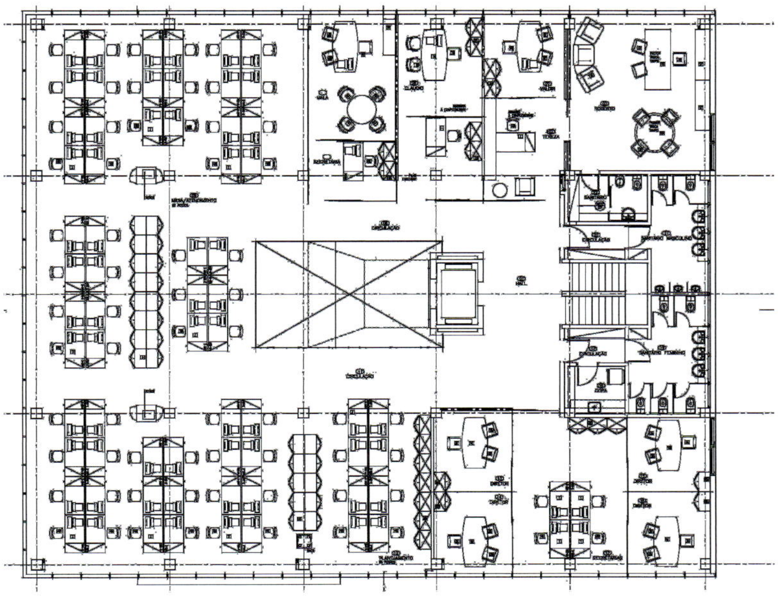

CITY São Paulo
COUNTRY Brazil
REGION South America
TYPOLOGY Office
COMPLETION 2004
WEBSITE www.npc-arq.com.br
ARCHITECTS NPC Grupo Arquitetura (Nucci, Pietraroia & Camargo)

MM HOUSE

The program of this house in São Paulo is distributed over 4 floors. What sets the house apart is that its appearance never seems closed-off or abandoned. Along the right façade, a long and narrow swimming pool stretches to the back wall of the plot while the large living/dining room opens with its entire width onto the terrace. Another special feature is the completely glazed volume on the first floor, enveloping the staircase, a bedroom and a bathroom. This solution was inspired by the client's wish to be able to come back to a lively place, which gives an impression of having lights on and people inside at any time.

01 View from northeast **02** View from the street **03** View on veranda **04** Floor plan **05** Interior view

Photos: Courtesy Domingos Pascali & Gisela Zilberman

CITY São Paulo
COUNTRY Brazil
REGION South America
TYPOLOGY Living
COMPLETION 2006
WEBSITE -
ARCHITECTS Domingos Pascali & Gisela Zilberman

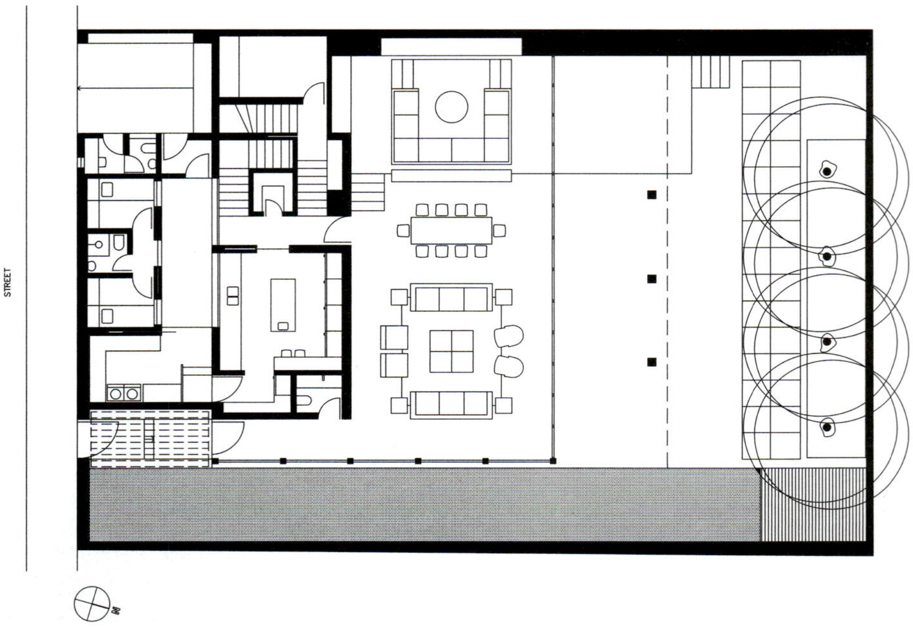

LAW FIRM

The legal firm headquarters in São Paulo designed by the architects Athie/Wohnharth and Reinach/Mendonça are characterized by a well that was created by the architects between three of the building's floors, and which are interconnected by a large glass-and-steel staircase. The reception area and meeting rooms are located on the middle floor; a beautiful, open-plan library occupies the lower floor while the cafeteria welcomes the building's employees on the upper level.

01 View into ground floor 02 Glass staircase 03 Staircase 04 Interior 05 Detail registration desk

Photos: Patricia Cardoso, Andrés Otero (01)

CITY São Paulo
COUNTRY Brazil
REGION South America
TYPOLOGY Office
COMPLETION 2007
WEBSITE www.rmaa.com.br
ARCHITECTS Henrique Reinach e Maurício Mendonça

CITY
São Paulo

COUNTRY
Brazil

REGION
South America

TYPOLOGY
Gastronomy

COMPLETION
2004

WEBSITE
www.rosenbaum.com.br

ARCHITECTS
Rosenbaum Design (architecture) / EPWWW (Graphic Design)

SHIMO RESTAURANTE

Inspired in the Shimokitazawa atmosphere, a bohemian location for students and artists in Tokyo, the Shimo is like a box of sensations caused by impacts and contrasts: the access through a steel walkway, the 11-meter vertical height, the collective table, the low armchairs, the strong colors and the fluorescent pink tunnel, the huge neon of the name sign. In this environment, everything is vibrant and nothing is impersonal.

01 Interior **02** Dining area **03** Section **04** Exterior view by night

Photos: Courtesy Rosenbaum Design

CASA ZULEIKA

The house is a private residence located in a quiet neighborhood of Sao Paolo. Both the façade and the interior layout feature predominantly curved lines and whimsical cut-outs. Cast-on-site concrete was used for load-carrying elements. Irregular perforations are playfully arranged on the otherwise closed-off main front is clad in local wood. Exterior terraces and the tropical garden integrate with the house via the glass curtain façade facing the back. The built-in furniture designed by the architect is in dialog with the structure, some of it also cast in concrete.

01 View from garden into interior **02** Front façade **03** View from stairs **04** Interior

Photos: Leonardo Finotti

CITY São Paulo
COUNTRY Brazil
REGION South America
TYPOLOGY Living
COMPLETION 2005
WEBSITE www.ruyohtake.com.br
ARCHITECTS Ruy Ohtake

CITY
São Paulo

COUNTRY
Brazil

REGION
South America

TYPOLOGY
Education

COMPLETION
2006

WEBSITE
www.spadoni.com.br

ARCHITECTS
Spadoni & Associados Arquitetura

MACKENZIE UNIVERSITY BUILDING

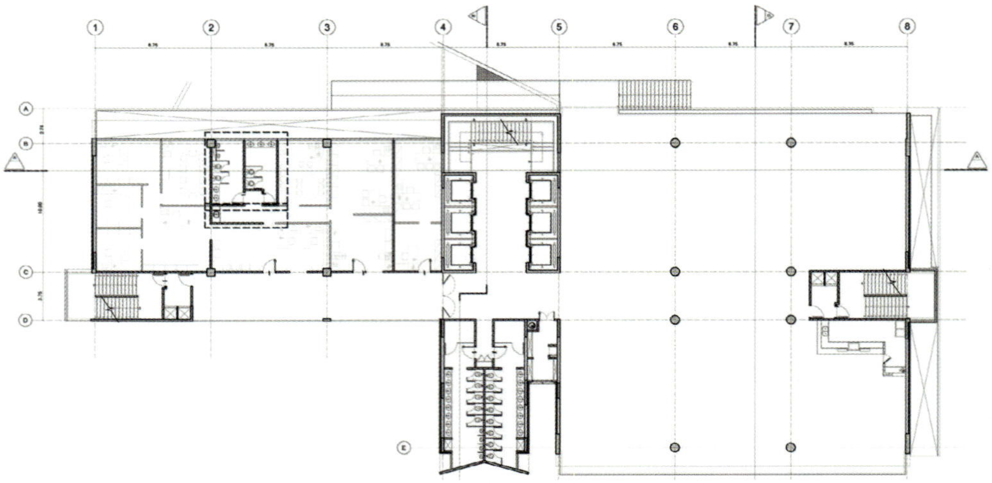

This building is the first project realized within the master plan developed by this architectural office for the remodeling of the Mackenzie University urban campus. The volume houses academic activities: classrooms, libraries, a sports center and administrative areas. The project is highlighted by its subtle integration with the dense set of existing buildings on campus, resolved by the creation of squares around it. Designed entirely in "in situ" concrete, the building reflects a tradition of Brazilian architecture, and suports a galvanized steel grid envelope.

01 Detail façade 02 Entrance area 03 Façade 04 Floor plan
05 Exterior view

Photos: Nelson Kon

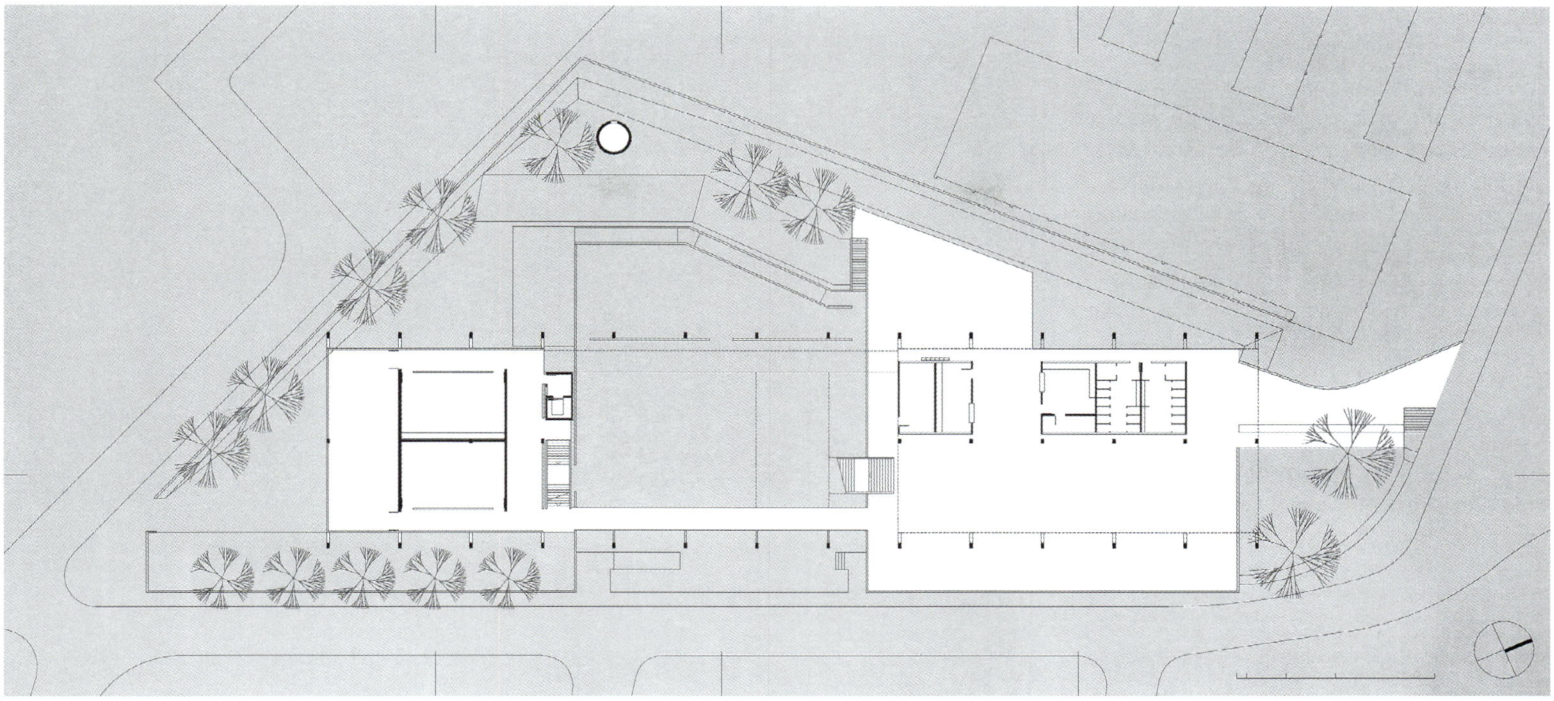

PUBLIC SCHOOL EE JARDIM ATALIBA LEONEL

The project for this secondary school for 650 students is part of a group of projects developed by the Foundation for the Development of Education (FDE) to define a standard school format and experiment with the application of a concrete prefabricated structural system. The dramatic topography where the school was built allowed a panoramically view of the whole neighborhood, especially to the opposite side of the valley, which is filled with preserved Atlantic nature. Three plateaus define clusters for administration, alumni access and the sport square, while the 15 classrooms are disposed in a unique elevated level.

01 Floor plan **02** Exterior view by night **03** Artwork panels **04** Detail sport area

Photos: Nelson Kon

CITY São Paulo
COUNTRY Brazil
REGION South America
TYPOLOGY Education
COMPLETION 2006
WEBSITE www.spbr.arq.br
ARCHITECTS Alvaro Puntoni and a Angelo Bucci / SPBR architects

LODUCCA

The brise-soleil figures – a traditional component of tropical architecture – is the center of this project. Located in an old neighborhood in São Paulo, the building emerges as a strong and organic 'incarnation' of the urban and natural aggressions (noise, solar radiation) from this tropical city and takes form by absorbing them. An organic and fluid brise-soleil membrane deforms itself under the effect of the sound waves, creating several internal light and temperature filters. All of the three floors are structured by the strong vertical element of the concrete staircase, while the back façade opens up to a tropical beach.

01 Frontal façade view **02** Transversal section **03** Frontal desk **04** Back façade view **05** Interior **06** Staircase to roof terrace

Photos: Fran Parente, Beto Consorte (03), Leonardo Finotti (05)

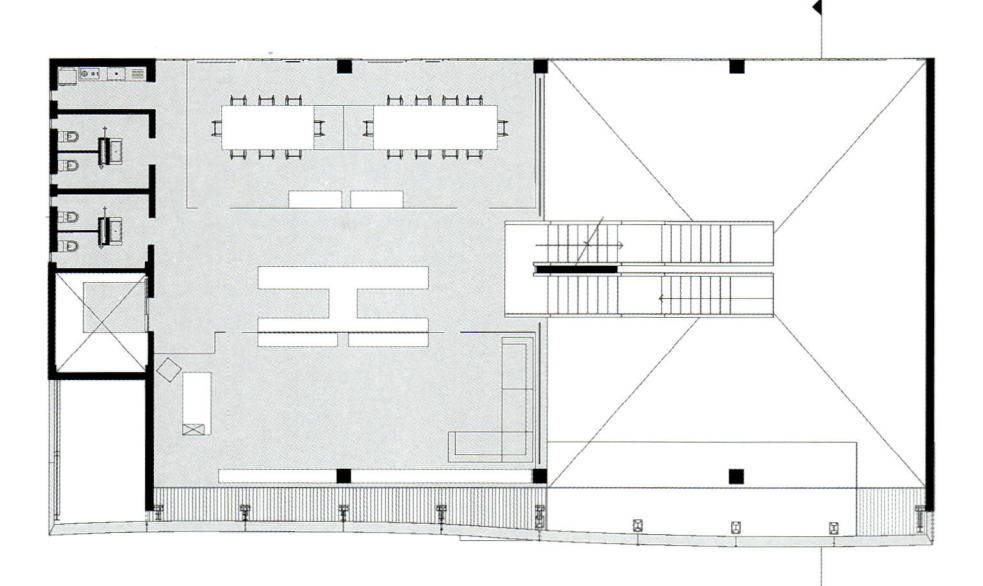

CITY São Paulo
COUNTRY Brazil
REGION South America
TYPOLOGY Commercial
COMPLETION 2007
WEBSITE www.triptyque.com
ARCHITECTS Triptyque (Greg Bousquet, Carolina Bueno, Guillaume Sibaud and Olivier Raffaelli)

HOUSE IN SÃO PAULO

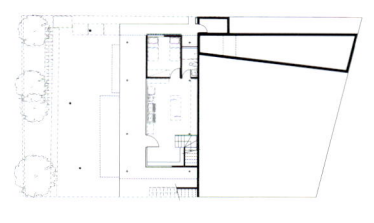

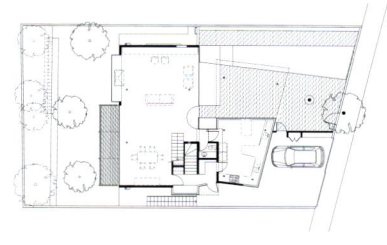

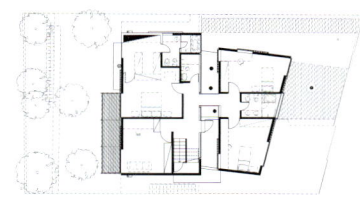

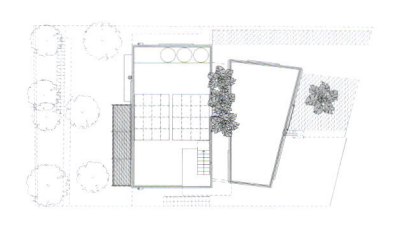

Located on a typical slope of Sao Paulo's landscape, this house is a compact volume with several floors that aims to make the best possible use of the site which presented greater-than-usual legal setbacks. Large existing palm trees were preserved, resulting in two rectangular blocks separated by a gap wide enough for the trees. The two volumes are linked to each other by short passages on each floor. The social area is located on the street level, leaving the services on the bottom floor. The bedrooms are on the upper floor, and the garden is found on the roof.

01 General view **02** Floor plans **03** Section **04** Pool **05** Inner courtyard

Photos: Courtesy André Vainer e Guilherme Paoliello Arquitetos

CITY
São Paulo

COUNTRY
Brazil

REGION
South America

TYPOLOGY
Living

COMPLETION
2003

WEBSITE
www.vainerepaoliello.com.br

ARCHITECTS
André Vainer e Guilherme Paoliello Arquitetos

IBIRAPUERA SPORTS COMPLEX

Constructed in the 1960's and urging renovation to keep with modern standards, this complex is the main sporting complex in the city of São Paulo. As a result of national competition, the project is faced with a challenge: conciliating new pragmatic necessities with the historical buildings and the exiguous expansion spaces. The proposal responds by maintaining the essence of original culture, overhauling existing structures to new sportive facilities and finally by providing identity and hierarchy back to the city. The program's objective is to host international and national prestigious competitions and events of various natures.

01 General view **02** Site plan **03** Interior view

Rendirings: Vigliecca&Assoc.

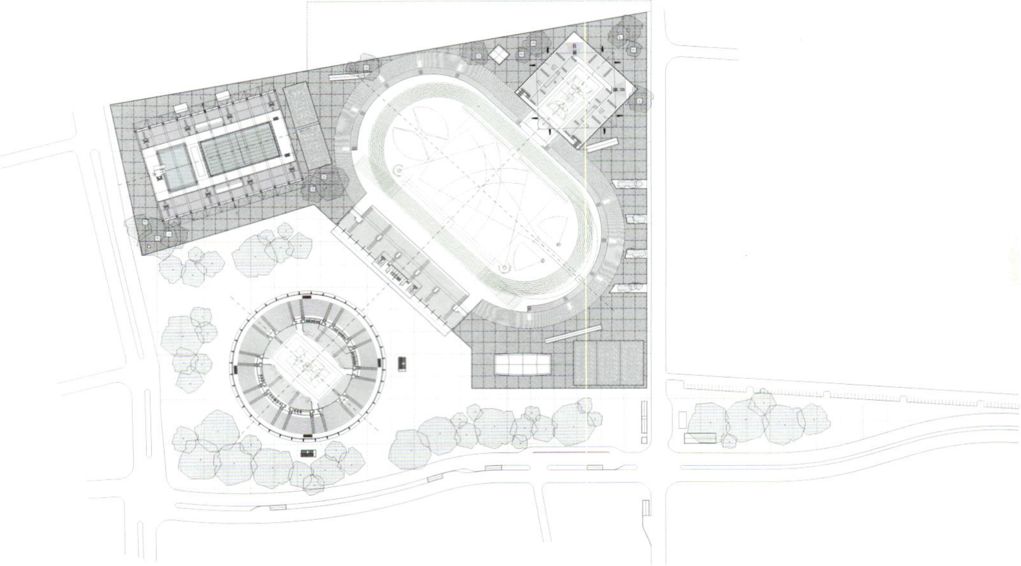

CITY São Paulo
COUNTRY Brazil
REGION South America
TYPOLOGY Leisure
COMPLETION in progress
WEBSITE www.vigliecca.com.br
ARCHITECTS Vigliecca&Assoc.

CASA P

The house was to accommodate a growing family that tired of living in the cramped quarters of an apartment. Social spaces were kept especially open for communal activities and friends; 6 m high ceilings were installed here. Middle levels enabled the block of bedrooms to have a height offering a unified city view. The metallic structure was conceived as porticos with framework built into the bedroom block's walls. The trusses permit light and ventilation to enter the house, and at the same time preserve the intimacy of the inhabitants. Perimeter beams of the upper floor that jut over the back façade serve to support the large face of shutter windows.

01 View to garden, reflecting wall **02** View into interior **03** Skylight **04** Wooden staircase **05** Main entrance

Photos: Leonardo Finotti

CITY: São Paulo
COUNTRY: Brazil
REGION: South America
TYPOLOGY: Living
COMPLETION: -
WEBSITE: www.bjaweb.com.br
ARCHITECTS: Bernardes + Jacobsen Arquitetura

MPM PROPAGANDA

The interior design of the MPM advertising agency, distributed on 3 double floors with mezzanines, is the embodiment of what the customer represents: dynamism, integration and objectivity. While the space is ethereal and has integrated forms, freijó wood panels separate the space, protecting the privacy necessary for each activity. In a minimalist way, the synthesis of finishings and standardization and modulation confer the dimension idea generation to the environment. The utility of the abstractly-formed furniture, also in freijó wood, is disclosed from the relation between itself and the user.

01 Interior view **02** Entrance hall **03** Façade of entrance hall **04** Entrance area

Photos: Leonardo Finotti

CITY: São Paulo
COUNTRY: Brazil
REGION: South America
TYPOLOGY: Office
COMPLETION: 2006
WEBSITE: www.bjaweb.com.br
ARCHITECTS: Bernardes + Jacobsen Arquitetura

CASA VERTICAL

The residence was designed for a single young man who desired a large program to be fit on a small plot. This requirement was resolved by building a house that evolves upwards on "half-levels", easing the climb up and down. Double and single-height spaces are stacked on top and inserted between floors. An indoor garden on the first floor has one tree, which grows vertically "through" the entire house. Although the house appears as a set of closed volumes from the street, each space has a view of exterior gardens and greenery. The roof terrace with all amenities for entertaining guests provides panoramic views of São Paulo.

01 Detail Façade 02 Exterior view 03 Living room 04 Detail outdoor pool and wall

Photos: Leonardo Finotti

CITY: São Paulo
COUNTRY: Brazil
REGION: South America
TYPOLOGY: Living
COMPLETION: –
WEBSITE: www.isayweinfeld.com
ARCHITECTS: Isay Weinfeld Arquitetura

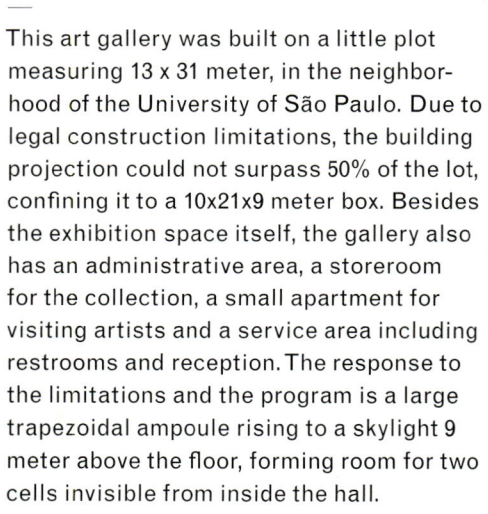

CITY	São Paulo
COUNTRY	Brazil
REGION	South America
TYPOLOGY	Culture
COMPLETION	2004
WEBSITE	–
ARCHITECTS	Paulo Mendes da Rocha

LEME´S GALLERY

This art gallery was built on a little plot measuring 13 x 31 meter, in the neighborhood of the University of São Paulo. Due to legal construction limitations, the building projection could not surpass 50% of the lot, confining it to a 10x21x9 meter box. Besides the exhibition space itself, the gallery also has an administrative area, a storeroom for the collection, a small apartment for visiting artists and a service area including restrooms and reception. The response to the limitations and the program is a large trapezoidal ampoule rising to a skylight 9 meter above the floor, forming room for two cells invisible from inside the hall.

01 Front view from street **02** Gallery space **03** Installation and outdoor area **04** Trapezoidal ampoule

Photos: Leonardo Finotti

PORTUGUESE LANGUAGE MUSEUM

This Museum was built in the existent installations of the administrative sector of the Railing Station of LUZ. The station is an important architectonic and urban building inaugurated in 1901 as the central station of São Paulo City. About 7,500 m² of its area was donated to the Cultural State Secretary in 2003 with the purpose of housing an important public institution – the Museum of Portuguese Language, in partnership with the state government and several enterprises. The main challenge was to provide an adequate relationship of the new program with the extremely high circulation due to adjacent train services.

01 View of entrance area **02** Interior auditorium **03** Interior, interactive totems **04** Interior wall exhibition

Photos: Leonardo Finotti

CITY: São Paulo
COUNTRY: Brazil
REGION: South America
TYPOLOGY: Culture
COMPLETION: 2004
WEBSITE: –
ARCHITECTS: Paulo Mendes da Rocha

CITY
São Paulo

COUNTRY
Brazil

REGION
South America

TYPOLOGY
–

COMPLETION
–

WEBSITE
www.ruyohtake.com.br

ARCHITECTS
Ruy Ohtake

CONDE DE SARZEDAS BUILDING

The 26-floor skyscraper stands as a blue, shining wall of water, a wave about to crash on a tiny 19th Century brick-colored structure in front of it. The listed castle, which now serves as the building's main entrance, was restored in the course of construction, and provides an improbable contrast in scale, material and color. The 11,750 m² undulating glass façade of the main office tower reflects a massive area of sky, proving a backdrop for the intricate structure in front of it. The tower has efficient systems of air circulation and lighting, adapting many modern sustainability standards.

01 Front façade **02** Exterior view by night **03** View towards front façade **04** Aerial view

Photos: Leonardo Finotti

SANTA CATARINA BUILDING

The building in the busy downtown section is an experiment in extreme volumetry using glass façades. The square cross-section measures 32.5 meters on the side and has rounded upper corners and sides. An inner core penetrates the entire length of the 17 floor building. The core is exposed at the level of the sixth floor, with offices measuring only 542 m² in area, or half of the others in the building. The entire volume is supported by four concrete columns 20 meters in height. A common room with 80-person capacity is located on the 18th floor.

01 View from the street **02** Front view **03** View from opposite building

Photos: Leonardo Finotti

CITY São Paulo
COUNTRY Brazil
REGION South America
TYPOLOGY Office
COMPLETION 2007
WEBSITE www.ruyohtake.com.br
ARCHITECTS Ruy Ohtake

EXPRESSO TIRADENTES

This is the city's main bus depot, well-connected by public transit system as well as for pedestrians. The futuristic design is typical of the architect's work, and the strong yellow and blue colors accentuate the desire to transform a mundane public terminal into a transcendental experience. The flattened cylindrical form of the main volume is elevated on stilts above the arrivals and departures area and houses two levels of program inside. The large skylight on the blue roof allows most of the interior space to receive natural light during the day. Two yellow ramps provide pedestrian access.

01 Bird´s eye view **02** Front façade **03** Interior view **04** View from upper platform

Photos: Leonardo Finotti

CITY: São Paulo
COUNTRY: Brazil
REGION: South America
TYPOLOGY: Transportation
COMPLETION: –
WEBSITE: www.ruyohtake.com.br
ARCHITECTS: Ruy Ohtake

SAHY HOUSE

The aim was to build a functional house using a rational construction process that prioritizes speed and low cost. Three modules were linearly arranged as bedrooms and bathrooms, and three other modules for living and service areas. Internal circulation is eliminated, with the function relegated to the external terrace; this optimizes area utilization and prevents space interference. A concrete platform was suspended from the ground to prevent absorption of soil humidity. To mitigate heat, an extended leveled roof corresponding to the plan was designed and "loosely" fitted, creating an open space for air circulation.

01 Sliding door façade with coulorful curtains **02** Extended levelled roof **03** Floor plan **04** External terrace

Photos: Courtesy Nitsche Arquitetos Associados

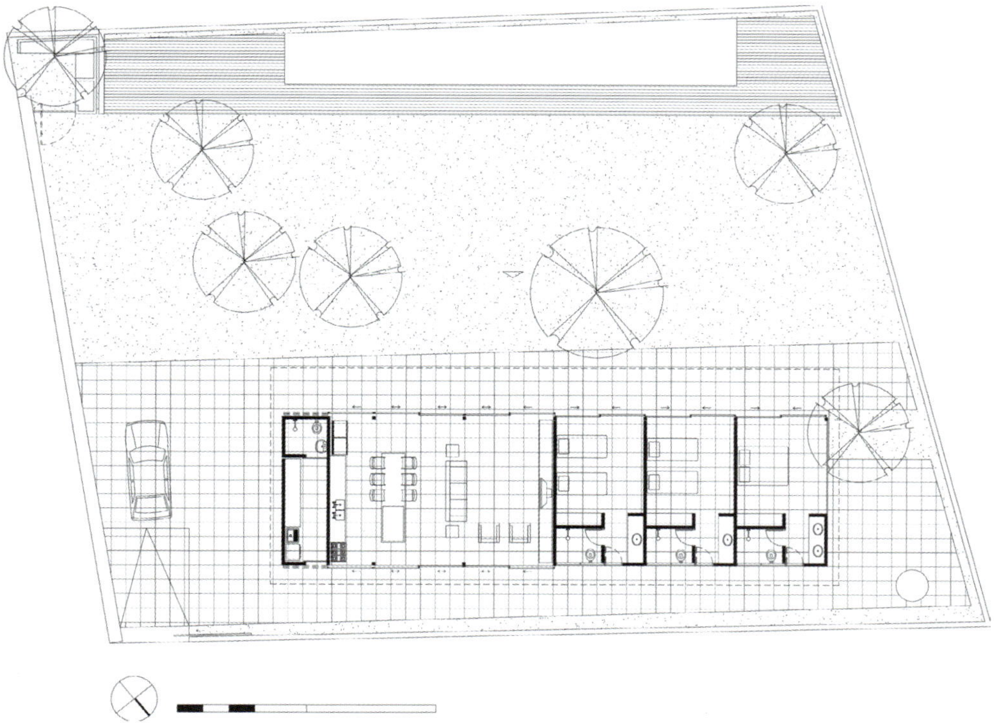

CITY São Sebastiao
COUNTRY Brazil
REGION South America
TYPOLOGY Living
COMPLETION 2002
WEBSITE –
ARCHITECTS Nitsche Arquitetos Associados.

CITY
São Sebastiao

COUNTRY
Brazil

REGION
South America

TYPOLOGY
Living

COMPLETION
2004

WEBSITE
www.arqdonini.com.br

ARCHITECTS
Donini Arquitetos Associados (ARQDONINI 10x10, Marco Donini / Francisco Zelesnikar)

JUNGLE/BEACH HOUSE SERTAO

Surrounded by a beach and waterfalls and almost concealed by the jungle, the location can be described as paradise on earth. The design recently won first prize awarded by "Planeta Casa Eco Awards." A variety of materials were chosen to create a system of pre-fabricated components in order to control waste and prevent damage to the environment. To enclose the iron structure, a "family" of glass and corrugated natural fiber panels and ready-made aluminum windows and doors were used. Few points of land contact add the feeling of flotation to the volume, complementing large amounts of natural light and great views.

01 Rear view **02** Interior view **03** Living room **04** Exterior view **05** Section

Photos: Francisco Zelenikar

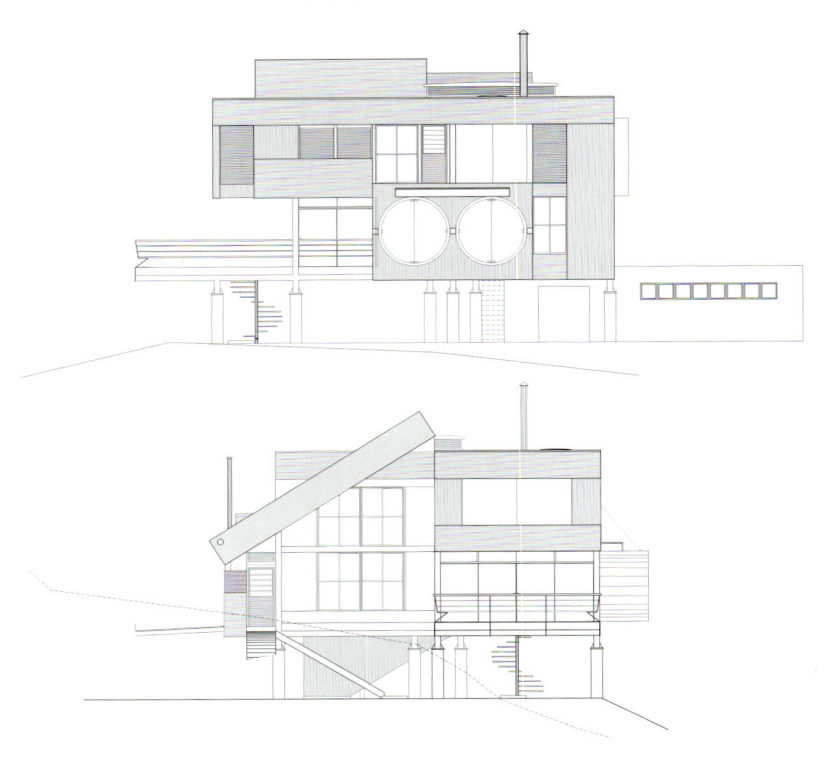

HOUSE OF SAIRAS

An imaginary line extends amid the forest, indicating rhythmic porches in laminated wood. A central void opens itself up as a terrace, linking public and private rooms. The whole space is inserted into a sea breeze-crisscrossed landscape. The central idea of the design lies in the multiple interactions between architecture and landscape, horizon and place, exteriority and intimacy, opacity and transparency, intense sunlight and tropical rain, lightness and consistency of the flight of the birds in the direction of the endless green of the forest. The house is but a point of color in the midst of this infinity.

01 View to deck **02** Exterior view by night **03** Floor plan **04** Detail façade

Photos: Sérgio Guerini

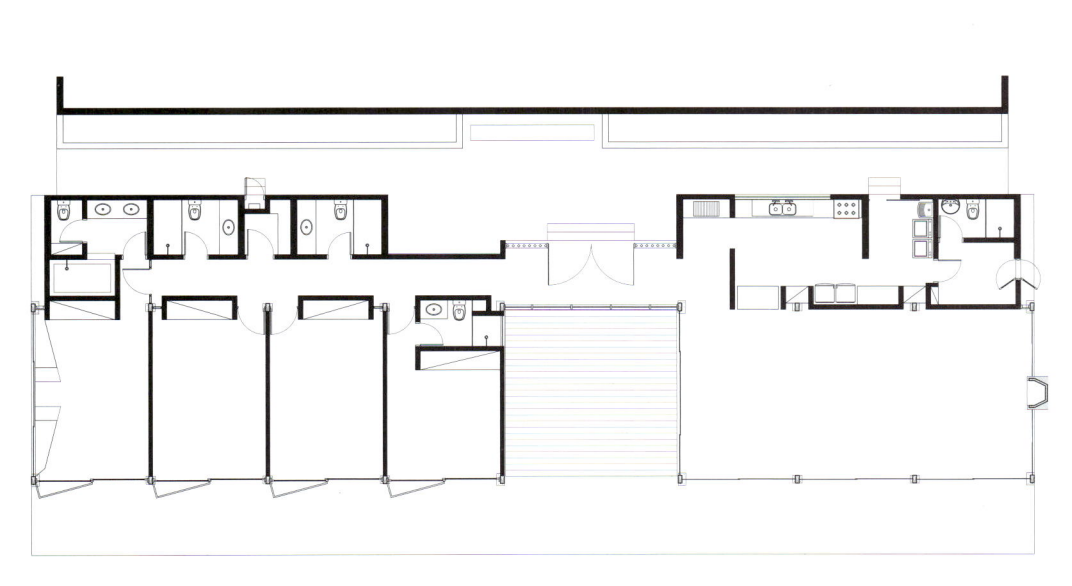

CITY
Ubatuba

COUNTRY
Brazil

REGION
South America

TYPOLOGY
Living

COMPLETION
2005

WEBSITE
www.kruchin.com.br

ARCHITECTS
Kruchin Arquitetura

CITY
Uberlândia

COUNTRY
Brazil

REGION
South America

TYPOLOGY
Living

COMPLETION
—

WEBSITE
—

ARCHITECTS
Finotti Arquitetura

LHF HOUSE

The aim pursued was a new interpretation of Brazilian traditional housing architecture with different materials as well as the integration of generously integrated and transparent spaces. This resulted in a construction of two floors with 400 square metres in a mixed constructive system: steel structure, metallic insulated roof, walls in brick masonry and gypsum, doors and windows in aluminium and temperated glass. The living and service areas are located in the entrance floor. The veranda is connected with the garage as some kind extension. The dining room is integrated with the kitchen space. In the upper floor are three bedrooms with bathrooms turned to the swimming pool and the backyard.

01 Front view by night **02** Veranda and outdoor pool **03** Detail deck and living room **04** Rear view of the building

Photos: Leonardo Finotti

JOAO NAVES DE AVILA BUS LANE

The eight kilometers-long city bus lane with 13 bus shelters spaced about every 500 meters is part of the Uberlândia public transport development plan. The system connects the city center to the southeast region and is used daily by 60,000 passengers. The lane is a wide avenue built over an old railway track which cut across the city until the middle of the 20th Century. The project defined enclosed bus shelters with automatic doors synchronized with the bus doors and controlled by the bus driver. The simple design with minimum urban impact results in bus shelters that interact with the scenery.

01 General view 02 Arrangement of the two buildings 03 Interior view 04 Rear view

Photos: Leonardo Finotti

CITY: Uberlandia
COUNTRY: Brazil
REGION: South America
TYPOLOGY: Public
COMPLETION: –
WEBSITE: www.modoarq.com.br
ARCHITECTS: modo arquitetura

CASA DIAS

Consisting of two nested white rectangular volumes, the house forms an "L" plan, intruding on an adjacent garden and pool. The internal and external leisure areas are integrated into each other, with the water surface acting as a reflecting pool for the house's geometry. The white color is continued on the interior, which features double-height living spaces and integrated layouts on the ground floor, and bedrooms on the upper, perpendicular-lying volume. The windows, doors and sun shades are made of untreated wood, which contrast against the stark monochrome façade.

01 Front pond by night **02** Front façade **03** Outdoor space with swimming pool **04** Floor plans **05** IView into living space from second level

Photos: Lin Zheng Li

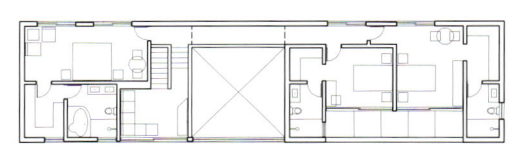

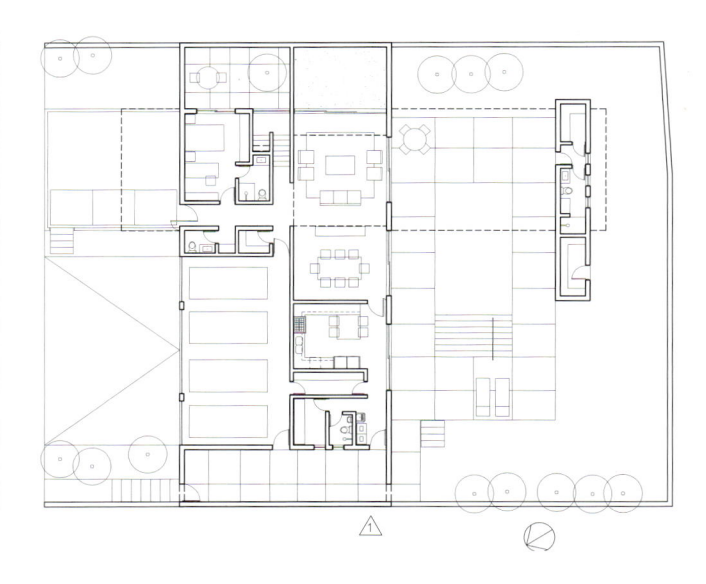

LAKESIDE HOUSE

The house is located in an essentially geographical scene, and the formal simplicity and rigor of the project were intended as means to achieve abstraction and establish a counterpoint with the landscape. Concomitantly, glass and steel were used in order to create lightness, transparence, and the impression of merging into the surrounding trees. The aim was to allow the dwellers to be in contact with nature even while inside the house. Three glass-encased green patios have been carefully laid out in the open plan, dividing it into different living areas. Vegetation on the patios articulates inner space with nature.

01 Bridge conntecting to nature **02** Front façade **03** Stone wall supporting 'crystal box' **04** View into glass-encsaed green patios **05** Elevation

Photos: Guy Wenborne

CITY Araucanía
COUNTRY Chile
REGION South America
TYPOLOGY Living
COMPLETION 2004
WEBSITE www.undurragadeves.cl
ARCHITECTS Undurragadeves Arquitectos

CITY
Cachagua

COUNTRY
Chile

REGION
South America

TYPOLOGY
Living

COMPLETION
2006

WEBSITE
www.ftres.cl

ARCHITECTS
Alejandro Dumay C.,
Nicolas Fones C.,
Francisco Vergara A.

CASA BOSQUE

The project, Forest House by **FTRES** Arquitectos, is located in a forest of Eucalyptus and Pine in the central coast of Chile. The order consists of a program with multifunctional spaces, with a capacity for 10 people in 3 dormitories, which optimize the 105 M2 where the relation between forest and house is fluid and dynamic. The location in favor of the level reduces the intervention in the land, and also eliminates the smaller amount of trees. Using some elements and materials appellants in the zone, one looks to rescue the historical image of the constructions of the development in a contemporary way.

01 Rear view **02** Stairs to entry **03** Detail **04** Deck **05** Stone and wooden panels façade

Photos: Ignacio Infante

BODEGAS VIÑA KINGSTON

The order consisted of designing a Wine Warehouse in Casablanca for a vine that is in its first years of export wine production. Although the objective is not to generate great volumes of wine, the project had to consider a growth in stages of three times its capacity. It was required that the wine production process was gravitational, that is to say, to occupy the gravity to move from one stage to another, avoiding the invasive use of pumps or mechanisms. The project, located in the lateral south-orients of a hill cord, takes advantage of the slope, creating a vine visual, allowing the building to be seen from the distance.

01 Perforated metal façade **02** North view **03** Site plan **04** Detail

Photos: Constanza Brünner Halpern

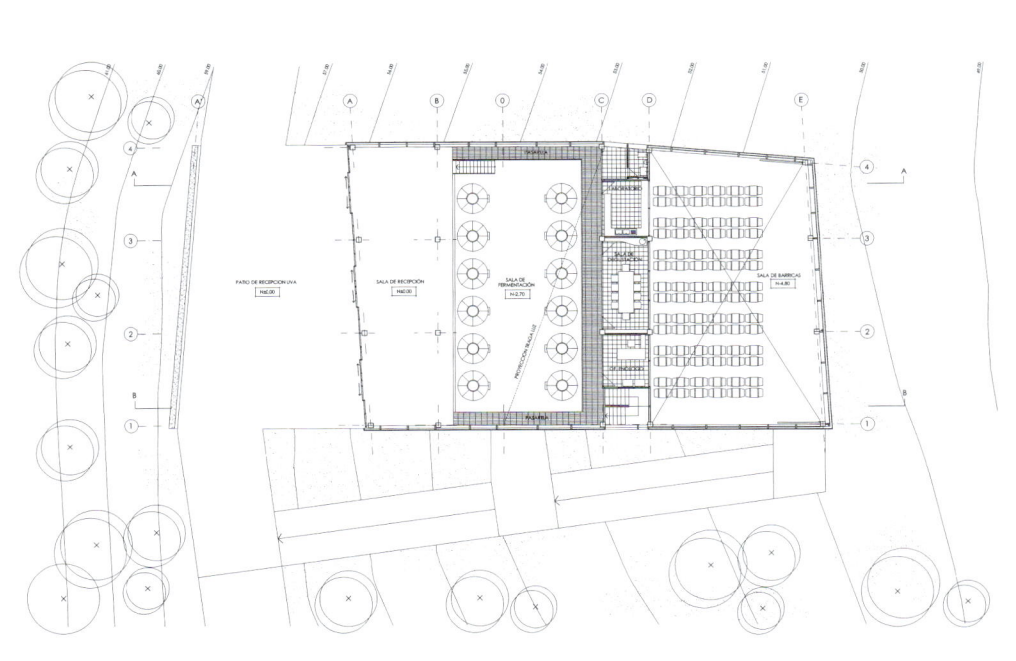

CITY Casablanca Fundo Sta. Rita
COUNTRY Chile
REGION South America
TYPOLOGY Industry
COMPLETION 2006
WEBSITE –
ARCHITECTS Juan Carlos Sabbagh & Gonzalo Cardemil Arquitectos

CITY Concepción
COUNTRY Chile
REGION South America
TYPOLOGY Education
COMPLETION 2008
WEBSITE cespedesizquierdo.cl
ARCHITECTS Céspedes + Izquierdo Arquitectos

COLEGIO CREACIÓN CONCEPCIÓN

The design of the school building aims to create ample interior space for student interaction during rainy winters. The regular three-storied volume houses classrooms, offices and bathrooms along its periphery. The center of the plan on all levels is reserved for vertical circulation, making the stairs the main sculptural object in the building, transforming them into public space where students can see each other when changing floors. To increase this effect, the ground floor was given 5 meter-high ceilings. The structure has diagonal load carriers to improve its ability to withstand seismic forces common in the area.

01 Exterior view **02** Skylight in staircase **03** Concrete constructions **04** Façade **05** Floor plan

Photos: Francisco Cespedes Schwerter

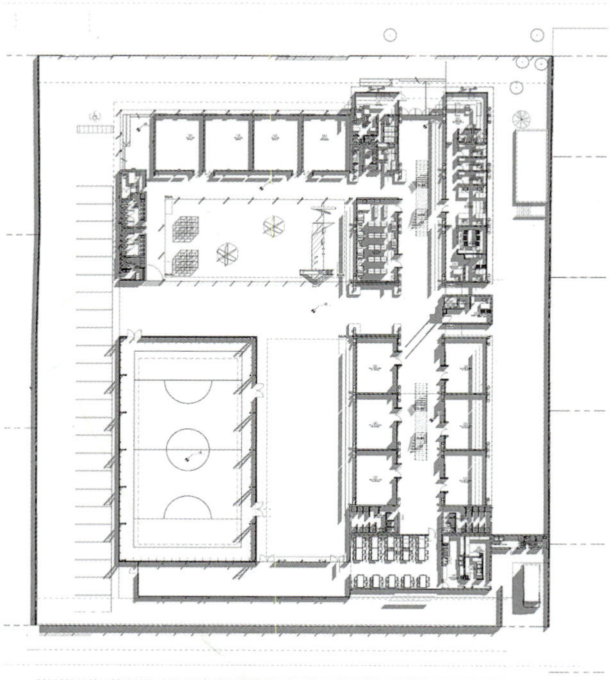

APUS RUPANCO HOUSE

Located in a remote and unpopulated area, this project explores the challenging topography of the landscape. Maintaining this original state of the location was fundamental. Four independent bodies (dormitories, public spaces, main dormitory and services) are connected by an 80 meter-long suspended gallery. Wood structures suspended on metal structures result in large eaves that protect the buildings from the region's abundant rainfall. The rigidity of the reinforced concrete used for all walls allowed the volumes' suspension above the ground with pillars. This suspended state creates a form that intersects with the beauty of the landscape.

01 Exterior view by night **02** Site plan **03** Elevations **04** Pillar construction **05** Hallway **06** View to seaside

Photos: Diego Aguiló, Rodrigo Pedraza

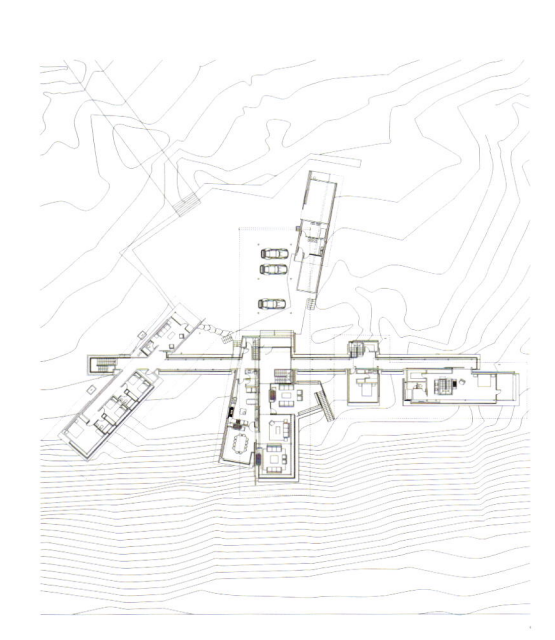

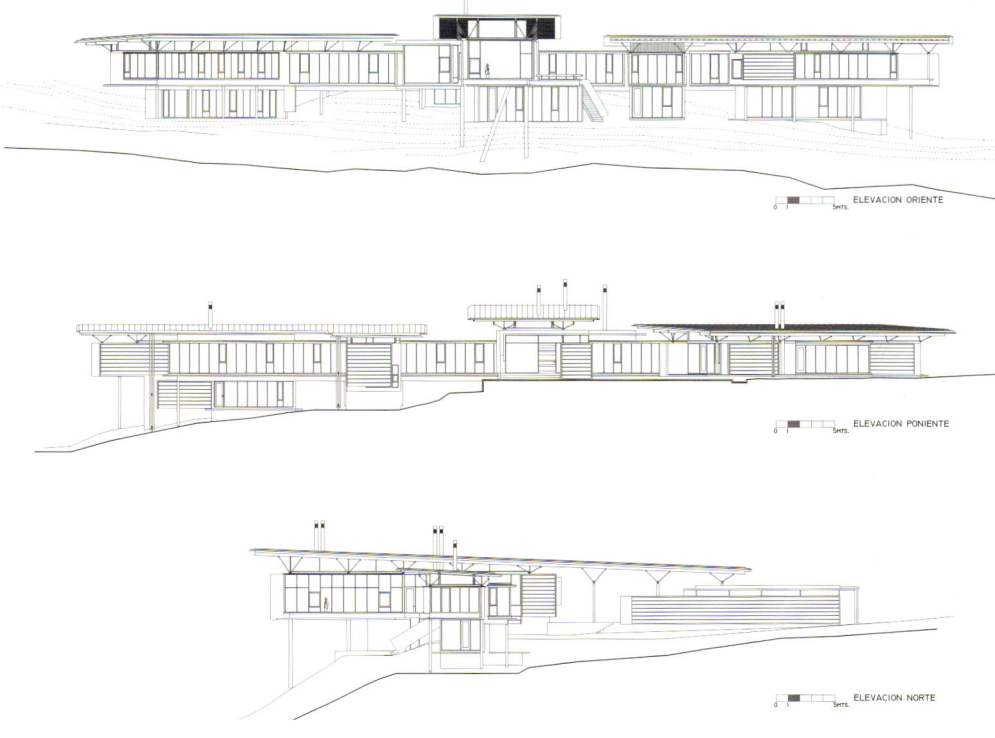

CITY Entre Lagos
COUNTRY Chile
REGION South America
TYPOLOGY Living
COMPLETION 2007
WEBSITE www.swinburnypedraza.cl
ARCHITECTS Swinburn & Pedraza

926

CITY
Iquique

COUNTRY
Chile

REGION
South America

TYPOLOGY
Living

COMPLETION
2006

WEBSITE
www.elementalchile.cl

ARCHITECTS
Elemental

QUINTA MONROY IQUIQUE

The government of Chile asked to solve a difficult situation: to come to the aid of 100 families who during the last 30 years had illegally occupied a terrain of 0.5 hectare in the center of Iquique, a city in the Chilean desert. The work was within the frame of a specific program called the Ministry of House Dynamic Social House without Debt (VSDsD) that is oriented towards society's poorest. To solve the problem, the solution was 1 house = 1 lot, even though this created small lots, in which only 30 families in the land could be fitted. In this case, each house then extended at least to double of its original surface.

01 Street side view **02** Front view **03** Entry view **04** View from courtyard

Photos: Cristobal Palma

CAPILLA RUPANCO

The work consists of an austere space, of only 21 m2, and with a capacity for 12 people, while using material of low cost. In its interior, the image of the altar is provided by its very own landscape, a lake and the mountain range, which defines the direction of the volume and its directionality. In the North facade, the feature of the shrine is placed with two niches for sculptures designed by the proprietor. Finally, the terrace which was prolonged from the access of the chapel, was conceived for the development of ceremonies on the outside, taking possession of the land extending the limits of the designed space.—

01 Front view **02** Side view **03** Area view **04** View to altar **05** Wooden panels façade **06** Section

Photos: Ignacio Infante

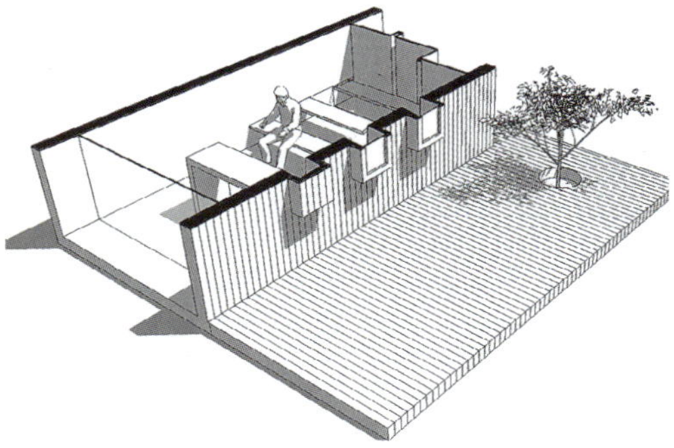

CITY: Lago Rupanco
COUNTRY: Chile
REGION: South America
TYPOLOGY: Culture
COMPLETION: 2006
WEBSITE: www.ftres.cl
ARCHITECTS: FTRES Arquitectos

CITY Laguna Verde
COUNTRY Chile
REGION South America
TYPOLOGY Living
COMPLETION –
WEBSITE –
ARCHITECTS Altamirano Armanet Bisball

CASA MERIZ MORENO

The house arises from a bet, where the challenge was to surpass it as much architectonically as economically. The foundation of the house leisurely arises like a main activity. The leisure is understood as a virtue and a way to inhabit, which is different from the way of life in the city. Seeing and living the surrounding scene, as much inner as external, is what makes the organization of the house have its different routes and atmospheres. The space is spent as much in the public spaces as in the exteriors, and consists of an over-sized gradería in the public space, and a gallery apt for the contemplation of the landscape.

01 View to deck **02** Seaside view **03** Wooden panels **04** Wooden column and façade

Photos: Andres Altamirano

GUESTS' HOUSE

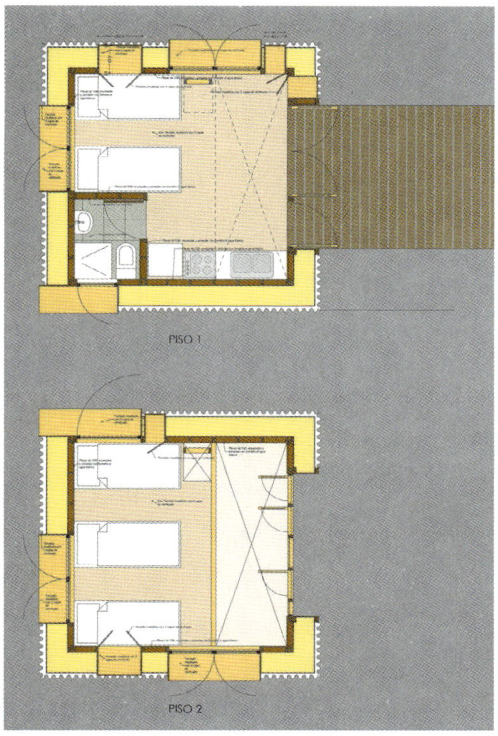

The assignment, a small cabin for visitors, is of wooden structure with two levels. The project takes into consideration low energy consumption, orientation, interior color, window location, and isolation. The isolation element provides a special characteristic to the façades, while the location of the windows allow for abundant sun light in the interior during winter and a crossed flow of air for ventilation during the summer. The green cover prevents wind to strike directly at the surface, while also providing heat, and the interior, painted white, allows natural light to bounce and diminish the use of artificial light.

01 View to green roof with pasture 02 Floor plans 03 Exterior view 04 Wooden structure and two-level glazing

Photos: impulsando.com

CITY: Licancheu
COUNTRY: Chile
REGION: South America
TYPOLOGY: Living
COMPLETION: 2006
WEBSITE: www.aata.cl
ARCHITECTS: AATA Associate Architects (Sebastián Cerda Pé)

CITY Los Vilos
COUNTRY Chile
REGION South America
TYPOLOGY Living
COMPLETION -
WEBSITE -
ARCHITECTS Cecilia Puga

LARRAIN HOUSE BAHIA AZUL

The structure, the last remaining railroad station on a north-bound line along Chile's coast orients toward the sea shore. All that is perishable has succumbed to the effects of time and disuse. The rectangular perforations in the house's walls are distributed along an imaginary line. The project was approached independently of the specific location and it was chosen to disintegrate the program separating the bedrooms to ensure their total independence. Three monolithic reinforced concrete containers were designed with a structured perforations that increased the location's versatility and the association between the volumes.

01 Garden view **02** Exterior construction **03** Deck and view inside **04** Living space **05** Exterior view

Photos: Cristobal Palma

ENVIRONMENTAL INFORMATION CENTER "FRAY JORGE"

The Environmental Information Center of the National Park Fray Forest Jorge is located in the Province of the Limarí, IV region of Coquimbo, and is placed within a plan of integration with the neighboring communities, for which a new access road was set out, including in its passage some bordering towns that now are part of the tourist and educative circuit of the zone. A landscape showing the nature and its different sizes is present, while the interior looks for a new approach. The bays in walls catch the fragmented landscape, while skies provide light and show the color and texture of the wood.

01 Information center in National Forest Park
02 Main entrance **03** Interior **04** Wooden façade

Photos: Nicolás Yazigi

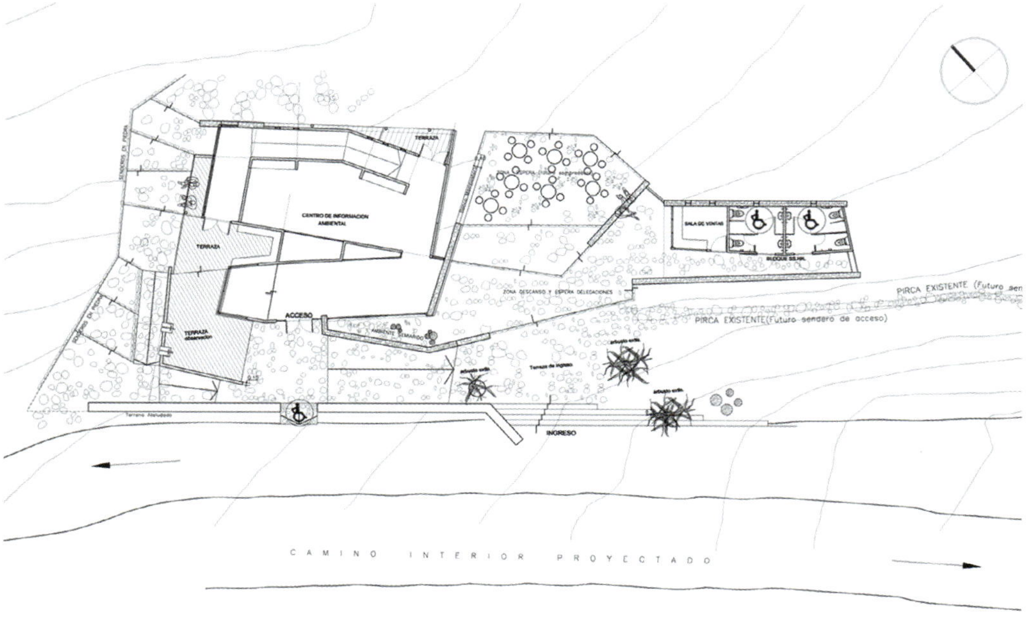

CITY La Serena
COUNTRY Chile
REGION South America
TYPOLOGY Public
COMPLETION 2006
WEBSITE www.3arquitectos.cl
ARCHITECTS 3arquitectos

CITY	La Reina
COUNTRY	Chile
REGION	South America
TYPOLOGY	Ecclesiastical
COMPLETION	2005
WEBSITE	www.antonioacosta.cl
ARCHITECTS	Antonio Acosta - Nicole Lyaudet Arquitectos

CAPILLA AVE MARIA

This chapel arises from the necessity of the community to complete a project initiated by the previous parish priest. Within the requirements that were asked for was to maintain part of the old construction and to propose a chapel to the liking of the community. The land insinuates a formal proposal of a wedge that is accentuated with the natural slope of the hill, where the main access to the chapel is generated in a sunken vestibule product, and is thought to be a welcoming encounter. Towards the back of the altar a multipurpose office is featured, while two other multipurpose rooms are used for community meetings.

01 Nave view **02** Exterior detail **03** Principal façade
04 Rear façade **05** Bell tower

Photos: AAP

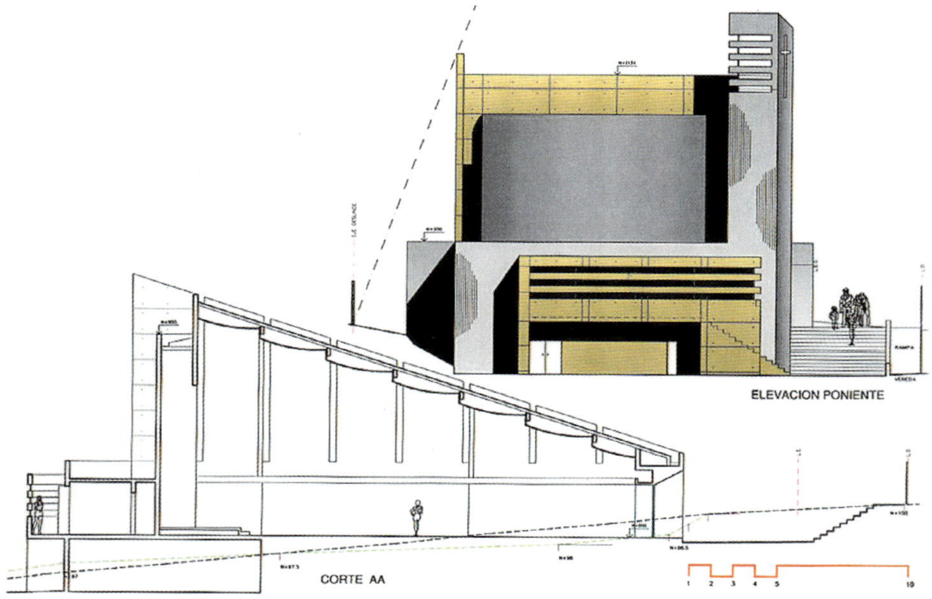

CASA POLGATTI-RIVAS

The order consists of a house in the outskirts of Santiago, in Chicureo, and needed to be extended with a low and repeatable constructive value in an area with similar topographic characteristics. The proposal consists of separating the public and private program in two volumes, perpendicularly placed on one another, relating both levels to the land in cuts. This allows for all enclosures of the house to always have a connection with the garden. The disposition of the volumes assures the view to the valley with maximum distance to the neighbors, while patios in the volume of dormitories aims to solve the possibility of growth.

01 Floor plan **02** Terrace with view to inner courtyard **03** View to pool and rear view **04** Exterior view **05** Concrete envelope with sliding glass doors

Photos: Marcos Mendizabal

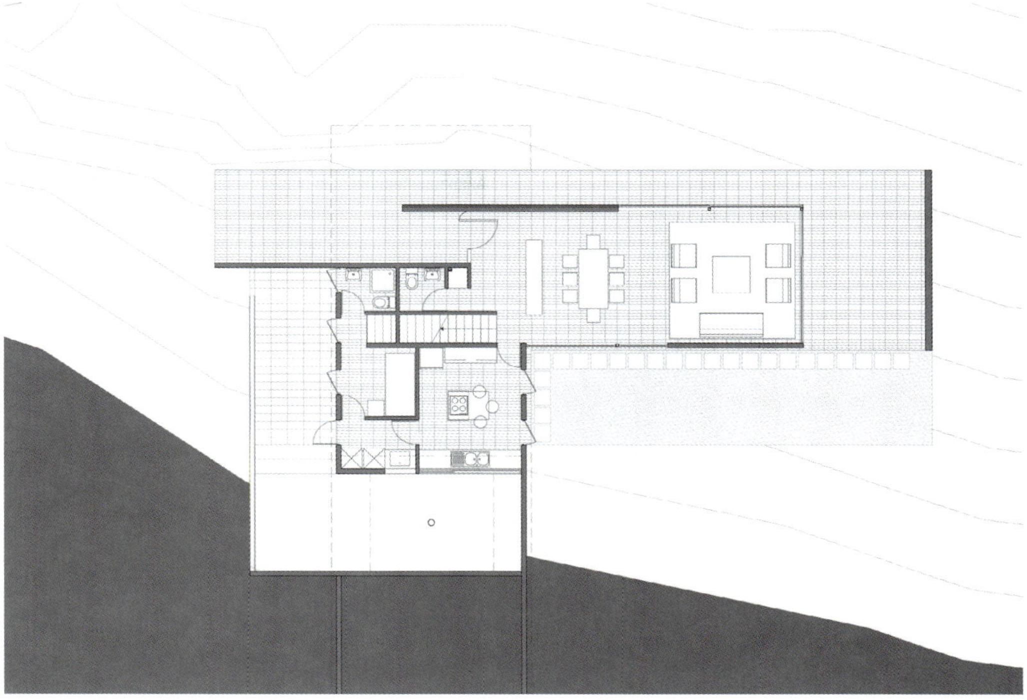

CITY La Reserva
COUNTRY Chile
REGION South America
TYPOLOGY Living
COMPLETION 2005
WEBSITE www.polidura-talhouk.com
ARCHITECTS Antonio Polidura, Marco Polidura

CITY: La Reserva
COUNTRY: Chile
REGION: South America
TYPOLOGY: Living
COMPLETION: 2007
WEBSITE: www.polidura-talhouk.com
ARCHITECTS: Antonio Polidura, Marco Polidura, Pablo Talhouk

CASA BINIMELIS-BARAHONA

The land of an 820 m² slope is in the Reserve, located in the sector of Chicureo, lies in the commune of Hill, Chile. The proposal consists of separating the public and private program in two volumes, while the enclosures of the house have a connection with the garden. The disposition of the volumes assures the view to the valley and the maximum distance to the neighbors. The incorporation of patios or emptiness's in the volume of dormitories aims to solve the possibility of growth, where the initial house was able to lodge 5 dormitories in 210 m². The area publishes of living and dining room and provides cooks with services.

01 Façade **02** Exterior view by night **03** Glazed sliding door **04** Floor plans

Photos: Aryeh Kornfeld

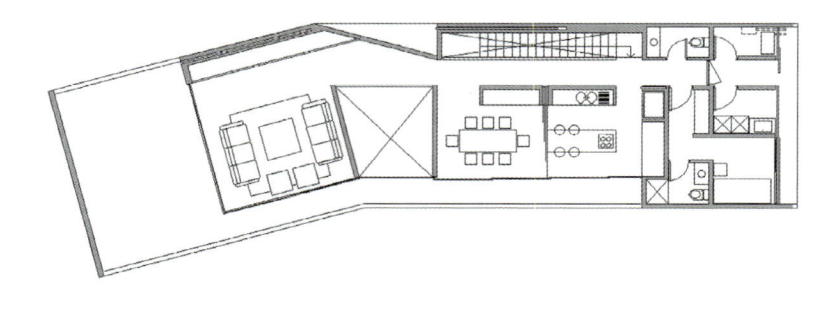

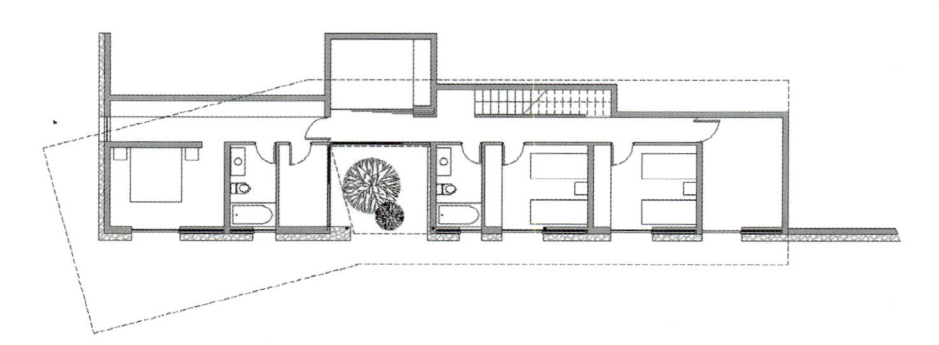

HOUSE IN MARBELLA

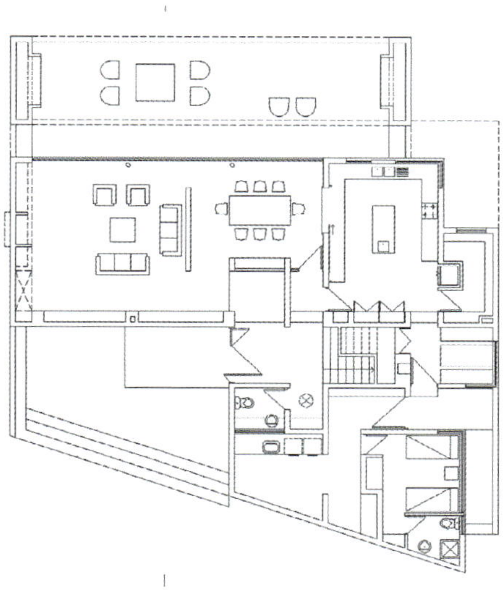

The house is located in a condominium that sets a styling standard, and has an excellent view over a distant landscape to the north. The idea is to focus that view through a "big eye" (terrace) that is detached from the ground with the purpose of bringing to the foreground what is at a distance. The house is a white and hermetic object from the outside, but well lit and warm from the inside. This is achieved by a combination of large glass planes to the north and specific light entry-points to the south, east and west. For weather protection, all windows have concrete awnings which contribute to extend the feeling of space.

01 View to deck **02** Exterior view **03** Floor plan **04** Street side view **05** Dining space

Photos: Guy Wenborne

CITY Marbella
COUNTRY Chile
REGION South America
TYPOLOGY Living
COMPLETION 2004
WEBSITE www.cristianolivos.com
ARCHITECTS Cristián Olivos arquitecto

CITY Osorno

COUNTRY Chile

REGION South America

TYPOLOGY Education

COMPLETION 2007

WEBSITE cespedesizquierdo.cl

ARCHITECTS Céspedes + Izquierdo Arquitectos

COLEGIO CREACIÓN OSORNO

The school in Osorno was designed on an unusual long, narrow site, which was resolved using two long parallel buildings that are shifted in relation to each other and whose façades sport strips of color that are the central theme of the ensemble. The use of strong color has roots in traditional Chilean architecture, which often features brightly painted wood to add cheer to the dark and rainy winters. In trying to incorporate these local design elements, the architects proposed a colorful central playground and garden with external corridors and stairs between the volumes in order to breakaway from the traditional school yard.

01 Main entry school yard **02** Detail **03** Section and elevation **04** Wooden and concrete hallway **05** Main yard interior façade

Photos: Carlos Izquierdo

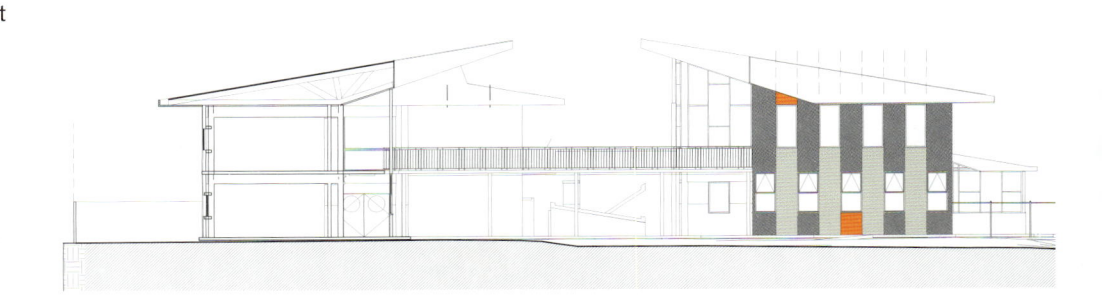

PITE HOUSE PUNTA PITE

From the temptation of being on the brink of establishing a strong inner-outer relationship, the project is exacerbated by the important presence of the ocean and an abrupt cliff, while developing through the articulation of the different spaces and zoning on the slope. The shape brings the spaces ever closer to the edge, where vertigo is present. The inner enclosures establish their form and position with a singular relation to the sea, while the central pavilion is suspended on the ocean, with carpentry of its windows, pavements and excellent frontal position help the interior to be understood as a raft.

01 Exterior view by night **02** View to pool **03** Seaside view **04** Side view **05** Dining space

Photos: Cristobal Palma

CITY Papudo
COUNTRY Chile
REGION South America
TYPOLOGY Living
COMPLETION —
WEBSITE —
ARCHITECTS Smiljan Radic

CITY Pinohuacho
COUNTRY Chile
REGION South America
TYPOLOGY Public
COMPLETION 2006
WEBSITE www.grupotalca.com
ARCHITECTS Rodrigo Sheward

PARADOR-MIRADOR EN PINOHUACHO

The project does not try to impose or merge, and marks an abstract, honest architectural form of finished materiality without the concrete made rock. It takes part in the landscape, respecting it, trying to be of importance to the site The project is solved in two pieces that articulate in the landscape; the inn that hangs of the rock and emerges towards the cliff, seized to the evenness of the floor and the other volume, and the other of the camping, receiving to the arrivals of automobiles. The skin/concrete structure generates the limits and hard edges of the work, generating the structure composition of the project.

01 Wooden façade **02** View inside **03** Elevation **04** View to snow covered hills **05** Exterior view

Photos: Heidy Ullrich (01), German Valenzuela (02, 05), Rodrigo Sheward (04)

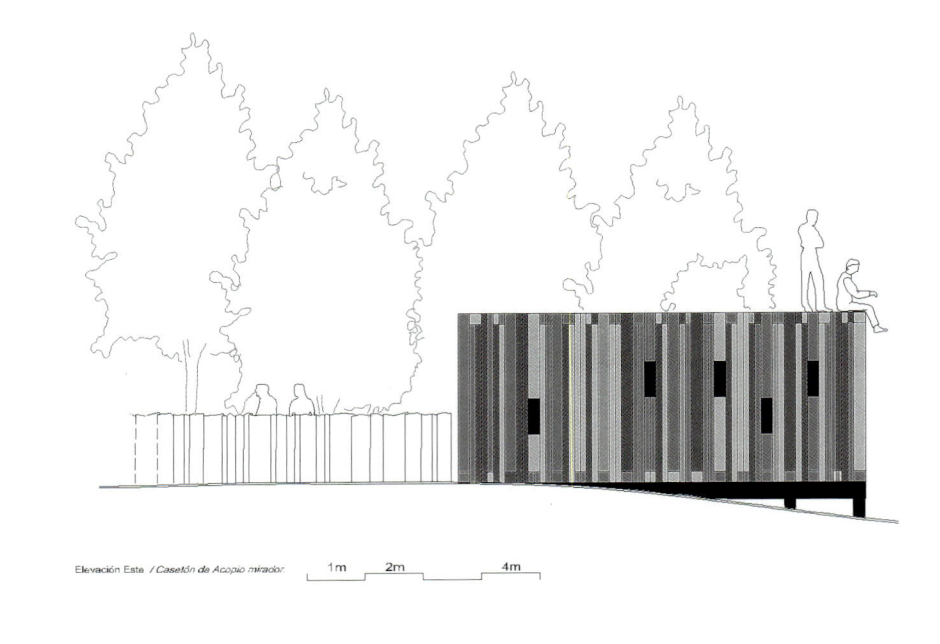

COLEGIO SANTA MARÍA DE PAINE

What formerly was the first Seminary of the Capucins, was carefully remodeled and gradually extended to welcome the structure of an average basic school. Pertaining to the Corporation of Social Development of the Rural Sector, it offers gratuitous education and of quality standard to the people of the field. This same philosophy takes maximum advantage of the limited resources, and really, is the base of the project for this school. The necessary and reduced budget did think about the construable building involving stages, in which without it, it could have easily seemed like a series of fragments.

01 Bird's eye view **02** First floor plan **03** Façade **04** Interior **05** Detail glazing

Photos: Cristián Barahona

CITY Paine
COUNTRY Chile
REGION South America
TYPOLOGY Education
COMPLETION 2007
WEBSITE www.claudiomagrini.com
ARCHITECTS Claudio Magrini / Marco Vidal Cabello

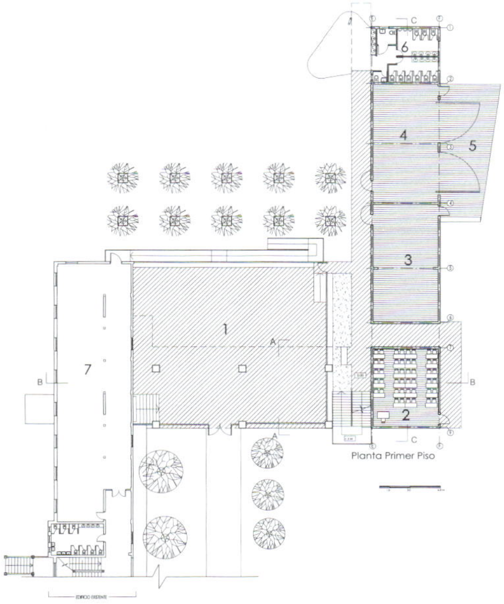

HOTEL REMOTA IN PATAGONIA

Inspired by the buildings used for many of the sheep farm works that are done inside due to wind and cold weather, Hotel Remota is placed in the midst of nature, an ancient Latin American cultural tradition, in the Patagonian plains. The wild grasses cover the roofs of the buildings, while the empty central courtyard introduces the vastness of Patagonia as the hotel's core. The ever-changing light of Patagonia penetrates the building and is captured by the bright colors of the fabrics that cover the dark wooden furniture, which was hand made by on-site carpenters using pieces of dead native wood.

01 Cross sections 02 Synthetic asphalt membrane 03 Planted roof 04 Floor-ceiling windows 05 Concrete structure of pillars

Photos: Guy Wenborne, Felipe Camus (02), Turek (05)

CITY
Puerto Natales

COUNTRY
Chile

REGION
South America

TYPOLOGY
Leisure

COMPLETION
2006

WEBSITE
www.germandelsol.cl

ARCHITECTS
German del Sol

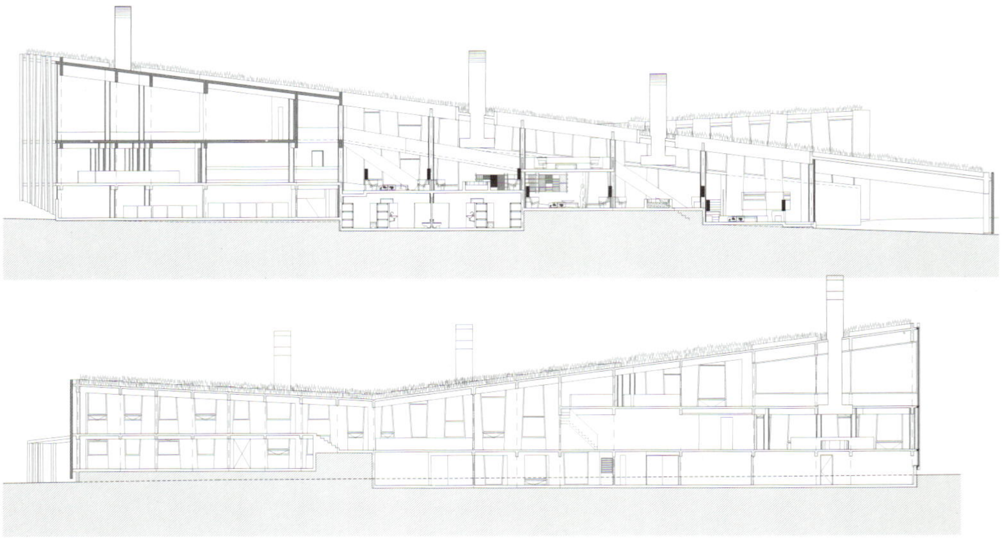

CITY: Puerto Natales
COUNTRY: Chile
REGION: South America
TYPOLOGY: Hospitality
COMPLETION: 2007
WEBSITE: www.sebastianirarrazaval.com
ARCHITECTS: Sebastián Irarrázával

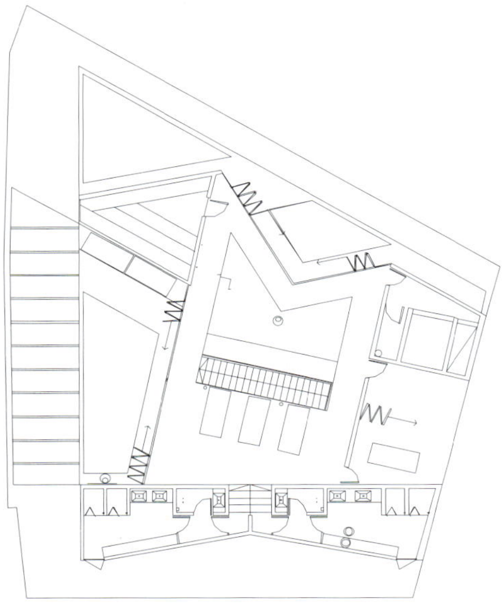

INDIGO PATAGONIA HOTEL

Situated along the maritime passage of Puerto Natales, which is the entrance to the Torres del Paine National Park, this hotel has six levels with 29 bedrooms and a Spa on top of the building. The project is organized around three main ideas: discovering the building as a voyager who experience places through continuous steps, to be sensitive with the site and its provincial character, and to radically differentiate the intimate space of the sleeping rooms from the monumental space of public areas. The work done consisted in voiding the core of the house and reinforcing the perimeter walls with a steel frame.

01 Rooftop pool **02** Exterior view from seaside **03** Sixth floor plan **04** Rooftop spa **05** Eucalyptus bars curtain **06** Interior

Photos: Cristobal Palma

CITY Rancagua
COUNTRY Chile
REGION South America
TYPOLOGY Gastronomy
COMPLETION 2002
WEBSITE www.emiliana.cl
ARCHITECTS José Cruz Ovalle / Hernán Cruz / Ana Turell

LOS ROBLES WINECELLAR

This organic wine cellar elaborates the wine in a bio dynamic process, which allows it to be free of pesticides and fungicides. Water and compost are continuously recycled, which is a new way to preserve the farmland and produce the grape harvest. The mass is built as a 1 on 1 relation to each stone, each adobe, and each piece of wood in order to feel the building through hands and body, much the same way a wine taster tastes the wine. The materials are selected from an architectonical point of view that situates the building from its edges through concave walls made of concrete-stone, adobe, and wood.

01 Exterior view by night **02** Concaved walls **03** Façade of concrete-stone, adobe and wood **04** Sections **05** Pillar construction

Photos: Juan Purcell, Ana Turell

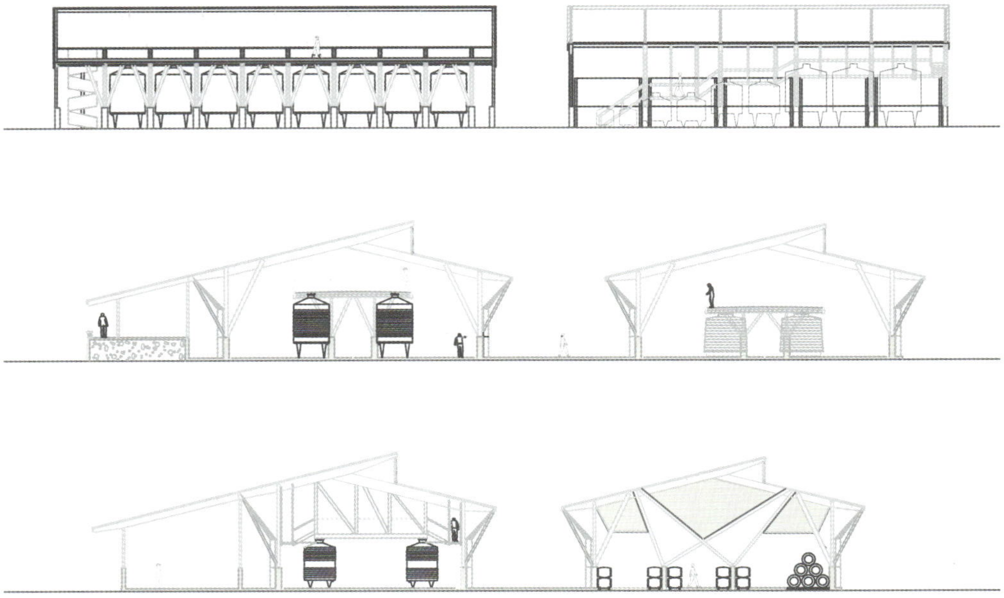

CASA WOLF ANDALUE

The houses with a mansarda element are habitual in this zone and these new suburbs. For many, it is the legal opening before the shortage of square meters that admits the DFL2, and raising three levels seems to be at a disadvantage. Besides occupying those residual deltas that leave the covers inclined, as in the inverted perspective of Hockney, the vertical body is faceted with slight deviations diagonals that do everything possible to avoid to their immediate and close neighbors. The program tries to solve the voluntary and dominant imprisonment finishes renewing its marriage and its paternity.

01 Windows' perforations and skylight **02** Exterior view
03 View from seaside **04** Living space **05** Fully open window and façade construction

Photos: Cristobal Palma

CITY San Pedro
COUNTRY Chile
REGION South America
TYPOLOGY Living
COMPLETION 2007
WEBSITE www.pezo.cl
ARCHITECTS Pezo von Ellrichshausen Architects

CITY
San Pedro de Atacama

COUNTRY
Chile

REGION
South America

TYPOLOGY
Leisure

COMPLETION
2000

WEBSITE
www.germandelsol.cl

ARCHITECTS
German del Sol

UN HOTEL EN ATACAMA

Natural and cultural Life, dispersed in Atacama's vastness, is present at the hotel and invites visitors to go out and experience its natural and cultural riches firsthand. Upon their return, the hotel allows guests to come back to comfort. The hotel is distant from existing settlements, and aims to found a new town in Atacama. It follows the pre-Columbian tradition of building in public squares, and creating towns without the use of streets. The building is a sequence of interior and exterior spaces, as is usual in other small towns in Atacama, where the public and the private are not very well defined.

01 Entry view **02** Wooden roof construction **03** Site plan **04** Guest room with wooden ceiling **05** Deck

Photos: Guy Wenborne

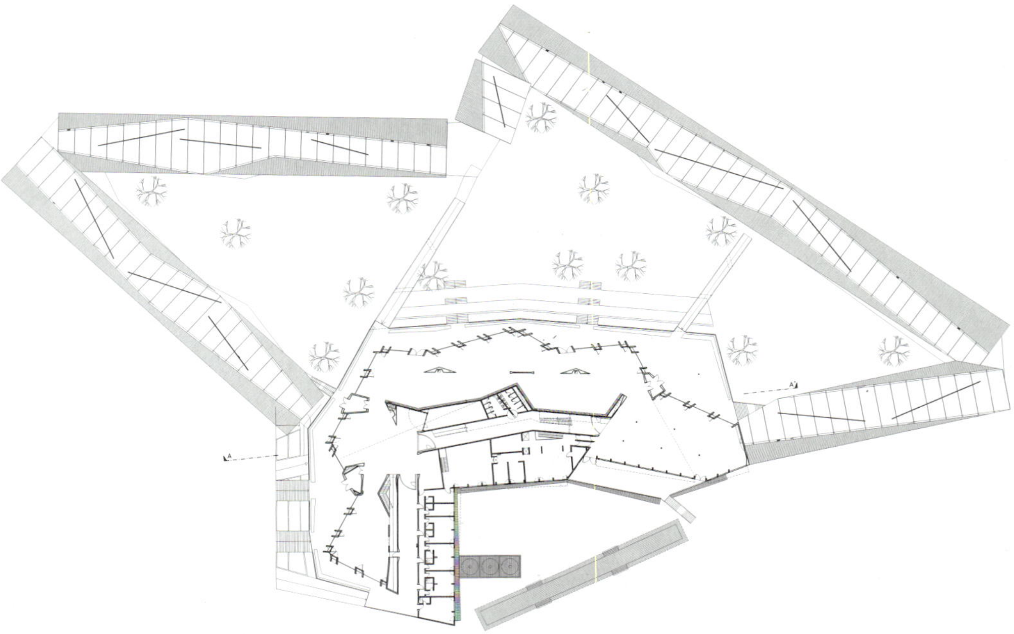

SAUNAS AND WATER RESERVOIRES IN ATACAMA

To dwell in this vast land, men and women build graceful stone structures along the roads in Atacama in order to get an insight into nature, and make it hospitable. These concrete landmarks in the landscape reveal the presence of water reservoirs used to irrigate the land, and allow visitors to swim and to open up new views to the immense wilderness around them. The water is kept still, flowing gently over the reservoir's edges to reflect the light, and the beauty of the place, against a dark slate coating.

01 Exterior view by night **02** View from pool side **03** General view **04** Elevations, floor plan **05** Relaxing space

Photos: Guy Wenborne

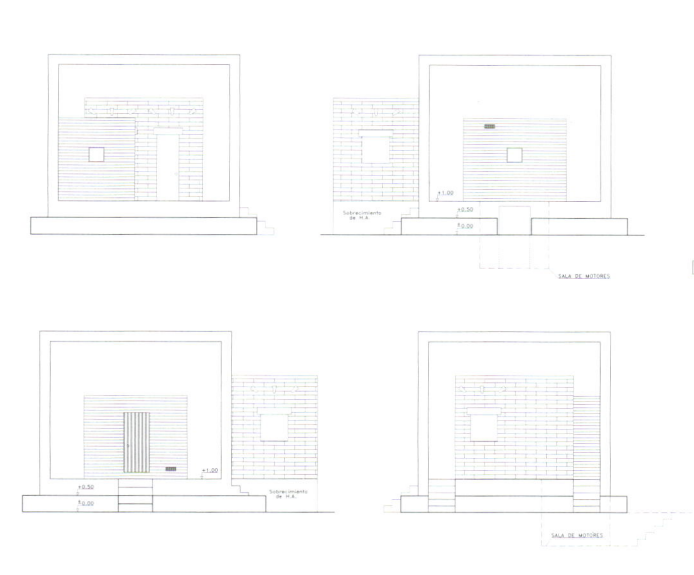

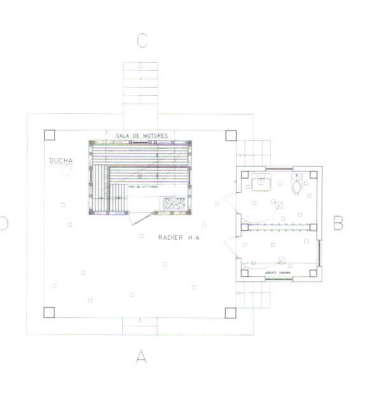

CITY San Pedro de Atacama
COUNTRY Chile
REGION South America
TYPOLOGY Leisure
COMPLETION 2000
WEBSITE www.germandelsol.cl
ARCHITECTS German del Sol

CITY
Santiago

COUNTRY
Chile

REGION
South America

TYPOLOGY
–

COMPLETION
2004

WEBSITE
www.masarquitectos.cl

ARCHITECTS
+arquitectos (Alex Brahm / David Bonomi / Maite Bartolomé / Marcelo Leturia / Alfredo Muñoz / Francisco Soto)

EDIFICIO CONSORCIO SUCRUSAL LA FLORIDA

This branch rose under a strict norm of not constructing on two floors of height, nor building more than 50% of the land. In order to fulfill the project, a building of three levels was designed, which consists of an underground one, leaving areas of attention to public parking concerning the street, while distributing offices on both remaining levels. With the purpose to make the dependencies attractive on the inferior level, the complete perimeter of the land was excavated creating a great patio reduced by the front skylights and inner patios. This solution allowed to give illumination and natural ventilation to the offices.

01 Interior sun screens **02** Glass façade **03** Wooden floor **04** Floor plan

Photos: Giuseppe Brucculeri

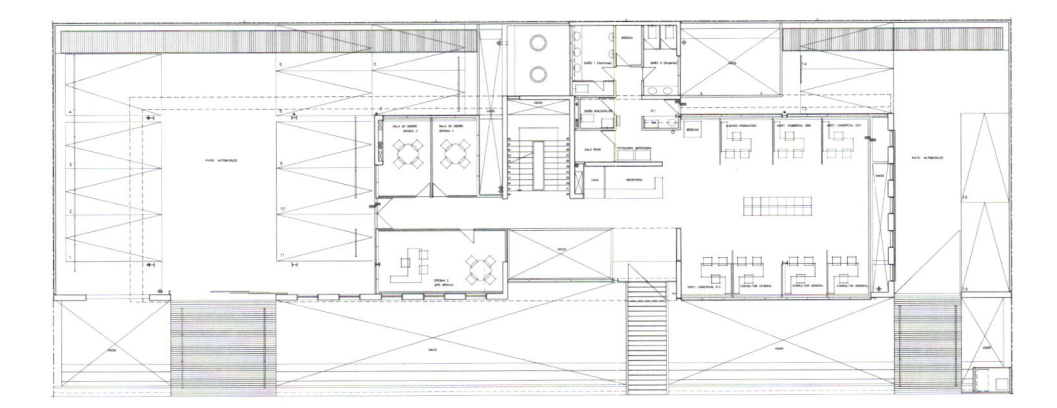

EDIFICO VESPUCIO SUR

This building, the Edifico Vespucio Sur, was projected to solve the operative needs of the concessionary company of the urban highway Freeway Américo South Vespucio. The project is conformed by a main building of seven levels that lodges the administrative offices, and one minor of three that lodge the technical rooms and of traffic control and toll. Both bodies lift a level on the ground, clearing the totality of the land to welcome the parking. This solution also contributes to emphasize the presence of the building on the concession highway, while granting greater height, providing another element to this project.

01 Fully glazed façade **02** Interior detail **03** Courtyard **04** Stair construction

Photos: Giuseppe Brucculeri

CITY Santiago
COUNTRY Chile
REGION South America
TYPOLOGY –
COMPLETION 2005
WEBSITE www.masarquitectos.cl
ARCHITECTS +arquitectos (Alex Brahm / David Bonomi / Maite Bartolomé / Marcelo Leturia / Alfredo Muñoz / Francisco Soto)

MERCAT RESTAURANT

The 250 m² restaurant is located on the east side of Santiago de Chile. The area, dominated by art and design exhibitions, has an intense pedestrian activity. The design strategy focuses on the visual continuity between the street and the interior patio; to achieve this effect, the perimeters of the public areas were surrounded by a continuous transparent strip. A fish pond reflects the sunlight onto the main saloon ceiling and helps to create a fresh atmosphere during the summer season. Choice of materials was reduced to a minimum – wood for the interior deck and main access, black stone as floor covering and white stucco walls.

01 Outdoor eating space **02** Fully glazed façade **03** Sections **04** View inside

Photos: 01AQ arquitectos asociados

CITY Santiago
COUNTRY Chile
REGION South America
TYPOLOGY Gastronomy
COMPLETION 2006
WEBSITE www.01arq.cl
ARCHITECTS 01ARQ arquitectos asociados (Cristian Winckler, Felipe Fritz, Pablo Saric)

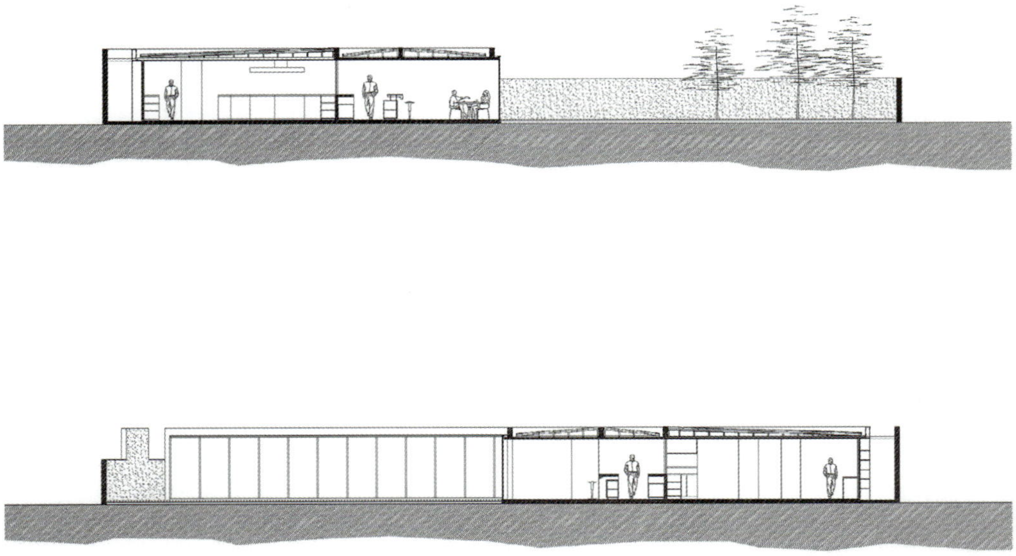

CONTEX HEADQUARTERS

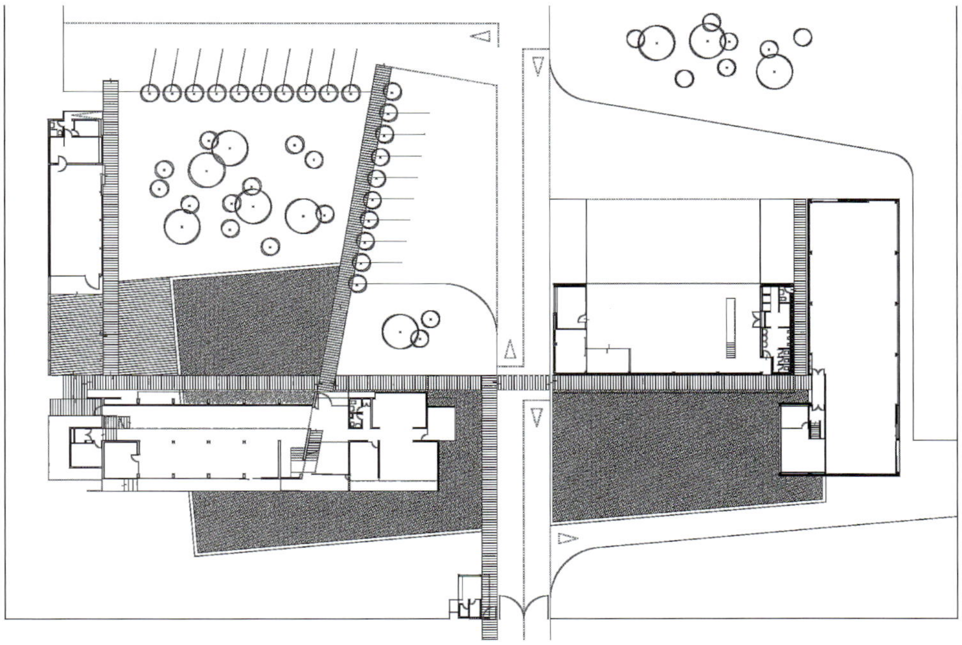

The assignment arises from a contest to build the dependencies of a construction company, with a diverse program of Warehouse, Workshop, Offices and Cafeteria. The proposal is based on taking the diversity of materials, the recognizable structures, and the basic shapes as architectonic elements that are present in the works of the company. The Warehouse is characterized by the wavy plate and by its steel structure, while the Workshop opens completely to the west, keeping equipment towards the edges. The Offices stand out for being constructed of pure concrete with steel lattices, while the Cafeteria appears as a glass pavilion.

01 Stoned courtyard 02 Exterior detail 03 Wooden hallway 04 Floor plan 05 Concrete façade

Photos: 57STUDIO

CITY Santiago
COUNTRY Chile
REGION South America
TYPOLOGY Office
COMPLETION 2004
WEBSITE www.57studio.com
ARCHITECTS 57STUDIO

CITY Santiago
COUNTRY Chile
REGION South America
TYPOLOGY Industrial
COMPLETION 2006
WEBSITE www.antonioacosta.cl
ARCHITECTS Antonio Acosta - Nicole Lyaudet Arquitectos

IMBRA

The industrial building serves as a storage warehouse, but also includes an area of offices in the interior. Defined its metallic structure, the warehouse responds of different forms from the orientation. Towards the north, it is closed by an inclined and isolated facade without windows, except in the corridor, which requires natural illumination. The south of the building is dominated by a superior window, while the façade of the east side forms the image of the company. Natural illumination is provided by windows in the roof.

01 Concrete façade, service building **02** Main façade facing street **03** North façade **04** Interior Corridor

Photos: AAP

FACULTAD DE ARQUITECTURA, ARTE Y DISEÑO UNIVERSIDAD DIEGO PORTALES

The previous building presented a series of problems in its use, and the opportunity was there to set out the municipality of authorizing the continuous facade. This allowed the creation of a whole back-to-back strip to the existing building, with the condition for releasing the first level towards the street. The project, given its great construction density, looks to make light enter on all the levels and to generate the greater amount of possible open spaces. Also, it was chosen to occupy the space under the patio in two levels that will lodge the rooms and laboratories of computation and an audience.

01 Façade 02 Transition zone 03 West elevation 04 inner courtyard 05 Planted courtyard

Photos: Guy Wenborne

CITY Santiago
COUNTRY Chile
REGION South America
TYPOLOGY Education
COMPLETION 2005
WEBSITE www.ricardoabuauad.cl
ARCHITECTS Ricardo Abuauad

CITY
Santiago

COUNTRY
Chile

REGION
South America

TYPOLOGY
Education

COMPLETION
2007

WEBSITE
www.ard-arquitectos.cl

ARCHITECTS
ARD Arquitectos - Alejandro Rojas Donoso

FACULTAD DE ODONTOLOGÍA, UNIVERSIDAD DE CHILE

The Clinical Building of Dental Medicine is born from the necessity to complete the Olive Campus which is the practical program of the race. The clinic, a concept of attention to the public, is a prime concern in the project. The program is divided in clear blocks; two power stations of sterilization, symmetrical within the building, connected with nuclei of sterilization, with reception of clean and dirty material only, on all the floors. The Building located in Av. La Paz with Olive trees, is conformed by 5 floors. The program of the Building can be summarized as floor socle, surrounded by English patios.

01 Detail **02** Exterior view by night **03** Street side view
04 Examination room **05** Glazed courtyard

Photos: Oliver Llaneza Hesse

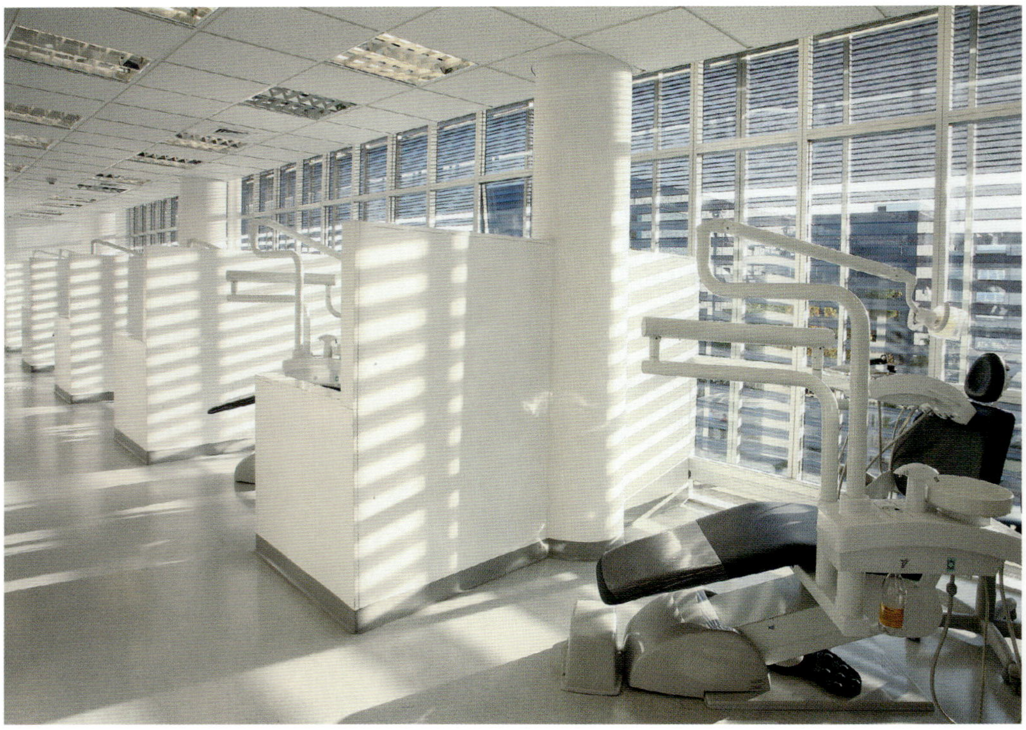

OFICINAS ECOPELLETS

The project is located in the Bosa zone industrial land. It consists of offices for a company of pellets of wood, which is a system of alternative energy. Order of low cost and fast execution raised a project of small scale in relation to the surroundings and a construction of uniform materiality, surrounding panel prefabricated, and of zinc emballetado, fusing it to the industrial context. The volume lodges two dissimilar programs; administrative offices and service of personnel that are expressed through Louvre windows, duplicating the scale of the project and generating advertising support structure.

01 Exterior view by night 02 Site plan 03 General view 04 Zinc façade 05 Entrance

Photos: Aryeh Kornfeld

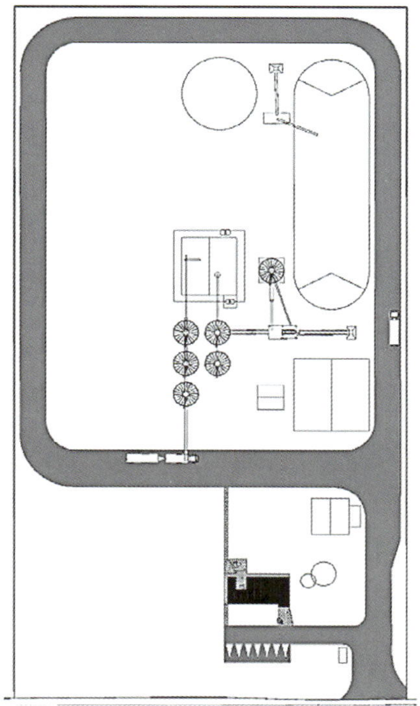

CITY: Santiago
COUNTRY: Chile
REGION: South America
TYPOLOGY: Office
COMPLETION: 2007
WEBSITE: www.ivanbravo.cl
ARCHITECTS: Iván Bravo

CITY: Santiago
COUNTRY: Chile
REGION: South America
TYPOLOGY: Public
COMPLETION: 2005
WEBSITE: –
ARCHITECTS: Cox & Ugarte Arquitectos (Carlos Ugarte – Arturo Cox – Matías Cordoba)

BIBLIOTECA DE SANTIAGO

In a declared building national monument, the Library of Santiago is considered to be like a great open space that is given to the city, where their citizens can be and interact. An esplanade that comes from the street welcomes the activities, while simultaneously being a public access to the project. One second place, excavated, more intimate and protégée of the activity on the street, generates a place with optimal conditions for exhibitions or events controlled outdoors. The project is framed as a new model of the library, which is an active space where the great educative project is carried out.

01 Front view **02** Patio **03** Glazed façade lining **04** Roofed transition **05** First floor plan

Photos: Rodrigo Opazo

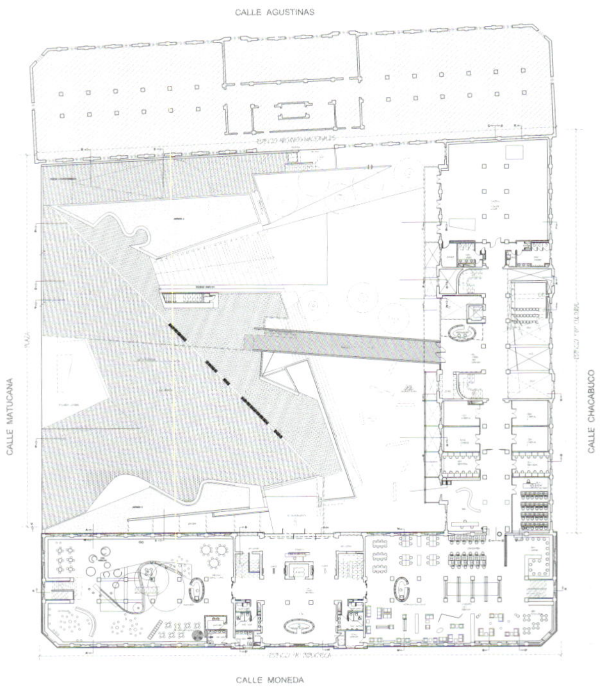

WALL HOUSE

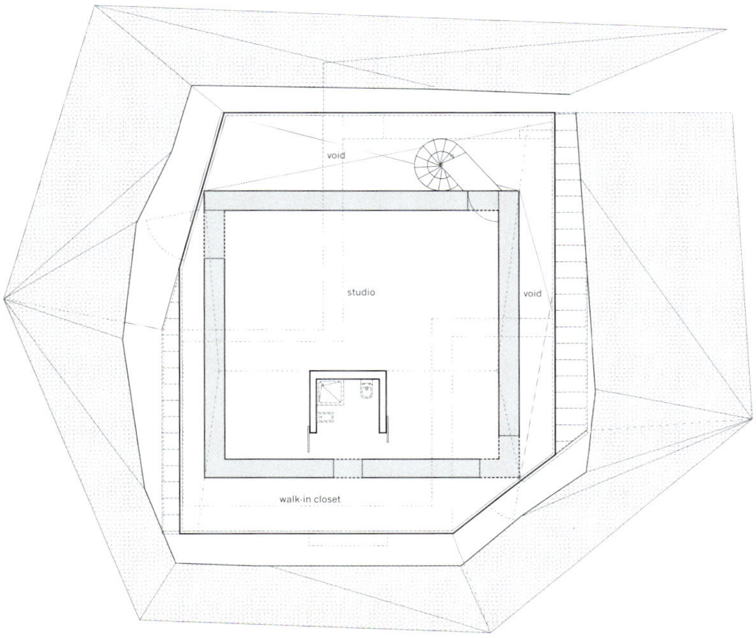

The project is a design investigation into how the qualitative aspects of the wall, as a complex membrane, structure our social interactions and climatic relationships. The project breaks down the "traditional" walls of a house into a series of four delaminated layers including concrete cave, stacked shelving, milky shell, and soft skin, where each is characterized by very specific atmospheric, structural, and functional properties. An energy screen typically used in greenhouse construction constitutes the outermost layer, creating a diffused lighting, a comfortably acclimatized zone inside, and a diamond-cut appearance.

01 General view by night **02** Fully glazed surface **03** Floor plan **04** Interior **05** Outer skin made of aluminum strips woven with polymer fibers

Photos: Cristobal Palma

CITY Santiago
COUNTRY Chile
REGION South America
TYPOLOGY Living
COMPLETION 2007
WEBSITE www.f-a-r.net
ARCHITECTS FAR Frohn&Rojas

CITY Santiago

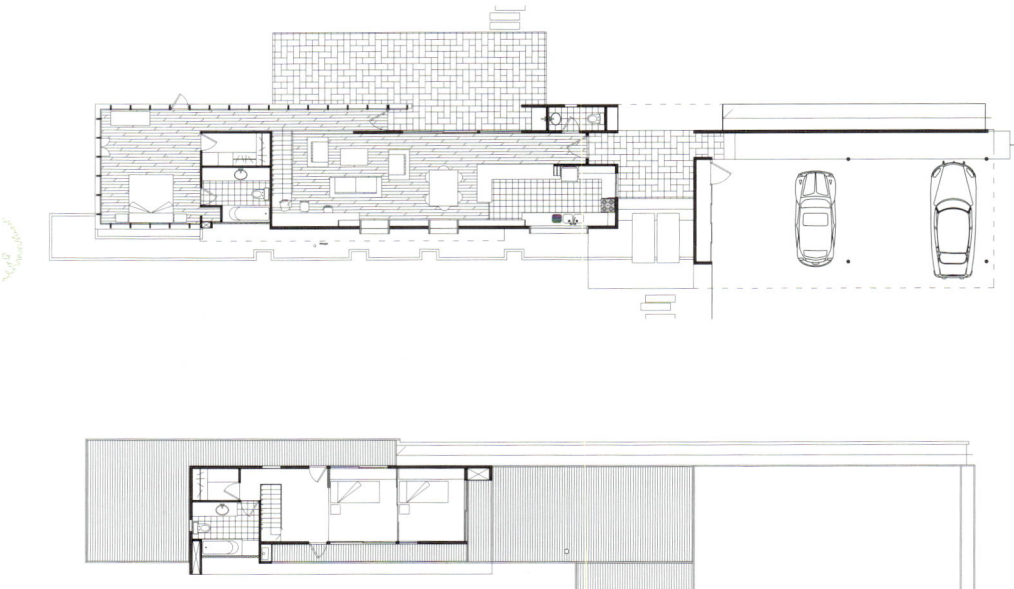

COUNTRY Chile

REGION South America

TYPOLOGY Living

COMPLETION 2004

WEBSITE www.funky.cl

ARCHITECTS funky (ignacio quintana + victor pellegrini)

CASA ALGARROBO IV

This house works open, like its owners, who receive with open arms and piscosour. It is a house without doors, and the celebration of the kitchen and the dining room are a reflection of the celebration of being. Fences do not exist or cross, nor do doors delay advances while walking through the spaces. If areas are not recognizable, it is because there is nothing to recognize. You look for a place and beams to do your own thing; read, sing or dance, and if you define your space, you have only gained. There are no horizons, no spiritual purposes, nor searches, only a great garage and a house that slopes down.

01 General view **02** Sun deck **03** First floor, second floor plan **04** Carport

Photos: Courtesy funky

PRINCIPADO

The house principality rises in front of the mountain range of the Andes, in the high part of Santiago, Chile, and watches the Re-ojo, a valley of Santiago. The house inserted in the land was constructed by its own drawing, created its own references, conquering the slope by means of suspended volumes, which provides the steep topography of the land. The interior inhabits different levels of height and privacy, and of equal measures, the cockpit for guests separates the main volume and changes materiality. The house is thought to receive many guests in festive events, therefore the interior responds to this requirement.

01 View to upper floor **02** Glass and stone façade **03** Interior wooden ceiling **04** Sections **05** Staircase

Photos: Courtesy g8vs architectos

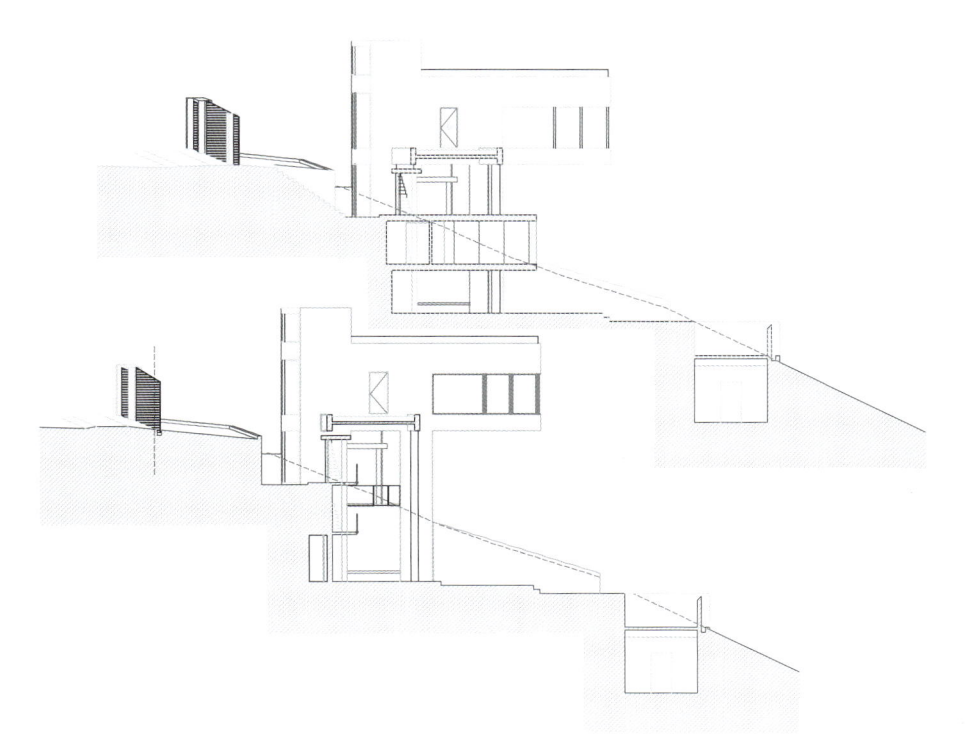

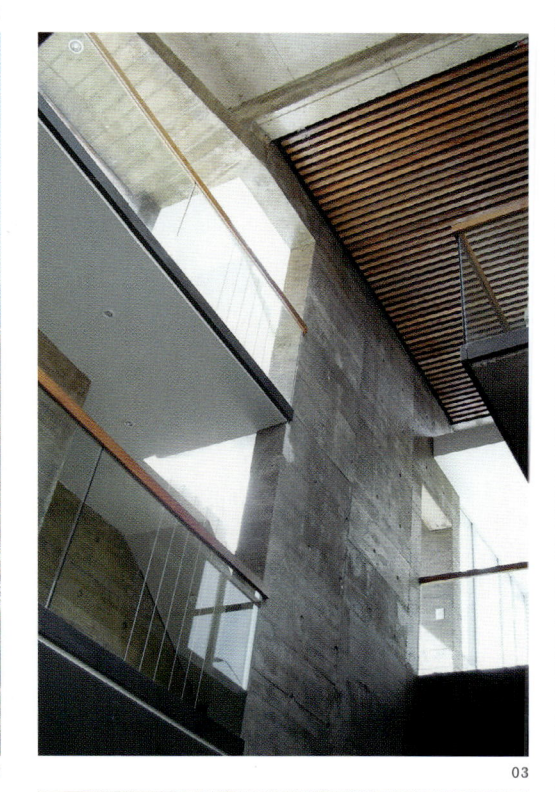

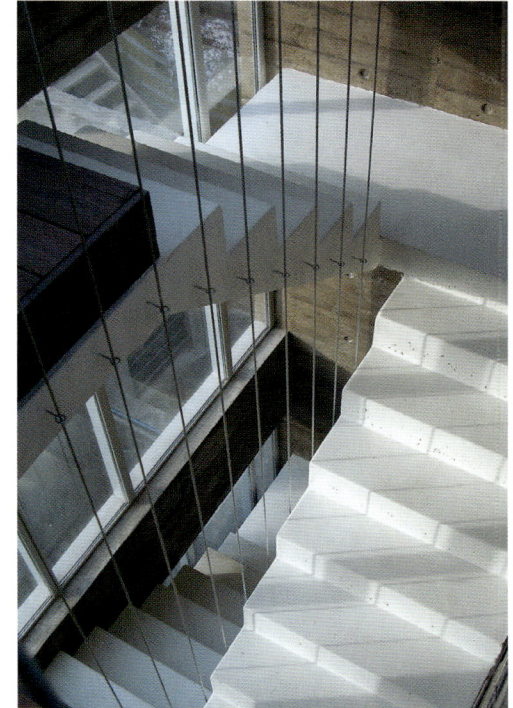

CITY Santiago
COUNTRY Chile
REGION South America
TYPOLOGY Living
COMPLETION 2007
WEBSITE www.g8vs.cl
ARCHITECTS g8vs arquitectos

CITY Santiago
COUNTRY Chile
REGION South America
TYPOLOGY Office
COMPLETION 2006
WEBSITE www.guillermohevia.cl
ARCHITECTS Guillermo Hevia H. / Francisco Carrión G.

CHILEXPRESS S.A.

The project, CHILEXPRESS S.A, is a corporative building for the offices of the Company and operations center. Both buildings are connected through the "place of the encounter", and is the access of all the personnel, finished off in a hall connection glass finish. The set has streets and patios of peripheral operations (circulation and security). A horizontal volume of three floors of height is suspended, and separated curtain walls of the facades are in crystal and steel. In the façade, perforated metallic panels were replaced, allowing to shift the solar radiation without clearing the transparencies.

01 Deatil window shades **02** Fully glazed façade **03** Exterior detail **04** Floor plan **05** Concrete structure

Photos: Courtesy Guillermo Hevia H. / Fransisco Carrión G.

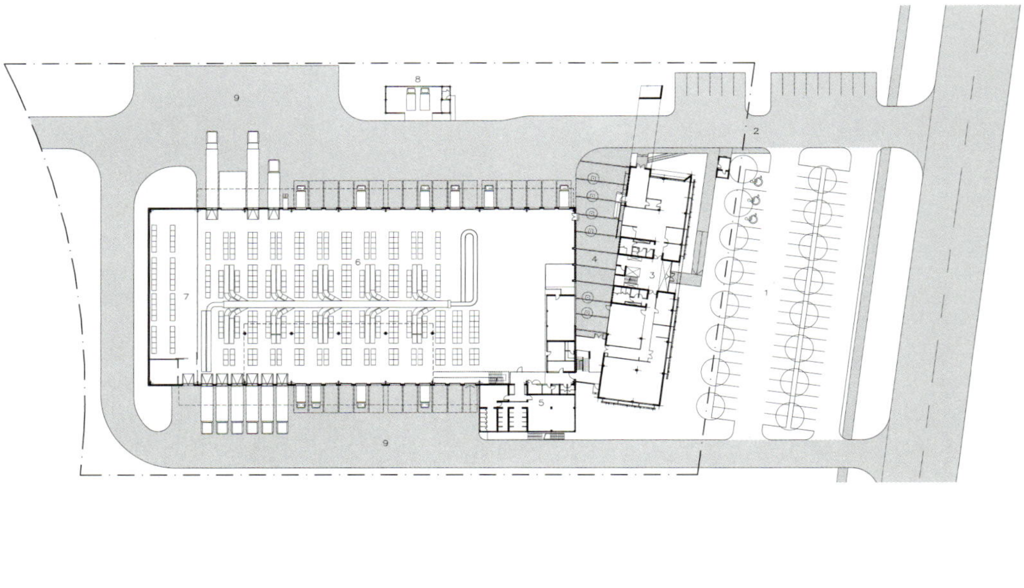

FARMACIAS AHUMADA

Alternate games of windows give movement to the facades, showing different readings from the corporative image of the company. During the day, the building is like a pure volume, a metallic body closed and drawn with fine horizontal windows, which is in contrast to the night where these transform into a blackout line floating in the dark. The incorporation of the BIOCLIMA for use in the inner atmospheres is an expression in architecture much like shining tubes that are born from the Earth. One tries saving and rational use of power resources, looking to improve the quality of life and the protection of the environment.

01 General view 02 View inside 03 Receiving platform, façade with light well 04 Building site

Photos: Courtesy Guillermo Hevia H. / Christián Pino I.

CITY Santiago
COUNTRY Chile
REGION South America
TYPOLOGY Industry
COMPLETION 2004
WEBSITE www.guillermohevia.cl
ARCHITECTS Guillermo Hevia H. / Cristán Pino I.

CITY: Santiago
COUNTRY: Chile
REGION: South America
TYPOLOGY: Education
COMPLETION: 2007
WEBSITE: www.uai.cl
ARCHITECTS: José Cruz Ovalle (José Cruz Ovalle + Hernán Cruz + Ana Turell + Juan Purcell)

ADOLFO IBÁÑEZ UNIVERSITY POST GRADE BUILDING

Situated on a steep plot between two river basins, the site aims to build space that follows the path of the basins through several levels. The architecture of this building is conceived as a void or inner space which follows nature, taking the freedom of a sightseeing walk. It provides the continuity for the foot to never lose a sure step and variety for the eye as if on an outdoor excursion. With stops and pauses, this excursion holds the relationship between study and contemplation. This is a continuous space, but never homogeneous: in it, twists, turns and size variations lead on the path through half-lit to illuminated places.

01 Outdoor cafeteria **02** Hallway **03** Bird's eye view **04** View inside and courtyard **05** Library

Photos: Courtesy of Juan Purcell

EDIFICIO ACCESO PARQUE METROPOLITANO SUR, CERRO CHENA

The Hill San Cristóbal, located in the city center of Santiago, lodges to the Metropolitan Park, visited by nearly 5,000,000 people a year. The order consisted of conforming vehicle and pedestrian accesses to the Park. In addition, it had to solve a program that included a house of information, toll, and public & personal baths. The project strategy was to differentiate the scales, creating a pavilion of access for the pedestrians and a cover for the vehicles. The existence of the toll house as an element isolated between two circulations fragmented the rest of the program in five volumes of large equal and proportions.

01 Exterior view **02** Light-passing staircase **03** Section **04** Stone and steel façade

Photos: Marcos Mendizabal

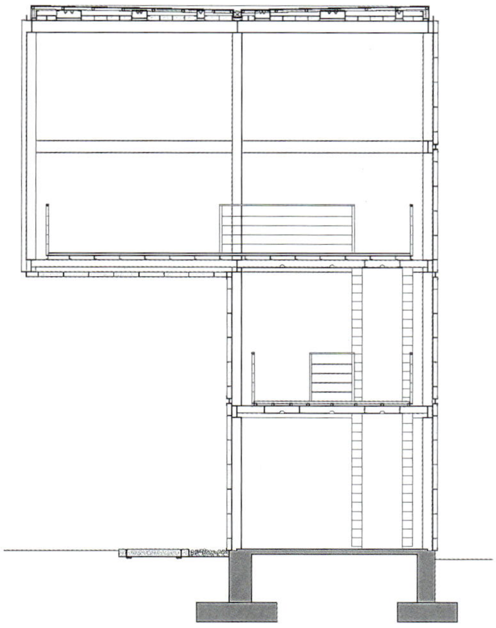

CITY Santiago
COUNTRY Chile
REGION South America
TYPOLOGY Public
COMPLETION 2005
WEBSITE www.polidura-talhouk.com
ARCHITECTS Polidura+Talhouk Arquitectos, Antonio Polidura / Pablo Talhouk

CITY
Santiago

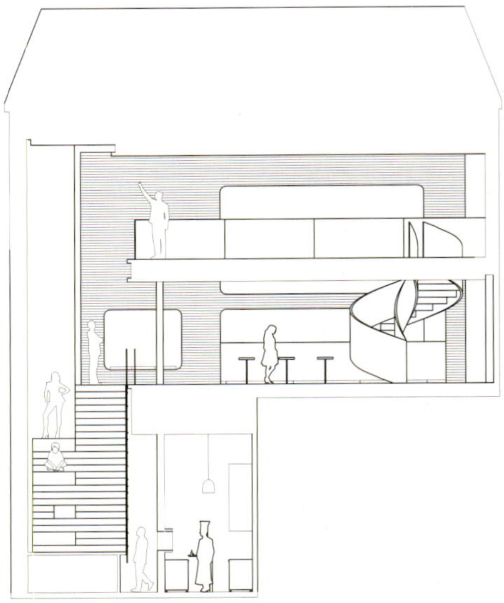

COUNTRY
Chile

REGION
South America

TYPOLOGY
Gastronomy

COMPLETION
2006

WEBSITE
www.tidy.cl

ARCHITECTS
Tidy Arquitectos (Albert Tidy + Ian Tidy)

DOMINGA

The proposal consists in designing the interior of a space composed by an access area, a double height volume located on the second level, and an exterior terrace. The enclosure is located in a well-known commercial complex in the city of Santiago, Chile, right in front of a motorway. At night, images are projected from the interior onto a large translucent crystal window, marking their presence in the complex. Gradations define the space, emphasizing double heights, free floors, and circulations, allowing the access stairs to turn into a "sloped plaza", the attic into a balcony, and the kitchen into an inviting shop window.

01 Interior 02 Section 3 Spiral staircase 04 Ebony ceiling
05 Upper floor seating

Photos: Sebastián Sepúlveda

FACULTAD ARTES VISUALES

The project was adjudged in concourse of antecedents summoned by the faculty of Arts to the faculty of Architecture of the University of Chile. The order consisted of rehabilitating a structure left in the present campus Juan Go'mez Milias of the Faculty of Art. The building was projected originally by Ricardo Architect Joy at the end of `60's ', in which it was unfinished and in an advanced state of deterioration. The managements of the faculty of arts managed to take on these several Mecesup projects with a common objective: to improve the precarious facilities existents to the benefit of the students.

01 Side view **02** Fully glazed façade **03** Exterior view by night **04** Hallway and staircase **05** Aula

Photos: Cristóbal Palma

CITY Santiago
COUNTRY Chile
REGION South America
TYPOLOGY –
COMPLETION –
WEBSITE www.tidy.cl
ARCHITECTS Abert Tidy + Emilio Marín

CITY Santiago (Las Condes)

COUNTRY Chile

REGION South America

TYPOLOGY Living

COMPLETION 2004

WEBSITE www.rdm.cl

ARCHITECTS Rodrigo Duque Motta

DUQUE HOUSE

The Mirador Hill House is located at the top of a small hill just in front of the Los Andes Mountain in Santiago, Chile. The idea was to maximize the frontal views of the mountains, while having a rich relation with the topography, generating a variety of exterior controlled spaces. The first floor of the house is like a base between both sides of the plot, while the second floor rests as a float, like an isolated pavilion. The pavilion is a square plan that combines interior and exterior spaces, with the staircase as its central nucleus. Located around are the living room, dinning room, kitchen, and entrance hall.

01 Exterior view by night **02** Entry with steel rods structure **03** Sections **04** Inner courtyard stone wall

Photos: Rodrigo Duque, Alaluf+Duque

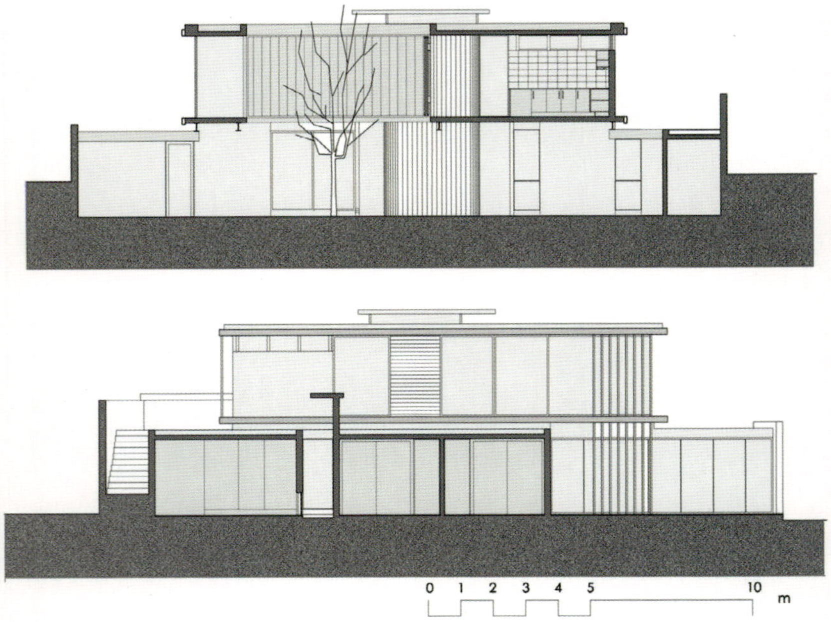

CENTRO DE ATENCION DE EMERGENCIAS SUR

The program of The Center of Attention of South Emergency lodges the Offices of the Personnel of Security and Maintenance, the Operations Center of Traffic, the Parking of Vehicles of Emergency, and the general warehouses of these programmatic areas. Located in the estate of the C.A.E, it complements the area of the preexisting Corporative Building, with a new terrain taken to the strip of the highway. Towards the freeway a facade composed by a concrete socle was considered, and a panel superior of industrial channels regulate the natural illumination of the west and the acoustics of the facilities.

01 Façade with lighting set **02** Stair construction **03** Street side view **04** Glazed balustrade

Photos: Giuseppe Brucculeri

CITY Santiago (San Bernardo)
COUNTRY Chile
REGION South America
TYPOLOGY –
COMPLETION 2004
WEBSITE www.masarquitectos.cl
ARCHITECTS +arquitectos (Alex Brahm / David Bonomi / Maite Bartolomé / Marcelo Leturia / Alfredo Muñoz

CITY
Santiago

COUNTRY
Chile

REGION
South America

TYPOLOGY
Education

COMPLETION
2006

WEBSITE
www.a2o.cl

ARCHITECTS
Alvano y Riquelme,
Renzo Alvano,
Pablo Riquelme

FACULTAD DERECHO UDP

The project is inserted within the plan of infrastructure renovation to the University Diego Vestibules, centrally located in the university district of Santiago. The new project for the Faculty of Right has initial complexity of a solved existing building of 2 floors with a stamp of style loaded with present solutions in the neoclassic language. The general strategy proposes the conservation of the existing construction releasing it of all decorative loads and reinforcing it like a great socle that receives the new proposal. The new construction becomes ordained concentrating the circulations towards the interior of the lot.

01 Urban sidewalk portal **02** Library interior skylight **03** Open staircase **04** Central civic yard **05** Sections **06** Street corner scorso view **07** Hallway

Photos: Fernando Gomez

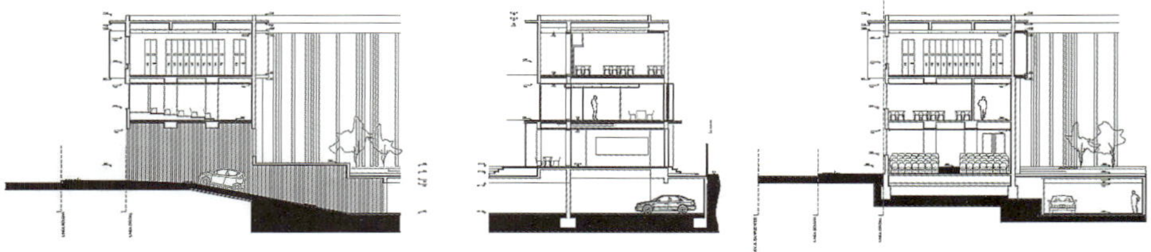

PORTERIAS LA RESERVA

The project deals with the construction of a set of porterías that accedes project ZODUC, the Reserve, in the Hill Commune. The Reserve comprises of the Hill Valley presented as a characteristic differentiating the presence of slopes, little vegetation, and a rocky ground constitution, all of which are part of the strategy of the location that attempts not to sweep the existing landscape. The project is located as an access door to the valley and provides a path to a linear park throughout a gorge. The general strategy was to construct a line of traverse, closing several stone walls of the place.

01 Bird's eye view **02** Stone and concrete texture **03** Gateway access plan **04** Portal view

Photos: Pablo Riquelme

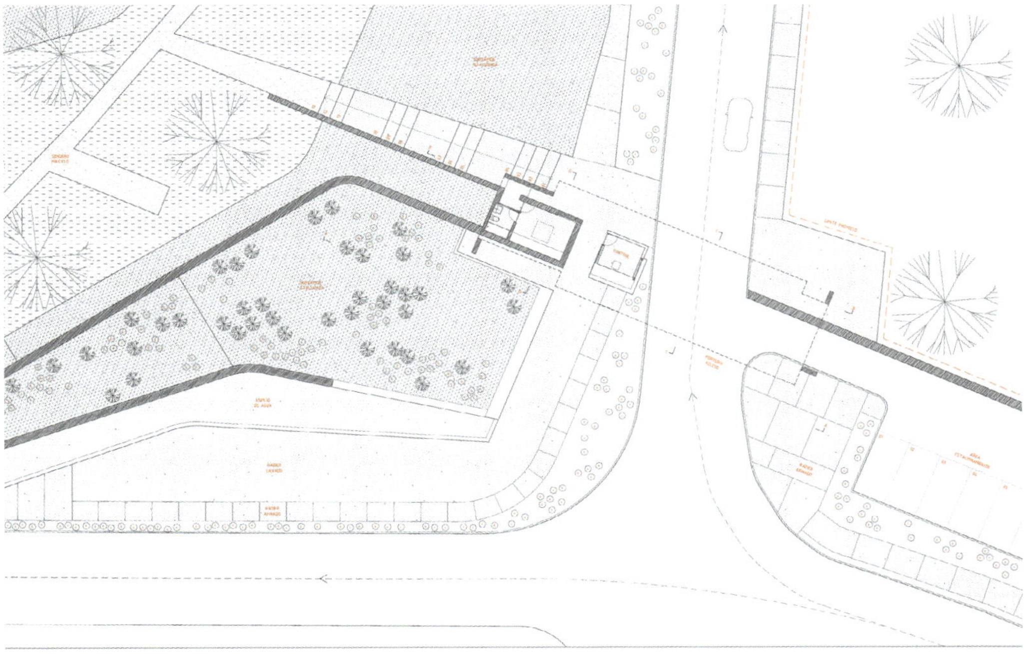

CITY Santiago
COUNTRY Chile
REGION South America
TYPOLOGY Urban
COMPLETION 2008
WEBSITE www.a2o.cl
ARCHITECTS Alvano y Riquelme / Renzo Alvano, Pablo Riquelme

CITY
Santiago

COUNTRY
Chile

REGION
South America

TYPOLOGY
—

COMPLETION
2004

WEBSITE
www.elementalchile.cl

ARCHITECTS
Alejandro Aravena

SIAMESE TOWERS

A glass tower was to host all IT-related programs of the university, which had reserved a 5,000 m² site for the project. As insufficient funds were available for a curtain wall, another sun protection was found. Two 'skins' were designed to each perform a single function – an outer glass skin to protect from weathering, and an inner fiber cement skin to avoid the greenhouse effect. The inner skin shields the interior from the sun's rays and allows the air pocket between the two to act as a perimeter chimney through which hot air leaves by convection through an opening above. Above the 7th floor, the tower is split into two volumes.

01 Wooden entrance area **02** Exterior view **03** Wooden flooring **04** Construction detail

Photos: Cristobal Palma

CRYPT SANTIAGO

A continuous white marble carpet was extended to the presbytery, which was widened to increase capacity; the stairs of the crypt were developed in a smooth line so that the processional routes could develop fluidly. The project explores the relation of layers (presbytery and crypt) like a system of levels on the floor of a ship, whose success of flotation is determined by spaciousness and materials. The marble slab dissolves between the ground of the presbytery and the flat sky of the new crypt, separating it like a membrane: a smooth and luminous white ground for the presbytery and the sky adorned with the crypt's caissons.

01 View to altar **02** Marble stair **03** Subdued light ceiling **04** Interior detail **05** Sanctuary

Photos: Cristobal Palma

CITY Santiago
COUNTRY Chile
REGION South America
TYPOLOGY Ecclesiastical
COMPLETION –
WEBSITE –
ARCHITECTS Perez de Arce-Mardones-Bianchi

CITY
Santiago

COUNTRY
Chile

REGION
South America

TYPOLOGY
Institution

COMPLETION
2006

WEBSITE
www.vsv.com.ar

ARCHITECTS
VSV - Vila-Sebastián-Vila Asociados Arquitectos

CENTRO DE JUSTICIA SANTIAGO – CHILE

The project, Centro de Justicia based in Santiago, Chile solves the set of buildings in an independent and efficient form, but it forms in its entirety, a complex of strong unit that defines the identity of the great public buildings who, like landmarks, order and redefine the urban plot. The set is organized around a great citizen place and a popular area for the everyday person known as Open Pie. This certain space is accessible to all the habitants and with an adapted massive scale.

01 Fully glazed façades **02** General view **03** Glass and concrete façade **04** View to inner courtyard

Photos: Courtesy VSV - Vila-Sebastián-Vila Asociados Arquitectos

NUEVO ACCESO AL PARQUE METROPOLITANO DE SANTIAGO

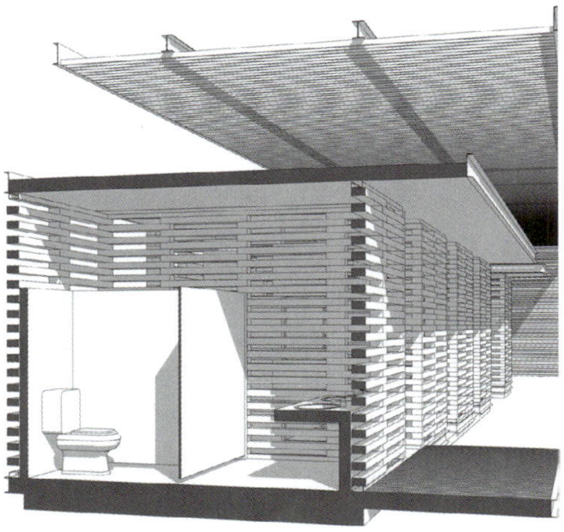

This project inserted the Green Plan Program of the Ministry of House and Urbanism of Chile and the Metropolitan Park of Santiago. The idea is to increase the amount of green areas by inhabitants in the South zone of the city, which is low compared to international standards. "An amiable city" must have about 9 to 10 M2 of green areas by inhabitants; Santiago counts less than five while the San Bernardo zone has approximately 2.8. With the professionals of the Metropolitan Park and multidisciplinary equipment, 37 hectares of the Hill Chena have been developed, creating the future of the South Metropolitan Park.

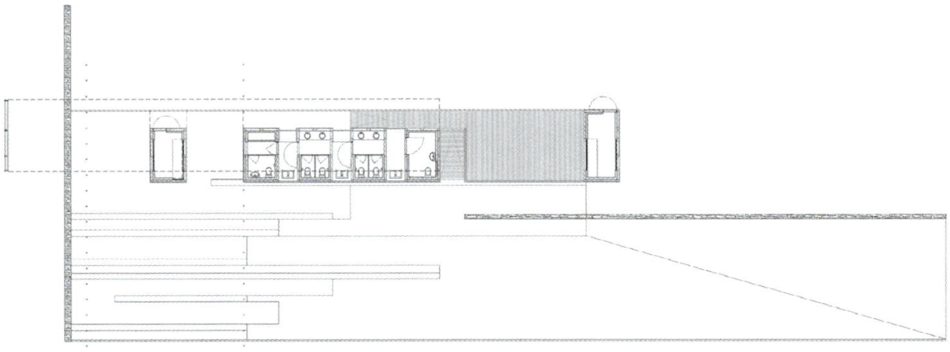

01 Wooden structure **02** Sketch **03** General view **04** Floor plan **05** Elevation

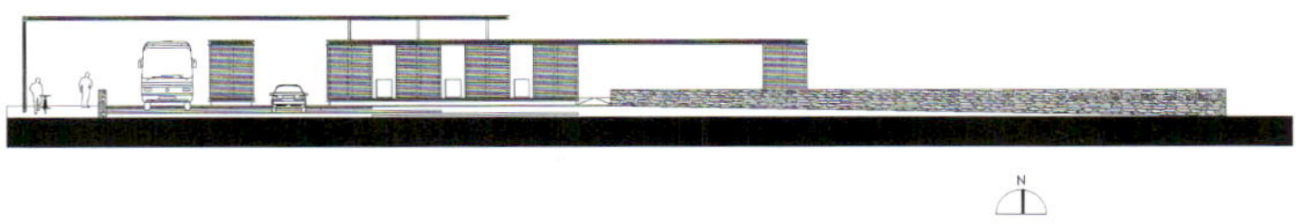

Photos: Marcelo Levy, Cristian Donoso

CITY Santiago
COUNTRY Chile
REGION South America
TYPOLOGY Public
COMPLETION 2003
WEBSITE www.polidura-tallhouk.com
ARCHITECTS Polidura + Talhouk Arquitectos. Antonio Polidura / Pablo Talhouk

SIMONETTI BUILDING

The simplicity of the open plan offices smoothly articulates the central staircase and the three-dimensional hall that provide circulation and social interaction. The main feature of the building is the enclosure panel, designed in response to the conventional technology of curtain walls. The design aims to create tension between tradition and avant-garde. The proposed translucent glass panel captures the first light of the morning and releases it in the course of the day; quartz filling the space between sheets of glass provides warmth while framing the landscape in transparent modules placed into the pattern of the façade.

01 Exterior view from street **02** Central staircase **03** Translucent glass panel **04** Quartz panel south façade **05** Hallway leading to offices

Photos: Guy Wenborne

CITY Santiago

COUNTRY Chile

REGION South America

TYPOLOGY Public

COMPLETION 2006

WEBSITE www.undurragadeves.cl

ARCHITECTS Undurragadeves Arquitectos + Alejandro Simonetti

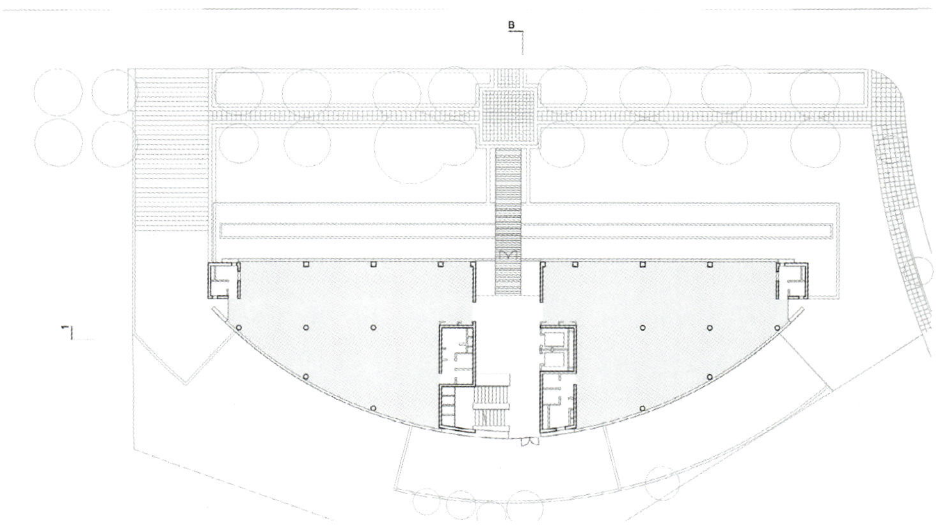

LAS CONDES TOWN COUNCIL BUILDING

This public housing building was added to the area with the intention of increasing its urban character in the face of predominantly autonomous structures surrounding it. Local bylaws led to the development of isolated volumes connected by a 7-meter-high unbroken baseboard. In order to promote urban continuity, the lower volume of the baseboard was covered with travertine marble, like that of the neighboring building. An outer diagonal steel beam structure balances the rigidity of an inner concrete core that contains all service areas. This solution also increased the seismic stability of the structure.

01 Front façade **02** Travertine marble baseboard **03** Staircase with skylight **04** Section **05** Curtain wall with diagonal beam structure

Photos: Guy Wenborne

CITY	Santiago
COUNTRY	Chile
REGION	South America
TYPOLOGY	Public
COMPLETION	2003
WEBSITE	www.undurragadeves.cl
ARCHITECTS	Undurragadeves Arquitectos

CITY Santiago
COUNTRY Chile
REGION South America
TYPOLOGY Living
COMPLETION 2002
WEBSITE www.undurragadeves.cl
ARCHITECTS Undurragadeves Arquitectos

EL MIRADOR HOUSE

Located on a gentle slope next to the Andes, the project was created as a single powerful volume of exposed concrete, scaled with the landscape. The same formal layout was used to close the house on the public side towards the street, and to open it up towards the mountains. The upper cornice on this side counterpoints the mountain silhouette, while the floor blends with the topography. The house adapts itself to the natural slope of the site with a ramp that articulates the main spaces. On the other hand, to open up views to the mountains, the roof remains as a single horizontal line with a logical height gain above interior spaces.

01 First level floor plan **02** Second level floor plan **03** Ramp **04** Side view with views to the Andean mountains **05** Ramp **06** Patio **07** Inner courtyard with staricase leading to rooftop

Photos: Guy Wenborne

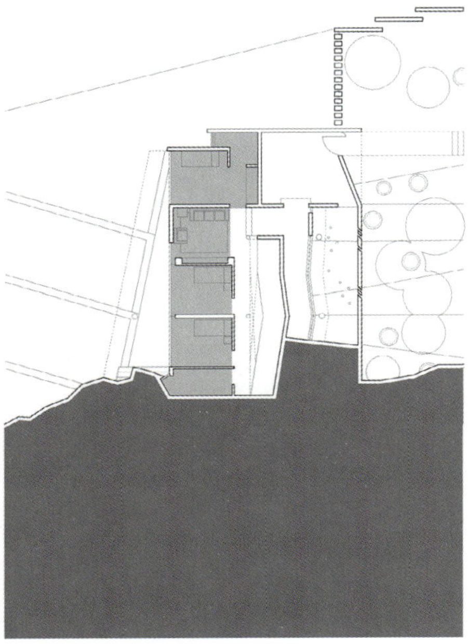

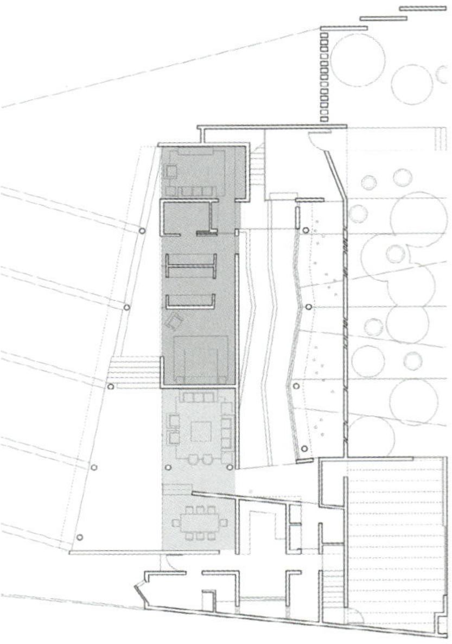

SANTIAGO MUSEUM OF VISUAL ARTS

The museum is located on a square in a small urban corner in the very heart of Santiago. A compact, austere concrete box shaped like a parallelepiped closes off the square, filling in the available space. Given the proximity of neo-Colonial structures, a meeting of contrasts occurs. The museum entrance crosses the arcade of an old house, turning it into the new building's atrium. The space extends vertically through facing half-stories that emphasize the three-dimensional character of the layout. The luminous central void establishes a pause and connects the various levels of the exhibition halls with freestanding stairs.

01 Luminous central void **02** Exhibition areas **03** Vertical half-story spaces **04** Longitudinal section **05** Installation art in courtyard

Photos: Guy Wenborne - Luis Poirot

CITY Santiago
COUNTRY Chile
REGION South America
TYPOLOGY Culture
COMPLETION 1999
WEBSITE www.undurragadeves.cl
ARCHITECTS Undurragadeves Arquitectos

CITY Santiago
COUNTRY Chile
REGION South America
TYPOLOGY Culture
COMPLETION 2005
WEBSITE www.undurragadeves.cl
ARCHITECTS Undurragadeves Arquitectos

SANTIAGO ARCHEOLOGICAL MUSEUM

This small museum is an extension of the Museum of Visual Arts. The collection is located on the second floor of an old neo-colonial house adjacent to it, and it is devoted to the arts and crafts of different Indian cultures that inhabited the remote Chilean landscapes before the Spanish conquest. In order to achieve a diffusely lit interior, we proposed a glass panel with an infill of dry wood sticks. The wicker placed vertically along horizontal glass panels filters light like a wicker basket. The sticks were placed in a simple and direct way, exposing the quality of the material.

01 Glass panel with an infill of dry wood sticks **02** Front façade **03** Art collection **04** Main entrance **05** Sections

Photos: Luis Poirot

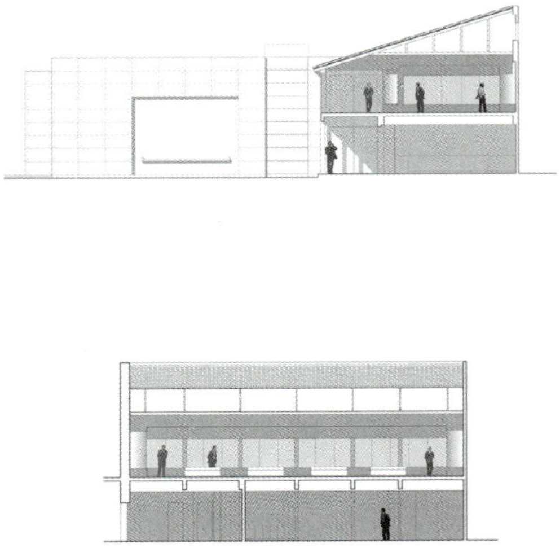

PATIO HOUSE

The project is developed as a single plan, with the spaces organized around a central patio with crystal and quartz walls. During the day, the walls capture sunlight and illuminate the main hall of circulation; in the evening the walls are artificially lit and give the patio an illuminated glow. Facing south, the public façade is closed, hiding the interior which is revealed only through the extension of the beams on the north façade. The interiors of the different enclosures are defined by walls that do not reach the ceiling, allowing wood beams pass, creating a visual continuity throughout the house.

01 Front façade **02** Interior courtyard **03** Floor plan **04** Main Entrance

Photos: Cristobal Palma

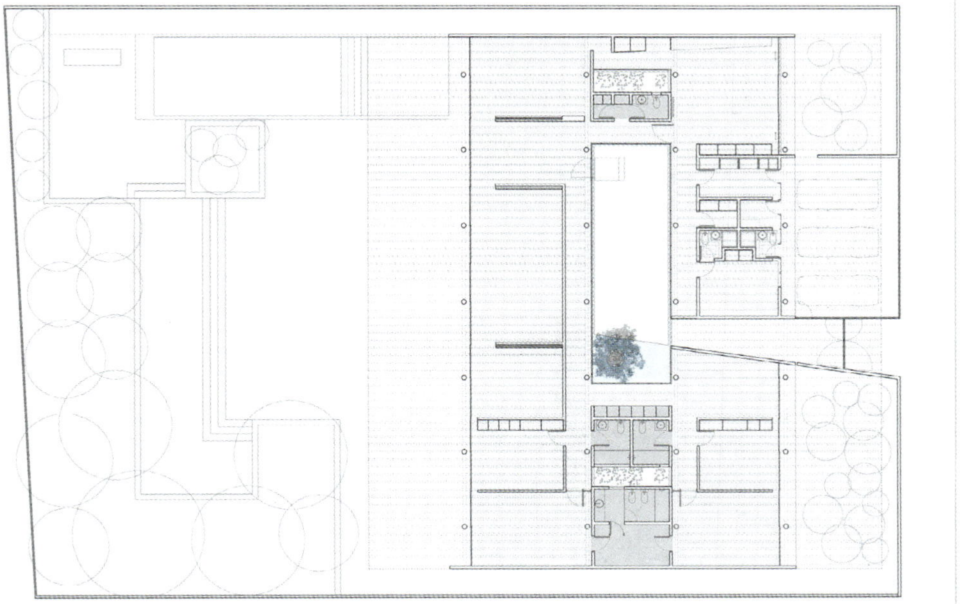

CITY Santiago
COUNTRY Chile
REGION South America
TYPOLOGY Living
COMPLETION 2007
WEBSITE www.undurragadeves.cl
ARCHITECTS Undurragadeves Arquitectos

SPENCE MINE STAGING

URO1.ORG understands their roll in the development of the country, much the same as the approach from a creative action, on the process of cultural transformation in a society. This action has concentrated in projects that try the development of functional models of utility, emotional and social oriented to serve as tools of cultural transformation. These models are developed from a multidisciplinary platform that ties on the one hand the observation and critic of the cultural reality, using tools of the art and social sciences, with the transference of new technologies to the scopes of planning, management, and design.

01 Floor plan **02** Interior construction **03** Stage and screens **04** Interior light construction **05** Detail

Photos: Valeria Zalaquett

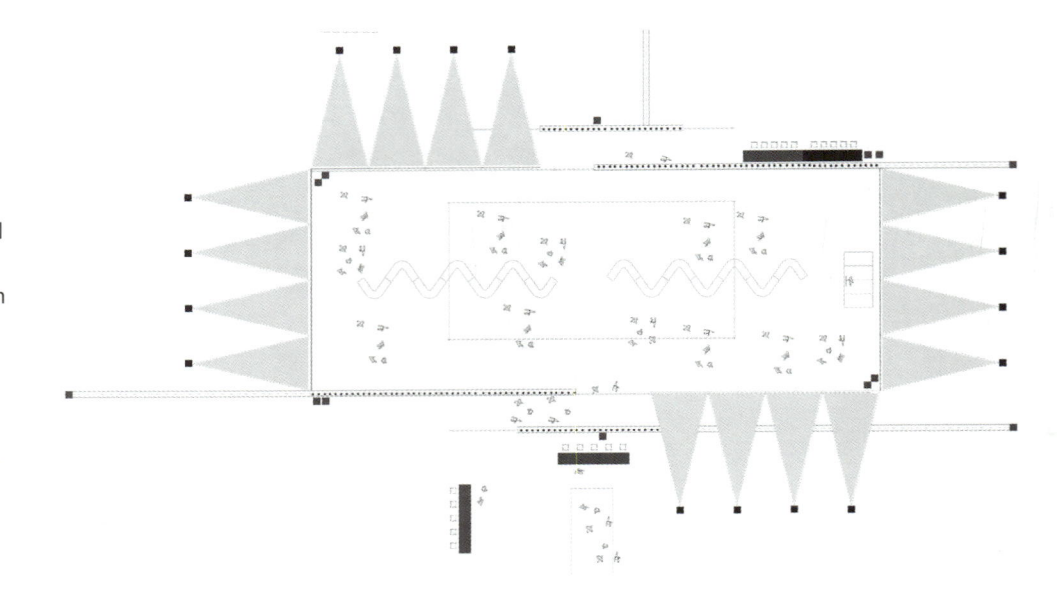

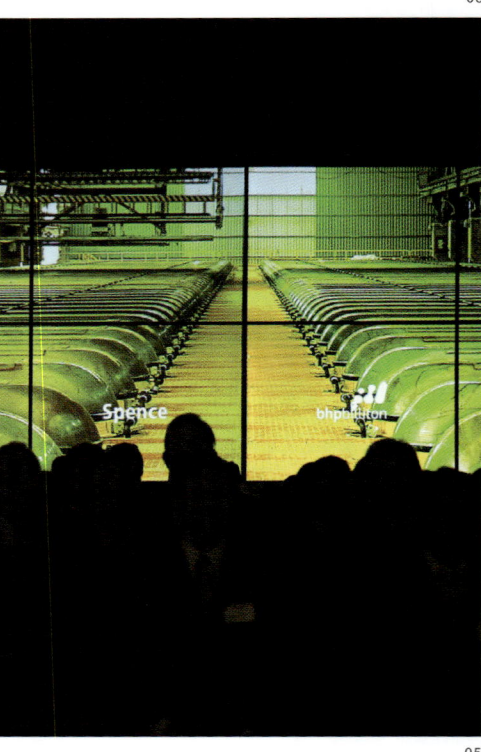

CITY Santiago
COUNTRY Chile
REGION South America
TYPOLOGY –
COMPLETION –
WEBSITE www.uro1.org
ARCHITECTS Cooperativa URO1.ORG

UCINF'S CORPORATIVE BUILDING

The order requests an emblematic building with a strong image, while being representative of the university's 10th anniversary. The program includes 38 class rooms, an aula magna (230 people), casino, library, laboratories and administration areas all placed in a very complex site with an extremely tight front and a very large background. The crystal treatment of the external layer is defined by the filter grade, where four crystals of similar conditions are placed in a geometric form in the building, providing a unique exterior skin, which offers light to the interior by a complex reflex of color and transparency.

01 Opaque and transparent glazing **02** Fully glazed façade **03** Exterior view by night **04** First floor plan **05** Unique cristal exterior skin

Photos: Gonzalo Donoso

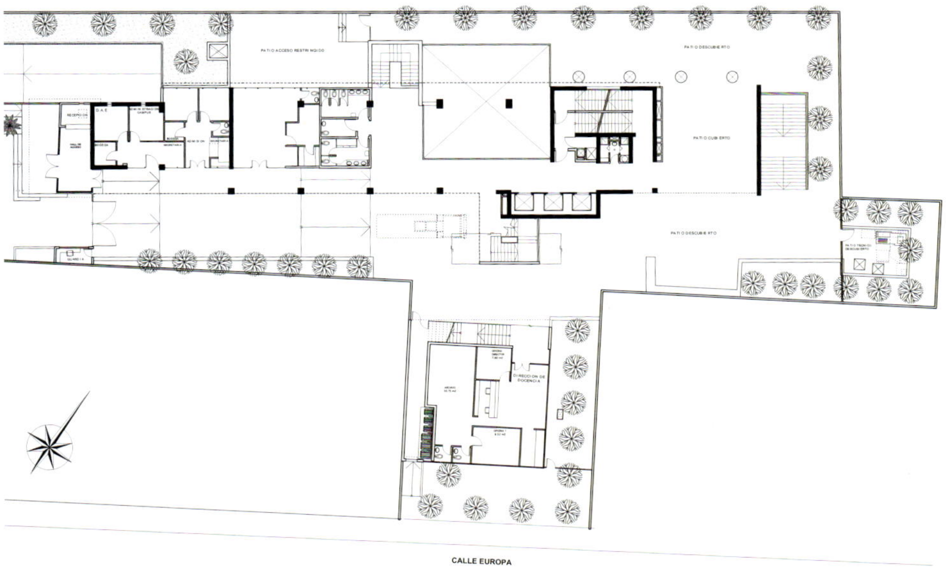

CITY Santiago
COUNTRY Chile
REGION South America
TYPOLOGY Education
COMPLETION 2007
WEBSITE www.maceiras.cl
ARCHITECTS maceiras y cia.ltda

DOUBLEVIEW HOUSE

The design process, as a test and a revision of the result, provided us with the house's geometry. The specific form of the house corresponds with its interior spaces, the structural and technical requirements, the needs and proposals of the clients, aesthetic considerations, agreements and modifications. The exterior two-level terrace is a great empty space which crosses the house connecting two situations, both the immediate and the distant. It is an interesting and quite unusual space, which ended up becoming the center of the project.

01 View inside **02** Exterior structure **03** Fenestration **04** Roofed courtyard **05** Fireplace

Photos: Macarena Alvarez

CITY Talca
COUNTRY Chile
REGION South America
TYPOLOGY Living
COMPLETION 2007
WEBSITE www.murua-valenzuela.com
ARCHITECTS Rodrigo Valenzuela - Benjamín Murúa

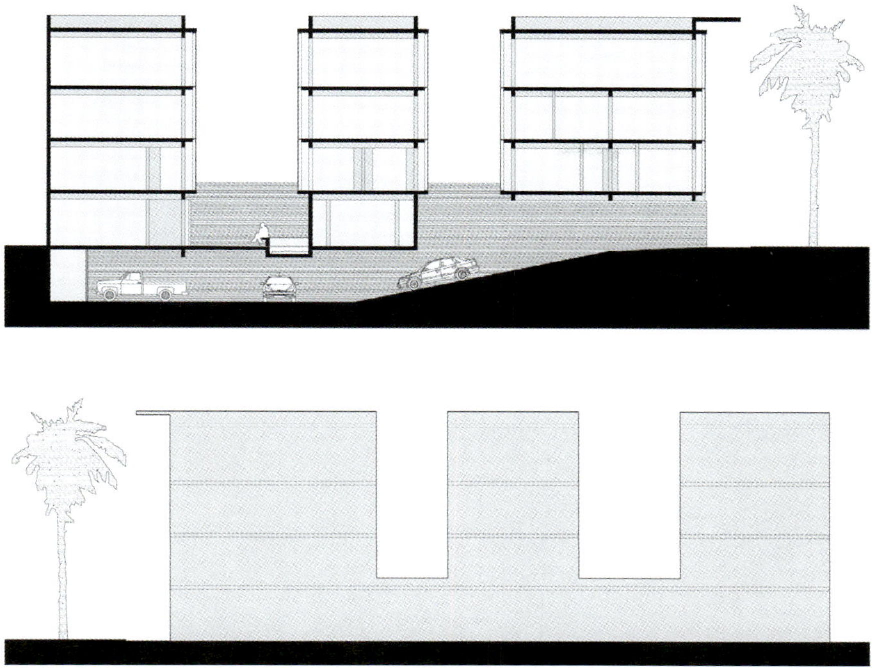

CAJA DE COMPENSACION LA ARAUCANA

The project is located in the Talca, Seventh Region, which is just south of Chile. The building of the equalization fund for Talca looks to group a series of independent services that participate within the same building, assuring in certain way, the independence of diverse programs including health and educational areas, and office space. As a general strategy proposed to the construction of three blocks, a reception block was put into place, allowing the independence of the circulations to accede to each program, to which it was added, on each side, while two volumes solve the zones of permanence.

01 Sections **02** Curtain wall façade laminated wood structure **03** Block connection **04** Intermediate block relation **05** Staircase detail **06** Exterior block façade

Photos: Fernando Gomez

CITY: Talca
COUNTRY: Chile
REGION: South America
TYPOLOGY: Institution
COMPLETION: 2007
WEBSITE: www.a2o.cl
ARCHITECTS: Alvano y Riquelme / Renzo Alvano, Pablo Riquelme

CITY Tunquen, Casablanca
COUNTRY Chile
REGION South America
TYPOLOGY Living
COMPLETION 2005
WEBSITE www.riescoyrivera.blogspot.com
ARCHITECTS Riesco + Rivera Arquitectos Asociados

CONTADOR-WELLER HOUSE

The Contador-Weller House, a weekend retreat in Valparaiso, was built using a Canadian timber fabrication system of pre-fab panels. The architects broke down the system and used the elements in different ways; panels as both structure and internal wall, with the modular units creating the basic grid for simplicity. 'This allowed us to generate a total expression of the house,' says Riesco, 'very distant from the classic Canadian model, but using the same system that was known by the builders.

01 Exterior view **02** Wooden façade **03** West view **04** Site plan

Photos: Sebastián Melo and Carlos Eguiguren

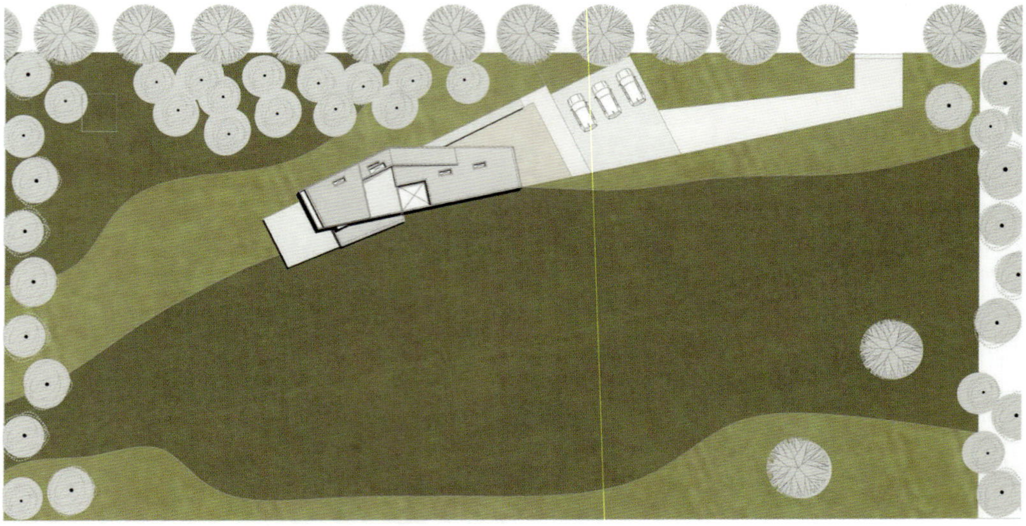

HOSPEDERÍA COLGANTE · CORPORACIÓN AMEREIDA

The Open City is an extension of 270 hectares located 4 km to the North of Concón, and was founded in 1970 by poets, philosophers, sculptors, painters, architects and designers. Today by means of the educational investigations that are realized within the lands of the open city, the students of the School of Architecture and Designs, PUCV, co-participate actively in the permanent construction. This project consists of a 180 m2 building, and provides an exhibition gallery made up of rooms of work (of projection and study), and an Annex for the lodging of the family to stay, known as a hospedería hanging.

01 Exterior view **02** View from below **03** Area view **04** Floor plan **05** Dining corner

Photos: Manuela Donoso

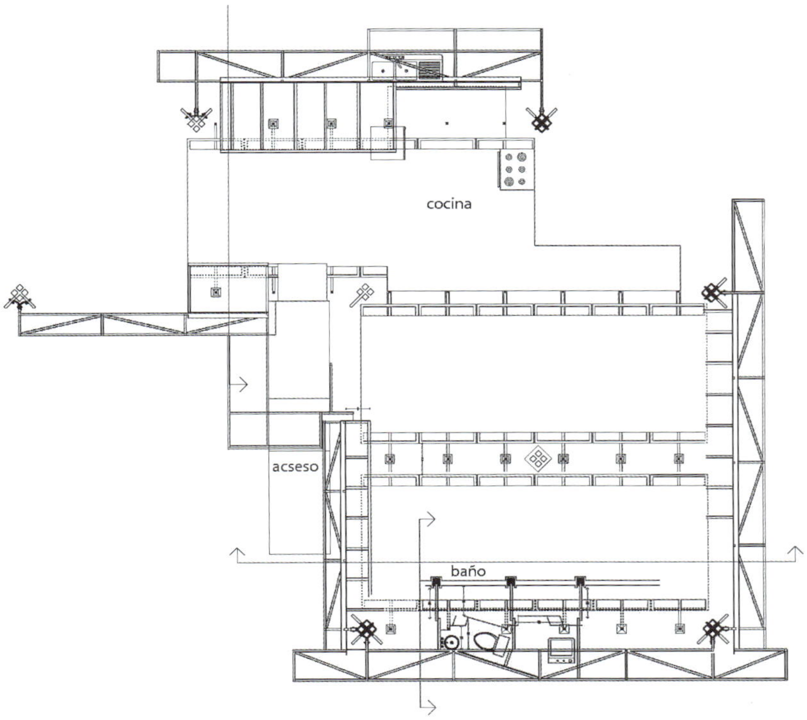

CITY
Valparaíso (Corporación Cultural Amereida)

COUNTRY
Chile

REGION
South America

TYPOLOGY
Hospitality

COMPLETION
2006

WEBSITE
www.corporacionamereida.cl

ARCHITECTS
David Luza - Open City (Amereida)

CITY Valparaíso
COUNTRY Chile
REGION South America
TYPOLOGY Living
COMPLETION 2006
WEBSITE www.rearquitectura.cl
ARCHITECTS Rearquitectura / Antonio Menéndez and Cristian Barrientos

LOFTS YUNGAY

Lofts Yungay is located on the outskirts of a World Heritage Site in Valparaíso, Chile. For this reason, this apartment building had to relate to its surroundings in a way that wouldn't disturb the architectural heritage. To accomplish this, the existing façade was reconstructed and the building was covered with a corrugated steel coating that is typical for the area. The layout of the apartments echoes classical colonial topology, with all units converging into a central court. The project contains two one-story apartments and 9 three-story lofts. Each unit has an area of about 50 square meters.

01 General view **02** Aerial view **03** Inner courtyard
04 Street side view **05** General floor plan

Photos: Antonio Corcuera

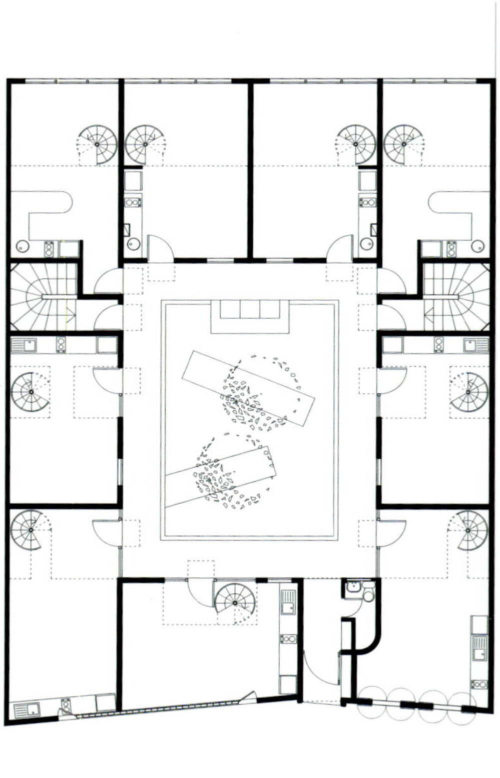

CASA PAINE

Based on a slope, The Casa Paine watches the Maipo River, in which the order consists of a wood cabin of low cost, and is developed on two levels. The first contains public spaces, while also communicating inner-outer elements. The second is of double height and contains living and dormitory space, all with views dominating the valley. A further surface generates a covered parking, while a sector roof is provided for roasts. A volume of single-wire lines, with perforations controlled towards the access, refuses to the street, and towards the interior, the house uses the slope in favor of the land.

01 General view **02** Wooden deck, upper floor **03** Elevations
04 Wrapped-around deck **05** Exterior view by night

Photos: Aryeh Kornfeld

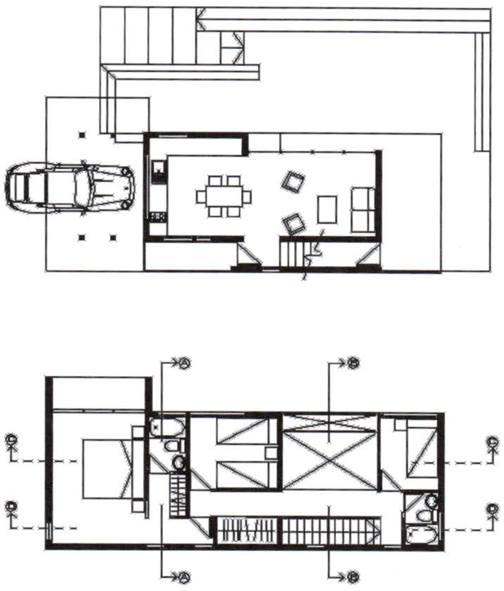

CITY Valdivia de Paine
COUNTRY Chile
REGION South America
TYPOLOGY Living
COMPLETION 2004
WEBSITE -
ARCHITECTS Iván Bravo

CASA ALTAVISTA

Located at the top of a hill in the middle of steep slope, the house is located valuing the deep space. The terrace with views to the sea passes to be the main space of the house. The plant of triangular form distributes the program in two volumes. The first volume follows the level of the hill, in the same plane of the terrace, and welcomes the programs more public space of the house: being, the dining room and the kitchen. The second volume is located against the slope, lowering next to four different levels, in which the dormitories are located. This way a protected center of the wind is obtained.

01 Rear view **02** Sun deck **03** Outdoor dining space **04** Floor plan **05** Fenestration to seaside

Photos: Felipe Durán Palma

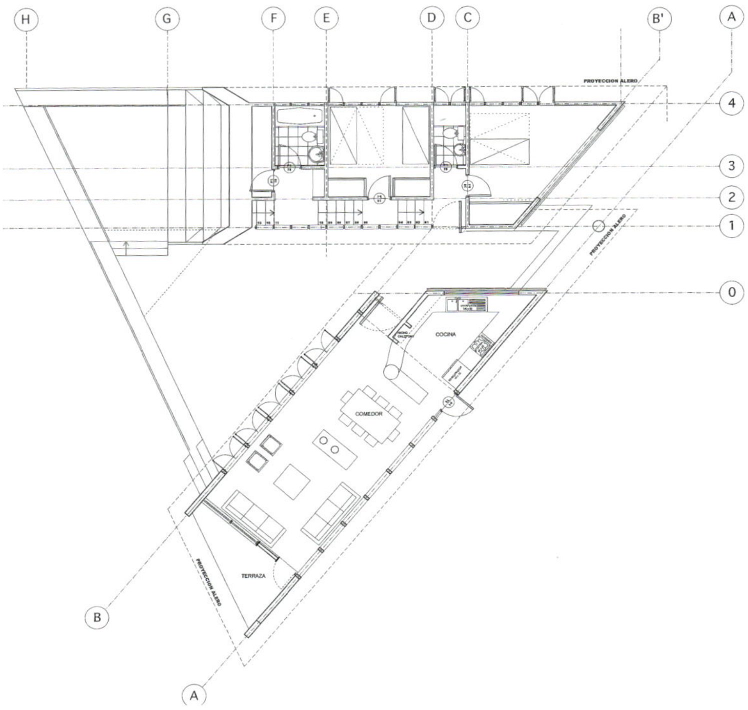

OMNIBUS HOUSE

This is space for life and leisure. To break up the typical areas of an urban house (kitchen, living and dining room and bedrooms) this house has a double circulation that deconstructs these areas into a set of complimentary places. This creates a way of inhabiting that moves away from a typical urban arrangement into a more playful one. To inhabit the exterior of a holiday house does not only imply direct interaction with the outside of the house, but also interaction throughout the house. This includes re-discovering new views from the terrace roof, from the back terrace through the living room, from the corridor, and so on.

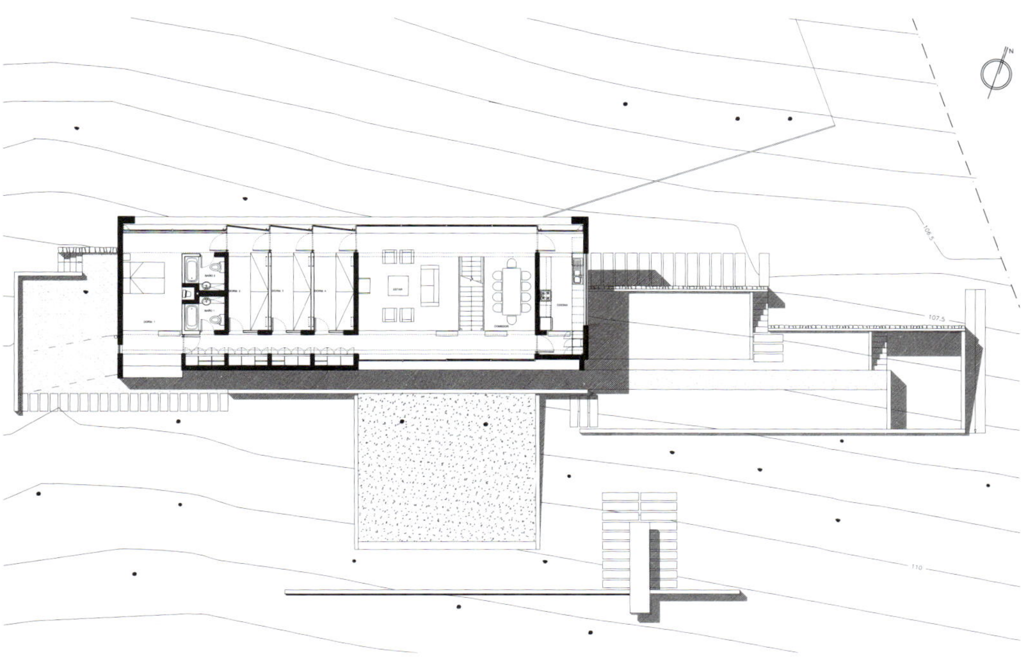

01 Rear façade with discreet windows **02** Glass-encased staircase **03** Hallway with view into sleeping rooms **04** Concrete 'box' with fully glazed façade **05** Floor plan

Photos: Marcos Mendizabal

CITY Zapallar
COUNTRY Chile
REGION South America
TYPOLOGY Living
COMPLETION 2003
WEBSITE www.gubbinsarquitectos.cl
ARCHITECTS Gubbins Arquitectos

CITY
Bogotá

COUNTRY
Colombia

REGION
South America

TYPOLOGY
Education

COMPLETION
2007

WEBSITE
www.daniel-bonilla.com

ARCHITECTS
Daniel Bonilla

EDIFICIO ADMINISTRATIVO COLEGIO LOS NOGALES

This project, located in the north area of Bogotá, is part of the master plan for the expansion of the school. It emerges from the need to develop a building for administrative offices, and from taking advantage of the strategic localization of the building, to set up the project as a main access to the institution. The upper box is composed of two sides made of ochre concrete, controlling the sun in the morning and afternoon. The two other sides, composed with opaque and color glass, are modulated to become elements that allow flexibility into the interior, without changing or loosing the image of the building.

01 Exterior view **02** Detail façade **03** Floor plans, ground floor & first floor **04** Front view **05** Staircase

Photos: Daniel Bonilla

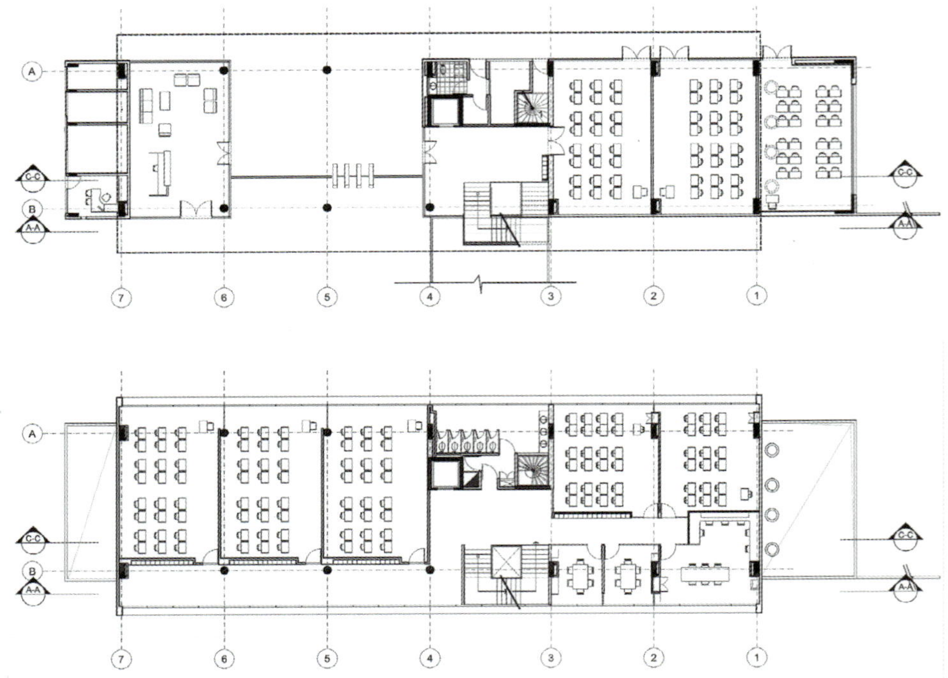

EDIFICIO JULIO MARIO SANTODOMINGO

The building is conceived as a new element that interconnects the campus of the University, concentrating various programs and integrating pedestrian flow spaces like the access plaza and the first-floor gallery. The mixed program that includes parking and postgraduate classrooms is represented in pure and forceful geometry which clearly expresses the duality through the materials used on the façade. This lowers the building's impact on the area as an intersection of university housing and mixed use. The terrace garden on the upper floors of the building creates welcoming contemplation areas.

01 Façade by night **02** Stairs, seventh floor **03** Interior **04** View on terrace garden **05** Longitudinal section

Photos: Daniel Bonilla

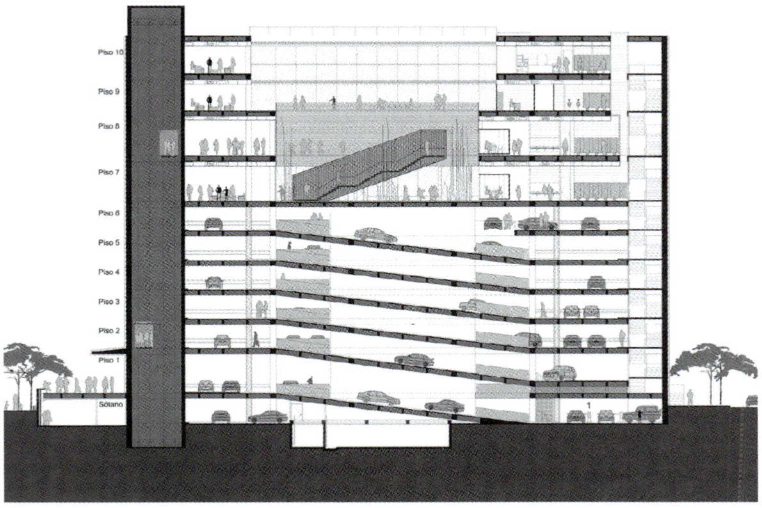

CITY Bogotá
COUNTRY Colombia
REGION South America
TYPOLOGY Education
COMPLETION 2007
WEBSITE www.daniel-bonilla.com
ARCHITECTS Daniel Bonilla

CASA SANTA ANA

This house, known as the Casa Santa Ana, and constructed by Rodriguez & Valencia Arquitectos, is of 650 m2, and is located in the means of the city, which proposes the permanent relation of inside and outside by the distinct features of inner patios and the gardens. The house is acceded by a foot-bridge that extends on a water mirror, leading to a patio which also takes you towards the appearance of the front door. The house is solved in two levels; on the first level, it takes the shape of being the social area, while on the second level, two alcoves are featured creating an interesting element for the house.

01 View from garden **02** Entrance area **03** View from roof terrace **04** Floor plans **05** View on first floor and terrace

Photos: Courtesy of Rodriguez & Valencia

CITY Bogotá
COUNTRY Colombia
REGION South America
TYPOLOGY Living
COMPLETION 2006
WEBSITE –
ARCHITECTS Rodriguez & Valencia Arquitectos

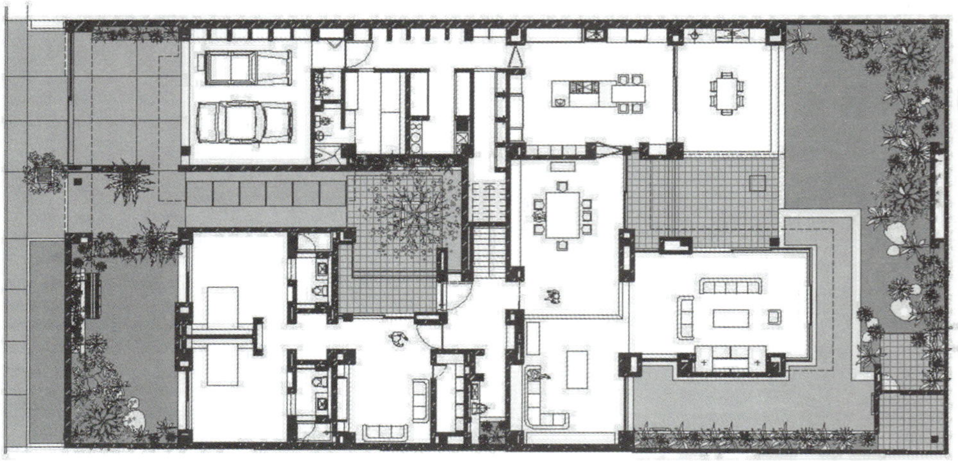

INTERNATIONAL CONVENTION CENTER

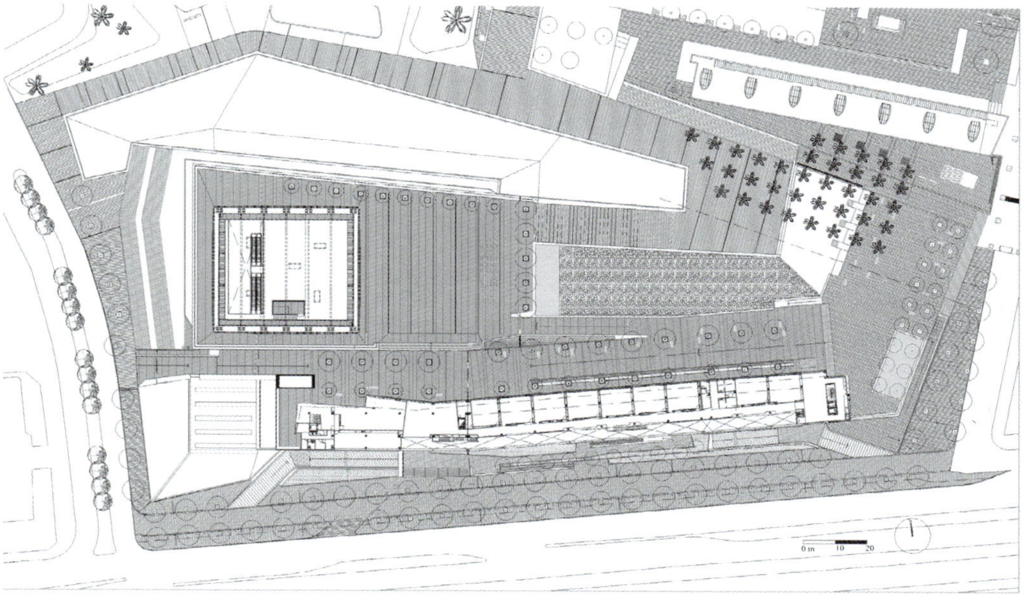

The Center of Medellín (C.I.C) is an urban complex featuring conference facilities, an office-retail building, and a parking lot. The urban quality of the complex creates a new feature in the city enhancing an eco-sustainable development that articulates the surrounding buildings and the urban structure. The C.I.C. is based upon the idea of open doors, going against the typical institutional building, which is isolated from the neighborhood. The inner space allows several transformations from a meeting place or open-covered and shadowed piazza, to a place for concerts and events, or space for a temporal gallery or fair.

01 General view **02** Bird`s eye view by night **03** Site plan
04 Corridor **05** Artwork on ceiling

Photos: Carlos Tobón

CITY Medellín
COUNTRY Colombia
REGION South America
TYPOLOGY Public
COMPLETION 2005
WEBSITE –
ARCHITECTS Daniel Bonilla, Giancarlo Mazzanti, Rafael Esguerra

CITY Medellín
COUNTRY Colombia
REGION South America
TYPOLOGY Education
COMPLETION 2004
WEBSITE –
ARCHITECTS Felipe Uribe de Bedout

BIBLIOTECA TEMATICA E.P.M.

Its location is part of a plan for the recovery of one of the degraded sectors in the city of Medellín. Elements of connection lead the user from the city through deambulatorio vestibular, folding themselves in inclines, while creating enclosures for the introspection or the coexistence. The books are the support of the building, distributed in shelves with structural bond; part of a set that reflects sophistication in the handling of the matter. Constructive innovation and bio-climatic criteria complete these values that do of the work a referring one, for the development of new educative and cultural typologies.

01 Front façade **02** Interior **03** Divided by departments
04 Pedestrian precint **05** Stairs to reading room **06** Floor pan

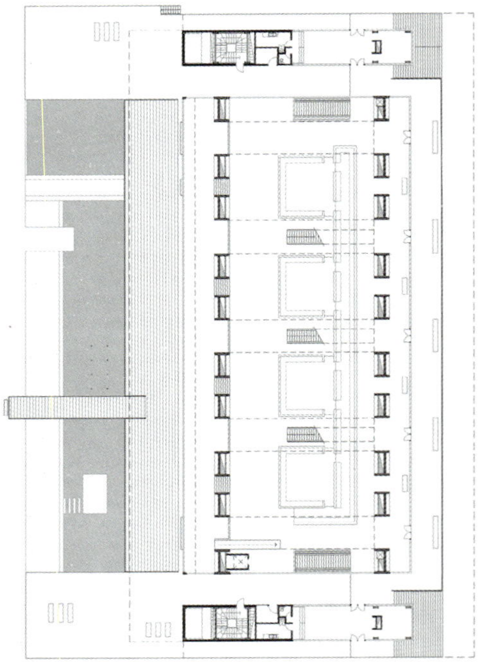

Photos: Sergio Gómez, Carlos Tobón, Gerardo Olave, Guillermina Abeledo

SUBURBAN HOUSE

Located in a suburb, this project is a one-family house that takes advantage of the surrounding environment and the possibilities offered by the terrain to generate an intense treatment of green areas. Two volumes (built using traditional techniques using handcrafted red brick, wood, glass and metal) are separated to confine intermediate spaces, patios as transitions and projections towards the distant landscape. The upper volume reinforces the composition, focusing on the impressive mountains and generating a flat roof that makes a more direct contact with a privileged background possible.

01 Side view **02** Rear view by night **03** Garden pont **04** Floor plans **05** Roof deck **06** Fireplace

Photos: Sebastián Crespo

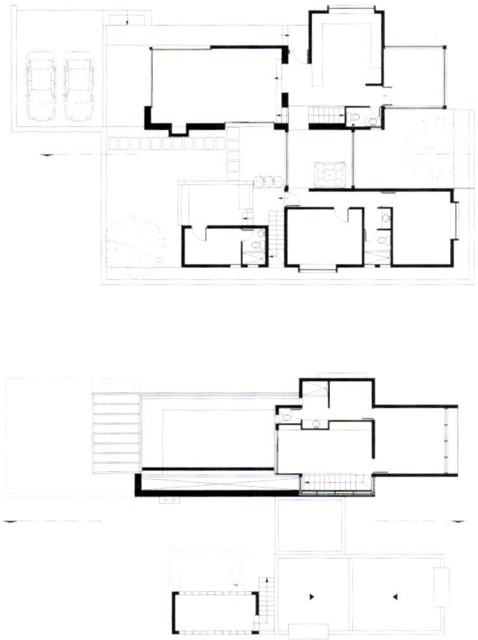

CITY Cuenca
COUNTRY Ecuador
REGION South America
TYPOLOGY Living
COMPLETION 2006
WEBSITE www.surrealestudio-arquitectura.com.ec
ARCHITECTS Pedro Espinosa, Carlos Espinoza, Alejandro Vanegas / surrealestudio arquitectura

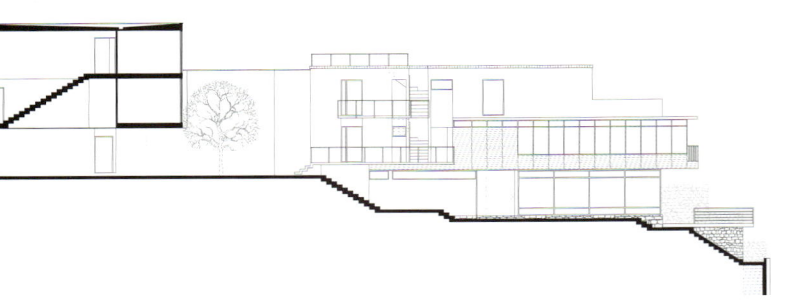

CITY Cuenca
COUNTRY Ecuador
REGION South America
TYPOLOGY Living
COMPLETION 2007
WEBSITE www.surrealestudio-arquitectura.com.ec
ARCHITECTS Pedro Espinosa, Carlos Espinoza, Alejandro Vanegas / surrealestudio arquitectura

HOUSE IN "EL BARRANCO"

This multifunctional project puts together compatible uses to generate a constant dynamism with its favorable connections to the urban scheme and small accommodation solutions on a minor scale. The building is fifty meters long, has a lateral street-like circulation which generates patios, retains original elements and eliminates a level difference of twelve meters. The façade faces a street with high levels of activity and the back of the building integrates with the emblematic zone of "El Barranco", projecting its openings towards the river and the lower part of the city.

01 First floor plan, section **02** Patio **03** Interior skylight **04** Exterior view

Photos: Sebastián Crespo (02, 04), Felipe Cobos (03)

CASA RX

The house is the first of a group of two. Designed for a young couple, this two-story house forms a white prism with a cut that breaks its south west corner. Through a concrete wall, the main entrance leads to the vertical circulation defined by an inclined skylight that juts out toward the sky. The large panes of glass with wooden carpentry and the bare concrete walls and ceiling of this space mark a contrast with the prism, which is closed in to protect against the strong sun. The concrete wall also defines the exterior space, a communal patio with interesting landscapes.

01 Concrete wall breaking south west corner **02** View from the garden **03** House forming white prism **04** Projected floorplan **05** Interior view from the upper floor

Photos: Pablo Moreira

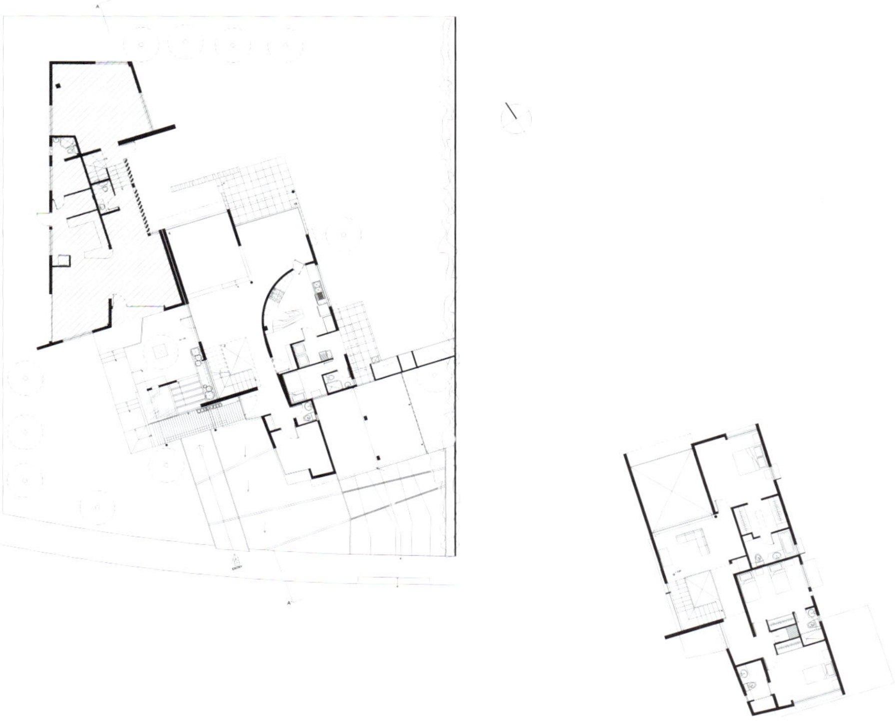

CITY Nayón, Quito
COUNTRY Ecuador
REGION South America
TYPOLOGY Living
COMPLETION 2006
WEBSITE –
ARCHITECTS MCM + A (Rubén Moreira, Natalia Corral + Pablo Moreira

CASA PENTIMENTO

The project involves a garden and a client, both fearless in their vision for an intense interaction. A barebones architecture that connects to its surroundings arises on this complicated plot in coexistence with greenery. Built using a single form of prefabricated concrete which can be stacked in four different ways for assembly resolved the entire house structure, separators, furniture, ladders, even a garden façade, which was the origin of the project. Outside is a neutral grid that is camouflaged like a fence or hedge. Inside, each wall is different and fits its scale needs, function, position, etc.

01 House decks with planting **02** Concrete interior construction with wooden work **03** Exterior view by night **04** Wooden interior construction **05** Floor plan with landscape

Photos: José María Sáez, Raed Gindeya

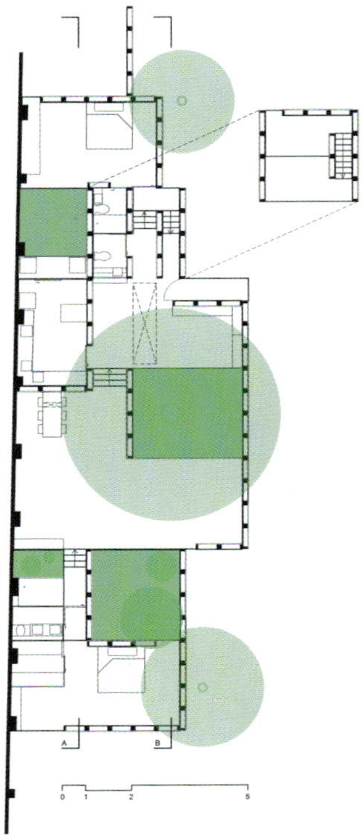

CITY Quito
COUNTRY Ecuador
REGION South America
TYPOLOGY Living
COMPLETION 2006
WEBSITE www.arqsaez.com
ARCHITECTS Jose María Sáez y David Barragan Arquitectos

CASA SAN JUAN

A house in Quito's historic Old Town turns its gaze on a private garden. On the old terrace, the new hall becomes a connector between the interior and the exterior. A continuous steel girder reaffirms the vocation of openness to the landscape, while its horizontality unifies the façade oriented to the garden. The extremities of the beam are delicately separated from the adobe (sun-dried mud brick) wall, barely tapping them. The mobile gallery allows for a wide range of openings towards the garden, and a selected room can regain its original condition as a terrace.

01 Exterior view by night **02** Exterior view **03** Floor plans **04** Roof deck, fully glazed wall **05** Garage door **06** Gallery with view outside **07** Brick staircase with celing lighting set

Photos: José María Sáez, Raed Gindeya

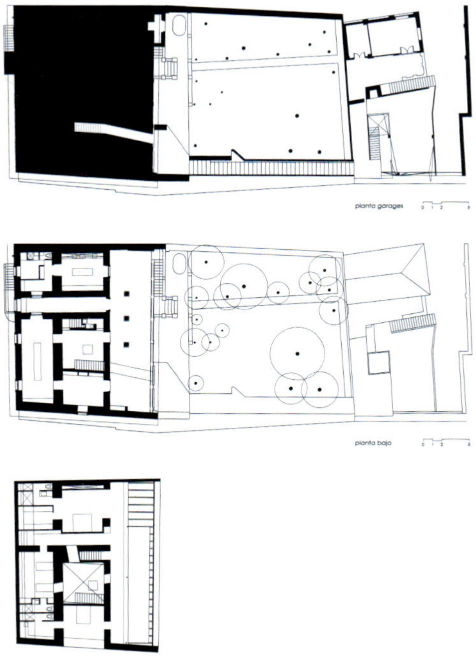

CITY Quito
COUNTRY Ecuador
REGION South America
TYPOLOGY Living
COMPLETION 2007
WEBSITE www.arqsaez.com
ARCHITECTS Jose María Sáez Arquitectos

CITY
Quito

COUNTRY
Ecuador

REGION
South America

TYPOLOGY
Retail / Office

COMPLETION
2005

WEBSITE
www.arquitecturax.com

ARCHITECTS
arquitectura x - Adrian Moreno
& Maria Samaniego

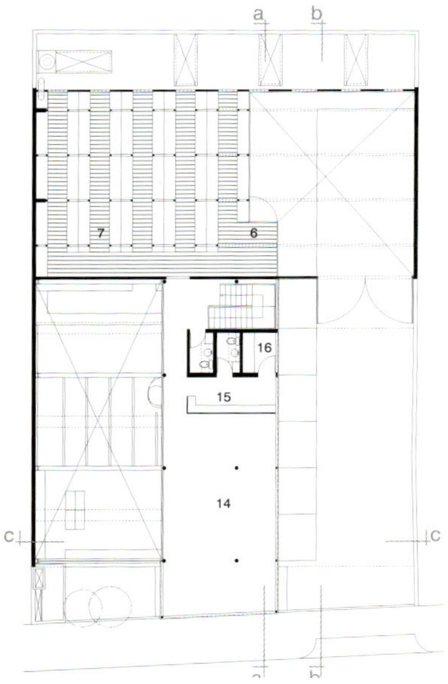

CASTILLO HNOS - HARDWARE STORE

The execution of the project was defined by the location of the store's storage facilities, delivery access and customer parking. Reducing the building's footprint and opening up the front and side of the lot to offer an alternative to the district's overly front-weighted occupation and urban decay were the architects' goals. Because the building had to occupy a large proportion of the lot, the resulting structure and choice of materials strove to reduce its weight by means of a cantilevered construction and through the use of different degrees of transparency to control incoming sunlight and act as a glowing display at night.

01 Upper level floor plan **02** White polycarbonate skin **03** Detail façade **04** Steel structure with polycarbonate façade **05** Interior with steel and wood display units and concrete floors

Photos: Sebastian Crespo

X-HOUSE

The house was designed without a specific site in mind, and a straight-forward scheme was produced that could be implemented either in Quito or in the valleys to the east. The form is abstract and anticipates a likely plot. The open-ended box structure delimited by the eastern or western range of the Andes exhibits a plan that separates the public and private spaces, which help define a patio. Service, circulati-on and functional elements are designed as a plug-in, and can be installed in several different ways according to the requirements of the plot.

01 Fully glazed wall facing east **02** Steel column construction **03** Translucent enclosure for service and circulation elements facing west **04** Floor plans **05** Patio **06** Kitchen from living room

Photos: Sebastian Crespo

CITY: Quito
COUNTRY: Ecuador
REGION: South America
TYPOLOGY: Living
COMPLETION: 2007
WEBSITE: www.arquitecturax.com
ARCHITECTS: arquitectura x - Adrian Moreno & Maria Samaniego

CITY Quito

COUNTRY Ecuador

REGION South America

TYPOLOGY Living

COMPLETION 2006

WEBSITE www.gdarquitectos.com

ARCHITECTS Gonzalo Diez Arquitectos
Gonzalo Diez P. - Felipe Muller B.

URBANA BUILDING

The project is developed in an urban residential zone in the city of Quito, and required a building of eleven exclusive departments to be developed in six floors of height, with two subsoil levels for parking. The land has an aggressive topography, and this location is one of the residential points, and therefore privileged with views. One is clear about the importance of the location in relation to the surroundings, recognizing the two corners and their fronts as important urban elements. A surrounding seen concrete element welcomes the duplex of the esquinero side and ends in a porch abierto on the terrace.

01 Regressed illumination and wooden floor **02** Street side view **03** Upper floor **04** Living space with floor height ceiling **05** Floor plans

Photos: Sebastián Crespo

CASA CRUZ

This 19th Century, post-colonial house represents the classic architectural style of historic Quito: adobe construction, „zaguán", central stone courtyard, and arcaded corridors. These elements were interpreted and adapted to the needs of its new owner. The restoration proposal called for contemporary features such as a curtain wall of equatorial wood replacing the rear wing which had little historical value, and a roof solarium viewing the old town complemented with hanging vegetation to soften the eastern sun and climate.

—
01 Roof terrace **02** Patio **03** Detail of kitchen **04** First floor **05** Second floor

Photos: Pablo Moreira

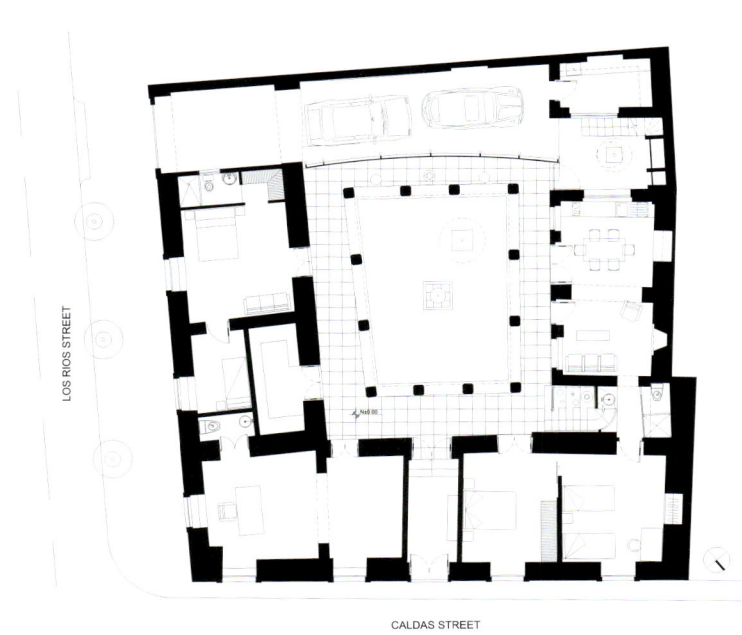

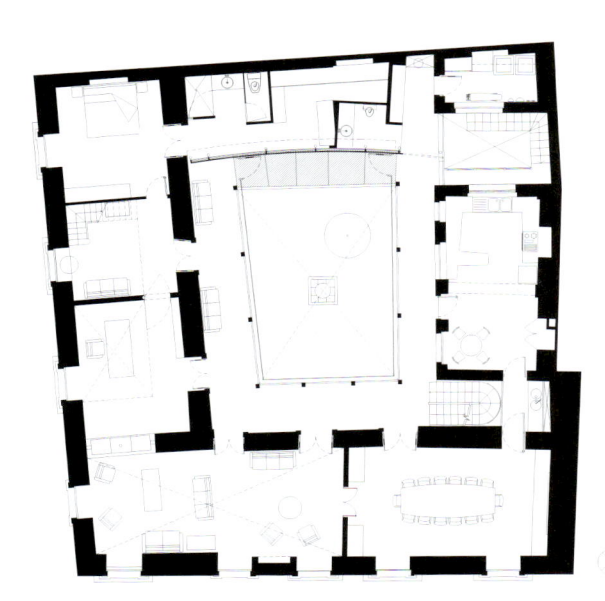

CITY Quito
COUNTRY Ecuador
REGION South America
TYPOLOGY Living
COMPLETION 2007
WEBSITE –
ARCHITECTS MCM + A (Pablo Moreira, Natalia Corral, Ruben Moreira)

CITY Asia
COUNTRY Peru
REGION South America
TYPOLOGY Living
COMPLETION 2005
WEBSITE www.juancarlosdoblado.com
ARCHITECTS Juan Carlos Doblado

LA ISLA BEACH HOUSE

The city of Lima has seen a peripheral increase in the development of new urbanizations along its coast. Near the district of Cañete, a suburb named Asia was discovered in the Andes foothills. Although the desert character of the zone, the climatic conditions are not extreme, providing a friendly environment to live in. This house attempts to evince the connection between abstract architecture and its environment, setting the relationship between man and nature, desert and sea. The lower level features bedrooms and a family room, while the upper level contains a living room, dining room, kitchen and terrace.

01 Kitchen view **02** Deck with pool **03** Balcony **04** Sections **05** Terrace

Photos: Alex Kornhuber

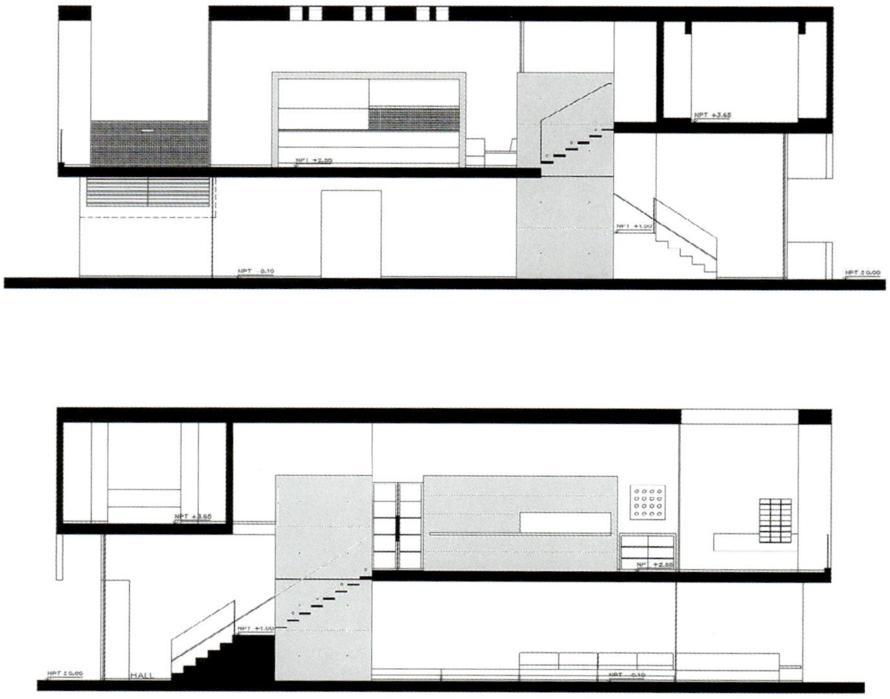

CASA EQUIS

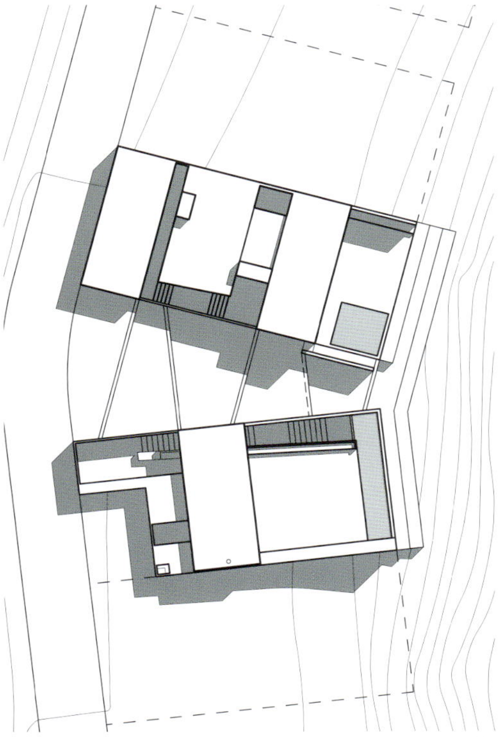

The house is located on a long strip of Peruvian desert between the Andes and the ocean. Because of its sea-level elevation, the conditions here are relatively temperate despite the arid landscape. The building was designed using 'subtractive' logic that entailed imagining a plain abstract volume and 'carving out' the theoretical solid, a technique reminiscent of a Columbian archaeological dig. The terrace facing the ocean acts as an artificial beach, and an open staircase beneath it leads to the bedrooms below. To prevent the house from visually aging, sand color was widely used to obscure layers of desert dust.

01 Entrance patio **02** Site plan **03** Ochre/sand color façade **04** Living space

Photos: Jean Pierre Crousse, Courtesy of Barclay & Crousse

CITY La Escondida Beach
COUNTRY Peru
REGION South America
TYPOLOGY Living
COMPLETION 2003
WEBSITE www.barclaycrousse.com
ARCHITECTS Barclay & Crousse

MULTIVACACIONES

This project creates offices and a showroom for a travel agency in Lima. The project challenges the usual Peruvian introverted architecture of fear, which yields buildings that are protected by walls and take the -entire lot away form the public domain. Using innovative low-tech solutions, the building improves its urban context with generous public spaces while generating a remarkable spatial interior through the design of its skin.

01 Fully glazed façade **02** Interior **03** Exterior with water ditch **04** Site plan **05** Wooden panneling

Photos: 51-1 arquitectos

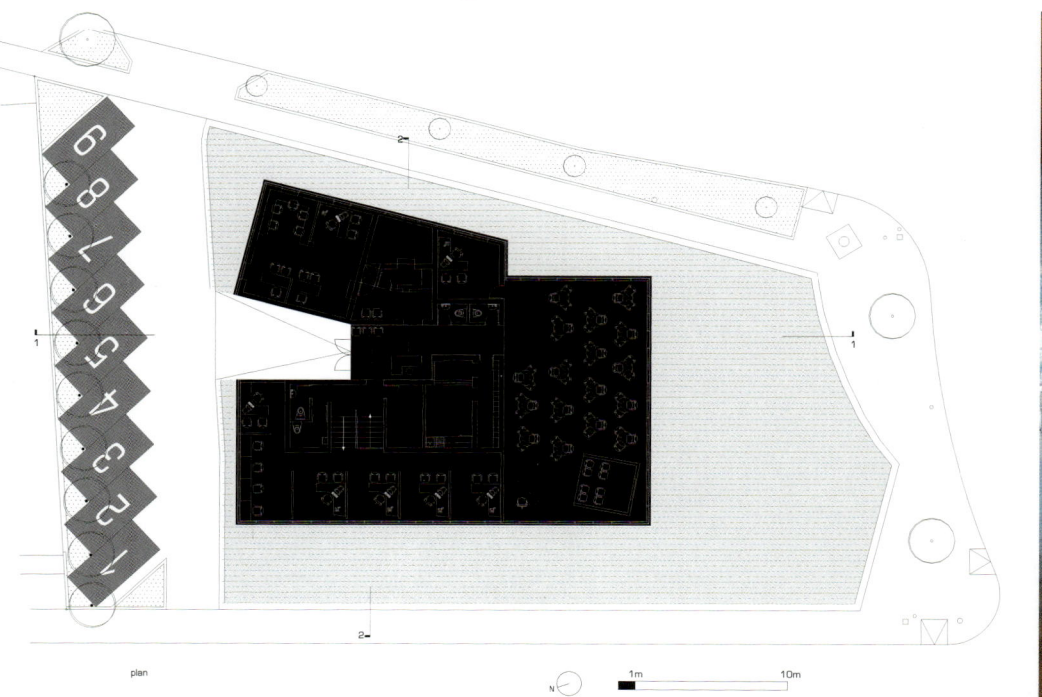

CITY Lima

COUNTRY Peru

REGION South America

TYPOLOGY Living

COMPLETION 2006

WEBSITE www.51-1.com

ARCHITECTS 51-1 arquitectos

ALVAR APARTMENT BUILDING

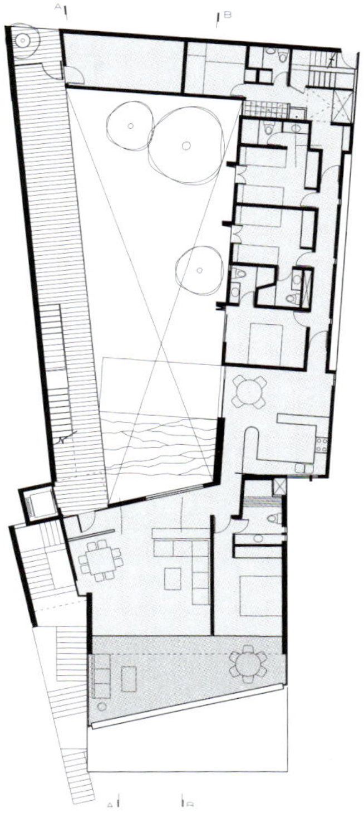

The desert coast of Peru with its beautiful and rugged topography inspired the execution of this project as an observatory. The five-unit family building steps back and sits on a cliff. The irregular shape of the site inspired the architects to design volumes that give a spatial order and fit with the eclectic surrounding buildings. The materials include whitewashed walls, carved stone, wooden floors and blinds, travertine floors. All were chosen to ensure integration into the landscape and of a construction process where craftsmanship is highly valued.

01 Exterior view by night **02** Pool **03** Floor plan **04** Exterior seating

Photos: Stella Watmough, Elsa Ramirez

CITY: Lima
COUNTRY: Peru
REGION: South America
TYPOLOGY: Living
COMPLETION: 2008
WEBSITE: www.ruthalvarado.com
ARCHITECTS: Ruth Alvarado

CITY
Lima

COUNTRY
Peru

REGION
South America

TYPOLOGY
Living

COMPLETION
2008

WEBSITE
www.ruthalvarado.com

ARCHITECTS
Ruth Alvarado -
Cynthia Watmough

LA HONDA BEACH CLUB

La Honda Beach is a small crescent cove. As the unearthed Inca remains indicate, this has been a fishing site for thousands of years. The program required boating and fishing facilities, as well as a social area for this small vacation community. The project integrates into the overwhelming surroundings of the desert coast of Peru in a subdued way. The curves were drawn following the shape of the natural terrain. These curves became stone-stepped walls. The materials used, as well as the curved stepped walls, sit gracefully, blending in with the site.

01 Curved walls **02** Wooden roofed patio **03** Section **04** Concept **05** Curved pool **06** Bird's eye view

Photos: Stella Watmough

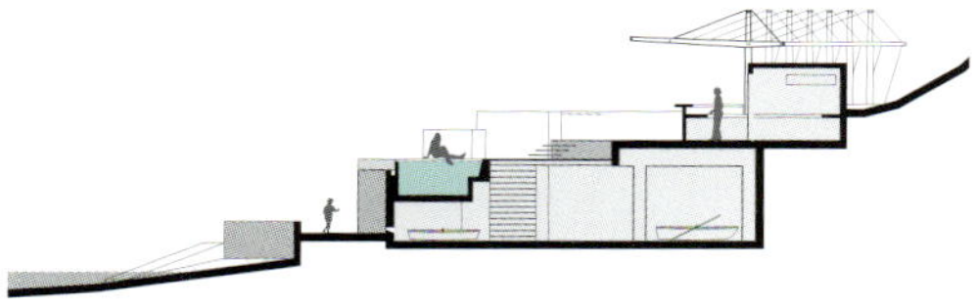

LAS ARENAS BEACH HOUSE

The project is a small house located on a beach 100 km south of Lima which conceptually explores the expansion of usual activities performed at a beach getaway. Created as an oversized container, a space that integrates the living-dining room with the terrace-swimming pool, the space contains diverse elements that have been designed to allow manifold applications. Architectonically, the volume has been strategically cut on some of its faces to achieve control of sunlight and certain visual effects, and has deliberately been suspended over the lawn to accomplish the effect of weightlessness and freedom.

01 Entrance view 02 Patio with pool 03 View inside by night 04 Floor plans 05 Side view

Photos: Alex Kornhuber

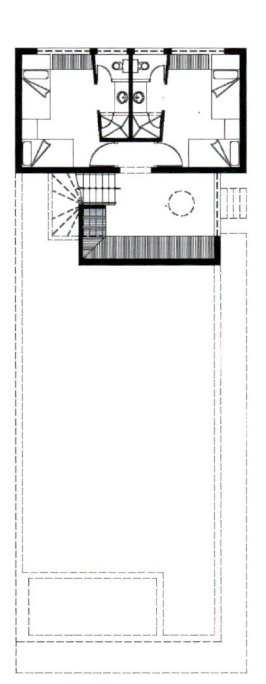

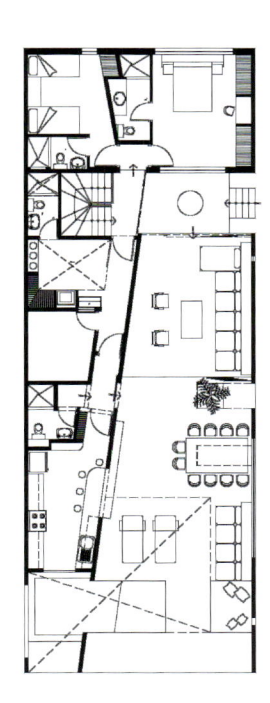

CITY Lima
COUNTRY Peru
REGION South America
TYPOLOGY Living
COMPLETION 2006
WEBSITE www.javierartadi.com
ARCHITECTS Javier Artadi (Artadi Arquitectos)

CITY	Cañete, Lima
COUNTRY	Peru
REGION	South America
TYPOLOGY	Living
COMPLETION	2007
WEBSITE	www.benwat.com
ARCHITECTS	Benavides + Watmough

CASA I

Sited on the second row, blocked from the ocean view, House-I is designed on a 12x17m flat site. To comply with the highly restrictive building codes and an extensive building program, it is partially buried. Luminous sculpted patios give the impression of the building being above ground. The lack of privacy and unexciting context led the architects to design a house partially closed to the outside but rich in interior views. Translucent glass panels accompanied by vegetation were used to control views while detaching the house from its context. From the exterior, the interiors are barely insinuated.

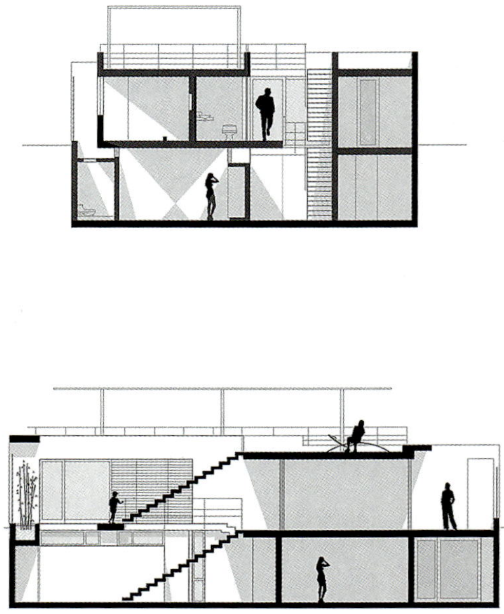

01 Opaque glazed façade **02** View to deck, glazed sliding doors **03** Façade **04, 05** Open staircase **06** Section

Photos: Stella Watmough, Avelina Crespo

CASA O

Located on a hilltop site with a panoramic view of Lima and the Pacific Ocean at a distance, the house continues the ascent of the hill partially suspended in a cantilever. An imaginary line parallel to the horizon accompanies the mass of the concrete house which is then carved out below for the best views and flow of space. Prone to strong southern winds, the terrace and garden are protected by the dwelling. A long structural wall supports a narrow 25 meter-long lap pool.

01 Site plan **02** View to roof **03** Garden view **04** Exterior **05** Perspective

Photos: Stella Watmough

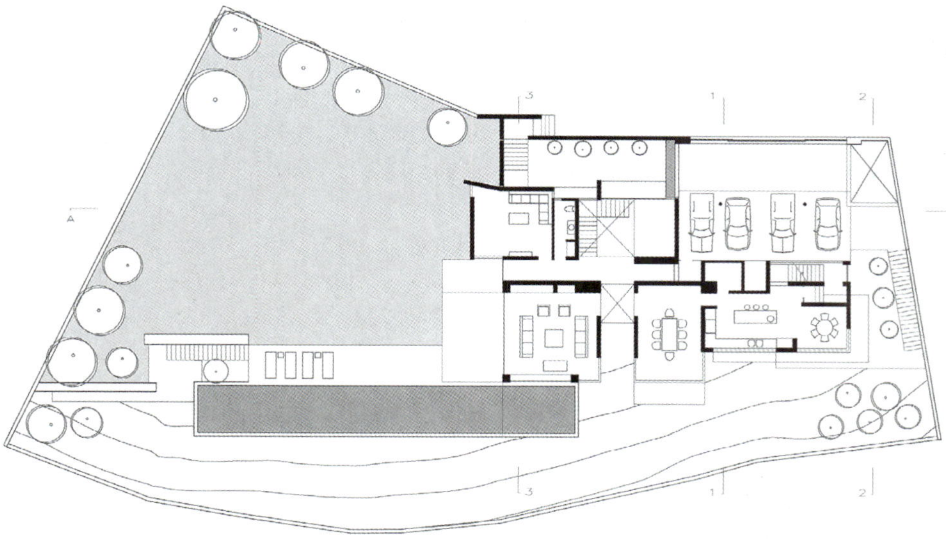

CITY
Lima

COUNTRY
Peru

REGION
South America

TYPOLOGY
Living

COMPLETION
2005

WEBSITE
www.benwat.com

ARCHITECTS
Benavides + Watmough

LEFEVRE HOUSE

Conceived as the meeting place of the arid Peruvian desert and the Pacific Ocean, this beach house located at Punta Misterio, 117 km south of Lima, is an intervention where the architecture's integration into the landscape was an important concern. Sand garden roofs act as the extension of the desert; sports and recreation pools connect the ocean with the house, while a glass box is suspended from the main structure, symbolizing architecture between sand and water.

01 Exterior view by night **02** Cube structure **03** General view
04 Living space with view outside **05** Floor Plans

Photos - renderings : Y. Jamis (01, 02), C. Bottger (03, 05) - C. Tamariz (04)

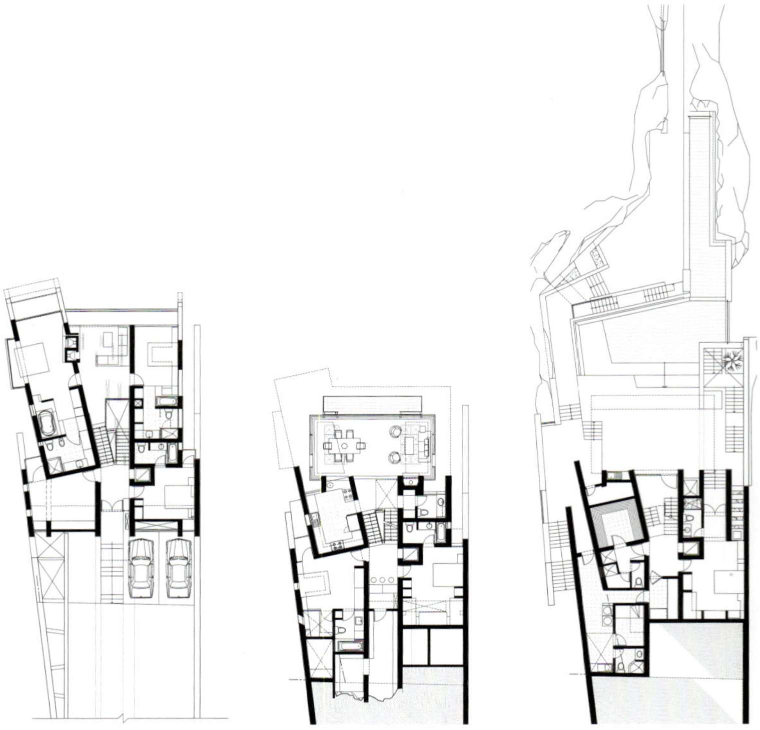

PACHACAMAC HILL HOUSE

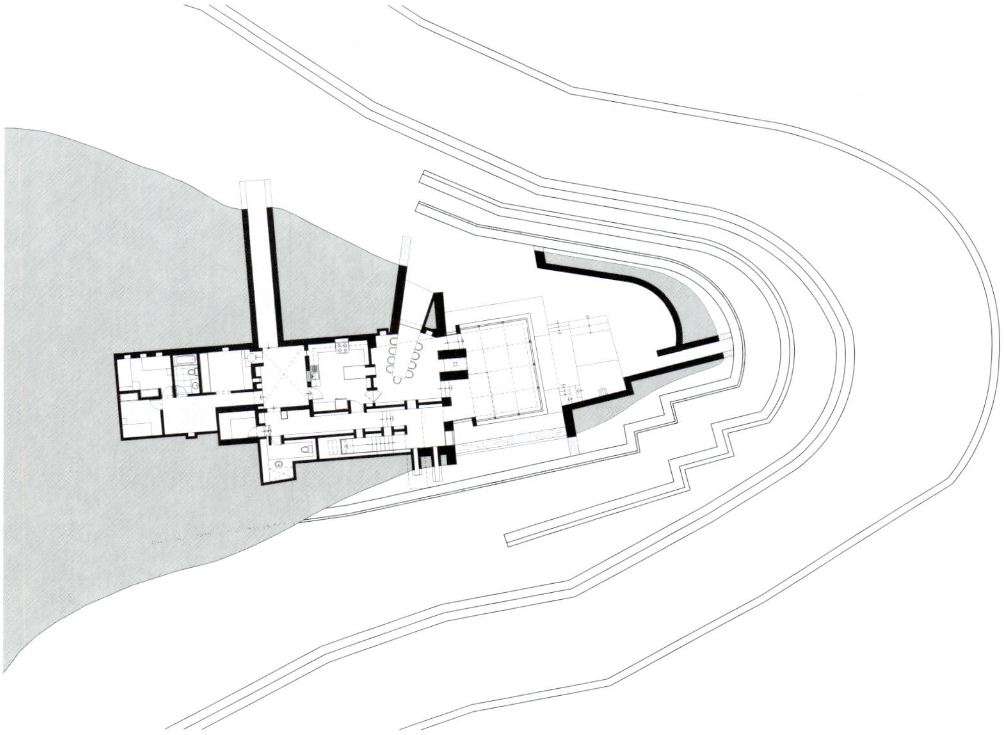

The Pachacamac hill on the coast of Peru, located 40 km south of Lima, is the site of a retirement home for a couple of prestigious philosophers. The response to the site was to bury the house inside the hill in an attempt to create a balanced dialog between architecture and landscape, where inside / outside becomes a constant interpretation of materiality, but nonetheless provides a strong sense of protection and appreciation of darkness and light. A glass box projects out of the hill, symbolizing architectural intervention that leaves nature untouched.

01 Side view **02** Concrete interior walls **03** Stone façade
04 First floor plan **05** Planted roof

Photos: L. Longhi, I. Loredo (04)

CITY: Lima
COUNTRY: Peru
REGION: South America
TYPOLOGY: Living
COMPLETION: 2008
WEBSITE: www.longhiarchitect.com
ARCHITECTS: Luis Longhi Architects

CITY Lima
COUNTRY Peru
REGION South America
TYPOLOGY Public
COMPLETION 2004
WEBSITE www.metropolisperu.com
ARCHITECTS Jose Orrego Herrera

CREMATORIO SANTA ROSA

The project was designed to honor the members of the meritorious police of Peru, where the name of the park cemetery corresponds to the Saint of the institution. The main idea was to create a dominant volume that organized a great extension of land so that it served as an axis to all the activities, events and homage of the police institution, and conceived to synthesize the silhouette of a bale so that its form is easily grateful to the different approaches of the structure.

A martial square has become a commemorative space that acts as an extension of the chapel when necessary to harbor a quantity of people.

01 General view **02** Interior chapel **03** Entrance view **04** Floor plan

Photos: Arquifoto

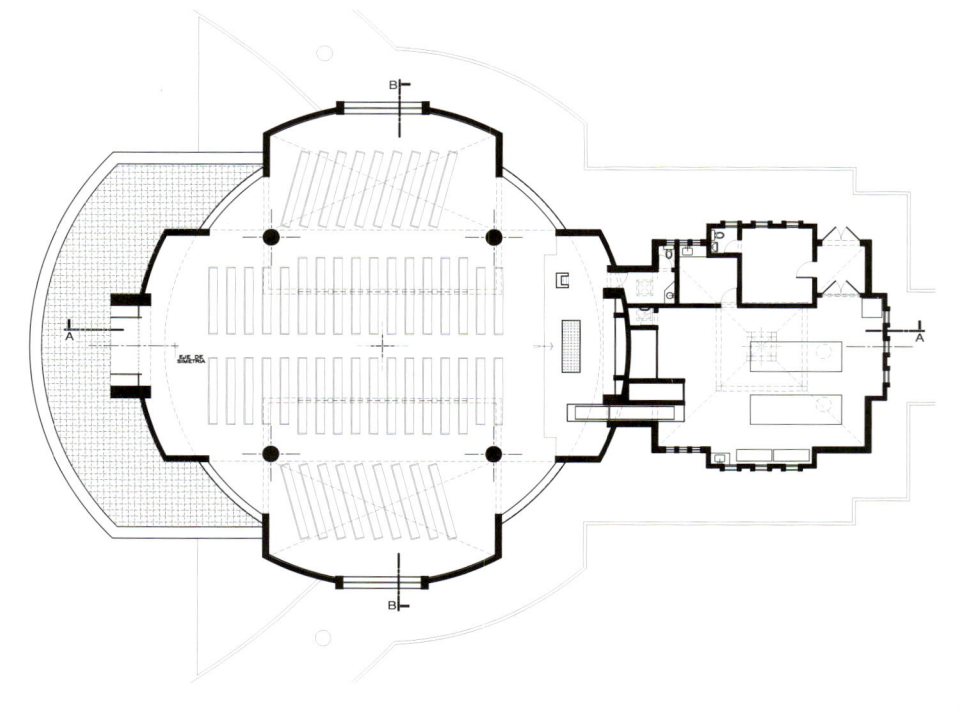

TANATORIO CHAPEL & CREMATORY JARDINES DE LA PAZ

The site is located on the outskirts of Lima, Peru. Close to the ocean and to a highway, it stands out on a raised plot of land. The complex is composed of a chapel, a crematorium, and a few spaces for vigil. The service areas include a coffee shop, administrative spaces and public restrooms. The buildings are situated around a circular plaza which establishes the organization of service buildings adjacent to the chapel. The clean design of the chapel is punctuated with non-linear openings, creating a playful yet somber quality inside the space. Complimenting the design is the strategically placed altar.

01 Entrance view **02** Narrow-light windows **03** Stone façade **04** Sections **05** Patio with skylight

Photos: Arquifoto

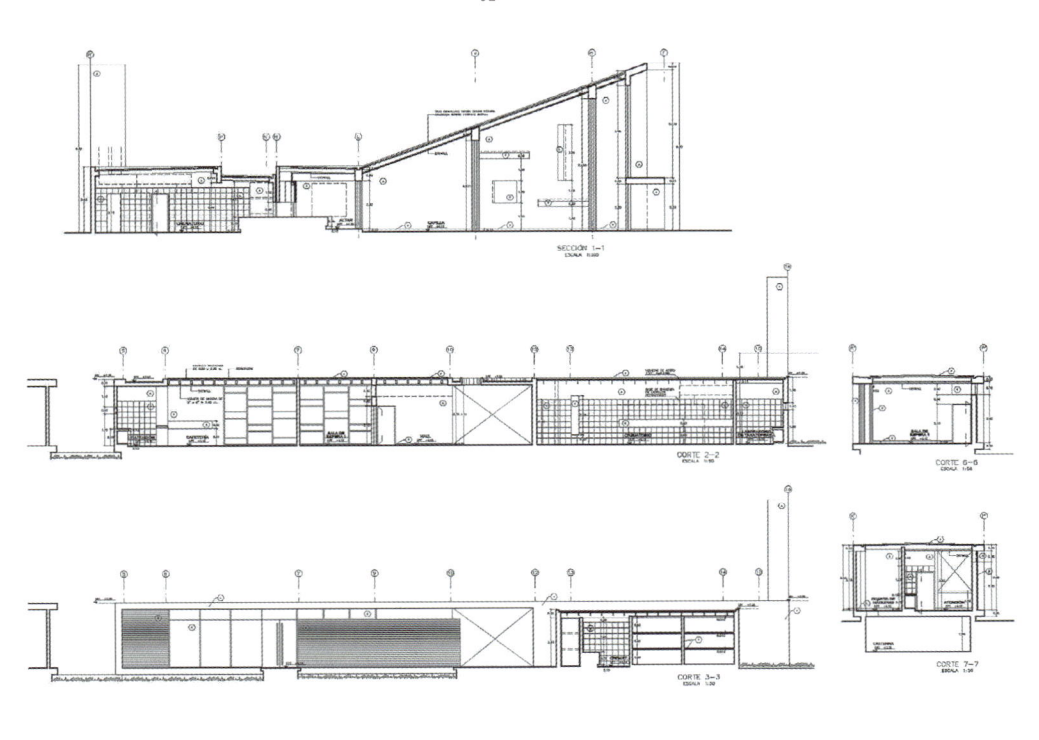

CITY Lima
COUNTRY Peru
REGION South America
TYPOLOGY Public
COMPLETION 2005
WEBSITE www.metropolisperu.com
ARCHITECTS Jose Orrego Herrera

1014

CITY
Lima

COUNTRY
Peru

REGION
South America

TYPOLOGY
Living

COMPLETION
2003

WEBSITE
www.ruthalvarado.com

ARCHITECTS
Ruth Alvarado

BEACH HOUSE AT LAS LOMAS TWO

The project's main theme is enjoying the available sea views. For this reason, the parti places a transparent volume on the sea front and two opaque elongated volumes on the back, describing a main axial circulation. While the transparent volume houses the social area, the opaque volumes on the back hold the private rooms. The master bedroom has a cave-shaped cutout on the wall, through which one can see the ocean, a poetic reference to the surrounding desert landscape of the Peru coast. Likewise, the concrete walls with its rugged texture resemble the surrounding rock cliffs.

01 Entrance view **02** Exterior detail **03** Patio with view to beach **04** Floor plan **05** Open interior space

Photos: Stella Watmough

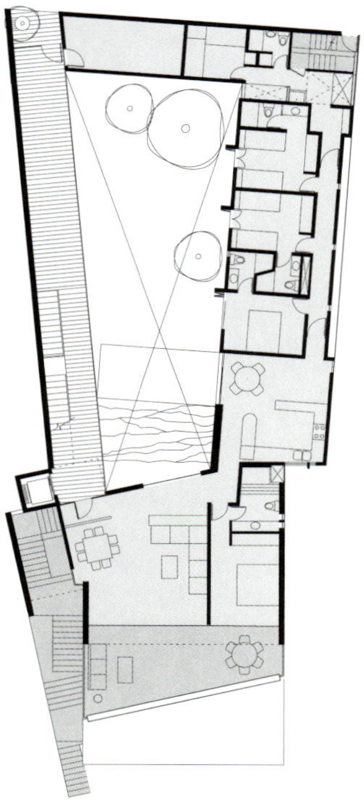

CASA EN LA PLANICIE, ALVARO BALLON

The house is situated on an unusually long, thin parcel of land. The architects explored the sense of verticality by letting the two volumes encounter one another independently. Strongly structured, the house creates a balance of sober concrete finish and transparency that tries to break the mass. At night, this volumetry becomes a "box of light" that lets itself be openly seen. The equilibrium is illustrated at the point the horizontal and vertical dimensions meet. Both forces cohabitate in the spatial richness of the organized circulation flow, especially in the spaces with double heights.

01 Exterior view by night **02** Construction detail **03** Wooden flooring and concrete walls **04** Skylight **05** Regressed luminaire

Photos: Sebastián Correa, Javier de la Flor

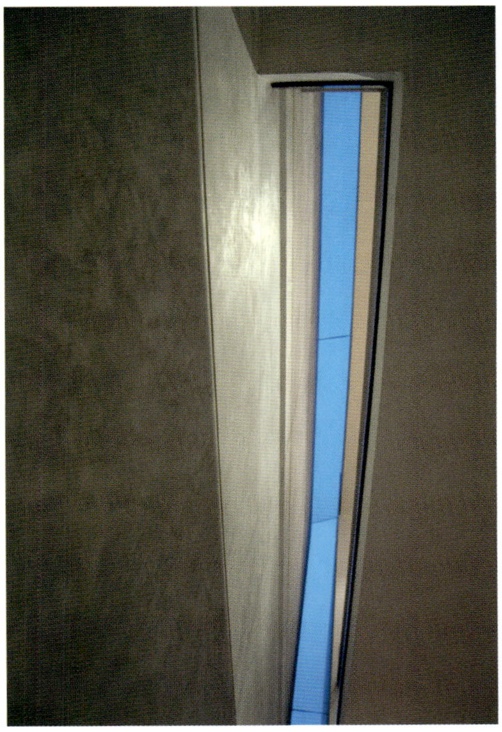

CITY Lima
COUNTRY Peru
REGION South America
TYPOLOGY Living
COMPLETION 2007
WEBSITE www.sacro.net
ARCHITECTS SACRO Arquitectos
Alvaro Ballón - Daniel Brenis

CITY
Salto del Penitente

COUNTRY
Uruguay

REGION
South America

TYPOLOGY
Public

COMPLETION
2004

WEBSITE
www.gualano.com.uy

ARCHITECTS
gualano+gualano, arquitectos // g+

PARADOR SALTO DEL PENITENTE

The project does not try to impose or merge, and marks an abstract, honest architectural form of finished materiality without the concrete made rock. It takes part in the landscape, respecting it, trying to be of importance to the site The project is solved in two pieces that articulate in the landscape; the inn that hangs of the rock and emerges towards the cliff, seized to the evenness of the floor and the other volume, and the other of the camping, receiving to the arrivals of automobiles. The skin/concrete structure generates the limits and hard edges of the work, generating the structure composition of the project.

01 Exterior view from river side **02** Sun deck **03** Bird's eye view **04** Interior with wooden floor and ceiling, concrete walls **05** Exterior balustrade

Photos: Ramiro Rodríguez Barilari

THE FIVE PATIO HOUSE

A large roof delimits the playful space where the collective life of the house comes together and later gives way to the individual volumes that shelter private spaces. A water patio acts as the entrance, sheltered by a sunlight filtered by a structural sieve. An oaken patio built from blocks is the dining area. A bamboo patio offers a quiet space for study. The kitchen stage is a central patio that turns its user into the main character. The family garden and pool area is the main living space in a house that is constructed as one large inhabited patio.

01 Exterior view **02** Sieve form façade as source of light
03 First floor plan **04** Ground floor plan

Photos: Ricardo Leon Jatem

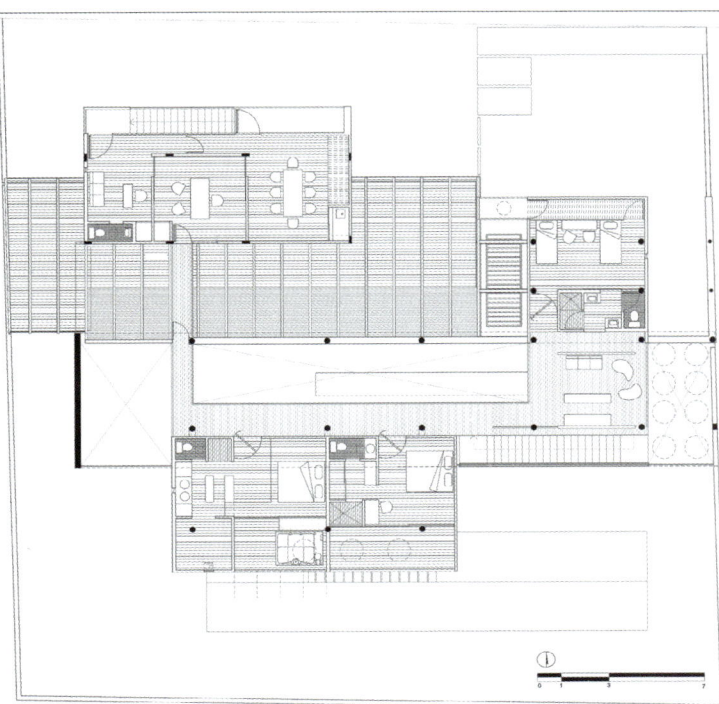

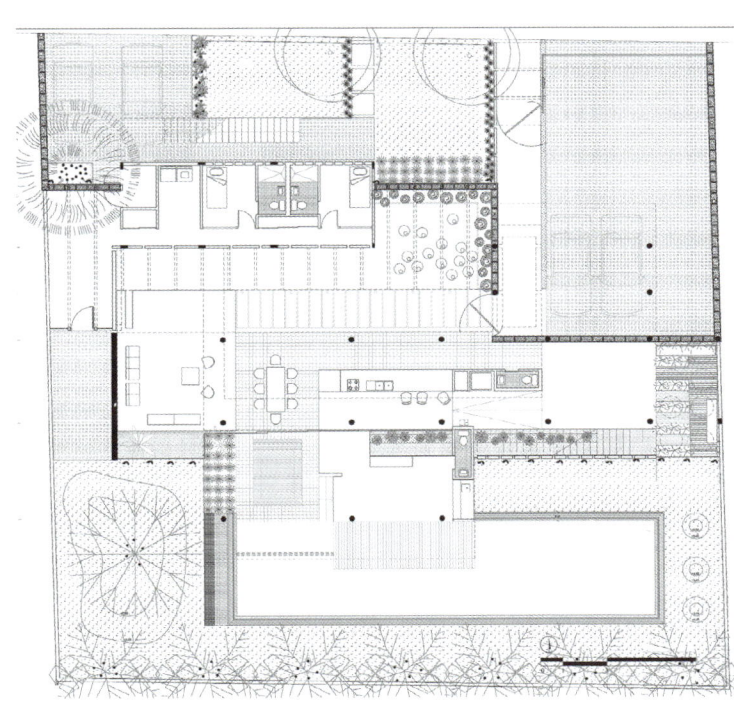

CITY Maracaibo
COUNTRY Venezuela
REGION South America
TYPOLOGY Living
COMPLETION in progress
WEBSITE www.nomadas.net
ARCHITECTS nomadas taller de arquitectura y diseño

INDEX

ARCHITECTS

1 2 3
+arquitectos **946, 947, 965**
01ARQ arquitectos asociados **948**
1100: Architect **439, 624**
212box **364**
2form Architecture **217**
3arquitectos **931**
51-1 arquitectos **1004**
57Studio **949**
7xa arquitectura / Ángel López.
  Carlos Ortiz **650, 755, 758**

A
A1 Arquitetura – Alessandra Pires e Carla Barranco **806**
AATA Associate Architects **929**
Abraham, Raimund **365**
Abuauad, Ricardo **951**
Acayaba, Marcos **832**
Acconci Studio **343**
Acton Ostry Architects Inc **115**
AD-11 **652–654**
adamo-faiden **786**
Adler, Jonathan **463**
AEdifica + Lapointe Magne **32**
Affleck + de la Riva Architects **51**
Aflalo & Gasperini Arquitetos **880**
agps architecture **482, 584**
Agraz Arquitectos di Vece Arquitectos **765**
Aidlin Darling Design **502, 546, 547**
Aja Aspil Cobelo Arqs S.A. **800**
Albert+Rachlin Architects **603**
Alatorre, Ramiro **750**
Alchemy Architects **507**
Alejandro Aptilon Arquitectos **668, 669**
Alejandro Ortiz Architects **299**
Aleks Istanbullu Architects **160, 180, 615**
Alexander Gorlin Architect **198, 383, 437**
Allen + Maurer Architects **50**
Allen + Philp Architects / Interiors **562**
Allied Works Architecture **579**
Alric Galindez Arquitectos **784**
Alsop Architects (U.K.) **94**
Altamirano Armanet Bisball **928**
Altius Architecture (Trevor McIvor) **29, 73, 74**
Alvano y Riquelme / Renzo Alvano, Pablo Riquelme **667, 966, 981**
Alvarado, Ruth **1005, 1006, 1014**
Alvares, Daniel **685**
Alvaro Puntoni anda Angelo Bucci / SPBR architects **903**
Alvaro Rojas / FoRo ARQUITECTOS **638**
Amantea, Michael **23**

Ancona Riestra, Roberto José **661, 664**
Anderson Anderson Architecture **359, 575**
Andersson•Wise Architects **585**
Andrade, Vinicius **840**
Andres Remy Arquitectos **799**
Antonio Acosta – Nicole Lyaudet Arquitectos **932, 950**
Aravena, Alejandro **968**
Arbona, Javier **429**
Archetonic, Arq. Jacobo Micha Mizrahi **658, 670**
Archimania **344–346**
Archi-Tectonics **181, 366, 430**
architectsAlliance **88**
Architectes Gallienne e Moisan **59**
Architects Cubed Inc **776**
Architectural Body Research Foundation –"Reversible Density" **212**
Architecture in Formation, PC **513**
Architekton **588, 589, 592**
ARCHI[TE]NSIONS / Alessandro Orsini **367**
Arcop Architects **48**
ARCOP Group **53**
ARD Arquitectos – Alejandro Rojas Donoso **952**
Arditti+RDT arquitectos **671**
Ariel Rojo Design Studio **706**
armE_studio – Pablo Velazquez **672**
Arquitectonica **157, 257, 491**
Arquitectura 911SC **715**
Arquitectura Organica – Javier Senosiain **710, 739**
arquitectura x – Adrian Moreno & Maria Samaniego **998, 999**
Arquitetos Associados do Brasil **876, 877**
Arrowstreet **164**
Ars atelier de arquitecturas **757, 766**
Arshia+Reza [null:lab] **310**
Artadi, Javier (Artadi Arquitectos) **1007**
assembledge+ **284, 285**
Asymptote **368**
at103 Julio Amezcua + Francisco Pardo **673, 676, 677, 754**
Atelier FABRIQ (Peart Bertrand Koch architectes) **377**
atelierT.A.G. **72**
Augusto Quijano Arquitectos, S.C.P. **762**
Axis Mundi **250, 426, 441, 500**

B
B+H Architects **95**
B+U, LLP Baumgartner & Uriu **311**
Baird Sampson Neuert Architects **10, 13, 70**
Ball-Nogues **161**
Banchini, Guillermo **796**
Barbosa & Corbucci Arquitetos Associados **881**

Barclay & Crousse **1003**
Barnstone, Robert **462**
Barq Julian Berdichevsky, Joaquin Sanchez Gomez **787**
Barragan, David **996**
Barton Myers Associates Inc. **589**
Barton Phelps & Associates **449, 451, 516**
Basiches, José Ricardo **837**
BCMF Arquitetos / Bruno Campos, Marcelo Fontes e Silvio Todeschi **858**
Becker Arquitectos **674, 716**
Behnisch Architekten **88, 168**
Bel Lobo & Bob Neri Arquitetos **859**
Belzberg Architects **269, 286, 612**
Ben Hansen Architect **369, 431, 432**
Benavides + Watmough **1008, 1009**
besonias almeida kruk arquitectos **797**
Bentel & Bentel, Architects **332, 370, 577**
Bernardes + Jacobsen Arquitetura **808, 833, 868, 907, 908**
Bertoldi, Marcos / Studio Bertoldi **826, 827**
Bettis Tarazi Arquitectos (David M. Bettis, Teofilo Tarazi) **768–772**
bgp arquitectura **651, 675–677**
Billes Architecture **363**
Bing Thom Architects **63, 66**
biselli + katchborian arquitetos associados **882**
Biselli, Mario **836**
BLAC – Backheuser e Leonídio Arquitetura e Cidade **860**
blank studio **481, 512**
BNIM, International Architects Atelier **266**
Bohlin Cywinski Jackson **152, 258, 573**
Bonilla, Daniel **988, 991**
BOORA Architects **185, 206, 333, 483**
Borsoi Arquitetura **846**
Boutros + Pratte **33**
Bodouva, William Nicholas & Associates **371**
Bozzola, Santiago **788**
Bratke, Carlos Ateliê de Arquitetura **821**
Brasil arquitectura – Francisco Fanucci e Marcelo Ferraz **818, 872**
Brasil, Alexandre **877**
Braverman, Louise **357**
Bravo, Iván **953, 985**
Bregman + Hamann Architects **25**
Brian Healy Architects **489**
Brière, Gilbert + associés, architectes **34**
Broissin, Gerardo **680, 717**
Brunzini Arquitectos & Asociados **798**
Buchanan Architecture **208**
Bunker Arquitectura **646**

Burdifilek Interior Design **75, 106**
Burka Varacalli Architects **31**
Busby Perkins + Will Architects Co. **35, 116, 117**

C
Caballero, Gerardo **802**
Cadaval & Solà-Morales Arquitectos **747**
Canales, Fernanda **740**
Cancian, Flavia **805**
Canda Gazaneo Ungar arquitectos **785**
Cardin+Ramirez & Associés, Architectes **49**
Carney Architects **259, 260, 335**
Carrión G., Francisco **958**
Carter + Burton Architecture **183, 184, 225, 613**
Cary Bernstein Architect **530**
Castaing, Gustavo y Malena (interior design) **804**
Cavagnero, Mark Associates **336**
CC Arquitectos **660, 678, 679**
CCS Architecture **219, 514, 552, 553**
Cee Architects **549**
Cengiz, Deger **373**
Central de Arquitectura **681, 751**
Céspedes + Izquierdo Arquitectos **924, 936**
Chong Partners Architecture **531**
Cibinel Architects **127**
Cigolle X Coleman, Architects **318, 467**
Cindy Rendely Architexture **78**
Circle West **563, 590**
Claudio Magrini / Marco Vidal Cabello **939**
COA: Central Office of Architecture **312, 319, 600**
Coburn Architecture **517**
Contemporary Architecture Practice **433**
COOP HIMMELB(L)AU **287**
Cooperativa URO1.ORG **978**
Core Architects Inc **77**
Coscia Day Architecture & Design **609**
Covarrubias, Gabriel **680**
Cox & Ugarte Arquitectos (Carlos Ugarte –Arturo Cox – Matias Cordoba) **954**
Croft Pelletier architectes **60, 67**
Croxton Collaborative Architects PC **488**
Cruz, Hernán **942, 960**
Cuarto Arquitectura y Diseño **656**
CUBE **221**
CUH2A **137**
C U P **479**

D
DA4 Arquitectos **986**
dan hisel design **170**
Daniel Ventura Arquitecto **794**
Daniel Vergara Architecture **313**

Daoust Lestage Inc. **45**
D'Arcy Jones Design Inc. **24**
DB Arquitectos **989**
DBB Architects (New York) **838**
DeBR Desenho Brasileiro / Washington Fajardo + Patricia Fendt **863, 864**
DDG Arquitetura **862**
DeBartolo architects **236, 473, 564, 631**
De Jauregui Salas **789**
DeJong, Constance (sculptor) **334**
De Leon + Primmer Architecture **327**
de Oliveira Rosa, Eduardo **873**
Dean Maltz Architect **413, 427, 506**
Deborah Berke & Partners Architects LLP **177, 331, 445**
Della Valle Bernheimer **169, 374, 586**
Dellekamp Architects **682**
DeMaria Design **494**
Design*21 / Roger Kurath **561**
DesignARC **328, 602**
DesignBuildBLUFF **492**
designLAB architects **172, 629**
Di Renzo, Guillermo **804**
dialogue38 **102**
Diametro Arquitectos **683, 684**
Dias, Pedro **885**
Diller Scofidio + Renfro **375, 381**
Doblado, Juan Carlos **1002**
Donald Chong Studio **100**
Donini Arquitetos Associados (ARQDONINI 10x10, Marco Donini / Francisco Zelesnikar) **875, 916**
Doug Jackson Design Office **271**
Drew Mandel Design **79–81**
dRW-build **320**
Duarte Aznar Arquitectos, S.C.P **665**
Dubbeldam Design Architects **68, 103**
Dumay C., Alejandro **922**
Duque Motta, Rodrigo **964**
Dussol, Francois-Xavier **865**
DVS, AA Diaz Varela Sartor, Arquitectos **790**

E
E. Cobb Architects **566**
E/Ye Design **261**
Easton+Combs **244, 248**
Echeverria, Iñaki **657, 736, 748**
Edwards and Daniels Architects **205**
EFM Design **27, 138**
EHDD Architecture **518**
Eight Inc. **376**
El dorado Architects **245, 246, 280**
Elemental **926**

Eleven Eleven Architecture 16
Elkus Manfredi Architects 358
EMERGENT Tom Wiscombe 288
Eric Rosen Architects 354
Ese Design (Edward S. Eglin) 234
Esguerra, Rafael 991
Eskew+Dumez+Ripple 930
Estilo Yucatan / Victor Cruz, Atahualpa Hernandez, Luis Estrada, Silvia Cuitun 662, 663
Ethan Gerard Architect 150, 442

F

Fabric arquitectura 718
Faccio, Paulo 885
FAR Frohn&Rojas 955
Farouk Noormohamed – FNDA Architecture, Inc. 121
Farrow Partnership Architects Inc. 30, 71
Faulders, Thom Architecture 544
FdM:Arch Francois de Menil 247, 378
Fernández, Maite 802
Fernando Vazquez Studio 308
Ferreira da Silva, Ana Catarina 820
FFKR Architects 448
Fichten Soiferman et Associés 47
Finotti Arquitetura 918
Fisher Friedman Associates 456
FO – Field Operations 381
Fones C., Nicolas 922
Form4 Architecture 498
Forte, Gimenes & Marcondes Ferraz 886
Fournier, Sylvia 636
Frank, Vladimir 158
Franke, Gottsegen, Cox Architects 380, 434, 435
Frederick Fisher and Partners Architects 220
Frederick Phillips and Associates 268
FRENTE arquitectura / Juan Pablo Maza 702, 719
Frentes Arquitetura / José Alves 887
Frits de Vries Architect Ltd 122
FTRES Arquitectos 927
Fullerton Diaz Architects 349, 641
Fung + Blatt Architects 155, 289, 315, 316
funky (Ignacio Quintana + Victor Pellegrini) 956
Furlanetto, Renata 805
Fúster + Partners, Architects, PSC, Nataniel Fúster 778
FX Fowle Architects PC 447

G

g8vs arquitectos 957
GA Grupo Arquitectura 685
Gabellini Sheppard Associates 440
Gage/Clemenceau Architects 281
Gangi Design + Build 238
Garduño Arquitectos 686, 687
Garofalo Architects 147, 187
Garrison Architects 340, 436
Gates Merkulova Architects 493
Gay Freed, Janet (interior designer) 158
GCP Arquitetos 838
German del Sol 940, 944, 945
Gerson Castelo Branco 822, 828, 874
GFa Gruppo Immobiliaro 689
GH3 Architects 82, 83
Giannone Associates Architects 107
Gigaplex 619
Gillespie & Steel Limited 780, 781
Glavovic Studio 222
GLHN 592
GLR architects 741
Gluck and Partners, Peter L. Architects 136, 143, 454
Gluckman Mayner Architects 382, 522
Goettsch Partners 188
Goldner, Daniel Architects 282
Goldsmith Borgal & Company Ltd. Architects 86
Gomes + Staub Architects 175
Gomez Crespo Arquitectos 690
Gonzalez de León, Teodoro 720, 721
Gonzalo Diez Arquitectos Gonzalo Diez P. –Felipe Muller B. 1000
Gordon Kipping (GTECTS) 385
Gow Hastings Archtiects Inc. 84
Gould Evans 474, 587
Gracia Studio / Jorge Gracia 760, 761
GRAFT 279, 362
Graham Downes Architecture 523
Gray Organschi Architecture 360
GRAYmatter Architecture 555, 605
Greden, Lara 429
Griffin Enright Architects 163, 342, 469
Griffiths Rankin Cook Architects 54
Grimshaw 743
Grupo de Diseño Urbano, Mario Schjetnan / José Luis Pérez 688
Grupo Taller de Arquitectura SC 763
Grupo ABV – Amsel-Boruchowicz-Vilamowski arquitectos 791
Grzywinski Pons Architects 384, 443
gualano+gualano, arquitectos // g+ 1016
guardia architects 601
Gubbins Arquitectos 987
Gustavo Penna Arquiteto & Associados 810, 845
Gutierrez-Alonso Arquitectura 642, 734
Guy Architects 128
Gwathmey Siegel & Associates Architects 487

H

Hal Ingberg Architecte 38
Handel Architects 224, 386
Hanganu, Dan 39
Hansen Architects, P. C. 499
Hariri & Hariri – Architecture 151, 213
Helliwell+Smith.Blue Sky Architecture 64
Hernández de la Garza, Jorge 680
Hevia H., Guillermo 958, 959
HGA Architects and Engineers 239, 355
Hipogeo 655
Hix, John 779
HKS, Inc. 207
hMa hanrahanMeyers architects 233, 387, 388
HNTB Architecture Inc. BNIM 266
Hodges, Anne 777
Hodgetts + Fung Design and Architecture 291, 314, 496
HOK 689
Holzman Moss Architecture 176
Hotson Bakker Boniface Haden architects + urbanistes 52, 61
Höweler + Yoon Architecture LLP 165, 166, 330

HS2 Architecture 623
Hughes Condon Marler 123
Hugh Newell Jacobsen 356
Hulanicki, Barbara 777
Huntsman Architectural Group 533
Hype Studio 848

I

Ibarra Rosano Design Architects 593, 596–599
Iglesia, Rafael 803
Imirzian, Marlene & Associates Architects 475
Indio da Costa Arquitetura e Design 857, 861
Inmobiliaria Brom (Arquitectos Brom Asociados) 691, 722
Intel-Arq 753
Irarrazával, Sebastián 941
Isay Weinfeld Arquitetura 819, 834, 869, 888, 909,
Iu + Bibliowicz Architects LLP 390
IwamotoScott Architecture 534

J

Jackson & Ryan Architects 515
James Carpenter Design Associates Inc. 372
JCNAME Arquitectos 767
Jensen Architects 227, 550, 554
JHG Jorge Hernández de la Garza 659, 745
Jim Jennings Architecture 171
Joachim, Mitchell 429
John Friedman Alice Kimm Architects 292, 322, 323, 556
John Lum Architecture 537, 551
Johnsen Schmaling Architects 504
Johnson Chou 76
Jones Studio 476
JSª (formerly Higuera + Sánchez) 692–695, 728
Juaçaba, Carla 866
Juan Carlos Sabbagh & Gonzalo Cardemil Arquitectos 923
Junk Architects 266

K

KAA Design Group, Inc. 240
Kalach, Alberto / Taller de Arquitectura X 732
Kanner Architects 468, 559
Kappe, Ray 557
Karin Payson architecture + design 535
Kasian Architecture Interior Design and Planning 119
Kazovsky, Alla (Designed Real Estate) 293
Kevin Hom + Andrew Goldman Architects, PC 224, 386
KieranTimberlake Associates 339
Klai Juba Architects 278
Klotz, Mathias 992
KNOBSDesign / Jose Salinas 391
Kogan, Marcio 812, 889, 890
Kohn Pedersen Fox Associates 392
Kohn Shnier Architects 96–99
Kongats Architects 18, 108
Kós, José 847
KPMB 47
Kroiz Architecture LLC 159
Krown Lab / Stefan Andren 484
Kruchin Arquitetura 917
Krueck + Sexton Architects 199
Kuth/Ranieri Architects 536
Kuwabara Payne McKenna Blumberg Architects (KPMB) 85, 86, 87
Kyu Sung Woo Architects 452

L

LA DALLMAN Architects 338
LADESIGN New York / Leonardo Annecca 393
Lagranha, Tais 851
Landa Arquitectos 742
Landon Bone Baker 200
Landry Design Group 325
Neumann Mendro Andrulaitis Architects 173
LAR / Fernando Romero 696, 719, 723
larkin architect limited 105
LCM / Fernando Romero 697
LeAP Laboratorio en Arquitectura Progresiva 746
Lee Burkhart Liu Architects 294
Leeser Architecture 394
Legat Architects 231
Legorreta + Legorreta 649, 749
Lehrer Architects 626
Leite, André 836
Lemay, Lapointe, Voyer, Architects & Associés 65
Leroy Street Studio 280
Les Architectes FABG 36, 37
Leven Betts Studio Architects 132, 395
Libeskind, Daniel 109, 209, 211, 396, 545
Lillepold Dowling Architects 19
Line and Space, LLC 477
Llonch+vidalle Architecture 179
Lloyd Russell 526, 527
Llussa, Julianaa 887
LMN Architects 574
LOHA (Lorcan O'Herlihy Architects) 627
Logan, Eric 617
Longhi, Luis Architects 1010, 1011
Longo, Eduardo 891
LOT-EK 428
Lourenço Sarmento Arquitetos 842
LTL Architects 140
Lucio Muniain et al Arquitectura & Urbanismo 699
Luza, David 1010, 1011
Lyn Rice Architects 397
Lynch / Eisinger Design 398

M

m2p arquitetura – Aurélio Meira, Joaquim Meira, Marci Pereira e Silvana Meira 809
maceiras y cia.ltda 979
Machado and Silvetti Associates 130, 154
Maciel, Carlos Alberto 877
Maclennan Jaunkalns Miller Architects 11
Macy Architecture 524
Mafra, Fred 811
Magnani, Luis 885
Mahlum 263
Make Architecture 497
Mantovani, Simone Arquitetura 892
Marble Fairbanks 490
Marc Boutin Architectural Collaborative 21
(M)Arch. 472
mareines+patalano 807

Marín, Emiliano 963
Mark Dziewulski Architects 182, 520, 521
Mark Horton/Architecture 353, 455, 576
Marlon Blackwell Architect 223, 256
Marmol Radziner and Associates 295, 296
Marván Arquitectos 643, 644
Maryann Thompson Architects 341, 509, 620
Matoso Macedo, Danilo 816
mayer sattler-smith 131
Mazzanti, Giancarlo 991
MCA Manoel Coehlo Arquitetura & Design 825
Mccrumarchitects 399
McFarland, Larry Architects 62
MCM + A 995, 1001
Mendes da Rocha, Paulo 855, 878, 910, 911
Menkes Shooner Dagenais LeTournex Architects 40, 41, 55, 114
Menicucci, Paulo 816
[merz]project 478
MESH Architectures 400
metro arquitetos associados 893
Metro Arquitetura 854
Michael Willis Architects 229
Mickey Muennig / Vladimir Frank (Expansion Rooms) 518
micro.arq / Herman Bottle H. + Mercedes Castro W. 756
Jaime Varon, Abraham Metta, Alex Metta / Migdal Arquitectos 698, 724
Min ! Day 464
Minarc 297
Minond, Edgardo 792
Miró Rivera Architects 142, 144
Mitnick Roddier Hicks 630
MMBB 894
modo arquitetura 919
Molenaar (Dan & Diane Molenaar) 20
Montalba Architects, Inc. 606
Montgomery Sisam Architects Inc. 57, 110, 113
Morettin, Marcelo 840
Moriyama & Teshima Architects 54
Morphosis / Thom Mayne 401
MOS: michael meredith, hilary sample 58
Muñoz Arquitectos Asociados S.C.P. 666
Murphy/Jahn 189
Murúa, Benjamín 980

N

n:dL [nocturnal design Lab] 298
nARCHITECTS 402
Nave Arquitetos Associados 895
NBBJ 235, 276
Neil M. Denari Architects, Inc. 309
Niemeyer, Oscar 815, 829, 870, 896
Nitsche Arquitetos Associados 835, 915
[NOA] Najmias Oficina de Arquitectura 793
nomadas taller de arquitectura y diseño 1017
Novelo, Zoreda 661
NPC Grupo Arquitetura (Nucci, Pietraroia & Camargo) 897
Núcleo de Arquitetura 839
Nuño, Mac Gregor y de Buen Arquitectos, S.C. 667
nurko arquitectos 725
Nurko, Ricardo 669

O

O Norte Oficina de Criação – Bruno Lima, Chico Rocha e Lula Marcondes 856
Obie G Bowman 232, 503
OBRA Architects 425
Ocean D 403
Office Feuerman 379
Office for Metropolitan Architecture (OMA), Rem Koolhaas, Ole Scheeren 574, 735
Office for Mobile Design (OMD) / Jennifer Siegal 610
Office of Charles F. Bloszies 548
Office of Richard Davignon, Architect Inc. (ORDA) 17
Oficina de Arquitetos 853
Ogawa Depardon Architects 423
Ohtake, Ruy 843, 879, 901, 912-914
OJMR Architects 471
Oliveira Jr. Arquiteto 830
Olivos, Cristián arquitecto 935
Openshop | Studio 404
Oppenheim 347, 348, 350–352
Orrego Herrera, Jose 1012, 1013
Osborn 139
Oshatz Harvey, Robert Architect 485, 486
Ovalle, José Cruz 942, 960
OWP/P 190
oyler wu collaborative 300

P

PXS (Linda Pollari, Robert Somol) 302
P.A.T.T.E.R.N.S. Marcelo Spina 321, 625,628,801
PARA 405
Paravant 301
Pardo, Francisco 673, 754
Paranhos, Paulo Henrique 817
Parsons + Fernandez-Casteleiro Architects 204
Pascal Arquitectos 700, 701, 726
Pascali, Domingos 834
Patel Architecture 470, 495
Patricia Motzkin Architecture 453
Paul Cha Architect 249
Paul Lukez Architecture 241
Paul Raff Studio 111
PEG Office of landscape + architecture 133
Pentagram 283
Perez de Arce-Mardones-Bianchi 969
Perkins Eastman 406
Peter Cardew Architects 124
Pezo von Ellrichshausen Architects 943
Pfau Architecture 538, 549
Philip Banta & Associates 329
Pino I., Christián 959
Piratininga Arquitetos Associados 824, 867
PLANT Architect Inc. 89
PleskowRael Architecture(s) 407
Plus Minus Studio 479
PLY Architecture 134
Polidura, Antonio 933, 934, 961, 971
Polidura, Marco 933, 934
Polshek Partnership Architects / Susan T. Rodriguez 153
Predock, Antoine Architect PC 141, 334
procter-rihl architects 149, 850
PRODUCTORA 702

Puga, Cecilia 930
Pugh + Scarpa 243, 519, 558
Purcell, Juan 960
Pushelberg, Yabu 39
PUUK arquitectos 703

Q

Qua'Virarch 201, 326
Quadrangle Architects Limited 90
Quijano Axle, Augusto 616

R

R+R arquitectura – Reinoso & Rodriguez 707
Radic, Smiljan 937
Rafael Viñoly Architects 135
Randy Brown Architects design / build 457–549
Rashid, Karim 408
RDZ + LARA arquitectura / Miguel Angel Navarro Robles 737
Rearquitectura / Antonio Menéndez and Cristian Barrientos 984
Rec Arquitectura / Gerardo Recoder 647, 648, 731
ReCURSO studio 704
reddymade design 409
Reinach, Henrique e Mauricio Mendonça 813, 814, 841, 899
Reis, Lair 890
Renzo Piano Building Workshop 447
Resolution 4: Architecture 262, 466
richard+bauer 178, 591, 595
Richardson Sadeki 278
Riesco + Rivera Arquitectos Asociados 982
Rios Clementi Hale Studios 303
Ripple Design 304
Rob Paulus Architects 594
Robbie Young + Wright / IBI Group Architects (Canada) 94
Rockhill+Associates / Studio 264, 265
Rodriguez & Valencia Arquitectos 990
Rodríguez + Guerra Arquitectos 764
Rodríguez, Gilberto L. / GLR architects 741
Rogers Marvel Architects 410
Rojkind Arquitectos 705
Ronald Frink Architects 228
Rose + Guggenheimer Studio 510
Rosenbaum Design 900
Rounthwaite Dick + Hadley Architects 112

S

Sacro Arquitectos 1015
Sáez, Jose María Arquitectos 996, 997
Safdie, Moshe 499
Sagan Piechota Architecture 539
Saia Barbarese Topouzanov Architectes 41, 42, 44, 46
Sam Trimble Design 419, 582
Sánchez Arquitectos y Asociados 708, 738
Sander Architects 202, 611, 616
sanjosereves/Djiego van der Laat 639
Sant Architects Inc. 607
Santos Prescott and Associates 501
Saroli Palumbo et Bergeron Thouin, Consortium Atelier d'Architecture 43
Sasaki Associates 273
Saucier and Perrotte Architects 40, 125
SCAP (Juan Carlos Alvear / Homero Hernández) 709
Schacht Aslani Architects 571
Schwartz, Frederic Architects 412
Sebastian Mariscal Studio 275, 529
Segal, Jonathan 277, 525, 528
Semple Brown Design 210, 216, 272
SH_Arc Scott Hughes Architects 242, 255
Sheward, Rodrigo 938
Shieh Arquitetos Asociados 920
Shigeru Ban Architects 413, 506
Shim-Sutcliffe Architects 22, 28
SHoP Architects 414
Shore Tilbe Irwin & Partners 92
Shubin + Donaldson Architects 560
Sica Palermo, Nicolás 851
Simonetti, Alejandro 971
Single Speed Design 270
Siza, Alvaro 852
Skidmore, Owings & Merrill LLP 511
Skylab Architecture 145
SLVK / Gustavo Slovik 729, 730
Smith & Thompson Architects 415
Solomon Cordwell Buenz 186, 196
Sordo Madaleno Arquitectos 727
Spadoni & Associados 902
Specht Harpman 618
SPF:architects Studio Pali Fekete architects 162, 203, 305, 306
SPG Architects 416
Stagno, Bruno 635, 637
Stanley Saitowitz / Natoma Architects Inc. 540, 541
Stantec Architecture Ltd., Architects 91
Starck, Phillip 871
Stephen B. Jacobs Group 411
Stephen Dynia Architects 260
Steven Ehrlich Architects 465, 604
Steven Holl Architects 251, 267, 446
Steven Lombardi, Architect 215
Stratton, G. Bruce Architects 12
Studio Arthur Casas 831, 883, 884
Studio D W E L L 191
Studio Gaia / Ilan Waisbrod 733
Studio Gang Architects 197
Studio Junction 101
Studio NminusOne 126
Studio Paralelo / Luciano Andrades + Rochelle Castro + Gabriel Gallina 849
Studio Shift 307
Studio ST Architects / Esther Sperber 417
Studiomake 526
StudioMDA 168, 438
STUDIOS Architecture 252, 614
Suárez, Mariel 795
superkül inc | architect 15
surrealestudio arquitectura / Pedro Espinosa, Carlos Espinoza, Alejandro Vanegas 993, 994
Suyama Peterson Deguchi 567
Swanke Hayden Connell Architects 418
Swatt Architects 274
Sweeny Sterling Finlayson & Co Architects 93
Swinburn & Pedraza 925
Synthesis Design Inc. 120

T

T3ARC Taller de Arte y Arquitectura / Alfredo Raymundo Cano Briceño 645
TAL (Taller de Agustín Landa R) / Agustín Landa and Rolando Martínez 759
Talhouk, Pablo 934, 961, 971
Taller 13 Arquitectos [elias cattan + patricio guerrero] 711
Taller de Arquitectura-Mauricio Rocha 712
Taylor Smyth Architects 26
Teeple Architects 14, 56, 69, 104, 118
TEN Arquitectos, Taller de Enrique Norten Arquitectos SC 713
Terreform 1 429
The Lawrence Group 578
Tidy Arquitectos (Albert Tidy + Ian Tidy) 963
Tighe Architecture 146, 317
Titton, Claudia 851
Tod Williams Billie Tsien Architects 480
Todeschi, Silvio 858
Toshiko Mori Architect 174
Touraine Richmond Architects 608
Trahan Architects 505
Travis Price Architects 621, 622
Triptyque 904
Turell, Ana 942, 960
Turett Collaborative Architects 421

U

UM + Two Ton 422
una arquitetos 823
Undurragadeves Arquitectos 921, 972–977
Uni 167
urban lab 192
Urban Office Architecture 581
Urban Works, Ltd 193
Uribe de Bedout, Felipe 992

V

Vainer, André e Guilherme Paoliello Arquitetos 905
Valenzuela, Rodrigo 980
Vandeventer+Carlander Architects 565, 568, 572
Vazio S/A Arquitetura – Carlos M Teixeira 844
Vergara, Francisco 922
Veverka Architects 542
Vidal Arquitectos 744
Vidarq 683
Viglieccа&Assoc. 906
VSV – Vila-Sebastián-Vila Asociados Arquitectos 970

W

Wannemacher Jensen Architects 450, 508
Watmough, Cynthia 1006
Weinstein A | U Architects+Urban Designers LLC 570
Weiss / Manfredi 569
Weisz + Yoes Architecture 156
WendellBurnetteArchitects 214
Westlake Reed Leskosky 461
wHY Architecture 230
Wijaya, Made 634
will bruder+PARTNERS 239
William Duff Architects 337, 532
Wolf Architecture 583
Wood + Zapata 194
Work Architecture Company 389
Workshop for Architecture 226
workshop/apd 361

X

Xefirotarch – Hernán Díaz Alonso 444
Ximenes, Bruna 836
XTEN Architecture 237, 290, 324, 460

Y

Yazdani Studio Cannon Design 148

Z

Zack / de Vito Architecture 543
ZD+A / Yuri Zagorin and Erik Carranza 714
Zeidler Partnership Architects 95
Zilberman, Gisela 898
Zimmer Gunsul Frasca Architects LLP 218, 253, 254, 597
Zoka Zola architecture + urban design 195
Zoreda Novelo, Jorge Carlos 661
Zurita Architecture 424

INDEX PROJECTS

1 2 3
- 541 1028 + 1022 Natoma Street
- 188 111 South Wacker
- 36 115 Studios pour le Cirque de Soleil
- 692 13 de Septiembre
- 368 166 Perry Street / Luxury Condominiums
- 17 1830 Bankview
- 191 2041 W Cortland
- 374 245 Tenth
- 559 26th Street Low Income Housing
- 275 2-Inns
- 326 300MAIN
- 411 325 Fifth Avenue
- 196 340 on the Park
- 547 351 11th Street
- 155 3ality Digital
- 431 471 Washington Street
- 91 51 Division Police Station
- 468 511 House
- 97 519 Church Street Community Centre
- 122 5230 Seaside Place
- 410 55 Water Street Plaza
- 434 59E59 Theaters
- 432 627 Greenwich Street
- 604 700 Palms
- 609 747 House
- 605 7ten Project
- 79 83a Marlborough Ave Residence
- 628 8746 Sunset Boutique Plastic Sensation

A
- 63 Aberdeen Centre
- 31 Absolute
- 832 Acayaba House
- 174 Addition to House on the Gulf of Mexico
- 483 Adidas America Headquarters
- 960 Adolfo Ibáñez University Post Grade Building
- 690 Adolfo Prieto 1369
- 652 Advertising Agency
- 851 Advocacia Fontana – Lawyers office
- 298 Aeroform – Subsidized Urban Living Module
- 248 Airport Parking Facility
- 607 AK Live/Work
- 309 Alan-Voo Family House
- 806 Aldeia da Serra House
- 375 Alice Tully Hall, Lincoln Center
- 803 Altamira Apartment Building
- 65 Aluminum Technology Centre
- 1005 Alvar Apartment Building
- 390 Alvin Ailey American Dance Foundation
- 678 Amatepec
- 753 Ampliacion de Oficinas Corporativas
- 711 Amsterdam 253
- 693 Amsterdam 315
- 719 Anexo a el Eco
- 307 Animo Film and Theatre Arts High School
- 227 Ann Hamilton Tower
- 818 Antaq Building
- 727 Antara Polanco
- 925 Apus Rupanco House
- 682 AR58
- 507 Arado weeHouse®
- 322 Aragon Avenue Elementary School-Classroom Building and Lunch Shelter
- 200 Archer Courts Phase 1
- 252 Architect's Point Reyes Residence
- 654 Aria Pavillion
- 172 Arkell Museum
- 435 Ars Nova Building
- 415 Art Gallerie & Architects' Studio
- 140 Arthouse
- 780 Arthur Lok Jack Graduate School of Business
- 164 Artists for Humanity EpiCenter
- 436 Artists in Residence: Student Housing for Pratt Institute
- 772 Arts Tower
- 655 Atenas 354
- 418 Atlantic Terminal
- 339 Atwater Commons, Middlebury College
- 138 Austerlitz House
- 141 Austin City Hall and Public Plaza
- 365 Austrian Cultural Forum
- 830 Auto Shopping Cidade Empresarial
- 676 Ave Fenix Fire Station

B
- 235 Banner Gateway Medical Center
- 285 Barsky Residence
- 278 Bathhouse Spa
- 488 Bay Educational Center
- 443 Bayside Residence
- 859 Bazzar Restaurant
- 1014 Beach House At Las Lomas Two
- 255 Beach Road 2
- 848 Beira-Rio Stadium Renovation and Urban Master Plan
- 151 Belmont House
- 163 Benedict Canyon House
- 263 Benjamin Franklin Elementary School
- 890 Berçário Primetime
- 305 Beuth Residence
- 768 Biblioteca Boquete
- 664 Biblioteca de Ciencias Sociales
- 667 Biblioteca de la Facultad de Medicina Ciudad Universitaria, UNAM
- 954 Biblioteca de Santiago
- 992 Biblioteca Tematica E.P.M.
- 732 Biblioteca Vasconcelos
- 824 Biblioteca y Ambulatório de Fisioterapia
- 60 Bibliothèque de Charlesbourg
- 270 Big Dig Building
- 355 Bigelow Chapel at United Theological Seminary
- 587 Biodesign Institute at Arizona State University, Building B
- 44 Biological Sciences Building, University of Québec in Montreal (UQAM)
- 212 Bioscleave House
- 57 Bird Studies Canada Headquarters
- 457 Bizarre
- 677 Black House
- 256 Blessings Golf Course
- 420 Blue
- 90 BMW Toronto
- 310 Bobco Metals
- 923 Bodegas Viña Kingston
- 150 Boomeranch
- 166 Boston City Hall 2.0
- 706 Boutique de Club Med en la Ciudad de México
- 154 Bowdoin College Museum of Art
- 184 Boxhead
- 11 Brampton Soccer Centre
- 858 Brazilian National Shooting Center, Pan American Games Rio 2007
- 855 Brennand Chapel
- 119 British Columbia Institute of Technology (BCIT) Aerospace Technology Campus
- 321 Broad Cafe @ SCI_Arc / Interstitial Sensations
- 558 Broadway Housing
- 156 Bronx Charter School for the Arts
- 157 Bronx Museum of the Arts Expansion, North Wing
- 168 Brooklyn Arts Tower
- 162 Brosmith Residence
- 299 Broughton Studio
- 318 Building 9, Wildwood Elementary School
- 14 Burlington Central Public Library

C
- 657 CA House
- 103 Cabbagetown Residence
- 516 Cabrillo Marine Aquarium
- 170 Cadyville Sauna
- 645 Café Cinco
- 981 Caja de Compensacion La Araucana
- 554 California College of the Arts Graduate Center
- 303 California Endowment
- 276 CalIT2, University of California San Diego
- 53 Canada Aviation Museum
- 86 Canada's National Ballet School Project Grand Jeté: Stage 1 – Jarvis Street Campus
- 82 Canadian Museum of Inuit Art
- 93 Canadian National Institute for the Blind Centre
- 54 Canadian War Museum
- 611 Canal House
- 106 Capezio Flagship
- 932 Capilla Ave Maria
- 927 Capilla Rupanco
- 349 Capital at Brickell
- 882 Cáritas School
- 956 Casa Algarrobo IV
- 845 Casa Alphaville
- 986 Casa Altavista
- 761 Casa Becerril
- 934 Casa Binimelis-Barahona
- 891 Casa Bola
- 922 Casa Bosque
- 819 Casa Brasilia
- 759 Casa Bravo
- 767 Casa BS
- 826 Casa Casagrande Bertoldi
- 799 Casa CH
- 1001 Casa Cruz
- 797 Casa de Hormigón
- 977 Casa del Patio
- 778 Casa Delpin
- 920 Casa Dias
- 822 Casa do Cumbuco
- 734 Casa Echegaray
- 805 Casa en Araçoiaba
- 1015 Casa en la Planicie
- 791 Casa en las Glorietas
- 1003 Casa Equis
- 756 Casa estudio B.C
- 807 Casa Folha
- 760 Casa GA
- 651 Casa GDL1
- 1008 Casa I
- 642 Casa Jade
- 659 Casa Los Amates
- 789 Casa MA – Estancia Abril
- 928 Casa Meriz Moreno
- 702 Casa Mixcoac
- 1009 Casa O
- 758 Casa OL-411
- 710 Casa Organica
- 762 Casa Pa'lmar
- 985 Casa Paine
- 996 Casa Pentimento
- 933 Casa Polgatti-Rivas
- 754 Casa Romero
- 827 Casa Roveda Carvalho
- 995 Casa RX
- 997 Casa San Juan
- 990 Casa Santa Ana
- 717 Casa Taanah Sak
- 672 Casa Tlalpuente
- 866 Casa Varanda
- 909 Casa Vertical
- 636 Casa Williamson
- 943 Casa Wolf Andalue
- 901 Casa Zuleika
- 786 Casas Lago
- 740 Casas M
- 998 Castillo HNOS – Hardware Store
- 433 Catalyst
- 132 CC01 House
- 455 CCA Dormitory
- 45 CDP Capital Centre Pedestrian Passage – Montreal Underground City
- 288 Cell House
- 108 Centennial College Visual Arts Centre
- 301 Center of Communities of Faith
- 66 Central City
- 287 Central Los Angeles Area High School #9 for the Visual and Performing Arts
- 769 Central Park Panama
- 49 Centre Communautaire Intergénérationnel d'Outremont
- 689 Centro Comunitario Ciudad de México
- 674 Centro Corporativo DIARQ
- 720 Centro Cultural Bella Época y la Librería
- 829 Centro Cultural Oscar Niemeyer
- 680 Centro Cultural Vladimir Kaspe
- 965 Centro de Atencion de Emergencias Sur
- 853 Centro de Ensino Cicero Dias
- 737 Centro de Investigacion y Biblioteca C.I.D.E.
- 970 Centro de Justicia Santiago – Chile
- 308 Centro del Pueblo
- 821 CEPEMA Environment Education and Research Center (Torres en Altura)
- 714 Cervantes
- 477 Cesar Chavez Library
- 456 Chabot Observatory
- 359 Chameleon House
- 588 Chandler-Gilbert Community College Student Center
- 646 Chapel in a Garden
- 426 Chatham House
- 543 Chattanooga Residence
- 215 Chelsea
- 198 Chicago Townhouse
- 585 Chihuly Bridge of Glass
- 472 Children's Center at Caltech's Outdoor Science Laboratory
- 697 Children's Room
- 509 Children's School
- 958 Chilexpress S.A.
- 409 Chocolate Bar
- 713 Chopo Museum
- 345 Christ Community Clinic Board Street
- 544 Chromogenic Dwelling
- 249 C-I House
- 653 CIME
- 862 Circo Voador
- 919 City Bus Lane – Joao Naves Avenue
- 662 CL53 House
- 96 Claude Watson School for the Arts
- 854 Club Nox
- 811 Club Roxy
- 924 Colegio Creación Concepción
- 936 Colegio Creación Osorno
- 656 Colegio El Roble
- 939 Colegio Santa María de Paine
- 424 Comfort Stations
- 236 Commons
- 336 Community School of Music and Arts
- 561 Concrete Panel House
- 787 Conde 3234
- 912 Conde de Sarzedas Building
- 728 CONDESA df

744 Condominos la Diana
982 Contador-Weller House
579 Contemporary Art Museum St. Louis
545 Contemporary Jewish Museum
949 Contex Headquarters
34 Coopérative d'habitation Au Pied du Courant
586 Copper House
350 Cor
577 Cor Jesu Academy
254 Cornell University, Duffield Hall
699 Corporate Headquarters Autofin
671 Corporativo Banorte
660 Corporativo Frexport
716 Corporativo Imagen
707 Corporativo Santa Rosalia
304 Courtyard House
101 Courtyard House
280 Courtyard Houses
580 Cox Communications, A New Distribution Center for
30 Credit Valley Hospital
1012 Crematorio Santa Rosa
969 Crypt Santiago
347 Cube Tower
450 Cypress Forest Park Recreation Center

D
75 Davids Flagship
300 Density Fields
211 Denver Art Museum Residences
518 Department of Global Ecology, Carnegie Institution for Science
178 Desert Broom Public Library
470 Diamond Residence
389 Diane von Fürstenberg Studio's new Headquarters
13 Discovery Landing
962 Dominga
804 Don Enrique Lodge
133 Double Jeopardy
980 Doubleview House
571 Douglass-Truth Branch of the Seattle Public Library
599 Downing Residence
400 Downtown Duplex
271 DRAPE Artist Residence and Gallery
563 Duke
681 Dumas + Horacio
73 Dunn Avenue Triplex
479 Duplex Residence
964 Duque House
466 Dwell Home

E
880 E Tower
619 Earl's Silo
421 East 61st Street Residence/NYC
169 East New York Affordable Housing
417 East Side Duplex
427 Eaton Residence
738 EBC Campus Tlalneplanta
849 E-Box Parking
876 EC House
128 Ecole Allain St-Cyr
43 École Primaire Mont – Jésus-Marie
961 Edificio Acceso Parque Metropolitano Sur, Cerro Chena
988 Edificio Administrativo Colegio Los Nogales
794 Edificio Argerich
802 Edificio Brown
946 Edificio Consorcio Sucrusal La Florida
798 Edificio Da Vinci
989 Edificio Julio Mario Santodomingo
730 Edificio Manantiales Polanco
729 Edificio Parque España 23
638 Edificio Van der Laat & Jimenez
947 Edificio Vespucio Sur
556 Ehrlich Residence
102 Eko
74 Ellis Park House
319 Elysian Park Residence
879 Emiliano (hotel)
857 Encosta do Corcovado
208 Envelope
573 Envelope Summer
931 Environmental Information Center "Fray Jorge"
329 Equinox House
742 Escuela de Medicina ITESM
752 Esencia
846 Espaço Ciência
893 Estúdio Leme
668 Etc. Building
679 Eugenio Sue
810 Expominas
914 Expresso Tiradentes
209 Extension to the Denver Art Museum, Frederic C. Hamilton Building
394 Eyebeam Atelier, Museum of Art & Technology

F
520 F65 Center Transit Village
429 Fab Tree Hab
963 Facultad Artes Visuales
951 Facultad de Arquitectura, Arte y Diseño Universidad Diego Portales
952 Facultad de Odontología, Universidad de Chile
966 Facultad Derecho UDP
354 Fairways Residence
625 Fake Plastic Tree
705 Falcon Headquarters
875 Farm Building / Sapucai
959 Farmacias Ahumada
567 Fauntleroy Residence
839 FDE School – Jardim Angélica III
485 Fennell Residence
504 Ferrous House
214 Field House
15 Fielding Estate Winery
570 Fire Station 10
731 Firefly
219 Firefly Grill
360 Firehouse 12 Recording Studio
112 First Leaside Financial Office Headquarters
1017 Five Patio House
279 Fix
892 FKL House
220 Flint Institute of Arts
58 Floating Boathouse
143 Floating Box House
669 Flow House
393 Flower House
224 Flushing Meadows Corona Park Natatorium & Ice Rink
29 Foreman Point Cottage
869 Forneria
217 Fox Hollow Residence
10 French River Visitor Centre
471 Fritz Residence
223 Fulbright Building
328 Fuller Residence
315 Fung+Blatt Residence
801 FYF Residence

G
703 Galileo 211
100 Galley House
598 Garcia Residence
111 Garden Pavilion
85 Gardiner Museum
627 Gardner 1050
346 GE 5 Condos
110 George and Kathy Dembroski Centre for Horticulture, Toronto Botanical Garden
137 Georgia Institute of Technology, Molecular Sciences and Engineering Building
222 Girls' Club
268 Glade House
748 Gladiolas 402
813 Glass House
490 Glen Oaks Branch Library
487 Glenstone Residence
673 Gm1607
777 Goldeneye
438 Governors Island Tower
241 Graham Residence
266 Grand Ballroom at the Kansas City Convention Center
230 Grand Rapids Art Museum
258 Grand Teton Discovery and Visitor Center
338 Great Lakes Future, Discovery World
790 Grecia 3191
369 Greene Street Loft
297 Greenfield Residence
159 Green-HAB
366 Greenwich Project
416 Greenwich Village Townhouse
441 Greenwich Village Townhouse
423 Grove Street Townhouse
181 GT Residence
833 Guarujá House
142 Guest House
929 Guests' House

H
120 Hanna Residence
77 Harbour View Estates Superclub
439 Harrison Street Residence
148 Hauptman-Woodward Structural Biology Research Center
553 Haus Martin
92 Hazel McCallion Academic Learning Centre
239 Hercules Public Library
18 Hespeler Library
381 High Line
491 High School for Construction Trades, Engineering and Architecture
404 Hive Loft
294 HNRT
246 Hodgdon Powder Company, An Office for
637 HOLCIM
233 Holley House
291 Hollywood Bowl
505 Holy Rosary Church Complex
130 Honan-Allston Branch of the Boston Public Library
478 Hoover House
983 Hospedería Colgante · Corporación Amereida
665 Hospital Regional de Alta Especialidad
763 Hotel Azúcar
751 Hotel Básico
871 Hotel Fasano
658 Hotel Marquis los Cabos
612 Hotel Ray
940 Hotel Remota in Patagonia, Chile
800 Hotel Territorio
562 Hotel Valley Ho
808 House AM
895 House at Vila Zelina
864 House Camboinhas
868 House CG
513 House for a Butcher and an Art Maven
709 House GG
994 House in "El Barranco"
883 House in Iporanga
935 House in Marbella
816 House in Nova Lima
784 House in Patagonia
649 House in San Miguel de Allende
905 House in São Paulo
873 House in São Pedro
601 House in Upstate New York
863 House Jardim Botanico
476 House of 5 Dreams
828 House of Fortim
917 House of Sairas
22 House on Hurricane Lake
27 House on Lake Erie
493 House on the Hill
907 House P
840 House RR
135 Howard Hughes Medical Institute Janelia Farm Research Campus
704 Huacal
84 Humer College Institute of Technology & Advanced Learning
187 Hyde Park Art Center
314 Hyde Park Miriam Matthews Branch Library
560 Hydraulx
226 Hynansky House

I
852 Iberê Camargo Museum
896 Ibirapuera Auditorium
906 Ibirapuera Sports Complex
796 Iblr House
189 IIT Student Housing
107 Il Fornello
176 ImaginOn: The Joe & Joan Martin Center
950 Imbra
617 Indian Paintbrush Residence
594 Indigo Modern
941 Indigo Patagonia Hotel
591 Interdisciplinary Science + Technology Building 2 – Arizona State University
991 International Convention Center
835 Iporanga Beach House I
834 Iporanga House
836 Iporanga House
282 Ironworkers Training Facility (II)
177 Irwin Union Bank
867 Itanhanga House
32 ITHQ – Tourisme Institute of Québec
841 Itu House

J
260 Jackson Hole Center for the Arts Performance Hall
534 Jellyfish House (Exhibition)
499 Jepson Center for the Arts at the Telfair Museum of Art
221 Jetty House
718 Jiva
357 Joe's Salon + Spa
62 John MS Lecky UBC Boathouse
229 Joseph Jensen Treatment Plant Ozonation Building
19 Joseph Studio
387 Juliana Curran Terian Pratt Pavillion
916 Jungle/Beach House-Setao

K
528 K Lofts
225 Kampschroer – Yoon
886 Kase Mooca
293 Kazovsky Renovation
216 Kent Denver Student Center for the Arts
126 Khyber Ridge House (aka the Boarding House)
115 King David Highschool
23 Kleinburg Pool Pavilion
510 Kripalu Center Housing Tower

L
683 L' Atelier
323 L.A. Design Center
779 La Casona
1006 La Honda Beach Club
1002 La Isla Beach House
640 La Lancha
317 LA Loft
686 La Loma II House
865 La Maison
749 La Purificadora
269 Lab at Belmar
459 Laboratory
144 Lady Bird Lake Hike and Bike Trail Restroom
419 Lady M Cake Boutique
160 Lago Vista Guest House
552 Lake Street Residence
565 Lake Union Floating Home
921 Lakeside House
182 Lakeside Studio
121 Lalji Residence
590 LandSource Tempe
98 Laneway House
118 Langara College Library and Classroom Building
55 Language Technologies Research Centre (LTRC) University of Quebec in Outaouais (UQO)
399 Larchmont Residence
930 Larrain House Bahia Azul
1007 Las Arenas Beach House
973 Las Condes Town Council Building
41 Lassonde Pavilions, École Polytechnique
335 Laurance S. Rockefeller Preserve, Grand Teton National Park
899 Law Firm
124 Leblanc House
1010 Lefevre House
152 Lehigh University Alumni Memorial Hall Entry Court and Parking Structure
910 Leme Art Gallery
549 Lesbian Gay Bisexual Transgender Community Center
918 LHF House
530 Liberty Street Residence
746 Library and Media Center Fernando del Paso
715 Libreria Porrua
538 Lick-Wilmerding High School
650 Linda Vista House
621 Linnean Family
136 Little Ajax Affordable Housing
190 Little Village High School, Chicago
272 Littleton Church of Christ
204 Littman Residence
192 Live + Work
557 LivingHomes model 1.0
888 Livraria da Vila
630 LL House
887 Llussá Marcenaria
842 LM House
904 Loducca
793 Loft 34
984 Lofts Yungay
736 Lope de Vega 324
942 Los Robles Winecellar
428 Lot-ek (CHK)
210 Lowenstein Retaill and Parking Garage
186 Loyola University Richard J. Klarcheck Information Commons
292 Lucky Devils
663 LW49 House

M
902 Mackenzie University Building
568 Mad Park
572 Madrona House
825 Main Library – Centro Universitario Positivo/UNICENP
180 Malibu Meadows
273 Manon Caine Russell and Kathryn Caine Wanlass Performance Hall
33 Marche d'Alimentation Adonis
614 Marconi Communications Corporate Campus
445 Marianne Boesky Gallery
473 Mariposa Residence
788 Market Square
331 Marlboro College Serkin Center
356 Mary and Howard Lester Wing, University of Oklahoma
332 Massapequa-Bar Harbor Public Library
861 Massimo – House in Rio de Janeiro II
42 Masterplan, Pierre Dansereau Science Complex, University of Québec in Montreal (UQAM)
50 Maurer House and Studio
47 McGill University – The Montreal Genomics and Proteomics Center
437 McKinley Houses Community Center
620 Meadow House
809 Medical Laboratory Dr. Paulo Azevedo
700 Meditation House
379 MEGAchurch
448 MegaPlex 13
595 Meinel Optical Sciences Building – University of Arizona
396 Memory Foundations / World Trade Center Design Study
343 Memphis Performing Arts Center Plaza
817 Mercado Design
712 Mercado San Pablo Oztotepec
948 Mercat Restaurant
533 Mercedes-Benz of San Francisco
333 Mesa Arts Center
755 Mesa de la Corona
243 Mill Center for the Arts
244 Mill Center for the Arts
334 Minnesota Gateway Landmark
51 Minton Hill House
974 Mirador House
741 Miravalle Tower
889 Mirindiba's House
257 Mississippi Telecommunications & Conference Center (MTCC)
395 Mixed Greens Gallery
385 Miyake Madison
316 Miyoshi Residence
765 ML House
898 MM House
361 Mod Set: From Transience to Permanence
203 Modaa Building
370 Modern
618 Modern Barn
265 Modular 3 Project
264 Modular 4 Project
578 Momentum Worldwide Headquarters St. Louis
206 Mondavi Center for the Arts
283 Montauk Residence Guesthouse
24 Mosewich House
403 Mountain Hut
262 Mountain Retreat
908 MPM Propaganda
16 MTech Building
1004 Multivacaciones
114 Musee Du FJORD
515 Museo Alameda del Smithsonian
721 Museo de Arte Popular
644 Museo de Historia Natural TAMux
743 Museo Del Acero
815 Museu Nacional Honestino Guimarães
522 Museum of Contemporary Art San Diego
392 Museum of Modern Art
28 Muskoka Boathouse
602 Mussel Shoals House

N
171 Napa House
643 NATHAI Natural History Museum
386 National September 11th Memorial at the World Trade Center
185 National Underground Railroad Freedom Center
145 NAU webfronts
495 Nautilus
739 Nautilus
475 Neighborhood Resource Center
358 Neiman Marcus at Natick Collection
267 Nelson-Atkins Museum of Art
452 Nerman Museum of Contemporary Art
401 New Academic Building for the Cooper Union for the Advancement of Science and Art
194 New Stadium at Soldier Field
531 New Sustainable California Academy of Sciences
37 New Theater – Dawson College
21 New Varscona Theatre
447 New York Times Building
383 New York Townhouse
600 Newfield House
398 Nike Shoe Laboratory
52 Nk'Mip Desert Cultural Centre
542 Noe Valley Residence
576 Nokia, New York Flagship Store
413 Nomadic Museum
408 Nooch
289 Noonan Residence
384 Norfolk Street Residences
35 Normand Maurice Building
508 North Shore Pool
139 Northview Middle School Gymnasium
626 Norton Towers-on-the-Court
312 (N)QMA: New Queens Museum of Art
971 Nuevo Acceso al Parque Metropolitano de Santiago
498 NVidia
378 NYC Townhouse
446 NYU Department of Philosophy

O
546 Ocean Beach Residence
76 Offices for Grip Limited
302 Off-Use
661 Oficinas Corporativas Constructora PROSER
953 Oficinas Ecopellets
569 Olympic Sculpture Park
987 Omnibus House
529 On Grape
382 One Kenmare Square
526 One Space (house/apartment)
608 One Window House
247 One Two Townhouse
391 Onishi Gallery / Gallery Memoria
237 Openhouse
39 Opus Hotel
575 Orchard House
232 Oregon Coast House
647 Origami
165 Outside-In Loft

P
1011 Pachacamac Hill House
104 Pachter House, Gallery and Studio
228 Pacific BMW Showroom
234 Painting Studio
38 Palais des Congrès, Montréal
474 Palo Verde Library & Maryvale Community Center
785 Pamacahua Housing
641 Panorama
1016 Parador Salto del Penitente
938 Parador-Mirador en Pinohuacho
134 Park House
351 Park Lane
536 Park Presidio Residence
670 Parral 67
592 Patrick K. Hardesty Midtown Multicenter-Service Center
766 Pavilion + Two Patios House
639 Pavilion for the Design Exhibition Su Casa en Vivo, Barrio Amon
20 Pavilion House YM
59 Pavillon Gene H. Kruger Quebec Laurent Goulard
497 Peach House Project
701 Pedregal Shopping Center
442 Penthouse 360
461 Peoria Center for the Performing Arts
635 Pergola Building
125 Perimeter Institute for Research in Theoretical Physics
648 Petatglass
847 Petropolis House
195 Pfanner Residence
131 Phelps/Burke Residence
480 Phoenix Art Museum Expansion
242 Pine School
362 Pink – Make It Right
937 Pite House Punta Pite
320 Pizza Rio
724 Plaza Residences
372 Podium Light Wall
342 Point Dume Residence
524 Point Loma Residence
341 Polly Hill Arboretum Visitors' Center
464 Poolhouse
870 Popular Theater
414 Porter House
967 Porterias La Reserva
482 Portland Aerial Tram
911 Portuguese Language Museum
158 Post Ranch Inn
622 Price Residence
957 Principado
325 Private Residence
666 Procuraduría General de Justicia del estado de Yucatán
277 Prospect
444 PS1 MoMa / Warm Up / "SUR"
425 PS1 MoMA BEATFUSE! Young Architects Program 2006 Winner
281 PS1/MOMA
463 PSYC at The Parker Palm Springs
903 Public School EE Jardim Ataliba Leonel
149 Pull House
684 Punta del Parque

Q
770 Q Tower
406 Queens Hospital Center Ambulatory Care Pavilion
25 Queens University – Beamish-Munro Hall
926 Quinta Monroy Iquique

R
527 R3 Triangle Building
685 Rancho el Ortigo
80 Ravine House
78 Ravine Residence
814 Red House
127 Red River College
494 Redondo Beach Container House
723 Reforma 222
48 Renovation And Expansion of Pierre-Elliott-Trudeau – Montreal International Airport
489 Renovations to Grant Hall, Brown University
363 Repairs and Renovations to the Louisiana Superdome
81 Residence at Evergreen Gardens
202 Residence for a Briard
837 Residência Acapulco
67 Residencia Cantin Collin
856 Residência Derby
831 Residência PK
453 Residential Remodel
113 Restoration Services Centre, Toronto and Region Conservation Authority
885 Restoring and Renovation Project of Ibirapuera's Planetarium
61 Richmond City Hall
284 Ridgewood Residence

245 Rieger Building Addition	377 SIXTY USA: Head Office and Showroom	405 Times Square Recruiting Center	**W**
860 Rio das Ostras Bridge		440 Top of the Rock Observation Deck at Rockefeller Plaza	207 W Dallas-Victory Hotel & Residences
521 River House	484 Skybox		733 W Mexico City
581 Robbins Elementary School	286 Skyline Residence	584 Topanga Ranch	12 W. Ross Macdonald School for the Blind
582 Robert's Residence	850 Slice House	735 Torre Bicentenario	
179 Rock Bridge Christian Church	757 SMO House	708 Torre de Ingeniería UNAM	884 W.K. Private Residence Alphaville
872 Rodin Museum	745 Smooth Building for Corponet	722 Torre Optima 3	465 Waldfogel
492 Rosie Joe House	313 Snake Coming Out of a Metal Cage	691 Torre Reforma 115	955 Wall House
109 Royal Ontario Museum	512 Social Condenser for Superior	688 Torre Siglum	296 Ward Residence
83 Russell Hill	566 Soma House	523 Tower 23	238 Water + Life Museums and Campus
469 Rustic Canyon Residence	306 Somis Hay Barn	467 TR-1 House and Studio	623 Watermill House
	503 Sonoma Coast House	56 Trent University Chemical Sciences Building	624 Watermill Houses
S	502 Sonoma Vineyard Residence		388 Waveline
812 S401 House	874 Sorocaba's House	330 Triple House	175 Webb Dotti House
878 Sabina School Park of Arts and Science	197 SOS Children's Villages Lavezzorio Community Center	550 Turner Duckworth Offices	250 Weekend Retreat for a Writer
		792 Turner International Studios	371 West Midtown Ferry Terminal
539 Sagan Piechota Architecture Office	696 Soumaya Museum	634 Turtle Inn	123 West Vancouver Aquatic Centre
213 Sagaponac House	311 Sound City		615 Westchester/Loyola Village Branch Library
506 Sagaponac House	978 Spence Mine Staging	**U**	
915 Sahy House	199 Spertus Institute of Jewish	340 U.S. Border Patrol Station	380 West-Park Presbyterian Church
698 Salón de Usos Múltiples Tarbut	147 Spring Prairie Residence	511 U.S. Census Bureau Headquarters	337 Wheeler Residence
764 San Angel House	537 Sproule-Rowen Residence	253 U.S. Food and Drug Administration. FDA at Irvine, Pacific Regional Laboratory-Southwest and Los Angeles District Office	261 W-House
616 Sander Tree House	105 St. Gabriel's Passionist Parish		486 Wilkinson Residence
913 Santa Catarina Building	205 St. John the Baptist Catholic Church		259 Wine Silo
976 Santiago Archeological Museum	535 Starfish House		593 Winter Residence
975 Santiago Museum of Visual Arts	412 Staten Island Ferry Terminal	979 UCINF'S Corporative Building	364 Wonderfactory
324 Sapphire	881 Stations for the Transport of São Paulo	695 UCSJ Center for Graduate and Continuous Education Studies	462 Wood Materials Engineering Laboratories, Annex Building
153 Sarah Lawrence College Monica A. and Charles A. Heimbold Jr. Visual Arts Center			
	631 Stone Ridge Church	548 Ultra-Sustainable Skyscraper	344 Woodbury Dermatology Center
	240 Strand Residence	99 Umbra Retail and Concept Store	89 Woodlawn and Footes Pond
945 Saunas and Water Reservoires in Atacama	993 Suburban House	944 Un Hotel en Atacama	68 Woodside House
	353 Sugar Bowl Residence	843 Unique Garden	629 World Headquarters for the International Fund for Animal Welfare
69 Scarborough Chinese Baptist Church	173 Sullivan-Cowan Residence	193 United Neighborhood Organization Archer Heights Charter School	
430 Schein Loft	26 Sunset Cabin		877 WP House
555 Schey Residence	551 Sunset Magazine Idea Home	231 University Center of Lake County	
454 Scholar's Library	407 Sunshine Cinema	597 University of Arizona, Chemical Sciences Building	**X**
823 School in Campinas	402 Switch Building		481 Xeros Residence
251 School of Art & Art History, University of Iowa	496 Sylmar Library	218 University of Oregon, Athletic Medicine Center	999 X-House
			167 XSmall
40 Schulich Pavilion of the McGill University Faculty of Music	**T**	781 University of the West Indies Lecture Theater & Classroom Building	
	583 Tampa		**Y**
46 Science Heart, University of Québec in Montreal (UQAM)	1013 Tanatorio Chapel & Crematory Jardines De La Paz	367 Upside Down Skyscraper	327 Yew Dell Gardens
		1000 Urbana Building	183 Yoga Studio
564 Scottsdale First Assembly	820 Tauana Hotel		95 York University General Academic and Performing Arts Building – Accolade Project
514 Seadrift Residence	747 TDA House	**V**	
574 Seattle Central Library	771 Telefonica Flagship Store	687 V-3 House	
576 Sebastopol Wine Barn	117 Telus House	519 Vail Grant House	897 Young & Rubicam
725 Shakespeare's Dwellings	694 Temístocles 12	838 Valeo VSS Plant – Guarulhos	87 Young Centre for the Performing Arts
64 Shalkai	589 Tempe Center for the Arts	606 Venice Properties	
94 Sharp Centre at Ontario College of Art & Design, Toronto	348 Ten Museum Park	373 Versadome Modular Building System	**Z**
	88 Terrence Donnelly Center for Cellular and Biomolecular Research	500 Vertical House	675 Zacatecas
540 Shaw Residence		290 Vhouse	
397 Sheila C Johnson Design Center / The New School	449 Thacher Arts Building	603 Victorville City Hall	
	517 Thai Style House	295 Vienna Way	
613 Shenandoah Retreat Teaser	596 The Six	844 Vila del Rey House	
726 Sheraton Centro Historico	422 The Station	894 Vila Romana Residence	
274 Shimmon Residence	525 The Union	352 Villa Allegra	
900 Shimo Restaurante	72 Théâtre du Vieux-Terrebonne	201 Villa_OR	
776 Shoestring	70 Thomas L Wells Public School	458 Village Pointe East	
610 ShowHouse	71 Thunder Bay Regional Health Sciences Centre	501 Village Street Loft	
968 Siamese Towers		795 Vivienda Unifamiliar en Kentucky Club de Campo	
116 Silver Sea	750 Tides Riviera Maya		
460 Silverspur	161 Tiffany		
972 Simonetti Building	146 Tigertail		
451 Sinquefield House	532 Timbuk2		

We thank all architects for providing us with their projects' material and collaboration throughout the production of this book.

We would also like to thank especially the following architects, hotel group and photographer for their expert advise:

Eduardo Cadaval / Cadaval & Solà-Morales Arquitectos (Mexico)
Habita Group Hotels, Mexico (CONDESA df, Hotel Azúcar, Hotel Básico, La Purificadora)
Alex Souza and Leonardo Finotti Photographer (Brazil)
Pablo Talhouk / Polidura + Talhouk Arquitectos (Chile)
Adrian Moreno / arquitectura x (Ecuador)

Special thanks to the following architecture and design websites for announcing the book to reach out to architects in the American continent:

Dwell Magazine (USA) – **www.dwell.com**

[purshpullbar]² Architecture + design forum – **www.pushpullbar.com**

Radio Arquitectura (Mexico) – **www.radioarquitectura.com**

Chile [arquitectura] (Chile) – **www.chilearq.com**

Also in this series

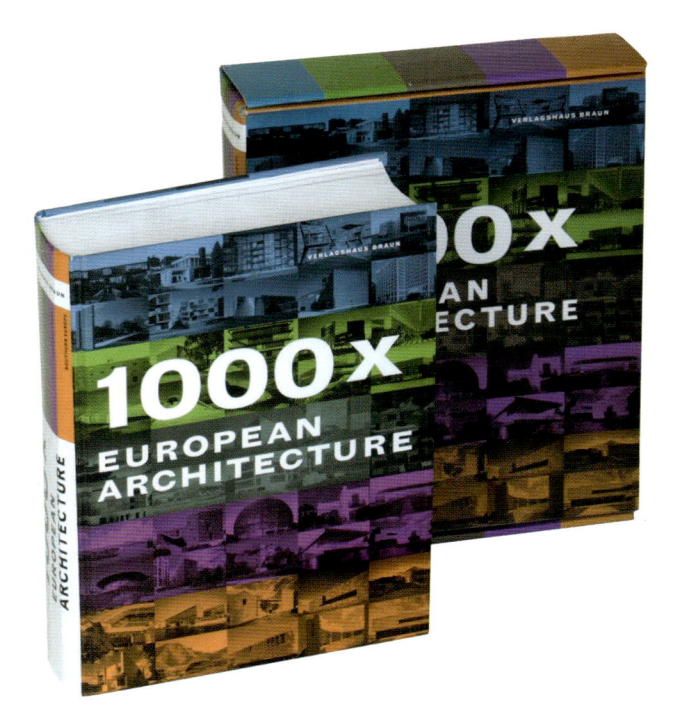

1000 x European Architecture
ISBN 978-3-938780-10-7

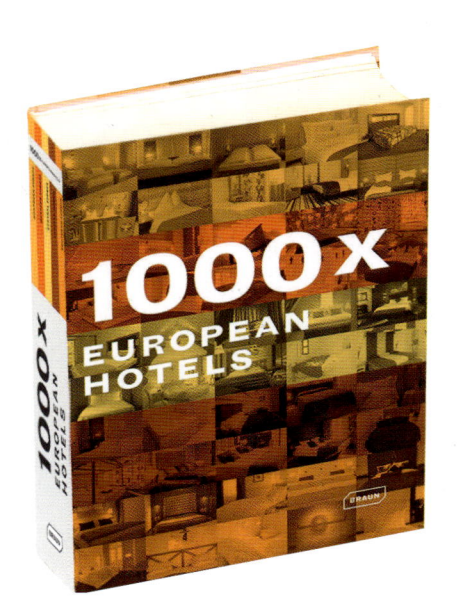

1000 x European Hotels
ISBN 978-3-938780-30-5

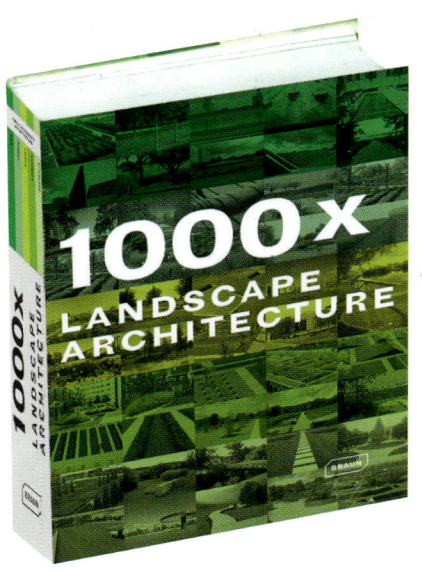

1000 x Landscape Architecture
ISBN 978-3-938780-60-2

www.verlagshaus-braun.com

BRAUN

Other series by Verlagshaus Braun

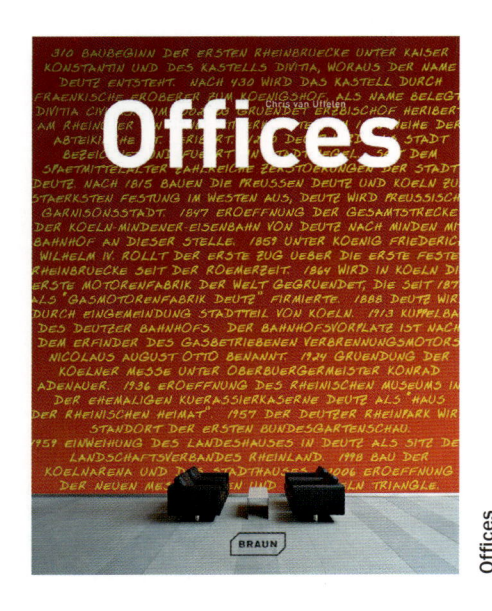

Offices
ISBN 978-3-938780-21-3

Also available in this series "Architecture in Focus"

Bath & Spa
ISBN 978-3-938780-39-8

Factory Design
ISBN 978-3-938780-75-6

Fair Design
Architecture for Exhibition
ISBN 978-3-938780-62-6

Hospital Architecture
ISBN 978-3-938780-26-8

INSIDE
Interiors of Concrete
Stone Wood
ISBN 978-3-938780-19-0

INSIDE
Interiors of Colour Fabric
Glass Light
ISBN 978-3-938780-40-4

Malls and Department Stores
ISBN 978-3-938780-27-5

New Landscape Architecture
ISBN 978-3-938780-25-1

Theme Hotels
ISBN 978-3-938780-24-4

Townhouses & more
ISBN 978-3-938780-57-2

Also available in this series "Architecture & Materials"

Clear Glass
Creating New Perspectives
ISBN 978-3-938780-63-3

Concrete Creations
Contemporary Buildings
and Interiors
ISBN 978-3-938780-32-9

In Full Colour
Recent Buildings and Interiors
ISBN 978-3-938780-33-6

Magic Metal
Buildings of Steel, Aluminium,
Copper and Tin
ISBN 978-3-938780-31-2

Set in Stone
Rethinking a Timeless Material
ISBN 978-3-938780-64-0

Touch Wood
The Rediscovery of a Building
Material
ISBN 978-3-938780-50-3

Pure Plastic
New Materials for Today's Architecture
ISBN 978-3-938780-51-0

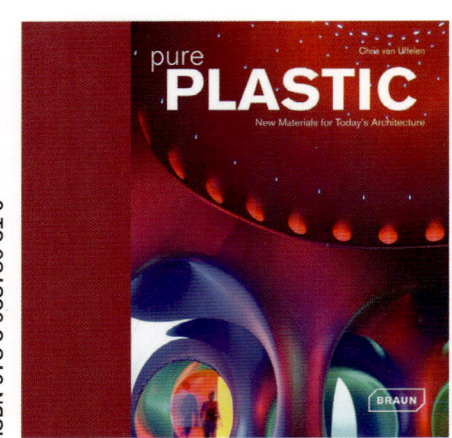

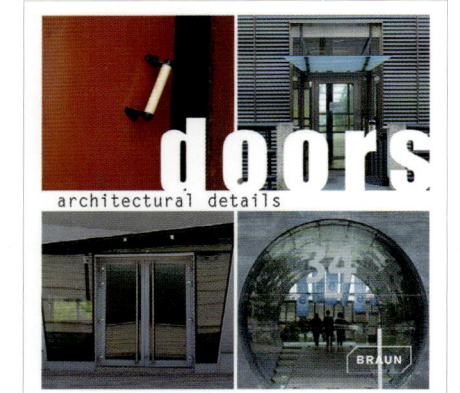

Architectural Details – Doors
ISBN 978-3-938780-36-7

Also available in this series "Architectural Details"

Architectural Details – Balconies
ISBN 978-3-938780-48-0

Architectural Details – Façades
ISBN 978-3-938780-38-1

Architectural Details – Pillars
ISBN 978-3-938780-47-3

Architectural Details – Stairs
ISBN 978-3-938780-46-6

Architectural Details – Windows
ISBN 978-3-938780-37-4

Home! Best of Living Design
ISBN 978-3-938780-54-1

Also available in this series "Best of…"

Eat! Best of Restaurant Design
ISBN 978-3-938780-69-5

Relax! Best of Bath Design
ISBN 978-3-938780-68-8

Work! Best of Office Design
ISBN 978-3-938780-55-8

BRAUN

www.verlagshaus-braun.com